SHEPPARD'S BOOK DEALERS
IN THE BRITISH ISLES

Companion Volumes

SHEPPARD'S DIRECTORIES

Directories of Antiquarian & Secondhand Book Dealers

SHEPPARD'S BOOK DEALERS IN EUROPE

SHEPPARD'S BOOK DEALERS IN JAPAN

SHEPPARD'S BOOK DEALERS IN AUSTRALIA & NEW ZEALAND

SHEPPARD'S BOOK DEALERS IN NORTH AMERICA

SHEPPARD'S BOOK DEALERS IN INDIA AND THE ORIENT

SHEPPARD'S BOOK DEALERS IN LATIN AMERICA & SOUTHERN AFRICA

Other Directories

SHEPPARD'S INTERNATIONAL DIRECTORY OF PRINT AND MAP SELLERS
A DIRECTORY OF BUSINESSES IN THIRTY-EIGHT COUNTRIES

SHEPPARD'S INTERNATIONAL DIRECTORY OF EPHEMERA DEALERS
A DIRECTORY OF BUSINESSES IN TWENTY-ONE COUNTRIES

SHEPPARD'S DEALERS IN COLLECTABLES (UK)
A DIRECTORY OF DEALERS IN NEW & REPRODUCTION AND OLD & ANTIQUE COLLECTABLES

SHEPPARD'S DEALERS IN COLLECTIBLES (USA)
A DIRECTORY OF DEALERS IN NEW & REPRODUCTION AND OLD & ANTIQUE COLLECTIBLES

SHEPPARD'S
BOOK DEALERS IN THE BRITISH ISLES

A DIRECTORY OF
ANTIQUARIAN AND SECONDHAND
BOOK DEALERS IN THE
UNITED KINGDOM,
THE CHANNEL ISLANDS,
THE ISLE OF MAN AND THE
REPUBLIC OF IRELAND

TWENTY-SEVENTH EDITION

RICHARD JOSEPH PUBLISHERS

First Edition published 1951
Twenty-seventh published 2003

**RICHARD JOSEPH PUBLISHERS LIMITED
P.O. BOX 15, TORRINGTON
DEVON EX38 8ZJ
ENGLAND
TEL: 01805 625750 FAX: 01805 625376
E-MAIL: rjoe01@aol.com**

I.S.S.N. 0950-0715
I.S.B.N. 1 872699 78 2

© **RICHARD JOSEPH PUBLISHERS LIMITED 2003**

MADE IN ENGLAND

Database advisors - John Withers, Kevin Grimshire
Printed and bound by
Antony Rowe Ltd, Bumpers Farm, Chippenham, Wiltshire SN14 6LH

Editor's Note. Whilst every care is taken to ensure that the information given in this Directory is as accurate and complete as possible, the Publishers cannot accept any responsibility for any inaccuracies that occur or for any relevant information that was not available to the Publishers or its professional advisors at the time of going to press.

CONTENTS

SPECIALITY HEADINGS	8
INTRODUCTION	12
MISCELLANEOUS INFORMATION	
Abbreviations	14
Sizes of Books	15
Metric Conversions	16
The British Book Trade	17
ANTIQUARIAN BOOKSELLERS' ASSOCIATIONS	20
PERIODICALS – Literary Magazines and Book Trade Papers	24
CURRENT REFERENCE BOOKS	28
SUPPLIES AND SERVICES	
Book Auctioneers	36
Book Display and Storage Equipment	37
Book Fair Organisers	37
Catalogue Printers	40
Craft Bookbinders	40
Packaging Materials Suppliers	44
Remainder Merchants	44
Logistics/Shipping Agents	45
Suppliers of Materials & Tools for Binding and Restoring	45
USE OF THE DIRECTORY	47
INDEX OF CITIES AND TOWNS	48
GEOGRAPHICAL DIRECTORY OF DEALERS	
ENGLAND (see following pages)	55
THE CHANNEL ISLANDS	257
ISLE OF MAN	258
NORTHERN IRELAND	259
SCOTLAND	261
REPUBLIC OF IRELAND	275
WALES	280
ALPHABETICAL INDEXES	
List of dealers by name of Business	291
List of dealers with Web Sites	311
List of dealers by name of Proprietor	322
Speciality Index (see following pages)	331
Booksearch Service	434
Large Print Books	437
DISPLAYED ADVERTISEMENT INDEX	438

CONTENTS

ENGLAND (by Counties)

BEDFORDSHIRE	55
BERKSHIRE	57
BRISTOL (incl. Unitary Authority of Bristol)	60
BUCKINGHAMSHIRE	62
CAMBRIDGESHIRE	64
CHESHIRE	69
CORNWALL	73
CUMBRIA	77
DERBYSHIRE	81
DEVON	83
DORSET	90
DURHAM (incl. Unitary Authorities of Darlington, Hartlepool & Stockton-on-Tees)	96
EAST SUSSEX	98
EAST YORKSHIRE (incl. Unitary Authorities of East Riding & Kingston-upon-Hull)	104
ESSEX	106
GLOUCESTERSHIRE (incl. Unitary Authority of South Gloucestershire)	111
GREATER MANCHESTER (incl. the Unitary Authorities of Bolton, Bury, Manchester, Oldham, Rochdale, Salford, Stockport, Tameside, Trafford & Wigan)	116
HAMPSHIRE	120
HEREFORDSHIRE	126
HERTFORDSHIRE	128
ISLE OF WIGHT	131
KENT	133
LANCASHIRE	140
LEICESTERSHIRE	143
LINCOLNSHIRE (incl. the Unitary Authorities of North East Lincolnshire) & North Lincolnshire)	146
LONDON (EAST POSTAL DISTRICTS)	151
LONDON (EAST CENTRAL POSTAL DISTRICTS)	152
LONDON (NORTH POSTAL DISTRICTS)	153
LONDON (NORTH WEST POSTAL DISTRICTS)	157
LONDON (SOUTH EAST POSTAL DISTRICTS)	160
LONDON (SOUTH WEST POSTAL DISTRICTS)	163
LONDON (WEST POSTAL DISTRICTS)	169
LONDON (WEST CENTRAL POSTAL DISTRICTS)	176
LONDON (OUTER)	180
MERSEYSIDE (incl. the Unitary Authorities of Knowsley, Liverpool, St. Helens, Sefton & Wirral)	185
NORFOLK	187
NORTH YORKSHIRE (incl. the Unitary Authorities of Cleveland, Middlesbrough, Redcar & York)	192
NORTHAMPTONSHIRE	198
NORTHUMBERLAND	200
NOTTINGHAMSHIRE	202
OXFORDSHIRE	204
SHROPSHIRE	211
SOMERSET (incl. the Unitary Authorities of Bath & North East Somerset & North Somerset)	214
SOUTH YORKSHIRE (incl. the Unitary Authorities of Barnsley, Doncaster, Rotherham & Sheffield)	220
STAFFORDSHIRE	222
SUFFOLK	224
SURREY	230

CONTENTS

TYNE AND WEAR (incl. the Unitary Authorities of Gateshead,
  Newcastle upon Tyne, North Tyneside, South Tyneside & Sunderland) 235
WARWICKSHIRE 236
WEST MIDLANDS (incl. the Unitary Authorities of Birmingham, Coventry,
  Dudley, Sandwell, Solihull, Walsall & Wolverhampton) 238
WEST SUSSEX 241
WEST YORKSHIRE (incl. the Unitary Authorities of Bradford, Calderdale,
  Kirklees, Leeds & Wakefield) 245
WILTSHIRE 250
WORCESTERSHIRE 254

ENGLAND (by Unitary Authorities)

To locate a dealer within a Unitary Authority, use the page references shown below in conjuction with the County Index shown above.

Barnsley	220	North Tyneside	235
Bath & North East Somerset	214	North Somerset	214
Birmingham	238	Oldham	116
Bolton	116	Redcar	192
Bradford	245	Rochdale	116
Bristol	60	Rotherham	220
Bury	116	St. Helens	185
Calderdale	245	Salford	116
Cleveland	192	Sandwell	238
Coventry	238	Sefton	185
Darlington	96	Sheffield	220
Doncaster	220	Solihull	238
Dudley	238	South Gloucestershire	111
East Riding	104	South Tyneside	235
Gateshead	235	Stockport	116
Hartlepool	96	Stockton-on-Tees	196
Kingston-upon-Hull	104	Sunderland	235
Kirklees	245	Tameside	116
Knowsley	185	Trafford	116
Leeds	245	Wakefield	245
Liverpool	185	Walsall	238
Manchester	116	Wigan	116
Middlesbrough	192	Wirral	185
Newcastle upon Tyne	235	Wolverhampton	238
North East Lincolnshire	146	York	192
North Lincolnshire	146		

SPECIALITY INDEX

The following list has been created from subjects nominated by dealers from entry forms or on their web page in Sheppard's Booksearch

Subject	Page
Academic/Scholarly	331
Advertising	332
Aeronautics	332
Africana	332
Agriculture	332
Alchemy	332
Almanacs	333
Alpinism/Mountaineering	333
Alternative Medicine	333
American Indians	333
Americana	333
Animals and Birds	333
Annuals	334
Anthologies	334
Anthropology	334
Anthroposophy	334
Antiquarian	334
Antiques	336
Apiculture	336
Applied Art	337
Archaeology	337
Architecture	337
Arms and Armour	338
Art	339
Art History	340
Art Reference	341
Arthurian	341
Artists	341
Arts, The	341
Assassinations	342
Astrology	342
Astronautics	342
Astronomy	342
Atlases	342
Author(s)	
– General	342
– Specific (A–Z)	343
– Local	350
– Women	350
Autobiography	350
Autographs	351
Avant-Garde	351
Aviation	351
Banking and Insurance	352
Beat Writers	352
Bell-Ringing (Campanology)	352
Bibles	352
Bibliography	352
Bindings	352
Biography	353
Biology	354
Black Studies	354
Book of Hours	354
Bookbinding	354
Books about Books	354
Botany	355
Brewing	355
Bridge	355
Broadcasting	355
Building and Construction	355
Bull Fighting	355
Buses/Trams	355
Business Studies	355
Byzantium	355
Calligraphy	355
Canadiana	355
Canals/Inland Waterways	356
Caricature	356
Carpets	356
Carriages and Driving	356
Cartography	356
Cartoons	356
Catalogues Raisonnés	356
Cats	356
Ceramics	356
Chemistry	356
Chess	357
Children's	
– General	357
– Illustrated	358
Christmas	358
Churchilliana	359
Cinema/Film	359
Circus	359
Cities	359
City of London	359
Civil Engineering	359
Classical Studies	359
Cockfighting	360
Collecting	360
Colonial	360
Colour-Plate	360
Comedy	360
Comic Books and Annuals	360
Comics	360
Company History	361
Computing	361
Conservation	361
Cookery/Gastronomy	361
Counterculture	361
Countries and Regions	
– Afghanistan	361
– Africa	361
– Albania	362
– Americas, The	362
– Andorra	362
– Antarctic, The	362
– Arabia	362
– Arctic, The	362
– Armenia	362
– Asia	362
– Asia Minor	362
– Australasia	362
– Australia	362
– Austria	362
– Balkans, The	362
– Balkan States	362
– Bermuda	362
– Burma	362
– Caribbean, The	362
– Central America	362
– Central Asia	363
– Channel Islands, The	363
– China	363
– Cuba	363
– Cyprus	363
– East Europe	363
– Egypt	363
– England	363
– Ethiopia	363
– Europe	363
– Far East, The	363
– France	363
– Germany	363
– Gibraltar	363
– Greece	363
– Greenland	363
– Himalayas, The	363
– Hungary	363
– Iceland	363
– India	363
– Iran	364
– Ireland	364
– Isle of Man	364
– Isle of Wight	364
– Isles of Scilly	364
– Italy	364
– Japan	364
– Kenya	364
– Korea	364
– Latin America	364
– Malaysia	364
– Malta	364
– Melanesia	364
– Mexico	364
– Middle East, The	364
– Mongolia	365
– Morocco	365
– Near East, The	365
– Nepal	365
– Pacific, The	365
– Pakistan	365
– Palestine	365

SPECIALITY INDEX

- Papua New Guinea 365
- Philippines, The 365
- Poland 365
- Polar 365
- Polynesia 365
- Portugal 365
- Puerto Rico 365
- Romania 365
- Russia 365
- Santo Domingo 365
- Sarawak 365
- Scotland 365
- Siam 366
- South Africa 366
- South America 366
- South Atlantic Islands 366
- South East Asia 366
- Spain 366
- Sri Lanka 366
- Straits Settlements, The 366
- Sudan, The 366
- Switzerland 366
- Tanzania 366
- Tibet 366
- Turkey 366
- U.S.A 366
- Vietnam 366
- Wales 366
- West Indies 366

Country Houses 366
Courtesy 366
Crafts 366
Crime (True) 367
Criminology 367
Crochet 367
Cryptozoology 367
Culture
- Foreign 367
- National 367

D.I.Y (Do It Yourself) 367
Dance 367
Decorative Art 367
Deep Sea Diving 368
Design 368
Diaries 368
Dictionaries 368
Divining 368
Documents - General 368
Dogs 368
Dolls and Dolls' Houses 368
Drama 369
Drawing 369
Drugs 369

Early Imprints 369
Earth Mysteries 369
Easter 369
Ecclesiastical History and
  Architecture 369
Ecology 369
Economics 369
Education & School 370

Egyptology 370
Emblemata 370
Embroidery 370
Encyclopaedias 370
Engineering 370
Engraving 370
Entertainment - General ... 370
Entomology 371
Environment, The 371
Erotica 371
Esoteric 371
Espionage 371
Ethnography 371
Ethnology 371
Etiquette 371
Evolution 371
Ex-Libris 371

Fables 372
Fairgrounds 372
Farming & Livestock 372
Farriers 372
Fashion and Costume 372
Feminism 372
Fiction
- General 372
- Crime, Detective, Spy,
  Thrillers 373
- Fantasy, Horror 374
- Historical 374
- Romantic 374
- Science Fiction 374
- Westerns 375
- Women 375
Fine and Rare 375
Fine Art 375
Fine Printing 376
Fire and Firefighters 376
Firearms/Guns 376
First Editions 376
Fishes 377
Flower Arranging 377
Folio Society, The 377
Folklore 377
Food and Drink 377
Fore-Edge Paintings 378
Foreign Texts 378
Forestry 378
Free Thought 378
Freemasonry and
  Anti-Masonry 378
Furniture 378

Gambling 378
Games 378
Gardening 378
Gemmology 379
Genealogy 379
Geography 379
Geology 379
Ghosts 379
Glamour 379
Glass 379

Gnostics 380
Graphics 380
Guide Books 380
Gynaecology 380
Gypsies 380

Health 380
Heraldry 380
Herbalism 380
Hermeticism 380
Herpetology 380
History
- General 380
- 19th Century 382
- American 382
- Anarchism 382
- Ancient 382
- British 382
- Byzantine 382
- Design 382
- European 382
- Guilds & Livery 383
- Industrial 383
- Irish 383
- Labour/Radical
  Movements 383
- Local 383
- Middle Ages 384
- National 384
- Renaissance, The 384
- Roman 384
- Women 384
History of Civilisation 384
History of Ideas 384
Hobbies 384
Holocaust 384
Homeopathy 384
Homosexuality and
  Lesbianism 384
Horizon Writers 384
Horology 394
Horticulture 385
Humanism 385
Humanities 385
Humour 385
Hydrography 385

Iconography 385
Illuminated Manuscripts 385
Illustrated 385
Imprints 387
Incunabula 387
Industry 387
Interior Design 387
International Affairs 387
Irish Interest 387

Jewellery 387
Journalism 387
Journals
- General 388
- Maritime 388
Judiaca 388

SPECIALITY INDEX

Juvenile 388

Knitting 388

Lace 388
Landscape 388
Languages
– African 388
– Foreign 388
– National 389
Law 389
Lepidopterology 389
Letters 389
Limited Editions 389
Linguistics 389
Literary Criticism 389
Literary Travel 390
Literature 390
Literature - Victorian 392
Literature in Translation ... 392
Locks and Locksmiths 392
Magic and Conjuring 392
Manual
– General 393
– Seamanship 393
Manuscripts 393
Marine Sciences 393
Maritime/Nautical 393
Maritime/Nautical Logbooks .. 394
Marque Histories
 (see also Motoring) 394
Marxism 394
Mathematics 394
Media 394
Medicine 394
Medicine - History of 394
Medieval 395
Memoirs 395
Memorabilia 395
Metaphysics 395
Meteorology 395
Microscopy 395
Military 395
Military History 396
Mind, Body and Spirit 397
Mineralogy 397
Miniature Books 397
Mining 397
Modern First Editions 397
Monographs 398
Motorbikes 398
Motoring 398
Moveable & 3D (See Pop Up) .. 399
Music
– General 399
– Classical 399
– Composers 399
– Folk and Irish Folk 399
– Jazz 400
– Music Hall 400
– Musicians 400
– Opera 400
– Political Songs and Ballads 400

– Popular 400
– Printed 400
– Rock 400
Musical Instruments 400
Mycology 400
Mysteries 400
Mysticism 400
Mythology 401

Natural Health 401
Natural History 401
Natural Sciences 402
Naturism 402
Naval 402
Navigation 402
Needlework 403
Neurology 403
New Age 403
New Naturalist 403
Newspapers - General 403
Nostalgia 403
Numismatics 403

Occult 403
Odd and Unusual 403
Oriental 403
Ornithology 404
Osteopathy 404
Ottoman Empire 404
Oxford Movement 404

Pacifism 404
Paganism 404
Painting 404
Palaeography 404
Palaeontology 404
Palmistry and Fortune
 Telling 404
Papermaking 404
Parapsychology 405
Parish Registers 405
Performing Arts 405
Periodicals and Magazines ... 405
Pharmacy/Pharmacology 405
Philately 405
Philology 405
Philosophy 405
Photography 406
Phrenology 406
Physical Culture 406
Physics 407
Plant Hunting 407
Plays 407
Poetry 407
Police Force Histories 408
Politics 408
Pop-Up, 3D, Cut Out and
 Movable (See Moveable) ... 408
Poultry 408
Prayer Books 408
Precious Metals - Silver 408
Pre-Raphaelite 408
Printing 408

Private Press 408
Proof Copies 409
Psychic 409
Psychoanalysis 409
Psychology/
 Psychiatry 409
Psychotherapy 409
Public Houses 409
Public Schools 409
Publishers
– General 410
– Batsford 410
– Black, A. and C. 410
– Blackie 410
– Chambers 410
– Curwen Press 410
– David and Charles 410
– Edinburgh
 University Press 410
– Foulis, T.N. 410
– Ghost Story Press 410
– Guinness Publishing Ltd. .. 410
– Hogarth Press 410
– Joseph Ltd., Michael 410
– Ladybird Books 410
– Oakwood Press 410
– Oxford University Press ... 410
– Pan 410
– Pelican 410
– Penguin 410
– Puffin 410
– Roundwood Press 410
– Studio, The 410
– Thames and Hudson 410
– Warnes 410
Publishing 411
Pulps 411
Puppets and Marionettes 411
Puzzles 411

Radical Issues 411
Radio/Wireless 411
Railways 411
Reference 412
Religion
– General 412
– Buddhism 412
– Christian 412
– Islam 412
– Jewish 413
– Methodism 413
– Oriental 413
– Quakers 413
– Roman Catholic 413
– Taoism 413
Religious Texts 413
Royalty
– General 413
– European 413
Rugs 413
Rural Life 413

Satire 414

SPECIALITY INDEX

School Registers/Rolls
  of Honour.................. 414
Science
– General....................... 414
– History of.................... 414
Scientific Instruments 414
Scottish Interest.............. 414
Scouts and Guides............ 415
Sculpture...................... 415
Self-Sufficiency 415
Sets of Books.................. 415
Sexology....................... 415
Sheep/Shepherding 415
Sherlockiana.................. 415
Ship Modelling................ 415
Shipbuilding 415
Shorthand..................... 415
Sigillography.................. 415
Signed Editions 415
Slavery........................ 416
Social History 416
Social Sciences 416
Socialism 416
Sociology...................... 416
Special Collections............ 416
Spiritualism 417
Sport
– General...................... 417
– American Football 417
– Angling/Fishing............. 417
– Archery 417
– Athletics.................... 417
– Badminton.................. 417
– Ballooning 417
– Big Game Hunting......... 417
– Billiards/Snooker/Pool..... 418
– Boxing...................... 418
– Canoeing/Kayaks........... 418
– Caving (Spelaeology) 418
– Climbing and Trekking.... 418
– Coursing 418
– Cricket 418
– Croquet 418
– Cycling 418
– Diving/Sub-Aqua........... 418
– Duelling.................... 418
– Falconry 418
– Fencing.................... 418
– Field Sports 418

– Football (Soccer) 419
– Golf......................... 419
– Greyhound Racing 419
– Highland Games........... 419
– Hockey 419
– Horse Racing (inc. Riding/
    Breeding/Equestrian) 419
– Hunting 419
– Martial Arts 419
– Motor Racing 419
– Olympic Games, The....... 419
– Pig-Sticking 419
– Polo 419
– Racket Sports 420
– Rowing 420
– Rugby 420
– Shooting.................... 420
– Skiing...................... 420
– Tennis 420
– Weightlifting/
    Bodybuilding................ 420
– Wrestling................... 420
– Yachting.................... 420
Stained Glass 420
Steam Engines 420
Supernatural 420
Surrealism 420

Tapestry 420
Taxidermy..................... 421
Technical 421
Technology.................... 421
Teddy Bears................... 421
Television..................... 421
Textiles....................... 421
Theatre....................... 421
Theology...................... 421
Theosophy.................... 422
Topography
– General..................... 422
– Local....................... 423
Town Planning 425
Toys.......................... 425
Traction Engines 425
Trade Unions 425
Transatlantic arts 425
Transport..................... 425
Travel
– General..................... 426

– Africa 428
– Americas................... 428
– Asia 428
– Australasia/Australia 428
– Europe..................... 428
– Middle East 429
– Polar 429
Tribal........................ 429
Typography 429

U.F.O.s 429
Unexplained, The............. 429
University Texts 429
Urban History 429

Vatican and Papal
  History, The................ 430
Ventriloquism 430
Veterinary 430
Victoriana 430
Vintage Cars 430
Vintage Paperbacks 430
Viticulture 430
Voyages and Discovery...... 430

War
– General 430
– American Civil War 431
– Boer, The.................. 431
– English Civil Wars 431
– Napoleonic................. 431
– Spanish Civil War.......... 431
– Vietnam 431
– World War I............... 431
– World War II.............. 432
Wargames 432
Weird and Wonderful 432
Welsh Interest............... 432
Whaling 432
Whisky...................... 432
Windmills and Watermills .. 432
Wine........................ 432
Witchcraft 432
Women...................... 432
Woodwork................... 432

Yoga......................... 433

Zoology 433

INTRODUCTION

Eighteen months ago we made a decision to migrate the database to a web site, which would not only provide an innovative BookSearch service, but one where dealers could update their business details on line – a quicker and more cost effective method for all concerned. The site also allows for constant updating as their details change, but to do this, dealers needed access to the Internet. In the last six years the number of dealers registering an e-mail address in Sheppard's has grown from a mere handful to over 2,000. It was reasonable for us to assume that dealers were making good use of this new method of communication. Therefore, following this logic, we assumed that dealers would regularly visit their page and update or amend their details. Thus, it would reduce the time taken to publish.

However, to our surprise and frustration we found that our messages, alerting dealers to go to their page, were apparently often ignored. Those dealers whose e-mail addresses we hold (and which are still correct) and have not yet heard from us, can be assured that we have e-mailed them on at least six occasions during the last seven months. And we know, because we have carried out special checks, that these have been sent out correctly. At one extreme, some dealers apparently do not visit their e-mail post box for months at a time, while others, those making regular and frequent use of the Internet have also failed to read our e-mails. There may be a good reason for the latter, many of whom suffer numerous and unsolicited e-mails, have installed one of the many anti 'spam' programmes currently available. These will block our messages if not permitted by the user but a few dealers admitted to deleting our e-mails! We ask dealers to look out for, and respond to, any e-mail from booksearch@sheppardsdirectories.com.

Although we have now provided this new service, our policy remains the same no response from a dealer means that we will not publish their full details and for this year only, where we have not had a reply, we publish only their name and address. They may well be trading, or they may not, and for users of this year's directory 'caveat emptor' will apply.

In almost every recent edition, we have specified a limit to the number of specialities stocked. If a dealer has a very small stock (less than 2,000 titles), the limit was five classifications and for those with a very large stock (more than 20,000 titles) we allowed twenty-five classifications. This made sense for a number of reasons, primarily users of the directory knew the subjects nominated were the dealers' major stocks, and we kept control of the size of the directory.

But by registering themselves on the web site, many dealers have taken advantage of the additional classifications as they will attract enquiries and orders through Sheppard's Booksearch. That is to be expected and we encourage this. However, in exporting this data to be typeset, there are clearly going to be too many headings many dealers have over fifty classifications and one has over 140!

We ask dealers to restrain themselves from adding every possible subject, as the logical result will be to make the directory uneconomic to produce in its present form. Had we created this directory with all these headings shown in the Geographical section the page extent would have been much greater and therefore an increase in the cover price would have been inevitable.

Users should therefore note that although all the headings registered do not appear in the Geographical Section *they are* included in the Speciality Classification Index.

Over forty-one new headings have appeared in this year's Speciality Index, including a number of sports – badminton, coursing and pig-sticking; a number of publishers – Hogarth Press, Pelican and Puffin; and countries Bermuda, Nepal and Pakistan.

Some statistics for the year are blurred by the paucity of information from dealers but overall there are 2,347 entries, 74 less than appeared in the last edition. However, other comparative figures for this year are not reliable other than the total number linked to the Internet which is 2,163. We will be refining the database during the next few months so that we can supply in the next edition a wider range of accurate statistics and therefore a more comprehensive picture of the trade.

The Sheppard's BookSearch web site is now live and working well. We remind dealers that to receive enquiries of books wanted or for sale, all they have to do is to register their details on the site and to reply through their page rather than by replying to the e-mail alerts.

To send searches and offers requires a subscription and details have been posted to our domestic web site (www.sheppardsdirectories.co.uk) but this is not to be confused with the site for Booksearch (www.sheppardsdirectories.com). Dealers who subscribe to BookSearch can also register a book theft free of charge a change to our initial marketing announcements

Sheppard's Booksearch is not just another database of titles that can be searched, it is a business to business link between the dealer searching and all dealers in that subject of the book being sought. It is pro-active as request alerts are mailed out. Thus, the service compliments all search engines (such as abebooks.com and biblion.com) as they rely on dealers uploading titles for matching against searches. *If you cannot find that title on these and other search engines then use Sheppard's Booksearch.*

From the orders and constant calls we have received in the last few months, we know that this directory is relied upon by a very large proportion of the trade so if we are to provide a comprehensive directory, we would hope that every dealer will keep in mind to maintain their details and for those not on the Internet, to keep us posted.

Richard Joseph
October 2003

Sheppard's Booksearch

A New Internet service

Linking booksellers to bookdealers
Linking bookdealers to bookdealers

Booksearch
A business-to-business Internet link enabling booksellers to send their customers' requirements selected by subject to relevant bookdealers. The service will allow bookdealers to send offers and searches by subject. The service will use Sheppard's unique library of e-mail addresses.

Book Theft
Dealers are now able to register the theft of any title - and Book Theft Alert will broadcast an alert to all others dealers registered with Sheppard's. The same data will appear on the Book Theft database - available to dealers 24/7. Dealers can protect their identity and upload digital images to aid identification.
Visit: www.sheppardsdirectories.com

For further details contact the Richard Joseph Publishers on rjoe01@aol.com

ABBREVIATIONS USED IN DESCRIBING BOOKS

Some booksellers and buyers use highly individualistic systems of abbreviations. The following are sufficiently well known to be generally used, but all other words should be written in full, and the whole typed if possible. Condition is described by the following scale:– Mint – Fine – Very good – Good – Fair – Poor.

A.D.	Autograph document	Lea.	Leather
A.D.s.	Autograph document, signed	Ll.	Levant Morocco
A.D.*	Autograph document with seal	Ll.	Leaves
A.e.g.	All edges gilt	L.P.	Large paper
A.L.s.	Autograph letter, signed	M.	Mint
a.v.	Authorized version	Mco., mor	Morocco
B.A.R.	Book Auction Records	M.e.	Marbled edges
Bd.	Bound	M.S.(S.)	Manuscripts
Bdg.	Binding	N.d.	No date
Bds.	Boards	n.ed.	new edition
B.L.	Black letter	n.p.	no place (of publication)
C., ca.	Circa (approximately)	Ob., obl.	Oblong
C. & p.	Collated and perfect	Oct.	Octavo
Cat.	Catalogue	O.p.	Out of print
Cent.	Century	P.	Page
Cf.	Calf	P.f.	Post free
C.I.F.	Cost, insurance and freight	Pict.	Pictorial
Cl.	Cloth	Pl(s).	Plate(s)
Col(d).	Colour(ed)	Port.	Portrait
C.O.D.	Cash on delivery	P.P.	Printed privately
Cont.	Contemporary	Pp.	Pages
C.O.R.	Cash on receipt	Prelims.	Preliminary pages
Cr. 8vo.	Crown octavo	Pseud.	Pseudonym(ous)
d.e.	Deckle edges	Ptd.	Printed
Dec.	Decorated	q.v.	Quod Vide (which see)
D-j., d-w.	Dust jacket, dust wrapper	Qto.	Quarto
E.D.L.	Edition de luxe	Rev.	Revised
Edn.	Edition	Rom.	Roman letter
Endp., e.p.	Endpaper(s)	S.L.	Sine loco (without place of publication)
Eng., engr.	Engraved, engraving		
Ex-lib.	Ex-library	Sgd.	Signed
Facs.	Facsimile	Sig.	Signature
Fcp.	Foolscap	S.N.	Sine nomine (without name of printer)
F.	Fine		
F.,ff.	Folio, folios	Spr.	Sprinkled
Fo., fol.	Folio (book size)	T.e.g.	Top edge gilt
F.O.B.	Free on board	Thk.	Thick
Fp., front.	Frontispiece	T.L.s.	Typed letter, signed
Free	Post Free	T.p.	Title page
G.	Good	T.S.	Typescript
G., gt.	Gilt edges	Unbd.	Unbound
G.L.	Gothic letter	Uncut	Uncut (pages not trimmed)
Hf. bd.	Half bound	Und.	Undated
Illum.	Illuminated	V.d.	Various dates
Ill(s).	Illustrated, illustrations	V.g..	Very good
Imp.	Imperial	Vol,	Volume
Impft.	Imperfect	W.a.f.	With all faults
Inscr.	Inscribed, inscription	Wraps.	Wrappers
Ital.	Italic letter		

SIZES OF BOOKS

These are only approximate, as trimming varies and all sizes ignore the overlap of a book case.

	Octavo (8vo)		Quarto (4to)	
	Inches	*Centimetres*	*Inches*	*Centimetres*
FOOLSCAP	$6^{3}/_{4}$ x $4^{1}/_{4}$	17.1 x 10.8	$8^{1}/_{2}$ x $6^{3}/_{4}$	21.5 x 17.1
CROWN	$7^{1}/_{2}$ x 5	19.0 x 12.7	10 x $7^{1}/_{2}$	25.4 x 19.0
LARGE POST	$8^{1}/_{4}$ x $5^{1}/_{4}$	20.9 x 13.3	$10^{1}/_{2}$ x $8^{1}/_{4}$	26.6 x 20.9
DEMY	$8^{3}/_{8}$ x $5^{5}/_{8}$	22.3 x 14.2	$11^{1}/_{4}$ x $8^{3}/_{4}$	28.5 x 22.2
MEDIUM	9 x $5^{3}/_{4}$	22.8 x 14.6	$11^{1}/_{2}$ x 9	29.2 x 22.8
ROYAL	10 x $6^{1}/_{4}$	25.4 x 15.8	$12^{1}/_{2}$ x 10	31.7 x 25.4
SUPER ROYAL	$10^{1}/_{4}$ x $6^{3}/_{4}$	26.0 x 17.5	$13^{3}/_{4}$ x $10^{1}/_{4}$	34.9 x 26.0
IMPERIAL	11 x $7^{1}/_{2}$	27.9 x 19.0	15 x 11	38.0 x 27.9
FOOLSCAP FOLIO			$13^{1}/_{2}$ x $8^{1}/_{2}$	34.2 x 21.5
METRIC A5	$8^{1}/_{4}$ x $5^{7}/_{8}$	21.0 x 14.8		
A4	$11^{3}/_{4}$ x $8^{1}/_{4}$	29.7 x 21.0		
'A' FORMAT PAPERBACK		17.8 X 11.1		
'B' FORMAT PAPERBACK		19.8 X 12.9		

BRITISH PAPER SIZES (untrimmed)

Sizes of Printing Papers

	Inches	*Centimetres*
Foolscap	17 x $13^{1}/_{2}$	43.2 x 34.3
Double Foolscap	27 x 17	68.6 x 43.2
Crown	20 x 15	50.8 x 38.1
Double Crown	30 x 20	76.2 x 50.8
Quad Crown	40 x 30	101.6 x 76.2
Double Quad Crown	60 x 40	152.4 x 101.6
Post	$19^{1}/_{4}$ x $15^{1}/_{2}$	48.9 x 39.4
Double Post	$31^{1}/_{2}$ x $19^{1}/_{2}$	80.0 x 49.5
Double Large Post	33 x 21	83.8 x 53.3
Sheet and $^{1}/_{2}$ Post	$23^{1}/_{2}$ x $19^{1}/_{2}$	59.7 x 49.5
Demy	$22^{1}/_{2}$ x $17^{1}/_{2}$	57.2 x 44.5
Double Demy	35 x $22^{1}/_{2}$	88.9 x 57.2
Quad Demy	45 x 35	114.3 x 88.9
Music Demy	20 x $15^{1}/_{2}$	50.8 x 39.4
Medium	23 x 18	58.4 x 45.7
Royal	25 x 20	63.5 x 50.8
Super Royal	$27^{1}/_{2}$ x $20^{1}/_{2}$	69.9 x 52.1
Elephant	28 x 23	71.1 x 58.4
Imperial	30 x 22	76.2 x 55.9

Available from Richard Joseph Publishers Ltd
Sheppard's Book Dealers in NORTH AMERICA

15th Edition   (Royal H/b plus CD-ROM)   £30.00 560pp

METRIC CONVERSIONS

SIZES				WEIGHTS	
inches	m.m.	inches	m.m.	lbs.	kgs.
1/4	6	7 3/4	197	1	0.45
1/2	13	8	203	2	0.91
3/4	19	8 1/4	210	3	1.36
1	25	8 1/2	216	4	1.81
1 1/4	32	8 3/4	222	5	2.27
1 1/2	38	9	229	6	2.72
1 3/4	44	9 1/4	235	7	3.18
2	51	9 1/2	241	8	3.63
2 1/4	57	9 3/4	248	9	4.08
2 1/2	64	10	254	10	4.54
2 3/4	70	10 1/4	260	11	4.99
3	76	10 1/2	267	12	5.44
3 1/4	83	10 3/4	273	13	5.90
3 1/2	89	11	279	14	6.35
3 3/4	95	11 1/4	286	15	6.80
4	102	11 1/2	292	16	7.26
4 1/4	108	11 3/4	298	17	7.71
4 1/2	114	12	305	18	8.16
4 3/4	121	12 1/4	311	19	8.62
5	127	12 1/2	318	20	9.07
5 1/4	133	12 3/4	324	21	9.53
5 1/2	140	13	330	22	9.98
5 3/4	146	13 1/4	337	23	10.43
6	152	13 1/2	343	24	10.89
6 1/4	159	13 3/4	349	25	11.34
6 1/2	165	14	356	26	11.79
6 3/4	171	14 1/4	362	27	12.25
7	178	14 1/2	368	28	12.70
7 1/4	184	14 3/4	375	56	25.40
7 1/2	191	15	381	112	50.80

To convert inches to millimetres multiply by 25.4. Millimetres to inches may be found by multiplying by .0394.

To convert pounds to kilogrammes multiply by .4536. Kilogrammes to pounds may be found by multiplying by 2.205.

Available soon from Richard Joseph Publishers Ltd
Sheppard's Book Dealers in EUROPE
11th Edition (Royal H/b)   £27.00

THE BRITISH BOOK TRADE

NEW BOOKS

In the United Kingdom, marketing of new books is well organised and controlled by individual publishers. However, the British Book Trade has two highly organised trade associations, The Publishers Association and The Booksellers Association which represent a vast majority of their respective parts of the trade.

The Booksellers Association publishes an annual directory of members, listing 3,300 members in the current edition. This is an essential reference source used by all publishers. In addition, the Booksellers Association publishes an annual directory of book publishers, distributors and wholesalers.

The directory of B.A. Members includes not only general booksellers, but businesses that concentrate on specific subjects. Although, in fact, it confers no right to buy books at trade terms, entry in this directory confirms to publishers that they are eligible for trade terms.

Bibliographic information is supplied to the book trade through Nielson Book Data Ltd. Publishers supply information on the titles they have published and this is disseminated to booksellers. Users of this directory will note the growing importance of this information in relation to the secondhand book trade.

THE BOOKSELLERS ASSOCIATION OF THE UNITED KINGDOM AND IRELAND LIMITED, 272 Vauxhall Bridge Road, London SW1V 1BA. Tel: (020) 7802 0802. Fax: (020) 7802 0803. E-Mail: mail@booksellers.org.uk. Web Site: www.booksellers.org.uk. Est: 1895 as the Associated Booksellers of Great Britain and Ireland and changed to its present name in 1999. Chief Executive: Tim Godfray. The Association's aims are: to provide services to help members increase book sales and develop the market for new books; to assist members to reduce costs; to improve distribution between publishers, booksellers and consumers; to represent booksellers' interests; and to provide a forum for members to discuss matters of common interest. It is not concerned with the secondhand or antiquarian trade: membership is open to all those engaged in the sale of new books, some of whom also sell secondhand and antiquarian books. It has about 3,300 members, and there are fifteen regional branches in which members hold meetings. The Association is governed by an Annual Conference and a Council which meets four times a year, delegating much work to specialist committees and encouraging members to join groups concerned with academic bookselling, Christian bookselling, children's bookselling etc. Book Tokens, batch.co.uk - an electronic clearing house for the payment of accounts, are some of the services provided for members. The Association is linked with similar bodies overseas.

THE PUBLISHERS ASSOCIATION, 29B Montague Street, London WC1B 5BH. Tel: (020) 7691 9191. Fax: 7691 9199. E-Mail: mail@publishers.org.uk. Est: 1896. President: John Clement. Chief Executive: Ronnie Williams. Including the Trade Publishers Council, International Division (BDCI), the Educational Publishers Council (School Books division), the Council of Academic and Professional Publishers and the Electronic Publishers Forum. The Association represents the interests of UK publishers of books, electronic publications and journals to governments, other bodies in the trade and the public at large. It seeks to promote the sales of British books by all suitable means, and provides members with a wide range of services and help on publishing problems and opportunities.

SECONDHAND AND ANTIQUARIAN BOOKS

Anyone who is so minded can enter this branch of the trade without any formality at all and, indeed, book lovers and collectors, buying items for their own libraries and selling duplicate or unwanted copies, have sometimes, almost unwittingly, drifted into a habit of rather casual regular dealing. This sounds easy and pleasant but, to enter seriously into business and make a profit in any way commensurate with the work involved, a great deal of expert knowledge is required.

Of course, many dealers have large and handsome premises, but most retail shops are still situated in the less expensive districts of their towns. Retail shops can be found almost everywhere but there are many more businesses run from private premises, where the stock, often including rare and much sought-after items, is stored in a spare room, or sold from stockrooms where the trade and general public are admitted only by appointment. In addition to these sales outlets, there are numerous book fairs of varying size around the country. While most dealers in secondhand and antiquarian books will try to obtain for a customer any required item which they do not have in stock, many specialists will now refer requests outside their speciality to other dealers. Perhaps a word of advice may be given here: if a book is required, ask for it from as many dealers as possible, but make it clear whether you wish the bookdealer to advertise for it, and ask only one to do this. If a book-buyer goes from dealer to dealer asking to see if they can get a copy of some book for him, the probability is that six advertisements for it will appear in the next week's trade journal; the law of supply and demand will begin to operate, and the man who has a copy will feel that he has put too low a price on a book that is so eagerly sought, and will increase it accordingly.

Requests are still dealt with through an elaborate system of reporting offers and requirements in trade journals such as the *Bookdealer*, though the bookdealers have embraced the Internet as a platform for searches and offers, so much so, that the secondhand book trade is one now one of the largest users. There are several international search engines devoted to dealers' stocks but few dealers have the time to upload all their titles. Nevertheless, the Internet has become a very useful tool to search for titles. Those seeking information about this aspect will find the new service *Sheppard's Booksearch* very useful.

Booksellers whose principal business is in new books must, nearly always, maintain a general stock. There are a few in large towns that do not, but, generally speaking, if anyone requires any recently published book, he goes to the nearest bookshop and it can be obtained as easily from there as from anywhere else; if it is not in stock it will come from the publishers in a few days at a known cost.

A distinctive feature of the secondhand book trade, however, is its high degree of specialisation. Almost every dealer has a particular interest, and some will be found who deal only in books on one subject, or indeed in the works of one author or group of authors. If one requires a secondhand or antiquarian book he should go or write directly to the specialist. This directory is intended to provide a handy guide that will enable the booklover to do this with the minimum of trouble.

There are two national trade associations for antiquarian book dealers:

THE ANTIQUARIAN BOOKSELLERS' ASSOCIATION, Sackville House, 40 Piccadilly, London W1J 0DR. Tel: (020) 7439-3118. Fax: 7439-3119. E-Mail: admin@aba.org.uk. Web Site: www.ABAinternational.com. Est: 1906. President: Adrian Harrington. Vice President: Jonathan Potter. Treasurer: Paul Minet. Administrators: John Critchley, Philippa Gibson, Marianne Harwood and Andrea Brown. The Antiquarian Booksellers' Association includes the leading dealers in antiquarian, fine and scarce secondhand books throughout Great Britain as well as in some other countries. It is the founding member of the twenty similar associations, scattered throughout Europe, the Americas, and the Far East which together form the International League of Antiquarian Booksellers.

The Association seeks to provide a comprehensive service to its members. It organises the prestigious and renowned Antiquarian Book Fair each June at Olympia, London and a more broadly-based Book Fair at Chelsea Town Hall every autumn. Branch fairs are also held in Edinburgh and Bath. All members receive an informative newsletter each month and there is a fine reference library ready to answer their bibliographical queries. Their interests are further looked after by representatives sitting on various government bodies and dealing with such subjects as the export of manuscripts, the future of the British Library, the National Book League, the monitoring of V.A.T. and customs regulations both here and in the Common Market. The Association organises, through the year, a series of events – sporting, social, and educational – aimed at promoting friendship and understanding among colleagues at both national and international levels. There is a Benevolent Fund upon which members may call in times of financial difficulty. Members may also benefit from advantageous rates on credit card processing, postal and delivery services and insurance negotiated on their behalf by the Association.

There are various ways in which the Association looks after the interest of the general public. By requiring of all its members a good experience of the trade, and high professional standards and ethics, it ensures that the public may approach with confidence any dealer displaying the A.B.A. badge. In rare cases of difficulty or dispute, the Association stands ready to arbitrate between dealer and client.

The public, especially institutions and public libraries, are further served by a sophisticated security system founded and developed by the Association and now copied throughout the world. It has already accounted for the apprehension of an impressive list of book-thieves and for the recovery and restoration to their rightful owners of many hundreds of stolen books.

From within its ranks, the Antiquarian Booksellers' Association can produce experts on most aspects of bibliography and book-collecting, and their collective expertise is available to the general public through the Association's office. A list of Members is published annually and is available on request from the Administrators.

PROVINCIAL BOOKSELLERS' FAIRS ASSOCIATION, The Old Coach House, 16 Melbourn Street, Royston, Hertfordshire SG8 7BZ. Tel: (01763) 248400. Fax: 248921. Fairs information line: 249212. E-Mail: info@pbfa.org. URL: www.pbfa.org. Est: 1974. Chairman: John Bonham. Vice-Chairman: Alex Alec Smith. Honorary Secretary: Tony Judd. Honorary Treasurer: Greg Way. Honorary Membership Secretary: Gill Tiffin. Administrator: Gina Dolan. Over 730 members.

The PBFA is the largest association of antiquarian and secondhand booksellers in Great Britain. With over 700 members it is also the largest in the world. It is non-profit making and co-operatively managed by its members through national and regional committees. The full-time administrative headquarters are in Royston.

The Association organises book fairs throughout the country – 140 in all – each year. Central to this programme are the monthly fairs held at the Hotel Russell in London and the international fairs held each June, at the Hotel Russell and Commonwealth Institute.

Support for members and their dependents is available at times of distress through the Association's own charity, the Richard Condon Memorial Fund. The size of the membership allows the PBFA to negotiate advantageous rates for credit card processing, postal services, insurance and bulk purchasing.

The PBFA caters for a wide range of book collecting interests and aims to promote a broader interest in antiquarian and secondhand books. The PBFA provides safeguards for the public buying from its members and is committed to maintaining the highest trading standards. In addition The Alice Brett Memorial Trust organises lectures and seminars of an educational nature on all aspects of books and the book trade for both members and the general public.

A monthly newsletter is published for members and an annual Directory of Members *(£3.00 inc. p&p)* and a nationwide calendar of book fairs *(free)* is available from the Royston office.

There is also an antiquarian and secondhand book-trade association for Wales:

WELSH BOOKSELLERS ASSOCIATION, c/o 44 Lion Street, Hay-on-Wye, Herefordshire HR3 5AA. Tel: (01497) 820322. Fax: 821150. Est: 1987. Chairman: Richard Booth. Secretary & Treasurer: Anna Cooper. The Association aims to encourage the development of antiquarian and secondhand bookselling in Wales. Books, maps, prints, manuscripts and ephemera all come within the scope of the Association. An annual leaflet giving details of each member is available from the Secretary, or from any member. Currently 29 members.

PRIVATE LIBRARIES ASSOCIATION, Ravelston, South View Road, Pinner, Middlesex HA5 3YD. Est: 1956. The Private Libraries Association is an international society of book collectors with about 650 private members (about one quarter of them in America) and about 150 institutional members. The Association publishes a quarterly journal (*The Private Library*, which contains articles, notes and other items), an annual checklist of Private Press Books, a quarterly *Newsletter and Exchange List*, a *Members' List*, and other books about various aspects of book collecting. Annual subscription £25.

ANTIQUARIAN BOOKSELLERS' ASSOCIATIONS

Australia and New Zealand
AUSTRALIAN AND NEW ZEALAND ASSOCIATION OF ANTIQUARIAN BOOKSELLERS, 69 Broadway, Nedlands 6009, Western Australia. Tel: (618) 9386-6103. Fax: (618) 9386-8211. E-mail: anzaab@iinet.net.au. Internet: www.anzaab.com.au/~anzaab. Est 1977. President: Robert Muir. Vice-Presidents: Leo Berkelouw and Anne McCormick. Secretary: Honka McGill. Treasurer: John Sainsbury. 62 members.

Austria
VERBAND DER ANTIQUARE ÖSTERREICHS, Gruënangergasse 4, A-1010 Wien, Austria. Tel: (01) 512 15 35. Fax: (01) 512 84 82. E-mail: sekretariat@hvb.at. Internet: http://www.buecher.at.

Belgium
CHAMBRE PROFESSIONNELLE BELGE DE LA LIBRAIRIE ANCIENNE ET MODERNE (C.L.A.M.). BELGISCHE BEROEPSKAMER VAN ANTIQUAREN (B.B.A.), Schildersstraat 2, B-2000 Antwerpen, Belgium. Tel: (03) 216 41 90. Fax: (03) 238 94 08. E-Mail: jan.ceuleers@pi.be. Est: 1946. President: Erick Speeckaert. Vice President: Johan Devroe. Treasurer: Wim De Goeij. Secretary: Jan Ceuleers. 56 members.

Brazil
ASSOCIAÇÃO BRASILEIRA DE LIVERIROS ANTIQUÁRIOS, Rua Santos Dumont 677 25625-090 Centro Petrópolis, Brazil. Tel: (242) 42 03 76. Fax: (242) 31 16 95. Est: 1961. President: Mrs Ana Maria Bocayuva de Miranda Jordão. E-mail: sebofino@uol.com.br. 5 members.

Canada
ANTIQUARIAN BOOKSELLERS' ASSOCIATION OF CANADA, (A.B.A.C). 2nd Floor, 489 Queen Street West, Toronto, M5V 2B4. President: Steven Temple. E-mail: temple@istar.ca. 68 members.

Czech Republic
SVAZ ANTIKVÁRU CR, Karlova 2, 110 00 Praha 1, Czech Republic. Tel: & Fax: (02) 22 22 02 86, 22 22 02 88. E-mail: info@meissner.cz.

Denmark
DEN DANSKE ANTIKVARBOGHANDLERFORENING, P.O. Box 2028, DK-1012 Copenhagen K, Denmark. E-mail: antikvar@vip.cybercity.dk. Internet: www.antikvar.dk. Est: 1920. President: Poul Jan Poulsen. 35 members.

PROVINCIAL BY NAME

The PBFA has been running quality book fairs for more than quarter of a century. From our first event, held in London in 1972, and intended as a shop window for provincial book dealers (hence the name), to our current programme of fairs all round the country we offer the book collecting public and the secondhand book trade an unparalleled range of events to suit every taste and every pocket - large fairs, small fairs, in the North and in the South; specialist fairs, and general fairs with books on all subjects at prices ranging from £5 to £5,000. A PBFA book fair, large or small, stands out by its quality - quality of presentation, quality of organisation and quality of items offered.

Our fairs in Le Méridien Russell have a well-deserved reputation as **the** place to buy books in London, but each area of the United Kingdom now boasts its own regular major event; from Aberdeeen through Edinburgh, York, Harrogate, Cambridge, Oxford and Bath.

Visit out web site www.pbfa.org to see our full programme of quality fairslists of exhibitors, detailed information and maps for all fairs Our published calendar is also available post free from our HQ address below.

All PBFA members are established bookdealers who abide by a code of practice. Their trading details are readily accessible in the Directory of Members available at £3.00 (p + p extra) and through our online directory.

The PBFA relies on volunteers to run its affairs, be it on committees, managing a fair, or helping out with putting up posters or clearing up afterwards. We could not function without these hardworking members and however large we grow, we will retain our founding principles of working co-operatively to sell quality books at quality events.

WORLDWIDE BY REPUTATION

For further information on our renowned book fairs or how to join the PBFA contact:
Gina Dolan, PBFA, The Old Coach House, 16 Melbourn St, Royston, Herts, SG8 7BZ.
Tel: 01763 248400, Fax: 01762 248921,
email: info@pbfa.org or visit our web site at www.pbfa.org

ANTIQUARIAN BOOKSELLERS' ASSOCIATIONS

Finland
SUOMEN ANTIKVARIAATTIYDISTYS RY. (Finska Antikvariatföreningen rf.), P.O. Box 144, FIN–00121 Helsinki, Finland. Tel: (09) 628 004. Est: 1941. President: Mr Timo Surojegin. E-mail: timo.surojegin@pp.inet.fi.

France
SYNDICAT NATIONAL DE LA LIBRAIRIE ANCIENNE ET MODERNE, 4 rue Gît-le-Cœur, F-75006 Paris, France. Tel: (01) 43 29 46 38. Fax: (01) 43 25 41 63. E-mail: slam@worldnet.fr. Internet: www.slam-livre.fr. Est: 1914. President: Mr Alain Marchiset. 220 members.

Germany
VERBAND DEUTSCHER ANTIQUARE e.V., P.O. Box 10 10 20, D-50450 Köln, Kreuzgasse 2-4, D-50667, Köln, Germany. Tel: (0221) 92 54 82 62. Fax: (0221) 92 54 82 82. E-mail: buch@antiquare.de. Internet: www.antiquare.de. Est: 1949. President: Mr Ulrich Hobbeling. Vice-President: Götz Kocher-Benzing. Treasurer: Sabine Keune. 278 members.

Italy
ASSOCIAZIONE LIBRAI ANTIQUARI D'ITALIA, via Jacopo Nardi 6, I-50132 Firenze, Italy. Tel: & Fax: (055) 24 32 53. E-mail: alai@dada.it. Internet: www.dada.it/alai. Est: 1947. President: Francesco Chellini. Vice President: Umberto Pregliasco. Treasurer: Piero Crini. 106 members.

Japan
THE ANTIQUARIAN BOOKSELLERS' ASSOCIATION OF JAPAN (ABAJ), 29 San-ei-cho, Shinjuku-ku, Tokyo 160, Japan. Tel: (03) 3357-1411. Fax: (03) 3351-5855. Est: 1963. President: Mr Noriaki Abe. E-mail: subun@ja2.so-net.ne.jp. 31 members.

Korea
ANTIQUARIAN BOOKSELLERS' ASSOCIATION OF KOREA (A.B.A.K.), 33, Gwan-Hoon-Dong, Chongro-Ku, 110-300 Seoul, Korea. Tel: & Fax: (02) 735 2772. President: Mr Jong-So Lee. 31 members.

Netherlands
NEDERLANDSCHE VEREENIGING VAN ANTIQUAREN, Noorderhaven 25, 9712 VG Groningen, Netherlands. Tel: (050) 318 9725. Fax: (050) 318 9321. Est: 1935. President: Mr Andre Swertz. E-mail: swertz@xs4all.nl. 76 members.

Norway
NORSK ANTIKVARBOKHANDLERFORENING, Anders Guldhaug, Postboks 3167, Elisenberg, 0208 Oslo, Norway. Tel: (47) 22 44 51 40. Internet: www.antikvariat.no. President: Anders Guldhaug. 21 members.

Spain
ADSCRIPTO IBERICA LIBRARIAE ANTIQUARIORUM (A.I.L.A.), San Miguel 12, E-07002 Palma de Mallorca, Spain. Tel: (971) 72 13 55. Fax: (971) 71 74 36. Internet: www.libreriaripoll.com.

ANTIQUARIAN BOOKSELLERS' ASSOCIATIONS

Sweden
SVENSKA ANTIKVARIATFÖRENINGEN, Box 22549, SE-104 22 Stockholm, Sweden. Tel: (08) 654 80 86. Fax: (08) 654 80 06. E-Mail: main@svaf.se. Internet: www.svaf.se.

Switzerland
VEREINIGUNG DER BUCHANTIQUARE UND KUPFER-STICHHÄNDLER IN DER SCHWEIZ (V.E.B.U.K.U.) / SYNDICAT DE LA LIBRARIE ANCIENNE ET DU COMMERCE DE L'ESTAMPE EN SUISSE (S.L.A.C.E.S.), Restelbergstr. 82, CH-8044 Zürich, Switzerland. Tel: (01) 350 14 41. Fax: (01) 350 14 43. E-mail: mail@fluehmann.com. Internet: www.vebuku..ch and www.slaces.ch. President: Timur Yüksel. Secretary: Dr. Adrian Flühmann. Treasurer: Gertrud Benz. 79 members.

United Kingdom
THE ANTIQUARIAN BOOKSELLERS' ASSOCIATION, Sackville House, 40 Piccadilly, London W1J 0DR. Tel: (020) 7439-3118. Fax: 7439-3119. E-Mail: admin@aba.org.uk. Web Site: www.ABAinternational.com. Est: 1906. President: Adrian Harrington. Director: John Critchley. Events Officer: Philippa Gibson. Administration: Marianne Harwood. Accounts: Andrea Brown.

PRIVATE LIBRARIES ASSOCIATION, Ravelston, South View Road, Pinner, Middlesex HA5 3YD. Est: 1956. The Private Libraries Association is an international society of book collectors with about 650 private members (about one third of them in America) and about 150 library members.

PROVINCIAL BOOKSELLERS FAIRS ASSOCIATION, The Old Coach House, 16 Melbourn Street, Royston, Hertfordshire SG8 7BZ. Tel: (01763) 248400. Fax: (01763) 248921. Fairs information line: (01763) 249212. E-Mail: info@pbfa.org. Web Site: www.pbfa.org. Est: 1974. Chairman: John Bonham. Vice-Chairman: Alex Alec Smith. Honorary Secretary: Tony Judd. Honorary Treasurer: Greg Way. Honorary Membership Secretary: Gill Tiffin. Administrator: Gina Dolan. Over 730 members.

WELSH BOOKSELLERS ASSOCIATION, c/o 44 Lion Street, Hay-on-Wye, Herefordshire HR3 5AA. Tel: (01497) 820322. Fax: 821150. E-Mail: WBA@richardbooth.demon.co.uk. Est. 1987. Chairman: Richard Booth. 29 members.

United States of America
ANTIQUARIAN BOOKSELLERS' ASSOCIATION OF AMERICA (A.B.A.A.), 20 West 44th Street, Fourth Floor, New York, N.Y. 10036-6604, U.S.A. Tel: (212) 944-8291. Fax: 944-8293. E-Mail: inquiries@abaa.org. Web Site: www.abaa.org. Est: 1949. President: Ken Lopez. Secretary: John Crichton. Treasurer: Donald A. Heald. Over 475 members.

The badge of the
INTERNATIONAL LEAGUE OF ANTIQUARIAN BOOKSELLERS (I.L.A.B.) to which most national associations belong. President: Kay Craddock, The Assembly Hall Building, 156 Collins St. Melbourne, VIC 3000 Australia. E-mail: kcraddoc@anzaab.com.au. Vice–President: Robert D. Fleck, 310 Delaware Street, Newcastle, DE 19720 USA. E-mail: oakknoll@oakknoll.com. Treasurer: Poul Jan Poulsen, P.O. Box 2028, DK-1012 Copenhagen K, Denmark. E-mail: p.j.p@mail.tele.dk. Secretary: Keith R. Fletcher, Wynches Barn, Much Hadham, Herts SG10 6BA. UK. E-mail: ilabsec@hmfletcher.co.uk.

PERIODICALS

Literary Magazines and Book Trade Papers

Please note that magazine prices and subscriptions are given as a guide only, and are liable to change. Those marked * we believe to be trading but have not received updated information.

ABR (Antiquarian Book Review). Magazine containing articles, book reviews, auction reports and listings, web directory, news and other relative information. Est: 1974. Subscription: £45 (U.K.), £55 (Europe), £65 (Rest of the World). Antiquarian Book Review, P.O. Box 97, High Wycombe, Buckinghamshire HP14 4GH. Tel: +44 (0)1494 562266. Fax: +44 (0)1494 565833.

THE AFRICAN BOOK PUBLISHING RECORD (ABPR). Covers new and forthcoming African publications, as well as publishing articles & news. Est: 1975. Quarterly. Subscription: EURO 328.00 (price for 2003). Editor: Cécile Lomer. Published by: K.G. Saur Verlag GmbH, Ortlerstrasse 8, 81373 Muenchen, Germany; Postfach 70 16 20, 81316 Muenchen, Germany. Tel: +49-89-76902-0; Fax: +49-89-76902-150; E-mail: info@saur.de. Subscription enquiries to K.G. Saur Verlag.

ALMANACCO DEL BIBLIOFILO. Yearly. Published at: Edizioni Rovello di Mario Scognamiglio, P.za Castello, 11, 20121 Milano, Italy. Tel: (02) 86464661 or 866532. Fax: 72022884. E-mail: edizovello@libero.it

ANTIQUES FAIRS AND CENTRES GUIDE. Six monthly. £1.50 per copy plus 50p p&p. (5 year subscription only £16.00 - as 4 year subscription). Published by: H.P. Publishing, 2, Hampton Court Road, Harborne, Birmingham B17 9AE. Tel: (0121) 681-8000 (Ad Sales); -8001 (Accounts); -8002 (Editorial). Subscriptions: Tel: (01562) 701001; Fax: (0121) 681-8005. E-Mail: subscriptions@antiquesmagazine.com. Web Site: www.antiquesfairsguide.com.

ANTIQUES MAGAZINE. Weekly or fortnightly. Subscription. £52.00 – 45 issues, plus 2 Antiques Fairs & Centres Guide (U.K.). Fortnightly £28.00 (U.K.); please call for overseas rates. Published by: H.P. Publishing, 2, Hampton Court Road, Harborne, Birmingham B17 9AE. Tel: (0121) 681-8000 (Ad Sales); -8001 (Accounts); -8002 (Editorial). Subscriptions: Tel: (01562) 701001; Fax: (0121) 681-8005. E-Mail: subscriptions@antiques magazine.com. Web Site: www.antiquesmagazine.com.

ANTIQUES TRADE GAZETTE. Contains comprehensive weekly reports on antiquarian book sales world-wide plus auction calendar. Est: 1971. Weekly. Subscription: £76.00 (£158.00 North America and rest of world, £120.00 Europe) a year. Published by: Metropress Ltd., 115 Shaftesbury Avenue, London WC2H 8AD. Tel: (020) 7420-6601. Editor: Ivan Macquisten. Antiquarian Books Editor: Ian McKay. Tel: (01795) 890475. Fax: 890014. E-mail: ianmackay@dircon.co.uk

AUS DEM ANTIQUARIAT. German journal on Antiquarian booktrade by subscription. Published six times a year by MVB Marketing- und Verlagsservice des Buchhandels GmbH, Grosser Hirschgraben 17-21, 60311 Frankfurt am Main (Postfach 100442, 60004 Frankfurt am Main), Germany.. Tel: +49 (69) 1306 469. Fax: 1306 394. E-Mail: antiquariat@mvb-online.de. Internet: www.buch-antiquariat.de.

BOOK AND MAGAZINE COLLECTOR. Biographies and bibliographies of collectable 19th and 20th century authors and illustrators, plus lists of books for sale and wanted. Est: 1984. Monthly. Subscription: £35.50 a year (U.K.), £40.00 (Europe, Airmail), £38.00 (Europe, Surface), £54.00 (U.S.A./Canada), £56.00 (Australia). Editor: Crispin Jackson. Publisher: John Dean. Published by: Diamond Publishing Group Ltd., 43–45 St. Mary's Road, Ealing, London W5 5RQ. Tel: (020) 8579-1082. Fax: 8566-2024. Email: info@dpgmags.co.uk

THE BOOK COLLECTOR. Est: 1952. Quarterly. Subscription: £40.00 (overseas £43.00, U.S. $68.00) a year. Editor: Nicolas Barker. Published by: The Collector Ltd., 20 Maple Grove, London NW9 8QY. Tel: & Fax: (020) 8200-5004. E-mail: info@thebookcollector.co.uk.

THE BOOKDEALER. Trade weekly for secondhand and antiquarian books for sale and wanted. £52.00 a year or £26.00 for six months (incl. p. & p. within U.K.). Editor: Barry Shaw. Published by: Alacrity, Eastern Wing, Banwell Castle, Weston-super-Mare BS29 6NX. Tel: (01934) 822971. Fax: 820682. E-mail: alacrity@ dial.pipex.com.

THE BOOKSELLER. Journal of the book trade in Great Britain. Weekly. Subscription: £170.00 a year (U.K.), £185.00 (overseas, airmail extra). Editor: Nicholas Clee. Published by: VNU Entertainment Media UK Ltd., 189 Shaftesbury Avenue, London WC2H 8TJ. Tel: (020) 7420-6006. Fax: 7420-6103.

PERIODICALS

BOOKS FROM FINLAND. English-language journal presenting Finnish literature and writers. Est: 1976. Editor-in-chief: Kristina Carlson. Editors: Soila Lehtonen & Hildi Hawkins. Quarterly. Subscription: 20 euros a year [about £31 @ 64p/1e] (Finland and Scandinavia), 27 euros [about £42] all other countries). Published by: Helsinki University Library, P.O. Box 15 (Unioninkatu 36) FIN-00014 University of Helsinki, Finland. Tel: & Fax: (09) 135-7942. E-Mail: bff@helsinki.fi. Web Site: www.lib.helsinki.fi/bff.

BOOK SOURCE MAGAZINE. Published since 1985, now the only magazine covering news, reviews and information for the secondhand/antiquarian book trade in the USA. Subscription bi-monthly: $20.00 (1st class USA); $24.00 (library rate, Canada and Mexico); $48/£28.00 (overseas airmail). Editor: John C. Huckans. Published at: 2007 Syossett Drive, Cazenovia, NY 13035-9753. Tel: & Fax: (315) 655-8499. E-Mail: books@dreamscape.com. Web Site: www.booksourcemagazine.com.

BOOK WORLD. Articles, reviews, advertisements and news of the book world in general. Monthly. Subscription: £25.00 (U.K.), $50.00 (surface mail U.S.), $75.00 (air mail U.S.). Published by: Christchurch Publishers Ltd., 2 Caversham Street, Chelsea, London SW3 4AH. Tel: & Fax: (020) 7351-4995.

CONTEMPORARY REVIEW. On politics, current affairs, theology, social questions, literature and the arts. Monthly. Subscription: £47.00 a year (U.K. surface mail), $184.00 (U.S.A. and Canada, airfreight), others on application. Editor: Dr. Richard Mullen. Published by: The Contemporary Review Co. Ltd., P.O. Box 1242, Oxford, OX1 4FJ, England. Tel: & Fax: (01865) 201529. E-mail: subscriptions@contemporaryreview.co.uk. Editorial office: editorial@contemporaryreview.co.uk.

L'ESOPO. Bibliophile magazine. Quarterly. Published at: Edizioni Rovello di Mario Scognamiglio, P.za Castello, 11, 20121 Milano, Italy. Tel: (02) 86464661 or 866532. Fax: 72022884. E-mail: edizovello@libero.it

FOLIO. Produced 3-4 times a year, to members only. Editor: Kit Shepherd. Published by: The Folio Society Ltd., 44 Eagle Street, London WC1R 4SF. Tel: (020) 7400-4222.

GAZZETTINO LIBRARIO. Requests and offers antiquarian and secondhand books. Est: 1958. 4 issues a year. Subscription: L. 85,000 a year. [about £25.00] Editor: Dr. Francesco Scala. Published by: Gazzettino Librario, via Jacopo Nardi 6, 50132 Firenze, Italy. Tel: (055) 243024.*

THE LITERARY REVIEW. Covers books, arts and poetry. Est: 1978. Monthly. Subscription: £32.00 a year (U.K.), £39.00 (Europe), £39.00 (U.S.A. & Canada Airspeed), £54.00 (rest of the world Air Mail). Editor: Nancy Sladek. Published by: The Literary Review, 44 Lexington Street, London W1F 0LW. Tel: (020) 7437-9392. Fax: (020) 7734-1844.

MINIATURE BOOK NEWS. Est: 1965. Quarterly. (Now incorporated in the Miniature Book Society Newsletter – Subscription to both: $30.00 oer year, US, $35.00 Canada and $45.00 Overseas). Editor: Julian I. Edison. Published at: 8 St. Andrews Drive, St. Louis, Missouri 63124, U.S.A.

THE PRIVATE LIBRARY. Established 1957. Quarterly. Distributed free to members of the Private Libraries Association, annual subscription £25.00 ($40.00). Editors: David Chambers & Paul W. Nash. Sample copy free on request. Published by: The Private Libraries Association, Ravelston, South View Road, Pinner, Middlesex HA5 3YD.

PRIVATE PRESS BOOKS. An annual bibliography of books printed by private presses in the English speaking world. 1991 edition: 78 pp, £20.00 or $40.00 (£13.50 or $27.00 to PLA members) 1994/8 edition: 206pages, £20.00 or $34.00 (£10.00 or $17.00 to PLA members) 1999, 2000 and 2001 expected early 2003. Editor: Paul W. Nash. Published by: The Private Libraries Association, Ravelston, South View Road, Pinner, Middlesex HA5 3YD.

QUILL AND QUIRE. Keeps its readers up-to-date on Canada's exciting book publishing scene and provides the earliest and most complete look at new Canadian books, with more than 500 titles reviewed each year. In addition, the Canadian Publishers Directory, which puts the book industry at your fingertips, is delivered free bi-annually. 12 issues a year for $64.15; USA and Overseas $95CDN (includes postage). Est: 1935. Editor-In-Chief: Scott Anderson. Published at: 70 The Esplanade, Suite 210, Toronto, Ontario M5E 1R2, Canada. Tel: (416) 360-0044. Fax: 955-0794. Email: subscriptions@quillandquire.com. Web Site: www.quillandquire.com.

SCOTTISH BOOK COLLECTOR. Est: 1987. 4 issues a year. Annual Subscription: individual/institutional: £14.00/£20.00 (U.K.), £15.50/£23.00 (Europe), £16.00/£25.00 (Rest of World). Editor: Jennie Renton. Published at: 8 Lauriston Street, Edinburgh EH3 9DJ. Tel: (0131) 228-4837. Fax: 228-3904. E-mail: jennie@scotbooksmag.demon.co.uk. Web Site: www.scotbooksmag.demon.co.uk.

TRIBUNE. Books Editor: Amanda Day. Published by: Tribune Publications Ltd., 9 Arkwright Road, London NW3 6AN. Tel: (020) 7433-6410. E-mail: george@tribpub.demon.co.uk.

The Book Collector

In its fifty years of publication THE BOOK COLLECTOR has firmly established itself as the most interesting and lively current journal for collectors, bibliographers, antiquarian booksellers and custodians of rare books. Leading authorities contribute regularly on all aspects of bibliophily, from medieval manuscripts to modern first editions and each issue offers new and original insight into the world of books

*Some back numbers of issues from 1956 to 1979 are available
We hold complete volumes from 1980 to date.*

Subscription rates and detailed list and prices from:
The Book Collector
20 MAPLE GROVE, LONDON NW9 8QY
Tel/fax 020-8200 5004
E-mail: info@thebookcollector.co.uk
Website: www.thebookcollector.co.uk

CURRENT REFERENCE BOOKS

ABC FOR BOOK COLLECTORS. By John Carter & new introduction by Nicolas Barker. 7th Edition. 224pp £12.95. Published by: Werner Shaw Ltd., Suite F22, Park Hall Estate, 40 Martell Road, West Dulwich, London SE21 8EN. Tel: & Fax: (020) 8761-5570. E-mail: wernershawltd@btinternet.com.

ABC OF BOOKBINDING. By Jane Greenfield. $39.95. Published by: Oak Knoll Press, 310 Delaware Street, New Castle, DE 19720, U.S.A. Tel: (302) 328-7232. Fax: 328-7274. E-Mail: oakknoll@oakknoll.com. Sales rights: Worldwide outside of UK. Available in the UK from The Plough Press.

AMERICAN BOOK PRICES CURRENT 2001. The auction season September 2000 to August 2001. $156.90. Published by: Bancroft Parkman Inc., P.O. Box 1236, Washington, CT 06793, U.S.A. Tel: (860) 868-7408. Fax: (860) 868-0080. E-Mail: abpc@snet.net. Web Site: http://www.bookpricescurrent.com.

AMERICAN BOOKS ON FOOD & DRINK. By William R. Cagle & Lisa Killron Stafford. $95.00. Published by: Oak Knoll Press, 310 Delaware Street, New Castle, DE 19720, U.S.A. Tel: (302) 328-7232. Fax: 328-7274. E-Mail: oakknoll@oakknoll.com.

AMERICAN BOOK TRADE DIRECTORY. Profiles retail and antiquarian book dealers plus book and magazine wholesalers, distributors and jobbers in the United States. 2002/2003: £231.00. Distributed in the UK by Bowker, Windsor Court, East Grinstead House, East Grinstead, West Sussex RH19 1XA. Tel: (01342) 336149. Fax: 336198/336192. E-mail: customer.servcies@bowker.co.uk. Web Site: www.bowker.co.uk.

THE ART & HISTORY OF BOOKS. By Norma Levarie. Paperback $29.95. Published by: Oak Knoll Press, 310 Delaware Street, New Castle, DE 19720, USA. Tel: (302) 328-7232. Fax: 328-7274. E-Mail: oakknoll@oakknoll.com.

THE ART OF BOOK-BINDING. By Edward Walker. $30.00. Published by: Oak Knoll Press, 310 Delaware Street, New Castle, DE 19720, U.S.A. Tel: (302) 328-7232. Fax: 328-7274. E-Mail: oakknoll@oakknoll.com.

AT HOME WITH BOOKS. How book lovers live with and care for their libraries. By: Estelle Ellis, Caroline Seebohm, Christopher Simon Sykes. 29.95. Published by: Thames & Hudson, 181A High Holborn, London WC1V 7QX. Tel: (020) 7845-5000. Fax: 7845-5050.E-mail: sales@thameshudson.co.uk.

BEFORE PHOTOCOPYING: THE ART & HISTORY OF MECHANICAL COPYING 1780 - 1938. By William Streeter & Barbara Rhodes. $75.00. Published by: Oak Knoll Press, 310 Delaware Street, New Castle, DE 19720, U.S.A. Tel: (302) 328-7232. Fax: 328-7274. E-Mail: oakknoll@oakknoll.com.

A & C BLACK COLOUR BOOKS. A collector's guide and bibliography 1900–1930. Author: Colin Inman. £30.00. Published in 1990 by Werner Shaw Ltd., Suite F22, Park Hall Estate, 40 Martell Road, West Dulwich, London SE21 8EN. Tel: & Fax: (020) 8761-5570. E-mail: wernershawltd@btinternet.com.

A BLOOMSBURY ICONOGRAPHY. By Elizabeth P. Richardson. $40.00. Published by: Oak Knoll Press, 310 Delaware Street, New Castle, DE 19720, U.S.A. Tel: (302) 328-7232. Fax: 328-7274. E-Mail: oakknoll@oakknoll.com.BOOKBINDING & CONSERVATION BY HAND: A working guide. Hardback $35.00. Paperback $24.95. Published by: Oak Knoll Press, 310 Delaware Street, New Castle, DE 19720, U.S.A. Tel: (302) 328-7232. Fax: 328-7274. E-Mail: oakknoll@oakknoll.com.

BOOKDEALING FOR PROFIT. By Paul Minet. The philosophy behind the business as well as a look into the future and how the Internet is having a major effect on the trade. Hardback £10.00. Published by Richard Joseph Publishers Ltd, P.O. Box 6123, Basingstoke, Hampshire RG25 2WE. UK. Tel: (01256) 811314. Fax: (01256) 336362. E-mail: rjoe01@aol.com. Web Site: www.sheppardsdirectories.co.uk.

BRITISH NATIONAL BIBLIOGRAPHY. Records new and forthcoming publications in the UK and Ireland. Options include: print (weekly list with cumulations), CD-ROM (monthly disc, fully cumulated) and MARC (weekly data file). Published by: The British Library, National Bibliographic Service, Boston Spa, Wetherby, West Yorkshire LS23 7BQ. ENGLAND. Tel: (01937) 546585. Fax: 546586. E-mail: nbs-info@bl.uk. Web Site: www.bl.uk. Orders and subscriptions: Turpin Distribution Services Ltd., Blackhorse Road, Letchworth, Herts SG6 1HN. ENGLAND. Tel: (01462) 672555. Fax: 480947. E-mail: turpin@turpinltd.com.

Bookdealer

The premier trade weekly for the second-hand & antiquarian book trade, **Bookdealer** *is the journal your business can't afford to overlook.*

and each week access thousands of Books Wanted or For Sale. Keep up to date through the magazine's features, reviews and editorials. All this for around £1 a week.

and know your ad will be seen by dealers throughout the UK and abroad. We can incorporate your existing artwork, or create an eye-catching display from scratch — free of charge!

Visit the new Bookdealer *website*

**www.alacrity.
dial.pipex.com**

For over thirty years **Bookdealer** *has been a valued companion to the bookdealing community. Find out why. Contact us for a free specimen copy and rate card. And ask about ...*

The *effective* **stock-matching programme for your PC**
- Is part or all of your stock on a computer database?
- Are you keen to maximise sales to the British trade?

If so then **BookMatch** is tailor-made for you. For less than £2 a week your stock is matched against the thousands of titles sought by dealers through the Books Wanted columns of *Bookdealer*.

It is incredibly simple. At the press of a few keys matches are made and can be edited on-screen prior to printing out for *Bookdealer*'s regular Wednesday free mailing — or e-mailed/faxed direct to the individual advertisers.

Contact us now for a FREE trial.

Published by **ALACRITY**
Eastern Wing • Banwell Castle • Banwell • Weston-super-Mare BS29 6NX
Tel: 01934-822971/820478 • Fax 01934-820682 • e-mail: alacrity@dial.pipex.com

CURRENT REFERENCE BOOKS

LEWIS CARROLL AND THE PRESS. By Charles Lovett. $35.00. Published by: Oak Knoll Press & The British Library. Information from: Oak Knoll Press, 310 Delaware Street, New Castle, DE 19720, U.S.A. Tel: (302) 328-7232. Fax: 328-7274. E-Mail: oakknoll@oakknoll.com.

CHILDREN'S BOOKS IN ENGLAND. By F.J. Harvey Darton. $49.95. Published by: The British Library & Oak Knoll Press. Information from: Oak Knoll Press, 310 Delaware Street, New Castle, DE 19720, U.S.A. Tel: (302) 328-7232. Fax: 328-7274. E-Mail: oakknoll@oakknoll.com. Sales Rights: North & South America; elsewhere, The British Library.

W.H. DAVIES, A BIBLIOGRAPHY. By Sylvia Harlow. $78.00. Published by: Oak Knoll Press, 310 Delaware Street, New Castle, DE 19720, U.S.A. Tel: (302) 328-7232. Fax: 328-7274. E-Mail: oakknoll@oakknoll.com.

DIRECTORY OF PUBLISHING: United Kingdom, Commonwealth and Overseas. 2003 28th Ed. 512pp £75.00. ISBN: 0-8264-6178-6. Published by Continuum, The Tower Building, 11 York Road, London SE1 7NX. ENGLAND. Tel: (020) 7922-0880. Fax: 7922-0881. Orders and distribution: The Orca Book Services, Stanley House, 3 Fleets Lane, Poole, Dorset BH15 3AJ. Tel: (01202) 665432.

THE ENCYCLOPEDIA OF PAPERMAKING AND BOOKBINDING: the definitive guide to making, embellishing and repairing paper and books by Heidi Reimer-Epp and Mary Reimer. 160 pages with 200m colour illustrations. Hardback £16.95. Published by The British Library; available from Turpin Distribution Ltd., Blackhorse Road, Letchworth, Hertfordshire SG6 1HN. E-mail turpin@tuirpinltd.com

THOMAS FROGNALL DIBDIN, 1776 - 1847: A BIBLIOGRAPHY. By John Windle & Karma Pippin. $85.00. Published by: Oak Knoll Press, 310 Delaware Street, New Castle, DE 19720, U.S.A. Tel: (302) 328-7232. Fax: 328-7274. E-Mail: oakknoll@oakknoll.com.

THE DICTIONARY OF 19TH CENTURY BOOK ILLUSTRATORS. By Simon Houfe. £39.50. Published by: Antique Collectors Club, Sandy Lane, Old Martlesham, Woodbridge, Suffolk IP12 4SD. Tel: (01394) 389950. Fax: 389999.

THE DICTIONARY OF 20TH CENTURY BRITISH BOOK ILLUSTRATORS. By Alan Horne. £45.00. Published by: Antique Collectors Club, Sandy Lane, Old Martlesham, Woodbridge, Suffolk IP12 4SD. Tel: (01394) 389950. Fax: 389999.

DIRECTORY OF RARE BOOK AND SPECIAL COLLECTIONS IN THE UNITED KINGDOM AND REPUBLIC OF IRELAND. Editor: B.C. Bloomfield. 1997. £98.00. Published by: Facet Publishing, 7 Ridgmount Street, London WC1E 7AE. Tel: (020) 7255-0590. Fax: 7255-0591. E-Mail: info@facetpublishing.co.uk. Web Site: www.facetpublishing.co.uk.

ENCYCLOPEDIA OF THE BOOK. By: Geoffrey Ashall Glaister. Hardcover $75.00, Paperback $49.75. Published by Oak Knoll Press, 310 Delaware Street, New Castle, DE 19720, U.S.A. Tel: (302) 328-7232. Fax: 328-7274. E-Mail: oakknoll@oakknoll.com.

THE ENGLISH AS COLLECTORS. By Frank Hermann. $49.95. Published by: Oak Knoll Press & John Murray Ltd. Information from: Oak Knoll Press, 310 Delaware Street, New Castle, DE 19720, U.S.A. Tel: (302) 328-7232. Fax: 328-7274. E-Mail: oakknoll@oakknoll.com. Sales rights: Worldwide outside of UK. Available in the UK from The Plough Press.

FIRST EDITIONS: A GUIDE TO IDENTIFICATION. 4th edition for 2001. $60.00. Editor: Edward N. Zempel. Published by: Spoon River Press, P.O. Box 3635, Peoria, IL 61614, U.S.A. Tel: (309) 672-2665.

T.N. FOULIS: THE HISTORY AND BIBLIOGRAPHY OF AN EDINBURGH PUBLISHING HOUSE. By Ian Elfick & Paul Harris. £30.00. Published in 1998 by: Werner Shaw Ltd., Suite F22, Park Hall Estate, 40 Martell Road, West Dulwich, London SE21 8EN. Tel: & Fax: (020) 8761-5570. E-mail: wernershawltd@btinternet.com.

ERIC GILL, A BIBLIOGRAPHY. By Evan Gill. $60.00. Published by: Oak Knoll Press, 310 Delaware Street, New Castle, DE 19720, U.S.A. Tel: (302) 328-7232. Fax: 328-7274.

GREATER LONDON HISTORY AND HERITAGE HANDBOOK: the millennium guide to historical, heritage and environmental networks and publications. 1999 edition, 189pp, £20 + £2p&p. Editor: Peter Marcan. Published by: Peter Marcan Publications, P.O. Box 3158, London SE1 4RA. Tel: (020) 7357-0368.

A GUIDE TO WORLD LANGUAGE DICTIONAIRIES. Andrew Dalby. 1998. £59.95. Published by Facet Publishing, 7 Ridgmount Street, London WC1E 7AE. Tel: (020) 7255 0590. Fax: (0)20 7255 0591. E-mail: info@facetpublishing.co.uk. Web Site: www.facetpublishing.co.uk.

What are they saying?

'It's for the intelligent reader.
It's not parochial.
it doesn't offer facile price guides'

'Whether you think books are for reading, browsing, buying or selling, it's a really interesting magazine'

That's what they're saying

£14 for four issues from
jennie@essbc.demon.co.uk
or Main Point Books, 8 Lauriston Street,
Edinburgh EH3 9DJ
+44 (0)131 228 4837

Scottish Book Collector
One of the few things in life that keeps getting better

CURRENT REFERENCE BOOKS

HISTORY OF ENGLISH CRAFT BOOKBINDING TECHNIQUE. By Bernard C. Middleton. $55.00. Published by: Oak Knoll Press, 310 Delaware Street, New Castle, DE 19720, U.S.A. Tel: (302) 328-7232. Fax: 328-7274. E-Mail: oakknoll@oakknoll.com. Sales Rights: Worldwide outside of UK. Available in the UK from The British Library

ELSPETH HUXLEY, A BIBLIOGRAPHY. By Robert Cass & Michael Perkin. $78.00. Published by: Oak Knoll Press, 310 Delaware Street, New Castle, DE 19720, U.S.A. Tel: (302) 328-7232. Fax: 328-7274. E-Mail: oakknoll@oakknoll.com.

THE ILLUSTRATIONS OF W. HEATH ROBINSON: A COMMENTARY AND BIBLIOGRAPHY. By Geoffrey Beare. The bibliography which follows the long introduction to Heath Robinson's work as an illustrator, was compiled from primary sources and is the first complete and detailed listing of the artist's work in books and magazines. 168pp. £18.95. Published by: Werner Shaw Ltd., Suite F22, Park Hall Estate, 40 Martell Road, West Dulwich, London SE21 8EN. Tel: & Fax: (020) 8761-5570. E-mail: wernershawltd@btinternet.com.

INTERNATIONAL DIRECTORY OF ANTIQUARIAN BOOKSELLERS. A world list of members of organisations belonging to the International League of Antiquarian Booksellers (I.L.A.B.). Published every 2 years: 2002 edition available late in 2002: £15.00 + £2.00 p&p. Published by: I.L.A.B. Distributed in the UK by: The Antiquarian Booksellers' Association, Sackville House, 40 Piccadilly, London W1J 0DR. Tel: (020 7439-3118. Fax: (020) 7439-3119. E-mail: admin@aba.org.uk.

BIBLIOGRAPHY OF HENRY JAMES. By Leon Edel & Dan Lawrence. $80.00. Published by: Oak Knoll Press, 310 Delaware Street, New Castle, DE 19720, U.S.A. Tel: (302) 328-7232. Fax: 328-7274. E-Mail: oakknoll@oakknoll.com.

LIBRARIES AND INFORMATION SERVICES IN THE UNITED KINGDOM AND REPUBLIC OF IRELAND, 2003. £39.95. Published by: Facet Publishing, 7 Ridgmount Street, London WC1E 7AE. Tel: (020) 7255-0590. Fax: 7255-0591. E-mail: info@facetpublishing.co.uk. Web Site: www.facetpublishing.co.uk.

CILIP: the Chartered Institute of. 2002–2003. £37.50. Compilers: Kathryn Beecroft (ed.). Published by: Facet Publishing, 7 Ridgmount Street, London WC1E 7AE. Tel: (020) 7255-0590. Fax: 7255-0591. E-Mail: info@facetpublishing.co.uk. Web Site: www.facetpublishing.co.uk..

LITERARY MARKET PLACE. The directory of the book publishing industry for America and Canada. Published annually. 2003 edition. Priced £199. Distributed in U.K. by: Bowker, Windsor Court, East Grinstead House, East Grinstead, West Sussex RH19 1XA. Tel: (01342) 336179. Fax: 336192.

LOCAL STUDIES LIBRARIANSHIP: A WORLD BIBLIOGRAPHY. Editor: Diana Dixon. 2001. £39.95. Published by Facet Publishing, 7 Ridgmount Street, London WC1E 7AE. Tel: (020) 7255 0590. Fax: (020) 7255 0591. E-mail: info@facetpublishing.co.uk. Web Site: www.facetpublishing.co.uk.

MARCAN HANDBOOK OF ARTS ORGANISATIONS: A compendium of information on the activities and publications of national (U.K. & Ireland), regional and international arts & cultural organisations. New 5th edition June 2001. £35 + £3.00 p&p. First published as 'Arts Address Book' in 1982. Published by: Peter Marcan Publications, P.O. Box 3158, London SE1 4RA. Tel: (020) 7357-0368.

A MATTER OF TASTE. By William R. Cagle & Lisa Killron Stafford. $95.00. Published by: Oak Knoll Press, 310 Delaware Street, New Castle, DE 19720, U.S.A. Tel: (302) 328-7232. Fax: 328-7274. E-Mail: oakknoll@oakknoll.com.

THOMAS BIRD MOSHER: PIRATE PRINCE OF PUBLISHERS. By Philip R. Bishop. $125.00. Published by: Oak Knoll Press & The British Library. Information from: Oak Knoll Press, 310 Delaware Street, New Castle, DE 19720, U.S.A. Tel: (302) 328-7232. Fax: 328-7274. Sales Rights: Worldwide outside of UK. Available in the UK from The British Library.

NEW SCIENCE OUT OF OLD BOOKS. Studies in manuscripts and early printed books in honour of A.I. Doyle. £72.50. Edited by: Richard Beadle and A.J. Piper. Published by: Ashgate Publishing Ltd., Gower House, Croft Road, Aldershot, Hampshire GU11 3HR. Distributed by Bookpoint. Tel: (01235) 827730. Fax: 400454.

NEW WORLDS IN OLD BOOKS. By Leona Rostenberg & Madeleine Stern. $29.95. Published by: Oak Knoll Press, 310 Delaware Street, New Castle, DE 19720, U.S.A. Tel: (302) 328-7232. Fax: 328-7274. E-Mail: oakknoll@oakknoll.com.

OLD BOOKS IN THE OLD WORLD. Reminiscences of book buying abroad. By: Leona Rostenburg and Madeleine B. Stern. $22.95. Published by Oak Knoll Press, 310 Delaware Street, New Castle, DE 19720, USA. Tel: (302) 328-7232. Fax: 328-7274. E-Mail: oakknoll@oakknoll.com.

CURRENT REFERENCE BOOKS

A POCKET GUIDE TO THE IDENTIFICATION OF FIRST EDITIONS. An essential guide to identifying first editions for collectors, dealers, librarians, cataloguers and auctioneers. 6th Edition $12.95 per copy plus $1 shipping 40% discount on 5 or more copies; shipping for 5 copies is $4 by Priority Mail. International orders: single copies shipping $2.50; five copies $6 by Air/Printed Matter. Published by: The Jumping Frog, McBride/Publisher, 141 South Street, West Hartford, CT 06110, U.S.A. Tel: (860) 523-1622. Web Site: www.mcbridepublisher.com.

PRINCE OF FORGERS. By Joseph Rosenblum. $39.95. Published by: Oak Knoll Press, 310 Delaware Street, New Castle, DE 19720, U.S.A. Tel: (302) 328-7232. Fax: 328-7274.

PROVENANCE RESEARCH IN BOOK HISTORY. By David Pearson. Hardback $49.95, paperback $29.95. Published by: Oak Knoll Press & The British Library. Information from: Oak Knoll Press, 310 Delaware Street, New Castle, DE 19720, U.S.A. Tel: (302) 328-7232. Fax: 328-7274. Sales Rights: North & South America; elsewhere, The British Library.

RESTORATION OF LEATHER BINDINGS. By Bernard C. Middleton. $39.95. Published by: Oak Knoll Press & The British Library. Information from: Oak Knoll Press, 310 Delaware Street, New Castle, DE 19720, U.S.A. Tel: (302) 328-7232. Fax: 328-7274. Sales Rights: North & South America; elsewhere, The British Library.

VITA SACKVILLE-WEST, A BIBLIOGRAPHY. By Robert Crass & Ann Ravenscroft Hulme. $80.00. Published by: Oak Knoll Press, 310 Delaware Street, New Castle, DE 19720, U.S.A. Tel: (302) 328-7232. Fax: 328-7274. E-Mail: oakknoll@oakknoll.com.

SIR WALTER SCOTT: A BIBLIOGRAPHY 1796 - 1832. By William B. Todd & Ann Bowden. $95.00. Published by: Oak Knoll Press, 310 Delaware Street, New Castle, DE 19720, U.S.A. Tel: (302) 328-7232. Fax: 328-7274. E-Mail: oakknoll@oakknoll.com.

STUDIES IN THE HISTORY OF BOOKBINDING. This book consists of articles on the history of bookbinding and related subjects. Grouped under seven headings ranging from general topics such as bookbinding as a subject for study and the need to preserve the book, to more detailed descriptions of individual bindings from the fifteenth to the twentieth century. £75.00. Published by: Ashgate Publishing Ltd., Gower House, Croft Road, Aldershot, Hampshire GU11 3HR. Distributed by Bookpoint. Tel: (01235) 827730. Fax: 400454.

JULIAN SYMONS, A BIBLIOGRAPHY. By John J. Walsdorf. $85.00. Published by: Oak Knoll Press, 310 Delaware Street, New Castle, DE 19720, U.S.A. Tel: (302) 328-7232. Fax: 328-7274

THE TARTARUS PRESS GUIDE TO FIRST EDITION PRICES 2002/3. Edited by: R.B. Russell. £14.99 inc. p&p. Published by: Tartarus Press, Coverley House, Carlton-in-Coverdale, Leyburn, North Yorks DL8 4AY. Tel: & Fax: (01969) 640399. E-Mail: tartarus@pavilion.co.uk.

J.R.R. TOLKIEN, A DESCRIPTIVE BIBLIOGRAPHY. By Wayne C. Hammond. $94.00. Published by: Oak Knoll Press, 310 Delaware Street, New Castle, DE 19720, U.S.A. Tel: (302) 328-7232. Fax: 328-7274. E-Mail: oakknoll@oakknoll.com.

TASHA TUDOR: THE DIRECTION OF HER DREAMS. By William John & Priscilla T. Hare. $85.00. A definitive bibliography; collector's guide. Published by: Oak Knoll Press, 310 Delaware Street, New Castle, DE 19720, U.S.A. Tel: (302) 328-7232. Fax: 328-7274.

WOMEN BOOKBINDERS 1880-1920. By: Marianne Tidcombe. 58.00. Published by: The British Library & Oak Knoll Press, 310 Delaware Street, New Castle, DE 19720, U.S.A. Tel: (302) 328-7232. Fax: 328-7274. E-Mail: oakknoll@oakknoll.com. Sales Rights: North & South America; elsewhere, The British Library.

LEONARD WOOLF, A BIBLIOGRAPHY. By Leila Luedeking & Michael Edmonds. $78.00. Published by: Oak Knoll Press, 310 Delaware Street, New Castle, DE 19720, U.S.A. Tel: (302) 328-7232. Fax: 328-7274. E-Mail: oakknoll@oakknoll.com.

Bonhams [1793]
NEW BOND STREET

Fine Art Auctioneers

Printed Books
Atlases & Maps
Autograph Letters
Historical Manuscripts

Ten sales each season

Bonhams, 101 New Bond Street, London W1S 1SR
Telephone 020 7468 8351, Fax 020 7465 0224
books@bonhams.com
www.bonhams.com

Please let me take a little of your time...

Insurance is one of those matters we would all rather not think about - until something goes wrong!

Insurance is a complicated matter. It all seems so simple to begin with, pay your premium and sleep easily; that's all there is to it.

When things go wrong however - for example a burglary, missing parcel or even accidental damage by fire or flood - then anxious scrutiny of the policy can reveal that (a) you are under insured or (b) that the small print excludes your circumstances.

T.L. Dallas *(City)* **Ltd (formerly Dowle Associates Ltd)** are insurance brokers who have worked for the book trade for over 20 years, and arrange insurance cover for the PBFA and its members.

We are experienced in the needs of the antiquarian and secondhand bookseller and the particular requirements of the private collector - general house contents policies are rarely sufficient for substantial collections.

We can provide a bespoke package to suit *your* requirements. Allow us to guide you through the jargon and supply you with a policy that is right for your circumstances.

Please allow **T. L. Dallas** *(City)* **Ltd** to give you a no obligation quotation.

You may be pleasantly surprised at the cost of true peace of mind.

T.L. DALLAS *(City)* **Ltd**
Ibex House, 42-47 Minories
London, EC3N 1DY
Tel: 020 7816 0210
Fax: 020 7488 2421
Email: dowle@tldallas.com

Discount for PBFA members

We are not just brokers for book insurance -
and can arrange all forms of insurance cover

SUPPLIES AND SERVICES

BOOK AUCTIONEERS

ACORN AUCTIONS, P.O. Box 152, Salford, Manchester M17 1BP. Tel: (0161) 877 8818. Fax: (0161) 877 8819. Web Site: www.invaluable.co.uk/acorn. *Regular Public Auctions of books, autographs, ephemera, postcards and cigarette cards at our premises in Trafford Park, Manchester.* Specimen catalogues and vendors' terms available. Contact: George Wewiora.

BLOOMSBURY BOOK AUCTIONS, 3 and 4 Hardwick Street, London EC1R 4RY. Tel: (020) 7833-2636/ 7 or 7923-6940. Fax: 7833-3954. E-Mail: info@bloomsbury-book-auct.com. Web site: www.bloomsbury-book-auct.com. *Thirty-two sales a year of books and manuscript material: four devoted to prints, drawings, maps and photographs, and modern first editions. (See display advertisement).*

BONHAMS, 101 New Bond Street, London W1S 1SR Tel: (020) 7468-8351. Fax: 7465-0224. E-Mail: d.park@bonhams.com. View our catalogues on-line at www.bonhams.com. *At least 10 sales each season on books, maps, photographs, autographs and historical manuscripts.* Enquiries to: David Park.

CAPES DUNN & CO., 38 Charles Street, Manchester M1 7DB. Tel: (0161) 273-1911. Fax: 273-3474. *Three to four sales per year. Catalogues can be accessed on* – www.ukauctioneers.com.

FINAN & CO., The Square, Mere, Wiltshire BA12 6DJ. Tel: (01747) 861411. Fax: 861944. E-Mail: post@finanandco.co.uk. Web Site: www.finanandco.co.uk. *4 auctions annually, including specialist books, manuscripts, photographs and ephemera.* Enquireis to Julia Haigh.

GEORGE KIDNER, The Old School, The Square, Pennington, Lymington, Hampshire SO41 8GN. Tel: (01590) 670070. Fax: 675167. E-Mail: info@georgekidner.co.uk. Web Site: www.georgekidner.co.uk. *3 sales a year, 200-300 lots per sale. Catalogues on subscription - £7 a year.* Enquiries to: Andrew Reeves.

GOLDING YOUNG & CO, Old Wharf Road, Grantham, Lincolnshire NG31 7AA. Tel: (01476) 565118. Fax: (01476) 561475. E-mail: enquiries@goldingyoung.com. Web Site: www.goldingyoung.com. Contact: Colin Young. *Established in 1900, Goldings currently hold 6 Fine Art sales per annum. Each sale has a dedicated book section. For vendors a Trade Rate Card is available upon request including some 0% commissions.*

HAMPTON & LITTLEWOOD AUCTIONEERS, The Auction Rooms, Alphin Brook Road, Alphington, Exeter, Devon EX2 8TH. Tel: (01392) 413100. Fax: (01392) 413110. E-Mail: enquiries@hampton andlittlewood.co.uk. Web Site: www.hamptonandlittlewood.co.uk.

KEYS AUCTIONEERS, 8 Market Place, Aylsham, Norwich, Norfolk NR11 6EH. Tel: (01263) 733195. Fax: 732140. E-mail: mail@aylshamsalerooms.co.uk. Web Site: www.aylshamsalerooms.co.uk.

LAMBRAYS, Polmorla Walk Galleries, The Platt, Wadebridge, Cornwall PL27 7AE. Tel: (01208) 813593. Fax: 814986. *Book auctions held as part of quarterly fine art auctions.* Enquiries to: Mr. R. Hamm.

LAWRENCE FINE ART LTD., Auctioneers and Valuers. South Street, Crewkerne, Somerset TA18 8AB. Tel: (01460) 73041. Fax: (01460) 270799. E-Mail: enquiries@lawrencec.co.uk. Web site: www.lawrences.co.uk. *General Sales every Wednesday, 4 catalogued Fine Art Sales per year, which includes two Book Sales.*

DAVID LAY, F.R.I.C.S., The Penzance Auction House, Alverton, Penzance, Cornwall TR18 4RE. Tel: (01736) 361414. Fax: 360035. E-Mail: david.lays@btopenworld.com. Web Site: catalogs.icollector.com/DLay. *2 book auctions a year in August & December.* Enquiries to: Mr. John Floyd.

MEALY'S LTD, Chatsworth Street, Castlecomer, County Kilkenny, Ireland. Tel: (056) 41229. Fax: (056) 41627. E-mail: info@mealys.com. Web site: www.mealys.com. *Irelands leading auctioneers of rare, interesting and valuable books.* Contact: Fonsie Mealy.

NEALES FINE ART AUCTIONEERS, 192 Mansfield Road, Nottingham, Nottinghamshire NG1 3HU. Tel: (0115) 962-4141. Fax: 985-6890. E-mail: books@neales-auctions.com. Web Site: www.neales-auctions.com

D.M. NESBIT & CO., 7 Clarendon Road, Southsea, Portsmouth, Hampshire PO5 2ED. Tel: (023) 9286-4321. Fax: 9229-5522. E-mail: auctions@nesbit.co.uk. Web Site: www.nesbit.co.uk. Contact: Mr John Cameron.

OUTHWAITE & LITHERLAND, Kingsway Galleries, Fontenoy Street, Liverpool L3 2BE. Tel: (0151) 236-6561. Fax: 236-1070. E-mail: auction@lots.uk.com. Web Site: www.lots.uk.com.

BONHAMS, 101 New Bond Street, London W1S 1SR. Tel: (020) 7468-8351. Fax: 7465-0224. E-mail: books@bonham.com.

BONHAMS, 1 Old King Street, Bath BA1 2JT. Tel: (01225) 788988. Fax: 446675.

BONHAMS, 39 Park End Street, Oxford OX1 1JD. Tel: (01865) 723524. Fax: 791064.

BONHAMS, 65 George Street, Edinburgh EH2 2JL. Tel: (0131) 225-2266.

SUPPLIES AND SERVICES

RIDDETTS OF BOURNEMOUTH, 177 Holdenhurst Road, Bournemouth BH8 8DQ. Tel: (01202) 555686. Fax: 311004. E-mail: auctions@riddetts.co.uk.

SCARBOROUGH PERRY FINE ARTS, Hove Auction Rooms, Hove Street, Hove, East Sussex BN3 2GL. Tel: (01273) 735266. Fax: 723813.

STRIDE & SON AUCTIONEERS, Southdown House, St. John's Street, Chichester, West Sussex PO19 1XQ. Tel: (01243) 780207. Fax: 786713. E-Mail: enquiries@stridesauctions.co.uk. Web Site: www.stridesauctions.co.uk or www.catmaker.co.uk. Appointment necessary for consultations. Book dept open Wednesdays 9am – 12.30pm for appointments. Buyers premium 15% + VAT. *3 auctions a year covering books, documents, ephemera, stamps & postcards.* Enquiries to: Derek White (ephemera) or Adriaan Van Noorden (books).

LAWRENCE TAUNTON LTD., Auctioneers & Valuers, The Corfield Hall, Magdalene Street, Taunton, Somerset TA1 1SG. Tel: (01823) 330567. Fax: (01823) 330596. E-Mail: enquiries.taunton@lawrence.co.uk. *Fine Art, Silver and Pictures. Sporting. Toys, Collectors and Militaria.*

THOMSON, RODDICK & MEDCALF, Coleridge House, Shaddongate, Carlisle CA2 5TU. Tel: (01228) 528939.

P.F. WINDIBANK, The Dorking Halls, Reigate Road, Dorking, Surrey RH4 1SG. Tel: (01306) 884556/876280. Fax: 884669. E-Mail: sjw@windibank.co.uk. Web Site: www.windibank.co.uk.

DOMINIC WINTER BOOK AUCTIONS, The Old School, Maxwell Street, Swindon, Wiltshire SN1 5DR. Tel: (01793) 611260. Fax: 491727. E-Mail: info@dominicwinter.co.uk. Web Site: www.dominicwinter.co.uk.

WOOLLEY & WALLIS, Book Dept. at 51-61 Castle Street, Salisbury, Wiltshire SP1 3FU. Head of Dept: Paul Viney. Direct Line: (01722) 339161. Direct Fax: (01722) 424508.

BOOK DISPLAY AND STORAGE EQUIPMENT, ETC

D AND M PACKAGING, 5a Knowl Road, Mirfield, West Yorkshire WF14 8DG. Tel: (01924) 495768. Fax: (01924) 491267. E-mail: packaging@dandmbooks.com. Web Site: www.bookcovers.co.uk. Contact: Daniel Hanson. *Suppliers of all types of covers for hardbacks, paperbacks and dust jackets. Also comprehensive range of packaging and book-care materials, adhesives, book cleaners, tapes, etc. Free catalogue on request. We supply both trade and private customers and have no minimum order.*

P.B.F.A., The Old Coach House, 16 Melbourn Street, Royston, Hertfordshire SG8 7BZ. Tel: (01763) 248400. Fax: 248921. *Folding bookshelves in natural beech and new books on book collecting and software for booksellers.*

POINT EIGHT LTD., Unit 14, Narrowboat Way, Blackbrook Valley Industrial Estate, Dudley, West Midlands DY2 0EZ. Tel: (01384) 238282. Fax: 455746. Web Site: www.point8.co.uk. *Bookshop and P.O.S. equipment designer and manufacture in wood, metal, plastic etc.*

SEALINE BUSINESS PRODUCTS LIMITED, Media House, 10 Greencotes, Hertford, Hertfordshire SG13 8AA. Tel: (01992) 558001. Fax: (01992) 304569. E-mail: sales@sealinemediastorage.com. Web Site: www.sealinemediastorage.com. Contact: Sarah White. Crown Media – *An attractive range of multi purpose cabinets designed to house a variety, or mix, of media types including CD, DVD, Video, Microfilm, DAT Tapes, Cassettes, Index Cards and much more. Complete with lock and anti-tilt in a choice of colour finishes. Shelving, mobile solutions and fire resistant storage compliment the range. Please visit our web site for full details.*

SIMPLEX, High Street, Oldland Common, Bristol BS30 9TA. Tel: (0117) 932-2279. Fax: 932-8800. *Wooden shelving storing units, bookcases and hi-fi units.*

BOOK-FAIR ORGANISERS

ANTIQUARIAN BOOKSELLERS ASSOCIATION. Est: 1906. International Book Fair held annually in London, in June, also in Chelsea (UK dealers only) in Autumn and, occasional book fairs elsewhere. *For complimentary tickets or handbook of members, please contact:* Antiquarian Booksellers' Association, Sackville House, 40 Piccadilly, London W1J 0DR. Tel: (020) 7439-3118. Fax: 7439-3119. E-Mail: admin@aba.org.uk. Web Site: www.abainternational.com.

BOOK COLLECTORS PARADISE. Est: 1986. *Enquiries to:* Trudy Ashford. Tel: (01442) 824440. Book fairs organiser for Buckinghamshire, Milton Keynes (and Wing Book Fair, 1st Sunday) each month – 10am to 4pm.

Bloomsbury Book Auctions
London's Specialist Auctioneers and Valuers

❦ For over eighteen years Bloomsbury Book Auctions has provided collectors, librarians and dealers with a specialised forum for buying and selling printed and graphic material.

❦ We are always pleased to advise on books, manusrcipts and historical documents, prints, drawings, photographs, maps, atlases, posters and printed ephemera.

❦ For further information on buying and selling *or* to receive a complimentary sample catalogue and sale calendar *or* for details of our catalogue/wants list subscription services please contact **Rupert Powell**.

Charles Fellows,
A Narrative of an Ascent to the Summit of Mount Blanc, 1827.
Sold for £40,350

The author's own copy, extra illustrated with eleven original watercolours and manuscripts.

Bloomsbury Book Auctions, 3 & 4 Hardwick Street, London EC1R 4RY
Tel: +44 20 7833 2636/7 & +44 20 7923 6940 Fax: +44 20 7833 3954
E-Mail: info@bloomsbury-book-auct.com
Internet: www.bloomsbury-book-auct.com

SUPPLIES AND SERVICES

BUXTON BOOK FAIRS, 75 Chestergate, Macclesfield, Cheshire SK11 6DG. Tel: (01625) 425352. *Enquiries to*: Sally Laithwaite. 10 fairs a year, held at Pavillion Gardens.

CIANA LTD., Lower Ground Floor, 4/5 Academy Buildings, Fanshaw Street, London N1 6LQ. Tel: (020) 7729-6044. Fax: 7729-3365. E-mail: enquiries@ciana.co.uk. Organisers of remainder and promotional book fairs, held in London in September and Brighton in January, and Bristol in June.

CLENT BOOKS OF BEWDLEY, Rose Cottage, Habberley Road, Bewdley, Worcs. DY12 1JA. Tel: (01299) - 401090. e-mail: clent.books@btopenworld.com. Web Site: www.abebooks.com/home/clentbooks. Co-organiser of Waverley Book Fair (est.1981). Third Sunday of each month at Kinver, Nr. Kidderminster. Contact: Ivor Simpson. (Member of P.B.F.A. and Francis Brett Young Soc.).

CODSALL BOOK FAIR. Held first Sunday, alternative months, commencing January, at Codsall Village Hall, Wolverhampton Road, Codsall, South Staffordshire. *Enquiries to:* John and Jean New, 11 Bryan Road, Walsall, West Midlands WS2 9DW. Tel: (01922) 639990.

THE EXHIBITION TEAM LTD (HD Bookfairs). Independent organisers for over 20 years, running the largest UK monthly Book Fairs in London – 140 plus exhibitors. Fairs in Farnham, Surrey and Kempton Park Racecourse – widest choice of books both Antiquarian and modern, as well as printed collectables. Pay us a visit! Free diary of events available on request; new exhibitors always welcome. Phone, fax or write to HD Book Fairs Ltd: Wendy Collyer or Peter Sheridan, 38 Fleetside, West Molesey, Surrey KT8 2NF. Tel: (020) 8224-3609 Fax: (020) 8224 3576. (See display advertisement).

FOREST BOOKS, 7 High Street West, Uppingham, Rutland LE15 9QB. Tel: & Fax: (01572) 821173. E-Mail: forestbooks@rutlanduk.fsnet.co.uk. Web Site: http://homepages.primex.co.uk/~forest. 6 Book Fairs organised annually: 4 at Farndon Memorial Hall, near Newark, Nottinghamshire and 2 at Uppingham School, Rutland. Please phone or e-mail for booking details. Maps & photos on our web site.

GERRARDS CROSS BOOK FAIR. Est: 1974. Fairs held at the Memorial Centre, East Common, Gerrards Cross, Bucks. Dates for 2004: 31 January; 28 February; 27 March; 8 May; 10 July; 11 September; 9 October; 13 November and 11 December. Enquiries to: Patty Lafferty on (01297) 21761. E-mail: patty@qxbooks.freeserve.co.uk

MISSING BOOK FAIRS. Est: 1994. Book fairs Cambridge (12 a year), Peterborough (6 a year), Orford (3 a year), Rayleigh (4 a year), Hatfield House (4 a year) and Dedham (4 a year). *Enquiries to:* Chris Missing, 'Coppers', Main Road, Great Leighs, Essex CM3 1NR. Tel: (01245) 361609.

NORTHWEST BOOK FAIRS. Many different venues throughout the year. *Enquiries to:* Greg Finn, 6 Knowsley View, Rainford, St Helens WA11 8SN. Tel: & Fax: (01744) 883780. E-mail: nwbookfairs@aol.co.uk. Also: V & C Finn; Specialists in Folio Society books, 1200 volumes, 3 catalogues a year. View by appointment; private premises.

PROVINCIAL BOOKSELLERS' FAIRS ASSOCIATION. Est: 1974. Fairs held in Central London (monthly) and in more than 100 other towns in Great Britain. *Enquiries to:* Gina Dolan (Administrator), Provincial Booksellers' Fairs Association, The Old Coach House, 16 Melbourn Street, Royston, Herts, SG8 7BZ. Tel: (01763) 248400. Fax: 248921. Fairs Information Service: (24 hrs) (01763) 249212. E-Mail: info@pbfa.org. Web Site: www.pbfa.org. (See display advertisement).

HD Book Fairs

Quality Fairs with a Friendly Atmosphere

Organisers of the Largest Monthly Book Fair in the U.K. Held at The Royal National Hotel Bloomsbury, London WC1.

Book fairs also held in Surrey & Middlesex

For further details write, 'phone, fax or e-mail
THE EXHIBITION TEAM LTD, 38 Fleetside, West Molesey, Surrey, KT8 2NF
Tel: 0208- 224 3609   Fax: 0208- 224 3576
E-mail: EXHIBITIONTEAM@aol.com

READING BOOK FAIR. Est: 1984. Fairs held at Our Lady of Peace, Catholic Church Hall, Wokingham Road, Earley, Reading, (4 a year). *Enquiries to:* John Creasey, Rural History Centre, University of Reading, Whiteknights, P.O. Box 229, Reading, RG6 6AG. Tel: (0118) 966-2458.

RYELAND BOOKS, 18 St. George's Place, Northampton. Tel: (01604) 716901. E-mail: amriley@ryeland. demon.co.uk. *Four fairs per year, fourteen dealers with select and changing stock. Held at St. Matthew's Parish Centre, Kettering Road, Northampton.* Contact: A & J Riley.

SUFFOLK BOOK MARKET at Long Melford. *10 weekend two-day high-attendance Book Markets are held each year at the Village Memorial Hall with around 30 book and ephemera dealers in attendance.* Exhibitor enquiries, dates etc. from the organisers:- K. McLeod, Boxford Books and Fairs, 3 Firs Farm Cottae, Boxford, Sudbury, Suffolk CO10 5NU. Tel: (01787) 210810. Fax: (01473) 823187.

TELFORD BOOK EVENTS. Fairs held in the indoor shopping centre junction 5 off the M54. Dates for 2003: 7-13 April; 14-20 July and 10-16 November. Enquiries to: Patty Lafferty on (01297) 21761.

TITLE PAGE BOOK FAIRS, 176 Elmbridge Avenue, Surbiton, Surrey KT5 9HF. Tel: & Fax: (020) 8399 8168. Mobile (07966) 162758. *Fairs in Surrey: Dorking 6 a year, Guildford 5 a year, Banstead 4 a year. Fairs in Kent: Bromley 6 a year. All fairs open 10–15.30 except Banstead 9.15–15.30.* Contact: Kieth Alexander.

WAVERLEY FAIRS, 9 Hayley Park, Hayley Green, Halesowen B61 1EJ. Tel: (0121) 550-4123. Kinver Book Fair established 1981, 3rd Sunday of every month. Also at Powick and Callow End Village Hall, Worcestershire.

WHITEHALL FAIRS, 3 Whitehall, Maybole, Ayrshire KA19 7AJ. Tel: & Fax: (01655) 883441. E-Mail: whitehallfairs@lineone.net. Fairs held at Alloway Village Hall, Alloway, Nr Ayr, Ayrshire. *Enquiries to:* Colin or Alexis.

WINCHESTER BOOK FAIRS, For details contact either Bill Jackson (02380) 812640, or Roly Hann (01962) 713929. E–mail: bill@bilberry.ndo.co.uk

WORLD WAR BOOKFAIRS, Oaklands, Camden Park, Tunbridge Wells, Kent TN2 5AE. Tel: & Fax: (01892) 538465. E-Mail: wwarbooks@btinternet.com. Contact: Tim Harper. *Specialist military, aviation and naval bookfairs organised in London, Tunbridge Wells, Marlborough, Chatham and other location from time to time.* Established in 1990, these are high quality fairs attracting some of the best specialist dealers in the UK.

CATALOGUE PRINTERS

THE DOLPHIN PRESS, 96 Whitehill Road, Whitehill Industrial Estate, Glenrothes, Fife. Tel: (01592) 771652. Fax: 630913. E-Mail: liz@dolphinpress.co.uk. Web Site: www.dolphinpress.co.uk *Catalogues and booklets printed.*

HOOVEY'S BOOKS, P.O. Box 27, St. Leonards-on-Sea, East Sussex TN37 6TZ. Tel & Fax: (01424) 753407. E-mail: hooveys@lineone.net. Web Site: www.hooveys.co.uk. We offer a budget-priced, 24 hour turnaround Catalogue Printing Service for book dealers – ask us to quote for your next catalogue – we aim to save you money. We are also suppliers of CoverClean the Trade cleaner for cloth covers, paperbacks and dust jackets (£5.95 inc. p&p), and LeatherBrite for cleaning/restoring leather bindings (£6.50 inc. p&p). Contact: Romney Hoovey.

JOSHUA HORGAN PRINT PARTNERSHIP, 246 Marston Road, Oxford OX3 0EL. Tel: (01865) 246762. Fax: (01865) 250555.

PARCHMENT PRINTERS, Printworks, Crescent Road, Cowley, Oxford OX4 2PB. Tel: (01865) 747547. Fax: 747551. Digital@ParchmentUK.com. Specialists in short run production. Contact: Ian Kinch. (See display advertisement).

CRAFT BOOKBINDERS

ROBERT ALLERTON BOOKBINDING, 45 Churchill Road, Shenstone, Lichfield, Staffordshire WS14 0LR. Tel & Fax: (01543) 480140. E-mail: robertallerton@clara.co.uk.

JOSEPHINE BACON, 179 Kings Cross Road, London WC1X 9BZ. Tel: (020) 7278 9490. Fax: 7278 2447. E-mail: bacon@americanization.com. *Specialist in foreign language material, judaica and cookery.*

Visiting London?
Think PBFA!

The monthly Russell Book Fairs are a major source
of fresh material for dealers, collectors and librarians
Keep ALL our London dates in mind when
planning your next visit to London

MONTHLY LONDON BOOK FAIRS

LE MÉRIDIEN RUSSELL
Russell Square, WC1

A mixture of one-day and quarterly two-day fairs

January	Sun 11	July	Sun 11
February	Sun 8	August	Sun 8
March	Sun/Mon 14-15	September	Sun/Mon 12-13
April	Sun 4	October	Sun 10
May	Sun 9	November	Sun 14

December Sun/Mon 12-13

Summer International Fairs
2 Fairs in 2 locations
Fair One: Le Méridien Russell   Sun/Mon 30-31 May
Fair Two: Commonwealth Institute
                    Kensington High Street   Fri/Sat 4-5 June

---

And for the specialists

Travel & Exploration Book Fair
Sunday April 18, 11-5
Royal Geographical Society, 1 Kensington Gore, SW7

Performing Arts Fairs
Saturdays April 3 & October 16

*Please note: all dates subject to change so please
check our website www.pbfa.org for latest information*

Organised by the PBFA
The Old Coach House, 16 Melbourn St.,
Royston, Herts, Great Britain, SG8 7BZ
Tel: 01763 248400, Fax: 01763 248921
email: info@pbfa.org
web: www.pbfa.org

SUPPLIES AND SERVICES

GEORGE BAYNTUN, incorporating Robert Riviere, Manvers Street, Bath BA1 1JW. Tel: (01225) 466000. Fax: 482122. E-mail: ebc@georgebayntun.com. Web Site: www.georgebayntun.com. *Fine binding in leather, restoration and case-making since 1894 (and Robert Riviere since 1829).*

CLIVE BOVILL, "Greenburn" River Lane, East Bilney, Dereham NR20 4HS. Tel: (01362) 860174. *Letterpress fine bindings, gold tooling and design. Special interest in conservation of 17th to 19th century books.*

BRISTOL BOUND BOOKBINDING, 300 North Street, Ashton Gate, Bristol BS3 1JU. Tel & Fax: (0117) 9663300. E-mail: information@bristolbound.couk. Web Site: www.bristolbound.co.uk. Rachel and Richard James. *We are a husband and wife team first established in 1986 when Rachel gained distinctions in bookbinding from Brunel Technical College, Bristol. We aim to offer a professional, yet friendly service to our customers, whilst maintaining a high standard of workmanship. We undertake new and restoration binding, thesis and dissertation binding, limited editions, corporate presentation binding, binding of newspapers, journals, magazines, personal memoirs, visitors books, photograph albums, wedding albums and much more.*

PHILIP N. BROOK (BOOKBINDER AND BOOK RESTORER), Bell Hill Farm, Lindale in Cartmel, Grange over Sands, Cumbria LA11 6LD. Tel: (01539) 534241. *Bookbinding, book restoration & conservation. To include single volume restorations, fine binding, short run (up to 1,000) publishers. Case work. All aspects of bookbinding work considered. Serving collectors, libraries and dealers for over twenty years.*

FRANCIS BROWN CRAFT BOOKBINDER, 24 Camden Way, Dorchester, Dorset DT1 2RA. Tel: (01305) 266039. *Francis Brown is a journeyman bookbinder who undertakes all kinds of binding work, ranging from simple repairs to the restoration of antiquarian volumes, fine limited editions or designed bindings. He has recently restored books for Balliol College, Wimborne Minster chained library and the Thomas Hardy Memorial Collection in the County Museum in Dorchester.*

FIONA CAMPBELL, 158 Lambeth Road, London SE1 7DF. Tel: & Fax: (020) 7928-1633. E-mail: fcampbell@britishlibrary.net. *Fine bookbinding.*

CEDRIC CHIVERS LTD., 1 Beaufort Trade Park, Pucklechurch, Bristol BS16 9QH. Tel: (0117) 937-1910. Fax: (0117) 937-1920. E-mail: info@cedricchivers.co.uk. Internet: www.cedricchivers.co.uk. Contact: Ivor Stone. *Binding, rebinding and repairing books since 1878. Conserving paper for a quarter of a century.*

COURTENAY BINDERY, Appleford, Abingdon OX14 4PB. Tel: (01235) 848319. *Specialist leather book restoration, especially early books (pre 1700). Purchase and sale of early books. Occasional Antiquarian books for sale, mainly history and theology for any who call by prior phone arrangement.*

NESTA RENDALL DAVIES, Studio C105, The Chocolate Factory, Clarendon Road, London N22 6XJ. Tel: (020) 8881-0881. E-mail: nesta@leafworks.co.uk. *Fine bookbinding and restoration. Boxes for books and prints. Commissions undertaken.*

CHRIS HICKS BOOKBINDER, 64 Merewood Avenue, Sandhills, Oxford OX3 8EF. Tel: (01865) 769346. E-Mail: chrishicksbookbinder@btinternet.com. Web Site: http://hicksbinder.cjb.net. *Binding, rebinding, repairs, theses, slipcases, solander cases, fine bindings, short-run edition binding, blank books etc.*

FELICITY HUTTON, Langore House, Langore, Launceston, Cornwall PL15 8LD. Tel: (01566) 773831. E-Mail: pandfhutton@hotmail.com. *Bookbinding and restoration.*

IPSLEY BINDERY, 10 Driffield Close, Ipsley, Redditch, Worcs. B98 0TH. Prop: Ray Beech. Tel: (01527) 521069. E-Mail: ipsleybind@aol.com. *Antiquarian & traditional craft bookbinding and restoration. Periodicals, theses, slipcases and book boxes.* Prompt Service. Telephone anytime.

Get your Booklet or Manual into Print

* No Minimum Quantity *

Digital print allows you the flexibility to order the exact quantity needed so there is no wastage, so you save money.

Add a full **COLOUR COVER** from **31p**

Call or email for a *FREE* sample booklet and price list

Parchment Printers
Printworks, Crescent Road
Cowley, Oxford OX4 2PB
Tel: 01865 747547 or
email: Digital@ParchmentUK.com

SUPPLIES AND SERVICES

JULIE JOHN, Borders Bindery, Birch House, High Street, Melrose, Roxburghshire TD6 9PB. Tel: (01896) 822391. *Hand bookbinding, repairs, restoration and library refurbishment.*

KINGSWOOD BOOKS, 17 Wick Road, Milborne Port, Sherborne, Dorset DT9 5BT. Tel: & Fax: (01963) 250280. E-mail: kingswoodbooks@btinternet.com. *Bookbinding & conservation.* Enquiries to A.J. Dollery.

NEW LEAF BINDERY, Unit B, 272 Montgomery Street, Sparkbrook, Birmingham B11 1DS. Tel: (0121) 773 1681. *Antiquarian and traditional bookbinding, slip cases, book boxes, portfolios, periodicals and theses, etc.* Contact: Julie Atkinson.

PERIOD BOOKBINDERS, Tollbridge House, Tollbridge Road, Batheaston, Bath BA1 7DF. Tel: (01225) 858217. Fax: 858975. E-mail: info@periodbookbinders.co.uk. Web Site: www.period bookbinders.co.uk. *Bookbinding, restoration and rebinding of antiquarian books.* (See display advertisement).

SALISBURY BOOKBINDERS, 45 St Andrews Road, Salisbury, Wilts SP2 9NT. Tel & Fax: (01722) 323488. E-mail: salisbury.bookbinders@virgin.net. Web Site: www.salisburybookbinders.co.uk. Contact: Nancy Winfield. Established in 1840. *Specialists in fine bindings, book repair and conservation, edge gilding using genuine gold leaf. Also bind small runs up to 1,000 copies.*

JOHN SMART BOOKBINDERS, The Old Waggon & Horses, Brinkworth, Chippenham, Wiltshire SN15 5AD. Tel: (01666) 510517. Fax: 510757. E-Mail: BkRestorer@aol.com. Web Site: oldenglish bindery.com. *Restoration of antique books & documents.*

THE STUDIO BINDERY, Unit 3, Nonsuch Industrial Estate, Kiln Lane, Epsom KT17 1DH. Tel: (01372) 747550. Fax: (01372) 747552. *Book restoration, rebinding in leather, cloth slip cases & boxes.* Contact: John Norman.

CHARLES SYMINGTON, 145 Bishopthorpe Road, York YO23 1NZ. Tel: (01904) 633995. *Bookbinding and restoration.*

JAYNE TANDY (CRAFT BOOKBINDING AND RESTORATION), Bowhayes Cross, Williton, Somerset TA4 4NL. Tel: (01984) 632293. *Bookbinding, book restoration, conservation and repair.*

COLIN TATMAN, 26 Westwood Road, Beverley, East Yorkshire HU17 8EJ. Tel: (01482) 880611. *Traditional craft bookbinding; paper repair; slipcases and book boxes; restoration and conservation.*

PERIOD BOOKBINDERS

Tollbridge House, Tollbridge Road, Batheaston,
Bath BA1 7DF
ENGLAND

Tel: 01225 858217. Fax: 01225 858975.
Web Site: www.periodbookbinders.co.uk
E-mail: info@periodbookbinders.co.uk

FINE & GENERAL BOOKBINDERS
Specialists in the Restoration
& Sympathetic Rebinding
of Antiquarian Books
Illustrated Brochure sent on request

FREE COLLECTION / DELIVERY
SERVICE TO MANY AREAS

SUPPLIES AND SERVICES

TEASDALE BOOKBINDERS, 103 Heath Road, Widnes, Cheshire WA8 7NU. Tel: (0151) 422-0747. E-Mail: catherinehore@bookbinder.fslife.co.uk. *Hand bookbinding and restoration. Prop: Catherine Hore.*

TEMPLE BOOKBINDERS, 10 Quarry Road, Headington, Oxford OX3 8NU. Tel: (01865) 451940. E-Mail: enquiries@templebookbinders.co.uk. Web Site: www.templebookbinders.co.uk. Mr. Ian Barnes. *Hand bookbinder in fine leathers, vellum, linens, cloth & buckrams. Quality restorer of antiquarian books.*

TRADITIONAL BOOKCRAFTS, Greenlea Cottage, 5 Ballgreen, Wigtown, Nr. Newton Stewart DG8 9HU. Tel: (01988) 402530. *Craft bookbinder, antique and modern book repair and restoration, boxes, slipcases, gold tooling, handmade and scribed books. Established: 1983. Limited edition bindings. Prices on request. Prop: Monica Thornton.*

PAUL TRONSON (MASTER BOOKBINDER), Yew Tree Farm Craft Centre, Wootton Wawen, Stratford Upon Avon B95 6BY. Tel: (01564) 793500. Fax: (01564) 779095. E-mail: paul@tronson.freeserve.co.uk. Internet: www.periodfinebindings.com. *Restorer of Antiquarian books using ancient formulae and period hand-made materials. Insurance of rare books can be provided linked to our unique DNA Coding System.*

LIZ YOUNG – BOOKBINDER, The Old Rectory, Buckland, Nr. Aylesbury, Buckinghamshire HP22 5HU. Tel: & Fax: (01296) 630461. *Traditional craft book-binding, restoration and photograph albums.*

PACKING MATERIALS SUPPLIERS

MACFARLANE GROUP PLC., **Group Head Office :** 21 Newton Place, Glasgow, G3 7PY. Tel: (0141) 333 9666. Fax: (0141) 333 1988. **PACKING CASE MANUFACTURERS: Dundee Branch:** Block 10, Myrekirk Road, Gourdie Industrial Esatate, Dundee DD2 4SH. Tel: (01382) 623328. Fax: (01382) 624469. **Glasgow Branch:** 249 Govan Road, Glasgow G51 2SH. Tel: (0141) 427 4044. Fax: (0141) 427 2577. **Grantham Branch:** PO Box 16, Alma Park Industrial Estate, Grantham, Lincolnshire NG31 9SF. Tel: (01476) 574747. Fax: (01476) 577444. **Renfrew Branch:** Kingsinch Road, Renfrew PA4 8XU. Tel: (0141) 886 1111. Fax: (0141 1019). **Sheffield Branch:** Daisy Spring Works, Green Lane, Sheffield S13 8SG. Tel: (0114) 276 3535. Fax: (0114) 276 3536. **Tyne & Wear Branch**: Unit 86/11 Alder Road, West Chirton Industrial Estate, North Shields, Tyne & Wear NE29 8SD. Tel: (0191) 258 5055. Fax: (0191) 257 6159. **Westbury Branch:** Quartermaster Road, West Wilts Trading Estate, Westbury, Wiltshire BA13 4JT. Tel: (01373) 858555. Fax: (01373) 858999. **PACKAGING MATERIALS: Bristol Branch:** Unit 7, Cribbs Causeway Centre, Cribbs Causeway, Bristol BS10 7TT. Tel: (0117) 959 4094. Fax: (0117) 959 3384. **Coventry Branch:** Siskin Parkway West, Middlemarch Business Park, Coventry, CV3 4PW. Tel: (02476) 217 000. Fax: (02476) 639 612. **Exeter:** Windsor Court, Manaton Close, Matford Business Park, Exeter EX2 8PF. Tel: (01342) 824994. Fax: (01392) 824131. **Glasgow Branch:** 249 Govan Road, Glasgow G51 2SH. Te: (0870) 150 4508. Fax: (0870 150 4509. **Grantham Branch:** PO Box 7219, Alma Park Industrial Estate, Grantham, Lincolnshire NG31 9WH. Tel: (0870) 150 4506. Rax: (0870) 150 4507. **Manchester Branch:** Empire Court, Trafford Park, Manchester M17 1TN. Tel: (0870) 150 4500. Fax: (0870) 150 4501. **Milton Keynes Branch:** Kingston Gateway, Whitehall Avenue, Milton Keynes MK10 0BU. Tel: (0870) 150 4502. Fax: (0870) 150 4503. **Telford Branch:** Unit D2, Horton Park Industrial Estate, Hortonwood 7, Telford, Shropshire TF7 4AP. Tel: (01952) 677256. Fax: (01952) 608057. **Tyne & Wear Branch**: Kingsway North, Team Valley, Gateshead, Tyne & Wear NE11 0JH. Tel: (0191) 482 2227. Fax: (0191) 482 3335. **Wakefield Branch:** Unit H, Brunel Road, Wakefield 41 Industrial Estate, Wakefield, WF2 0X6. (0870) 850 0118. Fax: (0870) 850 0119. **Wigan Branch:** Northgate Ditribution Centre, Caxton Close, Wheatlea Park Industrial Estate, Wigan WN3 6XU. Tel: (01942) 245686. Fax: (01942) 245422. *Macfarlane Group provides a complete range of packaging materials, including postal bags and Easywrap.*

D AND M PACKAGING, 5a Knowl Road, Mirfield, West Yorkshire WF14 8DQ. Tel: (01924) 495768. Fax: (01924) 491267. E-mail: packaging@dandmbooks.com. Web Site: www.bookcovers.co.uk. Contact: Daniel Hanson. *Suppliers of all types of covers for hardbacks, paperbacks and dust jackets. Also comprehensive range of packaging and book-care materials, adhesives, book cleaners, tapes, etc. Free catalogue on request. We supply both trade and private customers and have no minimum order.*

REMAINDER MERCHANTS

AWARD PUBLICATIONS LTD., 1st Floor, 27 Longford Street, London NW1 3DZ. Tel: (020) 7388-7800. Fax: 7388-7887. E-mail: anna@awardpublications.co.uk. *Genuine remainders for adults and children.*

BLAKETON HALL LTD., Unit 1, 26 Marsh Green Road, Marsh Barton, Exeter EX2 8PN. Tel: (01392) 210602. Fax: 421165. E-Mail: sales@blaketonhall.co.uk. *Remainders and overstocks, including scientific, technical, academic, gardening, crafts & children's.* Enquiries to: Martin Shillingford.

SUPPLIES AND SERVICES

ROY BLOOM LTD., Fanshaw House, 3/9 Fanshaw Street, London N1 6HX. Tel: (020) 7729-5373. Fax: 7729-2375. E-Mail: info@roybloom.com. www.roybloom.com. *General remainders. Exhibits at all major book fairs.*

BOOKMART LTD., Desford Road, Enderby, Leicester LE19 4AD. Tel: (0116) 275-1800. Fax: 275-0507. E-Mail: books@bookmart.co.uk. *Publisher & distributor of promotional books, reprints and remainders.*

GRANGE BOOKS PLC., The Grange, Units 1–6 Kingsnorth Industrial Estate, Hoo, Nr. Rochester, Kent ME3 9ND. Tel: (01634) 256000. Fax: 255500. E-Mail: sales@grangebooks.co.uk. *Distributors of remainders, and publisher of promotional books and reprints to the adult illustrated non-fiction and children's market.*

JIM OLDROYD BOOKS, 14/18 London Road, Sevenoaks, Kent TN13 1AJ. Tel: (01732) 463356. Fax: 464486. E-Mail: paula@oldroyd.co.uk. Web site: www.oldroyd.co.uk. *Adult and children's remainders.*

SANDPIPER BOOKS LTD., 24 Langroyd Road, London SW17 7PL. Tel: (020) 8767-7421. Fax: 8682-0280. Showroom: Lower Ground Floor, 4/5 Academy Buildings, Fanshaw Street, London N1 6LQ. Tel: (020) 7613-4446. Fax: 7613-4513. E-Mail: enquiries@sandpiper.co.uk. *Scholarly and literary remainders, academic reprints and mail order.*

LOGISTICS/SHIPPING AGENTS

BOOK SHIPPERS ASSOCIATION INC., Unit 3b, Questor, Hawley Road, Dartford, Kent DA1 1JS. Tel: (01322) 277414. Fax: (01322) 277415. E-mail: bookshipuk@btinternet.com. Contact: Duncan Scott. *International consolidator and small parcel distribution.*

SUPPLIERS OF MATERIALS AND TOOLS FOR BINDING AND RESTORING BOOKS, ETC.

EDGAR BACKUS (MR. H.T.H. TAYLOR), 22 Fairefield Crescent, Glenfield, Leicester LE3 8EH. Tel: (0116) 287-1095. *BACKUS LEATHER BINDING POLISH, cleans and restores leather bindings. BACKUS BOOKCLOTH CLEANER, restores and cleans buckram, linen, art and other bookcloths. Both sold in 500ml tins (U.K. only). Postal business only.*

FALKINER FINE PAPERS, 76 Southampton Row, London WC1B 4AR. Tel: (020) 7831-1151. Fax: 7430-1248. E-mail: falkiner@ic24.net. *PAPERS. Wide selection of papers for repairs, marbled papers and coloured end papers. LEATHERS AND BOOKCLOTHS for repairs and bindings. BOOKS in print on bookbinding, calligraphy, typography, papermaking and printing history. All items can be supplied by post. Price lists.*

FINE CUT GRAPHIC IMAGING LTD., Marlborough Road, Lancing Business Park, Lancing, West Sussex BN15 8UF. Tel: (01903) 751666. Fax: 750462. E-Mail: info@finecut.co.uk. Web Site: www.finecut.co.uk. *Manufacturers of bookbinders' finishing tools and accessories. 80 page catalogue available showing all styles of brass type, handle letters, hand tools and brass rolls supplied as standard. Special designs made to order. Tools designated into centuries to aid more authentic finishing.*

HARMATAN LEATHER LTD, Westfield Avenue, Higham Ferrers, Northamptonshire NN10 8AX. Tel: (01933) 412151. Fax: (01933) 412242. E-mail: marc@harmatan.co.uk. Web Site: www.harmatan.co.uk. Contact: Marc Lamb.

J. HEWIT AND SONS LIMITED, Unit 28, Park Royal Metro Centre, Britannia Way (off Coronation Road), London NW10 7PR. Tel: (020) 8965-5377. Fax: 8453-0414. E-Mail: sales@hewit.com. Web Site: www.hewit.com. *LEATHER CLEANING AND PRESERVING DRESSING, a non-ionic synthetic wax with properties similar to beeswax. Sold in 500ml bottles. BOOKBINDERS' TOOLS AND SUPPLIES, adhesive (paste, glue, P.V.A.), bone folders, brass type and type holders, brushes, knives, papers (marbled, etc.), presses, tapes, threads. BINDING LEATHERS. Basil, calf, goatskin, Moroccos, pigskin, skivers, etc, in a wide range of colours. BOOKCLOTHS, buckram, linen, cloth, mull, etc.*

HOOVEY'S BOOKS, P.O. Box 27, St. Leonards-on-Sea, East Sussex TN37 6TZ. Tel & Fax: (01424) 753407. E-mail: hooveys@lineone.net. Web Site: www.hooveys.co.uk. *Suppliers of CoverClean the Trade cleaner for cloth covers, paperbacks and dust jackets (£5.95 inc. p&p), and LeatherBrite for cleaning/restoring leather bindings (£6.50 inc. p&p). We also offer a budget-priced, 24 hour turnaround Catalogue Printing Service for book dealers – ask us to quote for your next catalogue – we aim to save you money.* Contact: Romney Hoovey.

ANN MUIR MARBLING, 1 St. Algar's Yard, West Woodlands, Frome, Somerset BA11 5ER. Tel: & Fax: (01985) 844786. E-mail: annmuir@marbling.freeserve.co.uk. *Web Site: www.annmuirmarbling.co.uk ANN MUIR makes*

SUPPLIES AND SERVICES

hand marbled paper in both modern and traditional patterns and colourways. She is happy to match old papers for restoration work and enjoys designing new papers for individual projects. Send for catalogue of samples and pricelist.

PAPERSAFE, 2 Green Bank, Adderley, Market Drayton TF9 3TH. Tel: (01630) 652217. E-Mail: philip@papersafe.demon.co.uk. Web Site: www.papersafe.demon.co.uk. *Suppliers of archival quality repair materials for book and paper collectors.*

PICREATOR ENTERPRISES LIMITED, 44 Park View Gardens, Hendon, London NW4 2PN. Tel: (020) 8202-8972. *Fine–art conservation and restoration materials. Manufacturers of Renaissance wax polish, Vulpex liquid soap and Groom/stick non–abrasive document dry cleaner. Bookdealers are increasingly undertaking basic cleaning and restorative treatment of books and paper. Picreator Enterprises supply professional products which are simple to use and advice is given on their application. The Company has held a Royal warrant of appointment to H.M. The Queen since 1984 as suppliers of products for (fine-art) restoration and conservation. It's Renaissance products are known and specified throught the world.*

RUSSELL BOOKCRAFTS, Great North Road, Wyboston, Bedfordshire MK44 3AB. Tel: (01480) 405464. Fax: 407105. E-Mail: john@russels.com. Web Site: www.russels.com. *Complete equipment to bookbinders, archivists and conservators. We are a major supplier of the very finest leathers. Our range includes the world renowned, and only genuine "OASIS" goatskin, "OASIS 400" goatskin, calf and sheepskin skivers. Our range of handmade bookbinders' equipment includes, specially designed work benches, nipping presses, lying presses, ploughs, sewing frames and Digby Stuart presses, all made in the finest wood. Our materials section offers a fine colour range of Buckrams and bookcloths. Mulls, Jaconette, tapes, threads and headbands. There is also a large selection of specialised papers and marbled end papers. Also Millboards and Dutch Grey Boards. Our excellent range of tools includes: finishing stoves, paring knives, bridled glue brushes, decorative hand tools and brass letters. Backing hammers, bone folders, burnishing agates and all types of bookbinders adhesives. We also have a wide variety of Archival and Conservation materials.*

Atlanticweb.co.uk

Wide ranging experience in the computer industry:

🖳 Bookdealer websites	▸ sell books online
	▸ secure sites

🖳 Database design	▸ online booksearches
	▸ stock control

🖳 Makeovers for existing sites

All enquiries to: sales@atlanticweb.co.uk
Telephone: (01598) 760404

USE OF THE DIRECTORY

This directory is divided into four sections. The first is the *Geographical Directory of Dealers*, in which full details, where supplied, are given for each business or private dealer. These are listed alphabetically by town in which the shop or business premises are located. The details, as supplied by dealers, are presented in the following manner:

Name of business.	As provided. ■ Indicates that the type of premises is a Shop.
Postal address.	(∗) Indicates the dealer's preference for indexing or where we have imposed current county boundaries.
Prop:	Name of proprietor(s).
Web Site:	Web Site address. Users should ignore the full point at the end of the entry.
Tel:	Dealer's telephone number, is followed by their fax number.
E-Mail:	Electronic mail address. Users should ignore the full point at the end of the entry.
Est:	Date at which business was established.
Type of premises occupied:	Shop, private, mail order/Internet, market stall or storeroom.
Opening times:	The 24 hour clock has been used for this edition where appropriate. Whether appointments to view stock are required; or if postal business only.
Normal level of total stock:	Very small (less than 2,000), small (2,000–5,000), medium (5,000–10,000), large (10,000–20,000) or very large (more than 20,000).
Spec:	Subjects in which dealer specialises. NB. Dealers list many more subjects on their web site than we can print in the Geographical Section. If a subject is listed in the Speciality Index, the dealer has a relatively large range of titles in that subject.
PR:	Price range of stock. This is intended as a guideline only.
CC:	Selection of Credit & Debit Cards eg. AE – American Express, DC – Diners Club, E – Eurocard, JCB – Japanese Credit Bureau, MC – Mastercard, V – Visa, SO – Solo, SW – Switch, and PayPal.
Important lines of business:	Other than secondhand antiquarian books.
Cata:	Frequency and subject of catalogues, if issued.
Corresp:	Languages, other than English, in which correspondence may be conducted.
Mem:	Membership of book trade organisations, eg. A.B.A. – Antiquarian Booksellers' Association B.A. – Booksellers Association of Great Britain & Ireland P.A. – Publishers Association P.B.F.A. – Provincial Booksellers' Fairs Association

The next section is an alphabetical *Index of Businesses*, giving full name and county with the page on which their full entry is to be found. Only the names and addressed for those dealers who have not replied for this edition are shown.

There is then a new section, the *Index of Web Sites,* which lists dealers alphabetically with their page reference and web site.

This is followed by an alphabetical *Index of Proprietors*, giving their name and trading name followed by their page reference.

The fourth section is the *Speciality Index*. This is presented in alphabetical order by subject heading, giving the dealer's name, county and page on which their details may be found.

INDEX OF CITIES AND TOWNS

Dealer locations listed alphabetically by country, city, town and village, as shown in the Geographical section.

ABERDEEN 265	BANK PLAIN 190	BLUNTISHAM 64
ABERFELDY 273	BARKING 180	BODMIN 73
ABERGAVENNY 283	BARNARD CASTLE 96	BOGNOR REGIS............ 241
ABERLOUR 266	BARNOLDSWICK 140	BOLNEY 241
ABERYSTWYTH............ 281	BARNSTAPLE................ 83	BOLTON 116
ABINGDON 204	BARROW–IN–FURNESS .. 77	BOOTLE........................ 185
ADARE........................... 278	BARTON–ON–HUMBER .. 146	BOURNEMOUTH 90
AIRDRIE........................ 270	BASINGSTOKE 121	BOURTON...................... 91
ALCESTER 236	BASSINGBOURN............ 64	BOWNESS–ON–
ALDRINGHAM 224	BATH 214	WINDERMERE......... 77
ALFRETON 81	BATLEY 245	BOXFORD...................... 224
ALLERTHORPE.............. 104	BEACONSFIELD............. 62	BRACKLEY 198
ALMONDSBURY 111	BEADNELL 200	BRADFORD................... 245
ALNWICK 200	BEAMINSTER 90	BRADFORD ON AVON.... 250
ALRESFORD 120	BECCLES 224	BRAINTREE 106
ALSAGER 69	BECKENHAM 133, 180	BRANSCOMBE................ 87
ALTON 120	BEDALE........................ 192	BRECON 285
ALTRINCHAM 116	BEDDINGTON 180	BRENTWOOD 106
ALVERSTOKE................ 120	BEDFORD 55	BRIDGE OF ALLAN........ 262
ALYSHAM...................... 187	BELFAST 259	BRIDGNORTH 211
ANDOVER..................... 120	BELPER 81	BRIDGWATER 215
ANSTRUTHER............... 264	BEMBRIDGE 131	BRIDLINGTON 104
APPLEBY–IN–	BERE ALSTON.............. 83	BRIDPORT 91
WESTMORLAND......... 77	BERKELEY................... 111	BRIERLEY HILL 239
ARBROATH................... 273	BERKHAMSTED 128	BRIGHOUSE 245
ARMAGH....................... 259	BERWICK–UPON–TWEED 200	BRIGHTON 98
ARUNDEL..................... 241	BETHESDA................... 283	BRISTOL 60
ASCOT........................... 57	BEULAH 284	BRIXHAM 84
ASHBOURNE................. 81	BEVERLEY 104	BROMLEY................ 133, 180
ASHBURNHAM............... 98	BEWDLEY..................... 254	BRUTON....................... 215
ASHBURTON................. 83	BEXHILL 98	BUCKINGHAM............... 62
ASHFORD 133	BICESTER 204	BUDE........................... 73
ASHPERTON 126	BIDDENDEN 133	BUDLEIGH SALTERTON. 84
ASHTEAD 230	BIDEFORD 83	BUNGAY 225
ASHTON........................ 74	BIGGAR........................ 271	BURES.......................... 225
ASHTON-UNDER-LYNE .. 116	BILLERICAY 106	BURES ST MARY 225
ASHURST...................... 120	BILLINGHAY 146	BURFORD...................... 204
ATTLEBOROUGH........... 187	BILLINGSHURST 241	BURTON UPON TRENT .. 222
AXMINSTER................... 83	BILSTON....................... 238	BURY............................ 140
AYLESBURY 62	BIRCH 106	BURY ST EDMUNDS 225
AYLSHAM..................... 187	BIRMINGHAM................ 238	BUSHEY 128
AYR.............................. 271	BISHOP AUCKLAND 96	BUILTH WELLS 284
	BISHOP'S CASTLE 211	BUXTON....................... 81
BADCOX........................ 216	BISHOP'S FROME........... 126	BYFLEET 230
BADMINTON................. 111	BISHOP'S STORTFORD ... 128	
BALA 283	BLACKBURN................. 140	CAERSWS 285
BALLATER.................... 266	BLACKPOOL 140	CAHIR.......................... 279
BALLINLOUGH 275	BLACKROCK 276	CAISTER–ON–SEA 187
BALLYDEHOB 275	BLAENAU FFESTINIOG .. 283	CALLANDER.................. 262
BALLYGOWAN 259	BLAENAVON 289	CALLINGTON................. 73
BALLYNAHINCH............ 260	BLAIR ATHOLL.............. 273	CALNE 250
BANBURY...................... 204	BLANDFORD FORUM 90	CAMBORNE 73
BANGOR, N IRELAND.... 260	BLEWBURY................... 204	CAMBRIDGE................. 64
BANGOR....................... 283	BLO NORTON................ 187	CAMPBELTOWN 271

INDEX OF CITIES AND TOWNS

CANNOCK 222	CORBRIDGE.................. 200	DUNMANWAY 276
CANTERBURY............... 133	CORSHAM 250	DUNSTABLE 55
CARDIFF....................... 280	COTHAM 60	
CARDIGAN.................... 281	COVENTRY.................... 239	EAGLE 147
CARLISLE..................... 77	COWES 131	EAST GRINSTEAD.......... 242
CARMARTHEN............... 280	COWFOLD 242	EAST HAGBOURNE........ 205
CARNDONAGH 276	CRANBROOK 134	EAST HORSLEY 231
CARNFORTH 140	CRAVEN ARMS 211	EAST LOOE 73
CARRICK–ON–SHANNON. 278	CREWE........................... 70	EAST MOLESEY............. 231
CARSHALTON................ 180	CREWKERNE 216	EAST RIDING................. 104
CARTMEL...................... 77	CRICCIETH 283	EASTBOURNE 100
CASTLE CARY................ 215	CRIEFF........................... 273	EASTHAM 185
CASTLE DOUGLAS......... 262	CROMER 187	ECCLESFIELD 220
CASTLETON 81	CROMFORD 82	ECKINGTON 220
CATERHAM 230	CROWBOROUGH 100	EDGWARE 180
CATTERICK VILLAGE.... 192	CROWTHORNE.............. 57	EDINBURGH 268
CAVAN........................... 275	CROYDON 180	EGERTON 135
CAVERSHAM 57	CULBOKIE 267	EGGINGTON 55
CHARD........................... 215		EGHAM 231
CHARLESTOWN 73	DACRE........................... 192	ELGIN 267
CHARMOUTH 91	DAGENHAM 107	ELLESMERE.................. 211
CHATHAM..................... 134	DALMELLINGTON......... 271	ELLON 267
CHATTERIS.................... 66	DARLINGTON 96	ELSTEAD 231
CHEADLE 69, 116	DARTFORD..................... 134	ELSTREE 128
CHELMSFORD................ 106	DARTMOUTH................. 84	ELY................................ 66
CHELTENHAM 111	DARWEN 141	EMSWORTH 121
CHESHAM...................... 62	DAWLISH 84	ENFIELD 181
CHESHUNT 128	DEAL 134	ENNISKILLEN 260
CHESTER........................ 69	DEBENHAM 226	EPPING.......................... 107
CHESTERFIELD............. 81	DEDDINGTON................ 205	EPSOM 231
CHICHESTER 241	DERBY 82	ESHER............................ 231
CHICKSANDS 55	DEREHAM 187	EXETER.......................... 84
CHIPPENHAM 250	DEVIZES 250	EXMOUTH 85
CHIPPING CAMPDEN..... 112	DIDCOT 205	EYE................................ 226
CHIPPING NORTON 204	DIDSBURY 117	
CHISWICK 172	DILWYN 126	FAIRFORD...................... 112
CHOBHAM 230	DINGWALL 267	FAKENHAM................... 188
CHORLEY 140	DITCHLING 100	FALMOUTH 74
CHRISTCHURCH 92	DOLGELLAU 283	FARINGDON 205
CHURCH STRETTON...... 211	DONAGHADEE............... 260	FARNBOROUGH............. 121
CIRENCESTER............... 112	DONCASTER 220	FARNBOROUGH............. 135
CLACTON–ON–SEA 106	DOOLIN.......................... 275	FARNHAM 232
CLAPTON–IN–	DORCHESTER 92	FAVERSHAM.................. 135
GORDANO 215	DORCHESTER ON	FELIXSTOWE 226
CLARE 225	THAMES 205	FELLING 235
CLEETHORPES 146	DORKING 230	FENCE............................ 141
CLEVEDON 215	DOUGLAS 258	FERNDOWN................... 92
CLEVELAND 96	DOVER 135	FILEY 192
CLITHEROE 141	DOWNDERRY 73	FLAMBOROUGH............ 104
CLONAKILTY 275	DOWNHAM MARKET..... 187	FLEET 121
COBHAM 230	DOWNPATRICK............. 260	FOCHABERS,.................. 267
COGGESHALL 106	DRIFFIELD 104	FOLKESTONE 135
COLCHESTER 107	DROITWICH 254	FOLKINGHAM 147
COLEFORD 112	DROITWICH SPA 254	FORDINGBRIDGE 121
COLERAINE 260	DUBLIN.......................... 277	FORFAR 273
COLNE 141	DUCKLINGTON............. 205	FORRES 267
COLWYN BAY 281	DUKINFIELD.................. 70	FORT WILLIAM 267
COLYTON 84	DULVERTON.................. 216	FOWEY........................... 74
CONWY 282	DUMFRIES 262	FRAMLINGHAM............. 226
COOKHAM 180	DUNDEE......................... 273	FRESHWATER................ 131
COOTEHILL 275	DUNFERMLINE.............. 265	FROME........................... 216

INDEX OF CITIES AND TOWNS

GALWAY 277	HEATHFIELD 101	KEMPSTON 55
GEDDINGTON............... 198	HEBDEN BRIDGE 245	KENDAL...................... 78
GIGGLESWICK 192	HELENSBURGH............. 272	KENILWORTH 236
GILLINGHAM 92	HELMSLEY 193	KENLEY 182
GIRVAN 271	HELSTON...................... 74	KENMARE 278
GLASBURY 126	HENLEY–IN–ARDEN 236	KENT 134
GLASGOW 271	HENLEY–ON–THAMES ... 206	KESWICK..................... 78
GLASTONBURY............. 216	HEREFORD.................. 126	KETTERING 198
GLOSSOP 82	HERNE BAY 136	KEW........................... 182
GLOUCESTER............... 112	HERTFORD.................. 129	KIBWORTH HARCOURT. 143
GODALMING 232	HEXHAM 200	KIDDERMINSTER.......... 255
GODMANCHESTER........ 66	HIGH WYCOMBE.......... 62	KILLIECRANKIE........... 273
GORING–BY–SEA........... 242	HILLSBOROUGH........... 260	KILMARNOCK 272
GORING–ON–THAMES ... 206	HINCKLEY................... 143	KINETON 236
GORLESTONE 188	HINDHEAD 232	KING'S LYNN............... 189
GOSPORT..................... 121	HINGHAM 188	KINGSBRIDGE 85
GRANGE–OVER–SANDS.. 78	HITCHIN..................... 129	KINGSCLERE 57
GRANTHAM 147	HOARWITHY............... 126	KINGSTON................... 182
GRASMERE................... 78	HOLBEACH 147	KINGSWINFORD 239
GRAVESEND................. 136	HOLMFIRTH 246	KINGTON 126
GREAT BARDFIELD....... 107	HOLT 188	KIRKBY LONSDALE....... 78
GREAT DRIFFIELD........ 104	HOLYHEAD 283	KIRKBY STEPHEN 78
GREAT DUNMOW.......... 107	HONITON 85	KIRKBY–IN–ASHFIELD .. 202
GREAT ELLINGHAM...... 188	HOOK NORTON............ 206	KIRKCALDY 265
GREAT LEIGHS 108	HORDLE...................... 122	KIRKCUDBRIGHT 263
GREAT MALVERN......... 254	HORNCASTLE 147	KIRKELLA 105
GREAT MISSENDEN....... 62	HORNCHURCH 108	KIRKSTALL 247
GREAT YARMOUTH 188	HORNDEAN 122	KIRKWALL 274
GREENFORD 181	HORSHAM 242	KIRTON....................... 148
GREENOCK................... 271	HORWICH 116	KNARESBOROUGH........ 193
GRIMSBY..................... 147	HOVE 101	KNIPTON..................... 147
GUERNSEY 257	HOYLAKE.................... 70	KNUTSFORD................. 70
GUILDFORD 232	HUDDERSFIELD........... 246	
GUISBOROUGH............. 192	HULL 105	LAMPETER 281
GUNTHORPE................. 202	HULME 117	LANCASTER................. 141
	HUNTINGDON 67	LANCING 243
HADDENHAM 67	HURLEY...................... 57	LANGPORT 216
HADDINGTON 270	HURST 57	LARBERT..................... 262
HALE 116	HYDE 70	LAUGHARNE 281
HALESOWEN................ 239	HYTHE 136	LAUNCESTON 74
HALIFAX 245		LAVENHAM 227
HALSTEAD 108	ILFORD 108, 182	LEALHOLM 193
HALTON...................... 141	ILKESTON 82	LEAMINGTON SPA 236
HALTWHISTLE............. 200	ILKLEY 246	LECHLADE 113
HAMPTON 181	ILMINSTER 216	LEDBURY 127
HAMPTON HILL 181	INGLETON................... 193	LEEDS 247
HARLESTON 187	INNERLEITHEN............ 261	LEICESTER 143
HARPENDEN................. 128	INVERNESS.................. 268	LEIGH 136
HARPLEY 188	IPSWICH 226	LEIGH–ON–SEA 108
HARROGATE 192	IRON BRIDGE 211	LEIGHTON BUZZARD 55
HARROW..................... 181	IRVINE 272	LEOMINSTER 127
HARWELL 206	ISLE OF ARRAN 272	LETHWORTH 129
HARWICH 108	ISLE OF COLONSAY 272	LEWES........................ 101
HASLEMERE 232	ISLEWORTH 182	LEYLAND 141
HASSOCKS................... 242	IVER 63	LICHFIELD 222
HASTINGS 100		LIMERICK 279
HATFIELD 128	JEDBURGH 261	LINCOLN..................... 148
HAWES........................ 193		LIPHOOK..................... 122
HAWORTH................... 245	KEIGHLEY................... 246	LISBURN 259
HAY–ON–WYE............... 285	KELSO 261	LISKEARD 75
HAYWARDS HEATH 242	KEMPSFORD................. 112	LITTLEBOROUGH.......... 117

INDEX OF CITIES AND TOWNS

LITTLEHAMPTON 243	MERRIOTT 217	NORTHWHICH 71
LIVERPOOL 185	MIDDLE CLAYDON 62	NORWICH 189
LIVERSEDGE 235	MIDDLETON-IN	NOTTINGHAM 202
LLANDUDNO 283	-TEESDALE 96	
LLANGAMMARCH WELLS 287	MIDHURST 243	OBAN 272
LLANGOLLEN 282	MIDLETON 276	OKEHAMPTON 86
LLANIDLOES 287	MIDSOMER NORTON 217	OLD COLWYN 282
LLANRWST 282	MILBORNE PORT 93	OLDBURY 239
LLANVAPLEY 283	MILLINGTON, YORK 105	OLDHAM 118
LOCHCARRON 268	MILTON KEYNES 63	ORLETON 212
LONDON (E) 151	MINCHINHAMPTON 113	ORPINGTON 137
LONDON (EC) 152	MINEHEAD 217	OSWESTRY 212
LONDON (N) 153	MIRFIELD 248	OTLEY 248
LONDON (NW) 157	MITCHAM 232	OUNDLE 198
LONDON (SE) 160	MODBURY 86	OVERTON 122
LONDON (SW) 163	MOFFAT 263	OXFORD 206
LONDON (W) 169	MOLD 282	OXTED 233
LONDON (WC) 176	MONTGOMERY 288	
LONDON (OUTER) 180	MONTROSE 267	PAIGNTON 86
LONDONDERRY 260	MOOR LANE 72	PAISLEY 272
LONG MELFORD 227	MOORLYNCH 217	PEASEDOWN ST. JOHN ... 217
LONGLEVENS 113	MORDEN 182	PENN 63
LOOE 75	MORETONHAMPSTEAD .. 86	PENRITH 78
LOUGHBOROUGH 144	MORETON-IN-MARSH ... 113	PENZANCE 75
LOUTH 148	MORPETH 201	PERSHORE 255
LOWESTOFT 227	MOTTRAM IN	PETERBOROUGH 67
LUDLOW 211	LONGDENDALE 118	PETERHEAD 267
LUTON 56	MOYARD 278	PETERSFIELD 122
LYDFORD 86	MUCH HADHAM 129	PETWORTH 243
LYME REGIS 92	MUCH WENLOCK 212	PICKERING 193
LYMINGE 136		PINNER 181
LYMINGTON 122	NAILSWORTH 113	PITLOCHRY 273
LYMPSTONE 86	NANTWICH 71	PLAISTOW 243
LYTHAM ST. ANNES 141	NEATH 284	PLEASLEY VALE 202
	NEW BARNET 182	PLYMOUTH 86
MACCLESFIELD 70	NEW MALDEN 232	PONTARDAWE 289
MACHYNLLETH 288	NEW MILTON 122	PONTYPRIDD 289
MADELEY, TELFORD 212	NEW ROSS 279	POOLE 93
MAIDENHEAD 57	NEW TREDEGAR 280	PORTSMOUTH 122
MAIDSTONE 136	NEWARK 149	PRESCOT 185
MALDON 108	NEWARK-ON-TRENT 202	PRESTEIGNE 288
MALMESBURY 250	NEWBURY 58	PRESTON 142
MALTON 193	NEWCASTLE UPON TYNE 235	PRUDHOE 201
MALVERN 255	NEWCASTLE-UNDER-	PUDDLETOWN 93
MANCHESTER 117	LYME 223	PURBROOK 123
MANNINGTREE 109	NEWENT 113	
MANSFIELD 202	NEWLYN 75	QUEEN CAMEL 217
MARAZION 75	NEWMARKET 227	
MARGATE 137	NEWNHAM ON SEVERN . 113	RADLETT 129
MARKET BOSWORTH 144	NEWPORT, I.O.W 131	RAINHAM 137
MARKET DRAYTON 212	NEWPORT ON TAY 265	RAINTON 194
MARKET HARBOROUGH 144	NEWPORT 284	RAINWORTH 203
MARKET RASEN 148	NEWTON ABBOT 86	RAMSBURY 252
MARLBOROUGH 251	NEWTOWN 288	RAMSGATE 137
MARSH GIBBON 206	NORMANTON 248	RAYLEIGH 109
MARYLEBONE 157	NORTH CHERITON 217	READING 58
MATLOCK 82	NORTH MARSTON 63	REDHILL 233
MAYBOLE 272	NORTH SHIELDS 235	REDRUTH 76
MELLOR 140	NORTH WALSHAM 189	REIGATE 233
MELROSE 261	NORTHAMPTON 198	RHOS-ON-SEA 282
MELTON MOWBRAY 145	NORTHLEIGH 86	RHYL 282

INDEX OF CITIES AND TOWNS

RICHMOND 194	SHARNBROOK 56	SUTTON 183, 234
RICHMOND–UPON–	SHEFFIELD 220	SUTTON COLDFIELD 240
THAMES 183, 233	SHENFIELD 109	SUTTON IN ASHFIELD ... 203
RICKMANSWORTH 129	SHERBORNE 93	SWANAGE 94
RINGWOOD 123	SHERINGHAM................ 190	SWANSEA 289
RIPON 194	SHIPLEY 248	SWANTON ABBOT........ 190
ROBERTSBRIDGE 102	SHOREHAM–BY–SEA 243	SWINDON 252
ROCHDALE................... 118	SHREWSBURY 213	SYSTON 145
ROMFORD 109	SIDMOUTH 87	
ROMSEY 123	SILVERSTONE 199	TADCASTER.................. 195
ROSCREA 279	SIMONSBATH 217	TALGARTH 288
ROSSCARBERY 276	SITTINGBOURNE........... 137	TAMWORTH 223
ROSSLARE HARBOUR.... 279	SKIBBEREEN................. 276	TARVIN 71
ROSS–ON–WYE 127	SKIPTON....................... 195	TAUNTON..................... 218
ROTHERHAM................. 220	SLEAFORD.................... 149	TAVISTOCK 87
ROTHLEY 145	SLIGO........................... 279	TEDDINGTON 183
RUGBY......................... 237	SLOUGH 58	TEIGNMOUTH............... 88
RUNCORN 71	SMARDEN 138	TELFORD 213
RUSHDEN 198	SMETHWICK 239	TETBURY 114
RUTHIN 282	SNETTISHAM 190	TEWKESBURY 114
RYDE 131	SOLIHULL 239	TEYNHAM 138
RYE 102	SOMERTON................... 218	THATCHAM 59
	SOUTH BRENT 87	THIRSK 195
SABDEN 142	SOUTH BURLINGHAM ... 190	THORNHILL................... 263
SAFFRON WALDEN 109	SOUTH QUEENSFERRY .. 270	THORNTON HEATH 183
SAINT ALBANS.............. 129	SOUTH SHIELDS 235	THORNTON 142
SAINT ANDREWS 265	SOUTHAMPTON 123	THORPE BAY 109
SAINT ANNES ON SEA ... 142	SOUTHEND–ON–SEA 109	THURCASTON 145
SAINT ASAPH................ 282	SOUTHPORT 186	TIBBERTON 114
SAINT AUSTELL 76	SOUTHSEA.................... 124	TICEHURST 103
SAINT HELENS......... 131, 185	SOUTHWOLD 228	TILLINGHAM 110
SAINT IVES 68, 76	SPALDING 149	TINTERN, ... 284
SAINT LEONARD'S–ON–	STAFFORD.................... 223	TISBURY....................... 252
SEA 102	STAITHES 195	TIVERTON 88
SAINT NEOTS 68	STALBRIDGE 94	TODMORDEN................. 248
SAINT PETER PORT 257	STAMFORD................... 149	TONBRIDGE.................. 138
SAINT TEATH................ 76	STAMFORD BRIDGE...... 195	TORQUAY..................... 88
SALFORD 142	STANFORD–LE–HOPE..... 109	TORRINGTON 88
SALISBURY 252	STANSTED 109	TOTNES 89
SALTBURN–BY–THE–SEA 194	STAPLEHURST 138	TOWCESTER 199
SALTHOUSE.................. 190	STEVENAGE.................. 130	TREGARON................... 281
SALTLEY 239	STEYNING 244	TRING 130
SANDIACRE.................. 203	STOCKPORT.................. 118	TRURO 76
SANDY 56	STOCKSFIELD 201	TUNBRIDGE WELLS....... 138
SAXMUNDHAM.............. 228	STOCKTON–ON–TEES..... 97	TWICKENHAM 183
SCARBOROUGH 194	STOKE SUB HAMDON 218	
SCHULL........................ 276	STOKE–ON–TRENT 223	ULVERSTON 79
SCONE......................... 273	STOKESLEY 195	UMBERLEIGH 89
SCUNTHORPE 149	STONESFIELD 209	UPPER CLAPTON........... 151
SEAFORD 103	STOURPORT-ON-	UPPER RISSINGTON 114
SEAHOUSES 201	SEVERN..................... 255	UPPINGHAM 145
SEASCALE 79	STOWMARKET.............. 228	UPTON BY CHESTER...... 69
SEATON....................... 87	STOW–ON–THE–WOLD ... 114	UPTON ST. LEONARDS... 115
SEAVIEW 131	STRATFORD–UPON–	URMSTON 118
SEDBERGH 79	AVON 237	UTTOXETER 223
SELBY 195	STROUD 114	
SELKIRK 261	STUDLEY...................... 237	VENTNOR..................... 131
SETTLE......................... 195	STURMINSTER NEWTON 94	VICARSTOWN 278
SEVENOAKS.................. 137	SUDBURY..................... 228	
SHAFTESBURY.............. 93	SUNBURY–ON–THAMES. 183	WADEBRIDGE............... 76
SHAMLEY GREEN 233	SURBITON 233	WADHURST 139

INDEX OF CITIES AND TOWNS

WALDERTON 244	WEST WICKHAM 68, 184	WIRRAL 186
WALLASEY 186	WESTBURY 252	WISBECH 68
WALLINGFORD............. 209	WESTBURY-ON-	WITHAM...................... 110
WALLINGTON............... 234	SEVERN...................... 115	WITHERSLACK.............. 80
WALSALL 240	WESTCLIFF-ON-SEA...... 110	WITNEY 210
WALSDEN...................... 248	WESTON-SUPER-MARE.. 218	WOKING....................... 234
WALSINGHAM 191	WETHERBY................... 249	WOKINGHAM 59
WALTON-ON-THAMES... 234	WEYBRIDGE 234	WOLVERHAMPTON 240
WALTON-ON-THE-	WEYMOUTH 94	WOMBOURN.................. 223
NAZE 110	WHITBY 196	WOMBWELL.................. 221
WANTAGE..................... 209	WHITCHURCH 213	WOODBRIDGE............... 229
WARBOROUGH 209	WHITEHAVEN............... 79	WOODFORD GREEN 110
WAREHAM 94	WHITHORN................... 263	WOODSTOCK 210
WARFIELD 59	WHITLEY BAY 235	WOOLER....................... 201
WARMINSTER................ 252	WHITSTABLE 139	WOOTTON BASSETT....... 253
WARRINGTON 71	WICKFORD.................... 110	WORCESTER 255
WARSASH...................... 124	WICKHAM BISHOPS,	WORTHING................... 244
WARWICK 237	WITHAM.................... 110	WRAGBY 150
WATFORD...................... 130	WIGAN.......................... 119	WREXHAM 290
WEDMORE..................... 218	WIGAN, LANCASHIRE.... 119	WYMONDHAM.............. 191
WELLING 184	WIGTON 79	WYVERSTONE................ 229
WELLINGBOROUGH 199	WIGTOWN 263	
WELLINGTON 218	WILLERBY..................... 105	YARM 196
WELLS-NEXT-THE-SEA.. 191	WILLINGTON................ 97	YARMOUTH.................. 132
WELSHPOOL 289	WIMBORNE................... 95	YEALMPTON..................89
WELTON........................ 79	WINCHESTER................ 124	YEOVIL 219
WEM 213	WINDERMERE 79	YORK........................... 196
WEOBLEY...................... 127	WINDLESHAM................ 234	YOUGHAL 276
WEST BALDWIN 258	WINDSOR 59	YOXALL 223
WEST KINGTON 252	WING 63	YOXFORD..................... 229
WEST LINTON............... 262	WINSFORD 72	
WEST PENNARD............ 218	WIRKSWORTH 82	ZEALS 253

OLYMPIC GAMES

Jeux Olympiques – Olympische Spiele – Giochi Olimpichi

1896 – 2004

Always Buying & Selling:

Official Reports - Programs - Books - Posters - Maps -
Tickets - Medals - Badges - Medallions - Collectables - etc.

Specializing in:
Olympic Games
History of Sport
Physical Education
Wrestling, Fencing
Rowing, Gymnastics
Sports & Athletics
Sport in Art
Sports Medicine
Graphic Illustrations of
   Sports & Athletics
Expositions & World's Fairs
1900 Paris, 1904 St. Louis

Historical research, writing & consulting services available.
Catalogs by subscription – Brokerage & Private Treaty sales.
Auctions – Consignments accepted – collection development.

HARVEY ABRAMS – BOOKS
P.O. Box 732 State College, P.A., U.S.A. 16804
Tel: (814) 237-8331 – Fax: (814) 237-8332
Email: Olympicbks@aol.com

BEDFORDSHIRE

BEDFORD

Books With Care, 7 Barford Road, Willington, Bedford, MK44 3QP. Prop: Gerald Ford. Tel: (01234) 831288. Fax: (01234) 831288. Website: www.bookswithcare.com. E-mail: gfbooks@bookswithcare.com. Est: 1996. Private premises; postal business only. Appointment necessary. Small general stock. PR: £1–200. CC: MC; V.

The Eagle Bookshop, ■ 103 Castle Road, Bedford, MK40 3QP. Prop: P.M. & M.M. Budek. Tel: (01234) 269295. Fax: (01234) 269295. Website: www.eaglebookshop.co.uk. E-mail: customers@eaglebookshop.co.uk. Est: 1991. Shop; open **M:** 10:00–17:30; **T:** 10:00–17:30; **Th:** 10:00–17:30; **F:** 10:00–17:30; **S:** 09:30–17:00. Very large stock. Spec: Mathematics; Physics; Science - General; Technology. PR: £1–2,000. CC: MC; V; SW.

Kingsmere Books, 41 Haylands Way, Bedford, MK41 9BY.

CHICKSANDS

Leslie H. Bolland Books, 1 Warren Court, Chicksands, SG17 5QB. Prop: Les & Anne Bolland. Tel: (01462) 815174. Fax: (01462) 814738. Website: www.bollandbooks.com. E-mail: lesbolland@aol.com. Est: 1997. Office &/or bookroom; Internet and postal. Appointment necessary. Large stock. Spec: Academic/Scholarly; Advertising; Assassinations; Author - Buckeridge, A.; Crime (True); Criminology; Police Force Histories; Sport - Angling/Fishing. PR: £2–500. CC: MC; V; SW. Also, a booksearch service. Mem: PBFA. VAT No: GB 806 1492 42.

DUNSTABLE

Adrian Walker, 107 Great Northern Road, Dunstable, LU5 4BW. Tel: (01582) 605824. E-mail: adrian-walker@supanet.com. Est: 1965. Private premises; postal business only. Very small stock. Spec: Sport - Falconry. PR: £1–250.

EGGINGTON

Robert Kirkman Ltd., Kings Cottage, Eggington, LU7 9PG. Tel: (01525) 210647. Fax: (01525) 211184. E-mail: robertkirkmanltd@btinternet.com. Est: 1987. Private premises; appointment necessary. Small stock. Spec: Antiquarian; Author - Bunyan, John; Author - Churchill, Sir Winston; Autographs; Bibles; Bindings; First Editions; Fore-Edge Paintings; Limited Editions; Literature; Sets of Books; Signed Editions. PR: £20–100. Also: Literary relics. Cata: occasionally.

KEMPSTON

Assinder Books, The Mill House, Riverview Way, Kempston, MK42 7BB. Prop: N.M. & I. Assinder. Tel: (01234) 841503. Website: www.abebooks.com. E-mail: assinbooks@aol.com. Est: 1992. Private premises; Internet and postal. Medium general stock. Spec: Children's - General; Military; Travel - General. PR: £2–300.

LEIGHTON BUZZARD

Behind the Lines, 40 Old Road, Linslade, Leighton Buzzard, LU7 2RE.

Dealers who need to update their entry should visit their page on
www.sheppardsdirectories.com

LUTON

Norman F. Hight, 121 Wardown Crescent, Luton, LU2 7JU. Tel: (01582) 402090. E-mail: norman.f.hight @care4free.net. Est: 1998. Private premises; appointment necessary. Small stock. Spec: Fiction - Crime, Detective, Spy, Thrillers; Fiction - Fantasy, Horror; Fiction - Science Fiction; Modern First Editions. PR: £1–200. CC: PayPal.

SANDY

H.J. Morgan, 47 Bedford Road, Sandy, SG19 1ES. Tel: (01767) 691383. Est: 1980. Private premises; postal business only and at book fairs. Small stock. Spec: Academic/Scholarly; History - General; Literature; Travel - General. VAT No: GB 467 3823 19.

SHARNBROOK

Ouse Valley Books, 16 Home Close, Sharnbrook, Bedford, MK44 1PQ. Prop: Barrie Farnsworth. Tel: (01234) 782411. Website: www.abebooks.com.home/ousevalleybooks. E-mail: ousevalleybooks @btinternet.com. Est: 1990. Private premises; Internet. Appointment necessary. Bookfairs. Very small stock. Spec: Academic/Scholarly; Art; Cartography; History - British; Sport - Cycling; Topography - General. PR: £5–500. CC: MC; V. Cata: Lists as required. Mem: PBFA.

BERKSHIRE

ASCOT

Ian Cross, 83 Gainsborough Drive, Ascot, SL5 8TA. Tel: (01344) 872100. Fax: (01344) 872544. E-mail: ccross@btconnect.com. Est: 1972. Spec: Art. PR: £25–500.

Melnick House Books, P.O. Box 306, Ascot, SL5 8TS.

CAVERSHAM

Caversham Emporium, ■ 10, Bridge Street,, Caversham, Reading, RG4 8AA. Prop: R.J. & E.M. Maggs, and S. Daniels. Tel: (0118) 946 2175. E-mail: sdaniels@cav-emp.freeserve.co.uk. Est: 1983. *Shop at:* Fosseway Cottage, Stratton-on-the-Fosse, Bath, Somerset, BA3 4RG. Open: **W:** 10:00–17:00; **Th:** 10:00–17:00; **F:** 10:00–17:00; **S:** 10:00–17:00; **Su:** 10:00–17:00. Medium stock. PR: £1–500 Mem: PBFA.

CROWTHORNE

Malcolm Applin, 21 Larkswood Drive, Crowthorne, Crowthorne, RG45 6RH. Tel: (01344) 776881. Est: 1993. Private premises; postal business only. Small stock. Spec: Biography; Fiction - General; Fiction - Women; Literary Criticism; Poetry. PR: £5–250. Cata: 6 a year.

HURLEY

Russell Jones Books, The Coach House, High Street, Hurley, SL6 5NB. Prop: Russell Jones. Tel: (01628) 824237. Est: 1958. Spec: Crafts; Engineering; Military; Mining; Railways; Rural Life; Steam Engines; Traction Engines; Vintage Cars. PR: £15–14,800. Also, booksearch service.

HURST

Christopher Edwards, Hatch Gate Farmhouse, Lines Road, Hurst, RG10 0SP. Prop: Christopher Edwards & Margaret Erskine. Tel: (0118) 934 0531. Fax: (0118) 934 0539. E-mail: chr.edwards@which.net. Spec: Early Imprints; History - General; Literature.

KINGSCLERE

Wyseby House Books, ■ Kingsclere Old Bookshop, 2a George Street, Kingsclere, Nr. Newbury, RG20 5NQ. Prop: Dr. T. Oldham. Tel: (01635) 297995. Fax: (01635) 297677. Website: www.wyseby.co.uk. E-mail: info@wyseby.co.uk. Est: 1978. Shop, Internet and postal. Open: **M:** 09:00–17:00; **T:** 09:00–17:00; **W:** 09:00–17:00; **Th:** 09:00–17:00; **F:** 09:00–17:00; **S:** 09:00–17:00. Very large stock. Spec: Applied Art; Architecture; Art; Art History; Art Reference; Artists; Arts, The; Biology; Botany; Decorative Art; Ecology; Fine Art; Gardening; Natural History; Natural Sciences; Ornithology; Science - History of; Zoology. PR: £1–1,000. CC: AE; JCB; MC. Cata: 12 on art, architecture, natural history, garden and science. Mem: PBFA. VAT No: GB 295 3261 54.

MAIDENHEAD

Derek Hayles Military Books, 35 St Marks Road, Maidenhead, SL6 6DJ. Tel: (01628) 639535. Fax: (01628) 788377. E-mail: derekhalyes@militarybooks.co.uk. Est: 1982. Private premises; appointment necessary. **M:** 09:00–21:00; **T:** 09:00–21:00; **W:** 09:00–21:00; **Th:** 09:00–21:00; **F:** 09:00–21:00; S: 09:00–21:00. Medium stock. Spec: Aviation; Biography; Military; Military History; Naval; War - General. PR: £10–500. CC: E; JCB; MC; V. Publishers of 'Blue List' listing 46 military specialists. Cata: 8 a year. VAT No: GB 491 8512 12.

Valerie Peel, t/a Kiandra Associates Ltd., 40 Culley Way, Cox Green, Maidenhead, SL6 3PX. Tel: (01628) 822439. Fax: (01628) 826118. E-mail: valerie_peel@dogbooks.freeserve.co.uk. Est: 1985. Private premises; postal business only. Small stock. Spec: Dogs. PR: £4–750. Free Booksearch. Cata: 2 – 6 monthly.

NEWBURY

Eastleach Books, Unit 34, New Horizon House, New Greenham Park, Newbury, RG19 6HT. Prop: Daniel Unwin. Tel: (01635) 817377. Website: www.abebooks.com/home/eastleach. E-mail: dan@bookville.freeserve.co.uk. Est: 1997. Warehouse; Internet and postal. Open: **M:** 09:00–18:00; **T:** 09:00–18:00; **W:** 09:00–18:00; **Th:** 09:00–18:00; **F:** 09:00–18:00; **S:** 09:00–18:00. Medium general stock. Spec: Academic/Scholarly; Alpinism/Mountaineering; Animals and Birds; Antiquarian; Archaeology; Architecture. PR: £2–4,500. CC: E; JCB; MC; V. Corresp: Little French.

Railway Book and Magazine Sear, The Warren, Curridge, Newbury, RG18 9DN. Prop: N.J. Bridger. Tel: (01635) 200507. Est: 1981. Private premises; postal business only. Very small general stock. Spec: Railways; Spiritualism. PR: £1–200. Also, booksearch. *Also at:* Nevis Railway Bookshop, Goring-on-Thames, Oxon (q.v.) and Nevis Railway Bookshop, Marlborough, Wiltshire (q.v.).

READING

Books & Bygones, ■ 40 Hollow Lane, Shinfield, Reading, RG2 9BT. Prop: John Lilly & Pamela Pither. Tel: (0118) 988-4346. Website: www.booksbygones.com. E-mail: booksbygones@btinternet.com. Est: 1992. *Shop at:* Lane End Farm, Shinfield, RG2 9BE. Open: **S:** 10:00–16:00; **Su:** 10:00–16:00. Very large general stock. Spec: Animals and Birds; Architecture; Artists; Arts, The; Astrology; Autobiography; Children's - General; Cookery/Gastronomy; Crafts; Fiction - Romantic; Fiction - Science Fiction; Fiction - Westerns; Firearms/Guns; First Editions; Food & Drink; Gardening. PR: £1–100. CC: MC; V; SW. Mem: Ibooknet.

K.C. Brown, 11 Easington Drive, Lower Earley, Reading, RG6 3XN. Tel: (0118) 966-7013. Est: 1991. Private premises; appointment necessary. Small general stock. Also, booksearch service.

Mary Butts Books, 219 Church Road, Earley, Reading, RG6 1HW. Tel: (0118) 926-1793. E-mail: mary@mbutts.fsnet.co.uk. Est: 1985. Private premises; Internet and postal. Appointment necessary: **M:** 09:00–17:00; **T:** 09:00–17:00; **W:** 09:00–17:00; **Th:** 09:00–17:00; **F:** 09:00–17:00; **S:** 09:00–17:00. Medium stock. Spec: Applied Art; Architecture; Art; Art History; Art Reference; Artists; Children's - General; Decorative Art; Illustrated; Literature; Painting; PR: £4–50. Corresp: French. Also, booksearch.

Footballana, 275 Overdown Road, Tilehurst, Reading, RG31 6NX. Prop: Bryan Horsnell. Fax: (0118) 942 4448. Private premises; postal business only. Very small stock. Spec: Sport - Football (Soccer); PR: £5–100. Also, pre-1950 football programmes and ephemera. Cata: occasionally.

J.B. Books, 3 Wenlock Edge, Charvil, Reading, RG10 9QG. Prop: John A. Baker. Tel: (0118) 934-0679. Website: www.balloonbooks.co.uk. E-mail: jb.books@btopenworld.com. Est: 1978. Private premises; postal business only. Small stock. Spec: Aviation; Sport - Ballooning. PR: £1–250. Corresp: French.

Keegan's Bookshop, ■ Merchant's Place, (off Friar Street), Reading, RG1 1DT. Prop: John & Judith Keegan. Tel: (0118) 958-7253. Fax: (0118) 958-5220. Est: 1979. Shop: open **M:** 09:00–17:30; **T:** 09:00–17:30; **W:** 09:00–17:30; **Th:** 09:00–17:30; **F:** 09:00–17:30; **S:** 09:00–17:30. Medium stock. Spec: Military; Railways; Topography - General. PR: £1–100.

Veronica Mayhew, Trewena, Behoes Lane, Woodcote, Reading, RG8 0PP. Tel: (01491) 680743. E-mail: veronica.mayhew@virgin.net. Est: 1972. Private premises; appointment necessary. Small stock. Spec: Animals and Birds; Apiculture; Cats; Farming & Livestock; Ornithology. PR: £1–500. Cata: 1 each on poultry, pigeons, cagebirds, farm livestock. VAT No: GB 537 6954 02.

SLOUGH

Edward Sanderson, 60a Upton Park, Slough, SL1 2DE. Prop: Edna Sanderson. Tel: (01753) 526601. Est: 1975. Spec: Anthropology; Antiquarian; Arts, The; Bibliography; Biography; Countries - Scotland; Ex-Libris; Music - Music Hall; Music - Opera; Music - Political Songs & Ballads; Music - Popular; Performing Arts; Printing; Scottish Interest; Theatre; Victoriana; PR: £10–500.

Dealers who need to update their entry should visit their page on
www.sheppardsdirectories.com

BERKSHIRE

THATCHAM
Goldsboro Books Limited, 59 Browning Close, Thatcham, RG18 3EF.

WARFIELD
Moss End Bookshop, Moss End Garden Centre, Moss End, Warfield, Nr. Bracknell, RG42 6EJ. Prop: K. & M.A. Precious. Tel: (01344) 422110. Est: 1981. Spec: Antiques; Rural Life; Sport - Field Sports. PR: £2–250.

WINDSOR
Brian Billing, 28 Athlone Square, Ward Royal, Windsor, SL4 1SS. Tel: (01753) 851343. Est: 1965. Private premises; postal business only. Small stock. Spec: Economics; Natural History; Travel - General. PR: £2–250. Cata: occasionally.

Eton Antique Bookshop, ■ 88 High Street, Eton, Windsor, SL4 6AF. Prop: Maurice Bastians. Tel: (01753) 855534. Est: 1975. Shop open: **M:** 12:00–17:00; **T:** 12:00–17:00; **W:** 12:00–17:00; **Th:** 12:00–17:00; **F:** 12:00–17:00; **S:** 12:00–17:00; **Su:** 12:00–17:00. Medium stock. Spec: Bindings; Public Schools; Sets of Books. PR: £3–1,000. CC: E; JCB; MC; V. Open mornings but hours variable - phone first. Also, bookbinding and booksearch. Corresp: Spanish. Mem: Eton Traders Assoc. VAT No: GB 787 1877 65.

WOKINGHAM
John Townsend, 95 Arbor Lane, Winnersh, Wokingham, RG41 5JE. Tel: (0118) 978-5463. Fax: (0118) 978-1875. Website: www.johntownsend.demon.co.uk. E-mail: john@johntownsend.demon.co.uk. Est: 1991. Private premises; Internet and postal. Appointment necessary. Medium stock. Spec: Genealogy; Heraldry; History - General; Manuscripts; Parish Registers; School Registers/Rolls of Honour; Topography - General; Topography - Local. PR: £10–200. Cata: 6 on Genealogy, Heraldry, British Local History. Corresp: French, German. VAT No: GB 591 8061 25.

BRISTOL

BRISTOL

Lesley Aitchison, 22 West Shrubbery, Redland, Bristol, BS6 6TA.

Ambra Books, 22 West Shrubbery, Redland, Bristol, BS6 6TA. Prop: Ivor Cornish. Tel: (0117) 907-6899. Fax: (0117) 974-1962. Website: www.localhistory.co.uk/ambra. E-mail: ambra@localhistory.co.uk. Est: 1972. Private premises; Internet and postal. Appointment necessary: **M:** 09:00–17:00; **T:** 09:00–17:00; **W:** 09:00–17:00; **Th:** 09:00–17:00; **F:** 09:00–17:00; **S:** 09:00–12:00. Small stock. Spec: Genealogy; History - Local; Topography - Local. PR: £10–3,000. CC: MC; V; SW. Cata: 6 on West Country topography. Corresp: French, Italian.

Anthroposophical Books, 12d Cotham Road, Cotham, Bristol, BS6 6DR. Prop: H. & A. Tandree. Tel: (0117) 923-7372. Fax: (0117) 923-7372. E-mail: herb@philosophy-books.co.uk. Est: 1988. Private premises; appointment necessary. Small general stock. Spec: Anthroposophy; Author - Steiner, Rudolf; Occult. PR: £8–50. CC: MC; V. Cata: 1 a year on Rudolf Steiner & anthroposophy. Corresp: French, German.

Avon Books, ■ 4 Waterloo Street, Clifton, Bristol, BS8 4BT. Prop: John Ray. Tel: (0117) 973-9848. E-mail: sales@avonbook.co.uk. Est: 1991. Shop; open **M:** 11:00–18:00; **T:** 11:00–18:00; **W:** 11:00–18:00; **Th:** 11:00–17:00; **F:** 11:00–18:00; **S:** 11:00–18:00. Medium general stock. PR: £2–200. CC: MC; V.

Gerald Baker, 28 Beaconsfield Road, Clifton, Bristol, BS8 2TS. Tel: (0117) 974-4319. Website: www.gwrpublicity.co.uk. E-mail: gwrpublicity@btinternet.com. Postal business only. Very small stock. Spec: Railways; PR: £5–200. Cata: 2 a year.

Beware of The Leopard Books, 66–69 & 77 The Covered Market, St. Nicholas Market, St Nicholas Street, Bristol, BS1 1LJ. Prop: David Jackson. Tel: (0117) 925-7277. Est: 1991. Market stand/stall **M:** 10:00–17:00; **T:** 10:00–17:00; **W:** 10:00–17:00; **Th:** 10:00–17:00; **F:** 10:00–17:00; **S:** 10:00–17:00. Very large general stock. Spec: Academic/Scholarly; Art; Biography; Chemistry; Computing; Economics; Fairgrounds; Fiction - General; First Editions; History - General; Humanities; Languages - Foreign; Law; Literature; Mathematics; Medicine; Music - General; Poetry; Politics; Religion - General; Science - General; Social History; Technical; Theology. PR: £1–75. CC: JCB; MC; V. VAT No: GB 520 0870 87.

Bishopston Books, ■ 259, Gloucester Rd, Bishopston, BS7 8NY. Prop: Bill Singleton. Tel: (0117) 944-5303. E-mail: bishopstonbooks@btinternet.com. Est: 1995. Shop; open **Th:** 10:00–17:30; **F:** 10:00–17:30; **S:** 09:30–16:30. Medium general stock. PR: £1–200. CC: JCB; V.

Bristol Books, 180b Cheltenham Road, Montpelier, Bristol, BS6 5RB.

Bristol Books Academic, 180c Cheltenham Road, Montpelier, Bristol, BS6 5RB.

James Burmester, Pipley Old Farm, North Stoke Lane, Upton Cheyney, Bristol, BS30 6NG. Prop: James & Rosamund Burmester. Tel: (0117) 932-7265. Fax: (0117) 932-7667. E-mail: james@libros.demon.co.uk. Est: 1985. Private premises; appointment necessary. Small stock. Spec: Agriculture. PR: £50–10,000. Cata: 3. VAT No: GB 404 6808 60.

Chandos Books, 8 Chandos Road, Redland, Bristol, BS6 6PE.

Cotham Hill Bookshop, 39a Cotham Hill, Cotham, BS6 6JY.

Court Hay Books, Court Hay, 26 Church Road, Easton-in-Gordano, Bristol, BS20 0PQ. Prop: Howard and Gilian Walters. Tel: (01275) 372751. Website: www.courthaybooks.co.uk. E-mail: courthay books@btconnect.com. Est: 1990. Private premises; Internet and postal. Appointment necessary. Small stock. Spec: Flower Arranging; Gardening; Horticulture. PR: £10–2,000. CC: AE; JCB; MC; V.

Darklair, 37 Lintern Crescent, Bristol, BS30 8GB.

Searching for a title - and cannot find it on any Internet database?
Then try **SheppardsBooksearch**

By selecting the subject classification – the request goes to all dealers who major in that subject.

BRISTOL 61

Deverell Books, 86a Memorial Road, Hanham, Bristol, BS15 3LA. Prop: Paul Deverell Hughes. Tel: (0117) 961-6234. Fax: (0117) 373-8786. E-mail: pdhbooks@hotmail.com. Est: 2001. Private premises; appointment necessary. Very small stock. Spec: Books about Books; Children's - General; Illustrated; Spiritualism. PR: £10–2,000. Cata: 1 annually.

R.A. Gilbert, 4 Julius Road, Bishopston, Bristol, BS7 8EU. Tel: (0117) 924-6936. Fax: (0117) 924-4937. Est: 1963. Private premises; appointment necessary. Small stock. Spec: Alchemy; Folklore; Freemasonry & Anti-Masonry; Gnostics; Occult; Psychic; Religion - General; Theology; Witchcraft. PR: £5–1,000. Cata: 1 on Freemasonry & occult, occasionally on others. Corresp: French. Mem: PBFA. VAT No: GB 138 9728 22.

Harlequin Books, ■ 122 High Street, Staple Hill, Bristol, BC16 5HH. Prop: Brian W. Ball. Tel: (0117) 970-1801. Fax: (0117) 970-1801. E-mail: harlequin.books@virgin.net. Est: 1984. Shop: open **M:** 09:30–16:30; **T:** 09:30–16:30; **W:** 09:30–16:30; **Th:** 09:30–16:30; **F:** 09:30–16:30; **S:** 09:30–16:30. Medium stock. Spec: Aviation; Military; Motoring; Railways; Topography - Local. PR: £2–200. CC: AE; JCB; MC; V.

Hawthorn Books, The Old Mill, Brices Farm, Westerleigh, Bristol, BS37 8QU. Prop: Anthony & Nora Aldridge. Tel: (01454) 319712. Website: www.hawthornbooks.co.uk. E-mail: hawthorn.books @btconnect.com. Est: 1980. Private premises; Internet. Medium stock. Spec: Modern First Editions; Sport - Golf. PR: £20–1,500. VAT No: GB 464 7940 13.

A.R. Heath, 62 Pembroke Road, Clifton, Bristol, BS8 3DX. Tel: (0117) 974-1183. Fax: (0117) 973-2901. Website: www.abebooks.com/home/arheath/. E-mail: heath.rare-books@dsl.pipex.comco.uk. Est: 1964. Spec: Fine & Rare; Manuscripts. PR: £50–10,000.

Herb Tandree Philosophy Books, 12d Cotham Road, BS6 6DR. Prop: Herb Tandree. Tel: (0117) 923 7372. Fax: (0117) 923 7372. Website: www.philosophy-books.co.uk. E-mail: herb@philosophy-books.co.uk. Est: 2000. Private premises; Internet and postal. Appointment necessary. Medium stock. Spec: Academic/Scholarly; Economics; History of Ideas; Philosophy; Religion - General. CC: AE; JCB; MC. Cata: 6 bi-monthly. Corresp: French, German. VAT No: GB 783 4154 17.

Arthur Hook, 54 Egerton Road, Bristol, BS7 8HL. Tel: (0117) 9144673. E-mail: hooksbooks@ blueyonder.co.uk. Est: 1997. Private premises; postal business only. Very small stock. Spec: Topography - General; Travel - General. Cata: 1 occasionally.

A.J. Kitley, 31 Perrys Lea, Bradley Stoke, BS32 0EE. Tel: (01454) 615261. Est: 1986. Private premises; postal business only. Very small stock. Spec: Musical Instruments. PR: £1–150. Cata: occasionally. Also, booksearch.

Rachel Lee Rare Books, The Old Bakery, 30 Poplar Road, Warmley, Bristol, BS30 5JU. Prop: Rachel Lee & Herb Tandree. Tel: (0117) 960-6891. Fax: (0117) 960-6935. Website: www.rleerarebooks.co.uk. E-mail: rachellee.books@virgin.net. Est: 1979. Private premises; Internet and postal. Appointment necessary. Small stock. Spec: Academic/Scholarly; Economics; History of Ideas; Philosophy. PR: £20–20,000. CC: AE; MC; V. Also, a booksearch service for philosophy only. Cata: 3. Mem: ABA. VAT No: GB 783 5078 02.

Paperbacks Plus, Regent Street Shopping Arcade, 98 Regent Street, Kingswood, Bristol, BS15 8HP. Prop: Mr. T. Nicholls. Tel: (0117) 9566232. Website: www.pbplus.freeserve.co.uk. E-mail: books@ pbplus.freeserve.co.uk. Est: 1994. Spec: Children's - General; Modern First Editions; Vintage Paperbacks. PR: £1–20.

S.P.C.K., 79 Park Street, Bristol, BS1 5PF.

Serendipity Books, 213 Easton Road, Bristol, BS5 0EH.

Morris & Juliet Venables, 270 Henbury Road, Bristol, BS10 7QR. Tel: (0117) 950-7362. Fax: (0117) 959-2361. E-mail: morris.venables@ukgateway.net. Est: 1970. Spec: Academic/Scholarly; Antiquarian; Art; Fine & Rare; Literary Criticism; Literature; Music - General; Poetry; Stained Glass. PR: £5–1,000.

The Wise Owl Bookshop, 4 Julius Road, Bishopston, Bristol, BS7 8EN. Prop: Mrs. Patricia Gilbert. Tel: (0117) 924-6936. Fax: (0117) 949-4937. Est: 1968. Private premises; appointment necessary. Small stock. Spec: Cats; Children's - General; Music - General. PR: £1–100. Cata: 1 each on children's and cats. Corresp: French.

BUCKINGHAMSHIRE

AYLESBURY

Bernwode Books, 48 Worminghall Road, Oakley, Aylesbury, HP18 9QY. Prop: Dr. S.R.J. Woodell. Tel: (01844) 238399. Est: 1984. Private premises; appointment necessary. Small stock. Spec: Botany; Evolution; Natural History; Science - General; Travel - General. PR: £2–400. Cata: occasionally. Corresp: French.

Peter Eaton (Booksellers) Ltd., 1 Sandhill House, Middle Claydon, MK18 2LD. Prop: M. Eaton. Tel: (01296) 738888. E-mail: margaret@peaton.plus.com. Est: 1944. Private premises; postal business only. Small general stock. Spec: Antiquarian. PR: £25–10,000. Corresp: French. Mem: ABA. VAT No: GB 238 7381 36.

Wendover Bookshop, 35 High Street, Wendover, Aylesbury, HP22 6DU.

BEACONSFIELD

Barn Books, Old Hay Barn, Holtspur Bottom, Beaconsfield, HP9 1BS. Prop: Elisabeth & Wolfgang Ansorge. Tel: (01494) 671122. Fax: (01494) 671122. E-mail: barnbooks@supanet.com. Spec: Archaeology; Art; Cinema/Film; Collecting; Crafts; History - General; Military; Natural History; Politics; Royalty - General; Voyages & Discovery. PR: £5–3,000. Also, booksearch.

BUCKINGHAM

Corvus Books, 11 Parsons Close, Winslow, Buckingham, MK18 3BX. Prop: Chris Corbett. Tel: (01296) 713393. Fax: (01296) 713393. E-mail: corvusbooks@btinternet.com. Est: 1990. Private premises; appointment necessary. Very small stock. Spec: Colour-Plate; Natural History; Travel - General. PR: £50–5,000. CC: Pay Pal. Also attends 10 fairs a year at the Hotel Russell, London. Mem: PBFA.

CHESHAM

David Mundy, ■ 9 Market Square, Chesham, HP5 1HG. Tel: (020) 7482 7087. Est: 2000. Shop. Very small stock. Spec: Art; Philosophy; Psychology/Psychiatry; Psychotherapy; Topography - General. PR: £1–50. CC: MC; V. *Also at:* (Postal Address) 3 Oakford Road, London NW5 1AJ.

Omniphil Prints, Germain's Lodge, Fullers Hill, Chesham, HP5 1LR. Tel: (01494) 771851. E-mail: omniphil@talk21.com. Private premises; appointment necessary. Spec: Periodicals & Magazines. Specialist stocks of Illustrated London News.

GREAT MISSENDEN

Martin Blackman, 6 Wychwood Rise, Great Missenden, HP16 0HB. Tel: (01494) 890839. Fax: (01494) 890839. E-mail: martin@mblackman.fsnet.co.uk. Est: 1993. Spec: First Editions; Modern First Editions. PR: £5–200.

HIGH WYCOMBE

Torsdag Books, 16 Hampden Road, High Wycombe, HP13 6SX. Prop: Clive Harper. Private premises; postal business only. Spec: First Editions; Occult. PR: £1–100.

Dealers who need to update their entry should visit their page on
www.sheppardsdirectories.com

Dealers without e-mail – post details

IVER

Pemberley Books, ■ 8 Bathurst Walk, Richings Park, Iver, SL0 9AZ. Prop: Ian A. Johnson. Tel: (01753) 631114. Fax: (01753) 631115. Website: www.pembooks.demon.co.uk. E-mail: ij@pembooks.demon.co.uk. Est: 1985. Shop; Internet and postal. Telephone first. Spec: Antiquarian; Botany; Entomology; Herpetology; Lepidopterology / Lepidoptery; Natural History; Ornithology; Zoology. PR: £5–8,000. CC: AE; E; JCB; MC; V. Also, new books on specialities. Cata: 2 . Corresp: German. Mem: PBFA. VAT No: GB 646 2266 34.

MILTON KEYNES

Andromeda Books, 4 Glovers Lane, Heelands, Milton Keynes, MK13 8LW. Prop: Annie & Mike Eynon. Tel: (01908) 312046. Fax: (01908) 312046. Website: www.m31books.co.uk. E-mail: andromedabooks@btopenworld.com. Est: 1998. Private premises; postal business only. Appointment necessary. Small stock. Spec: Art; Astronomy; Decorative Art. PR: £2–100. CC: AE; JCB; MC; V; SW. Cata: 4 – quarterly. Mem: FSB.

Butler Books, Castlethorpe Lodge, Hanslope Road, Castlethorpe, Milton Keynes, MK19 7HD.

Daeron's Books, ■ 3 Timor Court, Stony Stratford, Milton Keynes, MK11 1DG. Prop: Angela Gardner. Tel: (01908) 568989. Fax: (01908) 266092. Website: www.daerons.co.uk. E-mail: books@daerons.co.uk. Est: 1992. Shop; Internet, postal and shop at: The Office: 69 Malletts Close, Stony Stratford MK11 1DG. Open: **M:** 09:00–17:00; **T:** 09:00–17:00; **W:** 09:00–17:00. **F:** 09:00–17:00; **S:** 09:00–17:00. Medium stock. Spec: Author - Tolkien, J.R.R.; Fiction - Fantasy, Horror; Fiction - Science Fiction; Mythology. PR: £1–500. CC: AE; D; E; JCB; MC; V. Mem: FSB, SSBA. VAT No: GB 776 7066 85.

Fireside Books, 3 Naseby Court, Bradville, Milton Keynes, MK13 7EP. Prop: John and Catherine Coppock. Tel: (01908) 320100. Fax: (0870) 1617621. Website: www.firesidebooks.demon.co.uk. E-mail: john@firesidebooks.demon.co.uk. Est: 1998. Private premises; postal business only. Very small stock. Spec: Author - Morton, H.V.; History - General; Rural Life; Topography - General; Topography - Local; Travel - General. PR: £2–300. Also, Booksearch.

Periplus Books, ■ 2 Timor Court, Stony Stratford, Milton Keynes, MK11 1EJ. Prop: John Phillips. Tel: (01908) 263300. Fax: (01908) 663579. E-mail: info@periplusbooks.co.uk. Web site: www.periplusbooks.co.uk. Est: 1997. Shop open: **T:** 10:30–17:00; **W:** 10:30–17:00. **F:** 10:30–17:00; **S:** 10:30–17:00. Small general stock. Spec: Marine Sciences; Meteorology. Stock at shop is general. Titles on Oceanography, Marine Biology, Meteorology only by post and Internet. PR: £1–100.

NORTH MARSTON

Valerie Newby, Prices Cottage, 57 Quainton Road, North Marston, MK8 3PR. Tel: (01296) 670001. Fax: (01296) 670002. E-mail: valerie.newby@btopenworld.com. Est: 1996. Private premises; postal business only. Small stock. Spec: Antiquarian; Atlases; Cartography; Voyages & Discovery. PR: £5–1,000. CC: MC; V. Corresp: French, Spanish.

PENN

Penn Barn Bookshop, ■ By the Pond, Elm Road, Penn, HP10 8LB. Prop: P.J.M. Hunnings. Tel: (01494) 815691. Est: 1968. Shop; open: **T:** 10:30–14:00; **W:** 10:30–14:00; **Th:** 10:30–14:00; **F:** 10:30–14:00; **S:** 10:30–14:00. Small stock. Spec: Antiquarian; Art; Bindings; Illustrated; Topography - General. PR: £2–200.

WING

Book Collectors Paradise, 38 Windmill Way, Tring, HP23 4HH. Prop: Trudy Ashford. Tel: (01442) 824440. Est: 1985. Book fairs only: at Wing Village Hall, Buckinghamshire. Open: **Su:** 10:00–16:00. PR: £1–100. *Also at:* At Milton Keynes Shopping Centre.

CAMBRIDGESHIRE

BASSINGBOURN

David Bickersteth, 4 South End, Bassingbourn, SG8 5NG. Tel: (01763) 245619. Fax: (01763) 242969. E-mail: dlb.1930@virgin.net. Est: 1967. Private premises; appointment necessary. VAT No: GB 213 7868 52.

BLUNTISHAM

Bluntisham Books, Oak House, 4 East Street, Bluntisham, Huntingdon, PE28 3LS. Prop: D.W.H. & S. Walton. Tel: (01487) 840449. Fax: (01487) 840894. Website: www.bluntishambooks.co.uk. E-mail: contact@bluntishambooks.co.uk. Est: 1976. Private premises; postal business only. Small stock. Spec: Avant-Garde; Countries - Antarctic, The; Countries - Arctic, The; Countries - Greenland; Countries - Polar; Whaling. PR: £5–2,000. CC: MC; V. Also, publishers of Antarctic book, inc. reprints of classics. Cata: 3. VAT No: GB 344 2959 39.

CAMBRIDGE

Adab Books, P.O. Box 16, Cambridge, CB3 9QQ. Prop: Daphne Roper. Tel: (01223) 323047. Fax: (01223) 367190. E-mail: adab@adabbooks.co.uk. Est: 1971. Postal business only. Very small stock. Spec: Byzantium; Canals/Inland Waterways; Carriages & Driving; Countries - Africa; Countries - Asia; Countries - Balkans, The; Countries - Spain; Ottoman Empire; Religion - Islam. PR: £20–3,000. CC: AE; MC; V. Cata: 5. VAT No: GB 532 2307 85.

Book Barrow, 93 Cam Causeway, Chesterton, Cambridge, CB4 1TL. Tel: (01223) 424 429. E-mail: bookbarrow@btclick.com. Market stand/stall; Internet and postal. Open: **Th:** 09:30–16:00; **F:** 09:30–22:00. Spec: Academic/Scholarly; Advertising; Aeronautics; Africana; Agriculture; American Indians; Esoteric; First Editions; Modern First Editions; Satire; Signed Editions.

Books & Collectables Ltd., Unit 7/8, Railway Arches, Coldhams Road, Cambridge, CB1 3EW.

Books of Note, 19 Howard Close, Cambridge, CB5 8QU. Prop: Mark Richardson. Tel: (01223) 292280. Fax: (01223) 292280. Website: www.booksofnote.co.uk. E-mail: markcamb@gxn.co.uk. Est: 1996. Private premises; postal business only. Spec: Music - Folk & Irish Folk; Music - Popular. PR: £5–30.

The Bookshop, ■ 24 Magdalene Street, Cambridge, CB3 0AF. Prop: Peter Bright & Hugh Hardinge. Tel: (01223) 362457. E-mail: hardinge@btinternet.com. Est: 1996. Open: **M:** 10:30–17:30; **T:** 10:30–17:30; **W:** 10:30–17:30; **Th:** 10:30–17:30; **F:** 10:30–17:30; **S:** 10:30–17:30. Medium stock. Spec: Academic/Scholarly; Art; Children's - General; Literature; Poetry; Sport - Cricket; Topography - General. PR: £3–250. See also, P.G. Bright, 11 Ravens Court, Ely (q.v.) and Hugh Hardinge, Cambridge Market Square.

Bracton Books, 25 Lode Road, Lode, Cambridge, CB5 9ER. Prop: Mrs S.J. Harrison. Tel: (01223) 811976. Website: www.bractonbooks.co.uk. E-mail: bractonbooks@uk2.net. Est: 1981. Private premises; postal business only. Large stock. Spec: American Indians; Anthropology; Archaeology; Biology; Books about Books; Countries - Africa; Countries - Americas, The; Countries - Asia; Countries - Melanesia; Countries - Polynesia; Ethnography; Evolution; Folklore; History - General; Literary Criticsim; Literature; Medicine; Periodicals & Magazines, Poetry; Psychology/Psychiatry; Travel - General; Tribal; Zoology. PR: £2–100. Cata: occasionally. Computer listings on requests.

Harry Brett, Pepperpot Cottage, Bartlow Road, Castle Camps, Cambridge, CB1 6SX. Tel: (01799) 584515. Est: 1968. Private premises; postal business only. Small stock. PR: £2–500.

J. & J. Burgess Booksellers, 2 St Thomas's Road, Cambridge, CB1 3TF. Prop: John Burgess. Tel: (01223) 249037. E-mail: jandjburgess2@ntlworld.com. Est: 1997. Private premises; appointment necessary. Small general stock. Spec: Academic/Scholarly; Animals and Birds; Arms & Armour; Astrology; Author - General; Aviation; Buses/Trams; Children's - General; Maritime/Nautical; Medicine; Military; Natural History; New Age; Politics; Science - General; Witchcraft. PR: £4–150.

G. David, ■ 16 St. Edward's Passage, Cambridge, CB2 3PJ. Prop: D.C. Asplin, N.T. Adams & B.L. Collings. Tel: (01223) 354619. Fax: (01223) 324663. E-mail: gdavid.books@btinternet.com. Est: 1896. Shop; open **M:** 09:00–17:00; **T:** 09:00–17:00; **W:** 09:00–17:00; **Th:** 09:00–17:00; **F:** 09:00–17:00; **S:** 09:00–17:00. Medium stock. Spec: Antiquarian; Bindings; Children's - General; Early Imprints; Fine & Rare; Illustrated; Literature; Natural History; Travel - General. PR: £1–10,000. CC: JCB; MC; V. Large selection of remainders. Corresp: Japanese, Swedish. Mem: ABA; PBFA; BA.

CAMBRIDGESHIRE

Galloway & Porter Limited, ■ 30 Sidney Street, Cambridge, CB2 3HS. Tel: (01223) 367876. Fax: (01223) 360705. E-mail: galpor1@aol.com. Est: 1900. Shop; open **M:** 08:45–17:00; **T:** 08:45–17:00; **W:** 08:45–17:00; **Th:** 08:45–17:00; **F:** 08:45–17:00; **S:** 09:00–17:15. Large stock. Spec: Academic/Scholarly; Mythology. PR: £1–2,000. Also, remainders and bargain books. Mem: ABA; PBFA; BA; BT.

K.P. Hunter, Bookseller, 13, St. Margaret's Road, Girton, Cambridge, CB3 0LT. Tel: (01223) 529295. Website: www.abebooks.com. E-mail: kate.hunter1@ntlworld.com. Est: 1995. Private premises; Book fairs only. Very small stock. Spec: Academic/Scholarly; Author - 20th Century; Author - Lawrence, T.E.; Authors - Women; Bibliography; First Editions; Fishes; Gardening; Literature. PR: £5–500. Corresp: French. Mem: PBFA.

Sarah Key Books, ■ The Haunted Bookshop, 9 St. Edward's Passage, Cambridge, CB2 3PJ. Prop: Sarah Key & Phil Salin. Tel: (01223) 312913. E-mail: sarahkey@hauntedbooks.demon.co.uk. Est: 1985. Shop; open: **M:** 10:00–17:00; **T:** 10:00–17:00; **W:** 10:00–17:00; **Th:** 10:00–17:00; **F:** 10:00–17:00; **S:** 10:00–17:00. Medium stock. Spec: Academic/Scholarly; Aeronautics; Annuals; Authors: Brent-Dyer, E; Oxenham, E; Needham, V; Johns WE; Barker, CM; Attwell, ML; Mallory, C; Courtney, G; Crompton, R; Rackham, A; Wain, L; Blyton, E; Saville, M; Bruce, DF; Fitzroy, O. PR: £1–2,000. CC: AE; JCB; MC. Also, local interest items & a booksearch service. Cata: 1 – on children's & illustrated. Corresp: French. Mem: PBFA. VAT No: GB 572 9680 04.

Paul Kunkler Books, 6 Hardwick Street, Cambridge, CB3 9JA. Tel: (01223) 321419. Fax: (01223) 321419. Private premises; appointment necessary. Very small stock. Spec: Art History; Manuscripts.

Lund Theological Books, 1 Arbury Road, Cambridge, CB4 2JB. Prop: Philip Lund. Tel: (01223) 565303. Website: www.lundbooks.co.uk. E-mail: sales@lundbooks.co.uk. Est: 1983. Private premises; Internet and postal. Medium stock. Spec: Bibles; Ecclesiastical History & Architecture; History - Byzantine; History - Middle Ages; Medieval; Mysticism; Philosophy; Prayer Books; Religion - Buddhism; Religion - Christian; Religion - Islam; Religion - Jewish; Theology; Vatican and Papal History. PR: £5–300. CC: MC; V. Cata: – on specialities. Mem: IBooknet. VAT No: GB 386 0602 50.

Adam Mills Rare Books, 328 High Street, Cottenham, Cambridge, CB4 8TX. Tel: (01954) 250106. Fax: (01954) 250106. Website: www.abebooks.com. E-mail: adam@millsrb.freeserve.co.uk. Est: 1981. Private premises; Internet and postal. Open: Small stock. Spec: Bibliography; Books about Books; Fine Printing; Illustrated; Literature; Private Press; Typography. CC: MC; V. Cata: regularly. Corresp: French, Italian. Mem: PBFA.

Peter Moore, P.O. Box 66, 200a Perne Road, Cambridge, CB1 3PD. Prop: Peter Moore. Tel: (01223) 411177. Fax: (01223) 240559. Website: www.aus-pacbooks.co.uk. E-mail: aus-pacbooks@lineone.net. Est: 1970. Office &/or bookroom; Internet and postal. Appointment necessary. Small stock. Spec: Countries - Australia; Countries - Pacific, The; Countries - Papua New Guinea; Travel - Australasia/Australia. PR: £1–500. CC: MC; V. Cata: 2 occasionally. Mem: PBFA; BCSA.VAT No: GB 215 3610 02.

Mike Parker Books, 2 Mill Lane, Duxford, Cambridge, CB2 4PT. (*). Tel: (01223) 835935. Fax: (01223) 839737. E-mail: mjp@lineone.net. Est: 1995. Private premises; appointment necessary. Small stock. Spec: Academic/Scholarly; Advertising; Modern First Editions. PR: £5–500.

Plurabelle Books, 77 Garden Walk, Cambridge, CB4 3EW. Prop: Dr. Michael Cahn. Tel: (01223) 571105. Website: www.plurabelle.co.uk. E-mail: books@plurabelle.co.uk. Est: 1993. Warehouse; postal business only. Telephone first. Very large stock. Spec: Academic/Scholarly; Computing; Foreign Texts; Humanities; Linguistics; Literary Criticism; Literature; Philology; Philosophy; Science - History of. PR: £8–200. CC: MC; V. Corresp: German, Italian. Mem: Tom Folio; IBooknet. VAT No: GB 636 8493 00.

Quest Booksearch, 24 Hawthorne Road, Stapleford, Cambridge, CB2 5DU. Prop: Dr. Rosemary Scott. Tel: (01223) 844080. Fax: (01223) 844080. E-mail: qbs2@lineone.net. Est: 1997. Private premises; postal business only. Spec: Literature; Poetry. PR: £1–200. Also, booksearch.

Rupert Books, 58/59 Stonefield, Bar Hill, Cambridge, CB3 8TE. Prop: Paulina M. & R. Dixon Smith. Tel: (01954) 781861. Website: www.rupert-books.co.uk. E-mail: sales@rupert-books.co.uk. Est: 1984. Spec: Author - Conan Doyle, Sir Arthur; Crime (True); Sherlockiana. PR: £3–1,000.

Available from Richard Joseph Publishers Ltd
Sheppard's International Directory of
PRINT AND MAP SELLERS

4th Edition (Royal H/b)   £27.00 320pp

Ken Trotman, Unit 11, 135 Ditton Walk, Cambridge, CB5 8PY. Prop: Richard & Roz Brown. Tel: (01223) 211030. Fax: (01223) 212317. Website: www.kentrotman.com. E-mail: rlbtrotman@aol.com. Est: 1949. Postal business only. Spec: Military. PR: £5–1,500. CC: MC; V. Cata: 4 – quarterly. Corresp: French. Mem: PBFA. VAT No: GB 386 4614 23.

de Visser Books, 309 Milton Road, Cambridge, CB4 1XQ. Prop: Erik de Visser. Tel: (01223) 500909. Fax: (01223) 500909. E-mail: devisserbooks@hotmail.com. Est: 1989. Private premises; appointment necessary. Small stock. Spec: Biography; Countries - Albania; Countries - Austria; Countries - Germany; Countries - Hungary; Countries - Poland; Countries - Romania; Culture - Foreign; Economics; Foreign Texts; Literature; Military; Politics; Religion - Jewish. PR: £5–500. CC: E; MC; V. Also, a booksearch service. Cata: 5. Corresp: Dutch, French, German. VAT No: GB 493 3891 05.

Frances Wetherell, 8 Highworth Avenue, Cambridge, CB4 2BG. Tel: (01223) 363537. E-mail: frances.wetherell@talk21.com. Est: 1988. Private premises; postal business only. Very small general stock. Spec: Art; Economics; Literature; Social History. PR: £10–100. Also, a booksearch service.

David White, The Old Guildhall, 4 Church Lane, Linton, Cambridge, CB1 6JX. Prop: David White. Tel: (01223) 894447. Fax: (01223) 894449. Website: www.davidwhitebooks.co.uk. E-mail: david.white23@virgin.net. Est: 1987. Private premises; Internet and postal. Appointment necessary. Very small stock. Spec: Medicine; Medicine - History of; Pharmacy/Pharmacology. PR: £10–2,000. CC: MC; V. Cata: 1 a year. VAT No: GB 665 6605 10.

Peter Wood, 20 Stonehill Road, Great Shelford, Cambridge, CB2 5JL. Tel: (01223) 842419. Private premises; appointment necessary. Small stock. Spec: Art; Biography; Broadcasting; Cinema/Film; Entertainment - General; Music - General; Performing Arts; Photography; Puppets & Marionettes; Ventriloquism. PR: £10–100. CC: AE; JCB; MC; V. Cata: 4 a year. Mem: PBFA. VAT No: GB 214 4339 88.

CHATTERIS

Joan Stevens, ■ 3 High Street, Chatteris, PE16 6BE. Tel: (01354) 696874. Fax: (01354) 696874. Est: 1962. Shop; open **S:** 10:00–17:00. Medium stock. Spec: Art History; Art Reference; Artists; Arts, The; Feminism; Fiction - General; Illustrated; Literary Criticism; Literature; Literature in Translation; Music - General; Poetry; Politics; Social History; War - General; Women. PR: £5–100. Open at other times by appointment. Cata: 2 – a year on art, illustrated, literature, poetry.

ELY

P.G. Bright, 11 Ravens Court, Ely, CB6 3ED. Tel: (01353) 661727. E-mail: peter.bright@care4free.net. Est: 1982. Private premises; appointment necessary. Medium stock. Spec: Children's - General; Illustrated; Literature; Sport - Cricket. PR: £1–500. Mem: PBFA. *Also at:* The Bookshop, 24 Magdalene Street, Cambridge (q.v.).

Ely Books, 24 Downham Road, Ely, CB6 1AF. Prop: Michael G. Kousah. Tel: (01353) 661824. E-mail: elybooks@ntlworld.com. Est: 1986. Private premises; appointment necessary and bookfairs. Very small stock. Spec: Bindings; Children's - General; Illustrated; Travel - General. PR: £1–2,000. Mem: PBFA. VAT No: GB 572 9042 32.

Hereward Books, ■ 17 High Street, Haddenham, Ely, CB6 3XA. Prop: Roger J. Pratt. Tel: (01353) 740821. Fax: (01353) 741721. Website: www.herewardbooks.co.uk. E-mail: sales@herewardbooks.co.uk. Est: 1985. Shop; Internet and postal. Open: **M:** 10:00–16:00; **T:** 10:00–16:00. **Th:** 10:00–16:00; **F:** 10:00–13:00; **S:** 10:00–13:00. Medium stock. Spec: Bindings; Illustrated; Natural History; Sport - Angling/Fishing; Sport - Falconry; Sport - Field Sports; Travel - General. PR: £15–1,000. CC: MC; V & Debit. Cata: 2 – on field sports. Mem: PBFA. VAT No: GB 382 3886 03.

Octagon Books, ■ 14 Pilgrims Way, Ely, CB6 3DL. Prop: John & Jacqueline Williams. Tel: (01353) 610244. Website: www.cloistersantiques.co.uk/octagon. E-mail: octagonbooks@aol.com. Est: 1982. Shop at; Cloister's Antique Shop, 1A Lynn Road, Ely. Open: **M:** 10:00–16:30. **W:** 10:00–16:30; **Th:** 10:00–16:30; **F:** 10:00–16:30; **S:** 10:00–16:30; **Su:** 12:30–16:30. Small stock. Spec: Architecture; Art. Mem: PBFA. VAT No: GB 393 2186 39.

GODMANCHESTER

Godmanchester Books, Staughton House, 11 Post Street, Godmanchester, PE29 2BA. Prop: Doreen Lewis. Tel: (01480) 455020. Est: 1974. Private premises; appointment necessary. Small stock. Spec: History - Local; Topography - Local. PR: £1–100. Also, booksearch.

CAMBRIDGESHIRE

HADDENHAM

John Lewcock, 6 Chewells Lane, Haddenham, Ely, CB6 3SS. Prop: John Lewcock. Tel: (01353) 741960. Fax: (01353) 741710. Website: www.abebooks.com/home/maritime. E-mail: lewcock@maritime-bookseller.com. Est: 1984. Office &/or bookroom; Internet and postal. Telephone first. Medium stock. Spec: Academic/Scholarly; Animals and Birds; Deep Sea Diving; Manuals - Seamanship; Maritime/Nautical; Naval; Navigation; Shipbuilding; Sport - Yachting; Voyages & Discovery. PR: £5–1,500. CC: AE; E; JCB; MC; V; SW. Also, insurance & probate valuations. Cata: 4 – quarterly. Mem: ABA; PBFA; ILAB; CEng/IEE. VAT No: GB 410 5334 04.

HUNTINGDON

The Curiosity Shop, ■ 7 High Street, Huntingdon, PE29 3TE. Prop: D. Fletcher & A. Bowers. Tel: (01480) 411605. Est: 1982. Shop; open: **M:** 10:00–16:00; **T:** 10:00–16:00; **W:** 10:00–16:00; **Th:** 10:00–16:00; **F:** 10:00–16:00; **S:** 10:00–16:00. Small stock. Spec: Topography - General; Travel - General. PR: £1–75.

Roger Gaskell Rare Books, 17 Ramsey Road, Warboys, Huntingdon, PE28 2RW. Tel: (01487) 823059. Fax: (01487) 823070. Website: www.RogerGaskell.com. E-mail: roger@rogergaskell.com. Est: 1989. Private premises; postal business only. Appointment necessary. Very small stock. Spec: Medicine; Science - General; Technology. PR: £100–10,000. Cata: 2 a year. Mem: ABA; ILAB. VAT No: GB 550 6050 74.

MK Book Services, 7 East Street, Huntingdon, PE29 1WZ. Prop: Melvyn R King. Tel: (01480) 353710. Fax: (01480) 431703. E-mail: mkbooks@tiscali.co.uk. Est: 1983. Private premises; postal business only. Appointment necessary. Very small general stock. Spec: Authors - Local; Countries - Baltic States; Countries - South Atlantic Islands; Religion - Methodism; Sport - Horse Racing (all aspects). PR: £1–50. CC: E; MC; V; SW. Mem: BA. Also, booksearch.

John Robertshaw, 5 Fellowes Drive, Ramsey, Huntingdon, PE26 1BE. Tel: (01487) 813330. Fax: (01487) 711901. E-mail: robertshaw.books@virgin.net. Est: 1983. Office &/or bookroom; appointment necessary. *Shop at:* 24G Great Whyte Ramsey, Huntingdon, Cambridgeshire, PE26 1HA. Small general stock. Spec: Antiquarian; Foreign Texts; Languages - Foreign. Cata: 4 a year. Corresp: French, German. Mem: PBFA. VAT No: GB 360 1311 09.

PETERBOROUGH

Anglewise Books, 14 Green Walk, Market Deeping, Peterborough, PE6 8BQ.

Francis Bowers Chess Suppliers, 1 Marriott Court, Oxney Road, Peterborough, PE1 5NQ. Prop: Francis John Bowers. Tel: (01733) 897119. Website: home.aol.com/chessbower. E-mail: chessbower@aol.com. Est: 1991. Spec: Chess; Children's - General. PR: £1–1,000.

Broadway Books, 144 Broadway, Peterborough, PE1 4DG. Prop: Alan & Marion Peasgood. Tel: (01733) 565055. Est: 1997. Private premises; postal business only. Small general stock. PR: £1–25. Gallery has art books only - open 11:00–17:00. *Also at:* Gildenbergh Gallery, Broadway, Peterborough.

P. S. Brookbanks, 68 Grounds Way, Coates, Peterborough, PE7 2BU. Tel: (01733) 840482. E-mail: blacktoad@aol.com. Est: 1995. Postal and Internet only. Spec: Biography; Sport - Cricket; Sport - Football (Soccer).

Brian Cocks Books, 18 Woodgate, Helpston, Peterborough, PE6 7ED. Tel: (01733) 252791. Fax: (01733) 252791. E-mail: brianc@bookhouse.nildram.co.uk. Est: 1982. Private premises; appointment necessary. Small stock. Spec: Aviation. Cata: 2 a year. Corresp: French, German, Spanish. Also, booksearch. VAT No: GB 513 9334 31.

T.V. Coles, ■ 981 Lincoln Road, Peterborough, PE4 6AH. Tel: (01733) 577268. Est: 1982. Shop. Small stock. Spec: Military.

Available from Richard Joseph Publishers Ltd
MINIATURE BOOKS
by Louis W. Bondy

(A5 H/b)   221pp £24.00

DoublePlusBooks, 25 Princes Gardens, Peterborough, PE1 4DP. Prop: Richard Mankiewicz. Tel: (07092) 121 393. Fax: (07092) 121 393. Website: www.doubleplusbooks.com. E-mail: doubleplusbooks@ntlworld.com. Est: 2002. Private premises; Internet and postal. Appointment necessary. **M:** 10:00–20:00; **T:** 10:00–20:00; **W:** 10:00–20:00; **Th:** 10:00–20:00; **F:** 10:00–20:00; **S:** 10:00–18:00; **Su:** 10:00–16:00. Small stock. Spec: Antiquarian; Antiques; Applied Art; Architecture; Arms & Armour; Art; Art History; Art Reference; Author - General; Catalogues Raisonnes; Ceramics; Collecting; Crafts; Decorative Art; Design; Fiction - General; Fine & Rare; Firearms/Guns; Furniture; and others as listed in the Speciality Index. PR: £3–500. CC: Paypal. Free Booksearch, Books Bought or Sold on Commission. Corresp: Italian. *Also at:* Leicester Antiques Warehouse and Olney Antiques Centre.

Paul Green, 83b London Road, Peterborough, PE2 9BS. Est: 1998. Private premises; postal business only. Very small stock. Spec: Naturism; Poetry. PR: £2–50. Cata: 2 on naturism and poetry.

Peakirk Books, ■ Railway Cottage, 15 St Pegas Road, Peterborough, PE6 7NF. Prop: Heather and Jeff Lawrence. Tel: (01733) 253182. Website: www.peakirkbooks.com. E-mail: peakirkbooks@btinternet.com. Est: 1997. Shop; Internet and postal. Open: **W:** 14:00–17:00; **Th:** 09:30–17:00; **F:** 09:30–17:30; **S:** 09:30–17:00; **Su:** 12:00–16:00. Large stock. Spec: Academic/Scholarly; Annuals; Author - General; Children's - General; Fiction - General; Illustrated; Military; Natural History; Poetry; Publishers - Penguin; Railways; Topography - Local; War - General. PR: £1–500. CC: AE; MC; V; Debit cards. Available on internet/telephone every day except Tuesday. Also, booksearch.

Frank T. Popeley, 27 Westbrook Park Road, Woodston, Peterborough, PE2 9JG. Tel: (01733) 562386. Private premises; postal business only. Small stock. Spec: Animals and Birds; Countries - Africa; Countries - Kenya; Countries - Tanzania; Sport - Big Game Hunting; Tribal. PR: £1–1,000. Cata: 2 – general.

Wizard Books, 106 Church Street, Deeping St. James, Peterborough, PE6 8HB. Prop: Stephen Blessett. Tel: (01778) 343175. Fax: (01778) 380538. E-mail: wizardbooks@aol.com. Private premises; Internet and postal. Small general stock. Spec: Arms & Armour; Arthurian; Cryptozoology; Divining; Ghosts; Magic & Conjuring; Military; Military History; Mysteries; Mysticism; Mythology; Occult; Psychic; Psychology/Psychiatry; Religion - General; Spiritualism; U.F.O.s; Witchcraft. PR: £5–100. CC: JCB; MC; V.

SAINT IVES

Brunner Books, ■ 1 White Hart Court, St. Ives, PE27 5EA. Prop: Chris & Barbara Frances Coupland. Tel: (01480) 300032. Fax: (01480) 300032. Est: 1999. Shop; open **M:** 09:00–17:00; **T:** 09:00–17:00; **W:** 09:00–17:00; **Th:** 09:00–17:00; **F:** 09:00–17:00; **S:** 09:00–17:00. Spec: Fiction - General; Fiction - Crime, Detective, Spy, Thrillers; Fiction - Science Fiction; First Editions; Proof Copies. PR: £1–250. Also, new books. Mem: BA. VAT No: GB 716 6471 26.

SAINT NEOTS

Target Books, 200 Cambridge Street, St. Neots, PE19 1PX. Prop: Michael Gaadt. Tel: (01480) 351832. E-mail: m.gaadt@ntlworld.com. Est: 1982. Private premises; postal business only. Small stock. Spec: Biography; Health; History - General; Sport - Field Sports; Sport - Horse Racing (all aspects). PR: £1–300. Cata: 2 a year.

WEST WICKHAM

Elizabeth Spindel, Court Barn, Pond Meadow, West Wickham, CB1 6RY. Private premises. PR: £1–1,500. Cata: occasionally on modern first editions.

WISBECH

Oasis Booksearch, 88 Norfolk Street, Wisbech, PE13 2LF. Prop: R.G.M. & M.E. Welford. Tel: (01945) 420438. Website: www.ukbookworld.com/members/welford. E-mail: welford@pgen.net. Est: 1998. Warehouse; Internet and postal. Open: **T:** 09:00–17:00; **W:** 09:00–17:30; **Th:** 09:00–17:30; **F:** 09:00–17:30; **S:** 09:00–16:00. Small stock. Spec: Author - Ballantyne, Robert M.; Author - Lewis, C. S.; Author - Morton, H.V.; Bibles; Mind, Body & Spirit; Prayer Books; Religion - Christian; Religion - Methodism; Religion - Roman Catholic; Theology. Mem: PBFA; CBA.

CHESHIRE

ALSAGER

Cavern Books, 13 Birch Avenue, Alsager, ST7 2RD. Prop: Harry Madden. Tel: (01270) 873837. Website: www.cavernbooks.co.uk. E-mail: cavernbks@aol.com. Private premises; postal business only. Stock at: Biblion, London W. and through The Internet Bookshop (q.v.). Open: Large stock. Spec: Topography - General; Transport. PR: £1–150. Also on mobile (07712) 046873. *Also at:* The Arts Antiques Centre, Knutsford, Cheshire (q.v.) and and Booklore, Nantwich, Cheshire (q.v.).

CHEADLE

Geoff Booth (Booksearch Service), 2 Hastings Close, Cheadle Hulme, Cheadle, SK8 7BE. (*). Tel: (0161) 485-4246. Est: 1981. Small stock. Spec: Art; Autobiography; Aviation; Biography; Colour-Plate; Countries - Poland; Crime (True); Fiction - General; Magic & Conjuring; Modern First Editions; Natural History; Proof Copies; Topography - General. PR: £1–150. Cata: irregularly on specialities. Also, booksearch.

A. Browne, 8 Lincoln Avenue, Heald Green, Cheadle, SK8 3LJ. E-mail: abrowne@talk21.com. Est: 1998. Private premises; postal business only. Small stock. Spec: Geology; Mineralogy; Mining; Palaeontology. Cata: 4 – quarterly.

Tennis Collectables, 31 Syddall Avenue, Cheadle, SK8 3AA. Prop: Fiona & John Partington. Tel: (0161) 718-5378. Fax: (0161) 718-5378. E-mail: john@partbook.demon.co.uk. Private premises; postal business only. Very small stock. Spec: Periodicals & Magazines; Sport - Tennis. PR: £2–200. CC: JCB; MC; V. Also, a booksearch service. Cata: 3 a year. VAT No: GB 748 5252 10.

CHESTER

Gerald S. Grant, 16 Tintern Avenue, Upton by Chester, CH2 1SB. Tel: (01244) 312825. Est: 1974. Private premises; postal business only. Small stock. Spec: Architecture; Art; Art History; Artists; Author - Crane, Hall; Author - Gill, Eric; Author - Searle, Ronald; Bibliography; Books about Books; Decorative Art; Fine Printing; Illustrated; Private Press. PR: £10–100. Corresp: French, Italian.

A. Grieveson, 34 Pickmere Drive, Eastham, Chester, Wirral, CH62 9EW. Prop: Andrea Grieveson. Tel: (0151) 3280172. Website: www.alibris.com. E-mail: golden.frog@lineone.net. Est: 1988. Spec: Alternative Medicine; Astrology; Ghosts; Parapsychology; Philosophy; Psychic; Supernatural. PR: £3–100.

Richard Nicholson of Chester, Stoneydale, Pepper Street, Christleton, Chester, CH3 7AG. Tel: (01244) 336004. Fax: (01244) 336138. Website: www.antiquemaps.com. E-mail: richard@maps.u-net.com. Est: 1961. Postal business only. Very small stock. Spec: Atlases. PR: £10–3,000. CC: MC; V.

Stothert Old Books, ■ 4 Nicholas Street, Chester, CH1 2NX. Prop: Alan Checkley. Tel: (01244) 340756. Fax: (01829) 770628. E-mail: alancheckley@yahoo.com. Est: 1978. Shop; open **M:** 10:00–17:00; **T:** 10:00–17:00; **W:** 10:00–17:00; **Th:** 10:00–17:00; **F:** 10:00–17:00; **S:** 10:00–17:00. Medium stock. Spec: Antiquarian; Bindings; Children's - General; Fine & Rare; Literature; Private Press; Topography - General; Topography - Local; Transport; Travel - General; War - General. PR: £1–1,000. CC: JCB; MC; V. Corresp: French. VAT No: GB 691 9276 88.

Wheatsheaf Antiques, 57 Christleton Road, Chester, CW3 9BZ. Prop: Jeremy Marks. Tel: (01244) 403743. Website: www.antiquesonlineuk.com. E-mail: books@antiquesonlineuk.com. Est: 1990. Private premises; open: **M:** 11:00–16:00; **T:** 11:00–16:00; **W:** 11:00–16:00; **Th:** 11:00–16:00; **F:** 11:00–16:00; **S:** 11:00–16:00; **Su:** 12:00–16:00. Very small stock. Spec: Natural History; Nostalgia; Ornithology; Sport - Angling/Fishing; Topography - General. PR: £1–1,000.

Dealers who need to update their entry should visit their page on *www.sheppardsdirectories.com*

Words & Music, 2 City Walls, Northgate, Chester, CH1 2JG. Prop: Mr. S.M. Whitaker. Tel: (01244) 311910. Est: 1991. Spec: Art; Arts, The; Children's - General; Countries - Melanesia; Drama; First Editions; Food & Drink; History - General; Literature; Music - Composers; Music - Jazz; Music - Opera. PR: £1–100.

CREWE

Copnal Books, ■ 18 Meredith Street, Crewe. Prop: P.E. Ollerhead. Tel: (01270) 580470. Est: 1980. Shop; open **M:** 09:30–17:00; **F:** 09:30–17:00; **S:** 09:30–17:00. Large general stock. PR: £1–50. Open other times by appointment. Corresp: French.

Starlord Books, 72 Chester Avenue, Dukinfield, SK16 5BW. Prop: Starlord. Tel: 0161-338-8465. E-mail: Starlord@Starlord-Enterprises.freeserve.co.uk. Est: 1995. Private premises; Internet and postal. Appointment necessary. **M:** 10:00–18:00; **T:** 09:00–12:00; **W:** 10:00–18:00; **Th:** 10:00–16:00; **F:** 12:00–16:00; **S:** 10:00–16:00; **Su:** 12:00–16:00. Small stock. Spec: Academic/Scholarly; Alternative Medicine; Astrology; Autobiography; Biography; Comic Books & Annuals; Crime (True); Esoteric; Fiction - Crime, Detective, Spy, Thrillers; Fiction - Fantasy, Horror; Fiction - Science Fiction; Metaphysics; Mind, Body & Spirit - and others as listed in the Speciality Index. PR: £1–100.

HOYLAKE

Marine and Cannon Books, Naval & Maritime Dept., 'Nilcoptra', 3 Marine Road, Hoylake, Wirral, CH47 2AS. Prop: Michael & Vivienne Nash and Diane Churchill-Evans. Tel: (0151) 632-5365. Fax: (0151) 632-6472. E-mail: michael@marinecannon.com. Est: 1983. Private premises; Internet and postal. Appointment necessary. **M:** 09:00–18:00; **T:** 09:00–18:00; **W:** 09:00–18:00; **Th:** 09:00–18:00; **F:** 09:00–18:00; **S:** 09:00–17:00. Closed for lunch: 13:00–13:30. Medium stock. Spec: Antiquarian; Aviation; History - General; Manuscripts; Maritime/Nautical; Military; Military History; Naval; Shipbuilding; Transport; Voyages & Discovery; War - General; Whaling. PR: £10–20,000. CC: JCB; MC; V. Cata: 6 – One every 2 months. Mem: ABA; PBFA; ILAB. Also, booksearch.

HYDE

J.A. Heacock (Antiques and Books), ■ 155 Market Street, Hyde, SK14 1HG. Prop: Joseph Anthony Heacock. Tel: (0161) 366 5098. Est: 2000. Shop; telephone first. Medium stock. Spec: History - General; Literature; Natural History; Topography - General; Travel - General.

KNUTSFORD

BC Books, 12 Mallard Close, Knutsford, WA16 8ES. Prop: Brian Corrigan. Tel: (01565) 654014. E-mail: brian@corrigan.demon.co.uk. Est: 1993. Private premises; postal business only but contactable. Small general stock. Spec: First Editions; History - Ancient; History - British; Humour; Literature. PR: £1–250. Corresp: French.

Cavern Books, ■ 13 Birch Avenue, Alsager, ST7 2RD. Prop: Harry Madden. Tel: (01565) 654092. Website: www.cavernbooks.co.uk. E-mail: cavernbks@aol.com. *Shop at:* Knutsford Arts & Antiques Centre, 113 King St, Knutsford. Open: **T:** 10:00–17:00; **W:** 10:00–17:00; **Th:** 10:00–17:00; **F:** 10:00–17:00; **S:** 10:00–17:00; **Su:** 12:00–17:00. Small stock. Spec: Countries - Poland; Guide Books; Juvenile; Occult; Spiritualism; Topography - Local; Transport. PR: £1–250. Stock at Biblion, London W and through The Internet Bookshop (q.v.). *Also at:* Cavern, Alsager, Cheshire (q.v.) and Booklore, Natwich, Cheshire (q.v.).

Fiction First, The Old Chapel, Knolls Green Village, Knutsford, WA16 7BW. Tel: (01565) 872634. Fax: (01565) 872634. Website: www.abebooks.com. E-mail: richard.offer@virgin.net. Est: 1992. Private premises; Internet and postal. Appointment necessary. Small stock. Spec: Fiction - General; Fiction - Crime, Detective, Spy, Thrillers; Fiction - Fantasy, Horror; Fiction - Science Fiction; First Editions. PR: £10–2,000. Cata: 1 a year.

Richard Offer, The Old Chapel, Knolls Green Village, Knutsford Rd, Mobberley, Knutsford, WA16 7BW. Tel: (01565) 872634. Fax: (01565) 872634. E-mail: richard.offer@virgin.net. Est: 1992. Private premises; postal business only. Spec: Countries - Melanesia; Countries - Mexico; Fiction - General; Fiction - Science Fiction; First Editions. PR: £5–300.

MACCLESFIELD

Mereside Books, ■ 75 Chestergate, Macclesfield, SK11 6DG. Prop: Sally Laithwaite & Steve Kowalski. Shop (01625) 425352; Home (01625) 431160. Est: 1996. Shop; open **W:** 10:00–17:00; **Th:** 10:00–17:00; **F:** 10:00–17:00; **S:** 10:00–17:00. Small general stock. Spec: Illustrated. PR: £3–500. CC: E; JCB; MC; V. Organisers of Buxton Book Fairs.

Morten Books, Brooklands House, Padgbury Lane, Congleton, Macclesfield, CW12 4LP.

CHESHIRE

Roger J. Treglown, Sunderland House, Sunderland Street, Macclesfield, SK11 6JF. Tel: (01625) 618978. Fax: (01625) 618978. Website: www.rogerjtreglown.com. E-mail: roger@rogerjtreglown.com. Est: 1980. Spec: Antiquarian; Chess; Early Imprints; Esoteric; Odd & Unusual. PR: £2–2,000. Also, valuations for probate etc.

NANTWICH

Cavern Books, ■ 13 Birch Avenue, Nantwich, ST7 2RD. Prop: Harry Madden. Tel: (0771) 2046873. Website: www.cavernbooks.co.uk. E-mail: cavernbks@aol.com. *Shop at:* Booklore Shops, 3/4 Crafts Arcade, Dagfields Antiques, Walgherton, Nr Nantwich. Open: **M:** 10:00–17:00; **T:** 10:00–17:00; **W:** 10:00–17:00; **Th:** 10:00–17:00; **F:** 10:00–17:00; **S:** 10:00–17:00; **Su:** 10:00–17:00. Small stock. Spec: Entertainment - General; Military; Spiritualism; Topography - General; Transport. PR: £1–250. *Also at:* Cavern Books, Alsager and and Knutsford Antiques Centre, Knutsford and Biblion (q.v.).

Guildmaster Books, 81 Welsh Row, Nantwich, CW5 5ET. Tel: (01270) 629982. Fax: (01270) 629108. E-mail: guild.house@virgin.net. Bookroom; appointment necessary. Est: 1986. Spec: Agriculture; Antiquarian; Churchilliana; Culture - National; Firearms/Guns; Herbalism; History - British; Maritime/Nautical; Military History; Topography. PR: £10–20.

Leona Thomas (Books), 84, London Road, Nantwich, CW5 6LT. Prop: Leona Thomas. Tel: (01270) 627779. Website: www.leonathomas.co.uk. E-mail: books@leonathomas.co.uk. Est: 1990. Private premises. Telephone first. Small stock. Spec: Antiquarian; Antiques; Bindings; Books about Books; Folio Society, The; History - General; Poetry; Topography - Local; War - English Civil Wars. PR: £1–500. Cata: 4 – a year. Corresp: French. Mem: PBFA.

NORTHWICH

KSC Books, 48, Chapel Street, Castle, Northwich, CW8 1HD. Prop: K. Stuart Crook. Tel: (01606) 79975. Fax: by prior arrangement. E-mail: kscbooks@btinternet.com. Est: 1995. Private premises; Internet and postal. Telephone first. Small stock. Spec: Author - Laithwaite, Eric; Author - Raistrick, Arthur; Canals/Inland Waterways; Musical Instruments; Science - General; Technology. PR: £1–100. CC: MC; V; SW. Also, a booksearch service. VAT No: GB 798 2130 04.

RUNCORN

Kirk Ruebotham, 16 Beaconsfield Road, Runcorn, WA7 4BX. Tel: (01928) 560540. Website: www.abebooks.com/home/kirk61. E-mail: kirk.ruebotham@ntlworld.com. Est: 1993. Private premises; postal business only. Small stock. Spec: Crime (True); Fiction - Crime, Detective, Spy, Thrillers; Fiction - Fantasy, Horror; Fiction - Science Fiction; First Editions; Vintage Paperbacks. PR: £1–150. Cata: 4 a year.

TARVIN

Henry Wilson Books, 14 Broomheath Lane, Tarvin, Chester, CH3 8HB. Prop: J.M. Wilson. Tel: (01829) 740693. Fax: (01829) 749060. E-mail: hwrailwaybooks@aol.com. Est: 1983. Private premises; Internet and postal. Large stock. Spec: Author - Rolt, L.T.C.; Buses/Trams; Canals/Inland Waterways; History - Industrial; Railways; Steam Engines; Traction Engines; Transport. PR: £2–500. CC: MC; V; SW. New books & back issues of railway journals. Also, booksearch. Cata: 1 – on railways, transport and industrial history. Corresp: French, German. Mem: PBFA. VAT No: GB 439 7672 03.

WARRINGTON

Bookfinder–General, 21 Chester Avenue, Lowton, Warrington, WA3 2JF.

Halson Books, The Oaks, Farnworth Road, Penketh, Warrington, WA5 2TT. Tel: (01925) 726699. Website: www.users.zetnet.co.uk/halsongallery. E-mail: halson.gallery@zetnet.co.uk. Private premises; Internet and postal. Appointment necessary. Large stock. Spec: Colour-Plate; Dogs; Natural History. CC: PayPal. Cata: 12 – monthly.

Available from Richard Joseph Publishers Ltd

BOOKWORMS, THE INSECT PESTS
by N. Hickin

Revised Edition (A5 H/b)　　　　　　184pp £24.00

CHESHIRE

K. Books, 60 Mardale Crescent, Lymm, Warrington, WA13 9PJ. (*) Prop: Jef & Janet Kay. Tel: (01925) 755736. E-mail: jefkay@supanet.com. Est: 1994. Private premises; appointment necessary. Spec: Astronautics; Author - Blyton, Enid; Author - Charteris, Leslie; Children's - General; Comic Books & Annuals; Fiction - General; Fiction - Science Fiction; First Editions; Juvenile; Nostalgia. PR: £1–100. Mem: Followers of Rupert. VAT No: GB 161 1956 22.

Sensawunda Books, 59 Dunnock Grove, Birchwood, Warrington, WA3 6NW.

Dr. B. Shakeshaft, 15 Marlborough Crescent, Grappenhall, Warrington, WA4 2EE. Prop: B.L. Shakeshaft. Tel: (01925) 264790. E-mail: blsbooks@btopenworld.com. Est: 1999. Private premises; postal business only. Very small stock. Spec: Americana; Children's - General; Illustrated; Modern First Editions; Natural History. PR: £1–500. Attends Knutsford Book Fair.

David M. Shaw, 31 Newlands Drive, Lowton, Warrington, WA3 2RJ. Tel: (01942) 726319. Website: www.antiquemapsuk.com. E-mail: david@antiquemapsuk.com. Est: 1986. Postal business only. Spec: Atlases; Canals/Inland Waterways. PR: £1–1,000. Also, remainders. Mem: PBFA. VAT No: GB 153 1344 96.

Naomi Symes Books, 2 Pineways, Appleton Park, Warrington, WA4 5EJ. Prop: Naomi Symes. Tel: 44 (0)1925 602898. Fax: 44 (0)1925 602898. Website: www.naomisymes.com. E-mail: books@naomisymes.com. Est: 1994. Private premises; postal business only. Contactable **M:** 10:00–18:00; **T:** 10:00–18:00; **W:** 10:00–18:00; **Th:** 10:00–18:00; **F:** 10:00–18:00; **S:** 10:00–18:00; **Su:** 10:00–18:00. Small stock. Spec: Academic/Scholarly; Authors - Women; Feminism; Fiction - Women; History - General; History - 19th Century; History - British; History - Industrial; History - Labour/Radical Movements; Literary Criticism; Literature; Literature - Victorian; Social History; Women. PR: £5–500. CC: AE; D; E; JCB; MC; V; SW, S. Also: History A Level tuition; booksearch service; proof reading; copy editing and history resource centre on-line. Cata: 3 a year. Corresp: French. Mem: PBFA.

The Warrington Book Loft, Osnath Works, Lythgoes Lane, Warrington, WA2 7XE. Prop: Mrs Pat Devlin. Tel: (01925) 633907. Est: 1994. Spec: Academic/Scholarly; Fiction - General; University Texts. PR: £1–20.

WIDNES

Iain Campbell, Unit A5, Moor Lane Business Centre, Moor Lane, Widnes, WA8 7AQ. Tel: (0151) 420-5545. Storeroom; appointment necessary. Small stock. PR: £1–1,000. CC: D; MC; V. Mem: PBFA. VAT No: GB 166 7763 21.

WINSFORD

Blackman Books, 46 The Loont, Winsford, CW7 1EU. Prop: Margaret & Roger Blackman. Tel: (01606) 558527. Website: www.abebooks.com/home/rtmb. E-mail: books@blackmanbooks.freeserve.co.uk. Est: 1997. Private premises; Internet and postal. Appointment necessary. Very small stock. PR: £10–1,000. CC: JCB; MC; V; Da, S. Corresp: French.

CORNWALL

BODMIN

Dusty Miller, Bruach, Cassacawn Road, Blisland, Bodmin, PL30 4JF. Tel: (01208) 851220. Fax: (01208) 851554. E-mail: pamdus@aol.com. Spec: Biography; Children's - General; Crafts; Fiction - General.

BUDE

David Eastwood Books, Ardoch Poundstock, Bude, EX23 0DF. Tel: (01288) 361847. E-mail: d_eastwood37@hotmail.com. Spec: Antiques; Fine & Rare; Children's Illustrated; Illustrated; Limited editions; Literature. PR: £10–800. Mem: PBFA.

CALLINGTON

Music By The Score, South Coombe, Downgate, Callington, PL17 8JZ. Prop: Eileen Hooper–Bargery. Tel: (01579) 370053. Fax: (01579) 370053. Website: www.musicbythescore.com. E-mail: musicbythescore@yesmate.com. Est: 1993. Private premises; Internet and postal. Appointment necessary. **M:** 10:00–20:00; **T:** 10:00–20:00; **W:** 10:00–20:00; **Th:** 10:00–20:00; **F:** 10:00–20:00; **S:** 10:00–20:00. Large stock. Spec: Music - General; Music - Composers; Music - Music Hall; Music - Musicians; Music - Opera; Music - Political Songs & Ballads; Music - Popular. PR: £4–40. CC: MC; V; SW.

CAMBOURNE

Humanist Book Services, 15 Basset Street, Camborne, TR14 8SW. Prop: Linnea Timson. Tel: (01209) 716470. Fax: (0870) 125 8049. Website: www.cornwallhumanists.org.uk. E-mail: humbooks@ukgateway.net. Est: 1964. Spec: Evolution; Free Thought; Humanism; Philosophy. PR: £1–15.

CHARLESTOWN

BBNO, 10 Quay Road, Charlestown, PL25 3NX. Prop: J. S. Kinross. Est: 1971. Private premises; Contactable. Small stock. Spec: Apiculture; Children's - General; Crafts; Natural History. CC: MC; V.

DOWNDERRY

The Book Bungalow, Victoria Villa, Downderry, PL11 3LE. Prop: Simon and Janet Alloway. Tel: (01503) 250388. E-mail: email@bookbungalow.com. Est: 2000. Postal business only. Spec: Author - Cornwell, Bernard; Author - Fleming, Ian; Author - Rowling, J.K.; Biography; Children's - General; Crime (True); Fiction - Science Fiction; Illustrated; Modern First Editions; Signed Editions. PR: £2–1,500.

EAST LOOE

Bosco Books, ■ The Old Hall Bookshop, Chapel Court, Shutta Road, East Looe, PL13 1BJ. Prop: Mr. & Mrs. S. Hawes. Tel: (01503) 263700. Fax: (01503) 263700. E-mail: boscobooks@aol.com. Est: 1971. Shop; Internet and postal. Open: **M:** 10:30–17:00; **T:** 10:30–17:00; **W:** 10:30–17:00; **Th:** 10:30–17:00; **F:** 10:30–17:00; **S:** 10:30–17:00. Very large stock. Spec: Alpinism/Mountaineering; Archaeology; Architecture; Art; Art History; Art Reference; Biography; Crafts; Fiction - General; Gardening; Military; Ornithology; Transport; Victoriana. PR: £1–750. CC: MC; V; SW. Winter: closed Mondays and Sundays, please ring to confirm. Corresp: French, Italian.

Dealers who need to update their entry should visit their page on
www.sheppardsdirectories.com

CORNWALL

FALMOUTH

Browser's Bookshop, ■ 13, 14 & 15, St. George's Arcade, Falmouth, TR11 3DH. John Floyd. Tel: (01326) 313464. Est: 1985. Shop; open **M:** 10:00–17:00; **T:** 10:00–17:00; **W:** 10:00–17:00; **Th:** 10:00–17:00; **F:** 10:00–17:00; **S:** 10:00–17:00. Large stock. Spec: Maritime/Nautical; Odd & Unusual; Railways; Topography - General. PR: £1–200. CC: AE; V.

Isabelline Books, 2 Highbury House, 8 Woodlane Crescent, Falmouth, TR11 4QS. Prop: Michael Whetman. Tel: (01326) 210412. Fax: 0870 051 6387. Website: www.beakbook.demon.co.uk. E-mail: mikann@beakbook.demon.co.uk. Est: 1997. Private premises; Internet and postal. Appointment necessary. Very small stock. Spec: Ornithology. PR: £10–2,000. CC: JCB; V. Cata: 3.

FOWEY

Bookends of Fowey, ■ 4 South Street, Fowey, PL23 1AR. Prop: Ann Willmore. Tel: (01726) 833361. Fax: (01726) 833900. Website: www.bookendsoffowey.com. E-mail: alex@nder.com. Est: 1987. Shop; Internet and postal. Open: **M:** 09:30–17:30; **T:** 09:30–17:30; **W:** 09:30–17:30; **Th:** 09:30–17:30; **F:** 09:30–17:30; **S:** 09:30–17:30. Closed for lunch: 13:00–14:00. Large stock. Spec: Author - du Maurier, Daphne; Author - Quiller-Couch, Sir A.T.; History - Local; Illustrated; Literature; Maritime/Nautical; Travel - General; Voyages & Discovery. PR: £1–600. CC: MC; V; SW. Also, publish under the imprint of Alexander Associates.

Ronald C. Hicks, Ardwyn, 22 Park Road, Fowey, PL23 1ED. Tel: (01726) 832739. Est: 1964. Private premises; postal business only. Very small stock. Spec: Architecture; Art; History - Local. PR: £1–500. Cata: 1 – occasionally. Also, booksearch.

Sue Moore, 37 Passage Street, Fowey, PL23 1DE. Prop: Susan M. Moore. Tel: (01726) 832397. Est: 1986. Private premises; appointment necessary. Small stock. Spec: Modern First Editions. PR: £2–50. Also, booksearch.

HELSTON

Peter Clay, Heatherbank, North Corner, Coverack, Helston, TR12 6TH. Prop: Peter & Linda Clay. Tel: (01326) 280475. E-mail: ps.clay@virgin.net. Est: 1982. Private premises; Internet and postal. Appointment necessary. Open: **M:** 10:30–17:30; **T:** 10:30–17:30; **W:** 10:30–17:30; **Th:** 10:30–17:30; **F:** 10:30–17:30. Medium stock. Spec: Antiques; History - Local; Topography - Local. PR: £1–100. Corresp: French.

The Helston Bookworm, ■ 9 Church Street, Helston, TR13 8TA. Prop: Ann & Malcolm Summers. Tel: (01326) 565079. Website: www.users.dialstart.net/~helstonb. E-mail: helstonb@dialstart.net. Est: 1994. Shop; Internet and postal. Open: **M:** 10:00–17:30; **T:** 10:10–17:30; **W:** 10:00–17:30; **Th:** 10:00–17:30; **F:** 10:00–17:30; **S:** 10:00–14:00. Large general stock. Spec: Antiquarian; Topography - Local. PR: £1–300. CC: AE; MC; V. Mem: PBFA.

J.T. & P. Lewis, 'Leaway', Tresowes Green, Ashton, Nr. Helston, TR13 9SY. Prop: John T. & Pearl Lewis. Tel: (01736) 762406. Website: http://dogbert.abebooks.com/abep/il.dll?vci=228845. E-mail: JohnandPearl@aol.com. Est: 1990. Private premises; Internet and postal. Medium stock. Spec: Academic/Scholarly; Fiction - General; History - General; Modern First Editions; Odd & Unusual; Religion - General; Science - General; Theology; Topography - General; Travel - General; War - General. PR: £5–500. CC: Payment via Paypal using JohnandPearl@aol.com. VAT No: GB 803 4711 59.

LAUNCESTON

Charles Cox Rare Books, River House, Treglasta, Launceston, PL15 8PY. Tel: (01840) 261085. Fax: (01840) 261464. Website: www.abebooks.com. E-mail: charlescox@verso.fsnet.co.uk. Est: 1974. Private premises; Internet and postal. Appointment necessary. Small stock. Spec: Antiquarian; Autographs; Fiction - General; Fine & Rare; Literature; Poetry; Theatre. PR: £10–2,500. CC: Paypal. Cata: 3 a year. VAT No: GB 797 4887 40.

R. & B. Graham, ■ 10 Church Street, Launceston, PL15 8AP. Prop: Richard & Beryl Graham. Tel: (01566) 774107. Fax: (01566) 777299. Website: www.cookery-books-online.com. E-mail: thebookshop@eclipse.co.uk. Est: 1984. Shop; Internet and postal. Open; **M:** 09:30–16:30; **T:** 09:30–16:30; **W:** 09:30–16:30; **Th:** 09:30–16:30; **F:** 09:30–16:30; **S:** 09:30–16:30. Small stock. Spec: Authors - Local; Cookery/Gastronomy; History - Local; Natural History; Topography - General; Topography - Local. PR: £1–300. CC: AE; E; JCB; MC; V. Mem: BA. VAT No: GB 750 5071 55.

Wayfarer Books, 3 Highgrove, Trevadlock Hall, Launceston, PL15 7PW. Prop: Bob & Brenda Brown. Tel: (01566) 782325. Fax: (01566) 782325. Website: www.ukbookworld.com/members/wayfarer. E-mail: beebeebrownwayfarer@eclipse.co.uk. Est: 1985. Private premises; postal business only. Small stock. Spec: Antiquarian; Aviation; Bindings; History - General; Maritime/Nautical; Military; Puzzles; Topography - General. Also, booksearch. PR: £10–1,000. Cata: 3 – on specialities. Mem: PBFA.

LISKEARD

P. & K. Stanton, Trafalgar, Pensilva, Liskeard, PL14 5PH. Prop: Pam and Kent Stanton. Tel: (01579) 362448. Fax: (01579) 363376. E-mail: books@liskeard.demon.co.uk. Est: 1982. Private premises; appointment necessary. Very small stock. Spec: Author - Churchill, Sir Winston; Poetry. PR: £5–200. Major stocks of poet: Dr Charles Causely.

LOOE

A. & R. Booksearch, High Close, Lanreath, Looe, PL13 2PF. Prop: Avis & Robert Ronald. Tel: (01503) 220146. Fax: (01503) 220965. Website: www.musicbooksrus.com. E-mail: sales@musicbooksrus.com. Est: 1984. Postal business only. Small stock. Spec: Music - Popular. PR: £1–500. CC: MC; V, SW. VAT No: GB 187 4977 94.

MARAZION

Andrew Stewart, Castledene, Turnpike Hill, Marazion, TR170BZ. Tel: (01736) 794927. Fax: (01736) 719133. E-mail: espaceblue@btopenworld.com. Est: 1978. Private premises; appointment necessary. Small stock. Spec: Classical Studies; Medieval; Printing; Theology. PR: £20–500. Cata: 3. Corresp: French, German. Mem: PBFA. VAT No: GB 328 0066 78.

PENZANCE

Green Meadow Books, 2 Bellair House, Bellair Road, Madron, Penzance, TR20 8SP. Prop: Sue Bell. Tel: (01736) 351708. Fax: (01736) 351708. Website: www.greenmeadowbooks.co.uk. E-mail: sue@bell83.fsnet.co.uk. Est: 1982. Private premises; Internet and postal. Appointment necessary. Medium stock. Spec: Author - Blyton, Enid; Author - Saville, M.; Children's - General; Children's - Illustrated; Illustrated. CC: MC; V. Also, toys, games & a booksearch service. Cata: 5.

Mount's Bay Books, Sea Glimpses, Garth Road, Newlyn, Penzance, TR18 5QJ. Prop: Tim Scott. Tel: (01736) 351335. Website: www.mountsbaybooks.co.uk. E-mail: timscott@mountsbaybooks.co.uk. Est: 1994. Private premises; Internet and postal. Appointment necessary. Very small stock. Spec: Author - Tangye, D.; Natural History; Rural Life; Topography - Local. PR: £2–100. Cata: 6.

Newlyn & New Street Books, ■ New Street Bookshop, 4 New Street, Penzance, TR18 2LZ. Prop: Kelvin Hearn. Tel: (1736) 362758. E-mail: eankelvin@yahoo.com. Est: 1992. Shop; Internet and postal. Open: **M:** 10:00–17:00; **T:** 10:00–17:00; **W:** 10:00–17:00; **Th:** 10:00–17:00; **F:** 10:00–17:00; **S:** 10:00–17:00. Medium general stock. Spec: Art; Topography - General; Topography - Local. PR: £1–350. CC: MC; V.

Penzance Rare Books, ■ 43 Causewayhead, Penzance, TR18 2SS. Prop: Pat Johnstone. Tel: (01736) 362140. E-mail: pat@boscathnoe.free-online.co.uk. Est: 1990. Shop; open **M:** 10:00–17:00; **T:** 10:00–17:00; **W:** 10:00–17:00; **Th:** 10:00–17:00; **F:** 10:00–17:00; **S:** 10:00–17:00. Large general stock. Spec: Engineering; Steam Engines; Traction Engines. PR: £1–1,000. Cata: 2.

Searching for a title - and cannot find it on any Internet database?
Then try **SheppardsBooksearch**

By selecting the subject classification – the request goes to all dealers who major in that subject.

CORNWALL

REDRUTH

Anne Jones, Bryher, Barncoose Terrace, Redruth, TR15 3EP. Tel: (01209) 211180. Fax: (01209) 211180. E-mail: jones@bryherbooks.fsnet.co.uk. Est: 1989. Private premises; postal business only.Very small stock. Spec: Architecture; Bridge; Canals/Inland Waterways; Civil Engineering; Company History; Engineering; History - Industrial; Industry; Steam Engines; Technical; Technology; Traction Engines; PR: £5–250. CC: MC; V. Cata: 2.

recollectionsbookshop.co.uk, 8F Cardrew Industrial Estate, Redruth, Cornwall TR15 1SS. Tel: (01209) 219594. Prop: Valerie Frith & Ray Frith. E-mail: recollection@btconnect.com. Warehouse; Internet and postal only. Spec: Topography - Local. PR: £4–100.

SAINT AUSTELL

BMH Books, The Lodge, Rescorla, Saint Austell, PL26 8YT.

Neville Chapman, 24 Caudledown Lane, Stenalees, St. Austell, PL26 8TG. Tel: (01726) 850067. Website: www.abebooks.com/home/chapbooks. E-mail: chapbooks@aol.com. Est: 1992. Private premises; Internet and postal. Appointment necessary. Small stock. Spec: Topography - Local. PR: £1–50.

SAINT IVES

The Book Gallery, The Old Post Office Garage, Chapel Street, St. Ives, TR26 2LR. Prop: David & Tina Wilkinson. Tel: (01736) 793545. Website: www.abebooks.com/home/tinyworld. E-mail: books@book-gallery.co.uk. Est: 1991. Private premises; Internet and postal. Telephone first. Small stock. Spec: Art; Art History; Art Reference; First Editions; Topography - Local. PR: £5–2,500.

SAINT TEATH

Christopher Holtom, Aaron's, Treburgett, St. Teath, PL30 3LJ. Tel: (01208) 851062. Fax: (01208) 851062. Est: 1972. Private premises; appointment necessary. Medium stock. Spec: Antiquarian; Children's - General; Education & School; Fables; Folklore; Juvenile; Mathematics. PR: £3–150. Cata: 6 – 18th–20thC children's books and school text books. Corresp: French.

TRURO

Bonython Bookshop, 16 Kenwyn Street, Truro, TR1 3BU. Prop: R.D. Carpenter. Tel: (01872) 262886. E-mail: bonythonbooks@btconnect.com. Est: 1996. Spec: History - Local; Topography - Local. PR: £1–1,000. CC: D; E; JCB; MC; V. Also, booksearch.

Just Books, ■ 9 Pydar Mews, Truro, TR1 2UX. Prop: Jennifer Wicks. Tel: (01872) 242532. Est: 1987. Shop; open: **M:** 09:30–17:00; **T:** 09:30–17:00; **W:** 09:30–17:00; **Th:** 09:30–17:00; **F:** 09:30–17:00; **S:** 09:30–17:00. Medium stock. Spec: History - Local; Windmills & Watermills. PR: £1–200. CC: AE; E; JCB; MC; V. Cata: 1 – occasionally. VAT No: GB 789 3503 84.

Kenneth Langmaid, Glencairn House, Grampound Road, Truro, TR2 4EE. Tel: (01726) 882280. Est: 1966. Private premises; appointment necessary. Very large stock. Spec: Arts, The; General; Biography; Countries - France; Countries - Italy; Ecclesiastical History & Architecture; Fiction - General; First Editions; Guide Books; History - General; International Affairs; Law; Literature; Military; Music - General. PR: £1–200. Also, postcards. Cata: – occasionally, on theology and topography. Corresp: German.

WADEBRIDGE

Polmorla Books, ■ 1 Polmorla Road, Wadebridge, PL27 7NB. Prop: John Buck. Tel: (01208) 814399. Est: 1991. Shop; open: **M:** 10:30–17:00; **T:** 10:30–17:00; **W:** 09:30–17:00; **Th:** 10:30–17:00; **F:** 10:30–17:00; **S:** 10:30–17:00. Large general stock. Spec: Art; Drama; Fiction - General; History - General; History - Local; Literature; Military; Transport. PR: £1–50. Winter hours 10:30–16:30.

CUMBRIA

APPLEBY-IN-WESTMORLAND

Barry McKay Rare Books, Kingstone House, Battlebarrow, Appleby–in–Westmorland, CA16 6XT. Prop: Barry McKay. Tel: (01768) 352282. Fax: (01768) 352946. Website: www.abebooks.com/home/barrymckayrarebks. E-mail: barry.mckay@britishlibrary.net. Est: 1986. Office &/or bookroom; Internet and postal. Telephone first. Open: **M:** 09:00–17:00; **T:** 09:00–17:00; **W:** 09:00–17:00; **Th:** 09:00–17:00; **F:** 09:00–17:00; **S:** 09:00–17:00. Medium stock. Spec: Antiquarian; Bibliography; Bookbinding; Books about Books; Calligraphy; Fine Printing; Imprints; Palaeography; Papermaking; Printing; Publishing. PR: £5–500. CC: E; JCB; MC; V. Cata: 4 – quarterly. Corresp: French. Mem: PBFA. VAT No: GB 448 5469 09.

Major John R. McKenzie, Town End Farm, Brampton, Appleby–in–Westmorland, CA16 6JS. Prop: Major J.R. McKenzie & Susana Hunter. Tel: (01768) 351384. E-mail: mckenzie@militarybooks.freeserve.co.uk. Est: 1993. Private premises; postal business only. Spec: Military. PR: £10–1,000. Corresp: Spanish. Also, booksearch.

BARROW-IN-FURNESS

Americanabooksuk, 72 Park Drive, Barrow–in–Furness, LA13 9BB. Prop: Alan R. Beattie. Tel: (01229) 829722. Website: www.americanabooks.co.uk. E-mail: alan.rbeattie@virgin.net. Private premises. Contactable. Very small stock. Spec: American Indians; Americana; Art; Countries - U. S.A.; Fiction - Westerns; Firearms/Guns; History - American; Literature; Military History; Travel - Americas; Voyages & Discovery; War - American Civil War. PR: £3–150. Cata: 1. Also, booksearch.

BARROW-ON-WINDERMERE

Past & Presents, ■ Crag Brow, Bowness–on–Windermere, LA23 3BX. Prop: W.F. & C.R. Johnson. Tel: (01539) 445417. E-mail: billnchris.johnson@btinternet.com. Est: 1995. Shop; open **M:** 09:30–17:30; **T:** 09:30–17:30; **W:** 09:30–17:30; **Th:** 09:30–17:30; **F:** 09:30–17:30; **S:** 09:30–17:30; **Su:** 09:30–17:30. Very small general stock. Spec: Author - Ransome, Arthur. PR: £2–85. CC: AE; D; MC; V. VAT No: GB 652 1595 37.

CARLISLE

Maurice Dodd Books, Greenwood House, Thursby, Carlisle, CA5 6NU. Prop: R.J. McRoberts. Tel: (01228) 710456. Fax: (01228)710456. E-mail: doddrarebooks@btconnect.com. Est: 1945. Office &/or bookroom; telephone first. Bookroom at 44 Cecil Street, Carlisle CA1 1NT. Medium stock. Spec: Antiquarian; Bindings; History - General; History - Local; Illustrated; Literature; Science - General; Topography - Local; Travel - General. PR: £5–1,500. Cata: 2. Mem: PBFA. VAT No: GB 256 3359 47.

Anne Fitzsimons, 3 Croft Park, Wetheral, Carlisle, CA4 8JH. Tel: (01228) 562184. Fax: (01228) 562184. Est: 1978. Private premises; postal business only. Small stock. Spec: Cinema/Film; Circus; Dance; Magic & Conjuring; Music - General; Music - Music Hall; Music - Opera; Performing Arts; Puppets & Marionettes; Television; Theatre. Cata: 2 – a year. Mem: PBFA.

CARTMEL

Peter Bain Smith, ■ Bank Court, Market Square, Cartmel, LA11 6QB. Tel: (01539) 536369. Est: 1972. Shop; open **M:** 13:30–17:00; **T:** 13:30–17:00; **W:** 13:30–17:00; **Th:** 13:30–17:00; **F:** 13:30–17:00. Very large stock. Spec: Children's - General; Classical Studies; Topography - Local. PR: £1–400. Winter open, Wednesday to Sunday 13.30–16.30.

Dealers who need to update their entry should visit their page on
www.sheppardsdirectories.com

CUMBRIA

Norman Kerr Booksellers, Priory Barn, Cartmel, Grange–over–Sands, LA11 6PX. Prop: H. & J.M. Kerr. Tel: (015395) 36247/32508. Website: www.kerrbooks.co.uk. E-mail: enquiries@ kerrbooks.co.uk. Est: 1933. Shop &/or showroom; telephone first. *Also at:* Gatehouse Bookshop, The Square, Cartmel. Medium stock. Spec: Architecture; Arts, The; Engineering; Illustrated; Maritime/Nautical; Motoring; Natural History; Ornithology; Railways; Topography - Local; Transport; Travel - General. PR: £5–500. Alternative tel: (015395) 32508. Cata: occasionally. Mem: PBFA. VAT No: GB 312 3475 89.

GRANGE-OVER-SANDS

Over-Sands Books, The Old Waiting Room, The Station, Grange-Over-Sands, LA11 6EH.

GRASMERE

Yewtree Books, ■ The Lakes Crafts & Antiques Gallery, 3 Oakbank Broadgate, Grasmere, LA22 9TA. Prop: Joe and Sandra Arthy. Tel: (015394) 35037. Fax: (015394) 44271. E-mail: allbooks@globalnet.co.uk. Est: 1990. Shop; open **M:** 10:00–17:00; **T:** 10:00–17:00; **W:** 10:00–17:00; **Th:** 10:00–17:00; **F:** 10:00–17:00; **S:** 10:00–17:00; **Su:** 10:00–17:00. Spec: Alpinism/Mountaineering; Children's - General; Railways; Topography - General; Topography - Local; Travel - General. PR: £1–300. CC: JCB; MC; V.

KENDAL

The Riverside Bookshop, ■ Yard 39, Highgate, Kendal, LA9 4ED. Prop: Paul & Carole Lee. Tel: (01539) 735173. Fax: (0870) 124-8380. Website: www.riversidebooks.co.uk. E-mail: riversidebooks@aol.com. Est: 1993. Shop; Internet and postal. Open: **M:** 10:30–16:00; **T:** 10:30–16:00; **W:** 10:30–16:00. **F:** 10:30–16:00; **S:** 10:30–15:00. Medium stock. Spec: Academic/Scholarly; Advertising; Alpinism/ Mountaineering; Children's - General; Fiction - General; First Editions; Railways; Topography - Local. PR: £1–250. CC: JCB; MC; V. Mem: PBFA.

KESWICK

Jean Altshuler, 54 St. John Street, Keswick, CA12 5AB. Tel: (01768) 775745. E-mail: books@jopplety. demon.co.uk. Est: 1996. Private premises; appointment necessary. Small general stock. Spec: Children's - General; Fiction - Science Fiction. PR: £5–200.

Keswick Bookshop, ■ 4 Station Street, Keswick, CA12 5HT. Prop: Jane & John Kinnaird. Tel: (01228) 528567. Est: 1994. Shop; Telephone first. Open: **M:** 10:30–17:00; **T:** 10:30–17:00; **W:** 10:30–17:00; **Th:** 10:30–17:00; **F:** 10:30–17:00; **S:** 10:30–17:00. Medium stock. Spec: Antiques; Applied Art; Architecture; Art; Children's - General; Decorative Art; First Editions; Illustrated; Interior Design; Photography. PR: £1–500. CC: JCB; MC; V. Winter opening: Saturday only (Dec-March). Cata: 2 – a year on art, architecture and design. Mem: PBFA. VAT No: GB 531 4987 33.

KIRKBY LONSDALE

Beck Head Books, ■ 10 Beck Head, Kirkby Lonsdale, LA6 2AY. Mrs. Barbara French. Tel: (01524) 271314. Est: 1984. Shop; open **T:** 10:00–17:00. **Th:** 10:00–17:00; **F:** 10:00–17:00; **S:** 10:00–17:00. Medium stock. Spec: Antiquarian; Bindings; First Editions; Gardening; Juvenile; Literature; Poetry; Topography - Local. CC: E; MC; V. Not open on Tuesdays in winter.

KIRBY STEPHEN

The Book House, Ravenstonedale, Kirkby Stephen, CA17 4NG. Prop: Chris & Mary Irwin. Tel: (01539) 623634. Website: www.thebookhouse.co.uk. E-mail: mail@thebookhouse.co.uk. Est: 1963. Private premises; open: **M:** 09:00–17:00. **W:** 08:00–17:00; **Th:** 09:00–17:00; **F:** 09:00–17:00; **S:** 09:00–17:00. Large stock. Spec: Archaeology; Children's - General; Engineering; Fiction - General; Gardening; History - Industrial; Languages - Foreign; Mining; Railways; Technology; Transport. PR: £1–750. CC: E; MC; V. Also, booksearch. Cata: 24. Corresp: French, Italian. Mem: PBFA. VAT No: GB 113 8746 69.

Discourse Books, 1 Old Midland Cottages, Kirkby Stephen, CA17 4LF.

PENRITH

David A.H. Grayling, Verdun House, Main Street, Shap, Penrith, CA10 3NG. Tel: (01931) 716746. Fax: (01931) 716746. Website: www.davidgraylingbooks.co.uk. E-mail: graylingbook@fsbdial.co.uk. Est: 1970. Private premises; Internet and postal. Appointment necessary. Medium stock. Spec: Colour-Plate; Fine & Rare; Natural History; Scottish Interest; Sport - Angling/Fishing; Sport - Big Game Hunting; Sport - Field Sports; Sport - Shooting; Travel - Africa; Travel - Americas; Travel - Asia; Zoology. PR: £20–5,000. CC: AE; MC; V. Publishers of reprints of rare books. Cata: 8 – big game, field sports & natural history. Corresp: French, German. Mem: PBFA. VAT No: GB 154 6592 46.

G.K. Hadfield, Beck Bank, Great Salkeld, Penrith, CA11 9LN.

Phenotype Books, 39 Arthur Street, Penrith, CA11 7TT. Prop: J.E. Mattley. Tel: (01768) 863049. Fax: (01768) 890493. E-mail: phenobooks@btinternet.com. Est: 1985. Private premises; telephone first. Small stock. Spec: Agriculture; Animals and Birds; Carriages & Driving; Farming & Livestock; Farriers; Periodicals & Magazines; Veterinary. PR: £5–1,500. Cata: 3 – on subjects relating to the farm. Mem: PBFA. VAT No: GB 442 8614 47.

SEASCALE

Archie Miles Book Shop, ■ Beck Place, Gosforth, Seascale, CA20 1AT. Prop: Mrs. C. M. Linsley. Tel: (01946) 725792. Est: 1870. Shop; open **T:** 10:00–17:00; **W:** 10:00–17:00; **Th:** 10:00–17:00; **F:** 10:00–17:00; **S:** 10:00–17:00. Medium stock. Spec: Illustrated; Literature; Topography - General. PR: £1–1,000. Also, booksearch. Opening hours varied in winter, phone first.

SEDBURGH

R.F.G. Hollett and Son, ■ 6 Finkle Street, Sedbergh, LA10 5BZ. Prop: C.G. & R.F.G. Hollett. Tel: (01539) 620298. Fax: (01539) 621396. Website: www.holletts-rarebooks.co.uk. E-mail: hollett@sedbergh.demon.co.uk. Est: 1959. Shop; Internet and postal. Open **W:** 10:00–17:00; **Th:** 10:00–17:00; **F:** 10:00–17:00; **S:** 10:00–17:00. Closed for lunch: 12:00–13:50. Large stock. Spec: Alpinism/Mountaineering; Antiquarian; Antiques; Fine Art; Natural History; Sport - Field Sports; Topography - General; Topography - Local; Travel - General. PR: £30–50,000. CC: AE; E; JCB; MC; V; Solo. Valuations. Cata: – regularly. Mem: ABA. VAT No: GB 343 4391 63.

ULVERSTON

Bookfare, Lowick Hall, Ulverston, LA12 8ED. Prop: Dr. A.C.I. Naylor. Tel: (01229) 885240. Fax: (01229) 885240. Website: www.bookfare.co.uk. E-mail: ambookfare@aol.com. Est: 1977. Private premises; postal business only. Small general stock. PR: £6–300. Corresp: French.

Brogden Books, 11 Brogden Street, Ulverston, LA12 7AH.

WELTON

All Seasons Books, Sebergham Castle Mansion, Welton, Near Carlisle, CA5 7HG. Prop: Frank Grant. Tel: (01697) 476079. Fax: (01697) 476079. E-mail: FGrant7472@aol.com. Private premises; postal business only. Small stock. Spec: Alpinism/Mountaineering; Sport - Climbing & Trekking. PR: £2–500. Also, a booksearch service. Cata: 1 – on subjects listed.

WHITEHAVEN

Michael Moon's Bookshop, ■ 19 Lowther Street, Whitehaven, CA28 7AL. Prop: Michael & Sylvia Moon. Tel: (01946) 599010. Fax: (09146) 599010. Est: 1970. Shop; open **M:** 09:30–17:00; **T:** 09:30–17:00; **Th:** 09:30–17:00; **F:** 09:30–17:00; **S:** 09:30–17:00. Spec: Cinema/Film; History - Local; Topography - Local. Also, booksearch. Closed Wed - Jan to Easter. Publisher on Cumbrian history. Cata: 2 – on Cumbriana. Mem: PBFA; SBA. VAT No: GB 288 1073 42.

WIGTON

Chelifer Books, Todd Close, Curthwaite, Wigton, CA7 8BE. (*) Prop: Mike Smith & Deryn Walker. Tel: (01228) 711388. Website: www.militarybooks.net. E-mail: chelifer@militarybooks.net. Est: 1985. Private premises; Internet and postal. Appointment necessary. Small stock. Spec: American Indians; Antiquarian; Arms & Armour; Aviation; Military; Military History; War - General; Wargames. PR: £5–1,500. CC: MC; V; SW. Cata: 6.

Fine Art Catalogues, The Hollies, Port Carlisle, Wigton, CA7 5BU.

Rosley Books, Rosley Farmhouse, Rosley, Wigton, CA7 8BZ. Prop: Ian Blakemore. Tel: (016973) 49244. Fax: (016973) 45149. Website: www.rosleybooks.com. E-mail: sales@rosleybooks.com. Est: 2000. Private premises; appointment necessary. Medium stock. Spec: Academic/Scholarly; Antiquarian; Author - Belloc, Hilaire; Author - Bunyan, John; Author - Chesterton, G.K.; Author - Eliot, T. S.; Author - Inklings, The; Author - Lewis, C. S.; Author - MacDonald, George; Author - Ruskin, John; Author - Tolkien, J.R. PR: £5–5,000.

WINDERMERE

Bridge Books, 2 Sunnybrae Brook Road, Windermere.

Fireside Bookshop, ■ 21 Victoria Street, Windermere, LA23 1AB. Prop: Mr R.D. Sheppard. Tel: (015394) 45855. Website: www.firesidebookshop.co.uk. E-mail: firesidebookshop@btconnect.com. Est: 1977. Shop; open **M:** 11:00–17:00; **T:** 11:00–17:00; **W:** 11:00–17:00; **Th:** 11:00–17:00; **F:** 11:00–17:00; **S:** 11:00–17:00; **Su:** 11:00–17:00. Large stock. Spec: Academic/Scholarly; Alpinism/Mountaineering; Antiquarian; Art; Fiction - General; History - General; Humanities; Maritime/Nautical; Medicine - History of; Military; Natural History; Rural Life; Science - History of; Social History; Transport. PR: £1–1,000. CC: AE; JCB; MC; SW.

WITHERSLACK

Rosemary Dooley, Crag House, Witherslack, Grange–over–Sands, LA11 6RW. Prop: R.M. S. Dooley. Tel: (01539) 552286. Fax: (01539) 552013. Website: www.booksonmusic.co.uk. E-mail: musicbks@rdooley.demon.co.uk. Est: 1992. Private premises; postal business only. Appointment necessary. Medium stock. Spec: Music - General. PR: £3–400. CC: AE; E; MC; V. Cata: 6 – every 2 months. Mem: PBFA. VAT No: GB 393 1979 09.

DERBYSHIRE

ALFRETON

John Titford, Yew Tree Farm, Hallfieldgate, Higham, Alfreton, DE55 6AG. (*). Tel: (01773) 520389. Fax: (01773) 833373. E-mail: john@titford.freeserve.co.uk. Est: 1987. Private premises; postal business only. Appointment necessary. Small stock. Spec: Genealogy; History - General; Topography - General. PR: £2–1,000 Also, booksearch. Corresp: French.

ASHBOURNE

Pamela Elsom - Antiques, ■ 5 Church Street, Ashbourne, DE6 1AT. Tel: (01335) 343468. Est: 1963. Shop; open **Th:** 10:00–17:00; **F:** 10:00–17:00; **S:** 10:00–17:00. Small stock. PR: £1–50.

BELPER

Green Man Books, 12 The Scotches, Belper, DE56 2UE. Prop: N. Rigby. Tel: (01773) 828503. Est: 1984. Private premises; postal business only. Small stock. Spec: Literary Criticism; Literature; Natural History.

BUXTON

Birdnet Optics Ltd., 5 London Road, Buxton, SK17 9PA.

Scrivener's Books & Book Bindi, ■ 42 High St., Buxton, SK17 6HB. Prop: Alastair Scrivener. Tel: (01298) 73100. Est: 1990. Shop; open **M:** 09:00–17:00; **T:** 09:00–17:00; **W:** 09:00–17:00; **Th:** 09:00–17:00; **F:** 09:00–17:00; **S:** 09:00–17:00; **Su:** 12:00–16:00. Very large stock. Spec: Academic/Scholarly; Animals and Birds; Antiquarian; Archaeology; Art Reference; Children's - General; Cinema/Film; Comic Books & Annuals; Countries - Poland; Crafts; Dictionaries; Engineering; Farming & Livestock; Fiction - General; First Editions. PR: £1–2,000. CC: AE; D; E; JCB; MC; V.

Willmer Books, 5 The Glade, Buxton, SK17 6SL.

CASTLETON

Hawkridge Books, The Cruck Barn, Cross Street, Castleton, Hope Valley, S33 8WH.

CHESTERFIELD

Nigel Bradley, 91 Hawksley Avenue, Chesterfield, S40 4TJ.

Tilleys Vintage Magazine Shop, ■ 21 Derby Road, Chesterfield, S40 2EF. Prop: Antonius & Albertus Tilley. Tel: (01246) 563868. Website: www.tilleysmagazines.com. E-mail: tilleys281@aol.com. Est: 1978. Shop; telephone first. Very large stock. Spec: Comic Books & Annuals; Glamour; Newspapers - General; Periodicals & Magazines; PR: £1–100. CC: AE; MC; V. Mail order. 1 million + items in stock 1890s-present. Corresp: Dutch. *Also at:* 281 Shoreham Street, Sheffield (q.v.).

Dealers who need to update their entry
should visit their page on
www.sheppardsdirectories.com

Dealers without e-mail - post details to us

DERBYSHIRE

CROMFORD

Scarthin Books, ■ The Promenade, Scarthin, Cromford, DE4 3QF. Prop: Dr. D.J. Mitchell. Tel: (01629) 823272. Fax: (01629) 825094. Website: www.scarthinbooks.com. E-mail: clare@scarthinbooks.com. Est: 1974. Shop; open **M:** 09:30–18:00; **T:** 09:30–18:00; **W:** 09:30–18:00; **Th:** 09:30–18:00; **F:** 09:30–18:00; **S:** 09:30–18:00; **Su:** 12:00–18:00. Very large stock. Spec: Alpinism/Mountaineering; American Indians; Animals and Birds; Antiquarian; Architecture; Author - Uttley, Alison; History - Industrial; History - Local; Music - General; Topography - Local. PR: £1–5,000. CC: MC; V. Also, new books, publishers of local history and walking books, and booksearch. Corresp: French, German. Mem: BA; IPG. VAT No: GB 127 6427 64.

DERBY

R.A. Beck, 19 Lawrence Avenue, Derby, DE21 4RD.

Bob Mallory (Books), 14 Dean Close, Littleover, Derby, DE23 7EF.

GLOSSOP

Andrew's Books & Collectables, Glossop Antique Centre, Brookfield, Glossop.

T. Cleverley, 88 Simmondley Lane, Simmondley, Glossop, SK13 6LX.

The George Street Loft, ■ 31 George Street, Glossop, SK13 8AY. Prop: Andrew Hancock. Tel: (01457) 863413. Fax: (01457) 863413. Website: www.multifuel.com. Est: 1986. Shop; open **W:** 10:00–17:00; **Th:** 10:00–17:00; **F:** 10:00–17:00; **S:** 10:00–17:00. Medium general stock. PR: £1–100. CC: MC; V.

Brian Mills: Books, Beech House, 18 North Road, Glossop, SK13 7AS.

ILKESTON

Philip S. Woodrow, 50 Kniveton Park, Ilkeston, DE7 5FD.

MATLOCK

Hunter and Krageloh, Honeybee Cottage, In the Dale, Wensley, Matlock, DE4 2LL. Prop: J.A. Hunter & Michael Papworth. Tel: (01629) 732845. E-mail: hunterandkrageloh@btinternet.com. Est: 1993. Telephone first. Spec: Alpinism/Mountaineering; Cartoons; Plant Hunting; Sport - Climbing & Trekking; Travel - Asia; Travel - Polar. PR: £1–12,000. Mem: PBFA.

Jarvis Books (incorporating 'Gaston's Alpine Books'), ■ 57/59 Smedley Street East, Matlock, DE4 3FQ. Grant & Valerie Jarvis. Tel: (01629) 55322. Website: www.mountainbooks.co.uk. E-mail: bd@mountainbooks.co.uk. Est: 1979. Shop; open **M:** 09:30–17:30; **T:** 09:30–17:30; **W:** 09:30–17:30; **Th:** 09:30–17:30; **F:** 09:30–17:30; **S:** 09:30–17:30. Medium stock. Spec: Alpinism/Mountaineering. CC: AE; MC; V. Shop closing soon but will be trading via postal address. Cata: 5. Mem: PBFA. VAT No: GB 439 5226 36.

WIRKSWORTH

Pastmasters, ■ 15 The Causeway, Wirksworth, DE4 4DL.

DEVON

ASHBURTON

Ashburton Books, ■ 44 East Street, Ashburton, TQ13 7AX. Prop: J.C. Tasker. Tel: (01364) 654744. Shop; open **T:** 10:00–18:00; **Th:** 10:00–18:00; **F:** 09:00–18:00; **S:** 10:00–17:00. Small stock. Spec: Biography; Drama; Fiction - General; Music - General; Poetry.

The Dartmoor Bookshop, ■ 2 Kingsbridge Lane, Ashburton, TQ13 7DX. Prop: Mr. & Mrs. P.R. Heatley. Tel: (01364) 653356. Shop; open **M:** 09:30–17:30; **T:** 09:30–17:30; **W:** 09:30–17:30; **Th:** 09:30–17:30; **F:** 09:30–17:30; **S:** 09:30–17:30. Very large stock. Spec: Alpinism/Mountaineering; Antiquarian; Architecture; Art; Art History; Art Reference; Artists; Fiction - General; Fine & Rare; Gardening; Maritime/Nautical; Military; Military History; Natural History; Occult; Topography - General; Topography - Local. PR: £1–250. VAT No: GB 365 7662 17.

AXMINSTER

Bookquest, High Grange, Dalwood, Axminster, EX13 7ES. Prop: E.M. Chapman. Tel: (01404) 831317. Est: 1968. Private premises; postal business only. Also, booksearch.

W.C. Cousens, 'The Leat', Lyme Road, Axminster, EX13 5BL. Prop: William Clifford Cousens. Tel: (01297) 32921. Est: 1988. Private premises; appointment necessary. Small stock. Spec: Gardening; Topography - Local. PR: £1–200. Also, booksearch. Cata: 3 – a year. Mem: PBFA.

BARNSTAPLE

B. Butler – Books, 68 Gould Road, Barnstaple, EX32 8ET. Prop: Brian Butler. Tel: (01271) 371794. Fax: (01271) 343211. Est: 1982. Private premises; postal business only.Very small stock. Spec: Author - Byron, Lord. PR: £5–5,000. Cata: – rarely.

Golden Books, Blurridge, Ridge Hill, Combe Martin, Barnstaple, EX34 0NR.

Tarka Books, ■ 5 Bear Street, Barnstaple, North Devon, EX32 7BU. Prop: Fiona Broster. Tel: (01271) 374997. Website: www.tarkabooks.co.uk. E-mail: books@tarkabooks.co.uk. Est: 1988. Shop; open **M:** 09:45–17:00; **T:** 09:45–17:00; **W:** 09:45–17:00; **Th:** 09:45–17:00; **F:** 09:45–17:00; **S:** 09:45–17:00. Very large general stock. Spec: Author - Williamson, Henry. PR: £1–100. CC: V. Also, a booksearch service. Mem: BA; FSB. VAT No: GB 691 7763 87.

BERE ALSTON

The Victoria Bookshop, ■ 9 Fore Street, Bere Alston, PL20 7AA. Prop: Peter Churcher. Tel: (01822) 841638. Website: www.victoriabookshop.co.uk. E-mail: victoria_bookshop@btopenworld.com. Est: 2000. Shop and postal business. Open **T:** 10:30–16:30; **W:** 10:30–16:30; **Th:** 10:29–16:30; **F:** 10:30–16:30; **S:** 10:30–16:30; **Su:** 10:30–16:30. Very large stock. Spec: Academic/Scholarly; Occult; Psychology/Psychiatry. PR: £3–600. CC: AE; MC; V; SW.

BIDEFORD

Allhalland Books, ■ 7 Allhalland St., Bideford, EX39 2JD. Prop: J.P. Simpson O'Gara and S. Sutherland. Tel: (01237) 479301. Est: 1997. Shop; open **M:** 09:00–17:00; **T:** 09:00–17:00; **W:** 09:00–17:00; **Th:** 09:00–17:00; **F:** 09:00–17:00; **S:** 09:00–17:00. Small stock. Spec: Natural History; Topography - General. PR: £2–500. Also, bookbinding.

C. & D. Davis, 9 Great Burrow Rise, Northam, Bideford, EX39 1TB. Prop: Carol & Dennis Davis. Tel: (01237) 475165. E-mail: dddesigns@mailcity.com (Public Library PC). Est: 1994. Private premises; postal business only. Spec: Sport - Canoeing/Kayaks. PR: £1–100. Also, a booksearch service.

Dealers who need to update their entry should visit their page on
www.sheppardsdirectories.com

Discovery, ■ 8a Grenville Street, Bideford, EX39. Prop: Peter Christie. Tel: (01237) 473577. E-mail: pchristi@ndevon.ac.uk. Est: 1978. Shop; open **M:** 10:00–16:00; **T:** 10:00–16:00; **W:** 10:00–16:00; **Th:** 10:00–16:00; **F:** 10:00–16:00; **S:** 09:00–17:00. Small general stock. PR: £1–50. Also, secondhand records, tapes, compact discs, videos & comics.

Peter Hames, Old Bridge Antiques Centre, 19 Market Place, Bideford, EX39 1HG. Prop: Old Bridges Antiques Centre. Tel: (01237) 421065. Fax: (01237) 421065. E-mail: peterhames@hotmail.com. Est: 1980. Spec: Topography - Local. PR: £5–50.

Nicholas Nickleby, Old Gazette Building, 6 Grenville St., Bideford, EX39 2EA.

Porcupines, The Moorings, 11 Windmill Lane, Northam, Bideford, EX39 1BZ. Prop: Susan Lowe. Tel: (01271) 861158. Fax: (01271) 861158. Est: 1964. Private premises; appointment necessary. Small general stock. Spec: Art; Author - Cobbett, William; Author - Lear, Edward; Collecting; Countries - Malta; Dolls & Dolls' Houses; Illustrated; Numismatics; Topography - Local; Toys. PR: £1–500.

The Swan Bookshop, ■ 20 Buttgarden Street, Bideford, EX39 2AU. Prop: Christopher Brazier. Tel: +44(0)1237 420678. Fax: +44(0)1237 420678. E-mail: sales@swanbookshop.co.uk. Est: 1979. Shop; open **M:** 10:00–17:00; **T:** 10:00–17:00; **W:** 10:00–17:00; **Th:** 10:00–17:00; **F:** 10:00–17:00; **S:** 10:00–13:00. Very large stock. Spec: Academic/Scholarly; Alpinism/Mountaineering; Antiques; Author - General; Authors - Women; Autobiography; Biography; Canals/Inland Waterways; Farming & Livestock; Feminism; Fiction - General; Fiction - Women; Health; History - General; History - British - and others listed in Speciality Index. PR: £1–100. Bookfinding Service.

BRIXHAM

Kate Armitage (Booksearch), 5 Park Court, Heath Road, Brixham, TQ5 9AX.

Book Warren, ■ 9a Bolton Street, Brixham, TQ5 9BZ. Prop: Mrs. E.M. Dare. Tel: (01803) 858531. Est: 1987. Shop; open M: 10:00–16:30; **T:** 10:00–16:30; **W:** 10:00–16:30; **Th:** 10:00–16:30; **F:** 10:00–16:30; **S:** 10:00–16:30. Very large general stock. Spec: Autobiography; Children's - General; Cookery/Gastronomy; Criminology; Fiction - General; Fiction - Crime, Detective, Spy, Thrillers; History - General; Music - General; Natural History; Navigation; Sport - General; Topography - General and others listed in the Speciality Index. PR: £1–100. Oct. to May, closed Wednesday & 1st Monday and Tuesday of each month.

BUDLEIGH SALTERTON

The Book Shelf, 17 High Street, Budleigh Salterton, EX9 6LD.

COLYTON

Island Books, Shutes Farm, Northleigh, Colyton, EX24 6BL. Tel: (01404) 871600. Fax: (01404) 871601. E-mail: island@swauk.freeserve.co.uk. Est: 1974. Private premises; Internet and postal. Appointment necessary. Medium stock. Spec: Academic/Scholarly; Aeronautics; Agriculture; Animals and Birds; Antiquarian; Applied Art; Architecture; Author - 20th Century; Author - Austen, Jane; Author - Baring-Gould, S.; Author - Belloc, Hilaire; Author - Betjeman, Sir John; Author - Boswell; and others listed in the Speciality Index. PR: £10–10,000. CC: AE; JCB; MC; V.

DARTMOUTH

Chantry Bookshop & Gallery, ■ 11 Higher Street, Dartmouth, TQ6 9RB. Prop: M.P. Merkel. Tel: (01803) 832796. Est: 1948. Shop; open **M:** 10:30–17:00; **T:** 10:30–17:00; **W:** 10:30–17:00; **Th:** 10:30–17:00; **F:** 10:30–17:00. Medium stock. Spec: Antiquarian; Author - Dickens, Charles; Fine & Rare; First Editions. CC: AE; MC; V. Alternative Tel: (01803) 834208. Also, antique prints, pencil drawings and aquatints.

DAWLISH

Dawlish Books, ■ White Court, Beach Street, Dawlish, EX7 9PN. Prop: S. French. Tel: (01626) 866882. E-mail: dawlishbooks@fsmail.net. Est: 2000. Shop; open **M:** 10:30–16:30; **T:** 10:30–16:30; **W:** 10:30–16:30; **Th:** 10:30–16:30; **F:** 10:30–16:30; **S:** 10:30–16:30. Medium general stock. Spec: Alternative Medicine; Astrology; Mysteries; Mysticism; Natural Health; New Age; Occult; Psychic; U.F.O.s; Witchcraft. PR: £1–100. Open all week in summer.

EXETER

Mrs. Muriel J. Bryant, 5 Clipper Quay, The Quay, Exeter, EX2 4AP. Tel: (01392) 434674. Est: 1993. Private premises; appointment necessary. Small stock. PR: £2–20. Also, booksearch.

Lisa Cox Music, The Coach House,, Colleton Crescent, Exeter, EX 2 4DG. Prop: Ms. L. Cox. Tel: (01392) 490290. Fax: (01392) 277336. Website: www.lisacoxmusic.co.uk. E-mail: music@lisacoxmusic.co.uk. Est: 1984. Private premises; Internet and postal. Appointment necessary. Open **M:** 10:00–17:00; **T:** 10:00–17:00; **W:** 10:00–17:00; **Th:** 10:00–17:00; **F:** 10:00–12:00. Medium stock. Spec: Autographs; Manuscripts; Music - Printed. PR: £100–50,000. CC: MC; V. Cata: 3. Corresp: French. Mem: ABA. VAT No: GB 631 4239 64.

Exeter Rare Books, ■ 12a, Guildhall Shopping Centre, Exeter, EX8 5AX. R.C. Prop: Parry M.A. Tel: (01392) 436021. Est: 1977. Shop; open **M:** 10:00–17:00; **T:** 10:00–17:00; **W:** 11:00–17:00; **Th:** 10:00–17:00; **F:** 10:00–17:00; **S:** 10:00–17:00. Closed for lunch: 13:00–14:00. Medium stock. Spec: Topography - Local. PR: £2–500. CC: MC; V. Corresp: German. Mem: ABA; PBFA. VAT No: GB 142 3267 91.

John S. Hill, 78 Pinhoe Road, Exeter, EX4 7HL. Tel: (01392) 439753. Fax: (01392) 439753. E-mail: john@hill6383.fsnet.co.uk. Est: 1988. Private premises; Internet and postal. Appointment necessary. Small stock. Spec: Fiction - Crime, Detective, Spy, Thrillers; Fiction - Science Fiction; First Editions; Military. PR: £5–1,500. Also, booksearch. Cata: 1 – variable.

Pennies, 6 Marsh Green Road, Marsh Barton, Exeter.

Pennies, 40 Fore Street, Topsham, Exeter.

Joel Segal Books, ■ 27 Fore Street, Topsham, Exeter, EX3 0HD. Tel: (01392) 877895. Website: www.joelsegalbooks.eclipse.co.uk. E-mail: joelsegalbooks@eclipse.co.uk. Shop; open **M:** 10:30–17:00; **T:** 10:30–17:00; **W:** 10:30–17:00; **Th:** 10:30–17:00; **F:** 10:30–17:00; **S:** 10:30–17:00. Closed for lunch: 13:00–14:00. Very large stock. Spec: Arts, The; Literature; Natural History; Social History; Topography - General; Topography - Local; Transport. PR: £1–200. CC: MC; V. Also, an valuation service, and ephemera. Corresp: French.

EXMOUTH

Keverel Chess Books, Keverel Lodge, 40 Phillipps Avenue, Exmouth, EX8 3HZ.

HONITON

Ænigma Designs (Books), Whites Plot, Luppitt, Honiton, EX14 4RZ. Tel: (01404) 891560. Fax: (01404) 891560. Website: www.puzzlemuseum.com. E-mail: books@puzzlemuseum.com. Est: 1973. Internet and postal. Spec: Mathematics; Puzzles; Science - General. PR: £5–200. CC: PayPal.

High Street Books, ■ 150 High Street, Honiton, EX14 8JX. Prop: Geoff Tyson. Tel: (01404) 45570. Fax: (01404) 45570. Est: 1992. Shop; open **M:** 10:00–17:00; **T:** 10:00–17:00; **W:** 10:00–17:00; **Th:** 10:00–17:00; **F:** 10:00–17:00; **S:** 10:00–17:00. Large stock. Spec: Applied Art; Erotica; Maritime/Nautical; Military; Topography - General; Topography - Local; Travel - General. PR: £1–600.

Honiton Old Bookshop, ■ Felix House, 51 High Street, Honiton, EX14 1PW. Prop: Roger Collicott. Tel: (01404) 47180. E-mail: honitonoldbooks@ukonline.co.uk. Shop; open **M:** 10:00–16:30; **T:** 10:00–16:30; **W:** 10:00–17:30; **Th:** 10:00–17:30; **F:** 10:00–17:30; **S:** 10:00–17:30. Medium stock. Spec: Antiquarian; Bindings; Geology; Mineralogy; Science - History of; Topography - General; Topography - Local; Travel - Asia; War - English Civil Wars. CC: E; MC; V. Cata: 2 – British topography & early printed books. Mem: ABA; PBFA; ILAB. VAT No: GB 568 9200 11.

Graham York, 233 High Street, Honiton, EX14 1AH.

KINGSBRIDGE

Bookends of Devon, 41 Fore Street, Kingsbridge, TQ7 1PG. Tel: (01548) 854318. Website: www.bookends.free-online.co.uk. E-mail: carol@bookends.free-online.co.uk. Est: 1991. PR: £1–50.

Booktrace International, The Hald, Kernborough, Kingsbridge, TQ7 2LL. Prop: Richard Newbold. Tel: (01548) 511121. E-mail: booktrace@aol.com. Est: 1995. Private premises; postal business only. Small stock. PR: £5–200. Booksearch service is main line of business.

Searching for a title - and cannot find it on any Internet database?
Then try **Sheppard'sBooksearch**

By selecting the subject classification – the request goes to all dealers who major in that subject.

LYDFORD

Dean Byass, Tavistock Books, Rookwood, Lydford, EX20 4BW. Prop: Dean Byass. Tel: (01822) 820381. E-mail: byass@btopenworld.com. Est: 1994. Private premises; appointment necessary. Spec: Antiquarian; History of Ideas; Natural History; Natural Sciences; Science - History of. PR: £50–2,000. CC: AE; MC; V. VAT No: GB 799 9334 44.

LYMPSTONE

Reaveley Books, 1 Church Road, Lympstone, Nr Exmouth, EX8 5JU. Prop: Jane Johnson. Tel: (01395) 225462. Website: www.reaveleybooks.com. E-mail: jane@johnsgrj.demon.co.uk. Est: 1998. Private premises; telephone first. Small stock. Spec: Author - Murdoch, I.; Modern First Editions. PR: £5–500. CC: Paypal. Mem: FSB; FPBA.

MODBURY

Lamb's Tales Books, 63 Brownston Street, Modbury, Ivybridge, PL21 0RQ. Prop: James & Elizabeth Lamb. Tel: (01548) 830317. Website: www.lambstales.co.uk. E-mail: books@lambstales.co.uk. Est: 1988. Private premises; Internet and postal. Contactable. Small general stock. PR: £5–150. VAT No: GB 768 6509 77.

MORETONHAMSTEAD

Moreton Books, ■ 3a The Square, Moretonhampstead, TQ13 8NF. Tel: (01647) 441176. Est: 1994. Shop; open **M:** 10:00–17:00; **T:** 10:00–17:00; **W:** 10:00–17:00; **Th:** 10:00–17:00; **F:** 10:00–17:00; **S:** 10:00–17:00. Medium stock. Spec: Antiquarian; Art History; Art Reference; Autobiography; Literature; Modern First Editions; Natural History; Poetry; Railways; Topography - Local; Travel - General. PR: £1–500. CC: E; MC; V; SO, SW. Viewing times differ in winter.

NEWTON ABBOT

Wayfarers Books, 5 Cleaveland Rise, East Ogwell, Newton Abbot, TQ11 6FF.

Adrian Forman Books, P.O. Box 163, Braunton, North Devon, EX33 2YF.

NORTHLEIGH

Island Books, Shutes Farm, Northleigh, EX24 6BL. Prop: S.F.J. Westall. Tel: (01404) 871600. Fax: (01404) 871601. E-mail: island@swauk.freeserve.co.uk. Est: 1973. Private premises; appointment necessary. Medium stock. Spec: Author - Bates, H.E.; Author - Churchill, Sir Winston; Author - Cobbett, William; Author - Hardy, Thomas; Author - Jefferies, R.; Author - Morton, H.V.; Author - Sackville-West, Vita; Author - Sassoon, Siegfried; Author - Williamson, Henry; Bibliography and others listed in the Speciality Index. PR: £20–3,000. Also, a booksearch service. Cata: – irregularly. Corresp: French, German.

OKEHAMPTON

Ruth & Emma Delow, 5 Steddafords, Sticklepath, Okehampton, EX20 2NP.

PAIGNTON

Biddy's Bookshop, 99c Dartmouth Road, Goodrington, Paignton.

The Diver's & Watersportsman's, 10 Cedar Road, Preston, Paignton, TQ3 2DD. Prop: David Way. Tel: (01803) 390824. Est: 1990. Private premises; appointment necessary. Small stock. Spec: Deep Sea Diving; Sport - Angling/Fishing; Sport - Diving/Sub-Aqua. PR: £1–120. Cata: 2 – on specialities and carp.

The Old Celtic Bookshop, ■ 43 Hyde Road, Paignton, TQ4 5BP. Prop: Michael Sutton. Tel: (01803) 558709. E-mail: michael.sutton2@virgin.net. Est: 1989. Shop; open **M:** 09:00–18:00; **T:** 09:00–18:00; **W:** 09:00–18:00; **Th:** 09:00–18:00; **F:** 09:00–18:00; **S:** 09:00–18:00; **Su:** 09:00–18:00. Large stock. PR: £1–50. Extended opening until 21:30 June to September.

The Pocket Bookshop, ■ 159 Winner Street, Paignton, TQ3 3BP. Prop: Leon Corrall. Tel: (01803) 529804. Est: 1985. Shop; open **T:** 10:30–17:30; **W:** 10:30–17:30; **Th:** 10:30–17:30; **F:** 10:30–17:30; **S:** 10:30–17:30. PR: £1–50. Open Mondays in from July to September.

PLYMOUTH

Albion Books, 5 Quay Road, Plymouth, PL1 2JZ.

Anne Harris Books & Bags Books, 38 Burleigh Park Road, Peverell, Plymouth, PL3 4QH.

The Bookcupboard, 3 Mitre Court, Southside Street, Barbican,, Plymouth, PL1 2LD.

DEVON

Books2Books, 64 Glendower Road, Peverell, Plymouth, PL3 4LD.

Cornerstone Books, New Street Antiques Centre, 27 New Street, The Barbican, Plymouth, PL1 2NB. Prop: Mark Treece. Tel: (01752) 661165. Website: mark@streece.freeserve.co.uk. E-mail: mark@streece.freeserve.co.uk. Est: 1986. Market stand/stall; Internet and postal. *Shop at:* 11 Inverdene Peverell Plymouth Devon. PL3 4LE (postal only). Open: **M:** 09:00–17:00; **T:** 09:00–17:00; **W:** 09:00–17:00; **Th:** 09:00–17:00; **F:** 09:00–17:00; **S:** 09:00–17:00. Large general stock.

Jeremy Parrott, 53 Elm Road, Mannamead, Plymouth, PL4 7AZ.

Purple Haze Comics & Books, 38 Eastlake Walk, Drake Circus Shopping Centre, Plymouth, PL1 1BX.

Rods Books, 20–21 Southside Street, Barbican, Plymouth, PL1 2LD. Prop: R.P. Murphy. Tel: (01752) 253546. E-mail: rmurphy980@aol.com. Est: 1996. Spec: Countries - Mexico; Deep Sea Diving; Fiction - Science Fiction; Fiction - Westerns; History - General; History - Ancient; History - British; History - Local; Maritime/Nautical; Military; Military History; Naval; Navigation; Rural Life; Shipbuilding and others listed in the Specialities Index. PR: £2–40.

The Sea Chest Nautical Bookshop, ■ Queen Anne's Battery Marina, Coxside, Plymouth, PL4 0LP. Prop: R.A. Dearn. Tel: (01752) 222012. Fax: (01752) 252679. Website: www.seachest.co.uk. E-mail: sales@seachest.co.uk. Est: 1987. Shop; open **M:** 09:00–17:00; **T:** 09:00–17:00; **W:** 09:00–17:00; **Th:** 09:00–16:00; **F:** 09:00–17:00; **S:** 09:00–17:00. Small stock. Spec: Maritime/Nautical; Navigation; Sport - Yachting. PR: £2–750. CC: AE; MC; V. Also, new nautical books, pilots & charts, a booksearch service & British Admiralty chart agent. Mem: BA. VAT No: GB 501 5928 65.

SEATON

Gerrards Cross Books, 'Upwood', Old Beer Road, Seaton, EX12 2PX. Prop: Mrs. Patty Lafferty. Tel: (01297) 21761. Est: 1972. Private premises; postal business only. Very small general stock. PR: £1–100.

Hill House Books, Hill House, Highcliffe Crescent, Seaton, EX12 2PS.

Tantalus Antiques & Books, Holly Cottage, Watercombe, Branscombe, Seaton,, EX12 3BT. Prop: A. & B. Dustan-Smith. Tel: (0129) 680457. E-mail: tonydustansmith@onetel.net.uk. Est: 1971. Private premises. Small general stock. Spec: Antiques; Biography. PR: £3–150. CC: JCB; V. Mem: PBFA.

SIDMOUTH

Books Plus, ■ 91 High Street, Sidmouth, EX10 8DL. Prop: Robert Starling. Tel: (01395) 578199. E-mail: books.plus@btinternet.com. Est: 1999. Shop; open **M:** 09:00–17:00; **T:** 09:00–17:00; **W:** 09:00–17:00; **Th:** 09:00–17:00; **F:** 09:00–17:00; **S:** 09:00–17:00. Small general stock. Spec: Cinema/Film; Military; Music - Jazz. PR: £1–30. Also, videos & CDs.

Midnight Books, The Mount, Ascerton Road, Sidmouth, EX10 9BT.

SOUTH BRENT

P.M. Pollak, Moorview, Plymouth Road, South Brent, TQ10 9HT. Tel: (01364) 73457. Fax: (01364) 649126. Website: www.rarevols.co.uk. E-mail: patrick@rarevols.co.uk. Est: 1973. Private premises; Internet and postal. Telephone first. Small stock. Spec: Academic/Scholarly; Economics; Medicine; Natural Sciences; Photography; Science - General; Science - History of; Scientific Instruments; Social History; Technology. PR: £30–5,000. CC: AE; JCB; MC; V. Also, medical and scientific paintings. Cata: 6 – on history of medicine & science. Corresp: German, French. Mem: ABA; ILAB. VAT No: GB 267 5364 31.

Rosemary Stansbury, 25 Church Street, South Brent, TQ10 9AB. Tel: (01364) 72465. Est: 1985. Private premises; appointment necessary. Small stock. Spec: Children's - General. PR: £1–50. Cata: 3 – a year.

TAVISTOCK

Bookworm Alley, 36 Brook Street, Tavistock, PL19 0HE. Prop: Joan Williams. Tel: (01822) 617740. E-mail: bookworm-alley@freenet.co.uk. Est: 2000. Private premises; appointment necessary. Small stock. Spec: Religion - Christian. PR: £1–50.

Lee Furneaux Books, 6 Lopes Road, Dousland, Yelverton, Tavistock, PL20 6NX. Tel: (01822) 853243. Website: www.abebooks.com/home/madeleine. E-mail: lee@furneauxbooks.freeserve.co.uk. Est: 1987. Market stand/stall; Internet and postal. Telephone first. *Shop at:* Tavistock Pannier Market, Tavistock, Devon. Open: **T:** 08:30–16:00. **Th:** 08:30–16:00; **F:** 08:30–16:00; **S:** 08:30–16:00. Small stock. Spec: Art; Children's - General; Crafts; Gardening; History - General; Literature; Mind, Body & Spirit; Music - Popular; Music - Rock; Mysteries; Rural Life; Topography - Local; Travel - General. PR: £1–100.

TEIGNMOUTH

IKON, Magnolia House, New Road, Teignmouth, TQ14 8UD. Prop: Dr. Nicholas & Clare Goodrick–Clarke. Tel: (01626) 776528. Fax: (01626) 776528. E-mail: ikon@globalnet.co.uk. Est: 1982. Postal business only. Spec: Alchemy; Esoteric; Herbalism; History - European; Literature in Translation; Natural Health; New Age. PR: £10–75.

Quayside Bookshop, ■ 43 Northumberland Place, Teignmouth, TQ14 8DE. Prop: V.K. & E.C. Marston. Tel: (01626) 775436. Fax: (01626) 777023. Website: www.milestonebooks.co.uk. E-mail: quaybook@aol.com. Est: 1982. Shop; Internet and postal. Open **M:** 09:30–17:30; **T:** 09:30–17:30; **W:** 09:30–17:30. **F:** 09:30–17:30; **S:** 09:30–17:30. Closed for lunch: 13:30–14:00. Medium stock. Spec: Aviation; Buses/Trams; Maritime/Nautical; Naval; Navigation; Railways; Ship Modelling; Shipbuilding; Steam Engines; Transport; Voyages & Discovery. PR: £2–800. CC: AE; D; MC; V; SW. Also, new books on specialities. Cata: 2 – on maritime and aviation. Mem: BA. VAT No: 585 7083 03.

TIVERTON

Heartland Old Books, ■ 12–14 Newport Street, Tiverton, EX16 6NL. Prop: Jeremy Whitehorn. Tel: (01884) 254488. Website: www.heartlandoldbooks.co.uk. E-mail: jwhitehorn@heartlandoldbooks.co.uk. Est: 2001. Shop; open **M:** 10:00–17:00; **T:** 10:00–17:00; **W:** 10:00–17:00; **Th:** 10:00–17:00; **F:** 10:00–17:00; **S:** 10:00–17:00. Medium stock. Spec: Art; Cookery/Gastronomy; Military; Sport - Field Sports; Topography - Local; Travel - General. PR: £1–750. Easy parking in Pannier Market opposite. Mem: PBFA.

Kelly Books Limited, 6, Redlands, Tiverton, EX16 4DH. Props: Len & Lynda Kelly. Tel: (01884) 256170. Fax: (01884) 251063. Website: www.kellybooks.co.uk. E-mail: len@kellybooks.co.uk. Est: 1972. Private premises; Internet and postal. Appointment necessary. Open: **M:** 09:00–18:00; **T:** 09:00–18:00; **W:** 09:00–18:00; **Th:** 09:00–18:00; **F:** 09:00–18:00; **S:** 09:00–18:00. Medium stock. Spec: Academic/Scholarly; Advertising; Aeronautics; Broadcasting; Cinema/Film; Journalism; Media; Radio/Wireless; Television. PR: £5–500. CC: AE; MC; V; SW. Supply of back numbers of Radio Times. Cata: 2. VAT No: GB 799 7192 48.

TORQUAY

Colin Baker - Books for the Collector, 66 Marldon Road, Shiphay, Torquay, TQ2 7EH. Tel: (01803) 613356. Fax: (01803) 613356. E-mail: colinbakerbooks@yahoo.co.uk. Est: 1994. Private premises; postal business only. Spec: Author - Read, Miss; Author - Tangye, D.; Children's - General; Children's - Illustrated; Illustrated; Topography - General; Topography - Local. PR: £5–500.

Duncan's Books, ■ 176 Union Street, Torquay, TQ2 5QP. Prop: Duncan Campbell. Tel: (01803) 294081. Est: 1996. Shop; open **M:** 09:30–17:00; **T:** 09:30–17:00; **W:** 09:30–17:00; **Th:** 09:30–17:00; **F:** 09:30–17:00; **S:** 09:30–17:00. Small general stock. Spec: Music - General; Theology; Travel - General. PR: £1–20. Also, sheet music & memorabilia.

The Schuster Gallery, P.O. Box 139, Torquay, TQ1 2XX.

Westcountry Old Books, 215 Babbacombe Road, Babbacombe, Torquay, TQ1 3SX. Prop: Mr. D.A. Neil. Tel: (01803) 322712. E-mail: westcountryoldbooks@btopenworld.com. Est: 1989. Private premises; appointment necessary. Small stock. Spec: Antiquarian; Illustrated; Literature; Topography - Local. PR: £1–500. Also at Biblion, London W1K 5AB (q.v.). Mem: PBFA.

TORRINGTON

The Archivist, Priory Cottage, Frithelstock, Torrington, EX38 8JH. Tel: (01805) 625750. Fax: (01805) 625376. E-mail: rjoe01@aol.com. Est: 1990. Private premises; Internet and postal. Appointment necessary. Very small stock. Spec: Cats; Journalism; Literature; Publishers - Joseph Ltd., Michael. PR: £1–1,000.

River Reads Bookshop, ■ Unit 9, Pannier Market, Torrington, EX38 8HD. Tel: (01805) 625888. Fax: (01805) 622064. E-mail: keitarmshw@aol.com. Est: 2002. Shop; open **M:** 10:00–16:00; **T:** 10:00–16:00; **W:** 10:00–13:00; **Th:** 10:00–16:00; **F:** 10:00–16:00; **S:** 10:00–16:00. Medium stock. Spec: Art; Children's - General; Cookery/Gastronomy; Fishes; Gardening; Health; Hobbies; Natural History; Sport - Angling/Fishing. PR: £2–40. Also, vintage fishing tackle.

TOTNES

Collards Bookshop, ■ 4 Castle Street, Totnes, TQ9 5NU. Prop: Belle Collard. Tel: (01548) 550246. E-mail: collards@freeuk.com. Est: 1970. Shop; open **M:** 10:30–17:00; **T:** 10:30–17:00; **W:** 10:30–17:00; **Th:** 09:30–17:00; **F:** 10:30–17:00; **S:** 10:30–17:00. Small general stock. PR: £1–300. Hours vary midweek January to March.

Geoff Cox, Lower West Wing, Tristford House, Harberton, Totnes, TQ9 7RZ. Tel: (01803) 866181. Fax: (01803) 866181. E-mail: geoffcox46@hotmail.com. Est: 1978. Private premises; appointment necessary. Medium stock. Spec: Aviation; Canals/Inland Waterways; History - Industrial; Maritime/Nautical; Mining; Motoring; Railways; Social History; Steam Engines; Traction Engines; Vintage Cars. PR: £1–500.

Harlequin, ■ 41 High Street, Totnes, TQ9 5NP. Prop: Paul Wesley. Tel: (01803) 865794. Est: 1983. Shop; open **M:** 10:00–17:30; **T:** 09:00–17:30; **W:** 10:00–17:30; **Th:** 10:00–17:30; **F:** 10:00–17:30; **S:** 10:00–17:30. Medium general stock. PR: £1–50.

Pedlar's Pack Books, ■ 4 The Plains, Totnes, TQ9 5DR. Prop: Peter & Angela Elliott. Tel: (01803) 866423. E-mail: pedlar@aol.com. Est: 1981. Shop; Internet and postal. Open **M:** 09:00–17:00; **T:** 09:00–17:00; **W:** 09:00–17:00; **Th:** 09:00–17:00; **F:** 09:00–17:00; **S:** 09:00–17:00. Large stock. PR: £1–500. CC: AE; JCB; V; SW. Also, a booksearch service. Mem: PBFA.

UMBERLEIGH

D. & D.H.W. Morgan, Whitmore, Chittlehamholt, Umberleigh, EX7 9HB. Tel: (01769) 540214. Website: www.birdjournals.com. E-mail: stjamestree@btopenworld.com. Est: 1978. Private premises; postal business only. Appointment necessary. Medium stock. Spec: Botany; Gardening; Natural History; Ornithology; Periodicals & Magazines. PR: £1–100. Also, ornithological periodicals. Cata: 1. Corresp: French.

YEALMPTON

Lesley Evans Booksearch, The Old School House, 3 Chapel Road, Yealmpton, PL8 2LZ. Prop: Lesley Evans. Tel: (01752) 880386. E-mail: yealmptonbooks@aol.com. Est: 1996. Spec: Maritime/Nautical; Military History; Naval; Topography - Local. PR: £1–250. Also, booksearch.

DORSET

BEAMINSTER

John E. Spooner, 18 Glebe Court, Barnes Lane, Beaminster, DT8 3EZ. Tel: (01308) 862713. Est: 1975. Market stand/stall; Small stock. Spec: Aviation; Military; Naval. PR: £5–100.

BLANDFORD FORUM

Ancient & Modern Bookshop, (Basement) 84 Salisbury Street, Blandford Forum, DT11 7QE. Prop: Margaret A. Davey. Tel: (01258) 455276. Website: www.ancientandmodernbooks.co.uk. E-mail: pegdavey@tinyworld.co.uk. Est: 1989. Private premises. Open: **M:** 09:30–16:30; **T:** 09:30–16:30. **Th:** 09:30–16:30; **F:** 09:30–16:30; **S:** 09:30–16:30. Closed for lunch: 12:30–13:30. Large general stock. Spec: Academic/Scholarly; Alpinism/Mountaineering; Antiquarian; History - British; Science - General. PR: £1–100. CC: Cheque. Also, limited number of pictures, book rests, chairs & tables. Cata: – on request.

N. Trevor Armitage, 2 Deverill House, Salisbury Road, Blandford Forum, DT11 7QG.

The Dorset Bookshop, ■ 69 East Street, Blandford Forum, DT11 7DX. Ethan Golden. Tel: (01258) 452266. Est: 1950. Shop; open **M:** 10:00–17:00; **T:** 10:00–17:00; **W:** 10:00–17:00; **Th:** 10:00–17:00; **F:** 10:00–17:00; **S:** 10:00–17:00. Small general stock. PR: £1–100. Mem: BA.

Four Tees Booksearch, P.O. Box 2701, Blandford Forum, DT11 8YR. Prop: J.A. Davis. Tel: (01725) 516425. Est: 1996. Private premises; postal business only. Small general stock. PR: £1–120. Also, booksearch.

BOURNEMOUTH

Mary Bradley–Cox, 13 Lascelles Road, Bournemouth, BH7 6NF. Tel: (01202) 246160. Website: mbradleycox.com. E-mail: mbradleycox@aol.com. Est: 1992. Private premises; Internet and postal. Small stock. Spec: Crime (True); Fiction - Crime, Detective, Spy, Thrillers; Medicine; Politics; Psychotherapy; Sport - Golf. PR: £5–200. CC: AE; MC; V; SW; SO. VAT No: GB 797 8711 57.

Butler Books, 3 Denewood Road, Bournemouth, BH4 8EB. Prop: B.H. & M.E. Butler. Tel: (01202) 764185. Fax: (01202) 764185. E-mail: butler.books@lineone.net. Est: 1980. Private premises; postal business only. Appointment necessary. Medium general stock. Spec: History of Ideas; Oriental; Religion - General; Religion - Christian; Religion - Jewish; Theology. PR: £10–5,000. Cata: 3 – on theology and religion. Corresp: French, German.

Facet Books, ■ 67 Bennett Road, Bournemouth, BH8 8RH. Prop: Mr James Allinson and Mrs Margit Allinson. Tel: (01202) 269269. Website: www.jallinson.freeserve.co.uk. E-mail: jim@jallinson.freeserve.co.uk. Est: 1982. Shop; Internet and postal. Open: **M:** 10:00–17:30; **T:** 10:00–17:30; **W:** 10:00–17:30; **Th:** 10:00–17:30; **F:** 10:00–17:30; **S:** 09:30–16:00. Large general stock. Spec: Cartoons; Children's - General; Comedy; Comic Books & Annuals; Comics; Mysticism; Odd & Unusual; Psychic; Religion - Christian; Spiritualism; Supernatural; U.F.O.s. PR: £1–2,500. CC: MC; V; SW. Also, booksearch. Corresp: German. Mem: FSB.

Holdenhurst Books, ■ 275, Holdenhurst Road, Bournemouth, BH8 8BZ. R.W. Reese. Tel: (01202) 397718. Est: 1985. Shop; open **M:** 10:00–17:00; **T:** 09:00–17:00. **Th:** 10:00–17:00; **F:** 10:00–17:00; **S:** 10:00–17:00. Medium stock. Spec: Motorbikes; Motoring. PR: £5–150.

P.F. & J.R. McInnes, 59, Richmond Park Road, Bournemouth, BH8 8TU. Tel: (01202) 394609. Est: 1981. Private premises; appointment necessary. Very small stock. Spec: Sport - Boxing. PR: £1–3,000. Research facility on premises, with B&B offered.

**Dealers who need to update their entry
should visit their page on
*www.sheppardsdirectories.com***

H. & S.J. Rowan, ■ 459 Christchurch Road, Boscombe, Bournemouth, BH1 4AD. Tel: (01202) 398820. Est: 1969. Shop; open **M:** 09:00–18:00; **T:** 09:00–18:00; **W:** 09:00–18:00; **Th:** 09:00–18:00; **F:** 09:00–18:00; **S:** 09:00–18:00. Large general stock. Spec: Antiquarian; Antiques; Art; Aviation; Topography - Local. PR: £1–1,000. Also, booksearch. VAT No: GB 185 3287 39.

Sue Sims, 21 Warwick Road, Pokesdown, Bournemouth, BH7 6JW. Tel: (01202) 432562. Fax: (01202) 460059. E-mail: sue@sims.abel.co.uk. Est: 1978. Private premises; postal business only. Contactable. Very small stock. Spec: Author - Brent-Dyer, Elinor M.; Author - Fairlie–Bruce, D.; Author - Forest, A; Author - Oxenham, Elsie; Children's - General; Religion - Roman Catholic. PR: £1–500. Major stock of girl's books and school stories, and booksearch. Cata: 1 – Irregular. Corresp: French, German.

Yesterday Tackle & Books, 42 Clingan Road, Boscombe East, Bournemouth, BH6 5PZ. Prop: David & Alba Dobbyn. Tel: (01202) 476586. Est: 1983. Private premises; appointment necessary. Small stock. Spec: Sport - Angling/Fishing. PR: £1–100. CC: AE. Also, fishing tackle and related items. Cata: 1 – occasionally.

Yesterday's Books, 6 Cecil Avenue, Bournemouth, BH8 9EH. Prop: David & Jessica L. Weir. Tel: (01202) 522442. E-mail: djl.weir@btinternet.com. Est: 1974. Storeroom; Internet and postal. Telephone first. Open: **M:** 09:00–17:00; **T:** 09:00–17:00; **W:** 09:00–17:00; **Th:** 09:00–17:00; **F:** 09:00–17:00; **S:** 09:00–13:00. Medium stock. Spec: Anthropology; Countries - Africa; Egyptology; Ethnography; History - General; Literary Travel; Literature; Pacifism; Sport - Hockey; Travel - General; Travel - Africa; Tribal. PR: £5–500. CC: JCB; MC; V. Cata: 4 – on Africana. Corresp: French, German. Mem: PBFA.

BOURTON

Well–Head Books, The Old Vicarage, Bourton, Gillingham, SP8 5BJ. Prop: Stephen Mobsby. Tel: (01747) 840213. Fax: (01747) 840724. E-mail: Wellheadbk. Est: 1985. Postal business only. Spec: Crafts; Dolls & Dolls' Houses; Embroidery; Lace; Needlework; Textiles; Woodwork. PR: £5–500. Also, booksearch.

BRIDPORT

Clearwater Books, St. Bartholomew Cottage, Shipton Gorge, Bridport, DT6 4LU.

Far Horizons Books, Far Horizons, Ryall, Bridport, DT6 6EG. Prop: Mrs. C.E.M. Parr. Tel: (01297) 489046. Est: 1990. Private premises; Internet and postal. Contactable. Open: **M:** 10:00–19:30; **T:** 10:00–19:30; **W:** 10:00–19:30; **Th:** 10:00–19:30; **F:** 10:00–19:30. Medium general stock. Spec: Esoteric; Ghosts; Gnostics; Metaphysics; Mind, Body & Spirit; Mysticism; Occult; Parapsychology; Psychic; Religion - Buddhism; Religion - Christian; Religion - Islam; Spiritualism; Supernatural; Weird & Wonderful; Witchcraft; Yoga. PR: £4–100. Cata: 4 – a year on specialities.

Caroline Mactaggart, Manor Farmhouse, Swyre, Bridport, Dorchester, DT2 9DN. (*). Tel: (01308) 898174. E-mail: caroline@textbiz.com. Est: 1984. Private premises. *Shop at:* Bridport Old Books, 11 South Street, Bridport, Dorset. Very small stock. Spec: Scottish Interest. PR: £5–200. CC: MC; V. Mem: PBFA.

CHARMOUTH

Charmouth Bounty Books, 1 Maycroft, Higher Sea Lane, Charmouth, DT6 6BB. Prop: Louisa Mamakou. Tel: (01297) 560233. Website: www.clique.co.uk/members/charmouth. E-mail: louisa@charmouthbountybooks.fsnet.co.uk. Est: 2003. Private premises; Internet and postal. Appointment necessary. Very small general stock. Spec: Biography; Children's - General; Countries - Cyprus; Countries - Greece; Geology; Literature; Maritime/Nautical; Music - General; Natural History; Palaeontology; Slavery; Topography - General. PR: £1–250. CC: MC; V; (via Abe). Free Worldwide Booksearch. Cata: 3 – a year. Corresp: French, Greek.

Brian Kesterton, Freedom Heights, Westcliff Road, Charmouth, DT6 6BG.

Available from Richard Joseph Publishers Ltd
CLEANING, REPAIRING AND CARING FOR BOOKS
by Robert L. Shep

Revised Edition   148pp £12.00

CHRISTCHURCH

R.D. Hooker, 8 Friars Road, Christchurch, BH23 4EA.

DORCHESTER

The Dorchester Bookshop, ■ 3 Nappers Court, Charles Street, Dorchester, DT1 1EE. Prop: Michael J. Edmonds. Tel: (01305) 269919. Est: 1993. Shop; open: **T:** 10:00–17:00; **W:** 10:00–17:00; **Th:** 10:00–17:00; **F:** 10:00–17:00; **S:** 10:00–17:00. Medium general stock. PR: £1–500.

Julian Nangle, ■ 12 South Walks Road, Dorchester, DT1 1ED. Tel: (01305) 251919. Fax: (01305) 267872. E-mail: jnangle@tiscali.co.uk. Shop; open **M:** 10:00–17:30; **S:** 10:00–17:30. Large stock. Spec: First Editions; History - Local; Illustrated; Literature. PR: £10–1,000. Also, remainders and new books. Cata: 2 – occasionally. Mem: *Also at: Also at:* Words Etcetera, Dorset. (q.v.).

Judith Stinton, 21 Cattistock Road, Maiden Newton, Dorchester, DT2 OAG. Tel: (01300) 320778. Website: www.abebooks.com. E-mail: judithstinton@hardycountry.fsnet.co.uk. Est: 1989. Private premises; Internet and postal. Appointment necessary. Very small stock. Spec: Children's - General; Topography - Local. PR: £1–100.

Woolcott Books, Kingston House, Higher Kingston, Dorchester, DT2 8QE. Prop: H.M. & J.R. St. Aubyn. Tel: (01305) 267773. Fax: (01305) 751899. Est: 1978. Private premises; appointment necessary. Small stock. Spec: Colonial; Countries - Africa; Countries - India; History - National; Military; Travel - Africa; Travel - Asia; Travel - Middle East. PR: £3–300. Also, booksearch. Cata: 1 – a year.

Words Etcetera, ■ 2 Cornhill, Dorchester, DT1 1BA. Prop: Julian Nangle. Tel: (01258) 455940. Fax: (01258) 267872. E-mail: jnangle@tiscali.co.uk. Shop; open **M:** 09:30–17:30; **T:** 09:30–17:30; **W:** 09:30–17:30; **Th:** 09:30–17:30; **F:** 09:30–17:30; **S:** 09:30–17:30. PR: £1–1,000. *Also at:* Julian Nangle, Dorchester, Dorset (q.v.).

R.A. Yates, 9 Treves Road, Dorchester, DT1 2HD. Tel: (01305) 264336. Private premises; appointment necessary. Small stock. Spec: Academic/Scholarly; Humanities. PR: £1–100. Cata: 1 – occasionally.

FERNDOWN

Janet Cherry, Highbury, Woodside Road, West Moors, Ferndown, BH22 0LY. Prop: Stanley Cherry. Tel: (01202) 874372. Fax: (01202) 874370. Est: 1970. Private premises; appointment necessary. Very small stock. Spec: Antiquarian; Gardening; Horticulture; Voyages & Discovery; War - General. PR: £5–100. Corresp: French.

GILLINGHAM

Eden Books, PO Box 1562, Gillingham, SP8 4ZN. Prop: Grant & Tracey Eden. Tel: (01747) 831130. Website: www.edenbooks.com. E-mail: edenbooks@aol.com. Est: 1997. Private premises; Internet and postal. Spec: Publishers - Ladybird Books; Sport - Boxing; Sport - Football (Soccer); Sport - Rugby. CC: AE; E; JCB; MC; V. Mem: PBFA. VAT No: GB 762 3914 22.

Lilian Modlock, Southcote, Langham Lane, Wyke, Gillingham, SP8 5NT. Tel: (01747) 821875. Fax: (01747) 821875. E-mail: lmodlock@aol.com. Est: 1995. Private premises; postal business only. Appointment necessary. Medium stock. Spec: Biography; Children's - General; Cinema/Film; Cookery/Gastronomy; Illustrated; Landscape; Poetry; Topography - General; Topography - Local; Travel - General. PR: £3–400. Also, a booksearch service.

LYME REGIS

Lymelight Books & Prints, 1 Drakes Way, Lyme Regis, DT7 3QP.

Marine Workshop Bookshop, ■ The Cobb, Marine Parade, Lyme Regis, BT7 3JF. Prop: Lucy Forman. Tel: 901297) 444820. Est: 1996. Shop; open: **M:** 11:00–16:00; **T:** 11:00–16:00; **W:** 11:00–16:00; **Th:** 11:00–16:00; **F:** 11:00–16:00. Small stock. Spec: Fiction - General; Fiction - Crime, Detective, Spy, Thrillers; Publishers - Penguin. PR: £1–100. Open weekends in summer, phone first. Also, fossils.

Ingrid Mostyn Books, 27 Whalley Lane, Uplyme, Lyme Regis, DT7 3UR.

Sanctuary Bookshop, 65 Broad Street, Lyme Regis, DT7 3QF.

MILBOURNE PORT

Kingswood Books, 17 Wick Road, Milborne Port, Sherborne, DT9 5BT. Prop: Anne Rockall & Allan Dollery. Tel: (01963) 250280. Fax: (01963) 250280. Website: www.kingswoodbooks.btinternet.co.uk. E-mail: kingswoodbooks@btinternet.com. Est: 1985. Private premises; Internet and postal. Appointment necessary. Medium stock. Spec: Archaeology; Canals/Inland Waterways; Cartoons; History - National; Science - History of. PR: £1–500. CC: JCB; MC; V; SW. Bookbinders & restorers. See our web site. Cata: 2. Mem: PBFA. *Also at:* Various book fairs listed on our web site.

POOLE

Bookstand, 53 Kings Ave., Poole, BH14 9QQ. Prop: Eleanor Smith & Wendy Marten. Tel: (01202) 716229. Fax: (01202) 734663. Website: www.abebooks.com/home/bookstand. E-mail: bookstand@lineone.net. Est: 1997. Private premises; Internet. Appointment necessary. Small general stock. Spec: Author - Thelwell, N; Author - Wheatley, Dennis; Autographs; Humour; Illustrated; Manuscripts; Modern First Editions; Poetry; Private Press; Signed Editions. PR: £15–5,000. CC: V.

Branksome Books, 33a Kings Avenue, Poole, BH14 9QG. Prop: P.G. Bryer–Ash. Tel: (01202) 730235. Fax: (01202) 730235. Est: 1988. Private premises; appointment necessary. Very small general stock. Spec: Author - Lawrence, T.E.; Sport - Angling/Fishing; Sport - Field Sports; Travel - General. PR: £5–200. Corresp: French.

ECR Books, 4 Yarmouth Road, Branksome, Poole, BH12 1JN. Prop: John Aris. Tel: (01202) 537365. Est: 1989. Private premises; appointment necessary. Medium stock. Spec: Antiquarian; Bindings; Children's - General; Private Press; Theology; Typography. PR: £10–100. Also, booksearch. Cata: 1 – occasionally.

R.H. & P. Haskell, 64 Winston Avenue, Branksome, Poole, BH12 1PG. Tel: (01202) 744310. Fax: (01202) 744310. E-mail: reg.thebinder@talk21.com. Est: 1973. Private premises; appointment necessary. Very small stock. Spec: Architecture. PR: £5–1,000. Also, bookbinding service.

Christopher Williams, 19 Morrison Avenue, Parkstone, Poole, BH12 4AD. Prop: Christopher & Pauline Williams. Tel: (01202) 743157. Fax: (01202) 743157. Website: www.abebooks.com/home/cw. E-mail: cw4finebooks@lineone.net. Est: 1967. Private premises; Internet and postal. Appointment necessary. Very small stock. Spec: Arts, The; Bibliography; Cookery/Gastronomy; Crafts; Lace; Topography - Local. PR: £5–100. CC: MC; V. Cata: – occasionally. Mem: PBFA.

PUDDLETOWN

The Antique Map and Bookshop, ■ 32 High Street, Puddletown, DT2 8RU. Prop: C.D. & H.M. Proctor. Tel: (01305) 848633. Fax: (01305) 848992. Website: www.abebooks.com/home/proctorbooks. E-mail: proctor@puddletown.demon.co.uk. Est: 1976. Shop; open **M:** 09:00–17:00; **T:** 09:00–17:00; **W:** 09:00–17:00; **Th:** 09:00–17:00; **F:** 09:00–17:00; **S:** 09:00–17:00. Medium stock. Spec: Author - Conan Doyle, Sir Arthur; Author - Hardy, Thomas; Author - Henty, G.A.; Natural History. PR: £5–2,000. CC: MC; V; SW. Cata: 5. Corresp: German. Mem: ABA; PBFA; ILAB. VAT No: GB 291 7495 21.

SHAFTSBURY

Paul Goldman, Meadow View, East Orchard, Shaftesbury, SP7 0LG.

Not Just Books, 7A, High Street, Shaftesbury, SP7 8HQ. Tel: (01747) 850003. E-mail: ntrevor64@supanet.com.

SHERBORNE

Chapter House Books, Trendle Street, Sherborne, DT9 3NT. Prop: Robert & Carol Hutchison. Tel: (01935) 816262. E-mail: chapterhousebooks@tiscali.co.uk. Est: 1988. PR: £1–250. Also, works of art, booksearch, bookbinding & book repair services.

Keeble Antiques, 2 Tilton Court, Digby Road, Sherborne, DT9 3NL.

Available from Richard Joseph Publishers Ltd
BOOK DEALING FOR PROFIT
by Paul Minet

1st Edition 2000 (Quarto H/b)   £10.00 144pp

Grahame Thornton, Monghyr House, Spring Lane, Long Burton, Sherborne, DT9 5NZ. Tel: (01963) 210443. Fax: (01963) 210443. Website: www.grahamethornton.f9.co.uk. E-mail: grahame@grahamethornton.f9.co.uk. Private premises; Internet and postal. Telephone first. Small stock. Spec: Biography; Espionage; Fiction - General; History - General; History - 19th Century; Medicine; Military; Publishers - Penguin; Travel - General; War - World War I; War - World War II. CC: MC; V; SW, S. Also, booksearch.

Verandah Books, Stonegarth, The Avenue, Sherborne, DT9 3AH. Prop: Michael Hougham. Tel: (01935) 815900. Fax: (01935) 815900. Website: www.verandah.demon.co.uk. E-mail: mah@verandah.demon.co.uk. Est: 1992. Private premises; postal business only. Appointment necessary. Medium stock. Spec: Author - Kipling, Rudyard; Countries - Afghanistan; Countries - Burma; Countries - Himalayas, The; Countries - India; Countries - Nepal; Countries - Pakistan; Countries - South East Asia; Countries - Sri Lanka. PR: £10–500. Cata: 5.

STALBRIDGE

March House Books, March House, Thornhill Road, Stalbridge, DT10 2PS. Prop: Mrs. Barbara Fisher. Tel: (01963) 364405. Fax: (01963) 364405. Website: www.marchhousebooks.com. E-mail: books@marchhousebooks.com. Est: 1997. Private premises; Internet and postal. Small stock. Spec: Children's - General; Illustrated. PR: £5–650. CC: Paypal.

STURMINSTER NEWTON

Boris Books, ■ Boris Books, Market Place, Sturminster Newton, DT10 1AS. Prop: Pam Stevenson. Tel: (01258) 471912. Website: www.borisbooks.co.uk. E-mail: pam@borisbooks.fsnet.co.uk. Est: 1995. Shop; open **M:** 09:30–16:30; **T:** 09:30–16:30; **W:** 09:30–16:30; **Th:** 09:30–16:30; **F:** 09:30–16:30; **S:** 09:30–13:00. Closed for lunch: 13:15–14:15. Small general stock. Spec: Author - Heyer, Georgette; Children's - General; Fiction - General; Fiction - Historical; First Editions; Illustrated; Literature; Music - General; Music - Composers. PR: £1–500. CC: MC; V. Also, booksearch. Mem: PBFA; FSB. VAT No: GB 717 6806 15.

SWANAGE

New & Secondhand Books, 35 Station Road, Swanage, BH19 1AD. Prop: Jill & Mike Blanchard. Tel: (01929) 424088. PR: £1–100.

Reference Works Ltd., 9 Commercial Road, Swanage, BH19 1DF. Tel: (01929) 424423. Fax: (01929) 422597. Website: www.referenceworks.co.uk. E-mail: sales@referenceworks.co.uk. Est: 1984. Office &/or bookroom; telephone first. Small stock. Spec: Antiques; Ceramics; Decorative Art. PR: £5–800. CC: MC; V. Cata: 8.

WAREHAM

Calluna Books, c/o Syldata, Arne, Wareham, BH20 5BJ. Prop: Y. Gartshore & J. Day. Tel: (01929) 552560. Fax: (01929) 552560. E-mail: neil&yuki@onaga54.freeserve.co.uk. Est: 1997. Spec: Botany; Conservation; Entomology; Natural History; Ornithology. PR: £5–500.

Reads, Beehive Cottage, East Stoke, Wareham, BH20 4JW. Prop: Reg Read & Anthony Hessey. Tel: (01929) 554971. Est: 1998. Private premises; postal business only. Small stock. Spec: Architecture; Cinema/Film; Guide Books; Music - General; Performing Arts; Railways; Theatre; Topography - General; Topography - Local; Travel - General. PR: £5–1,000. Corresp: French. Mem: PBFA.

WEYMOUTH

Books & Bygones, ■ 26, Great George Street, Weymouth, DT4 7AS. Mrs. D. Nash. Tel: (01305) 777231. Est: 1983. Shop; open **M:** 12:00–17:00; **T:** 12:00–17:00; **W:** 12:00–17:00; **Th:** 12:00–17:00; **F:** 12:00–17:00; **S:** 12:00–17:00; **Su:** 12:00–17:00. Medium general stock. PR: £1–1,000.

Searching for a title - and cannot find it on any Internet database?

Then try **Sheppard's Booksearch**

By selecting the subject classification – the request goes to all dealers who major in that subject.

Books Afloat, ■ 66 Park Street, Weymouth, DT4 7DE. John Ritchie. Tel: (01305) 779774. Est: 1983. Shop; open **M:** 09:30–17:30; **T:** 09:30–17:30; **W:** 09:30–17:30; **Th:** 09:30–17:30; **F:** 09:30–17:30; **S:** 09:30–17:30. Large general stock. Spec: Author - Hardy, Thomas; Author - Powys Family, The; Aviation; Canals/Inland Waterways; Fiction - General; Maritime/Nautical; Military History; Navigation; Railways; Sport - Yachting; Topography - General; Topography - Local; Transport; Travel - General. PR: £1–140.

Bournes Bookworld, 15 Buxton Road, Rodwell, Weymouth, DT4 9PG.

Micelle Press, 10–12 Ullswater Crescent, Weymouth, DT3 5HE.

The Nautical Antique Centre, ■ 3a Cove Passage, Hope Square, Weymouth, DT4 8TR. Prop: Mr D.C. Warwick. Tel: (01305) 777838. Website: www.nauticalantiquesweymouth.co.uk. E-mail: nauticalantiques@tinyworld.co.uk. Est: 1989. Shop; appointment necessary. Open: **T:** 10:00–17:00; **W:** 10:00–17:00; **Th:** 10:00–17:00; **F:** 10:00–17:00. Closed for lunch: 13:00–14:00. Very small stock. Spec: Journals - Maritime; Manuals - Seamanship; Maritime/Nautical; Maritime/Nautical - Log Books; Naval; Navigation; Shipbuilding; Steam Engines. PR: £5–300. CC: MC; V.

WIMBORNE

John Graham, 52 Blandford Road, Corfe Mullen, Wimborne, BH21 3HQ. Prop: John Graham. Tel: (01202) 692397. Fax: (01202) 692397. Est: 1987. Private premises; postal business only. Small stock. Spec: Biography; History - General; History - Industrial; History - Local; History - National; Social History. PR: £1–100. Also, booksearch.

Minster Books, 12 Corn Market, Wimborne, BH21 1JL.

The Talking Dead, 12 Rosamund Avenue, Merley, Wimborne, BH21 1TE.

DURHAM

BARNARD CASTLE

Books on the Bank, ■ 3 The Bank, Barnard Castle, DL12 8PH. Prop: Colin and Cathy Robinson. Tel: (01833) 695123. Website: www.booksonthebank.co.uk. E-mail: enquiry@booksonthebank.co.uk. Est: 1999. Shop; open **T:** 10:00–16:00; **W:** 10:00–16:00; **Th:** 10:00–16:00; **F:** 10:00–16:00; **S:** 10:00–17:00. Medium general stock. Spec: Art Reference; Rural Life; Topography - Local. PR: £1–300. CC: E; JCB; MC; V. Internet sales via abebooks.com.

Curlews, 27 Horse Market, Barnard Castle, DL12 8LX.

Greta Books, Lodge Farm, Scargill, Barnard Castle, DL12 9SY. Prop: Gordon Thomson. Tel: (01833) 621000. Fax: (01833) 621000. E-mail: thomson2000@bigfoot.com. Postal business only. Spec: Farming & Livestock; Fiction - General; History - General; Maritime/Nautical. PR: £5–50.

BISHOP AUCKLAND

Vinovium Books, Wear Valley Business Centre, 27 Longfield Road, Bishop Auckland, DL14 6XB. Prop: Paul Hughes. Tel: (01388) 777770. Website: www.vinoviumbooks.co.uk. E-mail: enqrj@vinoviumbooks.co.uk. Est: 1996. Office &/or bookroom; Internet and postal. Appointment necessary. Medium stock. Spec: Academic/Scholarly; History - General; History - Local; Military History; Sport - Angling/Fishing; Sport - Field Sports; Topography - Local. PR: £5–3,000. CC: JCB; MC; V; SW. Mem: PBFA. VAT No: GB 746 9734 81.

DARLINGTON

Combat Arts Archive, 12 Berkeley Road, Darlington, DL1 5ED. Prop: Mr. J. Sparkes. Tel: (01325) 465286. E-mail: johnsparkes@ntlworld.com. Est: 1995. Private premises; postal business only. Appointment necessary. Small stock. Spec: Physical Culture; Sport - Boxing; Sport - Duelling; Sport - Fencing; Sport - Martial Arts,; Sport - Weightlifting/Bodybuilding; Sport - Wrestling. PR: £1–150. CC: JCB; MC; V. Cata: 4 – every 3 months.

Tony and Gill Tiffin, 144 Coniscliffe Road, Darlington, DL3 7RW. Prop: G.A. & M.G. Tiffin. Tel: (01325) 487274. E-mail: tony.tiffin@btinternet.com. Est: 1992. Private premises; book fairs only. Telephone first. Spec: Academic/Scholarly; Children's - General; Literature; Military; Military History; Poetry; School Registers/Rolls of Honour; Sport - Cricket; War - World War I. PR: £3–200. Mem: PBFA.

Jeremiah Vokes, ■ 61 Coniscliffe Road, Darlington, DL3 7EH. Prop: Jeremiah Vokes. Tel: (01325) 469449. Est: 1979. Shop; open M: 09:30–17:30; **T:** 09:30–17:30; **W:** 09:30–17:30; **Th:** 09:30–17:30; **F:** 09:30–17:30; **S:** 09:30–17:30. Medium general stock. Spec: Fiction - Crime, Detective, Spy, Thrillers; Sherlockiana. PR: £5–1,000. Also, booksearch.

MIDDLETON–IN–TEESDALE

The Village Bookshop, 36 Market Place, Middleton–in–Teesdale, DL12 0RJ. Prop: Susan and David Fielden. Tel: (01833) 640373. Fax: (01833) 640373. Website: www.villagebookshop.co.uk. E-mail: david.fielden@talk21.com. Est: 2000. Spec: Crafts; Rural Life; Topography - Local. PR: £1–50.

STOCKTON-ON-TEES

P.R. Brown (Books), 39 Sussex Walk, Norton–on–Tees, Cleveland, TS20 2RG. (*) Prop: P. Robinson–Brown. Tel: (01642) 871704. Est: 1975. Private premises; appointment necessary. Very small stock. Spec: Botany; History - Local; Ornithology. PR: £5–500.

**Dealers who need to update their entry
should visit their page on
*www.sheppardsdirectories.com***

Norton Books, 18 Wolviston Road, Billingham, Stockton–on–Tees, TS22 5AA. Prop: C. Casson. Tel: (01642) 649657. Fax: (01642) 649658. E-mail: sales@ricardmarketing.com. Est: 1981. Private premises; Internet and postal. Appointment necessary. Spec: Antiquarian; Author - Crosby, Harry & Caresse; Author - Cunard, Nancy; Author - Joyce, James; Author - Miller, Henry; Author - Nin, Anais; Author - Stein, Gertrude; Literature; Modern First Editions. PR: £10–2,000. Mem: PBFA.

D.B. Wilson (Books), Barnard Gallery, No. 2 Theatre, Yard, (behind Green Dragon Yard), Stockton-on–Tees, TS18 1AT.

WILLINGTON

John Turton, 83 High Street, Willington. *Also at:* 1–2 Cochrane Terrace, Willington (q.v.)

John Turton, 1–2 Cochrane Terrace, Willington, Crook, DL15 0HN. Tel: (01388) 745770. Fax: (01388) 746741. E-mail: johnturton@turtome.co.uk. Est: 1978. Spec: Antiquarian; Bindings; Ecclesiastical History & Architecture; Free Thought; Genealogy; Heraldry; Journals - General; Military History; Mining; Parish Registers; School Registers/Rolls of Honour; Topography - General; Topography - Local. PR: £5–2,000 Mem: *Also at:* 83 High Street, Willington (q.v.).

EAST SUSSEX

ASHBURNHAM

William Duck, Pay Cottage, The Furnace, Ashburnham, Battle, TN33 9PG. Tel: (01424) 838295. Fax: (01424) 838291. Est: 1963. Private premises; appointment necessary. Very small stock. Spec: Aeronautics; Architecture; Arms & Armour; Astronautics; Aviation; Building & Construction; Canals/Inland Waterways; Cities; Country Houses; Design; Engineering; Firearms/Guns; Gardening; Geology; History - Industrial; Industry; Landscape; Maritime/Nautical; and others as listed in the Speciality Index. Cata: 2 – on specialities.

BEXHILL–ON–SEA

Raymond Elgar, 6 Blackfields Avenue, Bexhill, TN39 4JL. Tel: (01424) 843539. Private premises; postal business only. Very small stock. Spec: Bindings; Magic & Conjuring; Music - General; Musical Instruments. Cata: 1 – bookbinding sundries and tools.

BRIGHTON

Breese Books Ltd, 10 Hanover Crescent, Brighton, BN2 9SB. Prop: Martin Breese. Tel: (01273) 687-555. Website: www.sherlockholmes.co.uk. E-mail: MBreese999@aol.com. Est: 1988. Private premises; postal business only. Small stock. Spec: Author - Blyton, Enid; Author - Crompton, Richmal; Author - Greene, Graham; Fiction - General; Magic & Conjuring; Sherlockiana. PR: £35–5,000. CC: MC; V. Also, specialist publishers.

Brighton Books, ■ 18 Kensington Gardens, Brighton, BN1 4AL. Prop: Paul Carmody & Catherine Clement. Tel: (01273) 693845. Fax: (01273) 693845. Est: 1996. Shop; open **M:** 10:00–18:00; **T:** 10:00–18:00; **W:** 10:00–18:00; **Th:** 10:00–18:00; **F:** 10:00–18:00; **S:** 10:00–18:00. Spec: Academic/Scholarly; Architecture; Art; Biography; Children's - General; Cinema/Film; Drama; Fiction - General; First Editions; Gardening; Illustrated; Mythology; Photography; Poetry. PR: £1–100. CC: AE; JCB; MC; V; SW. Corresp: French, German.

Cooks Books, 34 Marine Drive, Rottingdean, Brighton, BN2 7HQ. Prop: Tessa McKirdy. Tel: (01273) 302707. Fax: (01273) 301651. E-mail: tessamckirdy@hotmail.com. Est: 1975. Private premises; appointment necessary. Medium stock. Spec: Cookery/Gastronomy; Food & Drink. CC: D; E; JCB; MC; V. Cata: 2 - specialities. Corresp: French. VAT No: GB 509 0878 31.

K. Davies at Flair, P.O. Box 456, Hove, Brighton, BN3 1DY.

Dinnages Transport Publishing, P.O. Box 2210, Brighton, BN1 9WA. Prop: Mr. G. & Mrs. C. Dinnage. Tel: (01273) 601001. Fax: (07957) 602725. Website: www.transport-postcards.co.uk. E-mail: publishers@dinnages.org.uk. Est: 1989. Office &/or bookroom; Internet and postal. Appointment necessary. Very small stock. Spec: Buses/Trams; History - Local; Publishers - General; Railways; Transport. PR: £1–25. Also publish own nostalgic transport photographs and postcards.

Turner Donovan Military Books, 12 Southdown Avenue, Brighton, BN1 6EG. Tel: (01273) 566230. E-mail: tom@turnerdonovan.com. Est: 1985. Postal business only. Spec: Countries - India; Military; Military History; War - Napoleonic; War - World War II. PR: £15–2,500.

Fisher Nautical, Huntswood House, St. Helena Lane, Streat, Hassocks, Brighton, BN6 8SD. (*) Prop: S. & J. Fisher. Tel: (01273) 890273. Fax: (01273) 891439. Website: www.fishernauticalbooks.co.uk. E-mail: fishernautical@seabooks.fsnet.co.uk. Est: 1969. Private premises; postal business only. Very large stock. Spec: Maritime/Nautical. PR: £10–3,000. CC: MC; V. Also, booksearch. Cata: 12 – every 4-6 weeks on nautical. Mem: PBFA.

Dealers who need to update their entry should visit their page on
www.sheppardsdirectories.com

EAST SUSSEX

Invisible Books, Unit 8, 15-26 Lincoln Cottage Works, Lincoln Cottages, Brighton, BN2 9UJ. Prop: Bridget Penney & Paul Holman. Tel: (01273) 694574. Fax: (0870) 052 2755. E-mail: invisible@invisiblebooks.demon.co.uk. Est: 1994. Storeroom; Internet and postal. Appointment necessary. Small stock. Spec: Academic/Scholarly; Counterculture; New Age; Politics. PR: £1–1,000. Also, publishing small press/alternative.

Kenya Books, 31 Southdown Ave., Brighton, BN1 6EH. Prop: J. McGivney. Tel: (01273) 556029. Website: www.abebooks.com/home/kenyabooks. E-mail: info@kenyabooks.com. Private premises; Internet and postal. Small stock. Spec: Countries - Africa; Countries - Kenya; Travel - Africa. PR: £1–500.

Moviedrome, 8 Friar Crescent, Brighton, BN1 6NL. Prop: Don Shiach. Tel: (01273) 881611. E-mail: moviedrome@fastnet.co.uk. Est: 1993. Internet and postal. Contactable. Spec: Cinema/Film. PR: £1–500.

The Mulberry Bush, 9 George Street, Brighton, BN2 1RH.

Colin Page Antiquarian Books, ■ 36 Duke Street, Brighton, BN1 1AG. Prop: John Loska. Tel: (01273) 325954. E-mail: cpagebooks@aol.com. Est: 1969. Shop; open **M:** 09:30–17:30; **T:** 09:30–17:30; **W:** 09:30–17:30; **Th:** 09:30–17:30; **F:** 09:30–17:30; **S:** 09:30–17:30. Large stock. Spec: Bindings; Children's - General; Colour-Plate; Illustrated; Literature; Natural History; Topography - General; Travel - General. PR: £1–10,000. CC: AE; JCB; MC; V. Cata: 1 – on request. Mem: ABA.

Rainbow Books, ■ 28 Trafalgar Street, Brighton, BN1 4ED. Prop: Kevin Daly. Tel: (01273) 605101. Est: 1998. Shop; open **M:** 10:30–18:00; **T:** 10:30–18:00; **W:** 10:30–18:00; **Th:** 10:30–18:00; **F:** 10:30–18:00; **S:** 10:30–18:00. Very large general stock. PR: £1–20.

Savery Books, ■ 300 Ditchling Road, Brighton, BN1 6JH. Prop: James & Sarah Savery. Tel: (01273) 564899 and 503030. Est: 1990. Shop; open **W:** 10:00–16:30; **Th:** 10:00–16:30; **F:** 10:00–16:30. Very large stock. Spec: Academic/Scholarly; Art; Aviation; Biography; Business Studies; Chess; Children's - General; Cinema/Film; Cookery/Gastronomy; Countries - Poland; Crafts; Crime (True); Feminism; Fiction - General; Fore-Edge Paintings; Gardening; Health; History - General; and others as listed in the Speciality Index. PR: £1–20. CC: MC; V. Also, antiques & small furniture.

Liz Seeber, Old Vicarage, 3 College Road, Brighton, BN2 1JA. Tel: (01273) 684949. Website: www.lizseeberbooks.com. E-mail: seeber.books@virgin.net. Est: 1994. Private premises; postal business only. Appointment necessary. Small stock. Spec: Cookery/Gastronomy; Gardening PR: £5–2,000. Also, booksearch. CC: MC; V. Cata: 4 – Quarterly. VAT No: GB 629 3954 04.

Studio Bookshop, ■ 68 St. James's Street, Brighton, BN2 1PJ. Prop: Paul Brown. Tel: (01273) 691253. Website: www.abebooks.com/home/studiobookshop. E-mail: studiobookshop@btconnect.com. Est: 1995. Shop; open **M:** 11:00-17:00; **T:** 11:00–17:00; **W:** 11:00–19:00; **F:** 11:17–17:00; **S:** 11:00–17:00. Medium stock. Spec: Academic/Scholarly; Antiques; Applied Art; Architecture; Art; Art Reference; Ceramics; First Editions; Glass; History - General; Humanities; Literary Criticism; Literature; Literature in Translation; Modern First Editions; Stained Glass. PR: £5–450. CC: JCB; MC; V.

Templar Books, 8 Coldean Lane, Brighton, BN1 9GD.

The Trafalgar Bookshop, ■ 44 Trafalgar Street, Brighton. Prop: David Boland. Tel: (01273) 684300. Est: 1979. Shop; open. Medium stock. Spec: Colour-Plate; Journals - General; Literature; Sport - General; Sport - Horse Racing (all aspects). Also, booksearch.

Waxfactor, 24 Trafalgar Street, Brighton, BN1 4EQ.

Available from Richard Joseph Publishers Ltd
Sheppard's Book Dealers in Latin America and Southern Africa
1st Edition 2000 (A5 P/b)   87pp £21.00

CROWBOROUGH

Ray Hennessey Bookseller, Panfield House, Crowborough Hill, Crowborough, TN6 2HJ. Prop: Ray & Deanna Hennessey. Tel: (01892) 653704. Fax: (0870) 0548776. Website: www.bibliofind.com or www.bibliocity.com. E-mail: rayhen@books4.demon.co.uk. Est: 1954. Private premises; Internet and postal. Appointment necessary. *Shop at:* Olinda House Antiques Rotherfield East Sussex. Open: **M:** 10:10–17:17; **T:** 10:10–17:17; **W:** 10:10–17:17; **Th:** 10:00–17:00; **F:** 10:00–17:00; **S:** 10:00–17:00; **Su:** 11:00–16:00. Large stock. Spec: Africana; Antiquarian; Antiques; Applied Art; Art; Bibles; Canals/Inland Waterways; Children's - Illustrated; Gardening; Illustrated; Lace; Literature; Miniature Books; Needlework; Poetry; Publishers - Batsford; Sport - Golf; Tapestry; Textiles; Topography - Local. PR: £5–1,000. CC: AE; E; JCB; MC; V. Mem: PBFA.

Simply Read Books, Fielden Rd, Crowborough, TN6 2TR. Prop: W.L. & W.P. Banks. Tel: (01892) 664584. Website: www.abebooks.com/home/simplyread. E-mail: simplyreadbook@aol.com. Est: 1998. Private premises; Internet and postal. Telephone first. *Shop at:* Badgers Wood, Fielden Rd., Crowborough, East Sussex TN6 1TP. Spec: Countries - Melanesia; Crime (True); Modern First Editions; Travel - General. PR: £2–20. CC: MC; V. Also, booksearch.

DITCHLING

Autobooks Ltd., 2 South Street, Ditchling, Near Brighton, BN6 8UQ.

EASTBOURNE

Camilla's Bookshop, ■ 57 Grove Road, Eastbourne, BN21 4TX. Prop: Camilla Francombe & Stuart Broad. Tel: (01323) 736001. E-mail: c@millasbooks.fsnet.co.uk. Est: 1976. Shop; open **M:** 10:00–17:30; **T:** 10:00–17:30; **W:** 10:00–17:30; **Th:** 10:00–17:30; **F:** 10:00–17:30; **S:** 10:00–17:30. Very large stock. Spec: Antiques; Art; Aviation; Children's - General; Military; Motoring; Natural History; Needlework; Occult. PR: £1–1,000. CC: JCB; MC; V. Also, booksearch. VAT No: GB 583 7350 18.

Roderick Dew, 10 Furness Road, Eastbourne, BN21 4EZ. Tel: (01323) 720239. Est: 1975. Private premises; appointment necessary. Small stock. Spec: Applied Art; Architecture; Bibliography; Fine Art. PR: £5–500. Cata: 4 – on art and bibliography. Corresp: French, German.

A. & T. Gibbard, ■ 30 South Street, Eastbourne, BN21 4XB. Alan & Maria Tania Gibbard. Tel: (01323) 734128. Fax: (01323) 734128. Est: 1909. Shop; open **M:** 09:30–17:30; **T:** 09:30–17:30; **W:** 09:30–17:30; **Th:** 09:30–17:30; **F:** 09:30–17:30; **S:** 09:30–17:30. Very large stock. Spec: Literature; Natural History; Railways; Topography - Local; Transport. PR: £1–1,000. CC: AE; MC; V. Corresp: Italian, Spanish. Mem: PBFA. VAT No: 621 5744 53.

Green Man Bookshop & Gallery, 24 South Street, Eastbourne, BN21 4XB.

Berry Harper, Books, 4 Friston Downs, Friston, Eastbourne, BN20 0ET. Prop: Mrs. B. Harper. Tel: (01323) 423335. E-mail: berry@pavilion.co.uk. Est: 1986. Private premises; Internet and postal. Telephone first. Very small stock. Spec: Publishers - General; Publishers - Ladybird Books. PR: £1–50. Corresp: French, German.

London & Sussex Antiquarian Book & Print Services, Southwood, 15 Dittons Road, Eastbourne, BN21 1DR.

R. & A. Books, 4 Milton Grange, 6 Arundel Road, Eastbourne, BN21 2EL. Prop: Robert Manning and Alan Millard. Tel: (01323) 647690. Website: www.robert.manning.btinternet.co.uk/index.html. E-mail: robert.manning@btinternet.com. Private premises; Internet and postal. Small stock. Spec: Animals and Birds; Art; Biography; Children's - General; History - General; Literature; Modern First Editions; Reference; Topography - General. PR: £1–250.

HASTINGS

Calendula Horticultural Books, 3 Amherst Garden, Hastings, TN34 1TU. Prop: Heiko Miles. Tel: (01424) 437591. Website: www.calendulabooks.com. E-mail: heiko@calendulabooks.com. Est: 1987. Private premises; postal business only. Spec: Flower Arranging; Gardening; Herbalism; Horticulture; Landscape; Ornithology; Plant Hunting. PR: £5–10,000.

Chthonios Books, 7 Tamarisk Steps, Off Rock-a-Nores Road,, Hastings, TN34 3DN. Prop: Stephen Ronan. Tel: (01424) 433302. Website: www.esotericism.co.uk/index.htm. E-mail: service@esotericism.co.uk. Est: 1985. Private premises; Internet and postal. Telephone first. Small stock. Spec: Alchemy; Classical Studies; Earth Mysteries; Egyptology; Hermeticism; Humanism; Literature in Translation; Occult; Paganism; Philosophy; Religion - Christian; Spiritualism; Witchcraft. PR: £3–300. CC: MC; V; SW. SO. Also, booksearch. Cata: 8 – E-mail catalogues of new stock. Corresp: French.

Hoovey's Books, P.O. Box 27, St. Leonards–on–Sea, Hastings, TN37 6TZ. (*). Tel: (01424) 753407. Fax: (01424) 753407. Website: www.hooveys.co.uk. E-mail: books@hooveys.com. Est: 1968. Office &/or bookroom; appointment necessary. Small general stock. Catalogue printing, cleaning materials, jacket coverings. Also, booksearch. VAT No: GB 397 8504 94.

Howes Bookshop, ■ Trinity Hall, Braybrooke Terrace, Hastings, TN34 1HQ. Prop: Miles Bartley. Tel: (01424) 423437. Fax: (01424) 460620. Website: www.howes.co.uk. E-mail: rarebooks@howes.co.uk. Est: 1921. Shop; open **M:** 09:30–17:00; **T:** 09:30–17:00; **W:** 09:30–17:00; **Th:** 09:29–17:00; **F:** 09:30–17:00. Closed for lunch: 13:00–14:00. Very large stock. Spec: Academic/Scholarly; Antiquarian; Arts, The; Bibliography; Classical Studies; History - General; Literature; Philosophy; Theology; Travel - General. PR: £10–5,000. CC: MC; V. Cata: 5 – speciailities. Mem: ABA; PBFA; ILAB. VAT No: 201 2142 45.

Robert Mucci, ■ 68 High Street, Old Town, Hastings, TN34 3EW. Prop: Robert M. Mucci. Tel: (01424) 445340. Est: 1989. Shop; open **M:** 11:00–18:00; **T:** 11:00–18:00; **W:** 11:00–18:00; **Th:** 11:00–18:00; **F:** 11:00–18:00; **S:** 11:00–18:00; **Su:** 11:00–18:00. Very small general stock. PR: £1–8.

Olio Books, 43 Robertson Street, Hastings, TN34 1HL. Prop: Philip & Denise Rees. Tel: (01424) 428987. Est: 1981. Spec: Antiques; Art; Art Reference; Author - General; Children's - General; Fiction - General; History - General; Military; Music - General; Topography - General; Travel - General. PR: £1–100.

The Paperback Reader, ■ 82 Queens Road, Hastings, TN34 1RL. Prop: Rog and Amanda Read. Tel: (01424) 446749. Est: 1972. Shop; open **M:** 09:00–17:00; **T:** 09:00–17:00. **Th:** 09:00–17:00; **F:** 09:00–17:00; **S:** 09:00–17:00. Large stock. Spec: Comics. PR: £1–4.

Anthony Sillem, 9 Tackleway, Old Town, Hastings, TN34 3DE. Prop: Anthony Sillem. Tel: (01424) 446602. Fax: (01424) 446602. Website: tackletext@btopenworld.com. E-mail: tackletext@btopenworld.com. Est: 1994. Private premises; appointment necessary. Small stock. Spec: First Editions; Illustrated; Literature; Literature in Translation; Memoirs; Modern First Editions. PR: £10–2,000. CC: MC; V. Cata: 3. Mem: PBFA.

Underwater Books, 104d High Street, Hastings, TN24 3ES.

HEATHFIELD

Apteryx, Moon Cottage, Ghyll Road, Heathfield, TN21 0XL.

Botting & Berry, ■ 31 High Street, Heathfield, TN21 8HU. Prop: John Botting and Dave Berry. Tel: (01435) 868555. Est: 2001. Shop; open **M:** 10:00–17:00; **T:** 10:00–17:00; **W:** 10:00–17:00; **Th:** 10:00–17:00; **F:** 10:00–17:00; **S:** 10:00–17:00. Small stock. PR: £1–500. Fairs: Royal National, Bloomsbury, London.

HOVE

Bennetts Books, 14 Brunswick Square, Hove, BN3 1EH. D. Bennett. Tel: . Est: 1970. Private premises; postal business only. Medium stock. Spec: Gambling; Private Press; Sport - Greyhound Racing; Sport - Horse Racing (all aspects). Cata: 4 – by subject.

J.F. Holleyman, 3 Portland Avenue, Hove, BN3 5NP. Tel: (01273) 410915. Private premises; appointment necessary. Small stock. Spec: Photography. Cata: 4.

Whitehall Books, 3 Leighton Road, Hove, BN3 7AD.

LEWES

Richard Beaton, 24 Highdown Road, Lewes, BN7 1QD. Prop: Dr. Richard Beaton. Tel: (01273) 474147. Fax: (01273) 474147. Website: www.btinternet.com/~beaton.books. E-mail: beaton.books@btinternet.com. Est: 1996. Private premises; Internet and postal. Appointment necessary. Open: **M:** 09:00–18:00; **T:** 09:00–18:00; **W:** 09:00–18:00; **Th:** 09:00–18:00; **F:** 09:00–18:00; **S:** 09:00–18:00. Small stock. Spec: Fiction - General; Literature - Victorian. PR: £5–500. CC: MC; V; SW. Cata: 5 – Every 2 - 3 months. Corresp: French. Mem: PBFA.

John Beck, 29 Mill Road, Lewes, BN7 2RU. Tel: (01273) 477555. Est: 1982. Office &/or bookroom; postal business only. Appointment necessary. *Shop at:* The Boxroom, Needlemakers, Lewes. Open 7 days. **M:** 10:00–16:00; **T:** 10:00–16:00; **W:** 10:00–16:00; **Th:** 10:00–16:00; **F:** 10:00–16:00; **S:** 10:00–16:00; **Su:** 10:00–16:00. Small stock. Spec: Children's - General; Comic Books & Annuals; Comics; Juvenile. PR: £1–1,000.

EAST SUSSEX

Bow Windows Book Shop, ■ 175 High Street, Lewes, BN7 1YE. Prop: Alan & Jennifer Shelley. Tel: (01273) 480780. Fax: (01273) 486686. Website: www.bowwindows.com. E-mail: rarebooks@bowwindows.com. Est: 1964. Shop; open **M:** 09:30–17:00; **T:** 09:30–17:00; **W:** 09:30–17:00; **Th:** 09:30–17:00; **F:** 09:30–17:00; **S:** 09:30–17:00. Medium stock. Spec: Antiquarian; Author - Sackville-West, Vita; Countries - Japan; Geology; Literature; Natural History; Travel - Africa; Travel - Asia. PR: £1–5,000. CC: AE; MC; V. Cata: 4. Corresp: German. Mem: ABA; PBFA; ILAB. VAT No: GB 370 1163 88.

Brimstones, Unit 6, Sewells Farm, Birdhole Lane, Barcombe, Lewes, BN8 5TJ.

Caburn Books, 49 High Street, Lewes, BN7 2DD.

A. & Y. Cumming Limited, ■ 84 High Street, Lewes, BN7 1XN. Prop: A.J. Cumming. Tel: (01273) 472319. Fax: (01273) 486364. E-mail: a.y.cumming@ukgateway.net. Est: 1976. Shop; open **M:** 10:00–17:00; **T:** 10:00–17:00; **W:** 10:00–17:00; **Th:** 10:00–17:00; **F:** 10:00–17:00; **S:** 10:00–17:30. Very large stock. Spec: Art; Bindings; Illustrated; Literature; Natural History; Topography - General; Travel - General. Mem: ABA. VAT No: GB 412 4098 80.

The Fifteenth Century Bookshop, 99/100 High Street, Lewes, BN7 1XH.

Ruth Kidson, ■ 31 Western Road, Lewes, BN7 1RL. Prop: Mrs. G.R. Kidson. Tel: (01273) 487087. Fax: (01273) 487087. Website: www.ruth.kidson@virgin.net. E-mail: ruth.kidson@virgin.net. Est: 1992. Shop; Internet and postal. *Shop at:* open **T:** 11:00–16:00; **W:** 11:00–16:00; **Th:** 11:00–16:00; **F:** 11:00–16:30; **S:** 11:00–16:30. Small general stock. Spec: Medicine. PR: £2–1,000. CC: MC; V; Da. Opening times may vary, please phone ahead if coming any distance. Cata: 1. Mem: ABA; PBFA; ILAB. VAT No: GB 777 7852 58.

T.F. S. Scott, 37 St. Anne's Crescent, Lewes, BN7 1SB. Tel: (01273) 473619. Est: 1979. Private premises; appointment necessary. Small general stock. Spec: Fiction - General; First Editions; Literature; Memoirs; Topography - General; Topography - Local; Travel - Africa; Travel - Asia; Travel - Europe; Travel - Middle East. PR: £2–700. Mem: PBFA.

Derek Wise, Berewood House, Barcombe, Lewes, BN8 5TW. Tel: (01273) 400559. Fax: (01273) 400559. E-mail: derekwise@pavilion.co.uk. Est: 1986. Private premises; appointment necessary. Small stock. Spec: Author - Byron, Lord; Education & School; Literature; Maritime/Nautical; Military; Military History; Natural History; Naval; Public Schools; School Registers/Rolls of Honour. PR: £1–1,500. Cata: 1 – occasionally. Corresp: French. Mem: PBFA.

ROBERTSBRIDGE

Spearman Books, ■ The Old Saddlery Bookshop, 56 High Street, Robertsbridge, TN32 5AP. John & Janet Brooman. Tel: (01580) 880631. Fax: (01580) 880631. E-mail: saddlerybooks@aol.com. Est: 1970. Shop; open **M:** 10:00–17:00; **T:** 10:00–17:00; **W:** 10:00–17:00; **Th:** 10:00–17:00; **F:** 10:00–17:00; **S:** 09:00–17:00. Closed for lunch: 13:00–14:00. Medium general stock. Spec: Travel - General. PR: £1–500.

RYE

Chapter and Verse Booksellers, ■ 105 High Street, Rye, TN31 7JE. Prop: Spencer James Rogers. Tel: (01797) 222692. E-mail: chapterandverse@btconnect.com. Est: 1993. Shop; open **M:** 10:00–17:00; **T:** 10:00–17:00; **W:** 10:00–17:00. **F:** 10:00–17:00; **S:** 10:00–17:00. Medium stock. Spec: Antiquarian; Art; Art History; Art Reference; Author - Woolf, Virginia; Autobiography; Bindings; Biography; Colour-Plate; Topography - General; Topography - Local; Travel - General; War - General. PR: £10–27,500. CC: MC; V; SW. Also, a booksearch service.

The Meads Book Service, ■ 4 & 5 Lion Street, Rye, TN31 7LB.

The Book Jungle, ■ 24 North Street, St. Leonard's–on–Sea, TN38 0EX. Prop: Michael Gowen. Tel: (01424) 421187. E-mail: mrgowen@lineone.net. Est: 1990. Shop; open **T:** 10:00–16:00; **Th:** 10:00–16:00; **F:** 10:00–16:00; **S:** 10:00–16:00. Medium general stock. PR: £1–100.

Searching for a title - and cannot find it on any Internet database?

Then try **Sheppard's Booksearch**

By selecting the subject classification – the request goes to all dealers who major in that subject.

John Gorton Booksearch, 22 Charles Road, St. Leonard's-on-Sea, TN38 0QH. Est: 1981. Private premises; appointment necessary. Very small stock. Spec: Chess; History - General; Literature; Mathematics; Philosophy; Psychoanalysis. PR: £10–150. Also, booksearch.

Gerald Lee, Maritime Books, P.O. Box 7, St. Leonard's-on-Sea, TN38 8WX.

Patrick Vickers, 67a Church Road, St. Leonard's-on-Sea, TN37 6EE.

Raymond Kilgarriff, 15 Maze Hill, St. Leonards-on-Sea, TN38 0HN.

SEAFORD

Barn Collectors Market & Studi, Church Lane, Seaford, BN25 1HL.

TICEHURST

Piccadilly Rare Books, ■ Church Street, Ticehurst, TN5 7AA. Prop: Paul P.B. Minet. Tel: (01580) 201221. Fax: (01580) 200957. Website: www.picrare.com. E-mail: Picrare@btinternet.com. Est: 1972. Shop; open **M:** 10:00–17:00; **T:** 10:00–17:00; **W:** 10:00–17:00; **Th:** 10:00–17:00; **F:** 10:00–17:00; **S:** 10:00–18:00. Large general stock. Spec: Diaries; Royalty - General; Royalty - European. PR: £5–1,000. CC: AE; MC; V. Also, publishers of 'Royalty Digest' (monthly); 'British Diarist' (quarterly). Rates on request. Reprinters. Mem: PBFA; AVBA. VAT No: GB 583 9618 89.

EAST YORKSHIRE

ALLERTHORPE

K. Books, Waplington Hall, Allerthorpe, York, YO42 4RS. Prop: B.J. & S.M. Kaye, M.J. Rose. Tel: (01759) 302142. Fax: (01759) 305891. Website: www.kbooks.uk.com. E-mail: kaye@kbooks.uk.com. Est: 1966. Private premises; Internet and postal.Very large stock. Spec: Antiquarian; History - General; Literature; Natural History; Printing; Topography - General. PR: £10–2,000. CC: V. Also, a booksearch service. Corresp: French. Mem: ABA.

BEVERLEY

Beverley Old Bookshop, ■ 2 Dyer Lane, Beverley, HU17 8AE. Prop: Colin Tatman. Tel: (01482) 880611. Website: www.eastridingbooksandmusic.co.uk. E-mail: info@eastridingbooksandmusic.co.uk. Est: 1993. Shop; open **M:** 10:00–17:00; **T:** 10:00–17:00; **W:** 10:00–17:00; **Th:** 10:00–17:00; **F:** 10:00–17:00; **S:** 10:00–17:00. Medium general stock. Spec: Bookbinding; Children's - General; History - Local; Illustrated; Music - General; Theology. PR: £1–200. Also, book restoration.

Minster Garage Bookshop, 44 Eastgate, Beverley, HU17 0DT.

Peter Riddell, Hall Cottage, Main St., Cherry Burton, Beverley, HU17 7RF. Tel: (01964) 551453. E-mail: bkscherryb@aol.com. Est: 1989. Private premises; appointment necessary. Very small general stock. Spec: Alpinism/Mountaineering; Countries - Central Asia; Countries - Polar. PR: £1–250.

BRIDLINGTON

J.L. Book Exchange, ■ 72 Hilderthorpe Road, Bridlington, East Riding, YO15 3BQ. Prop: John Ledraw. Tel: (01262) 601285. Est: 1971. Shop; Open in summer. **M:** 08:30–18:00; **T:** 08:30–18:00; **W:** 08:30–18:00; **Th:** 08:30–18:00; **F:** 08:30–18:00; **S:** 08:30–18:00; **Su:** 08:30–18:00. Medium general stock. PR: £1–80. Winter opening: Mon-Sat 09.30–17.30. Mem: PBFA.

Family Favourites (Books), 51 First Avenue, Bridlington, YO15 2JR. Prop: Shirley Jackson. Tel: (01262) 606061. E-mail: shirleyjackson@telco4u.net. Est: 1989. Private premises; postal business only. Medium stock. Spec: Annuals; Autobiography; Biography; Drawing; Fiction - General; Modern First Editions; Ornithology; Topography - General. PR: £3–500. Also, booksearch.

Kilburn Books, 25 Trinity Road, Bridlington, YO15 2EZ.

DRIFFIELD

Solaris Books, Flat 4, 13 Lockwood St., Driffield, YO25 6RU.

FLAMBOROUGH

Resurgam Books, ■ The Manor House, Flamborough, Bridlington, York, YO15 1PD. Prop: Geoffrey Miller. Tel: (01262) 850943. Fax: (01262) 850943. Website: www.resurgambooks.co.uk. E-mail: gm@resurgambooks.co.uk. Est: 1998. Shop; Internet and postal. Open: **M:** 09:00–17:00; **T:** 09:00–17:00; **W:** 09:00–17:00; **Th:** 09:00–17:00; **F:** 09:00–17:00; **S:** 09:00–17:00; **Su:** 10:00–16:00. Very small stock. PR: £1–400. CC: E; JCB; MC; V.

GREAT DRIFFIELD

The Driffield Bookshop, ■ 21 Middle Street North, Great Driffield, YO25 6SW. Prop: G.R. Stevens. Tel: (01377) 254210. Est: 1981. Shop; open **M:** 10:00–17:30; **T:** 10:00–17:30; **W:** 10:00–17:30; **Th:** 10:00–17:30; **F:** 10:00–17:30; **S:** 10:00–17:30. Medium stock. Spec: Fiction - Science Fiction; History - General; Literature; Military History; Modern First Editions; Travel - General. PR: £1–150. Cata: 3.

Dealers who need to update their entry
should visit their page on
www.sheppardsdirectories.com

HULL

Cygnet Books, ■ 16 West End, Swanland, Hull, HU14 3PE. (*) Prop: Mrs. Jackie Kitchen. Tel: (01482) 634288. Website: www.abebooks.com. E-mail: jackie@cygnetbooks.com. Est: 1995. Shop and postal business. Please call before travelling any distance. Sometimes closed on a Wed. Open: **M:** 10:00–17:00; **T:** 10:00–17:00; **W:** 10:00–17:00; **Th:** 10:00–17:00; **F:** 10:00–17:00; **S:** 10:00–14:00. Small stock. Spec: Children's - General; Fine & Rare; Juvenile. PR: £2–80. Shop is 400 years old with original historic features. Also, booksearch.

Harry Holmes Books, 85 Park Avenue, Hull, HU5 3EP. Prop: H.H. & P.A. Purkis. Tel: (01482) 443220. Est: 1989. Private premises; appointment necessary. Small stock. Spec: Alpinism/Mountaineering; Biography; Countries - Scotland; Literature; Religion - Christian; Spiritualism; Topography - Local; Travel - Polar; Voyages & Discovery. PR: £1–100. Also, booksearch. Books on literary biography are also stocked. Cata: 5 – on Polar exploration and mountaineering. Corresp: French and German. Mem: PBFA.

Colin Martin - Bookseller, ■ 3 Village Road, Garden Village, Hull, HU8 8QP. Prop: Colin and Jane Martin, L.L.B., B.A. Tel: (01482) 585836. Website: www.colinmartinbooks.com. E-mail: enquiries@colinmartinbooks.com. Est: 1991. *Shop at:* 380 Holderness Road, Hull. Open: **M:** 10:00–16:00; **T:** 10:00–16:00; **W:** 10:00–16:00; **Th:** 10:00–16:00; **F:** 10:00–16:00. Very large stock. Spec: Applied Art; Archaeology; Architecture; Art; Art History; Art Reference; Artists; Arts, The; Ceramics; Design; Fashion & Costume; Glass; Interior Design; Publishers - Thames & Hudson; Sculpture. PR: £3–600. CC: AE; D; JCB; MC; V; SW, SO. Also, booksearch. Cata: 1 – occasionally. Corresp: French, German, Italian. VAT No: GB 780 4607 24.

Keith Stephenson, 50 Queen's Drive, Cottingham, Hull, HU16 4EL.

KIRKELLA

East Riding Books & Music, 13 Westland Road, Kirkella, HU10 7PH. Prop: Gill Carlile. Tel: (01482) 650674. Website: www.eastridingbooksandmusic.co.uk. E-mail: er.books@virgin.net. Private premises; Internet and postal. Small stock. Spec: Music - General; Music - Classical; Music - Composers; Music - Jazz; Music - Musicians; Music - Opera; Musical Instruments. PR: £1–200.

MILLINGTON

Quest Books, Harmer Hill, Millington, York, YO42 1TX. Prop: Dr. Peter Burridge. Tel: (01759) 304735. Fax: (01759) 306820. E-mail: questbyz@aol.com. Est: 1984. Private premises; postal business only. Appointment necessary. Very small stock. Spec: Academic/Scholarly; Archaeology; Architecture; Classical Studies; Countries - Arabia; Countries - Asia Minor; Countries - Balkans, The; Countries - Cyprus; Countries - Egypt; Countries - Greece; Countries - Iran; Countries - Turkey; Travel - General; Travel - Middle East. PR: £5–1,000. CC: JCB; MC; V. Cata: 2. Mem: PBFA.

WILLERBY

Countryman Books, 'Southrise', Great Gutter Lane West, Willerby, HU10 6DP.

ESSEX

BILLERICAY

Engaging Gear Ltd., Lark Rise, 14 Linkdale, Billericay, CM12 9QW. Prop: D.E. Twitchett. Tel: (01277) 624913. Est: 1965. Private premises; postal business only. Very small stock. Spec: Author - Moore, John; Horology; Sport - Cycling; Travel - General. PR: £5–500.

BIRCH

John Cowley, Auto–in–Print, Mill Lodge, Mill Lane, Birch, Colchester, CO2 0NG. Tel: (01206) 331052. Fax: (01206) 330438. Website: www.autoinprint.freeserve.co.uk. E-mail: cowley@autoinprint.freeserve.co.uk. Est: 1975. Private premises; Internet and postal. Appointment necessary. Very large stock. Spec: Motoring. Also, booksearch.

BRAINTREE

Lawful Occasions, 68 High Garrett, Braintree, CM7 5NT. Prop: M.R. Stallion. Tel: (01376) 551819. Fax: (01376) 326073. Website: www.lawfuloccasions.co.uk. E-mail: stallion@supanet.com. Est: 1997. Private premises; Internet and postal. Appointment necessary. Very small stock. Spec: Crime (True); Criminology; Police Force Histories. PR: £2–100. Credit/debit card payments via Paypal only. Publisher of bibliographies etc on police history. Cata: 4 – Quarterly. Corresp: French.

BRENTWOOD

Book End, ■ 36–38 Kings Road, Brentwood, CM14 4DW. Prop: G.E. & M.K. Smith. Est: 1980. Shop; open **M:** 10:00–17:30; **T:** 10:00–17:30; **W:** 10:00–17:30; **Th:** 10:00–13:00; **F:** 10:00–17:30. Medium general stock. PR: £1–100.

Fortune Books, 94 Shenfield Road, Brentwood, CM15 8ET. Prop: J.H. Jeffries. Est: 1980. Private premises; appointment necessary. Very small stock. Spec: Countries - Melanesia. PR: £1–150. Cata: 2.

CHELMSFORD

Christopher Heppa, 48 Pentland Avenue, Chelmsford, CM1 4AZ. Tel: (01245) 267679. E-mail: christopher@heppa4288.fsnet.co.uk. Est: 1982. Private premises; postal business only. Medium stock. Spec: Author - Bates, H.E.; Author - Buchan, John; Author - Wodehouse, P.G.; Children's - General; Fiction - Crime, Detective, Spy, Thrillers; Fiction - Historical; First Editions; Illustrated; Literature; Military History; Modern First Editions; Signed Editions; War - World War I. PR: £1–5,000. Cata: 4 – intermittently. Corresp: Spanish. Mem: PBFA.

CLACTON–ON–SEA

Bookworm, ■ 100 Kings Ave., Holland–on–Sea, Clacton-on-Sea, CO15 5EP. Prop: Mr Andrew M. M'Garry-Durrant. Tel: (01255) 815984. Fax: (01255) 815984. Website: www.bookwormshop.com. E-mail: question@bookwormshop.com. Est: 1994. Shop; open **M:** 09:00–17:00; **T:** 09:00–17:00; **W:** 09:00–17:00; **Th:** 09:00–17:00; **F:** 09:00–17:00; **S:** 09:00–17:00. Medium stock. Spec: Cinema/Film; Military; Modern First Editions; Sport - Motor Racing. PR: £5–15 CC: AE; JCB; MC; V.

COGGESHALL

Jeremy Dore, 18 Hitcham Road, Coggeshall, CO6 1QS.

Dealers who need to update their entry should visit their page on
www.sheppardsdirectories.com

John Lewis, 35 Stoneham Street, Coggeshall, CO6 1UH. Tel: (01376) 561518. Website: www.abebooks.com. E-mail: LewisLynet@aol.com. Est: 1985. Private premises; appointment necessary. Very small stock. Spec: Maritime/Nautical; Travel - General; Travel - Africa; Travel - Americas; Travel - Asia; Travel - Australasia/Australia; Travel - Europe; Travel - Middle East; Travel - Polar; Voyages & Discovery. PR: £25–2,000. CC: MC; V. Also, booksearch. Cata: – specialities. Corresp: French. Mem: PBFA.

COLCHESTER

Book–Worm International, 5 Pointwell Lane, Coggeshall Hamlet, Colchester, SS11 7PP. Prop: Donna Collins. Tel: (07754) 583759. Website: www.abebooks.com/home/donnasbookworm. E-mail: donna@bookworm.fsnet.co.uk. Est: 1999. Private premises; Internet and postal. Appointment necessary. Medium stock. Spec: Children's - General; Cookery/Gastronomy; Countries - Mexico; Crime (True); History - General; Humour; Literature; Modern First Editions; Poetry; Royalty - General. PR: £1–200. CC: E; MC; V; SW. Cata: – on request.

Castle Bookshop, ■ 40 Osborne St., Colchester, CO2 7DB. Prop: J.R. Green. Tel: (01206) 577520. Est: 1947. Shop; open **M:** 09:00–17:00; **T:** 09:00–17:00; **W:** 09:00–17:00; **Th:** 09:00–17:00; **F:** 09:00–17:00; **S:** 09:00–17:00. Very large stock. Spec: Archaeology; Aviation; First Editions; History - Local; Military; Modern First Editions; Topography - General; Topography - Local; Transport. PR: £1–1,000. CC: MC; V. Also, booksearch. Mem: PBFA. VAT No: GB 360 3502 89.

Farringdon Books, Shrubland House, 43 Mile End Road, Colchester, CO4 5BU. Prop: Alan Austin. Tel: (01206) 844218. E-mail: alan@farringdon-books.demon.co.uk. Est: 1984. Private premises. Small stock. Spec: Fiction - Crime, Detective, Spy, Thrillers; Fiction - Fantasy, Horror; Fiction - Science Fiction. PR: £1–200.

Greyfriars Books: the Colchester, ■ 92 East Hill, Colchester, CO1 2QN. Prop: Pauline & Simon Taylor. Tel: (01206) 563138. Website: www.greyfriarsbooks.co.uk. E-mail: simon@greyfriarsbooks.co.uk. Est: 1983. Shop; open **M:** 10:00–17:30; **T:** 10:00–17:30; **W:** 10:00–17:30; **Th:** 10:00–17:30; **F:** 10:00–17:30; **S:** 10:00–17:30. Large general stock. Spec: Academic/Scholarly; Archaeology; Architecture; Art; Art Reference; Gardening; History - Ancient; History - British; Literary Criticism; Literature; Mathematics; Natural History; Philosophy; Poetry; Psychology/Psychiatry; Science - General; Topography. PR: £2–200. Cata: – occasionally. Corresp: French. VAT No: GB 759 8699 37.

Keble Books, 1 Keble Close, Oxford Road, Colchester, CO3 3HL.

Quentin Books Ltd., 10 Brook Street, Wivenhoe, Colchester, CO7 9DS.

DAGENHAM

John Thorne, 19 Downing Road, Dagenham, RM9 6NR. Tel: (020) 8592-0259. Fax: (020) 8220-0082. E-mail: liquidliterature@aol.com. Est: 1985. Private premises; postal business only.Very small stock. Spec: Brewing; Public Houses; Viticulture; Whisky; Wine. PR: £1–300. CC: PayPal. Cata: 3.

EPPING

Browsers Bookshop, ■ 9 Station Road, Epping, CM16 4HA. Prop: Brian & Moira Carter. Tel: (01992) 572260. Est: 1990. Shop; open **M:** 10:00–17:00. **Th:** 10:00–17:00; **F:** 10:00–17:00; **S:** 10:00–17:00. Medium general stock. PR: £1–800.

GREAT BARDFIELD

Ken & Jenny Jacobson, 'Southcotts', Petches Bridge, Great Bardfield, CM7 4QN. Prop: Ken Jacobson. Tel: (01371) 810566. Fax: (01371) 810845. Website: www. jacobsonphoto.com. E-mail: ken@jacobsonphoto.com. Est: 1970. Private premises; Internet and postal. Appointment necessary. Very small stock. Spec: Photography. PR: £100–3,000. 19th century photographs. Corresp: French. Mem: AIPAD.

GREAT DUNMOW

Green Street Books (Mail Order), Yardley's, 12 Newbiggen Street, Thaxted, Great Dunmow, CM6 2QR.

ESSEX

Clive Smith, Brick House, North Street, Great Dunmow, CM6 1BA. Tel: (01371) 873171. Fax: (01371) 873171. E-mail: clivesmith@route56.co.uk. Est: 1975. Private premises; appointment necessary. Small stock. Spec: Antiquarian; Cookery/Gastronomy; Medicine; Military; Natural History; Topography - General; Topography - Local; Travel - General; Travel - Asia; Voyages & Discovery. PR: £10–500 Corresp: French, Indonesian. VAT No: GB 571 6001 67.

GREAT LEIGHS

Missing Books, 'Coppers', Main Road, Great Leighs, CM3 1NR. Prop: Chris Missing. Tel: (01245) 361609. E-mail: missingbooks@madasafish.com. Est: 1994. Private premises; Internet and postal. Small stock. Spec: Architecture; Biography; City of London; Countries - England; History - Local; Publishers - Black, A. & C.; Rural Life; Topography - General; Topography - Local. PR: £2–500. CC: MC; V. Mem: ABA.

HALSTEAD

Alhambra Books, Three Oaks, Toldish Hall Road, Gt. Maplestead, Halstead, CO9 2QZ.

Brad Books, 1st Floor, Townsford Mill Antique Centre, Halstead, CO9 1ET.

HARWICH

Harwich Old books, ■ 21, Market Street, Harwich, CO12 3DX. Prop: Peter J. Hadley. Tel: (01255) 551667. Fax: (01255) 554539. Website: books@hadley.co.uk. E-mail: books@hadley.co.uk. Est: 1982. Shop; open **F:** 10:00–17:00; **S:** 10:00–17:00; **Su:** 13:00–17:00. Medium stock. Spec: Academic/Scholarly; Architecture; Art Reference; Artists; Arts, The; Illustrated; Limited Editions; Literature. CC: MC; V; SW. Cata: 6 – Architecture / Literature. Corresp: French, Italian. Mem: ABA; PBFA; ILAB. VAT No: GB 489 0588 89.

HORNCHURCH

Talatin Books, 21 Parkstone Avenue, Emerson Park, Hornchurch, RM11 3LX.

ILFORD

June Rhoda, 43 Redbridge Lane East, Ilford, IG4 5EU. Prop: J.R. Arnold. Tel: (020) 8550-5256. Fax: (020) 8550-5256. Est: 1983. Private premises; postal business only. Very small stock. Spec: Alpinism/Mountaineering; History - Local. PR: £1–100.

LEIGH–ON–SEA

Eden's Books, 4 Rectory Grove, Leigh–on–Sea, SS9 2HE.

Leigh Gallery Books, ■ 135-137 Leigh Road, Leigh–on–Sea, SS9 1JQ. Prop: Barrie Gretton. Tel: (01702) 715477. Fax: (01702) 715477. Website: www.abebooks.com/home/BOO/. E-mail: leighgallerybooks@bigfoot.com. Est: 1983. Shop; open **T:** 10:00–17:00; **Th:** 10:00–17:00; **F:** 10:00–17:00; **S:** 10:00–17:00. Large general stock. Spec: Art; Illustrated; Literature; Topography - Local. PR: £1–200. CC: MC; V.

Othello's Bookshop, 1376 London Road, Leigh–On–Sea, SS9 2UH. Prop: F.G. Bush & M.A. Layzell. Tel: (01702) 473334. E-mail: othellos@hotmail.com. Est: 1999. PR: £6–100.

MALDON

All Books, ■ 2 Mill Road, Maldon, CM9 5HZ. Prop: Mr. Kevin Peggs. Tel: (01621) 856214. Website: www.allbooks.demon.co.uk. E-mail: kevin@allbooks.demon.co.uk. Est: 1970. Shop; Internet and postal. Open: **M:** 10:00–17:00; **T:** 10:00–17:00; **W:** 10:00–16:00; **Th:** 10:00–17:00; **F:** 10:00–16:00; **S:** 10:00–17:30; **Su:** 13:30–17:00. Very large stock. Spec: Arts, The; Aviation; History - General; Maritime/Nautical; Steam Engines. PR: £1–500. CC: MC; V.

Searching for a title - and cannot find it on any Internet database?
Then try **Sheppard's Booksearch**

By selecting the subject classification – the request goes to all dealers who major in that subject.

MANNINGTREE

John Drury Rare Books, Strandlands, Wrabness, Manningtree, CO11 2TX. Prop: David Edmunds. Tel: (01255) 886260. Fax: (01255) 880303. Website: www.johndrury.co.uk. E-mail: mail@ johndrury.co.uk. Est: 1971. Private premises; appointment necessary. Small stock. Spec: Antiquarian; Economics; Education & School; History of Ideas; Law; Manuscripts; Philosophy; Politics; Social History. PR: £30–3,000. CC: MC; V. Cata: – irregularly. Corresp: French. Mem: ABA. VAT No: GB 325 6594 41.

RAYLEIGH

Fantastic Literature, 35 The Ramparts, Rayleigh, SS6 8PY. Prop: Simon G. Gosden. Tel: (01268) 747564. Fax: (01268) 747564. Website: www.fantasticliterature.com. E-mail: sgosden@ netcomuk.co.uk. Est: 1984. Private premises; postal business only. Large stock. Spec: Author - Blackwood, A.; Author - King, Stephen; Author - Pratchett, Terry; Author - Wells, H.G.; Fiction - Crime, Detective, Spy, Thrillers; Fiction - Fantasy, Horror; Fiction - Historical; Fiction - Science Fiction; Publishers - Ghost Story Press; Unexplained, The. PR: £1–250. CC: E; MC; V; SW. Also, booksearch and scans available of any title. Cata: 6 – specialities. Corresp: French. Mem: IBN.

ROMFORD

J.V.A. Jones, 68 Sedgefield Crescent, Romford, RM3 9RS. Prop: John V.A. & Trudi Jones. Tel: (01708) 340864. E-mail: jvajones@aol.com. Est: 1994. Private premises; postal business only. Medium stock. Spec: Children's - General; Entertainment - General; Fiction - General. PR: £1–20.

Ken Whitfield, 5 Eugene Close, Romford, RM2 6DJ. Tel: (01708) 474763. E-mail: kenkwhitfield@ aol.com. Est: 1984. Private premises; Internet and postal. Contactable. Small stock. Spec: Art; Biography; Entertainment - General; Fiction - General; History - General; Military; Sport - Football (Soccer); Topography - General; Transport; Travel - General. PR: £2–80. Cata: 3.

SAFRON WALDEN

Lankester Antiques and Books, ■ The Old Sun Inn, Church Street and Market Hill, Saffron Walden, CB10 1HQ. Prop: Paul Lankester. Tel: (01799) 522685. Est: 1964. Shop; open **M:** 09:30–17:30; **T:** 09:30–17:30; **W:** 09:30–17:30; **Th:** 09:30–17:30; **F:** 09:30–17:30. Very large general stock. PR: £1–50.

SHENFIELD

Booknotes, 6 York Road, Shenfield, CM15 8JT.

SOUTHEND–ON–SEA

Tony Peterson, 11 Westbury Road, Southend–on–Sea, SS2 4DW. Prop: Tony Peterson. Tel: (01702) 462757. Website: www.chessbooks.co.uk. E-mail: tony@chessbooks.co.uk. Est: 1993. Private premises; Internet and postal. Appointment necessary. Very small stock. Spec: Chess. PR: £4–200. Cata: 4.

Gage Postal Books, P.O. Box 105, Westcliff–on–Sea, Southend-on-Sea, SS0 8EQ. (*) Prop: Simon A. Routh. Tel: (01702) 715133. Fax: (01702) 715133. Website: www.gagebooks.com. E-mail: gagebooks@clara.net. Est: 1971. Storeroom; Internet and postal. Appointment necessary. Very large stock. Spec: Ecclesiastical History & Architecture; Religion - General; Theology. PR: £3–1,000. CC: MC; V. Cata: 12. Corresp: German. Mem: PBFA.

STANFORD–LE–HOPE

Atticus Books, ■ 54 Bramleys, Stanford–Le–Hope, SS17 8AG. Prop: Robert Drake. Tel: Shop (01375) 371200. Est: 1981. *Shop at:* 8 London Road, Grays, Essex RM17 5XY. Open: **Th:** 09:00–16:00; **F:** 09:00–16:00; **S:** 09:00–16:00. Medium stock. Spec: Antiquarian; Arms & Armour; Aviation; Bindings; Dogs; Fiction - General; Firearms/Guns; History - Local; Maritime/Nautical; Military; Occult; Private Press; Spiritualism; Sport - Field Sports; Topography - Local. PR: £1–400. Also, booksearch.

STANSTEAD

Paul Embleton, 12 Greenfields, Stansted, CM24 8AH. Tel: (01279) 812627. Fax: (01279) 817576. Website: www.abebooks.com/home/embleton. E-mail: 106461.2742@compuserve.com. Est: 1994. Private premises; appointment necessary between Monday to Friday. Small stock. Spec: Illustrated. PR: £3–500. Also, a booksearch service. Cata: – List available.

THORPE BAY

Martin Garwood, 37 Willingale Way, Thorpe Bay, SS1 3SN.

TILLINGHAM
Youngs Antiquarian Books, Casey Lane, Tillingham, CM0 7ST.

WALTON–ON–THE–NAZE
Crispin's Day, Antiquarian and, 35, Woodside, Walton-on-the-Naze, CO14 8NP. Prop: Ian Capper. Tel: (01255) 679600. Est: 1990. Private premises; postal business only. Appointment necessary. Medium stock. Spec: Academic/Scholarly; Antiquarian; Arms & Armour; Fine & Rare; History - National; Military; Military History; War - General; War - American Civil War; War - Boer, The; War - English Civil Wars; War - World War I; War - World War II. PR: £10–100,000. Also, booksearch. Cata: 2 – a year.

WESTCLIFF–ON–SEA
Clifton Books, 34 Hamlet Court Road, Westcliff–on–Sea, SS0 7LX. Prop: John R. Hodgkins. Tel: (01702) 331004. Fax: (01702) 346304. Website: www.cliftonbooks.co.uk. E-mail: jhodgk9942@aol.com. Est: 1970. Private premises; Internet and postal. Appointment necessary. Large stock. Spec: Academic/Scholarly; Agriculture; Economics; History - British; Social History; Trade Unions; Transport. CC: AE; D; E; JCB; MC; V. Cata: 12 – one a month. Mem: PBFA.
Barrie E. Ellen, The Bookshop, ■ 262 London Road, Westcliff–on–Sea, SS0 7GJ. Tel: (01702) 338763. Website: www.abebooks.com/home/barrieellen. E-mail: barrie_ellen@hotmail.com. Est: 1976. Shop; Internet and postal. Open: **M:** 10:00–17:00; **T:** 10:00–17:00; **Th:** 10:00–17:00; **F:** 10:00–17:00; **S:** 10:00–17:00. Large stock. Spec: Chess; Games. PR: £1–400. CC: AE; E; JCB; MC; V; SW.
Marjon Books, 16 Mannering Gardens, Westcliff–on–Sea, SS0 0BQ. Prop: R.J. Cooper. Tel: (01702) 347119. Est: 1975. Private premises; appointment necessary. Very small stock. Spec: Countries - Melanesia; First Editions. PR: £2–120. Cata: 2 – on detective fiction.

WICKFORD
Mr. H. Macfarlane, 40 Chaucer Walk, Wickford, SS12 9DZ.

WITHAM
Baldwin's Scientific Books, 18, School Road, Wickham Bishops, Witham, CM8 3NU.
Phoenix Fine Books, Hatchcroft House, White Notley, Witham, CM8 1RG. Prop: Diane Barber. Tel: (01376) 326283. Est: 1972. Postal business only. Spec: Artists; Guide Books; Literature. PR: £5–500.
N.B. Williamson, 72 Constance Close, Witham, CM8 1XY.

WOODFORD GREEN
Handsworth Books, 8 Warners Close, Woodford Green, IG8 0TF. Prop: Stephen Glover. Tel: (07976) 329042. Fax: (0870) 0520258. Website: www.handsworthbooks.co.uk. E-mail: steve@handsworthbooks.demon.co.uk. Est: 1987. Postal business only. Medium general stock. Spec: Academic/Scholarly; Applied Art; Company History; Fine Art; History - General; Literary Criticism; Military History; Music - General; Philosophy; Religion - General; Topography - General; War - General. PR: £2–650. CC: AE; E; JCB; MC. Mem: PBFA.
Salway Books, 47 Forest Approach, Woodford Green, IG8 9BP.

GLOUCESTERSHIRE

ALMONDSBURY

Michael Garbett Antiquarian Books, 1 Over Court Mews, Over Lane, Almondsbury, BS32 4DG. Prop: Michael & Jeanne Garbett. Tel: (01454) 617376. Fax: (01454) 617376. Website: www.michaelgarbett. theanswer.co.uk. E-mail: migarb@overcourtmews.freeserve.co.uk. Est: 1965. Private premises; appointment necessary. Small stock. Spec: Bindings; Miniature Books. Cata: 1 – on miniature. Mem: ABA; PBFA. VAT No: GB 358 1080 58.

BADMINTON

Highfield Books Ltd., The Malt House, Park Street, Hawkesbury Upton, Badminton, GL9 1BA.

Mrs. P.A. Sheppard, 2 Rose Cottage, Hawkesbury Upton, Badminton, GL9 1AU. Tel: (01454) 238686. Website: http://ukbookworld.com/cgi-bin/search.pl?s_i_DLR_I. E-mail: annesbookroom@aol.com. Est: 1998. Private premises; Internet and postal. Appointment necessary. Small general stock. PR: £1–350. CC: PayPal.

BERKELEY

Volumes of Motoring, Hertsgrove, Wanswell, Berkeley, GL13 9RR. Prop: Terry Wills. Tel: (01453) 811819. Fax: (01453) 811819. E-mail: twills@breathemail.net. Est: 1979. Private premises; Internet and postal. Open: **M:** 08:00–22:00; **T:** 08:00–22:00; **W:** 08:00–22:00; **Th:** 08:00–22:00; **F:** 08:00–22:00; **S:** 08:00–21:00; **Su:** 09:00–22:00. Spec: Motoring; Sport - Motor Racing. PR: £2–60. CC: MC; V. Wide range of motoring remainders available to the trade.

CHELTENHAM

Abbey Antiquarian Books, Abbey Old House, Cowl Lane, Winchcombe, Cheltenham, GL54 5RA.

Anchor House Bookshop, 88 North Street, Winchcombe, Cheltenham, GL54 5PS.

R. Andrews, The Barn, Brockhampton, Cheltenham, GL54 5XL. Tel: (01242) 820904. Est: 1977. Private premises; appointment necessary. Medium stock. Spec: Crime (True); Fiction - Crime, Detective, Spy, Thrillers. Cata: – occasionally.

David Bannister, 26 Kings Road, Cheltenham, GL52 6BG. Tel: (01242) 514287. Fax: (01242) 513890. Website: www.antiquemaps.co.uk. E-mail: db@antiquemaps.co.uk. Est: 1963. Private premises; Internet and postal. Appointment necessary. Very small stock. Spec: Atlases; Cartography; Reference. PR: £10–5,000. CC: JCB; MC; V. Mem: PBFA. VAT No: GB 391 9317 27.

Cotswold Internet Books, Maida Vale Business Centre, Mead Road, Cheltenham, GL53 7ER. Prop: John & Caro Newland. Tel: (01242) 261428. E-mail: jnewland@v21mail.co.uk. Est: 1989. Warehouse; Internet and postal. Telephone first. Very large general stock. PR: £5–500. CC: JCB; MC. Mem: ABA. VAT No: GB 535 5039 51.

James Hawkes, 174 Old Bath Road, Cheltenham, GL53 7DR. Tel: (1242) 514202. Fax: (1242) 514202. Website: http://www.abebooks.com/home/JAMESHAWKES/. E-mail: scholarlybooks@aol.com. Private premises; Internet and postal. Appointment necessary. Small stock. Spec: Academic/Scholarly; Literary Criticism; Literature. PR: £20–500. CC: JCB; MC; SW. Cata: 3.

Lavender Fields Books, Kimberley, Bradley Road, Charlton Kings, Cheltenham, GL53 8DX.

Bruce Marshall Rare Books, Foyers, 20 Gretton Road, Gotherington, Cheltenham, GL52 9QU. Tel: (01242) 672997. Fax: (01242) 675238. E-mail: marshallrarebook@aol.com. Private premises; appointment necessary. Very small stock. Spec: Atlases; Colour-Plate; Natural History; Travel - General. Mem: ABA; ILAB.

Valerie Merritt, 174 Old Bath Road, Cheltenham, GL53 7DR. Tel: (01242) 514664. Est: 1975. Private premises; appointment necessary. Small stock. Spec: Gardening; Horticulture; Natural History; Plant Hunting; Travel - General. PR: £20–2,000. Also, garden design and history. Cata: 3 – on specialities.

Available from Richard Joseph Publishers Ltd

Sheppard's Book Dealers in
NORTH AMERICA

15th Edition   (Royal H/b, plus CD-ROM)   £30.00   560pp

Moss Books, ■ 8–9 Henrietta Street, Cheltenham, GL50 4AA. Prop: Christopher Moss. Tel: (01242) 222947. E-mail: chris.moss@virgin.net. Est: 1992. Shop; open **M:** 10:00–18:00; **T:** 10:00–18:00; **W:** 10:00–18:00; Th: 10:00–18:00; **F:** 10:00–18:00; **S:** 09:00–18:00. Large general stock. PR: £1–100. Corresp: Japanese. VAT No: GB 618 3105 62.

Peter Lyons Books, 11 Imperial Square, Cheltenham, GL50 1QB. Prop: Peter Lyons. Tel: (01242) 260345. Est: 2001. Spec: Applied Art; Art; Art History; Art Reference; Artists; Arts, The; Biography; Children's - General; Modern First Editions; Poetry. PR: £2–50.

Michael Rayner Bookseller, 11 St. Luke's Road, Cheltenham, GL53 7JQ.

F.W. Taylor, 15 The Nurseries, Bishops Cleeve, Cheltenham, GL52 8XB.

Nick Thorne, 6 Cleeveview Road, Cheltenham, GL52 5NH. Tel: . E-mail: the.thornes@btinternet.com. Est: 1994. Spec: Author - Carroll, Lewis; Children's - General; Sport - Boxing. PR: £1–250.

Robin Turner, 30 Great Norwood Street, Cheltenham, GL50 2BH. Tel: (01242) 234303. E-mail: robinturner@robamol.fsnet.co.uk. Est: 1987. Private premises; appointment necessary. Very small stock. Spec: History - General; Military; War - General. PR: £5–200 Mem: PBFA.

John Wilson (Autographs) Ltd., Painswick Lawn, 7 Painswick Road, Cheltenham, GL50 2EZ. Prop: John Wilson. Tel: (01242) 580344. Fax: (01242) 580355. Website: www.manuscripts.co.uk. E-mail: mail@manuscripts.co.uk. Est: 1976. Private premises; Internet and postal. Appointment necessary. Very large stock. Spec: Autographs; Documents - General; Manuscripts. PR: £20–30,000. CC: AE; MC; V. Cata: 1. Mem: ABA; PBFA; ILAB; PADA.

CHIPPING CAMPDEN

Draycott Books, 2 Sheep Street, Chipping Campden, GL55 6DX.

CIRENCESTER

Aviabooks, 8 Swan Yard, West Market Place, Cirencester, GL7 2NH.

The Bookroom, Cirencester Arcade, Market Place, Cirencester, GL7 2NX.

Books for Collectors, 9 The Pheasantry, Down Ampney, Cirencester, GL7 5RE. Prop: Jon Edgson. Tel: (01793) 750152. Website: www.booksforcollectors.co.uk. E-mail: jonedgson@aol.com. Private premises; appointment necessary. Small stock. Spec: Art; Design; Fashion & Costume; Illustrated; Interior Design; Performing Arts; Photography; Vintage Paperbacks. PR: £5–500. Regularly attends book fairs. Cata: 1 – occasionally on design, fashion, costume, photography. Mem: PBFA.

Country Hoard Books, 14 Trafalgar Road, Cirencester.

Taran Books, The Annexe, Mill Bank Cottage, Winson, Nr Cirencester, GL7 5EW

COLEFORD

Simon Lewis Transport Books, PO Box 9, Coleford, GL16 8YF. Prop: Simon Lewis. Tel: (01594) 839369. Website: www.simonlewis.com. E-mail: simon@simonlewis.com. Est: 1985. Office &/or bookroom; Internet and postal. Medium stock. Spec: Buses/Trams; Motorbikes; Motoring; Railways; Sport - Motor Racing; Steam Engines; Transport; Vintage Cars. PR: £1–500. CC: E; MC; V; D. Cata: 4 – quarterly. VAT No: GB 575 9030 21.

DURSLEY

Internet Bookshop UK Ltd., ■ 28–30 Long Street, Dursley, Gloucester, GL11 4HX.

FAIRFORD

Jacques Gander, 14 Keble Lawns, Fairford, GL7 4BQ.

Merryheart, Tudor Cottage, London Street, Fairford, GL7 4AQ.

KEMPSFORD

Ximenes Rare Books Inc., Kempsford House, Kempsford, GL7 4ET. Prop: Stephen Weissman. Tel: (01285) 810640. Fax: (01285) 810650. E-mail: steve@ximenes.com. Est: 1965. Small stock. Spec: Antiquarian. PR: £50–10,000. CC: MC; V. Cata: 3. Corresp: French. Mem: ABA; PBFA; ILAB; ABAA. VAT No: GB 672 4533 30.

LECHLADE

Evergreen Livres, The Old School, Kelmscot, Lechlade, GL7 3HG. Prop: N. S. O'Keeffe. Tel: (01367) 252558. Fax: (01367) 252558. E-mail: ocker@oxfree.com. Est: 1984. Private premises; postal business only. Very small stock. Spec: Dogs; Farming & Livestock; Gardening; Horticulture; Natural History. PR: £2–500.

Hairpin Books, 7 Abbots Walk, Lechlade, GL7 3DB. Prop: Paul Saddington. Tel: (01367) 253220. Website: www.hairpinbooks.co.uk. E-mail: paulsaddington@hotmail.com. Est: 1999. Private premises; Internet and postal. Telephone first. *Shop at:* Old Ironmongers Antiques Centre, 5 Burford Street, Lechlade, Glos. Open: **M:** 10:00–17:00; **T:** 10:00–17:00; **W:** 10:00–17:00; **Th:** 10:00–17:00; **F:** 10:00–17:00; **S:** 10:00–17:00; **Su:** 10:00–17:00. Small stock. Spec: Aviation; Buses/Trams; Motorbikes; Motoring; Railways; Shipbuilding; Transport; Vintage Cars. PR: £5–500. CC: JCB; MC; V; SW. Also, booksearch. Mem: ABA.

LONGLEVENS

Bevins & Colin, The Maples, 24 Old Cheltenham Road, Longlevens, GL2 0AW.

MINCHINHAMPTON

The Blue Penguin, 1 High Street, Minchinhampton, GL6 9BN.

MORETON–IN–MARSH

Jeffrey Formby Antiques, Orchard Cottage, East Street, Moreton–in–Marsh, GL56 0LQ. Tel: (01608) 650558. Fax: (01608) 650558. Website: www.formby-clocks.co.uk. E-mail: jeff@formby-clocks.co.uk. Est: 1993. Shop &/or gallery; telephone first. Shop; open **F:** 10:00–17:00; **S:** 10:00–17:00. Very small stock. Spec: Horology; Scientific Instruments. PR: £5–500. CC: JCB; MC; V. Cata: 2.

Four Shire Bookshops, ■ 17 High Street, Moreton–in–Marsh, GL56 0AF. Prop: Hazel & David Potten. Tel: (01608) 651451. Fax: (01608) 650827. E-mail: fourshirebooks@aol.com. Est: 1981. Shop; open **M:** 09:30–16:00; **T:** 09:30–16:00; **W:** 09:30–16:00; **Th:** 09:30–17:00; **F:** 09:30–17:00; **S:** 08:30–17:00. Closed for lunch: 13:00–14:00. Medium stock. Spec: Embroidery; History - Local; Needlework; Topography - Local. PR: £1–100. CC: E; JCB; MC. Cata: 2 – on embroidery & quilting. Also, booksearch.

NAILSWORTH

Recycling Books, Jubilee Road, Nailsworth, GL6 0EZ.

Keogh's Books, 26 Tynings Road, Nailsworth, Stroud, GL6 0EQ. Prop: J. Keogh. Tel: (01453) 834253. Fax: (01453) 834253. Website: www.keoghsbooks.co.uk. E-mail: joekeogh@keoghbooks.fsnet.co.uk. Est: 1985. Market stand/stall; Internet and postal; telephone first. Open: **M:** 09:30–17:00. Large stock. Spec: Art; Art History; Art Reference; Artists. PR: £2–200. CC: AE; MC; V; SW.

NEWENT

Oakwood Books, 37 Church Street, Newent, GL18 1AA. Prop: Jim Haslem, A.L.A. Tel: (01531) 821040. Website: www.abebooks.com/home/oakwoodbooks. E-mail: haslem@ukgateway.net. Est: 1987. Private premises; Internet and postal. Appointment necessary. Small stock. Spec: Topography - Local. PR: £1–450.

NEWNHAM ON SEVERN

Marcus Niner, Newnham Old Books, 48 High Street, Newnham on Severn, GL14 1AA. Tel: (01594) 516088. E-mail: ninerbooks@aol.com. Private premises; telephone first. Very small stock. Spec: Art; Literature; Topography - Local; Travel - General. PR: £10–2,000. CC: MC; V. Mem: PBFA.

Christopher Saunders (Orchard Books), Kingston House, High Street, Newnham on Severn, GL14 1BB.

Searching for a title - and cannot find it on any Internet database?

Then try Sheppard's Booksearch

By selecting the subject classification – the request goes to all dealers who major in that subject.

STOW-ON-THE-WOLD

Wychwood Books, ■ Sheep Street, Stow-on-the-Wold, GL54 1AA. Prop: Lucy & Henry Baggott. Tel: (01451) 831880. E-mail: wychwoodbooks@btopenworld.com. Est: 1985. Shop; open **T:** 10:00–17:30; **W:** 10:00–17:30; **Th:** 10:00–17:30; **F:** 10:00–17:30; **S:** 10:00–17:30. Large stock. Spec: Art; Biography; Literature; Natural History; Topography - General. PR: £3–300.

Paper Moon Books, 1 The Dell, Blockley, Moreton-in-Marsh, Stow-on-the-Wold, GL56 9DB.

STROUD

Ian Hodgkins and Company Limit, Upper Vatch Mill, The Vatch, Slad, Stroud, GL6 7JY. Prop: G.A. Yablon & I. Hoy. Tel: (01453) 764270. Fax: (01453) 755233. Website: www.ianhodgkins.com. E-mail: i.hodgkins@dial.pipex.com. Est: 1974. Private premises; Internet and postal. Appointment necessary. Medium general stock. Spec: Applied Art; Art; Art Reference; Artists; Author - Austen, Jane; Author - Brontes, The; Author - Crane, Walter; Author - Gaskell, E.; Author - Lang, Andrew; Author - Morris, William; Author - Potter, Beatrix; Author - Rossetti, C.; Author - Ruskin, and others as listed in the Speciality Index. PR: £5–5,000. CC: MC; V. Cata: 4. Mem: ABA.

Inprint, ■ 31 High Street, Stroud, GL5 1AJ. Prop: Joy & Mike Goodenough. Tel: (01453) 759731. Fax: (01453) 759731. Website: www.inprint.co.uk. E-mail: enquiries@inprint.co.uk. Est: 1978. Shop; Internet and postal. Open: **M:** 10:00–17:00; **T:** 10:00–17:00; **W:** 10:00–17:00; **Th:** 10:00–17:00; **F:** 10:00–17:00; **S:** 10:00–17:00. Medium stock. Spec: Applied Art; Cinema/Film; Fine Art; Gardening; Performing Arts. PR: £5–500. CC: AE; D; E; JCB; MC; V. Cata: 1 – irregularly.

Ruth Pyecroft, 56 Middle Street, Stroud, GL5 1DZ.

Surprise Books, 14 Padin Close, Chalford, Stroud, GL6 8FB.

Alan & Joan Tucker, Old Stationmaster's House, Station Road, Stroud, GL5 3AP.

TETBURY

Tetbury Old Books Limited, ■ 4, The Chipping, Tetbury, GL8 8ET. Prop: Tetbury Old Books Ltd. Tel: (01666) 504330. Fax: (01666) 504458. E-mail: oldbooks@tetbury.co.uk. Est: 1994. Shop; open **M:** 10:00–18:00; **T:** 10:00–18:00; **W:** 10:00–18:00; **Th:** 10:00–18:00; **F:** 10:00–18:00; **S:** 10:00–18:00; **Su:** 11:00–18:00. Small general stock. PR: £1–5,000. CC: JCB; MC; V. Mem: TADA. *Also at:* The Bookroom, Cirencester.

TEWKESBURY

Avonbridge Books, 8 Churchill Grove, Newtown, Tewkesbury, GL20 8EL. Tel: (01684) 295785. Fax: (01684) 291823. Website: www.avonbridgebooks.com. E-mail: libris@avonbridgebooks.com. Private premises; Internet and postal. Medium stock. Spec: Academic/Scholarly; Antiquarian; Books about Books; Maritime/Nautical. PR: £5–1,000. CC: JCB; MC; V; SW. Also, a booksearch service. Mem: PBFA.

Cornell Books, ■ 93 Church Street, Tewkesbury, GL20 5RS. Prop: D.W. Hall & G.T. & C.L. Cornell. Tel: (01684) 293337. Fax: (01684) 273959. E-mail: gtcornell@aol.com. Est: 1996. Shop; open **M:** 10:30–17:00; **T:** 10:30–17:00; **W:** 10:30–17:00; **Th:** 10:30–17:00; **F:** 10:30–17:00; **S:** 10:30–17:00. Large general stock. Spec: Author - Moore, John; Children's - General; Colour-Plate; Natural History; Topography - General; Topography - Local; Travel - General. PR: £1–500. CC: MC; V. Also, booksearch.

TIBBERTON

www.drivepast.com, Tibberton Court, Tibberton, GL19 3AF. Prop: Paul Veysey. Tel: (01452) 790672. Fax: (01452) 790672. Website: www.drivepast.com. E-mail: paul@drivepast.com. Est: 2000. Market stand/stall; Internet and postal. Appointment necessary. Spec: Cinema/Film; Marque Histories (see also motoring); Motoring; Sport - Motor Racing; Vintage Cars. CC: E; MC; V. Also, booksearch. Original Cinema Posters stocked, and found. Corresp: French.

UPPER RISSINGTON

Aquarius Books Ltd., Unit 132, Rissington Business Park, Upper Rissington, GL54 2QB. Prop: Mrs Valerie Dumbleton. Tel: (01451) 820352. Website: www.ukbookworld.com/members/aquarius. E-mail: aquarius.bks@virgin.net. Est: 1993. Office &/or bookroom; Internet and postal. Appointment necessary. Large general stock. PR: £2–750. CC: MC; V. Also, booksearch.

UPTON ST. LEONARDS

John Bush, Bookdealer, Hazel Grove House, Upton Hill, Upton St. Leonards, GL4 8DE. Tel: (01452) 814386. Fax: (01452) 814386. E-mail: john.bush@virgin.net. Est: 1990. Private premises; Internet and postal. Appointment necessary. Very large general stock. Spec: Academic/Scholarly; Antiquarian; Biography; Fiction - General; History - General; Limited Editions; Sport - Cricket. PR: £5–200.

WESTBURY–ON–SEVERN

Patricia Larkham Books, ■ Dive In, Lecture Hall, The Village, Westbury-on-Severn, GL14 1PA. Prop: Patricia Larkham. Tel: (01452) 760124. Fax: (01452) 760590. Website: www.diveinbooks.co.uk. E-mail: mydive@globalnet.co.uk. Est: 1975. Shop; Internet and postal. Telephone first. Open: **M:** 09:00–15:00; **T:** 09:00–15:00; **W:** 09:00–15:00; **Th:** 09:00–15:00; **F:** 09:00–15:00. Small stock. Spec: Archaeology; Deep Sea Diving; Maritime/Nautical; Natural History; Sport - Cycling; Travel - General. PR: £1–150. Also, underwater photographs.

GREATER MANCHESTER

ALTRINCHAM

Edward Yarwood Rare Books, 61 Fairywell Road, Timperley, Altrincham, WA15 6XB. Est: 1994. Private premises; postal business only. Medium stock. Spec: Author - Gurdjieff, W.I.; Author - Wilson, Colin; Biography; Philosophy. PR: £5–250. Also; book plates, manuscripts, booksearch and attends fairs. Cata: 4 – a year on Gurdjieff.

Christopher Baron, 15 Crossfield Road, Hale, Altrincham, WA15 8DU.

ASHTON–UNDER–LYNE,

Marathon Books, 12 Lytham Close, Ashton-under-Lyne, Lancashire, OL6 9ER.

BOLTON

Martin Bott (Bookdealers) Ltd., ■ 28-30 Lee Lane, Horwich, BL6 4JE. (*) Prop: M.L.R. & M.H. Bott. Tel: (01204) 691489. Fax: (01204) 698729. Website: www.bottbooks.com. E-mail: martin.bott@btinternet.com. Est: 1997. Shop; Internet and postal. Telephone first. Postal address - 6 St. Leonards Avenue, Lostock, Bolton, BL6 4JE. Open: **M:** 10:00–15:00; **T:** 10:00–15:00. **Th:** 10:00–15:00; **F:** 10:00–15:00; **S:** 10:00–16:00. Large stock. Spec: Aviation; Buses/Trams; Canals/Inland Waterways; Company History; Engineering; Geology; Industry; Maritime/Nautical; Mining; Naval; Railways; Steam Engines; Technology; Traction Engines; Transport. PR: £1–1,000. CC: AE; JCB; MC; V; SW. Booksearch for Railway & Industrial History titles only.

Delph Books, 437 Bury & Bolton Road, Radcliffe, Bolton, M26 4LJ. Prop: Frank Lamb. Tel: (0161) 764-4488. Est: 1979. Private premises; appointment necessary. Medium stock. Spec: Company History; Genealogy; Military; Parish Registers; Police Force Histories; School Registers/Rolls of Honour; Topography - Local. PR: £1–200. Also, booksearch.

Siri Ellis Books, ■ The Last Drop Village, Bromley Cross, Bolton, BL7 9PZ. Prop: Siri E. Ellis. Tel: (01204) 597511. Website: www.siriellisbooks.co.uk. E-mail: mail@siriellisbooks.co.uk. Est: 1998. Shop; open **M:** 12:00–17:00; **T:** 12:00–17:00; **W:** 12:00–17:00; **Th:** 12:00–17:00; **F:** 12:00–17:00; **S:** 10:00–17:00; **Su:** 10:00–17:00. Small stock. Spec: Children's - General; Children's - Illustrated; Illustrated. PR: £1–1,000. CC: AE; V; SW. Booksearch for childhood favourites. Mem: PBFA.

BURY

G. Hall, 377 Bolton Road, Bury, Lancashire, BL8 2PH. Tel: (0161) 764-3406. Est: 1967. PR: £1–50.

CHEADLE

Clifford Elmer Books, 8 Balmoral Avenue, Cheadle Hulme, Cheadle, SK8 5EQ. Prop: Clifford & Marie Elmer. Tel: (0161) 485-7064. Website: www.truecrime.co.uk. E-mail: sales@cliffordelmerbooks.com. Est: 1978. Private premises; appointment necessary. Medium stock. Spec: Crime (True); Criminology. PR: £3–500. CC: JCB; MC. Cata: 8. Mem: PBFA.

Mainly Fiction, 21 Tennyson Road, Cheadle, SK8 2AR.

DIDSBURY

Barlow Moor Books, 29 Churchwood Road, Didsbury, Manchester, M20 6TZ. Prop: Dr. Roger & Dr. L.A. Finlay. Tel: (0161) 434 5073. Fax: (0161) 448 2491. E-mail: books@barlowmoorbooks.com. Est: 1990. Private premises; postal business only. Very small general stock. Spec: Corresp: French. VAT No: GB 560 9236 38.

Dealers who need to update their entry
should visit their page on
www.sheppardsdirectories.com

E.J. Morten (Booksellers), ■ 6–9 Warburton Street, Didsbury, Manchester, M20 6WA. Prop: John A. Morten. Tel: (0161) 445-7329. Fax: (0161) 448-1323. E-mail: morten.booksellers@lineone.net. Est: 1959. Shop; open **M:** 10:00–17:30; **T:** 09:00–17:29; **W:** 10:00–17:30; **Th:** 10:00–17:30; **F:** 10:00–17:30; **S:** 10:00–00:30. Large stock. Spec: Military History; Sport - General; Travel - General. Cata: 2. Corresp: French, German. Mem: PBFA; BA; ILAB; BT; NBL. *Also at:* Morten Books, Congleton, Cheshire (q.v.).

HULME

The Bookshop, Hulme Market Hall, Hulme High Street, Hulme, M15 5JT.

LITTLEBOROUGH

George Kelsall, ■ The Bookshop, 22 Church Street, Littleborough, OL15 9AA. Tel: (01706) 370244. E-mail: kelsall@bookshop22.fsnet.co.uk. Est: 1979. Shop; open **M:** 11:00–17:00; **T:** 13:00–17:00; **W:** 10:00–17:00; **Th:** 10:00–17:00; **F:** 10:00–17:00; **S:** 10:00–17:00. Large stock. Spec: Art History; Art Reference; History - General; History - Industrial; Politics; Social History; Topography - Local; Transport. PR: £1–500. Mem: PBFA. VAT No: 306 0657 8.

MANCHESTER

The Bookshop, 441 Wilmslow Road, Withington, Manchester, M20 4AN.

Browzers, 2 Buckingham Road, Prestwich, Manchester, M25 9NE. Prop: Alan E. Seddon. Tel: (0161) 773-2327. Fax: (0161) 773-2327. Website: http://www.browzersbooks.co.uk. E-mail: sales@browzers.co.uk. Est: 1980. Private premises; postal business only. Small stock. Spec: Antiques; Collecting; Sport - Horse Racing (all aspects). PR: £1–300. CC: MC; V; SW. Cata: 2 – horse racing. Mem: PBFA.

Classic Crime Collections, 95a Boarshaw Road, Middleton, Manchester, M24 6AP. Prop: Rob Wilson. Tel: (0161) 653-4145. E-mail: Rob@mtwilson.freeserve.co.uk. Est: 1989. Private premises; postal business only. Small stock. Spec: Antiques; Author - Christie, Agatha; Author - Creasey, John; Author - Fleming, Ian; Author - Francis, Dick; Author - Ransome, Arthur; Author - Wodehouse, P.G.; Canals/Inland Waterways; Countries - Melanesia; Crime (True); Dogs; Fiction - Science Fiction, and others as listed in the Speciality Index. PR: £2–250. Also, a booksearch service.

Forest Books of Manchester, inside The Ginnel Gallery, 18–22 Lloyd Street, Manchester, M2 5WA.

Franks Booksellers, Suite 33, 4th Floor, St Margaret's Chambers, 5 Newton Street, Piccadilly, Manchester, M1 1HL. Tel: (0161) 237-3747. Est: 1960. Office &/or bookroom. Open: **M:** 10:00–14:00; **T:** 10:00–14:00; **W:** 10:00–14:00; **Th:** 10:00–14:00; **F:** 10:00–14:00. Small stock. Spec: Advertising; Autographs; Children's - General; Cinema/Film; Comic Books & Annuals; Magic & Conjuring; Performing Arts; Periodicals & Magazines; Private Press; Sport - Boxing; Sport - Football (Soccer); Sport - Rugby. PR: £1–1,000.

Gibbs Bookshop Ltd., ■ 10 Charlotte Street, Manchester, M1 4FL. Tel: (0161) 236-7179. Fax: (0161) 236-7179. Est: 1922. Shop; open **M:** 10:00–17:00; **T:** 10:00–17:00; **W:** 10:00–17:00; **Th:** 10:00–17:00; **F:** 10:00–17:00; **S:** 10:00–17:00. Large general stock. PR: £2–300. CC: D; E; JCB; MC; V. Mem: ABA.

Tim Kendall–Carpenter, 633 Wilmslow Road, Manchester, M20 6DF. Tel: (0161) 445-6172. Fax: (0161) 438-8445. E-mail: timkcbooks@aol.com. Est: 1996. Private premises; Internet and postal. Appointment necessary. Medium stock. Spec: First Editions; Modern First Editions; Poetry; Proof Copies. PR: £5–500. CC: MC; V. Cata: 3.

The Little Bookshop, ■ The Basement, Friends Meeting House, 6 Mount Street, Manchester, M2 5NS. Prop: Joseph McGarraghy. Tel: (0161) 773-4665. Est: 1989. *Shop at:* (use Bootle Street entrance). Open: **M:** 10:00–17:30; **T:** 10:00–17:30; **W:** 10:00–17:30; **Th:** 10:00–17:30; **F:** 10:00–17:30. Large stock. Spec: Archaeology; Architecture; Arts, The; Autobiography; Fiction - General; History - General; Motorbikes; Poetry; Religion - General. PR: £1–100. Contactable in evenings on (07815) 560872.

Philip Nevitsky, P.O. Box 364, Manchester, M60 1AL. Tel: (0161) 228-2947. Fax: (0161) 236-0390. Est: 1974. Storeroom; postal business only. Small stock. Spec: Cinema/Film; Entertainment - General; Music - Popular.

The Old Bookshop, The Prince of Wales Buildings, Ste. 5 (2nd Floor), 4 Newton St., Manchester, M1 2AW.

V.M. Riley Books, 3 Leyburn Avenue, Stretford, Manchester, M32 8DZ. Prop: Mrs. Valerie M. Riley. Tel: (0161) 865-6543. E-mail: val@rileyv.fsnet.co.uk. Est: 1989. Private premises; postal business only. Very small stock. PR: £1–50.

Don Swift Books, 9 Seymour Road, Mile End, Stockport, Manchester, SK2 6ES.

The Treasure Island, 4 Evesham Road, Blackley, Manchester, M9 7EH. Prop: Ray Cauwood. Tel: (0161) 795 7750. Website: www.abebooks.com/home/RAYJC2000. E-mail: ray@the-treasure-island.com. Est: 2003. Private premises; postal business only. Appointment necessary. Small stock. Spec: Animals and Birds; Art; Aviation; Languages - National; Maritime/Nautical; Medicine; Philately; Photography; Railways; Sport - Angling/Fishing; Sport - Cricket; Sport - Horse Racing (all aspects); Sport - Rugby; Travel - General. PR: £1–50. CC: V. Cata: 1 – a year.

MOTTRAM IN LONGDENDALE

Rose Books, 26 Roe Cross Green, Mottram in Longdendale, Hyde, SK14 6LP. (*) Prop: E. Alan Rose. Tel: (01457) 763485. Fax: (01457) 763485. Est: 1990. Private premises; appointment necessary. Very small stock. Spec: History - Local; Religion - Christian; Theology. PR: £2–150.

OLDHAM

Moorland Books, 1 Smithy Lane , Uppermill, Oldham, OL3 6AH. Prop: Mrs. C.M. Bennett & Mrs. C.L. Longton. Tel: (01457) 871306. E-mail: moorlandbooks@ntlworld.com. Est: 1982. PR: £1–100. Also, booksearch.

Oldham Bookshop, 65 George Street, Oldham, OL1 1LX. (*) Prop: Bob Lees. Tel: (0161) 628-4693. Est: 1994. Spec: History - Local. PR: £1–50.

Towpath Bookshop, ■ 27 High Street, Uppermill, Oldham, OL3 6HS. (*) Prop: Janet Byrom. Tel: (01457) 877078. Est: 1992. Shop; open **T:** 11:00–16:30; **W:** 10:30–17:00; **Th:** 10:30–17:00; **F:** 10:30–17:00; **S:** 10:30–17:00; **Su:** 11:00–17:00. Very small general stock.

ROCHDALE

Mrs. C. Crabtree, 35 Bankfield Lane, Norden, Rochdale, OL11 5RS.

Empire Books, 61 Broad Lane, Rochdale, OL16 4PL. Prop: Robert Oliver. Tel: (01706) 666678. Fax: (01706) 666678. Website: www.empiremilitarybooks.co.uk. E-mail: empirebooks@ boltblue.com. Est: 1993. Private premises; Internet and postal. Appointment necessary. Large stock. Spec: Arms & Armour; Aviation; Biography; Colonial; Countries - Australia; Espionage; Firearms/Guns; Maritime/Nautical; Memoirs; Military; Military History; Naval; Newspapers - General; War - General; War - American Civil War; War - Boer, The; War - English Civil Wars, and others as listed in the Speciality Index. PR: £1–200. CC: JCB; MC; V; SW. Also, Australian military specialist. Mem: PBFA. VAT No: GB 647 2977 92.

Rochdale Book Company, ■399 Oldham Road, Rochdale, OL16 5LN. Prop: J. S. & S.M. Worthy. Tel: (01706) 631136. Fax: (01706) 658300. E-mail: worthybooks@aol.com. Est: 1971. Shop; open **S:** 10:30–17:30. Large stock. Spec: Architecture; Canals/Inland Waterways; Children's - General; Company History; Countries - Poland; Fine & Rare; History - Industrial; Illustrated; Industry; Military History; Motoring; Railways; Topography - Local; Transport; Travel - General. CC: MC; V. Mem: PBFA.

STOCKPORT

Richard Coulthurst, 97 Green Pastures, Stockport, SK4 3RB. Tel: (0161) 431-3864. E-mail: richard. coulthurst@btinternet.com. Est: 1995. Private premises; postal business only. Very small stock. Spec: Canals/Inland Waterways; History - Industrial; Publishers - Oakwood Press; Railways; Steam Engines; Transport. PR: £5–100. Also, booksearch. Cata: 1.

Robin S. Hunt, 6 Alford Road, Heaton Chapel, Stockport, SK4 5AW.

Talisman Books, 42 Town Street, Marple Bridge, Stockport, SK6 5AA.

Crime Inc., Mount Melfort, Urmston, Manchester, M41 9EJ. Prop: Barry & Gail Turner. Tel: (0161) 748 9485. Est: 1982. Private premises; appointment necessary. Small stock. Spec: Fiction - Crime, Detective, Spy, Thrillers. PR: £1–20.

Searching for a title - and cannot find it on any Internet database?

Then try **Sheppard's Booksearch**

By selecting the subject classification – the request goes to all dealers who major in that subject.

WIGAN

R.D.M. & I.M. Price (Books), 25 Coniston Avenue, Whitley, Wigan, WN1 2EY. Prop: Robert and Irene Price. Tel: (01942) 242607. Est: 1997. Private premises; postal business only. Small stock. Spec: Autobiography; Biography; Colonial; Fiction - General. PR: £1–120. Also, booksearch.

Wiend Books & Collectables, ■ 8–12 The Wiend, Wigan, Lancashire, WN1 1PF. Prop: Paul Morris. Tel: (01942) 820500. Fax: (01942) 820500. Website: www.wiendbooks.co.uk. E-mail: wiendbooks@lycos.co.uk. Shop; open. Spec: Archaeology; Architecture; Art; Children's - General; Cinema/Film; Collecting; Company History; Cookery/Gastronomy; Countries - Melanesia; Fiction - Science Fiction; History - Ancient; Magic & Conjuring; Maritime/Nautical; Military History. PR: £3–250.

HAMPSHIRE

ALRESFORD

Bolton Books, 60 The Dean, Alresford, SO24 9BD. Prop: David A. Bolton. Tel: (01962) 734435. Fax: (01962) 734435. Est: 1997. Private premises; postal business only. Very small general stock. Spec: Colour-Plate; Illustrated; Magic & Conjuring; Publishers - Black, A. & C.; Topography - General. PR: £5–1,250. Cata: 6 – a year on A & C Black colour books. Mem: PBFA.

Laurence Oxley, The Studio Bookshop, 17 Broad Street, Alresford, Hampshire SO24 9AW

Open Hand Books, Arle Mill, The Weir, Alresford, SO24 9DG.

ALTON

Alton Secondhand Books, ■ 43 Normandy Street, Alton, GU34 1DQ. Prop: Mrs. J. Andrews. Tel: (01420) 89352. E-mail: joan.andrews@virgin.net. Est: 1989. Shop; open **M:** 09:30–17:30; **T:** 09:30–17:30; **W:** 09:30–17:00; **Th:** 09:30–17:30; **F:** 09:30–17:30; **S:** 09:30–17:00. Medium stock. PR: £1–50. Also, booksearch. VAT No: GB 631 9874 13.

Dance Books Ltd., The Old Bakery, 4 Lenten St., Alton, GU34 1HG.

Nebulous Books, Cromwell House, 11 Oliver Rise, Alton, GU34 2BN. Prop: Peter Bancroft. Tel: (01420) 89264. Est: 1986. Private premises; appointment necessary. Small stock. Spec: Canals/Inland Waterways; Railways; Transport. PR: £1–40.

Soldridge Books Ltd, Soldridge House, Soldridge Road, Medstead, Alton, GU34 5JF. Prop: Jan & John Lewis. Tel: (01420) 562811. Fax: (01420) 562811. Website: www.soldridgebooks.co.uk. E-mail: lewis@soldridgebooks.co.uk. Est: 1991. Private premises; Internet and postal. Appointment necessary. Medium stock. Spec: Aeronautics; Aviation; First Editions; Photography; Poetry. PR: £3–400. CC: MC; V; Delta. Cata: 6. Corresp: French. Mem: PBFA. VAT No: GB 799 6939 25.

ALVERSTOKE

Pioneer Books, 12 St Mark's Road, Alverstoke, Gosport, PO12 2DA. Prop: I. Forder. Tel: (023) 9252-7965. E-mail: forder@marksrd.freeserve.co.uk. Est: 1985. Private premises; postal business only. Spec: Free Thought; Humanism; Radical Issues. PR: £1–100. Also, a booksearch service.

ANDOVER

Armchair Auctions, 98 Junction Road, Andover, SP10 3JA. Prop: George Murdoch. Tel: (01264) 362048. Fax: (01264) 362048. Est: 1989. Private premises; Spec: Aviation; Military; Naval; War - World War I. PR: £5–200. CC: AE; MC; V. Also postal auctions and booksearch.

Countryside Books, Sleepers Cottage, Penton Mewsey, Nr. Andover, SP11 ORA.

Eve Magee Books, Lower House, Lower Chute, Andover, SP11 9EB. Tel: (01264) 730284. Fax: (01264) 730284. Website: www.abebooks.com/home/chute. E-mail: evemageebooks@yahoo.co.uk. Est: 1988. Private premises; appointment necessary. Medium general stock. PR: £5–50. *Also at:* Eve Magee Books, Marlborough, Wiltshire (q.v.).

ASHURST

Les Alpes Livres, 'Arcadia', Hazel Grove, Ashurst, SO40 7AJ. Prop: Tony Astill. Tel: (023) 8029 3767. Website: www.les-alpes-livres.co.uk. E-mail: alpes@supanet.com. Est: 1993. Private premises; Internet and postal. Telephone first. Small stock. Spec: Alpinism/Mountaineering; Bindings; Countries - Central Asia; Countries - Switzerland; Countries - Tibet. PR: £5–1,000. CC: D; MC; V. Cata: 4 – quarterly. Corresp: French. VAT No: GB 631 6744 41.

Dealers who need to update their entry should visit their page on
www.sheppardsdirectories.com

Nova Foresta Books, ■ 185 Lyndhurst Road, Ashurst, Southampton, SO40 7AR. Prop: Georgina Babey & Peter Roberts. Tel: (023) 8029-3389. Website: www.novaforestabooks.co.uk. E-mail: postmaster@novaforestabooks.co.uk. Est: 1994. Shop; open **T:** 10:00–17:30; **W:** 10:00–17:30; **Th:** 10:00–17:30; **F:** 10:00–17:30; **S:** 10:00–17:30. Medium stock. Spec: Art; Literature; Poetry; Topography - Local. PR: £1–1,000. Mem: PBFA.

BASINGSTOKE

A. O'Neill, 32 Milton Close, Basingstoke, RG24 9BY.

EMSWORTH

Bookends, ■ 7 High St., Emsworth, PO10 7AQ. Prop: Carol Waldron. Tel: (01243) 372154. E-mail: cawaldron@tinyworld.co.uk. Est: 1982. Shop; open **M:** 09:00–17:00; **T:** 09:00–17:00; **W:** 09:00–17:00; **Th:** 09:00–17:00; **F:** 09:00–17:00; **S:** 09:00–17:00; **Su:** 10:00–15:00. Large stock. PR: £1–300. Corresp: French.

Peter Hill, 3 Westbourne Avenue, Emsworth, PO10 7QT. Tel: (01243) 379956. Fax: (01243) 379956. E-mail: peterhill.books@btinternet.com. Est: 1986. Private premises; appointment necessary. Shop; open **M:** 09:00–17:00; **T:** 09:00–17:00; **W:** 09:00–17:00; **Th:** 09:00–17:00; **F:** 09:00–17:00. Small stock. Spec: Alpinism/Mountaineering; Classical Studies; Travel - General. PR: £10–2,000. Corresp: French. Mem: ABA; PBFA.

FARNBOROUGH

Books International, 101 Lynchford Road, Farnborough, GU14 6ET.

Bramble Books, 60 Caswell Close, Farnborough, GU14 8TD.

Farnborough Bookshop and Galle, 26 Guildford Road West, Farnborough, GU14 6PU. Prop: P.H. Taylor. Tel: (01252) 518033. Fax: (01252) 511503. Website: www.farnboroughgallery.co.uk. E-mail: peter-t@btconnect.com. Est: 1978. Shop &/or gallery; Internet and postal. Appointment necessary. Medium general stock. Spec: Art; First Editions; History - General; Military History. CC: AE; MC; V. Also, booksearch. Cata: 4 – military history, art, general railways. VAT No: GB 296 4807 13.

Malmo Books, 9 Leopold Avenue, Farnborough, GU14 8NL. Prop: D. & L. Pilborough. Tel: (01252) 510297. Est: 1983. Private premises; appointment necessary. Large stock. Spec: Aviation; Biography; Culture - Foreign; Dictionaries; Economics; Foreign Texts; Geography; Guide Books; History - General; Humanities; Languages - Foreign; Literature in Translation; Maritime/Nautical; Military History; Naval; Oriental; Politics; and others as listed in the Speciality Index. PR: £1–1,000. Cata: – occasionally on specialities.

FLEET

Booksave, 16 Malthouse Close, Church Crookham, Fleet, GU52 6TB.

War & Peace Books, 32 Wellington Ave., Fleet, GU51 3BF.

FORDINGBRIDGE

Bristow & Garland, ■ 45–47 Salisbury Street, Fordingbridge, SP6 1AB. Prop: David Bristow & Victoria Garland. Tel: (01425) 657337. Fax: (01425) 657337. Website: www.bristowandgarland.co.uk. E-mail: mail@bristowandgarland.co.uk. Est: 1970. Shop; open **M:** 10:00–17:00; **T:** 10:00–17:00; **W:** 10:00–17:00; **Th:** 10:00–13:00; **F:** 10:00–17:00; **S:** 10:00–17:00. Small general stock. Spec: Autographs; Fine & Rare; Manuscripts. PR: £5–5,000. CC: JCB; MC.

GOSPORT

Richard Martin Bookshop & Gall, ■ 19-23 Stoke Road, Gosport, PO12 1LS. Tel: (023) 9252-0642. Fax: (023) 9252-0642. Website: www.richardmartingallery.co.uk. E-mail: enquiries@richardmartgallery.co.uk. Est: 1976. Shop; open **T:** 10:30–16:30. **Th:** 10:30–16:30; **F:** 10:30–16:30; **S:** 10:30–13:00. Closed for lunch: 13:00–14:15. Medium stock. Spec: Illustrated; Maritime/Nautical; Topography - General; Travel - General. PR: £10–3,000. CC: MC; V. Also, restoration work, frames and mounts. Cata: – occasionally on thematic. Mem: PBFA. VAT No: GB 430 6603 81.

Sub Aqua Prints and Books, 3 Crescent Road, Alverstoke, Gosport, PO12 2DH. Prop: Kevin F. Casey. Tel: (023) 9252-0426. Website: www.subaquaprints.com. E-mail: k.casey@subaquaprints.com. Est: 1991. Private premises; Internet and postal. Appointment necessary. Small stock. Spec: Deep Sea Diving; Marine Sciences; Maritime/Nautical. PR: £5–500. CC: JCB; MC; V.

HAMPSHIRE

Alastor Books, 12 Wisbech Way, Hordle, SO41 0YQ. Prop: J.A. Eaton. Tel: (01425) 629756. E-mail: alastor.books@virgin.net. Internet and postal. Spec: Antiquarian; Bibliography; Books about Books; Travel - General. PR: £15–1,000. Mem: PBFA.

HORDEAN

Milestone Publications Goss &, 62 Murray Road, Horndean, PO8 9JL.

Tobo Books, 10 London Road, Horndean, Waterlooville, PO8 0BZ. Prop: Matthew Wingett. Tel: (023) 9259 6139. Website: www.tobo-books.com. E-mail: sheppards@tobo-books.com. Est: 2000. Office &/ or bookroom and Internet. Open: M: 09:00–17:00; **T:** 09:09–17:00; **W:** 09:09–17:00; **Th:** 09:09–17:00; **F:** 09:00–17:00. Small stock. Spec: Antiquarian; Architecture; Author - Byron, Lord; Author - Cruickshank, G.; Author - Dickens, Charles; Author - Fleming, Ian; Author - Greene, Graham; Author - Milne, A.A.; Author - Tolkien, J.R.R.; Author - Trollope, Anthony; Bindings; Fine & Rare; and others as listed in the Speciality Index. PR: £1–5,000. VAT No: GB 812 1985 36.

LIPHOOK

Pauline Harries Books, 4 Willow Close, Liphook, GU30 7HX. Tel: (01428) 723764. Fax: (01428) 722367. Website: www.abebooks.com/home/paulineharriesbooks. E-mail: paulineharriesbooks@lineone.net. Est: 1982. Private premises; appointment necessary. Medium general stock. PR: £2–1,000. CC: JCB; MC; V; Delta. Also, booksearch.

LYMINGTON

M. & B. Clapham, ■ 7 Emsworth Road, Lymington, SO41 9BL. Prop: Barbara & Peter Clapham. Tel: (01590) 673178. Est: 1978. *Shop at:* Lymington Antiques Centre, 75 High Street, Lymington. Open: **M:** 10:00–17:00; **T:** 10:00–17:00; **W:** 10:00–17:00; **Th:** 10:00–17:00; **F:** 10:00–17:00; **S:** 09:00–17:00. Medium stock. Spec: Music - General; Sport - Yachting. Cata: 1 – occasionally. Corresp: French, Italian.

Units 7 and 8, Lymington Antique Centre, 76 High Street, Lymington, SO41 9ZX.

NEW MILTON

J.H. Day, 33 Ashley Common Road, Ashley, New Milton, BH25 5AL. Prop: J.H. Day. Tel: (01425) 619406. Website: www.abebooks.com. E-mail: jamesjday@aol.com. Est: 1983. Private premises; appointment necessary. Medium general stock. Spec: Sport - Horse Racing (all aspects). PR: £10–100. Cata: 1 – occasionally. CC: Paypal.

OVERTON

P. & D. Doorbar, Quidhampton Mill, Station Road, Overton, RG25 3EA. Prop: Mr. K.P. & Mr. D.L. Doorbar. Tel: (01256) 771418. Fax: (01256) 770196. Website: www.doorbar.co.uk/books/. E-mail: books@doorbar.co.uk. Est: 1991. Private premises; Internet. Small stock. Spec: Art; Children's - General; Children's - Illustrated; Dogs; Gypsies; Illustrated; Rural Life. PR: £5–500 Mem: PBFA.

David Esplin, 30 High Street, Overton, RG25 3HA.

PETERSFIELD

The Petersfield Bookshop, ■ 16a Chapel Street, Petersfield, GU32 3DS. Prop: Frank, Ann, John & David Westwood. Tel: (01730) 263438. Fax: (01730) 269426. Website: www.petersfieldbookshop.com. E-mail: sales@petersfieldbookshop.com. Est: 1918. Shop; open **M:** 09:00–17:30; **T:** 09:00–17:30; **W:** 09:00–17:30; **Th:** 09:00–17:30; **F:** 09:00–17:30; **S:** 09:00–17:30. Spec: Sport - Angling/Fishing; Travel - General. PR: £1–2,000. CC: AE; D; MC; V. Also, maps, prints, new books, art materials, picture framing & a booksearch service. Cata: 4. Mem: ABA; PBFA; BA; ILAB. VAT No: GB 192 6013 72.

David Schutte, 'Waterside', 119 Sussex Road, Petersfield, GU31 4LB. Tel: (01730) 269115. Fax: (01730) 231177. Website: www.davidschutte.co.uk. E-mail: david.schutte@virgin.net. Est: 1980. Private premises; Internet and postal. Appointment necessary. Spec: Author - Blyton, Enid; Author - Buckeridge, A.; Author - Crompton, Richmal; Author - Johns, W.E.; Author - Wodehouse, P.G.; Children's - General. PR: £3–1,500. CC: MC; V. Cata: 6. Mem: PBFA.

SOUTHSEA

Abbey Bookshop, ■ 69 Fawcett Road, Southsea, Portsmouth, PO4 ODB. (*) Prop: Nick & Stella Purkis. Tel: (023) 9273-7077. Est: 1986. Shop; open **T:** 12:00–18:00. **Th:** 12:00–18:00; **F:** 12:00–18:00; **S:** 11:00–18:00. Very large stock. Spec: Chess; Children's - General; Countries - Melanesia; Esoteric; Fiction - Crime, Detective, Spy, Thrillers; First Editions; History - General; Literary Criticism; Literature; Maritime/Nautical; Military; Politics; Travel - General. Cata: 1.

Art Reference Books, 3 Portswood Road, Portsmouth, PO2 9QX. Prop: Andy Ralph. Tel: (02392) 790861. Fax: (02392) 650756. Website: www.artreferencebooks.com. E-mail: artreferencebooks@hotmail.com. Est: 1999. Private premises; Internet and postal. Appointment necessary. Medium general stock. Spec: Antiquarian; Antiques; Applied Art; Architecture; Art; Art History; Art Reference; Artists; Ceramics; Children's - Illustrated; Collecting; Country Houses; Decorative Art; Design; Dolls & Dolls' Houses; Fashion & Costume; Fine Art; Furniture; Glass; and others as listed in the Speciality Index. PR: £2–1,000.

Jade Mountain, ■ 17–19 Highland Road, Southsea, Portsmouth, PO4 9DA. Prop: Ian Stemp. Tel: (023) 92 732951. Website: www.jademountain.co.uk. E-mail: ianstemp@btinternet.com. Est: 1992. Shop; Internet and postal. Open: **M:** 09:30–17:30. **W:** 09:30–17:30. **F:** 09:30–17:30; **S:** 08:30–17:30. Large stock. Spec: Animals and Birds; Annuals; Dictionaries; Fiction - General; Food & Drink; Gardening; History - General; Languages - Foreign; Literature; Music - General; Poetry; Psychology/Psychiatry; Railways; Religion - General; Spiritualism; Theology; Topography - General; Transport; Travel - General. PR: £1–80.

Roadster Motoring Books, 33 Martin Road, Copnor, Portsmouth, PO3 6JZ. Prop: Peter Cockburn. Tel: (023) 9266-5632. Est: 1991. Private premises; appointment necessary. Small stock. Spec: Motorbikes; Motoring; Sport - Motor Racing; Vintage Cars. PR: £5–200.

PURBROOK

Hobgoblin Books, Goblin Brook, 66 Privett Road, Purbrook, PO7 5JW.

RINGWOOD

E. Chalmers Hallam, Trees, 9 Post Office Lane, St. Ives, Ringwood, BH24 2PG. Prop: Laura Hiscock. Tel: (01425) 470060. Fax: (01425) 470060. Website: www.hallam-books.co.uk. E-mail: laura@chalmershallam.freeserve.co.uk. Est: 1946. Private premises; appointment necessary. Large stock. Spec: Anthropology; Author - Watkins–Pitchford, Denys ('B.B.'); Cockfighting; Countries - Africa; Countries - India; Dogs; Firearms/Guns; Fishes; Sport - Angling/Fishing; Sport - Archery; Sport - Big Game Hunting; Sport - Coursing; Sport - Falconry; Sport - Fencing; and others as listed in the Speciality Index. PR: £5–5,000. CC: MC; V; Debit card. Cata: 2. Mem: PBFA.

ROMSEY

Bufo Books, 32 Tadfield Road, Romsey, SO51 5AJ. Prop: Ruth Allen & Peter Hubbard. Tel: (01794) 517149. Fax: (01794) 517149. Website: www.bufobooks.demon.co.uk. E-mail: bufo@bufobooks.demon.co.uk. Est: 1979. Private premises; Internet and postal. Appointment necessary. Medium stock. Spec: Children's - General; Military; War - General. PR: £1–200. CC: MC; V; Bartercard. Attends bookfairs. Cata: – occasionally. Corresp: French. Mem: PBFA. VAT No: GB 522 4988 32.

Ellwood Editions, 2 Benchmark Cottages, Kimbridge, Romsey, SO16 8AM. Prop: Mark Harrison and Helen Ford. Tel: (01794) 342390. E-mail: info@ellwoodbooks.com. Est: 2001. Private premises; appointment necessary. Small stock. Spec: Fiction - General; Fine & Rare; Modern First Editions; Poetry. PR: £5–30. CC: AE; MC; V. Attends HD and Winchester fairs. Cata: 1 – occasionally on specialities.

SOUTHAMPTON

Greg Alexander, 14 Blake Close, Nursling, Southampton, SO16 0TL.

Vincent G. Barlow, 24 Howerts Close, Warsash, Southampton, SO31 9JR. Tel: (01489) 582431. Est: 1981. Storeroom; appointment necessary. Small stock. Spec: Art Reference; Catalogues Raisonnes; Children's - General; Decorative Art; Fine Printing; Illustrated; Interior Design; Limited Editions; Monographs; Private Press. Attends monthly fairs at Royal National. Mem: PLA; IBIS. *Also at:* Words Etcetera, Dorchester.

Searching for a title - and cannot find it on any Internet database?

Then try Sheppard's Booksearch

By selecting the subject classification – the request goes to all dealers who major in that subject.

Broadwater Books, 62 Britannia Gardens, Hedge End, Southampton, SO30 2RP. Prop: J.B. & A.B. Dancy. Tel: (01489) 786035. Website: matchingbooks.co.uk. E-mail: john@jdancy.fsnet.co.uk. Est: 1988. Private premises; postal business only. Large stock. Spec: Countries - England; Countries - Melanesia; Countries - Scotland; History - General; Religion - General; Theology; Travel - General. PR: £1–400. Also, wants lists welcomed.

Centurion Books, 16 Emmett Road, Rownhams, Southampton, SO16 8JB.

Fountain Books, 9 Carthage Close, Chandlers Ford, Southampton, SO53 2BL.

W.E. Jackson, 6 Shepherds Close, Bartley, Southampton, SO40 2LJ. Prop: Bill Jackson. Tel: (02380) 812640. E-mail: bill@bilberry.ndo.co.uk. Est: 1988. Private premises; postal business only. Small general stock. PR: £1–100. Stock displayed at: The Shirley Bookshop, Southampton.

Morley Case, 24 Wildburn Close, Calmore, Southampton, SO40 2SG. Prop: David Case. Tel: (023) 8086-4264. Website: www.abebooks.com/home/case. E-mail: morleycase@aol.com. Est: 1973. Private premises; Internet and postal. Appointment necessary. Small general stock. Spec: Art; Aviation; Military; Sport - Golf. PR: £5–200.

Mr. Mac, Rose Cottage, Portsmouth Road, Old Netley, Southampton, SO31 8ET.

Peter Rhodes, Bookseller, ■ 21 Portswood Road, Southampton, SO17 2ES. Tel: (02380) 399003. E-mail: peterrhodes.books@virgin.net. Est: 1996. Shop; open **M:** 11:00–17:00; **T:** 11:00–17:00; **W:** 11:00–17:00; **Th:** 11:00–17:00; **F:** 11:00–17:00; **S:** 11:00–17:00; **Su:** 11:00–17:00. Large general stock. Spec: Anthropology; Author - 20th Century; Children's - Illustrated; Countries - India; Photography; Theatre. Also, insurance and probate valuation.

The Shirley Bookshop, ■ 2 Emsworth Road, Southampton, SO15 3LX. Prop: Mrs. V.A. Ford, J.H. Day, W.E. Jackson & L.D. Sweed. Tel: (023) 8051-0779. Est: 1992. Shop; open **M:** 10:30–17:30; **T:** 10:30–17:30; **W:** 10:30–17:30; **Th:** 10:30–17:30; **F:** 10:30–17:30; **S:** 10:00–17:00. Large general stock. PR: £1–500.

SOUTHSEA

Academy Books, 13 Marmion Road, Southsea, PO5 2AT.

Albion Books, 18 Sussex Road, Southsea, PO5 3EX.

Palladour Books, 23, Eldon Street, Southsea, PO5 4BS. Prop: Jeremy & Anne Powell. Tel: (02392) 826935. Fax: (02392) 826935. E-mail: palladour@powellj33.freeserve.co.uk. Est: 1985. Private premises; Internet and postal. Appointment necessary. Very small stock. Spec: First Editions; Literature; Military; Periodicals & Magazines; Poetry; School Registers/Rolls of Honour; War - General; War - World War I; War - World War II. PR: £1–500. Cata: 2 – Military Literature and Poetry of WWI. Also, booksearch.

WARSASH

Warsash Nautical Bookshop, ■ 6 Dibles Road, Warsash, Southampton, SO31 9HZ. Prop: Mr. Andrew Marshall. Tel: (01489) 572384. Fax: (01489) 885756. Website: www.nauticalbooks.co.uk. E-mail: orders@nauticalbooks.co.uk. Est: 1973. Shop; Internet and postal. Open: **M:** 09:00–17:45; **T:** 09:00–17:45; **W:** 09:00–17:45; **Th:** 09:00–17:45; **F:** 09:00–17:45; **S:** 09:30–17:00. Small stock. Spec: Maritime/Nautical; Maritime/Nautical - Log Books; Navigation. PR: £5–500. CC: AE; D; E; JCB; MC; V. Cata: 4 – Quarterly. VAT No: GB 108 3293 82.

WINCHESTER

John Barton, 84 Old Kennels Lane, Winchester, SO22 4JT. Tel: (01962) 866543. E-mail: jgbartonwin@ukgateway.net. Est: 1966. Private premises; postal business only. Very small stock. Spec: Archaeology; Architecture; History - General; History - Local; History - National; Topography - General. PR: £2–100 Mem: PBFA.

Peter M. Daly, 9 Lansdowne Court, Lansdowne Avenue, Winchester, SO23 9TJ. Prop: Peter M. Daly. Tel: (01962) 867732. E-mail: petermdaly@rarebooks.fsnet.co.uk. Est: 1984. Private premises; Internet and postal. Appointment necessary. Small general stock. Spec: Africana; Agriculture; Alpinism/Mountaineering; Animals and Birds; Countries - Arabia; Countries - Far East, The; Forestry; Gardening; History - Local; Natural History; Ornithology; Sport - Field Sports; Sport - Shooting; Travel - Africa; Travel - Asia; and others as listed in the Speciality Index. PR: £1–1,000. CC: JCB; MC; V; SW. Mem: PBFA. VAT No: GB 411 8630 76.

H.M. Gilbert & Son, 5 Rooks Down, Winchester, SO22 4QN. Prop: Richard Gilbert. Tel: (023) 8022-6420. E-mail: gilbookuk@yahoo.co.uk. Est: 1859. Private premises; appointment necessary. Small stock. Spec: Antiquarian; Literature; Topography - General; Topography - Local. PR: £1–500. CC: MC; V. Mem: PBFA.

Michael Green, 12 St. James Lane, Winchester, SO22 4NX.

Kingsgate Books & Prints, ■ Kingsgate Arch, Winchester, SO23 9PD. Prop: Michael Fowkes. Tel: (01962) 864710. Fax: (01962) 864710. Est: 1992. Shop; open **T:** 12:30–17:00; **W:** 12:30–17:00; **Th:** 12:30–17:00; **F:** 12:30–17:00; **S:** 10:00–17:00. Very small stock. Spec: Art History; Art Reference; History - Local; Literary Criticism; Literature; Natural History; Poetry. PR: £1–150. CC: MC; V. Corresp: French. Mem: BA.

Sen Books, 3 Long Barrow Close, South Wonston, Winchester, SO21 3ED. Prop: Andrew Duckworth. Tel: (01962) 884405. Est: 1974. Private premises; appointment necessary. Small general stock. Spec: Author - Trollope, Anthony; Author - White, Gilbert. PR: £1–200. Also, booksearch.

Winchester Antiquarian Books, 40 Bereweeke Avenue, Winchester, SO22 6BL. Prop: Robert Brown. Tel: (01962) 863483. Fax: by arrangement. E-mail: books.winchester@btinternet.com. Est: 1991. Private premises. Trading from: The Winchester Bookshop, Winchester (q.v.). Medium stock. Spec: Canals/Inland Waterways; Fiction - General; History - Industrial; Industry; Literary Criticism; Literature; Literature - Victorian; Modern First Editions; Steam Engines; Transport; Travel - Asia; Travel - Middle East.

The Winchester Bookshop, ■ (next to Ladbroke's), 10a St. George's Street, Winchester, SO23 8BG. Prop: J. Barton, R. Brown, D. Barnes & M. Green. Tel: (01962) 855630. E-mail: books.winchester@btinternet.com. Est: 1991. Shop; open **M:** 10:00–17:00; **T:** 10:00–17:00; **W:** 10:00–17:00; **Th:** 10:00–17:00; **F:** 10:00–17:00; **S:** 10:00–17:30. Medium general stock. Spec: Archaeology; Bindings; Literature; Sport - Angling/Fishing; Topography - General; Topography - Local. PR: £1–300. CC: MC; V. Corresp: German.

HEREFORDSHIRE

ASHPERTON

T. Bicknell, 1 Mudwalls, Bishop's Frome, Worcestershire, WR6 5DB. (*). Tel: (01885) 490723. E-mail: mail@bicknellbooks.freeserve.co.uk. Est: 2000. Private premises; Internet and postal. Very small stock. Spec: Bindings; Churchilliana. PR: £10–1,000.

Books for Content, Spring Grove Farm, Wood End, Ashperton, Ledbury, HR8 2RS. Prop: H.M. & M.G. Jones. Tel: (01432) 890279. Est: 1989. Private premises; postal business only. Small stock. Spec: Agriculture; Cookery/Gastronomy; Gardening; Rural Life. PR: £3–100.

DILWYN

Mary Bland, 3 Castle Barn, Dilwyn, HR4 8HZ. Tel: (01544) 318750. Est: 1978. Private premises; appointment necessary. Small stock. Spec: Botany; Gardening. PR: £1–200. Cata: 2 – occasionally.

GLASBURY

babelog books, Victoria House, Glasbury, Hereford, HR3 5NR. Prop: Simon Cartwright. Tel: (01497) 847190. Website: www.ukbookworld.com/members/mason. E-mail: babelog.books@ukgateway.net. Est: 2000. Private premises; postal business only. Appointment necessary. Very small stock. Spec: Literature; Literature in Translation; Modern First Editions; Poetry. PR: £5–1,000. *Also at:* www.babelog.books.ukgateway.net.

HAY–ON–WYE (SEE ALSO UNDER POWYS, WALES)

HEREFORD

Bournville Books, 95 Whitecross Road, Hereford, HR4 0DQ.

The New Strand Bookshop, ■ Eardisley, Hereford, HR3 6PW. (*) Prop: R. & A. Cardwell. Tel: (01544) 327285. Shop; open **W:** 09:30–18:00; **Th:** 09:30–18:00; **F:** 09:30–18:00; **S:** 09:30–18:00; **Su:** 09:30–18:00. Very large stock. Spec: Children's - General; Fiction - General; Fiction - Crime, Detective, Spy, Thrillers; Fiction - Science Fiction; Natural History. PR: £1–250.

B.A. & C.W.M. Pratt, Huntington House, Huntington Lane, Hereford, HR4 7RA. Tel: (01432) 350927. Est: 1967. Private premises; postal business only. Spec: Medicine.

David Warnes, One Pound Cottage, Yarkhill, Hereford, HR1 3TA.

HOARWITHY

Peter Huyton, Rockland House, Hoarwithy, HR2 6QR. Tel: (01423) 840703. E-mail: peterhuyton@hotmail.com. Est: 2002. Storeroom; Very small stock. Spec: Entomology; History - Local; Natural History. Corresp: French.

KINGTON

Castle Hill Books, ■ 12 Church Street, Kington, HR5 3AZ. Prop: Peter Newman. Tel: (01544) 231195. Fax: (01544) 231161. Website: www.castlehillbooks.co.uk. E-mail: sales@castlehillbooks.co.uk. Est: 1987. Shop; open **M:** 10:30–13:00; **T:** 10:30–13:00; **W:** 10:30–13:00; **Th:** 10:30–13:00; **F:** 10:30–13:00; **S:** 10:30–16:00. Large stock. PR: £3–15,000. CC: MC; V. Also, new books, and maps in stock. Cata: 1 – lists sent on request. VAT No: GB 489 2054 19.

Dealers who need to update their entry
should visit their page on
www.sheppardsdirectories.com

HEREFORDSHIRE

Courtyard Books, Gladestry, Kington, HR5 3NR. Prop: M Johnson. Tel: (01544) 370296. Website: www.courtyardbooks.org.uk. E-mail: info@courtyardbooks.org.uk. Est: 2002. Shop &/or showroom; Internet and postal. Telephone first. Open: **M** 10:00–17:00; **T:** 10:00–17:00; **W:** 10:00–17:00; **Th:** 10:00–17:00; **F:** 10:00–17:00. Very small stock. Spec: Author - 20th Century; Author - Cornwell, Bernard; Author - Hemingway, Ernest; Author - Kerouac, Jack; Author - Le Carre, John; Author - Pinter, Harold; Author - Rankin, Ian; Author - Rushdie, Salman; Espionage; Fiction - Crime, Detective, Spy, Thriller; and others as listed in the Speciality Index. PR: £8–300. CC: MC; V. Cata: 1. *Also at:* Fineart Photographer, Kington (q.v.).

Fineart Photographer, The Courtyard Barns, Gladestry, Kington, HR5 3NR. Prop: Michael Johnson. Tel: (01544) 370296. Website: www.fineart-photographer.com. E-mail: info@fineart-photographer.com. Est: 2002. Shop &/or showroom; Internet and postal. Telephone first. Open: **M:** 10:00–17:00; **T:** 10:00–17:00; **W:** 10:10–17:00; **Th:** 10:00–17:00; **F:** 10:00–16:00. Very small stock. Spec: Art; Art History; Fine Art; Illustrated; Photography. PR: £5–200. CC: MC; V. Cata: 1. *Also at:* Courtyard Books, Kington (q.v.).

LEDBURY

Castle Frome Books, 2 New House, Castle Frome, Ledbury, HR8 1HG. Prop: Mrs. G. McElroy. Tel: (01531) 640292. Fax: (01531) 640292. E-mail: c.f.books@btinternet.com. Est: 1988. Private premises; postal business only. Appointment necessary. Small stock. Spec: Academic/Scholarly; Autobiography; Biography; Diaries; Literary Criticism; Literature; University Texts. PR: £10–150. Cata: 4. Corresp: German.

David Thomas Motoring Books, ■ Redsul, Upperfields, Ledbury, HR8 1LE. Tel: (01531) 635114. Fax: (01531) 635114. Website: www.allautobooks.com. E-mail: davidthomas@tesco.net. Est: 1997. Shop; appointment necessary. New shop opening in Ledbury October 2003 - please contact for address. Medium stock. Spec: Motoring; PR: £3–500. CC: MC; V; SW. Corresp: French, German, Italian. Mem: FSB.

Keith Smith Books, ■ 78b The Homend, Ledbury, HR8 1BX. Prop: Keith Smith. Tel: Day (01531) 635336. E-mail: keith@ksbooks.demon.co.uk. Est: 1986. Shop; open **M:** 10:00–17:00; **T:** 10:00–17:00; **W:** 10:00–17:00; **Th:** 10:00–17:00; **F:** 10:00–17:00; **S:** 10:00–17:00. Medium general stock. Spec: Author - Dymock Poets, The; Author - Masefield, John; Embroidery; History - Local; Needlework; Poetry; Rugs; Topography - Local; War - World War I. PR: £1–250. CC: AE; E; JCB; V; De, SW. Cata: 4. Mem: PBFA.

LEOMINSTER

Lyndon Barnes - Books, 3 Mortimer Drive. Ludlow, Shropshire, Leominster, SY8 4JW. Tel: (01568) 780641. Fax: (01568) 780641. Website: www.abebooks.com. E-mail: lyndon7@aol.com. Est: 1987. Private premises; Internet and postal. Also on ukbookworld and alibris. Open: **M:** 09:00–17:00; **T:** 09:00–17:00; **W:** 09:00–17:00; **Th:** 09:00–17:00; **F:** 09:00–17:00; **S:** 09:00–17:00; **Su:** 09:00–17:00. Small general stock. PR: £2–120. Cata: 3 – a year, mostly non-fiction.

ROSS–ON–WYE

John Bevan Catholic Bookseller, St. Francis, Great Doward, Ross–on–Wye, HR9 6DY. Tel: (01600) 890878. Fax: (01600) 890888. Website: www.catholicbooks.co.uk. E-mail: johnbevan@catholicbooks.co.uk. Est: 1978. Storeroom; appointment necessary. Medium stock. PR: £1–100. CC: MC; V. Cata: 4. Corresp: French, German.

Ross Old Books & Prints, ■ 51 & 52 High Street, Ross–on–Wye, HR9 5HH. Prop: Phil Thredder. Tel: (01989) 567458. Fax: (01989) 567861. Website: www.antiqueprints.com. E-mail: enquiries@rossoldbooks.co.uk. Est: 1986. Shop; open **M:** 10:00–17:00; **T:** 10:00–17:00; **W:** 10:00–17:00; **Th:** 10:00–17:00; **F:** 10:00–17:00; **S:** 10:00–17:00. Medium stock. Spec: Folio Society, The; History - Local; Topography - General. PR: £1–500. CC: AE; MC; V; SW, SO. Also, British county maps. Mem: PBFA.

WEOBLEY

The Weobley Bookshop, ■ 5 Portland Street, Weobley, HR4 8SB. Tel: Shop (01544) 319292. Fax: (01544) 319292. E-mail: karen@grovedesign.co.uk. Est: 1999. *Shop at:* Broad Street Books, 18 Broad Street, Ludlow, Shropshire, SY8 1NG. Open: **T:** 10:00–17:00; **W:** 10:00–17:00; **Th:** 10:00–17:00; **F:** 10:00–17:00; **S:** 10:00–17:00. Medium stock. PR: £2–100. CC: MC; V. Also, booksearch. Mem: BA. VAT No: GB 489 1728 94.

HERTFORDSHIRE

BERKHAMSTED

Heritage Antiques, ■ 24 Castle Street, Berkhamsted, HP4 2DD. Prop: David Mundy. Tel: (020) 7482 7087. Est: 1994. Shop; open **M:** 10:00–17:30; **T:** 10:00–17:30; **W:** 10:00–17:30; **Th:** 10:00–17:30; **F:** 10:00–17:30; **S:** 10:00–17:30; **Su:** 10:00–17:30. Small stock. Spec: Antiques; Art; Military; Topography - General; Transport; Travel - General. PR: £1–50. CC: MC; V. Postal Address: 3 Oakford Road, London NW5 1AJ. *Also at:* Nooks & Crannies, Chesham, Bucks HP5 1HG (q.v.).

Richard Frost, 'Sunhaven', Northchurch Common, Berkhamsted, HP4 1LR. Tel: (01442) 862011. E-mail: frost.family@freeuk.com. Est: 1989. Spec: Biography; First Editions; History - General; Literary Criticism; Philately; Topography - General; Travel - General. PR: £1–200.

Red Star Books, 4 Hamilton Road, Berkhamsted, HP4 3EF. Prop: Conor Pattenden. Tel: (01442) 870775. Website: www.abebooks.com/home/conorpattenden. E-mail: redstarbooks@freeuk.com. Est: 2001. Private premises; Internet and postal. Appointment necessary. Medium stock. Spec: Academic/Scholarly; History - General; Marxism; Politics; Radical Issues; Social History; Socialism; Sport - Football (Soccer); Trade Unions; War - Spanish Civil War; PR: £2–500. Cata: occasionally.

James Wilson, 22 Castle Street, Berkhamsted, HP4 2DW.

BISHOP'S STORTFORD

Sheila Rainford, White Pine Cottage, High St., Henham, Bishop's Stortford, CM2 6AS.

Ray Smith, 'Lynwood', 111 Parsonage Lane, Bishop's Stortford, CM23 5BA.

Edwin Trevorrow, 5 Pryors Close, Bishop's Stortford, CM23 5JX. Tel: (01279) 652902. Est: 1994. Spec: Biography; Countries - Melanesia; Fiction - General; Fiction - Historical; Fiction - Science Fiction; First Editions; Literature; Modern First Editions; Vintage Paperbacks. PR: £1–200.

BUSHEY

Aviation Book Supply, ■ 10 Pasture Close, Bushey, WD23 4HP. Prop: R.K. Tomlinson. Tel: (020) 8950-1724. Est: 1996. Appointment necessary. *Shop at:* Hardwick Airfield, Denton, Norfolk. Open: Medium stock. Spec: Aviation. PR: £5–250. CC: MC; V. Cata: 2 – a year. VAT No: GB 232 6072 90.

CHESHUNT

Denis W. Amos, 10 Mill Lane, Cheshunt, Waltham Cross, EN8 0JH. Tel: (01992) 630486. Est: 1948. Private premises; postal business only. Large stock. Spec: Gambling; Sport - General; Sport - Football (Soccer); Sport - Horse Racing (all aspects); Sport - Olympic Games, The; Sport - Racket Sports; Sport - Tennis. Also, booksearch.

ELSTREE

Elstree Books, 12 West View Gardens, Elstree, WD6 3DD.

HARPENDEN

Mavis Eggle, 34 Cowper Road, Harpenden, AL5 5NG. Tel: (01582) 762603. Fax: (01582) 762603. Est: 1979. Private premises; appointment necessary. Small stock. Spec: Antiquarian; Social History; Sport - Angling/Fishing; Technology. PR: £1–500. Mem: PBFA.

HATFIELD

Edna Whiteson Ltd., 22 Cornflower Way, Hatfield, AL10 9FU. Tel: (01707) 647716. Fax: (01707) 647716. E-mail: ednawhiteson_books@lineone.net. Est: 1962. Private premises; appointment necessary. Medium stock. Spec: First Editions; Limited Editions; Modern First Editions; Signed Editions; Topography - General; Travel - General. Also, booksearch. Cata: 4. Mem: ABA; PBFA.

Available from Richard Joseph Publishers Ltd
Sheppard's Book Dealers in
AUSTRALIA & NEW ZEALAND
4th Edition   (Royal H/b)   £27.00   252pp

HERTFORD

G. Collins (Book & Print Dealer), 39 Byde Street, Hertford, SG14 3AR.

Gillmark Gallery, 25 Parliament Square, Hertford, SG14 1EX.

Stobart Davies Limited, Priory House, 2 Priory Street, Hertford, SG14 1RN.

HITCHIN

Adrem Books, 7/9 Bury End, Pirton, Hitchin, SG5 3QB.

The Bookbug, 1, The Arcade, Hitchin, SG5 1ED. Prop: T.W. & S. Jevon. Tel: (01462) 431309. Est: 1986. PR: £1–10.

Eric T. Moore Books, ■ 24 Bridge Street, Hitchin, SG5 2DF. Tel: (01462) 450497. E-mail: booksales@erictmoore.co.uk. Est: 1965. Shop; open **M:** 09:30–17:00; **T:** 09:30–17:00; **W:** 09:30–17:00; **Th:** 09:30–17:00; **F:** 09:30–17:00; **S:** 09:30–17:30. Very large stock. Spec: CC: MC; V. VAT No: GB 759 7801 77.

Phillips of Hitchin (Antiques), ■ The Manor House, Hitchin, SG5 1JW. Prop: Jerome Phillips. Tel: (01462) 432067. Est: 1884. Shop; open **M:** 09:00–17:30; **T:** 09:00–17:30; **W:** 09:00–17:30; **Th:** 09:00–17:30; **F:** 09:00–17:30. Medium stock. Spec: Antiques; Applied Art; Architecture; Interior Design; Woodwork. PR: £5–3,000. CC: AE; E; MC; V. Also, booksearch. Cata: 1 – a year. Corresp: French, German, Italian, Spanish, Russian, Portuguese. VAT No: GB 197 1842 28.

LETCHWORTH GARDEN CITY

Barry Meaden (Aviation Books), Silverbirch Cottage, 26 Station Road, Letchworth Garden City, SG6 3BE. Tel: (01462) 678912. Website: www.ukbookworld.com/members/spitfire. E-mail: barrymeaden@waitrose.com. Postal business only. Spec: Aviation; Military; Naval. PR: £5–150. Also, booksearch.

MUCH HADHAM

H.M. Fletcher, Wynches Barn, Much Hadham, SG10 6BA.

RADLETT

G.L. Green Ltd., 18 Aldenham Avenue, Radlett, WD7 8HX.

RICKMANSWORTH

Clive A. Burden Ltd., Elmcote House, The Green, Croxley Green, Rickmansworth, WD3 3HN. Tel: (01923) 778097. Fax: (01923) 896520. E-mail: info@caburden.com. Est: 1966. Appointment necessary. Spec: Academic/Scholarly; Atlases; Illustrated; Travel - General. PR: £5–10,000. Also, large print books. Mem: ABA; ILAB; IMCoS.

SAINT ALBANS

Thomas Thorp, 64 Lancaster Road, St Albans, AL1 4ET. Prop: J.H.Thorp. Tel: 01727 864778. Fax: (01727) 854778. Website: www.abebooks.com/home/thorpbooks. E-mail: thorpbooks@compuserve.com. Est: 1883. Private premises; Internet and postal. Appointment necessary. Very small stock. Spec: Antiquarian; Private Press. PR: £25–5,000. CC: MC; V. Cata: 1. Mem: ABA; PBFA; ILAB. VAT No: GB 211 9058 89.

L.M.S. Books, 28 Orchard Street, St. Albans, AL3 4HL. Prop: Chris Fruin. Tel: (01727) 864339. Website: www.lmsbooks.co.uk. E-mail: lmsbooks@hotmail.com. Est: 1993. Office &/or bookroom; appointment necessary. Medium stock. Spec: Author - Pratchett, Terry; Countries - Melanesia; Countries - Mexico; Fiction - General; First Editions; Literature; Modern First Editions; Mysteries; Signed Editions. PR: £10–350. CC: MC; V; SW. Also, a selection of stock at: Biblion, London W1. Cata: – bi-monthly.

Parrots Books, The Gate Cottage, 12 Frogmore, Park St., St. Albans, AL2 2LL.

Paton Books, 34 Holywell Hill, St. Albans, AL1 1DE.

RM Books, 18 Cornwall Road, St. Albans, AL1 1SH. Prop: Robert Moore. Tel: (01727) 830058. Website: www.rmbooks.co.uk. E-mail: rmbooks@verulamium94.freeserve.co.uk. Est: 1988. Private premises; postal business only. Very small stock. Spec: Medicine; Medicine - History of; Science - General; Science - History of. PR: £10–100. Cata: – on request. Mem: PBFA.

Spineage Books, P.O. Box 248, St. Albans, AL1 8TX.

STEVENAGE

F.D. Davies, 52 Jackdaw Close, Stevenage, SG2 9DB.

The Strong Oak Press, P.O. Box 47, Stevenage, SG2 8PF.

TRING

David Ford Books, Midwood, Shire Lane, Cholesbury, Tring, HP23 6NA. Tel: (01494) 758663. E-mail: dford.books@ukgateway.net. Est: 1985. Private premises; Internet. Telephone first. Large stock. Spec: Art History; History - General; Military; Topography - General; Topography - Local; Travel - General. PR: £1–500. CC: JCB; MC; V. Mem: PBFA. *Also at:* Hertford Antique Centre, St Andrews St., Hertford and The Gillmark Gallery, Parliament Square, Hertford.

WATFORD

G. & R. Leapman Ltd., 37 Hogarth Court, High Street, Bushey, Watford, WD23 1BT. (*) Prop: Gillian Leapman. Tel: (020) 8950-2995. Fax: (020) 8950-4131. E-mail: gleapman1@compuserve.com. Est: 1970. Private premises; appointment necessary. Very small stock. Spec: Countries - Caribbean, The; Travel - Americas. PR: £10–1,000. Also, booksearch.

Musicalania, 30 Chester Road, Watford, WD18 0RQ. Tel: (01923) 230111. E-mail: musicalania@btinternet.com. Est: 1973. Private premises; Internet and postal. Telephone first. Small stock. Spec: Music - General; Music - Composers; Music - Popular. PR: £1–50. Cata: 5.

Peter Taylor & Son, 1 Ganders Ash, Leavesden, Watford, WD25 7HE. Tel: (01923) 663325. E-mail: taylorbooks@clara.co.uk. Est: 1973. Storeroom; postal business only. Medium stock. Spec: Academic/Scholarly; Antiquarian; Archaeology; Art History; Bibliography; Biography; Ecclesiastical History & Architecture; Fine & Rare; Heraldry; History - British; History - Irish; History - Local; History of Civilisation; History of Ideas; and others as listed in the Speciality Index. PR: £15–200. Cata: 4 – on the Middle Ages, Renaissance & early modern Bri. Corresp: French.

Westons Booksellers Ltd., 44 Stratford Road, Watford, WD17 4NZ. Prop: Jeremy Weston. Tel: (01923) 229081. Fax: (01923) 243343. Website: www.westons.co.uk. E-mail: books@westons.co.uk. Est: 1977. Private premises; appointment necessary. Medium stock. Spec: Engineering; Medicine; Science - General; Technology. PR: £3–300. CC: E; MC; V. Cata: 11 – and on the Internet. VAT No: GB 225 0259 93.

Norman Wright, 60 Eastbury Road, Watford, WD19 4JL. Tel: (01923) 232383. Est: 1989. Private premises; postal business only. Small stock. Spec: Children's - General; Comic Books & Annuals; Comics. PR: £5–500. Cata: 4 – a year on specialities.

ISLE OF WIGHT

BEMBRIDGE

Black & White Books, 7 The Ruskins, King's Road, Bembridge, PO35 5NY. (*) Prop: M.T. Kirk. Tel: 01983 875494. Website: www.ukbookworld.com. E-mail: m.kirk@which.net. Est: 1990. Private premises; Internet and postal. Appointment necessary. Very small general stock. PR: £4–100. Also, booksearch. *Also at:* Books for sale at the Hungerford Arcade, Berkshire.

COWES

Curtle Mead Books, Curtle Mead, Baring Road, Cowes, PO31 8DS. Prop: John Lucas. Tel: (01983) 294312. E-mail: lucas@curtlemead.demon.co.uk. Est: 1999. Private premises; telephone first. Small stock. Spec: Archaeology; Botany; Gardening; History - General; Maritime/Nautical; Natural History; Naval; Navigation; Ornithology; Ship Modelling; Shipbuilding; Sport - Yachting; Topography - Local; Travel - General. PR: £1–500. Also, booksearch. Cata: 1 – occasional. Corresp: German. Mem: PBFA.

FRESHWATER

Cameron House Books, Dimbola Lodge, Terrace Lane, Freshwater, PO40 9QE.

Golden Hours Bookshop, 113 School Green Road, Freshwater, PO40 9AZ.

R. Danzig, P.O. Box 7, Newport, PO30 2PY.

NEWPORT

Firsts in Print, 95 St. John's Road, Newport, PO30 1LS. Prop: Peter Elliston. Tel: (01983) 521748. Fax: (01983) 521373. Website: firsts-in-print.co.uk. E-mail: peterelliston@aol.com. Est: 1984. Private premises; Internet and postal. Appointment necessary. Open: **M:** 09:00–17:00; **T:** 09:00–17:00; **W:** 09:00–17:00; **Th:** 09:00–17:00; **F:** 09:00–17:00. Medium stock. Spec: Countries - Melanesia; Literature; Modern First Editions; Proof Copies; Signed Editions. PR: £3–1,000. CC: MC; V; SW. Cata: 5 – Every two months. *Also at:* Corner House, Lugley Street, Newport, Isle of Wight. VAT No: GB 768 9507 66.

Heritage Books, ■ 7 Cross Street, Ryde, PO33 2AD. Prop: Rev. D.H. Nearn. Tel: (01983) 562933. Fax: (01983) 812634. E-mail: heritagebooksryde@btconnect.com. Est: 1978. Shop; open **T:** 10:00–17:00; **W:** 09:00–17:00. **F:** 09:00–17:00; **S:** 10:00–17:00. Medium stock. Spec: Countries - Africa; Countries - Isle of Wight; Theology. PR: £1–100. Corresp: French, Portuguese. VAT No: GB 339 0615 58.

The Ryde Bookshop, ■ 135 High Street, Ryde, PO33 2RJ. Prop: M.D. Sames. Tel: (01983) 565227. Est: 1988. Shop; open **M:** 08:30–17:45; **T:** 08:30–17:45; **W:** 08:30–17:45; **Th:** 08:30–17:45; **F:** 08:30–17:45; S: 08:30–17:45. Very large general stock. Spec: CC: AE; E; JCB; MC; V. Also, new books.

P. & R. Gardiner, Rock Cottage, Oakhill Road, Seaview, PO34 5AL.

SAINT HELENS

Mother Goose Bookshop, West Green House, Upper Green Road, St. Helens. Prop: Valerie Edmondson. Tel: (01983) 874063. E-mail: mothergoosebooks@lycos.com. Est: 1980. Spec: Alpinism/Mountaineering; Author - General; Maritime/Nautical; Military. PR: £300–3,000.

VENTNOR

Emporium Books, 58 High Street, Ventnor, PO38 1LT.

Dealers who need to update their entry should visit their page on *www.sheppardsdirectories.com*

Shirley Lane Books, St. Lawrence Dene, Undercliff Drive, Ventnor, PO38 1XJ. Prop: Shirley Lane. Tel: (01983) 852309. Website: www.ukbookworld.com/members/Shirleylane. E-mail: shirleylane@talk21.com. Est: 1976. Private premises; Internet and postal. Appointment necessary. Small stock. Spec: Authors - Women; Children's - General; Cookery/Gastronomy; Feminism; Needlework; Women. PR: £1–500. Corresp: French.

Ventnor Rare Books, ■ 32 Pier Street, Ventnor, PO38 1SX. Prop: Nigel & Teresa Traylen. Tel: (01983) 853706. Fax: (01983) 854706. E-mail: vrb@andytron.demon.co.uk. Est: 1989. Shop; open **M:** 10:00–17:00; **T:** 10:00–17:00. **Th:** 10:00–17:00; **F:** 10:00–17:00; **S:** 10:00–17:00. Medium stock. Spec: Academic/Scholarly; Antiquarian; Art Reference; Bibliography; Bindings; Fiction - General; Literature; Military History; Royalty - General; Topography - General; Topography - Local; Transport. PR: £1–500. CC: MC; V; SW. Corresp: French. Mem: ABA; PBFA; ILAB. VAT No: GB 566 5246 19.

Alan Argent, Two Ways, Sconce Road, Norton, Yarmouth, PO41 0RT. Tel: (01983) 760851. Private premises; appointment necessary. Small stock. Spec: Sport - Yachting. PR: £3–100.

KENT

ASHFORD

D.R. & A.K. Flawn, 42 Magazine Road, Ashford, TN24 8NT.

Woodside Books, 1 Woodside Cottages, Westwell Lane, Ashford, TN26 1JB. Prop: Ann Gipps. Tel: (01233) 624495. Fax: (01233) 643926. E-mail: ann.gipps@btinternet.com. Est: 1991. Private premises; Internet and postal. Appointment necessary. Very small stock. Spec: Botany; Entomology; Natural History; Ornithology. PR: £1–500. CC: MC; V. Cata: 4 – 3 monthly.

BECKENHAM

Julia Sesemann, 10 Kemerton Road, Beckenham, BR3 6NJ. Tel: (020) 8658-6123. Est: 1977. Private premises; appointment necessary. Very small stock. Spec: Author - Blyton, Enid; Children's - General; Comic Books & Annuals; Illustrated; Juvenile. PR: £2–250. Cata: 1 – occasionally.

BIDDENDEN

P.R. & V. Sabin (Printed Works), Saxton House, The Nightingales, Biddenden, TN27 8HN. Tel: (01580) 715603. Fax: (01580) 714603. E-mail: paulsabin@btopenworld.com. Private premises; appointment necessary. Medium stock. Spec: Bibliography; Illustrated; Limited Editions; Manuscripts; Papermaking; Printing; Private Press. Also, booksearch. Mem: PBFA.

BROMLEY

Barry Chambers, 55 Recreation Road, Shortlands, Bromley, BR2 0DY. (*). Tel: (020) 8464-7354. E-mail: barrychambers@onetel.net.uk. Est: 1997. Private premises; postal business only. Very small stock. Spec: Natural History; Ornithology.

CANTERBURY

The Canterbury Bookshop, ■ 37 Northgate, Canterbury, CT1 1BL. Prop: David Miles. Tel: (01227) 464773. Fax: (01227) 780073. Website: canterburybookshop @btconnect.com. E-mail: canterburybookshop@btconnect.com. Est: 1980. Shop; open **M:** 10:00–17:00; **T:** 10:00–17:00; **W:** 10:00–17:00; **Th:** 10:00–17:00; **F:** 10:00–17:00; **S:** 10:00–17:00. Small stock. Spec: Children's - General; Illustrated; Juvenile; Typography. PR: £1–2,000. CC: MC; V. Fairs attended: all London, ABA, Olympia, Chelsea and in USA. Cata: 1 – occasionally. Mem: ABA; PBFA; ILAB.

The Chaucer Bookshop, ■ 6 & 7 Beer Cart Lane, Canterbury, CT1 2NY. Prop: Sir Robert Sherston–Baker, Bt. Tel: (01227) 453912. Fax: (01227) 451893. Website: www.chaucer-bookshop.co.uk. E-mail: chaucerbooks@btconnect.com. Est: 1956. Shop; open **M:** 10:00–17:00; **T:** 10:00–17:00; **W:** 10:00–17:00; **Th:** 10:00–17:00; **F:** 10:00–17:00; **S:** 10:00–17:00. Large stock. Spec: Antiquarian; Archaeology; Art; Bindings; Biography; History - General; Topography - General; Topography - Local. PR: £5–150. CC: AE; D; E; JCB; MC; V; SW. Mem: ABA; PBFA. VAT No: GB 332 9825 44.

Elham Valley Bookshop, St. Mary's Road, Elham, Canterbury, CT4 6TH.

Little Stour Books, North Court House, West Stourmouth, Nr Preston, Canterbury, CT3 1HT. Prop: Colin Button. Tel: (01227) 722371. Fax: (01227) 722021. Website: www.littlestourbooks.com. E-mail: sales@littlestourbooks.com. Est: 1996. Private premises; Internet and postal. Appointment necessary. Large stock. Spec: Author - Blyton, Enid; Author - Buckeridge, A.; Author - Crompton, Richmal; Author - Henty, G.A.; Author - Johns, W.E.; Author - Maclean, Alistair; Author - Oxenham, Elsie; Author - Rackham, Arthur; Author - Wodehouse, P.G.; Children's - General; and others as listed in the Speciality Index. PR: £6–500. CC: JCB; MC; V; SW; SO. Cata: 4. Mem: PBFA.

Dealers who need to update their entry should visit their page on
www.sheppardsdirectories.com

Oast Books, 1 Denstead Oast, Chartham Hatch, Canterbury, CT4 7SH. Prop: Bill & Jennie Reading. Tel: (01227) 730808. Fax: (01227) 730808. Website: members.aol.com/oastbooks/home.htm. E-mail: oastbooks@aol.com. Est: 1997. Postal business only. Small stock. Spec: Psychoanalysis; Psychology/ Psychiatry; Psychotherapy. PR: £2–40.

Periwinkle Press, ■ 197 Ashford Road, Canterbury, CT1 3XS. Prop: Antony & Clare Swain. Tel: (01227) 768516. E-mail: cswain1805@aol.com. Est: 1968. Shop; Internet and postal. *Shop at:* Faversham Antique Centre,7 Court Street, Faversham, (01795) 591471. Open: **M:** 10:00–17:00; **T:** 10:00–17:00; **W:** 10:00–14:00; **Th:** 10:00–17:00; **F:** 10:00–17:00; **S:** 10:00–17:00. Medium general stock. Spec: Author - Ardizzone, Edward; Children's - General; Self-Sufficiency; Topography - Local. PR: £1–100. CC: AE; JCB; V. Also, print and picture restoration. Picture Framing.

Tiger Books, Yew Tree Cottage, Westbere, Canterbury, CT2 0HH. Prop: Dr. Bryan & Mrs. Sylvia Harlow. Tel: (01227) 710030. Fax: (01227) 712066. E-mail: tiger@sharlow.fsbusiness.co.uk. Est: 1988. Private premises; appointment necessary. Large stock. Spec: Antiquarian; Author - Dickens, Charles; Fiction - Women; Literary Travel; Literature; Literature in Translation; Periodicals & Magazines. PR: £10–5,500. CC: E; JCB; MC; V. Also, a booksearch service. Cata: 6 – as specialities. Mem: ABA; BA; ILAB.

CHATHAM

Roadmaster Books, P.O. Box 176, Chatham, Kent, ME5 9AQ. Prop: Malcolm & Sue Wright. Tel: (01634) 862843. Fax: (01634) 201555. E-mail: susanwright@blueyonder.co.uk. Est: 1976. postal business only. Spec: Canals/Inland Waterways; Company History; Conservation; Dolls & Dolls' Houses; Flower Arranging; Geography; Geology; Motoring; Publishers - David & Charles; Publishing; Railways; Rural Life; Shipbuilding; Social History; Steam Engines; Topography - Local; and others as listed in the Speciality Index. PR: £1–350.

Sandstone Books, 14 Seymour Road, Chatham, ME5 7AE. Tel: (01634) 306437. Website: www.sandstonebooks.co.uk. E-mail: verne@sandstonebooks.co.uk. Est: 1989. Private premises; Internet and postal. Appointment necessary. Open: **M:** 09:00–20:00; **T:** 09:00–20:00; **W:** 09:00–20:00; **Th:** 09:00–20:00; **F:** 09:00–20:00; **S:** 09:00–20:00; **Su:** 09:00–20:00. Small stock. Spec: Modern First Editions. PR: £10–500. Cata: 4.

Sylvia Taylor, 45 Henry Street, Chatham, ME4 5NR.

CRANBROOK

Roundabout Books, 10 Campion Crescent, Cranbrook, TN17 3QJ.

DARTFORD

Douglas Biswell, 3 Keith Ave., Sutton at Hone, Dartford, DA4 9HH. Tel: (01322) 225522. E-mail: dougrbiswell@aol.com. postal business only. Very small stock. Spec: Astronomy. PR: £1–1,000.

Third Reich Books, 34 Walnut Tree Avenue, Dartford, DA1 1LJ. Prop: Mr. Jeremy Dixon. Tel: (01322) 279026. Fax: (01322) 279026. Website: www.thirdreichbooks.com. E-mail: trbooks@aol.com. Est: 1991. Private premises; postal business only. Telephone first. Very small stock. Spec: Holocaust; Memoirs; Military History; War - World War II. PR: £5–300. Also, a booksearch (Nazi Germany only).

DEAL

Books, ■ 168 High Street, Deal, CT14 6BQ. Prop: Peter Ritchie. Tel: (01304) 368662. Shop; open **Th:** 10:00–17:00; **F:** 10:00–17:00; **S:** 10:00–17:00. Medium stock. Spec: Antiques; Architecture; Art; Collecting. PR: £2–300.

J. Clarke–Hall Limited, 75 Middle Street, Deal, CT14 6HN. Prop: S.M. Edgecombe. Tel: (01304) 375467. Est: 1934. Private premises; appointment necessary. Very small general stock. PR: £5–750. Attends Bonnington Fair in June. Cata: 1 – occasionally on Samuel Johnson and his world.

The Golden Hind Bookshop, ■ 85 Beach Street, Deal, CT14 6JB. Prop: Josephine & Colin Whittington. Tel: (01304) 375086/37553. Fax: (01304) 375533. E-mail: goldenhind@freeuk.co.uk. Est: 1989. Shop; open **Th:** 10:30–17:00; **F:** 10:30–17:00; **S:** 10:30–17:00; **Su:** 10:30–17:00; Medium general stock. Spec: Biography; Children's - General; Countries - Melanesia; Fiction - General; History - General; Humour; Military; Poetry; Topography - General; Topography - Local; War - General. PR: £1–100. Corresp: French, Spanish, German, Italian.

McConnell Fine Books, 11 The Beach, Walmer, Deal, CT14 7HE. Prop: Nick McConnell. Tel: (01304) 368708. Website: www.abebooks.com/home/sandwichfinebooks. E-mail: mcconnellbooks@aol.com. Est: 1975. Private premises; appointment necessary. Small stock. Spec: Antiquarian; Bindings. PR: £20–10,000. CC: MC; V. Corresp: French, Russian. Mem: ABA; PBFA; ILAB.

DOVER

Pat Castleton, 26 Kearsney Avenue, Dover, CT16 3BU. Prop: Pat Castleton. Tel: (01304) 330371. E-mail: patriciacastleton@hotmail.com. Est: 1992. Private premises; Book fairs only. Appointment necessary. Very small stock. Spec: Animals and Birds; Author - General; Author - Dahl, Roald; Autobiography; Biography; Children's - General; Children's - Illustrated; Christmas; Gardening; Natural History; Pop-Up, 3D, Cut Out & Movable; Publishers - Ladybird Books; Publishers - Puffin; Sport - Angling/Fishing; Topography - General; Topography - Local. PR: £5–50. Regular stand at local markets,Country Fairs etc. Corresp: French.

EGERTON

Mindreaders Books, Forstal Corner Cottage, Egerton, TN27 9EH. Prop: Ali Jones. Tel: (01233) 756490. E-mail: info@mindreaders.co.uk. Est: 2000. Private premises; Internet and postal. Small stock. Spec: Psychotherapy. PR: £1–50. CC: MC; V.

FARNBOROUGH

Lewis First Editions, 9 Ferndale Way, Farnborough, BR6 7EL. Prop: David Fordyce. Tel: (01689) 854261. Website: www.abebooks.com/home/davidfordyce/. E-mail: lewisfirsteditions@hotmail.com. Est: 2000. Internet and postal. Small stock. Spec: Author - Lewis, C. S.; Author - Saville, M.; Author - Shute, Neville; Modern First Editions. PR: £5–2,000.

FAVERSHAM

Faversham Antique Centre, ■ 7 Court Street, Faversham, ME13 QBS. Prop: Antony Swain. Tel: (01795) 591471. Website: cswain1805@aol.com. E-mail: cswain1805@aol.com. Est: 1968. Shop; Internet and postal. Shop at: Periwinkle Press , 197 Ashford Road, Canterbury, Kent. CT1 3XS. Open: **M:** 10:00–17:00; **T:** 10:00–17:00; **W:** 10:00–14:30; **Th:** 10:00–17:00; **F:** 10:00–17:00; **S:** 10:00–17:00. Very small general stock. Spec: Topography - Local. PR: £1–100. Also, booksearch. CC: MC; V.

Faversham Books, 49 South Road, Faversham, ME13 7LS. Prop: Mr. & Mrs. C.M. Ardley. Tel: (01795) 532873. Est: 1979. Postal business only. Spec: Author - Kipling, Rudyard. PR: £1–500.

John O'Kill, 'Coulthorn Lodge', 9 Ospringe Road, Faversham, ME13 7LJ.

FOLKESTONE

Jenny Hurst, (formerly Bookstop), The Old Coach House, Rectory Lane, Lyminge, Folkestone, CT18 8EG.

G. & D. Marrin & Sons, ■ 149 Sandgate Road, Folkestone, CT20 2DA. Prop: John & Patrick Marrin. Tel: (01303) 253016. Fax: (01303) 850956. Website: www.marrinbook.clara.net. E-mail: marrinbook @clara.co.uk. Est: 1940. Shop; Internet and postal. Open: **T:** 09:30–17:30; **W:** 09:30–17:30; **Th:** 09:30–17:30; **F:** 09:30–17:30; **S:** 09:30–17:30. Medium stock. Spec: Topography - Local; War - World War I. PR: £1–5,000. CC: MC; V; Debit. Cata: 4 – on Kent topography & First World War. Mem: ABA; PBFA. VAT No: 316 6132 80.

Selling Books, Brandon Farm, Woodlands, Lyminge, Folkestone, CT18 8DP.

Searching for a title - and cannot find it on any Internet database?
Then try **Sheppard's Booksearch**

By selecting the subject classification – the request goes to all dealers who major in that subject.

Nick Spurrier, ■ 45 The Old High Street, Folkestone, CT20 1RN. Tel: (01303) 246100. Fax: (01303) 245800. Website: www.nick-spurrier.co.uk. E-mail: spurrier@btconnect.com. Est: 1977. Shop; appointment necessary. Medium stock. Spec: Black Studies; Company History; Economics; Feminism; History - General; Marxism; Pacifism; Philosophy; Politics; Psychology/Psychiatry; Radical Issues; Socialism; Trade Unions; War - General; Women. PR: £1–50. CC: JCB; MC. Also, booksearch. Cata: 8 – on economic history & other specialities. VAT No: GB 362 1931 64.

GRAVESEND

Hummingbird Books, 30 Laurel Avenue, Gravesend, DA12 5QP. Prop: Jill Gibbs. Tel: (01474) 537671. Fax: (01474) 537671. Website: hummingbirdbooks@btinternet.com. E-mail: hummingbirdbooks@btinternet.com. Est: 2001. Private premises; Internet. Appointment necessary. Small stock. Spec: Illustrated; Military History; Natural History; Needlework; Topography - General.

Manor Books, 1 Manor View, Spring Croft, Hartley, Longfield, Gravesend, DA3 8BA.

HERNE BAY

Barber Music, 85 Sea Street, Herne Bay, CT6 8QQ. Prop: Denis M. Allen. Tel: (01227) 375341. Est: 2000. Spec: Dance; Music - General; Musical Instruments. PR: £1–20.

Herne Bay Books, 2 Stanley Road, Herne Bay, CT6 5SH.

HYTHE

MilitaryHistoryBooks.com, ■ 27 High Street, Hythe, CT21 5AD. Prop: Ian H. & Gillian M. Knight. Tel: (01303) 237883. Fax: (01303) 268149. Website: www.militaryhistorybooks.com. E-mail: info@militaryhistorybooks.com. Est: 1970. Shop; Internet and postal. Open: **M:** 10:00–17:00; **T:** 10:00–17:00; **W:** 10:00–17:00; **Th:** 10:00–17:00; **F:** 10:00–17:00; **S:** 09:00–14:00. Large stock. Spec: Arms & Armour; Aviation; Espionage; Firearms/Guns; Military; Military History; War - General; Wargames. PR: £10–500. CC: AE; D; E; JCB; MC; V; SW. Also, booksearch. Cata: 4 – quarterly. VAT No: GB 770 7124 36.

The Old Gallery Bookshop, ■ 125 High Street, Hythe, CT21 5JJ. Prop: David & Philippa Hadaway. Tel: (01303) 269339. Est: 1990. Shop; open **M:** 10:00–17:00; **T:** 10:00–17:00; **W:** 10:00–13:00; **Th:** 10:00–17:00; **F:** 10:00–17:00; **S:** 09:00–17:00. Medium stock. Spec: Aviation; Maritime/Nautical; Military; Motoring; Ornithology; Railways; Transport. PR: £1–400. CC: E; MC; V. Winter: open 10:00 to 16:00 and closed Wednesday and Sunday.

LEIGH

Peter Davis, Old Farm Cottage, Lealands Avenue, Leigh, Tonbridge, TN11 8QU. Tel: (01732) 832275. Est: 1984. Private premises; appointment necessary. Small stock. Spec: Circus; Entertainment - General; Fairgrounds; Magic & Conjuring; Music - Music Hall; Performing Arts; Puppets & Marionettes. PR: £2–100. *Also at:* Kent Book Fairs. Corresp: French, German.

LYMINGE

Scott Brinded, 17 Greenbanks, Lyminge, CT18 8HG. Tel: (01303) 862258. Est: 1991. Private premises; postal business only. Small stock. Spec: Antiquarian; Bibliography; Books about Books; Literature; Palaeography; Papermaking; Printing; Topography - General; Typography. PR: £1–5,000. CC: MC; V. Cata: 2 – a year.

MAIDSTONE

Peter Blest, Little Canon Cottage, Wateringbury, Maidstone, ME18 5PJ. Prop: Peter & Jan Blest. Tel: (01622) 812940. Est: 1974. Private premises; postal business only. Very large stock. Spec: Agriculture; Animals and Birds; Botany; Cockfighting; Entomology; Flower Arranging; Gardening; Herbalism; Herpetology; Horticulture; Natural History; New Naturalist; Ornithology; Plant Hunting; Poultry; Rural Life; Sport - Angling/Fishing; Sport - Shooting; Taxidermy; Zoology. PR: £5–5,000. CC: E; MC; V. Cata: 1 – on natural history, gardening, field sports. Mem: PBFA.

Cobnar Books, 567 Red Hill, Wateringbury, Maidstone, ME18 5BE. Prop: Larry Ilott. Tel: (01622) 813230. Fax: (0870) 0567232. Website: books@cobnar.co.uk. E-mail: books@cobnar.demon.co.uk. Private premises; postal business only. Appointment necessary. Spec: Antiquarian; Bibliography; Printing; Topography - Local. PR: £10–2,000. CC: MC; V. Cata: – occasionally. Mem: PBFA. VAT No: GB 702 4681 56.

Jill Howell, Photographic Book, Hopview Cottage, 1, Hilltop, Hunton, Maidstone, ME15 0QP. Prop:Jill Howell. Tel: (01622) 820899. Fax: (01622) 820899. E-mail: jillphotobooks@aol.com. Est: 1993. Private premises; postal business only. Appointment necessary. Small stock. PR: £3–1,000. Also, a booksearch service in specialist subject only. Cata: 3. Corresp: French. Mem: PBFA.

MARGATE

Ian Stewart, 72 Northumberland Avenue, Margate, CT9 3LY. Tel: (01843) 230790. Fax: (0709) 2024636. E-mail: ianstewart@baroka.freeserve.co.uk. Est: 1999. Private premises; Internet. Appointment necessary. Small stock. Spec: Architecture; Civil Engineering; History - Design; Interior Design. PR: £3–200.

ORPINGTON

Roland Books, 60 Birchwood Road, Petts Wood, Orpington, BR5 1NZ. Prop: A.R. Hughes. Tel: (01689) 838872. Fax: (01689) 838872. E-mail: py32@dial.pipex.com. Private premises; postal business only. Open: **M:** 09:00–17:00; **T:** 09:00–17:00; **W:** 09:00–17:00; **Th:** 09:00–17:00; **F:** 09:00–17:00. Medium general stock. Spec: Architecture; Art; Buses/Trams; Business Studies; Crime (True); Entertainment - General; Fiction - General; History - General; Military History; Motoring; Music - Rock; Natural History; Philosophy; Railways; Sport - General; Transport; Travel - General. PR: £2–75. CC: MC; V; SW.

RAINHAM

The Book Mark, Unit 15c, Rainham Shopping Centre, Rainham, ME8 9HW. Prop: G. Harrison. Tel: (01634) 365987. Est: 1992. PR: £1–30.

RAMSGATE

Arcady Books, 5 Chatham Street, Ramsgate.

michaelsbookshop.com, ■ 72 King St., Ramsgate, CT11 8NY. Prop: Michael Child. Tel: (01843) 589500. Website: www.michaelsbookshop.com. E-mail: michaelsbookshop@aol.com. Est: 1984. Shop; Internet and postal. Open: **M:** 09:30–17:30; **T:** 09:30–17:30; **W:** 09:30–17:30; **Th:** 09:30–17:30; **F:** 09:30–17:30; **S:** 09:30–17:30; **Su:** 11:00–16:00. Very large general stock. PR: £1–100. CC: MC; V.

Yesteryear Railwayana, Stablings Cottage, Goodwin Road, Ramsgate, CT11 0JJ. Prop: Patrick & Mary Mullen. Tel: 01843 587283. Fax: (01843) 587283. Website: www.yesrail.co.uk. E-mail: mullen@yesrail.com. Est: 1978. Private premises; Internet and postal. Large stock. Spec: Railways. PR: £1–500. CC: AE; JCB; MC. Cata: 9 – Every six weeks.

SEVENOAKS

Roderick M. Barron, The Antique Map Specialist, P.O. Box 67, Sevenoaks, TN13 3WW. Tel: (01732) 742558. Fax: (01732) 742558. Website: www.barron.co.uk. E-mail: rod@barron.co.uk. Est: 1989. Postal business only. Spec: Atlases. PR: £100–10,500.

Garwood & Voigt, 55 Bayham Road, Sevenoaks, TN13 3XE.

Geophysical Books, 82 Granville Road, Sevenoaks, TN13 1HA.

Chas J. Sawyer, P.O. Box 170, Sevenoaks, TN13 3QF. Tel: (01732) 457262. Fax: (01732) 742026. E-mail: cjsbks@compuserve.com. Est: 1894. Private premises; appointment necessary. Very small stock. Spec: Africana; Bibliography; Bindings; Churchilliana; City of London. PR: £20–5,000. CC: AE; MC; V. Cata: 1 – occasionally. Stock also at: Jonathan Potter Ltd, London W. (q.v.).

Martin Wood Cricket Books, 1c Wickenden Road, Sevenoaks, TN13 3PJ. Tel: (01732) 457205. Fax: (01732) 457205. Est: 1970. Private premises; appointment necessary. Small stock. Spec: Sport - Cricket. PR: £1–500. Cata: 1 – on cricket every January.

SITTINGBOURNE

J. & J. Fox Books, 48 Woodstock Road, Sittingbourne, ME10 4HN. Prop: M.V. Fox. Tel: (01795) 470310. Fax: (01795) 470310. E-mail: jjfoxbooks@clara.net. Est: 1981. Storeroom; appointment necessary. Small stock. Spec: Antiquarian; Cookery/Gastronomy; Maritime/Nautical; Military; Typography. PR: £10–1,500. CC: AE; D; E; JCB; MC; V. Cata: 1 – occasionally. Corresp: French, Portugese, Spanish. Mem: PBFA.

Underwater Antiques, 123 Peregrine Drive, Sittingbourne, ME10 4UG. Tel: (01795) 472664. E-mail: philsidey@aol.com. Postal business only. Spec: Antiquarian; Author - Cecil, H; Crime (True); Maritime/Nautical; Modern First Editions; Sport - Diving/Sub-Aqua. PR: £3–300.

SMARDEN

Mrs Janet Cameron, The Meeting House, Smarden, TN27 8NR. Est: 1992. Private premises; postal business only. Small general stock.

STAPLEHURST

Stained Glass Books, 17, Marden Road, Staplehurst, TN12 0NF. Prop: K.R. & S.J. Hill. Tel: (01580) 891692. Website: www.glassconservation.com. E-mail: bookmail@glassconservation.com. Est: 1987. Private premises; postal business only. Very small stock. PR: £5–500.

TEYNHAM

Colin Barnard, 54 London Road, Teynham, Sittingbourne, ME9 9QN. Tel: (01795) 521167. E-mail: cgb@dcs.qmw.ac.uk. Est: 1990. Postal business only. Medium stock. PR: £1–200. Also, a booksearch service.

TONBRIDGE

C. & A.J. Barmby, 140 Lavender Hill, Tonbridge, TN9 2AY. Prop: Chris & Angela Barmby. Tel: (01732) 771590. Fax: (01732) 771590. Website: bookpilot@aol.com. E-mail: bookpilot@aol.com. Est: 1981. Storeroom; Internet and postal. Appointment necessary. Medium stock. Spec: Antiquarian; Antiques; Applied Art; Archaeology; Art; Art Reference; Carpets; Ceramics; Collecting; Decorative Art; Gemmology; Glass; Horology; Jewellery; Maritime/Nautical; Musical Instruments; Sport - Cricket; Stained Glass; Topography - Local; and others as listed in the Speciality Index. PR: £2–500. CC: MC; V; SW. VAT No: GB 367 4200 58.

Grant Demar Books, 15 White Cottage Road, Tonbridge, TN10 4PX. Tel: (01732) 360208. Est: 1977. Private premises; appointment necessary. Small stock. Spec: Animals and Birds; Conservation; Entomology; Natural History; Ornithology; Zoology. PR: £1–1,000. Cata: 2 – a year.

Invicta Booksearch, 63 Weald View Road, Tonbridge, TN9 2NQ.

Tony Skelton, The Old School House, Shipbourne, Tonbridge, TN11 9PB. Prop: D.A.L. Skelton. Tel: (01732) 810481. E-mail: tskelt@waitrose.com. Est: 1992. Private premises; Internet and postal. Open **M:** 09:30–17:00; **T:** 09:09–20:20; **W:** 09:00–19:00. Small stock. Spec: Countries - Ireland; Literature; Modern First Editions; Publishers - Penguin. PR: £5–500. Also booksearch. Corresp: French, German. Mem: PBFA. VAT No: GB 796 5067 79.

P. & F. Whelan, 68 The Drive, Tonbridge, TN9 2LR. Prop: Tony & Mary Whelan. Tel: (01732) 354882. Fax: (01732) 354882. E-mail: whelanirishbooks@lineone.net. Est: 1986. Private premises; postal business only. Small stock. Spec: Countries - Ireland; History - National; Irish Interest. PR: £5–250. Cata: 3 – on history of Ireland, Irish literature & guidebooks.

Anthony Whittaker, Four Seasons, Chillmill Green, Brenchley, Tonbridge, TN12 7AL. Tel: (01892) 723494. E-mail: bookant@hotmail.com. Est: 1980. Private premises and book fairs only. Appointment necessary. Spec: CC: MC; V. Mem: PBFA.

TUNBRIDGE WELLS

Hall's Bookshop, ■ 20–22 Chapel Place, Tunbridge Wells, TN1 1YQ. Prop: Sabrina Izzard. Tel: (01892) 527842. Fax: (01892) 527842. Est: 1869. Shop; open **M:** 09:30–17:00; **T:** 09:30–17:00; **W:** 09:30–17:00; **Th:** 09:30–17:00; **F:** 09:30–17:00; **S:** 08:30–17:00. Large stock. Spec: Art; Bindings; Biography; History - General; Literature; Natural History; Topography - General; Travel - General. Also, booksearch. Mem: PBFA.

The Old Bank Bookshop, The Old Bank, Station Road, Groombridge, Tunbridge Wells, TN3 9QY.

Dealers who need to update their entry should visit their page on
www.sheppardsdirectories.com

World War Books, Oaklands, Camden Park, Tunbridge Wells, TN2 5AE. Prop: Tim Harper. Tel: (01892) 538465. Fax: (01892) 538465. E-mail: wwarbooks@btinternet.com. Est: 1993. Private premises; Internet and postal. Medium stock. Spec: Aviation; Holocaust; Maritime/Nautical; Military; School Registers/Rolls of Honour; War - General. PR: £10–5,000. CC: MC; V. Cata: 2. Mem: PBFA; OMRS.

WADHURST

Riseden Books, Old Snape House, Snape, Wadhurst, East Sussex, TN5 6NX.

WHITSTABLE

Ancient History Books, 96 Applegarth Park, Seasalter Lane, Seasalter, Whitstable, CT5 4BZ.

Alan & Margaret Edwards, 10 Meteor Avenue, Whitstable, CT5 4DH. Tel: (01227) 262276. Fax: (01227) 261158. E-mail: a.m.books@lineone.net. Est: 1988. Private premises; postal business only. Small stock. Spec: Ecclesiastical History & Architecture; Theology. PR: £1–500. Cata: 3. Corresp: French, German.

David B. Revell, 47 Saddleton Road, Whitstable, CT5 4JH.

LANCASHIRE

BARNOLDSWICK
Collector's Corner, 13 Wellhouse Road, Barnoldswick, BB8 6DB.

BLACKBURN
The Bookshelf, c/o 10 Pendle Road, Great Harwood, Blackburn, BB6 7TN. Prop: Jeff & Jean Taylor. Tel: (01254) 884242. Fax: (01254) 876233. Website: abebooks.com. E-mail: thebshelf@aol.com. Est: 1998. Private premises; Internet. Small stock. PR: £1–50. CC: AE; MC; V.

Neil Summersgill, Pigeon Hall, Abbott Brow, Mellor, Nr. Blackburn, BB2 7HT. Tel: (01254) 813559. Fax: (01254) 813559. E-mail: summersgill@worldonline.co.uk. Est: 1984. Private premises; Internet and postal. Appointment necessary. Very small stock. Spec: Antiquarian; Atlases; Autographs; Bindings; Letters; Manuscripts; Natural History; Sport - Field Sports; Travel - General. PR: £10–3,000. Mem: PBFA.

BLACKPOOL
Book Mad, 151 Church Street, Blackpool, FY1 3NX.

Chevet Supplies Ltd., 157 Dickson Road, Blackpool, FY1 2EU.

Bob Dobson, 3 Staining Rise, Staining, Blackpool, FY3 0BU. Tel: (01253) 895678. Fax: (01253) 895678. E-mail: bobdobson@amserve.com. Est: 1969. Private premises; appointment necessary. Large stock. Spec: History - Local; Topography - Local. PR: £1–100. Incl: books on Lancashire, Yorkshire and Cheshire. Also publishes as Landy Publishing. Cata: 6 – 2 each year on Lancashire, Yorkshire, Cheshire. VAT No: GB 534 3982 30.

John McGlynn, 173 Newton Drive, Blackpool, FY3 8ND.

BURY
Richard Byrom Textile Bookroom, 3 Hawkshaw Lane, Bury, BL8 4JZ. Tel: (01204) 880155. Fax: (01204) 880155. Est: 1984. Private premises; appointment necessary. Medium stock. Spec: Carpets; Company History; Crochet; Embroidery; Fashion & Costume; Industry; Knitting; Lace; Sheep/Shepherding; Social History; Tapestry; Textiles; Trade Unions. PR: £1–500.

CARNFORTH
The Carnforth Bookshop, ■ 38–42 Market Street, Carnforth, LA5 9JX. Prop: P. & G. Seward. Tel: (01524) 734588. Fax: (01524) 735893. Website: www.carnforthbooks.co.uk. E-mail: carnforth bkshop@aol.com. Shop; Internet and postal. Open: **M:** 09:00–17:30; **T:** 09:00–17:30; **W:** 09:00–17:30; **Th:** 09:00–17:30; **F:** 09:00–17:30; **S:** 09:00–17:30. Very large stock. Spec: Alpinism/Mountaineering; Art; Art History; Biography; Classical Studies; Fiction - General; Fine & Rare; Gardening; History - General; History - Local; History - National; Languages - Foreign; Literature; Military History; Music - General; and others as listed in the Speciality Index. PR: £1–500. CC: AE; E; MC; V. Also, Booksearch. Mem: BA. VAT No: GB 306 8293 93.

F.N. Crack (Books), 2 Sawmill Cottages, Burton–in–Lonsdale, Carnforth, LA6 3JS. Prop: Noel Crack. Tel: (015242) 61244. Est: 1978. Private premises; appointment necessary. Small stock. Spec: Animals and Birds; Botany; Entomology; Gardening; Natural History; Natural Sciences; Ornithology; Sport - Falconry; Sport - Field Sports; Taxidermy. PR: £2–600. Cata: 2 – a year. Mem: PBFA.

Philip Vernon, 47 Slyne Road, Bolton–le–Sands, Carnforth, Lancashire, LA5 8AQ.

CHORLEY
Liz Berry Books, 5 Rylands Road, Chorley, PR7 2DN.

Bowland Bookfinders, 88 Bury Lane, Withnell, Chorley, PR6 8SD. (*) Prop: D. S. Suttie. Tel: (01254) 830619. E-mail: david@bookfind.freeserve.co.uk. Est: 1987. Private premises; postal business only. appointment necessary. Also, booksearch.

Browse Books, 10 Silverdale Close, Worden Park, Leyland, Chorley, PR5 2BY.

Modern Firsts Etc., Emminster House, 114 School Lane, Brinscall, Chorley, PR6 8PU. Prop: R.J. Leek. Tel: (01254) 830861. Fax: (01254) 830861. Est: 1985. Private premises; postal business only.Very small stock. Spec: Autographs; First Editions; Painting. PR: £1–500.

Bowdon Books, ■ 33 Lowergate, Clitheroe, BB7 1AD. Prop: Gordon & Gillian Hill. Tel: (01200) 425333. Fax: (01200) 443490. E-mail: gor15@dial.pipex.com. Est: 1987. Shop; open **T:** 10:00–17:00. **Th:** 10:00–17:00; **F:** 10:00–17:00; **S:** 10:00–17:00. Medium general stock. Spec: Fashion & Costume; Needlework; Textiles; Topography - Local. PR: £5–500. CC: JCB; MC; V; SW. Also, book fairs. Mem: PBFA.

CLITHEROE

Moorside Books, ■ Moorside Cottage, Whalley Old Road, Billington, Clitheroe, BB7 9JF. Prop: David Sedgwick. Tel: (01254) 824104. E-mail: dsbooks@easynet.co.uk. Est: 1985. Shop; open **T:** 10:00–17:00. **Th:** 10:00–17:00; **F:** 10:00–17:00; **S:** 10:00–17:00. Spec: Astronomy; Author - Lawrence, T.E.; Bindings; Physics; Science - General; Science - History of; Travel - Asia; Travel - Middle East. PR: £5–2,500. CC: MC; V; SW. Cata: 1. Mem: PBFA; *Also at:* 29 Moor Lane, Clitheroe, Lancs.

Roundstone Books, 29 Moor Lane, Clitheroe, BB7 1BE. Prop: Jo Harding. Tel: (01200) 444242. Website: www.roundstonebooks.co.uk. E-mail: joharbooks@aol.com. Est: 1995. Spec: Academic/Scholarly; Alternative Medicine; Biography; Children's - General; Countries - Poland; Drama; Feminism; First Editions; History - General; Languages - Foreign; Literary Criticism; Literature; Poetry; Travel - General. PR: £1–100. Also, free booksearch.

COLNE

Liber Books, 3 Hartington Street, Winewall, Colne, BB8 8DB.

DARWEN

Bygone Books, 27 Glenshiels Avenue, Hoddlesden, Darwen, BB3 3LS. Prop: Gordon French. Tel: (01254) 703077. Website: www.bygonebooks.fsnet.co.uk. E-mail: gordonandjen@bygonebooks.fsnet.co.uk. Est: 1992. Private premises; Internet and postal. Telephone first. Very small stock. Spec: Children's - General; Fiction - General; First Editions; Topography - General. PR: £2–80. CC: MC; V. Also, booksearch. Mem: PBFA.

Red Rose Books, 478, Bolton Road, Darwen, BB3 2JR. Prop: K.M. Tebay. Tel: (01254) 776767. Website: www.cricketsupplies.com/books. E-mail: redrosebooks@btinternet.com. Est: 1993. Private premises; Internet and postal. Appointment necessary. Small stock. Spec: Sport - Cricket. PR: £1–1,000. CC: AE; MC; V. Cata: 5. Mem: PBFA. VAT No: GB 693 2135 32.

FENCE

Pendleside Books, 359 Wheatley Lane Road, Fence, Nr. Burnley, BB12 9QA. Prop: Edward Sutcliffe. Tel: (01282) 615617. Est: 1974. Private premises; appointment necessary. Small stock. Spec: Entomology; Mycology; Topography - Local. CC: JCB; MC; V.

HALTON

Mark Towers, 45 Beech Road, Halton, LA2 6QQ.

LANCASTER

Austwick Hall Books, Austwick Hall, Austwick, Near Settle, Lancaster, LA2 8BS. Tel: (015242) 51794. E-mail: austwickhall@btinternet.com. Spec: Animals and Birds; Anthropology; Biology; Botany; Conservation; Countries - Iceland; Entomology; Evolution; Farriers; Fine & Rare; First Editions; Medicine; Natural History; Phrenology; Science - General; Voyages & Discovery. PR: £5–2,000. Also, booksearch.

Daemon Books, 9 King's Arcade, King St., Lancaster, LA1 1LE.

Interstellar Master Traders, 33 North Road, Lancaster, LA1 1NS.

PRESTON

Great Grandfather's, ■ 82 Towngate, Leyland, Preston, PR25 2LR. Prop: Greg D. Smith. Tel: (01772) 422268. E-mail: books@greatgrandfathers.fsnet.co.uk. Est: 1985. Shop; open **T:** 10:00–17:30. **Th:** 10:00–16:30; **F:** 10:00–17:30; **S:** 10:00–17:30. Large stock. Spec: Natural History; Topography - Local. PR: £1–200. Open other times by appointment. Corresp: French, German. Mem: PBFA.

LYTHAM ST. ANNES

Dobel's Books, 18 Orchard Road, St. Annes on Sea, Lytham St. Annes.

Bygone Tunes, 19 Churchside, New Longton, Preston, PR4 4LU. Prop: Jean Billington. Tel: (01772) 613729. E-mail: jean@bygonetunes.com. Est: 1975. Private premises; postal business only. Large general stock. Spec: Music - General; Music - Jazz; Music - Printed. PR: £3–10.

PRESTON

V.J. Moss Antiquarian Books, 83 Chaigley Road, Longridge, Preston, PR3 3TQ. Tel: (01772) 782943. Fax: (01772) 782943. E-mail: vjmoss@onetel.net.uk. Est: 1982. Private premises; Internet and postal. Appointment necessary. Large stock. Spec: Bibliography; Bindings; Books about Books; Collecting; Papermaking; Printing; Publishing; Typography. PR: £10–2,000. Also, booksearch. Cata: 2 – books about books. VAT No: GB 604 5317 68.

O'Connor Fine Books, 9 Garrison Road, Fulwood, Preston, PR2 8AL. Prop: John and Evelyn O'Connor. Tel: (01772) 719359. E-mail: oconnorfinebooks@hotmail.com. Est: 2002. Private premises; appointment necessary. Very small stock. Spec: Bibliography; Bindings; Collecting; Design; Illustrated; Papermaking; Printing; Private Press; Publishing; Typography. Cata: 2 – a year. Corresp: French.

Pamona Books, 28 Canberra Road, Leyland, Preston, PR5 2JH.

Preston Book Company, ■ 68 Friargate, Preston, PR1 2ED. Prop: M. Halewood. Tel: (01772) 252613. E-mail: prestonrarebooks@halewood221b.freeserve.co.uk. Est: 1960. Shop; Internet and postal. Open: **M:** 10:00–17:00; **T:** 10:00–17:00; **W:** 10:00–17:00; **Th:** 10:00–17:00; **F:** 10:00–17:00; **S:** 10:00–17:00. Large general stock. Spec: Americana; Atlases; Author - Conan Doyle, Sir Arthur; Colour-Plate; Sherlockiana; Travel - General. PR: £10–1,000. CC: JCB; MC.

SARDEN

Mayflower Books, 67 Whalley Road, Sabden, BB7 9ED.

SAINT ANNES ON SEA

BookstopUK, 47 St. David's Road North, Saint Annes on Sea, FY8 2BS. Prop: Ian & Jackie Allen. Tel: (01253) 721676. Fax: (0870) 129 4686. Website: www.bookstopuk.co.uk. E-mail: bookstopuk@clara.co.uk. Est: 2000. Private premises; Internet and postal. Appointment necessary. Very small general stock. Spec: Academic/Scholarly; Advertising; Aeronautics; Fiction - General; Fiction - Crime, Detective, Spy, Thrillers; Fiction - Fantasy, Horror; Fiction - Historical; Fiction - Science Fiction; Modern First Editions; Proof Copies.

SALFORD

Coffee Gourmet, 30 Holden Road, Salford, Greater Manchester, M7 4LR.

THORNTON

Seabreeze Books, 39 Woodfield Road, Thornton, Cleveleys, FY5 4EQ.

Dealers who need to update their entry should visit their page on
www.sheppardsdirectories.com

LEICESTERSHIRE

HINCKLEY

Caduceus Books, 28 Darley Road, Burbage, Hinckley, LE10 2RL. Prop: Ben Fernee. Tel: (01455) 250542. Fax: (0870) 055-2982. Website: www.io.com/~albion/caduceus/ or www.cadu.demon.co. E-mail: ben@cadu.demon.co.uk. Est: 1989. Private premises; appointment necessary. Very small stock. Spec: Alchemy; Astrology; Esoteric; Occult; Supernatural; Witchcraft. PR: £1–1,000. CC: MC; V. Also, manuscripts, associated items.

KIBWORTH HARCOURT

The Countryman's Gallery, ■ , Kibworth Harcourt, LE8 0NE. Prop: Pamela M. Turnbull. Tel: (0116) 279-3211. Fax: (0116) 279-2437. Shop; appointment necessary. Small stock. Spec: Dogs; Illustrated; Private Press; Rural Life; Sport - Field Sports; Sport - Hunting; Topography - General. PR: £1–500. CC: MC; V. Cata: – on request.

LEICESTER

Aucott & Thomas, 45 Mount Ave., Barwell, Leicester, LE9 8AJ.

Black Cat Bookshop, ■ 90 Charles St., Leicester, LE1 1GE. Prop: Philip & Karen Woolley. Tel: (0116) 251-2756. Fax: (0116) 281-3545. Website: www.blackcatbookshop.com. E-mail: blackcatuk@ aol.com. Est: 1987. Shop; Internet and postal. *Shop at:* www.blackcatbookshop.com. Open: M: 09:30–17:00; T: 09:30–17:00; W: 09:30–17:00; Th: 09:30–17:00; F: 09:30–17:00; S: 09:30–17:00. Large general stock. Spec: Author - Conan Doyle, Sir Arthur; Author - Fleming, Ian; Children's - General; Comic Books & Annuals; Comics; Counterculture; Countries - Melanesia; Countries - Mexico; Fiction - General; Fiction - Historical; Fiction - Science Fiction; Music - Pop; and others as listed in the Speciality Index. PR: £1–500. CC: E; JCB; MC; V; SW, De. Cata: 5 – various subjects 2-3 times a years.

Cottage Books, Gelsmoor, Coleorton, Leicester, LE67 8HR. (*) Prop: Jennifer M. Boyd–Cropley. Tel: . Est: 1970. Private premises; postal business only. Medium stock. Spec: Agriculture; Architecture; Canals/Inland Waterways; Crafts; Fairgrounds; Folklore; Gypsies; History - Local; Landscape; Rural Life; Scottish Interest; Social History; Traction Engines; Windmills & Watermills. PR: £1–2,000. Cata: 10 – 6 on rural subjects & 4 on Gypsies and fairs.

Cyclamen Books, P.O. Box 69, Leicester, LE1 9EW. Prop: D. & Y. Abramski. Fax: (0116) 270-4623. E-mail: rara@cyclamenbooks.com. Est: 1976. Storeroom; postal business only. *Shop at:* 18 Ashclose Avenue, Leicester LE2 3WA. Very large general stock. Spec: Academic/Scholarly; Advertising; Africana; Countries - Balkans, The; Countries - Central Asia; Countries - East Europe; Countries - France; Countries - Middle East, The; Countries - Russia; Criminology; Feminism; Languages - Foreign; Media; Pacifism. PR: £10–100. Corresp: French.

Rebecca Dearman Rare Books, ■ 2 Francis Street, Stonygate, Leicester, LE2 BD. Tel: (0116) 270-9666. Website: rebeccadearmanrarebooks.co.uk. E-mail: rebeccadearman@hotmail.com. Est: 1967. Shop; Internet and postal. Open: **T:** 09:00–17:30; **W:** 09:00–17:30; **Th:** 09:00–17:30; **F:** 09:00–17:30; **S:** 09:00–18:00. Large general stock. PR: £1–1,000. Cata: 3.

Ice House Books, 19 Hall Road, Leicester, LE7 9SY. Prop: Eleanor S. Davidson. Tel: (0116) 292 1964. E-mail: eleanor@icehousebooks.co.uk. Web Site: www.icehousebooks.co.uk. Warehouse, Internet and postal. Appointment necessary. Open **M:** 09:00–19:00; **T:** 09:00–19:00; **W:** 09:00–19:00; **Th:** 09:00–19:00; **F:** 09:00–19:00; **S:** 09:00–17:00; **Su:** 10:00–17:00. Closed for lunch: 12:00–13:00. Large stock. Spec: Academic/Scholarly; Animals and Birds; Anthropology; Art; Arts, The; Biography; Biology; Botany; Building & Construction; Business Studies; and others as listed in the Speciality Index. PR: £5–2,000. Cata: weekly web updates.

Bruce Main–Smith & Co. Ltd., 132, Saffron Road, Wigston, Leicester, LE18 4UP. (*) Prop: D.R. & M.E. Mitchell (Directors). Tel: (0116) 277-7669. Fax: (0116) 277-7669. Website: www.brucemainsmith.com. E-mail: sales@brucemainsmith.com. Est: 1972. Spec: Motorbikes. PR: £4–100. CC: MC; V; SW. Also, virtually a complete stock of all new motor cycle books, plus 4,000 photocopied manuals, spares lists & brochures.

Maynard & Bradley, 1 Royal Arcade, Silver Street, Leicester, LE1 5YW.

Pooks Motor Books, ■ Unit 4, Fowke Street, Rothley, Leicester, LE7 7PJ. (*) Prop: Barrie Pook & John Pook. Tel: (0116) 237-6222. Fax: (0116) 237-6491. E-mail: pooks.motorbooks@virgin.net. Shop; open **M:** 09:00–17:00; **T:** 09:00–17:00; **W:** 09:00–17:00; **Th:** 09:00–17:00; **F:** 09:00–17:00. Very large stock. Spec: Biography; Marque Histories (see also motoring); Motorbikes; Motoring; Transport; Vintage Cars. PR: £3–1,000. CC: MC; V. Also, sales catalogues for cars & motorcycles.

Rosanda Books, 11 Whiteoaks Road, Oadby, Leicester, LE2 5YL. Prop: David Baldwin BA, M. Phil. & Joyce Baldwin. Tel: (0116) 2713880. E-mail: dbaldwin@themutual.net. Est: 1994. Private premises; appointment necessary. Spec: History - Ancient; History - British; History - European; History - Middle Ages. PR: £2–50. Cata: 3 – History.

Tin Drum Books, 68 Narborough Road, Leicester, LE3 0BR.

Treasure Trove Books, 21 Mayfield Road, Leicester, LE2 1SR.

Tony Yates Antiquarian Books, 3 Melton Avenue, Leicester, LE4 7SE. Tel: (0116) 266-1891. E-mail: tonyyatesbooks@btopenworld.com. Est: 1989. Private premises; appointment necessary. Small stock. Spec: Antiquarian; Children's - General; Education & School; Illustrated; Literature; Topography - Local. PR: £2–1,000. Cata: 1 – a year.

LOUGHBOROUGH

Booklore, ■ 6 The Green, East Leake, Loughborough, LE12 6ld. (*) Prop: Ralph & Simon Corbett. Tel: (01509) 852614. Fax: (01509) 852614. E-mail: Ralphcorbett@aol.com. Shop; open **M:** 09:30–17:30; **T:** 09:30–17:30; **W:** 09:30–17:30; **Th:** 09:30–17:30; **F:** 09:30–17:30; **S:** 09:00–16:00. Small stock. Spec: Antiquarian; Bindings. PR: £10–5,000. Mem: PBFA.

Eric Goodyer, Natural History, Hathern, Loughborough, LE12 5LE. Prop: Sue Duerdoth & Eric Goodyer. Tel: (01509) 844473. Fax: (01509) 844473. E-mail: eg@dmu.ac.uk. Est: 1992. Spec: Antiquarian; Natural History. PR: £5–300.

Malcolm Hornsby, Antiquarian and Seconhand Books, ■ 41 Churchgate, Loughborough, LE11 1UE. Prop: Malcolm Hornsby. Tel: (01509) 269860. Website: hornsbybooks.co.uk. E-mail: info@hornsbybooks.co.uk. Est: 1993. Shop; open **M:** 10:00–17:30; **T:** 10:00–17:30; **W:** 10:00–17:30; **Th:** 10:00–17:30; **F:** 10:00–17:30; **S:** 10:00–17:30. Medium general stock. Spec: Academic/Scholarly; Antiquarian; Art; Aviation; History - General. CC: AE; E; JCB; MC; V. Corresp: French, German, Greek.

Magis Books, 64 Leopold Street, Loughborough, LE11 5DN. Prop: Tom Clarke. Tel: (01509) 210626. Fax: (01509) 238034. Website: www.magis.co.uk. E-mail: enquiries@magisbooks.com. Est: 1975. Private premises; Internet and postal. Telephone first. Spec: Alchemy; Astrology; Earth Mysteries; Esoteric; Folklore; Fore-Edge Paintings; Freemasonry & Anti-Masonry; Ghosts; Mysticism; Mythology; New Age; Occult; Paganism; Philosophy; Psychic; Spiritualism; Witchcraft. PR: £1–1,200. CC: AE; D; MC; V. Also, distributor of new books & publishers (Thoth Publications). Mem: PBFA.

Wolds Book Services, 24 Barrow Road, Burton–on–the–Wolds, Loughborough, LE12 5TB. (*) Prop: Arthur L. Whitwell. Tel: (01509) 880755. Fax: (01509) 880755. E-mail: arthurwhitwell@btinternet.com. Est: 1992. Private premises; postal business only. Appointment necessary. Small stock. Spec: Animals and Birds; Anthropology; Antiquarian; Antiques; Apiculture; Arms & Armour; Art; Arts, The; Computing; History - General; Incunabula; Topography - General; War - General; War - World War II. PR: £2–1,000. CC: AE; JCB; MC; V; Delta. Also, custom book-binding & restoration.

MARKET BOSWORTH

Michael D. Raftery (Books), Whitemoors Antique Centre, Shenton, Market Bosworth.

MARKET HARBOROUGH

Aquarius Books, 17 St. Mary's Road, Market Harborough, LE16 7DS.

Bowden Books, 14 Station Road, Great Bowden, Market Harborough, LE16 7HN. Prop: Terry Bull. Tel: (01858) 466832. Est: 1986. Private premises; postal business only.Very small stock. Spec: Architecture; Art; Colour-Plate; Publishers - Black, A. & C.; Topography - General; Travel - General. PR: £5–750 Corresp: French, Italian. Mem: PBFA.

Christine's Book Cabin, ■ Rear of 7–9 Coventry Road, Market Harborough, LE16 9BX. Prop: Malcolm & Christine Noble. Tel: (01858) 433233. Website: www.bookcabin.co.uk. E-mail: bookcabin@harborough.uk.com. Est: 1997. Shop; open **M:** 10:00–16:30; **T:** 10:00–16:30. **Th:** 10:00–16:30; **F:** 10:00–16:30; **S:** 10:00–16:30. Small general stock. PR: £1–300. CC: AE; JCB; MC; V; SW. Also, a booksearch service. See also Malcolm and Christine Noble. Cata: – catalogue available on website.

Malcolm & Christine Noble, 1 Stuart Crescent, Lubenham, Market Harborough, LE16 7RL. Tel: (01858) 434671. Website: www.bookcabin.co.uk. E-mail: malcolm@bookcabin.co.uk. Est: 1992. Private premises; postal business only. Spec: Entertainment - General; Nostalgia; Periodicals & Magazines; Topography - Local. CC: AE; JCB; MC; V. Also, booksearch.

MELTON MOBRAY

Witmehá Productions, The Orchard, Wymondham, Melton Mowbray, LE14 2AZ.

ROTHLEY

Whig Books Ltd., 11 Grangefields Drive, Rothley. Prop: Dr. J. Pollock & Mrs. A. Hinchliffe. Tel: (0116) 237-4420. Est: 1985. Private premises; appointment necessary. Very small stock. Spec: Art; History - General; Literature. PR: £1–500. Cata: 1 – occasionally. Mem: PBFA.

SYSTON

Booksearch Ltd., 72 High Street, Syston, LE7 1GQ. Tel: (0116) 260-4442. Fax: (0116) 260-1396. E-mail: booksearch@outofprintbooks.co.uk. Est: 1998. Spec: History - General.

THURCASTON

Ian Kilgour (Sporting Books), 3 Hall Farm Road, Thurcaston, LE7 7JF. Prop: Ian Kilgour. Tel: (0116) 235-0025. E-mail: sportingbooks@ntlworld.com. Est: 1972. Private premises; Internet and postal. Appointment necessary. Small stock. Spec: Cockfighting; Dogs; Farming & Livestock; Firearms/ Guns; Rural Life; Sport - Angling/Fishing; Sport - Field Sports; Sport - Hunting; Sport - Shooting. PR: £2–500. Cata: 8.

UPPINGHAM

Forest Books, 7 High Street West, Uppingham, Rutland, LE15 9QB.

Goldmark Books, 14 Orange Street, Uppingham, Rutland, LE15 9SQ.

LINCOLNSHIRE

BARTON–ON–HUMBER

Humber Books, Rozel House, 4 St. Mary's Lane, Barton–on–Humber, DN18 5EX. Prop: Peter M. Cresswell. Tel: (01652) 634958 (Answ. Fax: (01652) 634965. Website: www.humberbooks.co.uk. E-mail: pmc@humberbooks.co.uk. Est: 1972. Spec: Antiquarian; Bibles; Religion - Christian; Theology. PR: £15–2,000.

Roger & Sylvia Shakeshaft, Pinewoods, High Street, South Ferriby, Barton–upon–Humber. Tel: (01652) 661185. Est: 1995. Private premises; appointment necessary. Very small general stock. Spec: Americana; Children's - Illustrated; Illustrated; Modern First Editions; Natural History. PR: £1–25. Corresp: French.

BILLINGHAY

Not JUST Books, 27-29 High Street, Billinghay, Lincoln LN4 4AU. Prop: Maggy Browne. Tel: (01526) 860294. Fax: (0870) 7059623. Website: www.notjustbooks.f9.co.uk. E-mail: books@notjustbooks.f9.co.uk. Est: 1981. Private premises; Internet and postal. Appointment necessary. Medium general stock. Spec: Biography; Crime (True); Fiction - General; Fire & Firefighters; History - General; Police Force Histories; Politics; Publishers - Chambers; Publishers - Guinness Publishing Ltd.; Radio/Wireless; Religion - General; Social History; Television. PR: £1–50. CC: AE; JCB; MC; SW. Also, booksearch, props for Theatre, Film and TV. Mem: FSB.

BOSTON

Libra Books, Church House, Wigtoft, Boston, PE20 2NJ. Prop: Paul & Linda Daunter. Tel: (01205) 460829. Fax: (01205) 460829. Website: : http://www.ukbookworld.com/members/LibraBooks. E-mail: libra.books@btinternet.com. Est: 1994. Private premises; Internet and postal. Telephone first. Large general stock. Spec: Biography; Ex-Libris; Fiction - General; Fiction - Crime, Detective, Spy, Thrillers; Fiction - Historical; Fiction - Science Fiction; Fiction - Women; Gardening; History - General; Juvenile; Memoirs; Modern First Editions; Music - General; and others as listed in the Speciality Index. PR: £1–100.

CLEETHORPES

Soccer Books Limited, 72 St Peters Avenue, Cleethorpes, DN35 8HU. Prop: John Robinson. Tel: (01472) 696226. Fax: (01472) 698546. Website: www.soccer-books.co.uk. E-mail: info@soccer-books.co.uk. Est: 1983. Office &/or bookroom; postal business only. Appointment necessary. Open: **M:** 09:00–17:00; **T:** 09:00–17:00; **W:** 09:00–17:00; **Th:** 09:00–17:00; **F:** 09:00–17:00. Small stock. Spec: Sport - Football (Soccer). PR: £1–500. CC: AE; E; JCB; MC; V. Mem: PBFA. VAT No: GB 546 5008 49.

THEOLOGY & BIBLES
PRINTED BEFORE 1700

Regular Catalogues issued free (including later works)

Specialising in the Protestant Reformation, Puritanism & Nonconformity

Books also purchased

HUMBER BOOKS

4 ST MARY'S LANE, BARTON-ON-HUMBER, DN18 5EX.
Tel: (01652) 634958 Fax: (01652) 634965.
Email: pmc@humberbooks.co.uk Website: www.humberbooks.co.uk

EAGLE

J. & J. Books, Holly Cottage, 14 Scarle Lane, Eagle, LN6 4EJ.

FOLKINGHAM

David Strauss, The White House, 25 Market Place, Folkingham, NG34 0SE. Prop: David & Victoria Strauss. Tel: (01529) 497298. Fax: (01529) 497298. Website: www.abebooks.com/home/davidstrauss. E-mail: david.strauss@btinternet.com. Est: 1977. Private premises; Internet and postal. Telephone first. Medium stock. Spec: Academic/Scholarly; Architecture; Art History; History - General; Literary Criticism; Philosophy; Theology. PR: £8–3,500. CC: MC; V; SW.

GRANTHAM

Bookwyze, 42 Castlegate, Grantham, NG31 6SS. Prop: Tony Midgley. Tel: (01476) 579887. Website: www.bookwyze.co.uk. E-mail: tony.midgley@talk21.com. Est: 1990. Private premises; Internet and postal. Telephone first. Medium general stock. Spec: Academic/Scholarly; Advertising; Antiquarian; Bibles; Bindings; Fine & Rare; First Editions; History - General; Illuminated Manuscripts; Illustrated; Manuscripts; Topography - General; Travel - General. PR: £10–1,000. CC: Paypal. Also, booksearch. Corresp: French, Latin, German.

CHC Books, 88 Edward Street, Grantham, NG31 6JG.

Forest Books, 2 Nursery Lane, Knipton, Grantham, NG32 1RF. Prop: W.R.H. Laywood. Tel: (01476) 870224. Fax: (01476) 870198. Website: www.forestbooks.co.uk. E-mail: bib@forestbooks.co.uk. Est: 1979. Private premises; Internet and postal. Appointment necessary. Medium stock. Spec: Bibliography; Bindings; Books about Books; Papermaking; Printing; Sport - Football (Soccer); Sport - Rugby. PR: £5–10,000. CC: MC; V. Cata: 6. Mem: PBFA.

Gravity Books, 110 Harrowby Road, Grantham, NG31 9DS. Prop: Mr. P.N. Emery. Tel: (01476) 564233. Website: www.gravitybooks.co.uk. E-mail: gravitybks@aol.com. Est: 1999. Private premises; Internet and postal. Appointment necessary. Large stock. Spec: Architecture; Music - Popular; Music - Rock; Sport - General. PR: £2–200. CC: MC; V; SW. Also, booksearch. Corresp: French.

Midas Books & Prints, Hillside House, Beacon Lane, Grantham, NG31 9DQ. Prop: Tricia Daniels and Carolin Midgley. Tel: (01476) 566730. Fax: (01476) 566730. Est: 1990. Storeroom; appointment necessary. Very small stock. Spec: Art; Children's - General; Design. PR: £5–100. Corresp: French. *Also at:* Broad Street Book Centre, Hay-on-Wye, Hereford.

GRIMSBY

Ian Barfield, P.O. Box 233, Grimsby, DN31 3XF.

HOLBEACH

P. Cassidy (Bookseller), ■ 1 Boston Road, Holbeach, PE12 7LR. Tel: (01406) 426322. E-mail: bookscass @aol.com. Est: 1975. Shop; open **M:** 10:00–17:30; **T:** 10:00–17:30; **W:** 10:00–17:30; **Th:** 10:00–17:30; **F:** 10:00–17:30; **S:** 10:00–17:30. Medium general stock. Spec: Topography - Local. PR: £1–250. CC: AE; MC; V. Also, a picture-framing service.

HORNCASTLE

Roger Lucas, 44 Queen Street, Horncastle, LN9 6BG. Tel: (01507) 522261. E-mail: rogerbks@aol.com. Est: 1984. Private premises; appointment necessary. Medium general stock. Spec: Literature. PR: £1–150. CC: MC; V. *Also at:* The Bookshop in the Prison, Lincoln. Mem: PBFA.

Available from Richard Joseph Publishers Ltd
BOOKDEALING FOR PROFIT
by Paul Minet

1st Edition 2000 (Quarto H/b)   £10.00 144pp

LINCOLNSHIRE

KIRKTON

D.C. Books, Parker House, 61a Horseshoe Lane, Kirton, Boston, PE20 1LW. Prop: D.J. & C. Lidgett. Tel: (01205) 724507. Fax: (01205) 724507. E-mail: dcbooks@lineone.net. Est: 1984. Private premises; postal business only. Very small stock. Spec: Travel - General. PR: £3–5. Also, booksearch.

LINCOLN

Autumn Leaves, ■ 19 The Green, Nettleham, Lincoln, LN2 2NR. Prop: Ian & Sue Young. Tel: (01522) 750779. E-mail: leaves@onetel.net.uk. Est: 1997. Shop; open **T:** 09:15–16:30; **W:** 09:30–16:30; **Th:** 09:30–16:30; **F:** 09:15–17:00; **S:** 09:15–12:30. Medium stock. Spec: Antiques; Art; Cookery/Gastronomy; Drama; Entertainment - General; Fiction - General; Health; History - General; Humour; Knitting; Languages - Foreign; Literary Criticism; Literature; Music - General; Natural History; Sport - General; Transport PR: £2–30. CC: AE; JCB; MC; V; SW, SO. Corresp: French, German, Swedish. VAT No: GB 737 8648 80.

Berwick Books, 23–25 Queens Crescent, Lincoln, LN1 1LR.

Bookshop at the Plain, 6 West Parade, Lincoln, LN1 1JT.

Chapter & Verse, 17 Queensway, Lincoln, LN2 4AJ. Prop: Roy Fines. Tel: (01522) 523202. E-mail: roy@fines18.freeserve.co.uk. Est: 1977. Private premises; Internet and postal. Appointment necessary. Open: **M:** 09:00–18:00; **T:** 09:00–18:00; **W:** 09:00–18:00; **Th:** 09:00–18:00; **F:** 09:00–18:00; **S:** 09:00–18:00; **Su:** 09:00–18:00; Very small stock. Spec: Antiquarian; Topography - Local. PR: £1–5,000. CC: AE; MC; V; SW. Corresp: German.

Golden Goose Books, ■ 20–21 Steep Hill, Lincoln, LN2 1LT. Prop: Mrs Anna Cockram & Richard West–Skinn. Tel: (01522) 522589. E-mail: harlequin@acockram.fsbusiness.co.uk. Est: 1984. Shop; Internet. Open: **M:** 11:00–17:00; **T:** 11:00–17:00; **Th:** 11:00–17:00; **F:** 11:00–17:00; **S:** 11:00–17:15. Spec: Antiques; Art; Illustrated. Mem: PBFA; *Also at:* Harlequin Gallery, 20-22, Steep Hill, Lincoln (q.v.).

Harlequin Gallery, 22 Steep Hill, Lincoln, LN2 1LT.

Orlando Booksellers, 1 Rasen Lane, Lincoln, LN1 3EZ. Prop: Alison Smith & Christopher McKee. Tel: (01522) 510828. Fax: (01522) 544322. Website: www.abebooks.com/home/ORLAN_DO/. E-mail: orlando@booksellers.fsworld.co.uk. Est: 1994. Private premises; Internet and postal. Small stock. Spec: Beat Writers; Fine & Rare; Literature; Modern First Editions; Photography; Poetry; Publishers - Hogarth Press; Publishers - Pan; Publishers - Penguin; Women. PR: £20–1,000. CC: AE; JCB; MC; V; SW. VAT No: GB 629 3707 21.

Readers Rest, ■ 13–14 Steep Hill, Lincoln, LN2 1LT. Prop: Nick Warwick. Tel: (01522) 543217. Est: 1982. Shop; open **M:** 09:30–16:00; **T:** 09:30–16:00; **W:** 09:30–16:00; **Th:** 09:30–16:00; **F:** 09:30–16:00; **S:** 09:30–16:00; **Su:** 11:00–16:00; Very large general stock. PR: £1–50. *Also at:* Readers Rest Hall of Books, Steep Hill, Lincoln.

Smallwood Books, 37 Cranwell Street, Lincoln, LN5 8BH. Prop: Thomas & Steven Smallwood. Tel: (01522) 822834. Website: www.smallwoodbooks.co.uk. E-mail: admin@smallwoodbooks.co.uk. Est: 1995. Private premises; Internet and postal. Appointment necessary. Medium stock. Spec: Academic/Scholarly; Antiquarian; Fore-Edge Paintings; Literary Criticism; Topography - Local. PR: £1–5,000. CC: AE; MC; V. Corresp: Italian French. *Also at:* Astra Antiques Centre, Old RAF Hemswell, Lincolnshire.

LOUTH

Booksleuth, 64 Legbourne Road, Louth, LN11 8ER.

MARKET RASEN

Croft Selections, ■ Corner Croft, Main St., Bishop Norton, Market Rasen, LN8 2BE. Prop: Bob Mould and Christine Pawson. Tel: (01633) 818711. Fax: (01633) 818711. Website: www.croft-selections.co.uk. E-mail: croftselections@btinternet.com. Est: 1999. Shop; open **M:** 08:00–19:00; **T:** 08:00–19:00; **W:** 08:00–19:00; **Th:** 08:00–19:00; **F:** 08:00–19:00; **S:** 08:00–19:00; **Su:** 08:00–19:00. Large general stock. Spec: Art; Biography; Children's - General; Crime (True); Dogs; Fiction - General; Gardening; History - General; Military; Music - General; Politics; Royalty - General; Travel - General; U.F.O.s. PR: £10–100. CC: AE; JCB; MC; V. Also, booksearch.

NEWARK

Gaslight Books, Gaslight Cottage, 1 and 2 Gas Street, Horncastle, Newark, LN9 6AH. Prop: Richard & Sarah Ingram-Hill. Tel: (01507) 524415. Fax: (01507) 524415. Website: www.gaslightbooks.com. E-mail: books@gaslightbooks.com. Est: 1997. Private premises. Open: **M:** 09:00–17:00; **T:** 09:00–17:00; **W:** 09:00–17:00; **Th:** 09:00–17:00; **F:** 09:00–17:00; **S:** 09:00–17:00; **Su:** 09:00–16:00. Very small general stock. PR: £5–1,000. CC: MC; V. Trade callers only between Monday and Friday. *Also at:* Pickering Antiques Centre, North Yorks and Antiques Trade space, Brunel Drive, Newark.

SCUNTHORPE

Butterwick Books, The Old Chapel, 33 West Street, West Butterwick, Scunthorpe, DN17 3JZ. Prop: John Hardy. Website: www.ukbookworld.com/members/butterbooks. E-mail: butterwickbooks@hotmail.com.

Richard Williams (Bookdealer), 15 High Street, Dragonby, Scunthorpe, DN15 0BE. Prop: Richard Williams. Tel: (01724) 840645. Website: www.freespace.virgin.net/rah.williams/. E-mail: rah.williams@virgin.net. Est: 1975. Private premises; appointment necessary. Very large stock. Spec: Author - Wallace, Edgar; Bibliography; Cinema/Film; Crime (True); Fiction - General; Fiction - Crime, Detective, Spy, Thrillers; Fiction - Fantasy, Horror; Fiction - Romantic; Fiction - Science Fiction; Fiction - Women; First Editions; Periodicals and Magazines; Television. PR: £3–100. CC: MC; V. www.freespace.virgin.net/rah.williams/. Cata: 4. Corresp: French, German.

SLEAFORD

Phillip Austen, 50 Main Street, Ewerby, Sleaford, NG34 9PJ. Tel: (01529) 461074. E-mail: phillip-austen@militarybooks.f9.co.uk. Est: 1989. Private premises; postal business only. Medium stock. Spec: Military. Cata: 2. Mem: PBFA.

Early Cinema, 11 River Lane, Anwick, Sleaford, NG34 9SP.

Julian Roberts Fine Books, Hill House, Braceby, Sleaford, NG34 0TA. Tel: (01529) 497271. Fax: (01529) 497271. Website: www.abebooks.com/home/JULIANROBERTS/. E-mail: jrfinebooks@aol.com. Private premises; appointment necessary. Small stock. Spec: Author - Blyton, Enid; Author - Crompton, Richmal; Author - Dahl, Roald; Author - Johns, W.E.; Children's - General; Fables; Fiction - General; Fiction - Crime, Detective, Spy, Thrillers; Fiction - Fantasy, Horror; Fiction - Historical; Fiction - Science; Modern Firsts. PR: £10–5,000. CC: MC; V. Mem: PBFA.

Westgate Bookshop, ■ 45 Westgate, Sleaford, NG34 7PU. Prop: Geoffrey Almond. Tel: (01529) 304276. Website: www.abebooks.com/home/WESTGATEBOOKSHOP/. E-mail: geoff.almond@btinternet.com. Est: 1986. Shop; open **M:** 10:00–17:00; **T:** 10:00–17:00; **W:** 10:00–17:00. **F:** 10:00–17:00; **S:** 10:00–17:00. Small stock. PR: £1–15. CC: MC; V.

SPALDING

Anchor Books, 51 Langwith Gardens, Holbeach, Spalding, PE12 7JJ. Prop: Mr. C.R. Dunn. Tel: 01476 550103. E-mail: c.r.dunn@btinternet.com. Est: 1990. Private premises; postal business only. Medium stock. Spec: Aeronautics; Aviation; Canals/Inland Waterways; History - General; Maritime/Nautical; Military; Naval. CC: MC; V. Corresp: German. Mem: PBFA.

Robin Peake, 26 Balmoral Avenue, Spalding, PE11 2RN.

Michael Prior, 34 Fen End Lane, Spalding, PE12 6AD. Tel: (01775) 761851. Fax: (01775) 761733. E-mail: mick.prior@tiscali.co.uk. Est: 1970. Private premises; Internet and postal. Appointment necessary. Medium stock. Spec: Advertising; Aeronautics; Author - Churchill, Sir Winston; Author - Forester, C. S.; Author - Masefield, John; Aviation; Maritime/Nautical; Military; Military History; Naval; Nostalgia; Ship Modelling; Shipbuilding; Sport - Yachting; Transport; Voyages & Discovery; and others as listed in the Speciality Index. PR: £10–250. Cata: – irregularly. Corresp: French.

Alexander Rogoyski (Old and Rare Books), 22 Market Street, Long Sutton, Spalding, PE12 9DF. Tel: (01406) 364111. Est: 1964. Private premises; appointment necessary. Very small stock. Spec: Antiquarian. Also, uncommon pre-1850 European. Corresp: French.

STAMFORD

Andrew Burroughs, 34 St. Martins, Stamford, PE9 2LJ.

St. Mary's Books & Prints, ■ 9 St. Mary's Hill, Stamford, PE9 2DP. Prop: N.A.M., M.G.D. P.A. Tyers. G.R. Tyers. Tel: (01780) 763033. Website: www.stmarysbooks.com. E-mail: orders@stmarysbooks.com. Est: 1971. Shop; Internet and postal. Open: **M:** 08:00–18:30; **T:** 08:00–18:30; **W:** 08:00–18:30; **Th:** 08:00–18:30; **F:** 08:00–18:30; **S:** 08:00–18:30; **Su:** 09:00–18:30; Spec: Academic/Scholarly; Almanacs; Archaeology; Architecture; Author - Fleming, Ian; Author - Rackham, Arthur; Author - Rowling, J.K.; Author - Watkins–Pitchford, Denys ('B.B.'); Bell-Ringing (Campanology); Bindings; Children's - General; Fine & Rare; and others as listed in the Speciality Index. PR: £10–25,000. CC: AE; D; E; JCB; MC; V. Corresp: German, Latin, French.

Staniland (Booksellers), ■ 4/5 St. George's Street, Stamford, PE9 2BJ. Prop: V.A. & B.J. Valentine Ketchum. Tel: (01780) 755800. Fax: (01780) 755800. E-mail: stanilandbooksellers@btinternet.com. Est: 1972. Shop; Internet. Open: **M:** 10:00–17:00; **T:** 10:00–17:00; **W:** 10:00–17:00; **F:** 10:00–17:00; **S:** 10:00–17:00. Closed for lunch: 13:00–14:00. Large stock. Spec: Academic/Scholarly; Applied Art; Archaeology; Architecture; Art; Art History; Art Reference; Bindings; Building & Construction; Country Houses; Ecclesiastical History & Architecture; Gardening; History - General; Interior Design; Literary Criticism PR: £1–3,000. CC: MC; V. Mem: PBFA. VAT No: GB 200 8434 08.

Undercover Books, ■ 30 Scotgate, Stamford, PE9 2YQ.

WRAGBY

The Book Haven, Victoria Street, Wragby, LN8 5PF.

Dealers who need to update their entry should visit their page on
www.sheppardsdirectories.com

LONDON
(EAST LONDON POSTAL DISTRICTS)

Bibliophile Books, 5 Thomas Road, London, E14 7BN.

Birchden Books, 3 Edith Road, East Ham, London, E1 1DE. Prop: Michael Vetterlein. Tel: (020) 8472-3654. E-mail: mike@mvetterlain.freeserve.co.uk. Est: 2001. Spec: Architecture; Ecclesiastical History & Architecture; Illuminated Manuscripts; Sculpture; Stained Glass.

Crimes Ink, 35 Moreton Close, Upper Clapton, London, E5 9EP. Prop: Nigel S. Piercy. Tel: (020) 8806-1895. E-mail: crimesink@q-serve.com. Est: 1987. Private premises; appointment necessary. Medium stock. Spec: Assassinations; Crime (True); Criminology; Espionage; Fiction - General; Fiction - Crime, Detective, Spy, Thrillers; Fiction - Science Fiction; Law; Police Force Histories. PR: £1–150. Corresp: French.

Dalian Books, 81 Albion Drive, London Fields, London, E8 4LT.

Flora Books, 10 Wotton Court, 6 Jamestown Way, London, E14 2DB. Prop: Barrie Macey. Tel: (07785) 525685. E-mail: flora.books@btinternet.com. Est: 1998. Postal business only. Spec: Antiquarian; Bibliography; Gardening. PR: £2–1,000. CC: MC; V; SW; SO.

Goldhold Ltd., 55 Ravenscroft Road, Canning Town, London, E16 4AF. Prop: A. McKenzie. Tel: (020) 7473-5091. Website: www.goldhold.co.uk. E-mail: sales@goldhold.co.uk.

David Houston - Bookseller, 26 North Birkbeck Road, London, E11 4JG. Tel: (020) 8556-9048. Fax: (020) 8556-9048. Website: www.abebooks.com/home/dghbooks. E-mail: scotsbooks@aol.com. Est: 1997. Private premises; postal business only. Small stock. Spec: Scottish Interest. PR: £5–100. CC: MC; V. Cata: 4. Corresp: French.

Left on The Shelf, 7 Hambledon House, Cricketfield Road, London, E5 8NT. Prop: Dave Cope. Tel: (020) 8985-2090. Website: www.abebooks.com/home/leftontheshelf. E-mail: leftontheshelf@cricketfield.demon.co.uk. Est: 1992. Private premises; postal business only. Large stock. Spec: History - Labour/Radical Movements; Marxism; Pacifism; Radical Issues; Socialism; Trade Unions; War - Spanish Civil War. PR: £2–150. CC: MC; V. Also, booksearch. Cata: 3. Corresp: French.

M.A. Stroh, Riverside House, Leaside Road, Upper Clapton, E5 9LU. Tel: (0208) 806 3690. Fax: (0208) 806 3690. Website: www.webspawner.com/users/Buttonbook/. E-mail: patent@stroh.demon.co.uk. Est: 1956. Storeroom; appointment necessary. Very large stock. Spec: Mathematics; Medicine; Science - General; Technology. PR: £10–1,000. Cata: 1 – occasionally. Corresp: French.

Brian Troath Books, 106 Graham Road, London, E8 1BX. Tel: (020) 7254-2912. Fax: (020) 7254-2912. Website: www.ukbookworld.com/members/ariel. E-mail: briantroathbooks@onetel.net.uk. Est: 1970. Private premises; Internet and postal. Appointment necessary. Medium stock. Spec: Books about Books; Cinema/Film; Classical Studies; Drama; Fine & Rare; First Editions; History - General; Limited Editions; Literary Criticism; Literature; Performing Arts; Periodicals & Magazines; Poetry; Private Press. PR: £10–1,000. Cata: – very occasionally.

Searching for a title - and cannot find it on any Internet database?
Then try **Sheppard's Booksearch**

By selecting the subject classification – the request goes to all dealers who major in that subject.

LONDON
(EAST CENTRAL POSTAL DISTRICTS)

The Amwell Book Company, 53 Amwell St., London, London, EC1R 1UR. Prop: Charlotte Robinson. Tel: (020) 7837 4891. E-mail: sixrobins@aol.com. Est: 1980. Spec: Applied Art; Architecture; Children's - Illustrated; Fashion & Costume; Fiction - Crime, Detective, Spy, Thrillers; Fiction - Women; Fine & Rare; Juvenile; Modern First Editions; Photography. PR: £5–1,000. CC: MC; V; SW. Mem: PBFA; *Also at:* Biblion, Davies Street, London W1.

Ash Rare Books, 153 Fenchurch Street, London, EC3M 6BB. Prop: Laurence Worms. Tel: (020) 7626-2665. Fax: (020) 7623-9052. Website: www.ashrare.com. E-mail: books@ashrare.com. Est: 1946. Office &/or bookroom; Internet and postal. Appointment necessary. Open: **M:** 10:00–17:00; **T:** 10:00–17:00; **W:** 10:00–17:00; **Th:** 10:00–17:00; **F:** 10:00–17:00. Small stock. Spec: Bibliography; City of London; First Editions; Poetry. PR: £20–5,000. CC: AE; D; E; JCB; MC; V. Cata: 6. Mem: ABA; ILAB. VAT No: GB 244 2896 45.

Elizabeth Crawford, 5 Owen's Row, London, EC1V 4NP. Tel: (020) 7278-9479. Fax: (020) 7278-9479. E-mail: E.Crawford@sphere20.freeserve.co.uk. Est: 1984. Postal business only. Spec: Authors - Women; Women. PR: £5–5,000.

Andrew Sclanders (Beatbooks), Apt. 32 St Paul's View, 15 Amwell Street, London, EC1R 1UP. Tel: (020) 7278-5034. Fax: (020) 7278-5034. Website: www.beatbooks.com. E-mail: sclanders@beatbooks.com. Est: 1990. Spec: Author - Burroughs, William; Author - Kerouac, Jack; Avant-Garde; Beat Writers; Counterculture; Music - Rock. PR: £5–1,500.

Dealers who need to update their entry should visit their page on *www.sheppardsdirectories.com*

LONDON
(NORTH POSTAL DISTRICTS)

Abbey Books, ■ c/o Skywalkers, 209 Park Road, London, N8 8JG. Prop: S. Magill. Tel: (020) 8889 1674. E-mail: spencermagill@aol.com. Est: 1991. Shop; open **M:** 10:00–17:30; **T:** 10:00–17:30; **W:** 10:00–17:30; **Th:** 09:00–17:30; **F:** 10:00–17:30; **S:** 10:00–17:30. Large stock. Spec: Arts, The; Bindings; Fiction - General; Irish Interest; Literature; Occult. PR: £1–500.

Alpha Books, 60 Langdon Park Road, London, N6 5QG. Prop: Tony Maddock. Tel: (020) 8348-2831. Fax: (020) 8348-2831. E-mail: alpha@dircon.co.uk. Est: 1983. Private premises; appointment necessary. Medium stock. Spec: Academic/Scholarly; Alchemy; Astrology; Egyptology; Esoteric; Folklore; Freemasonry & Anti-Masonry; Hermeticism; Metaphysics; Mythology; Occult; Palmistry & Fortune Telling; Psychic; Theosophy; Travel - Asia; U.F.O.s; Witchcraft. PR: £1–500. CC: MC; V. Cata: 4. Mem: PBFA.

G.W. Andron, 162a Brunswick Park Road, London, N11 1HA. Tel: (020) 8361-2409. Est: 1972. Private premises; postal business only. Medium general stock. Spec: Aeronautics; Aviation; Bibliography; Bookbinding; Books about Books; Maritime/Nautical; Military; Military History; Natural History; Naval; Printing; Topography - General; Topography - Local; Travel - General; Typography; War - General. PR: £1–100. Cata: 2 – one general & one military/naval or travel & topography; and others as listed in the Speciality Index.

Antique Prints of the World, 6 Livingstone Road, Palmers Green, London, N13 4SD.

Atlas, 17 Pitfield Street, London, N1 6HB.

The Aviation Bookshop, ■ 656 Holloway Road, London, N19 3PD. Prop: David Hatherell. Tel: (020) 7272-3630. Fax: (020) 7272-9761. E-mail: info@aviation-bookshop.com. Est: 1948. Shop; open **M:** 09:30–17:30; **T:** 09:30–17:30; **W:** 09:30–17:30; **Th:** 09:30–17:30; **F:** 09:30–17:30; **S:** 09:30–17:30. Large stock. Spec: Aviation. PR: £1–200. CC: AE; D; E; JCB; MC; V. Mem: BA.

Church Street Bookshop, 142 Stoke Newington, Church Street, London, N16 0JU. Prop: Tim Watson. Tel: (0171) 241-5411. Est: 1984. Spec: Academic/Scholarly. PR: £1–50.

Michael Cuddy Books, 29 Highwood Avenue, London, N12 8QL. Tel: (020) 8445-7768. Est: 1977. Private premises; postal business only. Small stock. Spec: Aviation; Maritime/Nautical; Military. PR: £3–100. Also, booksearch. Cata: 1 – occasionally. Corresp: French.

De Swartes Ltd., 36 Church Lane, London, N2 8DT.

Erian Books, 24 Woodside Avenue, Highgate, London, N6 4SS.

Fantasy Centre, ■ 157 Holloway Road, London, N7 8LX. Prop: Ted Ball & Erik Arthur. Tel: (020) 7607-9433. Fax: (020) 7607-9433. Website: www.fantasycentre.demon.co.uk. E-mail: books@fantasycentre.biz. Est: 1972. Shop; open **M:** 10:00–18:00; **T:** 10:00–18:00; **W:** 10:00–18:00; **Th:** 10:00–18:00; **F:** 10:00–18:00; **S:** 10:00–18:00. Medium stock. Spec: Fiction - Fantasy, Horror; Fiction - Science Fiction. CC: E; MC; V. *Also see:* website: fantasycentre.biz and - abe.books.com Cata: 5.

Fisher & Sperr, ■ 46 Highgate High Street, London, N6 5JB. Tel: (020) 8340-7244. Fax: (020) 8348-4293. Est: 1939. Shop; open **M:** 10:00–17:00; **T:** 10:00–17:00; **W:** 10:00–17:00; **Th:** 10:00–17:00; **F:** 10:00–17:00; **S:** 10:00–17:00. Very large stock. Spec: Art; Art History; Folio Society, The; Literary Criticism; Philosophy; Sets of Books; Topography - General. PR: £1–10. Corresp: French. Mem: ABA; ILAB.

Walter H. Gardner & Co., 16 Chalton Drive, London, N2 0QW. Tel: (020) 8458-3202. Fax: (020) 8458-8499. Est: 1978. Storeroom; appointment necessary. Small stock. Spec: Applied Art; Art Reference; Decorative Art; Economics; Journals - General; Periodicals & Magazines; Reference; Science - History of. Also, remainders and back issues of journals. Corresp: German. VAT No: GB 756 6751 89.

Gate Memorabilia, 35 Nether Close, Finchley, London, N3 1AA. Prop: Jon Baldwin. Tel: (020) 8346 1090. Website: ukbookworld.com/members/Jonnyb. E-mail: jonny.b@tesco.net. Est: 1981. Private premises; Internet and postal. Appointment necessary. Very small general stock. Spec: Animals and Birds; Annuals; Archaeology; Art; Autobiography; Biography; Cinema/Film; Dance; Drama; Fiction - Crime, Detective, Spy, Thrillers; Fiction - Women; First Editions; History - General; Juvenile; Literature; Memorabilia; Music - General; Performing Arts; War - General. PR: £3–500. CC: MC; V.

Nancy Sheiry Glaister, Fine & Rare Books, 18 Huntingdon Street, London, N1 1BS.

Nicholas Goodyer, ■ 15 Calabria Road, Highbury Fields, London, N5 1JB. Tel: (020) 7226-5682. Fax: (020) 7354-4716. Website: www.nicholasgoodyer.com. E-mail: email@nicholasgoodyer.com. Shop; Telephone first. Open: **M:** 10:00–17:00; **T:** 10:00–17:00; **W:** 10:00–17:00; **Th:** 10:00–17:00; **F:** 10:00–17:00. Medium stock. Spec: Animals and Birds; Architecture; Art; Botany; Colour-Plate; Decorative Art; Fashion & Costume; Gardening; Illustrated; Natural History; Ornithology; Topography - General; Travel - General. CC: AE; MC; V. Open other times by appointment. Cata: 1 – regularly. Corresp: French, German, Italian, Spanish, Portuguese. Mem: ABA; PBFA. VAT No: GB 629 6750 05.

The Greek Bookshop, Zenos Book, 57a Nether Street, North Finchley, London, N12 7NP.

F. & J. Hogan, 31 Tranmere Road, Edmonton, London, N9 9EJ. Prop: Frederick & Joan Hogan. Tel: (020) 8360-6146. Website: www.fjhogan.freeuk.com. E-mail: fjhogan@freeuk.com. Est: 1969. Postal business only. Spec: Atlases; Caricature; Cartography. PR: £5–1,000.

Idle Genius Books, 115 Cluse Court, St. Peter Street, London, N1 8PE. Prop: Philip Obeney. Tel: (020) 7704-3193. E-mail: p.obeney@btopenworld.com. Est: 2000. Storeroom. Small stock. Spec: Archaeology; Literature; Modern First Editions; Topography - Local. PR: £5–400. Attends HD Book Fairs. Also, ephemera on London in wartime.

InterCol London, ■ 43 Templars Crescent, London, N3 3QR. Prop: Yasha Beresiner. Tel: (020) 8349-2207. Fax: (020) 8346-9539. Website: www.intercol.co.uk. E-mail: yasha@compuserve.com. Est: 1981. *Shop at:* 114 Islington High Street (in Camden Passage), Islington. Open: **T:** 10:30–17:00; **W:** 10:30–17:00; **Th:** 10:30–17:00; **F:** 10:30–17:00; **S:** 10:30–17:00. Small stock. Spec: Banking & Insurance; Cartography; Erotica; Freemasonry & Anti-Masonry; Gambling; Games; Numismatics; Topography - General. PR: £5–500. CC: AE; E; JCB; MC; V. Corresp: French, Italian, Spanish, Turkish, Hebrew. Mem: ANA; IBNS; IMCoS; IPCS. VAT No: GB 350 6069 69.

M.E. Korn Books, 5 Dolphin Court, 42 Carleton Road, London, N7 0ER. Prop: Eric Korn. Tel: (020) 7609-7100. Fax: (020) 7609-7100. E-mail: eric@mekornbooks.freeserve.co.uk. Est: 1969. Private premises; Book fairs only. Small stock. Spec: Children's - General; Natural History; Science - General. PR: £5–500. Also, a booksearch service. Cata: – very seldom. Corresp: French Russian. Mem: ABA; PBFA. VAT No: GB 234 2420 04.

Judith Lassalle, 7 Pierrepont Arcade, Camden Passage, London, N1 8EF.

Manor House Books/John Trotter, ■ 80 East End Road, Finchley, London, N3 2SY. Prop: John Trotter. Tel: (020) 8349-9484. Fax: (020) 8346-7430. Website: www.bibliophile/John-Trotter-Books.html. E-mail: jtrotter@freenetname.co.uk. Est: 1983. Shop; open **M:** 09:30–16:30; **T:** 09:30–16:30; **W:** 09:30–16:30; **Th:** 08:30–16:30; **F:** 09:30–13:00. **Su:** 09:30–13:00; Medium stock. Spec: Archaeology; Assassinations; Bibles; Countries - Egypt; Countries - Middle East, The; Judaica; Religion - Christian; Religion - Islam; Religion - Jewish. PR: £5–1,000. CC: AE; E; JCB; MC. Cata: 2. Mem: PBFA; BA. Also, booksearch, and at: John Trotter Books, London N3 (q.v.). VAT No: GB 370 7855 29.

Barrie Marks Limited, 24 Church Vale, Fortis Green, London, N2 9PA. Tel: (020) 8883-1919. Spec: Fine & Rare; Illustrated; Limited Editions; Literature; Private Press.

Ian McKelvie, 45 Hertford Road, London, N2 9BX. Tel: (020) 8444-0567. Fax: (020) 8444-0567. E-mail: ianmckelvie@supanet.com. Est: 1969. Private premises; Internet and postal. Appointment necessary. Large stock. Spec: Author - Bloomsbury Group, The; Fiction - General; Fiction - Crime, Detective, Spy, Thrillers; First Editions; Limited Editions; Literature; Modern First Editions; Plays; Poetry; Proof Copies; Signed Editions. CC: AE; JCB; MC. Cata: 4.

Mountaineering Books, 6 Bedford Road, London, N8 8HL. Prop: Mr. R. & Mrs. A. Court. Tel: (020) 8340-1953. Est: 1990. Private premises; appointment necessary. Very small stock. Spec: Alpinism/Mountaineering. PR: £10–1,500. Cata: 2 – a year on alpinism/mountaineering.

Newton Books, Flat 3, 74 Marquess Road, London, N1 2PY.

Nicolas - Antiquarian Booksell, 59 Fallowcourt Avenue, London, N12 0BE.

Norton & Roberts, 18 Mildmay Grove South, London, N1 4RL.

Dealers who need to update their entry
should visit their page on
www.sheppardsdirectories.com

Pendleburys Bookshop, Church House, Portland Avenue, Stamford Hill, London, N16 6HJ.

Pholiota Books, 3 Caledonian Road, London, N1 9DX.

John Price, 8 Cloudesley Square, London, N1 0HT. Tel: (020) 7837-8008. Fax: (020) 7278-4733. Website: www.johnpriceantiquarianbooks.com. E-mail: books@jvprice.com. Est: 1988. Private premises; appointment necessary. Very small stock. Spec: Antiquarian; Cookery/Gastronomy; History of Ideas; Literature; Music - General; Performing Arts; Philosophy; Scottish Interest. PR: £45–4,500. CC: AE; MC; V. Corresp: French, German. Mem: ABA; PBFA; ILAB.

Ripping Yarns, ■355 Archway Road, London, N6 4EJ. Tel: (020) 8341-6111. Fax: (020) 7482-5056. Website: www.rippingyarns.co.uk. E-mail: yarns@rippingyarns.co.uk. Est: 1984. Shop; open **Tu**: 11:00–17:00; **W**: 11:00–17:00; **Th**: 11:00–17.00; **F**: 11:00–17.00; **S**: 10:00–17:00; **S**: 11:00-16:00. Large stock. Spec: Childrens' Illustrated; Childrens; General. Corresp: French, German. Mem: PBFA.

Robbie's Bookshop, 118a Alexandra Park Road, London, N10 2AE.

Susanne Schulz–Falster, 22 Compton Terrace, London, N1 2UN. Prop: Susanne Schulz-Falster. Tel: (020) 7704-9845. Fax: (020) 7354-4202. E-mail: sfalster@btinternet.com. Est: 1997. Private premises; appointment necessary. Very small stock. Spec: Antiquarian; Early Imprints; Economics; History of Ideas; Linguistics; Philosophy. PR: £100–10,000. CC: MC; V. Also, booksearch, building collections, valuations. Cata: 3. Corresp: German, Italian, French. Mem: ABA; ILAB; VDA.

John Singleton, 8 Gladsmuir Road, London, N19 3JX. Tel: (020) 7263-9179. Website: jsingl1920@aol.com. E-mail: jsingl1920@aol.com. Est: 1995. Private premises; Internet and postal. Appointment necessary. Large stock. Spec: Children's - General; Cinema/Film; Modern First Editions; Performing Arts; Poetry. PR: £5–300.

George B. Skelly, 24 Cloudesley Square, London, N1 0HN. Tel: (020) 7833-1555. Private premises; postal business only. Medium stock. Spec: Literature; Maritime/Nautical; Theology. PR: £3–150. CC: MC; V. Also, booksearch. Cata: 4 – a year, two on theology, 2 on maritime.

Stanhope Bibliophiles, P.O. Box 6754, London, N3 3NT. Prop: Mr. Smith. Tel: (withheld). Est: 1975. Private premises; postal business only. Very small stock. Spec: Atlases; Cartography; Dictionaries; Military History; Parish Registers; Railways; Steam Engines; Topography - Local; Urban History. PR: £5–500.

STM Books, 2 Castle Mews, North Finchley, London, N12 9EH. Tel: 020 8492 7324. Website: www.stmbooks.co.uk. E-mail: sales@stmbooks.co.uk. Est: 1984. Shop &/or showroom; Internet and postal. Telephone first. Open: **M**: 08:00–16:00; **T**: 08:00–16:00; **W**: 08:00–16:00; **Th**: 08:00–16:00; **F**: 08:00–16:00. Very small stock. Spec: Medicine; Medicine - History of; Veterinary. PR: £10–500. CC: AE; D; JCB; MC. Also, new books. Mem: PBFA.

Robert Temple, 65 Mildmay Road, London, N1 4PU. Prop: P.J. Allen. Tel: (020) 7254-3674. Fax: (020) 7254-3674. Website: www.telinco.co.uk/RobertTemple/. E-mail: roberttemple@telinco.co.uk. Est: 1977. Warehouse; Internet and postal. Appointment necessary. Medium stock. Spec: Academic/Scholarly; Anthologies; Antiquarian; Fiction - General; Fiction - Crime, Detective, Spy, Thrillers; Fiction - Fantasy, Horror; Fiction - Historical; Fiction - Science Fiction; Fiction - Women; First Editions; Journals - General; Juvenile; and others as listed in the Speciality Index. PR: £5–6,000. CC: PayPal. Credit and Debit cards taken via the PayPal secure server only (VISA, non-corporate AmEx, MasterCard, Discover, SW, Solo). Corresp: French. VAT No: GB 292 2648 41.

Richard Thornton Books, 116 Osidge Lane, Southgate, London, N14 5DN. Tel: (020) 8368-2816. Website: www.abebooks.com/home/NEVILLE/. E-mail: richard.thorntonbooks@btinternet.com. Est: 1994. Private premises; appointment necessary. Small stock. Spec: Children's - General; Literature; Modern First Editions; Sport - General. PR: £10–500. CC: AE; MC; V. Also on ukbookworld.com/members/payton14. Mem: PBFA.

Ripping Yarns (Celia Mitchell)

355 Archway Road
London N6 4EJ
Tel: 020 8341 6111
Fax: 020 7482 5056

Antiquarian & secondhand stock bought and sold
All subjects but especially **CHILDREN'S**
Highgate Tube. Free car parking (1 hour) just north of shop in Archway Road
Email: yarns@rippingyarns.co.uk. Web site: www.rippingyarns.co.uk

Weekdays 10.30-5.30
Saturdays 10.00-5.00
Sundays 11.00-4.00

John Trotter Books, 80 East End Road, London, N3 2SY. Prop: John Trotter. Tel: (020) 8349-9484. Website: www.bibliophile.net/John-Trotter-Books.htm. E-mail: jtrotter@freenetname.co.uk. Est: 1973. Office &/or bookroom; Internet and postal. Open: **M:** 09:00–17:00; **T:** 09:09–17:00; **W:** 09:00–17:00; **Th:** 09:00–17:00. **Su:** 10:00–13:00; Large stock. Spec: Countries - Middle East, The; History - Ancient; Religion - Jewish; Travel - Middle East. PR: £5–1,500. CC: AE; MC; V. Also, booksearch. Mem: PBFA; BA.

Tyger Press, 41 Cheverton Road, London, N19 3BA.

Graham Weiner, 78 Rosebery Road, London, N10 2LA. Tel: (020) 8883-8424. Fax: (020) 8444-6505. E-mail: graham_weiner@msn.com. Est: 1973. Private premises; Internet and postal. Appointment necessary. Medium stock. Spec: Chemistry; Geology; History - General; Medicine; Physics; Science - General; Science - History of; Technology; Transport. PR: £15–2,500. CC: MC; V. Cata: 1. Corresp: French. Mem: IEE. VAT No: 230 6110 23.

Woburn Books, 5 Caledonian Road, London, N1 9DX. Prop: Andrew Burgin. Tel: (020) 7263 5196. Fax: (020) 7263-5196. E-mail: woburn@burgin.freeserve.co.uk. Est: 1991. Office &/or bookroom; Internet and postal. Medium stock. Spec: Academic/Scholarly; Africana; Anthropology; Antiquarian; Architecture; Art; Arts, The; Avant-Garde; Beat Writers; Black Studies; Economics; Health; History - Labour/Radical Movements; Marxism; Pacifism; Philosophy; Photography; Poetry; Politics; and others as listed in the Speciality Index. PR: £1–500. CC: JCB; V; SW. Mem: PBFA.

LONDON
(NORTH WEST POSTAL DISTRICTS)

Archive Books & Music, ■ 83 Bell Street, London, Marylebone, London, NW1 6TB. Prop: Tim Meaker. Tel: (020) 7402-8212. Website: www.archivebookstore.com. Est: 1973. Shop; open M: 10:30–18:00; T: 10:30–18:00; W: 10:30–18:00; Th: 10:30–18:00; F: 10:30–18:00; S: 10:30–18:00. Medium stock. Spec: Antiquarian; Music - General; Music - Classical; Music - Popular. PR: £1–150. CC: MC; V.

Aurelian Books, 31 Llanvanor Road, London, NW2 2AR. Prop: David Dunbar. Tel: (020) 8455 9612. E-mail: dgldunbar@aol.com. Est: 1970. Private premises; appointment necessary. Small stock. Spec: Colour-Plate; Conservation; Entomology; Lepidopterology / Lepidoptery; Natural History. PR: £5–5,000. CC: MC; V; SW. Cata: 2. Mem: PBFA.

H. Baron, 121 Chatsworth Road, London, NW2 4BH. Prop: Christel Wallbaum. Tel: (020) 8459-2035. Fax: (020) 8459-2035. Est: 1949. Private premises; postal business only. Spec: Autographs; Iconography; Letters; Music - General. CC: E; JCB; MC; V. Cata: 2 – antiquarian music, books on music, autographs. VAT No: GB 227 1452 82.

Black–Bird Books, 24 Grampian Gardens, London, NW2 1JG. Prop: James T. Lay. Tel: (020) 8455-3069. Website: www.laybooks.com. E-mail: lorettalay@hotmail.com. Spec: Fiction - Crime, Detective, Spy, Thrillers. PR: £5–1,000.

The Book Depot, 111 Woodcote Avenue, Mill Hill, London, NW7 2PD. Prop: Conrad Wiberg. Tel: (020) 8906-3708. E-mail: conrad@adword.fsnet.co.uk. Est: 1980. Postal business only. PR: £5–10. Also, booksearch.

Cranhurst Books, 20 Cranhurst Road, Willesden Green, London, NW2 4LN. Prop: Heidi Stransky. Tel: (020) 845-27845. E-mail: HStransky@aol.com. Spec: Children's General; Comic Books & Annuals; Modern First Editions. Est: 1997. Private premises; appointment necessary. Small stock. PR: £5–2,500.

P.G. de Lotz Books, 20 Downside Crescent, Belsize Park, London, NW3 2AP. Tel: (020) 7794-5709. Est: 1968. Private premises; appointment necessary. Medium stock. Spec: Aviation; Bibliography; Maritime/Nautical; Military; War - General. Cata: 1.

Keith Fawkes, ■ 1–3 Flask Walk, Hampstead, London, NW3 1HJ. Tel: (020) 7435-0614. Est: 1970. Shop; open **M:** 10:00–18:00; **T:** 09:00–18:00; **W:** 10:00–18:00; **Th:** 09:00–18:00; **F:** 10:00–18:00; **S:** 10:00–18:00; **Su:** 13:00–18:00. Large general stock. PR: £1–100.

Fishburn Books, 43 Ridge Hill, London, NW11 8PR. Prop: Jonathan Fishburn. Tel: (0208) 455-9139. Fax: (0208) 922-5008. E-mail: fishburnbooks@yahoo.co.uk. Est: 2000. Private premises; appointment necessary. Spec: Judaica. PR: £15–5,000. CC: AE; MC; V. Cata: 3. Mem: PBFA. VAT No: GB 805 4965 16.

Fortune Green Books, 74 Fortune Green Road, London, NW6 1DS. Prop: Eric Stevens & Jane Bell. Tel: (020) 7435-7545. Fax: (020) 7794 4937. E-mail: belleric@dircon.co.uk. Est: 1992. Office &/or bookroom; Internet and postal. Appointment necessary. Medium stock. Spec: Academic/Scholarly; Art; Feminism; Fiction - General; Fiction - Women; Literary Criticism; Literature; Women. PR: £1–50. CC: MC; V. Mem: PBFA.

Stephen Foster, ■ 95 Bell Street, London, NW1 6TL. Prop: Stephen Foster. Tel: (020) 7724-0876. Fax: (020) 7724-0927. Website: www.sfbooks.co.uk. E-mail: stephen.foster@sfbooks.co.uk. Est: 1987. Shop; open **M:** 10:00–18:00; **T:** 10:00–18:00; **W:** 10:00–18:00; **Th:** 10:00–18:00; **F:** 10:00–18:00; **S:** 10:00–18:00. Medium stock. Spec: Antiquarian; Antiques; Architecture; Art History; Art Reference; Artists; Arts, The; Decorative Art; History - General; Iconography; Interior Design; Literature. PR: £1–1,000. CC: AE; D; JCB; MC; V; SW. Also, a booksearch service ; new books at a discount. Mem: ABA; PBFA; ILAB; ibooknet. *Also at:* stock at Biblion, Davies Mews. VAT No: GB 521 5504 81.

Grenville Books, PO Box 22884, London, NW9 7ZL.

Otto Haas (A. Rosenthal), 49 Belsize Park Gardens, London, NW3 4JL.

Available from Richard Joseph Publishers Ltd
Sheppard's Book Dealers in JAPAN
1st Edition (A5 H/b) £24.00 200pp

Hellenic Bookservices, ■ 91 Fortess Road, Kentish Town, London, NW5 1AG. Prop: M. Williams & Andrew Stoddart. Tel: (020) 7267-9499. Fax: (020) 7267-9498. Website: www.hellenicbookservice.com. E-mail: info@hellenicbookservice.com. Est: 1966. Shop. Large stock. Spec: Academic/Scholarly; Byzantium; Classical Studies; Countries - Cyprus; Countries - Greece; Foreign Texts; Guide Books; Literary Criticism; Poetry; Theology. CC: AE; JCB; MC; V. Also, a booksearch service, school supplies – all subjects. Corresp: Modern Greek. Mem: PBFA.

Hindsight Books, P.O. Box 18644, London, NW3 1ZW.

Hosains Books, 12 Honeybourne Road, West Hampstead, London, NW6 1JJ.

C.R. Johnson Rare Book Collect, 4a Keats Grove, Hampstead, London, NW3 2RT. Prop: C.R. Johnson & C.A. Forster. Tel: (020) 7794-7940. Fax: (020) 7433-3303. Website: www.crjohnson.com. E-mail: mail@crjohnson.com. Est: 1970. Private premises; appointment necessary. Very large general stock. Spec: Authors - Women; Fiction - General; Literature. PR: £25–5,000. CC: MC; V. Cata: 1. Mem: PBFA.

Terence Kaye - Bookseller, 52 Neeld Crescent, London, NW4 3RR. Tel: (020) 8202-8188. Fax: (020) 8202-8188. E-mail: kforbook@onetel.net.uk. Est: 1996. Office &/or bookroom; appointment necessary. Open: **M:** 09:00–20:00; **T:** 09:00–20:00; **W:** 09:00–20:00; **Th:** 09:00–20:00; **F:** 09:00–18:00; **S:** 10:00–20:00; **Su:** 10:00–20:00. Small stock. Spec: Cinema/Film; Circus; Drama; Entertainment - General; Fairgrounds; Music - Music Hall; Performing Arts; Television; Theatre. PR: £10–200. Also, a booksearch service (specialist subjects only), and library/collection development. Corresp: Hebrew. Mem: Ephemera Society.

Loretta Lay Books, 24 Grampian Gardens, London, NW2 1JG. Tel: (020) 8455-3069. Website: www.laybooks.com. E-mail: lorettalay@hotmail.com. Est: 2001. Private premises; postal business only. Appointment necessary. Very small stock. Spec: Crime (True); Criminology. PR: £5–1,000. CC: JCB; MC; V; SW. *Also at:* Black-Bird Books, 24 Grampian Gardens, London.

Richard Lucas, 114 Fellows Road, London, NW3 3JH. Tel: (020) 7749-9431. Est: 1975. Private premises; appointment necessary. Medium stock. Spec: Brewing; Etiquette; Food & Drink; Herbalism; Public Houses; Travel - General. PR: £10–1,000. Cata: 1 – occasionally.

Nicholas Morrell (Rare Books), 77 Falkland Road, London, NW5 2XB. Tel: (020) 7485-5205. Fax: (020) 7485-2376. Website: www.morbook.com. E-mail: morbook@aol.com. Est: 1982. Private premises; appointment necessary. Very small stock. Spec: Travel - General. PR: £5–5,000. Cata: 1. Corresp: French, German. Mem: ABA; PBFA. VAT No: GB 370 7735 39.

Moss Books, 14 Manor Park Gardens, Edgware, London, HA8 7NA. Tel: (020) 8386-2707. Fax: (020) 8386-2707. E-mail: moss.books@ntlworld.com. Est: 2002. Market stand/stall; Internet and postal. Appointment necessary. Medium stock. Spec: Archaeology; Architecture; Ceramics; Ecclesiastical History & Architecture; Lepidopterology / Lepidoptery; Odd & Unusual; Ornithology; Pacifism; Religion - General; Theology. PR: £5–800. CC: PayPal. VAT No: GB 805 4666 26.

Neil's Books, 151 Fordwych Road, London, NW2 3NG.

Primrose Hill Books, 134 Regents Park Road, London, NW1 8XL.

Paul Rassam, Flat 5, 18 East Heath Road, London, NW3 1AJ. Tel: (020) 7794-9316. Fax: (020) 7794-7669. E-mail: paul@rassam.demon.co.uk. Est: 1976. Private premises; appointment necessary. Very small stock. Spec: Autographs; First Editions; Literature; Manuscripts. CC: MC; V. Cata: 1 – occasionally. Mem: ABA.

San Expedito Books, 18 Wentworth Mansions, Keats Grove, London, NW3 2RL. Prop: Dr. J.Q.C. Mackrell. Tel: (020) 7794-8414. Fax: (020) 7794-8414. E-mail: jqcmackrell@hotmail.com. Est: 1998. Private premises. Also, booksearch.

Dealers who need to update their entry
should visit their page on
www.sheppardsdirectories.com

Sevin Seydi Rare Books, 13 Shirlock Road, London, NW3 2HR. Prop: Sevin Seydi & Maurice Whitby. Tel: (020) 7485-9801. Fax: (020) 7428-9313. E-mail: sevin@seydi.fsnet.co.uk. Est: 1970. Private premises; appointment necessary. Medium stock. Spec: Architecture; Art History; Bindings; Classical Studies; Countries - Greece; Countries - Italy; Countries - Turkey; Early Imprints; Emblemata; History of Ideas; Illustrated; Incunabula; Manuscripts; Philology. CC: MC; V. Cata: 3 – irregularly on specialities. Corresp: French, Turkish. Mem: PBFA.

Walden Books, ■ 38 Harmood Street, London, NW1 8DP. Prop: David Tobin. Tel: (020) 7267-8146. Fax: (020) 7267-8147. Website: www.ukbookworld/members/waldenbooks. E-mail: waldenbooks@lineone.net. Est: 1979. Shop; open **Th:** 10:30–18:30; **F:** 10:30–18:30; **S:** 09:30–18:30; **Su:** 10:30–18:30; Medium stock. Spec: Architecture; Art; Literature; Philosophy. PR: £1–350. CC: AE; MC; V. Also, booksearch. Mem: PBFA. VAT No: GB 564 4805 26.

Eva M. Weininger, Antiquarian Bookseller, 79 Greenhill, London, NW3 5TZ. Tel: (020) 7435-2334. Est: 1979. Private premises; appointment necessary. Very small stock. Spec: Courtesy; Culture - Foreign; Culture - National; Etiquette; History of Ideas; Social History. PR: £10–150.

Mike Wells, 28 Laurier Road, London, NW5 1SG.

J. & S. Wilbraham, 1 Wise Lane, Mill Hill, London, NW7 2RL. Prop: John and Shahin Wilbraham. Tel: (0208) 959-3709. Website: www.wilbraham.demon.co.uk. E-mail: john@wilbraham.demon.co.uk. Est: 1981. Private premises; postal business only. Very small stock. Spec: Antiquarian; Children's - General; Literature; Music - General. PR: £10–1,000. Cata: 4. Corresp: French.

LONDON
(SOUTH EAST POSTAL DISTRICTS)

BBSJ Rare Books, 21 Southwood Road, New Eltham, London, SE9 3QE.

Beaumont Travel Books, Unit 6.2.9, Skillion Com. Centre, 49 Greenwich High Road, London, SE10 8JL.

Bookshop Blackheath, ■ 74 Tranquil Vale, Blackheath, London, SE3 0BW. Prop: Richard Platt. Tel: (020) 8852-4786. E-mail: tboth@btopenworld.com. Shop; open **M:** 10:00–18:00; **T:** 10:00–18:00; **W:** 10:00–18:00; **Th:** 10:00–18:00; **F:** 10:00–18:00; **S:** 09:00–18:00; **Su:** 11:00–17:00. Large general stock. Spec: Author - Fleming, Ian; Children's - General; Fiction - Crime, Detective, Spy, Thrillers; Modern First Editions; Topography - Local.

Brockwells Booksellers, Unit F11A1, 40 Martell Road, London, SE21 8EN. Prop: Richard Peace. Tel: (0208) 766 0077. Website: www.brockwells.co.uk. E-mail: richard@brockwells.co.uk. Est: 1997. Storeroom; Internet and postal. Appointment necessary. *Shop at:* Old Forge, Aisby, Lincolnshire NG32 3NF. Large stock. Spec: Antiquarian; Books about Books; Engineering; History - General; Military History; Politics; Travel - General; Voyages & Discovery; War - General. PR: £5–1,700. CC: AE; MC; V; SW, DE. Prints and maps selling.

Fiona Campbell, 158 Lambeth Road, London, SE1 7DF. Tel: (020) 7928-1633. Fax: (020) 7928-1633. E-mail: fcampbell@britishlibrary.net. Est: 1970. Private premises; appointment necessary. Small stock. Spec: Countries - Italy; Travel - General; Travel - Europe. CC: JCB; MC; V. Also, a booksearch service, and bookbinding. Cata: 2 – a year. Corresp: French, German and Italian. Mem: ABA; PBFA.

Marcus Campbell Art Books, ■ 43 Holland Street, Bankside, London, SE1 9JR. Prop: Marcus Campbell. Tel: (020) 7261-0111. Fax: (020) 7261-0129. Website: www.marcuscampbell.demon.co.uk. E-mail: campbell@marcuscampbell.demon.co.uk. Est: 1998. Shop; Internet and postal. Open: **M:** 10:30–18:30; **T:** 10:30–18:30; **W:** 10:30–18:00; **Th:** 10:30–18:06; **F:** 10:30–18:30; **S:** 10:30–18:30; **Su:** 12:00–18:00. Very large stock. Spec: Art; Art Reference; Artists; Monographs. PR: £2–2,000. CC: E; MC; V; SW. Cata: 1 – infrequent. Corresp: French. Mem: PBFA. VAT No: GB 605 8695 15.

Cassidy's Gallery, ■ 20 College Approach, Greenwich, London, SE10 9HY.

Chapter Two, Fountain House, Conduit Mews, London, SE18 7AP. Manager: Miss P. Brachotte. Tel: (020) 8316-5389. Website: www.chaptertwo.org.uk. E-mail: chapter2uk@aol.com. Est: 1976. Office &/or bookroom; appointment necessary. Large stock. Spec: Bibles; Religion - Christian. PR: £2–100. Also, publisher/retailer of new books & foreign language Christian literature, Bible distributor, archive & booksearch service.

Nigel A. Clark, 28 Ulundi Road, Blackheath, London, SE3 7UG. Tel: (020) 8858-4020. Est: 1975. Private premises; postal business only. Appointment necessary. Very small stock. Spec: Antiques; Art History; Art Reference; Artists; Ceramics; Collecting; Horology; Numismatics; Philately; Theatre. PR: £1–100. Also, booksearch.

Collectable Books, 15 West Park, London, SE9 4RZ. Partners: Tom & Sue Biro. Tel: (020) 8851-8487. Website: www.collectablebooks.co.uk. E-mail: biro@collectablebooks.co.uk. Est: 1992. Private premises; appointment necessary. Very small stock. Spec: Antiquarian; Architecture; Arts, The; Food & Drink; Health; Medicine; Natural History; Religion - General; Travel - General; Wine. PR: £10–20,000. CC: E; JCB; MC; V; SO, SW. Corresp: French, German, Italian, Hungarian, Portuguese. Mem: PBFA. VAT No: GB 299 3282 10.

Peter Ellis, Bookseller, ■ 28 Granville Park, London, SE13 7EA. Tel: (020) 8318-4748. Fax: (020) 8318-4748. Website: www.peter-ellis.co.uk. E-mail: ellisbooks@lineone.net. Est: 1999. *Shop at:* 18 Cecil Court, London WC2 4HE. Open: **M:** 10:00–17:00; **T:** 10:00–17:00; **W:** 10:00–17:00; **Th:** 10:00–17:00; **F:** 10:00–17:00; **S:** 10:00–17:00. Medium stock. Spec: Art; Artists; Arts, The; Beat Writers; Biography; Children's - General; Fiction - General; First Editions; Gardening; Limited Editions; Literary Criticism; Literature; Modern First Editions; Private Press; Signed Editions; Surrealism. PR: £10–1,000. CC: AE; MC; V. Cata: 6. Corresp: French, German. Mem: ABA. VAT No: GB 751 8751 12.

Enscot Books, 17 Crantock Road, Catford, London, SE6 2QS.

S.C. Fordham, 8 Old James Street, London, SE15 3TS.

Jane Gibberd, ■ 20 Lower Marsh, London, SE1 7RJ. Tel: (020) 7633-9562. Est: 1968. Shop; open **W:** 11:00–19:00; **Th:** 11:00–19:00; **F:** 11:00–19:00. Small general stock. PR: £1–25.

Gilham Books, 4 St. Austell Road, London, SE13 7EQ. Prop: Margaret Mendel. Tel: (020) 8852-1905. Fax: (020) 8852-1905. E-mail: mendel@gilhambooks.fsnet.co.uk. Est: 1983. Private premises; appointment necessary. Small stock. Spec: Music - General; Music - Composers; Music - Opera; Musical Instruments. PR: £1–300. Also, a booksearch service. Cata: 2 – a year on music, literature, some scores (not sheet music). Corresp: French, Italian, Greek.

Hava Books, 110 Aspinall Road, Brockley, London, SE4 2EG. Prop: John Havercroft. Tel: (020) 7639-8339. Website: www.havabooks.com. E-mail: jhavercroft@rmplc.co.uk. Est: 2000. Office &/or bookroom; Internet. Appointment necessary. *Shop at:* Jasmine House, 55 Jasmine Grove, London SE20 8JY. Small stock. Spec: Academic/Scholarly; Antiquarian; Atlases; Books about Books; Illustrated; Languages - Foreign; Literature - Victorian; Literature in Translation; Travel - General. PR: £10–3,000. CC: Paypal. Corresp: French, Spanish. Mem: PBFA. VAT No: GB 782 4918 92.

King Books, 147 Camberwell Road, London, SE5 0HB.

Kirkdale Bookshop, ■ 272 Kirkdale, Sydenham, London, SE26 4RS. Prop: Ms. Geraldine A. Cox. Tel: (020) 8778-4701. Fax: (020) 8776-6293. E-mail: kirkdalebookshop@hotmail.com. Est: 1966. Shop; open **M:** 09:00–17:30; **T:** 09:00–17:30; **W:** 09:00–17:30; **Th:** 09:00–17:30; **F:** 09:00–17:30; **S:** 09:00–17:30. Medium general stock. Spec: CC: MC; V. Also, new books, & greetings cards. Mem: BA.

David Koos, Flat 4, Chester Way, London, SE11 4UT.

Peter Marcan, Bookseller, P.O. Box 3158, London, SE1 4RA. Tel: (020) 7357 0368. Est: 2000. Private premises; appointment necessary. Open: **M:** 10:00–19:00; **T:** 10:00–19:00; **W:** 10:00–19:00; **Th:** 10:00–19:00; **F:** 10:00–19:00; **S:** 10:00–19:00. Very small stock. Spec: Architecture; Arts, The; Cities; Horticulture; Music - Classical; Social History; Urban History. PR: £3–50. Publishing - reprints, directories, catalogues. Cata: 3 – a year.

Marcet Books, ■ 4a Nelson Road, Greenwich, London, SE10 9JB. Prop: Martin Kemp. Tel: (020) 8853-5408. Fax: (020) 8853-5408. Website: www.marcetbooks.co.uk. E-mail: info@marcetbooks.co.uk. Est: 1980. Shop: open **M:** 10:00–18:00; **T:** 10:00–18:00; **W:** 10:00–18:00; **Th:** 10:00–18:00; **F:** 10:00–18:00; **S:** 10:00–18:00; **Su:** 10:00–18:00. Medium stock. Spec: Art; Bibliography; Fiction - Crime, Detective, Spy, Thrillers; First Editions; Maritime/Nautical; Naval; Sport - Cricket; Sport - Yachting; Topography - General; Travel - General. PR: £1–100. CC: AE; D; MC; V. Attends book fairs monthly at Russell Hotel, London. Cata: 1 – on foreign travel. Mem: PBFA.

Sheila Markham, P.O. Box 214, London, SE3 9XS.

Military Bookworm, P.O. Box 235, London, SE23 1NS. Prop: David W. Collett. Tel: (020) 8291-1435. Fax: (020) 8291-1435. Website: www.militarybookworm.co.uk. E-mail: info@militarybookworm.co.uk. Est: 1975. Storeroom; Internet. Medium stock. Spec: Military; Military History; School Registers/Rolls of Honour; PR: £5–300. CC: MC; V.

Herbert Murch Booksend, 258/260 Creek Road, Greenwich, London, SE10 9SW.

Richard Platt Rare Books, 84 Red Lion Lane, Shooters Hill, London, SE18 4LE. Tel: (020) 8856-4202. Fax: (020) 8856-4211. Website: www.abebooks.com/home/richardplatt. E-mail: richardplatt.books@btinternet.com. Est: 1997. Private premises; appointment necessary. Small stock. Spec: Author - Christie, Agatha; Author - Conan Doyle, Sir Arthur; Author - Fleming, Ian; Author - Freeman, R A; Author - Gilbert, Michael; Author - Rankin, Ian; Fiction - Crime, Detective, Spy, Thrillers; First Editions; Signed Editions. PR: £10–3,000. *Also at:* Biblion and at Bookshop Blackheath, London SE3.

Hilary Rittner Booksearch, 30 Crooms Hill, Greenwich, London, SE10 8ER. Prop: Hilary Rittner. Tel: (020) 8858-7759. Private premises; postal business only. Spec: Artists; Author - Ardizzone, Edward; Illustrated. Also, booksearch.

John Rolfe, 39 Combe, Blackheath, London, SE3 7PZ. Prop: John Rolfe. Tel: (020) 8858-3349. Website: abebooks.com/home/johnrolfe. E-mail: johnrolfebooks@tinyworld.co.uk. Private premises; Internet and postal.Very small stock. Spec: Dogs. PR: £5–500.

Ruskin Books, 49 Dighton Court, John Ruskin Street, London, SE5 0PR. Prop: Frederick W. Lidyard. Tel: (020) 7703 0567. E-mail: lidfred@aol.com. Also, a booksearch service.

The Saint Austin Press, 296 Brockley Road, London, SE4 2RA.

Michael Silverman, P.O. Box 350, London, SE3 0LZ. Tel: (020) 8319-4452. Fax: (020) 8856-6006. Website: www.michael-silverman.com. E-mail: ms@michael-silverman.com. Est: 1989. Private premises; postal business only. Appointment necessary. Medium stock. Spec: Art; Autographs; Documents - General; History - General; Letters; Literature; Manuscripts. CC: AE; MC; V. Cata: 2 – a year. Mem: ABA; ILAB. VAT No: GB 532 9017 59.

Spread Eagle Bookshop, ■ 8 Nevada Street, Greenwich, London, SE10. Prop: Richard F. Moy. Tel: (020) 8305-1666. Fax: (020) 8305 0447. Website: www.spreadeagle.org. E-mail: books@spreadeagle.org. Est: 1960. Shop; open **M:** 10:00–17:00; **T:** 10:00–17:00; **W:** 10:00–17:00; **Th:** 10:00–17:00; **F:** 10:00–17:00; **S:** 10:00–17:00; **Su:** 10:00–17:00; Closed for lunch: 13:00–14:00. Large stock. Spec: Advertising; Animals and Birds; Antiquarian; Arts, The; Author - Churchill, Sir Winston; Bindings; Children's - General; Children's - Illustrated; Cinema/Film; City of London; Collecting; D.I.Y (Do It Yourself); Decorative Art; Documents - General; and others as listed in the Speciality Index. PR: £3–100. CC: AE; D; E; JCB; MC; V. Also, ephemera, picture framing and restoration, collectables and antiques. Corresp: French, Italian.

Stephen E. Tilston, 37 Bennett Park, Blackheath, London, SE3 9RA.

Tower Bridge Books, 72 Gainsford Street, Tower Bridge Square, London, SE1 2NB. Prop: Tom Hoffman. Tel: (020) 7403-5485. Fax: (020) 7403-5485. Est: 1990. Private premises; appointment necessary. Small stock. Spec: Antiquarian; Fine & Rare; History - Guilds and Livery Companies; Sport - Rowing. PR: £5–500. Cata: 2 – on rowing.

LONDON
(SOUTH WEST POSTAL DISTRICTS)

Adam & Eve Books, 18a (Basement) Redcliffe Square, London, SW10 9JZ.

Allsworth Rare Books Ltd, P.O.Box 134, 235 Earls Court Road, London, SW5 9FE. Tel: (020) 7377-0552. Fax: (020) 7377-0552. E-mail: jenny@allsworthbooks.com. Est: 2002. Private premises; appointment necessary. Spec: Africana; Photography; Sport - Big Game Hunting; Travel - General; Travel - Asia; Travel - Middle East; Voyages & Discovery. Mem: PBFA.

Ancient Art Books, 34 East Sheen Ave., East Sheen, London, SW14 8AS. Prop: D.G. Giles. Tel: (020) 8878-8951. Fax: (020) 8878-9201. E-mail: ancientartbooks@aol.com. Est: 1999. Private premises; postal business only. Small stock. Spec: Glass. PR: £10–5,000. *Also at:* Biblion, London.

Chris Beetles Ltd., 8 & 10 Ryder Street, St. James's, London, SW1Y 6QB. Prop: Chris Beetles. Tel: (020) 7839-7551. Website: www.chrisbeetles.com. E-mail: gallery@chrisbeetles.com. Est: 1981. Spec: Art; Art History; Art Reference; Artists; Dictionaries; Fine Art; Humour; Illustrated. PR: £5–500. CC: AE; MC; V. Mem: BA.

Bodyline Books, 150a Harbord Street, London, SW6 6PH. Prop: G.R. Lyon Esq. Tel: (020) 7385-2176. Fax: (020) 7610-3314. Website: www.bodylinebooks.com. E-mail: info@bodylinebooks.com. Est: 1996. Private premises; Internet and postal. Appointment necessary. Small general stock. Spec: Sport - Cricket. PR: £4–10,000. CC: MC; V. Cata: 3.

Book Mongers, 439 Coldharbour Lane, London, SW9 8LN.

Bookseekers, 4 Manor Road, London, SW20 9AE. Prop: R. & J. Mernane. Fax: (020) 8542-2448. Est: 1981. Private premises; postal business only. Spec: Judaica; Religion - Jewish; Sport - Cricket. Also, booksearch. Corresp: French, German, Hebrew.

Ron Chapman, 12 Bolton Gardens Mews, off Little Boltons, London, SW10 9LW. Tel: (020) 7373-8370. Est: 1970. Private premises; appointment necessary. Large stock. Spec: Architecture; First Editions; Literature. PR: £5–1,000. *Also at:* Tindley & Chapman, London WC2N 4HE (q.v.).

Classic Bindings, ■ 61 Cambridge Street, Pimlico, London, SW1V 4PS. Prop: Mr. Sasha Poklewski–Koziell. Tel: (020) 7834-5554. Fax: (020) 7630-6632. Website: www.classicbindings.net. E-mail: info@classicbindings.net. Est: 1988. Shop; open **M:** 09:30–17:30; **T:** 09:30–17:30; **W:** 09:30–17:30; **Th:** 09:30–17:30; **F:** 09:30–17:30. Large stock. Spec: Architecture; Art; Bindings; Biography; Foreign Texts; History - General; Poetry; Religion - Christian; Topography - General; Topography - Local. PR: £10–5,000. CC: E; MC; V. Cata: – on request. VAT No: GB 562 2080 66.

Robin de Beaumont, 25 Park Walk, Chelsea, London, SW10 0AJ. Tel: (0207) 352-3440. Fax: (0207) 352-1260. Website: www.abebooks.com/home/RDEBOOKS. E-mail: rdebooks@aol.com. Est: 1980. Private premises; Internet and postal. Telephone first. Small stock. Spec: Architecture; Art; Bindings; Illustrated; Victoriana. PR: £20–3,000. CC: JCB; V. Corresp: French. Mem: ABA; ILAB.

The Earlsfield Bookshop, ■ 513 Garratt Lane, Wandsworth, London, SW18 4SW. Prop: Charles Dixon. Tel: (020) 8946-3744. Est: 1995. Shop; open **M:** 16:00–18:00; **T:** 16:00–18:00; **W:** 16:00–18:00; **Th:** 16:00–18:00; **F:** 11:00–18:00; **S:** 10:00–17:00. Small general stock. PR: £1–50.

Harfield Books of London, 81 Replingham Road, Southfields, London, SW18 5LU. Prop: P.V. Eastman. Tel: (020) 8871-0880. Fax: (020) 8871-0880. Website: www.harfieldbooks.com. E-mail: internet@harfieldbooks.com. Est: 1989. Warehouse; Internet and postal. Appointment necessary. Very large stock. Spec: Academic/Scholarly. Also, a booksearch service & academic publishers.

Europa Books, 15 Luttrell Avenue, Putney, London, SW15 6PD. Prop: Paul Hetherington PhD., F. S.A. Tel: (020) 8788-0312. Fax: (020) 8788-0312. E-mail: europabooks@ukonline.co.uk. Est: 1985. Private premises; appointment necessary. Small stock. Spec: Antiquarian; Architecture; Art; Art History; Art Reference; Decorative Art; Theatre. PR: £10–2,000. CC: E; JCB; MC; V. Appointments can be made at most times. Cata: – occasionally. Corresp: French, German, Italian. Mem: PBFA.

Available from Richard Joseph Publishers Ltd
Sheppard's International Directory of
EPHEMERA DEALERS

2nd Edition (A5 H/b) £24.00 342pp

LONDON SOUTH WEST POSTAL DISTRICTS

Exedra Booksearch Ltd., 40 Peterborough Road, London, SW6 3BN. Prop: Jonathan Tootell. Tel: (020) 7731-8500. Fax: (020) 7731-8400. Website: www.exedra.co.uk. E-mail: info@exedra.co.uk. Est: 1999. Postal business only. Contactable. Open: **M:** 09:00–18:00; **T:** 09:00–18:00; **W:** 09:00–18:00; **Th:** 09:00–18:00; **F:** 09:00–18:00; **S:** 09:00–14:00. Very small general stock. Spec: booksearch. CC: MC; V. Corresp: French.

Folios Limited, Flat 5, 193/195 Brompton Road, London, SW3 1LZ.

Paul Foster Bookshop, ■ 119 Sheen Lane, London, SW14 8AE. Tel: (020) 8876-7424. E-mail: paulfosterbooks@btinternet.com. Est: 1990. Shop; Internet and postal. Open: **W:** 10:30–18:00; **Th:** 10:30–18:00; F: 10:30–18:00; S: 10:30–18:00. Medium stock. Spec: Academic/Scholarly; Antiquarian; Art; Bindings; Children's - General; First Editions; Illustrated. PR: £5–10,000. CC: JCB; MC; V. Cata: 2. Mem: ABA; PBFA; ILAB.

Geneva Books, 58 Elms Road, London, SW4 9EW.

Gloucester Road Bookshop, ■ 123 Gloucester Road, London, SW7 4TE. Prop: Nick Dennys. Tel: (020) 7370-3503. Fax: (020) 7373-0610. Website: www.gloucesterbooks.co.uk. E-mail: nick.dennys@gloucesterbooks.co.uk. Est: 1983. Shop; open **M:** 09:30–22:30; **T:** 09:30–22:30; **W:** 09:30–22:30; **Th:** 09:30–22:30; **F:** 09:30–22:30; **S:** 10:30–18:30; **Su:** 10:30–18:30. Large stock. Spec: Antiques; Architecture; Art; Author - Greene, Graham; Children's - General; Fiction - General; History - General; Literature; Music - General; Natural History; Performing Arts; Philosophy; Poetry; Travel - General. PR: £1–5,000. CC: E; MC; V. Also, booksearch. Cata: 2 – occasionally on modern first editions, literature.

Michael Graves–Johnston, P. O. Box 532, 54 Stockwell Park Road, LONDON, SW9 0DR. Tel: (0207) 274-2069. Fax: (0207) 738-3747. Website: www.graves-johnston.com. E-mail: Books@gravesjohnston.demon.co.uk. Est: 1978. Private premises; appointment necessary. Large stock. Spec: Africana; Anthropology; Archaeology; Classical Studies; Colonial; Countries - Africa; Egyptology; Ethnography; Ethnology; Travel - Africa; Travel - Americas; Travel - Australasia/Australia; Travel - Polar; Voyages & Discovery. PR: £10–10,000. CC: AE; E; MC; V. Cata: 4. Mem: ABA; ILAB. VAT No: GB 238 2333 72.

Grays of Westminster, 40 Churton Street, Pimlico, London, SW1V 2LP.

Robin Greer, 434 Fulham Palace Road, London, SW6 6HX. Prop: Robin Greer. Tel: (020) 7381-9113. Fax: (020) 7381-6499. Website: www.rarerobin.com. E-mail: rarities@rarerobin.com. Est: 1966. Private premises; appointment necessary. Small stock. Spec: Children's - General; Illustrated; Travel - General. PR: £1–5,000. CC: MC; V. Cata: 5. Corresp: Spanish. Mem: ABA; PBFA; ILAB.

Hanshan Tang Books, Unit 3 Ashburton Centre, 276 Cortis Road, London, SW15 3AY.

Peter Harrington Antiquarian B, ■ 100 Fulham Road, Chelsea, London, SW3 6HS. Tel: (020) 7591-0220. Fax: (020) 7225-7054. Website: www.peter-harrington-books.com. E-mail: mail@peter-harrington-books.com. Shop. Very large general stock. Spec: Antiquarian; Architecture; Atlases; Autographs; Bibles; Bindings; Botany; Children's - General; Churchilliana; Colour-Plate; Fine & Rare; First Editions; Fore-Edge Paintings; Geography; Illustrated; Literature; Maritime/Nautical; Sets of Books; and others as listed in the Speciality Index. PR: £10–100,000. CC: AE; E; JCB; MC; V. SW, SO. Corresp: Polish, Spanish. VAT No: GB 701 5578 50.

Thomas Heneage Art Books, ■ 42 Duke Street St. James's, London, SW1Y 6DJ. Tel: (020) 7930-9223. Fax: (020) 7839-9223. Website: www.heneage.com. E-mail: artbooks@heneage.com. Est: 1977. Shop; open **M:** 09:30–18:00; **T:** 09:30–18:00; **W:** 09:30–18:00; **Th:** 09:30–18:00; **F:** 09:30–18:00. Spec: Antiques; Applied Art; Archaeology; Arms & Armour; Art; Art History; Carpets; Catalogues Raisonnes; Ceramics; Collecting; Conservation; Decorative Art; Fine Art; Firearms/Guns; Furniture; Glass; Interior Design; Jewellery; Lace; Monographs; Needlework; and others as listed in the Speciality Index. PR: £2–30,000. CC: MC; V. Also, a booksearch service and publishers of Art Book Survey. Open at other times by appointment..

Hesketh & Ward Ltd., 31 Britannia Road, London, SW6 2HJ.

Dealers who need to update their entry should visit their page on
www.sheppardsdirectories.com

Hünersdorff Rare Books, P.O. Box 582, London, SW10 9RP. Prop: Richard von Hünersdorff. Tel: (020) 7373-3899. Fax: (020) 7370-1244. Website: www.abebooks.com/hunersdorff/home. E-mail: huner.rarebooks@dial.pipex.com. Est: 1969. Spec: Architecture; Countries - South America; Gardening; Landscape; Languages - Foreign; Literature; Medicine; Science - General. PR: £25–100,000. CC: MC; V. Cata: 2. Corresp: German, Spanish, French. Mem: ABA; ILAB.

Andrew Hunter–Rare Books, Box 9, 34 Buckingham Palace Road, London, SW1W 0RH. Tel: (020) 7834-4924. Fax: (020) 7834-4924. Website: www.rarebookhunter.com. E-mail: andrew@rarebookhunter.com. Est: 2001. Private premises; appointment necessary. Very small stock. Spec: Literature; Medicine; Science - General; Scottish Interest. PR: £200–25,000. Cata: 2. Corresp: French, Spanish. VAT No: GB 782 2863 04.

The Illustrated Book, 4 Haverhill Road, Balham, London, SW12 0HA. Prop: Mr J. Pearson. Tel: (020) 8675-5177. Fax: (020) 8675-5177. Website: www.theillustratedbook.co.uk. E-mail: joe@jpearson51.freeserve.co.uk. Est: 2000. Postal business only. Very small stock. Spec: Art History; Art Reference; Children's - General; Design; Illustrated; Printing; Private Press; Publishers - Curwen Press; Publishers - Penguin; Transatlantic arts; Typography; Vintage Paperbacks. PR: £1–1,000.

Iris Books, 218a Merton Road, Wimbledon, London, SW19 1EQ.

J.K. Bookfinders, 40 Amesbury Avenue, Streatham Hill, London, SW2 3AA. Prop: John Kinsella. Tel: (020) 8671-4462. Website: www.abebooks.com. E-mail: jk.bookfinders@virgin.net. Est: 1989. Private premises. Medium stock. Spec: Americana; Author - Barker, Cecily M.; Author - Burroughs, William; Author - Carroll, Lewis; Author - Fleming, Ian; Children's - General; Countries - Arctic, The; Modern First Editions. Also, a booksearch service.

Dick Laurie, 27 Clarendon Drive, Putney, London, SW15 1AW.

Romilly Leeper, 12 Bolton Garden Mews, London, SW10 9LW. Tel: (020) 7373-8370. Fax: (020) 7370-3226. Est: 1986. Private premises; appointment necessary. Small stock. Spec: Sport - Horse Racing (all aspects); Travel - Asia. PR: £6–100. Corresp: Fench, German, Portuguese.

David Loman, Oriental Books & Manuscripts, 12 Suffolk Road, London, SW13 9NB. Prop: D.E.F. Loman. Tel: (020) 8748-0254. Fax: (020) 8563-7806. Est: 1970. Private premises; appointment necessary. Small stock. Spec: Academic/Scholarly; Antiquarian; Byzantium; Classical Studies; Dictionaries; Languages - Foreign; Linguistics; Oriental; Ottoman Empire; Travel - Middle East. Mem: ABA.

Londonline Books, Suite 53, 95 Wilton Road, London, SW1V 1BZ. Prop: Trudy Cutts and David Campbell. Tel: (020) 7976-6670. Fax: (020) 7630-8124. Website: www.londonlinebooks.co.uk. E-mail: trudycutts@aol.com. Est: 1993. Warehouse; Internet and postal. Appointment necessary. Large general stock. Spec: Aviation; Countries - Australia; Countries - Central Asia; Countries - India; Countries - Japan; Countries - Korea; Countries - Polar; Maritime/Nautical. PR: £5–1,000. CC: AE; JCB; MC. Corresp: French, Spanish, Japanese.

H.D. Lyon, 18 Selwood Terrace, London, SW7 3QG.

The Map House, 54 Beauchamp Place, Knightsbridge, London, SW3 1NY.

Nicholas Meinertzhagen, 82 Ritherdon Road, London, SW17 8QG. Tel: (020) 8672-2288. Est: 1978. Private premises; appointment necessary. Small stock. Spec: Countries - Europe; Countries - Hungary; Countries - Poland; Economics; Fine & Rare; Foreign Texts; History - European; Philosophy; Science - General. History of Eastern Europe; paintings drawings. Cata: – occasionally.

My Back Pages, 8–10 Balham Station Road, London, SW12 9SG.

Nibris Books, 14 Ryfold Road, Wimbledon Park, London, SW19 8BZ. Prop: Nigel Israel. Tel: (020) 8946-7207. Fax: (020) 8946-7207. E-mail: nibris_books@yahoo.com. Est: 1980. Private premises; appointment necessary. Small stock. Spec: Gemmology; Horology; Jewellery; Mineralogy. PR: £10–500. VAT No: GB 446 2021 80.

O'Donoghue Books, Unit F23, 72 Farm Lane, London, SW6 1QA. Prop: Sean O'Donoghue. Tel: (020) 7610-3004. Fax: (078160) 821745. Website: www.intertextuality.com. E-mail: odonoghue.books@virgin.net. Est: 1994. Private premises; postal business only. Large stock. Spec: Academic/Scholarly; Biography; Philosophy; Politics; Psychology/Psychiatry; Social Sciences. PR: £5–50. CC: MC; V; SW. VAT No: GB 751 8509 19.

Old World Books, 40 Peterboough Road, London, SW6 3BN. Prop: John Francis Phillimore. Tel: (020) 7352-3590. Website: www.oldworldbooks.com. E-mail: venicebooks@yahoo.co.uk. Est: 2003. Private premises. *Shop at:* Cannaregio 1190, Venezia 30121, Italy. Open: **M:** 10:00–19:00; **T:** 10:00–19:00; **W:** 10:00–19:00; **Th:** 10:00–19:00; **F:** 10:00–19:00. **Su:** 15:00–19:00. Closed for lunch: 13:00–15:00. Small stock. Spec: Literary Travel; Travel - Europe. PR: £5–1,500. CC: V. Also, books about Venice. Cata: occasionally. Corresp: Italian. Mem: PBFA. VAT No: GB 602 8936 37.

Paul Orssich, 2 St. Stephen's Terrace, South Lambeth, London, SW8 1DH. Tel: (020) 7787-0030. Fax: (020) 7735-9612. Website: www.orssich.com. E-mail: paulo@orssich.com. Est: 1980. Private premises; Internet and postal. Spec: Atlases; Author - Cervantes Saavedra, Miguel de; Bull Fighting; Cartography; Countries - Andorra; Countries - Central America; Countries - Gibraltar; Countries - Mexico; Countries - Morocco; Countries - Portugal; Countries - Puerto Rico; and others as listed in the Speciality Index. PR: £25–5,000. CC: AE; MC; V. Open any time by appointment. Cata: 4 – 3 months. Corresp: Spanish, Catalán, French, German, Italian. Mem: PBFA. VAT No: GB 442 4102 94.

Hugh Pagan Limited, P.O. Box 4325, London, SW7 1DD. Tel: (020) 7589-6292. Fax: (020) 7589-6303. Website: www.hughpagan.com. E-mail: pagan@mistral.co.uk. Est: 1987. Spec: Architecture; Fine Art.

Petersham Books, Unit 67, 56 Gloucester Road, London, SW7 4UB. Prop: Kate Stewart. Tel: (020) 7581-9147. Fax: (020) 7581-9147. Website: www.modernfirsts.co.uk. E-mail: ks@modernfirsts.co.uk. Private premises; Internet and postal. Contactable. Small stock. Spec: Children's - General; Children's - Illustrated; Modern First Editions. PR: £15–5,000. CC: JCB; MC; V. Corresp: Italian, French.

Nigel Phillips, 5 Burleigh Place, Cambalt Road, Putney Hill, London, SW15 6ES. Tel: (020) 8788-2664. Fax: (020) 8780-1989. Website: www.nigelphillips.com. E-mail: nigel@nigelphillips.com. Est: 1981. Private premises; appointment necessary. Medium stock. Spec: Antiquarian; History of Ideas; Medicine; Science - General; Science - History of; Technology. PR: £15–50,000. CC: MC; V. Cata: 2. Mem: ABA; ILAB.

Philologus–Fine & Rare Books, 83 Stanthorpe Road, London, SW16 2EA. Prop: G. Frydberg & U.K.H. Polczynski. Tel: (020) 8677-2076. Est: 1984. Postal business only. Spec: Antiquarian; Art Reference; Bibliography; Foreign Texts; Languages - Foreign; Philosophy; Science - History of. PR: £10–2,000. Also, booksearch.

Politico's, ■ 8 Artillery Row, London, SW1P 1RZ. Prop: Iain Dale. Tel: (020) 7828-0010. Fax: (020) 7828-8111. Website: www.politicos.co.uk. E-mail: bookstore@politicos.co.uk. Est: 1996. Spec: Autobiography; Autographs; Biography; History - National; Memoirs; Politics. PR: £1–1,000. CC: AE; MC; V; SW. Also, new books.

John Rees Rare Books, 242 Merton Road, London, SW18 5JQ.

SPAIN

and all aspects of **HISPANIC STUDIES** including

Mexico, Central and South America, Philippines and Pyrenees.
Travel, Literature, Translations, Literary Criticism
Bullfighting, Peninsula War, Carlist Wars
& Spanish Civil War.

Internet: www.orssich.com

Paul Orssich

Established 1980
2 St. Stephen's Terrace, South Lambeth, LONDON SW8 1DH
Tel: 020 7787 0030   **Fax: 020 7735 9612**
E-mail: paulo@orssich.com

Mandalay Bookshop, 36c Sisters Avenue, London, SW11 5SQ. Prop: Nicholas Greenwood. Tel: (020) 7223-8987. Fax: (020) 7223-8987. Website: www.mandalaybookshop.biz. E-mail: mandalaybookshop @aol.com. Est: 1991. Private premises; Internet and postal. Small stock. Spec: Countries - Burma. PR: £1–1,000. CC: PayPal. Also, booksearch. Corresp: French, German, Burmese, Thai.

Art Rubino & Co [USA] Numismat, 233 Wandsworth Bridge Road, London, SW6 2TU.

Russell Rare Books, ■ 239A Fulham Road, Chelsea, London, SW3 6HY. Tel: (020) 7351-5119. Fax: (020) 7376-7227. Website: www.russellrarebooks.com. E-mail: c.russell@russellrarebooks.com. Est: 1977. Shop; open **M:** 14:00–18:00; **T:** 14:00–18:00; **W:** 14:00–18:00; **Th:** 14:00–18:00; **F:** 14:00–18:00. Very small stock. Spec: Atlases; Bindings; Natural History; Social History; Travel - General. PR: £200–10,000. CC: V. *When closed:* telephone (07768) 004152 for appointment. Also, large print books. Mem: ABA; PBFA.

Sandpiper Books Ltd., 24 Langroyd Road, London, SW17 7PL.

Sims Reed Limited, 43a Duke Street, St. James's, London, SW1Y 6DD. Prop: Max Reed. Tel: (020) 7493-5660. Fax: (020) 7493-8468. Website: www.simsreed.com. E-mail: info@simsreed.com. Spec: Art; Artists; Illustrated.

Snowden Smith Books, 17 Cadogan Court, Draycott Avenue, London, SW3 3BX. Prop: Gillian Bickford-Smith & Jane Deyong. Tel: (020) 7581-8665. Fax: (020) 7581-0031. E-Mail: snowsmithbooks@hotmail.com. Est: 1974. Private premises; appointment necessary. Very small stock. PR: £5–500. Cata: 1 a year on 20th century travel, anthropology and related subjects.. Alternative tel: (01428) 641363. Corresp: French.

Victor Sutcliffe, 36 Parklands Road, London, SW16 6TE. Tel: (020) 8769-8345. Fax: (020) 8769-6446. Website: www.victorsutcliffe.demon.co.uk. E-mail: v@victorsutcliffe.demon.co.uk. Est: 1969. Private premises; Internet and postal. Appointment necessary. Very small stock. Spec: Military History. PR: £5–1,000. CC: JCB; V. Cata: 1.

John Thornton, ■ 455 Fulham Road, London, SW10 9UZ. Tel: (020) 7352-8810. Est: 1975. Shop; open **M:** 10:00–17:30; **T:** 10:00–17:30; **W:** 10:00–17:30; **Th:** 10:00–17:30; **F:** 10:00–17:30; **S:** 10:00–17:30. Medium stock. Spec: Religion - Roman Catholic. PR: £1–300. CC: MC; V; SW.

TSB Booksearch, 17 Gilbert Road, Wimbledon, London, SW19 1BP.

Twiggers Booksearch, 42 Charles St, Barnes, London, SW13 0NZ. Prop: T. Finn. Tel: (020) 8878-8644. Fax: (020) 8878-7826. Website: www.twiggers.com. E-mail: booksearch@twiggers.com. Est: 1980. Private premises; postal business only. Open: **M:** 09:00–17:30; **T:** 09:00–17:30; **W:** 09:00–17:30; **Th:** 09:00–17:30; **F:** 09:00–17:30; **S:** 10:00–16:00. Very small general stock. CC: SW. Also, booksearch.

Steve Walker Fine Books, 29 Ormeley Road, London, SW12 9QF. Tel: (0771) 448-1730. E-mail: vectaphile@hotmail.com. Est: 1985. Private premises; postal business only. Appointment necessary. Very small general stock. Spec: Languages - Foreign; Languages - National; Literature; Religion - General; Social History; Topography - General. PR: £5–500.

Mary Wells, 24 Minehead Road, London, SW16 2AW. Tel: (020) 8769-0778. Fax: (020) 8769-0778. Est: 1980. Market stand/stall; book fairs only. Small stock. PR: £1–500. Also, booksearch. Attends Bloomsbury Fair, Royal National.

Whistler's Books, 11 Ashbourne Terrace, Wimbledon, London, SW19 1QX.

World's End Bookshop, 357 King's Road, Chelsea, London, SW3 5ES.

SNOWDEN SMITH BOOKS

Props: Jane Deyong & Gillian Bickford-Smith

17 Cadogan Court, Draycott Avenue,
London SW3 3BX
Tel: 020 7581 8665 & 020 8870 2067
Fax: 020 7581 0031.

TRAVEL, ANTHROPOLOGY, ETHNOLOGY,
TRIBAL ART & GENERAL FOREIGN AFFAIRS

Relating especially to the Middle East,
Africa, Asia, Australia & the Pacific.
Catalogues on request. Postal business only.

We also list books on:
www.ukbookworld.com/members/chaplin

Wykeham Books, 64 Ridgway, Wimbledon, London, SW19 4RA. Prop: H. S.G. Mather. Tel: (020) 8879-3721. Website: www.bibliographies.co.uk. E-mail: wykbooks@msn.com. Est: 1976. Private premises; postal business only. Small stock. Spec: Bibliography; Books about Books. PR: £5–3,000.

LONDON
(WEST POSTAL DISTRICTS)

Al Saqi Books, 26 Westbourne Grove, London, W2 5RH.

Altea Antique Maps & Books, Third Floor, 91 Regent St., London, W1B 4EL. Prop: Mr. Massimo De Martini. Tel: (020) 7494-9060. Fax: (020) 7287-7938. Website: www.alteamaps.com. E-mail: info@alteamaps.com. Est: 1993. Shop &/or gallery; Internet and postal. Telephone first. Open: **M:** 10:00–18:00; **T:** 10:00–18:00; **W:** 10:00–18:00; **Th:** 10:00–18:00; **F:** 10:00–18:00. Small general stock. Spec: Astronomy; Atlases; Topography - General; Topography - Local; Travel - General; Voyages & Discovery. PR: £20–5,000. CC: AE; E; JCB; MC; V . Also, map search, colouring & restoration. Cata: 4 – Quarterly. Corresp: Italian. Mem: ABA; PBFA; ILAB; IMCoS. VAT No: GB 649 5809 86.

Archive of Modern Conflict, Flat 2, Tower House, Candover Street, London, W1P 7PQ.

Baskerville Books, 39 Scarsdale Villas, London, W8 6PU.

David Batterham, 36 Alexander Street, London, W2 5NU. Tel: (020) 7229-3845. Fax: (020) 7243-2421. E-mail: david.batterham@virgin.net. Est: 1966. Private premises; appointment necessary. Small stock. Spec: Applied Art; Architecture; Caricature; Fashion & Costume; Illustrated; Journals - General; Technology; Typography. PR: £5–5,000. CC: MC; V. Cata: 6. Corresp: French.

Nicholas Bernstein (Rare Books, 2 Vaughan Avenue, London, W6 0XS.

Biblical Heritage Collection, P.O. Box 646, London, W8 7PP.

Biblion Ltd, ■ 1–7 Davies Mews, London, W1K 5AB. Director: Leo Harrison. Manager: Stephen Poole. Tel: (020) 7629-1374. Fax: (020) 7629-1374. Website: www.biblion.com. E-mail: info@biblion.co.uk. Est: 1999. Shop; Internet and postal. Open: **M:** 10:00–18:00; **T:** 10:00–18:00; **W:** 10:00–18:00; **Th:** 10:00–18:00; **F:** 10:00–18:00; **S:** 10:00–18:00. Large stock. Spec: Antiquarian; Applied Art; Art; Bibliography; Bindings; Children's - General; Colour-Plate; Countries - Melanesia; Countries - Mexico; Countries - Poland; Engineering; Fine & Rare; History - Irish; Illuminated Manuscripts; Illustrated; Limited Editions; and others as listed in the Speciality Index. PR: £10–50,000. CC: E; JCB; MC; V.

J. & S.L. Bonham, Flat 14, 84 Westbourne Terrace, London, W2 6QE. Prop: John & Suzanne Bonham. Tel: (020) 7402-7064. Fax: (020) 7402-0955. Website: www.bonbooks.dial.pipex.com. E-mail: bonbooks@dial.pipex.com. Est: 1976. Private premises; Internet and postal. Appointment necessary. Medium stock. Spec: Alpinism/Mountaineering; Countries - Africa; Countries - Australia; Countries - Polar; Topography - General; Travel - General; Travel - Africa; Travel - Americas; Travel - Asia; Travel - Australasia/Australia; Travel - Europe; Travel - Middle East; Travel - Polar. PR: £10–2,000. CC: MC; V; SW, SO. Valuations. Cata: 1 – occasionally. Corresp: German. Mem: ABA; PBFA; ILAB. VAT No: GB 362 1962 53.

The Book Business, 90 Greenford Avenue, London, W7 3QS.

Books for Cooks, 4 Blenheim Crescent, London, W11 1NN.

Books & Things, P.O. Box 17768, London, W8 6ZD. Prop: M.M. Steenson. Tel: (020) 7370-5593. Fax: (020) 7370-5593. Website: www.booksandthings.co.uk. E-mail: martin@booksandthings.co.uk. Est: 1972. Warehouse; Internet and postal. Small stock. Spec: Advertising; Applied Art; Art Reference; Children's - Illustrated; Decorative's Art; Illustrated; Modern First Editions; Periodicals & Magazines; Photography; Private Press; Publishers - Studio, The. PR: £20–1,000. CC: E; JCB; MC. Also, a booksearch service. Cata: 1 – on specialities. Mem: ABA; PBFA; ILAB.

Julian Browning, P.O. Box 4005, London, W9 1XF. Tel: (020) 7286-6034. Fax: (020) 7286-1919. Website: www.jbautographs.com. E-mail: browning@jbautographs.com. Est: 1992. Private premises; appointment necessary. Medium stock. Spec: Autographs; Documents - General; Manuscripts. PR: £20–2,000. CC: AE; MC; V. Cata: 1 – on autograph letters, manuscripts & historical documents.

Available from Richard Joseph Publishers Ltd
BOOK DEALING FOR PROFIT
by Paul Minet

1st Edition 2000 (Quarto H/b) £10.00 144pp

biblion

BOOKSHOP OF BOOKSHOPS

biblion *mayfair* -&- biblion.com

Europe's leading marketplace for rare, antiquarian and out of print books

Nr. Bond St. tube station
Biblion, 1-7 Davies Mews, Mayfair, London.   Tel: 020 7629 1374   Fax: 020 7493 7158
Email: info@biblion.com   Web: www.biblion.com

ADRIAN HARRINGTON
ANTIQUARIAN BOOKSELLER
A wide ranging stock of antiquarian books, prints and maps

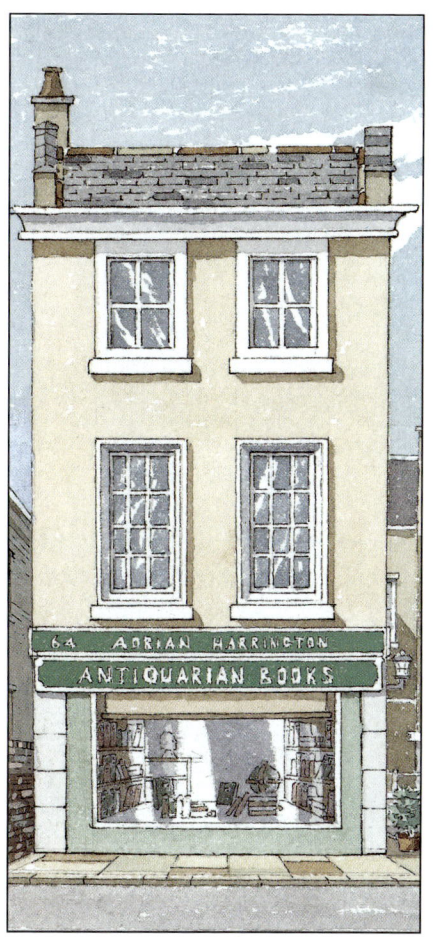

Specialising in:
Literature, first editions and bound library sets. Voyages and travel, atlases, colourplate and illustrated books. Children's books, fore edge paintings and fine and rare books in all fields.

We are just 5 minutes walk from both High Street Kensington and Notting Hill tube stations.

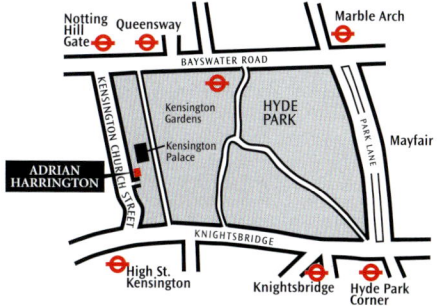

64A Kensington Church Street, Kensington, London W8 4DB
tel 020 7937 1465 · fax 020 7368 0912
e-mail: rare@harringtonbooks.co.uk
Visit our website: www.harringtonbooks.co.uk
Opening Hours: Monday to Saturday: 10.00am - 6.00pm. Out of hours by appointment

Chiltern Books, 9 York Mansions, 84 Chiltern Street, London, W1U 5AL. Prop: Georges Lannois. Tel: (020) 7935-8641. Est: 1965. Private premises; appointment necessary. Small stock. Spec: Foreign Texts; Languages - Foreign; Modern First Editions; Publishers - Penguin; Travel - General. PR: £1–40. Corresp: French, Portuguese.

W.H. Collectables, 500 Chesham House, 150 Regent Street, London, W1R 5FA. Prop: Michael A. Wheeler. Tel: (01394) 385021. Est: 1981. Storeroom; appointment necessary. Very large general stock. Spec: Alpinism/Mountaineering; Animals and Birds; Antiquarian; Aviation; Banking & Insurance; Brewing; Canals/Inland Waterways; Comic Books & Annuals; Erotica; Manuscripts; Maritime/Nautical; Military History; Mining; Motoring; Physical Culture; Railways. PR: £10–500. CC: AE; MC; V. Cata: 4 – a year.

Cusack Books, P.O. Box 17696, London, W12 8WR. Prop: Elaine M. Cusack-O'Connell. Tel: (020) 8743-0517. Website: www.cusackbooks.com. E-mail: davidoconnell@tesco.net. Est: 1998. Private premises; Internet and postal. Very small stock. Spec: Cinema/Film; Music - Popular; Music - Rock; Television. PR: £5–250. CC: D; E; JCB; MC; V.

Marc–Antoine du Ry Medieval M, medievalmodern, 14 Bulstrode Street, London, W1U 2JG. Tel: (07770) 888116. Fax: (020) 7419-0395. Website: www.medievalart.uk.com. E-mail: info@marcdury.co.uk. Est: 1995. Shop &/or gallery. Open: **W:** 11:00–18:00; **Th:** 11:00–18:00; **F:** 11:00–18:00; **S:** 11:00–18:00. Spec: Book of Hours; Illuminated Manuscripts; Manuscripts; Medieval. PR: £100–100,000. Cata: 1. Corresp: French; Italian. VAT No: GB 735 7640 16.

Elton Engineering Books, 27 Mayfield Avenue, London, W4 1PN. Prop: Julia Elton. Tel: (020) 8747-0967. Website: www.bibliopoly.com & www.ilab-lila.com. E-mail: elton_engineering_books@compuserve.com. Est: 1985. Private premises; Internet and postal. Appointment necessary. Small stock. Spec: Architecture; Building & Construction; Civil Engineering; Engineering; Railways; Technology; Transport. PR: £50–3,000. CC: MC; V. Cata: 1. Corresp: French, German. Mem: ABA; ILAB. VAT No: GB 429 7966 90.

Faircross Books, 46 Devonshire Road, Chiswick, W4 2HD.

James Fergusson Books & Manusc, 39 Melrose Gardens, London, W6 7RN. Tel: (020) 7602-3536. Fax: (020) 7602-0502. E-mail: jamesfergusson@btinternet.com. Est: 1986. Private premises; postal business only. Apointment necessary. Very small stock. Spec: Letters; Manuscripts. Also, 19th & 20th century literary association copies, autographs and photographs. Cata: – occasionally.

Simon Finch Rare Books Ltd., 53 Maddox Street, London, W1S 2PN. Tel: (020) 7499-0974. Fax: (020) 7499-0799. Website: www.simonfinch.com. E-mail: rarebooks@simonfinch.com. Est: 1981. Spec: Art; Autographs; Bindings; Design; Early Imprints; Literature; Manuscripts; Medicine; Modern First Editions; Photography; Printing; Science - General. PR: £1–500,000. CC: AE; MC; V; SW.

First State Books, 35 Talbot Road, London, W2 5JG. Prop: Euan Stuart. Tel: (020) 7792-2672. Fax: (020) 7792-2672. Website: www.firststatebooks.com. E-mail: euan.stuart@firststatebooks.com. Est: 2001. Private premises; Internet and postal. Very small stock displayed at: Biblion, London W1K 5AB. Spec: Fiction - General; First Editions. PR: £15–100.

Sam Fogg Ltd, ■ 15d Clifford Street, London, W1S 4JZ. Tel: (020) 7534-2100. Fax: (020) 7534-2122. Website: www.samfogg.com. E-mail: info@samfogg.com. Est: 1978. Shop; appointment necessary. Open: **M:** 09:29–17:30; **T:** 09:30–17:30; **W:** 09:30–17:30; **Th:** 09:30–17:30; **F:** 09:30–17:30. Small stock. Spec: Manuscripts. CC: MC; V. Cata: 1. Corresp: French, German. Mem: ABA. VAT No: GB 467 6893 80.

Richard Ford, 70 Chaucer Road, London, W3 6DP. Tel: (020) 8993-1235. Fax: (020) 8752-1431. E-mail: richard.rmford@btopenworld.com. Est: 1982. Private premises; appointment necessary. Very small stock. Spec: Autographs; Bibliography; Documents - General; Manuscripts; Publishing. PR: £10–1,000. Also, historical documents. Cata: – rarely on book history. Corresp: French, Italian. Mem: PBFA.

Fosters Bookshop, ■ 183 Chiswick High Road, London, W4 2DR. Prop: W.A. & M.A. Foster. Tel: (020) 8995-2768. Est: 1968. Shop; open **Th:** 10:30–17:30; **F:** 10:30–17:30; **S:** 10:30–17:30. Medium general stock. Spec: Applied Art; Architecture; Art; Bindings; Children's - General; First Editions; Illustrated; Sets of Books; Signed Editions; Travel - General. PR: £2–1,000.

Arthur Freeman Rare Books and, 5 Bryanston Square, London, W1H 2DH.

Fuller D'Arch Smith, 37b New Cavendish Street, London, W1G 8JR. Prop: Jean Overton Fuller & Timothy D'Arch Smith. Tel: (020) 7722-0063. Fax: (020) 7722-0063. Est: 1969. Private premises; appointment necessary. Very small general stock. PR: £5–500. Cata: – occasionally. Corresp: French, German, Italian, Russian.

Golfiana, Grays in the Mews B24, Davies Mews, London, W1.

Hab Books, 35 Wellington Road, Ealing, London, W5 4UJ. Prop: T. Habraszewski. Tel: (020) 8932-5058. Fax: (020) 8932-5058. E-mail: tom@habbks.freeserve.co.uk. Est: 1981. Private premises; postal business only. Spec: Biography; Countries - East Europe; Countries - Russia; Foreign Texts; Politics; Theology. Cata: – occasionally.

Adrian Harrington, 64a Kensington Church Street, Kensington, London, W8 4DB. Tel: (020) 7937-1465. Fax: (020) 7368-0912. Website: www.harringtonbooks.co.uk. E-mail: rare@harringtonbooks.co.uk. Est: 1971. Spec: Antiquarian; Art; Author - General; Author - Churchill, Sir Winston; Author - Conan Doyle, Sir Arthur; Author - Cornwell, Bernard; Author - Dickens, Charles; Author - Fleming, Ian; Author - Greene, Graham; Author - Johns; Author - Rowling, JK; and others as listed in the Speciality Index. PR: £10–50,000. CC: AE; MC; V. Also, bookbinding. Mem: ABA; PBFA.

Harrison's Books, ■ Biblion, 1–7 Davies Mews, London, W1K 5AB. Prop: Leo Harrison. Tel: (020) 7629-1374. Fax: (020) 7493-7158. Website: www.biblion.co.uk. E-mail: leo@ebiblion.co.uk. Est: 1967. *Shop at:* Biblion. Open: **M:** 10:00–18:00; **T:** 10:00–18:00; **W:** 10:00–18:00; **Th:** 10:00–18:00; **F:** 10:00–18:00; **S:** 10:00–18:00. Very small stock. Spec: Bindings; Children's - General; Illustrated; Sport - Angling/Fishing. PR: £20–5,000. CC: JCB; MC; V. Cata: 2.

G. Heywood Hill Limited, ■ 10 Curzon Street, London, W1J 5HH. Tel: (020) 7629-0647. Fax: (020) 7408-0286. Website: www.gheywoodhill.com. E-mail: old@gheywoodhill.com. Est: 1936. Shop; open **M:** 09:00–17:30; **T:** 09:00–17:30; **W:** 09:00–17:30; **Th:** 09:00–17:30; **F:** 09:00–17:30; **S:** 09:00–12:30. Medium general stock. Spec: Architecture; Children's - General; History - General; Illustrated; Literature; Natural History. PR: £5–10,000. CC: MC; V; SW. Also, new books & a booksearch service. Cata: 4 – Occasional. Corresp: French, German, Spanish, Italian. Mem: ABA; BA.

Judith Hodgson, 11 Stanwick Road, London, W14 8TL. Tel: (020) 7603-7414. Fax: (020) 7602-1431. E-mail: judithghodgson@supanet.com. Est: 1986. Private premises; postal business only. Appointment necessary. Small stock. Spec: Antiquarian. Cata: 1. Corresp: French, Spanish, Portuguese. Mem: ABA; ILAB. VAT No: GB 446 0649 44.

Don Kelly Books, Admiral Vernon, 141-149 Portobello Rd, London, W11. Prop: Don Kelly. Tel: (020) 7731-0482. Fax: (020) 7731-0482. E-mail: donkellybooks@btinternet.com. Est: 1981. Market stand/stall. *Postal address:* P.O. Box 44132, London SW6 2WN. Open: **S:** 07:00–16:00. Medium stock. Spec: Antiques; Applied Art; Fine Art. PR: £5–1,000. CC: JCB; MC. International mail order, booksearch.

Robert J. Kirkpatrick, 6 Osterley Park View Road, London, W7 2HH. Tel: (020) 8567-4521. E-mail: rkirkpatrick.molesworth@virgin.net. Est: 1986. Private premises; postal business only. Appointment necessary. Very small stock. Spec: Juvenile; Memoirs; Public Schools. PR: £1–100. Cata: 1.

Kitty Liebreich Antique Maps & Prints, 5 Monk's Drive, London, W3 0EG. Tel: (020) 8992-5104. Fax: (020) 8992-5104. Website: www.kittyprint.com. E-mail: kitty@liebreich.co.uk. Est: 1972. Private premises; Internet and postal. Appointment necessary. Small stock. Spec: Animals and Birds; Antiquarian; Pacifism; Topography - General; Topography - Local. PR: £20–500.

Bjorn Lowendahl Rare Books, 34–36 Maddox Street, London, W1S 1PD.

Maggs Brothers Limited, 50 Berkeley Square, London, W1J 5BA. Tel: (020) 7493-7160. Fax: (020) 7499-2007. Website: www.maggs.com. E-mail: postmaster@maggs.com. Est: 1853. Spec: Autographs; Bibliography; Bindings; Early Imprints; Fine Printing; Illuminated Manuscripts; Letters; Literature; Manuscripts; Military History; Natural History; Travel - General.

Carol Manheim, 31 Ennismore Avenue, London, W4 1SE. Tel: (020) 8994-9740. Fax: (0709) 239-4665. E-mail: art.photo@lineone.net. Est: 1982. Spec: Art History; Art Reference (20-21st C); Artists; Fashion & Costume; Photography. PR: £20–1,000. CC: MC; V.

Marlborough Rare Books Ltd, ■ 144/146 New Bond Street, London, W1S 2TR. Prop: Jonathan Gestetner. Tel: (020) 7493-6993. Fax: (020) 7499-2479. E-mail: sales@mrb-books.co.uk. Est: 1948. Shop; open **M:** 09:30–17:30; **T:** 09:30–17:30; **W:** 09:30–17:30; **Th:** 09:30–17:30; **F:** 09:30–17:30. Medium stock. Spec: Architecture; Bibliography; Bindings; Colour-Plate; Country Houses; Fine Art; Illustrated; Landscape; Literature; Topography - General. PR: £50–50,000. CC: MC; V. Cata: 6 – on art & architecture, travel & topography. Corresp: French, German. Mem: ABA; ILAB.

Orbis Books (London) Ltd., 206 Blythe Road, London, W14 0HH.

Paralos Ltd., 4th Floor, 23/24 Margaret Street, London, W1W 8RU. Prop: Panagiotis Chantziaras, Louise Bryan & Tim Bryars. Tel: (020) 7637-0796. Fax: (020) 7637-0819. Website: www.paralos.co.uk. E-mail: paralos@paralos.co.uk. Est: 1997. Office &/or bookroom; appointment necessary. Very large stock. Spec: Antiquarian; Atlases; Cartography; Classical Studies; Countries - Greece; Early Imprints; Fine & Rare; Natural History; Topography - General; Travel - General; Voyages & Discovery. PR: £10–30,000. CC: MC; V. Mem: ABA; ILAB; IAMA. VAT No: GB 697 3682 71.

Diana Parikian, Rare Books, 3 Caithness Road, London, W14 0JB. Tel: (020) 7603-8375. Fax: (020) 7602-1178. E-mail: dparikian@aol.com. Est: 1960. Private premises; appointment necessary. Spec: Emblemata; Fine & Rare; Foreign Texts; Iconography. PR: £200–10,000. Cata: 2.

Pickering & Chatto, 36 St. George Street, London, W1R 9FA.

William Poole, 97 New Bond Street, London, W1S 1SL. Tel: (020) 7629-8738. Est: 1979. Private premises; appointment necessary. Small stock. Spec: Academic/Scholarly; Classical Studies; Fine & Rare; Foreign Texts; Humanism; Publishers - General. Cata: 2 – European & British Books pre-1800, Classical Studies.

Portobello Books, 328 Portobello Road, London, W10 5RU. Prop: Mr. L. Thompson. Tel: (020) 8964-3166. Fax: (020) 8266-1993. E-mail: sales@portobello-books.com. Est: 1992. PR: £1–100.

Jonathan Potter Ltd., 125 New Bond Street, London, W1S 1DY. Tel: (020) 7491-3520. Fax: (020) 7491-9754. Website: www.jpmaps.co.uk. E-mail: jpmaps@attglobal.net. Est: 1975. Shop &/or gallery. Open: **M:** 10:00–18:00; **T:** 10:00–18:00; **W:** 10:00–18:00; **Th:** 10:00–18:00; **F:** 10:00–18:00. Spec: Atlases; Cartography; Reference. PR: £30–30,000. CC: AE; D; JCB; V. Also, reference books on the history of cartography & framing & paper restoration services. Mem: ABA; ILAB.

Quadrille at Delehar, ■ 146 Portobello Road, London, W11 2DZ. Prop: Valerie Jackson–Harris. Tel: (01923) 829079. Fax: (01923) 825207. Est: 1965. Shop; open **S:** 09:00–16:00. Medium stock. Spec: Antiques; Dance; Performing Arts; Royalty - General. PR: £5–5,000. CC: AE; MC; V. Also, Valentines, Christmas cards. Mem: ABA; PBFA; ES.

Bernard Quaritch Ltd., ■ 5-8 Lower John Street, Golden Square, London, W1F 9AU. Prop: Lord Parmoor. Tel: (020) 7734-2983. Fax: (020) 7437-0967. Website: www.quaritch.com. E-mail: rarebooks@quaritch.com. Est: 1847. Shop; open **M:** 09:30–17:30; **T:** 09:30–17:30; **W:** 09:30–17:30; **Th:** 09:30–17:30; **F:** 09:30–17:30. Large stock. Spec: Alchemy; Antiquarian; Architecture; Art; Bibliography; Cookery/Gastronomy; Early Imprints; Economics; Incunabula; Literature; Manuscripts; Medicine; Philosophy; Photography; Religion - Islam; Science - General; Travel - General. PR: £100–500,000. CC: AE; MC; V; SW. Cata: 12. Corresp: French, German, Italian, Spanish, Russian. Mem: ABA; PBFA; ILAB; SLAM; VDA; BADA. VAT No: GB 539 0733 36.

Leslie Robert, 74 Devonport, Southwick Street, London, W2 2QH.

Robert G. Sawers, P.O. Box 4QA, London, W1A 4QA.

A.F. Sephton, 16 Bloemfontein Avenue, Shepherds Bush, London, W12 7BL. Tel: (020) 8749-1454. Est: 1966. Private premises; appointment necessary. Small general stock. Spec: Artists; Colour-Plate; Illustrated; Social History. PR: £10–100.

Bernard J. Shapero Rare Books, ■ 32 St. George Street, London, W1R 0EA. Tel: (020) 7493-0876. Fax: (020) 7229-7860. Website: www.shapero.com. E-mail: info@shapero.com. Est: 1979. Shop; Internet and postal. Open: **M:** 09:30–18:30; **T:** 09:30–18:30; **W:** 09:30–18:30; **Th:** 09:30–18:30; **F:** 09:30–18:30; **S:** 11:00–17:00. Large stock. Spec: Academic/Scholarly; Africana; Alchemy; Alpinism/Mountaineering; American Indians; Americana; Animals and Birds; Anthropology; Antiquarian; Architecture; Arms & Armour; Art; Art History; Astrology; Atlases; Author - 20th Century; Bibliography; Children's Illustrated; and others as listed in the Speciality Index. PR: £50–100. CC: AE; D; E; JCB; MC; V; SW. Cata: 1 – regularly on specialities. Corresp: French, German, Italian, Spanish, Dutch. Mem: ABA; PBFA; ILAB. VAT No: GB 466 5294 16.

Sokol Books Ltd.,, P.O. Box 2409, London, W1A 2SH. Prop: C.J. Sokol. Tel: (020) 7499-5571. Fax: (020) 7629-6536. E-mail: books@sokol.co.uk. Est: 1977. Viewing by appointment only. Spec: Antiquarian; Classical Studies; Early Imprints; Early Manuscripts; Fine & Rare; History of Ideas; Incunabula; Literature; Science - History of; Travel - General. PR: £100–100,000. Mem: ABA; ILAB.

Searching for a title - and cannot find it on any Internet database?
Then try **SheppardsBooksearch**

By selecting the subject classification – the request goes to all dealers who major in that subject.

Henry Sotheran Limited, ■ 2–5 Sackville Street, Piccadilly, London, W1S 3DP. Tel: (020) 7439-6151. Fax: (020) 7434-2019. Website: www.sotherans.co.uk. E-mail: sotherans@sotherans.co.uk. Est: 1761. Spec: Architecture; Art; Bindings; Children's - General; Churchilliana; Illustrated; Literature; Natural History; Private Press; Sets of Books; Travel - General. PR: £20–100,000. CC: AE; MC; V. Mem: ABA.

Sue Lowell Natural History Boo, 101 Cambridge Gardens, London, W10 6JE. Prop: Sue Lowell. Tel: (020) 8960-4382. Fax: (020) 8968-7910. Website: Abebooks.com. E-mail: sue4382@aol.com. Est: 1972. Private premises; Internet and postal. Open: **M:** 10:00–19:00; **T:** 10:00–19:00; **W:** 10:00–19:00; **Th:** 10:00-19:00; **F:** 10:00–19:00; **S:** 09:00–13:00; **Su:** 10:00–16:00. Medium stock. Spec: Academic/Scholarly; Alpinism/Mountaineering; American Indians; Animals and Birds; Art Reference; Botany; Gardening; Medicine - History of; Natural History; New Naturalist; Ornithology; Science - History of; Travel - General; Zoology. PR: £10–4,000. CC: MC; V. Booksearch. Corresp: French.

Melvin Tenner, 51 Gayford Road, London, W12 9BY. Tel: (020) 8740-6677. Fax: (020) 8740-6960. E-mail: tenner@abelgratis.com. Est: 1980. Private premises; appointment necessary. Very small stock. Spec: International Affairs. PR: £1–200. Also, a booksearch service. Corresp: French.

The Travel Bookshop, 13-15 Blenheim Crescent, Notting Hill, London, W11 2EE.

Patrick Tuft, The Vicarage, Chiswick Mall, London, W4 2PJ. Private premises; postal business only. Very small stock. Spec: Bibles; Bibliography; History - General; Religion - Christian; Vatican and Papal History, The.

C.R. White, 22 Denbigh Terrace, London, W11 2QJ. Tel: (020) 7228-7317. Fax: (020) 7598 1248. E-mail: crwhite@globalnet.co.uk. Postal business only. Very small stock. Spec: Travel - Africa; Travel - Polar.

Mrs. Teresa White, Flat 4, 79 St. Helen's Gardens, London, W10 6LJ. Private premises; postal business only. Small stock. PR: £1–100. Cata: 52 – weekly.

LONDON
(WEST CENTRAL POSTAL DISTRICTS)

Any Amount of Books, 56 Charing Cross Road, London, WC2H 0BB.

Atlantis Bookshop, ■ 49a Museum Street, London, WC1A 1LY. Prop: Caroline Wise & Matthew Goulding. Tel: (020) 7405-2120. Website: www.atlantisbookshop.demon.co.uk. E-mail: atlantis@theatlantisbookshop.com. Est: 1922. Shop; open **M:** 10:30–18:00; **T:** 10:30–18:00; **W:** 10:30–18:00; **Th:** 10:30–18:00; **F:** 10:30–18:00; **S:** 10:30–18:00. Small stock. Spec: Archaeology; Fore-Edge Paintings; Mythology; Occult; Parapsychology. PR: £4–40. CC: AE; MC; V; SW.

Bertram Rota Ltd., ■ 31 Long Acre (First Floor), Covent Garden, London, WC2E 9LT. Tel: (020) 7836-0723. Fax: (020) 7497 9058. Website: www.bertramrota.co.uk. E-mail: bertramrota@compuserve.com. Est: 1923. Shop; open **M:** 09:30–17:30; **T:** 09:30–17:30; **W:** 09:30–17:30; **Th:** 09:30–17:30; **F:** 09:30–17:30. Medium stock. Spec: Antiquarian; Autographs; First Editions; Literature; Modern First Editions; Private Press. CC: D; E; JCB; MC; V. Also, a booksearch service. Mem: ABA; ILAB.

Bosphorus Books, 6 Whidborne Street, London, WC1H 8EU. Prop: Sinan A. Erhun. Tel: (020) 7713-6827. Fax: (020) 7837-4876. Website: www.bosphorusbooks.co.uk. E-mail: searhun@btopenworld.com. Est: 2000. Private premises; Internet and postal. Very small stock. Spec: Countries - Balkans, The; Countries - Middle East, The; Countries - Turkey; Ottoman Empire. CC: MC; V; D, SW. Corresp: French, Turkish.

Steve Burak, ■ 18, Leigh Street, off Judd Street, London, WC1H 9EW. Prop: Steve Burak. Tel: (020) 7388-1153. E-mail: SteveBurakLondon@yahoo.com. Est: 2002. *Shop at:* Ground Floor, 18 Leigh Street, London WC1H 9EW. Open: **M:** 11:00–19:00; **T:** 11:00–19:00; **W:** 11:00–19:00; **Th:** 11:00–19:00; **F:** 11:00–19:00; **S:** 11:00–19:00. Medium general stock. Spec: Academic/Scholarly; Antiquarian. PR: £5–1,000.

The Cinema Bookshop, ■ 13–14 Great Russell Street, London, WC1B 3NH. Prop: Fred Zentner. Tel: (020) 7637-0206. Fax: (020) 7436-9979. Est: 1969. Shop; open **M:** 10:30–17:30; **T:** 10:30–17:30; **W:** 10:30–17:29; **Th:** 10:30–17:30; **F:** 10:30–17:30; **S:** 10:30–17:30. Large stock. Spec: Cinema/Film. PR: £8–75. CC: E; JCB; MC; V. VAT No: GB 232 6938 54.

Collinge & Clark, ■ 13 Leigh Street, London, WC1H 9EW.

Lewis Davenport, 7 Charing Cross, Underground Concourse, The Strand, London, WC2N 4HZ.

Delectus Books, 27 Old Gloucester Street, London, WC1N 3XX. Prop: Michael R. Goss. Tel: (020) 8963-0979. Fax: (020) 8963-0502. Website: www.delectusbooks.co.uk. E-mail: mgdelectus@aol.com. Est: 1987. Private premises; Internet and postal. Very large stock. Spec: Anthropology; Astrology; Author - Blackwood, A.; Author - Machen, Arthur; Countries - Mexico; Countries - Middle East, The; Criminology; Dictionaries; Drugs; Economics; Erotica; Ethnography; Ethnology; Feminism; Folklore; Gambling; Gypsies; History - Anarchism; and others as listed in the Speciality Index. PR: £20–5,000. CC: D; JCB; MC; V; SW, SO. Cata: 2 – occasionally. Corresp: French, German, Spanish, Dutch. VAT No: GB 532 3080 82.

David Drummond at Pleasures of Past Times, 11 Cecil Court, Charing Cross Road, London, WC2N 4EZ. Prop: David Drummond. Tel: (020) 7836-1142. Fax: (020) 7836-1142. E-mail: drummond@popt.fsnet.co.uk. Est: 1967. Spec: Children's - General; Circus; Illustrated; Magic & Conjuring; Performing Arts. PR: £10–500. Also, juvenile illustrated. VAT No: GB 239 7395 19.

Dealers who need to update their entry should visit their page on
www.sheppardsdirectories.com

Francis Edwards (London) Limit, ■ 13 Great Newport Street, Charing Cross Road, London, WC2H 7JA. Tel: (020) 7379-7669. Fax: (020) 7836-5977. Website: www.francisedwards.co.uk. E-mail: sales@femilitary.demon.co.uk. Est: 218. Shop; Internet and postal. Open: **M:** 10:00–18:30; **T:** 10:00–18:30; **W:** 10:00–18:30; **Th:** 10:00–18:30; **F:** 10:00–18:30; **S:** 10:00–18:30. Small general stock. Spec: Art; Aviation; Bindings; Literature; Military; Naval; Voyages & Discovery. PR: £15–1,000. CC: AE; MC; V. Cata: – Regularly. Mem: ABA; PBFA; ILAB.

Fine Books Oriental Ltd., ■ 38 Museum Street, London, WC1A 1LP. Prop: Jeffrey Somers. Tel: (020) 7242-5288. Fax: (020) 7242-5344. Website: www.finebooks.demon.co.uk. E-mail: oriental@finebooks.demon.co.uk. Est: 1977. Shop; open **M:** 09:30–17:30; **T:** 09:30–17:30; **W:** 09:30–17:30; **Th:** 09:30–17:30; **F:** 09:30–17:30; **S:** 11:00–17:00. Medium stock. Spec: Aviation; Canals/Inland Waterways; Cartoons; Countries - Asia; Countries - India; Countries - Japan; Psychic; Religion - Oriental; Spiritualism; Travel - Asia; Travel - Middle East. PR: £3–15,000. CC: AE; D; JCB; MC; V; SW, SO. Corresp: Japanese. Mem: PBFA.

Michael Finney Antique Books &, ■ 31 Museum St., London, WC1A 1LG. Tel: (020) 7631-3533. Fax: (020) 7637-1813. Website: www.michaelfinney.co.uk. E-mail: prints@michaelfinney.co.uk. Est: 1979. Shop; open **M:** 10:00–18:00; **T:** 10:00–18:00; **W:** 10:00–18:00; **Th:** 10:00–18:00; **F:** 10:00–18:00; **S:** 10:00–18:00. Large general stock. Spec: Architecture; Illustrated; Natural History; Social History; Travel - General. PR: £20–5,000. CC: AE; MC; V. Cata: 6. Corresp: Spanish, French, Italian. Mem: ABA; PBFA. VAT No: GB 577 8997 48.

Robert Frew Limited, ■ 106 Great Russell Street, London, WC1B 3NB. Tel: (020) 7580-2311. Fax: (020) 7580-2313. Website: www.robertfrew.com. E-mail: shop@robertfrew.com. Est: 1993. Shop; open **M:** 10:00–18:00; **T:** 10:00–18:00; **W:** 10:00–18:00; **Th:** 10:00–18:00; **F:** 10:00–18:00; **S:** 10:00–14:00. Spec: Antiquarian; Atlases; Author - Churchill, Sir Winston; Bindings; Cartography; Encyclopaedias; History - General; Illustrated; Literature; Sets of Books; Sport - Skiing; Travel - General. PR: £10–30,000. CC: AE; D; E; JCB; MC; V. Mem: ABA; PBFA; ILAB. VAT No: GB 625 8877 92.

Gay's The Word, 66 Marchmont Street, London, WC1N 1AB.

R.A. Gekoski, ■ Pied Bull Yard, 15a Bloomsbury Square, London, WC1A 2LP. Prop: R.A. Gekoski, P.A. Grogan & J.A.M. Irvine. Tel: (020) 7404-6676. Fax: (020) 7404-6595. Website: www.gekoski.com. E-mail: rick@gekoski.com. Est: 1982. Shop; open **M:** 10:00–17:30; **T:** 10:00–17:30; **W:** 10:00–17:30; **Th:** 10:00–17:30; **F:** 10:00–17:30. Small stock. Spec: First Editions; Letters; Manuscripts. PR: £100–1,000. CC: MC; V. Cata: 1 – occasionally. Mem: ABA. VAT No: GB 418 5464 40.

Griffith & Partners Ltd., The Bookshop, 31–35 Great Ormond Street, London, WC1N 3HZ.

Grosvenor Prints, 28 Shelton Street, Covent Garden, London, WC2H 9JE.

Jarndyce Antiquarian Bookselle, 46 Great Russell Street, (opp. British Museum), London, WC1B 3PA. Prop: Brian Lake & Janet Nassau. Tel: (020) 7631-4220. Fax: (020) 7631-1882. Website: www.jarndyce.co.uk. E-mail: books@jarndyce.co.uk. Est: 1969. Shop &/or showroom. Open: **M:** 11:00–17:00; **T:** 11:00–17:00; **W:** 11:00–17:00; **Th:** 11:11–17:00; **F:** 11:00–17:00. Large stock. Spec: Antiquarian; Author - Austen, Jane; Author - Byron, Lord; Author - Cobbett, William; Author - Dickens, Charles; Economics; Education & School; First Editions; Literature; Literature - Victorian; Performing Arts; Plays; Politics; Social History; and others as listed in the Speciality Index. PR: £5–5,000. CC: AE; MC; V. Cata: 6. Corresp: French. Mem: ABA; PBFA. VAT No: 524 0890 57.

Judd Books, 82 Marchmont Street, London, WC1N 1AG.

The Maghreb Bookshop, 45 Burton Street, London, WC1H 9AL.

The Marchmont Bookshop, 39 Burton Street, London, WC1H 9AL.

Marchpane, 16 Cecil Court, Charing Cross Road, London, WC2N 4HE.

Murder One, ■ 71–73 Charing Cross Road, London, WC2H 0AA. Prop: M. Jakubowski & N. Landau. Tel: (020) 7734-3483. Fax: (020) 7734-3429. Website: www.murderone.co.uk. E-mail: murder_london@compuserve.com. Est: 1989. Shop; open **M:** 10:00–19:00; **T:** 10:00–19:00; **W:** 10:00–19:00; **Th:** 10:00–20:00; **F:** 10:00–20:00; **S:** 10:00–20:00. Very large stock. Spec: Countries - Melanesia; Countries - Mexico; Fiction - Romantic; Fiction - Science Fiction. PR: £1–500. CC: AE; E; JCB; MC; V. Corresp: French, Spanish, German & Italian.

Museum Bookshop, ■ 36 Great Russell Street, London, WC1B 3QB. Prop: Ashley Jones. Tel: (020) 7580-4086. Fax: (020) 7436-4364. Website: www.museumbookshop.org.uk/. E-mail: mbooks@btconnect.com. Est: 1979. Shop; Internet and postal. Open: **M:** 10:00–17:30. **S:** 10:00–17:30. Spec: Antiquarian; Archaeology; Classical Studies; Countries - Egypt; Egyptology; History - Ancient; Travel - Middle East. PR: £5–300. CC: AE; D; JCB; MC; V. Also, new books & back-numbers of journals, & a booksearch service.

Rees & O'Neill, ■ 27 Cecil Court, London, WC2N 4EZ. Tel: (020) 7836-3336. Website: admin@rees-oneill.com. E-mail: admin@rees-oneill.com. Est: 2002. Shop; open **M:** 10:00–18:00; **T:** 10:00–18:00; **W:** 10:00–18:00; **Th:** 10:00–18:00; **F:** 10:00–18:00; **S:** 10:00–17:00. Medium stock. Spec: Antiques; Art; Illustrated; Literature; Modern First Editions. CC: E; MC; V. Cata: 6. Mem: ABA; PBFA; ILAB.

Photo Books International, ■ 99 Judd Street, London, WC1H 9NE. Prop: Bill Herbert & Jasper Howard. Tel: (020) 7813-7363. Fax: (020) 7813-7363. Website: www.pbi-books.com. E-mail: pbi@britishlibrary.net. Est: 1998. Shop; Internet and postal. Open: **W:** 11:00–18:00; **Th:** 11:00–18:00; **F:** 11:00–18:00; **S:** 11:00–18:00. Medium stock. Spec: Photography. PR: £5–200. CC: AE; MC; V. Mem: PBFA; BA. VAT No: GB 730 6914 40.

Henry Pordes Books Ltd., 58–60 Charing Cross Road, London, WC2H 0BB.

Arthur Probsthain, 41 Great Russell Street, London, WC1B 3PE. Tel: (020) 7636-1096. Fax: (020) 7636-1096. E-mail: ap@oriental-african-books.com. Est: 1902. Spec: Countries - Africa; Oriental.

Quinto of Charing Cross Road, 48a Charing Cross Road, London, WC2H 0BB.

Red Snapper Books, ■ 22 Cecil Court, London, WC2N 4NE. Prop: James Allen. Tel: (020) 7240-2075. Fax: (01227) 277963. Website: www.redsnapperbooks.com. E-mail: james@redsnapperbooks.com. Est: 1996. Shop; open **M:** 10:00–17:30; **T:** 10:00–17:30; **W:** 10:00–17:30; **Th:** 10:00–17:30; **F:** 10:00–17:30; **S:** 10:00–17:30. Very small stock. Spec: Beat Writers; First Editions; Photography. PR: £10–20,000. CC: MC; V. Cata: 3 – a year on beat/American, literature.

Rees & O'Neill Rare Books, ■ 27 Cecil Court, London, WC2N 4EZ. Prop: Angus O'Neill. Tel: (020) 7836-3336. Website: www.rees-oneill.com. E-mail: admin@rees-oneill.com. Est: 2002. Spec: Antiques; Art Reference; First Editions; Illustrated; Literature. CC: D: E; JCB; MC; V. Mem: ABA; PBFA.

Reg & Philip Remington, 18 Cecil Court, London, WC2N 4HE.

Shipley Specialist Art Booksellers, ■ 70 Charing Cross Road, London, WC2H 0BQ. Prop: Ian Shipley. Tel: (020) 7836-4872. Fax: (020) 7379-4358. Website: www.artbook.co.uk. E-mail: sales@artbook.co.uk. Est: 1979. Shop; Internet and postal. Open: **M:** 10:00–18:00; **T:** 10:00–18:00; **W:** 10:00–18:00; **Th:** 10:00–18:00; **F:** 10:00–18:00; **S:** 10:00–18:00. Spec: Advertising; Antiques; Applied Art; Architecture; Art; Art History; Art Reference; Artists; Book of Hours; Carpets; Catalogues Raisonnes; Ceramics; Conservation; Decorative Art; Ecclesiastical History & Architecture; Fashion & Costume; Fine Art; and others as listed in the Speciality Index. PR: £1–200. CC: AE; E; JCB; MC; V. Also, new books on the arts and a booksearch service. VAT No: GB 242 7752 54.

Skoob Russell Square, 10 Brunswick Centre, (off Bernard Street), London, WC1N 1AE.

Spink & Son Limited, 69 Southampton Row, Bloomsbury, London, WC1B 4ET. Tel: (020) 7563-4000. Fax: (020) 7563-4068. Website: www.spink-online.com. E-mail: info@spinkandson.com. Est: 1666. Spec: Military; Numismatics. PR: £1–5,000.

Stage Door Prints, ■ 9 Cecil Court, Charing Cross Road, London, WC2N 4EZ. Prop: A.L. Reynold. Tel: (020) 7240-1683. Fax: (020) 7379-5598. Est: 1982. Shop; open **M:** 11:00–18:00; **T:** 11:00–18:00; **W:** 11:00–18:00; **Th:** 11:00–18:00; **F:** 11:00–18:00; **S:** 11:30–18:00. Medium stock. Spec: Autographs; Cinema/Film; Magic & Conjuring; Music - General; Performing Arts. CC: E; MC; V; D, E, SW.

Tindley & Chapman, ■ 4 Cecil Court, London, WC2N 4HE. Prop: James Tindley, Ron Chapman. Tel: (020) 7240-2161. Fax: (020) 7370-1062. Est: 1975. Shop; open **M:** 10:00–17:30; **T:** 10:00–17:30; **W:** 10:00–17:30; **Th:** 10:00–17:30; **F:** 10:00–17:30; **S:** 11:00–17:00. Medium stock. Spec: Fiction - General; Fiction - Crime, Detective, Spy, Thrillers; Fiction - Women; First Editions; Literature; Poetry. PR: £10–5,000. CC: MC; V. Mem: PBFA. *Also at:* Ron Chapman, London SW10 9LW (q.v.).

Travis & Emery Music Bookshop, 17 Cecil Court, Charing Cross Road, London, WC2N 4EZ.

Ulysses, ■ 40 Museum Street, London, WC1 1LU. Prop: Peter Jolliffe. Tel: (020) 7831-1600. Fax: (020) 7419-0070. E-mail: ulyssesbooks@fsbdial.co.uk. Est: 1990. Shop; open **M:** 10:30–18:00; **T:** 10:30–18:00; **W:** 10:30–18:00; **Th:** 10:30–18:00; **F:** 10:30–18:00; **S:** 10:30–18:00. Large stock. Spec: Illustrated; Modern First Editions. PR: £5–1,000. CC: AE; MC; V. Cata: 5. Mem: ABA; PBFA.

Unsworths Booksellers Ltd., ■ 12 Bloomsbury Street, London, WC1B 3QA. Prop: Charlie Unsworth & Sue Coe. Tel: (020) 7436-9836. Fax: (020) 7637-7334. Website: www.unsworths.com. E-mail: books@unsworths.com. Est: 1986. Shop; open **M:** 10:00–20:00; **T:** 10:00–20:00; **W:** 10:00–20:00; **Th:** 10:00–20:00; **F:** 10:00–20:00; **S:** 10:00–20:00; **Su:** 11:00–19:00. Very large stock. Spec: Academic/Scholarly; Anthropology; Antiquarian; Archaeology; Architecture; Art; Bibliography; Bindings; Books about Books; Byzantium; Cinema/Film; Classical Studies; Early Imprints; Ecclesiastical History & Architecture; Egyptology; Fiction - General; and others as listed in the Speciality Index. PR: £1–3,000. CC: AE; D; JCB; MC; V. Cata: 2. Mem: ABA; PBFA; BA; ILAB; *Also at:* 15 Turl St, Oxford. (q.v.). VAT No: GB 480 1145 75.

Waterstone's, ■ 82 Gower Street, London, WC1E 6EQ. Prop: HMV Media Group. Tel: (020) 7636-1577. Fax: (020) 7580-7680. Website: www.waterstones.co.uk/gowerst. E-mail: sh.gower.waterstones @lineone.net. Est: 1936. Shop; open **M:** 09:30–20:00; **T:** 10:00–20:00; **W:** 09:30–20:00; **Th:** 09:30–20:00; **F:** 09:30–20:00; **S:** 09:30–19:00; **Su:** 12:00–18:00. Medium stock. Spec: Academic/Scholarly. CC: AE; D; MC; V. Dept. also sells academic remainders and is situated within large, well-known bookshop.

Watkins Books Ltd., 19–21 Cecil Court, off Charing Cross Road, London, WC2N 4EZ.

Wildy & Sons Ltd., Lincoln's Inn Archway, Carey Steet, London, WC2A 2JD.

Nigel Williams Rare Books, ■ 25 Cecil Court, Charing Cross Road, London, WC2N 4EZ. Tel: (020) 7836-7757. Fax: (020) 7379-5918. Website: www.nigelwilliams.com. E-mail: sales@nigelwilliams.com. Est: 1989. Shop; open **M:** 10:00–18:00; **T:** 10:00–18:00; **W:** 10:00–18:00; **Th:** 10:00–18:00; **F:** 10:00–18:00; **S:** 10:00–18:00. Large stock. Spec: Author - Christie, Agatha; Author - Fleming, Ian; Author - Greene, Graham; Author - Joyce, James; Author - Wodehouse, P.G.; Countries - Melanesia; Countries - Mexico; Fiction - General; Fiction - Historical; First Editions; Literature; Manuscripts. PR: £5–10,000. CC: AE; D; E; JCB; MC; V. Cata: 20. Mem: ABA; PBFA; ILAB. VAT No: GB 574 3776 05.

LONDON
(GREATER LONDON, OUTER)

BARKING

James Smith Booksellers, Vicarage Field Shopping Centre, Ripple Road, Barking, 1G11 8DQ. Prop: D.R. Bird. Tel: (020) 8591-9090. Fax: (020) 8591-9937. Website: www.jsbooks.co.uk. E-mail: op@jsb.org.uk. Est: 1926. Spec: Computing. PR: £5–50. Also, new titles & a booksearch service, export & schools book supply.

BECKENHAM

Conquistador Mail Order, 158 Kent House Road, Beckenham, Kent, BR3 1JY.

BEDDINGTON

Mrs. Patricia Clear, 33 Cedars Road, Beddington, Surrey, CR0 4PU.

BROMLEY

Geoff Shaw, 4 Hammelton Court, London Road, Bromley, BR1 3QY.

CARSHALTON

Crosby Nethercott Books, 16 Kings Avenue, Carshalton, Surrey, SM5 4NX. (*) Prop: D.W. Beer. Tel: (020) 8643 4124. E-mail: crosbybooks@cwcom.net. Est: 1991. Private premises; Internet and postal. Appointment necessary. Medium stock. Spec: Author - Rolt, L.T.C.; Canals/Inland Waterways; Company History; History - Industrial; Railways. PR: £5–100. Also, a booksearch service. Corresp: French, German.

Croydon Bookshop, ■ 304 Carshalton Road, Carshalton, SM5 3QB. Prop: Mrs. P.F. Reding & P.J. Rogers. Tel: (020) 8643-6857. Est: 1954. Shop; open **T:** 10:30–17:30; **W:** 10:30–17:30; **Th:** 10:30–17:30; **F:** 10:30–17:30; **S:** 09:30–17:30. Medium stock. PR: £2–100. Corresp: French, German, Spanish.

Japan Books (Y & S Company Ltd, P.O. Box 693, Carshalton, SM5 3ZN. (*) Prop: Sammy I. Tsunematsu. Tel: Office (020) 8773-25. Fax: (020) 8286-8003. Website: www.yandscompany.co.uk/ japanbooks.htm. E-mail: jbooksuk@aol.com. Est: 1975. Spec: Children's - General; Countries - Japan; Illustrated. PR: £20–7,500. *Shop at:* Biblion, 1–7 Davies Mews, London WC1Y 2LP.

COOKHAM

Jean Hedger, Poultons, Lower Road, Cookham Rise, Cookham, SL6 9HW.

CROYDON

D.P. Hyland, 25 Russell Hill Road, Purley, Surrey, Croydon, CR8 2LF.

Steve Archer, 11 Bedford Place, Croydon, Surrey, CR0 2BS. (*). Tel: (020) 8686 3736. Fax: (020) 8686 3736. Website: www.ukbookworld.com/members/stevearcher. E-mail: stevearcher2000@ yahoo.co.uk. Est: 2000. Private premises; postal business only. Small stock. Spec: Autobiography; Biography; Canals/Inland Waterways; Literary Travel; Literature; Modern First Editions; Sport - Cricket. PR: £2–100. CC: Paypal.

Peter Howard (Books), 2 Park View Road, Addiscombe, Croydon, Surrey, CR0 7DE. (*). Tel: (020) 8656-8302. E-mail: barpeth@clara.co.uk. Est: 1979. Private premises; appointment necessary. Very small stock. PR: £5–200.

EDGWARE

Two Jays Bookshop, ■ 119 High Street, Edgware, HA8 7DB. Prop: Joyce and Mark Matthews. Tel: (020) 8952-1349. Est: 1977. Shop; open **T:** 09:00–17:00; **W:** 09:00–17:00; **F:** 09:00–17:00; **S:** 09:00–17:00. Large general stock. PR: £2–100.

Louise Grant, 65 Parkside Drive, Edgware, Middlesex, HA8 8JU.

Reedmore Books, 10 Redhill Dr., Edgware, Middlesex, HA8 5JN.

ENFIELD

Terence J. McGee, 20 Slades Close, Enfield, Middlesex, EN2 7EB. Prop: T.J. & J.I. McGee. Tel: (020) 8366-5727. E-mail: tmcgee@globalnet.co.uk. Est: 1972. Private premises and market stand; appointment necessary. Open: **S:** 09:00–19:00; **Su:** 09:00–19:00. Small stock. Spec: Cinema/Film; Comics; Counterculture; Education & School; Music - General; Nostalgia; Performing Arts; Science - General; Science - History of; Television; Theatre. PR: £1–500. Also, sound recordings & record tapes (inc. 78s). Cata: 1 – occasionally. Corresp: French, German, Italian, Spanish.

Oak Tree Books, 69 Landseer Road, Bush Hill Park, Enfield, Middlesex, EN1 1DP. Prop: Mr R.L. Conrich.

Felicity J. Warnes, ■ 82 Merryhills Drive, Enfield, Middlesex, EN2 7PD. Prop: F. J. Warnes. Tel: (020) 8367-1661. Fax: (020) 8372-1035. E-mail: felicity@fjwarnes.u-net.com. Est: 1978. Shop; appointment necessary. *Shop at:* The Old Bookshop, 36 Gordon Road, Enfield. Open: Large stock. Spec: Embroidery; Fashion & Costume; Jewellery; Knitting; Lace; Military; Social History; Textiles. PR: £5–200. CC: MC; V. Cata: 4. Mem: PBFA; ES.

GREENFORD

Jack Ben–Nathan, 22 Teignmouth Gardens, Perivale, Greenford, UB6 8BX. (*). Tel: (020) 8997-6574. E-mail: jack.ben-nathan@the-sun.co.uk. Est: 1980. Private premises; appointment necessary. Very small stock. Spec: Sport - Billiards/Snooker/Pool. PR: £3–300. Also, booksearch. Cata: 1 – on billiards.

Books B.C., 58 Elton Avenue, Greenford, Middlesex, UB6 0PP. (*) Prop: Martin McCrory. Tel: (020) 8864-0580. Est: 1987. Private premises; appointment necessary. Very small stock. PR: £1–500. Cata: 1 – occasionally on Egyptology, Ancient History.

HAMPTON

R. W. Clements, 114 High Street, Hampton, Middlesex, TW12 2ST. Prop: R. W. Clements. Tel: (020) 8979-3069. Est: 1992. Private premises; appointment necessary. Large general stock. Spec: Archaeology; Art; Autobiography; Biography; Children's - General; Drama; Fiction - General; History - General; Irish Interest; Literature; Music - General; Poetry; Sport - General; Transport; Travel - General. PR: £5–1,000. Also, ephemera and prints related to Ireland. Cata: 4.

R. S. and P.A. Scowen, 9 Birchwood Grove, Hampton, Middlesex, TW12 3DU.

HAMPTON HILL

Bates Books, 95 High Street, Hampton Hill, Middlesex, TW12 1NH. Prop: Garry and Jackie Bates. Tel: (020) 8941-6782. E-mail: garry@devilla97.freeserve.co.uk. Private premises; postal business only. Telephone first. Small stock. Spec: Children's - General; Education & School; First Editions; Illustrated. PR: £2–30.

HAMPTON–ON–THAMES

Ian Sheridan's Bookshop, ■ 34 Thames Street, Hampton–on–Thames, Middlesex, TW12 2DK. (*) Prop: Ian Sheridan. Tel: (020) 8979-1704. Est: 1960. Shop; open **M:** 10:30–17:00; **T:** 10:30–17:00; **W:** 10:00–17:00; **Th:** 10:00–17:00; **F:** 10:00–17:00; S: 10:00–17:00; Su: 09:00–17:00. Very large general stock. PR: £2–500. Closes at dusk in winter. Corresp: French, German.

HARROW

Mary Chapman Books, c/o Guido's Collectables, 39 Station Road, Harrow, HA2 7SU.

medievalbookshop, 118 Vaughan Road, West Harrow, Harrow, Middlesex, HA1 4ED.

HATCH END

B. Heyman, 27 Sherington Avenue, Hatch End, Pinner, Middlesex, HA5 4DU. (*). Private premises; postal business only. Small stock. Spec: Art; Drama; History - General; Literary Criticism; Theatre.

Unicorn Books, 56 Rowlands Avenue, Hatch End, Pinner, HA5 4BP. (*) Prop: Sheila Feller. Tel: (020) 8420-1091. Fax: (020) 8428-0125. Website: www.unicornbooks.co.uk. E-mail: unicorn@btinternet.com. Est: 1980. Private premises; Internet and postal. Telephone first. Very small stock. Spec: Children's - Illustrated. PR: £10–1,000. CC: MC; V. Cata: 8 – children's illustrated and original illustration. Corresp: French, Italian. Mem: ABA. VAT No: GB 370 8103 71.

HAYES

Mark Weber, 25a Station Road, Hayes, Middlesex, UB3 4BD.

LONDON (OUTER)

HIGH BARNET

Andrew Hind, 11 Byng Road, High Barnet, Hertfordshire, London, EN5 4NW.

ICKENHAM

Hayes Bookshop (C. & B. Glover, 6 Glebe Avenue, Ickenham, Middlesex, UB10 8PB.

ILFORD

Book Basket, 25a Meath Road, Ilford, Essex, IG1 1JA. (*) Prop: Peter Arnold. Tel: (0208) 514-5362. E-mail: peterarnoldiv@hotmail.com. Private premises; postal business only. Spec: Academic/Scholarly; Africana; Almanacs; Alpinism/Mountaineering; Alternative Medicine; American Indians; Americana; Annuals; Anthologies; Anthropology; Antiquarian; Antiques; Archaeology; Architecture; Arms & Armour; Art; Art History; Art Reference; and others as listed in the Speciality Index. PR: £15–1,000.

The London Bookworm, 77 Eton Road, Ilford, IG1 2UD.

Porcupine Books, 37 Coventry Road, Ilford, Essex, IG1 4QR. (*) Prop: Brian Ameringen. Tel: (020) 8554-3799. Website: www.porcupine.demon.co.uk. E-mail: brian@porcupine.demon.co.uk. Est: 1998. Private premises; Internet and postal. Appointment necessary. Open: **M:** 08:00–21:00; **T:** 08:00–21:00. **Su:** 08:00–21:00. Medium stock. Spec: Fiction - Crime, Detective, Spy, Thrillers; Fiction - Fantasy, Horror; Fiction - Science Fiction. PR: £1–2,500. Cata: 4.

ISLEWORTH

Chaters Motoring Booksellers, 8 South Street, Isleworth, Middlesex, TW7 7DH. (*) Prop: F.P.A. Stroud. Tel: (020) 8568-9750. Fax: (020) 8569-8273. Website: www.chaters.co.uk. E-mail: books@chaters.co.uk. Est: 1957. Spec: Motorbikes; Motoring. PR: £1–500. Also, new books in specialities & a booksearch service.

KENLEY

David & Lynn Smith, The Hermitage, 21 Uplands Road, Kenley, Surrey, CR8 5EE. Tel: (020) 8660-9908. Fax: (020) 8660-9908. E-mail: smithbookskenley@tiscali.co.uk. Est: 1980. Storeroom; appointment necessary. Small stock. Spec: Biology; Medicine; Medicine - History of; Pharmacy/Pharmacology; Science - General; Science - History of; Scientific Instruments. PR: £10–500. CC: JCB; MC; V. Cata: 1. Mem: PBFA.

KEW

Criterion Books, 6 Nylands Avenue, Kew, Richmond, TW9 4HH. (*) Prop: Terence Crimmings. Tel: (020) 8876-1773. E-mail: terry.crimmings@tinyworld.co.uk. Est: 1992. Private premises; postal business only. Appointment necessary. Spec: Author - Bloomsbury Group, The; Author - Durrell, Lawrence; Author - Lehmann, J; Biography; First Editions; Horizon Writers; Illustrated; Literary Travel; Literature; Modern First Editions; Poetry. PR: £10–200.

MORDEN

A. Burton–Garbett, 35 The Green, Morden, Surrey, SM4 4HJ. Tel: (020) 8540-2367. Fax: (020) 8540-4594. Est: 1959. Private premises; appointment necessary. Medium stock. Spec: Countries - Caribbean, The; Countries - Central America; Countries - Mexico; Countries - Portugal; Countries - South America; Countries - Spain.

NEW BARNET

Chandos Books, 111 Park Road, New Barnet, Hertfordshire, EN4 9QR.

ForensicSearch, 17 Greenacres, Glyn Avenue, New Barnet, EN4 9PJ.

NEW MALDEN

Modern First Editions, 32 Woodlands Avenue, New Malden, Surrey, Kingston, KT3 3UQ.

PINNER

The Eastcote Bookshop, ■ 156/160 Field End Road, Pinner, Middlesex, HA5 1RH. Prop: Eileen & David May. Tel: (020) 8866-9888. Fax: (020) 8905-9387. Est: 1993. Shop; open **T:** 12:00–16:00; **W:** 12:00–16:00. **F:** 10:30–17:00; **S:** 10:30–17:00. Very large stock. Spec: Alpinism/Mountaineering; American Indians; Annuals; Antiques; Art; Canals/Inland Waterways; Children's - General; Cinema/Film; Colour-Plate; Crime (True); Esoteric; Fiction - General; First Editions; Horticulture; Humour; Illustrated; Motoring; and others as listed in the Speciality Index. PR: £2–500. CC: MC; V. Occasional fairs. Mem: PBFA.

RICHMOND–UPON–THAMES

W. & A. Houben, 2 Church Court, Richmond–upon–Thames, TW9 1JL. (*) Prop: Mr. Chris Dunlop. Tel: (020) 8940-1055. E-mail: chrisdunlop1@aol.com. Est: 1963. PR: £1–500. Also, new books & secondhand CDs.

SUNBURY–ON–THAMES

Cecilia Marsden, 98 Manor Lane, Sunbury–on–Thames, Middlesex, TW16 6JB. (*).

SUTTON

Books at Sixpence, 9 Garden Court, 71 Grange Road, Sutton, Surrey, SM2 6SP.

Mike Park, 351 Sutton Common Road, Sutton, Surrey, SM3 9HZ. (*) Prop: Mike Park & Ian Smith. Tel: (020) 8641-7796. Fax: (020) 8641-3330. Est: 1974. Private premises; appointment necessary. Small stock. Spec: Botany; Flower Arranging; Forestry; Gardening; Herbalism; Horticulture; Landscape; Natural History; Plant Hunting; Rural Life. PR: £1–1,000. CC: AE; E; MC; V. Also, booksearch. Cata: 2 – specialities. Mem: PBFA.

TEDDINGTON

Chris Hollingshead, 10 Linden Grove, Teddington, TW11 8LT.

Bill Luckman, 31 Grosvenor Court, Fairfax Road, Teddington, TW11 9BT. (*). Tel: (020) 8977 0609. E-mail: luckman@mailbox.co.uk. Est: 1984. Private premises; postal business only. Appointment necessary. Small general stock. PR: £3–400. Also, booksearch.

THORNTON HEATH

Udo K.H. Polczynski, 29 Kingswood Avenue, Thornton Heath, Surrey, CR7 7HR. (*). Tel: (020) 8689-6274. Fax: (020) 8684-2751. Est: 1984. Private premises; appointment necessary. Medium stock. Spec: Anthropology; Archaeology; Classical Studies; Folklore; Journals - General; Medieval. PR: £10–5,000. *Also at:* Philologus - Fine & Rare Books, London SW16. Cata: 2. Corresp: French, German, Malay, Polish, Russian, Spanish.

TWICKENHAM

Books on Spain, P.O. Box 207, Twickenham, TW2 5BQ. (*) Prop: Keith Harris. Tel: (020) 8898-7789. Fax: (020) 8898-7789 (24 hours). Website: www.books-on-spain.com. E-mail: keithharris@books-on-spain.com. Est: 1993. Private premises; Internet and postal.Very large stock. Spec: Antiquarian; Bull Fighting; Countries - Andorra; Countries - Central America; Countries - Cuba; Countries - Gibraltar; Countries - Latin America; Countries - Mexico; Countries - Morocco; Countries - Portugal; Countries - Puerto Rico; Countries - South America; and others as listed in the Speciality Index. PR: £5–1,000. CC: JCB; MC; V; SW. Corresp: Spanish Portuguese French. Mem: PBFA. VAT No: GB 720 5623 63.

Philip Dawson (Modern First Ed, 35 Napoleon Road, St. Margarets, Twickenham, TW1 3EW. (*). Tel: (020) 8892-0511. E-mail: philip@poppysplace.fsnet.co.uk. Est: 1993. Private premises; Internet and postal. Appointment necessary. Open: **M:** 09:00–21:00; **T:** 09:00–21:00; **W:** 09:00–21:00; **Th:** 09:00–21:00; **F:** 09:00–21:00; **S:** 09:00–21:00; **Su:** 09:00–21:00. Medium stock. Spec: Children's - General; Literature; Modern First Editions; Natural History; Proof Copies. PR: £10–18,000. CC: AE; E; JCB; MC; V. Also, booksearch. Corresp: French, German.

Available from Richard Joseph Publishers Ltd

Sheppard's Book Dealers in Latin America and Southern Africa

1st Edition 2000 (A5 P/b)   87pp £21.00

Anthony C. Hall, Antiquarian B, ■ 30 Staines Road, Twickenham, Middlesex, TW2 5AH. Prop: Anthony C. Hall. Tel: (020) 8898-2638. Fax: (020) 8893-8855. Website: www.hallbooks.co.uk. E-mail: achallbooks@intonet.co.uk. Est: 1966. Shop; open **M:** 10:00–17:00; **T:** 10:00–17:00. **Th:** 10:00–17:00; **F:** 10:00–17:00. Small general stock. Spec: Countries - Africa; Countries - Asia; Countries - East Europe; Countries - Middle East, The; Countries - Russia; History - Industrial; Travel - Africa; Travel - Asia; Travel - Europe; Travel - Middle East. CC: MC; V. Corresp: French, German, Russian, Spanish. Mem: ABA; PBFA. VAT No: GB 224 2699 61.

John Ives Bookseller, 5 Normanhurst Drive, St. Margarets, Twickenham, TW1 1NA. (*). Tel: (020) 8892-6265. Fax: (020) 8744-3944. Website: www.ukbookworld.com/members/johnives. E-mail: jives@btconnect.com. Est: 1978. Private premises; appointment necessary. Medium stock. Spec: Antiques; Architecture; Art Reference; Ceramics; Collecting; Fashion & Costume; Glass; Jewellery; Needlework; Textiles. PR: £5–500. CC: JCB; MC; V. Cata: 3. Corresp: French, German. Mem: PBFA. VAT No: GB 409 8526 30.

John Prescott - The Bookseller, ■ Paul Hoffmann House, 57 York Street, Twickenham, TW1 3LP. Prop: John Prescott. Tel: (020) 8940-3066. E-mail: johnprescott@avdv.demon.co.uk. Est: 1998. Shop; open **F:** 10:30–18:00; **S:** 10:30–18:00. Medium general stock. Spec: Antiques; Archaeology; Architecture; Art; Art History; Cinema/Film; Countries - South America; Fables; Fiction - General; First Editions; Folio Society, The; Health; Military History; Music - Classical; Photography; Poetry; Sport - Cricket; Theatre. PR: £1–100. *NB: Shop sales only.* Corresp: German, French, Spanish, Dutch.

Stephen Miller, 19 Clifden Road, Twickenham, Middlesex, TW1 4LU. Tel: (020) 8892-0331. Est: 1981. Private premises. Very small general stock. Spec: Antiquarian. PR: £1–500 Corresp: French.

WELLING

Falconwood Transport & Militar, ■ 5 Falconwood Parade, The Green, Welling, DA16 2PL. (*) Prop: A.M. Doran. Tel: (020) 8303-8291. Fax: (020) 8303-8291. E-mail: falconw@globalnet.co.uk. Est: 1985. Shop; open **Th:** 09:30–17:30; **F:** 09:30–17:30; **S:** 09:30–17:30. Medium stock. Spec: Aviation; Engineering; Maritime/Nautical; Military; Motorbikes; Motoring; Railways; Traction Engines; Transport; Vintage Cars. PR: £5–50. CC: E; JCB; MC; V. Cata: 1 – on aviation, road transport, military vehicles. VAT No: GB 427 0309 76.

WEST WICKHAM

West Wickham Bookshop, 5 Bell Parade, Wickham Court, West Wickham, Kent, BR4 0RH.

MERSEYSIDE

BOOTLE

AH Books, 65 Springwell Road, Bootle, L20 6LU.

EASTHAM

Andrea Grieveson, 34 Pickmere Drive, Eastham, CH62 9EW. Prop: Andrea Grieveson. Tel: (0151) 328 0172. Website: golden.frog@lineone.net. E-mail: golden.frog@lineone.net. Est: 1983. Private premises; Internet and postal. Telephone first. Small stock. Spec: New Age. PR: £3–100. Corresp: French.

LIVERPOOL

Black Voices, 67 Hilberry Avenue, Liverpool, L13 7ET. Prop: T. Aitman. Tel: (0151) 228-1097. E-mail: tonyaitman@blackvoices.freeserve.co.uk. Est: 1992. Private premises; Internet and postal. Appointment necessary. Very small stock. Spec: Black Studies. PR: £3–2,000. Also booksearches in specialist subjects.

The Boydell Galleries, 48 Dowhills Road, Blundellsands, Liverpool, L23 8SW.

Gradwell Concepts, 197 Brodie Avenue, Mossley Hill, Liverpool, L18 4RQ. Prop: Rev. Eric G. Davies. Tel: (0151) 724-1219. Est: 1987. Private premises; appointment necessary. Small stock. Spec: Bibles; Ecclesiastical History & Architecture; Religion - Christian; Theology. PR: £1–20. Also, booksearch. Cata: 1 – occasionally on specialities. Mem: ECBA.

Hylton Booksearch, 23 Chelsea Court, West Derby, Liverpool, L12 6RS. Prop: Mr. R.A. Hylton. Tel: (0151) 259-5163. E-mail: hylton.booksearch@btinternet.com. Est: 1992. Postal business only. Very small stock. Spec: Modern First Editions. CC: PayPal. Also, booksearch.

J. & E.M. Macnamara, 56 Church Road, Liverpool, L13 2BA. Prop: John & Eileen M. MacNamara. Tel: (0151) 254-1722. Est: 1986. PR: £5–300.

Modern Welsh Publications Ltd., 32 Garth Drive, Liverpool, L18 6HW. Prop: Professor D. Ben Rees. Tel: (0151) 724 1989. Fax: (0151) 724-5691. E-mail: ben@garthdrive.fsnet.co.uk. Est: 1962. Private premises; postal business only. Medium stock. Spec: Countries - Wales; History - General; Literature in Translation; Politics; Theology. Corresp: Welsh.

Reid of Liverpool, 105 Mount Pleasant, Liverpool, L3 5TB.

PRESCOT

Nostalgia Unlimited, 19 Dunbeath Avenue, Rainhill, Prescot, L35 0QH. Tel: (0151) 426-2046. Est: 1988. Private premises; postal business only. Small stock. Spec: Christmas; Collecting; Comic Books & Annuals; Comics; Newspapers - General; Nostalgia; Periodicals & Magazines. PR: £1–35.

SAINT HELENS

V. & C. Finn, 6 Knowsley View, Rainford, St. Helens, WA11 8SN. Tel: (01744) 883780. Est: 1992. Private premises; appointment necessary. Small stock. Spec: Folio Society, The. PR: £1–200. Cata: 3 – a year.

Harvest Books, 25, Thickwood Moss Lane, Rainford, St. Helens, WA11 8QL. Prop: Mrs. Janet Christie. Tel: (01744) 885747. E-mail: harvestbooks@btinternet.com. Est: 1998. Private premises; Internet and postal. Appointment necessary. Very small stock. Spec: Authors - Women; Cookery/Gastronomy; Food & Drink; Rural Life; Social History. PR: £5–100. Also, booksearch. Cata: 4 – Quarterly. Mem: PBFA.

Dealers who need to update their entry should visit their page on
www.sheppardsdirectories.com

MERSEYSIDE

SOUTHPORT

Britannia Books, 72 Ryder Crescent, Birkdale, Southport, PR8 3AF.

Broadhurst of Southport Ltd., 5 & 7 Market Street, Southport, PR8 1HD. Prop: Laurens R. Hardman. Tel: (01704) 532064 & 534. Fax: (01704) 542009. Website: www.ckbroadhurst.com. E-mail: litereria@aol.com. Est: 1926. Spec: Architecture; Art; Bibliography; Biography; Children's - General; Fiction - General; Fine & Rare; History - General; Literary Criticism; Literature; Maritime/Nautical; Modern First Editions; Natural History; Private Press; Topography - General; Travel - General; and others as listed in the Speciality Index. PR: £5–5,000. Also, bookbinding & restoration service, new books on all subjects & a booksearch service.

Celtic Antiquarian Books, 48 Clairville, Lulworth Road, Southport, PR8 2FA.

Cover to Cover, 252 Balmoral Drive, Southport, PR9 8QA. Tel: (01704) 231443. Website: www.covers.freeuk.com. E-mail: covers@freeuk.com. Est: 1996. Private premises; Internet and postal. Telephone first. Spec: Applied Art; Architecture; Art; Ceramics; Cinema/Film; Circus; Crafts; Crochet; Decorative Art; Design; Dolls & Dolls' Houses; Embroidery; Fairgrounds; Gypsies; Knitting; Lace; Needlework; Performing Arts; Radio/Wireless; Rugs; Rural Life; Television. PR: £1–300.

Kernaghans, ■ 57–65 Wayfarers Arcade, Lord Street, Southport, PR8 1NT. Prop: Alwyn & Bryan Kernaghan. Tel: (01704) 546329. Fax: (01704) 546329. E-mail: kernaghanbooks@hotmail.com. Est: 1972. Shop; open **M:** 10:00–17:00; **T:** 10:00–17:00; **W:** 10:00–17:00; **Th:** 10:00–17:00; **F:** 10:00–17:00; **S:** 10:00–17:00. Very large stock. Spec: Countries - Ireland; Fine & Rare; Irish Interest; Moveable & 3D; Natural History; Pop-Up, 3D, Cut Out & Movable; Religion - Christian; Theology; Topography - Local; Travel - General. PR: £5–5,000. CC: AE; MC; V. Mem: PBFA.

Parkinsons, 359–363 Lord Street, Southport, PR8 1NH.

Rosemary Books, 27 Cedar Street, Southport, PR8 6NQ. Prop: Eileen M. Golborn. Tel: (01704) 542134. Est: 1983. Private premises; appointment necessary. Very small stock. Spec: Books about Books; Children's - General; Countries - Melanesia; Fiction - General; First Editions; Juvenile; Poetry; Religion - Christian.

Les Wilson (Motoring Books), 32 Beach Priory Gardens, Southport, PR8 1RT.

WALLASEY

Mill Lane Books, 56 Mill Lane, Liscard, Wallasey, CH44 5UG.

WIRRAL

Thin Read Line, 11 St. Andrews Road, Claughton, Prenton, Wirral, CH43 1TB. Prop: Dr. R.A. Dutton. Tel: (0151) 652-4483. Fax: (0151) 652-4483. Est: 1999. Private premises; postal business only. Medium stock. Spec: Aeronautics; Antiques; Arms & Armour; Aviation; Botany; Colonial; Firearms/Guns; Gardening; Horticulture; Maritime/Nautical; Military; Military History; Naval; War - General; War - World War II. PR: £3–100. Also, booksearch. Attends military fairs. Cata: 1 – on demand. Corresp: Dutch.

NORFOLK

ATTLEBOROUGH
By The Book, ■ Queens Square, Attleborough, NR17 2AF.

AYLSHAM
Abbey Books, Gothic House, 51 Hungate Street, Aylsham, NR11 6AA. Prop: Bruce & Jill Tulloch. Tel: (01263) 732861. Fax: (01263) 732861. E-mail: abbey.books@btinternet.com. Est: 1978. Private premises and book fairs only. Appointment necessary. *Shop at:* Red Lion Antiques, 44 Red Lion Street, Aylesham. Open: **S:** 09:00–17:00. Small stock. Spec: Academic/Scholarly; Art; Art Reference; History - General; Social History. Home tel: (01263) 732851. Corresp: French, German, Portuguese, Spanish. Mem: PBFA. VAT No: GB 322 2751 99

Burebank Books, 46 Red Lion Street, Aylsham, NR11 6ER.

Mayhew Books, 8 Sears Close, Aylsham, NR11 6JB. Prop: John & Linda Mayhew. Tel: (01263) 731305. Est: 1989. Private premises; postal business only. Very small general stock. PR: £1–100. Also, booksearch. Cata: 1 – on request.

CAISTER–ON–SEA
Brian Beighton, Garfield Villa, Garfield Terrace, Caister–on–Sea, NR30 5DQ. Tel: (withheld). Private premises; appointment necessary. Small stock. Spec: Almanacs; Sport - Cricket.

CROMER
Bookworms, ■ 9 New Street, Cromer, NR27 9HP. Prop: Susan & Ted Liddell & I.R. Petrie. Tel: (01263) 515078. Fax: (01263) 519008. Website: www.susanlid.freeserve.co.uk. E-mail: bookworms@susanlid.freeserve.co.uk. Est: 1987. Shop; open **M:** 10:00–17:00; **T:** 10:00–17:00; **W:** 10:00–17:00; **Th:** 10:00–17:00; **F:** 10:00–17:00; **S:** 10:00–17:00; **Su:** 10:00–17:00. Large stock. Spec: Art; Aviation; Biography; Children's - General; History - General; Literature; Music - General; Natural History; Sport - General; Topography - General; Transport; Travel - General; War - General. PR: £1–100. CC: AE.

DEREHAM
Village Books, 20a High Street, Dereham, NR19 1DR.

DISS
Riderless Horse Books, Oakfields, Redgrave Road, Blo Norton, Diss, IP22 2JA. (*) Prop: Richard B. Hamburger. Tel: (01379) 898481. E-mail: rhbooks@dircon.co.uk. Est: 1991. Private premises; Internet and postal. Appointment necessary. Small stock. Spec: First Editions; Literary Criticism; Literature; Literature in Translation; Periodicals & Magazines; Poetry. PR: £2–1,000. CC: MC; V. Cata: 2 – Poetry, Modern literature. Corresp: French. Mem: PBFA.

Michael Taylor Rare Books, Hoblins, One Eyed Lane, Weybread, Diss, IP21 5TT. Tel: (01379) 853889. Fax: (01379) 853889. E-mail: michael@hoblins.demon.co.uk. Est: 1984. Private premises; appointment necessary. Small stock. Spec: Bibliography; Calligraphy; Illustrated; Private Press; Typography. PR: £5–1,000. CC: MC; V. Cata: 4. Mem: PBFA.

DOWNHAM MARKET
Richard Everett, Sandfield House, 58 Lynn Road, Downham Market, PE38 9NN. Prop: Richard & Jenny Everett. Tel: (01366) 382074. Est: 1983. Office &/or bookroom; appointment necessary. Large stock. Spec: Children's - General; Illustrated; Topography - Local. PR: £2–400. Mem: PBFA. *Also at:* Southwold Antiques Centre, Suffolk (q.v.).

Dealers who need to update their entry should visit their page on
www.sheppardsdirectories.com

The King Street Bookshop, ■ c/o Gorlestone Bookstore, Unit 10, Longs Industrial Estate, Englands Lane, Gorlestone, NR31 6NE.

FAKENHAM

The Dancing Goat Bookshop, ■ 5 Oak Street, Fakenham, NR21 9DX. Prop: Michael Goss. Tel: (01328) 855757. E-mail: dancinggoatbooks@talk21.com. Est: 1998. Shop; open **M:** 10:00–16:00; **T:** 10:00–16:00; **W:** 10:00–16:00; **Th:** 10:00–16:00; **F:** 10:00–16:00; **S:** 10:00–16:00. Medium stock. Spec: American Indians; Americana; Folklore; Music - Folk & Irish Folk; Music - Popular; Music - Rock; Ornithology; Poetry; Vintage Paperbacks. PR: £1–100. Also a coffee shop (coffee, tea, home made cakes & light lunches).

GREAT ELLINGHAM

John Knowles, Brick Kiln Farm, Hingham Road, Great Ellingham, Nr. Attleborough, NR17 1JE. Prop: John Knowles. Tel: (01953) 452257. Fax: (01953) 452733. Website: knowlesbooks.com. E-mail: enquire@johnknowlesbooks.com. Est: 1985. Private premises; Internet and postal. Appointment necessary. Small stock. Spec: Marque Histories (see also motoring); Motoring; Sport - Motor Racing; Transport. PR: £5–1,000. CC: E; MC; V; SW. Cata: 2 – specialist subjects. Corresp: French, German.

GREAT YARMOUTH

Black Cat Books, Meadow Cottage, High Road, Wortwell, Harleston, IP20 0EN. Prop: Ann Morgan–Hughes. Tel: (01986) 788826. Fax: (01986) 788826. Website: www.blackcatbooks.co.uk. E-mail: ann@blackcatbooks.co.uk. Est: 1984. Storeroom; appointment necessary. Small stock. Spec: Cookery/Gastronomy; Embroidery; Fashion & Costume; Knitting; Lace; Needlework; Periodicals & Magazines; Social History; Textiles; Women. PR: £10–2,000. CC: MC; V. Cata: 4 – on specialities. Corresp: French, German, Greek, Russian. Mem: ABA; PBFA. VAT No: GB 446 3847 25.

David Ferrow, ■ 77 Howard Street South, Great Yarmouth, NR30 1LN. Tel: (01493) 843800. Est: 1940. Shop; open **M:** 10:00–17:00; **T:** 10:00–17:00; **W:** 10:00–17:00. **F:** 10:00–17:00. Large stock. Spec: Topography - Local. PR: £1–10,000. CC: MC; V. Appointment required for Thursdays. Mem: ABA; PBFA.

R.F. & C. Ward, 27 Kent Square, Great Yarmouth, NR30 2EX. P

HARLESTON

Riviera Books, ■ 9 Market Place, Harleston, IP20 9AD. Prop: David Chatten. Tel: (01379) 855123. E-mail: rivierabooks@fsmail.net. Est: 1999. Shop; open **T:** 10:00–16:30; **W:** 10:00–16:30; **Th:** 10:00–13:00; **F:** 10:00–16:30; **S:** 10:00–16:30. Large stock. Spec: Art; History - American. PR: £2–200. CC: MC; V. Corresp: French.

HARPLEY

Martin Keene, Chasewood, Church Lane, Harpley, King's Lynn, PE31 6TX.

HINGHAM

K. Anthony Ward, ■ Fairland Bookshop, 2 Fairland Court, Hingham, NR9 4HN. Prop: K.A. & V.J. Ward. Tel: (01953) 850006. E-mail: wardbooks@castleacre.fsbusiness.co.uk. Est: 1963. Shop; open **T:** 11:00–16:00; **W:** 11:00–16:00; **Th:** 11:00–16:00; **F:** 11:00–16:00; S: 11:00–16:00. Small general stock. Spec: Bibliography; Books about Books; Limited Editions; Literature; Modern First Editions. PR: £5–500. CC: MC; V. Mem: PBFA.

HOLT

Fullerton's Booksearch, 'Branta' 2 Maisons Bienvenues, High Street, Cley, Holt, NR25 7RR. Prop: Humphrey Boon. Tel: (01263) 740682. E-mail: fullertonsbooks@aol.com. Est: 1991. Postal business only. Spec: Booksearch. PR: £15–7,000.

Simon Gough Books Limited, 3/5 Fish Hill, Holt, NR25 6BD.

Heathfield Books, Candlestick Lane, Holt, NR25 6SU. Tel: (01263) 711531. Website: heathfield.books@get-the-web.com. E-mail: heathfield.books@get-the-web.com. Est: 1999. Storeroom; Internet and postal. Appointment necessary. Small stock. Spec: First Editions. PR: £5–100.

Jackdaw Books, ■ 10 New Street, Holt, NR25 6JJ. Prop: Mick & Eleanor Finn. Tel: (01263) 711658. Fax: (01263) 710056. Website: www.jackdawbooks.co.uk. E-mail: eleanor.finn@btopenworld.com. Est: 1997. Shop; Internet and postal. Open: **M:** 09:00–16:00; **T:** 09:00–16:00; **W:** 09:00–16:00. **F:** 09:00–16:00; **S:** 09:00–16:00. Large general stock. Spec: Academic/Scholarly; Animals and Birds; Antiquarian; Archaeology; History - General; History - British. PR: £5–2,000. CC: MC; V; SW.

TRJ Books, 44 Pineheath Road, High Kelling, Holt, NR25 6QF.

KINGS' LYNN

Brazenhead Ltd., Greenside, Market Place, Burnham Market, King's Lynn, PE31 8HD.

Elliot's Shelf, Beechwood, Bagthorpe Road, King's Lynn, PE31 8RA.

John Lowe, 7 Orchard Grove, West Lynn, King's Lynn, PE34 3LE. Tel: (01553) 661271. E-mail: john@lowebooks.fsnet.co.uk. Est: 1982. Spec: Academic/Scholarly; Archaeology; Folklore; History - British; Topography - General. PR: £2–200 Mem: PBFA.

NORTH WALSHAM

Angel Books, ■ 4 Aylsham Road, North Walsham, NR28 0BH. Prop: Mr. W., Ms., M., & Mrs. O.D. Green. Tel: (01692) 404054. E-mail: angelbooks@onetel.net.uk. Est: 1989. Shop; open **Th:** 09:00–17:00; **F:** 09:00–17:00; **S:** 09:00–16:00. Medium stock. Spec: History - Local; Sport - Cycling; Topography - Local. PR: £1–500. Also, booksearch. Cata: 1. Mem: PBFA.

C.J. Murphy, 5 Burton Avenue, North Walsham, NR28 0EW.

NORWICH

Bookshelf – Aviation Books, St. Catherines, The Green, Hickling, Norwich, NR12 0XR.

Carlton Books, 44 Langley Road, Chedgrave, Norwich, NR14 6HD. Prop: A.P. Goodfellow. Tel: (01508) 520124. Est: 1974. Private premises; appointment necessary. Small stock. Spec: History - Local; Natural History; Ornithology; Topography - Local. PR: £1–500 Mem: PBFA.

J. & D. Clarke, ■ St Michael at Plea Church, Redwell Street, Norwich, NR2 4SN. Prop: Joy Clarke. Tel: Shop (01603) 617700. Est: 1985. Shop; open **M:** 10:00–16:30; **T:** 10:00–16:30; **W:** 10:00–16:30; **Th:** 10:00–16:30; **F:** 10:00–16:30; **S:** 10:00–16:30. Medium general stock. Spec: Children's - General; Topography - General; Topography - Local. PR: £1–2,000. CC: AE; MC; V; D, SW. Attends PBFA fairs and Burnham Market. Mem: PBFA.

Peter Crowe Antiquarian Books, 75 & 77 Upper St. Giles Street, Norwich, NR2 1AB.

John Debbage, 28 Carterford Drive, Norwich, NR3 4DW. Tel: (01603) 488015. Fax: (01603) 788933. E-mail: norvicsales@btopenworld.com. Spec: Topography - Local.

J.R. & R.K. Ellis, ■ 53 St. Giles Street, Norwich, NR2 1JR. Tel: (01603) 623679. Est: 1960. Shop; open **M:** 08:30–17:30; **T:** 08:30–17:30; **W:** 08:30–17:30; **Th:** 08:30–17:30; **F:** 08:30–17:30; **S:** 08:30–17:30 Large general stock. PR: £1–100. Also, Market Stalls.

Freya Books & Antiques, St. Mary's Farm, Cheney's Lane, Tacolneston, Norwich, NR16 1DB. (*) Prop: Colin Lewsey. Tel: (01508) 489252. Website: www.freyaantiques.co.uk. E-mail: freyaantiques@ic24.net. Est: 1971. Storeroom. Medium stock. Spec: Fiction - General; Juvenile. PR: £1–50. CC: MC; V. Also, 3,000sq ft antique furniture. Corresp: French, Danish.

Peter J. Hadley Bookseller, ■ 29 Surrey Street, Norwich, NR1 3NX.

Hawes Books, 8 Keswick Road, Cringleford, Norwich, NR4 6UG. Prop: T.L.M. & H.J. Hawes. Tel: (01603) 452043. Est: 1980. Private premises; appointment necessary. Large stock. Spec: Genealogy; History - Local; History - National; Topography - General. PR: £2–200. VAT No: GB 342 4870 57.

Katnap Arts, 1 Whitefields, Norwich Road, Saxlingham Nethergate, Norwich, NR15 1TP. Prop: Margaret Blake. Tel: (01508) 498323. Fax: (01508) 498908. Website: www.katnaparts.fsbusiness.co.uk. E-mail: mail@katnaparts.fsbusiness.co.uk. Est: 1999. Private premises; postal business only. Medium general stock. Spec: Annuals; Architecture; Art; Art History; Art Reference; Children's - General; Entertainment - General; First Editions; History - General; Literature; Natural History; Typography; Vintage Paperbacks. PR: £5–250. CC: MC; V.

David Lake, 36 Colney Lane, Cringleford, Norwich, NR4 7RE. Tel: (01603) 453814. Fax: (01603) 453814. E-mail: djl@netcom.co.uk. Est: 1990. Private premises; postal business only. Spec: Antiquarian; Children's - Illustrated; Colour-Plate; Topography - Local. PR: £5–500.

LyngHeath Books, 51 Pightle Way, Lyng, Norwich, NR9 5RL. Prop: Tim Holt. Tel: (01603) 879037. Website: www.lyngheathbooks.co.uk. E-mail: lyngheathbooks@hotmail.com. Est: 1999. Private premises; Internet and postal. Appointment necessary. Open: **M:** 08:00–20:00; **T:** 08:00–20:00; **W:** 08:00–20:00; **Th:** 08:00–20:00; **F:** 08:00–20:00; **S:** 08:00–20:00; **Su:** 10:00–17:00. Small stock. Spec: Dogs; Sport - Football (Soccer). PR: £2–300. Also, booksearch. Corresp: French. *Also at:* Village Books, 20a High Street, East Dereham.

Joseph Mason Bookseller, 10 Shooters Close, Taverham, Norwich, NR8 6RD.

Nubec, 37 Lindley Street, Norwich, NR1 2HF.

Saint Michael at Plea Bookshop, Antiques Centre, St. Michael at Plea Church, Bank Plain, Norwich, NR2 4SN.

Terry Smith, Balwyn House, Freethorpe, Norwich, NR13 3LY.

Tasburgh Books, 20 Henry Preston Road, Tasburgh, Norwich, NR15 1NU. Prop: Janet Lamb & David Newton. Tel: (01508) 471921. E-mail: tasburgh@dircon.co.uk. Est: 1995. Private premises; Internet and postal. Telephone first. Small stock. Spec: Applied Art; Architecture; Art History; Art Reference; Decorative Art; Fine Art; Folio Society, The. CC: AE; MC; V. Cata: 4. Mem: ABA.

Tombland Bookshop, 8 Tombland, Norwich, NR3 1HF.

Touchstone Books, 1 Fairstead Road, Sprowston, Norwich, NR7 8XG. Prop: Robert Illsley. Tel: (01603) 401284. Est: 1985. Private premises; postal business only. Very small stock. Spec: Literature; Modern First Editions.

D.B. Waters, 11 Rectory Road, Dickleburgh, Diss, Norwich, IP21 4NW.

Michael Watson Books, Sea Mere, Hingham, Norwich, NR9 4LP. Tel: (01953) 850217. Est: 1995. Postal business only.

SALTHOUSE

John Hart, Salt Barn, Bard Hill, Salthouse, NR25 7XB. Tel: (01263) 741380. Fax: (01263) 741700. E-mail: johnhartbks@btopenworld.com. Est: 1987. Private premises; appointment necessary. Small stock. Spec: Literature. PR: £20–2,000. CC: MC; V. Cata: 5. Corresp: French. Mem: ABA; PBFA. VAT No: GB 529 2455 28.

SHERINGHAM

R.L. Cook, 12 Sycamore Grove, Sheringham, NR26 8PG. Tel: (01263) 822050. Est: 1950. Private premises; appointment necessary. Very small stock. Spec: Antiquarian; Juvenile; Literature; Travel - General. PR: £20–250.

Peter Pan Bookshop, ■ 5 The Courtyard, Station Road, Sheringham, NR26 8RF. Prop: Peter Cox. Tel: (01263) 824411. Est: 1994. Shop; open **M:** 10:30–17:00; **T:** 10:30–17:00; **W:** 10:30–17:00; **Th:** 10:30–17:00; **F:** 10:30–17:00; **S:** 10:30–17:00; **Su:** 12:00–16:00; Small general stock. PR: £1–20. Secondhand books published after 1980. *Also at:* Peter's Bookshop, 19 St Peter's Road (q.v.).

Peter's Bookshop, ■ 19 St. Peter's Road, Sheringham, NR26 8QY. Prop: Peter Cox. Tel: (01263) 823008. Est: 1984. Shop; open **M:** 10:00–17:30; **T:** 10:00–17:30; **W:** 10:00–17:30; **Th:** 10:00–17:30; **F:** 10:00–17:30; **S:** 10:00–17:30; **Su:** 13:00–17:00. Very large stock. Spec: Children's - General; Fiction - General; Literature. PR: £1–100. CC: E; MC; V. Winter hours: (Nov. to Mar.) Mon./Tue. & Thurs. to Sat. 10:30–16:30. Corresp: French. *Also at:* The Peter Pan Bookshop, Sheringham, Norfolk (q.v.).

SNETTISHAM

Torc Books, ■ 9 Hall Road, Snettisham, King's Lynn, PE31 7LU. Prop: Heather Shepperd. Tel: (014585) 541188. Est: 1977. Shop; open **F:** 10:00–16:00; **S:** 10:00–16:00. Medium general stock. PR: £1–100. Open other times by appointment.

SOUTH BURLINGHAM

Mermaid Books (Burlingham), Old Hall, Norwich Road, South Burlingham, NR13 4EY.

SWANTON ABBOT

Hamish Riley–Smith, Swanton Abbot Hall, Swanton Abbot, NR10 5DJ. Prop: Hamish Riley-Smith. Tel: (01692) 538244. Fax: (01692) 538696. Website: www.riley-smith.com. E-mail: hamish@riley-smith.co.uk. Est: 1974. Private premises; Internet and postal. Telephone first. Very small stock. Spec: Academic/Scholarly; Antiquarian; Economics; Fine & Rare; Foreign Texts; Letters; Literature; Manuscripts; Philosophy; Science - General; Scottish Interest. PR: £100–20,000. Also, manuscripts & signed autograph letters. Cata: 1 – infrequent. VAT No: GB 342 4732 69.

WALSINGHAM
Pilgrim's Progress Bookshop, 63 High Street, Walsingham, NR22 6BZ.

WELLS–NEXT–THE–SEA
The Old Station Pottery & Book, 2/4 Maryland, Wells–Next–The–Sea, NR23 1LX. Prop: Thom Borthwick. Tel: (01328) 710847. Fax: (01328) 711566. E-mail: oldstation.books@btinternet.com. Est: 1996. Spec: Children's - General; Topography - General. PR: £1–50.

WYMONDHAM
The Bookshop, ■ 1 Town Green, Wymondham, NR18 OPN. Prop: M. & A.C. Thompson. Tel: (01953) 602244. Est: 1975. Shop; open **M:** 09:45–16:50; **T:** 10:30–16:50; **W:** 10:30–16:50; **Th:** 10:30–16:50; **F:** 10:30–16:50. Large general stock. Spec: Comics; Entertainment - General; Music - General; Topography - General. PR: £1–300.

Turret House, ■ 27 Middleton Street, Wymondham, Norfolk, NR18 0AB. Prop: Dr. D.H. & R.A. Morgan. Tel: (01953) 603462. E-mail: hughmorgan@turrethouse.demon.co.uk. Est: 1972. Shop; Telephone first. Very small general stock. Spec: Astronomy; Mathematics; Medicine; Microscopy; Natural Sciences; Science - General; Science - History of; Scientific Instruments. PR: £1–1,000. CC: MC; V. Mem: PBFA. VAT No: GB 282 1349 63.

NORTH YORKSHIRE

BEDALE

Sugen & Co., Southwood House, Well, Bedale, DL8 2RL. Prop: K. Sugen. Tel: (01677) 470079. Website: http://www.film-tvtieins.co.uk. E-mail: sugenbooks@ukf.net. Est: 1993. Private premises; Internet and postal. Medium stock. PR: £3–100. Cata: 5 – 2 months approx.

CATTERICK VILLAGE

Brock Books, 43 High Street, Catterick Village, DL10 7LL. Prop: Jude Haslam. Tel: (01748) 818729. Website: www.brockbooks.com. E-mail: judehaslam@hotmail.com. Est: 2002. Private premises; Internet and postal. Appointment necessary. Open: **M:** 09:00–17:30; **T:** 09:00–17:30; **W:** 09:00–17:30. **F:** 11:00–17:00; **S:** 09:00–17:00; **Su:** 09:00–16:00. Very small stock. Spec: Art; Biography; Books about Books; Design; Literature; Literature - Victorian; Natural History; Textiles; Theatre; Topography - General. PR: £5–500. CC: PayPal. Cata: 1.

DACRE

Theatreshire Books, Dacre Hall, Dacre, HG3 4ET. Prop: Catherine Shire. Tel: (01423) 780497. Fax: (01423) 781957. E-mail: theatreshire@theatresearch.co.uk. Est: 2000. Private premises; Internet and postal. Appointment necessary. Small stock. Spec: Engineering; Fire & Firefighters; Performing Arts; Theatre. PR: £1–3,000. Cata: 1.

FILEY

Professional Book Services, 10 Hope St., Filey, YO14 9DL. Prop: Peter Jacques. Tel: (01723) 515170. Fax: (01723) 515133. Website: www.bookspluspictures.com. E-mail: books@bookspluspictures.com. Est: 1996. Private premises; postal business only.

GIGGLESWICK

Post Horn Books, ■ Belle Hill, Giggleswick, BD24 0BA. Prop: Patricia & Edward Saunders. Tel: (01729) 823438. Website: www.abebooks.com/home/posthorn. E-mail: posthornbooks@btinternet.com. Est: 1979. Shop; open **T:** 10:30–17:30; **W:** 09:30–17:30; **Th:** 10:30–17:30; **F:** 10:30–17:30; **S:** 10:30–17:30. Closed for lunch: 12:00–14:00. Medium general stock. Spec: Alpinism/Mountaineering; Countries - Africa; Countries - Asia; Environment, The; Religion - Quakers; Sport - Caving (Spelaeology); Topography - Local. PR: £1–200.

GUISBOROUGH

K.A. McCaughtrie, 7 Grosvenor Square, Guisborough, Cleveland, TS14 6PB. Tel: (01287) 633663. Est: 1986. Private premises; postal business only. Appointment necessary. Very small stock. Spec: Biography; Crime (True); Fiction - Crime, Detective, Spy, Thrillers. PR: £1–50.

HARROWGATE

Richard Axe Rare & Out of Print Books, 12 Cheltenham Crescent, Harrogate, HG1 1DH.

Books (For All), ■ 23a Commercial Street, Harrogate, HG1 1UB. Prop: Jenny Todd. Tel: (01423) 561982. E-mail: booksforall@amserve.net. Est: 1998. Shop; open **M:** 10:30–17:00; **T:** 10:30–17:00; **W:** 10:30–17:00; **Th:** 10:30–17:00; **F:** 10:30–17:00; **S:** 10:30–17:00. Large stock. Spec: Art History; Biography; Children's - General; Cookery/Gastronomy; Esoteric; Fiction - Science Fiction; History - General; Horticulture; Literature; Music - General; Natural History; Religion - General; Topography - General. PR: £1–100. CC: MC; V; SW.

Dealers who need to update their entry should visit their page on
www.sheppardsdirectories.com

Books at the Warehouse, 32 Glebe Avenue, Harrogate, HG2 0LT. Prop: Jo Lunt. Tel: (01423) 523656. E-mail: jolunt@amserve.net. Est: 1993. Private premises; postal business only. Appointment necessary. Open: **M:** 10:00–17:00; **T:** 10:00–17:00; **W:** 10:00–17:00; **Th:** 10:00–17:00; **F:** 10:00–17:00; **S:** 10:00–17:00; **Su:** 10:00–16:00. Medium stock. Spec: Art Reference; Ceramics; Publishers - Penguin. PR: £1–100. A free 3-month search facility, collections of Penguin Books sold on commission. Corresp: French, German.

Bookstop Bookshop, 28 Mayfield Grove, Harrogate, HG1 5HB. Prop: J.K. Shackleton. Tel: (01423) 505817. E-mail: bookstopbookshop@aol.com. Est: 1986. Spec: History - General; Military History. PR: £1–100. Also, board games.

Macbuiks, 7 Leadhall Crescent, Harrogate, HG2 9NG.

Oval Books, 7 Chantry Court, Ripley, Harrogate, HG3 3AD. Prop: M. S. Spark. Tel: (01423) 772346. Est: 1985. Private premises; appointment necessary. Very small stock. Spec: Sport - Rugby. PR: £1–150. Cata: 3 – a year. Corresp: French.

HAWES

Kit Calvert's Bookshop, Burnside, Burtersett Road, Hawes, DL8 3NT.

HELMSLEY

Helmsley Antiquarian & Secondhand Books, ■ The Old Fire Station, Borogate, Helmsley, YO62 5BN. Prop: Myles Moorby. Tel: (01439) 770014. Est: 1985. Shop; open: **M:** 10:00–17:00; **T:** 10:00–17:00; **W:** 09:00–17:00; **Th:** 10:00–17:00; **F:** 10:00–17:00; **S:** 10:00–17:00; **Su:** 12:00–17:00. Medium stock. Spec: Architecture; Art; Topography - Local. PR: £1–100. CC: MC; V.

INGLETON

John Killeen, 16 Main Street, Ingleton, LA6 3HF. Tel: (015242) 41021. Est: 1974. Private premises; appointment necessary. Spec: Literature; Marxism; Philosophy; Politics; Religion - Roman Catholic; Topography - Local; Travel - General. PR: £1–300. Attends fairs in Northern England. Corresp: French. Mem: PBFA.

KNARESBOROUGH

Pennymead Books, 1 Brewerton Street, Knaresborough, HG5 8AZ. Prop: David Druett. Tel: (01423) 865962. Fax: (01423) 547057. Website: www.pennymead.com. E-mail: pennymead@aol.com. Est: 1984. Private premises; Internet and postal. Telephone first. Small stock. Spec: Carriages & Driving; Colonial; Countries - Bermuda; Countries - Caribbean, The; Countries - Cuba; Countries - Puerto Rico; Countries - Santo Domingo; Countries - West Indies, The; Philately; Sport - Badminton; Sport - Hockey. PR: £5–5,000. CC: JCB; MC; V. Also, postage stamp auctioneer. Cata: 1. Mem: PBFA. VAT No: GB 387 9262 94.

LEALHOLM

Stepping Stones Bookshop, ■ Stepping Stones, Lealholm, near Whitby. Prop: Judith & Lawrence Davies. Tel: (01947) 897382. Est: 1970. Shop; open **M:** 10:00–17:00; **T:** 10:00–17:00; **W:** 10:00–17:00; **Th:** 09:00–17:00; **F:** 10:00–17:00; **S:** 10:00–17:00; **Su:** 10:00–17:00 Medium general stock. PR: £1–100.

MALTON

Old Talbot Gallery, 9 Market Street, Malton, YO17 7LY.

OTLEY

Otley Maypole Rare Books, 98 Boroughgate, Otley, LS21 1AE. Prop: John Hepworth. Tel: (01943) 468899.

PICKERING

Alan Avery, 15 Middleton Road, Pickering, YO18 8AL. Prop: Alan Avery. Tel: (01751) 476863. Fax: (01751) 476863. Website: www.abebooks.com/home/avery. E-mail: avery_uk@yahoo.com. Est: 1988. Private premises; appointment necessary. Small stock. Spec: Folio Society, The. PR: £5–60.

Sybil Buckley, ■ Pickering Antique Centre, Southgate, Pickering, YO18 8BN. Tel: (01751) 477210. E-mail: buckleysbooks@lineone.net. Est: 1998. *Shop at:* 37a Westagte, Pickering, North Yorkshire, YO18 8BA. Open: **M:** 10:00–17:00; **T:** 10:00–17:00; **W:** 10:00–17:00; **Th:** 10:00–17:00; **F:** 10:00–17:00; **S:** 10:00–17:00; **Su:** 10:00–17:00. Small general stock. PR: £1–200. CC: MC; V; DELTA.

Cobweb Books, ■ Ye Olde Corner Shoppe, 1 Pickering Road, Thornton–Le–Dale, Pickering, YO18 7LG. Prop: Robin & Sue Buckler. Tel: (01751) 476638. Website: www.cobwebbooks.co.uk. E-mail: robin@cobweb-books-yorks.fsnet.co.uk. Est: 1979. Shop; open M: 10:00–17:00; **T:** 10:00–17:00; **W:** 10:00–17:00; **Th:** 10:00–17:00; **F:** 10:00–17:00; **S:** 10:00–17:00; **Su:** 10:00–17:00. Very large stock. Spec: Antiquarian; Aviation; First Editions; Illustrated; Military; Motoring; Railways; Topography - General; Transport. PR: £1–1,000. CC: AE; JCB; MC; V; SW.

Inch's Books, 6 Westgate, Pickering, YO18 8BA. Prop: Peter & Eleanor Inch. Tel: (01751) 474928. Fax: (01751) 475939. Website: www.inchsbooks.co.uk. E-mail: inchs.books@dial.pipex.com. Est: 1986. Office &/or bookroom. Telephone first. Open: **M:** 09:00–17:00; **T:** 09:00–17:00; **W:** 09:00–17:00; **Th:** 09:00–17:00; **F:** 09:00–17:00. Medium stock. Spec: Architecture; Building & Construction; Cities; Design; History - Design; Landscape; Town Planning; Urban History. PR: £10–1,500. CC: JCB; MC. Cata: 8 – 1-2 months. Corresp: French. Mem: ABA; PBFA; ILAB. VAT No: GB 412 1286 94.

RAINTON

Pandion Books, 10 Carr Close, Rainton, Thirsk, YO7 3QE.

RICHMOND

Ian Dyer Cricket Books, 29 High Street, Gilling West, Richmond, DL10 5JG. Prop: Michael & Jennie Gauntlett. Tel: (01748) 822786. Fax: (01748) 822786. Website: www.cricketbooks.co.uk. E-mail: iandyer@cricketbooks.co.uk. Est: 1979. Private premises; Internet and postal. Telephone first. Medium stock. Spec: Sport - Cricket. PR: £2–3,500. CC: MC; V; SW, S. Mem: PBFA; Cricket Society/CMA. VAT No: GB 698 9620 57.

Richmond Books, ■ 25 Silver Meadows, Barton, Richmond, DL10 4QN. Prop: Bob & Gail Ions. Tel: (01325) 377332. Fax: evenings. E-mail: richmondbooks@ions.fsbusiness.co.uk. Est: 1995. Shop; open **M:** 09:30–16:30; **T:** 09:30–16:30; **W:** 09:30–16:30; **Th:** 09:30–16:30; **F:** 09:30–16:30; **S:** 09:30–16:30; **Su:** 10:00–16:30. Medium stock. Spec: Biography; Countries - Melanesia; History - General; Literature; Military History; Poetry; Topography - Local. PR: £1–200.

Vokes Books Ltd., Linton House, 43 Bargate, Richmond.

RIPON

Hornseys', ■ 3 Kirkgate, Ripon, HG4 1PA. Prop: Bruce, Susan & Daniel Hornsey. Tel: (01765) 602878. Fax: (01765) 601692. E-mail: daniel@rarebooks.freeserve.co.uk. Est: 1990. Shop; open **M:** 09:00–17:30; **T:** 09:00–17:30; **W:** 09:00–17:30; **Th:** 09:00–17:30; **F:** 09:00–17:30; **S:** 09:00–17:30; **Su:** 09:00–17:30. Medium stock. Spec: Alpinism/Mountaineering; Architecture; Aviation; Children's - General; Fashion & Costume; History - General; Military History; Motoring; Sport - General; Topography - General; Topography - Local. PR: £1–1,500. CC: MC; V; SW. We stock prints and engravings on a variety of subjects.

SALTBURN–BY–SEA

Saltburn Bookshop, ■ 3 Amber Street, Saltburn–by–the–Sea, TS12 1DT. Prop: Jösef Thompson. Tel: (01287) 623335. E-mail: josefthompson@freeuk.com. Est: 1978. Shop; open **M:** 11:00–17:00; **T:** 11:00–17:00; **W:** 11:00–17:00; **Th:** 11:00–17:00; **F:** 11:00–17:00; **S:** 11:00–17:00. Closed for lunch: 13:00–14:00. Winter opening hours: Mon to Sat 11:00–16:00. (Closed for lunch 13:00–14:00). Medium stock. PR: £1–100. Also, a booksearch service.

SCARBOROUGH

Antiquary Ltd., (Bar Bookstore) ■ 4 Swanhill Road, Scarborough, YO11 1BW. Prop: Michael Chaddock. Tel: (01723) 500141. Website: www.ukbookworld.com/members/Barbooks. E-mail: antiquary@btinternet.com. Est: 1976. Shop; open **T:** 10:30–17:00; **W:** 10:30–17:00; **Th:** 10:30–17:00; **F:** 10:30–17:00; **S:** 10:30–18:00. Medium general stock. Spec: Academic/Scholarly; Art; Author - Housman, A.E.; History - General; Literature; Topography - General; Topography - Local. PR: £1–200. Also, booksearch. Cata: – occasional. Mem: PBFA.

The Bookshelf, ■ 6 Victoria Road, Scarborough, YO11 1SD. Prop: Mrs. Leslie Anne Stones. Tel: (01723) 381677. Website: www.bookshelf.scarborough.co.uk. E-mail: leslie_stones@hotmail.com. Est: 2000. Shop; open **M:** 10:00–17:00; **T:** 10:00–17:00; **W:** 10:00–17:00; **Th:** 10:00–17:00; **F:** 10:00–17:00; **S:** 10:00–17:00. Small general stock. PR: £1–100. Corresp: some French.

Richard Dalby, 4 Westbourne Park, Scarborough, YO12 4AT. Tel: (01723) 377049. Est: 1976. Private premises; postal business only. Very small stock. Spec: Fiction - Fantasy, Horror; Literature. Cata: 2. Mem: PBFA.

Mrs. Lofthouse's Secondhand Book Emporium, 2 Queen Street, Scarborough,
W.H. Reeves (Technical Books), Quarry House, Quarry Road, Burniston, Scarborough, YO13 0DJ.
Scarborough Books, 55 Castle Road, Scarborough, YO11 1BH.

SELBY
Anthony Vickers, 23 Baffam Gardens, Selby, YO8 9AY.

SETTLE
Anderson Slater Antiques, ■ 6 Duke Street, Settle, BD24 9DW. Prop: Kenneth C. Slater. Tel: (01729) 822051. Fax: (01969) 663751. Est: 1998. Shop; open **M:** 10:00–17:00; **T:** 10:00–17:00; **W:** 10:00–17:00; **Th:** 10:00–17:00; **F:** 10:00–17:00. Medium stock. Spec: Animals and Birds; Antiques; Art; Arts, The; Biography; Fiction - General; First Editions; Literary Criticism; Music - General; Poetry; Travel - General. PR: £3–60. VAT No: GB 160 0763 92.
Peter M. Thornber, 3 School Hill, Settle, BD24 9HB. Tel: (01729) 824067. Est: 1997. Private premises; appointment necessary. Small stock. Spec: Agriculture; Antiquarian; Ecclesiastical History & Architecture; Farming & Livestock; Modern First Editions; Religion - Christian; Theology. PR: £5–500. Also, valuations, consultancy and researcher, commissions at auctions. Corresp: French.

SKIPTON
Alley Books, 6a Sheep Street, Skipton, BD23 1JH.
Grove Rare Books, ■ The Old Post Office, Bolton Abbey, Skipton, BD23 6EX. Prop: Andrew & Janet Sharpe. Tel: (01756) 710717. Fax: (01756) 710717. Website: www.grovebookshop.co.uk. E-mail: antiquarian@groverarebooks.co.uk. Est: 1984. Shop; open **T:** 10:00–17:00; **W:** 10:00–17:00; **Th:** 10:00–17:00; **F:** 10:00–17:00; **S:** 10:00–17:00. Closed for lunch: 13:00–14:00. Medium stock. Spec: Bindings; Fiction - General; Illustrated; Literature; Rural Life; Sets of Books; Sport - Angling/Fishing; Sport - Field Sports; Sport - Hunting; Topography - General; Topography - Local. PR: £10–1,000. CC: JCB; MC; V; SW, SO. Formerly of the Grove Bookshop, Ilkley. Cata: 2 – a year. Mem: ABA; PBFA.
C.L. Hawley, 26 Belgrave Street, Skipton, West Riding of Yorkshire, BD23 1QB. (*) Prop: Catherine Hawley. Tel: (01756) 792380. Website: www.clhawley.co.uk. E-mail: clh@clhawley.co.uk. Est: 2000. Private premises; postal business only. Small general stock. Spec: Arts, The; Biography; Children's - General; History - General; Humanities; Literary Criticism. PR: £2–250. Also, a booksearch service. Mem: Ibooknet.

STAITHES
John L. Capes (Books, Maps & Prints), Church Street, Staithes, Cleveland, TS13 5DB. Tel: (01947) 840-790. Fax: (0870) 127-2061. Website: www.johncapes.co.uk. E-mail: capes@staithes.fsbusiness.co.uk. Est: 1969. Private premises; appointment necessary. Very small general stock. Spec: Academic/Scholarly; Antiquarian; Fine Art; Topography - Local. PR: £10–2,000 Mem: PBFA.

STAMFORD BRIDGE
Batterdale Books, 32 Godwin's Way, Stamford Bridge, YO41 1DB. Prop: Gordon B. & Fleur L. Steven. Tel: (01759) 372616. Website: http://hometown.aol.com/GBSteven. E-mail: GBSteven@aol.com. Est: 1994. Private premises; postal business only. Small stock. Spec: Banking & Insurance; Canals/Inland Waterways; Company History; Industry; Railways; Steam Engines. PR: £1–100. Cata: 4 – a year on railways.

STOKESLEY
Sansovino Books, Faceby Lodge Farm, Stokesley, TS9 7DP.

TADCASTER
Roy Allport, Bramblings, 120 Wighill Lane, Tadcaster, LS24 8HE. Tel: (01937) 834176. Fax: (01937) 834176. Website: www.abebooks.com/home/ROYPORT. E-mail: royport@clara.co.uk. Est: 1991. Private premises; Internet. Appointment necessary. Very small stock. Spec: Academic/Scholarly; Folklore; Gypsies; Rural Life; Social History; Traction Engines; Windmills & Watermills. PR: £2–200.

THIRSK
Book & Stamp Shop, 7 Westgate, Thirsk, YO7 1QR.
Hambleton Books, 43 Market Place, Thirsk, YO7 1HA.
Potterton Books, The Old Rectory, Sessay, Thirsk, YO7 3LZ.

WHITBY

Allan Clewlow, Bookseller, 46 Baxtergate, Whitby, YO21 1BL.

Endeavour Books, 1 Grape Lane, Whitby, YO22 4BA.

John R. Hoggarth, Thorneywaite House, Glaisdale, Whitby, YO21 2QU. Tel: (01947) 897338. Fax: (01947) 897061. Website: www.johnrhoggarth.co.uk. E-mail: john@johnrhoggarth.co.uk. Est: 1978. Private premises; Internet and postal. Appointment necessary. Small stock. Spec: Author - Baden-Powell, Lord Robert; Children's - General; History - General; Scouts & Guides. PR: £1–100. CC: PayPal. Cata: 6.

Naughty Nostalgia, P O Box 23, Whitby, YO21 3YT.

Old Chapel Books, Chapel Street, Whitby, Robin Hoods Bay, YO22 4SQ.

YARM

Richard J. Hodgson (Books), Manor Farm, Kirklevington, Yarm, TS15 9PY.

YORK

Barbican Bookshop, ■ 24 Fossgate, York, YO1 9TA. Prop: Christian Literature Stalls Ltd,. Tel: (01904) 653643. Fax: (01904) 653643. Website: barbicanbookshop.co.uk. E-mail: mail@barbicanbookshop.co.uk. Est: 1960. Shop; open **M:** 09:00–17:30; **T:** 09:15–17:30; **W:** 09:00–17:30; **Th:** 09:00–17:30; **F:** 09:15–17:30; **S:** 09:00–17:30. Large general stock. Spec: Aeronautics; Bibles; Canals/Inland Waterways; Ecclesiastical History & Architecture; Folio Society, The; History - General; History - Industrial; History - Local; Literature; Military; Military History; Prayer Books; Railways; Religion - Christian. PR: £1–500. CC: E; JCB; MC; V. Also, new books, remainders, cards & videos. Cata: 2 – Theology. Mem: PBFA; BA.

Boer War Books, 8 Mill Lane, Heworth, York, YO31 7TE. Prop: E.A. Hackett. Tel: (01904) 415829. Fax: (01904) 415829. Est: 1969. Private premises; postal business only. Spec: Countries - South Africa; Rural Life. PR: £1 plus. Cata: 1 – on Boer War.

Courtney & Hoff, Hutton Hall Farm, Long Marston, York, YO26 7LZ.

Jack Duncan Books, 36 Fossgate, York, YO1 9TF.

Empire Books, 12 Queens Staith Mews, York, YO1 6HH. Prop: Colin Hinchcliffe. Tel: (01904) 610679. Fax: (01904) 641664. E-mail: colin@empires.demon.co.uk. Est: 1990. Private premises; Internet and postal. Appointment necessary. Large stock. Spec: Travel - General; Travel - Africa; Travel - Americas; Travel - Asia; Travel - Australasia/Australia; Travel - Europe; Travel - Middle East; Travel - Polar. PR: £3–500. CC: MC; V. Cata: 4 – quarterly.

Mark Kelly Books, 68 Alma Terrace, Fulford Road, York, YO10 4DJ.

Knapton Bookbarn, Back Lane, Knapton, York, YO26 6QJ.

Lucius Books Ltd, 15 Main Street, Wilberfoss, York, YO41 5NN. (*) Prop: James Hallgate. Tel: (0759) 380960. E-mail: james@luciusbooks.fsnet.co.uk. Est: 1993. Private premises; appointment necessary. Very small stock. Spec: Author - Christie, Agatha; Author - Fleming, Ian; Author - Johns, W.E.; Children's - General; Children's - Illustrated; Fine & Rare; First Editions; Illustrated. PR: £30–20,000. CC: JCB; MC; V. Cata: 3. Mem: ABA; PBFA; ILAB. VAT No: GB 766 9110 08.

Philip Martin Music Books, 22 Huntington Road, York, YO31 8RL.

Minster Gate Bookshop, ■ 8 Minster Gates, York, YO1 7HL. Prop: Nigel Wallace. Tel: (01904) 621812. Fax: (01904) 622960. Website: www.minstergatebooks.co.uk. E-mail: rarebooks@minstergatebooks.co.uk. Est: 1970. Shop; Internet and postal. Open: **M:** 10:00–17:30; **T:** 10:00–17:30; **W:** 10:00–17:30; **Th:** 10:00–17:30; **F:** 10:00–17:30; **S:** 10:00–17:30; **Su:** 11:00–19:00. Large general stock. Spec: Arthurian; Children's - General; Folklore; Illustrated; Literature. PR: £1–500. CC: MC; V. Also, a free booksearch service. Corresp: French. Mem: PBFA. VAT No: GB 450 7122 78.

Mr. Christmas Books, 3 Macdonald Court, Pocklington, York, YO4 2GH.

Nicholson's Books, The Coach House, Wiganthorpe, Terrington, York, YO60 6NU.

Nostalgia Publications Ltd., ■ 91–93 Nunnery Lane, York, YO23 1AH. Prop: Jim Barker. Tel: (01904) 624901. Fax: (01904) 654925. Website: www.nostalgia-publications.co.uk. E-mail: jim@products.demon.co.uk. Est: 1983. Shop; Internet and postal. *Shop at:* 1 Victoria Street, off Nunnery Lane, York (side of the office). Open: **T:** 11:00–17:30; **W:** 11:00–17:30; **Th:** 11:00–17:30; **F:** 11:00–17:30; **S:** 11:00–17:30. Medium stock. Spec: Glamour; Periodicals & Magazines. PR: £1–100. CC: MC; V. Mailorder. Cata: 1 – bi-monthly.

Oblong Books, ■ 36 Fossgate, York, YO19TF. Prop: Alex Helstrip. Tel: (01904) 641389. E-mail: alexhelstrip@hotmail.com. Est: 1992. Shop; open **M:** 10:00–17:30; **T:** 10:00–17:30; **W:** 10:00–17:30; **Th:** 10:00–17:30; **F:** 10:00–17:30; **S:** 10:00–17:30. Large stock. Spec: Academic/Scholarly; Antiquarian; Arts, The; Aviation; Biography; Children's - General; Cinema/Film; Fiction - General; First Editions; Folio Society, The; History - General; Literary Criticism; Literature; Maritime/Nautical; Military; Music - General; and others as listed in the Speciality Index. PR: £2–500. CC: MC; V. Cata: 2 – the Folio Society. Corresp: Spanish.

Janette Ray Rare and Out of Print, 8 Bootham, York, YO30 7BL.

Rose Fine Art & Antiques, Fox Inn Farm, Easingwold Road, Stillington, York.

Ken Spelman, ■ 70 Micklegate, York, YO1 6LF. Prop: Peter Miller & Tony Fothergill. Tel: (01904) 624414. Fax: (01904) 626276. Website: www.kenspelman.com. E-mail: rarebooks@kenspelman.com. Est: 1948. Shop; open **M:** 09:00–17:30; **T:** 09:00–17:30; **W:** 09:00–17:30; **Th:** 09:00–17:30; **F:** 09:00–17:30; **S:** 09:00–17:30. Very large general stock. Spec: Academic/Scholarly; Antiquarian; Fine Art; History - General; Horticulture; Literature. PR: £1–10,000. CC: E; MC; V; SW. Also, valuations & a booksearch service & on-line search and ordering. Cata: 3. Mem: ABA; PBFA; ILAB.

Jeffrey Stern Antiquarian Book, Little Hall, Heslington, York, YO10 5EB.

Stone Trough Books, ■ 38 Fossgate, York, YO1 9TF. Prop: George Ramsden. Tel: (01904) 670323. Fax: (01944) 768465. E-mail: george@stonetrough.demon.co.uk. Est: 1981. Shop; open **T:** 10:00–17:30; **W:** 10:00–17:30; **Th:** 10:00–17:30; **F:** 10:00–17:30; **S:** 10:00–17:30. Small general stock. Spec: Literature. PR: £2–200. CC: V. Cata: 2 – Literature. Corresp: French, German. VAT No: GB 237 5500 70.

WestField Books, 28 Easthorpe Drive, Nether Poppleton, York, YO26 6NR. Prop: Henry Parker. Tel: (01904) 794711. E-mail: westfieldbooks@btopenworld.com. Est: 1990. Private premises; Internet and postal. Medium stock. Spec: Antiquarian. PR: £5–5,000.

NORTHAMPTONSHIRE

BRACKLEY
The Old Hall Bookshop, 32 Market Place, Brackley, NN13 7DP.

GEDDINGTON
Cooksweb, Dukes Farm, 39 Queen Street, Geddington, NN14 1AZ. Prop: Natalie Miller. Tel: (01536) 460991. Fax: (01536) 741704. Website: www.cooksweb.co.uk. E-mail: info@cooksweb.co.uk. Est: 1999. Private premises; Internet and postal. Appointment necessary. Open: **M:** 09:30–15:00; **T:** 09:30–15:00; **W:** 09:30–15:00; **Th:** 09:30–15:00; **F:** 09:30–15:00. Small stock. Spec: Brewing; Christmas; Cookery/Gastronomy; Crafts; Embroidery; Etiquette; Fashion & Costume; Flower Arranging; Food & Drink; Gardening; Horticulture; Viticulture; Whisky; Wine. CC: MC; V; Debit. Cata: 6 – Food & Drink. Corresp: French, German. VAT No: GB 745 9304 20.

KETTERING
Donald S. King, 41 Cottesmore Avenue, Barton Seagrave, Kettering, NN15 6QU.

NORTHAMPTON
Hickey Books, 17 Overslade House, Overslade Close, East Hunsbury, Northampton, NN4 0RZ.

Occultique, 30 St. Michael's Avenue, Northampton, NN1 4JQ. Prop: M. John Lovett. Tel: (01604) 627727. Fax: (01604) 603860. Website: www.occultique.co.uk. E-mail: enquiries@occultique.co.uk. Est: 1973. Private premises; Internet and postal. Appointment necessary. Medium stock. Spec: Alchemy; Alternative Medicine; American Indians; Astrology; Author - Crowley, Aleister; Author - Spare, Austin Osman; Earth Mysteries; Egyptology; Erotica; Esoteric; Fiction - Fantasy, Horror; Folklore; Freemasonry & Anti-Masonry; Ghosts; Herbalism; and others as lsited in the Speciality Index. PR: £1–1,000. CC: PayPal. Also, new books, essential oils, herbs & occult paraphernalia. Cata: 2 – fairly frequent.

Mr. M. Quinnell, 116 Lutterworth Road, Northampton, NN1 5JL.

W. Reid Books, 1 Compton Close, Earls Barton, Northampton, NN6 0PN. Tel: 01604 812090. E-mail: bill.reid@btinternet.com.

Roosterbooks, 7 Elysium Terrace, Northampton, NN2 6EN. Prop: Roy Sheffield. Tel: (01604) 720983. Fax: (01604) 720983. E-mail: roosterbooks@themail.com. Est: 1997. Private premises; Internet and postal. Medium stock. Spec: Biography; History - General; Mind, Body & Spirit; Modern First Editions. PR: £1–800. CC: JCB; MC. VAT No: GB 655 1461 40.

Ryeland Books, 18 St. George's Place, Northampton, NN2 6EP. Prop: Alan & Joy Riley. Tel: (01604) 716901. E-mail: amriley@ryeland.demon.co.uk. Est: 1998. Private premises; appointment necessary. Small stock. Spec: Architecture; Art History; History - General; Literary Criticism; Literature; Natural History; Theology. PR: £3–1,000. Cata: 3.

OUNDLE
Geraldine Waddington Books & P, 3 West Street, Oundle, PE8 4EJ. Tel: (01832) 275028. Fax: (01832) 275028. E-mail: g.waddington@dial.pipex.com. Est: 1984. Spec: Art Reference; Engraving; Ex-Libris; Folio Society, The; Illustrated; Private Press. PR: £2–500.

RUSHDEN
Booksmart, 4 Manning Rise, Rushden, NN10 0LY. Prop: Andy Wagstaff. Tel: (01933) 357416. Website: www.booksmart.co.uk. E-mail: wagstaa@hotmail.com. Est: 1990. Postal business only. PR: £1–10.

Dealers who wish to update their entry should visit their page on
www.sheppardsdirectories.com

SILVERSTONE

Collectors Carbooks, ■ 2210 Silverstone Technolgy Park, Silverstone Circuit, Silverstone, NN12 8TN. Prop: Chris Knapman. Tel: (01327) 855888. Fax: (01327) 855999. Website: www.collectorscarbooks.com. E-mail: sales@collectorscarbooks.com. Est: 1993. Shop; Internet and postal. Open: **M:** 09:00–17:00; **T:** 09:00–17:00; **W:** 09:00–17:00; **Th:** 09:00–17:00; **F:** 09:00–17:00; **S:** 08:30–02:33. Large stock. Spec: Marque Histories; Motorbikes; Motoring; Sport - Motor Racing; Transport; Vintage Cars. PR: £1–1,200. CC: MC; V. Open race Saturdays 08:30–14:30. Also, a free booksearch service. Attends historic motor racing events. VAT No: GB 649 2588 91.

TOWCESTER

Mr. Pickwick of Towcester, Lavender Cottage, Shutlanger, Towcester, NN12 7RR. Prop: William Mayes. Tel: (01604) 862006. Fax: (01604) 862006. Website: www.yell.co.uk/sites/pickwickbookfinders. Est: 1972. Private premises; postal business only. Very large stock. Spec: Author - Dickens, Charles; Biography; Books about Books; Fiction - General; Literature; Memoirs; Newspapers - General; Periodicals & Magazines; Sport - General; Television. PR: £3–300. Also, booksearch. Cata: – occasionally.

WELLINGBOROUGH

R.C. Brett, 32 Abbots Way, Wellingborough, NN8 2AG. Tel: (01933) 224502. E-mail: joe.brett@btinternet.com. Private premises; postal business only. Appointment necessary. Very small stock. Spec: Sport - Athletics; Sport - Olympic Games, The. PR: £1–75. Cata: – occasionally.

The Park Gallery & Bookshop, ■ 16 Cannon Street, Wellingborough, NN8 4DJ. Prop: J.A. Foster. Tel: (01933) 222592. Website: www.ukbookworld.com/members/parkbookshop. E-mail: judy@parkbookshop.freeserve.co.uk. Est: 1979. Shop; Internet and postal. Open: **M:** 10:00–17:30; **T:** 10:00–17:30; **W:** 10:00–17:30; **Th:** 10:00–14:30; **F:** 10:00–17:30; **S:** 10:00–18:00. Medium stock. Spec: Antiquarian; Antiques; Author - Bates, H.E.; Biography; Children's - General; Fiction - General; Military; Railways; Topography - General; Topography - Local. PR: £1–500. Also, a booksearch service, collectables, ephemera, prints & maps, plus picture framing.

NORTHUMBERLAND

ALNWICK

Barter Books, ■ Alnwick Station, Alnwick, NE66 2NP. Prop: Stuart & Mary Manley. Tel: (01665) 604888. Fax: (01665) 604444. Website: www.barterbooks.co.uk. E-mail: bb@barterbooks.co.uk. Est: 1991. Shop; open **M:** 09:00–19:00; **T:** 09:00–19:00; **W:** 09:00–19:00; **Th:** 09:00–19:00; **F:** 09:00–19:00; **S:** 09:00–19:00; **Su:** 09:00–19:00. Very large general stock. PR: £1–6,000. CC: AE; D; E; JCB; MC; V. Open rest of the year, Mon-Sun 09:00–17.00. Corresp: French. *Also at:* Barter Books, Seahouses, Northumberland. VAT No: GB 414 3504 88.

BEADNELL

Shearwater Bed & Books (formerly John Lumby Nat. History Bks), Shearwater, 78 Harbour Road, Beadnell, Northumberland, NE67 5BE. Prop: John Lumby. Tel: (01665) 720654. E-mail: johnspaullumby@yahoo.co.uk. Private premises; appointment necessary. Small stock. Spec: Animals and Birds; Entomology; Lepidopterology / Lepidoptery; Natural History; Ornithology; Plant Hunting. PR: £3–600. Also, booksearch and B&B. Attends British Bird Watching Fair - and bookbinding work.

BERWICK–UPON–TWEED

Bridge Street Bookshop, ■ 41 Bridge Street, Berwick–upon–Tweed, TD15 1ES. Prop: Christopher & Do Shaw. Tel: (01289) 304986. Fax: (01289) 304986. Est: 1993. Shop; open **M:** 09:15–17:00; **T:** 09:15–17:00; **W:** 09:15–17:00; **Th:** 09:15–13:00; **F:** 09:15–17:00; **S:** 08:00–17:00. Small general stock. Spec: History - Local; Rural Life. PR: £1–150. CC: MC; V.

Anne Hattle, 31 Church Street, Berwick–upon–Tweed, TD15 1EE. Tel: (01289) 331502. Est: 1984. Spec: History - General; Scottish Interest; Topography - General. PR: £1–100.

CORBRIDGE

Cheyne Books, 8 Cheyne Road, Prudhoe, Corbridge, NE42 6PE.

HALTWHISTLE

Newcastle Bookshop@Haltwhistle, ■ Market Square, Haltwhistle, NE49 OBG. Prop: Valerie Levitt. Tel: (01434) 320 103. Website: www.newcastlebookshop.com. E-mail: newcstlbk@aol.com. Est: 1975. Shop; open **F:** 11:00–17:00; **S:** 11:00–17:00. Medium stock. Spec: Art; Art History; Art Reference; Illustrated; Photography. PR: £1–500. CC: AE; JCB; MC; V; SW. Also, old prints.

HEXHAM

Alex Fotheringham, East Chesterhope, West Woodburn, Hexham, NE48 2RQ. Tel: (01434) 270046. Fax: (01434) 632931. Private premises; appointment necessary. Very small stock. Spec: Antiquarian; Architecture; Art; Bibliography; Literature; Theology. PR: £20–2,500. Cata: 6 – a year. Mem: ABA; PBFA. VAT No: GB 646 1882 17.

Hencotes Books & Prints, ■ 8 Hencotes, Hexham, NE46 2EJ. Prop: Penny Pearce. Tel: (01434) 605971. E-mail: hencotesbooks@btinternet.com. Est: 1972. Shop; open **M:** 10:30–17:00; **T:** 10:30–17:00; **W:** 10:30–17:00. **F:** 10:30–17:00; **S:** 10:30–17:00. Medium general stock. PR: £1–500. CC: JCB; MC; V; SW. Also, booksearch service & attends P.B.F.A. fairs. Mem: PBFA.

Dealers who need to update their entry should visit their page on
www.sheppardsdirectories.com

Newgate Books, 3 Quatre Bras, Hexham, NE46 3JY. Prop: John Dwyer. Tel: (01434) 607650. Fax: (01434) 607650. E-mail: newgate.books@virgin.net. Est: 1987. Private premises; postal business only. Telephone first. Open: **M:** 09:00–17:00; **T:** 09:00–17:00; **W:** 09:00–17:00; **Th:** 09:00–17:00; **F:** 09:00–12:00; **S:** 09:00–12:00. Closed for lunch: 13:00–14:30. Small general stock. Spec: Music - General. PR: £5–100. Also, a booksearch service. Corresp: French.

Priestpopple Books, ■ 9b Priestpopple, Hexham, NE46 1PF.

MORPETH

Appleby's Bookshop, 60 Newgate Street, Morpeth, NE61 1BE.

Intech Books, 14 Bracken Ridge, Morpeth, NE61 3SY. Prop: Mr. D. J. Wilkinson. Tel: (01670) 519102. Fax: (01670) 515815. E-mail: djwintech@talk21.com. Est: 1981. Private premises; Internet and postal. Appointment necessary. Small stock. Spec: Children's - General; Comic Books & Annuals; Fiction - General; First Editions; Sport - Golf; Topography - Local . PR: £1–100. Also, a booksearch service.

PRUDHOE

Arcanum, 1 Carnaby Close, Castlefields, Prudhoe, NE42 5QY.

SEAHOUSES

Barter Books, 67 Main Street, Seahouses.

STOCKSFIELD

Leaf Ends, Ridley Mill, Stocksfield, NE43 7QU. Prop: Mrs Moira Tait. Tel: (01661) 844261. Fax: (01661) 844261. Website: www.abebooks.com. E-mail: alexander.tait@virgin.net. Postal business only. Large general stock. Spec: Children's - General. PR: £2–800. CC: MC; V. Also, booksearch. VAT No: GB 747 2468 08.

WOOLER

Hamish Dunn Antiques & Books, ■ 17 High Street, Wooler, NE71 6BU. Tel: (01668) 281341. Est: 1986. Shop; open **M:** 09:00–16:00; **T:** 09:00–16:00; **W:** 09:00–16:00; **Th:** 09:00–12:00; **F:** 09:00–16:00; **S:** 09:00–16:00. Small general stock. PR: £1–100. CC: AE; D; V.

NOTTINGHAMSHIRE

GUNTHORPE
Letterbox Books, The Coach House, Gunthorpe, NG14 7ES.

KIRKBY-IN-ASHFIELD
Kyrios Books, ■ 11 Kingsway, Kirkby-in-Ashfield, NG17 7BB. Prop: Keith Parr. Tel: (01623) 452556. Website: www.kyriosbooks.co.uk. E-mail: keith@kyriosbooks.co.uk. Est: 1989. Shop; Internet and postal. Telephone first. Open: **M:** 10:30–14:30; **T:** 10:30–14:30; **Th:** 10:30–14:30; **F:** 10:30–14:30; **S:** 10:30–14:30. Closed for lunch: 12:00–13:00. Medium stock. Spec: Autobiography; Ecclesiastical History & Architecture; Philosophy; Prayer Books; Religion - General; Religion - Christian; Theology. PR: £1–100. Cata: 6 – Bi-monthly - Random Stock Selection. Mem: FSB.

MANSFIELD
R. W. Price, 19 Park Avenue, Mansfield, NG18 2AU. Prop: Mr G.D. Price. Tel: (01623) 629858. Website: www.snap.to/uk. E-mail: gdp@gdprice.freeserve.co.uk. Est: 1986. Private premises; Internet and postal. Very large general stock. Spec: Beat Writers; Children's - General; Comedy; Erotica; Espionage; Fiction - General; Fiction - Crime, Detective, Spy, Thrillers; Fiction - Fantasy, Horror; Fiction - Romantic; Fiction - Science Fiction; Fiction - Westerns; First Editions; Modern Firsts; and others as listed in the Speciality Index. PR: £1–100. Cata: 4.

NEWARK-ON-TRENT
Jandee Books, Melrose, Old Hall Lane, East Markham, Newark-on-Trent, NG22 0RF. Tel: (01777) 871759. Website: www.ukbookworld.com/members/jandee. E-mail: andrewcampbell@skynow.net. Private premises; Internet and postal. Very small general stock. PR: £1–500.

NOTTINGHAM
Artco, 6 Grantham Road, Radcliffe on Trent, Nottingham, NG12 2HD. Prop: Mr. H. Boehm. Tel: (0115) 933-3530. Fax: (0115) 911-9746. Est: 1970. Private premises; appointment necessary. Small stock. Spec: Applied Art; Art; Art Reference; Artists; Arts, The; Colour-Plate; Foreign Texts; Illustrated; Limited Editions; Literature; Private Press. PR: £10–1,000. CC: MC; V. Cata: – occasional lists. Corresp: German.

Geoffrey Blore's Bookshop, ■ 484 Mansfield Road, Sherwood, Nottingham, NG5 2BF. Tel: (0115) 969-1441. Est: 1987. Shop; open **M:** 10:30–17:00; **T:** 10:30–17:00; **W:** 10:30–17:00; **Th:** 10:30–17:00; **F:** 10:30–17:00; **S:** 10:30–17:00. Very large general stock.

Caron Books, 29 Clarence Road, Attenborough, Nottingham, NG9 5HY. Prop: Steve Caron. Tel: (0115) 925-4851. Website: www.caronbooks.co.uk. E-mail: caronbooks@btclick.com. Est: 2000. Spec: Fiction - General. PR: £3–150.

Guy Davis, Antiquarian Books, 61 Bakerdale Road, Bakersfield, Nottingham, NG3 7GJ.

A. Holmes, 82 Highbury Avenue, Nottingham, NG6 9DB.

Jermy & Westerman, ■ 203 Mansfield Road, Sherwood, Nottingham, NG1 3FS.

C.J. Martin, 45 New Mill Lane, Mansfield Woodhouse, Nottingham, NG19 9BU.

Maynard & Bradley, 30 Friar Lane, Nottingham, NG1 6DQ.

Stephen Rigley, 23 Woodthorpe Drive, Nottingham, NG5 4FT.

Frances Wakeman Books, Unit 13, Carlton Business Centre, Station Road, Carlton, Nottingham, NG4 3AA. Prop: Frances & Paul Wakeman. Tel: (0115) 956-6850. Fax: (0115) 956-6944. Website: www.fwbooks.com. E-mail: info@fwbooks.com. Est: 1970. Office &/or bookroom; Internet and postal. Appointment necessary. Small stock. Spec: Bibliography; Books about Books; Papermaking; Printing; Private Press; Publishing; Typography. PR: £1–5,000. CC: AE; E; JCB; MC; V. Also, publishing books about books. Cata: 8 – every other month. Mem: PBFA. VAT No: GB 685 4226 14.

PLEASLEY VALE
Caroline Hartley Books, Mill 3, Unit J2, Pleasley Vale Business Park, Pleasley Vale, NG19 8RL. Prop: Caroline Hartley. Tel: (01246) 558481. Website: www.abebooks.com/home/carolinehartley. E-mail: carohartley@aol.com. Est: 1985. Warehouse; Internet and postal. Large stock. Spec: Odd & Unusual. PR: £3–100. CC: MC; V.

RAINWORTH
Lynda Mallett/Scottish Booksea, 'Fernlea', 106 Southwell Road East, Rainworth, Mansfield, NG21 0EL.

SANDIACRE
A.E. Beardsley, 14 York Avenue, Sandiacre, NG10 5HB.

SUTTON IN ASHFIELD
Ashfield Books and Records, ■ 110 Outram Street, Sutton in Ashfield, NG17 4FS. Prop: Stephen & Susan Cooke. Tel: daytime (01623) 5536. E-mail: stephen@cooke5.fsnet.co.uk. Est: 1990. Shop; open **M:** 10:00–17:00; **T:** 10:00–17:00; **W:** 10:00–17:00; **Th:** 10:00–17:00; **F:** 10:00–17:00; **S:** 10:00–17:00. Small general stock. Spec: Art; Cinema/Film; History - General; Medicine; Music - General; Politics; Psychology/Psychiatry; Theatre; Topography - General; Transport; Travel - General; War - General. CC: JCB; MC; SW. Also, booksearch, Naxos CDs, Sheet Music, Cassette Tapes, Vinyl Records. VAT No: GB 797 2060 05.

Kingfisher Book Service, 6 Ash Grove, Skegby, Sutton in Ashfield, NG17 3FH. Prop: Malcolm Walters. Tel: (01623) 552530. Fax: (01623) 552530. Website: www.kingfisher-books.co.uk. E-mail: quotes@kingfisher-books.co.uk. Est: 1991. Private premises; postal business only. Very small general stock. Spec: Fiction - General; Military. PR: £3–100. CC: E; JCB; MC; V.

OXFORDSHIRE

ABINGDON

Bennett & Kerr Books, Millhill Warehouse, Church Lane, Steventon, Abingdon, OX13 6SW.

Courtenay Bookroom, Appleford, Abingdon, OX14 4PB.

Mary Mason, 55 Winterborne Road, Abingdon, OX14 1AL.

BANBURY

'Books', The Old Forge, Upper Brailes, Banbury, OX15 5AT.

Seckworth Books, 36 Wykham Lane, Bodicote, Banbury, OX15 4BW.

BICESTER

The Bookshop Down The Lane, ■ 14 Wesley Lane, Bicester, OX26 6JU. Prop: Tony Simcock. Tel: (01869) 360085 or 34. Est: 2000. Shop; open **M:** 10:00–17:00; **T:** 10:00–17:00; **W:** 10:00–17:00; **Th:** 10:00–17:00; **F:** 10:00–16:00. Closed for lunch: 13:00–14:00. Medium general stock. PR: £1–100. CC: E; JCB; MC; V.

DaSilva Puppet Books, 63 Kennedy Road, Bicester, OX26 8BE. Prop: Ray DaSilva. Tel: (01869) 245793. Fax: (01869) 245793. Website: www.puppetbooks.co.uk. E-mail: dasilva@puppetbooks.co.uk. Est: 1986. Private premises; Internet and postal. Appointment necessary. Very small stock. Spec: Entertainment - General; Performing Arts; Puppets & Marionettes; Theatre. PR: £1–200. CC: MC; V; SW. Also, new specialist books & consultancy on Puppet Theatre. Cata: 2. Corresp: French. VAT No: GB 119 7586 34.

BLEWBURY

Blewbury Antiques, Applethorpe, London Road, Blewbury, OX11 9NX.

BURFORD

Quill Books, The Old Forge, 24 Lower High Street, Burford, OX18 4RR.

CHIPPING NORTON

Greensleeves, P.O. Box 156, Chipping Norton, OX7 3XT. Prop: P.R. & C. Seers. Tel: (01608) 676140. Fax: (01608) 676140. Website: www.greensleevesbooks.co.uk. E-mail: greensleeves@v21mail.co.uk. Est: 1982. Private premises; postal business only. Medium stock. Spec: Alternative Medicine; Anthroposophy; Astrology; Esoteric; Health; Herbalism; Homeopathy; Metaphysics; Mysticism; Mythology; Natural Health; New Age; Occult; Parapsychology; Psychic; Psychology/Psychiatry; Psychotherapy; Religion - Christian; Religion; and others as listed in the Speciality Index. PR: £1–500. CC: MC; V. Also, new books and booksearch service. Cata: 8 – specialities. Mem: BA. VAT No: GB 596 3357 96.

Kellow Books, ■ 6 Market Place, Chipping Norton, OX7 5NA. Prop: Peter & Jan Combellack. Tel: (01608) 644293. Est: 1998. Shop; open **M:** 10:00–16:30; **T:** 10:00–16:30; **W:** 10:00–16:30; **Th:** 10:00–16:30; **F:** 10:00–16:30. Medium general stock. Spec: Children's - General; Company History; Fiction - General; Maritime/Nautical; Military History; Natural History; Ornithology; Topography - General; Topography - Local. PR: £2–800. CC: AE; D; E; JCB; MC; V; all cards.

Dealers who need to update their entry should visit their page on *www.sheppardsdirectories.com*

OXFORDSHIRE

DEDDINGTON

Brian Carter, 13 High Street, Deddington, OX15 0SJ. Prop: Brian Carter. Tel: (01869) 337341. E-mail: carterbe@lineone.net. Est: 1974. Private premises; postal business only. Small stock. Spec: Ecclesiastical History & Architecture; Oxford Movement; Philosophy; Theology. PR: £5–500. CC: MC; V.

K.R. Clark, Manor Flat, Deddington Manor, New Street, Deddington, OX15 0SS. Tel: (01869) 338543. Market stand/stall. *Shop at:* Oxford Antique & Craft Market, Gloucester Green, Oxford. Open: **Th:** 08:00–15:00. Spec: Art; Bindings; Literature; Topography - Local. Mem: PBFA; *Also at:* Oxford Antique & Craft Mkt, Gloucester Green.

Andrew Jones, Monks Court, Castle Street, Deddington, Banbury, OX15 OTE.

DIDCOT

The Parlour Bookshop, ■ 30 Wantage Road, Didcot, OX11 0BT. Prop: Roy Frank Burton. Tel: (01235) 818989. Fax: (01235) 814494. Est: 1995. Shop; open **T:** 10:00–16.00; **W:** 10:00–16:00; **Th:** 10:00–16:00; **F:** 10:00–16:00; **S:** 10:00–16:00. Closed for lunch: 12:45–13:45. Medium general stock. PR: £1–50. Closed Bank Holidays, Good Friday : Easter Monday, Christmas Eve to 4 January.

Wayside Books & Cards, Wayside Wellshead, Harwell, Didcot, OX11 0HD. Prop: J.A.B. & J.L. Gibson. Tel: (01235) 835256. E-mail: gibsonjab@aol.com. Est: 1985. Private premises; postal business only. Open in summer. Spec: Astronomy; Biography; Countries - Melanesia; Fiction - Science Fiction; Journals - General; Law; Physics; Religion - General; Science - General; Science - History of. PR: £1–50.

DUCKLINGTON

Demetzy Books, Manor House, Ducklington, Oxfordshire, OX29 7UX.

DORCHESTER ON THAMES

Pablo Butcher, Overy Mill, Dorchester on Thames, OX10 7JU. Tel: (01865) 341445. Fax: (01865) 341445. Est: 1974. Storeroom; appointment necessary. Small stock. Spec: Art; Ethnography; Photography; Travel - Africa; Travel - Americas; Travel - Asia. Cata: 1 – occasionally. Mem: ABA; PBFA; ILAB.

EAST HAGBOURNE

E.M. Lawson & Company, Kingsholm, East Hagbourne, OX11 9LN. Prop: W.J. & K.M. Lawson. Tel: (01235) 812033. Est: 1919. Private premises; appointment necessary. Very small stock. Spec: Antiquarian; Countries - Africa; Countries - Americas, The; Countries - Australasia; Economics; Literature; Medicine; Science - General; Voyages & Discovery. Cata: 1 – occasionally. Mem: ABA.

FARINGDON

E.W. Classey Limited, P.O. Box 93, Faringdon, SN7 7DR.

N.W. Jobson, 8 Weston Cottages, Buscot Wick, Faringdon, SN7 8DN. Prop: Nigel Jobson. Tel: (01367) 252240. E-mail: jobbobookfinder@tiscali.co.uk. Est: 1981. Private premises; postal business only. Small stock. PR: £1–70. Also, a booksearch service.

PROJECT PORTMANTEAUX - EVERY MAN A DEBTOR

Give thought - Virtue can be fun

Project Portmanteaux the outcome of the creative thinking of Gordon Rattray-Taylor is a project which brings hope to the excluded young. In the first instance the gifted who by misfortune have missed their footing on the upper rungs of the educational ladder. While mammon demands that we fund raise, our immediate plangent need is for fine minds willing to help keep the good ship charity on course. Mind Tune the young. Let your educational success endow theirs.

Be a mentor on the net:

mind-a-mind.com   guru-4u.com   entente-serieurse.com

This advertisement is sponsored by Game Advice, 71 Rose Hill, OX4 4JR GB

GORING–ON–THAMES

Nevis Railway Books, ■ Barbara's, The Orchard, Goring–on–Thames, RG8 9HB. Prop: N.J. Bridger. Tel: (01491) 873032. Est: 1992. Shop; open **M:** 10:00–17:00; **T:** 10:00–17:00; **W:** 10:00–17:00; **Th:** 10:00–17:00; **F:** 10:00–17:00; **S:** 10:00–17:00. Closed for lunch: 13:00–14:15. Very small stock. Spec: Railways. PR: £1–50. *Also at:* Railway Book & Magazine Search, Newbury, Berks. (qv.) and Nevis railway Bookshops, Marlborough, Wilts (q.v).

HARWELL

Wayside Books and Cards, Wayside, Wellshead, Harwell, Didcot, OX11 OHD. Tel: (01235) 835256. Fax: (01235) 835256. Website: gibsonjab@aol.com. E-mail: gibsonjab@aol.com. Est: 1985. Private premises; Internet and postal. Appointment necessary. Small general stock. Spec: Academic/ Scholarly; Astronomy; Author - Greene, Graham; Author - Haggard, Sir Henry Rider; Author - Simenon, Georges; Author - Wodehouse, P.G.; Law; Science - History of. PR: £1–50.

HENLEY–ON–THAMES

Jonkers Rare Books, ■ 24 Hart Street, Henley–on–Thames, RG9 2AU. Prop: Christiaan & Sam Jonkers. Tel: (01491) 576427. Fax: (01491) 573805. Website: www.jonkers.co.uk. E-mail: books@jonkers.co.uk. Est: 1990. Shop; open **M:** 10:00–17:30; **T:** 10:00–17:30; **W:** 10:00–17:30; **Th:** 10:00–17:30; **F:** 10:00–17:30; **S:** 10:00–17:30. Small stock. Spec: Author - Fleming, Ian; Author - Potter, Beatrix; Children's - General; Illustrated; Literature; Modern First Editions; Topography - Local. PR: £20–5,000,000. CC: AE; MC; V. Cata: 4 – occasionally, on modern firsts, illustrated, children's. Corresp: French, Italian, Spanish. Mem: ABA; PBFA; ILAB.

Richard J. Kingston, ■ 95 Bell Street, Henley–on–Thames, RG9 2BD. Tel: (01491) 574535. Est: 1911. Shop; open **M:** 09:30–17:00; **T:** 09:30–17:00; **W:** 09:30–17:00; **Th:** 09:30–17:00; **F:** 09:30–17:00; **S:** 09:30–17:00. Small stock. Spec: Maritime/Nautical; Navigation; Topography - General; Travel - General.

Richard Way Booksellers, ■ 54 Friday Street, Henley–on–Thames, RG9 1AH. Prop: Richard Way & Diana Cook. Tel: (01491) 576663. Fax: (01491) 576663. E-mail: waybooks@btconnect.com. Est: 1978. Shop; open **M:** 10:00–17:30; **T:** 10:00–17:30; **W:** 10:00–17:30; **Th:** 10:00–17:30; **F:** 10:00–17:30; **S:** 10:00–17:30. Small general stock. Spec: Sport - Rowing. PR: £1–200. CC: JCB; V. Mem: ABA.

HOOK NORTON

Orangeberry Books, Rowan House, Queens Street, Hook Norton, Banbury, OX15 5PH. Prop: Paul Tranter. Tel: (01608) 737928. Fax: (01608) 730810. Website: www.orangeberry.co.uk. E-mail: books@orangeberry.co.uk. Est: 1995. Private premises; Internet and postal. Telephone first. Medium stock. Spec: Literature; Poetry; Science - General; Technology; Travel - General. PR: £5–1,000. CC: E; MC; V; SW. Corresp: French. Mem: IBN. VAT No: GB 800 0734 85.

MARSH GIBBON

Dusty Old Books Ltd., 7 Pear Tree Farm, Marsh Gibbon, OX27 0GB.

OXFORD

Arcadia, ■ 4 St. Michael's Street, Oxford, OX1 2DU. Tel: (01865) 241757. Est: 1975. Shop; open **M:** 10:00–18:00; **T:** 10:00–17:00; **W:** 10:00–18:00; **Th:** 09:00–18:00; **F:** 10:00–18:00; **S:** 10:00–18:00. Very small general stock. PR: £1–50.

Ars Artis, 31 Abberbury Road, Oxford, OX4 4ET. Prop: G.B. & H.J. Lowe. Tel: (01865) 770714. Est: 1976. Private premises; appointment necessary. Large stock. Spec: Applied Art; Architecture; Art History; Art Reference; Artists; Catalogues Raisonnes; Fine Art; Photography. PR: £1–5,000 Corresp: French, German. VAT No: GB 119 1785 58.

Blackwell's Music Shop, 23–25 Broad Street, Oxford, OX1 3AX.

Blackwell's Rare Books, 48–51 Broad Street, Oxford, OX1 3BQ. Prop: Blackwell Retail Ltd. Tel: (01865) 333555. Fax: (01865) 794143. Website: www.rarebook.blackwell.co.uk. E-mail: rarebooks@ blackwell.co.uk. Est: 1879. Spec: Children's - General; First Editions; Illustrated; Literature; Modern First Editions; Poetry; Private Press; Sets of Books; Topography - General. Also, booksearch on speciality subjects. Mem: PBFA.

Robert Clark Fine Books, 6a King Street, Oxford, OX2 6DF.

The Classics Bookshop, 3 Turl Street, Oxford, OX1 3DQ.

Roy Davids Ltd., The Old Forge, Rectory Road, Great Haseley, Oxford, OX44 7JG. Prop: Roy Davids. Tel: (01844) 279154. Fax: (01844) 278221. Website: www.roydavids.com. E-mail: manuscripts@roydavids.com. Est: 1994. Private premises. Spec: Autographs; History - General; Letters; Manuscripts; Music - General. PR: £50–100,000. CC: MC; V. Also, portraits and related artefacts. Cata: 1 – occasionally. Mem: ABA; ILAB.

Game Advice, 71 Rose Hill, Oxford, OX4 4JR. Prop: Alick Elithorn & Karen Stevenson. Tel: (01865) 777317. Fax: (01865) 433050. Website: www.game-advice.com. E-mail: a.elithorn@ntlworld.com. Est: 1975. Private premises; Internet and postal. Telephone first. Large general stock. Spec: Academic/Scholarly; Anthropology; Children's - General; Computing; Education & School; Fore-Edge Paintings; Games; History of Ideas; Juvenile; Linguistics; Magic & Conjuring; Medicine; Medicine - History of; Neurology; Philosophy; Psychoanalysis; and others as listed in the Speciality Index. PR: £3–9,000. Also, chess sets, antique games & puzzles, chess prints, educational software, computer & personal consultancy, booksearch & loan. Cata: 2 – bi-annual. Corresp: French.

Adrian Greenwood, 2 Union St., Oxford, OX4 1JP.

Hanborough Books, The Foundry, Church Hanborough, Nr. Witney, Oxford, OX29 8AB. Prop: Dennis Hall. Tel: (01993) 881260. Fax: (01993) 883080. Website: www.parrotpress.co.uk. Est: 1970. Private premises; appointment necessary. Small stock. Spec: Antiquarian; Illustrated; Limited Editions; Private Press; Typography. PR: £5–650. CC: MC; V. Cata: 4. VAT No: GB 490 6827 17.

The Inner Bookshop, ■ 111 Magdalen Road, Oxford, OX4 1RQ. Prop: R.E. Ashcroft & A. S. Cheke. Tel: (01865) 245301. Fax: (01865) 245521. Website: www.innerbookshop.com. E-mail: mail@innerbookshop.com. Est: 1982. Shop; Internet and postal. Open: **M:** 10:00–17:45; **T:** 10:00–17:45; **W:** 10:00–17:45; **Th:** 10:00–17:45; **F:** 10:00–17:45; **S:** 10:00–17:45. Large stock. Spec: Alchemy; Alternative Medicine; American Indians; Anthroposophy; Arthurian; Astrology; Cryptozoology; Earth Mysteries; Esoteric; Folklore; Fore-Edge Paintings; Freemasonry & Anti-Masonry; Ghosts; Health; Herbalism; Hermeticism; Judaica; Magic & Conjuring; and others as listed in the Speciality Index. PR: £1–1,000. CC: E; MC; V; SW, SO. Also, new books on specialities & tarot cards, New Age music, bargain books and a passive booksearch service. Mem: PBFA.

Islamic Books - A.R. Bullock, 62 Kelburne Road, Oxford, OX4 3SH.

FEELING IS BELIEVING

GAME ADVICE IS UP AND WITHIT

at

.GAME-ADVICE.   .OXFORD-BOOKS.

and

.OXFORD-4U.

Not the centre of the universe but certainly every bookophile's must do. Oxford, a mongrel City, is mixing it with the best and will serve you well.

To find out how just add to the above your suffix **www** and your telling tail **com** and plan your next visit.

At oxford-books.com whether you sit on the shoulders of giants; an MX5; or trudge in the footprints of Karl, you will find out just how.

The Oxford Antique book trail offers a wide and wise choice

Warm previews from: **+44 (0)1865 433050** or **71 Rose Hill, Oxford OX4 4JR**

a.elithorn@ntlworld.com

Jeremy's, 98 Cowley Road, Oxford, OX4 1JE.

Jericho Books, ■ 48 Walton Street, Oxford, OX2 6AD. Prop: Frank Stringer. Tel: (01865) 511992. Fax: (0870) 1315166. Website: www.jerichobooks.com. E-mail: shop@jerichobooks.com. Est: 1997. Shop; open **M:** 10:30–18:00; **T:** 10:30–18:00; **W:** 10:30–18:00; **Th:** 10:30–18:00; **F:** 10:30–18:00; **S:** 10:30–18:00; **Su:** 11:00–17:30. Large stock. Spec: Academic/Scholarly; Antiquarian; Art; Cinema/Film; Classical Studies; Fiction - Fantasy, Horror; Fine & Rare; First Editions; History - General; Literature; Mind, Body & Spirit; Odd & Unusual; Philosophy; Politics; Religion - General; Theology; and others as listed in the Speciality Index. PR: £2–1,000. CC: MC; V. Also, a booksearch service. Cata: 1 – occasionally. Corresp: French. Italian. Mem: ABA; PBFA. VAT No: GB 717 9092 13.

Leabeck Books, Meadowbrook Farm, Sheepwash Lane, Steventon, Oxford, OX13 6SD. Prop: Tony Sloggett. Tel: (01235) 820914. E-mail: tony.sloggett@britishlibrary.net. Est: 1993. Private premises; Internet and postal. Appointment necessary. Small stock. Spec: Antiques; Art; Children's - General; First Editions; History - General; Literature. PR: £5–200. Corresp: French, German. *Also at:* Antiques on High, 85 High Street, Oxford, OX1 1BG.

Magna Gallery, ■ 85 High Street, Oxford, OX1 4BG. Prop: Martin Blant. Tel: (01285) 750753. Fax: (01285) 750753. Website: www.magna-gallery.com. E-mail: info@magna-gallery.com. Est: 1969. Shop; open **M:** 10:00–17:00; **T:** 10:00–17:00; **W:** 10:00–17:00; **Th:** 10:00–17:00; **F:** 10:00–17:00; **S:** 10:00–17:00; **Su:** 11:00–17:00. Small stock. PR: £5–1,000. CC: AE; MC; V. Corresp: French.

Joe McCann Ltd., 4240 Nash Court, Oxford Business Park South, Oxford, OX4 2RU. Tel: (01865) 337405 or 77. Fax: (01865) 337433. Website: www.joemccann.com. E-mail: joe@joemccann.com. Est: 1988. Office &/or bookroom. Telephone first. Small stock. Spec: Author - Beckett, S.; Author - Joyce, James; Author - Pinter, Harold; Author - Steadman, Ralph; Author - Stoker, B.; Author - Wilde, Oscar; Author - Yeats, W.B.; Countries - Ireland; First Editions; Irish Interest; Limited Editions; Literature; and others as listed in the Speciality Index. PR: £5–5,000. Cata: 3. Mem: PBFA; RIPGCS.

Roger Middleton, P.O. Box 16, Wheatley, Oxford, OX33 1RD. T

Chris Morris, 67 Home Close, Wolvercote, Oxford, OX2 8PT. Tel: (01865) 557806. Fax: (0709) 2126589. E-mail: chris@books1.demon.co.uk. Est: 1990. Postal business only. Spec: Cinema/Film; Countries - Melanesia; Modern First Editions; Motoring; Music - Popular; Sport - Motor Racing; Television. PR: £2–200.

M. & D. Reeve, P.O. Box 16, Wheatley, Oxford, OX33 1RD. Prop: Dr. Margarita Reeve. Tel: (01865) 874383. Fax: (01865) 872442. Website: www.reevebooks.com. E-mail: mdreeve@btinternet.com. Est: 1981. Private premises; postal business only. Medium stock. Spec: Children's - General; Illustrated; Juvenile. PR: £20–3,000. CC: MC; V. Cata: 4. Corresp: Italian, French. Mem: ABA; PBFA; ILAB.

A. Rosenthal Limited, P.O. Box 801, Oxford, OX1 3BX.

St Philip's Books, ■ 82 St. Aldates, Oxford, OX1 1RA. Prop: Christopher James Zealley. Tel: (01865) 202182. Fax: (01865) 202184. Website: www.stphilipsbooks.co.uk. E-mail: sales@stphilipsbooks.co.uk. Est: 1995. Shop; Internet and postal. Open **M:** 10:00–17:00; **T:** 10:00–17:00; **W:** 10:00–17:00; **Th:** 10:00–17:00; **F:** 10:00–17:00; **S:** 10:00–17:00. Large stock. Spec: Academic/Scholarly; Antiquarian; Art History; Author - Inklings, The; Author - Lewis, C. S.; Author - Newman, Cardinal; Bibles; Ecclesiastical History & Architecture; History - General; History - British; History - European; Literature; Religion - General; and others as listed in the Speciality Index. PR: £1–2,000. CC: MC; V; SO, SW. Books bought nationwide. Cata: 4. Mem: PBFA. VAT No: GB 717 9250 21.

Sanders of Oxford Limited, ■ Salutation House, 104 High Street, Oxford, OX1 4BW. Prop: The Hon. C.A. Lennox–Boyd. Tel: (01865) 242590. Fax: (01865) 721748. Website: www.oxlink.co.uk/antiques/sanders.html. E-mail: soxinfo@btclick.com. Est: 1840. Shop; open **M:** 10:00–18:00; **T:** 10:00–18:00; **W:** 10:00–18:00; **Th:** 10:00–18:00; **F:** 10:00–18:00; **S:** 10:00–18:00. Very large stock. Spec: Topography - Local. PR: £1–10,000. CC: AE; MC; V. Mem: PBFA.

Thorntons of Oxford Ltd., 11 Broad Street, Oxford, OX1 3AR.

M. & D. REEVE CHILDREN'S BOOKS

4 catalogues a year, sent world-wide

PO Box 16, Wheatley, Oxford OX33 1RD. Tel: 01865 874383 Fax: 01865 872442
Email: MDReeve@btinternet.com   Web site: www.reevebooks.com

Tooley, Adams & Co., PO Box 174, Wallingford D.O., Oxford, OX10 0YT. (*) Prop: Stephen Luck. Tel: (01491) 838298. Fax: (01491) 834616. Website: www.tooleys.co.uk. E-mail: steve@tooleys.co.uk. Est: 1982. Private premises; postal business only. Spec: Atlases. PR: £10–10,000. CC: AE; D; MC; V. Mem: ABA; I.A.M.A.

S.P. Tuohy, 45 Warwick Street, Oxford, OX4 1SZ.

Unsworths Booksellers Ltd., ■ 15 Turl St, Oxford, OX1 3DQ. Prop: Charlie Unsworth & Susan Coe. Tel: (01865) 727928. Fax: (01865) 727206. Website: www.unsworths.com. E-mail: books@unsworths.com. Est: 1986. Shop; open **M:** 10:00–18:00; **T:** 10:00–18:00; **W:** 10:00–18:00; **Th:** 10:00–18:00; **F:** 10:00–18:00; **S:** 10:00–18:00; **Su:** 12:00–17:00. Very large stock. Spec: Academic/Scholarly; Antiquarian; Art; Early Imprints; History - General; Humanities; Literature. PR: £1–2,000. CC: AE; MC; V. Cata: – one or two annually. Mem: ABA; PBFA; BA; ILAB; *Also at:* 12 Bloomsbury St, WC1 (q.v.). VAT No: GB 480 1145 75.

Waterfield's, ■ 52 High Street, Oxford, OX1 4AS. Prop: Robin Waterfield Ltd,. Tel: (01865) 721809. Est: 1973. Shop; open **M:** 09:45–17:45; **T:** 09:45–17:45; **W:** 09:45–17:45; **Th:** 08:45–17:45; **F:** 09:45–17:45; **S:** 09:45–17:45. Large stock. Spec: Academic/Scholarly; Antiquarian; Arts, The; First Editions; History - General; Humanities; Literary Criticism; Literature; Philosophy. PR: £1–5,000. CC: E; MC; V. Cata: 4 – Eng Lit, history, philosophy, and on 17th and 18thC books. Corresp: French. Mem: ABA; PBFA. VAT No: GB 195 8007 39.

STONESFIELD

Austin Sherlaw-Johnson, Woodland View, Churchfields, Stonesfield, OX29 8PP. Tel: (01993) 898223. E-mail: austin.sherlaw-johnson@virgin.net. Est: 2001. Private premises; appointment necessary. Open: **M:** 09:00–17:00; **T:** 09:00–17:00; **W:** 09:00–17:00; **Th:** 09:00–17:00; **F:** 09:00–17:00. Medium stock. Spec: Music - General; Music - Composers; Music - Opera; Musical Instruments. PR: £1–500. Cata: 4 – occasionally. *Also at:* Malvern Bookshop, Malvern, Worcestershire and Antiques on High, 85 High Street, Oxford.

WALLINGFORD

Toby English, ■ 10 St. Mary's Street, Wallingford, OX10 0EL. Tel: (01491) 836389. Fax: (01491) 836389. Website: www.tobyenglish.com. E-mail: toby@tobyenglish.com. Est: 1981. Shop; open **M:** 09:30–16:45; **T:** 09:30–16:45; **W:** 09:30–17:00; **Th:** 09:30–16:45; **F:** 09:30–16:45; **S:** 09:30–17:00. Large stock. Spec: Academic/Scholarly; Architecture; Art; Author - Inklings, The; First Editions; Private Press; Topography - Local; Typography. PR: £1–500. CC: AE; JCB; MC; V; SW. Also, a booksearch service. Cata: 2 – Art and Architecture, Renaissance Studies. Mem: PBFA.

WANTAGE

Parrott Books, ■ Regent Mall, Newbury Street, Wantage, OX12 8BU. Prop: Howard Preene. Tel: (01367) 820251. Fax: (01367) 820210. Website: www.abebooks.com/home/hpbooks. E-mail: parrottbooks@aol.com. Est: 1996. Shop; open **M:** 08:30–17:30; **T:** 08:30–17:30; **W:** 08:30–17:30; **Th:** 08:30–17:30; **F:** 08:30–17:30; **S:** 08:30–17:00. Very large stock. Spec: Cookery/Gastronomy; Gardening; Military History; Private Press; Topography - General. PR: £5–20.

Postaprint, Bethesda House, West Hanney, Wantage, Oxfordshire OX12 0LR. Prop: Anna Roderick. Tel: (01235) 867592. Website: www.postaprint.co.uk. E-mail: sales@postaprint.co.uk. Est: 1970. Private premises; Internet only. Very large stock. Spec: Atlases; Colour-Plate; Engraving. PR: £10–5,000. CC: MC; V. Also, web site includes on-line inventory, searchable databases & wants list matching service.

WARBOROUGH

Nineteenth Century Books, St. Mary's Cottage, 61 Thame Road, Warborough, Wallingford, OX10 7EA. Prop: Dr. Ann M. Ridler. Tel: (01865) 858379. Fax: (01865) 858575. Website: www.ukbookworld.com/members/papageno. E-mail: annridlersoutter@warboro.fsnet.co.uk. Est: 1984. Private premises; Internet and postal. Small stock. Spec: Biography; Books about Books; History - General; Literature; Natural History; Philology; Poetry; Topography - General. PR: £5–500. CC: MC; V. Also, booksearch. Corresp: French, Spanish. Mem: PBFA.

WITNEY

Church Green Books, ■ 46 Market Square, Witney, OX28 6AL. Prop: Roger & Margaret Barnes. Tel: (01993) 700822. Website: www.churchgreen.co.uk. E-mail: books@churchgreen.co.uk. Est: 1992. Shop; open **M:** 10:00–16:00; **T:** 10:00–16:00; **W:** 10:00–16:00; **Th:** 10:00–16:00; **F:** 10:00–16:00. Medium stock. Spec: Bell-Ringing (Campanology); Music - Folk & Irish Folk; Topography - Local. PR: £1–300. CC: MC; V. Valuations of Bell-ringing books. Cata: 2 – Church Bells & Bell-ringing. Mem: PBFA.

WOODSTOCK

Cranmer Books, 1a Farm End, Old Woodstock, Woodstock, OX20 1XN. Prop: Michael C. Millard. Tel: (01993) 813368. Fax: (01993) 813368. E-mail: millard@cranmerbooks.co.uk. Est: 1998. Private premises; postal business only. Very small stock. Spec: Ecclesiastical History & Architecture; History - General; Theology. PR: £3–100. Cata: 3 – on specs.

The Woodstock Bookshop, ■ 3 Market Place, Woodstock, OX20 1SY. Prop: Mark Wratten. Tel: (01993) 811005. Website: www.abebooks.com. Est: 1989. Shop; open **M:** 10:00–17:00; **T:** 10:00–17:00; **W:** 10:00–17:00; **Th:** 10:00–17:00; **F:** 10:00–17:00. Closed for lunch: 13:00–14:15. Small stock. Spec: Academic/Scholarly; Alpinism/Mountaineering; Architecture; Art; Literature; Natural History; Travel - General. CC: MC; V. Also, selection of stock on abebooks.com. Corresp: French. Mem: PBFA.

SHROPSHIRE

BISHOP'S CASTLE
Autolycus, ■ 10 Market Square, Bishop's Castle, SY9 5DN. Prop: David & Jay Wilkinson. Tel: (01588) 630078. Fax: (01588) 630078. Website: www.booksonline.uk.com. E-mail: autolycusbc@aol.com. Est: 1996. Shop; Internet and postal. Open: **M:** 11:00–16:30; **T:** 11:00–16:30; **W:** 11:00–16:30; **Th:** 11:00–16:30; **F:** 11:00–16:30; **S:** 10:30–15:00. Medium stock. Spec: Antiquarian; Children's - Illustrated; Illustrated; Modern First Editions; Topography - General; Travel - General. PR: £3–2,000. CC: MC; V. Cata: 2 – Infrequent. Corresp: French, German. VAT No: GB 771 9717 90.

Milestones Bookshop, 38/40 High Street, Bishop's Castle, SY9 5BQ.

Yarborough House Bookshop, ■ Yarborough House, The Square, Bishop's Castle, SY9 5BN. Prop: Carol Wright. Tel: (01588) 638318. Est: 1980. Shop; open **T:** 10:00–17:30. **Th:** 10:00–17:30; **F:** 10:00–17:30; **S:** 09:00–17:30; **Su:** 10:00–17:00. Medium stock. PR: £1–20. Also, secondhand classic records.

BRIDGNORTH
The Bookpassage, 57a High Street, Bridgnorth, WV16 4DX.

Bookstack & D.J. Creece (Bookbinder), The Bindery Book Store, 3 Castle Terrace, Bridgnorth, WV16 4AH. Prop: Elizabeth Anderton (Books), Dermott Creece (Binder). Tel: (01746) 768008. E-mail: bookstack@ntlworld.com. Est: 1975. Storeroom; appointment necessary. Very small stock. Spec: Pre-Raphaelite. PR: £1–200.

CHURCH STRETTON
Church Stretton Books, Victoria House, 48 High Street, Church Stretton, SY6 6BX.

CRAVEN ARMS
Black Hill Books, The Wain House, Black Hill, Clunton, Craven Arms, SY7 0JD.

ELLESMERE
Glyn's Books, 6 The Avenue, Lyneal, Ellesmere, SY12 OQJ.

IRON BRIDGE
Philip Spark Books, 47 Church Hill, Iron Bridge, TF8 7QB.

LUDLOW
Judith Adams, ■ The Art Bookshop, 3 Quality Square, off Castle Sq., Ludlow, SY8 1AR. Tel: (01584) 872758. Shop; open **F:** 10:00–17:00; **S:** 10:00–17:00. Medium stock. Spec: Architecture; Art; Art History; Art Reference; Artists; Decorative Art; Fine Art; Gardening; Textiles. PR: £2–300. CC: MC; V. Mem: PBFA.

Ampersand Books, Ludford Mill, Ludlow, SY8 1PR.

M. & M. Baldwin, ■ 24 High Street, Cleobury Mortimer, Kidderminster, Ludlow, DY14 8BY. (*). Tel: (01299) 270110. Fax: (01299) 270110. E-mail: mb@mbaldwin.free-online.co.uk. Est: 1978. Shop; open **W:** 14:00–18:00. **S:** 10:14–13:18. Closed for lunch: 13:00–14:00. Medium stock. Spec: Author - Rolt, L.T.C.; Aviation; Canals/Inland Waterways; Crafts; Cryptography; Espionage; Maritime/Nautical; Military; Military History; Motoring; Railways; Sport - Canoeing/Kayaks; Sport - Yachting; Transport; Vintage Cars; War - World War II. PR: £1–500. CC: AE; MC; V. Also, publisher of books.

Dealers who need to update their entry should visit their page on *www.sheppardsdirectories.com*

SHROPSHIRE

Lyndon Barnes - Books, 3 Mortimer Drive, Ludlow, SY8 4JW.

Bookshop Bookfair, 56 Mill Street, Ludlow, SY8 1BB.

Innes Books, 22 Julian Road, Ludlow, SY8 1HA. Prop: Pat & Trevor Innes. Tel: (01584) 878146. Website: www.abebooks.com/home/innesbooks. E-mail: patricia@innesbooks.fsnet.co.uk. Est: 1997. Postal business only. Spec: Academic/Scholarly; Children's - General; Fiction - General; Illustrated; Literature; Modern First Editions. PR: £2–400.

Peter Lloyd, 28 Mill Street, Ludlow, SY8 1BG.

Offa's Dyke Books, Old School House, Downton-on-the Rock, Ludlow, SY8 2HX. Prop: S.R. Bainbridge. Tel: (01584) 856212. E-mail: books@offas-dyke.fsnet.co.uk. Est: 1972. Private premises; appointment necessary. Spec: Antiquarian; Art; Literature.

Olynthiacs, 19 Castle View Terrace, Ludlow, SY8 2NG. Prop: Neil MacGregor. Tel: (01584) 872671. Website: www.ukbookworld.com/members/olynthiacs. E-mail: neil@nandmmacgregor.fsnet.co.uk. Est: 1948. Storeroom; postal business only. Medium stock. Spec: Author - Wodehouse, P.G.; Biography; Classical Studies; Ecclesiastical History & Architecture; Fiction - General; History - General; Linguistics; Philology; Theology. PR: £5–500.

MADELEY

C.R. Moore, Park House, Park Lane, Madeley, Telford, TF7 5HF.

MARKET DRAYTON

Reg Bladen, Pinewood Drive, Ashley Heath, Market Drayton, TF9 4PA.

MUCH WENLOCK

Good Books, Hill Top Farm, Hill Top, Much Wenlock, TF13 6DJ.

P.J. Mead, 6 Blakeway Hollow, Much Wenlock, TF13 6AR. Tel: (01952) 727591. Fax: (01952) 727591. E-mail: meadbooks@yahoo.com. Est: 1976. Private premises; postal business only. Spec: Antiquarian; Bibliography; Bindings; Books about Books; Juvenile; Miniature Books; Sport - General. PR: £10–1,000 Mem: PBFA. VAT No: GB 349 3412 50.

Wenlock Books, 12 High Street, Much Wenlock, TF13 6AA.

ORLETON

P. Rulton Books, 3 Hallets Well, Orleton, SY8 4HH. Prop: Peter Rulton. Tel: (01568) 780860. E-mail: pjrulton@hotmail.com. Est: 1994. Private premises; Internet and postal. Telephone first. Small stock. Spec: Fiction - General; Fiction - Crime, Detective, Spy, Thrillers; Fiction - Science Fiction; Illustrated; Literature; Modern First Editions. PR: £5–10,000. CC: JCB; V.

OSWESTRY

Arcadia, 6 Upper Brook Street, Oswestry, SY10 2TB. Prop: Joyce & Rod Whitehead. Tel: (01691) 655622. Est: 1997. Spec: Antiquarian; Arts, The; History of Ideas; Illustrated; Literary Criticism; Literature; Needlework; Philosophy; Poetry; Topography - General. PR: £1–25.

Bookworld, ■ 32 Beatrice Street, Oswestry, SY11 1QG. Prop: John Cranwell. Tel: (01691) 657112. Fax: (01691) 657112. Website: www.tgal.co.uk/bookworld. E-mail: john.cranwell@jcbookworld.co.uk. Est: 1993. Shop; open **M:** 09:00–17:30; **T:** 09:00–17:30; **W:** 09:00–17:30; **Th:** 08:00–17:30; **F:** 09:00–17:30; **S:** 09:00–17:30. Medium general stock. Spec: Alpinism/Mountaineering; Antiques; Autobiography; Children's - General; Cookery/Gastronomy; Crafts; Dictionaries; Gardening; Guide Books; Humour; Maritime/Nautical; Sport - Hockey; Travel - General. PR: £2–250.

John Read Antiques, 59 Church Street, Oswestry, SY11 2SZ.

SHREWSBURY

Candle Lane Books, ■ 28 & 29, Princess Street, Shrewsbury, SY1 1LW. John & Margaret Thornhill. Tel: (01743) 365301. Est: 1974. Shop; open **M:** 09:30–17:00; **T:** 09:00–17:00; **W:** 09:00–17:00; **Th:** 09:00–17:00; **F:** 09:00–17:00; **S:** 09:00–17:00. Very large stock. PR: £1–3,000. CC: MC; V. Also, booksearch.

Len Lewis, Shrewsbury Antique Centre, Princess Street, Shrewsbury.

Oriental and African Books, 33 Whitehall Street, Shrewsbury, SY2 5AD. Prop: Paul D. Wilson. Tel: (01743) 352575. Fax: (01743) 363432. Website: www.africana.co.uk. E-mail: paul@africana.co.uk. Est: 1982. Office &/or bookroom; Internet and postal. Telephone first. Large stock. Spec: Academic/Scholarly; Africana; Black Studies; Countries - Africa; Countries - Middle East, The; Travel - Africa; Travel - Middle East. PR: £25–2,000. CC: E; JCB; MC; V. Cata: 3. Corresp: French, Arabic. Mem: PBFA. VAT No: GB 434 0550 82.

Roundwood Books, ■ 24 Claremont Hill, Shrewsbury, SY1 1RD. Prop: Andrew Cork. Tel: (01743) 244833. E-mail: roundwoodbooks@btinternet.com. Est: 1995. Shop; open **T:** 10:00–17:00; **W:** 10:00–17:00; **Th:** 10:00–17:00; **F:** 10:00–17:00; **S:** 10:00–17:00. Medium stock. PR: £1–50. CC: MC; V. Mem: DTMFC.

Colin Snowdon, 7 Bank Drive, Dorrington, Shrewsbury, SY5 7JH. T

TELFORD

Fin Rare Books, 27 Deepfield Road, Dawley, Telford, TF4 3EH. Prop: Stephen H. Dawes (Sam). Tel: (01952) 591711. Website: www.finrarebooks.co.uk. E-mail: info@finrarebooks.co.uk. Est: 1985. Private premises; Internet. Appointment necessary. Small general stock. Spec: Academic/Scholarly; Autobiography; Biography; Children's - General; Cookery/Gastronomy; First Editions; Gardening; History - General; Hobbies; Illustrated; Industry; Military; Modern First Editions; Music - Rock; Natural History; Religion - General; and others as listed in the Speciality Index. PR: £1–500.

WEM

Black Five Books, 54 High Street, Wem, SY4 5DW. Prop: Ken Simpson. Tel: (01939) 233993. Website: www.black5books.co.uk. E-mail: black5books@wemshropshire.freeserve.co.uk. Est: 1984. Spec: Aviation; Biography; Children's - General; Education & School; Fiction - General; Fiction - Historical; History - General; History - Ancient; History - British; History - Local; Horticulture; Humour; Literature; Military History; Railways; Sport - Cricket; Transport; Travel - General. PR: £1–100.

WHITCHURCH

Barn Books, Pear Tree Farm, Norbury, Whitchurch, SY13 4HZ. Prop: Mary Perry. Tel: (01948) 663742. Fax: (01948) 663742. Website: www.barnbooks.co.uk. E-mail: barnbooks@barnbooks.co.uk. Est: 1985. Spec: Agriculture; Farming & Livestock; Gardening; History - Local; Horticulture; Rural Life; Topography - Local. PR: £1–500.

Robert Downie Fine Books Ltd., Lord Hill House, Dobsons Bridge, Whixall, Whitchurch, SY13 2QQ. Tel: (01948) 710345. Fax: (01948) 710776. Website: www.booksets.com. E-mail: sales@booksets.com. Est: 1974. Postal business only. Spec: Academic/Scholarly; Banking & Insurance; Biography; Calligraphy; Cinema/Film; Company History; Computing; Crime (True); Economics; Education & School; Entertainment - General; History - General; History of Ideas; Journals - General; Mathematics; and others as listed in the Speciality Index. PR: £25–5,000.

SOMERSET

BATH

Bankes Books, 5 Margaret's Buildings, Bath, BA1 2LP.

Bath Book Exchange, ■ 35 Broad Street, Bath, BA1 5LP. Mr. L.M. Turner. Tel: (01225) 466214. Est: 1959. Shop; open **M:** 09:30–17:00; **T:** 09:30–17:00; **W:** 09:30–17:00; **Th:** 09:30–17:00; **F:** 09:30–17:00; **S:** 09:30–17:00. Closed for lunch: 12:00–13:00. Medium general stock. PR: £1–10. Also, booksearch.

Bath Old Books, 9c Margaret's Buildings, Bath, BA1 2LP.

George Bayntun, ■ Manvers Street, Bath, BA1 1JW. Prop: E.W.G. Bayntun–Coward. Tel: (01225) 466000. Fax: (01225) 482122. Website: www.georgebayntun.com. E-mail: isabelle@georgebayntun.com. Est: 1894. Shop; open **M:** 09:00–17:30; **T:** 09:00–17:30; **W:** 09:00–17:30; **Th:** 09:00–17:30; **F:** 09:00–17:30; **S:** 09:30–13:00. Closed for lunch: 13:00–14:00. Small stock. Spec: Bindings; Children's - General; Children's - Illustrated; Fine & Rare; First Editions; Illustrated; Literature; Poetry. PR: £10–5,000. CC: MC; V; SW, SO. Also, bindery incorporating the famous binding firm of Robert Riviere & Son, est. 1829. Corresp: French. Mem: ABA; PBFA. VAT No: GB 137 5073 71.

Camden Books, ■ 146 Walcot Street, Bath, BA1 5BL. Prop: Victor & Elizabeth Suchar. Tel: (01225) 461606. Fax: (01225) 461606. Website: www.camdenbooks.com. E-mail: suchcam@msn.com. Est: 1984. Shop; Internet and postal. Open: **M:** 11:00–16:00; **T:** 11:00–16:00; **W:** 11:00–16:00; **Th:** 11:00–16:00; **F:** 11:00–16:00; **S:** 11:00–16:00. Large general stock. Spec: Academic/Scholarly; Architecture; Art History; Biography; Civil Engineering; Classical Studies; Company History; Diaries; Economics; History - Byzantine; History - Middle Ages; History of Civilisation; Letters; Literature; Mathematics; Philosophy; and others as listed in the Speciality Index. PR: £10–2,000. CC: JCB; MC. Mem: PBFA.

Janet Clarke, 3 Woodside Cottages, Freshford, Bath, BA2 7WJ. Tel: (01225) 723186. Fax: (01225) 722063. E-mail: janetclarke@ukgateway.net. Est: 1973. Private premises; postal business only. Small stock. Spec: Cookery/Gastronomy; Food & Drink; Wine. PR: £5–3,000. Cata: 1.

Peter Goodden, 7 Clarendon Villas, Widcombe Hill, Bath, BA2 6AG.

George Gregory, ■ Manvers Street, Bath, BA1 1JW. Prop: Charlotte Bayntun-Coward. Tel: (01225) 466000. Fax: (01225) 482122. E-mail: isabelle@georgebayntun.com. Est: 1846. Shop &/or gallery. Open: **M:** 09:00–17:30; **T:** 09:00–17:30; **W:** 09:00–17:30; **Th:** 09:00–17:30; **F:** 09:00–17:30; **S:** 08:30–13:00. Closed for lunch: 13:00–14:00. Large general stock. Spec: Literature. PR: £1–50. CC: MC; V. Engraved portraits and views.

Pathway Books, 23 Pera Place, Bath, BA1 5NX.

Patterson Liddle, ■ 10 Margaret's Buildings, Brock Street, Bath, BA1 2LP. John Patterson & Steve Liddle. Tel: (01225) 426722. Fax: (01225) 426722. Website: www.pattersonliddle.com. E-mail: mail@pattersonliddle.com. Est: 1982. Shop; open **M:** 10:00–17:30; **T:** 10:00–17:30; **W:** 10:00–17:30; **Th:** 10:00–17:30; **F:** 10:00–17:30; **S:** 10:00–17:30. Medium stock. Spec: Architecture; Art; Aviation; Bindings; Canals/Inland Waterways; History - Local; Illustrated; Railways; Topography - General; Travel - General. PR: £1–5,000. CC: MC; V. Cata: – occasionally on aviation, canals & British railways. Mem: ABA; PBFA; ILAB. VAT No: GB 358 0633 48.

Robert & Susan Pyke, 2 Beaufort Villas, Claremont Road, Bath, BA1 6LY. Tel: (01225) 311710. Fax: (01225) 311710. Website: www.abebooks.com/home/pykemaritime. E-mail: robert.pyke@virgin.net. Est: 1974. Private premises; appointment necessary. Medium stock. Spec: Maritime/Nautical; Sport - Yachting. PR: £7–2,000. CC: MC; V; SW. Cata: 2 – a year. Mem: PBFA.

Dealers who need to update their entry should visit their page on *www.sheppardsdirectories.com*

Hugh Ashley Rayner, 4 Malvern Buildings, Fairfield Park, Bath, BA1 6JX. Prop: Hugh A. Rayner. Tel: (01225) 463552. Fax: (01225) 463552. Website: www.indiabooks.co.uk. E-mail: hughrayner@indiabooks.co.uk. Private premises; Internet and postal. Appointment necessary. Open: **M:** 10:00–19:00; **T:** 10:00–19:00; **W:** 10:00–19:00; **Th:** 10:00–19:00; **F:** 10:00–19:00; **S:** 10:00–19:00; **Su:** 12:00–18:00. Small stock. Spec: Countries - Asia; Countries - Burma; Countries - Central Asia; Countries - Himalayas, The; Countries - India; Countries - Sri Lanka; Photography; Travel - Asia. PR: £35–500. CC: AE; D; JCB; MC; V. Valuations, Library Cataloguing. Cata: 1 – India & The Orient. Corresp: German. Mem: PBFA.

G. Charles Robinson, 10a Widcombe Crescent, Bath, BA2 6AH.

Louise Ross & Company Ltd., Mulberry House, 8 Mount Road, Lansdown, Bath, BA1 5PW.

The Traveller's Bookshelf, Canal House, Murhill, Limpley Stoke, Bath, BA2 7FQ. Prop: Jenny Steadman. Tel: (01225) 722589. Fax: (01225) 723262. E-mail: jenny@travellersbookshelf.co.uk. Est: 1991. Private premises; Internet and postal. Spec: Countries - Afghanistan; Countries - Albania; Countries - Arabia; Countries - Armenia; Countries - Asia Minor; Countries - Balkans, The; Countries - Central Asia; Countries - China; Countries - Ethiopia; Countries - Far East, The; Countries - Greece; and others as listed in the Speciality Index. PR: £20–5,000. CC: MC; V; SW. Cata: 3. Mem: ABA; PBFA; ILAB. VAT No: GB 779 2193 85.

BRIDGWATER

Wembdon Books, 112 Wembdon Hill, Bridgwater, TA6 7QA.

BRUTON

Abaris Books, 12 Priory Mead, Bruton, BA10 0DZ.

CASTLE CARY

Bailey Hill Bookshop, Fore Street, Castle Cary, BA7 7BG. Prop: Peter Booth. Tel: (01963) 350917. Fax: (01963) 351230. Website: www.baileyhillbookshop.co.uk. E-mail: books@baileyhillbookshop.co.uk. Est: 1978. Open: **M:** 09:30–18:00; **T:** 09:30–18:00; **W:** 09:30–18:00; **Th:** 09:30–18:00; **F:** 09:30–18:00; **S:** 09:30–17:00. Small general stock. PR: £1–100. CC: AE; JCB; MC. Also, new books and greetings cards. Mem: PBFA. VAT No: GB 501 6633 79.

CHARD

P.J. Baron - Scientific Book S, Lakewood,, Chard, TA20 4AJ. Prop: Dr. P. Baron. Tel: (01460) 66319. Fax: (01460) 66319. Website: www.barons.clara.net. E-mail: barons@clara.net. Est: 1975. Private premises; Internet and postal. Small stock. Spec: Biology; Botany; Chemistry; Computing; Ecology; Engineering; Mathematics; Medicine; Natural History; Science - General; Zoology. PR: £5–150. CC: MC; V; SW. Cata: 6 – on science; computing/medicine; separate catalogue. Corresp: French. VAT No: GB 549 4779 82.

CLAPTON–IN–GORDANO

Avonworld Books, 1 Swancombe, Clapton–in–Gordano, BS20 7RR. Prop: Michael C. Ross. Tel: (01275) 842531. Fax: (01275) 849221. Website: www.avonworld-booksource.co.uk. E-mail: books@avonworld.demon.co.uk. Est: 1984. Office &/or bookroom; Internet and postal. Appointment necessary. Open: **M:** 09:00–18:00; **T:** 09:00–18:00; **W:** 09:00–18:00; **Th:** 09:00–18:00; **F:** 09:00–18:00. Closed for lunch: 13:00–14:00. Small stock. Spec: Art; Author - Buchan, John; Author - Coward, Noel; Author - Graves, Robert; Author - Kipling, Rudyard; Author - Sayers, Dorothy; Literature; Modern First Editions. PR: £1–500. CC: MC; V. Valuations for insurance or probate of private collections in our author specialities. Cata: – Author or Category stock print-outs on request. Corresp: German (post only, not e-mail). Mem: PBFA. VAT No: GB 496 6867 66.

CLEVEDON

Clevedon Books, Canbourne Cottage, 6 Seavale Road, Clevedon, BS21 7QB.

K.W. Cowley, Bookdealer, Trinity Cottage, 153 Old Church Road, Clevedon, BS21 7TU. Tel: (01275) 872247. E-mail: kencowley@blueyonder.co.uk. Est: 1987. Private premises; postal business only. Spec: Anthologies; Books about Books; Cinema/Film; Fiction - Crime, Detective, Spy, Thrillers; Fiction - Fantasy, Horror; Fiction - Science Fiction; Ghosts; Pulps; Supernatural; Vintage Paperbacks. PR: £1–100. Cata: 2 – Occasional.

CREWKERNE

Books Galore, ■ 1 The Old Warehouse, North Street, Crewkerne, TA18 7AJ. Prop: Bryan & Helen Hall. Tel: (01460) 74465. Fax: (01460) 74465. E-mail: hallbook@aol.com. Est: 1968. Shop; open **M:** 10:00–17:00; **T:** 10:00–17:00; **W:** 10:00–17:00; **Th:** 10:00–17:00; **F:** 10:00–17:00; **S:** 10:00–17:00. Closed for lunch: 12:00–13:00. Large stock. Spec: Art; Biography; Children's - General; Natural History; Rural Life; Sport - General; Topography - General. PR: £1–50.

Gresham Books, ■ 31 Market Street, Crewkerne, TA18 7JU. Prop: James Hine. Tel: (01460) 77726. Fax: (01460) 52479. Website: www.greshambooks.co.uk. E-mail: jameshine@gresham-books.demon.co.uk. Est: 1972. Shop; open **M:** 10:00–17:00; **T:** 10:00–17:00; **W:** 10:00–17:00; **Th:** 10:00–17:00; **F:** 10:00–17:00; **S:** 10:00–17:00. Medium general stock. Spec: Antiquarian; Antiques; Architecture; Cookery/Gastronomy; Fashion & Costume; Food & Drink; Needlework; Sport - Golf; Wine. PR: £1–1,000. CC: AE; MC; V; SW. Mem: ABA; PBFA.

Anne Hine / Gresham Books, ■ 31 Market Street, Crewkerne, TA18 7JU. Tel: (01460) 77726. Fax: (01460) 52479. E-mail: annehine@gresham-books.demon.co.uk. Est: 1994. Shop; open **M:** 10:00–17:00; **T:** 10:00–17:00; **W:** 10:00–17:00; **Th:** 10:00–17:00; **F:** 10:00–17:00; **S:** 10:00–17:00. Very small stock. Spec: Publishers - Warnes. CC: AE; MC; V.

Sacketts Books on Crafts and Restoration, Rose Cottage, Higher Chillington, Ilminster, Somerset, Crewkerne, TA19 0PT.

DULVERTON

Rothwell and Dunworth, ■ 2 Bridge Street, Dulverton, TA22 9HJ. Prop: Caryl Rothwell. Tel: (01398) 323169. Fax: (01398) 331161. E-mail: Rothwellm@aol.com. Est: 1975. Shop; Internet and postal. Spec: Biography; Literature; Military History; Natural History; Sport - Angling/Fishing; Sport - Big Game Hunting; Sport - Field Sports; Sport - Hunting; Sport - Shooting; Voyages & Discovery. PR: £1–1,000. CC: MC; V. Cata: 2. Mem: ABA; PBFA.

FROME

Parbury House Books, 98 Vallis Road, Frome, BA11 3EN. Prop: David & Susan Kemp. Tel: (01373) 463043. Fax: (01373) 453449. E-mail: davidkemp@cogeco.ca. Est: 1997. Office &/or bookroom; appointment necessary. Large stock. Spec: Americana; Art; Arts, The; Author - General; Autobiography; Biography; Canadiana; Cartoons; Cinema/Film; Culture - National; Dance; Drama; Entertainment - General; Fine Art; Humour; Modern First Editions; Music - General; Performing Arts; Signed. PR: £1–500. Also, B & B in private cottage. Cata: 1 – occasionally. Corresp: French, German. Mem: *Also at:* Parbury House Books, Kingston, Ontario Canada K7M 6P6.

Upper–Room Books, ■ Above Antiques & Country Living, Vallis Way, Badcox, Frome, BA11 3BA. Prop: Victor Adams. Tel: (01373) 467125. Fax: (01373) 467125. Website: www.vabooks.com. E-mail: victoradams@vabooks.co.uk. Est: 1990. Shop; open **M:** 09:30–17:30; **T:** 09:30–17:30; **W:** 09:30–17:30; **Th:** 09:30–17:30; **F:** 09:30–17:30; **S:** 09:30–17:30. Medium general stock. Spec: Art; Artists; Author - Morris, William; Crafts; Furniture; Woodwork. PR: £5–1,000. CC: MC; V. Mem: PBFA.

GLASTONBURY

Book Barn Ltd., 17-18 Market Place, Glastonbury, BA6 9HL. Prop: Derek Bolton. Tel: (01458) 835698. Website: www.bookbarn.co.uk. E-mail: bookbarn@netcomuk.co.uk.

ILMINSTER

David Clarke Books, P.O. Box 24, Ilminster, TA19 0YU.

LANGPORT

The Old Bookshop, ■ Bow Street, Langport, TA10 9PQ. Prop: Heather Ridgway. Tel: (01458) 252644. E-mail: heatherridgway@gofree.co.uk. Est: 1984. Shop; open **W:** 09:00–17:00; **Th:** 09:00–17:00; **F:** 09:00–17:00; **S:** 09:00–17:00. Medium stock. Spec: Autobiography; Biography; Crafts; Literature; Natural History; Ornithology; Rural Life; Social History; Topography - Local; Travel - General. PR: £1–100. Also, a booksearch service, large print books & Listen for Pleasure Tapes.

MERRIOTT

Richard Budd, The Coach House, Glebelands, Merriott, TA16 5RE. Prop: Richard Budd. Tel: (01460) 78297. E-mail: richardbudd@btconnect.com. Est: 1972. Private premises; postal business only. Appointment necessary. Small stock. Spec: Author - Beckett, S.; First Editions; Limited Editions; Literary Criticism; Literature; Poetry. PR: £10–5,000. CC: E; MC; V. Also, attends 50 bookfairs a year. Cata: 6 – Every two months. Corresp: French. Mem: ABA; PBFA; ILAB.

MIDSOMER NORTON

Tom Randall, Welton Hill Cottage, Welton Grove, Midsomer Norton, Radstock, BA3 2TS. (*).

MINEHEAD

Rare Books & Berry, ■ High Street, Porlock, Minehead, TA24 8PT. Prop: Mike Berry and Christopher Ondaatje. Tel: (01643) 863255. Fax: (01643) 863092. Website: www.rarebooksandberry.co.uk. E-mail: search@rarebooksandberry.co.uk. Est: 1992. Shop; open **M:** 09:30–17:00; **T:** 09:30–17:00; **W:** 09:30–17:00; **Th:** 09:30–17:00; **F:** 09:30–17:00; **S:** 09:30–17:00. Closed for lunch: 13:00–14:00. Medium stock. Spec: Author - Edwards, Lionel; Sport - Angling/Fishing; Sport - Hunting; Topography - Local. PR: £1–1,000. CC: MC; V; S; SW. Cata: 1 – occasionally.

MOORLYNCH

Arnold Desmond, Polden, Moor Road, Moorlynch, TA7 9BU. Tel: (01458) 210911. Fax: (01458) 210911. E-mail: desmond@morlynch.globalnet.co.uk. Postal business only. Small general stock. Spec: Academic/Scholarly; Author - Arnold, Matthew. PR: £4–100.

NORTH CHERITON

Paper Pleasures, Holt Farm, North Cheriton, BA8 OAQ. Lesley Tyson. Tel: (01963) 33718. E-mail: lesley@paperpleasures.bchip.com. Est: 1998. Private premises; postal business only. Small stock. Spec: Erotica; Glamour; Homosexuality & Lesbianism; Periodicals & Magazines; Photography; Sexology. PR: £5–2,000. CC: SW. Cata: 2. *Also at:* Bath Old Books, Bath.

PEASEDOWN ST. JOHN

BookLovers, The Post Office, 12 Bath Road, Peasedown St. John, BA2 8DH. Prop: Heather Spence. Tel: 0870 1200 970. Fax: 0870 1200 980. Website: www.booklovers.co.uk. E-mail: dgs@booklovers.co.uk. Est: 1998. Shop &/or showroom; Internet and postal. Telephone first. Large stock. Spec: Biography; Gambling; History - General; Modern First Editions. PR: £1–100. CC: AE; D; E; JCB; MC; SW, DE. Cata: – occasional.

QUEEN CAMEL

Steven Ferdinando, The Old Vicarage, Queen Camel, Nr. Yeovil, BA22 7NG. Tel: (01935) 850210. E-mail: stevenferdinando@onetel.net.uk. Est: 1977. Office &/or bookroom; telephone first. Medium stock. Spec: Agriculture; Author - Hardy, Thomas; Author - Powys Family, The; Illustrated; Irish Interest; Literature; Topography - Local; Travel - General. PR: £4–400. CC: MC; V. Mem: PBFA; *Also at:* Bath Old Books, Bath. (q.v.).

SIMONSBATH

Spooner & Co., Mead Cottage, Honeymead, Simonsbath, TA24 7JX. Prop: Brian John Spooner. Tel: (01643) 831562. Fax: (01643) 831562. E-mail: spoonerb@supanet.com. Est: 1985. Private premises; appointment necessary. Small stock. Spec: Antiquarian; Archaeology; Architecture; Bibliography; Ecclesiastical History & Architecture; Genealogy; Heraldry; History - Local; Theology; Topography - Local. PR: £3–230. Also, booksearch, bookbinding and repairs.

Searching for a title - and cannot find it on any Internet database?
Then try **SheppardsBooksearch**

By selecting the subject classification – the request goes to all dealers who major in that subject.

SOMERTON

Simon's Books, ■ Broad Street, Somerton. Prop: Bryan Ives. Tel: (01458) 272313. Est: 1978. Shop; open **M:** 10:00–16:30; **T:** 10:00–16:30; **W:** 09:00–16:30; **Th:** 09:00–16:30; **F:** 10:00–16:30; **S:** 10:00–16:30. Large general stock. PR: £1–100.

STOKE SUB HAMDON

R.G. Watkins, Book and Print Room, 9 North Street Farm Workshops, Stoke Sub Hamdon, TA14 6QR.

TAUNTON

Badger Books, 11 Salisbury Street, Taunton, TA2 6NA. Prop: Janet & Nic Tall. Tel: (01823) 323180. Website: www.badgerbooks.co.uk. E-mail: janetnic@badgerbooks.co.uk. Est: 2002. Private premises; Internet and postal. Appointment necessary. Spec: Author - Brent-Dyer, Elinor M.; Author - Forest, A; Author - Johns, W.E.; Author - Saville, M.; Children's - General. PR: £1–100. Also, wants lists accepted & children's booksearch offered. Cata: 3. Corresp: German.

Bookshop Gallery, 13a Paul Street, Taunton, TA1 3PF.

Boxwood Books & Prints, Ashbrook House, Winsford, Minehead, Taunton, TA24 7HN. (*)

Dene Barn Books & Prints, Brackenbury, Ash Priors, Taunton, TA4 3NF. Tel: (01823) 433103. Est: 1990. Private premises; appointment necessary. Very small general stock. Spec: Botany; Natural History; Topography - Local. PR: £10–500. Picture Framing.

The Eastern Traveller, 52 Mountway Road, Bishops Hull, Taunton, TA1 5LS. Prop: Geoffrey Mullett. Tel: (01823) 327012. Est: 1979. Postal business only. Spec: History - General; Military; Military History; Travel - General; Travel - Africa; Travel - Asia; Travel - Middle East; Voyages & Discovery. PR: £5–50.

C & P Munro, Springs, Taunton, TA2 8HR.

Russell Needham Books, 5 Silver St., Milverton, Taunton, TA4 1LA.

Russell Books, 2 Mount Nebo, Taunton, TA1 4HG. Prop: D.R. & E.M. Kerr. Tel: (01823) 330887. E-mail: russellbooks@ukonline.co.uk. Est: 1997. Private premises; Internet and postal. Contactable. Spec: Art; Children's - General; Countries - Melanesia; Fiction - General; Fiction - Science Fiction; First Editions; History - General; Humour; Military; Poetry; Religion - General; Topography - General; War - General. PR: £1–100. CC: JCB; MC. Also, booksearch. Corresp: French, Japanese, Latin.

WEDMORE,

Max Gate Books, Max Gate, Theale, Wedmore, BS28 4SN. Prop: Mrs. J.M. Dupont. Tel: (01934) 712267. Est: 1983. Postal business only. Spec: Cookery/Gastronomy; Crafts; Embroidery; Gardening; Needlework; Women. PR: £5–100.

WELLINGTON

Peter J. Ayre, Greenham Hall, Greenham, Wellington, TA21 0JJ. Tel: (01823) 672603. Fax: (01823) 672307. E-mail: peterjayre@aol.com. Est: 1980. Private premises; Internet and postal. Appointment necessary. Small stock. Spec: Countries - Africa; Natural History; Natural Sciences; Sport - Big Game Hunting; Travel - Africa. PR: £10–1,000. CC: JCB; MC; V. Also, a booksearch service. Cata: 4 – Quarterly.

WEST PENNARD

Eddie Baxter - Books, The Old Mill House, West Pennard, BA6 8ND. Prop: Josie Matthews. Tel: (01749) 890369. Fax: (01749) 890369. Est: 1956. Private premises; postal business only. Very small stock. Spec: Dance; Music - General; Music - Jazz. Also, booksearch. Cata: 1 – occasionally on specialities.

WESTON–SUPER–MARE

Chris Crook, ■ P.O. Box 180, Weston–Super–Mare, BS22 9SS. Prop: Chris Crook. Tel: (01225) 422244. Fax: (01963) 33718. Est: 1980. *Shop at:* Bath Old Books, Margarets Buildings, Brock Street, Bath. Open: **M:** 10:00–17:00; **T:** 10:00–17:00; **W:** 10:00–17:00; **Th:** 10:00–17:00; **F:** 10:00–17:00; **S:** 10:00–17:00. Small stock. Spec: Architecture; Art; Art History; Art Reference; Natural History. PR: £8–300 Mem: PBFA.

Manna Bookshop, ■ 30 Orchard Street, Weston–Super–Mare, BS23 1RQ. Prop: Peter Fairnington. Tel: (01934) 636228. Est: 1981. Shop; open **M:** 10:00–17:00; **T:** 10:00–17:00; **W:** 10:00–17:00; **Th:** 10:00–17:00; **F:** 10:00–17:00; **S:** 10:00–17:00. Large general stock. PR: £1–100. (Sometimes closed on Thursday).

Sterling Books, ■ 43a Locking Road, Weston-Super-Mare, BS23 3DG. Prop: David Nisbet. Tel: (01934) 625056. Website: www.abe.com. E-mail: sterling.books@talk21.com. Est: 1966. Shop; open **T:** 10:00–17:30; **W:** 10:00–17:30; **Th:** 10:00–13:00; **F:** 10:00–17:30; **S:** 10:00–17:30. Very large general stock. Spec: Antiquarian; Art; Bindings; Crafts; History - General; Theology; Topography - General; Travel - General. PR: £1–1,500. CC: AE; D; E; JCB; MC; V . Also, bookbinding & restoration, picture-framing & a booksearch service. Mem: ABA; PBFA; ILAB.

YEOVIL

Cook the Books, 34 Lower Odcombe, Yeovil, BA22 8TX.

SOUTH YORKSHIRE

DONCASTER

Hedgerow Books, 10 Whitbeck Close, Wadworth, Doncaster, DN11 9DZ. Prop: Peter & Elizabeth Hedge. Tel: (01302) 856311. Fax: (01302) 856311. Website: www.hedgerowbooks.com. E-mail: sales@hedgerowbooks.com. Est: 1988. Private premises; Internet and postal. Appointment necessary. Open: **M:** 09:00–21:00; **T:** 09:00–21:00; **W:** 09:00–21:00; **Th:** 09:00–21:00; **F:** 09:00–21:00; **S:** 09:00–12:30. Closed for lunch: 12:30–14:00. Small stock. Spec: Sport - Boxing; Sport - Football (Soccer). PR: £1–300. CC: MC; V; SW. Cata: 4 – Boxing & Football. Mem: PBFA. VAT No: GB 657 8581 80.

ECCLESFIELD

Compost (Books), 243 The Wheel, Ecclesfield, Sheffield, S35 9ZA.

ECKINGTON

The Bibliophile, P.O. Box 1175, Sheffield, Eckington, S21 4XZ.

ROTHERHAM

Anthony Singleton, 6 Birkwood Terrace, Braithwell, Rotherham, S66 7AE.

SHEFFIELD

Annie's Books, 7 Spout Copse, Sheffield, S6 6FB. Prop: Christine Wren. Tel: (0114) 234 0199. Fax: (0114) 232-0866. Website: www.abebooks.com/home/chriswren. E-mail: wrentrading@talk21.com. Est: 1999. Private premises; postal business only. Appointment necessary. Open: **M:** 09:00–17:00; **T:** 09:00–17:00; **W:** 09:00–17:00; **Th:** 09:00–17:00; **F:** 09:00–17:00. Small stock. Spec: Animals and Birds; Cats; Children's - General; Modern First Editions; Royalty - General. PR: £1–200. CC: AE; MC; V; SW. Also, booksearch. Cata: 2.

Baedekers & Murray Guides, 11 St. Quentin Drive, Sheffield, S17 4PN.

Biff Books & Records, 11 Commonside, Sheffield, S10 1GA.

The Book and Art Shop, 204 West Street, Sheffield, S1 4EU.

Chantrey Books, 24 Cobnar Road, Sheffield, S8 8QB.

Alan Hill Books, Unit 4, Meersbrook Works, Sheffield, S8 9FT.

The Porter Bookshop, ■ 227 Sharrowvale Road, Sheffield, S11 8ZE. Prop: Margot Armitage. Tel: (0114) 266-7762. Est: 1988. Shop; telephone first. Medium stock. Spec: Academic/Scholarly; Crime (True); Humanities; Literature.

Rare & Racy, 164–166 Devonshire Street, Sheffield, S3 7SG.

Margaret Riccetti, 303 Uperthorpe, Sheffield, S6 3NG. Prop: Margaret Riccetti. Tel: (0114) 266-6305. Website: www.riccetti.freeserve.co.uk. E-mail: maggie@riccetti.freeserve.co.uk. Est: 1997. Private premises; Internet. Appointment necessary. Small stock. Spec: Antiquarian; Art; Art History; Atlases; Collecting. PR: £5–500. CC: Paypal. Corresp: Italian, French. Mem: *Also at:* Court House Antiques, 2-6 Town End Road, Ecclesfield.

John D. Staley, 4 Clumber Rise, Aston, Sheffield, S26 2ES.

Tilleys Vintage Magazine Shop, ■ 281 Shoreham Street, Sheffield, S1 4SS. Prop: Antonius & Albertus Tilley. Tel: (0114) 275-2442. Website: www.tilleysmagazines.com. E-mail: tilleys281@aol.com. Est: 1978. Shop; open **T:** 10:00–16:30; **W:** 10:00–16:30; **Th:** 10:00–16:30; **F:** 10:00–16:30; **S:** 10:00–16:30. Very large stock. Spec: Comic Books & Annuals; Comics; Periodicals & Magazines; Spiritualism. PR: £1–200. CC: AE; MC; V. *Also at:* 21 Derby Road, Chesterfield (q.v.).

John Webb Books, 68 Harwood Gardens, Waterthorpe, Sheffield, S20 7LE. Tel: (0114) 248-8669. Fax: (0114) 248-8669. E-mail: john-webb@altair.co.uk. Est: 1997. Private premises; postal business only. Very small stock. Spec: Author - Bramah, Ernest; Author - Rand, Ayn; Author - Shute, Neville; First Editions. PR: £10–1,000.

YSF Books, ■ 365 Sharrowvale Road, Hunters Bar, Sheffield, S11 8ZG. Prop: J. & R. Eldridge. Tel: (0114) 268-0687. Website: www.ysfbooks.com. E-mail: ysfbooks@ysfbooks.com. Est: 1986. Shop; Internet and postal. Open: **M:** 09:30–17:00; **T:** 09:30–17:00; **W:** 09:30–17:00; **Th:** 09:30–17:00; **F:** 09:30–17:00; **S:** 09:30–17:00. Large general stock. Spec: Aeronautics; Alpinism/Mountaineering; Applied Art; Art History; Arts, The; Aviation; Food & Drink; Gardening; Maritime/Nautical; Military; Music - General; Natural History; Photography; Religion - General; Social History; Topography - General; and others as listed in the Specilaity Index. PR: £1–300.

WOMBWELL

Bijou Books, Nimrod, 55 Aldham House Lane, Wombwell, S73 8RG. Prop: Maureen Firth, Dr. Gregory Firth (Assistant). Tel: (01226) 755012. Fax: (01226) 755012. E-mail: maureenfirth@blueyonder.co.uk. Est: 1982. Private premises; postal business only. Small stock. Spec: Art Reference; Arts, The; Biography; Ceramics; Cookery/Gastronomy; Illustrated; Limited Editions; Literature; Memoirs; Philosophy; Photography; Private Press; Travel - General. PR: £1–500. Also, booksearch.

Available from Richard Joseph Publishers Ltd
Sheppard's Book Dealers in
NORTH AMERICA
15th Edition (Royal H/b, plus CD-ROM)   £30.00 560pp

STAFFORDSHIRE

BURTON UPON TRENT

Michael Morris, Weavers Green, Tutbury Road. Needham, Burton upon Trent, DE13 9PQ. Tel: (01283) 575344. Est: 1993. Private premises; postal business only. Spec: Antiquarian; Atlases; Cartography; Country Houses; Documents - General; Illustrated; Topography - General. PR: £5–1,500. Also, charts and plans. VAT No: GB 694 6934 73.

Ian J. Sherratt, Rhoslyn, Victoria St. Yoxall, Burton upon Trent, DE13 8NG. Est: 1989. Private premises; postal business only. Small general stock. PR: £1–20.

CANNOCK

Roger J. Knowles - Antiquary, 26 Church Road, Norton Canes, Cannock, WS11 3PD.

LICHFIELD

Mike Abrahams, 9 Burton Old Road, Streethay, Lichfield, WS13 8LJ. Tel: (01543) 256200. Est: 1979. Spec: Antiques; Banking & Insurance; Canals/Inland Waterways; Children's - General; Collecting; Comic Books & Annuals; Cookery/Gastronomy; Crime (True); Earth Mysteries; Fashion & Costume; Guide Books; Gypsies; History - Local; Magic & Conjuring; Motoring. PR: £1–500.

Steve Brown (Books), 2 Curborough Cottages, Watery Lane, Lichfield, WS13 8ER. Prop: Steve Brown. Tel: (01543) 264498. Website: www.abebooks.com/home/sbbooks. E-mail: steve.brown26@virgin.net. Est: 1992. Private premises; Internet and postal. Appointment necessary. Small general stock. Spec: Sport - Horse Racing (all aspects). PR: £5–500. Corresp: French. Mem: PBFA. *Also at:* Curborough Antiques Centre, Watery Lane, Lichfield.

Burntwood Bookshop, ■ Farewell Lane, Burntwood, Lichfield, WS7 9DP. (*) Prop: Kenneth Hayward & Royden Smith. Tel: (01543) 682217. Est: 1972. Shop; open **M:** 09:00–17:00; **T:** 09:00–17:00; **W:** 09:00–17:00; **Th:** 09:00–17:00; **F:** 09:00–17:00; **S:** 09:00–17:00. Very large general stock. PR: £1–200.

David Clegg, 6 Longbridge Road, Lichfield, WS14 9EL. Tel: (01543) 252117. Est: 1984. Private premises; postal business only. Very small general stock. Spec: Occult; Religion - General; Travel - General. PR: £5–20.

Terry W. Coupland, 15 Harwood Road, Lichfield, WS13 7PP. Tel: (01543) 256599. Est: 1980. Private premises; appointment necessary. Small stock. Spec: Bookbinding; Children's - General; Illustrated; Juvenile; Papermaking; Printing; Private Press; Publishing; Sport - Golf. PR: £5–1,500. Attends PBFA fairs. Cata: 3 – a year on printing, typography, private press. Mem: PBFA.

Fair Reader, 186 Walsall Road, Lichfield, WS13 8AH.

Images, The Staffs Bookshop, 4 and 6 Dam Street, Lichfield, WS13 6AA.

Colin Shakespeare Books, 3 Chestnut Drive, Shenstone, Lichfield, WS14 OJH. Prop: Colin & Lilian Shakespeare. Tel: (01543) 480978. Est: 1991. Private premises; postal business only. Contactable. Open: **M:** 09:00–21:00; **T:** 09:00–21:00; **W:** 09:00–21:00; **Th:** 09:00–21:00; **F:** 09:00–21:00. Medium general stock. Spec: Topography - General. PR: £3–1,500. Cata: 1 – occasionally on topography.

The Staffs Bookshop, ■ 4 & 6 Dam Street, Lichfield, WS13 6AA. Prop: Stephanie Hawkins. Tel: (01543) 264093. E-mail: contact@staffsbookshop.co.uk. Est: 1938. Shop; open **M:** 09:30–17:30; **T:** 09:30–17:30; **W:** 09:30–17:30; **Th:** 09:30–17:30; **F:** 09:30–17:30; **S:** 09:30–17:30. Very large stock. Spec: Author - Johnson, Samuel; Children's - General; Dolls & Dolls' Houses; History - General; Literature; Theology; Topography - Local. PR: £1–1,000. Also, art display.

Dealers who need to update their entry should visit their page on
www.sheppardsdirectories.com

STAFFORDSHIRE

NEWCASTLE–UNDER–LYME

Pomes Penyeach, 25 Curzon Street, Basford, Newcastle–under–Lyme, ST5 0PD. Prop: Paul Robinson. Tel: (01782) 630729. Website: www.abebooks.com. E-mail: books@pomes-penyeach.co.uk. Est: 1985. Private premises; appointment necessary. Small general stock. Spec: Academic/Scholarly; Children's - General; First Editions; History - General; Literary Criticism; Literature; Modern First Editions; Philosophy; Poetry; Psychology/Psychiatry; Science - General; University Texts. PR: £1–500. CC: AE; MC; V; Delta. Also, a booksearch service. Mem: PBFA.

Keith Twigg, 27 Lansdell Avenue, Porthill, Newcastle-under-Lyme, ST5 8ET.

STAFFORD

(Abacus) Books and Cards, ■ 56–60 Millrise Road, Milton, Stoke–on–Trent, ST2 7BW. Prop: Dave & Margaret Mycock. Tel: (01782) 543005. Est: 1980. Shop; open **M:** 09:00–17:00; **T:** 09:00–17:00; **W:** 09:00–17:00; **Th:** 09:00–17:00; **F:** 09:00–17:00; **S:** 09:00–16:00. Medium stock. Spec: Art; Autobiography; Bindings; Biography; Ceramics; Cookery/Gastronomy; Fiction - General; Gardening; History - General; Military; Music - General; Natural History; New Age; Photography; Poetry; Railways; Sport - General; Topography - General; and others as listed in the Speciality Index. PR: £1–200. Also, attends Buxton Book Fairs. VAT No: GB 478 7684 71.

Cartographics, 49 Grange Road, Biddulph, Stoke–on–Trent, ST8 7RY. Prop: R.J. & S.W. Dean. Tel: (01782) 513449. Website: www.cartographics.co.uk. E-mail: carto@tesco.net. Est: 1969. Private premises; Internet and postal. Appointment necessary. Very large stock. Spec: Canals/Inland Waterways; Cartography. PR: £1–500. Map drawing-repair-mounting-conservation. Historical research from cartographic sources. Corresp: French (limited!). VAT No: GB 318 9820 32.

Ray Roberts (Booksellers), Whiston Hall Mews, Whiston Hall, Whiston, Nr. Penkridge, Stafford, ST19 5QH. (*). Tel: (01785) 712232. Fax: (01785) 712232. Est: 1980. Private premises; appointment necessary. Medium stock. Spec: Aviation; Motorbikes; Motoring; Sport - Ballooning; Sport - Cycling; Steam Engines; Transport. Also: publishing 'Bentley Specials & Special Bentleys in 2003' and booksearch. Cata: 1 – Bentley and Rolls Royce.

STOKE-ON-TRENT

Acumen Books, Rushton House, 167 Nantwich Road, Audley, Stoke-on-Trent, ST7 8DL. Managing Director: C.B. Pearson. Tel: (01782) 720753. Fax: (01782) 720798. Website: www.acumenbooks.co.uk. E-mail: shep@acumenbooks.co.uk. Est: 1978. Spec: Sport - Cricket. PR: £1–20. CC: MC; V. Cata: 1 – Cricket Umpiring and Scoring. Mem: ACU&S MCIArb.

TAMWORTH

G. & J. Chesters, ■ 14 Market Street, Polesworth, Tamworth, B78 1HW. (*) Prop: Geoff & Jean Chester. Tel: (01827) 894743. Website: www.abebooks.com/home/geoffchesters. E-mail: gandjchesters @tiscali.co.uk. Est: 1970. Shop; open **M:** 10:00–17:00; **T:** 10:00–17:00. **Th:** 10:00–17:00; **F:** 10:00–17:00; **S:** 10:00–17:00. Very large general stock. Spec: Academic/Scholarly; Anthropology; Criminology; Economics; Education & School; Geography; Geology; History - General; Linguistics; Literary Criticism; Mathematics; Medicine - History of; Music - Classical; Philosophy; Politics; Psychology/Psychiatry. PR: £1–1,000. CC: AE; MC; V; SW. Mem: PBFA. VAT No: GB 112 6448 93.

UTTOXETER

J.O. Goodwin, Woodcrofts Farm, Highwood, Uttoxeter, ST14 8PS. Tel: (01889) 562792. Est: 1965. Private premises; appointment necessary. Small general stock. PR: £1–200. VAT No: GB 125 9041 83.

WOMBOURN

Rookery Bookery, 39 Rookery Road, Wombourn, WV5 0JH. Prop: Colin Hardwick. Tel: (01902) 895983. Est: 1987. Private premises; appointment necessary. Very small general stock. PR: £1–250. Cata: – occasionally. Corresp: French.

YOXALL

Ray Sparkes (Books), The Hollies, Bond End, Yoxall, DE13 8NH. (*). Tel: (01543) 472274. Fax: (01543) 472274. Est: 1987. Private premises; appointment necessary. Small stock. Spec: History - Local; Reference; Topography - General. PR: £2–3,000. Cata: 4 – on British directories. Mem: PBFA. VAT No: GB 478 2190 24.

SUFFOLK

ALDRINGHAM

Aldringham Books, Aldringham House, Aldringham, IP16 4PT.

BECCLES

Besleys Books, ■ 4 Blyburgate, Beccles, NR34 9TA. Prop: Piers & Gabby Besley. Tel: (01502) 715762. Fax: (01502) 675649. Website: www.besleysbooks.demon.co.uk. E-mail: piers@besleysbooks.demon.co.uk. Shop; open **M:** 09:30–17:00; **T:** 09:30–17:00. **Th:** 09:30–17:00; **F:** 09:30–17:00; **S:** 09:30–17:00. Large stock. Spec: Gardening; Illustrated; Natural History. PR: £1–1,000. CC: MC; V. Cata: 2 – biennial. Mem: ABA; PBFA.

BOXFORD

Dolphin Books, Old Coach House, Broad Street, Boxford, CO10 5DX. Prop: Rita Watts. Tel: (01787) 211630. Website: dolphinbooks@lineone.net. E-mail: dolphinbooks@lineone.net. Est: 1988. Private premises; Internet and postal. Appointment necessary. Small general stock. Spec: Authors - Women; Autobiography; Biography; Diaries; History - General; History - Women; Literature; Performing Arts; Politics; Rural Life; Women. PR: £5–50. Also, a booksearch service.

BARDSLEY'S BOOKS

ANTIQUARIAN
& SECONDHAND
BOOKS
BOUGHT & SOLD

Catalogues Issued
New Books to Order
Book - Search

(01986) 892077

22 Upper Olland Street
Bungay, Suffolk NR35 1BH

antonybardsley@easynet.co.uk

BUNGAY

Bardsley's Books, ■ 22 Upper Olland Street, Bungay, NR35 1BH. Prop: W.N.A. & D.H. Bardsley. Tel: (01986) 892077. Website: www.bardsleysbooks.co.uk. E-mail: antonybardsley@easynet.co.uk. Est: 1998. Shop; open **M:** 10:00–17:30; **T:** 10:00–17:30; **Th:** 10:00–17:30; **F:** 10:00–17:30; **S:** 10:00–17:30. Very large general stock. Spec: Antiquarian; Art; Bibles; Books about Books; Cinema/Film; Countries - Mexico; Countries - Poland; Ecclesiastical History & Architecture; Fine Printing; History - General; Iconography; Illuminated Manuscripts; Music - General; Mysticism; and others as listed in the Specialitity Index. PR: £1–250. Also, cards, O.S. Maps, CDs & new books to order.

Beaver Booksearch, 33 Hillside Road East, Bungay, NR35 1JU. Prop: Sarah Coulthurst & Nicholas Watts. Tel: (01986) 896698. Fax: (01986) 896698. Website: www.booksearch.u-net.com. E-mail: nick@beaverbooksearch.co.uk. Est: 1995. Private premises; postal business only. Small stock. Spec: Bridge. PR: £1–50. CC: MC; V; SW. Also, a booksearch service.

Scorpio Books, Autumn Cottage, Low Street, Ilketshall St. Margaret, Bungay, NR35 1QZ. Prop: Lorna & Patrick Quorn. Tel: (01986) 781721. Fax: (01986) 781721. E-mail: scorpiobooks@clara.co.uk. Est: 1988. Private premises; Internet and postal. Appointment necessary. Medium stock. Spec: Art; Aviation; Military; Music - Jazz; War - General; Women. PR: £1–500. CC: JCB; MC; V. Corresp: French, Spanish. Mem: PBFA.

BURES

Major Iain Grahame, Daws Hall, Lamarsh, Bures, CO8 5EX. Prop: Iain Grahame. Tel: (01787) 269213. Fax: (01787) 269634. Website: www.IainGrahameRareBooks.com. E-mail: majorbooks@compuserve.com. Est: 1979. Private premises; Internet and postal. Telephone first. Open: **M:** 09:00–21:00; **T:** 09:00–21:00; **W:** 09:00–21:00; **Th:** 09:00–21:00; **F:** 09:00–21:00; **S:** 09:00–17:00; **Su:** 09:00–17:00. Medium stock. Spec: Natural History; Sport - Field Sports. PR: £5–50,000. CC: AE; MC; V. Also, a booksearch service. Cata: 2 – Sporting, Natural History & Africana. Corresp: French and Italian. Mem: ABA. VAT No: GB 341 7566 51.

BURES ST. MARY

Trevor J. Giddings, Coopers Lodge, 1 Church Terr., Nayland Road, Bures St Mary, CO8 5ED.

BURY ST. EDMUNDS

Bury Bookshop, ■ 28a Hatter Street, Bury St. Edmunds, IP33 1NE. Prop: Joe & Sheila Wakerley. Tel: (01284) 703107. Fax: (01284) 755936. Est: 1980. Shop; open **M:** 09:00–17:30; **T:** 08:00–17:30; **W:** 09:00–17:30; **Th:** 08:00–17:30; **F:** 09:00–17:30; **S:** 09:00–17:30. Medium general stock. PR: £1–100. CC: AE; MC; V.

Janet Carters, 40 Church Lane, Barton Mills, Bury St. Edmunds, IP28 6AY. Tel: (01638) 717619. Est: 1978. Private premises; appointment necessary. Small stock. Spec: Sport - Horse Racing (all aspects). PR: £2–500. Cata: 3. VAT No: GB 334 0238 92.

John Crawford - Rare and Secondhand Books, 55 Avenue Approach, Bury St. Edmunds, IP32 6BA.

Guy Pratt, Guildhall Street Antiques, 27 Guildhall Street, Bury St. Edmunds, IP33 1QD.

Sally Smith Books, 13 Manor Garth, Pakenham, Bury St Edmunds, IP31 2LB. Tel: (01359) 230431. Website: www.sallysmithbooks.co.uk. E-mail: sally@sallysmithbooks.co.uk. Est: 1989. Private premises; Internet. Appointment necessary. Medium general stock. Spec: Antiques; Bibliography; Biography; Children's - General; Crafts; Fiction - General; Literature - Victorian; Natural History; Publishing; Travel - General; War - General. PR: £1–300. Corresp: French.

CLARE

Trinders' Fine Tools, ■ Malting Lane, Clare, CO10 8NW. Prop: Rosemary Trinder. Tel: (01787) 277130. Fax: (01787) 277677. Website: www.trindersfinetools.co.uk/. E-mail: peter@trindersfinetools.co.uk. Est: 1975. Shop; Internet and postal. Open: **M:** 10:00–17:00; **T:** 10:00–17:00; **W:** 10:00–17:00; **Th:** 10:00–17:00; **F:** 10:00–17:00; **S:** 10:00–12:00. Small stock. Spec: Antiques; Applied Art; Architecture; Art; Art Reference; Artists; Arts, The; Building & Construction; Carpets; Collecting; Conservation; Crafts; Crime (True); D.I.Y (Do It Yourself); Decorative Art; Design; Dolls & Dolls' Houses; Ecclesiastical History; and others as listed in the Speciality Index. PR: £2–500. CC: AE; JCB; MC; V. NB. Please phone before travelling lest we be closed! Also, quality hand-tools, especially British infill planes. Mem: PBFA. VAT No: GB 299 6575 77.

SUFFOLK

DEBENHAM

David Shacklock (Books), ■ 27 High St., Debenham, IP14 6QN. Prop: David Shacklock. Tel: (01728) 861286. E-mail: riley01@globalnet.co.uk. Est: 1986. Shop; open **T:** 10:00–17:00. **F:** 14:00–20:00; **S:** 10:00–16:00. Medium stock. Spec: Annuals; Anthologies; Author - Baring-Gould, S.; Author - Henty, G.A.; Biography; Fiction - General; Guide Books; History - General; Juvenile; Military; Reference; Royalty - General; Theology; Topography - General; Victoriana. PR: £1–150. Also, booksearch. Closed Tuesday 13:00–14:00. *Also at:* Townsend Mill, Halstead.

EYE

Rosalind Brewer, 29 Castle Street, Eye, IP23 7AW.

Thomas Rare Books, Valley Farm House, Yaxley, Eye, IP23 8BX. Prop: G.L. Thomas. Tel: (01379) 783288. Fax: (01379) 788517. Website: www.abebooks.com. E-mail: thomasrarebooks@btinternet.com. Est: 1978. Private premises; postal business only. Spec: Antiquarian. PR: £10–5,000.

FELIXSTOWE

Books Only, 84 Garrison Lane, Felixstowe, IP11 7RQ. Prop: Colin E. Sharman. Tel: (01394) 285546. E-mail: colinbooksonly@msn.com. Est: 1980. Spec: Cookery/Gastronomy; Photography; Politics; Topography - Local; Trade Unions. PR: £1–150.

Poor Richard's Books, ■ 17 Orwell Road, Felixstowe, IP11 7EP. Prop: Dick Moffat. Tel: (01394) 283138. E-mail: moffatsfx@aol.com. Est: 1997. Shop; open **M:** 09:00–17:00; **T:** 09:00–17:00; **W:** 09:00–17:00; **Th:** 09:00–17:00; **F:** 09:00–17:00; **S:** 09:00–17:00. Very large stock. PR: £1–500. CC: AE; MC; V; SW, SO. Mem: PBFA.

The Treasure Chest, ■ 61 Cobbold Road, Felixstowe, IP11 7BH. Prop: Robert Green. Tel: (01394) 270717. Est: 1982. Shop; open **M:** 09:30–17:30; **T:** 09:30–17:30; **W:** 09:30–17:30; **Th:** 09:30–17:30; **F:** 09:30–17:30; **S:** 09:30–17:30. Very large stock. Spec: Aviation; Cinema/Film; Topography - Local. PR: £1–500.

FRAMLINGHAM

Mrs. V. S. Bell (Books), ■ 19 Market Hill, Framlingham, Nr. Woodbridge, IP13 9BB. Tel: (01728) 723046. Est: 1974. Shop; open **M:** 10:00–16:00; **T:** 10:00–16:00; **W:** 10:00–12:00; **Th:** 10:00–16:00; **F:** 10:00–16:00; **S:** 09:00–16:00. Small stock. Spec: Fiction - Crime, Detective, Spy, Thrillers. PR: £2–75. Also, booksearch.

Mrs. A. Kent (Books), ■ 19 Market Hill, Framlingham, Nr. Woodbridge, IP13 9BB. Tel: (01728) 723046. Est: 1974. Shop; open **M:** 10:00–16:00; **T:** 10:00–16:00; **W:** 10:00–12:00; **Th:** 10:00–14:00; **F:** 10:00–14:00; **S:** 09:00–16:00. Closed for lunch: 13:00–14:00. Medium stock. Spec: Fiction - Crime, Detective, Spy, Thrillers. PR: £1–100. Also, booksearch.

IPSWICH

Roy Arnold, ■ 77 High Street, Needham Market, Ipswich, IP6 8AN. Tel: (01449) 720110. Fax: (01449) 722498. Website: www.royarnold.com. E-mail: ra@royarnold.com. Est: 1976. Shop; open **M:** 10:10–17:17; **T:** 10:10–17:17; **W:** 10:10–17:17; **Th:** 10:10–17:17; **F:** 10:10–17:17; **S:** 10:00–17:00. Spec: Antiquarian; Antiques; Applied Art; Rural Life; Scientific Instruments; Windmills & Watermills; Woodwork. PR: £4–3,000. CC: MC; V. Also, new books on specialities & a booksearch service. Cata: 1. Mem: PBFA; TATHS, SOT, EAIA, MWTCA. VAT No: GB 334 0169 85.

The Art Book Company, 35 Belstead Road, Ipswich, IP2 8AU.

Claude Cox Old & Rare Books, ■ College Gateway Bookshop, 3 & 5 Silent Street, Ipswich, IP1 1TF. Prop: Anthony Brian Cox. Tel: (01473) 254776. Fax: (01473) 254776. Website: www.claudecox.co.uk. E-mail: books@claudecox.co.uk. Est: 1944. Shop; open **W:** 10:00–17:00; **Th:** 10:00–17:00; **F:** 10:00–17:00; **S:** 10:00–17:00. Medium general stock. Spec: Antiquarian; Art Reference; Bibliography; Bindings; Books about Books; Ex-Libris; Fine Printing; Fore-Edge Paintings; History - General; Illuminated Manuscripts; Illustrated; Limited Editions; Literature; Military; Natural History; and others as listed in the Speciality Index. CC: JCB; MC; V; SW. Binding Repairs Suffolk Prints & Maps. Cata: 6 – Antiquarian and Printing & the Art of the Book. Mem: ABA; PBFA; ILAB; PLA, PHS. VAT No: GB 304 7952 56.

Footrope Knots, 501 Wherstead Road, Ipswich, IP2 8LL. Prop: Des & Liz Pawson. Tel: (01473) 690090. E-mail: knots@footrope.fsnet.co.uk. Est: 1981. Spec: Crafts; Maritime/Nautical; Sport - Yachting. PR: £1–100.

Gippeswic Books, 21 Belmont Road, Ipswich, IP2 9RJ. Prop: Martin L. Crook. Tel: (01473) 682302. Fax: (01473) 682302. Est: 1991. Private premises; postal business only. Small general stock. Spec: History - General; Military History; Topography - Local; Travel - General. PR: £2–300. Attends bookfairs. Mem: PBFA.

The Idler, ■ 37 High Street, Hadleigh, Ipswich, . Prop: Bryan & Jane Haylock. Tel: (01473) 827752. Est: 1980. Shop; open **M:** 09:30–17:30; **T:** 09:30–17:30; **W:** 09:30–12:30; **Th:** 09:30–17:30; **F:** 09:30–17:30; **S:** 09:30–17:00. Medium stock. Spec: Art. Also, booksearch.

LAVENHAM,

R.G. Archer, ■ 7 Water Street, Lavenham, Sudbury, CO10 9RW. Tel: (01787) 247229. Est: 1970. Shop; open **M:** 10:00–17:00; **T:** 10:00–17:00. **Th:** 09:00–17:00; **F:** 10:00–17:00; **S:** 10:00–17:00; **Su:** 10:00–17:00. Medium general stock. PR: £1–1,000. Open all bank holidays.

LONG MELFORD

Lime Tree Books, Hall Street, Long Melford, CO10 9JF.

LOWESTOFT

The Bookseller, 6 Pekefield Road, Lowestoft, NR33 0HS. Prop: Christopher John Chambers. Tel: (01502) 581011. Fax: (01502) 574891. Website: www.abfa.co.uk. E-mail: reasons@interdart.co.uk. Est: 1994. Private premises; postal business only. Open: **M:** 10:00–17:00; **T:** 10:00–17:00; **W:** 10:00–16:00; **Th:** 10:00–12:30; **F:** 10:00–17:00; **S:** 10:00–17:00. Closed for lunch: 12:30–13:30. Medium stock. Spec: Author - Heyer, Georgette; Fiction - Romantic; History - Local; Naval; Topography - Local; War - World War II. PR: £5–500. CC: MC; V; D, SW, SO. Corresp: French. Mem: IBN.

A Book for All Reasons, Rockville House, 6 Pakefield Road, Lowestoft, NR33 0HS. Prop: G.A. Michael Sims. Tel: (01502) 581011. Fax: (01502) 574891. Website: www.abfar.co.uk. E-mail: reasons@interdart.co.uk. Est: 1994. Private premises; Internet and postal. Medium stock. Spec: Author - Heyer, Georgette; Author - Yates, Dornford; Fiction - General; Fiction - Historical; Fiction - Romantic; History - Local; Naval; Topography - Local; War - World War II. PR: £5–500. CC: MC; V; SW. Mem: ibooknet. VAT No: GB 770 1056 57.

R. W. Lamb, Talbot House, 158 Denmark Road, Lowestoft, NR32 2EL. Tel: (01502) 564306. Fax: (01502) 564306. E-mail: talbot@rwlamb.co.uk. Est: 1972. Private premises; Internet and postal. Appointment necessary. Spec: Classical Studies. Cata: 2.

John Rolph, ■ The Coach–House Bookstore, Pakefield Street, Lowestoft, NR33 0JT. Tel: (01502) 572039. Est: 1952. Shop; open **T:** 11:00–17:00; **W:** 11:00–17:00; **F:** 11:00–17:00; **S:** 11:00–17:00. Closed for lunch: 13:00–14:30. Medium stock. PR: £1–100.

NEWMARKET

Miles Apart, 5 Harraton House, Exning, Newmarket, CB8 7HF.

C.D. Paramor, 25 St. Mary's Square, Newmarket, CB8 0HZ. Tel: (01638) 664416. Fax: (01638) 664416. Est: 1974. Private premises; appointment necessary. Medium stock. Spec: Cinema/Film; Dance; Entertainment - General; Music - General; Performing Arts; Television; Theatre. PR: £1–350. Also, booksearch. Cata: 6.

R.E. & G.B. Way, Brettons, Burrough Green, Newmarket, CB8 9NA. Tel: (01638) 507217. Fax: (01638) 508058. Website: http://www.geocities.com/regbway. E-mail: waybks@msn.com. Est: 1958. Private premises. Telephone first. Open: **M:** 08:30–17:30; **T:** 08:30–17:30; **W:** 08:30–17:30; **Th:** 08:30–17:30; **F:** 08:30–17:30; **S:** 08:30–12:00. Spec: Animals and Birds; Natural History; Private Press; Sport - Big Game Hunting; Sport - Field Sports. CC: MC; V. Mem: ABA; PBFA; BA. VAT No: GB 103 4378 02.

Dealers who need to update their entry should visit their page on *www.sheppardsdirectories.com*

SAXMUNDHAM

Roger Ballantyne–Way, Kiln House, Benhall Low Street, Saxmundham, IPI7 1JQ. Prop: Roger Ballantyne-Way. Tel: (01728) 604711. E-mail: ballantyne.way@virgin.net. Est: 1979. Private premises; Internet and postal. Appointment necessary. Medium stock. Spec: Architecture; Art; Art History; Art Reference; Artists; Arts, The; Decorative Art; Design; Fashion & Costume; Illustrated; Printing; Private Press. PR: £5–1,000. CC: AE; MC; V. Also, booksearch on Suffolk writers. Cata: 1 – art. Mem: PBFA.

Chapel Books, ■ Westleton, Saxmundham, IP17 3AA. Prop: Robert Jackson. Tel: (01728) 648616. Website: www.chapelbooks.com. E-mail: bob.thechapel@virgin.net. Est: 1982. Shop; open **M:** 12:00–17:00; **T:** 12:00–17:00; **W:** 12:00–17:00; **Th:** 12:00–17:00; **F:** 12:00–17:00; **S:** 12:00–17:00; **Su:** 12:00–17:00. Large general stock. PR: £1–500. CC: AE; MC; V; SW. VAT No: 811 7652 39.

Keith A. Savage, ■ 35 High Street, Saxmundham, IP17 1AJ. Tel: 01728 604538. Fax: 01986 872231(answerphone). Est: 1992. Shop; open **M:** 10:30–13:00; **T:** 10:30–17:00; **W:** 10:30–17:00. **F:** 10:30–17:00; **S:** 10:30–13:00. Small general stock. Spec: Children's - General; Comic Books & Annuals; Comics. PR: £1–150.

Sax Books, ■ 4a High St., Saxmundham, IP17 1DF. Prop: Richard W.L. Smith, M.V.O. Tel: (01728) 605775. E-mail: richard@saxbooks.co.uk. Est: 2000. Shop; open **W:** 10:00–16:00; **Th:** 10:00–16:00; **F:** 10:00–16:00; **S:** 10:00–16:00; **Su:** 10:00–16:00. Medium general stock. Spec: Art; Autobiography; Biography; Churchilliana; Fiction - General; History - General; Military History; Railways; Religion - General; Royalty - General; Sport - Cricket; Topography - Local. PR: £1–100. Sunday opening : Summer months only. Mem: PBFA.

Steven Simpson Natural History, Rising Sun, Kelsale, Saxmundham, IP17 2QY.

SOUTHWOLD

Pinkneys Lane Bookshop, 9 Pinkneys Lane, Southwold, IP18 6EW.

Southwold Antiques Centre, ■ Buckenham Mews, 83 High Street, Southwold, IP18 6DS. Tel: (01502) 723060. Shop; open **M:** 09:00–17:00; **T:** 09:00–17:00; **W:** 09:00–17:00; **Th:** 09:00–17:00; **F:** 09:00–17:00; **S:** 09:00–17:00; **Su:** 09:00–17:00. Small stock. Spec: Publishers - Warnes. PR: £2–50 Mem: PBFA. *Also at*, Downham Market, Norfolk (q.v.).

STOWMARKET

H.G. Pratt, Harvesters, Rectory Road, Wyverstone, Stowmarket, IP14 4SH. Tel: (01449) 781372. Private premises; postal business only. Open: **M:** 09:00–17:00; **T:** 09:00–17:00; **W:** 09:00–17:00; **Th:** 09:00–17:00; **F:** 09:00–17:00. Small stock. Spec: History - Local; Photography; Religion - Christian; Rural Life; Topography - Local. PR: £10–400. Also, booksearch. VAT No: GB 496 7023 16.

SUDBURY

Beckham Books Ltd., Chilton Mount, Newton Road, Sudbury, CO10 2RS. Prop: Mrs. J.E. Beckham. Tel: (01787) 373683. Fax: (01787) 375441. Website: www.beckhambooks.com. E-mail: sales@beckhambooks.co.uk. Est: 1994. Private premises; telephone first. Open: **M:** 09:00–18:00; **T:** 09:00–18:00; **W:** 09:00–18:00; **Th:** 09:00–18:00; **F:** 09:00–18:00; **S:** 09:00–18:00; **Su:** 10:00–17:00. Large general stock. Spec: Antiquarian; Bibles; Bindings; Biography; Ecclesiastical History & Architecture; History - General; Languages - Foreign; Prayer Books; Religion - General; Religion - Methodism; Religion - Methodism; Religious Texts; Theology. PR: £1–2,000. CC: AE; E; JCB; MC. Free booksearch service. Mem: ABA. VAT No: GB 750 9305 36.

Suffolk Rare Books, ■ The Bookshop, 7 New Street, Sudbury, CO10 6JB.

Searching for a title - and cannot find it on any Internet database?
Then try SheppardsBooksearch

By selecting the subject classification – the request goes to all dealers who major in that subject.

Derek Vanstone - Aviation Book, Tymperley Farm, Great Henny, Sudbury, CO10 7LX. Tel: (01787) 269291. Fax: (01787) 269291. Website: www.aircraftbooks.com. E-mail: derek.vanstone@lineone.net. Est: 1996. Private premises; Internet and postal. Open: **M:** 09:00–18:00; **T:** 09:00–18:00; **W:** 09:00–18:00; **Th:** 09:00–18:00; **F:** 09:00–18:00; **S:** 09:00–13:00. Small stock. Spec: Aviation; Maritime/Nautical; Military. PR: £1–200. CC: AE; MC; V. Cata: 3. Mem: PBFA. VAT No: GB 711 3364 72.

WOODBRIDGE

Blakes Books, ■ 88 The Thoroughfare, Woodbridge, IP12 1AL. Prop: Robert Green. Tel: (01394) 380302. Est: 1983. Shop; open **M:** 09:30–17:00; **T:** 09:30–17:00; **W:** 09:30–17:00; **Th:** 09:30–17:00; **F:** 09:30–17:00; **S:** 09:30–17:00. Medium general stock. PR: £1–100. CC: MC; V. Mem: PBFA.

WYVERSTONE

H.G. Pratt, Harvesters, Rectory Road, Wyverstone, Stowmarket, IP14 4SH.

YOXFORD

Garden House Books, The High Street, Yoxford, IP17 3ER.

SURREY

ASHTEAD

Bagot Books, 2 Bagot Close, Ashtead, KT21 1NS. Prop: Nigel Smith. Tel: (01372) 272517. Fax: (01372) 272517. E-mail: bagotbooks@nigelsmyth.fsnet.co.uk. Est: 2000. Private premises; postal business only. Small stock. PR: £1–250 Mem: IBN.

Nigel Smith Books, 2 Bagot Close, Ashtead, KT21 1NS.

BYFLEET

Joppa Books Ltd., ■ 68 High Road, Byfleet, KT14 7QL. Prop: Nadeem M. Elissa. Tel: (01932) 336777. Fax: (01932) 348881. Website: www.joppabooks.com. E-mail: joppa@joppabooks.com. Est: 1989. Shop; Internet and postal. Open: **M:** 10:00–14:00; **T:** 10:00–16:00; **W:** 10:00–16:00; **Th:** 10:00–16:00; **F:** 10:00–16:00. Closed for lunch: 12:00–14:00. Large stock. Spec: Academic/Scholarly; Antiquarian; Archaeology; Canals/Inland Waterways; Carriages & Driving; Countries - Middle East, The; Egyptology; History - National; Military; Oriental; Politics; Religion - Islam; Travel - Africa; Travel - Asia; Travel - Middle East. PR: £5–5,000. CC: AE; MC; V; SW. Cata: 24 – every two weeks. Corresp: Arabic, French. Mem: PBFA. VAT No: GB 493 7403 24.

CATERHAM

Chaldon Books & Records, 1 High Street, Caterham, CR3 5UE. Prop: K. Chesson. Tel: (01883) 348583. Est: 1994. PR: £1–200. Also, booksearch.

Corrie Ball, 116 Stanstead Road, Caterham, CR3 6AE.

CHOBHAM

Glenwood Books, Highlands, Cedar Road, Hook Heath, Chobham, Woking, GU22 0JJ.

Nectar Books, P.O. Box 263, Cobham, KT11 2YZ. Prop: T.G. Kent. Tel: (01932) 865637. E-mail: sales@nectarbooks.co.uk. Est: 1976. Private premises; postal business only. Appointment necessary. Very small general stock. Spec: Broadcasting; Cinema/Film; Drama; Entertainment - General; Erotica; Genealogy; Memorabilia; Music - General; Performing Arts. PR: £5–200. Also, a booksearch service.

DORKING

A.J. Coombes, 24 Horsham Road, Dorking, RH4 2JA. Prop: John Coombes. Tel: (01306) 880736. Fax: (01306) 743641. E-mail: john.coombes@ukgateway.net. Est: 1967. Private premises; appointment necessary. Small stock. Spec: Architecture; History - General; History - British; History - Local; Topography - General; Topography - Local. Cata: 3 – on British local history & topography. Corresp: German. Mem: ABA. VAT No: GB 210 5273 14.

T. S. Hill Books, ■ 9 Falkland Road, Dorking, RH4 3AB. Prop: Tim Hill. Tel: (01306) 886468. Est: 1987. Shop; appointment necessary. Open: **M:** 09:00–17:00; **T:** 09:00–17:00; **W:** 09:00–17:00; **Th:** 09:00–17:00; **F:** 09:00–17:00. Very small general stock. PR: £5–500.

C.C. Kohler, 12 Horsham Road, Dorking, RH4 2JL. Tel: (01306) 881532. Fax: (01306) 742438. E-mail: cornflwr@cornflwr.demon.co.uk. Est: 1963. Storeroom; appointment necessary. Medium stock. Spec: Special collections. Corresp: German. Mem: ABA; ILAB. VAT No: GB 293 7862 08.

Dealers who need to update their entry should visit their page on
www.sheppardsdirectories.com

EAST HORSLEY

Emjay Books, Ashdene, High Park Avenue, East Horsley, KT24 5DF. Prop: M. Gardner. Tel: (01483) 283373. E-mail: emjaybooks@lineone.net. Est: 1990. Private premises; Internet and postal. Appointment necessary. Large stock. Spec: American Indians; Author - Bates, H.E.; Author - Byron, Lord; Author - Christie, Agatha; Author - Francis, Dick; Author - Tangye, D; Motoring; Private Press; Reference. PR: £5–3,000. CC: V. Also, a booksearch service.

Rowan House Books, Rowans, Norrels Ride, East Horsley, KT24 5EH. Prop: George Spranklins. Tel: (01483) 282482. Fax: (01483) 285924. Website: abebooks.com. E-mail: gsprankling@aol.com. Est: 1995. Private premises; Internet and postal. Appointment necessary. Medium stock. Spec: Children's - General; First Editions; Illustrated. PR: £10–500. CC: MC; V.

EAST MOLESEY,

Books Bought & Sold Ltd, ■ 68 Walton Road, East Molesey, KT8 0DL. Prop: P.J. Sheridan & W.J. Collyer. Tel: (020) 8224-3609. Fax: (020) 8224-3576. Website: www.books.keyuk.com. E-mail: sheridan@books.keyuk.com. Est: 1985. Shop; open **T:** 10:00–17:00; **W:** 10:00–17:00; **Th:** 10:00–17:00; **F:** 10:00–17:00; **S:** 10:00–17:00. Medium stock. Spec: Aeronautics; Aviation; Children's - General; History - General; Illustrated; Military; Motoring; Railways; Topography - Local. PR: £1–900. CC: D; E; JCB; MC; V. Organisers of HD Book Fairs. VAT No: GB 644 1831 46.

Cecil Books, ■ Nostradamus II Antiques Centre, 53 Bridge Road, East Molesey, KT8 9ER. Prop: Desmond & Ruth Cecil. Tel: Shop: (020) 8783 059. Fax: (020) 8224-5856. E-mail: ruthcecil@dial.pipex.com. Est: 1996. Shop; open **T:** 10:00–17:00; **W:** 10:00–17:00; **Th:** 10:00–17:00; **F:** 10:00–17:00; **S:** 10:00–17:00; Su: 11:00–17:00; Small general stock. Spec: Antiquarian; Biography; Poetry; Travel - General. PR: £5–500 Also, booksearch. Corresp: French, German, Italian.

EGHAM

Blacklock's, ■ 8 Victoria Street, Englefield Green, Egham, Surrey, TW20 0QY. Prop: Graham Dennis. Tel: (01784) 438025. Est: 1988. Shop; open **M:** 09:00–17:00; **T:** 09:00–17:00; **W:** 09:00–17:00; **Th:** 09:00–17:00; **F:** 09:00–17:00; **S:** 09:00–17:00. Closed for lunch: 13:00–14:00. Small general stock. Spec: Sport - Polo. PR: £1–100. CC: MC; V. Cata: 2 – on polo.

Corfe Books, ■ 'Corfe', Mount Lee, Egham, TW20 9PD. Prop: Mark Hayhoe. Tel: (01932) 850674. Est: 2001. *Shop at:* 163 Station Road, Adlestone, Surrey. Open: **M:** 10:00–16:30; **T:** 10:00–16:30; **W:** 10:00–16:30; **Th:** 10:00–16:30; **F:** 10:00–17:45; **S:** 10:00–17:45. Large stock. Spec: Aeronautics; Animals and Birds; Antiques; Archaeology; Architecture; Espionage; Fiction - General; History - General; Military History; Modern First Editions; Motoring; Naval; Railways; Signed Editions. PR: £1–300. Also, booksearch.

L.M. Fenton, 25 Lynwood Avenue, Egham, TW20 9RE.

ELSTEAD

Brian P. Martin (Books and Pictures), Honeypot Antiques, Milford Road, Elstead, Nr. Godalming.

EPSOM

J.W. McKenzie Ltd, ■ 12 Stoneleigh Park Road, Epsom, KT19 0QT. (*). Tel: (0208) 3937700. Website: www.mckenzie-cricket.co.uk. E-mail: jwmck@netcomuk.co.uk. Est: 1971. Shop; open **M:** 09:00–16:00; **T:** 09:00–17:00; **W:** 08:00–17:00; **Th:** 09:00–17:00; **F:** 09:00–17:00; **S:** 10:00–13:00. Closed for lunch: 13:00–14:00. Medium stock. Spec: Sport - Cricket. CC: E; JCB; MC; V. Cata: 1 – occasionally.

Vandeleur Antiquarian Books, 6 Seaforth Gardens, Stoneleigh, Epsom, KT19 0NR. Prop: E.H. Bryant. Tel: (020) 8393-7752. Fax: (020) 8393-7752. Est: 1971. Private premises; appointment necessary. Medium stock. Spec: Alpinism/Mountaineering; Antiquarian; Bindings; Sport - Big Game Hunting; Sport - Rowing; Travel - Africa; Travel - Americas; Travel - Asia; Travel - Europe; Travel - Polar; Voyages & Discovery. PR: £5–2,000. Attends bookfairs. Mem: PBFA.

ESHER

Charnwood Books, 44 Stevens Lane, Claygate, Esher, KT10 0TH.

Elizabeth Gant, 8 Sandon Close, Esher, KT10 8JE. Prop: Elizabeth Gant. Tel: (020) 8398-0962. Fax: (020) 8398-5107. Website: www.bookline.co.uk. E-mail: egant@bookline.co.uk. Est: 1982. Private premises; appointment necessary. Small stock. Spec: Children's - General; Illustrated. PR: £1–800. CC: JCB; V. Cata: 3 – Four monthly. Mem: ABA; PBFA.

FARNHAM

Derek Burden, 1 Boundstone Road, Wrecclesham, Farnham, GU10 4TH. Prop: Derek Burden. Tel: (01252) 793615. Fax: (01252) 794789. E-mail: dweburden@aol.com. Est: 1967. Private premises; Internet and postal. Appointment necessary. Large stock. Spec: Graphics; Illustrated. PR: £1–1,000.

Oxfam, ■ 3 The Woolmead, Farnham, GU7 9TX. Tel: (01252) 726951. Fax: (01252) 726951. Est: 1943. Shop; open **M:** 09:30–16:30; **T:** 09:30–16:30; **W:** 09:30–16:30; **Th:** 09:30–16:30; **F:** 09:30–16:30; **S:** 09:30–16:29. Very small general stock. PR: £1–3. CC: MC; V; SW.

GODALMING

Catalyst Booksearch Services, 1 Weston House, Ballfield Road, Godalming, GU7 2HB. Prop: Patrick Blosse. Tel: 01483 428500. Fax: 01483 428500. Website: www.abebooks.com/home/PATBLOSSE/. E-mail: books@catalystbs.com. Est: 1997. Private premises; Internet and postal. Appointment necessary. Large stock. Spec: Animals and Birds; Annuals; Author - General; Biography; Children's - General; Children's - Illustrated; Cinema/Film; Crime (True); Drama; Fiction - General; Fiction - Crime, Detective, Spy, Thrillers; First Editions; History - General; Natural History; and others as listed in the Speciality Index. PR: £2–250.

Crouch Rare Books, Syringa, Tuesley Lane, Godalming, GU7 1SB. Prop: A. S. Crouch. Tel: (01483) 420390. Fax: (01483) 421371. Website: www.crbooks.co.uk. E-mail: efrosyne@crbooks.co.uk. Est: 1970. Storeroom; Internet and postal. Telephone first. Open: **M:** 09:00–17:30; **T:** 09:00–17:30; **W:** 09:00–17:30; **F:** 09:00–17:30; **S:** 09:00–17:30. Closed for lunch: 13:00–14:00. Medium stock. Spec: Academic/Scholarly; Antiquarian; Archaeology; Canals/Inland Waterways; Classical Studies; Countries - Greece; Crafts; Ecclesiastical History & Architecture; Egyptology; Embroidery; Foreign Texts; History - General; History of Civilisation; Lace; and others as listed in the Speciality Index. PR: £2–800. CC: AE; D; MC; V; SW. Also, publishers. Cata: 3. Corresp: French and Greek. VAT No: GB 417 6129 55.

Brian Martin (Books & Pictures), 4 Upper Birtley, Haslemere Road, Brook, Godalming, GU8 5LB.

GUILDFORD

Apocalypse Books, Albert Villas, 55 Stoke Fields, Guildford, GU1 4LT.

HASLEMERE

Anglo-American Rare Books, Galleons Lap, P.O. Box 71, Haslemere, GU27 1YT. Prop: Jack Laurence and David Purt. Tel: (01428) 606462. Fax: (01428) 606462. E-mail: anglobooks@aol.com. Est: 1995. Private premises; postal business only. Small stock. Spec: Americana; Author - General; Author - Eliot, T. S.; Author - Greene, Graham; Author - Hemingway, Ernest; Author - James, Henry; Author - Mailer, Norman; Author - Murdoch, I.; Author - Sassoon, Siegfried; Fiction - General; Journalism; Literature; and others as listed in the Speciality Index. PR: £5–2,000. Also, a booksearch service. Mem: PBFA.

HINDHEAD

Beacon Hill Bookshop, ■ Beacon Hill Road, Hindhead, GU26 6QL. Prop: Stan & Cherie Jenks. Tel: (01428) 606783. Est: 1970. Shop; open **M:** 09:00–17:00; **T:** 09:00–17:00. **Th:** 09:00–17:00; **F:** 09:00–17:00; **S:** 09:00–17:00. Large general stock. Cata: 52 – to trade only.

MITCHAM

J.G. Natural History Books, 149 Sherwood Park Road, Mitcham, CR4 1NJ. Prop: J. Greatwood. Tel: (020) 8764-4669. Fax: (020) 8764-4669. Website: www.reptilebooks.com. E-mail: jgbooks@btinternet.com. Est: 1969. Spec: Gemmology; Herpetology. PR: £10–500. CC: MC; V. Also, new books. Cata: 12 – on new herpetological books only.

Kay Books Ltd., 88 Glebe Court, Mitcham, CR4 3NG. Tel: (020) 8640-7779. Fax: (020) 8640-7779. E-mail: jacqui@degnanj.fsnet.co.uk. Est: 1968. Telephone first. Spec: Bindings; Topography - General; Travel - General. Mem: PBFA.

NEW MALDEN

Steve Baxter, 13 Westbury Road, New Malden, KT3 5BE. Tel: (020) 8942-4431. Fax: (020) 8942-2249. E-mail: baxterfinebooks@aol.com. Private premises; postal business only. Small stock. Spec: Antiquarian; Bindings; Churchilliana; Fine & Rare; First Editions; History - General; Literature; Sets of Books. Mem: PBFA. Also, booksearch. VAT No: GB 711 1425 88.

Safina Books, 20 Manor Drive North, New Malden, KT3 5PB.

OXTED

"Books in the Basement", ■ 80-84 Station Road East, Oxted, RH8 0PG. Tel: (01883) 723131. Est: 1999. Shop; open **M:** 09:00–17:00; **T:** 09:00–17:00; **W:** 09:00–17:00; **Th:** 09:00–17:00; **F:** 09:00–17:00. Medium general stock. PR: £1–300. *Also at:* Secondhand Bookshop, Oxted, Surrey (q.v.).

Postings, P.O. Box 1, Oxted, RH8 0FD. Prop: R.N. Haffner. Tel: (01883) 722646. Fax: (01883) 722646. Est: 1992. Private premises; postal business only. Very small stock. Spec: Aviation; Philately; Railways; Sport - Ballooning; Topography - Local; Transport. PR: £5–300. CC: E; JCB; MC; V. Cata: 2 – a year on postal history, memorabilia, civil aviation. Mem: PTS, PTA.

Secondhand Bookshop, ■ 56 Station Road West, Oxted, RH8 9EU. Tel: (01883) 715755. Est: 1993. Shop; open **M:** 10:00–17:00; **T:** 10:00–17:00; **W:** 10:00–17:00; **Th:** 10:00–17:00; **F:** 10:00–17:00; **S:** 09:00–17:00. Medium general stock. PR: £1–400. Also, at home, by appointment. *Also at:* Books in the Basement, Oxted (q.v.) and Browsers's Coffee Shop, Lingfield, Surrey.

REDHILL

Ivelet Books Ltd., 18 Fairlawn Drive, Redhill, RH1 6JP.

REIGATE

Reigate Galleries, ■ 45a Bell Street, Reigate, RH2 7AQ. Prop: K. & J. Morrish. Tel: (01737) 246055. Est: 1948. Shop; open **M:** 09:00–17:30; **T:** 09:00–17:30; **W:** 09:00–12:30; **Th:** 09:00–17:30; **F:** 09:00–17:30; **S:** 09:00–17:30. Medium stock. Spec: Illustrated; Topography - General; Travel - General. PR: £1–200. CC: MC; V. Mem: PBFA. VAT No: GB 211 0178 27.

Reigate Rare Books, 26 Cornfield Road, Reigate, RH2 7HE.

RICHMOND-UPON-THAMES

T.A. Cherrington Rare Books Lt, 1a Church Court, Richmond-upon-Thames, TW9 1JL.

SHAMLEY GREEN

Eric Thompson, Hullhatch, Shamley Green, Guildford, GU5 0TG. Tel: (01483) 893694. Fax: (01483) 892219. Est: 1978. Private premises; appointment necessary. Large stock. Spec: Motoring. PR: £5–750. Also, booksearch. Cata: 1 – motoring.

SURBITON

The Bookroom, ■ 146 Chiltern Drive, Surbiton, KT5 9HF. Prop: Keith Alexander. Tel: (020) 8404-6644. Fax: (020) 8399-8168. E-mail: kmabooks@aol.com. Est: 2002. Shop; open **W:** 11:00–18:00; **Th:** 11:00–18:00; **F:** 11:00–18:00; **S:** 11:00–18:00. Large stock. Spec: Academic/Scholarly; Advertising; Aeronautics; Agriculture; Antiques; Architecture; Art; Biography; Children's - General; Cinema/Film; Fiction - General; Health; History - General; Modern First Editions; Music - General; Plays; Poetry. PR: £1–30. Fair organiser. See Title Page Book Fairs in prelims.

Caissa Books, 5 Pembroke Avenue, Berrylands, Surbiton, KT5 8HN. Prop: Mike Sheehan. Tel: (020) 8399 6591. Fax: (020) 8399 6591. E-mail: caissa.books@tinyworld.co.uk. Est: 1980. Postal business only. Contactable. Open: **M:** 14:14–20:20; **T:** 14:14–20:20; **W:** 14:14–20:20; **Th:** 14:14–20:20; **F:** 14:14–20:20. Small stock. Spec: Chess. PR: £3–3,000. CC: MC; V. Cata: 1 – annual. Corresp: French and German.

Fun in Books, 120 Ewell Road, Surbiton, KT6 6HA. Prop: Michael J. White. Tel: (020) 8390-5566. Fax: (020) 8390-6443. E-mail: mail@melitzer.co.uk. Est: 1994. Storeroom; postal business only. Spec: Freemasonry & Anti-Masonry; Glamour; Humour. PR: £5–100.

Available from Richard Joseph Publishers Ltd
Sheppard's Book Dealers in
AUSTRALIA & NEW ZEALAND

4th Edition (Royal H/b)   £27.00   252pp

SURREY

SUTTON

Nonsuch Books, 176 Mulgrave Road, Cheam, Sutton, SM2 6JS. (*) Prop: Robert and Lynette Gleeson. Tel: (020) 8770 7875. E-mail: nonsuch.books@virgin.net. Est: 1990. Private premises; postal business only. Appointment necessary. Open: **M:** 09:00–17:00; **T:** 09:00–17:00; **W:** 09:00–17:00; **Th:** 09:00–17:00; **F:** 09:00–17:00; **S:** 09:00–17:00. Small stock. Spec: Archaeology; Architecture; Art; Art History; Art Reference; History - General; Illustrated; Literature. PR: £5–200.

WALLINGTON

A.R. Wright, 34 Burleigh Avenue, Wallington, SM6 7JG.

WALTON–ON–THAMES

Grey House Books, 2 Wilton Lodge, 35 Rydens Road, Walton–on–Thames, KT12 3DX. Prop: Camille Wolff. Tel: (01932) 245610. Est: 1972. Spec: Crime (True); Criminology.

Fred Lake, 104 Kings Road, Walton–on–Thames, KT12 2RE. Tel: (01932) 227824. Private premises; postal business only. Very small stock. Spec: Periodicals & Magazines; Sport - Archery; Sport - Field Sports. PR: £1–150.

WEYBRIDGE

Mrs. D.M. Green, 7 Tower Grove, Weybridge, KT13 9LX. Tel: (01932) 241105. Est: 1974. Private premises; appointment necessary. Very small stock. Spec: Atlases; Topography - General. PR: £1–3,500. Cata: 1 – occasionally on British county maps. Mem: IMCos.

WINDLESHAM

Cold Tonnage Books, 22 Kings Lane, Windlesham, GU20 6JQ.

WOKING

Glenwood Books, Highlands, Cedar Road, Hook Heath, Woking, GU22 0JJ.

Goldsworth Books & Prints Ltd, ■ 47 Goldsworth Road, Woking, GU21 6JY. Prop: Brian & Joyce Hartles. Tel: (01483) 767670. Fax: (01483) 767670. E-mail: brian@goldsworthbooks.com. Est: 1986. Shop; open **T:** 10:00–17:00; **W:** 10:00–17:00; **Th:** 10:00–17:00; **F:** 10:00–17:00; **S:** 09:30–16:30. Very large stock. PR: £1–1,000. CC: JCB; V. Also, booksearch. Mem: PBFA. VAT No: GB 641 2513 73.

Peter Kennedy, ■ 2 Shirley Place, Knaphill, Woking, GU21 2PL. Tel: (01483) 797293. Fax: (01483) 488006. Est: 1972. *Shop at:* at 87 Portobello Road, London W11. Open: **S:** 08:00–16:00. Spec: Atlases; Botany; Illustrated; Natural History. CC: V. Also, antique maps. Appointment necessary: Monday to Friday (home address). Mem: ABA.

World War II Books, P.O. Box 55, Woking, GU22 8HP.

TYNE & WEAR

FELLING
Worley Publications & Booksell, 10 Rectory Road East, Felling, NE10 9DN.

LIVERSEDGE
Heckmondwike Book Shop, ■ 66 Union Road, Liversedge, WF15 7JF. Prop: David Sheard. Tel: (01924) 505666. E-mail: david.sheard@ntlworld.com. Est: 1984. Shop; Internet and postal. Open: **S:** 10:00–17:00. Large stock. Spec: Author - Wheatley, Dennis; Fiction - General; Fiction - Crime, Detective, Spy, Thrillers; Fiction - Science Fiction; Publishers - Pan; Publishers - Penguin; Publishers - Puffin; Vintage Paperbacks. PR: £0–100. Will open shop at other times by arrangement. VAT No: GB 427 5900 45.

NEWCASTLE UPON TYNE
Arcanum Books, 11 Lockerbie Road, Cramlington, Northumberland, Newcastle upon Tyne, NE23 8DH.
Frank Smith Maritime Aviation, ■ 98–100 Heaton Road, Newcastle upon Tyne, NE6 5HL. Prop: Alan Parker. Tel: (0191) 265-6333. Fax: (0191) 224-2620. E-mail: books@franksmith.freeserve.co.uk. Est: 1981. Shop; Internet and postal. Open: **M:** 10:00–16:00; **T:** 10:00–16:00; **W:** 10:00–16:00; **Th:** 10:00–16:00; **F:** 09:00–16:00; **S:** 10:00–13:00. Large stock. Spec: Aviation; Maritime/Nautical; Motoring; Shipbuilding; Sport - Yachting. PR: £4–1,000. CC: E; JCB; MC; V. Cata: 24 – Monthly on Aviation & Maritime. Corresp: German, French, Dutch. Mem: PBFA. VAT No: 297 9302 12.
Robert D. Steedman, ■ 9 Grey Street, Newcastle upon Tyne, NE1 6EE. Prop: D.J. Steedman. Tel: (0191) 232-6561. Est: 1907. Shop; open **M:** 09:00–17:00; **T:** 09:00–17:00; **W:** 09:00–17:00; **Th:** 09:00–17:00; **F:** 09:00–17:00; **S:** 09:00–12:30. Large general stock. PR: £1–5,000. CC: JCB; MC; V; S, SW. Cata: 1 – occasionally. Mem: ABA; BA. VAT No: GB 177 1638 41.

NORTH SHIELDS
Keel Row Books, ■ 11 Fenwick Terrace, Preston Road, North Shields, NE29 0LU. Tel: Withheld. Est: 1980. Shop; open **M:** 10:30–17:00; **T:** 10:30–17:00. **Th:** 10:30–17:00; **F:** 10:30–17:00; **S:** 10:30–17:00; **Su:** 11:00–16:00. Very large stock. Spec: Alpinism/Mountaineering; Art; Children's - General; Cinema/Film; Comic Books & Annuals; Crime (True); Military; Military History; Politics; Railways; Theatre; Voyages & Discovery; War - General. PR: £1–700.

SOUTH SHIELDS
W.L. Smith, 23 Fraser Close, South Shields, NE33 5AT.

WHITLEY BAY
R. Allen, 27 Deneholm, Monkseaton, Whitley Bay, NE25 9AU. Tel: (0191) 252-4516. Fax: (0191) 252-4516. E-mail: rb27allen@aol.com. Very small stock. Spec: Author - Haggard, Sir Henry Rider; Author - Heyer, Georgette; Author - Stoker. PR: £2–300. Also, a booksearch service and Editor/Founder of the Rider Haggard Society. Cata: – on request. Corresp: French, Spanish.
Christopher Handley, 38 Hamilton Drive, Whitley Bay, NE26 1JQ.
Olivers Bookshop, ■ 48a Whitley Road, Whitley Bay, NE26 2NF. Prop: John Oliver. Tel: (0191) 251-3552. Est: 1987. Shop; open **M:** 11:00–17:00. **Th:** 11:00–17:00; **F:** 11:00–17:00. Medium stock. PR: £1–500. Mobile (0771) 8392830.

Dealers who need to update their entry should visit their page on
www.sheppardsdirectories.com

WARWICKSHIRE

ALCESTER

Home Farm Books, 44 Evesham Road, Cookhill, Alcester, B49 5LJ. Prop: Tony Read. Tel: (01789) 763115. Fax: (01789) 766086. E-mail: readbk@globalnet.co.uk. Est: 1979. Private premises; postal business only. Small stock. Spec: Cockfighting; Dogs; Firearms/Guns; Natural History; Rural Life; Sport - Angling/Fishing; Sport - Big Game Hunting; Sport - Falconry; Sport - Field Sports; Taxidermy. PR: £2–400. Also, a booksearch service. Cata: 4 – on specialities.

HENLEY–IN–ARDEN

Arden Books & Cosmographia, ■ 11 Pound Field, Wootton Wawen, Henley–in–Arden, B95 6AQ. Prop: David Daymond. Tel: (01564) 793476. Est: 1998. *Shop at:* Yew Tree Farm Craft Centre, Wootton Wawen. Open: **T:** 10:00–17:00; **W:** 10:00–17:00; **Th:** 10:00–17:00; **F:** 10:00–17:00; **S:** 10:00–17:00; **Su:** 10:00–17:00. Small general stock. Spec: Antiques; Art; Biography; Canals/Inland Waterways; Children's - General; Crafts; Food & Drink; Gardening; Guide Books; History - General; History - Local; Maritime/Nautical; Natural History; Needlework; Poetry; Railways; Rural Life; Topography - General; and others as listed in the Speciality Index. PR: £1–50. Winter: open November to March 10:30–16.00 and Bank Holidays 09:00:18:00. Corresp: French, German.

KENILWORTH

LSA Books, 45 Randall Road, Kenilworth, CV8 1JX. Prop: Les Anscombe. Tel: (01926) 850580. Website: www.ukbookworld.com/members/lesanscombe. E-mail: lesanscombe@lineone.net. Est: 1998. Private premises; Internet. Appointment necessary. Small general stock. Spec: Biography; Literature; Performing Arts. PR: £10–50.

KINETON

Kineton Books, ■ Bookshop, Southam Street, Kineton, CV35 0LP. Prop: J Neal. Tel: (01926) 640700. Website: www.kinetonbooks.co.uk. E-mail: josie@kinetonbooks.co.uk. Est: 1998. *Shop at:* 25 Shortacres, Kineton, Warwickshire, CV35 0LH. Open: **W:** 10:00–17:00; **Th:** 10:00–17:00; **F:** 10:00–17:00; **S:** 10:00–16:00. Medium stock. Spec: Annuals; Author - Milligan, Spike; Children's - General; Illustrated; Publishers - Ladybird Books. PR: £1–200.

LEAMINGTON SPA

Alexander's Books, 58 Greatheed Road, Leamington Spa, CV32 6ET.

Books do Furnish a Room, 18 Warwick St., Leamington Spa, CV32 5LL.

Nial Devitt Books, Merrion House, 217 Leam Terrace, Leamington Spa, CV31 1DW. Prop: Margaret & Nial Devitt. Tel: (01926) 315533. Website: www.devittbooks.com. E-mail: margaret@devittbooks.com. Est: 1974. Private premises; Internet and postal. Appointment necessary. Small general stock. Spec: Children's - General; Ex-Libris; Illustrated; Literature; Printing; Private Press. PR: £30–1,000. CC: AE; D; MC; V. Wide range. Bookbinding; valuations for probate & insurance. Corresp: French, Italian, German.

Elaine Lonsdale Books, 11 Church Terrace, Cubbington, Leamington Spa, CV32 7JX.

Portland Books Ltd., 7 Campion Terrace, Leamington Spa, CV32 4SU.

**Dealers who need to update their entry
should visit their page on
*www.sheppardsdirectories.com***

Derek Slavin Rare and Collectable Books, 4 Ravensgate House, 46 Willes Road, Leamington Spa, CV31 1BY. Tel: (01926) 882419. Fax: (01926) 882419. Website: www.leamingtonbooks.co.uk. E-mail: derek@leamingtonbooks.co.uk. Est: 1992. Private premises; Internet and postal. Contactable. Small stock. Spec: Antiquarian; Author - Aldin, Cecil; Author - Durrell, Lawrence; Author - Flint, William Russell; Author - Francis, Dick; Author - Greene, Graham; Author - Priestley, J.B.; Author - Rackham, Arthur; Author - Sitwell Family; Author - Wells, H.G.; Childen's - Illustrated; and others as listed in the Speciality Index. PR: £10–2,000. CC: JCB; MC; V. Mem: PBFA; Ibooknet.

RUGBY

J & M Books, 3 Pendred Road, Rugby, CV22 7BS. Prop: Jonathan & Amanda Sewell. Tel: (01788) 542482. Fax: (01788) 578688. Website: www.abebooks.com/home/jmbooks2. E-mail: jmbooks2@aol.com. Est: 1998. Office &/or bookroom; Internet and postal. Appointment necessary. Large stock. Spec: Countries - Melanesia; Countries - Mexico; Fiction - Crime, Detective, Spy, Thrillers; Fiction - Science Fiction; First Editions; Modern First Editions. PR: £1–2,000. CC: AE; E; MC; V; SW. Cata: 4 – quarterly.

STRATFORD–UPON–AVON

Chaucer Head Bookshop, ■ 21 Chapel Street, Stratford–upon–Avon, CV37 6EP. Prop: Richard & Vanessa James. Tel: (01789) 415691. Website: www.stratford-upon-avonbooks.co.uk. E-mail: books@stratford-upon-avonbooks.co.uk. Shop; open **M:** 10:00–18:00; **T:** 10:00–18:00; **W:** 10:00–18:00; **Th:** 10:10–18:00; **F:** 10:00–18:00; **S:** 10:00–18:00; **Su:** 11:00–16:00. Spec: Author - Corelli, Marie; Author - Shakespeare, William; Topography - Local. PR: £2–200. CC: MC; V; SW. Corresp: French.

Paul Meekins Books, 34 Townsend Road, Tiddington, Stratford–upon–Avon, CV37 7DE. Prop: Paul Meekins. Tel: (01789) 295086. Fax: (01789) 295086. Website: www.paulmeekins.co.uk. E-mail: paul@paulmeekins.co.uk. Est: 1989. Private premises; Internet and postal. Appointment necessary. Medium stock. Spec: Arms & Armour; Fashion & Costume; Firearms/Guns; History - General; History - Ancient; History - British; Medieval; Military; Military History; Rural Life; War - General; War - American Civil War; War - English Civil Wars; War - World War I; and others as listed in the Speciality Index. PR: £2–200. Cata: – By subject, and listed on website. See website for details of shows we attend.

The Stratford Bookshop, 45a Rother Street, Stratford–upon–Avon, CV37 6LT.

STUDLEY

Brewin Books Ltd., Doric House, 56 Alcester Road, Studley, B80 7NP. Director: K.A.F. Brewin. Tel: (01527) 854228. Fax: (01527) 852746. Website: www.brewinbooks.com. E-mail: admin@brewinbooks.com. Est: 1973. Office &/or bookroom; Internet and postal. Telephone first. Open: **M:** 09:00–17:00; **T:** 09:00–17:00; **W:** 09:00–17:00; **Th:** 09:00–17:00; **F:** 09:00–17:00. Closed for lunch: 13:00–14:00. Medium stock. Spec: Aviation; Genealogy; Motoring; Railways; Steam Engines; Topography - Local; Transport; Vintage Cars. Also, publishers of local history books. Cata: 1 – annually. VAT No: GB 705 0077 73.

WARWICK

Duncan M. Allsop, ■ 68 Smith Street, Warwick, CV34 4HU. Tel: (01926) 493266. Fax: (01926) 493266. Website: www.clique.co.uk/abe.htm. E-mail: duncan.allsop@btopenworld.com. Est: 1966. Shop; open **M:** 09:30–17:30; **T:** 09:30–17:30; **W:** 09:30–17:30; **Th:** 09:30–17:30; **F:** 09:30–17:30; **S:** 09:30–17:30. Large stock. Spec: Antiquarian; Bindings; Fine & Rare. PR: £5–3,000. CC: MC; V; SW, SO. Mem: ABA.

Anticus, 5 Bridge Street, Kineton, Warwick, CV35 0HP. Prop: M. & A.M. Valiadis. Tel: (01926) 640400. Est: 1980. Private premises; Very small general stock. Spec: Private Press; Publishers - Roundwood Press. PR: £1–100. CC: AE; D; JCB; MC; V. Corresp: French. Mem: PBFA. VAT No: GB 273 8090 44.

Eastgate Bookshop, 11 Smith Street, Warwick, CV34 4JA.

J. & R.K. Foort, 52 Station Road, Hatton, Warwick, CV35 8XJ.

Phillip Robbins, 3 Normandy Close, Hampton Magna, Warwick, CV35 8UB. Prop: Phillip John Robbins. Tel: (01926) 494368. E-mail: phillrobbins@yahoo.co.uk. Est: 1990. Private premises; Internet and postal. Contactable. Small stock. Spec: Author - Moore, John; Conservation; Entomology; Magic & Conjuring; Manuals - General; Manuals - Seamanship; Manuscripts; Marine Sciences; Maritime/Nautical; Natural History. PR: £3–50. Also, booksearch. Mem: PBFA.

WEST MIDLANDS

BILSTON

Christine M. Chalk (Old & Out, 17 Regent Street, Bilston, WV14 6AP. Tel: (01902) 403978. Fax: (01902) 403978. E-mail: chrischalkbks@gofornet.co.uk. Est: 1996. Private premises; postal business only. Small stock. Spec: Art; Artists; Decorative Art; Illustrated; Literature; Poetry. PR: £1–200. Cata: 1 – occasionally.

BIRMINGHAM

Afar Books International, 11 Church Place, 135 Edward Road, Balsall Heath, Birmingham, B12 9JQ. Prop: Alf Richardson. Tel: (0121) 440-3918. Est: 1990. Private premises; postal business only. Medium stock. Spec: Anthropology; Black Studies; Colonial; Countries - Africa; Countries - Caribbean, The; Countries - Egypt; Egyptology; Voyages & Discovery. PR: £1–300. Also, booksearch. Cata: 1. Only telephone evenings or Sunday.

Andromeda Bookshop, 2–5 Suffolk Street, Birmingham, B1 1LT.

Armchair Books, 11 Squires Gate Walk, Castle Vale, Birmingham, B35 7JN. Prop: I.M. & L.E. Loader. Tel: (0121) 747-0958. Est: 1988. Private premises; postal business only. Small general stock. PR: £1–150. Cata: 2 – a year. Also, booksearch..

Robin Doughty Fine Books, 100a Frederick Road, Stechford, Birmingham, B33 8AE. Tel: (0121) 783-7289. E-mail: robin.doughty@btinternet.com. Est: 1994. Postal business only. Small general stock. Spec: Antiquarian; Illustrated; Literature; Private Press; Topography - General. PR: £1–2,500. Mem: PBFA.

Elmfield Books, 24 Elmfield Crescent, Moseley, Birmingham, B13 9TN. Prop: Liz Palmer. Tel: (0121) 689-6246. Website: www.elmfieldbooks.co.uk. E-mail: elmfieldbooks@blueyonder.co.uk. Est: 1999. Private premises; Internet and postal. Small stock. Spec: Cookery/Gastronomy; Food & Drink; Illustrated; Natural History; Topography - General; Topography - Local. PR: £5–500. CC: MC; V. Mem: PBFA.

Haven Booksearch, 260 Haslucks Green Road, Shirley, Solihull, Birmingham, B90 2LR. (*) Prop: M.L. Prickett. Tel: (0121) 744-4671. Est: 1972. Private premises; appointment necessary. Also, booksearch. Corresp: French.

Heritage, P.O. Box 3075, Edgbaston, Birmingham, B15 2EW. Prop: Gill & Jem Wilyman. Tel: (0121) 440-2734. E-mail: heritagebook@aol.com. Est: 1985. Private premises; appointment necessary. Medium stock. Spec: Antiquarian; Atlases; Cartography; Ex-Libris; Heraldry; Illustrated; Motoring; Private Press; Royalty - General; Topography - Local. PR: £10–500. Mem: PBFA.

J.K. Maddison, 45 Seymour Close, Selly Wick Road, Birmingham, B29 7JD. Prop: J.K. Maddison & C.J. Murtagh. Tel: (0121) 472-8356. Website: www.anvilbookshalesowen.co.uk. E-mail: jkm@anvilbookshalesowen.co.uk. Private premises; postal business only. Spec: Canals/Inland Waterways; History - Industrial; Maritime/Nautical; Railways; Topography - Local; Transport. PR: £1–250. Also, a booksearch service. *Also at:* Anvil Books, Halesowen, W. Midlands. (q.v.).

Mood Indigo Books, 22 Sterling Court, 48 Newhall Hill, Birmingham, B1 3JN. Prop: K. Rajput. Tel: (07817) 225345. E-mail: moodindigobooks@hotmail.com. Private premises; Postal business only. Very small stock. Spec: Languages - Foreign; Literature; Religion - Islam. PR: £15–200. Also, Internet booksellers. Corresp: Farsi, French. *Also at:* Maryland, USA

Moseley Books, 7 Cornerstone, Birmingham, B13 8EN. Tel: (0121) 442 6062. Website: www.moseleybooks.co.uk. E-mail: john@moseleybooks.co.uk. Est: 2002. Storeroom; Internet and postal. Very small stock. Spec: Classical Studies; Philosophy; Politics. PR: £2–20.

Dealers who need to update their entry
should visit their page on
www.sheppardsdirectories.com

Taplin's Bookshop, 62 Station Road, Marston Green, Birmingham, B37 7BA.

Kelvin Watson, 616 Pershore Road, Birmingham, B29 7HG.

Whonotes, 65 Jacoby Place, Edgbaston, Birmingham, B5 7UW.

Stephen Wycherley, ■ 508 Bristol Road, Selly Oak, Birmingham, B29 6BD. Prop: Stephen & Elizabeth Wycherley. Tel: (0121) 471-1006. Est: 1971. Shop; open **Th**: 10:00–17:00; **F**: 10:00–17:00; **S**: 10:00–17:00. Large general stock. PR: £1–500. Winter opening: Mon-Sat 10:00–17:00, Wed closed 13:00.

BRIERLEY HILL

David Hill (Fine Glass), 96 Commonside, Pensnett, Brierley Hill, DY5 4AJ. T

COVENTRY

Armstrongs Books & Collectable, ■ 178 Albany Road, Earlsdon, Coventry, CV5 6NG. Prop: Colin Rowe Armstrong. Tel: (024) 7671-4344. Est: 1983. Shop; open **M**: 10:00–18:00; **T**: 10:00–18:00; **W**: 10:00–18:00; **Th**: 10:00–18:00; **F**: 10:00–18:00; **S**: 10:00–18:00. Medium stock. Spec: Comic Books & Annuals; Comics; Fiction - Science Fiction; First Editions; Publishers - Penguin. PR: £1–100.

Malcolm Harris (Books), 154 Avon Street, Coventry, CV2 3GP. Tel: (withheld). Private premises; postal business only. Very small stock. Spec: Autobiography; Fiction - Crime, Detective, Spy, Thrillers; Modern First Editions; Signed Editions; Theatre. Cata: 1 – as requested.

Silver Trees Books, Silver Trees Farm, Balsall St., Balsall Common, Coventry, CV7 7AR. Prop: Brian and Elaine Hitchens. Tel: (01676) 533143. Fax: (01676) 533143. Website: www.abebooks.com. E-mail: brian.hitchens@tesco.net. Private premises; postal business only. Telephone first. Small stock. Spec: Ceramics; Children's - General; Gardening; Military; Modern First Editions. PR: £3–1,500. CC: AE; JCB; MC; V; SW.

HALESOWEN

Anvil Books, ■ 52 Summer Hill, Halesowen, B63 3BU. Prop: J.K. Maddison & C.J. Murtagh. Tel: (0121) 550-0600. Website: www.anvilbookshalesowen.co.uk. E-mail: jkm@anvilbookshalesowen.co.uk. Est: 1997. Shop; Internet and postal. Telephone first. Open: **T**: 10:00–17:00. **Th**: 10:00–17:00. **S**: 10:00–17:00. Medium stock. Spec: Art; Author - Young, Francis Brett; Canals/Inland Waterways; Industry; Maritime/Nautical; Navigation; Railways; Shipbuilding; Topography - Local; Transport; PR: £1–200. Also, a booksearch service. *Also at:* J.K. Maddison, Birmingham. (q.v.).

Janus Books, Newlands, 9 Hayley Park, Hayley Green, Halesowen, B61 1EJ. Prop: Royston Thomas Slim. Tel: (0121) 550-4123. Est: 1968. Private premises; postal business only. Small stock. Also, book fair organiser – see prelims.

Jim Reading (Weaponry Books), 101 Alexandra Road, Hasbury, Halesowen, B63 4BP.

KINGSWINFORD

Wright Trace Books, 70 Ash Crescent, Kingswinford, DY6 8DH. Prop: Colin Micklewright and Pam Wright. Tel: (01384) 341211. E-mail: colinpams@cs.com. Est: 2001. Postal business only. Spec: Animals and Birds; Annuals; Dogs; Modern First Editions. Also, booksearch.

OLDBURY

Anthony Dyson, 57 St John's Road, Oldbury, B68 9SA. Tel: (0121) 544-5386. Est: 1973. Private premises; appointment necessary. Small stock. Spec: Fashion & Costume; Fiction - Crime, Detective, Spy, Thrillers; Literary Criticism; Literature. Cata: 1 – frequently.

SALTLEY

Albion Books, Beechcroft, 15 Woodlands Road, Saltley, B8 3AG. Prop: John Bentley. Tel: (0121) 328 2878. Est: 1999. Private premises; postal business only. Small stock. Spec: Military; Military History; War - General; War - World War I. PR: £1–100. Also, booksearch. Other subjects: origins of the Great War; international politics.

SMETHWICK

Bearwood Bookshop, Bearwood Indoor Market, 509 Bearwood Road, Smethwick, B66 4BE.

SOLIHULL

Fifth Element, 15 St. Lawrence Close, Knowle, Solihull, B93 0EU.

Helion & Company Ltd, 26 Willow Road, Solihull, B91 1UE. Tel: (0121) 705-3393. Fax: (0121) 711-4075. Website: www.helion.co.uk. E-mail: books@helion.co.uk. Est: 1992. Private premises; postal business only. Very large stock. Spec: Academic/Scholarly; Archaeology; Arms & Armour; Aviation; Countries - Germany; Firearms/Guns; History - General; History - 19th Century; History - American; History - Anarchism; History - Ancient; History - British; History - Byzantine; History - European; and others as listed in the Speciality Index. PR: £1–3,500. CC: AE; E; JCB; MC; V; SW. Also, a free booksearch service. Cata: 4 – Quarterly. Corresp: German, French, Spanish. VAT No: GB 797 4185 72.

SUTTON COLDFIELD

Bearwood Bookshop, P.O. Box 4606, Sutton Coldfield, B73 5DT. P

Patrick Walcot, 60 Sunnybank Road, Sutton Coldfield, B73 5RJ.

WALSALL

Margaret & Geoff Adkins, 7 Boscobel Road, Walsall, WS1 2PL. Prop: Margaret Adkins. Tel: (01922) 622641 (answerphone). Est: 1995. Private premises; postal business only. Small stock. Spec: Rural Life; Transport. PR: £1–100. Attends book fairs.

A.J. Mobbs, 65 Broadstone Avenue, Walsall, WS3 1JA. Tel: (01922) 477281. Fax: (01922) 477281. Website: www.mobbs.birdbooks.btinternet.co.uk. E-mail: mobbs.birdbooks@btinternet.com. Est: 1982. Private premises; Internet and postal. Appointment necessary. Small stock. Spec: Entomology; Herpetology; Natural History; Ornithology. PR: £1–200.

J. & M.A. Worrallo, 29 Trees Road, The Delves, Walsall, WS1 3JU.

WOLVERHAMPTON

Books & Bygones (Pam Taylor), ■ 19 Hollybush Lane, Penn, Wolverhampton, WV4 4JJ. Tel: (01902) 334020. Fax: (01902) 334747. Est: 1987. Shop; open **S:** 08:30–17:00; **Su:** 08:30–17:00. Medium stock. Spec: Authors - Women; Autographs; Dictionaries; Fiction - Science Fiction; History - General; History - Industrial; Magic & Conjuring; Performing Arts; Poetry; Scouts & Guides; Transport; Women. PR: £1–10. Open other times by appointment only.

R. & S. Crombie, 73 Griffiths Drive, Wednesfield, Wolverhampton, WV11 2JN. Tel: (01902) 733462. E-mail: royandsheila@rcrombie.freeserve.co.uk. Est: 1995. Private premises. Book fairs only. Telephone first. PR: £1–100.

Mogul Diamonds, 17 High Street, Albrighton, Wolverhampton, WV7 3JT.

The Old Bookshop, ■ 53 Bath Road, Wolverhampton, WV1 4EL. Prop: Kate Lee. Tel: (01902) 421055. E-mail: theoldbookshop@btopenworld.com. Est: 1967. Shop; open **M:** 13:00–15:00; **T:** 10:10–15:15; **W:** 10:00–15:00; **Th:** 10:00–15:00; **F:** 10:00–15:00; **S:** 10:00–17:00. Very large stock. Spec: Art; Embroidery; History - General; Literature; Needlework; Theology; Topography - Local. PR: £1–200. CC: MC; V.

WEST SUSSEX

ARUNDEL

Arundel Bookshop, ■ 10 High Street, Arundel, BN18 9AB. Prop: Mrs L.L Flowers. Tel: (01903) 882680. E-mail: kimsbookshop@hotmail.com. Est: 1977. Shop; open **M:** 10:00–17:00; **T:** 10:00–17:00; **W:** 10:00–17:00; **Th:** 10:00–17:00; **F:** 10:00–17:00; **S:** 10:00–17:30; **Su:** 10:30–17:00. Large stock. Spec: Aeronautics; Archaeology; Artists; Astrology; Author - General; Books about Books; Comics; Company History; Diaries; Folio Society, The; Food & Drink; Gardening; History - General; Letters; Literary Criticism; Literature; Music - General; Needlework; and others as listed in the Speciality Index. PR: £1–1,000. VAT No: GB 193 1791 43.

Baynton–Williams Gallery, 37a High Street, Arundel, BN18 9AB.

BILLINGSHURST

Books and Things, 58–62 High Street, Billingshurst, RH14 9NY. Prop: Jean Lawson. Tel: (01403) 785131. Est: 1976. PR: £1–100. Also, booksearch.

BOGNOR REGIS

Donald Gildea, 15 Shelley Road, Bognor Regis. Tel: (01243) 821266. Est: 1966. Private premises; appointment necessary. Small stock. Spec: Bibliography; Biography; Memoirs. PR: £10–100. Also, diaries, letters and antique needlework pictures. Cata: 1 – occasionally.

Meadowcroft Books, 21 Upper Bognor Road, Bognor Regis, PO21 1JA. Prop: Emma Laing & Anthony Parry. Tel: (01243) 868614 (24hr). Fax: (01243) 868714 (24hr). Website: www.meadowcroftbooks.demon.co.uk. E-mail: quotes@meadowcroftbooks.demon.co.uk. Est: 1996. Private premises; appointment necessary. Very small stock. PR: £1–50. CC: MC; V; SW. Primarily a booksearch service. VAT No: GB 699 0227 01.

BOLNEY

Mary Sharpe, Thornfield, 1 Springfield Cottages, Top Street, Bolney, RH17 5PN. Tel: (01444) 881217. Est: 1995. Private premises; postal business only. Small general stock. Spec: Author - Austen, Jane; Author - Bloomsbury Group, The; Author - Brontes, The; Author - Burney, Fanny; Author - Eliot, G.; Author - Gaskell, E.; Author - Hardy, Thomas; Author - Potter, Beatrix; Author - Woolf, Virginia; Children's - General; Illustrated; Literature; Topography - General. Attends bookfairs. Cata: 2 – to 3 a year. Mem: PBFA.

CHICHESTER

Canon Gate Bookshop (formerly, 28 South Street, Chichester, PO19 1EL.

The Chichester Bookshop, 39 Southgate, Chichester, West Sussex, PO19 1DP. Prop: Nicholas Howell. Tel: (01243) 785473. E-mail: chibooks@fsbdial.co.uk. Est: 1994. Spec: Railways; Topography - Local. Also, booksearch.

Chichester Gallery, 39 East Street, Chichester, PO19 1HX.

Peter Hancock, 40–41 West Street, Chichester, PO19 1RP. Tel: (01243) 786173. Fax: (01243) 778865. Est: 1969. Storeroom. Open: **T:** 10:00–17:30; **W:** 10:00–17:30; **Th:** 10:00–17:30; **F:** 10:00–17:30. Closed for lunch: 13:00–14:00. Small general stock. PR: £1–300. CC: AE; E; JCB; MC; V. VAT No: GB 192 8554 28.

Dealers who need to update their entry
should visit their page on
www.sheppardsdirectories.com

WEST SUSSEX

Stride & Son, Southdown House, St. John's Street, Chichester, PO19 1XQ. Prop: Mark Hewitt & others. Tel: (01243) 780207. Fax: (01243) 786713. Website: www.stridesauctions.co.uk. E-mail: enquiries@stridesauctions.co.uk. Est: 1890. Office &/or bookroom; Internet and postal. Appointment necessary. Open: **W:** 09:30–01:00. Spec: Advertising; Anthropology; Antiquarian; Archaeology; Architecture; Arms & Armour; Art; Atlases; Author - General; Autobiography; Churchilliana. PR: £10–10,000. CC: MC; V. Cata: 3 – 3 Sales per year. Mem: RICS. VAT No: GB 193 0045 83.

COWFOLD

Michael Phelps, Allfreys House, Bolney Road, Cowfold, RH13 8AZ. Tel: (01403) 864049. Fax: (01403) 864730. E-mail: phelobooks@tiscali.co.uk. Est: 1974. Spec: Aeronautics; Alchemy; Astronomy; Aviation; Botany; Brewing; Chemistry; Engineering; Geology; Herbalism; Homeopathy; Hydrography; Mathematics; Medicine; Medicine - History of; Microscopy; Mineralogy; Mining; Natural History; Natural Sciences; and others as listed in the Speciality Index. PR: £10–100.

EAST GRINSTEAD

The Bookshop, ■ Tudor House, 22 High Street, East Grinstead, RH19 3AW. Prop: J. & H. Pye. Tel: (01342) 322669. Shop; open **M:** 09:00–17:30; **T:** 09:00–17:30; **W:** 09:00–17:30; **Th:** 09:00–17:30; **F:** 09:00–17:30; **S:** 09:00–17:30. Medium stock. Spec: History - General. CC: AE; D; MC; V. Mem: BA. VAT No: GB 472 9663 08.

GORING–BY–SEA

Barry Jones, Daymer Cottage, 28 Marine Crescent, Goring–by–Sea, BN12 4JF. Tel: (01903) 244655. Fax: (01903) 244655. Est: 1990. Private premises; appointment necessary. Small stock. Spec: Buses/Trams; Canals/Inland Waterways; Railways; Traction Engines; Transport. Appointments only between 09:00 and 21:00. Cata: 1 – a year on railways.

HASSOCKS

Doro Books, Lower Sands, Brighton Road, Hassocks, BN6 9LY. Prop: D. & R. Franklin. Tel: (01273) 843293. Est: 1985. Private premises; postal business only. Very large stock. Spec: Company History; Illustrated; Industry; Juvenile. PR: £1–500. Cata: 1 – occasionally. Corresp: Most European. Mem: PBFA.

Post Mortem Books, 58 Stanford Ave, Hassocks, BN6 8JH. Prop: Ralph Spurrier. Tel: (01273) 843066. Fax: (0870) 161-7332. Website: www.myebsite.com/pmbooks. E-mail: ralph@pmbooks.demon.co.uk. Est: 1979. Spec: Fiction - Crime, Detective, Spy, Thrillers. PR: £5–100.

B. & C. Seago, Flat 2, 107 Keymer Road, Keymer, Hassocks, BN68 8QL. Prop: Brian and Chris Seago. Tel: (01273) 841429. Est: 1974. Private premises; appointment necessary. Small general stock. PR: £20–1,000. Also, prints and maps.

HAYWARDS HEATH

Fine Art, P.O. Box 461, Haywards Heath, RH17 6YY. Prop: Robert Walker. Tel: (01444) 401100. Fax: (01444) 401100. Website: www.fineart.tm. E-mail: sheppards@fineart.tm. Est: 1991. Private premises; Internet and postal. Appointment necessary. Open: **M:** 10:00–21:00; **T:** 10:00–21:00; **W:** 10:00–21:00; **Th:** 10:00–21:00; **F:** 10:00–21:00; **S:** 10:00–17:00; **Su:** 10:00–12:00. Small general stock. Spec: Antiquarian; Arts, The; Bindings; Colour-Plate; Early Imprints; First Editions; Fore-Edge Paintings; Illuminated Manuscripts; Illustrated; Incunabula; Limited Editions; Natural History; Topography - General; Topography - Local. PR: £100–20,000. CC: AE; MC; V.

Halcyon Bookshop, ■ 11 The Broadway, Haywards Heath, RH16 3AQ. Prop: Jonathan Wilson. Tel: (01444) 412785. Fax: (01444) 443509. E-mail: halcyonbookshop@aol.com. Est: 1902. Shop; open **M:** 09:30–17:30; **T:** 09:30–17:30; **W:** 09:30–17:30; **Th:** 09:30–17:30; **F:** 09:30–17:30; **S:** 09:30–17:30. Small general stock. PR: £1–150. CC: MC; V.

HORSHAM

Horsham Bookshop, ■ 4 Park Place (off Piries Place), Horsham, RH12 1DG. Prop: Nick, Tom & Christine Costin. Tel: (01403) 252187. Website: www.horshambookshop.com. E-mail: sales@horshambookshop.com. Est: 1986. Shop; open **T:** 09:30–17:00; **W:** 09:30–17:00; **Th:** 09:30–17:00; **F:** 09:30–17:00; S: 09:30–17:00. Very large general stock. Spec: Antiquarian; Art; Aviation; Bindings; Biography; History - General; History - Local; Military; Motoring; Topography - Local. PR: £10–10,000. CC: MC; V; SW. Mem: PBFA.

Merlin Books, P.O. Box 153, Horsham, RH12 2YG. Prop: Mike Husband. Tel: (01403) 257626. Fax: (01403) 257626. Website: www.merlinbooks.com. E-mail: info@merlinbooks.com. Est: 1990. Private premises; Internet and postal. Telephone first. Very small stock. Spec: Motorbikes. PR: £2–60. CC: E; JCB; MC; V. Also, a booksearch service. Cata: 8.

Murray and Kennett, Bookseller, 102 The Bishopric, Horsham, RH12 1QN.

LANCING

Paul Evans Books, 13 Berriedale Drive, Sompting, Lancing, BN15 OLE.

LITTLEHAMPTON

Buckland Books, Holly Tree House, 18 Woodlands Road, Littlehampton, BN17 5PP. Prop: Mr. Chris Blanchett. Tel: (01903) 717648. Fax: (01903) 717648. Website: www.tiles.org/pages/bookshlf.htm. E-mail: cblanchett@lineone.net. Est: 1991. Private premises; postal business only. Appointment necessary. Small stock. Spec: Antiques; Architecture; Building & Construction; Ceramics; Collecting; Decorative Art; Interior Design. PR: £2–300. CC: MC; V; SW. Also, new books from around the world. Cata: 2 – 6 monthly. VAT No: GB 630 8660 43.

JB Books & Collectables, 14 Kingsmead, Thornlea Park, Littlehampton, BN17 7QS. Prop: Mrs J. Brittain. Tel: (01903) 725819. Fax: (01903) 725819. Website: www.jbbooks.co.uk. E-mail: jan@jbbooks.co.uk. Est: 1997. Private premises; Internet and postal. Open: **M:** 09:00–17:17; **T:** 09:00–17:00; **W:** 09:00–17:00; **Th:** 09:00–17:00; **F:** 09:00–17:00; **S:** 09:00–17:00. Closed for lunch: 13:00–14:00. Small general stock. Spec: Children's - General; Illustrated. PR: £1–500. CC: AE; MC; V; SW. Mem: PBFA.

Chris Adam Smith Modern First, 9 Western Road, Littlehampton, BN17 5NP. Tel: (01903) 722392. Fax: (01903) 722392. Website: www.adamsmithbooks.com. E-mail: chrisadamsmith@btinternet.com. Est: 1993. Private premises; Internet and postal. Appointment necessary. Small stock. Spec: Children's - General; Fiction - Crime, Detective, Spy, Thrillers; Fiction - Historical; Fiction - Science Fiction; Maritime/Nautical; Modern First Editions. PR: £10–4,000. CC: AE; E; JCB; MC; SW.

South Downs Book Service, Garden Cottage, 39c Arundel Road, Littlehampton, BN17 7BY. Prop: Ms. J.A. Bristow. Tel: (01903) 723401. Mon. Est: 1994. Private premises; postal business only. Appointment necessary. Small stock. Spec: Academic/Scholarly; Antiquarian; Diaries; Ecclesiastical History & Architecture; Economics; History - Industrial; History - Local; History - National; Maritime/Nautical; Social History. PR: £4–400.

MIDHURST

Beech Rural Books, 7 Station Yard, Elsted, Midhurst, GU29 0JT. P

Wheeler's Bookshop, ■ Red Lion Street, Midhurst, GU29 9PB. Prop: Mr. Simon Wheeler. Tel: (01730) 817666. Website: www.abebooks.com/home/SIMONWHEELER. E-mail: info@wheelersbookshop.co.uk. Shop. Medium stock. CC: E; MC; V. Also, booksearch.

PETWORTH

Tim Boss, North Street, Petworth, GU28 0DD. Tel: (01798) 343170. Est: 1993. Market stand/stall; postal business only. Small stock. PR: £1–350. Also, 10,000 inexpensive prints; and bookfairs.

Muttonchop Manuscripts, ■ The Playhouse Gallery, Lombard Street, Petworth, GU28 0AG. Prop: Roger Clarke. Tel: (01798) 344471. Fax: (01798) 344471. E-mail: rogmutton@aol.com. Est: 1992. Shop; open **T:** 10:00–16:00; **W:** 10:00–16:00; **Th:** 10:00–16:00; **F:** 10:00–16:00; **S:** 10:00–17:00. Medium stock. Spec: Agriculture; Antiquarian; Bibliography; Bindings; Books about Books; Erotica; Fables; Farming & Livestock; Firearms/Guns; Glamour; Manuscripts; Odd & Unusual; Traction Engines; Transport. PR: £5–5,000. CC: D; E; JCB; MC; V; SW; S. Corresp: French. Mem: PBFA. VAT No: GB 704 6864 26.

Petworth Antique Market (Bookroom), East Street, Petworth, GU28 0AB.

PLAISTOW

Explorer Books, Fallow Chase, Durfold Wood, Plaistow, RH14 OPL. Prop: J.I. & S.J. Simper. Tel: (01483) 200286. Fax: (01483) 200286. E-mail: explbooks@aol.com. Est: 1985. Spec: Countries - Antarctic, The; Countries - Arctic, The; Countries - Greenland; Countries - Polar; Travel - Polar; Voyages & Discovery. PR: £10–1,000.

SHOREHAM–BY–SEA

Bookworms of Shoreham, 4 High Street, Shoreham–by–Sea, BN43 5DA.

Sansovino Books, 9 Mill Lane, Shoreham–By–Sea, BN43 5AG. Prop: Q. & R. Barry. Tel: (01273) 455753. Est: 1991. Storeroom; appointment necessary. Medium stock. Spec: First Editions; Literature; Maritime/Nautical; Military; Private Press. PR: £5–200. Also, booksearch. Cata: 3 – general. *Also at:* Sansovino, Stokelsy, Cleveland.

A.C. Seddon, 53 Old Fort Road, Shoreham–by–Sea, BN43 5RL. Tel: (01273) 461501. Est: 1978. Private premises; appointment necessary. Small stock. Spec: Author - Swinburne, A.C.; Literature; Modern First Editions; Vintage Paperbacks.

STEYNING

dgbbooks, 15 Ingram Road, Steyning, BN44 3PF. Prop: Denise Bennett. Tel: (01903) 814895. E-mail: dgbbooks@talk21.com. Internet. Spec: Authors - Women; Biography; Fiction - General. PR: £5–50.

WALDERTON

John Henly, Brooklands, Walderton, Chichester, PO18 9EE. Tel: (023) 9263-1426. Fax: (023) 9263-1544. E-mail: johnhenly1@compuserve.com. Est: 1986. Private premises; postal business only. Appointment necessary. Spec: Geology; Mineralogy; Natural History; Palaeontology. CC: MC; V. Cata: 4. Mem: PBFA. VAT No: GB 582 5689 92.

WORTHING

Badgers Books, ■ 8–10 Gratwicke Road, Worthing, BN11 4BH. Prop: Ray Potter & Meriel Cocks. Tel: (01903) 211816. Est: 1982. Shop; open **M:** 09:00–17:30; **T:** 09:00–17:30; **W:** 09:00–17:30; **Th:** 09:00–17:30; **F:** 09:00–17:30; **S:** 09:00–18:00. Large general stock. CC: E; JCB; MC; V.

Mrs. Mary Corin, 29 Shirley Drive, Worthing, BN14 9AY.

Sheila Driver, 14 Gorse Avenue, Worthing, BN14 9PG.

Kim's Bookshop, ■ 19 Crescent Road, Worthing, BN11 1RL. Prop: Mrs. M.L. Francombe & Mrs. L.L. Flowers. Tel: (01903) 206282. E-mail: kimsbookshop@hotmail.com. Est: 1972. Shop; open **M:** 09:30–17:30; **T:** 09:30–17:30; **W:** 09:30–17:30; **Th:** 09:30–17:30; **F:** 09:30–17:30; **S:** 09:00–17:30. Very large stock. Spec: Antiques; Arts, The; Music - General; Natural History; Transport. PR: £1–1,000. Also, sheet music. Book stock approx 45,000 titles. *Also at:* 10 High Street, Arundel, West Sussex BN18 9AB.

Optimus Books Ltd, ■ 8 Ann Street, Worthing, BN11 1NX. Tel: (01903) 205895. Fax: (01903) 213438. E-mail: optimusbooks@easynet.co.uk. Est: 1975. Shop; Internet and postal. Open: **M:** 09:00–17:30; **T:** 09:00–17:30; **W:** 09:00–17:30; **Th:** 09:00–17:30; **F:** 09:00–17:30; S: 09:00–17:30. Medium general stock. CC: AE; MC; V. Mem: PBFA. VAT No: GB 193 7839 11.

Satara Books, 105 Hayling Rise, High Salvington, Worthing, BN13 3AQ. Prop: Phyl Tate. Tel: (01903) 267173. Est: 1987. Private premises; postal business only. Very small stock. Spec: Autobiography; Children's - General; Cinema/Film; First Editions; Guide Books; Modern First Editions; Topography - General; Topography - Local; Windmills & Watermills. PR: £10–200. Attends Southampton Book Fairs.

Jamie Sturgeon, 14 Longlands, Worthing, BN14 9NT. Tel: (01903) 201910. E-mail: jamie.s@clara.net. Private premises; appointment necessary. Small stock. Spec: Fiction - Crime, Detective, Spy, Thrillers. PR: £1–100. Also, a booksearch service. Cata: 4 – a year.

Searching for a title - and cannot find it on any Internet database?
Then try **SheppardsBooksearch**

By selecting the subject classification – the request goes to all dealers who major in that subject.

WEST YORKSHIRE

BATLEY

Vintage Motorshop, ■ 749 Bradford Road, Batley, WF17 8HZ. Prop: R. & C. Hunt. Tel: (01924) 470773. Fax: (01924) 470773. Website: www.vintagemotorshop.co.uk. E-mail: books@vintagemotorshop.co.uk. Est: 1976. Shop; open **Th:** 11:00–17:00; **F:** 11:00–17:00; **S:** 11:00–17:00. Medium stock. Spec: Magic & Conjuring; Motorbikes; Motoring; Traction Engines; Transport; Vintage Cars. PR: £1–30. CC: MC; V.

BRADFORD

Derek Bryant Brooks, 592 Thornton Road, Thornton, Bradford, BD13 3PS.

The Idle Booksellers, 7 Town Lane, Idle, Bradford, BD10 8PR. Prop: Ros Stinton & Michael Compton. Tel: (01274) 613737. E-mail: idlebooks@bd108pr.freeserve.co.uk. Est: 1990. Spec: Author - Brontes, The; Author - Gissing, George; Genealogy; Topography - Local. PR: £1–600.

Woodbine Books, 15 Stone Street, Bradford, BD15 9JR. Prop: Colin Neville. Tel: (01274) 824759. Website: www.abebooks.com/home/woodbine. E-mail: woodbine@blueyonder.co.uk. Private premises; Internet and postal. Appointment necessary. Very small stock. Spec: Artists; Author - Webb, Mary; Bindings; Engraving; Fine & Rare; First Editions; History - General; Illustrated; Natural History; Poetry; Private Press; Rural Life; Signed Editions. PR: £5–700. Mem: PBFA; FPBA; PLA.

BRIGHOUSE

Northern Herald Books, 5 Close Lea, Rastrick, Brighouse, HD6 3AR. Prop: R.W. Jones. Tel: (01484) 721845. E-mail: bobjones_nhb@talk21.com. Est: 1985. Private premises; postal business only. Large stock. Spec: Academic/Scholarly; Economics; Free Thought; Politics; Social History; Social Sciences; Socialism; Trade Unions; Women. PR: £1–100. Corresp: French. Mem: PBFA.

HALIFAX

M.R. Clark, 18 Balmoral Place, Halifax, HX1 2BG. Tel: (01422) 357475. Est: 1981. Private premises; appointment necessary. Medium stock. Spec: Gardening; Natural History. Also, booksearch. Cata: 4 – on gardening.

Bruce Holdsworth Books, 26 Lane Ends Green, Hipperholme, Halifax, HX3 8EZ. Prop: Bruce Holdsworth. Tel: (01422) 203307. Website: www.bruceholdsworthbooks.com. E-mail: Bruce@bruceholdsworthbooks.com. Est: 1993. Private premises; Internet and postal. Medium stock. Spec: Art; Art History; Art Reference; Arts, The; Crafts; Decorative Art; Fine Art; Sculpture. PR: £15–5,000. CC: AE; JCB; MC; V. Also, booksearch. Cata: 12 – Monthly. Mem: PBFA. VAT No: GB 686 9604 74.

HAWORTH

Hatchard & Daughters, 91 Main Street, Haworth.

HEBDEN BRIDGE

The Architecture Bookshop, Bridge Mill, Bridge Gate, Hebden Bridge, HX7 8EX.

Christopher I. Browne, Hawdon Hall, Hebden Bridge, HX7 7AL. Tel: (01422) 844744. Fax: (01422) 844744. E-mail: sales@gilbertandsullivanonline.com. Spec: Music - Opera.

Dealers who need to update their entry should visit their page on
www.sheppardsdirectories.com

The Glass Key, ■ 16 Market Street, Hebden Bridge, HX7 6AA. Prop: James Fraser. Tel: (01422) 846265. E-mail: jfraser@glasskey.prestel.co.uk. Est: 1991. Shop; open **F:** 11:30–17:30; **S:** 11:30–17:30; **Su:** 11:30–17:30. Small stock. Spec: Fiction - Crime, Detective, Spy, Thrillers; First Editions; Literature. PR: £1–100. Cata: 2 – on specialities. Corresp: French.

Hatchard & Daughters, 56 Market Street, Hebden Bridge, HX7 6HJ.

HOLMFIRTH

Beardsell Books, ■ Toll House Bookshop, 32–34 Huddersfield Road, Holmfirth, HD9 2JS. Prop: Elaine V. Beardsell. Tel: (01484) 686541. Fax: (01484) 688406. Website: www.toll-house.co.uk. E-mail: tollhouse.bookshop@virgin.net. Est: 1977. Shop; Internet and postal. Open: **M:** 09:00–17:00; **T:** 09:00–17:00; **W:** 09:00–17:00; **Th:** 09:00–17:00; **F:** 09:00–17:00; **S:** 09:00–17:30; **Su:** 13:00–17:00. Spec: Antiquarian; History - General; History - Local. CC: MC; V. Mem: PBFA; BA.

Daisy Lane Books, ■ Towngate, Holmfirth, HD9 1HA. Prop: J. & B. Townsend–Cardew. Tel: (01484) 688409. Website: www.area5.co.uk/daisy-lane-books. Shop; open **M:** 09:00–17:00; **T:** 09:00–17:00; **W:** 09:00–17:00; **Th:** 09:00–17:00; **F:** 09:00–17:00; **S:** 09:00–17:00; **Su:** 09:00–17:00. Very large general stock. Winter open: 09:30–16:30. Monday to Sunday.

Madalyn S. Jones, Horsegate Hill House, 3 Town End Road, Wooldale, Holmfirth, HD9 1AH. Prop: Madalyn S. Jones. Tel: (01484) 681580. Fax: (01484) 681580. Website: www.madalynjonesbooks.co.uk. E-mail: madalyn@jonesbooks.freeserve.co.uk. Est: 1979. Private premises; Internet and postal. Appointment necessary. Very small stock. Spec: Sculpture. PR: £1–500. Also, booksearch service & some P.B.F.A. fairs attended. Mem: PBFA.

HUDDERSFIELD

Aphra Books, Briar Cottage, 2 Top of the Hill, Thurstonland, Huddersfield, HD4 6XZ.

Childrens Bookshop, ■ 37/39 Lidget Street, Lindley, Huddersfield, HD3 3JF. Prop: Sonia & Barry Benster. Tel: (01484) 658013. Fax: (01484) 460020. Website: www.ukbookworld.com/members/benster. E-mail: barry@hudbooks.demon.co.uk. Est: 1975. Shop; open **M:** 09:00–17:30; **T:** 09:00–17:30; **W:** 09:00–17:30; **Th:** 09:00–17:30; **F:** 09:00–17:30; **S:** 09:00–17:00. Small stock. Spec: Author - Dickens, Charles; Children's - General; Medicine; Medicine - History of. CC: JCB; MC. Mem: BA.

William H. Roberts, The Crease, 113 Hill Grove, Salendine Nook, Huddersfield, HD3 3TL.

Susan Taylor Books, Briar Cottage, 2 Top of the Hill, Thurstonland, Huddersfield, HD4 6XZ. Tel: (01484) 662120. E-mail: richard@mosleyr.freeserve.co.uk. Est: 1986. Private premises; postal business only. Appointment necessary. Small stock. Spec: Women. PR: £1–150. Also, a booksearch service. Corresp: French, German. *Also at:* these premises - Aphra Books (q.v.).

Nick Tozer Railway Books, 62 Parkgate, Huddersfield, HD4 7NG. Prop: Nick Tozer. Tel: (01484) 663811 (9am-). Fax: (01484) 663811. Website: www.railwaybook.com. E-mail: nick@railwaybook.com. Est: 1997. Postal business only. Medium stock. Spec: Railways. PR: £1–50. Also, booksearch.

ILKLEY

Rupert Cavendish Books, 10 Elmete Grange, Main Street, Menston, Ilkley, LS29 6LA. Tel: (01943) 884228. E-mail: 100654.463@compuserve.com. Est: 1994. Private premises; postal business only. Small stock. Spec: Sport - General. PR: £5–500.

Greenroom Books, 9 St. James Road, Ilkley, LS29 9PY.

Skyrack Books, ■ 20 Skipton Road, Ilkley, LS29 9EJ. Prop: Steven Dyke. Tel: (01943) 601598. Fax: (01943) 601598. Est: 2000. Shop; open **T:** 10:00–17:00; **W:** 10:00–17:00; **Th:** 10:00–17:00; **F:** 10:00–17:00; **S:** 10:00–17:00. Closed for lunch: 13:00–14:00. Medium stock. Spec: Canals/Inland Waterways; History - Industrial; History - Local; Railways; Topography - Local. PR: £1–100. Also, booksearch. And stocks on Yorkshire. Cata: 1 – occasional. Mem: BA.

Mark Sutcliffe, 14 St. John's Avenue, Addingham, Ilkley, LS29 0QB. Tel: (01943) 830117. Fax: (01943) 830117. Website: www.abebooks.com/home/marksutcliffe/. E-mail: msfe@btinternet.com. Est: 1996. Private premises; Internet and postal. Appointment necessary. Very small stock. Spec: Author - Blake, N.; Author - Carr, John Dickson; Author - Crofts, Freeman Wills; Fiction - Crime, Detective, Spy, Thrillers; First Editions. PR: £5–3,000. CC: JCB; MC; V. Cata: – Detective fiction, some modern firsts and children's. Mem: PBFA.

KEIGHLEY

Birchwood Books, ■ 39 Church Street, Keighley, BD22. Tel: (01535) 692349. E-mail: andrew.darling@tesco.net. Est: 2001. Shop; open **Th:** 10:00–17:00; **F:** 10:00–17:00; **S:** 10:00–16:00. Large stock. Spec: Music - General; Music - Folk & Irish Folk.

KIRKSTALL

The Bookshop, Kirkstall, ■ 10 Commercial Road, Kirkstall, Leeds, LS5 3AQ. Prop: R.A. & P.P. Brook. Tel: (0113) 278-0937. Fax: (0113) 267-2889. E-mail: book.shop@btinternet.com. Est: 1982. Shop; open **M:** 10:15–17:30; **T:** 10:15–17:30; **W:** 10:15–15:30; **Th:** 10:15–17:00; **F:** 10:15–17:30; **S:** 10:15–17:30. Large general stock. Spec: Antiquarian. PR: £1–2,000. CC: MC; V.

LEEDS

Almar Books, 50 Vesper Road, Kirkstall, Leeds, LS5 3NX. Prop: Alan & Marjorie Jones. Tel: (0113) 275-5611. Est: 1974. Private premises; postal business only. Small stock. Spec: Bindings; Fine & Rare; First Editions; Illustrated; Literature. PR: £5–500. Mem: PBFA.

Bates & Hindmarch, 2 Cumberland Road, Headingley, Leeds, LS6 2EF. Prop: Jeffery Bates. Tel: (0113) 278-3306. Website: www.abebooks.com. E-mail: jefferybates@aol.com. Est: 1987. Private premises; appointment necessary. Small stock. Spec: Antiquarian; Bindings; Cartoons; Countries - Afghanistan; Countries - Asia; Countries - Central Asia; Countries - India; Countries - Tibet; Sport - Big Game Hunting; Travel - Asia. PR: £20–1,000. CC: AE; JCB; MC. Cata: 6. Mem: PBFA. VAT No: GB 417 9947 06.

John Blanchfield, 5 Stanmore Place, Leeds, LS4 2RR. Prop: John Blanchfield. Tel: (0113) 274-2406. E-mail: john@blanchfield.demon.co.uk. Est: 1984. Private premises; Internet and postal. Appointment necessary. Medium stock. Spec: Academic/Scholarly; History - Industrial; Industry. PR: £5–500. CC: JCB; V. Cata: 1 – issued October. Mem: PBFA. VAT No: GB 405 5743 61.

John Bonner, 82a Allerton Grange Rise, Moortown, Leeds, LS17 6LH. Tel: (0113) 269-0213. E-mail: johnbonner@btinternet.com. Est: 1990. Private premises; postal business only. Small stock. Spec: Aviation; Biography; Military. PR: £1–100.

The Book Academy, 14 Eldon Terrace, Leeds, LS2 9AB.

Bryony Books, 11 Woodhall Avenue, Leeds, LS5 3LH. Prop: Joan & Bill Martin. Tel: (0113) 258-7283. Est: 1976. Private premises; appointment necessary. Very small stock. Spec: Children's - General. PR: £2–100.

Coracle Books, 88 Ash Road, Leeds, LS6 3HD. Prop: Paul Hudson. Tel: (0113) 278-2531. Fax: (0113) 278-2531. E-mail: madmountaineer@madasafish.com. Est: 1980. Private premises; postal business only. Appointment necessary. Very small stock. Spec: Alpinism/Mountaineering; Poetry; Sport - Climbing & Trekking. PR: £5–80. Cata: 1.

Elephant Books, ■ off Midland Road, Nr. Hyde Park Corner, Leeds, LS6 1BQ. Prop: Neil Whitworth. Tel: (0113) 274-4021. Est: 1987. Shop; open **M:** 10:00–18:00; **T:** 10:00–18:00; **W:** 10:00–18:00; **Th:** 10:00–18:00; **F:** 10:00–18:00; **S:** 10:00–18:00. Large stock. Spec: Arts, The; Philosophy; Psychology/Psychiatry. PR: £1–100. CC: AE; D; E; JCB; MC; V; SO.

Find That Book, 74 Oxford Avenue, Guiseley, Leeds, LS20 9BX. Prop: David Herries. Tel: (01943) 872699. Website: www.findthatbook.demon.co.uk. E-mail: david@findthatbook.demon.co.uk. Est: 1991. Private premises; postal business only. Also, booksearch.

Leeds Bookseller, 3 Wedgewood Drive, Roundhay, Leeds, LS8 1EF. Prop: J.B. Wilkinson. Tel: (0113) 266-7183. Est: 1980. Private premises; postal business only. Very small stock. Spec: Academic/Scholarly; Languages - National; Palaeography. PR: £1–8.

The Old Book Company, Christopher Court, 4 Christopher Road, Leeds, LS6 2JX.

Parkfield Music, 178 Otley Road, West Park, Leeds, LS16 5LG.

Peregrine Books (Leeds), 27 Hunger Hills Avenue, Horsforth, Leeds, LS18 5JS. Prop: J. & M.A. Whitaker. Tel: (0113) 258-5495. Est: 1986. Private premises; appointment necessary. Small stock. Spec: Natural History; Travel - General. PR: £5–3,000. Cata: 1 – occasionally.

Use **Sheppard's Booksearch**
to offer a title for sale

By selecting the subject classification – the offer goes to all dealers who major in that subject.

David Spenceley Books, 75 Harley Drive, Leeds, LS13 4QY. Prop: David Spenceley. Tel: (0113) 257-0715 (24h. Website: www.abebooks.com/home/davidspenceleybooks. E-mail: davidspenceley@email.com. Est: 1990. Private premises; postal business only. Appointment necessary. Medium stock. Spec: Academic/Scholarly; Arms & Armour; Country Houses; Ecclesiastical History & Architecture; History - British; History - Middle Ages; History - Renaissance, The; History - Women; Languages - National; Medieval; War - English Civil Wars. PR: £5–200. Also, booksearch.

Graham Sykes, 81 Gledhow Park Grove, Leeds, LS7 4JW. Tel: (0113) 262-1547. Est: 1985. Private premises; postal business only. Small general stock. Spec: Fine Art; First Editions; History - General; Natural History; Palaeontology; Photography; Topography - General; Travel - General. Cata: 3 – a year on photography. Mem: PBFA.

Woodlands Books, 65 Gledhow Wood Road, Leeds, LS8 4DG. Prop: Bill & Valerie Astbury. Tel: (0113) 266-7834. Est: 1986. Private premises; postal business only. Small stock. Spec: Brewing; Music - General; Music - Musicians; Public Houses. PR: £2–150. Cata: 2 – on specialities.

MIRFIELD

D. & M. Books, 49 Park Drive, Mirfield, WF14 9HN. Prop: Daniel & Mary Hanson. Tel: (01924) 495768. Fax: (01924) 491267. Website: www.dandmbooks.com. E-mail: daniel@dandmbooks.com. Est: 1989. Spec: Cartoons; Children's - General; Comic Books & Annuals; Comics. PR: £10–1,000.

NORMANTON

Andrew Warrender, 4 West Street, Normanton, WF6 2AP.

OTLEY

Chevin Books, 19 Manor Square, Otley, LS21 3AP. Tel: (01943) 466599. E-mail: chevinbooks@yahoo.co.uk. Est: 1996. Spec: Architecture; Art; Fiction - Crime, Detective, Spy, Thrillers; Fiction - Fantasy, Horror; Fiction - Science Fiction; Folio Society, The; History - General; Literature; Military History; Natural History; Sport - General; Topography - General; Topography; and others as listed in the Speciality Index. PR: £1–200.

SHIPLEY

Derek Bryant Books, 592 Thornton Road, Thornton, Bradford, Shipley, BD13 3PS.

TODMORDEN

The Border Bookshop, ■ 61a & 63 Halifax Road, Todmorden, OL14 5BB. Prop: Victor H. Collinge. Tel: (01706) 814721. Website: www.borderbookshop.co.uk. E-mail: collinge@borderbookshop.fsnet.co.uk. Est: 1980. Shop; open **M:** 10:00–17:00. **W:** 10:00–17:00; **Th:** 10:00–17:00; **F:** 10:00–17:00; **S:** 10:00–17:00. Closed for lunch: 13:00–14:00. Large general stock. Spec: Children's - General; Comic Books & Annuals; Comics; Nostalgia; Periodicals & Magazines; Sport - Cricket; Sport - Football (Soccer). CC: E; JCB; MC; V. Also, new books, book tokens & book ordering service. Corresp: French. Mem: PBFA.

John Eggeling Books, Claremont South, Burnley Road, Todmorden, OL14 5LH. Prop: John Eggeling. Tel: (01706) 816487. Fax: (01706) 816487. Website: www.ndirect.co.uk/~todmordenbooks. E-mail: todmordenbooks@ndirect.co.uk. Est: 1972. Private premises; Internet and postal. Appointment necessary. Medium stock. Spec: Anthologies; Calligraphy; Colonial; Countries - Australasia; Fables; Fiction - General; Fiction - Crime, Detective, Spy, Thrillers; Fiction - Fantasy, Horror; Fiction - Historical; Fiction - Romantic; Fiction - Science Fiction; Fiction - Women; Periodicals & Magazines; Social History; Supernatural; Vintage Paperbacks. PR: £2–1,000. CC: MC; V. Also, a booksearch service. Cata: 6.

Magpie Books, Mellor Barn Farm, Peel Cottage Road, Walsden, Todmorden, OL14 7QJ. Tel: (01706) 815005. Website: http://www.ibooknet.co.uk/seller/magpie.htm. E-mail: magpie@mellorbarn.co.uk. Private premises; Internet and postal. Appointment necessary. Medium stock. PR: £5–2,000. CC: AE; JCB; MC; V. Mem: Ibooknet.

Judith Mansfield, Claremont South, Burnley Road, Todmorden, OL14 5LH. Tel: (01706) 816487. Fax: (01706) 816487. Website: www.ndirect.co.uk/~todmordenbooks. E-mail: todmordenbooks@ndirect.co.uk. Est: 1983. Private premises; Internet and postal. Appointment necessary. Medium stock. Spec: Crochet; Embroidery; Fashion & Costume; Knitting; Lace; Needlework; Textiles. PR: £2–500. CC: MC; V. Cata: 9 – 6 a year on embroidery & lace, 3 on costume & fash. Mem: PBFA.

The Military Collector, The Manse, East Lee Lane, Eastwood, Todmorden, OL14 8RW. Prop: Ian Wilkinson. Tel: (01706) 839690. Fax: (01706) 839690. Website: www.sonic.net/~bstone/military. E-mail: military.collector@virgin.net. Est: 1978. Storeroom; postal business only. Appointment necessary. Medium stock. Spec: Aeronautics; Alchemy; American Indians; Arms & Armour; Aviation; Colonial; Espionage; Firearms/Guns; Holocaust; Maritime/Nautical; Military; Military History; School Registers/Rolls of Honour; War - General; War - American Civil War; War - Boer; and others as listed in the Speciality Index. PR: £1–100. CC: AE; D; JCB; MC; V; Paypal. Also, a booksearch service. VAT No: GB 461 2500 84.

WETHERBY

Steve Schofield Golf Books, 29 Nichols Way, Wetherby, LS22 6AD.

WILTSHIRE

BRADFORD ON AVON

Ex Libris, ■ 1 The Shambles, Bradford on Avon, BA15 1JS. Prop: Roger Jones. Tel: (01225) 863595. Fax: (01225) 863595. Website: www.ex-librisbooks.co.uk. E-mail: roger.jones@ex-librisbooks.co.uk. Est: 1980. Shop; Internet and postal. Open: **M:** 09:00–17:30; **T:** 09:00–17:30; **W:** 09:00–17:30; **Th:** 09:00–17:30; **F:** 09:00–17:30; **S:** 09:00–17:30. PR: £1–10. CC: AE; JCB; MC. Also, new books publishing as Ex Libris Press. Mem: PBFA.

CALNE

Clive Farahar & Sophie Dupré, Horsebrook House, XV The Green, Calne, SN11 8DQ. Tel: (01249) 821121. Fax: (01249) 821202. Website: www.faraharduprc.co.uk. E-mail: sophie@faraharduprc.co.uk. Est: 1978. Private premises; Internet and postal. Appointment necessary. Open: **M:** 09:14–13:18; **T:** 09:14–13:18; **W:** 09:14–13:18; **Th:** 09:14–13:18; **F:** 09:14–13:18; **S:** 10:00–13:00. Closed for lunch: 13:00–14:00. Large stock. Spec: Antiquarian; Autographs; Documents - General; Letters; Literature; Manuscripts; Photography; Royalty - General; Signed Editions; Sport - Big Game Hunting; Travel - General; Travel - Africa; Travel - Americas; Travel - Asia; Travel - Australasia. PR: £10–10,000. CC: AE; JCB; MC; V. Cata: 2. Corresp: French. Mem: ABA; ILAB; PADA; Manuscript Society. VAT No: GB 341 0770 87.

CHIPPENHAM

Vernon Askew Books, Preston East Farm, Nr. Lyneham, Chippenham, SN15 4DX. Prop: Vernon Askew. Tel: (01249) 892177. Est: 1997. Storeroom; appointment necessary. Very large stock. Spec: Alpinism/Mountaineering; Aviation; Bibliography; Biography; Bull Fighting; Byzantium; Churchilliana; Countries - Cyprus; Dictionaries; History - General; Literary Travel; Military History; Modern First Editions; Private Press; Pulps; Religion - Christian; and others as listed in the Speciality Index. PR: £3–75. Corresp: Swedish.

Chris Phillips, 28 Round Barrow Close, Colerne, Chippenham, SN14 8EF. Tel: (01225) 742755. Fax: (0870) 831 2098. E-mail: batholdbooks@hotmail.com. Est: 1997. Private premises; postal business only. Medium stock. Spec: Academic/Scholarly; Antiquarian; Art; Irish Interest; Topography - General. PR: £1–700. CC: JCB; MC; V. Corresp: French. Mem: PBFA. *Also at:* Bath Old Books, 9c Margaret's Buildings, Bath.

CORSHAM

Ashwell Books, Lower Leaze House, Box, Nr. Corsham, SN13 8DU.

DEVIZES

D'Arcy Books, The Chequers, High Street, Devizes, SN10 1AT.

Garton & Co., Roundway House, Devizes, SN10 2EG. Prop: Robin Garton. Tel: (01380) 729624. Fax: (01380) 728886. Website: www.gartonandco.com. E-mail: info@gartonandco.com. Est: 1973. Spec: Catalogues Raisonnes; Fine Art. PR: £100–50,000.

MALMESBURY

Batstone Books, 12 Gloucester Street, Malmesbury, SN16 0AA. Tel: (01666) 822145. Est: 1982. Private premises; appointment necessary. Small stock. Spec: History - General; Maritime/Nautical; Philosophy; Religion - General. PR: £2–200. Cata: 1 – occasionally. Corresp: French.

Dealers who need to update their entry should visit their page on *www.sheppardsdirectories.com*

Earth Science Books, Old Swan House, Swan Barton, Sherston, Malmesbury, SN16 0LJ. Prop: Geoff Carss. Tel: 01666 840995. Website: www.earthsciencebooks.com. E-mail: geoff@earthsciencebooks.com. Est: 2002. Private premises; Internet and postal. Contactable. Very small stock. Spec: Geology. PR: £3–10,000. Cata: 6 – Geology - specialist catalogues released occasionally.

Richard Hatchwell, Cleeve House, Rodbourne Bottom, Malmesbury, SN16 0EZ. Tel: (01666) 823261. Est: 1952. Private premises; Small stock. Spec: Antiquarian; Early Imprints; Manuscripts; Topography - Local. Corresp: French, Italian.

MARLBOROUGH

Eve Magee Books, 6 London Road, Marlborough, SN8 1PH. Prop: Eve Magee. Tel: (01672) 516512. Fax: (01672) 516512. E-mail: evemageebooks@yahoo.co.uk. Est: 2003. Shop &/or showroom. Open: **M:** 10:00–17:00; **T:** 10:00–17:00; **W:** 10:00–17:00; **Th:** 10:00–17:00; **F:** 10:00–17:00; **S:** 10:00–17:00. Very small stock. PR: £3–50. CC: MC; V. Mem: PBFA. *Also at:* Lower House, Lower Chute, Andover SP11 9EB (q.v.).

Katharine House Gallery, ■ Katharine House, The Parade, Marlborough, SN8 1NE. Prop: Christopher Gange. Tel: (01672) 514040. Est: 1983. Shop; open **M:** 10:00–17:30; **T:** 10:00–17:30; **W:** 10:00–17:30; **Th:** 10:00–17:30; **F:** 10:00–17:30; **S:** 10:00–17:30. Medium stock. Spec: Antiques; Art; Illustrated; Modern First Editions. PR: £3–300. CC: MC; V. Mem: PBFA.

Military Parade Bookshop, The Parade, Marlborough, SN8 1NE.

Nevis Railway Bookshops, ■ Katharine House Gallery, The Parade, Marlborough, SN8 1NE. Prop: N.J. Bridger. Tel: Shop (01672) 514040. Est: 1988. Shop; open **M:** 10:00–17:30; **T:** 10:00–17:30; **W:** 10:00–17:30; **Th:** 10:00–17:30; **F:** 10:00–17:30; **S:** 10:00–17:30. Closed for lunch: 13:00–14:15. Medium stock. Spec: Railways; Spiritualism. PR: £1–75. *Also at:* Railway Book and Magazine Search, Newbury, Berks (q.v.) and Nevis Railway Bookshop, Goring-on-Thames, Oxon (q.v.).

Anthony Spranger, ■6 Kinsbury Street, Marlborough, SN8 1HU. Tel: (01672) 514105. E-mail: spranger@btinternet.com. Shop: open **W:** 10–17:00; **Th:** 10:00–17:00; **F:** 10:00–17:00; **S:** 10:00–17:00. Medium stock. Spec: Alpinism/Mountaineering, autobiography; biography; performing arts. CC: AE; D; JCB; MC; V. Corresp: French. Mem: PBFA.

ANTHONY SPRANGER

Secondhand and Collectable Books
Member of the Provincial Booksellers Fairs Association

6 Kingsbury Street • Marlborough
Wiltshire SN8 1HU
Telephone: 01672-514105

Shop Open Wednesday to Saturday 10am-5pm

Browse at Leisure — Buy for Pleasure

We stock a large selection of books on the Performing Arts

RAMSBURY

Heraldry Today, Parliament Piece, Ramsbury, Nr. Marlborough, SN8 2QH.

SALISBURY

Badger, Boxwood, Broadchalke, Salisbury, SP5 5EP. Prop: Peter Bletsoe. Tel: (01722) 326033. Est: 1987. Market stand/stall; at Antique Market, 37 Catherine Street, Salisbury. Open: **M:** 09:00–17:00; **T:** 09:00–17:00; **W:** 09:00–17:00; **Th:** 09:00–17:00; **F:** 09:00–17:00. Small general stock. CC: AE; D; E; JCB; MC; V.

Water Lane Bookshop ■ 24 Water Lane, Salisbury, SP2 7TE. Prop: P.J. Shouler. Tel: (01722) 337929. Website: www.drbooks.euro.bell.co.uk. E-mail: drbooks@eurobell.co.uk. Est: 1981. Shop; Internet and postal. Open: **M:** 10:00–17:00; **T:** 10:00–17:00; **W:** 10:00–17:00; **Th:** 10:00–17:00; **F:** 10:00–17:00; **S:** 10:00–17:00. Medium stock. Spec: Academic/Scholarly; Antiquarian; Architecture; Art; Art History; Art Reference; Artists; Arts, The; Aviation; Bindings; Catalogues Raisonnes; Fine & Rare; Fine Art; Illustrated; Military; Topography - General; Topography - Local; Travel - General. PR: £1–2,000. CC: JCB; MC; V. Mem: PBFA. VAT No: GB 723 3951 38.

Trevan's Old Books, ■ 30 Catherine Street, Salisbury, SP1 2DA. Prop: John & Trevan Cocking. Tel: (01722) 325818. Fax: (01722) 341181. Website: www.abebooks.com/home/trevan. E-mail: john.cocking@virgin.net. Est: 1999. Shop and Internet. Open: **M:** 09:30–17:30; **T:** 09:30–17:30; **W:** 09:30–17:30; **Th:** 09:30–17:30; **F:** 09:30–17:30; **S:** 09:30–17:30. Large stock. PR: £1–1,000. CC: AE; E; JCB; MC; V; SW, SO.

SWINDON

Bookmark (Children's Books), Fortnight, Wick Down, Broad Hinton, Swindon, SN4 9NR. Prop: Anne & Leonora Excell. Tel: (01793) 731693. Fax: (01793) 731782. E-mail: leonora.excell@btinternet.com. Est: 1973. Private premises; appointment necessary. Open: **M:** 09:00–18:00; **T:** 09:00–18:00; **W:** 09:00–18:00; **Th:** 09:00–18:00; **F:** 09:00–18:00; **S:** 10:00–18:00; **Su:** 10:00–16:00. Medium stock. Spec: Author - Aldin, Cecil; Author - Ardizzone, Edward; Author - Brent-Dyer, Elinor M.; Author - Crane, Walter; Author - Dahl, Roald; Author - Henty, G.A.; Author - Keeping, Charles; Author - Potter, Beatrix; Author - Uttley, Alison; Children's - General; and others as listed in the Speciality Index. PR: £5–1,500. CC: E; JCB; MC; V. Also, a specialist booksearch service. Cata: 3 – a year on children's books and related juvenilia. Mem: PBFA.

Collectors Corner, ■ 227 Kingshill, Swindon, SN1 4NG. Prop: Fred Stevens. Tel: (01793) 521545. Est: 1986. Shop; open **M:** 10:30–16:45; **T:** 10:30–16:45. **Th:** 10:30–16:45; **F:** 10:30–16:45; **S:** 10:30–16:45. Very small general stock. Spec: Collecting; Military; Railways; Topography - Local; Transport. PR: £1–100.

Victoria Bookshop, 30 Wood Street, Old Town, Swindon, SN1 4AB.

John Williams, 93 Goddard Avenue, Swindon, SN1 4HT.

TISBURY

Heatons, ■ 2–3 High Street, Tisbury, SP3 6PS. Prop: Ros King. Tel: (01747) 873025. Fax: (01747) 870059. Website: www.heatons-of-tisbury.co.uk. E-mail: rosking@freenetname.co.uk. Shop; Internet and postal. Open: **M:** 09:30–16:30. **F:** 09:30–16:30; **S:** 09:30–16:30. Very large stock. PR: £1–2,000. Also, engravings, maps, arts & crafts, Art Deco furniture & commemorative items.

WARMINSTER

Sturford Books, Landfall, 35 Corton, Warminster, BA12 0SY. Prop: Maria & Robert Mayall. Tel: (01985) 850478/85058. E-mail: robert_mayall@sturfordbooks.freeserve.co.uk. Est: 1993. Spec: Architecture; Art; Fiction - General; Foreign Texts; Literature; Poetry; Travel - General. PR: £5–800. Also, booksearch.

WEST KINGTON

Peter Barnitt, Latimer Lodge, West Kington, Chippenham, SN14 7JJ.

WESTBURY

Aardvark Books, 50 Bratton Road, Westbury, BA13 3EP. Prop: Clive & Caroline Williams. Tel: (01225) 867723. Fax: (01225) 863479. Website: www.sonic.net/~bstone/aardvarkbooks. E-mail: aardvarkbooks@blueyonder.co.uk. Est: 1998. Private premises; postal business only. Large stock. Spec: Military History; War - World War I; War - World War II. PR: £5–250. CC: MC; V; SW.

WILTSHIRE

Zardoz Books, 20 Whitecroft, Dilton Marsh, Westbury, BA13 4DJ. Prop: M. & L. Flanagan. Tel: (01373) 865371. Fax: (01373) 303984. Website: www.zardozbooks.co.uk. E-mail: 100124.262@compuserve.com. Est: 1990. Warehouse; Internet and postal. Appointment necessary. Very large stock. Spec: Books about Books; Comic Books & Annuals; Countries - Melanesia; Countries - Mexico; Crime (True); Early Imprints; Fiction - General; Fiction - Science Fiction; Glamour; Publishers - General; War - General. PR: £2–100. CC: MC; V. Also, importers, distributors of books & magazines about paperbacks, pulp, comics, illustrators, collectables, and publisher on specialities. Cata: 4.

WOOTTON BASSETT

G. Jackson, 10 Dryden Place, Wootton Bassett, SN4 8JP. Prop: Geoffrey Jackson. Tel: (01793) 849660. Fax: (01793) 849660. E-mail: geoff.jackson@tinyworld.co.uk. Est: 1992. Postal business only. Small stock. Spec: Antiquarian; Fiction - Crime, Detective, Spy, Thrillers; Fiction - Fantasy, Horror; Fiction - Science Fiction; Irish Interest; Literature; Military; Natural History; Topography - General; Travel - General. PR: £10–5,000.

ZEALS

Hurly Burly Books, 47 Zeals Rise, Zeals, BA12 6PL. Prop: Moira Lord. Tel: (01747) 840691. E-mail: hurlyburlybook@clara.co.uk. Est: 1995. Storeroom; appointment necessary. Small stock. Spec: Children's - General; Children's - Illustrated; Illustrated. CC: AE; D; E; JCB; MC; V. *Also at:* Words Etc, Dorchester, Dorset.

WORCESTERSHIRE

BEWDLEY

Abacus Books, 4 Merrick's Close, Bewdley, DY12 2PF.

Clent Books of Bewdley, Rose Cottage, Habberley Road, Bewdley, DY12 1JA. Prop: Ivor Simpson. Tel: (01299) 401090. Website: www.abebooks.com/home/clentbooks. E-mail: clent.books@btopenworld.com. Est: 1977. Private premises; Internet and postal. *Shop at:* Kinver Book Fair every third Sunday in the month. Medium stock. Spec: Antiquarian; Fine & Rare; History - Local; Military; Topography - Local. PR: £10–150. Book Fair Organiser. Mem: PBFA.

George J. Harris, Heathview, Habberley Road, Bewdley, DY12 1JH. Tel: (01299) 402413. Est: 1976. Private premises; appointment necessary. Medium stock. Spec: Aviation; Military; Military History; Naval; War - General; War - American Civil War; War - World War I; War - World War II. PR: £5–500. Attends PBFA fairs. Cata: 2 – on military/naval aviation. Corresp: French. Mem: PBFA.

Lion Books, ■ 28 Load Street, Bewdley, DY12 2AS. Prop: Colin Raxter. Tel: (01299) 401660. Website: www.lionbooks.com. E-mail: lionbooks2@aol.com. Est: 1989. Shop; Internet and postal. Open: **T:** 10:30–17:00; **W:** 10:30–17:00; **Th:** 10:30–17:00; **F:** 10:30–17:00; **S:** 10:30–17:00; **Su:** 12:30–16:30. Medium stock. Spec: Sport - Angling/Fishing; Sport - Cricket; Sport - Football (Soccer); Sport - Motor Racing; Sport - Rugby; Topography - Local. PR: £1–200. CC: JCB; MC; V; SW. Also, internet trade through ABE. Mem: PBFA.

DROITWICH

Grant Books, The Coach House, New Road, Cutnall Green, Droitwich, WR9 0PQ. Prop: Bob & Shirley Grant. Manager: Maureen Jones. Tel: (01299) 851588. Fax: (01299) 851446. Website: www.grantbooks.co.uk. E-mail: golf@grantbooks.co.uk. Est: 1972. Office &/or bookroom. Open: **M:** 09:00–17:00; **T:** 09:00–17:00; **W:** 09:00–17:00; **Th:** 09:00–17:00; **F:** 09:00–17:00. Small stock. Spec: Antiquarian; Sport - Golf. PR: £5–2,500. CC: AE; D; MC; V. Open at other times by appointment. Cata: 3 – on golf. Mem: PBFA; BGCS; GCS(USA). VAT No: GB 275 8638 10

M. & D. Books, ■ 16 High Street, Droitwich Spa, WR9 8EW. Prop: Mike Hebden. Tel: (01905) 775814. Est: 1996. Shop; open **T:** 10:00–17:00; **W:** 10:00–17:00; **Th:** 10:00–17:00; **F:** 10:00–17:00; **S:** 09:30–17:00. Medium general stock. Spec: Topography - Local. PR: £1–250. CC: AE; MC; V; SW.

GREAT MALVERN

The Malvern Bookshop, ■ 7 Abbey Road, Great Malvern,, WR14 3ES. Prop: Howard G. Hudson. Tel: (01684) 575915. Fax: (01684) 577357. E-mail: browse@malvern-bookshop.co.uk. Est: 1953. Shop; open **M:** 10:00–17:00; **T:** 10:00–17:00; **W:** 10:00–17:00; **Th:** 10:00–17:00; **F:** 10:00–17:00; **S:** 10:00–17:00. Closed for lunch: 10:00–17:00. Large general stock. Spec: Academic/Scholarly; Advertising; Antiques; Archaeology; Architecture; Art; Aviation; Bindings; Biography; Books about Books; Children's - General; Design; Literature; Military; Music - General; Natural History; Performing Arts; Poetry; Topography - Local; Transport; Travel - General. PR: £1–500. Also, a booksearch service.

Dealers who need to update their entry
should visit their page on
www.sheppardsdirectories.com

WORCESTERSHIRE

Wildside Books, Rectory House, 26 Priory Road, Great Malvern, WR14 3DR. Prop: Chris & Christine Johnson. Tel: (01684) 562 818. Fax: (01684) 566 491. Website: www.onthewildside.co.uk. E-mail: enquire@onthewildside.co.uk. Est: 1982. Private premises; Internet and postal. Appointment necessary. Small stock. Spec: Animals and Birds; Botany; Ecology; Fine & Rare; Fishes; Gardening; Horticulture; Landscape; Lepidopterology / Lepidoptery; Mycology; Natural History; Natural Sciences; New Naturalist; Ornithology; Plant Hunting; Rural Life; Sport - Falconry; Zoology. PR: £15–10,000. CC: E; MC; V; SW. Gallery: specialising in wildlife and botanical art from 18th-21st Century. Cata: 4 – 3 months. Mem: *Also at:* Gallery: 32 Church Street, Great Malvern.

KIDDERMINSTER

Bewdley Fine Books, 64 Trimpley Drive, Kidderminster, DY11 5LB.

Salsus Books, Elderfield Gardens, 42 Coventry Street, Kidderminster, DY10 2BT. Prop: Dr. D.T. Salt. Tel: (01562) 742081. Fax: (01562) 824583. E-mail: salsus@books93.freeserve.co.uk. Est: 1991. Private premises; Internet and postal. Appointment necessary. Medium stock. Spec: Ecclesiastical History & Architecture; Religion - General; Theology. PR: £1–250. CC: JCB; MC; V; SW. Cata: 4. Mem: PBFA.

MALVERN

Golden Age Books, PO Box 45, Malvern, WR14 1XT. Tony Byatt, Adrian and Gillian Ainge. Tel: mail order only. Website: www.goldenagebooks.co.uk. E-mail: info@goldenagebooks.co.uk. Est: 1981. Private premises; Internet and postal. Appointment necessary. Small stock. Spec: Bibles; Religion - General; Religion - Christian; Religion - Jewish; Theology. PR: £1–1,000. CC: E; JCB; MC; V; SW. Also, new Biblical books. Cata: 5.

St. Ann's Books, Rectory House, 26 Priory Road, Malvern, WR14 3DR.

PERSHORE

Coach House Books, ■ 17a Bridge Street, Pershore, WR10 1AJ. Prop: Michael & Sue Ellingworth. Tel: (01386) 554633. Fax: (01386) 554633. E-mail: sue.chb@virgin.net. Est: 1982. Shop; telephone first. Medium stock. Spec: Architecture; Art Reference; Author - Lawrence, T.E.; Folio Society, The; Horticulture; Limited Editions; Military; Ornithology; School Registers/Rolls of Honour; Sport - Cricket; Topography - General; Topography - Local. PR: £5–2,000. CC: AE; D; MC; V. Also, new books, picture framing, artists materials and a booksearch service. Corresp: French. Mem: BA; *Also at:* 46 High Street, Pershore, Worcestershire WR10 1DP. VAT No: GB 396 2460 27.

Ian K. Pugh Books, 40 Bridge Street, Pershore, WR10 1AT.

Sedgeberrow Books & Framing, ■ Retail Market, Cherry Orchard, Pershore, WR10 1EY. Prop: Mrs. Jayne Winter. Tel: (01386) 751830. Website: www.abebooks.com/home/SEDGEBERROW. E-mail: jayne@sedgeberrowbooks.fsnet.co.uk. Est: 1985. Shop; open **W:** 09:00–17:00; **Th:** 09:00–17:00; **F:** 09:00–17:00. Medium stock. Spec: History - Local; Railways. PR: £1–100.

Slaughter & Garratt Rare Books, P.O. Box 43, Pershore, WR10 3YH. Prop: June Slaughter and Christopher Garratt. Tel: (01386) 751477. Fax: (01386) 750052. E-mail: slaughter-garratt@amserve.net. Est: 1971. Private premises. Small stock. Spec: Art; Bindings; Sport - Big Game Hunting; Sport - Croquet; Travel - General; Voyages & Discovery. Cata: 1 – Occasionally. Mem: PBFA.

Wigley Books, Morewood House, Abbey Place, Pershore, WR10 1JE. Prop: Geoffrey Whatmore. Tel: (01386) 554125. Fax: (01386) 556555. Est: 1984. Private premises; appointment necessary. Small stock. Spec: Sport - Angling/Fishing. PR: £5–1,000. CC: MC; V. Cata: 2 – a year. Corresp: French.

STOURPORT-ON-SEVERN

P. and P. Books, Dairy Cottage, Yarhampton, Stourport, Stourport-on-Severn, DY13 0UY. Prop: J. S. Pizey. Tel: (01299) 896996. Fax: (01299) 896996. E-mail: pandpbooks_jim@compuserve.com. Est: 1982. Private premises; postal business only. Appointment necessary. Spec: Egyptology. PR: £5–2,000. CC: JCB. Valuations undertaken. Cata: 3 – Archaeology and travel in The Middle East and Egyptology. Mem: ABA; PBFA; ILAB. VAT No: GB 441 7426 59.

WORCESTER

Bookworms of Evesham, ■ 81 Port Street, Evesham, Worcester, WR11 3LF. Prop: T.J. Sims. Tel: (01386) 45509. Fax: (01386) 45509. Est: 1971. Shop; open **T:** 10:00–17:00; **W:** 10:00–17:00; **Th:** 10:00–17:00; **F:** 10:00–17:00; **S:** 10:00–17:00. Medium stock. Spec: Art; History - General; Literature; Military; Topography - Local; Transport; Travel - General. Fairs attended: Cheltenham, Bath, Cirencester; and Churchdown Book Fair. Cata: – occasionally on Gloucestershire topography. Mem: PBFA.

Capuchins, ■ 37 Sidbury, Worcester, WR1 2HT. Prop: Jo Cross. Tel: (01905) 21141. E-mail: capuchins@hotmail.com. Est: 1998. Shop; open **T:** 10:00–17:00; **W:** 10:00–17:00; **Th:** 10:00–17:00; **F:** 10:00–17:00; **S:** 10:00–17:00; **Su:** 11:30–14:30. Small general stock. PR: £1–50. Also, coffee house.

Ann & Mike Conry, 14 St. George's Square, Worcester, WR1 1HX. Tel: (01905) 25330. E-mail: irishallsorts@aol.com. Est: 1998. Postal business only. Spec: Irish Interest; Literary Travel; Modern First Editions; Sport - Football (Soccer). PR: £2–400.

Davies Fine Books, 21 Droitwich Road, Worcester, WR3 7LG. Prop: Richard Davies. Tel: (01905) 23919. Website: www.daviesfinebooks.biblion.com. E-mail: daviesfinebooks@yahoo.co.uk. Est: 2002. Private premises; Internet and postal. Contactable. Small stock. Spec: Antiquarian; Illustrated; Travel - General. Corresp: French.

Graduate Books, 5 Rectory Lane, Shrawley, Worcester, WR6 6TW. Tel: (01905) 620786. E-mail: davidrobertvirr@aol.com. Est: 1985. Private premises; Internet and postal. Appointment necessary. Very small stock. Spec: Esoteric; Mind, Body & Spirit; Music - Popular; Philosophy; Psychology/Psychiatry; Topography - Local. PR: £3–200. Corresp: French.

Priory Books, ■ 10 Church Walk, Malvern, Worcester, WR14 2XH. Prop: M. & L.P. Kelly. Tel: (01684) 560258. E-mail: paul@priorybooks.fsnet.co.uk. Est: 1985. Shop; open **M:** 09:30–17:15; **T:** 09:30–17:15; **W:** 09:30–17:15; **Th:** 09:30–17:15; **F:** 09:30–17:15; **S:** 09:00–17:15. Small stock. Spec: History - Local; Poetry; Railways; Topography - General. PR: £1–400. CC: JCB; MC; V.

Restormel Books, 1 East Comer, St. John's, Worcester, WR2 6BE. Prop: Roy Slade. Tel: (01905) 422290. Est: 1978. Display/stand. *Shop at:* Reindeer Court Antiques, Mealchealen Street, Worcester. Open: **M:** 10:00–17:00; **T:** 10:00–17:00; **W:** 10:00–17:00; **Th:** 10:00–17:00; **F:** 10:00–17:00; **S:** 10:00–17:00. Small stock. Spec: Collecting; Topography - Local. PR: £1–50. Attends PBFA fairs in Midlands. Corresp: French, Spanish. Mem: PBFA.

John Scott (Sporting Books), The Beeches, Wynniatts Way, Abberley, Worcester, WR6 6BZ. Tel: (01299) 896779. Fax: (01299) 896060. E-mail: books4hunters@btinternet.com. Est: 1990. Private premises; postal business only. Appointment necessary. Small stock. Spec: Author - Hemingway, Ernest; Cockfighting; Conservation; Dogs; Firearms/Guns; Fishes; Rural Life; Sport - Angling/Fishing; Sport - Archery; Sport - Big Game Hunting; Sport - Falconry; Sport - Field Sports; Sport - Hunting; Sport - Pig-Sticking; and others as listed in the Speciality Index. PR: £1–750. CC: E; JCB; MC; V; SW. Cata: 6. Mem: PBFA; BASC, CA. VAT No: GB 473 8334 26.

Worcester Rare Books, c/o Flat 3, Coach House Lodge, Old Palace Gardens, Deansway, Worcester, WR1 2JD. Prop: D.Ieuan Lloyd. Tel: (01905) 28780. E-mail: rareboks@worcester74.freeserve.co.uk. Est: 1972. Private premises; Internet and postal. Appointment necessary. Medium stock. Spec: Academic/Scholarly; Advertising; Antiquarian; Medicine; Philosophy; Science - General; Science - History of. PR: £10–1,000. CC: MC; V. Cata: 6. Corresp: French German. Mem: PBFA.

CHANNEL ISLANDS

GUERNSEY

ST. PETER PORT
Channel Islands Galleries Limited, Trinity Square Centre, Trinity Square, St. Peter Port, Guernsey, GY1 1LX.

SAINT SAMPSON
The Old Curiosity Shop, ■ Commercial Road, The Bridge, St. Sampson, Guernsey. Prop: Mrs. Adele Stevens Cox. Tel: (01481) 45324. Est: 1978. Shop; open **F:** 14:00–16:30. Small stock. Spec: Countries - Channel Islands, The. PR: £1–2,000 Corresp: French, German.

ISLE OF MAN

DOUGLAS

Garretts Antiquarian Books, 4 Summerhill, Douglas, IM2 4PJ. Prop: Mr. Jonathon Hall. Tel: (01624) 675065. Website: www.isleofmanbooks.com. E-mail: garrettsbooks_iom@yahoo.co.uk. Est: 1987. Private premises; Internet and postal. Telephone first. Small general stock. Spec: Countries - Isle of Man; History - Local; Topography - Local. PR: £1–1,000. CC: JCB; MC; V. Mem: PBFA.

WEST BALDWIN
Manx Printed Collectibles, The Rhyne, West Baldwin, IM4 5HD.

NORTHERN IRELAND

CO. ANTRIM

BELFAST (BEAL FEIRSIDE)

Belfast Book Search, ■ Unit A201, Portview Trade Center, 310 Newtonards Road, Belfast, Co. Antrim, BT4 1HE. Prop: Mr. William Burlingham. Tel: (028) 9045-1385. Fax: (028) 9045-1385. E-mail: belfastbooksearch@dnet.co.uk. Est: 1998. Storeroom; Internet and postal. Telephone first. Shop; open daily at Unit 9 North St Arcade Belfast City Centre. Open: **M:** 11:00–17:00; **T:** 11:00–17:00; **W:** 11:00–17:00; **Th:** 11:00–17:00; **F:** 11:00–17:00; **S:** 11:00–17:00. Medium stock. Spec: Irish Interest. PR: £1–50. CC: JCB; MC; V; SW. Also, booksearch.

The Bell Gallery, 13 Adelaide Park, Belfast, Co. Antrim, BT9 6FX. Prop: James Nelson Bell. Tel: (028) 9066-2998. Website: www.bellgallery.com. E-mail: bellgallery@btinternet.com. Est: 1965. Spec: Countries - Ireland; Irish Interest. PR: £10–100. Also, Irish paintings & sculpture.

Botanic Books, 19 Botanic Avenue, Belfast, Co. Antrim, BT7 1JG.

Emerald Isle Books, 539 Antrim Road, Belfast, Co. Antrim, BT15 3BU. Prop: Mr. & Mrs. John Gamble. Tel: (028) 9037-0798. Fax: (029) 9037-7288. Est: 1963. Private premises; appointment necessary. Very large stock. Spec: Antiquarian; Bindings; Countries - Ireland; Ecclesiastical History & Architecture; Fine & Rare; History - General; Irish Interest; Literature; Religion - Christian; Sets of Books; Social History; Travel - General. CC: MC; V. Mem: ABA; ILAB.

Evangelical Bookshop, 15 College Square East, Belfast, Co. Antrim, BT1 6DD.

T.H. Irwin, 32 Ravensdene Crescent, Ravenhill, Belfast, Co. Antrim, BT6 0DB.

P. & B. Rowan, Carleton House, 92 Malone Road, Belfast, Co. Antrim, BT9 5HP. Prop: Peter & Briad Rowan. Tel: (028) 9066-6448. Fax: (028) 9066-3725. E-mail: peter@pbrowan.thegap.com. Est: 1973. Private premises; appointment necessary. Large stock. Spec: Economics; Fine & Rare; History - General; Irish Interest; Law; Literature; Manuscripts; Medicine - History of; Philosophy; Science - History of; Travel - General; Voyages & Discovery. PR: £25- upwards. Cata: 3. Corresp: French. Mem: PBFA; IADA.

Stacks Bookshop, 67 Comber Road, Dundonald, Belfast, Co. Antrim, BT16 0FF. Prop: Jim Tollerton. Tel: (028) 9048-6880. Est: 1992. Spec: Academic/Scholarly; Animals and Birds; Antiquarian; Autobiography; Children's - General; Fiction - Historical; Military; Religion - Christian; Social History; Transport; War - General. PR: £3–5.

LISBURN

Jiri Books, 11 Mill Road, Lisburn, Co. Antrim, BT27 5TT. Prop: Jim & Rita Swindall. Tel: (028) 9082-6443. Fax: (028) 9082-6443. Website: http://www.abebooks.com/home/WJS/. E-mail: jiri.books@dnet.co.uk. Est: 1978. Private premises; postal business only. Appointment necessary. Medium stock. Spec: Antiquarian; Irish Interest; Literature; Poetry; Travel - General. CC: MC; V. Organise Annual Belfast Book Fair. Next fair 8th November 2003.

CO. ARMAGH

Craobh Rua Books, 12 Woodford Gardens, Armagh, Co. Armagh, BT60 2AZ. Prop: James Vallely. Tel: (028) 3752-6938. E-mail: craobh@btinternet.com. Est: 1990. Private premises; Internet and postal. Appointment necessary. Medium stock. Spec: Antiquarian; First Editions; History - National; Irish Interest; Literature; Topography - General; Travel - General. PR: £1–400. CC: MC; V. Also, a booksearch service. Cata: 12 – monthly. Corresp: French. Mem: PBFA.

CO. DOWN

BALLYGOWAN,

Saintfield Antiques & Fine Books, 68 Main Street, Saintfield, Ballygowan, Co. Down, BT24 7AB.

BALLYNAHINCH

Davidson Books, 34 Broomhill Road, Ballynahinch, Co. Down, BT24 8QD. Prop: Arthur Davidson. Tel: (028) 9756-2502. Fax: (028) 9756-2502. Est: 1958. Private premises; appointment necessary. Medium stock. Spec: History - National; Irish Interest; Literature; Topography - Local. Cata: 3 – a year.

BANGOR

Books Ulster, 12 Bayview Road, Bangor, Co. Down, BT19 6AL. Prop: D.A. Rowlinson. Tel: (028) 914-70310. Website: www.booksulster.com. E-mail: orders@booksulster.com. Est: 1995. Private premises; postal business only. Very small stock. Spec: Irish Interest. PR: £1–500.

Pages Bookshop, 12 High Street, Bangor, Co. Down, BT20 5AY.

DONAGHADEE

Prospect House Books, Prospect House, 4 Millisle Road, Donaghadee, Co Down, BT21 0HY. Prop: M.C. McAlister & J.M. Binney. Tel: (028) 9188-2990. Fax: (028) 9188-2990. Website: www.antiquarianbooksellersd.co.uk. E-mail: rarebooks.phb@btopenworld.com. Est: 1983. Private premises; Internet and postal. Appointment necessary. Large stock. Spec: Antiquarian; Bibliography; Biography; Countries - Ireland; Economics; Gardening; Geology; Irish Interest; Medicine; Natural History; Philology; Philosophy; Poetry; Religion - General; Scottish Interest; Theology; Travel - Africa; Travel - Asia; and others as listed in the Speciality. CC: MC; V.

DOWNPATRICK,

Bookline, 35 Farranfad Road, Downpatrick, Co. Down, BT30 8NH.

HILLSBOROUGH

Hillsborough BookHunters, 'Anna Livia', 6 Millvale Road, Hillsborough, Co. Down, BT26 6HR. Prop: Peter C. Hunter. Tel: (028) 9268-2635. Fax: (028) 9268-2268. E-mail: bookhunter@hillsborough0.demon.co.uk. Est: 1997. Private premises; appointment necessary. Small general stock. PR: £1–800.

CO. FERMANAGH

ENNISKILLEN

John Gowan Books, Drumaraw, Springfield, Enniskillen, Co. Fermanagh, BT74 8AS.

CO. LONDONDERRY

COLERAINE

The Coleraine Bookshop, 5 Stone Row, Coleraine, Co. Londonderry, BT52 1EP.

Foyle Books, ■ 12 Magazine Street, Londonderry, Co. Derry, BT48 6HH. Prop: Ken Thatcher & Art Byrne. Tel: (028) 7137-2530. Website: www.foylebooks.freeserve.co.uk/index.html. E-mail: ken@thatcher30.freeserve.co.uk. Est: 1984. Shop; open **M:** 11:00–17:00; **T:** 11:00–17:00; **W:** 11:00–17:00; **Th:** 11:11–17:17; **F:** 11:00–17:00; **S:** 10:00–19:00. Very large stock. Spec: Academic/Scholarly; Advertising; Countries - Ireland; Foreign Texts; History - National; Irish Interest; Theology. PR: £1–200. Also, a booksearch service. Corresp: French.

SCOTLAND

Including the Unitary Authorities of Aberdeenshire, Angus, Argyll & Bute, Borders, Clackmannan, Dumfries & Galloway, Dumbarton & Clydebank, Dundee, East Ayrshire, East Dunbartonshire, East Lothian, East Renfrewshire, Edinburgh, Falkirk, Fife, Glasgow, Highland, Inverclyde, Mid Lothian, Moray, North Ayrshire, North Lanarkshire, Orkney Islands, Perthshire & Kinross, Renfrewshire, Shetland Islands, South Ayrshire, South Lanarkshire, Stirling, Western Isles and West Lothian.

BORDERS

INNERLEITHEN,

Spike Hughes Rare Books, Willow Bank, Damside, Innerleithen, Borders, EH44 6HR. Tel: (01896) 830019. Fax: (01896) 831499. E-mail: spike@buik.demon.co.uk. Est: 1981. Private premises; Internet and postal. Appointment necessary. Small general stock. Spec: Countries - Scotland; Fine & Rare; History - General; History - Local; History - National; Literature; Philosophy; Social History. PR: £10–1,000. CC: MC; V. Cata: 6. Mem: ABA. VAT No: GB 345 4470 55.

JEDBURGH

G. & R. Stone, Hap House, 5 Allerton Court, Jedburgh, TD8 6RT. Prop: Gillian & Ralph Stone. Tel: (01835) 864147. Fax: (01835) 864147. E-mail: grstone@macunlimited.net. Est: 1972. Spec: Agriculture; Antiquarian; Natural History; Poetry; Women. PR: £5–100.

KELSO

Border Books, The Bookshop, 47–51 Horsemarket, Kelso, Borders, TD5 7AA.

Saints & Scholars, Linton Bankhead, Kelso, Borders, TD5 8AF.

MELROSE

The Old Storytellers Bookshop, ■ The Old School, Bowden, Melrose, Borders, TD6 0SS. Prop: Brian & Carolyn Boardman. Tel: (01835) 822228. Website: www.theoldschooltearoom.co.uk. Est: 1988. Shop; open **M:** 10:00–17:00; **T:** 10:00–17:00; **W:** 10:00–17:00; **Th:** 10:00–17:00; **F:** 10:00–17:00; **S:** 10:00–17:00. Small stock. Spec: Autobiography; Biography; Fiction - General; First Editions; History - British; Illustrated; Poetry; Scottish Interest; Topography - General; Topography - Local. PR: £2–150. CC: JCB; MC; V; DE, SW. Winter (Nov-Mar) 11:00 to 16:00 every day.

Stroma Books, Charlesfield, St. Boswells, Melrose, Borders, TD6 0HH. Tel: (01835) 824169. Website: www.stromabooks.co.uk. E-mail: kenny@stromabooks.fsnet.co.uk. Est: 2000. Private premises; postal business only. Medium stock. Spec: Biography; Entertainment - General; Military; Modern First Editions; Scottish Interest; Travel - General. CC: JCB; MC; V; M, SW, SO.

SELKIRK

Wheen O'Books, Glyndwr, Mill St., Selkirk, Borders, TD7 5AE. Prop: Margaret Tierney. Tel: (01750) 21009. E-mail: megtie@aol.com. Est: 1997. Private premises; Internet. Telephone first. PR: £2–1,500.

Dealers who need to update their entry should visit their page on
www.sheppardsdirectories.com

SCOTLAND

WEST LINTON

Linton Books, ■ Deanfoot Road, West Linton, Borders, EH46 7DY. Prop: Derek Watson. Tel: (01968) 660339. Fax: (01968) 661701. Est: 1994. Shop; open **M:** 10:30–17:30; **T:** 10:30–17:30; **W:** 10:30–17:30; **Th:** 10:30–17:30; **F:** 10:30–17:30; **S:** 09:30–17:30; **Su:** 12:00–17:00. Small stock. Spec: Mythology; Scottish Interest. PR: £1–150. CC: E; MC; V. Winter opening: Closed Thursdays and Sunday morning.

CENTRAL

BRIDGE OF ALLAN

Bridge of Allan Books, ■ 2 Henderson Street, Bridge of Allan, Central, FK9 4HT. Prop: Dr Andrew Jennings. Tel: (01786) 834483. Website: www.bridgeofallanbooks.com. E-mail: books@bridgeofallanbooks.com. Est: 1985. Shop; Internet and postal. Open: **M:** 10:00–17:00; **T:** 10:00–17:00; **W:** 10:00–17:00; **Th:** 10:00–17:00; **F:** 10:00–17:00; **S:** 10:00–17:00. Large stock. Spec: Academic/Scholarly; Alpinism/Mountaineering; Anthroposophy; Antiquarian; Countries - Scotland; History - Local; Literature; Topography - Local. PR: £1–700. Scottish history and Gaelic culture research, free booksearch service.

CALLANDER

HP bookfinders, Mosslaird, Brig O'Turk, Callander, Central, FK17 8HT. Tel: (01877) 376377. Fax: (01877) 376377. Website: www.hp-bookfinders.co.uk. E-mail: martin@hp-bookfinders.co.uk. Est: 1986. Private premises; Internet and postal. Contactable. Very small stock. CC: E; JCB; MC; V; SW.

LARBERT

Dave Simpson, Lorne Villa, 161 Main Street, Larbert, Central, FK5 4AL. Tel: (01324) 558628. Fax: (01324) 558628. Website: dave.simpson3@virgin.net. E-mail: dave.simpson3@virgin.net. Est: 2000. Private premises; Internet and postal. Contactable. Small general stock. Spec: Antiquarian; Children's - General; Literature; Modern First Editions; Signed Editions. PR: £10–300. CC: E; JCB; MC; V; SW.

DUMFRIES & GALLOWAY

CASTLE DOUGLAS

Douglas Books, 207 King Street, Castle Douglas, Kirkcudbrightshire, DG7 1DT.

Benny Gillies, ■ 31–33 Victoria Street, Kirkpatrick Durham, Castle Douglas, Kircudbrightshire, DG7 3HQ. Prop: Benny Gillies. Tel: (01556) 650412. Website: www.bennygillies.co.uk. E-mail: benny@bennygillies.co.uk. Est: 1979. Shop; open **M:** 10:00–17:00; **T:** 10:00–17:00; **W:** 10:00–17:00; **Th:** 10:00–17:00; **F:** 10:00–17:00; **S:** 10:00–18:00. Small stock. Spec: Countries - Scotland; Rural Life; Scottish Interest; Topography - Local. PR: £1–500. CC: MC; V. Cata: 2. Corresp: French. Mem: PBFA. VAT No: GB 499 0638 93.

DUMFRIES

Crescent Books, ■ 32 Church Crescent, Dumfries, Dumfries & Galloway, DG1 1DF. Prop: Martin Close. Tel: (01387) 261137. E-mail: crescent.books@virgin.net. Est: 1994. Shop; open **T:** 11:00–17:00; **W:** 11:00–17:00; **Th:** 11:00–17:00; **F:** 11:00–17:00; **S:** 11:00–17:00. Small general stock. PR: £1–50. CC: MC; V; SW. Also, secondhand records.

Hen Hoose Bookshop, ■ Tynron, Nr. Thornhill, Dumfries, Dumfries & Galloway, DG3 4LB. Prop: J. McGregor. Tel: (01848) 200418. Est: 1994. Shop; open **T:** 11:00–17:00; **W:** 11:00–17:00; **Th:** 11:00–17:00; **F:** 11:00–17:00; **S:** 11:00–17:00; **Su:** 11:00–17:00. Medium general stock. Spec: Art History; Art Reference. PR: £1–50. CC: V. Also, booksearch.

SCOTLAND

GATEHOUSE OF FLEET

Anwoth Books, ■ Mill on the Fleet, Gatehouse of Fleet, Dumfries, Dumfries & Gallway, DG7 2HS. Prop: Anwoth Books Ltd. Tel: (01557) 814774. Est: 1991. Shop; open **M:** 10:30–17:00; **T:** 10:30–17:00; **W:** 10:30–17:00; **Th:** 10:30–17:00; **F:** 10:30–17:00; **S:** 10:30–17:00; **Su:** 10:30–17:00. Large general stock. Spec: Art; Children's - General; Ornithology; Poetry; Scottish Interest. PR: £1–50. CC: JCB; MC; V. Winter opening: November to March open Friday to Sunday only.

KIRKCUDBRIGHT

Vailima Books, 61 High Street, Kirkcudbright, Dumfries & Galloway, DG6 4JZ.

MOFFAT

Moffat Book Exchange, 5 Well Street, Moffat, Dumfries & Galloway, DF10 9DP. Prop: Andy Armstrong. Tel: (01683) 220059. Fax: (01683) 220059. E-mail: dandrewarmstrong@aol.com. Est: 1998. Spec: Fiction - General; Fiction - Westerns. PR: £1–25.

THORNHILL

Addair, The Lamp, Burnhead, Thornhill, Dumfries & Galloway, DG3 4AD.

Addendum Books, The Lamp, Burnhead, Thornhill, Dumfries & Galloway, DG3 4AD. Prop: Dr. F.A. Ashton. Tel: (01848) 331523. E-mail: addendumbooks@aol.com. Est: 1996. Private premises; Internet and postal. Appointment necessary. Medium stock. Spec: Aviation; Children's - General; Design; Illustrated; Scottish Interest; Technical. PR: £10–700. CC: JCB; MC; V; SW. Mem: PBFA.

WHITEHORN

Wyche Books, ■ 58 George Street, Whithorn, Dumfries & Galloway, DG8 9PA. Prop: John & Kathleen Turner. Tel: (01988) 500720. E-mail: kaytee@wychebooks.demon.co.uk. Est: 2002. Shop; open **M:** 09:00–17:00; **T:** 09:00–17:00; **W:** 09:00–17:00; **Th:** 09:00–17:00; **F:** 09:00–17:00; **S:** 09:00–17:00; **Su:** 11:00–16:00. Medium general stock. Spec: Occult. PR: £1–20. Also, booksearch. Winter (November to Easter), please telephone first.

WIGTOWN

AA1 Books, ■ Unit 3, Duncan Park, Wigtown, Dumfries & Galloway, DG8 9JD. Prop: Marion Richmond. Tel: (01988) 402653. Website: www.bookavenue/hosted/AA1. E-mail: AA1books@supanet.com. Est: 2001. Shop; open **M:** 10:00–17:00; **T:** 10:00–17:00; **W:** 10:00–17:00; **Th:** 10:00–17:00; **F:** 10:00–17:00; **S:** 08:00–17:00; **Su:** 11:00–15:00. Very large stock. Spec: Children's - General; Espionage; Fiction - Crime, Detective, Spy, Thrillers; Fiction - Fantasy, Horror; Fiction - Science Fiction; Fiction - Westerns; Ghosts; History - General; Literature in Translation; Music - General; Natural History; Naval. PR: £1–150. CC: AE; MC; V. Also, new books. In association with Ming Books and Sign of the Dragon. Corresp: French, German.

Artyfacts, 14 North Main St., Wigtown, Dumfries & Galloway, DG8 9HL.

A.P. & R. Baker Limited, The Laigh House, Church Lane, Wigtown, Dumfries & Galloway, DG8 9HT. Prop: Anthony P. & Rosemary Baker. Tel: (01988) 403348. Fax: (01988) 403443. Website: www.apandrbaker.co.uk. E-mail: rosemary@apandrbaker.co.uk. Est: 1974. Spec: Archaeology; History - General. PR: £2–500.

Book Corner, ■ 2 High Street, Wigtown, Dumfries & Galloway, DG8 9HQ. Prop: Angela Langford. Tel: (01988) 402010. Website: www.book-corner.co.uk. E-mail: ian@book-corner.co.uk. Est: 1997. Shop; Internet and postal. Open **M:** 10:00–17:00; **T:** 10:00–17:00; **W:** 10:00–17:00; **Th:** 10:00–17:00; **F:** 10:00–17:00; **S:** 10:00–17:00. Very large general stock. Spec: Animals and Birds; Antiques; Art; Aviation; Botany; Conservation; Cookery/Gastronomy; Ecology; Entomology; Fiction - General; Food & Drink; Gardening; Horticulture; Lepidopterology / Lepidoptery; Motoring; Natural History; New Naturalist; Ornithology; and others as listed in the Speciality Index. PR: £1–150. CC: MC; V; SW. Also, wildlife art by major UK artists.

The Book Shop, 17 North Main Street, Wigtown, Dumfries & Galloway, DG8 9HL.

Books 'n' Looks, 15 South Main Street, Wigtown, Dumfries & Galloway, DG8 9EH.

The Box of Frogs, ■ 18 North Main Street, Wigtown, Dumfries & Galloway, DG8 9HL. Prop: Fiona Murphie. Tel: (01988) 402255. Fax: (01988) 402255. Website: www.froggybox.co.uk. E-mail: fiona@froggybox.co.uk. Est: 1998. Shop; open **M:** 10:00–16:30; **T:** 10:00–16:30; **W:** 10:00–16:30; **Th:** 10:00–16:30; **F:** 10:00–16:30; **S:** 10:00–16:30; **Su:** 12:00–16:00. Medium stock. Spec: Children's - General. PR: £1–100. CC: JCB; MC; V; SW. Mem: WBTA.

Byre Books, ■ 24 South Main St., Wigtown, Dumfries & Galloway, DG8 9EH. Prop: Laura Mustian and Chris Ballance. Tel: (01988) 402133. Website: www.byrebooks.co.uk. E-mail: info@byrebooks.co.uk. Est: 2000. Shop; Internet and postal. Open: **M:** 10:00–17:00; **T:** 10:00–17:00; **W:** 10:00–17:00; **Th:** 10:00–17:00; **F:** 10:00–17:00; **S:** 10:00–17:00. Small stock. Spec: Arthurian; Cinema/Film; Drama; Fables; Folklore; Mythology; Scottish Interest; Television; Theatre. PR: £3–100. CC: E; MC; V. From Nov-Mar irregular opening hours, phone first. Cata: 2. Corresp: Spanish, French. Mem: Wigtown Book Trades Ass. VAT No: GB 789 1742 76.

G C Books, ■ The Old Bank, 7 South Main Street, Wigtown, Dumfries & Galloway, DG8 9EH. Tel: (01988) 402688. Fax: (01988) 402688. Website: www.gcbooks.demon.co.uk. E-mail: sales@gcbooks.demon.co.uk. Est: 1990. Shop; Internet and postal. Open: **M:** 09:00–17:00; **T:** 09:00–17:00; **W:** 09:00–17:00; **Th:** 09:00–17:00; **F:** 09:00–17:00; **S:** 09:00–17:00. Large general stock. Spec: Academic/Scholarly; Architecture; Author - Niall, Ian; History - European; History - Local; History - National; Military History; Religion - General; Scottish Interest; War - World War II. PR: £1–1,000. CC: MC; V. Corresp: French. Mem: PBFA.

The Gleniffer Press, Benvoir, Wigtown, Dumfries & Galloway, DG8 9EE.

M.E. McCarty, Bookseller, 13 North Main St., Wigtown, Dumfries & Galloway, DG8 9HL.

Menavaur Books, Aberglass, Main Street, Kirkinner, Newton Stewart, Wigtown, Dumfries & Galloway, DG8 9AN. Prop: Paul & Carolle Oram. Tel: (01988) 840665. Website: www.abebooks.com. E-mail: menbks@globalnet.co.uk. Est: 1993. Private premises; postal business only. Contactable. Small stock. Spec: Academic/Scholarly; Advertising; Countries - Isles of Scilly; Fables; Fairgrounds; Illuminated Manuscripts; Illustrated; Maritime/Nautical; Satire; Scottish Interest; Travel - General. PR: £5–1,000. CC: MC; V. Cata: 4. Mem: PBFA.

Tim J. M'Garva, Barwhanny Farm, Whauphill, Wigtown, Dumfries & Galloway, DG8 9NU.

Ming Books, Beechwood House, Acre Place, Wigtown, Scotland, DG8 9DU. Prop: Mrs Marion Richmond. Tel: (01988) 402653. Fax: (0709) 221-8017. Website: www.mingbooks.com. E-mail: mingbooks@supanet.com. Est: 1982. Office &/or bookroom; Internet and postal. Open: **M:** 10:00–18:00; **T:** 10:00–18:00; **W:** 10:00–18:00; **Th:** 10:00–18:00; **F:** 10:00–18:00; **S:** 10:00–18:00; **Su:** 11:00–15:00. Closed for lunch: 12:00–13:00. Very large stock. Spec: Crime (True); Espionage; Fiction - Crime, Detective, Spy, Thrillers; History - General; Modern First Editions; Scottish Interest; Sherlockiana. PR: £4–1,000. CC: AE; MC; V; SW. Corresp: German and French. Mem: Wigtown Book Town. VAT No: GB 432 9993 15.

Reading Lasses, 17 South Main Street, Wigtown, Dumfries & Galloway, DG8 9EH. Prop: Angela Everitt. Tel: (01988) 403266. Fax: (01988) 403266. Website: www.wigtown-booktown.co.uk. E-mail: books@reading-lasses.com. Est: 1997. Spec: Academic/Scholarly; Authors - Women; Autobiography; Biography; Criminology; Diaries; Education & School; Feminism; Fiction - Women; Health; Homosexuality & Lesbianism; Psychology/Psychiatry; Religion - General; Scottish Interest; Social History; Travel - General; Women. PR: £1–50.

The Textile Book Bazaar, 6 South Main Street, Wigtown, Dumfries & Galloway, DG8 9EH. Tel: (01988) 402080.

Transformer, ■ 26 Bladnoch, Wigtown, Dumfries & Galloway, DG8 9AB. Prop: C.A. Weaver. Tel: (01988) 403455. E-mail: c.a.weaver@caweaver.freeserve.co.uk. Est: 1998. Shop; Internet and postal. Open in summer: **M:** 14:00–17:00; **T:** 14:00–17:00; **W:** 14:00–17:00; **Th:** 14:00–17:00; **F:** 14:00–17:00; **S:** 14:00–17:00; **Su:** 14:00–17:00. Large stock. Spec: Academic/Scholarly; Fiction - Science Fiction; Languages - Foreign; Science - General. PR: £1–300. Corresp: French.

FIFE

ANSTRUTHER

Rising Tide Books, 51 John Street, Cellardyke, Anstruther, Fife, KY10 3BA. Prop: Stephen Checkland. Tel: (01333) 310948. Fax: (01333) 310948. E-mail: stevecheckland@risingtidebooks.com. Est: 1997. Private premises; Type: Book fairs only. Appointment necessary. Very small stock. Spec: Illustrated; Modern First Editions; Scottish Interest. PR: £5–500. Mem: PBFA.

SCOTLAND

DUNFERMLINE,

Larry Hutchison (Books), 27 Albany Street, Dunfermline, Fife, KY12 OQZ. Tel: (01383) 725566. Fax: (01383) 620394. Website: www.larryhutchisobooks.com. E-mail: larry@larryhutchisonbooks.com. Est: 1987. Private premises; appointment necessary. Medium stock. Spec: Antiquarian; Countries - Scotland; Fine & Rare; Folklore; Genealogy; History - General; Literature; Military; Topography - Local. PR: £5–5,000. CC: AE; MC; V. Also, a booksearch service. Cata: 6. Corresp: most major European. Mem: PBFA. VAT No: GB 716 9500 30.

KIRKCALDY

R. Campbell Hewson Books, 6 West Albert Road, Kirkcaldy, Fife, KY1 1DL. Tel: (01592) 262051. Est: 1996. Private premises; appointment necessary. Small stock. Spec: Author - Burton, R.F.; Ethnography; Rural Life; Sport - Big Game Hunting; Travel - Africa; Voyages & Discovery. PR: £10–3,500.

Alistair Gibb, 17 Floors Place, Kirkcaldy, Fife, KY2 5SF.

NEWPORT ON TAY

Gordon Bettridge, 4 Myrtle Terrace, Newport on Tay, Fife, DD6 8DN.

Mair Wilkes Books, 3 St. Mary's Lane, Newport on Tay, Fife, DD6 8AH. Tel: (01382) 542260. Fax: (01382) 542260. E-mail: mairwilkes.books@zoom.co.uk. Est: 1969. Storeroom; open **T:** 10:00–16:30; **W:** 10:00–16:30; **Th:** 10:10–16:30; **F:** 10:00–16:30; **S:** 10:00–17:00. Closed for lunch: 12:30–14:00. Spec: Academic/Scholarly; Bindings; Fine & Rare; History of Ideas; Medicine - History of; Modern First Editions; Neurology; Psychology/Psychiatry; Science - History of; Scottish Interest; Topography - Local. PR: £2–1,000. CC: AE; V; SW. Cata: 3 – a year on Scottish Intererst. Mem: PBFA. *Also at:* Scottish Antiques Ctre, Abernyte, Inchture, Perthshire. VAT No: GB 397 9923 69.

ST. ANDREWS

The Quarto Bookshop, ■ 8 Golf Place, St. Andrews, Fife, KY16 9JA. Prop: M. Squires. Tel: (01334) 474616. E-mail: quartobooks@tesco.net. Est: 1969. Shop; open **M:** 10:00–17:30; **T:** 10:00–17:30; **W:** 10:00–17:30; **Th:** 10:00–17:30; **F:** 10:00–17:30; **S:** 10:00–17:30; **Su:** 12:00–17:00. Medium stock. Spec: Countries - Scotland; History - Local; Sport - Golf; Topography - Local. PR: £1–500. CC: MC; V. Also, a booksearch service. Corresp: French, Spanish. Mem: BA.

GRAMPIAN

ABERDEEN

Buchan Collectibles, South Meiklemoss, Collieston, Ellon, Aberdeen, Grampian, AB41 8SB. Tel: (+44) 1358 751774. Website: http://www.buchancollect.com. E-mail: enquiries@buchancollect.com. Est: 2000. Private premises; Internet and postal. Appointment necessary. Large general stock. Spec: Animals and Birds; Annuals; Biology; Botany; Children's - General; Comic Books & Annuals; Comics; Conservation; Entomology; Evolution; Fiction - General; Natural History; Ornithology; Poetry; Scottish Interest. PR: £3–500. CC: AE; JCB; MC; V. Also, booksearch. Mem: FSB.

Elizabeth Ferguson, 34 Woodburn Avenue, Aberdeen, Grampian, AB15 8JQ. Tel: (01224) 315949. Fax: (01224) 315949. E-mail: efergusonbooks@aol.com. Est: 2000. Postal business only. Small stock. PR: £5–500. Also, booksearch. Cata: – occasionally, on childrens, natural history. Corresp: French, German.

Grampian Books, South Monkshill, Fyvie, Turriff, Aberdeen, Grampian, AB53 8RQ. Prop: David Fleming. Tel: (01651) 891524. Fax: (01651) 891524. E-mail: dfleming@grampianbooks.sol.co.uk. Est: 1990. Private premises; appointment necessary. Medium stock. Spec: Academic/Scholarly; History of Ideas; Scottish Interest. PR: £2–1,000. CC: AE; MC; V. Corresp: French, Spanish. Mem: PBFA.

Kevin S. Ogilvie Modern First, 11 Wallacebrae Walk, Danestone, Aberdeen, Grampian, AB22 8YL. Tel: (07778) 637366. E-mail: kevinsogilvie@cwcom.net. Est: 1991. Postal business only. Spec: Children's - General; Countries - Melanesia; Countries - Mexico; First Editions; Modern First Editions. PR: £7–100.

Clifford Milne Books, 6 Hillcrest Place, Aberdeen, Grampian, AB2 7BP. Tel: (01224) 697654. Est: 1994. Private premises; postal business only. Small stock. Spec: Art; Countries - Scotland; Modern First Editions; Sport - Golf. PR: £1–100. Mem: PBFA.

Winram's Bookshop, ■ 32/36 Rosemount Place, Aberdeen, Grampian, AB25 2XB. Prop: Mrs. Margaret Davidson. Tel: (01224) 630673. Fax: (01224) 631532. Est: 1977. Shop; open **M:** 10:00–17:30; **T:** 10:00–17:30; **W:** 10:00–13:00; **Th:** 10:00–17:30; **F:** 10:00–17:30; **S:** 10:00–17:30. Medium general stock. Spec: Scottish Interest. PR: £1–1,000.

ABERLOUR

Speyside Books, 126 High Street, Aberlour, Grampian, AB38 9NX.

BALLATER

Deeside Books, ■ Station Square, Ballater, Aberdeenshire, AB35 5QB. Prop: Bryn Wayte. Tel: (01339) 754080. E-mail: deesidebk@aol.com. Est: 1998. Shop; open **M:** 10:00–17:00; **T:** 10:00–17:00; **W:** 10:00–17:00; **Th:** 10:00–17:00; **F:** 10:00–17:00; **S:** 10:00–17:00; **Su:** 12:00–17:00. Large stock. Spec: Military; Scottish Interest; Sport - Angling/Fishing; Sport - Field Sports; Topography - General; Topography - Local; Travel - General. PR: £1–100. CC: AE; JCB; MC; V. Mem: PBFA.

McEwan Fine Books, Glengarden, Ballater, Aberdeenshire, AB35 5UB. Prop: Dr. Peter McEwan. Tel: (01339) 755429. Fax: (01339) 755995. Website: www.rhodmcewan.com. E-mail: pjmm@easynet.co.uk. Est: 1968. Private premises; postal business only. Medium stock. Spec: Academic/Scholarly; Countries - Antarctic, The; Countries - Polar; Heraldry; Literature; Natural History; Ornithology; Sport - Angling/Fishing; Sport - Big Game Hunting; Sport - Cricket; Sport - Field Sports. PR: £5–5,000. Also, works of art. Cata: 4 – quarterly. *Also at:* Rhod McEwan Golf Books (q.v.).

Rhod McEwan Golf Books, Glengarden, Ballater, Aberdeenshire, AB35 5UB. Tel: (013397) 55429. Fax: (013397) 55995. Website: www.rhodmcewan.com. E-mail: teeoff@rhodmcewan.com. Est: 1985. Private premises; appointment necessary. Medium stock. Spec: Sport - Golf. PR: £3–5,000. CC: MC; V. Also, golf posters and paintings. Cata: 2. Corresp: German, Hungarian, Spanish. Mem: ABA. *Also at:* (At same premises:) McEwan Fine Books. (q.v.). VAT No: GB 605 2115 89.

RHOD McEWAN GOLF BOOKS

Specialist dealer in antiquarian, out-of-print and elusive books on golf

Annuals
Architecture
Biographies
Cigarette Cards
Club Histories
Ephemera
Essays
Fiction
Handbooks

Histories
Humour
Instructionals
Magazines
Rules
Tournament Histories
Turf Management
Upkeep
Women's Golf

I am always looking to purchase golf books in any quantity

Ballater, Royal Deeside, Aberdeenshire AB35 5UB
Telephone: (013397) 55429   Fax: (013397) 55995
E-mail: teeoff@rhodmcewan.com   www.rhodmcewan.com

ELGIN

Marianne Simpson, ■ 61/63 High Street, Fochabers, Elgin, Moray, IV32 7DU. Tel: (01343) 821192. Est: 1990. Shop; open **M:** 10:00–16:00; **T:** 10:00–16:00; **W:** 10:00–16:00; **Th:** 10:00–16:00; **F:** 10:00–16:00; **S:** 10:00–16:00. Closed for lunch: 13:00–14:00. Small general stock. PR: £1–100. Winter opening: Oct to Easter - Tues, Thurs & Sat 10:00-16:00. Closed lunch.

ELLON

Aberdeen Rare Books & Caledonian Books, Slains House, Collieston, Ellon, Grampian, AB41 8RT. Prop: A. J. & Mrs. P.M. Campbell. Tel: (01358) 751275. Est: 1977. Private premises; appointment necessary. Medium stock. Spec: Archaeology; Countries - Scotland; Fine & Rare; Heraldry; History - Local; Journals - General; Law; Music - General; Periodicals & Magazines; Poetry; Topography - Local. PR: £3–3,000. Cata: 1 – occasionally. Mem: PBFA. VAT No: GB 297 2352 32.

FOCHABERS

Alba Books, High Street, Fochabers, Moray, IV32 7DU. Prop: Mike Seton. Tel: (01343) 820575. Fax: (01343) 820780. Website: www.abebooks.com/home/albabooks. E-mail: Albabooks@dial.pipex.com. Office &/or bookroom; Internet and postal. Appointment necessary. Very large stock. Spec: Alternative Medicine; Art; Biology; Gynaecology; Literature; Maritime/Nautical; Medicine; Medicine - History of; Neurology; Pharmacy/Pharmacology; Psychoanalysis; Psychology/Psychiatry; Psychotherapy; Science - General; Scottish Interest; Veterinary; Zoology. PR: £2–200. CC: AE; E; MC; V; SW. Mem: IBooknet. VAT No: GB 751 3324 56.

FORRES

The Moray Bookshop, ■ Logie Steading Visitor Centre, Dunphail, Forres, IV36 2QN. Prop: Pierce Roche. Tel: (01309) 611373. Website: www.themoraybookshop.co.uk. E-mail: info@moraybookshop.co.uk. Est: 1999. Shop; (Shop sometimes closed January & February). Open: **M:** 11:00–17:00; **T:** 11:00–17:00; **W:** 11:00–17:00; **Th:** 11:00–17:00; **F:** 11:00–17:00; **S:** 11:00–17:00; **Su:** 11:00–17:01. Large general stock. Spec: Anthroposophy; Author - Walsh, M.; Cookery/Gastronomy; Countries - Scotland; Food & Drink; Scottish Interest; Whisky. PR: £1–500. CC: JCB; MC; V; SW. Cata: – Occasional. Mem: PBFA.

MONTROSE

Devanha Military Books, 4 Castle Terrace, Inverbervie, Montrose, Angus, DD10 0RE. Prop: Nick Ducat. Tel: (01561) 361387. E-mail: nickducat@devbooks.fsnet.co.uk. Est: 2001. Private premises; postal business only. Small stock. Spec: Military; Military History; War - General. PR: £5–350.

PETERHEAD

Vikings Books and Antiques, The Vikings, Auchiries, Cruden Bay, Peterhead, Aberdeenshire, AB42 0PE.

HIGHLAND

CULBOKIE

Tom Coleman, 2 Schoolcroft, Culbokie, Highland, IV7 8LB.

DINGWALL

Mercat Books, ■ 6 Church Street,, Dingwall, Highland, IV15 9SB. Prop: Hazel MacMillan. Tel: (01349) 865593. Fax: (01349) 865593. E-mail: mercat.books@zetnet.co.uk. Est: 1995. Shop; telephone first. Spec: Architecture; Fiction - General; Food & Drink; Gardening; Humour; Natural History; Poetry; Rural Life; Scottish Interest; Transport; War - General. PR: £1–100. Also, a booksearch service.

FORT WILLIAM

Don McGavin, 14 Lanark Place, Fort William, Inverness–shire, PH33 6UD. Tel: (01397) 703157. Private premises; appointment necessary. Very small general stock. PR: £1–100. Corresp: French.

Creaking Shelves, Arkaig Cottage, Fort William, Inverness-shire, Highland, PH33 6RN.

INVERNESS,

Leakey's Bookshop, ■ Greyfriars Hall, Church Street, Inverness, Highland, IV1 1EY. Prop: Charles Leakey. Tel: (01463) 239947. Est: 1979. Shop; open **M:** 10:00–17:30; **T:** 10:00–17:30; **W:** 10:00–17:30; **Th:** 10:00–17:30; **F:** 10:00–17:30; **S:** 10:00–17:30. Very large general stock. CC: E; JCB; MC; V.

LOCHCARRON

Blythswood Bookshop, ■ Main Street, Lochcarron, Ross-shire, IV54 8YD. Blythswood Trade. Tel: (01520) 722337. Fax: (01520) 722264. Website: www.blythswood.org. E-mail: blythswoodbookshop@lineone.net. Est: 1984. Shop; open **M:** 10:00–16:00; **T:** 10:00–16:00; **W:** 10:00–16:00; **Th:** 10:00–16:00; **F:** 10:00–16:00. Medium stock. Spec: Biography; First Editions; Religion - General; Religion - Christian; Theology. PR: £2–200. CC: MC; V. Also, new books. Mem: BA. *Also at:* Portree, Isle of Skye. Dingwell, Ross-shire. and Stornoway, Isle of Lewis, and Cromer, Norfolk. VAT No: GB 742 9279 06.

LOTHIAN

EDINBURGH,

Archways Sports Books, P.O. Box 13018, Edinburgh, Lothian, EH14 2YA. Prop: Iain C. Murray. Tel: (07990) 527942. E-mail: archways@blueyonder.co.uk. Est: 1992. Private premises; postal business only. Small stock. Spec: Health; Physical Culture; Sport - General. CC: AE; MC; V.

Armchair Books, 72 West Port, Edinburgh, Lothian, EH1 2LE. Prop: David Govan. Tel: (0131) 229-5927. E-mail: wlytle@ireland.com. Large general stock. Spec: Africana; Annuals; Art; Author - Buchan, John; Author - Chesterton, G.K.; Author - Lewis, C. S.; Countries - Ireland; Countries - Scotland; Esoteric; Fiction - Science Fiction; First Editions; History - Irish; Literature; Military History; Philosophy. PR: £1–200. CC: MC; V.

BOOKS

Antiquarian Books
Maps & Prints

Old & rare books on Fine Art,
Architecture, Scotland,
Edinburgh & Literature

Maps and Prints from the
17th–19th century

Open 10.30am–5.45pm Mon–Sat

The Old Town Bookshop

8 Victoria Street, Edinburgh
Tel: 0131 225 9237
www.oldtownbookshop.co.uk

SCOTLAND

Peter Bell, ■ 68 West Port, Edinburgh, Lothian, EH1 2LD. Tel: Home (0131) 556-2198. Fax: (0131) 558-9305. Website: www.peterbell.net. E-mail: books@peterbell.demon.co.uk. Est: 1980. *Shop at:* (Please ring if visiting on a Monday. Shop tel: (0131) 229-0562.) Open: **M:** 10:00–17:00; **T:** 10:00–17:00; **W:** 10:00–17:00; **Th:** 10:00–17:00; **F:** 10:00–17:00; **S:** 10:00–17:00. Small stock. Spec: Academic/Scholarly; Antiquarian; Biography; History - British; Literature; Philosophy; Publishers - Edinburgh University Press; Religion - Christian; Scottish Interest; Social History. PR: £1–200. CC: MC; V. Stock listed on abebooks.com and a selection of stock on show at Biblion, 7 Davies Mews, London W1K 5AB. Cata: – occasionally. Mem: ABA. VAT No: GB 416 0959 50.

Blacket Books, 1 Leadervale Terrace, Edinburgh, Lothian, EH16 6NX. Prop: Elizabeth Laing. Tel: (0131) 666-1542. Website: www.blacketbooks.co.uk. E-mail: liz@blacketbooks.co.uk. Est: 1985. Private premises; Internet and postal. Telephone first. Small general stock. Spec: Children's - General; Military; Scottish Interest. PR: £10–1,500. CC: JCB; MC; V. Mem: PBFA.

Bon Accord Enterprises, 14 Pentland Avenue, Colinton, Edinburgh, Lothian, EH13 0HZ. Tel: (0131) 441-6808. Est: 1987. Private premises; postal business only. Spec: Military. PR: £1–20. Cata: 1 – occasionally.

The Book Swop, 28 Bruntsfield Place, Edinburgh, Lothian, EH10 4HJ.

Broughton Books, ■ 2a Broughton Place, Edinburgh, Lothian, EH1 3RX. Prop: Peter Galinsky. Tel: (0131) 557-8010. Est: 1963. Shop; open **T:** 12:00–18:00; **W:** 12:00–18:00; **Th:** 12:00–18:00; **F:** 12:00–18:00; **S:** 09:30–17:30. Large stock. Spec: History - General; Humanities; Literature. PR: £2–250. Corresp: Flemish, French, Frisian, German, Dutch, Spanish.

Anna Buxton Books, Redcroft, 23 Murrayfield Road, Edinburgh, Lothian, EH12 6EP. Prop: A. Buxton. Tel: (0131) 337-1747. Fax: (0131) 337-8174. E-mail: annabuxtonb@aol.com. Est: 1989. Private premises; Internet and postal. Appointment necessary. Very small stock. Spec: Botany; Gardening; Landscape; Plant Hunting. PR: £12–1,000. CC: MC; V; SW. Cata: 1. Corresp: French, Italian. Mem: PBFA.

Duncan & Reid, 5 Tanfield, Edinburgh, Lothian, EH3 5DA.

Edward Fenwick, 3 Thirlestane Lane, Edinburgh, Lothian, EH9 1AJ.

Ferrial Books, 33 Bellfield Street, Edinburgh, Lothian, EH15 2BR.

Grant & Shaw Ltd., 62 West Port, Edinburgh, Lothian, EH1 2LD.

Jay Books, Rowll House, Roull Grove, Edinburgh, Lothian, EH12 7JP. Prop: D.J. Brayford. Tel: (0131) 316-4034. Fax: (0131) 467-0309. Website: www.jaybooks.demon.co.uk. E-mail: djb@jaybooks.demon.co.uk. Est: 1977. Private premises; Internet and postal. Appointment necessary. Open: **M:** 09:00–21:00; **T:** 09:00–21:00; **W:** 09:00–21:00; **Th:** 09:00–21:00; **F:** 09:00–21:00; **S:** 09:00–21:00; **Su:** 09:00–21:00. Small stock. Spec: Botany; Gardening; Natural History; Science - General; Science - History of; Technology. PR: £20–1,000. CC: MC; V. Also, valuations. Cata: 3. Corresp: Spanish, German, French. Mem: ABA; PBFA; ILAB.

Domhnall MacCormaig, 19 Braid Crescent, Edinburgh, Lothian, EH10 6AX. Prop: Domhnall MacCormaig. Tel: (0131) 447-2889. Fax: (0131) 447-9496. E-mail: grenitote@aol.com. Est: 1976. Private premises; postal business only. Medium stock. Spec: Countries - Scotland; Culture - National; History - Local; Literature in Translation; Scottish Interest; Topography - Local. PR: £10–5,000. Cata: 8 – a year on specialities. Mem: ABA.

Main Point Books, ■ 8 Lauriston Street, Edinburgh, Lothian, EH3 9DJ. Prop: Richard Browne. Tel: (0131) 228 4837. Fax: (0131) 228 4837. Est: 2001. Shop; open **T:** 11:00–17:00; **W:** 11:00–17:00; **Th:** 11:00–17:00; **F:** 11:00–17:00; **S:** 11:00–17:00. Medium stock. Spec: Alpinism/Mountaineering; Esoteric; Fiction - General; Literature; Poetry; Scottish Interest; Sport - Climbing & Trekking; Theology.

McFeely's Bookstore, 30 Buccleuch Street, Edinburgh, Lothian, EH15 1HZ.

McNaughtan's Bookshop, ■ 3a and 4a Haddington Place, Leith Walk, Edinburgh, Lothian, EH7 4AE. Prop: Elizabeth A. Strong. Tel: (0131) 556-5897. Fax: (0131) 556 8220. E-mail: mcnbooks@btconnect.com. Est: 1957. Shop; open **T:** 09:30–17:30; **W:** 09:30–17:30; **Th:** 09:30–17:30; **F:** 09:30–17:30; **S:** 09:30–17:30. Very large stock. Spec: Antiquarian; Architecture; Art; Children's - General; Literature; Scottish Interest. PR: £1–3,500. CC: MC; V. Mem: ABA; ILAB.

Robert S. Murray, 5 Briery Bauks, The Pleasance, Edinburgh, Lothian, EH8 9TE.

The Old Children's Bookshelf, 175 Canongate, Royal Mile, Edinburgh, Lothian, EH8 8BN.

SCOTLAND

The Old Town Bookshop, ■ 8 Victoria Street, Edinburgh, Lothian, EH1 2HG. Prop: Ronald Wilson. Tel: (0131) 225-9237. Fax: (0131) 229-1503. Website: www.oldtownbookshop.co.uk. E-mail: otb@ntlworld.com. Est: 1992. Shop; open **M:** 10:30–17:45; **T:** 10:30–17:45; **W:** 10:30–17:45; **Th:** 10:30–17:45; **F:** 10:30–17:45; **S:** 10:00–17:45. Medium stock. Spec: Antiquarian; Architecture; Art; Illustrated; Literature; Scottish Interest. PR: £1–5,000. CC: JCB; MC; V; D, SW. Mem: PBFA.

David Page, 47 Spottiswoode Road, Edinburgh, Lothian, EH9 1DA. Tel: (0131) 447-4553. Fax: (0131) 447-4553. E-mail: page@47spot.freeserve.co.uk. Private premises; telephone first. Small stock. Spec: Alpinism/Mountaineering; Natural History; Plant Hunting; Travel - General; Travel - Africa; Travel - Asia; Travel - Middle East; Travel - Polar. Corresp: French, German.

Pinnacle Books, 13 Westgarth Avenue, Edinburgh, Lothian, EH13 0BB.

Andrew Pringle Booksellers, ■ 39 Dundas Street, Edinburgh, Lothian, EH3 6QQ. Tel: (0131) 556-9698. Website: www.pringlebooks.co.uk. E-mail: andrew@pringlebooks.co.uk. Est: 1988. Shop; Medium stock. Spec: Antiquarian; Biography; History - National; Literature; Modern First Editions; Scottish Interest. PR: £3–500. CC: JCB; V. Corresp: French. Mem: PBFA.

Second Edition, ■ 9 Howard Street, Edinburgh, Lothian, EH3 5JP. Prop: Mrs. Maureen E. and W.A. Smith. Tel: (0131) 556-9403. Website: www.secondeditionbookshop.co.uk. E-mail: secondedition@tiscali.co.net. Est: 1979. Shop; open **M:** 10:29–17:30; **T:** 10:29–17:30; **W:** 10:30–17:30; **Th:** 10:30–17:30; **F:** 10:30–17:30; **S:** 09:30–17:30. Large stock. Spec: Children's - General; Fine Art; First Editions; Illustrated; Literature; Military History; Scottish Interest; Travel - General. PR: £10–10,000.Corresp: Croatian, French, German, Serbian, Slovenian, Spanish.

Till's Bookshop, ■ 1 Hope Park Crescent, (Buccleugh Street), Edinburgh, Lothian, EH8 9NA. Tel: (0131) 667-0895. E-mail: tillsbookshop@hotmail.com. Est: 1986. Shop; open **M:** 12:00–19:30; **T:** 12:00–19:30; **W:** 12:00–19:30; **Th:** 12:00–19:30; **F:** 12:00–19:30; **S:** 11:00–18:00; **Su:** 12:00–17:30. Large stock. Spec: Academic/Scholarly; Children's - General; Cinema/Film; Counterculture; Countries - Mexico; Crime (True); Drama; Entertainment - General; Feminism; Fiction - Crime, Detective, Spy, Thrillers; Fiction - Fantasy, Horror; Fiction - Science Fiction; Fiction - Westerns; and others as listed in the Speciality Index. PR: £1–100. CC: E; MC; V; DE, SW, SO.

John Updike Rare Books, 7 St. Bernard's Row, Edinburgh, Lothian, EH4 1HW. Prop: John S. Watson & Edward G. Nairn. Tel: (0131) 332-1650. Fax: (0131) 332-1347. Est: 1965. Private premises; appointment necessary. Medium general stock. Spec: Books about Books; Children's - General; Churchilliana; Drama; Fine & Rare; Fine Printing; First Editions; Illustrated; Irish Interest; Limited Editions; Literature; Literature in Translation; Periodicals & Magazines; Poetry; Private Press; and others as listed in the Speciality Index. Cata: 2 – a year on specialities. Mem: ABA.

West Port Books, 145 West Port, Edinburgh, Lothian.

HADDINGTON

Yeoman Books, 37 Hope Park Crescent, Haddington, East Lothian, EH41 3AN. Prop: D.A. Hyslop. Tel: (01620) 822307. Fax: (01620) 822307. E-mail: yeomanbooks@talk21.com. Est: 1924. Private premises; appointment necessary. Very small stock. Spec: Aviation; Military; Military History; Motorbikes; Motoring; War - General. PR: £5–150. Mem: PBFA.

SOUTH QUEENSFERRY

Marion Shearer, 41 Moubray Grove, South Queensferry, West Lothian, EH30 9PB. Tel: (0131) 331-1978. Private premises; postal business only. Very small general stock. PR: £2–200.

STRATHCLYDE

AIRDRIE

Brown-Studies, Woodside Cottage, Longriggend, Airdrie, Strathclyde, ML6 7RU. (*) Prop: Mr. M.G. & Mrs. B.J. Brown. Tel: (01236) 843826. Fax: (01236) 842545. Website: www.brown-studies.co.uk. E-mail: brownstudies@clara.co.uk. Est: 1990. Private premises; Internet and postal. Appointment necessary. Open: **M:** 09:00–20:00; **T:** 09:00–20:00; **W:** 09:00–20:00; **Th:** 09:00–20:00; **F:** 09:00–20:00; **S:** 09:00–20:00; **Su:** 09:00–20:00. Very large stock. Spec: Artists; Author - Read, Miss; Building & Construction; Cookery/Gastronomy; D.I.Y (Do It Yourself); Ecology; Gardening; Herbalism; Knitting; Needlework; Woodwork. PR: £3–300. CC: E; MC; V; SW. Mem: Ibooknet. VAT No: GB 556 6923 05.

AYR

Ainslie Books, ■ 1 Glendoune St., Girvan, Ayrshire, KA26 0AA. (*) Prop: Agnes & Gordon Clark. Tel: (01465) 715453. Fax: (01465) 715453. Website: www.ainsliebooks.co.uk. E-mail: ainslie.books@btopenworld.com. Shop; Internet and postal. Open: **M:** 10:00–17:00; **T:** 10:00–17:00; **W:** 10:00–17:00; **Th:** 10:00–17:00; **F:** 10:00–17:00; **S:** 10:00–17:00. Large general stock. Spec: Academic/Scholarly; Advertising; Aeronautics; Africana; Shorthand. PR: £1–200. CC: MC; V. Also, booksearch.

Village Books, 7 Alloway, Ayr, Strathclyde, KA7 4PY.

BIGGAR

Karen Thomson, South Lindsaylands, Biggar, Strathclyde, ML12 6NR. Tel: (01899) 221991. Fax: (01899) 221955. Est: 1987. Private premises; postal business only. Very small stock. Spec: Academic/Scholarly; Antiquarian; Dictionaries; Medieval; Philology. Cata: 6. Corresp: French, German.

CAMPBELTOWN

The Old Bookshelf, ■ 8 Cross Street, Campbeltown, Strathclyde, PA28 6HU. Prop: David and Davina Tomlinson. Tel: (01586) 551114. Website: www.theoldbookshelf.co.uk. E-mail: theoldbookshelf@aol.com. Est: 2001. Shop; Internet and postal. Open: **M:** 11:00–17:00; **T:** 11:00–17:00; **W:** 11:00–17:00; **Th:** 11:00–17:00; **F:** 11:00–17:00; **S:** 10:00–16:00. Large stock. CC: AE; D; E; JCB; MC; SW, SO. Mem: ibooknet. VAT No: GB 808 8668 81.

DALMELLINGTON

Wheen O'Blethers Bookshop, Unit 1, Dame Helen Bookcentre, 18c Ayr Road, Dalmellington, Strathclyde, KA6 7SJ. Prop: Ron Gabbott. Tel: (01292) 531723. Est: 2000. Spec: Biography; Calligraphy; Company History; Folklore; Industry; Linguistics; Private Press. PR: £1–500.

GLASGOW

Alba Secondhand Music, ■ Otago Street, Glasgow, Strathclyde, G12 8PQ. Prop: Robert Lay. Tel: (01389) 875996. Website: www.albamusick.co.uk. E-mail: robert@albamusick.fsnet.co.uk. Est: 1994. Shop; open **M:** 11:00–17:30; **T:** 11:00–17:30; **W:** 11:00–17:30; **Th:** 11:00–17:30; **F:** 11:00–17:30; **S:** 11:00–17:30. Large stock. Spec: Music - Classical. CC: MC; V. Shop located behind Otago café & open at other times by appointment.

Jack Baldwin, 34 Hamilton Park Avenue, Glasgow, Strathclyde, G12 8DT.

Caledonia Books, 483 Great Western Road, Kelvinbridge, Glasgow, Strathclyde, G12 8HL. Prop: Maureen Smillie & Charles McBride. Tel: (0141) 334-9663. Fax: (0141) 334-9663. Website: www.caledoniabooks.co.uk. E-mail: caledoniabooks@aol.com. Est: 1984. Spec: Art; Art History; Bibliography; Biography; Cinema/Film; Countries - Poland; Drama; Fiction - General; History - General; Irish Interest; Literary Criticism; Literature; Modern First Editions; Philosophy; Scottish Interest. PR: £2–200. CC: MC; V.

Cooper Hay Rare Books, ■ 182 Bath Street, Glasgow, Strathclyde, G2 4HG. Tel: (0141) 333-1992. Fax: (0141) 333-1992. Website: www.abebooks.com/home/haybooks. E-mail: chayrbooks@aol.com. Est: 1985. Shop; open **M:** 10:00–17:30; **T:** 10:00–17:30; **W:** 10:00–17:30; **Th:** 10:00–17:30; **F:** 10:00–17:30; **S:** 10:00–13:00. Closed for lunch: 13:00–14:15. Medium stock. Spec: Art; Bindings; Countries - Scotland; Juvenile; Scottish Interest. PR: £5–10,000. CC: MC; V. Cata: 2. Mem: ABA; ILAB.

Eddie's Books and Cards, Argyle Market Centre, 28 Argyle Street, Glasgow, Strathclyde, G2 8AD. Prop: Edward E. Cowan. Tel: (0141) 226-3050. Est: 1982. Market stand/stall. Open: **M:** 09:30–17:00; **T:** 09:30–17:00; **W:** 09:30–17:00; **Th:** 09:30–17:00; **F:** 09:30–17:00; **S:** 09:30–17:30. Medium stock. PR: £1–6. Also, greetings cards, remainders, calendars and jigsaws.

Erasmus Books, 34 Hamilton Park Avenue, Glasgow, Strathclyde, G12 8DT.

The Studio, De Courcy's Arcade, S. 21 Cresswell Lane, Glasgow, Strathclyde, G12 8AA.

Word of Mouth, c/o Moon, 10 Ruthven Lane, Glasgow, Strathclyde, G12 9BG. E-mail: ianmrry@aol.com.

Thistle Books, 61 Otago Street, Glasgow, Strathclyde, G12 8PQ. Prop: Robert Dibble. Tel: (0141) 334 8777. Est: 1997. PR: £1–50.

GREENOCK

Westwords, 14 Newton Street, Greenock, Strathclyde, PA16 8UJ.

HELENSBURGH

Brian Annesley Books of Scottish Interest, 26 Duchess Drive, Helensburgh, Dunbartonshire, G84 9PR. Tel: (01436) 676222. Fax: (0870) 0568922. Website: www.scotbooks.demon.co.uk. E-mail: brian@scotbooks.demon.co.uk. Est: 1983. Internet and postal. Small stock. Spec: Academic/Scholarly; Countries - Scotland. PR: £5–500. CC: MC; V.

McLaren Books, 22 John Street, Helensburgh, Dunbartonshire, G84 8BA. Tel: (01436) 676453. Fax: (01436) 673747. Website: www.mclarenbooks.co.uk. E-mail: mclarenbooks@breathe.co.uk. Est: 1976. Office &/or bookroom. Open: **F:** 10:00–17:00; **S:** 10:00–17:00. Medium stock. Spec: Manuals - Seamanship; Maritime/Nautical; Maritime/Nautical - Log Books; Naval; Navigation; Ship Modelling; Shipbuilding; Sport - Canoeing/Kayaks; Sport - Rowing; Sport - Yachting; Whaling. PR: £5–1,000. CC: MC; V; SW. Cata: 10. Mem: ABA; PBFA; ILAB. VAT No: GB 293 0008 81.

IRVINE

D. Webster, 43 West Road, Irvine, Ayrshire, KA12 8RE. Tel: (01294) 272257. Fax: (01294) 276322. E-mail: davidpwebster@hotmail.com. Est: 1958. Private premises; appointment necessary. Small stock. Spec: Circus; Physical Culture; Sport - Highland Games; Sport - Weightlifting/Bodybuilding; Sport - Wrestling. PR: £5–40. Also, booksearch. Cata: 2.

ISLE OF ARRAN

Barnhill Books, Old Schoolhouse, Kilmory, Isle of Arran, Strathclyde, KA27 8PQ. Prop: John Rhead. Tel: (01770) 870368. E-mail: rheadz@btinternet.com. Est: 1985. Private premises; postal business only. Spec: Alpinism/Mountaineering; Gardening; Natural History; Ornithology; Plant Hunting; Sport - Big Game Hunting; Sport - Falconry; Sport - Field Sports; Travel - General. PR: £5–2,000. Cata: 1.

Johnston's Marine Stores, Old Pier, Lamlash, Isle of Arran, Strathclyde, KA27 8JN.

Audrey McCrone, Windyridge, Whiting Bay, Isle of Arran, Strathclyde, KA27 8QT. Tel: (01770) 700564. Fax: (01770) 700564. Website: www.ukbookworld.com/members/finora. E-mail: a.mccrone@btinternet.com. Est: 1980. Private premises; Internet and postal. Telephone first. Small stock. Spec: Animals and Birds; Anthologies; Antiquarian; Archaeology; Art History; Astronomy; Biography; Children's - General; Crafts; Divining; Earth Mysteries; History - General; Illustrated; Literature; Military; Military History; Modern First Editions; and others as listed in the Speciality Index. PR: £5–200. Cata: 24.

ISLE OF COLONSAY

Colonsay Bookshop, ■ Isle of Colonsay, Argyll, Isle of Colonsay, Strathclyde, PA61 7YR. Prop: Kevin & Christa Byrne. Tel: (01951) 200232. Fax: (01951) 200232. Website: www.colonsay.org.uk. E-mail: bookshop@colonsay.org.uk. Est: 1988. Shop open in summer. Very small stock. Spec: Countries - Scotland; Scottish Interest. PR: £1–300. CC: MC; V; SW. Also, new books & publisher.

KILMARNOCK

Richard Roberts Bookseller, 8 Main Road, Waterside, Kilmarnock, Strathclyde, KA3 6JB.

MAYBOLE

ARC Books, 3 Whitehall, Maybole, Ayrshire, KA19 7AJ. Prop: Colin C. Galloway. Tel: (01655) 883441. E-mail: whitehallfairs@aol.com. Est: 1985. Postal business only. Very small stock. Spec: Children's - General; Fiction - General; Hobbies. PR: £3–20. Attends fairs at Alloway Village Hall, Ayr & Book Vaults in Wigtown.

Whitehall Antiques & Fairs, 3 Whitehall, Maybole, Ayrshire, HA19 7AJ. Tel: (01655) 883441. E-mail: whitehallfairs@aol.com. Est: 1996. Private premises; postal business only. Small stock. Spec: Children's - General; Countries - Scotland; Hobbies.

OBAN

Bygone Books, Terok Nor, Ardconnel Hill, Oban, Strathclyde, PA34 5DY. Prop: Simon D. Phillips. Tel: (01631) 563928. E-mail: simonph@hotmail.com. Est: 1987. Private premises; postal business only. Appointment necessary. Spec: Occult. PR: £5–100.

PAISLEY

Paisley Fine Books, 17 Corsebar Crescent, Paisley, Renfrewshire, PA2 9QA.

Barry Thurston, 3a Durrockstock Crescent, Paisley, Renfrewshire, PA2 0AW. Prop: Barry Thurston. Tel: (07986) 118480. Est: 2000. Market stand/stall at London Road Market, The Barras, Glasgow. Open: **S:** 09:30–16:00; **Su:** 09:30–16:00. Medium stock. Spec: Children's - General; Natural History; Ornithology; Scottish Interest. PR: £2–500. Fairs: Glasgow and North of England.

TAYSIDE

ABERFELDY
Freader's Books, 8 Dunkeld Street, Aberfeldy, Perthshire, Tayside, PH15 2DA.

ARBROATH
J. & M. Wilson, 94 Brechin Road, Arbroath, Angus, DD11 1SX. Prop: Janine Wilson. Tel: (01241) 877552. Fax: (08700) 529822. Website: jandmwilson.demon.co.uk. E-mail: books@jandmwilson.demon.co.uk. Est: 1986. Private premises; Internet and postal. Small stock. Spec: Author - Brent-Dyer, Elinor M.; Author - Buckeridge, A.; Author - Crompton, Richmal; Author - Dahl, Roald; Author - Needham, V; Author - Oxenham, Elsie; Children's - General; Fiction - Crime, Detective, Spy, Thrillers; Illustrated; Modern First Editions. PR: £1–500. Cata: 3 – Children's.

BLAIR ATHOLL
Atholl Browse, ■ by the Station, Blair Atholl, Perthshire, PH18 5SG. Prop: John & Mary Herdman. Tel: (01796) 481530. Est: 1989. Shop; open **M:** 10:00–18:00; **T:** 10:00–18:00; **W:** 10:00–18:00; **Th:** 10:00–18:00; **F:** 10:00–18:00; **S:** 10:00–18:00; **Su:** 12:00–18:00. Small stock. Spec: Scottish Interest. PR: £1–30. Nov - March 12:00 till 17:00 Mon - Sun. Closed Jan, Feb. Free Coffee. Corresp: French.

CRIEFF
Strathearn Books, Argyle House, Commissioner Street, Crieff, Tayside, PH7 3AY.

DUNDEE
Meadowside Bookshop, ■ 75 Meadowside, Dundee, Tayside. Prop: St. Mary Magdalene's Church. Tel: (01382) 223510. Website: www.marymagdalene.freeserve.co.uk. Est: 1985. Shop; open **M:** 10:30–17:30; **T:** 10:30–17:30; **W:** 10:30–17:30; **Th:** 10:30–17:30; **F:** 10:30–17:30. Small general stock. PR: £1–8. Corresp: French.

FORFAR
Hilary Farquharson, Deuchar Farm, Fern, Forfar, Tayside, DD8 3QZ. Prop: H. Farquharson. Tel: (01356) 650278. Fax: (01356) 650417. E-mail: deuchar-farm@fsmail.net. Est: 1992. Private premises; Type: Book fairs only. Appointment necessary. Open: **M:** 08:00–21:00; **T:** 08:00–21:00; **W:** 08:00–21:00; **Th:** 08:00–20:00; **F:** 08:00–21:00; **S:** 08:00–21:00; **Su:** 21:00–22:00. Medium stock. Spec: Agriculture; Antiquarian; Countries - Scotland; Genealogy; Motoring; Scottish Interest; Topography - General; Topography - Local. PR: £5–1,000. CC: JCB; V. Mem: PBFA.

KILLIECRANKIE
Atholl Fine Books, Clunemore Farm, Killiecrankie, by Pitlochry, PH16 5LS. Prop: Nancy Cameron. Tel: (01796) 473470. Fax: (01796) 473030. E-mail: nancy.foy@btinternet.com. Est: 1989. Private premises; postal business only. Very small stock. Spec: Antiquarian; Bindings; Countries - Scotland; Fine & Rare; Scottish Interest; Travel - General. PR: £20–300. CC: MC; V. Cata: 1 – see Atholl Books on abebooks.com. Mem: Soc. of Bookbinders. *Also at:* same premises - Atholl Bindery. E-mail: jcfcameron@btopenworld.com.

PITLOCHRY
Glacier Books, Ard–Darach, Strathview Terrace, Pitlochry, Perthshire, Tayside, PH16 5AT. Prop: Chris Bartle. Tel: (01796) 470056. Fax: (01796) 470056. Website: www.glacierbooks.com. E-mail: sales@glacierbooks.com. Est: 1999. Private premises; Internet and postal. Telephone first. Medium stock. Spec: Alpinism/Mountaineering; Travel - Polar; Voyages & Discovery. PR: £1–3,000. Cata: 3.

SCONE
Bookseeker, 5 Isabella Place, Scone, Tayside, PH2 6TE.

WESTERN ISLES

KIRKWALL

M.E.McCarty, Bookseller, ■ 54 Junction Road, Kirkwall, Western Isles, KW15 1AG. Prop: Moi McCarty. Tel: (01988) 402062. Fax: (01988) 402062. E-mail: moi@orkneybooks.co.uk. Est: 1986. Shop; postal business only. Appointment necessary. Open: **M:** 10:30–17:00; **T:** 10:30–17:00; **W:** 10:30–17:00; **Th:** 10:30–17:00; **F:** 10:30–17:00; **S:** 10:30–17:00; **Su:** 12:00–17:00. Closed for lunch: 13:00–16:00. Medium general stock. PR: £1–100. Corresp: French, German, Norwegian. Mem: PBFA; *Also at:* 13 North Main Street, Wigtown, Scotland (q.v.) and The Book Vaults, Wigtown Scotland (q.v.).

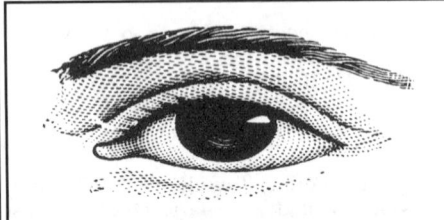

CAROL HOGBEN

Trade Catalogues

Industries & Arts

Manufacturers' pattern books, well illustrated wholesalers' price lists, big stores' general catalogues, interesting sales brochures etc., esp. 1840-1940

Berthlas Chapel Cottage,
Trefeglwys, nr Caersws,
Powys, SY17 5QG
Tel: 01686-430653
Fax: 01686-430447

REPUBLIC OF IRELAND

CO. CARLOW

Barrow Books, Raheen, Old Leighlin, Co. Carlow.

CO. CAVAN

CAVAN

Cavan Book Centre, Main Street, Cavan, Co. Cavan. Prop: Beatrice Maloney. Tel: (049) 436-2882. Est: 1984. Spec: Archaeology; Biography; Irish Interest; Maritime/Nautical; Religion - General; Transport; Travel - General. PR: £1–200. Also, booksearch.

COOTEHILL

Sillan Books, Drumgreen, Cootehill, Co. Cavan.

CO. CLARE

DOOLIN

Doolin Dinghy Books, ■ Fisher Street, Doolin, Co. Clare. Prop: Cynthia Sinnott Griffin. Tel: (065) 70 74449. Est: 1982. Shop; open **M:** 09:00–21:00; **T:** 09:00–21:00; **W:** 09:00–21:00; **Th:** 09:00–21:00; **F:** 08:00–21:00; **S:** 08:00–21:00. Small stock. Spec: Art; Biography; Children's - General; Fiction - General; Folklore; History - National; Languages - National; Literature; Travel - Europe. PR: £1–150. Open only March-October. Other times call for appointment. Cata: 1 – annually on Irish interests. Corresp: French. Mem: ASBI.

CO. CORK

BALLINLOUGH

Royal Carbery Books Ltd., Lissadell, 36 Beechwood Park, Ballinlough, Co. Cork. Prop: G. & M. Feehan. Tel: (021) 4294191. Fax: (021) 4294191. E-mail: mgfeehan@eircom.net. Est: 1976. Private premises; appointment necessary. Medium stock. Spec: Folklore; Guide Books; History - General; History - Local; Irish Interest; Literary Travel; Military; Music - Folk & Irish Folk; Topography - General. Cata: 4 – Irish interest.

BALLYDEHOB

Schull Books, , Ballydehob, Co.Cork. Prop: Barbara & Jack O'Connell. Tel: (+353) [0]28 37317. Fax: (+353) [0]28 37317. Website: www.schullbooks.com. E-mail: schullbooks@eircom.net. Est: 1981. Office &/or bookroom; appointment necessary. Regular exhibitor at Dublin bookfairs; contact for details. Open: **M:** 10:00–19:00; **T:** 10:00–19:00; **W:** 10:00–19:00; **Th:** 10:00–19:00; **F:** 10:00–19:00; **S:** 10:00–19:00. Medium stock. Spec: Irish Interest; Military History. PR: £10–500. CC: E; MC; V. Cata: 3 – Irish interest and military history. Corresp: French, German, Irish.

CLONAKILTY

Delaney's Books, Spillers Lane, Clonakilty, Co. Cork. Prop: Sheila Delaney. Tel: (023) 34363. Spec: Author - Orwell, George. PR: £1–100. Also, booksearch.

DUNMANWAY

Darkwood Books, Darkwood, Dunmanway, Co. Cork, . Prop: Annette Sheehan. Tel: (023) 55470. Fax: (023) 55224. Website: www.abebooks.com/homepage/darkwoodbooks/. E-mail: darkwood@indigo.ie. Est: 2000. Private premises; postal business only. Medium general stock. Spec: Architecture; Art; Art History; Art Reference; Artists; Biography; Countries - Ireland; History - General; History - Irish; Irish Interest; Sport - Angling/Fishing; Sport - Hunting; Sport - Shooting. PR: £1–500. CC: MC; V. Cata: 2.

MIDLETON

Gerald Mac Sweeney, East Ferry Cottage, Midleton, Co. Cork.

ROSSCARBERY

C.P. Hyland, ■ The Square, Rosscarbery, Co. Cork. Prop: Cal & Joan Hyland. Tel: (023) 48063. Fax: (023) 48658. Website: www.cphyland.com. E-mail: calbux@iol.ie. Est: 1966. Shop; Internet and postal. Telephone first. Open: **M:** 10:00–17:30; **T:** 10:00–17:30; **W:** 10:00–17:30; **Th:** 10:00–17:30; **F:** 10:00–17:30; **S:** 10:00–17:30; **Su:** 12:00–17:30. Large stock. Spec: Countries - Ireland; Irish Interest; Languages - National. PR: £1–10,000. CC: MC; V. Also, a restaurant on the premises. Cata: 4. Corresp: Gaelic.

SCHULL

Fuchsia Books, Main Street, Schull, Co. Cork. Prop: Mary Mackey. Tel: (028) 28016. Fax: (028) 28016. Website: www.fuchsiabooks.com. E-mail: shop@fuchsiabooks.com. Open: **M:** 10:00–17:00; **T:** 10:00–17:00; **W:** 10:00–17:00; **Th:** 10:00–17:00; **F:** 10:00–17:00; **S:** 10:00–17:00. Closed for lunch: 13:00–14:00. Small general stock. Spec: History - National; Irish Interest. PR: £1–200. Also, a booksearch service.

SKIBBEREEN

Fine Irish Books, P.O.Box 19, Skibbereen, Co. Cork. Prop: Michael Richards & Eve Chambers. Tel: (086) 8535365. Website: www.fineirishbooks.com. E-mail: bookskib@eircom.net. Est: 1995. Private premises; Internet and postal. Appointment necessary. Small stock. Spec: Antiquarian; Countries - Ireland; Fine & Rare; History - Irish; Irish Interest; Limited Editions; Private Press. PR: £100–10,000. CC: AE; MC; V; Paypal. Corresp: French, German, Spanish, Italian, Dutch, Japanese.

YOUGHAL

Alan Prim, ■ 6 South Main St., Youghal, Co. Cork. Prop: Alan Prim. Tel: (0035) 324 92781. E-mail: waprim@hotmail.com. Est: 1998. Shop; open **M:** 10:00–18:00; **T:** 10:00–18:00; **W:** 10:00–18:00; **Th:** 10:00–18:00; **F:** 10:00–18:00; **S:** 10:00–18:00; **Su:** 14:00–17:30. Closed for lunch: 13:30–14:00. Medium general stock. PR: £3–100. CC: AE; MC; V. Corresp: French, Spanish.

CO. DONEGAL

CARNDONAGH

The Bookshop, ■ Court Place, Carndonagh, Co. Donegal. Prop: Michael Herron. Tel: (07493) 74389. Est: 1989. Shop; open **M:** 14:00–18:00; **T:** 14:00–18:00. **Th:** 14:00–18:00; **F:** 14:00–18:00; **S:** 14:00–18:00; **Su:** 14:00–18:00. Very large general stock. Spec: Antiquarian; First Editions; History - Local; Irish Interest; Medicine; Philosophy; Religion - Christian; Science - General; Theology; Topography - Local; Travel - General. PR: £1–100. Also, half price sales in August, December and Easter. Cata: 3 – a year.

CO. DUBLIN

BLACKROCK

Carraig Books Ltd., 73 Main Street, Blackrock, Co. Dublin.

DUBLIN

Cathach Books Ltd., ■ 10 Duke Street, Dublin 2, Dublin, Co. Dublin. Prop: Enda Cunningham. Tel: (01) 671-8676. Fax: (01) 671-5120. Website: www.rarebooks.ie. E-mail: cathach@rarebooks.ie. Shop; open **M:** 09:30–17:45; **T:** 09:30–17:45; **W:** 09:30–17:45; **Th:** 09:30–17:45; **F:** 09:30–17:45; **S:** 09:30–17:45. Small stock. Spec: Academic/Scholarly; Archaeology; Irish Interest. PR: £5–10,000. CC: AE; MC; V. Also, a booksearch service. Cata: 4 – Irish History & Literature. Mem: Irish Antique Dealers.

Chapters Bookstore, ■ 108/109 Middle Abbey Street, Dublin, Co. Dublin, Dublin 1. Prop: William Kinsella. Tel: (01) 872-3297. Fax: (01) 972-3044. Est: 1982. Shop; open **M:** 09:00–19:00; **T:** 09:00–19:00; **W:** 09:00–19:00; **Th:** 09:00–20:00; **F:** 09:00–19:00; **S:** 13:00–18:30. Very large general stock. PR: £1–1,000. CC: MC. Also, booksearch. (Alternate Tel: (01) 872-0773, 872-3024) Mem: BA. VAT No: IE 658 7410 A.

De Burca Rare Books, 'Cloonagashel', 27 Priory Drive, Blackrock, Dublin, Co. Dublin. Prop: Eamonn & Vivien de Burca. Tel: (01) 288-2159. Fax: (01) 283-4080. Website: www.indigo.i.e/~deburca. E-mail: deburca@indigo.ie. Est: 1979. Private premises; appointment necessary. Large stock. Spec: Bindings; Countries - Ireland; Culture - National; Genealogy; History - National; Incunabula; Irish Interest; Literature; Manuscripts; Topography - General. PR: £5–20,000. Also, manuscripts of Irish interest, a worldwide mail order service & publishers of fine historical books. Cata: 3 – a year on Irish related subjects. Corresp: French, German, Italian. Mem: ABA. VAT No: IE 161 9333 3M

James Fenning, 12 Glenview, Rochestown Avenue, Dun Laoghaire, Dublin, Co. Dublin. Prop: Jim & Chris Fenning. Tel: (01) 285-7855. Fax: (01) 285-7919. E-mail: fenning@indigo.ie. Est: 1969. Private premises; appointment necessary. Small stock. Spec: Antiquarian. PR: £20–100. CC: V. Cata: 6 – a year. Mem: ABA. VAT No: IE 9T568850.

Glenbower Books, 46 Howth Road, Clontarf, Dublin, Co. Dublin, Dublin 3. Prop: Martin Walsh. Tel: (01) 833-5305. Fax: (01) 833-5305. Website: www.abebooks.com/home/GLENBOWERBOOKS. E-mail: oldbook@eircom.net. Private premises; postal business only. Medium general stock. Spec: Academic/Scholarly; Antiquarian. PR: £3–340. CC: MC; V.

Greene's Bookshop Ltd., 16 Clare Street, Dublin, Co. Dublin, Dublin 2.

Naughton Booksellers, 8 Marine Terrace, Dun Laoghaire, Dublin, Co. Dublin. Prop: Susan Naughton. Tel: +353 1 280-4392. Website: www.naughtonsbooks.com. E-mail: sales@naughtonsbooks.com. Est: 1976. Office &/or bookroom; Internet and postal. Telephone first. Large stock. Spec: Archaeology; Art; Countries - Ireland; Fiction - General; Fiction - Historical; First Editions; History - General; History - National; Irish Interest; Literature; Literature in Translation; Poetry; Travel - General. PR: £1–1,500. CC: AE; E; MC; V. Also, a booksearch service.

Neptune Gallery Limited, 1st Floor, 41 South William Street, Dublin, Co. Dublin, Dublin 2.

Phelan Books, 7 May Street, Drumcondra, Dublin 3, Dublin, Co. Dublin.

Read Ireland, ■ 342 North Circular Road, Dublin, Co. Dublin, Dublin 7. Prop: Gregory Carr. Tel: (00353) 18309828. Fax: (00353) 18302997. Website: www.readireland.com. E-mail: gregcarr@readireland.ie. Est: 1988. Shop; Internet and postal. Open: **M:** 10:00–17:00; **T:** 10:00–17:00; **W:** 10:00–17:00; **Th:** 10:00–17:00; **F:** 10:00–17:00; **S:** 12:00–17:00. Large stock. Spec: Irish Interest. PR: £3–500. CC: AE; MC; V. VAT No: IE 5093937G

Stokes Books, 19 Market Arcade, South Great George's Street, Dublin 2.

The Winding Stair Bookshop & Café, 40 Lower Ormond Quay, Dublin 1.

CO. GALWAY

GALWAY

Charlie Byrne's Bookshop, ■ Middle Street, Galway, Co. Galway, GW1. Tel: (0035) 391 561766. Fax: (0035) 391 561766. Website: www.charliebyrne.com. E-mail: info@charliebyrne.com. Shop; Internet and postal. Open: **M:** 09:00–18:00; **T:** 09:00–18:00; **W:** 09:00–18:00; **Th:** 09:00–18:00; **F:** 09:00–20:00; **S:** 09:00–18:00.

Kenny's Book Export Co., Kilkerrin Park, Liosban, Tuam Road, Galway, Co. Galway. Tel: (091) 709350. Fax: (091) 709351. E-mail: terri@kennys.ie. Est: 1999. Office &/or bookroom. Open: **M:** 09:00–17:00; **T:** 09:00–17:00; **W:** 09:00–17:00; **Th:** 09:00–17:00; **F:** 09:00–17:00. Very large stock. PR: £2–16,000. CC: AE; D; JCB; MC; V. Mem: ABA. *Also at:* Kenny's Bookshop & Art Gallery, Galway (q.v). VAT No: IE 6328356V.

Kennys Bookshops and Art Galle, ■ Art Galleries Ltd, High Street, Galway, Co. Galway. Prop: Managing Director: Mr. Conor Kenny. Tel: (091) 562739, 534760. Fax: (091) 568544. Website: www.kennys.ie and www.kennyscollections.com. E-mail: conor@kennys.ie. Est: 1940. Shop; open **M:** 09:00–18:00; **T:** 09:00–18:00; **W:** 09:00–18:00; **Th:** 09:00–18:00; **F:** 09:00–18:00; **S:** 09:00–18:00. Very large stock. Spec: Americana; Anthropology; Archaeology; Architecture; Art Reference; Author - 20th Century; Authors - Women; Bindings; Cinema/Film; Colonial; Countries - Africa; Countries - Arabia; Countries - Asia; Countries - Balkans, The; Countries - China; and others as listed in the Speciality Index. PR: £1–5,000. CC: AE; D; E; JCB; MC; V; Laser. Also, a booksearch service, in-house fine bindings & large comtemporary Irish Art Gallery. Cata: 99. Corresp: French, Italian. Mem: ABA; ILAB. *Also at:* Kennys Export Book Co., Galway (q.v). VAT No: IE 2238521A

MOYARD

The House of Figgis Ltd, Ross House, Moyard, Co. Galway. Prop: Neville Figgis. Tel: (095) 41092. Fax: (095) 41261. E-mail: figgisbooks@eircom.net. Private premises; appointment necessary. Small stock. Spec: Early Imprints; Irish Interest; Literature; Modern First Editions. CC: MC; V. Cata: 2 – on rare books and Irish interest. VAT No: IE 9 N543 415

CO. KERRY

KENMARE

Noel and Holland Books, ■ 3 Bridge Street, Kenmare, Co. Kerry, n/a. Prop: Dr. Noel Fursman and Ms. Julia Holland. Tel: (064) 42464. Fax: (064) 42464. Website: www.kenmare.com. E-mail: noelholland@eircom.net. Est: 1998. Shop; open **M:** 10:30–17:00; **T:** 10:30–17:00; **W:** 10:30–17:00; **Th:** 10:30–17:00; **F:** 10:30–17:00; **S:** 10:00–17:00. Medium general stock. Spec: Biography; Children's - General; Crime (True); History - General; Irish Interest; Military; New Naturalist; Politics; Transport. PR: £1–200. CC: AE; MC; V. Also, booksearch. Cata: occasionally. Corresp: Spanish, French, Irish.

CO. LAOIS

VICARSTOWN

Courtwood Books, Vicarstown, Stradbally, Vicarstown, Co. Laois. Prop: P.J. Tynan. Tel: (0502) 26384. Fax: (0502) 26298. E-mail: lbloom@eircom.net. Est: 1984. Private premises; Internet and postal. Appointment necessary. Medium stock. Spec: Academic/Scholarly; Advertising; Author - Joyce, James; Engineering; History - Local; Irish Interest; Topography - Local. PR: £1–500. CC: MC; V. Also, organiser of annual Kilkenny book fair (August). Cata: 2.

CO. LEITRIM

CARRICK–ON–SHANNON

Trinity Rare Books, Bridge Street, Carrick–on–Shannon, Co. Leitrim.

CO. LIMERICK

ADARE

George Stacpoole, , Adare, Co. Limerick.

LIMERICK

The Celtic Bookshop, ■ 2 Rutland Street, Limerick, Co. Limerick. Prop: Caroline O'Brien. Tel: (061) 401155. E-mail: celticbk@iol.ie. Est: 1982. Shop; Internet and postal. Telephone first. Open: **M:** 10:00–17:00; **T:** 10:00–17:00; **W:** 10:00–17:00; **Th:** 10:00–17:00; **F:** 10:00–17:00; **S:** 10:00–17:00. Medium stock. Spec: Academic/Scholarly; Antiquarian; Countries - Ireland; Fiction - General; History - General. PR: £3–1,000. CC: MC; V. Cata: 1 – Irish. Corresp: Irish. VAT No: IE 322566i

O'Brien Books & Photo Gallery, ■ 26 High Street, Limerick, Co. Limerick. Prop: John O'Brien. Tel: (061) 412833. E-mail: ob.books@oceanfree.net. Est: 1988. Shop; open **M:** 10:30–17:30; **T:** 10:30–17:30; **W:** 10:30–00:17; **Th:** 10:30–17:30; **F:** 10:30–17:30; **S:** 10:00–17:30. Closed for lunch: 13:00–13:30. Medium stock. Spec: Art; Biography; Cinema/Film; Countries - Poland; Fiction - General; History - General; Irish Interest; Literature; Military History; Photography. PR: £1–400. CC: AE; D; E; JCB; MC; V. VAT No: IE 192620 9a

CO. SLIGO

SLIGO
The Winding Stair Bookshop & Café, Hyde Bridge House, Sligo, Co. Sligo.

CO. TIPPERARY

CAHIR

Glengall Books, 4/5 The Square, Cahir, Co. Tipperary. Prop: Joan Walsh. Tel: (353) 52 42896. Fax: (353) 52 42899. E-mail: jwalsh@biotipp.com. Spec: Antiques; Archaeology; Architecture; Art; Author - Baden-Powell, Lord Robert; Countries - Ireland; Genealogy; Geography; History - General; Irish Interest; Military; Military History; Royalty - General; Travel - General.

ROSCREA

Roscrea Bookshop, Downeys, Rosemary Square, Roscrea, Co. Tipperary, N/A. Prop: Thomas Deegan. Tel: 00-353-505-22894. Fax: 00-353-505-22895. Website: www.newroad.ie. E-mail: info@roscreabookshop.com. Est: 1997. Postal business only.

CO. WEXFORD

NEW ROSS

Britons Catholic Library, Riverview, Arthurstown, New Ross, Co. Wexford. Prop: Mr. N.M. Gwynne. Tel: (51) 389111. E-mail: riverview@esatclear.ie. PR: £2–100.

ROSSLARE HARBOUR
Anton O'Broin, Kilrane, Rosslare Harbour, Co. Wexford.

WALES

The Unitary Authorities of Caerphilly, Cardiff, Carmarthenshire, Ceredigion, Conwy, Denbighshire, Dyfed, Flintshire, Gwynedd, Monmouthshire, Neath Port Talbot, Newport, Powys, Rhondda Cynon Taff, Swansea and Wrexham.

CAERPHILLY

NEW TREDEGAR
Tom Saunders, 9 Woodland Terrace, New Tredegar, Caerphilly, NP24 6LL. (*). Tel: (01443) 836946. Fax: (02920) 371921. E-mail: saunderst@cardiff.ac.uk. Est: 1989. Private premises; postal business only. Telephone first. Small stock. Spec: Academic/Scholarly; Biography; Chess; Children's - General; Education & School; Politics; Religion - General; Sport - American Football; Sport - Rugby; Topography - General. PR: £3–50.

CARDIFF

CARDIFF
Bookmark, 27 Fairoak Road, Cardiff, CF23 5HH.
Capital Bookshop, ■ 27 Morgan Arcade, Cardiff, CF1 2AF. Prop: A.G. Mitchell. Tel: (029) 2038-8423. E-mail: capitalbooks@cardiffwales.fsnet.co.uk. Est: 1981. Shop; open **M:** 10:00–17:30; **T:** 10:00–17:30; **W:** 10:00–17:30; **Th:** 10:00–17:30; **F:** 10:00–17:30; **S:** 10:00–17:30. Large stock. Spec: Antiquarian; Countries - Wales. PR: £1–500. Also, a booksearch service. Mem: ABA.
Jim Cronin, 154 Arabella Street, Cardiff, CF24 4SY. Tel: Evenings (029) 2048-8423. Est: 1977. Private premises; postal business only. Very small stock. Spec: History - General; Music - General; Politics; Sport - Cycling. PR: £2–30.
Len Foulkes, 28 St. Augustine Road, Heath, Cardiff, CF14 4BE. Tel: (029) 2062-7703. Est: 1971. Private premises; postal business only. Very large general stock. PR: £5–100. Now semi-retired.
Whitchurch Books Ltd., ■ 67 Merthyr Road, Whitchurch, Cardiff, CF14 1DD. Prop: Mr. G.L. Canvin. Tel: (029) 2052-1956. Fax: (029) 2062-3599. E-mail: whitchurchbooks@btopenworld.com. Est: 1994. Shop; open **T:** 10:00–17:30; **W:** 10:00–17:30; **Th:** 10:00–17:30; **F:** 10:00–17:30; **S:** 10:00–17:30. Very large stock. Spec: Anthropology; Archaeology; Art History; Arthurian; Byzantium; Cookery/Gastronomy; Countries - Wales; Ecclesiastical History & Architecture; Egyptology; Geology; History - General; History - 19th Century; History - Ancient; History - British; and others as listed in the Speciality Index. PR: £1–100. CC: AE; D; E; JCB; MC; V; SW; S; EL. Also, a booksearch service. Cata: 8. Mem: WBA. VAT No: GB 648 3263 23.
Nicholas Willmott Bookseller, 97 Romilly Road, Canton, Cardiff, CF5 1FN. Prop: Nicholas Willmott & Judith Wayne. Tel: (029) 2037-7268. Fax: (029) 2037-7268. Website: members.lycos.co.uk/nicholaswillmott/id17.htm. E-mail: willmott_wayne@hotmail.com. Est: 1982. Private premises; postal business only. Contactable. Large general stock. Spec: Authors - Women; Autobiography; Biography; Drama; Feminism; Fiction - General; History - General; Humour; Literature; Modern First Editions; Music - General; Music - Classical; Music - Composers; Music - Musicians; Music - Opera; Music - Popular; and others as lsited in the Speciality Index. PR: £2–500. Freelance tenor. Corresp: French. VAT No: GB 368 3564 19.

CARMARTHENSHIRE

CARMARTHEN
Sue Lloyd-Davies, ., 94 St. Catherine Street, Carmarthen, Carmarthenshire, SA31 1RF. Prop: Sue Lloyd-Davies. Tel: (01267) 235462. Fax: (01267) 235462. E-mail: sue@lloyd-davies.fsnet.co.uk. Est: 1979. Private premises; Internet and postal. Telephone first. Medium stock. Spec: Children's - General; Children's - Illustrated; First Editions; Illustrated; Literature; Travel - General. PR: £5–2,000. CC: E; JCB; MC; V; SW. Also, a booksearch service. Corresp: French Japanese Welsh. Mem: PBFA.

LAUGHARNE,
Corran Books Limited, King Street, Laugharne, Carmarthenshire, SA33 4RY.

CEREDIGION

ABERYSTWYTH

Ystwyth Books, ■ 7 Princess Street, Aberystwyth, Ceredigion, SY23 1DX. Prop: Mrs. H.M. Hinde. Tel: (01970) 639479. Est: 1976. Shop; open **M:** 10:00–17:00; **T:** 10:00–17:00; **W:** 10:00–17:00; **Th:** 10:00–17:00; **F:** 10:00–17:00; **S:** 10:00–17:00. Medium stock. Spec: Countries - Wales; History - Industrial; Technology; Topography - Local. PR: £2–100. CC: AE; D; E; JCB; MC; V. Mem: BA. VAT No: GB 124 7218 86.

Doggie Hubbard Bookshop, Bancrug, Buarth Road, Aberystwyth, Ceredigion, SY23 1NB.

Colin Hancock, Ty'N–Y–Llechwedd Hall, Llandre, Aberystwyth, Ceredigion, SY24 5BX. Tel: (01970) 828709. Fax: (01970) 828709. E-mail: colin-hancock@wales-books.demon.co.uk. Est: 1998. Private premises; postal business only. Appointment necessary. Small stock. Spec: Antiquarian; Archaeology; Countries - Wales; Culture - National; History - Local; Languages - National; Music - General; Topography - Local; Welsh Interest. PR: £1–2,000. Also, booksearch, and maps. Corresp: French, Welsh. Mem: Welsh Booksellers Assoc.

Economia Books, 61 Danycoed, Aberystwyth,Ceredigion, SY232hd. Prop: Peter Pavli. Tel: (01970) 624540. Website: www.abebooks.com. E-mail: peter@pavli28.freeserve.co.uk. Est: 1992. Private premises; postal business only. Appointment necessary. Small stock. Spec: Economics; Philosophy; Politics; Science - General; Social History. PR: £5–200. CC: MC; V.

CARDIGAN

Books in Cardigan, Guildhall Market, College Row, Cardigan, Ceredigion.
Books in Cardigan, 2 Pwll Hai, Cardigan, Cardigan, Ceredigion, SA43 1BZ.
The Cavers' Bookshelf, Duncavin, Riverside Mews, Cardigan, SA43 1DN.

LAMPETER

Roger Bray, Preswylfa, Ciliau Aeron, Lampeter, Ceredigion, SA48 7SH.
Barry Thomas, The Vicarage, Felinfach, Lampeter, Ceredigion, SA48 8AE.

TREGARON

Nigel Bird (Books), Bryn Hir, Llwynygroes, Tregaron, SY25 6PY. Prop: Nigel Bird. Tel: (01974) 821281. Fax: (01974) 821548. Website: www.nigelbirdbooks.co.uk. E-mail: nigelbird.books@virgin.net. Est: 1986. Private premises; appointment necessary. Medium stock. Spec: Author - Rolt, L.T.C.; Canals/Inland Waterways; Railways; Transport. PR: £1–100. Also, a booksearch service.

CONWY

COLWYN BAY

Bay Bookshop, 14 Seaview Road, Colwyn Bay, Conwy, LL29 8DG.

Colwyn Books, ■ 66 Abergele Road, Colwyn Bay, Conwy, LL29 7PP. Prop: John Beagan. Tel: (01492) 530683. E-mail: lindaandjohn@davies-beagan.freeserve.co.uk. Shop; open **M:** 09:30–17:30; **T:** 09:30–17:30; **W:** 09:30–13:00; **Th:** 09:30–17:30; **F:** 09:30–17:30; **S:** 09:30–17:00. Closed for lunch: 13:00–13:30. Very small stock. Spec: Countries - France; Foreign Texts; Theology. PR: £1–15. Also, catalogue of books in French, mostly fiction and literature, and booksearch. Cata: 2 – annually, Theology and French. Corresp: French, Welsh. Mem: Welsh Booksellers Assoc.

Rhos Point Books, ■ 85 The Promenade, Rhos–on–Sea, Colwyn Bay, Conwy, LL28 4PR. Prop: Gwyn & Beryl Morris. Tel: (01492) 545236. Fax: (01492) 540862. Website: www.ukbookworld.com/members/brynglas. E-mail: rhos.point@btinternet.com. Est: 1986. Shop; Internet and postal. Open: **M:** 10:00–17:30; **T:** 10:00–17:30; **W:** 10:00–17:30; **Th:** 10:00–17:30; **F:** 10:00–17:30; **S:** 10:00–17:30; **Su:** 10:00–17:30. Medium general stock. Spec: Antiquarian; Welsh Interest. PR: £1–300. CC: AE; MC; V. Corresp: Welsh.

Yesterday's News, 43 Dundonald Road, Colwyn Bay, Conwy, LL29 7RE.

CONWY
Bookshop Conwy, 21 High Street, Conwy, Conwy, LL32 8DE.

LLANRWST
Prospect Books, 10 Trem Arfon, Llanrwst, Conwy, LL26 0BP. Prop: M.R. & M.R. Dingle. Tel: (01492) 640111. Fax: (01492) 640111. Website: www.gunbooks.co.uk. E-mail: prospectbooks@aol.com. Est: 1986. Private premises; Internet and postal. Appointment necessary. Small stock. Spec: Arms & Armour; Firearms/Guns; Sport - Duelling; Sport - Shooting. PR: £1–700. CC: MC; V; SW. Cata: 4. VAT No: GB 625 4838 25.

OLD COLWYN
J V Owen, 13 Wynn Drive, Old Colwyn, Conwy, LL29 9DE. Tel: (01492) 516600. Fax: (01492) 516600. E-mail: owenbooks65@hotmail.com. Est: 2003. Private premises; appointment necessary. PR: £1–100. Specialises in European languages, and others. Corresp: French, German.

E. Wyn Thomas, Old Quarry, 9 Miners Lane, Old Colwyn, Conwy, LL29 9HG. Tel: (01492) 515336. Est: 1947. Private premises; appointment necessary. Small stock. Spec: Countries - Wales; Fiction - General; History - Local; Natural History; Topography - Local. PR: £1–1,000. Corresp: French, Welsh.

RHOS-ON-SEA
Bay Bookshop, Unit 2, Hadden Court, Penrhyn Avenue, Rhos-on-Sea, Colwyn Bay, Conwy, LL28 4NH.

DENBIGHSHIRE

LLANGOLLEN,
Books, ■ 17 Castle Street, Llangollen, Denbighshire, LL20 8NY. Prop: Mrs. K. Sever. Tel: (01978) 860334. Website: www.llangollen.org.uk/pages/books.htm. E-mail: books@easynet.co.uk. Est: 1983. Shop; open **M:** 10:00–17:00; **T:** 10:00–17:00; **W:** 10:00–17:00; **Th:** 10:00–17:00; **F:** 10:00–17:00; **S:** 10:00–17:00; **Su:** 10:00–17:00. Spec: Alpinism/Mountaineering; American Indians; Art; Astrology; Cinema/Film; Countries - Melanesia; Folklore; Gardening; History - General; Literary Criticism; Military; Music - General; Occult; Oriental; Philosophy; Photography; Poetry; Politics; Reference; and others as listed in the Speciality Index. PR: £3–50. CC: AE; JCB; V.

RHYL
Siop y Morfa, ■ 109 Stryd Fawr, Rhyl, Sir Ddinbych/Denbighshire, LL18 1TR. Prop: Dafydd Timothy. Tel: (01745) 339197. Website: www.siopymorfa.com. E-mail: dafydd@siopymorfa.com. Est: 1980. Shop; Internet and postal. Open: **M:** 09:30–17:30; **T:** 09:30–17:30; **W:** 09:30–17:30; **Th:** 09:30–17:30; **F:** 09:30–16:30; **S:** 09:30–17:30. Closed for lunch: 13:00–14:00. Small stock. Spec: History - National; Literature; Welsh Interest. PR: £5–200. CC: AE; JCB; MC; V; SO. Corresp: French, Welsh. Mem: PBFA. VAT No: GB 771 0696 20.

RUTHIN
Spread Eagle Books, The Spread Eagle, 3 Upper Clwyd Street, Ruthin, Denbighshire, LL15 1HY. Prop: Janet Kenyon–Thompson. Tel: (01824) 703840. Est: 1978. Spec: Biography; History - Local; Topography - Local; Travel - General; Welsh Interest. PR: £5–200. Also booksearch.

ST. ASAPH
Howard Gilmartin, Ridgemere, Upper Denbigh Road, St. Asaph, Denbighshire, LL17 0RR.

FLINTSHIRE

MOLD
BOOKS4U, 7 The Firs, Mold, Flintshire, CH7 1JX. Prop Norman MacDonald. Tel: (01352) 751121. E-mail: norman_macdonald@btinternet.com. Spec: Academic/Scholarly; Annuals; Antiquarian; Author - Buchan, John; Author - Conrad, Joseph; Author - Durrell, Lawrence; Author - Edwards, Lionel; Author - Fowles, John; Author - Gissing, George; Author - Greene, Graham; Author - Haggard, Sir Henry Rider; and others as listed in the Speciality Index. PR: £4–1,500.

Scott Lloyd, 1 Maes Gwyn, Graianrhyd, Mold, Flintshire, CH7 4QP.

GWYNEDD

BALA
White House Bookshop, ■ 99 High Street, Bala, Gwynedd, North Wales, LL23 7AE. Prop: Iona Lewis Bown. Tel: (01678) 520208. Fax: (01678) 520208. Est: 2001. Shop; open **M:** 10:00–16:30; **T:** 10:00–16:30; **W:** 10:00–12:00; **Th:** 10:00–16:30; **F:** 10:00–16:30; **S:** 10:00–16:30. Closed for lunch: 13:00–14:00. Medium general stock. Spec: Natural History.

BANGOR
musebookshop, ■ 43 Holyhead Road, Bangor, Gwynedd, LL57 2EU. Prop: Nigel Jones. Tel: (01248) 362062. Fax: (01248) 362042. E-mail: musebookshop@supanet.com. Est: 1991. Shop; open **M:** 09:30–17:00; **T:** 09:30–17:00; **W:** 09:30–17:00; **Th:** 09:29–18:00; **F:** 09:30–17:00; **S:** 10:00–16:00. Medium general stock. Spec: Academic/Scholarly; Alpinism/Mountaineering; Natural History; New Naturalist; Travel - General. PR: £1–500. CC: MC; V. Also, new books. Mem: BA. VAT No: GB 560 0796 45.

BETHESDA
A.E. Morris, ■ 40 High Street, Bethesda, Gwynedd, LL57 3AN. Tel: (01248) 602533. Est: 1987. Shop; open **M:** 10:00–17:00; **T:** 10:00–17:00; **W:** 10:00–17:00; **Th:** 10:00–17:00; **F:** 10:00–17:00; **S:** 10:00–17:00. PR: £1–100.

BLAENAU FFESTINIOG
Siop Lyfrau'r Hen Bost, 45 High Street, Blaenau Ffestiniog, Gwynedd, LL41 3AA.

CRICCIETH
Capel Mawr Collectors Centre, 21 High Street, Criccieth, Gwynedd, LL52 0BS.

DOLGELLAU
Cader Idris Books, ■ 2 Maldwyn House, Finsbury Square, Cader Road, Dolgellau, Gwynedd, LL40 1TR. Prop: Barbara Beeby & Son. Tel: (01654) 703849. Website: www.abebooks.com/home/dvbookshop. E-mail: beeb@dvbookshop.fsnet.co.uk. Est: 1997. Medium general stock. Spec: Modern First Editions; Welsh Interest. PR: £1–500. CC: AE; JCB; MC; V. Please telephone before calling. Cata: 4 – quarterly. Mem: PBFA. *Also at:* Dyfi Valley Bookshop, 6, Doll St., Machynlleth, Powys.

HOLYHEAD
Janet Box, Llanfachraeth, Holyhead, Gwynedd, LL65 4UU.

LLANDUDNO
More Books, 102 Upper Mostyn Street, Llandudno, Gwynedd, LL30 2SW.

MONMOUTHSHIRE

ABERGAVENNY
Books for Writers, 'Avondale', 13 Lansdown Drive, Abergavenny, Monmouthshire, NP7 6AW. Prop: Ms. Sonia A. Conway. Tel: (01873) 853967. Est: 1999. Private premises; postal business only. Very small general stock. Spec: Biography; Fiction - General; Reference. PR: £2–50. Cata: 3 – a year on writing guides, biographies, short stories.

Monmouth House Books, Monmouth House, Llanvapley, Abergavenny, Monmouthshire, NP7 8SN. Prop: Richard Sidwell. Tel: (01600) 780236. Fax: (01600) 780532. Website: www.monmouthhousebooks.co.uk. E-mail: monmouthhousebooks@compuserve.com. Est: 1985. Private premises; postal business only. Appointment necessary. Small stock. Spec: Architecture. PR: £5–1,000. Also, booksearch & stock lists on architecture only. Publishes facsimile reprints of early architectural books. Cata: 6 – Architecture & related subjects. VAT No: GB 615 8003 63.

WALES

TINTERN

Stella Books, ■Monmouth Road, Tintern, Monmouthshire, NP16 6SE. Prop: Chris Tomaszewski. Tel: (01291) 689755. Fax: (01291) 689998. Website: www.stellabooks.com. E-mail: enquiry@stellabooks.com. Est: 1990. Shop; open **M:** 09:30–17:00; **T:** 09:30–17:00; **W:** 09:30–17:00; **Th:** 09:30–17:00; **F:** 09:30–17:00; **S:** 09:30–17:00; **Su:** 09:30–17:00. Very large stock. Spec: children's; illustrated; Topography - Local; Topography - National; Natural History; Railways. Mem: PBFA. Corresp: French.

NEATH PORT TALBOT

NEATH

Rugby Relics Ltd, 61 Leonard Street, Neath, West Glamorgan, SA11 3HW. (*) Prop: Dave Richards. Tel: (01639) 646725. Fax: (01639) 638142. Website: www.rugbyrelics.com. E-mail: sales@rugbyrelics.com. Est: 1991. Private premises; postal business only. Very small stock. Spec: Sport - Boxing; Sport - Cricket; Sport - Football (Soccer); Sport - Golf; Sport - Rugby. PR: £2–200.

NEWPORT

NEWPORT

Carningli Centre, East Street, Newport, Newport, SA42 0SY.

POWYS

BEULAH

Myra Dean Illustrated Books, Crossways, Beulah, Powys, LD5 4UB. Tel: (01591) 620647. Fax: (01591) 620647. Website: www.btinternet.com/~myra.dean/index.html. E-mail: myra.dean@btinternet.com. Est: 1984. Private premises; Internet and postal. Telephone first. Very small stock. Spec: Children's - General; Illustrated; Private Press. PR: £5–2,000. CC: MC; V; SW. Cata: 9 – 6 weeks. Mem: PBFA.

BUILTH WELLS

Louise Boer, Arthurian Books, The Rectory, Rhosgoch, Builth Wells, Powys, LD2 3JU. Prop: Louise Boer. Tel: (01497) 851260. Fax: (01497) 851260. E-mail: louise.boer@btinternet.com. Est: 1996. Private premises; Internet and postal. Contactable. Medium general stock. Spec: Academic/Scholarly; Arthurian; Business Studies; Literary Criticism. PR: £2–150. CC: AE; MC; V. Corresp: Dutch.

Open 7 Days
Catalogues by E-mail
Books Bought
Wants Match Service
Visa/Amex

Stella BOOKS

Monmouth Road
Tintern
Monmouthshire
NP16 6SE
01291 689755

Rare and out of Print Books

Specialists in UK Topography, Childrens and Illustrated Books
Member UK online booksellers cooperative www.ibooknet.co.uk
Email: enquiry@stellabooks.com   Web: www.stellabooks.com

BRECON

Michael Rainger Books, 3 Usk Terrace, St. Michael Street, Brecon, Powys, LD3 9AA. Prop: Michael & Jane Rainger. Tel: (01874) 622817. Website: www.raingerbooks.co.uk. E-mail: michael@raingerbooks.co.uk. Est: 1993. Private premises; Internet and postal. Appointment necessary. Open: **M:** 09:00–18:00; **T:** 09:00–18:00; **W:** 09:00–18:00; **Th:** 09:00–18:00; **F:** 09:00–18:00; **S:** 09:00–18:00; **Su:** 10:00–16:00. Closed for lunch: 13:00–14:00. Medium stock. Spec: Astrology; Esoteric; Fore-Edge Paintings; Gnostics; Mysticism; Occult; Railways; Spiritualism; Witchcraft. PR: £3–150. CC: MC; V. Also, booksearch. Cata: 3. Mem: ABA.

A.G. & W. Wakeley, 7 The Struet, Brecon, Powys, LD3 7LL. Tel: (01874) 622714. Est: 1973. Spec: Countries - Wales; Culture - National; Topography - Local.

CAERSWS

Dead Mens Minds.co.uk, Brambles, Trefeglwys, Caersws, Powys, SY17 5QG. Prop: Tristan Winston-Smith. Tel: (01686) 430702. Website: www.deadmensminds.co.uk. E-mail: deadmensminds@aol.com. Est: 2000. Private premises; Internet and postal. Very small stock. Spec: Antiquarian. PR: £10–2,000. CC: MC; V; SW. Corresp: Translator.

Carol Hogben, Berthlas Chapel Cottage, The Waen, Trefeglwys, Caersws, Powys, SY17 5QG. Tel: (01686) 430653. Fax: (01686) 430447. Est: 1986. Private premises; postal business only. Very small stock. Spec: Applied Art; Architecture; Decorative Art; Fashion & Costume; Industry; Interior Design. PR: £10–1,000. Also, trade catalogues 1840-1960. Mem: PBFA. VAT No: GB 448 7214 32.

HAY–ON–WYE (SEE ALSO, HAY–ON–WYE, HEREFORDSHIRE)

The Addyman Annexe, 27 Castle Street, Hay–on–Wye, HR3 5DF. Tel: (01497) 821600. E-mail: madness@hay-on-wyebooks.com.

Addyman Books, ■ 39 Lion Street, Hay–on–Wye, HR3 5AA. Prop: Derek Addyman & Anne Brichto. Tel: (01497) 821136. Fax: (01497) 821732. Website: www.hay-on-wyebooks.com. E-mail: madness@hay-on-wyebooks.com. Est: 1987. Shop; Internet and postal. Open: **M:** 10:00–17:30; **T:** 10:00–17:30; **W:** 10:00–17:30; **Th:** 10:00–17:30; **F:** 10:00–17:30; **S:** 10:00–17:30; **Su:** 10:30–17:30. Large general stock. Spec: Anthologies; Antiquarian; Archaeology; Architecture; Art; Arthurian; Arts, The; Astronomy; Beat Writers; Bibles; Bindings; Book of Hours; Books about Books; History - General; Literature; Military; Modern First Editions; Poetry; Theatre; Theology; and others as listed in the Speciality Index. PR: £1–10,000. CC: MC; V; De, SW. NB: add ' via Hereford' after Hay-on-Wye when sending by post. *Also at:* Murder & Mayhem, 5 Lion St., Hay-on-Wye (q.v) and The Addyman Annexe, 27 Castle St., Hay-on-Wye, (q.v.).

C Arden, Bookseller, 'Radnor House', Church Street, Hay–on–Wye, HR3 5DQ.

Arthurian Book, Broad St. Antique & Book Centre, 6 Broad Street, Hay–on–Wye, HR3 5DB. Prop: Louise Boer. Tel: (01497) 820653. Fax: (01497) 820653. E-mail: louise.boer@btinternet.com. Est: 1997. Spec: Arthurian; Biography; Maritime/Nautical.

B. and K. Books, Riverside, Newport Street, Hay–on–Wye, HR3 5BG. Prop: Betty & Karl Showler. Tel: (01497) 820386. Website: www.hay-on-wye.co.uk/bkbooks. Est: 1966. Private premises; appointment necessary. Small stock. PR: £6–600. Also at storeroom. Cata: 1 – a year.

Dealers who need to update their entry should visit their page on
www.sheppardsdirectories.com

Dealers without e-mail - post details

WALES

Booth Books, ■ 44 Lion Street, Hay–on–Wye, HR3 5AA. Director: Mr. Richard Booth. Tel: (01497) 820322. Fax: (01497) 821150. Website: www.richardbooth.demon.co.uk. E-mail: postmaster@richardbooth.demon.co.uk. Est: 1961. Shop; open **M:** 09:00–20:00; **T:** 09:00–20:00; **W:** 09:00–20:00; **Th:** 09:00–20:00; **F:** 09:00–20:00; **S:** 09:00–20:00; **Su:** 11:00–16:00. Very large stock. Spec: Agriculture; Archaeology; Atlases; Children's - General; Cookery/Gastronomy; Countries - Mexico; Economics; Fiction - Science Fiction; Genealogy; History - General; Languages - Foreign; Law; Literature; Military; Natural History; Performing Arts; and others as listed in the Speciality Index. PR: £1–1,000. CC: AE; D; MC; V. Also, paperbacks & magazines. NB: add 'via Hereford' after Hay-on-Wye when sending by post. Mem: WBA. *Also at:* Hay Castle, Hay-on-Wye. (q.v.).

Booth Books, ■ Hay Castle, Hay–on–Wye, HR3 5DL. Prop: Hope Booth (Richard Booth Bookshops Ltd.). Tel: (01497) 820503. Fax: (01497) 821314. Website: www.richardboothbookseller.com. E-mail: inquiry@richardboothbookseller.com. Est: 1987. Shop; open **M:** 09:30–17:30; **T:** 09:30–17:30; **W:** 09:30–17:30; **Th:** 09:30–17:30; **F:** 09:30–17:30; **S:** 09:30–17:30; **Su:** 09:30–17:30. Very large stock. Spec: American Indians; Antiquarian; Antiques; Architecture; Art; Aviation; Bindings; Cinema/Film; Crafts; Decorative Art; Design; Humour; Illustrated; Maritime/Nautical; Motoring; Photography; Railways; Transport. PR: £1–2,500. CC: AE; MC; V; SW, SO. Also, photographic images from 1850s onwards. NB: add 'via Hereford' after Hay-on-Wye when sending by post. Corresp: French. Mem: WBA. *Also at:* 44 Lion Street, Hay–on–Wye (q.v.).

Janice Bowen, 13 Begwyns Bluff, Clyro, Powys, Hay–on–Wye, HR3 5SR. Tel: (01497) 821032. Fax: (01497) 821032. Est: 1983. Private premises; postal business only. Small stock. Spec: Academic/Scholarly; Anthropology; Ethnography; Travel - Africa; Travel - Americas; Travel - Asia; Travel - Australasia/Australia; Tribal. PR: £2–200. Cata: 2.

Boz Books, ■ 13a Castle Street, Hay–on–Wye, HR3 5DF. Prop: Peter Harries. Tel: (01497) 821277. Fax: (01497) 821277. Website: www.bozbooks.co.uk. E-mail: peter@bozbooks.demon.co.uk. Est: 1988. Shop; Internet and postal. Open **M:** 10:00–17:00; **T:** 10:00–17:00; **W:** 10:00–17:00; **Th:** 10:00–17:00; **F:** 10:00–17:00; **S:** 10:00–17:00. Closed for lunch: 13:00–14:00. Medium stock. Spec: Author - Dickens, Charles; Literature. PR: £1–10,000. CC: JCB; MC; V. NB :add ' via Hereford' after Hay-on-Wye when sending by post. Mem: ABA.

The Children's Bookshop, Toll Cottage, Pontvaen, Hay–on–Wye, HR3 5EW.

The Children's Bookshop No. 2, The Backfold, Hay-on-Wye, Hereford, HR3 5DL.

Marijana Dworski Books, Travel, 21 Broad Street, Hay–on–Wye, HR3 5DB.

davidleesbooks.com, ■ Marches Gallery, Lion Street, Hay–on–Wye, HR3 5AA. Prop: David Lees. Tel: (01497) 822969. Fax: (01568) 780468. Website: www.davidleesbooks.com. E-mail: julie@davidleesbooks.com. Est: 1985. Shop; Internet. Open **M:** 11:00–17:00; **T:** 11:00–17:00; **W:** 11:00–17:00; **Th:** 11:00–17:00; **F:** 11:00–17:00; **S:** 11:00–17:00; **Su:** 11:00–17:00. Medium general stock. PR: £1–1,000. CC: AE; MC; V; Debit Cards. VAT No: GB 488 7008 07.

Francis Edwards in Hay–on–Wye, ■ The Old Cinema, Castle Street, Hay–on–Wye, HR3 5DF. Prop: Hay Cinema Bookshop Ltd. Tel: (01497) 820071. Fax: (01497) 821900. Website: www.francisedwards.co.uk. E-mail: sales@francisedwards.demon.co.uk. Est: 1855. Shop; open **M:** 09:00–19:00; **T:** 09:00–19:00; **W:** 09:00–19:00; **Th:** 09:00–19:00; **F:** 09:00–19:00; **S:** 09:00–19:00; **Su:** 11:30–17:30. Medium general stock. Spec: Art; Economics; Law; Literature; Medicine; Military; Natural History; Naval; Philosophy; Travel - General. PR: £20–1,000. CC: AE; MC; V; SW. NB: add 'via Hereford' after Hay-on-Wye when sending by post. Cata: – Regularly. Mem: ABA; PBFA; ILAB.

Hancock & Monks Music Emporium, ■ 15 Broad Street, Hay–on–Wye, HR3 5DB. Prop: Eric Hancock & Jerry Monks. Tel: (01591) 821784. Fax: (01591) 610778. Website: www.hancockandmonks.co.uk. E-mail: jerry@hancockandmonks.co.uk. Est: 1974. Shop; Internet and postal. Open **M:** 10:30–16:30. **W:** 10:30–16:30; **Th:** 10:30–16:30; **F:** 10:30–16:30; **S:** 10:30–17:00. Medium stock. Spec: Music - General; Music - Classical; Music - Composers; Music - Jazz; Music - Music Hall; Music - Musicians; Music - Opera; Musical Instruments. PR: £1–250. CC: AE; MC; V. Also, classical CDs, DVDs, sheet music & scores. VAT No: GB 139 8108 51.

Hay Cinema Bookshop Ltd., ■ Castle Street, Hay–on–Wye, HR3 5DF. Tel: (01497) 820071. Fax: (01497) 821900. Website: www.haycinemabookshop.co.uk. E-mail: sales@haycinemabookshop. co.uk. Est: 1982. Shop; open **M:** 09:00–19:00; **T:** 09:00–19:00; **W:** 09:00–19:00; **Th:** 09:00–19:00; **F:** 09:00–19:00; **S:** 09:00–19:00; **Su:** 11:30–17:30. Very large general stock. PR: £1–25. CC: AE; D; JCB; MC; V. Fine and Antiquarian books in all subjects via our sister business Francis Edwards. Mem: ABA; PBFA. *Also at:* Quinto, 48a Charing Cross Road, London WC2H 0BB (q.v.) and Quinto, 63 Great Russell Street, London WC1B 3BF. VAT No: GB 594 2720 23.

HCB Wholesale, Unit 2, Forst Road Enterprise Park, Hay–on–Wye, HR3 5DS. Prop: Andrew Cooke. Tel: (01497) 820333. Fax: (01497) 821192. E-mail: sales@hcbwholesale.co.uk. Est: 2002. Storeroom; Open: **M:** 09:00–18:00; **T:** 09:00–18:00; **W:** 09:00–18:00; **Th:** 09:00–18:00; **F:** 09:00–18:00. Very large stock. CC: AE; D; E; JCB; MC; V. Main stock: publishers' returns, academic overstocks, and remainders. NB: add 'via Hereford' after Hay-on-Wye when sending by post. Cata: 1 – on demand, please ask.

Lion Fine Arts and Books, ■ 19 Lion Street, Hay–On–Wye, HR3 5AD. Prop: Charles Spencer. Tel: (01497) 821726. Website: www.ruralwales.org.uk/haybookshops/home/lion. Est: 1996. Shop; open **M:** 10:00–17:00; **T:** 10:00–17:00; **W:** 10:00–17:00; **Th:** 10:00–17:00; **F:** 10:00–17:00; **S:** 10:00–17:00. Small general stock. Spec: Antiquarian; Antiques; Architecture; Arms & Armour; Art; Collecting; Ecclesiastical History & Architecture; Military History; Musical Instruments; Natural History; Ornithology; Theology. PR: £1–300. NB: Add 'via Hereford' after Hay–on–Wye to address in all items posted.

Lion Street Books, 1 St. John's Place, Lion Street, Hay–on–Wye, HR3 5BN. T

Murder & Mayhem, 5 Lion Street, Hay–on–Wye, HR3 5AA.

Outcast Books, ■ 15a Broad St., Hay–on–Wye, HR3 5DB. Prop: David Howard. Tel: (01497) 820265. Website: www.ukbookworld.com/members/outcastbooks. E-mail: outcastbooks@supanet.com. Est: 1993. Shop; open **M:** 10:30–17:00; **T:** 10:30–17:00; **W:** 10:30–17:00; **Th:** 10:30–17:00; **F:** 10:30–17:00; **S:** 11:30–17:00; **Su:** 12:00–14:00. Small stock. Spec: Academic/Scholarly; Alternative Medicine; Medicine; Psychoanalysis; Psychology/Psychiatry; Psychotherapy; Social Sciences. PR: £1–150. NB: add 'via Hereford' after Hay-on-Wye when sending by post.

The Poetry Bookshop, ■ The Ice House, Brook Street, Hay–on–Wye, HR3 5BQ.

Rose's Books, ■ 14 Broad Street, Hay–on–Wye, HR3 5DB. Prop: Maria Goddard. Tel: (01497) 820013. Fax: (01497) 820031. Website: www.rosesbooks.com. E-mail: enquiry@rosesbooks.com. Est: 1982. Shop; Internet and postal. Open: **M:** 09:30–17:00; **T:** 09:30–17:00; **W:** 09:30–17:00; **Th:** 09:30–17:00; **F:** 09:30–17:00; **S:** 09:30–17:00; **Su:** 09:30–17:00. Large stock. Spec: Children's - General; Children's - Illustrated. PR: £3–500. CC: AE; MC; V; SW.

West House Books, Broad Street, Hay–on–Wye, HR3 5DB.

Mark Westwood Books, ■ High Town, Hay–on–Wye, HR3 5AE. Tel: (01497) 820068. Fax: (01497) 821641. E-mail: books@markwestwood.demon.co.uk. Est: 1975. Shop; open **M:** 11:00–17:00; **T:** 11:00–17:00; **W:** 11:00–17:00; **Th:** 11:00–17:00; **F:** 11:00–17:00; **S:** 11:00–18:00; **Su:** 11:00–17:00. Large stock. Spec: Antiquarian; Art; Economics; Geology; History - General; Mathematics; Medicine - History of; Philosophy; Psychology/Psychiatry; Science - General; Technology. PR: £5–1,000. CC: E; JCB; MC; V. NB: add 'via Hereford' after Hay-on-Wye when sending by post. Mem: ABA; PBFA; ILAB.

LLANGAMMARCH WELLS,

Cammarch Books, Cammarch House, Llangammarch Wells, Powys, LD4 4EB.

Dally Books & Collectables, Berthllwyd, Beulah, Llangammarch Wells, Powys, LD5 4UN. Prop: Andrew Dally. Tel: (01591) 610892. Website: www.dallybooks.com. E-mail: andrew@thedallys.com. Est: 2001. Market stand/stall; Internet and postal. Contactable. Small stock. Spec: Memorabilia; Military; Military History; War - General; War - World War I; War - World War II; Welsh Interest. PR: £1–200.

LLANIDLOES,

Dusty Books, The Old Woollen Mill, Shortbridge Street, Llanidloes, Powys, SY18 6AD. Prop: Bernard Conwell. Tel: (01686) 411247. Fax: (01686) 411248. Website: www.dustybooks.co.uk. E-mail: scribe@dustybooks.co.uk. Postal business only. Spec: Author - Farnol, Jeffery; Author - Forester, C. S.; Author - Heyer, Georgette; Author - Sabatini, R.; Author - Shute, Neville; Cookery/Gastronomy; Crafts; Food & Drink; Gardening; Rural Life; Sport - Angling/Fishing; Welsh Interest; Wine. PR: £5–250. Also, booksearch.

The Great Oak Bookshop, ■ Great Oak Street, Llanidloes, Powys, SY18 6BW. Prop: K. Reiter & B. Boswell. Tel: (01686) 412959. Website: www.midwales.com/gob. E-mail: greatoak@europe.com. Est: 1988. Shop; Internet and postal. Open: **M:** 09:30–17:30; **T:** 09:30–17:30; **W:** 09:29–17:30; **Th:** 09:31–17:30; **F:** 09:30–17:30; **S:** 09:31–16:30. Very large general stock. Spec: Autobiography; Biography; Countries - Wales; Welsh Interest. PR: £1–50. Also, new books, a booksearch service & greetings cards. Corresp: German, French. Mem: BA; WBA.

MACHYNLLETH

Coch-y-Bonddu Books, ■ Papyrus, Pentrerhedyn Street, Machynlleth, Powys, SY20 8DJ. Prop: Paul Morgan. Tel: (01654) 702837. Fax: (01654) 702857. Website: www.anglebooks.com. E-mail: paulmorgan@anglebooks.com. Est: 1982. Shop; Internet and postal. Open: **M:** 09:00–17:00; **T:** 09:00–17:00; **W:** 09:00–17:00; **Th:** 09:00–17:00; **F:** 09:00–17:00; **S:** 09:00–17:00. Large stock. Spec: Animals and Birds; Cockfighting; Conservation; Dogs; Fishes; Forestry; Natural History; Ornithology; Rural Life; Self-Sufficiency; Sport - Angling/Fishing; Sport - Falconry; Sport - Hunting; Welsh Interest. PR: £1–2,000. CC: AE; D; E; JCB; MC; V. We stock new books in our fields, as well as remainders, s/hand and antiquarian. Cata: – occasional. Corresp: French, German, Spanish, Portuguese, Welsh. Mem: PBFA; BA.

Dyfi Valley Bookshop, ■ 6 Doll Street, Machynlleth, Powys, SY20 8BQ. Prop: Barbara Beeby & Son. Tel: (01654) 703849. Website: www.abebooks.com/home/dvbookshop. E-mail: beeb@dvbookshop.fsnet.co.uk. Est: 1988. Shop; open **M:** 09:30–17:00; **T:** 09:30–17:00; **W:** 09:30–17:00; **Th:** 09:30–17:00; **F:** 09:30–17:00; **S:** 09:30–17:00. Closed for lunch: 12:00–12:30. Medium general stock. Spec: Firearms/Guns; Literature; Rural Life; Sport - Archery; Sport - Field Sports; Sport - Shooting. PR: £1–300. CC: AE; E; JCB; MC; V. Cata: 4 – quarterly. Mem: PBFA; WBA. *Also at:* Cader Idris Bookshop, Finsbury Square, Dolgellau.

Martin's Books, Zion Chapel, Llanwrin, Machynlleth, Powys, SY20 8QH.

MONTGOMERY

Castle Bookshop, The Old Rectory, Llandyssil, Montgomery, Powys, SY15 6LQ. Prop: C.N., E.J. & S.J. Moore. Tel: (01686) 668484. Fax: (01686) 668842. Website: www.archaeologybooks.co.uk. E-mail: castlebooks@dial.pipex.com. Est: 1987. Office &/or bookroom; telephone first. Large stock. Spec: Archaeology; Architecture; Countries - Wales; Welsh Interest. PR: £5–1,000. CC: MC; V; SW. Cata: 10 – Archaeology, Architecture, Wales. Mem: ABA; PBFA; ILAB. VAT No: GB 482 4054 51.

NEWTOWN

David Archer, The Pentre, Kerry, Newtown, Powys, SY16 4PD. Prop: David Archer & Alison Brown. Tel: (01686) 670382. Fax: (01686) 670551. Website: www.david-archer-maps.co.uk. E-mail: david@david-archer-maps.co.uk. Est: 1985. Private premises; Internet and postal. Telephone first. Open: **M:** 08:30–20:00; **T:** 08:30–20:00; **W:** 08:30–20:00; **Th:** 08:30–20:00; **F:** 08:30–20:00; **S:** 09:00–16:00. Very large stock. Spec: Academic/Scholarly; Cartography; Geography; Geology; Transport. PR: £1–50. Mem: Welsh Booksellers Assoc.

Carta Regis, 327 Dinas, Treowen, Newtown, Powys, SY16 1NW. Prop: David Pugh. Tel: (01686) 627610. Fax: (01686) 627610. Website: www.davidp@cartaregis.com. E-mail: davidp@cartaregis.com. Est: 1997. Private premises; Internet and postal. Open: **M:** 10:00–17:00; **T:** 10:00–17:00; **W:** 10:00–17:00; **Th:** 10:00–17:00; **F:** 10:00–17:00; **S:** 10:00–17:00. Medium stock. Spec: Academic/Scholarly; Agriculture; Alpinism/Mountaineering; Animals and Birds; Antiques; Arts, The; First Editions; Fore-Edge Paintings; Literary Criticism; Literature; Medicine; Modern First Editions; Music - General; Religion - General; and others as listed in the Speciality Index. CC: AE; E; MC; V. New Books. Alternative web site: www.cartaregisbooks.co.uk.

D.M. Newband, Drefor Cottage, Kerry, Newtown, Powys, SY16 4PQ. Prop: D.M. Newband. Tel: (01686) 670205. Fax: (01686) 670928. Website: www.davidnewbandbooks.co.uk. E-mail: davidnewband@ukgateway.net. Est: 1983. Office &/or bookroom; Internet and postal. Appointment necessary. Open: **M:** 09:00–19:00; **T:** 09:00–19:00; **W:** 09:00–19:00; **Th:** 09:00–19:00; **F:** 09:00–19:00; **S:** 09:00–19:00; **Su:** 10:00–18:00. Small stock. Spec: Railways; Steam Engines; Transport. PR: £1–200. CC: Paypal. Also, a booksearch service; valuation service railways only. Cata: 2 – January & July.

PRESTEIGNE

The Chaucer Head, Broadheath House, Presteigne, Powys, LD8 2HG.

Kingshead Books, ■ 45 High St., Presteigne, Powys. Prop: Ivan Monckton. Tel: (01547) 560100. Est: 1983. Shop; open **M:** 10:00–17:00; **T:** 10:00–17:00; **W:** 09:00–17:00; **Th:** 10:00–17:00; **F:** 10:00–17:00; **S:** 10:00–17:00. Medium stock. Spec: Natural History; Welsh Interest. PR: £1–250. Open as above in summer. Winter: Saturdays & various others. Phone first.

TALGARTH

The Strand Bookshop, ■ Regent Street, Talgarth, Powys, LD3 0DB. Prop: Mr. & Mrs. I. Perry. Tel: (01874) 711195. Shop; open **M:** 09:00–17:00. **Th:** 09:00–17:00; **F:** 09:00–17:00; **S:** 09:00–17:00; **Su:** 09:00–17:00. Medium general stock. PR: £1–50. *Also at:* The New Strand Bookshop, Eardisley.

WELSHPOOL

Len Lewis, Plas Y Coed, 3 Smithy Meadow, Guilsfield, Welshpool, Powys, SY21 9ND. Tel: (01938) 552023. E-mail: len.lewis5@virgin.net. Est: 1986. Private premises; postal business only. Telephone first. Very small stock. Spec: Sport - Athletics; Topography - Local. Booksearch service for any subject.

D. & J. Young, Fairview Cottage, Groes Llwyd, Welshpool, Powys, SY21 9BZ. Prop: David & Joy Young. Tel: (01938) 553149. Website: www.abebooks.com. E-mail: joy_young@lineone.net. Private premises; postal business only. Small stock. Spec: Calligraphy; Embroidery; Fashion & Costume; Knitting; Lace; Textiles. PR: £1–100.

RHONDA CYNON TAFF

PONTYPRIDD

Joseph Biddulph, 32 Stryd Ebeneser, Pontypridd, Rhonda Cynon Taff, CF37 5PB. Prop: Joseph Biddulph B.A. Hons. & Amicus Linguarum. Tel: (01443) 662559. Est: 1986. Private premises; Internet and postal.Very small stock. Spec: Academic/Scholarly; Heraldry; Languages - African; Languages - Foreign; Languages - National. PR: £5–40. Also, African cultures, incl: Creole and African Diaspora - and publishing. Corresp: Esperanto, Welsh.

SWANSEA

SWANSEA

Mollie's Loft Books., 31 Cilmaengwyn, Pontardawe, Swansea, SA8 4QL. Prop: M.J.P. Evans. Tel: (01792) 863556. Website: www.Molliesloft.com. E-mail: books@mollies.freeserve.co.uk. Est: 1998. Private premises; Internet and postal. Appointment necessary. Small stock. Spec: Science - General; Technology; Welsh Interest. PR: £5–150. CC: MC; V; SW. Corresp: French.

Dead Zone Books, 23 Quarry Road, Treboeth, Swansea, SA5 9DJ. Prop: Stephen Mallory. Tel: (01792) 795509. E-mail: stephenmallory@hotmail.com. Private premises; postal business only. Very small stock. Spec: Academic/Scholarly; Advertising; Aeronautics; Author - King, Stephen; Countries - Melanesia; Countries - Mexico; Fiction - Science Fiction. PR: £10–1,000.

Dylans Bookstore, ■ Salubrious Passage, Swansea, SA1 3RT. Prop: Jeff & Elizabeth Towns. Tel: (01792) 655255 & 360. Fax: (01792) 655255. Website: www.dylans.com. E-mail: jefftowns@dylans.com. Est: 1970. Shop; appointment necessary. Spec: Antiquarian; Author - Thomas, Dylan; Erotica; Folklore; History - Local; History - National; Literature; Topography - Local. PR: £5–500. CC: MC; V. Mem: PBFA. *Also at:* Dylans Thomas Centre,Somerset Place,Swansea,SA1 1RR.

J.M. Farringdon, Ariel Cottage, 8 Hadland Terrace, West Cross, Swansea, SA3 5TT. Prop: M.G. Farringdon. Tel: (01792) 405267. Fax: (01792) 405267. E-mail: bellbooks@aol.com. Est: 1970. Private premises; Internet and postal. Appointment necessary. Very small stock. Spec: Antiquarian; Author - Masefield, John; Author - Ransome, Arthur; Bell-Ringing (Campanology). PR: £20–1,000. Also, a booksearch service & publishing as 'Ariel House Publications'. Cata: 4. VAT No: GB 558 2330 40.

D. Ieuan Lloyd, 452 Mumbles Road, Mumbles, Swansea, SA3 4BY. Tel: (01792) 363175. Fax: (01792) 366747. Website: www.ukbookworld.com/members/dilloyd. E-mail: dilloyd@rbooks.fsnet.co.uk. Est: 1974. Private premises; appointment necessary. Small stock. Spec: Academic/Scholarly; Antiquarian; Philosophy. PR: £15–5,000. CC: MC; V. Cata: 1 – regularly. Corresp: French. Mem: PBFA.

TORFAEN

BLAENAVON

Blaenavon Books, ■ 86 Broad Street, Blaenavon, Torfaen, NP4 9HA. Prop: James Hanna. Tel: (01495) 793093. E-mail: fci2@ix.netcom.com. Est: 2003. Shop; open **M:** 10:00–17:00; **T:** 10:00–17:00; **W:** 10:00–17:00; **Th:** 10:00–17:00; **F:** 10:00–17:00; **S:** 09:00–17:00; **Su:** 10:00–17:00. Spec: Art; Design; Photography. PR: £1–100. CC: MC; V; SW, SO.

Broadleaf Books, ■ 12 Broad Street, Blaenavon, Torfaen, NP4 9ND. Prop: Joanna Chambers and Latagrifrith-Unny. Tel: (01495) 792852. E-mail: broadleaf12@aol.com. Est: 2003. Shop; open **M:** 10:00–17:00; **T:** 10:00–17:00; **W:** 10:00–17:00. **F:** 10:00–17:00; **S:** 10:00–17:00; **Su:** 11:00–16:00. Medium stock. Spec: Children's - General; Design; Natural History; Photography. PR: £1–50. CC: V.

Browning Books, ■ 33 Broad Street, Blaenavon, Torfaen, NP4 9NF. Prop: Stephanie and Andrew Nummelin. Tel: (01495) 790089. E-mail: info@browningbooks.co.uk. Shop; open **M:** 10:00–17:00; **T:** 09:00–17:00; **W:** 10:00–17:00; **Th:** 10:00–17:00; **F:** 10:00–17:00. **S:** 10:00–17:00; **Su:** 11:00–14:00. Medium general stock. Spec: Children's - General; Children's - Illustrated; Languages - National; Transport. PR: £1–150. CC: E; JCB; MC; V; MAE, ELEC.

Celtica Crafts, ■ 80 Broad Street, Blaenavon, Torfaen, NP4 9NF. Tel: (01495) 791406. Fax: (01495) 791406. E-mail: rick@celticacrafts.co.uk. Est: 2003. Shop; open **M:** 10:00–17:00; **T:** 10:00–17:00; **W:** 10:00–17:00; **Th:** 10:00–17:00; **F:** 10:00–17:00; **S:** 10:00–17:00; **Su:** 11:00–16:00. Very small stock. Spec: Crafts. PR: £1–12.

Chatterton's Books, ■ 35 Broad Street, Blaenavon, Torfaen, NP4 9NF. Prop: Jo Wyborn. Tel: (01495) 793141. Website: www.booktownblaenafon.com. E-mail: jo@chattertonsbooks.co.uk. Est: 2003. Shop; open **M:** 10:00–17:00; **T:** 10:00–17:00. **Th:** 10:00–17:00; **F:** 10:00–17:00; **S:** 10:00–17:00; **Su:** 11:00–16:00. Small general stock. Spec: Drama; Erotica; Fiction - General; Fiction - Romantic; Health; History - General; Homosexuality & Lesbianism; Humanities; Literary Criticism; Literature; Poetry; Politics; Sexology; Welsh Interest; Women. PR: £1–100. CC: MC; V; SW, SO.

The Left Bank, ■ 10 Broad Street, Blaenavon, Torfaen, NP4 9ND. Prop: Mark Bennett. Tel: (01495) 791300. Website: www.leftbank.org.uk. E-mail: leftbankents@aol.com. Est: 2003. Shop; open **M:** 09:30–17:30; **T:** 09:30–17:30; **W:** 09:30–17:30; **Th:** 09:30–17:30; **F:** 09:30–17:30; **S:** 09:30–17:30; **Su:** 11:00–16:00. Spec: Cinema/Film; Entertainment - General; Fiction - General; Fiction - Science Fiction; Music - General; Television; Theatre. PR: £1–150.

Llyfraufflur Books, ■ 63 Broad Street, Blaenavon, Torfaen. Prop: Alan Phillips. E-mail: alaniphillips@hotmail.com. Spec: Biography; Culture - National; Travel - General.

The Railway Shop, ■ 13a Broad Street, Blaenavon, Torfaen, NP4 9ND. Prop: Peter Hunt. Tel: (01495) 792263. E-mail: railway@pontypoolandblaenavon.freeserve.co.uk. Est: 1998. Shop; open **M:** 11:00–17:30; **T:** 11:00–17:30; **W:** 11:00–17:30; **Th:** 11:00–17:30; **F:** 11:00–17:30; **S:** 11:00–16:00. Small general stock. Spec: Aviation; Railways; Shipbuilding; Transport. PR: £1–20. Also: model railways, jigsaws and Thomas toys.

The Battle of New Orleans, ■ 56 Broad Street, Blaenavon, Torfaen, NP4 9NH. Tel: (01495) 792417. Est: 2003. Shop; open **M:** 06:00–17:00; **T:** 06:00–18:00; **W:** 06:00–18:00; **Th:** 06:00–18:00; **F:** 06:00–18:00; **S:** 06:00–18:00; **Su:** 05:00–18:00. Large general stock. PR: £1–60. Also, toys, new magazines, groceries.

WREXHAM

WREXHAM

Eileen Hewson, 22 Grove Lodge Close, Poster Road, Wrexham, LL11 2PB.

J.C. Poole Books, 7 Stonewalls, Rossett, Wrexham, LL12 0LG. Tel: (01244) 571557. E-mail: john@cooperpoole.freeserve.co.uk. Est: 1999. Private premises; appointment necessary. Spec: Antiquarian; Bindings; Fine Printing; Media; Military. PR: £5–250.

ALPHABETICAL INDEX BY NAME OF BUSINESS
Entries shown in *italics* indicate that the entry contains only their name and address

A. & R. Booksearch, Cornwall	75
Æenigma Designs (Books), Devon	85
AA1 Books, Scotland	263
Aardvark Books, Wiltshire	252
Abacus Books, Worcestershire	254
Abacus Gallery / The Village Bookshop, Staffordshire	223
Abaris Books, Somerset	215
Abbey Antiquarian Books, Gloucestershire	111
Abbey Books, London (N)	153
Abbey Books, Norfolk	187
Abbey Bookshop, Hampshire	122
Aberdeen Rare Books & Caledonian Books, Scotland	267
Abrahams (Mike), Staffordshire	222
Academy Books, Hampshire	124
Acumen Books, Staffordshire	223
Adab Books, Cambridgeshire	64
Adam & Eve Books, London (SW)	163
Adams (Judith), Shropshire	211
Addair, Scotland	263
Addendum Books, Scotland	263
Addyman Annexe (The), Wales	285
Addyman Books, Wales	285
Adkins (Margaret & Geoff), W Mids	240
Adrem Books, Hertfordshire	129
Afar Books International, W Mids	238
AH Books, Merseyside	185
Ainslie Books, Scotland	271
Aitchison (Lesley), Bristol	60
Al Saqi Books, London (W)	169
Alan Prim, Republic Of Ireland	276
Alastor Books, Hampshire	122
Alba Books, Scotland	267
Alba Secondhand Music, Scotland	271
Albion Books, Devon	86
Albion Books, Hampshire	124
Albion Books, W Mids	239
Aldringham Books, Suffolk	224
Alexander (Greg), Hampshire	123
Alexander's Books, Warwickshire	236
Alhambra Books, Essex	108
All Books, Essex	108
All Seasons Books, Cumbria	79
Allen (R.), Tyne & Wear	235
Alley Books, N Yorks	195
Allhalland Books, Devon	83
Allport (Roy), N Yorks	195
Allsop (Duncan M.), Warwickshire	237
Allsworth Rare Books Ltd., London (SW)	163
Almar Books, W Yorks	247
Alpes Livres (Les), Hampshire	120
Alpha Books, London (N)	153
Altea Antique Maps & Books, London (WC)	169
Alton Secondhand Books, Hampshire	120
Altshuler (Jean), Cumbria	78
Ambra Books, Bristol	60
Americanabooksuk, Cumbria	77
Amos (Denis W.), Hertfordshire	128
Ampersand Books, Shropshire	211
Amwell Book Company (The), London (EC)	152
Anchor Books, Lincolnshire	149
Anchor House Bookshop, Gloucestershire	111
Ancient & Modern Bookshop, Dorset	90
Ancient Art Books, London (SW)	163
Ancient History Books, Kent	139
Anderson Slater Antiques, N Yorks	195
Andrews (R.), Gloucestershire	111
Andrew's Books & Collectables, Derbyshire	82
Andromeda Books, Buckinghamshire	63
Andromeda Bookshop, W Mids	238
Andron (G.W.), London (N)	153
Angel Books, Norfolk	189
Anglewise Books, Cambridgeshire	67
Anglo-American Rare Books, Surrey	232
Anne Harris Books & Bags Booksearch, Devon	86
Annesley Books of Scottish Interest (Brian), Scotland	272
Annie's Books, S Yorks	220
Anthroposophical Books, Bristol	60
Anticus, Warwickshire	237
Antiquary Ltd., (Bar Bookstore), N Yorks	194
Antique Map and Bookshop (The), Dorset	93
Antique Prints of the World, London (N)	153
Anvil Books, W Mids	239
Anwoth Books, Scotland	263
Any Amount of Books, London (WC)	176
Aphra Books, W Yorks	246
Apocalypse Books, Surrey	232
Appleby's Bookshop, Northumberland	201
Applin (Malcolm), Berkshire	57
Apteryx, East Sussex	101
Aquarius Books, Leicestershire	144
Aquarius Books Ltd., Gloucestershire	114
ARC Books, Scotland	272
Arcadia, Oxfordshire	206
Arcadia, Shropshire	212
Arcady Books, Kent	137
Arcanum, Northumberland	201
Arcanum Books, Tyne & Wear	235
Archer (David), Wales	288
Archer (R.G.), Suffolk	227
Archer (Steve), London, Outer	180
Architecture Bookshop (The), W Yorks	245
Archive Books & Music, London (NW)	157
Archive of Modern Conflict, London (W)	169
Archivist (The), Devon	88
Archways Sports Books, Scotland	268
Arden Books & Cosmographia, Warwickshire	236
Arden, Bookseller (C.), Wales	285
Argent (Alan), Isle of Wight	132
Armchair Auctions, Hampshire	120
Armchair Books, W Mids	238

Armchair Books, Scotland 268
Armitage (Booksearch), (Kate), Devon 84
Armitage (N. Trevor), Dorset..................... 90
Armstrongs Books & Collectables, W Mids...... 239
Arnold (Roy), Suffolk............................... 226
Ars Artis, Oxfordshire 206
Art Reference Books, Hampshire 123
Artco, Nottinghamshire 202
Arthurian Book, Wales 285
Artyfacts, Scotland................................. 263
Arundel Bookshop, West Sussex.................... 241
Ash Rare Books, London (EC) 152
Ashburton Books, Devon 83
Ashfield Books and Records,
   Nottinghamshire 203
Ashwell Books, Wiltshire 250
Askew Books (Vernon), Wiltshire.................. 250
Assassin Books, W Mids 238
Assinder Books, Bedfordshire 55
Atholl Browse, Scotland............................ 273
Atholl Fine Books, Scotland........................ 273
Atlantis Bookshop, London (WC).................. 176
Atlas, London (N) 153
Atticus Books, Essex................................ 109
Aucott & Thomas, Leicestershire.................. 143
Aurelian Books, London (NW).................... 157
Austen (Phillip), Lincolnshire....................... 149
Austwick Hall Books, N Yorks 141
Autobooks Ltd., East Sussex 100
Autolycus, Shropshire............................... 211
Autumn Leaves, Lincolnshire....................... 148
Avery (Alan), N Yorks 193
Aviabooks, Gloucestershire........................ 112
Aviation Book Supply, Hertfordshire 128
Aviation Bookshop (The), London (N)........... 153
Avon Books, Bristol................................. 60
Avonbridge Books, Gloucestershire 114
Avonworld Books, Somerset....................... 215
Axe Rare & Out of Print Books (Richard),
   N Yorks... 192
Ayre (Peter J.), Somerset 218
B. and K. Books, Wales 285
babelog.books, Herefordshire....................... 126
Badger, Wiltshire.................................... 252
Badger Books, Somerset............................ 218
Badgers Books, West Sussex....................... 244
Baedekers & Murray Guides, S Yorks 220
Bagot Books, Surrey 230
Bailey Hill Bookshop, Somerset.................... 215
Baker - Books for the Collector (Colin),
   Devon.. 88
Baker (Gerald), Bristol.............................. 60
Baker Limited (A.P. & R.), Scotland.............. 263
Baldwin (Jack), Scotland........................... 271
Baldwin (M. & M.), Shropshire 212
Baldwin's Scientific Books, Essex 110
Ballantyne–Way (Roger), Suffolk 228
Bankes Books, Somerset 214
Bannister (David), Gloucestershire 111
Barber Music, Kent 136
Barbican Bookshop, N Yorks 196
Bardsley's Books, Suffolk 225
Barfield (Ian), Lincolnshire....................... 147
Barlow (Vincent G.), Hampshire................... 123
Barlow Moor Books, Greater Manchester 116

Barmby (C. & A.J.), Kent.......................... 138
Barn Books, Shropshire 213
Barn Books, Buckinghamshire...................... 62
*Barn Collectors Market & Studio
   Bookshop*, East Sussex 103
Barnard (Colin), Kent 138
Barnes - Books (Lyndon), Herefordshire 127
Barnes - Books (Lyndon), Shropshire 212
Barnhill Books, Scotland 272
Barnitt (Peter), Wiltshire 252
Baron - Scientific Book Sales (P.J.), Somerset ... 215
Baron (Christopher), Greater Manchester..... 116
Baron (H.), London (NW).......................... 157
Barron - The Antique Map Specialist
   (Roderick M.), Kent.............................. 137
Barry Meaden (Aviation Books),
   Hertfordshire 129
Barter Books, Northumberland 201
Barter Books, Northumberland 200
Barton (John), Hampshire 124
Baskerville Books, London (W) 169
Bass (Ben), Somerset 215
Bates & Hindmarch, W Yorks 247
Bates Books, London, Outer....................... 181
Bath Book Exchange, Somerset 214
Bath Old Books, Somerset........................ 214
Batstone Books, Wiltshire.......................... 250
Batterdale Books, N Yorks......................... 195
Batterham (David), London (W)................... 169
Battle of New Orleans /Pearce (The), Wales 290
Baxter - Books (Eddie), Somerset 218
Baxter (Steve), Surrey 232
Bay Bookshop, Wales 281
Bay Bookshop (Rhos), Wales..................... 282
Baynton–Williams Gallery, West Sussex........ 241
Bayntun (George), Somerset....................... 214
BBSJ Rare Books, London (SE).................. 160
BC Books, Cheshire 70
Beacon Hill Bookshop, Surrey 232
Beardsell Books, W Yorks 246
Beardsley (A.E.), Nottinghamshire 203
Bearwood Bookshop, W Mids.................... 240
Bearwood Bookshop, W Mids.................... 239
Beaton (Richard), East Sussex 101
Beaumont Travel Books, London (SE) 160
Beaver Booksearch, Suffolk........................ 225
Beck (John), East Sussex 101
Beck (R.A.), Derbyshire 82
Beck Head Books, Cumbria 78
Beckham Books, Suffolk............................ 228
Bee Books New and Old, Cornwall 73
Beech Rural Books, West Sussex................. 243
Beetles Ltd., (Chris), London (SW)............... 163
Behind the Lines, Bedfordshire 55
Beighton (Brian), Norfolk.......................... 187
Belfast Book Search, Northern Ireland 259
Bell (Books) (Mrs. V.S.), Suffolk................... 226
Bell (Peter), Scotland................................ 269
Bell Gallery (The), Northern Ireland 259
Ben–Nathan (Jack), London, Outer............... 181
Bennett & Kerr Books, Oxfordshire 204
Bennetts Books, East Sussex....................... 101
Bernstein (Rare Books) (Nicholas),
   London (W)....................................... 169
Bernwode Books, Buckinghamshire 62

ALPHABETICAL INDEX: Business (B – B)

Berry Books (Liz), Lancashire 140
Bertram Rota Ltd., London (WC) 176
Berwick Books, Lincolnshire 148
Besleys Books, Suffolk 224
Bettridge (Gordon), Scotland 265
Bevan (John), Herefordshire 127
Beverley Old Bookshop, East Yorkshire 104
Bevins & Colin, Gloucestershire 113
Beware of The Leopard Books, Bristol 60
Bewdley Fine Books, Worcestershire 255
Biblical Heritage Collection, London (W) 169
Biblion, London (W) 169
Bibliophile (The), S Yorks 220
Bibliophile Books, London (E) 151
Bickersteth (David), Cambridgeshire 64
Bicknell, (T.), Herefordshire 126
Biddulph (Joseph), Wales 289
Biddy's Bookshop, Devon 86
Biff Books & Records, S Yorks 220
Billing (Brian), Berkshire 59
Birchden Books, London (E) 151
Birchwood Books, W Yorks 246
Bird Books (Nigel), Wales 281
Birdnet Optics Ltd., Derbyshire 81
Bishopston Books, Bristol 60
Biswell, (Douglas), Kent 134
Black & White Books, Isle of Wight 131
Black Cat Books, Norfolk 188
Black Cat Bookshop, Leicestershire 143
Black Five Books, Shropshire 213
Black Hill Books, Shropshire 211
Black Voices, Merseyside 185
Black–Bird Books, London (NW) 157
Blacket Books, Scotland 269
Blacklock's, Surrey 231
Blackman (Martin), Buckinghamshire 62
Blackman Books, Cheshire 72
Blackwell's Music Shop, Oxfordshire 206
Bladen (Reg), Shropshire 212
Blaenavon Books, Wales 289
Blakes Books, Suffolk 229
Blanchfield (John), W Yorks 247
Bland (Mary), Herefordshire 126
Blest (Peter), Kent 136
Blewbury Antiques, Oxfordshire 204
Blore's Bookshop (Geoffrey),
  Nottinghamshire 202
Blue Penguin (The), Gloucestershire 113
Bluntisham Books, Cambridgeshire 64
Blythswood Bookshop, Scotland 268
BMH Books, Cornwall 76
Bodyline Books, London (SW) 163
Boer (Louise), Arthurian Books, Wales 284
Boer War Books, N Yorks 196
Bolland Books (Leslie H.), Bedfordshire 55
Bolton Books, Hampshire 120
Bon Accord Enterprises, Scotland 269
Bonham (J. & S.L.), London (W) 169
Bonner (John), W Yorks 247
Bonython Bookshop, Cornwall 76
Book & Stamp Shop, N Yorks 195
Book Academy (The), W Yorks 247
Book and Art Shop (The), S Yorks 220
Book Barn Ltd., Somerset 216
Book Barrow, Cambridgeshire 64
Book Basket, London, Outer 182
Book Bungalow (The), Cornwall 73
Book Business (The), London (W) 169
Book Collectors Paradise,
  Buckinghamshire 63
Book Corner, Scotland 263
Book Depot (The), London (NW) 157
Book End, Essex 106
Book for All Reasons (A.), Suffolk 227
Book Gallery (The), Cornwall 76
Book Haven (The), Lincolnshire 150
Book House (The), Cumbria 78
Book Jungle (The), East Sussex 102
Book Mad, Lancashire 140
Book Mark (The), Kent 137
Book Mongers, London (SW) 163
Book Shelf (The), Devon 84
Book Shop (The), Scotland 263
Book Swop (The), Scotland 269
Book Warren, Devon 84
Bookbug (The), Hertfordshire 129
Bookcupboard (The), Devon 86
Bookends, Hampshire 121
Bookends of Devon, Devon 85
Bookends of Fowey, Cornwall 74
Bookfare, Cumbria 79
Bookfinder–General, Cheshire 71
Bookline, Northern Ireland 260
Booklore, Leicestershire 144
BookLovers, Somerset 217
Bookmark, Wales 280
Bookmark (Children's Books), Wiltshire 252
Booknotes, Essex 109
Bookpassage (The), Shropshire 211
Bookquest, Devon 83
Bookroom (The), Surrey 233
Bookroom (The), Gloucestershire 112
Books, Kent 134
Books, Wales 282
Books & Bygones, Dorset 94
Books & Bygones, Berkshire 58
Books & Bygones (Pam Taylor), W Mids 240
Books & Collectables Ltd.,
  Cambridgeshire 64
Books & Things, London (W) 169
Books (For All), N Yorks 192
Books 'n' Looks, Scotland 263
Books Afloat, Dorset 95
Books and Things, West Sussex 241
Books at Sixpence, London, Outer 183
Books at the Warehouse, N Yorks 193
Books B.C., London, Outer 181
Books Bought & Sold, Surrey 231
Books do Furnish a Room,
  Warwickshire 236
Books for Collectors, Gloucestershire 112
Books for Content, Herefordshire 126
Books for Cooks, London (W) 169
Books for Writers, Wales 283
Books Galore, Somerset 216
Books in Cardigan, Wales 281
Books in Cardigan, Wales 281
Books in the Basement, Surrey 233
Books International, Hampshire 121
Books of Note, Cambridgeshire 64

ALPHABETICAL INDEX: Business (B – B)

Books on Spain, London, Outer 183
Books on the Bank, Durham 96
Books Only, Suffolk 226
Books Plus, Devon 87
Books Ulster, Northern Ireland 260
Books With Care, Bedfordshire 55
'Books', Oxfordshire 204
Books2Books, Devon 87
BOOKS4U, Wales 282
Booksave, Hampshire 121
Booksearch Ltd., Leicestershire 145
Bookseeker, Scotland 273
Bookseekers, London (SW) 163
Bookseller (The), Suffolk 227
Bookshelf – Aviation Books, Norfolk 189
Bookshelf (The), Lancashire 140
Bookshelf (The), N Yorks 194
Bookshop (The), Greater Manchester 117
Bookshop (The), Norfolk 191
Bookshop (The), Republic Of Ireland 276
Bookshop (The), Cambridgeshire 64
Bookshop (The), West Sussex 242
Bookshop (The), Greater Manchester 117
Bookshop at the Plain, Lincolnshire 148
Bookshop Blackheath, London (SE) 160
Bookshop Bookfair, Shropshire 212
Bookshop Conwy, Wales 282
Bookshop Down The Lane (The),
  Oxfordshire 204
Bookshop Gallery, Somerset 218
Bookshop, Kirkstall (The), W Yorks 247
Booksleuth, Lincolnshire 148
Booksmart, Northamptonshire 198
Bookstack & D.J. Creece (Bookbinder),
  Shropshire 211
Bookstand, Dorset 93
Bookstop Bookshop, N Yorks 193
Bookstop UK, Lancashire 142
Booktrace International, Devon 85
Bookworld, Shropshire 212
Bookworm, Essex 106
Bookworm Alley, Devon 87
Book–Worm International, Essex 107
Bookworms, Norfolk 187
Bookworms of Evesham, Worcestershire 255
Bookworms of Shoreham, West Sussex 243
Bookwyze, Lincolnshire 147
Booth (Booksearch Service), (Geoff), Cheshire .. 69
Booth Books, Wales 286
Border Books, Scotland 261
Border Bookshop (The), W Yorks 248
Boris Books, Dorset 94
Bosco Books, Cornwall 73
Bosphorus Books, London (WC) 176
Boss (Tim), West Sussex 243
Botanic Books, Northern Ireland 259
Bott, (Bookdealers) Ltd., (Martin), Greater
  Manchester 116
Botting & Berry, East Sussex 101
Bournes Bookworld, Dorset 95
Bournville Books, Herefordshire 126
Bow Windows Book Shop, East Sussex 102
Bowden Books, Leicestershire 144
Bowdon Books, Lancashire 141
Bowen (Janice), Wales 286

Bowers Chess Suppliers (Francis),
  Cambridgeshire 67
Bowland Bookfinders, Lancashire 140
Box (Janet), Wales 283
Box of Frogs (The), Scotland 263
Boxwood Books & Prints, Somerset 218
Boydell Galleries (The), Merseyside 185
Boz Books, Wales 286
Bracton Books, Cambridgeshire 64
Brad Books, Essex 108
Bradley (Nigel), Derbyshire 81
Bradley–Cox (Mary), Dorset 90
Bramble Books, Hampshire 121
Branksome Books, Dorset 93
Bray (Roger), Wales 281
Brazenhead Ltd., Norfolk 189
Breese Books Ltd., East Sussex 98
Brett (Harry), Cambridgeshire 64
Brett (R.C.), Northamptonshire 199
Brewer (Rosalind), Suffolk 226
Brewin Books Ltd., Warwickshire 237
Bridge Books, Cumbria 79
Bridge of Allan Books, Scotland 262
Bridge Street Bookshop, Northumberland 200
Bright (P.G.), Cambridgeshire 66
Brighton Books, East Sussex 98
Brimstones, East Sussex 102
Brinded (Scott), Kent 136
Bristol Books, Bristol 60
Bristol Books Academic, Bristol 60
Bristow & Garland, Hampshire 121
Britannia Books, Merseyside 186
Britons Catholic Library, Republic Of Ireland .. 279
Broadhurst of Southport Ltd., Merseyside 186
Broadleaf Books, Wales 290
Broadwater Books, Hampshire 124
Broadway Books, Cambridgeshire 67
Brock Books, N Yorks 192
Brockwells Bookshop, London (SE) 160
Brogden Books, Cumbria 79
Brookbanks (P.S.), Cambridgeshire 67
Broughton Books, Scotland 269
Brown (Books) (P.R.), Durham 96
Brown (Books) (Steve), Staffordshire 222
Brown (K.C.), Berkshire 58
Browne (A.), Cheshire 69
Browne (Christopher I.), W Yorks 245
Browning (Julian), London (W) 169
Browning Books, Wales 290
Brown-Studies, Scotland 270
Browse Books, Lancashire 140
Browsers Bookshop, Essex 107
Browser's Bookshop, Cornwall 74
Browzers, Greater Manchester 117
Brunner Books, Cambridgeshire 68
Bryant (Mrs. Muriel J.), Devon 84
Bryant Books (Derek), W Yorks 245, 248
Bryony Books, W Yorks 247
Buchan Collectibles, Scotland 265
Buckland Books, West Sussex 243
Buckley (Sybil), N Yorks 193
Budd (Richard), Somerset 217
Bufo Books, Hampshire 123
Burak (Steve), London (WC) 176
Burden Ltd., (Clive A.), Hertfordshire 129

ALPHABETICAL INDEX: Business (B – C)

Burebank Books, Norfolk 187
Burgess Booksellers, (J. & J.), Cambridgeshire .. 64
Burmester (James), Bristol 60
Burntwood Bookshop, Staffordshire 222
Burroughs (Andrew), Lincolnshire 149
Burton–Garbett (A.), London, Outer 182
Bury Bookshop, Suffolk 225
Bush, Bookdealer (John), Gloucestershire 115
Butcher (Pablo), Oxfordshire 205
Butler – Books (B.), Devon 83
Butler Books, Dorset 90
Butler Books, Buckinghamshire 63
Butterwick Books, Lincolnshire 149
Butts Books (Mary), Berkshire 58
Buxton Books (Anna), Scotland 269
By The Book, Norfolk 187
Bygone Books, Scotland 272
Bygone Books, Lancashire 141
Bygone Tunes, Lancashire 142
Byre Books, Scotland 264
Byrom Textile Bookroom (Richard),
  Lancashire 140
Caburn Books, East Sussex 102
Cader Idris Books, Wales 283
Caduceus Books, Leicestershire 143
Cahir Cosy Corner Bookshop,
  Republic Of Ireland 279
Caissa Books, Surrey 233
Caledonia Books, Scotland 271
Calendula Horticultural Books, East Sussex 100
Calluna Books, Dorset 94
Calvert's Bookshop (Kit), N Yorks 193
Camden Books, Somerset 214
Cameron (Mrs Janet), Kent 138
Cameron House Books, Isle of Wight 131
Camilla's Bookshop, East Sussex 100
Cammarch Books, Wales 287
Campbell (Fiona), London (SE) 160
Campbell (Iain), Cheshire 72
Campbell Art Books (Marcus), London (SE) 160
Campbell Hewson Books (R.), Scotland 265
Candle Lane Books, Shropshire 213
*Canon Gate Bookshop (formerly St. Peter's
  Bookshop)*, West Sussex 241
Canterbury Bookshop (The), Kent 133
Capel Mawr Collectors Centre, Wales 283
Capes (Books, Maps & Prints) (John L.),
  N Yorks 195
Capital Bookshop, Wales 280
Capuchins, Worcestershire 256
Carlton Books, Norfolk 189
Carnforth Bookshop (The), Lancashire 140
Carningli Centre, Wales 284
Caron Books, Nottinghamshire 202
Carraig Books Ltd., Republic Of Ireland 276
Carta Regis, Wales 288
Carter, (Brian), Oxfordshire 205
Carters (Janet), Suffolk 225
Cartographics, Staffordshire 223
Cassidy (Bookseller) (P.), Lincolnshire 147
Cassidy's Gallery, London (SE) 160
Castle Bookshop, Wales 288
Castle Bookshop, Essex 107
Castle Frome Books, Herefordshire 127
Castle Hill Books, Herefordshire 126

Castleton (Pat), Kent 135
Catalyst Books, Surrey 232
Cathach Books Ltd., Republic Of Ireland 277
Cavan Book Centre, Republic Of Ireland 275
Cavendish Books (Rupert), W Yorks 246
Cavern Books, Cheshire 69, 70, 71
Cavers' Bookshelf (The), Wales 281
Cecil Books, Surrey 231
Celtic Antiquarian Books, Merseyside 186
Celtic Bookshop (The), Republic Of Ireland 279
Celtica Crafts, Wales 290
Centurion Books, Hampshire 124
Chaldon Books & Records, Surrey 230
Chalk (Old & Out of Print Books)
  (Christine M.), W Mids 238
Chalmers Hallam (E.), Hampshire 123
Chambers (Barry), Kent 133
Chandos Books, London, Outer 182
Chandos Books, Bristol 60
Channel Islands Galleries Limited,
  Channel Islands 257
Chantrey Books, S Yorks 220
Chantry Bookshop & Gallery, Devon 84
Chapel Books, Suffolk 228
Chapman (Neville), Cornwall 76
Chapman (Ron), London (SW) 163
Chapman Books (Mary), London, Outer 181
Chapter & Verse, Lincolnshire 148
Chapter and Verse Booksellers, East Sussex 102
Chapter House Books, Dorset 93
Chapter Two, London (SE) 160
Chapters Bookstore, Republic Of Ireland 277
Charlie Byrne's Bookshop,
  Republic Of Ireland 277
Charmouth Bookstore, Dorset 91
Charnwood Books, Surrey 231
Chaters Motoring Booksellers,
  London, Outer 182
Chatterton's Books, Wales 290
Chaucer Bookshop (The), Kent 133
Chaucer Head (The), Wales 288
Chaucer Head Bookshop, Warwickshire 237
CHC Books, Lincolnshire 147
Chelifer Books, Cumbria 79
Cherrington Rare Books Ltd. (T.A.),
  Surrey 233
Cherry (Janet), Dorset 92
Chesters (G. & J.), Staffordshire 223
Chevet Supplies Ltd., Lancashire 140
Chevin Books, W Yorks 248
Cheyne Books, Northumberland 200
Chichester Bookshop (The), West Sussex 241
Chichester Gallery, West Sussex 241
Childrens Bookshop, W Yorks 246
Children's Bookshop (The), Wales 286
Children's Bookshop No. 2 (The), Wales 286
Chiltern Books, London (W) 172
Christine's Book Cabin, Leicestershire 144
Chthonios Books, East Sussex 100
Church Green Books, Oxfordshire 210
Church Street Bookshop, London (N) 153
Church Stretton Books, Shropshire 211
Cinema Bookshop (The), London (WC) 176
Clapham (M. & B.), Hampshire 122
Clark (K.R.), Oxfordshire 205

ALPHABETICAL INDEX: Business (C – D)

Clark (M.R.), W Yorks.................................. 245
Clark (Nigel A.), London (SE)....................... 160
Clark Fine Books (Robert), Oxfordshire 206
Clarke (J. & D.), Norfolk 189
Clarke (Janet), Somerset............................... 214
Clarke Books (David), Somerset 216
Clarke–Hall (J.) Limited, Kent....................... 134
Classey Limited (E.W.), Oxfordshire........... 205
Classic Bindings, London (SW) 163
Classic Crime Collections, Greater
  Manchester... 117
Classics Bookshop (The), Oxfordshire 206
Clay (Peter).. 74
Clear (Mrs. Patricia), London, Outer 180
Clearwater Books, Dorset 91
Clegg (David), Staffordshire 222
Clements (R.W.), London, Outer 181
Clent Books, Worcestershire........................ 254
Clevedon Books, Somerset......................... 215
Cleverley (T.), Derbyshire 82
Clewlow, Bookseller (Allan), N Yorks 196
Clifton Books, Essex 110
Coach House Books, Worcestershire.............. 255
Cobnar Books, Kent 136
Cobweb Books, N Yorks.............................. 194
Coch-y-Bonddu Books, Wales...................... 288
Cocks Books (Brian), Cambridgeshire 67
Coffee Gourmet, Lancashire........................ 142
Cold Tonnage Books, Surrey...................... 234
Coleman (Tom), Scotland.......................... 267
Coleraine Bookshop (The),
  Northern Ireland 260
Coles (T.V.), Cambridgeshire 67
Collards Bookshop, Devon 89
Collectable Books, London (SE).................... 160
Collectables (W.H.), London (W)................. 172
Collectors Carboks, Northamptonshire......... 199
Collectors Corner, Wiltshire........................ 252
Collector's Corner, Lancashire 140
Collinge & Clark, London (WC)................. 176
Collins (Book & Print Dealers) (G.),
  Hertfordshire 129
Colonsay Bookshop, Scotland...................... 272
Colwyn Books, Wales.................................. 281
Combat Arts Archive, Durham 96
Compost (Books), S Yorks 220
Conquistador Mail Order, London, Outer 180
Conry (Ann & Mike), Worcestershire........... 256
Cook (R.L.), Norfolk.................................. 190
Cook the Books, Somerset......................... 219
Cooks Books, East Sussex 98
Cooksweb, Northamptonshire...................... 198
Coombes (A.J.), Surrey................................ 230
Cooper Hay Rare Books, Scotland................. 271
Copnal Books, Cheshire 70
Coracle Books, W Yorks.............................. 247
Corfe Books, Surrey.................................... 231
Corin (Mrs. Mary), West Sussex................. 244
Cornell Books, Gloucestershire..................... 114
Cornerstone Books, Devon 87
Corran Books Limited, Wales..................... 281
Corrie Ball, Surrey 230
Corvus Books, Buckinghamshire 62
Cotham Hill Bookshop, Bristol 60
Cotswold Internet Books, Gloucestershire...... 111

Cottage Books, Leicestershire 143
Coulthurst (Richard), Greater Manchester 118
Country Hoard Books, Gloucestershire........ 112
Countryman Books, East Yorkshire............. 105
Countrymans Gallery (The), Leicestershire...... 143
Countryside Books, Berkshire..................... 120
Coupland (Terry W.), Staffordshire.............. 222
Court Hay Books, Bristol............................. 60
Courtenay Bookroom, Oxfordshire 204
Courtney & Hoff, N Yorks 196
Courtwood Books, Republic Of Ireland 278
Courtyard Books, Herefordshire 127
Cousens (W.C.), Devon................................ 83
Cover to Cover, Merseyside 186
Cowley, Auto–in–Print (John), Essex 106
Cowley, Bookdealer (K.W.), Somerset 215
Cox (Geoff), Devon.................................... 89
Cox Music (Lisa), Devon............................. 85
Cox Old & Rare Books (Claude), Suffolk 226
Cox Rare Books (Charles), Cornwall 74
Crabtree (Mrs. C.), Greater Manchester........ 118
Crack (Books) (F.N.), Lancashire 140
Cranhurst Books, London (NW)................. 157
Cranmer Books, Oxfordshire 210
Craobh Rua Books, Northern Ireland 259
Crawford (Elizabeth), London (EC).............. 152
*Crawford (John) - Rare and Secondhand
  Books*, Suffolk 225
Creaking Shelves, Scotland........................ 267
Crescent Books, Scotland 262
Crime Inc, Greater Manchester 118
Crimes Ink, London (E).............................. 151
Crispin's Day, Antiquarian and
  Out of Print Military Books, Essex 110
Criterion Books, London, Outer 182
Croft Selections, Lincolnshire...................... 148
Crombie (R. & S.), W Mids 240
Cronin (Jim), Wales 280
Crook (Chris), Somerset............................. 218
Crosby Nethercott Books, London, Outer 180
Cross (Ian), Berkshire.................................. 57
Crouch Rare Books, Surrey......................... 232
Crowe Antiquarian Books (Peter), Norfolk ... 189
Croydon Bookshop, London, Outer............... 180
Cuddy Books (Michael), London (N)............ 153
Cumming Limited (A. & Y.), East Sussex........ 102
Curiosity Shop (The), Cambridgeshire 67
Curlews, Durham....................................... 96
Curtle Mead Books, Isle of Wight................ 131
Cusack Books, London (W)........................ 172
Cyclamen Books, Leicestershire.................... 143
Cygnet Books, East Yorkshire 105
D. & M. Books, W Yorks........................... 248
D.C. Books, Lincolnshire 148
Daemon Books, Lancashire........................ 141
Daeron's Books, Buckinghamshire 63
Daisy Lane Books, W Yorks 246
Dalby (Richard), N Yorks 194
Dalian Books, London (E) 151
Dally Books & Collectables, Wales............... 287
Daly (Peter M.), Hampshire 124
Dance Books Ltd., Hampshire.................... 120
Dancing Goat Bookshop (The), Norfolk 188
Danzig (R.), Isle of Wight......................... 131
D'Arcy Books, Wiltshire 250

Darklair, Bristol 60
Darkwood Books, Republic Of Ireland 276
Dartmoor Bookshop (The), Devon 83
DaSilva Puppet Books, Oxfordshire 204
Davenport (Lewis), London (WC) 176
David (G.), Cambridgeshire 64
David Thomas Motoring Books, Herefordshire 127
davidleesbooks.com, Wales 286
Davids Ltd., (Roy), Oxfordshire 207
Davidson Books, Northern Ireland 260
Davies (F.D.), Hertfordshire 130
Davies at Flair (K.), East Sussex 98
Davies Fine Books, Worcestershire 256
Davis (C. & D.), Devon 83
Davis (Peter), Kent 136
Davis, Antiquarian Books (Guy), Nottinghamshire 202
Dawlish Books, Devon 84
Dawson (Modern First Editions), (Philip), London, Outer 183
Day (J.H.), Hampshire 122
de Beaumont (Robin), London (SW) 163
De Burca Rare Books, Republic Of Ireland ... 277
de Lotz Books (P.G.), London (NW) 157
De Swartes Ltd., London (N) 153
Dead Mens Minds.co.uk, Wales 285
Dead Zone Books, Wales 289
Dean Byass, Tavistock Books, Devon 86
Dean Illustrated Books (Myra), Wales 284
Dearman Rare Books (Rebecca), Leicestershire 143
Debbage (John), Norfolk 189
Deeside Books, Scotland 266
Delaney's Books, Republic Of Ireland 275
Delectus Books, London (WC) 176
Delow (Ruth & Emma), Devon 86
Delph Books, Greater Manchester 116
Demar Books (Grant), Kent 138
Demetzy Books, London (W) 172
Dene Barn Books & Prints, Somerset 218
Desmond (Arnold), Somerset 217
Devanha Military Books, Scotland 267
Deverell Books, Bristol 61
Devitt Books (Nial), Warwickshire 236
Dew (Roderick), East Sussex 100
dgbbooks, West Sussex 244
Dinnages Transport Publishing, East Sussex 98
Discourse Books, Cumbria 78
Discovery, Devon 84
Diver's & Watersportsman's Library (The), Devon 86
Dobel's Books, Lancashire 141
Dobson (Bob), Lancashire 140
Dodd Books (Maurice), Cumbria 77
Doggie Hubbard Bookshop, Wales 281
Dolphin Books, Suffolk 224
Donovan Military Books (Tom), East Sussex 98
Dooley (Rosemary), Cumbria 80
Doolin Dinghy Books, Republic Of Ireland 275
Doorbar (P. & D.), Hampshire 122
Dorchester Bookshop (The), Dorset 92
Dore (Jeremy), Essex 106
Doro Books, West Sussex 242
Dorset Bookshop (The), Dorset 90
Dorset Rare Books, Wiltshire 252
DoublePlusBooks, Cambridgeshire 68
Doughty Fine Books (Robin), W Mids 238
Douglas Books, Scotland 262
Downie Fine Books Ltd., (Robert), Shropshire 213
Draycott Books, Gloucestershire 112
Driffield Bookshop (The), East Yorkshire 104
Driver (Sheila), West Sussex 244
Drummond Pleasures of Past Times (David), London (WC) 176
Drury Rare Books (John), Essex 109
Du Ry Medieval Manuscripts (Marc–Antoine), London (W) 172
Duck (William), East Sussex 98
Duncan & Reid, Scotland 269
Duncan Books (Jack), N Yorks 196
Duncan's Books, Devon 88
Dunn Antiques & Books (Hamish), Northumberland 201
Dusty Books, Wales 287
Dusty Old Books Ltd., Oxfordshire 206
Dworski Books, Travel & Language Bookshop (Marijana), Wales 286
Dyer Cricket Books (Ian), N Yorks 194
Dyfi Valley Bookshop, Wales 288
Dylans Bookstore, Wales 289
Dyson (Anthony), W Mids 239
Eagle Bookshop (The), Bedfordshire 55
Earlsfield Bookshop (The), London (SW) 163
Early Cinema, Lincolnshire 149
Earth Science Books, Wiltshire 251
East Riding Books & Music, East Yorkshire 105
Eastcote Bookshop (The), London, Outer 183
Eastern Books of London, London (SW) 163
Eastern Traveller (The), Somerset 218
Eastgate Bookshop, Warwickshire 237
Eastleach Books, Berkshire 58
Eastwood Books (David), Cornwall 73
Eaton (Booksellers) Limited (Peter), Buckinghamshire 62
Economia Books, Wales 281
ECR Books, Dorset 93
Eddie's Books and Cards, Scotland 271
Eden Books, Dorset 92
Eden's Books, Essex 108
Edwards (Alan & Margaret), Kent 139
Edwards (Christopher), Berkshire 57
Edwards (London) Limited (Francis), London (WC) 177
Edwards in Hay–on–Wye (Francis), Wales 286
Eggeling Books (John), W Yorks 248
Eggle (Mavis), Hertfordshire 128
Elaine Lonsdale Books, Warwickshire 236
Elephant Books, W Yorks 247
Elgar (Raymond), East Sussex 98
Elham Valley Bookshop, Kent 133
Ellen, The Bookshop (Barrie E.), Essex 110
Elliot's Shelf, Norfolk 189
Ellis (J.R. & R.K.), Norfolk 189
Ellis, Bookseller (Peter), London (SE) 160
Ellwood Editions, Hampshire 123
Elmbury Books, Warwickshire 237
Elmer Books, (Clifford), Greater Manchester 116
Elmfield Books, W Mids 238

ALPHABETICAL INDEX: Business (E – G)

Elsom - Antiques (Pamela), Derbyshire 81
Elstree Books, Hertfordshire 128
Elton Engineering Books, London (W) 172
Ely Books, Cambridgeshire 66
Embleton (Paul), Essex 109
Emerald Isle Books, Northern Ireland 259
Emjay Books, Surrey 231
Empire Books, Greater Manchester 118
Empire Books, N Yorks 196
Emporium Books, Isle of Wight 131
Endeavour Books, N Yorks 196
Engaging Gear Ltd., Essex 106
English (Toby), Oxfordshire 209
Enscot Books, London (SE) 160
Erasmus Books, Scotland 271
Erian Books, London (N) 153
Esplin (David), Hampshire 122
Eton Antique Bookshop, Berkshire 59
Europa Books, London (SW) 163
Evangelical Bookshop, Northern Ireland 259
Evans Books (Paul), West Sussex 243
Evans Booksearch, (Lesley), Devon 89
Eve Magee Books, Wiltshire 251
Everett (Richard), Norfolk 187
Evergreen Livres, Gloucestershire 113
Ex Libris, Wiltshire 250
Exedra Booksearch Ltd., London (SW) 164
Exeter Rare Books, Devon 85
Explorer Books, West Sussex 243
Facet Books, Dorset 90
Fair Reader, Staffordshire 222
Faircross Books, London (W) 172
Falconwood Transport & Military Bookshop,
 London, Outer 184
Family Favourites (Books), East Yorkshire 104
Fantastic Literature, Essex 109
Fantasy Centre, London (N) 153
Far Horizons Books, Dorset 91
Farahar & Dupré (Clive & Sophie),
 Wiltshire 250
Farnborough Bookshop and Gallery,
 Hampshire 121
Farquharson, (Hilary), Scotland 273
Farringdon (J.M.), Wales 289
Farringdon Books, Essex 107
Faversham Antiques Centre, Kent 135
Faversham Books, Kent 135
Fawkes (Keith), London (NW) 157
Fenning (James), Republic Of Ireland 277
Fenton (L.M.), Surrey 231
Fenwick (Edward), Scotland 269
Ferdinando (Steven), Somerset 217
Ferguson (Elizabeth), Scotland 265
Fergusson Books & Manuscripts (James),
 London (W) 172
Ferrial Books, Scotland 269
Ferrow (David), Norfolk 188
Fiction First, Cheshire 70
Fifteenth Century Bookshop (The),
 East Sussex 102
Fifth Element, W Mids 239
Fin Rare Books, Shropshire 213
Finch Rare Books Ltd. (Simon), London (W)... 172
Find That Book, W Yorks 247
Fine Art, West Sussex 242
Fine Art Catalogues, Cumbria 79
Fine Books Oriental Ltd., London (WC) 177
Fine Irish Books, Republic Of Ireland 276
fineart-photographer, Herefordshire 127
Finn (V. & C.), Merseyside 185
Finney Antique Books & Prints (Michael),
 London (WC) 177
Fireside Books, Buckinghamshire 63
Fireside Bookshop, Cumbria 80
First State Books, London (W) 172
Firsts in Print, Isle of Wight 131
Firth (Bijou Books & Photography)
 (Maureen), S Yorks 221
Fishburn Books, London (NW) 157
Fisher & Sperr, London (N) 153
Fisher Nautical, East Sussex 98
Fitzsimons (Anne), Cumbria 77
Fletcher (H.M.), Hertfordshire 129
Flora Books, London (E) 151
Fogg Rare Books & Manuscripts (Sam),
 London (W) 172
Folios Limited, London (SW) 164
Foort (J. & R.K.), Warwickshire 237
Footballana, Berkshire 58
Footrope Knots, Suffolk 226
Ford (Richard), London (W) 172
Ford Books (David), Hertfordshire 130
Fordham (S.C.), London (SE) 160
ForensicSearch, London, Outer 182
Forest Books, Lincolnshire 147
Forest Books, Leicestershire 145
Forest Books of Manchester,
 Greater Manchester 117
Forman Books (Adrian), Devon 86
Formby Antiques (Jeffrey), Gloucestershire 113
Fortune Books, Essex 106
Fortune Green Books, London (NW) 157
Foster (Stephen), London (NW) 157
Foster Bookshop (Paul), London (SW) 164
Fosters Bookshop, London (W) 172
Fotheringham (Alex), Northumberland 200
Foulkes (Len), Wales 280
Fountain Books, Hampshire 124
Four Shire Bookshops, Gloucestershire 113
Four Tees Booksearch, Dorset 90
Fox Books (J. & J.), Kent 137
Foyle Books, Northern Ireland 260
Franks Booksellers, Greater Manchester 117
Freader's Books, Scotland 273
*Freeman Rare Books and Manuscripts
 (Arthur)*, London (W) 172
Frew Limited (Robert), London (WC) 177
Freya Books & Antiques, Norfolk 189
Frost (Richard), Hertfordshire 128
Fuchsia Books, Republic Of Ireland 276
Fuller D'Arch Smith, London (W) 172
Fullerton's Booksearch, Norfolk 188
Fun in Books, Surrey 233
Furneaux Books (Lee), Devon 87
G C Books, Scotland 264
Gage Postal Books, Essex 109
Galloway & Porter Limited,
 Cambridgeshire 65
Game Advice, Oxfordshire 207
Gander, (Jacques), Gloucestershire 112

ALPHABETICAL INDEX: Business (G – H)

Gant (Elizabeth), Surrey............................ 231
Garbett Antiquarian Books (Michael), Bristol... 111
Garden House Books, Suffolk...................... 229
Gardiner (P. & R.), Isle of Wight.............. 131
Gardner & Co., (Walter H.), London (N)........ 153
Garretts Antiquarian Books, Isle of Man 258
Garton & Co., Wiltshire........................... 250
Garwood & Voigt, Kent............................ 137
Garwood (Martin), Essex 109
Gaskell Rare Books (Roger), Cambridgeshire ... 67
Gaslight Books, Lincolnshire...................... 149
Gate Memorabilia, London (N).................... 153
Gay's The Word, London (WC) 177
Gekoski (R.A.), London (WC)..................... 177
Geneva Books, London (SW)..................... 164
Geophysical Books, Kent......................... 137
George Street Loft (The), Derbyshire 82
Gerrards Cross Books, Devon...................... 87
Gibb (Alistair), Scotland 265
Gibbard (A. & T.), East Sussex 100
Gibberd (Jane), London (SE)...................... 160
Gibbs Bookshop Ltd., Greater Manchester 117
Giddings (Trevor J.), Suffolk.................... 225
Gilbert (R.A.), Bristol.............................. 61
Gilbert and Son (H.M.), Hampshire............... 124
Gildea (Donald), West Sussex 241
Gilham Books, London (SE) 161
Gillies (Benny), Scotland 262
Gillmark Gallery, Hertfordshire................. 129
Gilmartin (Howard), Wales...................... 282
Gippeswic Books, Suffolk.......................... 227
Glacier Books, Scotland 273
Glaister, Fine & Rare Books (Nancy Sheiry),
 London (N).. 153
Glass Key (The), W Yorks......................... 246
Glenbower Books, Republic Of Ireland........... 277
Gleniffer Press, (The), Scotland 264
Glenwood Books, Surrey 230
Glenwood Books, Surrey 234
Gloucester Road Bookshop, London (SW) 164
Glyn's Books, Shropshire 211
Godmanchester Books, Cambridgeshire 66
Golden Age Books, Worcestershire................ 255
Golden Books, Devon............................. 83
Golden Goose Books, Lincolnshire................ 148
Golden Hind Bookshop (The), Kent 134
Golden Hours Bookshop, Isle of Wight 131
Goldhold Ltd., London (E)......................... 151
Goldman (Paul), Dorset...........................93
Goldmark Books, Leicestershire................. 145
Goldsboro Books Limited, Berkshire 59
Goldsworth Books & Prints, Surrey............... 234
Good Books, Shropshire......................... 212
Goodden (Peter), Somerset 214
Goodwin (J.O.), Staffordshire..................... 223
Goodyer (Nicholas), London (N).................. 154
Goodyer, Natural History Books (Eric),
 Leicestershire 144
Gorton Booksearch (John), East Sussex 103
Gough Books Limited (Simon), Norfolk........ 188
Gowan Books (John), Northern Ireland 260
Graduate Books, Worcestershire................... 256
Gradwell Concepts, Merseyside 185
Graham (John), Dorset............................. 95
Grahame (Major Iain), Suffolk..................... 225
Grampian Books, Scotland 265
Grant & Shaw Ltd., Scotland 269
Grant (Gerald S.), Cheshire.........................69
Grant (Louise), London, Outer.................. 180
Grant Books, Worcestershire 254
Graves–Johnston (Michael), London (SW)....... 164
Gravity Books, Lincolnshire....................... 147
Grayling (David A.H.), Cumbria 78
Grays of Westminster, London (SW) 164
Great Grandfather's, Lancashire................... 141
Great Oak Bookshop (The), Wales 287
Greek Bookshop, Zenos Booksellers (The),
 London (N)....................................... 154
Green (Michael), Hampshire..................... 125
Green (Mrs. D.M.), Surrey 234
Green (Paul), Cambridgeshire 68
Green Ltd. (G.L.), Hertfordshire................ 129
Green Man Books, Derbyshire 81
Green Man Bookshop & Gallery, East Sussex. 100
Green Meadow Books, Cornwall 75
Green Street Books (Mail Order), Essex 107
Greene's Bookshop Ltd., Republic Of Ireland. 277
Greenroom Books, W Yorks 246
Greensleeves, Oxfordshire.......................... 204
Greenwood, (Adrian), Oxfordshire.............. 207
Greer (Robin), London (SW)...................... 164
Gregory (George), Somerset 214
Grenville Books, London (NW) 157
Gresham Books, Somerset 216
Greta Books, Durham 96
Grey House Books, Surrey......................... 234
Greyfriars Books, Essex 107
Grieveson (A.), Cheshire........................... 69
Grieveson (Andrea), Merseyside 185
Griffith & Partners Ltd., London (WC) 177
Grosvenor Prints, London (WC) 177
Grove Bookshop (The), N Yorks.................. 195
Guildmaster Books, Cheshire...................... 71
Haas (A. Rosenthal) (Otto),
 London (NW).................................... 157
Hab Books, London (W)........................... 173
Hadfield (G.K.), Cumbria........................ 79
Hadley Bookseller (Peter J.), Norfolk 189
Hairpin Books, Gloucestershire 113
Halcyon Bookshop, West Sussex.................. 242
Hall (G.), Greater Manchester 116
Hall, (Anthony C.) Antiquarian Bookseller,
 London, Outer.................................... 184
Hall's Bookshop, Kent............................ 138
Halson Books, Cheshire............................ 71
Hambleton Books, N Yorks...................... 195
Hames (Peter), Devon 84
Hanborough Books, Oxfordshire 207
Hancock & Monks, Wales 286
Hancock (Colin), Wales 281
Hancock (Peter), West Sussex 241
Handley (Christopher), Tyne & Wear.......... 235
Handsworth Books, Essex.......................... 110
Hanshan Tang Books, London (SW)........... 164
Harlequin, Devon.................................. 89
Harlequin Books, Bristol 61
Harlequin Gallery, Lincolnshire................. 148
Harper, Books (Berry), East Sussex 100
Harries (Pauline), Hampshire...................... 122
Harrington (Adrian), London (W)................. 173

ALPHABETICAL INDEX: Business (H – I)

Harrington Antiquarian Bookseller (Peter), London (SW) 164
Harris (Books), (Malcolm), W Mids 239
Harris (George J.), Worcestershire 254
Harrison's Books, London (W) 173
Hart (John), Norfolk 190
Hartley Books (Caroline), Nottinghamshire 202
Harvest Books, Merseyside 185
Harwich Old Books, Essex 108
Haskell (R.H. & P.), Dorset 93
Hatchard & Daughters, W Yorks 245, 246
Hatchwell (Richard), Wiltshire 251
Hattle (Anne), Northumberland 200
Haven Booksearch, W Mids 238
Havercroft Antiquarian Books, London (SE) 161
Hawes Books, Norfolk 189
Hawkes (James), Gloucestershire 111
Hawkridge Books, Derbyshire 81
Hawley (C.L.), N Yorks 195
Hawthorn Books, Bristol 61
Hay Cinema Bookshop Ltd., Wales 286
Hayes Bookshop (C. & B. Glover), London, Outer 182
Hayles Military Books (Derek), Berkshire 57
HCB Wholesale, Wales 287
Heartland Old Books, Devon 88
Heath (A.R.), Bristol 61
Heathfield Books, Norfolk 188
Heatons, Wiltshire 252
Heckmondwike Book Shop, W Yorks 235
Hedger (Jean), London, Outer 180
Hedgerow Books, S Yorks 220
Helion & Company, W Mids 240
Hellenic Bookservices, London (NW) 158
Helmsley Antiquarian & Secondhand Books, N Yorks 193
Helston Bookworm (The), Cornwall 74
Hen Hoose Bookshop, Scotland 262
Hencotes Books & Prints, Northumberland 200
Heneage Art Books (Thomas), London (SW) 164
Henly (John), West Sussex 244
Hennessey Bookseller (Ray), East Sussex 100
Heppa (Christopher), Essex 106
Heraldry Today, Wiltshire 252
Herb Tandree Philosophy Books, Bristol 61
Hereward Books, Cambridgeshire 66
Heritage, W Mids 238
Heritage Books, Isle of Wight 131
Herne Bay Books, Kent 136
Hesketh & Ward Ltd., London (SW) 164
Hewson (Eileen), Wales 290
Heyman (B.), London, Outer 181
Heywood Hill Limited (G.), London (W) 173
Hickey Books, Northamptonshire 198
Hicks (Ronald C.), Cornwall 74
High Street Books, Devon 85
Highfield Books Ltd., Gloucestershire 111
Hight (Norman F.), Bedfordshire 56
Hill (Fine Glass) (David), W Mids 239
Hill (John S.), Devon 85
Hill (Peter), Hampshire 121
Hill Books (Alan), S Yorks 220
Hill Books (T.S.), Surrey 230
Hill House Books, Devon 87
Hillsborough Bookhunters, Northern Ireland 260
Hillside House, Lincolnshire 147
Hind (Andrew), London, Outer 182
Hindsight Books, London (NW) 158
Hine (Anne), Somerset 216
Hobgoblin Books, Hampshire 123
Hodgkins and Company Limited (Ian), Gloucestershire 114
Hodgson (Books) (Richard J.), N Yorks 196
Hodgson (Judith), London (W) 173
Hogan (F. & J.), London (N) 154
Hogben (Carol), Wales 285
Hoggarth (John R.), N Yorks 196
Holdenhurst Books, Dorset 90
Holdsworth Books (Bruce), W Yorks 245
Hollett and Son (R.F.G.), Cumbria 79
Holleyman (J.F.), East Sussex 101
Hollingshead (Chris), London, Outer 183
Holmes (A.), Nottinghamshire 202
Holmes Books (Harry), East Yorkshire 105
Holtom (Christopher), Cornwall 76
Home Farm Books, Warwickshire 236
Honiton Old Bookshop, Devon 85
Hook (Arthur), Bristol 61
Hooker (R.D.), Dorset 92
Hoovey's Books, East Sussex 101
Hornsby, Antiquarian and Secondhand Books (Malcolm), Leicestershire 144
Hornsey's, N Yorks 194
Horsham Bookshop (The), West Sussex 242
Hosains Books, London (NW) 158
Houben (W. & A.), London, Outer 183
House of Figgis Ltd (The), Republic Of Ireland 278
Houston - Bookseller, (David), London (E) 151
Howard (Books) (Peter), London, Outer 180
Howell, Photographic Books (Jill), Kent 137
Howes Bookshop, East Sussex 101
HP Bookfinders, Scotland 262
Hünersdorff Rare Books, London (SW) 165
Hughes Rare Books (Spike), Scotland 261
Humanist Book Services, Cornwall 73
Humber Books, Lincolnshire 146
Hummingbird Books, Kent 136
Hunt (Robin S.), Greater Manchester 118
Hunter and Krageloh, Derbyshire 82
Hunter, Bookseller, (K.P.), Cambridgeshire 65
Hunter–Rare Books (Andrew), London (SW) ... 165
Hurly Burly Books, Wiltshire 253
Hurst (Jenny), Kent 135
Hutchison (Books) (Larry), Scotland 265
Huyton (Peter), Herefordshire 126
Hyland (C.P.), Republic Of Ireland 276
Hyland (D.P.), London, Outer 180
Hylton Booksearch, Merseyside 185
Ian Johnson Natural History Books, Buckinghamshire 63
Ice House Books, Leicestershire 143
Idle Booksellers (The), W Yorks 245
Idle Genius Books, London (N) 154
Idler (The), Suffolk 227
IKON, Devon 88
Illustrated Book (The), London (SW) 165
Images, Staffordshire 222
Inch's Books, N Yorks 194
Inner Bookshop (The), Oxfordshire 207
Innes Books, Shropshire 212

ALPHABETICAL INDEX: Business (I – L)

Inprint, Gloucestershire................................ 114
Intech Books, Northumberland 201
InterCol London, London (N) 154
Internet Bookshop UK Ltd., Gloucestershire.. 112
Interstellar Master Traders, Lancashire 141
Invicta Booksearch, Kent 138
Invisible Books, East Sussex 99
Iris Books, London (SW).......................... 165
Irwin (T.H.), Northern Ireland.................. 259
Isabelline Books, Cornwall........................... 74
Islamic Books - A.R. Bullock, Oxfordshire 207
Island Books, Devon.......................... 84, 86
Ivelet Books Ltd., Surrey 233
Ives Bookseller (John), London, Outer............ 184
J & M Books, Warwickshire........................ 237
J. & J. Books, Lincolnshire 147
J.A. Heacock (Antiques and Books), Cheshire .. 70
J.B. Books, Berkshire 58
J.C. Poole Books, Wales............................ 290
J.G. Natural History Books, Surrey................ 232
J.K. Bookfinders, London (SW)..................... 165
J.L. Book Exchange, East Yorkshire.............. 104
Jackdaw Books, Norfolk 189
Jackson (M.W.), Wiltshire 253
Jackson (W.E.), Hampshire 124
Jacobson (Ken & Jenny), Essex 107
Jade Mountain, Hampshire 123
Jandee Books, Nottinghamshire.................... 202
Janus Books, W Mids............................... 239
Japan Books (Y & S Company Ltd.), Surrey.... 180
Jarndyce Antiquarian Booksellers,
 London (WC) 177
Jarvis Books (incorporating 'Gaston's Alpine
 Books'), Derbyshire 82
Jay Books, Scotland................................. 269
JB Books & Collectables, West Sussex............ 243
Jeremy's, Oxfordshire 208
Jericho Books, Oxfordshire......................... 208
Jermy & Westerman, Nottinghamshire......... 202
Jiri Books, Northern Ireland........................ 259
Jobson (N.W.), Oxfordshire......................... 205
John Read Antiques, Shropshire.................. 212
Johnson Rare Book Collections (C.R.),
 London (NW)................................... 158
Johnston's Marine Stores, Scotland 272
Jones (Andrew), Oxfordshire..................... 205
Jones (Anne), Cornwall.............................. 76
Jones (Barry), West Sussex........................ 242
Jones (J.V.A.), Essex 109
Jones (Madalyn S.), W Yorks 246
Jones Books (Russell), Berkshire................... 57
Jonkers Rare Books, Oxfordshire................. 206
Joppa Books Ltd., Surrey.......................... 230
Judd Books, London (WC)....................... 177
Julie Parker, Gloucestershire 112
Just Books, Cornwall 76
K. Books, East Yorkshire........................... 104
K. Books, Cheshire 72
Katharine House Gallery, Wiltshire 251
Katnap Arts, Norfolk................................ 189
Kay Books Ltd., Surrey 232
Kaye - Bookseller (Terence), London (NW) 158
Keble Books, Essex................................. 107
Keeble Antiques, Dorset............................. 93
Keegan's Bookshop, Berkshire 58

Keel Row Books, Tyne & Wear.................... 235
Keene (Martin), Norfolk.......................... 188
Kellow Books, Oxfordshire 204
Kelly Books, Devon................................. 88
Kelly Books (Don), London (W) 173
Kelly Books (Mark), N Yorks.................... 196
Kelsall (George), Greater Manchester............ 117
Kendall–Carpenter (Tim), Greater Manchester.. 117
Kennedy (Peter), Surrey 234
Kenny's Book Export Co., Republic Of Ireland. 277
Kenny's Bookshops and Art Galleries Ltd,
 Republic Of Ireland 278
Kent (Books) (Mrs. A.), Suffolk 226
Kent T. G., Surrey 230
Kenya Books, East Sussex 99
Keogh's Books, Gloucestershire.................... 113
Kernaghans, Merseyside............................ 186
Kerr (Norman), Cumbria 78
Kesterton (Brian), Dorset 91
Keswick Bookshop, Cumbria....................... 78
Keverel Chess Books, Devon 85
Kevin S. Ogilvie Modern First Editions,
 Scotland 265
Key Books (Sarah), Cambridgeshire............... 65
Kidson (Ruth), East Sussex........................ 102
Kilburn Books, East Yorkshire.................. 104
Kilgarriff (Raymond), East Sussex 103
Kilgour (Sporting Books) (Ian), Leicestershire... 145
Killeen (John), N Yorks 193
Kim's Bookshop, West Sussex..................... 244
Kineton Nooks, Warwickshire 236
King (Donald S.), Northamptonshire 198
King Books, London (SE) 161
King Street Bookshop (The), Norfolk......... 188
Kingfisher Book Service, Nottinghamshire....... 203
Kingsgate Books & Prints, Hampshire............ 125
Kingshead Books, Wales 288
Kingsmere Books, Bedfordshire 55
Kingston (Richard J.), Oxfordshire................ 206
Kingswood Books, Dorset 93
Kirkman Ltd., (Robert), Bedfordshire 55
Kirkpatrick (Robert J.), London (W) 173
Kitley (A.J.), Bristol................................. 61
Knapton Bookbarn, N Yorks..................... 196
Knockhundred Bookshop, West Sussex........... 243
Knowles - Antiquary (Roger J.),
 Staffordshire 222
Knowles (John), Norfolk 188
Kohler (C.C.), Surrey 230
Koos (David), London (SE) 161
Korn Books, (M.E.), London (N) 154
KSC Books, Cheshire................................ 71
Kunkler Books (Paul), Cambridgeshire........... 65
Kyrios Books, Nottinghamshire.................... 202
L.M.S. Books, Hertfordshire 129
Lake (David), Norfolk.............................. 189
Lake (Fred), Surrey 234
Lamb (R.W.), Suffolk.............................. 227
Lamb's Tales, Devon................................ 86
Lane Books (Shirley), Isle of Wight 132
Langmaid (Kenneth), Cornwall 76
Lankester Antiques and Books, Essex............ 109
Larkham Books (Patricia), Gloucestershire 115
Lassalle (Judith), London (N) 154
Laurie (Dick), London (SW).................... 165

ALPHABETICAL INDEX: Business (L– M)

Lavender Fields Books, Gloucestershire 111
Lawful Occasions, Essex 106
Lawson & Company (E.M.), Oxfordshire 205
Lawton (J.), Surrey 232
Lay Books (Loretta), London (NW) 158
Leabeck Books, Oxfordshire 208
Leaf Ends, Northumberland 201
Leakey's Bookshop, Scotland 268
Leapman Ltd. (G. & R.), Hertfordshire 130
Lee Rare Books (Rachel), Bristol 61
Lee, Maritime Books (Gerald), East Sussex .. 103
Leeds Bookseller, W Yorks 247
Leeper (Romilly), London (SW) 165
Lees Books.com, (David), Wales 287
Left Bank (The), Wales 290
Left on The Shelf, London (E) 151
Leigh Gallery Books, Essex 108
Letterbox Books, Nottinghamshire 202
Lewcock (John), Cambridgeshire 67
Lewis (J.T. & P.), Cornwall 74
Lewis (John), Essex 107
Lewis (Len), Wales 289
Lewis (Len), Shropshire 213
Lewis First Editions, Kent 135
Liber Books, Lancashire 141
Liebreich Antique Maps & Prints (Kitty),
  London (W) 173
Lime Tree Books, Suffolk 227
Linton Books, Scotland 262
Lion Books, Worcestershire 254
Lion Fine Arts and Books, Wales 287
Lion Street Books, Wales 287
Little Bookshop (The), Greater Manchester 117
Little Stour Books, Kent 133
Lloyd (D. Ieuan), Wales 289
Lloyd (Peter), Shropshire 212
Lloyd (Scott), Wales 283
Lloyd-Davies (Sue), Wales 280
Llyfraufflur Books, Wales 290
Lofthouse's Secondhand Book Emporium
  (Mrs.), N Yorks 195
Loman, Oriental Books & Manuscripts
  (David), London (SW) 165
London & Sussex Antiquarian Book & Print
  Services, East Sussex 100
London Bookworm, (The), London, Outer 182
Londonline Books, London (SW) 165
Lowe (John), Norfolk 189
Lowendahl Rare Books, (Bjorn),
  London (W) 173
LSA Books, Warwickshire 236
Lucas (Richard), London (NW) 158
Lucas (Roger), Lincolnshire 147
Lucius Books, N Yorks 196
Luckman (Bill), London, Outer 183
Lund Theological Books, Cambridgeshire 65
Lymelight Books & Prints, Dorset 92
LyngHeath Books, Norfolk 190
Lyon (H.D.), London (SW) 165
M. & D. Books, Worcestershire 254
Mac Sweeney (Gerald),
  Republic Of Ireland 276
Macbuiks, N Yorks 193
MacCormaig (Domhnall), Scotland 269
Macfarlane (Mr. H.), Essex 110

Macnamara (J. & E.M.), Merseyside 185
Mactaggart (Caroline), Dorset 91
Maddison (J.K.), W Mids 238
Magee Books (Eve), Hampshire 120
Maggs (R.J.), Berkshire 7
Maggs Brothers Limited, London (W) 173
Maghreb Bookshop (The), London (WC) 177
Magis Books, Leicestershire 144
Magna Gallery, Oxfordshire 208
Magpie Books, W Yorks 248
Main Point Books, Scotland 269
Mainly Fiction, Greater Manchester 116
Main–Smith & Co. Ltd. (Bruce),
  Leicestershire 143
Mair Wilkes Books, Scotland 265
Mallett/Scottish Booksearch (Lynda),
  Nottinghamshire 203
Mallory (Books) (Bob), Derbyshire 82
Malmo Books, Hampshire 121
Malvern Bookshop (The), Worcestershire 254
Manheim (Carol), London (W) 173
Manna Bookshop, Somerset 218
Manor Books, Kent 136
Manor House Books/John Trotter Books,
  London (N) 154
Mansfield (Judith), W Yorks 248
Manx Printed Collectibles, Isle of Man 258
Map House (The), London (SW) 165
Marathon Books, Greater Manchester 116
Marcan, Bookseller (Peter), London (SE) 161
Marcet Books, London (SE) 161
March House Books, Dorset 94
Marchmont Bookshop (The),
  London (WC) 177
Marchpane, London (WC) 177
Marine and Cannon Books, Cheshire 70
Marine Workshop Bookshop, Dorset 92
Marjon Books, Essex 110
Markham (Sheila), London (SE) 161
Marks Limited (Barrie), London (N) 154
Marlborough Rare Books Ltd., London (W) 173
Marrin & Sons (G. & D.), Kent 135
Marsden (Cecilia), London, Outer 183
Marshall Rare Books (Bruce),
  Gloucestershire 111
Martin - Bookseller (Colin), East Yorkshire 105
Martin (Books and Pictures), (Brian P).,
  Surrey 231
Martin (Brian), Surrey 232
Martin (C.J.), Nottinghamshire 202
Martin Bookshop & Gallery (Richard),
  Hampshire 121
Martin Music Books (Philip), N Yorks 196
Martin's Books, Wales 288
Mason (Mary), Oxfordshire 204
Mason Bookseller (Joseph), Norfolk 190
Max Gate Books, Somerset 218
Mayflower Books, Lancashire 142
Mayhew (Veronica), Berkshire 58
Mayhew Books, Norfolk 187
Maynard & Bradley, Nottinghamshire 202
Maynard & Bradley, Leicestershire 143
McCann (Joe), Oxfordshire 208
McCarty, Bookseller (M.E.), Scotland 274
McCarty, Bookseller (M.E.), Scotland 264

ALPHABETICAL INDEX: Business (M – N)

McCaughtrie (K.A.), N Yorks 192
McConnell Fine Books, Kent....................... 135
McCrone (Audrey), Scotland 272
McEwan Fine Books, Scotland.................... 266
McEwan Golf Books (Rhod), Scotland........... 266
McFeely's Bookstore, Scotland 269
McGavin (Don), Scotland........................... 267
McGee (Terence J.), London, Outer............... 181
McGlynn (John), Lancashire 140
McInnes (P.F. & J.R.), Dorset 90
McKay Rare Books (Barry), Cumbria 77
McKelvie (Ian), London (N).......................... 154
McKenzie (J.W.), Surrey 231
McKenzie (Major John R.), Cumbria.............. 77
McNaughtan's Bookshop, Scotland 269
Mead (P.J.), Shropshire............................. 212
Meadowcroft Books, West Sussex 241
Meadowside Bookshop, Scotland.................. 273
Meads Book Service (The), East Sussex 102
Meekins Books (Paul), Warwickshire 237
Meinertzhagen (Nicholas), London (SW)......... 165
Melnick House Books, Berkshire................. 57
Menavaur Books, Scotland 264
Mercat Books, Scotland............................. 267
Mereside Books, Cheshire.......................... 70
Merlin Books, West Sussex 243
Mermaid Books (Burlingham), Norfolk........ 190
Merritt (Valerie), Gloucestershire 111
Merryheart, Gloucestershire 112
M'Garva (Tim J.), Scotland...................... 264
Micelle Press, Dorset 95
michaelsbookshop.com, Kent....................... 137
Middleton (Roger), Oxfordshire 208
Midnight Books, Devon........................... 87
Miles Apart, Suffolk 227
Miles Book Shop (Archie), Cumbria 79
Milestone Publications Goss & Crested China,
  Hampshire... 122
Milestones Bookshop, Shropshire 211
Military Bookworm, London (SE)................. 161
Military Collector (The), W Yorks 249
Military Parade Bookshop, Wiltshire 251
MilitaryHistoryBooks.com, Kent 136
Mill Lane Books, Merseyside..................... 186
Miller (Stephen), London, Outer................... 184
Miller, (Dusty), Cornwall 73
Mills Rare Books (Adam), Cambridgeshire 65
Mills: Books (Brian), Derbyshire 82
Milne Books (Clifford), Scotland 265
Mindreaders Books, Kent 135
Ming Books, Scotland 264
Minster Books, Dorset 95
Minster Garage Bookshop, East Yorkshire 104
Minster Gate Bookshop, N Yorks.................. 196
Missing Books, Essex 108
MK Book Services, Cambridgeshire............... 67
Mobbs (A.J.), W Mids............................... 240
Modern First Editions, London, Outer 182
Modern Firsts Etc., Lancashire 140
Modern Welsh Publications Ltd., Merseyside.... 185
Modlock (Lilian), Dorset............................ 92
Moffat Book Exchange, Scotland.................. 263
Mogul Diamonds, W Mids 240
Mollie's Loft, Wales.................................. 289
Monmouth House Books, Wales................... 283

Moon's Bookshop (Michael), Cumbria 79
Moore (C.R.), Shropshire......................... 212
Moore (Eric T.), Hertfordshire 129
Moore (Peter), Cambridgeshire..................... 65
Moore (Sue), Cornwall 74
Moorland Books, Greater Manchester............ 118
Moorside Books, Lancashire....................... 141
Moray Bookshop (The), Scotland 267
More Books, Wales 283
Moreton Books, Devon.............................. 86
Morgan (D. & D.H.W.), Devon 89
Morgan (H.J.), Bedfordshire....................... 56
Morley Case, Hampshire 124
Morrell (Nicholas) Rare Books,
  London (NW)....................................... 158
Morris (A.E.), Wales 283
Morris (Chris), Oxfordshire 208
Morris (Michael), Staffordshire.................... 222
Morten (Booksellers) (E.J.), Greater Manchester 117
Morten Books, Cheshire 70
Moseley Books, W Mids 238
Moss Antiquarian Books (V.J.), Lancashire 142
Moss Books, London (NW) 158
Moss Books, Gloucestershire....................... 112
Moss End Bookshop, Berkshire.................... 59
Mostly Medieval, London, Outer................ 181
Mostyn Books (Ingrid), Dorset 92
Mother Goose Bookshop, Isle of Wight.......... 131
Mountaineering Books, London (N) 154
Mount's Bay Books, Cornwall 75
Moviedrome, East Sussex 99
Mr. Christmas Books, N Yorks 196
Mr. Mac, Hampshire.............................. 124
Mr. Pickwick of Towcester, Northamptonshire.. 199
Mucci (Robert), East Sussex 101
Mulberry Bush (The), East Sussex.............. 99
Mundy (David), Hertfordshire 128
Mundy (David), Buckinghamshire 62
Munro (C & P), Somerset 218
Murch Booksend, (Herbert), London (SE).... 161
Murder & Mayhem, Wales 287
Murder One, London (WC) 177
Murphy (C.J.), Norfolk............................. 189
Murray (Robert S.), Scotland.................... 269
Murray and Kennett (Booksellers),
  West Sussex... 243
musebookshop, Wales 283
Museum Bookshop, London (WC)................ 177
Music By The Score, Cornwall 73
Musicalania, Hertfordshire 130
Muttonchop Manuscripts, West Sussex 243
My Back Pages, London (SW)................... 165
Nangle (Julian), Dorset............................. 92
Naughton Booksellers, Republic Of Ireland...... 277
Naughty Nostalgia, N Yorks..................... 196
Nautical Antique Centre (The), Dorset 95
Nebulous Books, Hampshire 120
Needham Books, (Russell), Somerset........... 218
Neil's Books, London (NW) 158
Neptune Gallery Limited,
  Republic Of Ireland 277
Nevis Railway Books, Oxfordshire 206
Nevis Railway Bookshops (The Antique & Book
  Collector), Wiltshire................................ 251
Nevitsky (Philip), Greater Manchester 117

ALPHABETICAL INDEX: Business (N – P)

New & Secondhand Books, Dorset 94
New Strand Bookshop (The), Herefordshire 126
Newband (D.M.), Wales 288
Newby (Valerie), Buckinghamshire 63
Newcastle Bookshop, Northumberland 200
Newgate Books, Northumberland 201
Newlyn & New Street Books, Cornwall 75
Newton Books, London (N) 154
Nibris Books, London (SW) 165
Nicholson of Chester (Richard), Cheshire 69
Nicholson's Books, N Yorks 196
Nickleby, (Nicholas), Devon 84
Nicolas - *Antiquarian Booksellers & Art
   Dealers*, London (N) 154
Niner (Marcus), Gloucestershire 113
Nineteenth Century Books, Oxfordshire 209
Noble (Malcolm & Christine), Leicestershire..... 145
Noel and Holland Books, Republic Of Ireland .. 278
Nonsuch Books, Surrey 234
Northern Herald Books, W Yorks 245
Norton & Roberts, London (N) 154
Norton Books, Durham 97
NostalGia Publications Ltd., N Yorks 196
Nostalgia Unlimited, Merseyside 185
Not Just Books, Dorset 93
Nova Foresta Books, Hampshire 121
Nubec, Norfolk 190
Oak Tree Books, London, Outer 181
Oakwood Books, Gloucestershire 113
Oasis Booksearch, Cambridgeshire 68
Oast Books, Kent 134
Oblong Books, N Yorks 197
O'Brien Books & Photo Gallery, Republic
   Of Ireland 279
O'Broin (Anton), Republic Of Ireland 279
Occultique, Northamptonshire 198
O'Connor Fine Books, Lancashire 142
Octagon Books, Cambridgeshire 66
O'Donoghue Books, London (SW) 165
Offa's Dyke Books, Shropshire 212
Offer (Richard), Cheshire 70
O'Kill (John), Kent 135
Old Bank Bookshop *(The)*, Kent 138
Old Book Company, (The), W Yorks 247
Old Bookshelf (The), Scotland 271
Old Bookshop (The), Somerset 216
Old Bookshop (The), Greater Manchester 117
Old Bookshop (The), W Mids 240
Old Celtic Bookshop (The), Devon 86
Old Chapel Books, N Yorks 196
Old Children's Bookshelf (The), Scotland 269
Old Curiosity Shop (The), Channel Islands 257
Old Gallery Bookshop (The), Kent 136
Old Hall Bookshop (The),
   Northamptonshire 198
Old Station Pottery & Bookshop (The),
   Norfolk 191
Old Storytellers Bookshop (The), Scotland 261
Old Talbot Gallery, N Yorks 193
Old Town Bookshop (The), Scotland 270
Old World Books (Tre Archi), London (SW).... 165
Olio Books, East Sussex 101
Olivers Bookshop, Tyne & Wear 235
Olynthiacs, Shropshire 212
Omniphil Prints, Buckinghamshire 62

O'Neill (A.), Hampshire 121
O'Neill (Angus), London (WC) 178
Open Hand Books, Hampshire 120
Optimus Books Ltd, West Sussex 244
Orangeberry Books, Oxfordshire 206
Orbis Books (London) Ltd., London (W) 173
Oriental and African Books, Shropshire 213
Orlando Booksellers, Lincolnshire 148
Orssich (Paul), London (SW) 166
Othello's Bookshop, Essex 108
Otley Maypole Rare Books, N Yorks 193
Ouse Valley Books, Bedfordshire 56
Outcast Books, Wales 287
Oval Books, N Yorks 193
Over-Sands Books, Cumbria 78
Owen (J.V.), Wales 282
Oxley (Laurence), Hampshire 120
P. and P. Books, Worcestershire 255
Pagan Limited (Hugh), London (SW) 166
Page (David), Scotland 270
Page Antiquarian Books (Colin), East Sussex ... 99
Pages Bookshop, Northern Ireland 260
Paisley Fine Books, Scotland 272
Palladour Books, Hampshire 124
Pamona Books, Lancashire 142
Pandion Books, N Yorks 194
Paper Moon Books, Gloucestershire 114
Paper Pleasures, Somerset 217
Paperback Reader (The), East Sussex 101
Paperbacks Plus, Bristol 61
Paralos Ltd., London (W) 173
Paramor (C.D.), Suffolk 227
Parbury House Books, Somerset 216
Parikian, Rare Books (Diana), London (W) 174
Park (Mike), London, Outer 183
Park Gallery & Bookshop (The),
   Northamptonshire 199
Parker Books (Mike), Cambridgeshire 65
Parkfield Music, W Yorks 247
Parkinsons, Merseyside 186
Parlour Bookshop (The), Oxfordshire 205
Parrots Books, Hertfordshire 129
Parrott (Jeremy), Devon 87
Parrott Books, Oxfordshire 209
Past & Presents, Cumbria 77
Pastmasters, Derbyshire 82
Pathway Books, Somerset 214
Paton Books, Hertfordshire 129
Patterson Liddle, Somerset 214
Peake (Robin), Lincolnshire 149
Peakirk Books, Cambridgeshire 68
Pedlar's Pack Books, Devon 89
Peel (Valerie), t/a Kiandra Associates Ltd.,
   Berkshire 57
Pendleburys Bookshop, London (N) 155
Pendleside Books, Lancashire 141
Penn Barn Bookshop, Buckinghamshire 63
Pennies, Devon 85
Pennymead Books, N Yorks 193
Penzance Rare Books, Cornwall 75
Peregrine Books (Leeds), W Yorks 247
Periplus Books, Buckinghamshire 63
Periwinkle Press, Kent 134
Peter Lyons Books, Gloucestershire 112
Peter Pan Bookshop, Norfolk 190

ALPHABETICAL INDEX: Business (P – R)

Peter's Bookshop, Norfolk 190
Petersfield Bookshop (The), Hampshire 122
Petersham Books, London (SW) 166
Peterson (Tony), Essex 109
Petworth Antique Market (Bookroom),
   West Sussex 243
Phelan Books, Republic Of Ireland 277
Phelps (Michael), West Sussex 242
Phenotype Books, Cumbria 79
Phillips (Chris), Wiltshire 250
Phillips (Nigel), London (SW) 166
Phillips of Hitchin (Antiques) Ltd.,
   Hertfordshire 129
Philologus–Fine & Rare Books, London (SW) .. 166
Phoenix Fine Books, Essex 110
Pholiota Books, London (N) 155
Photo Books International, London (WC) 178
Photographery at Soldridge Books, Hampshire . 120
Piccadilly Rare Books, East Sussex 103
Pickering & Chatto, London (W) 174
Pilgrim's Progress Bookshop, Norfolk 191
Pinkneys Lane Bookshop, Suffolk 228
Pinnacle Books, Scotland 270
Pioneer Books, Hampshire 120
Platt Rare Books (Richard), London (SE) 161
Plurabelle Books, Cambridgeshire 65
Pocket Bookshop (The), Devon 86
Poetry Bookshop (The), Wales 287
Polczynski (Udo K.H.), London, Outer 183
Politico's, London (SW) 166
Pollak (P.M.), Devon 87
Polmorla Books, Cornwall 76
Pomes Penyeach, Staffordshire 0
Pooks Motor Books, Leicestershire 144
Poole (William), London (W) 174
Poor Richard's Books, Suffolk 226
Popeley (Frank T.), Cambridgeshire 68
Porcupine Books, London, Outer 182
Porcupines, Devon 84
Pordes Books Ltd., (Henry), London (WC) .. 178
Porter Bookshop (The), S Yorks 220
Portland Books Ltd., Warwickshire 236
Portobello Books, London (W) 174
Post Mortem Books, West Sussex 242
Postaprint, Oxfordshire 209
Post–Horn Books, N Yorks 192
Postings, Surrey 233
Potter Limited (Jonathan), London (W) 174
Potterton Books, N Yorks 195
Pratt (B.A. & C.W.M.), Herefordshire 126
Pratt (Guy), Suffolk 225
Pratt (H.G.), Suffolk 228, 229
Premier Books & Prints, Lincolnshire 146
Prescott - The Bookseller (John),
   London, Outer 184
Preston Book Company, Lancashire 142
Price (John), London (N) 155
Price (R.D.M. & I.M.) (Books),
   Greater Manchester 119
Price (R.W.), Nottinghamshire 202
Priestpopple Books, Northumberland 201
Primrose Hill Books, London (NW) 158
Pringle Booksellers (Andrew), Scotland 270
Prior (Michael), Lincolnshire 149
Priory Books, Worcestershire 256

Probsthain (Arthur), London (WC) 178
Professional Book Services, N Yorks............ 192
Prospect Books, Wales............................. 282
Prospect House Books, Northern Ireland 260
Pugh Books (Ian K.), Worcestershire 255
Purple Haze Comics & Books, Devon 87
Pyecroft (Ruth), Gloucestershire................ 114
Pyke (Robert & Susan), Somerset................ 214
Quadrille at Delehar, London (W)................ 174
Quaritch Ltd., (Bernard), London (W)........... 174
Quarto Bookshop (The), Scotland 265
Quayside Bookshop, Devon 88
Quentin Books Ltd., Essex 107
Quest Books, East Yorkshire 105
Quest Booksearch, Cambridgeshire 65
Quill Books, Oxfordshire 204
Quinnell, (Mr. M.),
   Northamptonshire 198
Quinto of Charing Cross Road,
   London (WC) 178
R M Books, Hertfordshire 129
R. & A. Books, East Sussex 100
R. & B. Graham, Cornwall 74
Raftery Books (Michael D.), Leicestershire... 144
Railway Book and Magazine Search, Berkshire. 58
Railway Shop (The), Wales 290
Rainbow Books, East Sussex 99
Rainford (Sheila), Hertfordshire 128
Rainger Books (Michael), Wales 285
Randall (Tom), Somerset........................ 217
Rare & Racy, S Yorks 220
Rare Books & Berry, Somerset................... 217
Rassam (Paul), London (NW).................... 158
*Ray Rare and Out of Print Books
   (Janette)*, N Yorks 197
Rayner (Hugh Ashley), Somerset 215
Rayner Bookseller (Michael),
   Gloucestershire 112
Read Ireland, Republic Of Ireland 277
Readers Rest, Lincolnshire........................ 148
Reading (Weaponry Books) (Jim), W Mids.. 239
Reading Lasses, Scotland......................... 264
Reads, Dorset 94
Reaveley Books, Devon 86
Recollections Bookshop, Cornwall 76
Recycling Books, Gloucestershire............... 113
Red Rose Books, Lancashire 141
Red Snapper Books, London (WC) 178
Red Star Books, Hertfordshire 128
Reedmore Books, London, Outer 180
Rees & O'Neill Rare Books, London (WC)...... 178
Rees Rare Books (John), London (SW) 166
Reeve (M. & D.), Oxfordshire..................... 208
Reeves (Technical Books) (W.H.),
   N Yorks 195
Reference Works Ltd., Dorset.................... 94
Reid Books, (W.), Northamptonshire 198
Reid of Liverpool, Merseyside 185
Reigate Galleries, Surrey 233
Reigate Rare Books, Surrey 233
Remington (Reg & Philip), London (WC) 178
Restormel Books, Worcestershire 256
Resurgam Books, East Yorkshire................. 104
Revell (David B.), Kent 139
Rhoda (June), Essex................................ 108

Rhodes, Bookseller (Peter), Hampshire 124
Rhos Point Books, Wales 281
Riccetti (Margaret), S Yorks........................ 220
Richmond Books, N Yorks 194
Riddell (Peter), East Yorkshire..................... 104
Riderless Horse Books, Norfolk 187
Right Now Books (Burma), London (SW)....... 167
Rigley (Stephen), Nottinghamshire 202
Riley Books (V.M.), Greater Manchester......... 117
Riley–Smith (Hamish), Norfolk 190
Ripping Yarns, London (N) 155
Riseden Books, Kent 139
Rising Tide Books, Scotland........................ 264
Rittner Booksearch (Hilary), London (SE)....... 161
River Reads Bookshop, Devon....................... 88
Riverside Bookshop (The), Cumbria 78
Riviera Books, Norfolk.............................. 188
Roadmaster Books, Kent............................ 134
Roadster Motoring Books, Hampshire............ 123
Robbie's Bookshop, London (N) 155
Robert (Leslie), London (W)....................... 174
Roberts (Booksellers), (Ray), Staffordshire...... 223
Roberts (Fine Books) (Julian), Lincolnshire 149
Roberts (William H.), W Yorks.................. 246
Roberts Bookseller (Richard), Scotland........ 272
Robertshaw (John), Cambridgeshire............... 67
Robinson (G. Charles), Somerset 215
Rochdale Book Company,
  Greater Manchester 118
Rods Books, Devon................................... 87
Rogoyski (Old and Rare Books) (Alexander),
  Lincolnshire....................................... 149
Roland Books, Kent 137
Rolfe (John), London (SE).......................... 161
Rolph (John), Suffolk............................... 227
Rookery Bookery, Staffordshire.................... 223
Roosterbooks, Northamptonshire.................. 198
Rosanda Books, Leicestershire 144
Roscrea Bookshop, Republic Of Ireland.......... 279
Rose Books, Greater Manchester.................. 118
Rose Fine Art & Antiques, N Yorks 197
Rosemary Books, Merseyside...................... 186
Rosenthal Limited (A.), Oxfordshire 208
Rose's Books, Wales 287
Rosley Books, Cumbria 79
Ross & Company Ltd., (Louise), Somerset.... 215
Ross Old Books & Prints, Herefordshire 127
Rothwell and Dunworth, Somerset 216
Roundabout Books, Kent 134
Roundstone Books, Lancashire 141
Roundwood Books, Shropshire..................... 213
Rowan (H. & S.J.), Dorset........................... 91
Rowan (P. & B.), Northern Ireland 259
Rowan House Books, Surrey 231
Royal Carbery Books Ltd., Republic Of Ireland 275
*Rubino & Co [USA] Numismatic & Philatelic
  Books of Santa Fe*, London (SW) 167
Ruebotham (Kirk), Cheshire........................ 71
Rugby Relics, Wales 284
Rupert Books, Cambridgeshire..................... 65
Ruskin Books, London (SE)........................ 161
Russell (Charles), London (SW)................... 167
Russell Books, Somerset............................ 218
Ryde Bookshop (The), Isle of Wight 131
Ryeland Books, Northamptonshire................ 198

S.P.C.K., Bristol...................................... 61
Sabin (Printed Works) (P.R. & V.), Kent 133
Sacketts Books on Crafts and Restoration,
  Somerset.. 216
Safina Books, Surrey............................... 232
St Ann's Books, Worcestershire 255
St Austin Press, (The), London (SE)............ 161
St Mary's Books & Prints, Lincolnshire 150
St Michael at Plea Bookshop, Norfolk 190
St Philip's Books, Oxfordshire..................... 208
Saintfield Antiques & Fine Books,
  Northern Ireland 259
Saints & Scholars, Scotland...................... 261
Salsus Books, Worcestershire 255
Saltburn Bookshop, N Yorks....................... 194
Salway Books, Essex 110
San Expedito Books, London (NW).............. 158
Sanctuary Bookshop, Dorset 92
Sanders of Oxford Limited, Oxfordshire.......... 208
Sanderson (Edward), Berkshire.................... 58
Sandpiper Books Ltd., London (SW) 167
Sandstone Books, Kent 134
Sansovino Books, N Yorks 195
Sansovino Books, West Sussex 244
Satara Books, West Sussex......................... 244
Saunders (Orchard Books) (Christopher),
  Gloucestershire................................... 113
Saunders (Tom), Wales 280
Savage (Keith A.), Suffolk 228
Savery Books, East Sussex 99
Sawers (Robert G.), London (W) 174
Sawyer (Chas. J.), Kent............................. 137
Sax Books, Suffolk.................................. 228
Scarborough Books, N Yorks 195
Scarthin Books, Derbyshire........................ 82
Schofield Golf Books (Steve), W Yorks........ 249
Schull Books, Republic Of Ireland 275
Schulz–Falster Rare Books (Susanne),
  London (N) 155
Schuster Gallery (The), Devon 88
Schutte (David), Hampshire 122
Sclanders (Beatbooks), (Andrew), London (EC) 152
Scorpio Books, Suffolk 225
Scott (Sporting Books) (John), Worcestershire .. 256
Scott (T.F.S.), East Sussex 102
Scowen (R.S. and P.A.), London, Outer 181
Scrivener's Books & Book Binding, Derbyshire . 81
Sea Chest Nautical Bookshop (The), Devon..... 87
Seabreeze Books, Lancashire 142
Seago (B. & C.), West Sussex..................... 242
Seckworth Books, Oxfordshire................... 204
Second Edition, Scotland........................... 270
Secondhand Bookshop, Surrey 233
Seddon (A.C.), West Sussex 244
Sedgeberrow Books & Framing, Worcestershire 255
Seeber (Liz), East Sussex 99
Segal Books (Joel), Devon 85
Selling Books, Kent 135
Sen Books, Hampshire............................. 125
Sensawunda Books, Cheshire..................... 72
Sephton (A.F.), London (W) 174
Serendipity Books, Bristol 61
Sesemann (Julia), Kent 133
Seydi Rare Books (Sevin), London (NW) 159
Shacklock Books (David), Suffolk 226

ALPHABETICAL INDEX: Business (S – S)

Shakeshaft (Dr. B.), Cheshire......................... 72
Shakeshaft (Roger & Sylvia), Lincolnshire 146
Shakespeare Books (Colin), Staffordshire......... 222
Shapero Rare Books (Bernard J.), London (W) .. 174
Sharpe (Mary), West Sussex 241
Shaw (David M.), Cheshire 72
Shaw (Geoff), London, Outer..................... 180
Shearer (Marion), Scotland 270
Shearwater Bed & Books (formerly John Lumby Nat. History Bks), Northumberland .. 200
Sheppard (Mrs. P.A.), Gloucestershire............. 111
Sheridan's Bookshop (Ian), London, Outer 181
Sherlaw-Johnson (Austin), Oxfordshire 209
Sherratt (Ian J.), Staffordshire...................... 222
Shipley Specialist Art Booksellers, London (WC) 178
Shirley Bookshop (The), Hampshire............... 124
Sidey, Bookdealer (Philip), Kent................... 137
Sillan Books, Republic Of Ireland............... 275
Sillem (Anthony), East Sussex...................... 101
Silver Trees Books, W Mids 239
Silverman (Michael), London (SE) 161
Simon Lewis Transport Books, Gloucestershire . 112
Simon's Books, Somerset............................ 218
Simply Read, East Sussex 100
Simpson (Dave), Scotland........................... 262
Simpson (Marianne), Scotland 267
Simpson Natural History Books (Steven), Suffolk... 228
Sims (Sue), Dorset................................... 91
Sims Reed Limited, London (SW)................. 167
Singleton (Anthony), S Yorks..................... 220
Singleton, (John), London (N) 155
Siop Lyfrau'r Hen Bost, Wales................... 283
Siop y Morfa, Wales 282
Siri Ellis Books, Greater Manchester.............. 116
Skelly (George B.), London (N).................... 155
Skoob Russell Square, London (WC).......... 178
Skyrack Books, W Yorks 246
Slaughter & Garratt Rare Books, Worcestershire...................................... 255
Slavin Rare and Collectable Books (Derek), Warwickshire....................................... 237
Smallwood Books, Lincolnshire.................... 148
Smith (Clive), Essex 108
Smith (David & Lynn), London, Outer........... 182
Smith (Peter Bain), Cumbria........................ 77
Smith (Ray), Hertfordshire....................... 128
Smith (Terry), Norfolk........................... 190
Smith (W.L.), Tyne & Wear 235
Smith Books (Keith), Herefordshire............... 127
Smith Books, (Nigel), Surrey.................... 230
Smith Books, (Sally), Suffolk 225
Smith Booksellers (James), London, Outer....... 180
Smith Maritime Aviation Books (Frank), Tyne & Wear 235
Smith Modern First Editions, (Chris Adam), West Sussex....................................... 243
Snowden Smith Books, London (SW).......... 167
Snowdon (Colin), Shropshire.................... 213
Soccer Books Limited, Lincolnshire 146
Sokol Books (A.), London (W) 174
Solaris Books, East Yorkshire.................... 104
Sotheran Limited (Henry), London (W) 175
South Downs Book Service, West Sussex........ 243

Southwold Antiques Centre, Suffolk 228
Spark Books (Philip), Shropshire 211
Sparkes (Books) (Ray), Staffordshire.............. 223
Spearman Books, East Sussex 102
Spelman (Ken), N Yorks............................. 197
Spenceley Books (David), W Yorks 248
Speyside Books, Scotland......................... 266
Spindel (Elizabeth), Cambridgeshire............... 68
Spineage Books, Hertfordshire 129
Spink & Son Limited, London (WC)............. 178
Spooner & Co., Somerset 217
Spooner (John E.), Dorset 90
Spranger (Anthony), Wiltshire...................... 251
Spread Eagle Books, Wales 282
Spread Eagle Bookshop, London (SE)............ 162
Spurrier (Nick), Kent 136
Stacks Bookshop, Northern Ireland 259
Stacpoole (George), Republic Of Ireland...... 278
Staffs Bookshop (The), Staffordshire.............. 222
Stage Door Prints, London (WC).................. 178
Stained Glass Books, Kent.......................... 138
Staley (John D.), S Yorks 220
Stanhope Bibliophiles, London (N)................ 155
Staniland (Booksellers), Lincolnshire.............. 150
Stansbury (Rosemary), Devon...................... 87
Stanton, (P. & K.), Cornwall 75
Starlord Books, Cheshire............................ 70
Steedman (Robert D.), Tyne & Wear 235
Stella Books, Wales 284
Stephenson (Keith), East Yorkshire 105
Stepping Stones Bookshop, N Yorks............... 193
Sterling Books, Somerset........................... 219
Stern Antiquarian Bookseller (Jeffrey), N Yorks.. 197
Stevens (Joan), Cambridgeshire 66
Stewart (Andrew), Cornwall 75
Stewart (Ian), Kent................................... 137
Stinton (Judith), Dorset 92
STM Books, London (N) 155
Stobart Davies Limited, Hertfordshire.......... 129
Stokes Books, Republic Of Ireland............. 277
Stone Trough Books, N Yorks...................... 197
Stone, (G.& R.), Scotland........................... 261
Stothert Old Books, Cheshire....................... 69
Strand Bookshop (The), Wales 288
Stratford Bookshop (The), Warwickshire...... 237
Strathearn Books, Scotland 273
Strauss (David), Lincolnshire....................... 147
Stride & Son, West Sussex 242
Stroh (M.A.), London (E)........................... 151
Stroma Books, Scotland............................. 261
Strong Oak Press (The), Hertfordshire......... 130
Studio (The), Scotland............................ 271
Studio Bookshop, East Sussex...................... 99
Sturford Books, Wiltshire 252
Sturgeon (Jamie), West Sussex 244
Sub Aqua Prints and Books, Hampshire 121
Sue Lowell Natural History Books, London (W) 175
Suffolk Rare Books, Suffolk..................... 228
Sugen & Co., N Yorks............................... 192
Summersgill (Neil), Lancashire..................... 140
Surprise Books, Gloucestershire................. 114
Sutcliffe (Mark), W Yorks 246
Sutcliffe (Victor), London (SW).................... 167
Swan Bookshop (The), Devon...................... 84

ALPHABETICAL INDEX: Business (S –W)

Swift Books *(Don)*, Greater Manchester 117
Sykes (Graham), W Yorks 248
Symes Books (Naomi), Cheshire 72
Talatin Books, Essex 108
Talisman Books, Greater Manchester 118
Talking Dead (The), Dorset 95
Tantalus Antiques & Books, Devon 87
Taplin's Bookshop, W Mids 239
Target Books, Cambridgeshire 68
Tarka Books, Devon 83
Tasburgh Books, Norfolk 190
Taylor & Son (Peter), Hertfordshire 130
Taylor (F.W.), Gloucestershire 112
Taylor (Sylvia), Kent 134
Taylor Books (Susan), W Yorks 246
Taylor Rare Books (Michael), Norfolk 187
Templar Books, East Sussex 99
Temple (Robert), London (N) 155
Tenner (Melvin), London (W) 175
Tennis Collectables, Cheshire 69
Tetbury Old Books, Gloucestershire 114
Textile Book Bazaar (The), Scotland 264
Theatreshire Books, N Yorks 192
Thin Read Line, Merseyside 186
Third Reich Books, Kent 134
Thistle Books, Scotland 271
Thomas (Barry), Wales 281
Thomas (Books) (Leona), Cheshire 71
Thomas (E. Wyn), Wales 282
Thomas Rare Books, Suffolk 226
Thompson (Eric), Surrey 233
Thomson (Karen), Scotland 271
Thornber (Peter A.), N Yorks 195
Thorne (John), Essex 107
Thorne (Nick), Gloucestershire 112
Thornton (Grahame), Dorset 94
Thornton (John), London (SW) 167
Thornton Books (Richard), London (N) 155
Thorntons of Oxford Ltd., Oxfordshire 208
Thorp (Thomas), Hertfordshire 129
Thurston (Barry), Scotland 273
Tiffin (Tony and Gill), Durham 96
Tiger Books, Kent 134
Tilleys Vintage Magazine Shop, Derbyshire 81
Tilleys Vintage Magazine Shop, S Yorks 220
Till's Bookshop, Scotland 270
Tilston (Stephen E.), London (SE) 162
Tin Drum Books, Leicestershire 144
Tindley & Chapman, London (WC) 178
Titford (John), Derbyshire 81
Tobo Books, Hampshire 122
Tombland Bookshop, Norfolk 190
Tony Skelton, Kent 138
Tooley, Adams & Co., Oxfordshire 209
Torc Books, Norfolk 190
Torsdag Books, Buckinghamshire 62
Touchstone Books, Norfolk 190
Tower Bridge Books, London (SE) 162
Towers (Mark), Lancashire 141
Townsend (John), Berkshire 59
Towpath Bookshop,
      Greater Manchester 118
Tozer Railway Books (Nick), W Yorks 246
Trafalgar Bookshop (The), East Sussex 99
Transformer, Scotland 264

Travel Bookshop (The), London (W) 175
Traveller's Bookshelf (The), Somerset 215
Travis & Emery Music Bookshop,
      London (WC) 178
Treasure Chest (The), Suffolk 226
Treasure Island (The), Greater Manchester 118
Treasure Trove Books, Leicestershire 144
Treglown (Roger J.), Cheshire 71
Trevan's Old Books, Wiltshire 252
Trevorrow (Edwin), Hertfordshire 128
Trinders' Fine Tools, Suffolk 225
Trinity Rare Books, Republic Of Ireland 278
TRJ Books, Norfolk 189
Troath Books (Brian), London (E) 151
Trotman (Ken), Cambridgeshire 66
Trotter Books (John), London (N) 156
TSB Booksearch, London (SW) 167
Tucker (Alan & Joan), Gloucestershire 114
Tuft (Patrick), London (W) 175
Tuohy (S.P.), Oxfordshire 209
Turner (Robin), Gloucestershire 112
Turret House, Norfolk 191
Turton (John), Durham 97
Twigg (Keith), Staffordshire 223
Twiggers Booksearch, London (SW) 167
Two Jays Bookshop, London, Outer 180
Tyger Press, London (N) 156
Ulysses, London (WC) 178
Undercover Books, Lincolnshire 150
Underwater Books, East Sussex 101
Unicorn Books, London, Outer 181
Units 7 and 8, Hampshire 122
Unsworths Booksellers Ltd., London (WC) 178
Unsworths Booksellers Ltd., Oxfordshire 209
Updike Rare Books (John), Scotland 270
Upper–Room Books, Somerset 216
Vailima Books, Scotland 263
Vandeleur Antiquarian Books, Surrey 231
Vanstone - Aviation Books, (Derek), Suffolk 229
Venables (Morris & Juliet), Bristol 61
Ventnor Rare Books, Isle of Wight 132
Verandah Books, Dorset 94
Vernon (Philip), Lancashire 140
Vickers (Anthony), N Yorks 195
Vickers (Patrick), East Sussex 103
Victoria Bookshop, Wiltshire 252
Victoria Bookshop (The), Devon 83
Vikings Books and Antiques, Scotland 267
Village Books, Scotland 271
Village Books, Norfolk 187
Village Bookshop (The), Durham 96
Vinovium Books, Durham 96
Vintage Motorshop, W Yorks 245
Visser Books (de), Cambridgeshire 66
Vokes (Jeremiah), Durham 96
Vokes Books Ltd., N Yorks 194
Volumes of Motoring, Gloucestershire 111
Waddington Books & Prints (Geraldine),
      Northamptonshire 198
Wakeley (A.G. & W.), Wales 285
Wakeman Books (Frances), Nottinghamshire ... 202
Walcot (Patrick), W Mids 240
Walden Books, London (NW) 159
Walker (Adrian), Bedfordshire 55
Walker Fine Books (Steve), London (SW) 167

War & Peace Books, Hampshire 121
Ward (K. Anthony), Norfolk 188
Ward (R.F. & C.), Norfolk 188
Warnes (David), Herefordshire 126
Warnes (Felicity J.), London, Outer 181
Warrender (Andrew), W Yorks 248
Warrington Book Loft (The), Cheshire 72
Warsash Nautical Bookshop, Hampshire 124
Water Lane Books, Wiltshire 252
Waterfield's, Oxfordshire 209
Waters (D.B.), Norfolk 190
Waterstone's, London (WC) 179
Watkins (R.G.), Somerset 218
Watkins Books Ltd., London (WC) 179
Watson (Kelvin), W Mids 239
Watson Books (Michael), Norfolk 190
Waxfactor, East Sussex 99
Way (R.E. & G.B.), Suffolk 227
Way Booksellers (Richard), Oxfordshire 206
Wayfarer Books, Cornwall 75
Wayfarers Books, Devon 86
Wayside Books and Cards, Oxfordshire 205, 206
Webb Books (John), S Yorks 220
Weber (Mark), London, Outer 181
Webster (D.), Scotland 272
Weiner (Graham), London (N) 156
Weininger Antiquarian Books (Eva M.),
  London (NW) 159
Well–Head Books, Dorset 91
Wells (Mary), London (SW) 167
Wells (Mike), London (NW) 159
Wembdon Books, Somerset 215
Wendover Bookshop, Buckinghamshire 62
Wenlock Books, Shropshire 212
Weobley Bookshop (The), Herefordshire 127
West House Books, Wales 287
West Port Books, Scotland 270
West Wickham Bookshop, London, Outer 184
Westcountry Old Books, Devon 88
WestField Books, N Yorks 197
Westgate Bookshop, Lincolnshire 149
Westons, Hertfordshire 130
Westwood Books (Mark), Wales 287
Westwords, Scotland 271
Wetherell (Frances), Cambridgeshire 66
Wheatsheaf Antiques, Cheshire 69
Wheen O'Blethers Bookshop, Scotland 271
Wheen O'Books, Scotland 261
Whelan (P. & F.), Kent 138
Whig Books Ltd., Leicestershire 145
Whistler's Books, London (SW) 167
Whitchurch Books Ltd., Wales 280
White (C.R.), London (W) 175
White (David), Cambridgeshire 66
White (Mrs. Teresa), London (W) 175
White House Bookshop, Wales 283
Whitehall Books, East Sussex 101
Whiteson Ltd., (Edna), Hertfordshire 128
Whitfield (Ken), Essex 109
Whittaker (Anthony), Kent 138
Whonotes, W Mids 239
Wiend Books & Collectables, Gr Manchester ... 119
Wigley Books, Worcestershire 255
Wilbraham (J. & S.), London (NW) 159
Wildside Books, Worcestershire 255

Wildy & Sons Ltd., London (WC) 179
Williams (Bookdealer), (Richard), Lincolnshire . 149
Williams (Christopher), Dorset 93
Williams (John), Wiltshire 252
Williams Rare Books (Nigel), London (WC) 179
Williamson (N.B.), Essex 110
Willmer Books, Derbyshire 81
Willmott Bookseller (Nicholas), Wales 280
Wilson (Autographs) Ltd., (John), Glos 112
Wilson (Books) (D.B.), Durham 97
Wilson (J. & M.), Scotland 273
Wilson (James), Hertfordshire 128
Wilson (Motoring Books) (Les), Merseyside .. 186
Wilson Books (Henry), Cheshire 71
Winchester Antiquarian Books, Hampshire 125
Winchester Bookshop (The), Hampshire 125
Winding Stair Bookshop & Café (The),
  Republic Of Ireland 277, 279
Windmill Bookshop, Lancashire 0
Winram's Bookshop, Scotland 266
Wise (Derek), East Sussex 102
Wise Owl Bookshop (The), Bristol 61
Witmehá Productions, Leicestershire 145
Wizard Books, Cambridgeshire 68
Woburn Books, London (N) 156
Wolds Book Services, Leicestershire 144
Wood (Peter), Cambridgeshire 66
Wood Cricket Books (Martin), Kent 137
Woodbine Books, W Yorks 245
Woodlands Books, W Yorks 248
Woodrow (Philip S.), Derbyshire 82
Woodside Books, Kent 133
Woodstock Bookshop (The), Oxfordshire 210
Woodstock Fabrics & Books, Shropshire 212
Woolcott Books, Dorset 92
Worcester Rare Books, Worcestershire 256
Word of Mouth, Scotland 271
Words & Music, Cheshire 70
Words Etcetera, Dorset 92
World War Books, Kent 139
World War II Books, Surrey 234
World's End Bookshop, London (SW) 167
Worley Publications & Booksellers, Tyne
  & Wear 235
Worrallo (J. & M.A.), W Mids 240
Wright (A.R.), Surrey 234
Wright (Norman), Hertfordshire 130
Wright Trace Books, W Mids 239
www.drivepast.com, Gloucestershire 114
Wyche Books, Scotland 263
Wycherley (Stephen), W Mids 239
Wychwood Books, Gloucestershire 114
Wykeham Books, London (SW) 168
Wyseby House Books, Berkshire 57
Ximenes Rare Books Inc., Gloucestershire 112
Yarborough House Bookshop, Shropshire 211
Yarwood Rare Books (Edward), Cheshire 116
Yates (R.A.), Dorset 92
Yates Antiquarian Books (Tony), Leicestershire 144
Yeoman Books, Scotland 270
Yesterday Tackle & Books, Dorset 91
Yesterday's Books, Dorset 91
Yesterday's News, Wales 281
Yesteryear Railwayana, Kent 137
Yewtree Books, Cumbria 78

York (Graham), Devon............................ 85
Young (D. & J.), Wales 289
Youngs Antiquarian Books, Essex................ 110
YSF Books, S Yorks................................ 221
Ystwyth Books, Wales............................. 281
Zardoz Books, Wiltshire............................ 253

ALPHABETICAL INDEX OF DEALERS WITH WEB SITES

A. & R. Booksearch, (See page 75) .... www.musicbooksrus.com
Ænigma Designs (Books), (See page 85) .... www.puzzlemuseum.com
AA1 Books, (See page 263) www.bookavenue/hosted/AA1
Aardvark Books, (See page 252) .... www.sonic.net/~bstone/aardvarkbooks
Acumen Books, (See page 223) .... www.acumenbooks.co.uk
Addyman Books, (See page 285) .... www.hay-on-wyebooks.com
Ainslie Books, (See page 271) .... www.ainsliebooks.co.uk
Alba Books, (See page 267) .... www.abebooks.com/home/albabooks
Alba Secondhand Music, (See page 271) .... www.albamusick.co.uk
All Books, (See page 108) .... www.allbooks.demon.co.uk
Allport (Roy), (See page 195) .... www.abebooks.com/home/ROYPORT
Allsop (Duncan M.), (See page 237) .... www.clique.co.uk/abe.htm
Alpes Livres (Les), (See page 120) .... www.les-alpes-livres.co.uk
Altea Antique Maps & Books, (See page 169) .... www.alteamaps.com
Ambra Books, (See page 60) .... www.localhistory.co.uk/ambra
Americanabooksuk, (See page 77) .... www.americanabooks.co.uk
Ancient & Modern Bookshop, (See page 90) .... www.ancientandmodernbooks.co.uk
Andromeda Books, (See page 63) www.m31books.co.uk
Annesley Books of Scottish Interest (Brian), (See page 272) .... www.scotbooks.demon.co.uk
Annie's Books, (See page 220) .... www.abebooks.com/home/chriswren
Antiquary Ltd., (Bar Bookstore), (See page 194) .... www.ukbookworld.com/members/Barbooks
Antique Map and Bookshop (The), (See page 93) .... www.abebooks.com/home/proctorbooks
Anvil Books, (See page 239) .... www.anvilbookshalesowen.co.uk
Aquarius Books Ltd., (See page 114) .... www.ukbookworld.com/members/aquarius
Archer (David), (See page 288) .... www.david-archer-maps.co.uk
Archer (Steve), (See page 180) .... www.ukbookworld.com/members/stevearcher
Archive Books & Music, (See page 157) .... www.archivebookstore.com
Arnold (Roy), (See page 226) .... www.royarnold.com
Art Reference Books, (See page 123) .... www.artreferencebooks.com
Ash Rare Books, (See page 152) .... www.ashrare.com
Assinder Books, (See page 55) .... www.abebooks.com
Atlantis Bookshop, (See page 176) .... www.atlantisbookshop.demon.co.uk
Autolycus, (See page 211) .... www.booksonline.uk.com
Avery (Alan), (See page 193) .... www.abebooks.com/home/avery
Avonbridge Books, (See page 114) .... www.avonbridgebooks.com
Avonworld Books, (See page 215) .... www.avonworld-booksource.co.uk
B. and K. Books, (See page 285) .... www.hay-on-wye.co.uk/bkbooks.
babelog.books, (See page 126) .... www.ukbookworld.com/members/mason
Badger Books, (See page 218) .... www.badgerbooks.co.uk
Bailey Hill Bookshop, (See page 215) .... www.baileyhillbookshop.co.uk
Baker (Gerald), (See page 60) .... www.gwrpublicity.co.uk
Baker Limited (A.P. & R.), (See page 263) .... www.apandrbaker.co.uk
Bannister (David), (See page 111) .... www.antiquemaps.co.uk
Barbican Bookshop, (See page 196) .... barbicanbookshop.co.uk
Bardsley's Books, (See page 225) .... www.bardsleysbooks.co.uk
Barmby (C. & A.J.), (See page 138) .... bookpilot@aol.com
Barn Books, (See page 213) .... www.barnbooks.co.uk
Barnes - Books (Lyndon), (See page 127) .... www.abebooks.com
Baron - Scientific Book Sales (P.J.), (See page 215) .... www.barons.clara.net
Barron - The Antique Map Specialist (Roderick M.), (See page 137) .... www.barron.co.uk
Barry Meaden (Aviation Books), (See page 129) .... www.ukbookworld.com/members/spitfire
Barter Books, (See page 200) .... www.barterbooks.co.uk
Bates & Hindmarch, (See page 247) .... www.abebooks.com
Batterdale Books, (See page 195) .... http://hometown.aol.com/GBSteven
Bayntun (George), (See page 214) .... www.georgebayntun.com
Beardsell Books, (See page 246) .... www.toll-house.co.uk
Beaton (Richard), (See page 101) .... www.btinternet.com/~beaton.books
Beaver Booksearch, (See page 225) .... www.booksearch.u-net.com
Beckham Books, (See page 228) .... www.beckhambooks.com
Beetles Ltd., (Chris), (See page 163) .... www.chrisbeetles.com

Bell (Peter), (See page 269)	www.peterbell.net
Bell Gallery (The), (See page 259)	www.bellgallery.com
Bertram Rota Ltd., (See page 176)	www.bertramrota.co.uk
Besleys Books, (See page 224)	www.besleysbooks.demon.co.uk
Bevan (John), (See page 127)	www.catholicbooks.co.uk
Beverley Old Bookshop, (See page 104)	www.eastridingbooksandmusic.co.uk
Biblion, (See page 169)	www.biblion.com
Bird Books (Nigel), (See page 281)	www.nigelbirdbooks.co.uk
Black & White Books, (See page 131)	www.ukbookworld.com
Black Cat Books, (See page 188)	www.blackcatbooks.com
Black Cat Bookshop, (See page 143)	www.blackcatbookshop.com
Black Five Books, (See page 213)	www.black5books.co.uk
Black–Bird Books, (See page 157)	www.laybooks.com
Blacket Books, (See page 269)	www.blacketbooks.co.uk
Blackman Books, (See page 72)	www.abebooks.com/home/rtmb
Bluntisham Books, (See page 64)	www.bluntisahmbooks.co.uk
Blythswood Bookshop, (See page 268)	www.blythswood.org
Bodyline Books, (See page 163)	www.bodylinebooks.com
Bolland Books (Leslie H.), (See page 55)	www.bollandbooks.com
Bonham (J. & S.L.), (See page 169)	www.bonbooks.dial.pipex.com
Book Barn Ltd., (See page 216)	www.bookbarn.co.uk
Book Corner, (See page 263)	www.book-corner.co.uk
Book for All Reasons (A.), (See page 227)	www.abfar.co.uk
Book Gallery (The), (See page 76)	www.abebooks.com/home/tinyworld
Book House (The), (See page 78)	www.thebookhouse.co.uk
Bookends of Devon, (See page 85)	www.bookends.free-online.co.uk
Bookends of Fowey, (See page 74)	www.bookendsoffowey.com
Bookfare, (See page 79)	www.bookfare.co.uk
BookLovers, (See page 217)	www.booklovers.co.uk
Books, (See page 282)	www.llangollen.org.uk/pages/books.htm
Books & Bygones, (See page 58)	www.booksbygones.com
Books & Things, (See page 169)	www.booksandthings.co.uk
Books Bought & Sold, (See page 231)	www.books.keyuk.com
Books for Collectors, (See page 112)	www.booksforcollectors.co.uk
Books of Note, (See page 64)	www.booksofnote.co.uk
Books on Spain, (See page 183)	www.books-on-spain.com
Books on the Bank, (See page 96)	www.booksonthebank.co.uk
Books Ulster, (See page 260)	www.booksulster.com
Books With Care, (See page 55)	www.bookswithcare.com
Bookseller (The), (See page 227)	www.abfa.co.uk
Bookshelf (The), (See page 140)	abebooks.com
Bookshelf (The),, (See page 194)	www.bookshelf.scarborough.co.uk
Booksmart, (See page 198)	www.booksmart.co.uk
Bookstand, (See page 93)	www.abebooks.com/home/bookstand
Bookstop UK, (See page 142)	www.bookstopuk.co.uk
Bookworld, (See page 212)	www.tgal.co.uk/bookworld
Bookworm, (See page 106)	www.bookwormshop.com
Book–Worm International, (See page 107)	www.abebooks.com/home/donnasbookworm
Bookworms, (See page 187)	www.susanlid.freeserve.co.uk
Bookwyze, (See page 147)	www.bookwyze.co.uk
Booth Books, (See page 286)	www.richardbooth.demon.co.uk
Booth Books, (See page 286)	www.richardboothbookseller.com
Border Bookshop (The), (See page 248)	www.borderbookshop.co.uk
Boris Books, (See page 94)	www.borisbooks.co.uk
Bosphorus Books, (See page 176)	www.bosphorusbooks.co.uk
Bott, (Bookdealers) Ltd., (Martin), (See page 116)	www.bottbooks.com
Bow Windows Book Shop, (See page 102)	www.bowwindows.com
Bowers Chess Suppliers (Francis), (See page 67)	home.aol.com/chessbower
Box of Frogs (The), (See page 263)	www.froggybox.co.uk
Boz Books, (See page 286)	www.bozbooks.co.uk
Bracton Books, (See page 64)	www.bractonbooks.co.uk
Bradley–Cox (Mary), (See page 90)	mbradleycox.com
Breese Books Ltd., (See page 98)	www.sherlockholmes.co.uk
Brewin Books Ltd., (See page 237)	www.brewinbooks.com
Bridge of Allan Books, (See page 262)	www.bridgeofallanbooks.com

ALPHABETICAL INDEX: Web Sites (B – C)

Bristow & Garland, (See page 121) .... www.bristowandgarland.co.uk
Broadhurst of Southport Ltd., (See page 186) .... www.ckbroadhurst.com
Broadwater Books, (See page 124).. matchingbooks.co.uk
Brock Books, (See page 192) .... www.brockbooks.com
Brockwells Bookshop, (See page 160) .... www.brockwells.co.uk
Brown (Books) (Steve), (See page 222) .... www.abebooks.com/home/sbbooks
Browning (Julian), (See page 169) .... www.jbautographs.com
Brown-Studies, (See page 270) .... www.brown-studies.co.uk
Browzers, (See page 117) .... http://www.browzersbooks.co.uk
Buchan Collectibles, (See page 265) .... http://www.buchancollect.com
Buckland Books, (See page 243) .... www.tiles.org/pages/bookshlf.htm
Bufo Books, (See page 123) .... www.bufobooks.demon.co.uk
Butterwick Books, (See page 149) .... www.ukbookworld.com/members/butterbooks
Bygone Books, (See page 141) .... www.bygonebooks.fsnet.co.uk
Byre Books, (See page 264) .... www.byrebooks.co.uk
Cader Idris Books, (See page 283) .... www.abebooks.com/home/dvbookshop
Caduceus Books, (See page 143) .... www.io.com/~albion/caduceus/ or www.cadu.demon.co.
Caledonia Books, (See page 271)... www.caledoniabooks.co.uk
Calendula Horticultural Books, (See page 100).. www.calendulabooks.com
Camden Books, (See page 214) .... www.camdenbooks.com
Campbell Art Books (Marcus), (See page 160) .... www.marcuscampbell.demon.co.uk
Canterbury Bookshop (The), (See page 133).. canterburybookshop@btconnect.com
Capes (Books, Maps & Prints) (John L.), (See page 195).. www.johncapes.co.uk
Carnforth Bookshop (The), (See page 140).. www.carnforthbooks.co.uk
Caron Books, (See page 202) .... www.caronbooks.co.uk
Carta Regis, (See page 288).. www.davidp@cartaregis.com
Cartographics, (See page 223) .... www.cartographics.co.uk
Castle Bookshop, (See page 288)... www.archaeologybooks.co.uk
Castle Hill Books, (See page 126)... www.castlehillbooks.co.uk
Catalyst Books, (See page 232) .... www.abebooks.com/home/PATBLOSSE/
Cathach Books Ltd., (See page 277) .... www.rarebooks.ie
Cavern Books, (See pages 69, 70, 71) .... www.cavernbooks.co.uk
Chalmers Hallam (E.), (See page 123) .... www.hallam-books.co.uk
Chapel Books, (See page 228) .... www.chapelbooks.com
Chapman (Neville), (See page 76)... www.abebooks.com/home/chapbooks
Chapter Two, (See page 160) .... www.chaptertwo.org.uk
Charlie Byrne's Bookshop, (See page 277) .... www.charliebyrne.com
Charmouth Bookstore, (See page 91) .... www.clique.co.uk/members/charmouth
Chaters Motoring Booksellers, (See page 182)... www.chaters.co.uk
Chatterton's Books, (See page 290)... www.booktownblaenafon.com
Chaucer Bookshop (The), (See page 133).. www.chaucer-bookshop.co.uk
Chaucer Head Bookshop, (See page 237).. www.stratford-upon-avonbooks.co.uk
Chelifer Books, (See page 79) .... www.militarybooks.net
Chesters (G. & J.), (See page 223) .... www.abebooks.com/home/geoffchesters
Childrens Bookshop, (See page 246)... www.ukbookworld.com/members/benster
Christine's Book Cabin, (See page 144)... www.bookcabin.co.uk
Chthonios Books, (See page 100) .... www.esotericism.co.uk/index.htm
Church Green Books, (See page 210) .... www.churchgreen.co.uk
Classic Bindings, (See page 163)... www.classicbindings.net
Clent Books, (See page 254) .... www.abebooks.com/home/clentbooks
Clifton Books, (See page 110) .... www.cliftonbooks.co.uk
Cobnar Books, (See page 136)... books@cobnar.co.uk
Cobweb Books, (See page 194) .... www.cobwebbooks.co.uk
Coch-y-Bonddu Books, (See page 288)... www.anglebooks.com
Collectable Books, (See page 160) .... www.collectablebooks.co.uk
Collectors Carbooks, (See page 199) .... www.collectorscarbooks.com
Colonsay Bookshop, (See page 272) .... www.colonsay.org.uk
Cooksweb, (See page 198) .... www.cooksweb.co.uk
Cooper Hay Rare Books, (See page 271) .... www.abebooks.com/home/haybooks
Cornerstone Books, (See page 87) .... mark@streece.freeserve.co.uk
Court Hay Books, (See page 60) .... www.courthaybooks.co.uk
Courtyard Books, (See page 127) .... www.courtyardbooks.org.uk
Cover to Cover, (See page 186) .... www.covers.freeuk.com
Cowley, Auto–in–Print (John), (See page 106)... www.autoinprint.freeserve.co.uk
Cox Music (Lisa), (See page 85) .... www.lisacoxmusic.co.uk

ALPHABETICAL INDEX: Web Sites (C – F)

Cox Old & Rare Books (Claude), (See page 226) .... www.claudecox.co.uk
Cox Rare Books (Charles), (See page 74) .... www.abebooks.com
Croft Selections, (See page 148) .... www.croft-selections.co.uk
Crouch Rare Books, (See page 232) .... www.crbooks.co.uk
Cusack Books, (See page 172) .... www.cusackbooks.com
Cygnet Books, (See page 105) .... www.abebooks.com
D. & M. Books, (See page 248) .... www.dandmbooks.com
Daeron's Books, (See page 63) .... www.daerons.co.uk
Daisy Lane Books, (See page 246) www.area5.co.uk/daisy-lane-books
Dally Books & Collectables, (See page 287) .... www.dallybooks.com
Darkwood Books, (See page 276) .... www.abebooks.com/homepage/darkwoodbooks/
DaSilva Puppet Books, (See page 204) .... www.puppetbooks.co.uk
David Thomas Motoring Books, (See page 127) .... www.allautobooks.com
davidleesbooks.com, (See page 286) .... www.davidleesbooks.com
Davids Ltd., (Roy), (See page 207) .... www.roydavids.com
Davies Fine Books, (See page 256) .... www.daviesfinebooks.biblion.com
Day (J.H.), (See page 122) .... www.abebooks.com
de Beaumont (Robin), (See page 163) .... www.abebooks.com/home/RDEBOOKS
Dead Mens Minds.co.uk, (See page 285) .... www.deadmensminds.co.uk
Dean Illustrated Books (Myra), (See page 284) .... www.btinternet.com/~myra.dean/index.html
Dearman Rare Books (Rebecca), (See page 143) .... rebeccadearmanrarebooks.com
Delectus Books, (See page 176) .... www.delectusbooks.co.uk
Devitt Books (Nial), (See page 236) .... www.devittbooks.com
Dinnages Transport Publishing, (See page 98) .... www.transport-postcards.co.uk
Dolphin Books, (See page 224) .... dolphinbooks@lineone.net
Dooley (Rosemary), (See page 80) .... www.booksonmusic.co.uk
Doorbar (P. & D.), (See page 122) .... www.doorbar.co.uk/books/
Dorset Rare Books, (See page 252) .... www.drbooks.eurobell.co.uk
DoublePlusBooks, (See page 68) .... www.doubleplusbooks.com
Downie Fine Books Ltd., (Robert), (See page 213) .... www.booksets.com
Drury Rare Books (John), (See page 109) .... www.johndrury.co.uk
Du Ry Medieval Manuscripts (Marc–Antoine), (See page 172) .... www.medievalart.uk.com
Dusty Books, (See page 287) .... www.dustybooks.co.uk
Dyer Cricket Books (Ian), (See page 194) .... www.cricketbooks.co.uk
Dyfi Valley Bookshop, (See page 288) .... www.abebooks.com/home/dvbookshop
Dylans Bookstore, (See page 289) .... www.dylans.com
Eagle Bookshop (The), (See page 55) .... www.eaglebookshop.co.uk
Earth Science Books, (See page 251) .... www.earthsciencebooks.com
East Riding Books & Music, (See page 105) .... www.eastridingbooksandmusic.co.uk
Eastern Books of London, (See page 163) .... www.harfieldbooks.com
Eastleach Books, (See page 58) .... www.abebooks.com/home/eastleach
Economia Books, (See page 281) .... www.abebooks.com
Eden Books, (See page 92) .... www.edenbooks.com
Edwards (London) Limited (Francis), (See page 177) .... www.francisedwards.co.uk
Edwards in Hay-on-Wye (Francis), (See page 286) .... www.francisedwards.co.uk
Eggeling Books (John), (See page 248) .... www.ndirect.co.uk/~todmordenbooks
Ellen, The Bookshop (Barrie E.), (See page 110) .... www.abebooks.com/home/barrieellen
Ellis, Bookseller (Peter), (See page 160) .... www.peter-ellis.co.uk
Elmer Books, (Clifford), (See page 116) .... www.truecrime.co.uk
Elmfield Books, (See page 238) .... www.elmfieldbooks.co.uk
Elton Engineering Books, (See page 172) .... www.bibliopoly.com & www.ilab-lila.com
Embleton (Paul), (See page 109) .... www.abebooks.com/home/embleton
Empire Books, (See page 118) .... www.empiremilitarybooks.com
English (Toby), (See page 209) .... www.tobyenglish.com
Ex Libris, (See page 250) .... www.ex-librisbooks.co.uk
Exedra Booksearch Ltd., (See page 164) .... www.exedra.co.uk
Facet Books, (See page 90) .... www.jallinson.freeserve.co.uk
Fantastic Literature, (See page 109) .... www.fantasticliterature.com
Fantasy Centre, (See page 153) .... www.fantasycentre.demon.co.uk
Farahar & Dupré (Clive & Sophie), (See page 250) .... www.farahardupre.co.uk
Farnborough Bookshop and Gallery, (See page 121) .... www.farnboroughgallery.co.uk
Faversham Antiques Centre, (See page 135) .... cswain1805@aol.com
Fiction First, (See page 70) .... www.abebooks.com
Fin Rare Books, (See page 213) .... www.finrarebooks.co.uk
Finch Rare Books Ltd. (Simon), (See page 172) .... www.simonfinch.com

ALPHABETICAL INDEX: Web Sites (F – H)

Name	Web Site
Find That Book, (See page 247)	www.findthatbook.demon.co.uk
Fine Art, (See page 242)	www.fineart.tm
Fine Books Oriental Ltd., (See page 177)	www.finebooks.demon.co.uk
Fine Irish Books, (See page 276)	www.fineirishbooks.com
fineart-photographer, (See page 127)	www.fineart=photographer.com
Finney Antique Books & Prints (Michael), (See page 177)	www.michaelfinney.co.uk
Fireside Books, (See page 63)	www.firesidebooks.demon.co.uk
Fireside Bookshop, (See page 80)	www.firesidebookshop.co.uk
First State Books, (See page 172)	www.firststatebooks.com
Firsts in Print, (See page 131)	firsts-in-print.co.uk
Fisher Nautical, (See page 98)	www.fishernauticalbooks.co.uk
Fogg Rare Books & Manuscripts (Sam), (See page 172)	www.samfogg.com
Forest Books, (See page 147)	www.forestbooks.co.uk
Formby Antiques (Jeffrey), (See page 113)	www.formby-clocks.co.uk
Foster (Stephen), (See page 157)	www.sfbooks.com
Foyle Books, (See page 260)	www.foylebooks.freeserve.co.uk/index.html
Frew Limited (Robert), (See page 177)	www.robertfrew.com
Freya Books & Antiques, (See page 189)	www.freyaantiques.co.uk
Fuchsia Books, (See page 276)	www.fuchsiabooks.com
Furneaux Books (Lee), (See page 87)	www.abebooks.com/home/madeleine
G C Books, (See page 264)	www.gcbooks.demon.co.uk
Gage Postal Books, (See page 109)	www.gagebooks.com
Game Advice, (See page 207)	www.game-advice.com
Gant (Elizabeth), (See page 231)	www.bookline.co.uk
Garbett Antiquarian Books (Michael), (See page 111)	www.michaelgarbett.theanswer.co.uk
Garretts Antiquarian Books, (See page 258)	www.isleofmanbooks.com
Garton & Co., (See page 250)	www.gartonandco.com
Gaskell Rare Books (Roger), (See page 67)	www.RogerGaskell.com
Gaslight Books, (See page 149)	www.gaslightbooks.com
Gate Memorabilia, (See page 153)	ukbookworld.com/members/Jonnyb
Gekoski (R.A.), (See page 177)	www.gekoski.com
George Street Loft (The), (See page 82)	www.multifuel.com
Gillies (Benny), (See page 262)	www.bennygillies.co.uk
Glacier Books, (See page 273)	www.glacierbooks.com
Glenbower Books, (See page 277)	www.abebooks.com/home/GLENBOWERBOOKS
Gloucester Road Bookshop, (See page 164)	www.gloucesterbooks.co.uk
Golden Age Books, (See page 255)	www.goldenagebooks.co.uk
Goldhold Ltd., (See page 151)	www.goldhold.co.uk
Goodyer (Nicholas), (See page 154)	www.nicholasgoodyer.com
Grahame (Major Iain), (See page 225)	www.IainGrahameRareBooks.com
Grant Books, (See page 254)	www.grantbooks.co.uk
Graves–Johnston (Michael), (See page 164)	www.graves-johnston.com
Gravity Books, (See page 147)	www.gravitybooks.com
Grayling (David A.H.), (See page 78)	www.davidgraylingbooks.co.uk
Great Oak Bookshop (The), (See page 287)	www.midwales.com/gob
Green Meadow Books, (See page 75)	www.greenmeadowbooks.co.uk
Greensleeves, (See page 204)	www.greensleevesbooks.co.uk
Greer (Robin), (See page 164)	www.rarerobin.com
Gresham Books, (See page 216)	www.greshambooks.co.uk
Greyfriars Books, (See page 107)	www.greyfriarsbooks.co.uk
Grieveson (A.), (See page 69)	www.alibris.com
Grieveson (Andrea), (See page 185)	golden.frog@lineone.net
Grove Bookshop (The), (See page 195)	www.grovebookshop.co.uk
Hairpin Books, (See page 113)	www.hairpinbooks.co.uk
Hall, (Anthony C.) Antiquarian Bookseller, (See page 184)	www.hallbooks.co.uk
Halson Books, (See page 71)	www.users.zetnet.co.uk/halsongallery
Hanborough Books, (See page 207)	www.parrotpress.co.uk
Hancock & Monks, (See page 286)	www.hancockandmonks.co.uk
Handsworth Books, (See page 110)	www.handsworthbooks.co.uk
Harries (Pauline), (See page 122)	www.abebooks.com/home/paulineharriesbooks
Harrington (Adrian), (See page 173)	www.harringtonbooks.co.uk
Harrington Antiquarian Bookseller (Peter), (See page 164)	www.peter-harrington-books.com
Harrison's Books, (See page 173)	www.biblion.co.uk
Hartley Books (Caroline), (See page 202)	www.abebooks.com/home/carolinehartley
Harwich Old Books, (See page 108)	books@hadley.co.uk

ALPHABETICAL INDEX: Web Sites (H – J)

Havercroft Antiquarian Books, (See page 161) .... www.havabooks.com
Hawkes (James), (See page 111) .... http://www.abebooks.com/home/JAMESHAWKES/
Hawley (C.L.), (See page 195) .... www.clhawley.co.uk
Hawthorn Books, (See page 61) .... www.hawthornbooks.co.uk
Hay Cinema Bookshop Ltd., (See page 286) .... www.haycinemabookshop.co.uk
Heartland Old Books, (See page 88) .... www.heartlandoldbooks.co.uk
Heath (A.R.), (See page 61) .... www.abebooks.com/home/arheath/
Heathfield Books, (See page 188) .... heathfield.books@get-the-web.com
Heatons, (See page 252) .... www.heatons-of-tisbury.co.uk
Hedgerow Books, (See page 220) .... www.hedgerowbooks.com
Helion & Company, (See page 240) .... www.helion.co.uk
Hellenic Bookservices, (See page 158) .... www.hellenicbookservice.com
Helston Bookworm (The), (See page 74) .... www.users.dialstart.net/~helstonb
Heneage Art Books (Thomas), (See page 164) .... www.heneage.com
Hennessey Bookseller (Ray), (See page 100) .... www.bibliofind.com or www.bibliocity.com
Herb Tandree Philosophy Books, (See page 61) .... www.philosophy-books.co.uk
Hereward Books, (See page 66) .... www.herewardbooks.co.uk
Heywood Hill Limited (G.), (See page 173) .... www.gheywoodhill.com
Hodgkins and Company Limited (Ian), (See page 114) .... www.ianhodgkins.com
Hogan (F. & J.), (See page 154) .... www.fjhogan.freeuk.com
Hoggarth (John R.), (See page 196) .... www.johnrhoggarth.co.uk
Holdsworth Books (Bruce), (See page 245) .... www.bruceholdsworthbooks.com
Hollett and Son (R.F.G.), (See page 79) .... www.holletts-rarebooks.co.uk
Hoovey's Books, (See page 101) .... www.hooveys.co.uk
Hornsby, Antiquarian and Secondhand Books (Malcolm), (See page 144) .... hornsbybooks.co.uk
Horsham Bookshop (The), (See page 242) .... www.horshambookshop.com
Houston - Bookseller, (David), (See page 151) .... www.abebooks.com/home/dghbooks
Howes Bookshop, (See page 101) .... www.howes.co.uk
HP Bookfinders, (See page 262) .... www.hp-bookfinders.co.uk
Hünersdorff Rare Books, (See page 165) .... www.abebooks.com/hunersdorff/home
Humanist Book Services, (See page 73) .... www.cornwallhumanists.org.uk
Humber Books, (See page 146) .... www.netguides.co.uk/uk/humber.html
Hummingbird Books, (See page 136) .... hummingbirdbooks@btinternet.com
Hunter, Bookseller, (K.P.), (See page 65) .... www.abebooks.com
Hunter–Rare Books (Andrew), (See page 165) .... www.rarebookhunter.com
Hutchison (Books) (Larry), (See page 265) .... www.larryhutchisobooks.com
Hyland (C.P.), (See page 276) .... www.cphyland.com
Ian Johnson Natural History Books, (See page 63) .... www.pembooks.demon.co.uk
Ice House Books, (See page 143) .... www.incehousebooks.co.uk
Illustrated Book (The), (See page 165) .... www.theillustratedbook.co.uk
Inch's Books, (See page 194) .... www.inchsbooks.co.uk
Inner Bookshop (The), (See page 207) .... www.innerbookshop.com
Innes Books, (See page 212) .... www.abebooks.com/home/innesbooks
Inprint, (See page 114) .... www.inprint.co.uk
InterCol London, (See page 154) .... www.intercol.co.uk
Isabelline Books, (See page 74) .... www.beakbook.demon.co.uk
Ives Bookseller (John), (See page 184) .... www.ukbookworld.com/members/johnives
J & M Books, (See page 237) www.abebooks.com/home/jmbooks2
J.B. Books, (See page 58) .... www.balloonbooks.co.uk
J.G. Natural History Books, (See page 232) .... www.reptilebooks.com
J.K. Bookfinders, (See page 165) .... www.abebooks.com
Jackdaw Books, (See page 189) .... www.jackdawbooks.co.uk
Jacobson (Ken & Jenny), (See page 107) .... www.jacobsonphoto.com
Jade Mountain, (See page 123) .... www.jademountain.co.uk
Jandee Books, (See page 202) .... www.ukbookworld.com/members/jandee
Japan Books (Y & S Company Ltd.), (See page 180) .... www.yandscompany.co.uk/japanbooks.htm
Jarndyce Antiquarian Booksellers, (See page 177) .... www.jarndyce.co.uk
Jarvis Books (incorporating 'Gaston's Alpine Books'), (See page 82) .... www.mountainbooks.co.uk
Jay Books, (See page 269) .... www.jaybooks.demon.co.uk
JB Books & Collectables, (See page 243) .... www.jbbooks.co.uk
Jericho Books, (See page 208) .... www.jerichobooks.com
Jiri Books, (See page 259) .... http://www.abebooks.com/home/WJS/
Johnson Rare Book Collections (C.R.), (See page 158) .... www.crjohnson.com
Jones (Madalyn S.), (See page 246) .... www.madalynjonesbooks.co.uk
Jonkers Rare Books, (See page 206) .... www.jonkers.co.uk

ALPHABETICAL INDEX: Web Sites (K – M)

Joppa Books Ltd., (See page 230) .... www.joppabooks.com
K. Books, (See page 104) .... www.kbooks.uk.com
Katnap Arts, (See page 189) .... www.katnaparts.fsbusiness.co.uk
Kelly Books, (See page 88) .... www.kellybooks.co.uk
Kenny's Bookshops and Art Galleries Ltd, (See page 278)... www.kennys.ie and www.kennyscollections.com
Kenya Books, (See page 99) .... www.abebooks.com/home/kenyabooks
Keogh's Books, (See page 113) .... www.keoghsbooks.co.uk
Kerr (Norman), (See page 78) .... www.kerrbooks.co.uk
Kidson (Ruth), (See page 102) .... www.ruth.kidson@virgin.net
Kineton Nooks, (See page 236) .... www.kinetonbooks.co.uk
Kingfisher Book Service, (See page 203) .... www.kingfisher-books.co.uk
Kingswood Books, (See page 93) .... www.kingswoodbooks.btinternet.co.uk
Knockhundred Bookshop, (See page 243) .... www.abebooks.com/home/SIMONWHEELER
Knowles (John), (See page 188) .... knowlesbooks.com
Kyrios Books, (See page 202) .... www.kyriosbooks.co.uk
L.M.S. Books, (See page 129) .... www.lmsbooks.co.uk
Lamb's Tales, (See page 86) .... www.lambstales.co.uk
Lane Books (Shirley), (See page 132) .... www.ukbookworld.com/members/Shirleylane
Larkham Books (Patricia), (See page 115) .... www.diveinbooks.co.uk
Lawful Occasions, (See page 106) .... www.lawfuloccasions.co.uk
Lay Books (Loretta), (See page 158) .... www.laybooks.com
Leaf Ends, (See page 201) .... www.abebooks.com
Lee Rare Books (Rachel), (See page 61) .... www.rleerarebooks.co.uk
Lees Books.com, (David), (See page 287) .... www.davidleesbooks.com
Left Bank (The), (See page 290) .... www.leftbank.org.uk
Left on The Shelf, (See page 151) .... www.abebooks.com/home/leftontheshelf
Leigh Gallery Books, (See page 108) .... www.abebooks.com/home/BOO/
Lewcock (John), (See page 67) .... www.abebooks.com/home/maritime
Lewis (J.T. & P.), (See page 74) .... http://dogbert.abebooks.com/abep/il.dll?vci=228845
Lewis (John), (See page 107) .... www.abebooks.com
Lewis First Editions, (See page 135) .... www.abebooks.com/home/davidfordyce/
Liebreich Antique Maps & Prints (Kitty), (See page 173) .... www.kittyprint.com
Lion Books, (See page 254) .... www.lionbooks.com
Lion Fine Arts and Books, (See page 287) .... www.ruralwales.org.uk/haybookshops/home/lion
Little Stour Books, (See page 133) .... www.littlestourbooks.com
Lloyd (D. Ieuan), (See page 289) .... www.ukbookworld.com/members/dilloyd
Londonline Books, (See page 165) .... www.londonlinebooks.co.uk
LSA Books, (See page 236) .... www.ukbookworld.com/members/lesanscombe
Lund Theological Books, (See page 65) .... www.lundbooks.co.uk
LyngHeath Books, (See page 190) .... www.lyngheathbooks.co.uk
Maddison (J.K.), (See page 238) .... www.anvilbookshalesowen.co.uk
Magee Books (Eve), (See page 120) .... www.abebooks.com/home/chute
Maggs Brothers Limited, (See page 173) .... www.maggs.com
Magis Books, (See page 144) .... www.magis.co.uk
Magna Gallery, (See page 208) .... www.magna-gallery.com
Magpie Books, (See page 248) .... http://www.ibooknet.co.uk/seller/magpie.htm
Main–Smith & Co. Ltd. (Bruce), (See page 143) .... www.brucemainsmith.com
Manor House Books/John Trotter Books, (See page 154) ...... www.bibliophile.net/John-Trotter-Books.html
Mansfield (Judith), (See page 248) .... www.ndirect.co.uk/~todmordenbooks
Marcet Books, (See page 161) .... www.marcetbooks.co.uk
March House Books, (See page 94) .... www.marchhousebooks.com
Marrin & Sons (G. & D.), (See page 135) .... www.marrinbook.clara.net
Martin - Bookseller (Colin), (See page 105) .... www.colinmartinbooks.com
Martin Bookshop & Gallery (Richard), (See page 121) .... www.richardmartingallery.com
McCann (Joe), (See page 208) .... www.joemccann.com
McConnell Fine Books, (See page 135) .... www.abebooks.com/home/sandwichfinebooks
McCrone (Audrey), (See page 272) .... www.ukbookworld.com/members/finora
McEwan Fine Books, (See page 266) .... www.rhodmcewan.com
McEwan Golf Books (Rhod), (See page 266) .... www.rhodmcewan.com
McKay Rare Books (Barry), (See page 77) .... www.abebooks.com/home/barrymckayrarebks
McKenzie (J.W.), (See page 231) .... www.mckenzie-cricket.co.uk
McLaren Books, (See page 0) .... www.mclarenbooks.co.uk
Meadowcroft Books, (See page 241) .... www.meadowcroftbooks.demon.co.uk
Meadowside Bookshop, (See page 273) .... www.marymagdalene.freeserve.co.uk
Meekins Books (Paul), (See page 237) .... www.paulmeekins.co.uk

Menavaur Books, (See page 264)	www.abebooks.com
Merlin Books, (See page 243)	www.merlinbooks.com
michaelsbookshop.com, (See page 137)	www.michaelsbookshop.com
Military Bookworm, (See page 161)	www.militarybookworm.co.uk
Military Collector (The), (See page 249)	www.sonic.net/~bstone/military
MilitaryHistoryBooks.com, (See page 136)	www.militaryhistorybooks.com
Mills Rare Books (Adam), (See page 65)	www.abebooks.com
Ming Books, (See page 264)	www.mingbooks.com
Minster Gate Bookshop, (See page 196)	www.minstergatebooks.co.uk
Mobbs (A.J.), (See page 240)	www.mobbs.birdbooks.btinternet.co.uk
Mollie's Loft, (See page 289)	www.Molliesloft.com
Monmouth House Books, (See page 283)	www.monmouthhousebooks.co.uk
Moore (Peter), (See page 65)	www.aus-pacbooks.co.uk
Moray Bookshop (The), (See page 267)	www.themoraybookshop.co.uk
Morgan (D. & D.H.W.), (See page 89)	www.birdjournals.com
Morley Case, (See page 124)	www.abebooks.com/home/case
Morrell (Nicholas) Rare Books, (See page 158)	www.morbook.com
Moseley Books, (See page 238)	www.moseleybooks.co.uk
Mount's Bay Books, (See page 75)	www.mountsbaybooks.co.uk
Mr. Pickwick of Towcester, (See page 199)	www.yell.co.uk.sites/pickwickbookfinders
Murder One, (See page 177)	www.murderone.co.uk
Museum Bookshop, (See page 177)	www.museumbookshop.org.uk/
Music By The Score, (See page 73)	www.musicbythescore.com
Naughton Booksellers, (See page 277)	www.naughtonsbooks.com
Nautical Antique Centre (The), (See page 95)	www.nauticalantiquesweymouth.co.uk
Newband (D.M.), (See page 288)	www.davidnewbandbooks.com
Newcastle Bookshop, (See page 200)	www.newcastlebookshop.com
Nicholson of Chester (Richard), (See page 69)	www.antiquemaps.com
Nineteenth Century Books, (See page 209)	www.ukbookworld.com/members/papageno
Noble (Malcolm & Christine), (See page 145)	www.bookcabin.co.uk
Noel and Holland Books, (See page 278)	www.kenmare.com
NostalGia Publications Ltd., (See page 196)	www.nostalgia-publications.co.uk
Nova Foresta Books, (See page 121)	www.novaforestabooks.co.uk
Oakwood Books, (See page 113)	www.abebooks.com/home/oakwoodbooks
Oasis Booksearch, (See page 68)	www.ukbookworld.com/members/welford
Oast Books, (See page 134)	members.aol.com/oastbooks/home.htm
Occultique, (See page 198)	www.occultique.co.uk
Octagon Books, (See page 66)	www.cloistersantiques.co.uk/octagon
O'Donoghue Books, (See page 165)	www.intertextuality.com
Old Bookshelf (The), (See page 271)	www.theoldbookshelf.co.uk
Old Storytellers Bookshop (The), (See page 261)	www.theoldschooltearoom.co.uk
Old Town Bookshop (The), (See page 270)	www.oldtownbookshop.co.uk
Old World Books (Tre Archi), (See page 165)	www.oldworldbooks.com
Olynthiacs, (See page 212)	www.ukbookworld.com/members/olynthiacs
O'Neill (Angus), (See page 178)	admin@rees-oneill.com
Orangeberry Books, (See page 206)	www.orangeberry.co.uk
Oriental and African Books, (See page 213)	www.africana.co.uk.
Orlando Booksellers, (See page 148)	www.abebooks.com/home/ORLAN_DO/
Orssich (Paul), (See page 166)	www.orssich.com
Ouse Valley Books, (See page 56)	www.abebooks.com.home/ousevalleybooks
Outcast Books, (See page 287)	www.ukbookworld.com/members/outcastbooks
Pagan Limited (Hugh), (See page 166)	www.hughpagan.com
Paperbacks Plus, (See page 61)	www.pbplus.freeserve.co.uk
Paralos Ltd., (See page 173)	www.paralos.co.uk
Park Gallery & Bookshop (The), (See page 199)	www.ukbookworld.com/members/parkbookshop
Parrott Books, (See page 0)	www.abebooks.com/home/HPBOOKS
Parrott Books, (See page 209)	www.abebooks.com/home/hpbooks
Patterson Liddle, (See page 214)	www.pattersonliddle.com
Peakirk Books, (See page 68)	www.peakirkbooks.com
Pennymead Books, (See page 193)	www.pennymead.com
Petersfield Bookshop (The), (See page 122)	www.petersfieldbookshop.com
Petersham Books, (See page 166)	www.modernfirsts.co.uk
Peterson (Tony), (See page 109)	www.chessbooks.co.uk
Phillips (Nigel), (See page 166)	www.nigelphillips.com
Photo Books International, (See page 178)	www.pbi-books.com

ALPHABETICAL INDEX: Web Sites (P – S)

Photographery at Soldridge Books, (See page 120)	www.soldridgebooks.co.uk
Piccadilly Rare Books, (See page 103)	www.picrare.com
Platt Rare Books (Richard), (See page 161)	www.abebooks.com/home/richardplatt
Plurabelle Books, (See page 65)	www.plurabelle.co.uk
Politico's, (See page 166)	www.politicos.co.uk
Pollak (P.M.), (See page 87)	www.rarevols.co.uk
Pomes Penyeach, (See page 0)	www.abebooks.com
Porcupine Books, (See page 182)	www.porcupine.demon.co.uk
Post Mortem Books, (See page 242)	www.myebsite.com/pmbooks
Post–Horn Books, (See page 192)	www.abebooks.com/home/posthorn
Potter Limited (Jonathan), (See page 174)	www.jpmaps.co.uk
Premier Books & Prints, (See page 146)	www.notjustbooks.f9.co.uk
Price (John), (See page 155)	www.johnpriceantiquarianbooks.com
Price (R.W.), (See page 202)	www.snap.to/uk
Pringle Booksellers (Andrew), (See page 270)	www.pringlebooks.co.uk
Professional Book Services, (See page 192)	www.bookspluspictures.com
Prospect Books, (See page 282)	www.gunbooks.co.uk
Prospect House Books, (See page 260)	www.antiquarianbooksellersd.co.uk
Pyke (Robert & Susan), (See page 214)	www.abebooks.com/home/pykemaritime
Quaritch Ltd., (Bernard), (See page 174)	www.quaritch.com
Quayside Bookshop, (See page 88)	www.milestonebooks.co.uk
R M Books, (See page 129)	www.rmbooks.co.uk
R. & A. Books, (See page 100)	www.robert.manning.btinternet.co.uk/index.html
R. & B. Graham, (See page 74)	www.cookery-books-online.com
Rainger Books (Michael), (See page 285)	www.raingerbooks.co.uk
Rare Books & Berry, (See page 217)	www.rarebooksandberry.co.uk
Rayner (Hugh Ashley), (See page 215)	www.indiabooks.co.uk
Read Ireland, (See page 277)	www.readireland.com
Reading Lasses, (See page 264)	www.wigtown-booktown.co.uk
Reaveley Books, (See page 86)	www.reaveleybooks.com
Red Rose Books, (See page 141)	www.cricketsupplies.com/books
Red Snapper Books, (See page 178)	www.redsnapperbooks.com
Red Star Books, (See page 128)	www.abebooks.com/home/conorpattenden
Rees & O'Neill Rare Books, (See page 178)	www.rees-oneill.com
Reeve (M. & D.), (See page 208)	www.reevebooks.com
Reference Works Ltd., (See page 94)	www.referenceworks.co.uk
Resurgam Books, (See page 104)	www.resurgambooks.co.uk
Rhos Point Books, (See page 281)	www.ukbookworld.com/members/brynglas
Riccetti (Margaret), (See page 220)	www.riccetti.freeserve.co.uk
Right Now Books (Burma), (See page 167)	www.mandalaybookshop.biz
Riley–Smith (Hamish), (See page 190)	www.riley-smith.com
Ripping Yarns, (See page 155)	www.rippingyarns.co.uk
Riverside Bookshop (The), (See page 78)	www.riversidebooks.co.uk
Roberts (Fine Books) (Julian), (See page 149)	www.abebooks.com/home/JULIANROBERTS/
Rolfe (John), (See page 161)	abebooks.com/home/johnrolfe
Roscrea Bookshop, (See page 279)	www.newroad.ie
Rose's Books, (See page 287)	www.rosesbooks.com
Rosley Books, (See page 79)	www.rosleybooks.com
Ross Old Books & Prints, (See page 127)	www.antiqueprints.com
Roundstone Books, (See page 141)	www.roundstonebooks.co.uk
Rowan House Books, (See page 231)	ABEBooks.com
Ruebotham (Kirk), (See page 71)	www.abebooks.com/home/kirk61
Rugby Relics, (See page 284)	www.rugbyrelics.com
Rupert Books, (See page 65)	www.rupert-books.co.uk
Russell (Charles), (See page 167)	www.russellrarebooks.com
Saint Mary's Books & Prints, ****, (See page 150)	www.stmarysbooks.com
Saint Philip's Books,***, (See page 208)	www.stphilipsbooks.co.uk
Sanders of Oxford Limited, (See page 208)	www.oxlink.co.uk/antiques/sanders.html
Sandstone Books, (See page 134)	www.sandstonebooks.co.uk
Scarthin Books, (See page 82)	www.scarthinbooks.com
Schull Books, (See page 275)	www.schullbooks.com
Schutte (David), (See page 122)	www.davidschutte.co.uk
Sclanders (Beatbooks), (Andrew), (See page 152)	www.beatbooks.com
Sea Chest Nautical Bookshop (The), (See page 87)	www.seachest.co.uk
Second Edition, (See page 270)	www.secondeditionbookshop.co.uk

ALPHABETICAL INDEX: Web Sites (S – T)

Sedgeberrow Books & Framing, (See page 255).................. www.abebooks.com/home/SEDGEBERROW
Seeber (Liz), (See page 99).. www.lizseeberbooks.co.uk
Segal Books (Joel), (See page 85).. www.joelsegalbooks.eclipse.co.uk
Shapero Rare Books (Bernard J.), (See page 174)... www.shapero.com
Shaw (David M.), (See page 72).. www.antiquemapsuk.com
Sheppard (Mrs. P.A.), (See page 111).................. http://ukbookworld.com/cgi-bin/search.pl?s_i_DLR_I
Shipley Specialist Art Booksellers, (See page 178).. www.artbook.co.uk
Sillem (Anthony), (See page 101).. tackletext@btopenworld.com
Silver Trees Books, (See page 239)... www.abebooks.com
Silverman (Michael), (See page 161).. www.michael-silverman.com
Simon Lewis Transport Books, (See page 112).. www.simonlewis.com
Simply Read, (See page 100).. www.abebooks.com/home/simplyread
Simpson (Dave), (See page 262)... dave.simpson3@virgin.net
Sims Reed Limited, (See page 167).. www.simsreed.com
Singleton, (John), (See page 155).. jsingl1920@aol.com
Siop y Morfa, (See page 282)... www.siopymorfa.com
Siri Ellis Books, (See page 116).. www.siriellisbooks.co.uk
Slavin Rare and Collectable Books (Derek), (See page 237)........................... www.leamingtonbooks.co.uk
Smallwood Books, (See page 148).. www.smallwoodbooks.co.uk
Smith Books, (Sally), (See page 225).. www.sallysmithbooks.co.uk
Smith Booksellers (James), (See page 180)... www.jsbooks.co.uk
Smith Modern First Editions, (Chris Adam), (See page 243).................... www.adamsmithbooks.com
Soccer Books Limited, (See page 146)... www.soccer-books.com
Sotheran Limited (Henry), (See page 175)... www.sotherans.co.uk
Spelman (Ken), (See page 197)... www.kenspelman.com
Spenceley Books (David), (See page 248)......................... www.abebooks.com/home/davidspenceleybooks
Spink & Son Limited, (See page 178).. www.spink-online.com
Spread Eagle Bookshop, (See page 162).. www.spreadeagle.org
Spurrier (Nick), (See page 136)... www.nick-spurrier.co.uk
Stained Glass Books, (See page 138)... www.glassconservation.com
Stella Books, (See page 284).. www.stellabooks.com
Sterling Books, (See page 219)... www.abe.com
Stinton (Judith), (See page 92)... www.abebooks.com
STM Books, (See page 155).. www.stmbooks.co.uk
Strauss (David), (See page 147)... www.abebooks.com/home/davidstrauss
Stride & Son, (See page 242)... www.stridesauctions.co.uk
Stroh (M.A.), (See page 151)... www.webspawner.com/users/Buttonbook/
Stroma Books, (See page 261).. www.stromabooks.co.uk
Studio Bookshop, (See page 99).. www.abebooks.com/home/studiobookshop
Sub Aqua Prints and Books, (See page 121).. www.subaquaprints.com
Sue Lowell Natural History Books, (See page 175)... Abebooks.com
Sugen & Co., (See page 192).. http://www.film-tvtieins.co.uk
Sutcliffe (Mark), (See page 246)... www.abebooks.com/home/marksutcliffe/
Sutcliffe (Victor), (See page 167)... www.victorsutcliffe.demon.co.uk
Symes Books (Naomi), (See page 72)... www.naomisymes.com
Tarka Books, (See page 83).. www.tarkabooks.co.uk
Temple (Robert), (See page 155).. www.telinco.co.uk/RobertTemple/
Third Reich Books, (See page 134).. www.thirdreichbooks.com
Thomas (Books) (Leona), (See page 71)... www.leonathomas.co.uk
Thomas Rare Books, (See page 226).. www.abebooks.com
Thornton (Grahame), (See page 94)... www.grahamethornton.f9.co.uk
Thornton Books (Richard), (See page 155)... www.abebooks.com/home/NEVILLE/
Thorp (Thomas), (See page 129)... www.abebooks.com/home/thorpbooks
Tilleys Vintage Magazine Shop, (See pages 81, 220)....................................... www.tilleysmagazines.com
Tobo Books, (See page 122)... www.tobo-books.com
Tooley, Adams & Co., (See page 209).. www.tooleys.co.uk
Townsend (John), (See page 59).. www.johntownsend.demon.co.uk
Tozer Railway Books (Nick), (See page 246).. www.railwaybook.com
Treasure Island (The), (See page 118)... www.abebooks.com/home/RAYJC2000
Treglown (Roger J.), (See page 71).. www.rogerjtreglown.com
Trevan's Old Books, (See page 252)... www.abebooks.com/home/trevan
Trinders' Fine Tools, (See page 225).. www.trindersfinetools.co.uk/
Troath Books (Brian), (See page 151)... www.ukbookworld.com/members/ariel
Trotman (Ken), (See page 66)... www.kentrotman.com
Trotter Books (John), (See page 156)................................. www.bibliophile.net/John-Trotter-Books.htm

Twiggers Booksearch, (See page 167)	www.twiggers.com
Unicorn Books, (See page 181)	www.unicornbooks.co.uk
Unsworths Booksellers Ltd., (See page 178)	www.unsworths.com
Unsworths Booksellers Ltd., (See page 209)	www.unsworths.com
Upper–Room Books, (See page 216)	www.vabooks.com
Vanstone - Aviation Books, (Derek), (See page 229)	www.aircraftbooks.com
Verandah Books, (See page 94)	www.verandah.demon.co.uk
Victoria Bookshop (The), (See page 83)	www.victoriabookshop.co.uk
Village Bookshop (The), (See page 96)	www.villagebookshop.co.uk
Vinovium Books, (See page 96)	www.vinoviumbooks.co.uk
Vintage Motorshop, (See page 245)	www.vintagemotorshop.co.uk
Wakeman Books (Frances), (See page 202)	www.fwbooks.com
Walden Books, (See page 159)	www.ukbookworld/members/waldenbooks
Warsash Nautical Bookshop, (See page 124)	www.nauticalbooks.co.uk
Waterstone's, (See page 179)	www.waterstones.co.uk/gowerst
Way (R.E. & G.B.), (See page 227)	http://www.geocities.com/regbway
Wayfarer Books, (See page 75)	www.ukbookworld.com/members/wayfarer
Wayside Books and Cards, (See page 206)	gibsonjab@aol.com
Westgate Bookshop, (See page 149)	www.abebooks.com/home/WESTGATEBOOKSHOP/
Westons, (See page 130)	www.westons.co.uk
Wheatsheaf Antiques, (See page 69)	www.antiquesonlineuk.com
Wheldon & Wesley Limited, (See page 0)	www.users.dircon.co.uk/~wheldwes
White (David), (See page 66)	www.davidwhitebooks.co.uk
Wiend Books & Collectables, (See page 119)	www.wiendbooks.co.uk
Wilbraham (J. & S.), (See page 159)	www.wilbraham.demon.co.uk
Wildside Books, (See page 254)	www.onthewildside.co.uk
Williams (Bookdealer), (Richard), (See page 149)	www.freespace.virgin.net/rah.williams/
Williams (Christopher), (See page 93)	www.abebooks.com/home/cw
Williams Rare Books (Nigel), (See page 179)	www.nigelwilliams.com
Willmott Bookseller (Nicholas), (See page 280)	members.lycos.co.uk/nicholaswillmott/id17.htm
Wilson (Autographs) Ltd., (John), (See page 112)	www.manuscripts.co.uk
Wilson (J. & M.), (See page 273)	jandmwilson.demon.co.uk
Woodbine Books, (See page 245)	www.abebooks.com/home/woodbine
Woodstock Bookshop (The), (See page 210)	www.abebooks.com
www.drivepast.com, (See page 114)	www.drivepast.com
Wykeham Books, (See page 168)	www.bibliographies.co.uk
Wyseby House Books, (See page 57)	www.wyseby.co.uk
Yesteryear Railwayana, (See page 137)	www.yesrail.com
Young (D. & J.), (See page 289)	www.abebooks.com
YSF Books, (See page 221)	www.ysfbooks.com
Zardoz Books, (See page 253)	www.zardozbooks.co.uk

ALPHABETICAL INDEX BY NAME OF PROPRIETOR

Abramski (D. & Y.) = Cyclamen Books........... 143
Adams (N.T.) = G. David 64
Adams (V.) = Upper–Room Books 216
Addyman (D.) = Addyman Books 285
Ainge (G.) = Golden Age Books..................... 255
Aitman (T.) = Black Voices........................... 185
Aldridge (A. & N.) = Hawthorn Books 61
Alexander (C.) = Bookends of Fowey 74
Alexander (K.) = The Bookroom 233
Allcoat (K.) = Tarka Books 83
Allen (D.M.) = Barber Music 136
Allen (I. & J.) = Bookstop UK 142
Allen (J.) = Red Snapper Books 178
Allen (P.J.) = Robert Temple........................ 155
Allen (R.) = Bufo Books 123
Allinson (J. & M.) = Facet Books 90
Alloway (S.& J.) = The Book Bungalow 73
Almond (G.) = Westgate Bookshop................ 149
Ameringen (B.) = Porcupine Books 182
Anderton (E.) = Bookstack & D.J. Creece........ 211
Andrews (Mrs. J.) = Alton Secondhand Books... 120
Anscombe (L.) = LSA Books.......................... 236
Ansorge (E. & W.) = Barn Books 62
Archer (D.) = David Archer.......................... 288
Ardley (C.M.) = Faversham Books................. 135
Aris (J.) = ECR Books 93
Armitage (M.) = The Porter Bookshop............ 220
Armstrong (A.) = Moffat Book Exchange 263
Arnold (J.R.) = June Rhoda.......................... 108
Arnold (P.) = Book Basket 182
Arthur (E.J.L.) = Fantasy Centre................... 153
Ashcroft (R.E.) = The Inner Bookshop............ 207
Ashford (T.) = Book Collectors Paradise.......... 63
Ashton (Dr. F.A.) = Addendum Books 263
Asplin (D.C.) = G. David 64
Astbury (B. & V.) = Woodlands Books 248
Astill (T.) = Les Alpes Livres........................ 120
Austin (A.) = Farringdon Books..................... 107
Babey (G.) = Nova Foresta Books 121
Baggott (L. & H.) = Wychwood Books........... 114
Bainbridge (S.R.) = Offa's Dyke Books 212
Baker (J.A.) = J.B. Books............................. 58
Baldwin (D. & J.) = Rosanda Books............... 144
Baldwin (J.) = Gate Memorabilia................... 153
Ball (B.W.) = Harlequin Books 61
Ball (E.W.) = Fantasy Centre 153
Ballance (C.) = Byre Books........................... 264
Bancroft (P.) = Nebulous Books..................... 120
Banks (W.L. & W.P.) = Simply Read,............ 100
Barber (D.) = Phoenix Fine Books 110
Barker (J.) = NostalGia Publications Ltd. 196
Barnes (R. & M.) = Church Green Books 210
Barry (Q. & R.) = Sansovino Books 244
Bartle (C.) = Glacier Books........................... 273
Bartley (M.) = Howes Bookshop 101
Barton (J.) = The Winchester Bookshop 125
Bastians(M) = Eton Antique Bookshop 59
Bates (G. & J.) = Bates Books 181
Bates (J.) = Bates & Hindmarch 247
Bayntun-Coward (C.) = George Gregory......... 214

Bayntun–Coward (G.) = George Bayntun......... 214
Beattie (A.) = Americanabooksuk 77
Beckham (J.E.) = Beckham Books 228
Beeby (B.) = Dyfi Valley Bookshop................ 288
Beeby (B. & Son) = Cader Idris Books 283
Beer (D.W.) = Crosby Nethercott Books.......... 180
Bell (J.) = Fortune Green Books..................... 157
Bell (S.) = Green Meadow Books.................... 75
Belton (D.) = Book Barn............................... 216
Bennett (Mrs. C.M.) = Moorland Books 118
Bennett (D.) = dgbbooks............................... 244
Benster (S. & B.) = Childrens Bookshop 246
Bentley (J.) = Albion Books 239
Beresiner (Y.) = InterCol London 154
Berry (D.) = Botting & Berry 101
Berry (M.) = Rare Books & Berry.................. 217
Billington (J.) = Bygone Tunes...................... 142
Binney (J.M.) = Prospect House Books........... 260
Bird (D.R.) = James Smith Booksellers........... 180
Biro (T. & S.) = Collectable Books................. 160
Blackman (M. & R.) = Blackman Books.......... 72
Blake (M.) = Katnap Arts 189
Blakemore (I.) = Rosley Books 79
Blanchard (J. & M.) = New &
 Secondhand Books 94
Blanchett (C.) = Buckland Books.................... 243
Blant (M.) = Magna Gallery 208
Blessett (S.) = Wizard Books,....................... 68
Bletsoe (P.) = Badger 252
Boardman (B. & C.) = The Old Storytellers
 Bookshop.. 261
Boehm (H.) = Artco 202
Boer (L.) = Arthurian Book 285
Boland (D.) = The Trafalgar Bookshop 99
Boon (H.) = Fullerton's Booksearch 188
Booth (P.M.) = Bailey Hill Bookshop 215
Borthwick (T.) = The Old Station Pottery &
 Bookshop.. 191
Boswell (B.) = The Great Oak Bookshop 287
Botting (J.) = Botting & Berry 101
Bowers (A.) = The Curiosity Shop 67
Bown (I.L.) = White House Bookshop 283
Boyd–Cropley (J.M.) = Cottage Books 143
Brayford (D.J.) = Jay Books 269
Brazier (C.) = The Swan Bookshop 84
Brichto (A.) = Addyman Books...................... 285
Bridger (N.J.) = Nevis Railway Books............ 206
Bridger (N.J.) = Nevis Railway Bookshops...... 251
Bridger (N.J.) = Railway Book and
 Magazine Search 58
Bright (P.) = The Bookshop 64
Bristow (J.A.) = South Downs Book Service 243
Brittain (J.) = JB Books & Collectables 243
Broad (S.) = Camilla's Bookshop................... 100
Brook (R.A. & P.P.) = The Bookshop, Kirkstall 247
Brooman (J. & J.) = Spearman Books 102
Brown (A.) = David Archer 288
Brown (B. & B.) = Wayfarer Books................ 75
Brown (M.G. & B.J.) = Brown-Studies........... 270
Brown (P.) = Studio Bookshop 99

ALPHABETICAL INDEX: Proprietor (B – D)

Brown (R.) = The Winchester Bookshop 125
Brown (R.) = Winchester Antiquarian Books 125
Brown (R. & R.) = Ken Trotman 66
Browne (M.) = Premier Books & Prints 146
Browne (R.) = Main Point Books 269
Bryan (L.) = Paralos Ltd. 173
Bryant (E.H.) = Vandeleur Antiquarian Books .. 231
Bryer–Ash (P.G.) = Branksome Books 93
Buck (J.) = Polmorla Books 76
Buckler (R. & S.) = Cobweb Books 194
Budek (P.M. & M.M.) = The Eagle Bookshop... 55
Bull (T.) = Bowden Books 144
Burden (D.) = J. Lawton 232
Burgin (A.) = Woburn Books 156
Burlingham (W.) = Belfast Book Search........... 259
Burridge (Dr. Peter) = Quest Books................. 105
Burton (R.F.) = The Parlour Bookshop 205
Bush (F.) = Othello's Bookshop 108
Button (C.) = Little Stour Books 133
Buxton (A.) = Anna Buxton Books 269
Byatt (T.) = Golden Age Books..................... 255
Byrne (A.) = Foyle Books............................ 260
Byrne (K. & C.) = Colonsay Bookshop 272
Byrom (J.) = Towpath Bookshop................... 118
Whitworth (N.) = Bookside.......................... 247
Cahn (M.) = Plurabelle Books 65
Cameron (J.C.F.) = Atholl Fine Books............ 273
Campbell (A.J. & Mrs. P.M.) = Aberdeen
    Rare Books 267
Campbell (D.) = Londonline Books................ 165
Campbell (D.) = Duncan's Books 88
Canvin (G.L.) = Whitchurch Books Ltd........... 280
Capper (I.) = Crispin's Day.......................... 110
Cardwell (R. & A.) = The New Strand Bookshop. 126
Carlile (G.) = East Riding Books & Music 105
Carmody (P.) = Brighton Books.................... 98
Carter (B. & M.) = Browsers Bookshop........... 107
Cartwright (S.) = babelog.books.................... 126
Case (D.) = Morley Case............................. 124
Casey (K.F.) = Sub Aqua Prints and Books...... 121
Casson (C.) = Norton Books........................ 97
Cauwood (R.) = The Treasure Island.............. 118
Cecil (D. & R.) = Cecil Books 231
Chaddock (M.) = Antiquary Ltd.
    (Bar Bookstore) 194
Chambers (C.J.) = The Bookseller.................. 227
Chambers (J.) = Broadleaf Books 290
Chantziaras (P.) = Paralos Ltd...................... 173
Chapman (E.M.) = Bookquest 83
Chapman (R.) = Tindley & Chapman 178
Chatten (D.) = Riviera Books....................... 188
Checkland (S.) = Rising Tide Books 264
Checkley (A.) = Stothert Old Books 69
Cheke (A.S.) = The Inner Bookshop 207
Chesson (K.) = Chaldon Books & Records 230
Child (M.) = michaelsbookshop.com............... 137
Christian Literature Stalls = Barbican Bookshop .. 196
Christie (J.) = Harvest Books........................ 185
Christie (P.) = Discovery 84
Churcher (P.R.) = The Victoria Bookshop........ 83
Churchill–Evans (D.) = Marine and
    Cannon Books 70
Clark (A. & G.) = Ainslie Books 271
Clarke (J.) = St. Michael at Plea Bookshop...... 190
Clarke (R.) = Muttonchop Manuscripts 243
Clarke (T.) = Magis Books 144
Clement (C.) = Brighton Books..................... 98
Close (M.) = Crescent Books........................ 262
Cockburn (P.) = Roadster Motoring Books 123
Cocking (J. & T.) = Trevan's Old Books.......... 252
Cockram (A.) = Golden Goose Books............. 148
Cocks (M.) = Badgers Books........................ 244
Coe (S.) = Unsworths Booksellers Ltd............. 209
Coe (S.) = Unsworths Booksellers Ltd............. 178
Collett (D.W.) = Military Bookworm.............. 161
Collicott (R.) = Honiton Old Bookshop........... 85
Collinge (V.H.) = The Border Bookshop 248
Collins (D.) = Book–Worm International, ... 107
Collyer (W.J.) = Books Bought & Sold............ 231
Combellack (P. & J.) = Kellow Books............. 204
Compton (M.) = The Idle Booksellers 245
Conway (Ms. S.A.) = Books for Writers 283
Conwell (B.) = Dusty Books,........................ 287
Cook (D.) = Richard Way Booksellers 206
Cooke (A.) = HCB Wholesale....................... 286
Cooke (S. & S.) = Ashfield Books and Records.. 203
Cooper (R.J.) = Marjon Books 110
Cope (D.) = Left on The Shelf 151
Coppock (C.) = Fireside Books 63
Corbett (R.) = Booklore.............................. 144
Corbett (S.) = Booklore 144
Cork (A.) = Roundwood Books 213
Cornell (G.T. & C.L.) = Cornell Books 114
Cornish (I.) = Ambra Books 60
Corrall (L.) = The Pocket Bookshop............... 86
Costin (C. & T.) = The Horsham Bookshop...... 242
Coulthurst (S.) = Beaver Booksearch 225
Coupland (C. & B.F.) = Brunner Books 68
Court (R. & A.) = Mountaineering Books 154
Cowan (E.E.) = Eddie's Books and Cards 271
Cox (A.B.) = Claude Cox Old & Rare Books 226
Cox (P.) = Peter's Bookshop 190
Cox (P.) = Peter Pan Bookshop..................... 190
Cranwell (J.) = Bookworld........................... 212
Cresswell (P.M.) = Humber Books 146
Crimmings (T.) = Criterion Books.................. 182
Crook (K.S.) = KSC Books 71
Crook (M.) = Gippeswic Books..................... 227
Cross (E.) = Chapter Two 160
Cross (J.) = Capuchins 256
Crouch (A.S.) = Crouch Rare Books 232
Cunningham (E.) = Cathach Books Ltd........... 277
Cusack-O'Connell (E.M.) = Cusack Books 172
Cutts (T.) = Londonline Books 165
Dale (I.) = Politico's 166
Daly (K.) = Rainbow Books 99
Dancy (J.E. & A.B.) = Broadwater Books 124
Daniels (T.) = Midas Books & Prints 147
D'Arch Smith (T.) = Fuller D'Arch Smith 172
Dare (Mrs. E.M.) = Book Warren 84
Darling (A.) = Birchwood Books 246
Davey (M.A.) = Ancient & Modern Bookshop .. 90
Davidson (E.S.) = Ice House Books................ 143
Davidson (D.) = Winram's Bookshop.............. 266
Davies (Rev. E.) = Gradwell Concepts 185
Davies (J. & L.) = Stepping Stones Bookshop.... 193
Davis (J.A.) = Four Tees Booksearch.............. 90
Dawes (S.H.) = Fin Rare Books.................... 213
Day (J.) = Calluna Books............................ 94
Day (J.H.) = The Shirley Bookshop............... 124

Daymond (D.) = Arden Books & Cosmographia .. 236
Dean (R.J. & S.W.) = Cartographics 223
Dearn (R.A.) = The Sea Chest
 Nautical Bookshop 87
Deegan (T.) = New Road Books, ... 279
De Martini (M.) = Altea Antique Maps
 & Books 169
Dennis (G.) = Blacklock's 231
Dennys (N.) = Gloucester Road Bookshop 164
Devlin (Mrs P.) = The Warrington Book Loft ... 72
Dingle (M.R. & M.R.) = Prospect Books 282
Dixon (C.) = The Earlsfield Bookshop 163
Dixon (J.) = Third Reich Books 134
Dobbyn (D. & A.) = Yesterday Tackle
 and Books 91
Dollery (A.) = Kingswood Books 93
Doran (A.) = Falconwood Transport & Military
 Bookshop 184
Drake (R.) = Atticus Books 109
Druett (D.) = Pennymead Books 193
Ducat (N.) = Devanha Military Books 267
Duckworth (A.) = Sen Books 125
Duerdoth (S.) = Eric Goodyer, Natural History
 Books 144
Dumbleton (V.) = Aquarius Books Ltd 114
Dunbar (D.) = Aurelian Books 157
Dunlop (C.) = W. & A. Houben 183
Dunn (C.R.) = Anchor Books 149
Dupont (J.M.) = Max Gate Books 218
Dutton (Dr. R.A.) = Thin Read Line 186
Dwyer (J.) = Newgate Books 201
Dyke (S.) = Skyrack Books 246
Eastman (P.V.) = Eastern Books of London 163
Eaton (J.A.) = Alastor Books 122
Eden (G. & T.) = Eden Books 92
Edgecombe (S.M.) = J. Clarke–Hall Limited 134
Edgson (J.) = Books for Collectors 112
Edmonds (M.J.) = The Dorchester Bookshop, ... 92
Edmondson (V.) = Mother Goose Bookshop 131
Edmunds (D.R.D.) = John Drury Rare Books ... 109
Edwards (C.) = Christopher Edwards 57
Eldridge (J. & R.) = YSF Books 221
Elissa (N.M.) = Joppa Books Ltd. 230
Elithorn (A.) = Game Advice 207
Ellingworth (M. & S.) = Coach House Books.... 255
Elliott (P. & A.) = Pedlar's Pack Books 89
Elliston (P.) = Firsts in Print, ... 131
Emery (P.N.) = Gravity Books 147
Erhun (S.A.) = Bosphorus Books 176
Erskine (M.) = Christopher Edwards 57
Evans (M.) = Mollie's Loft 289
Everitt (A.) = ReadingLasses 264
Excell (A. & L.F.) = Bookmark
 (Children's Books) 252
Eynon (A. & M.) = Andromeda Books 63
Fairnington (P.) = Manna Bookshop 218
Farnsworth (B.) = Ouse Valley Books 56
Feehan (G. & M.) = Royal Carbery Books Ltd.. 275
Feller (S.) = Unicorn Books 181
Fernee (D.) = Caduceus Books 143
Fielden (S.&D.) = The Village Bookshop 96
Figgis (N.) = The House of Figgis Ltd 278
Finlay (Dr. R. & Dr L.A.) = Barlow Moor
 Books 116
Finn (M. & E.) = Jackdaw Books 189
Finn (T.) = Twiggers Booksearch 167
Gregory (Dr G.) = Bijou Books 221
Firth (M.) = Bijou Books 221
Fishburn (J.) = Fishburn Books 157
Fisher (B.) = March House Books 94
Flanagan (M. & L.) = Zardoz Books 253
Fleming (D.) = Grampian Books 265
Fletcher (D.) = The Curiosity Shop 67
Flowers (L.L.) = Kim's Bookshop 244
Floyd (J.) = Browser's Bookshop 74
Ford (G.) = G.F. Book Services 55
Ford (V.A.) = The Shirley Bookshop 124
Forder (I.) = Pioneer Books 120
Fordyce (D.) = Lewis First Editions 135
Forman (L.) = Marine Workshop Bookshop..... 92
Forster (C.A.) = C.R. Johnson Rare
 Book Collections 158
Foster (J.A.) = The Park Gallery & Bookshop... 199
Fothergill (T.) = Ken Spelman 197
Fowkes (M.) = Kingsgate Books & Prints 125
Foy Cameron (N.) = Atholl Browse 273
Francombe (C.) = Camilla's Bookshop 100
Francombe (M.L.) = Kim's Bookshop 244
Franklin (D. & R.) = Doro Books 242
Fraser (J. & P.) = The Glass Key 246
Freeman (J.G. & A.H.) = Tombland Bookshop . 190
French (Mrs. B.) = Beck Head Books 78
French (G.) = Bygone Books 141
French (S.) = Dawlish Books 84
Fruin (C.) = L.M.S. Books 129
Frydberg (G.) = Philologus-Fine & Rare Books . 166
Fursman (Dr. N.) = Noel and Holland Books,... 278
Gaadt (M.) = Target Books 68
Gabbott (R.) = Wheen O'Blethers Bookshop..... 271
Galinsky (P.) = Broughton Books 269
Galloway (C.C.) = ARC Books 272
Gamble (Mr. & Mrs. J.) = Emerald Isle Books .. 259
Gange (C.) = Katharine House Gallery 251
Gardner (A.) = Daeron's Books 63
Gardner (M.) = Emjay Books 231
Gartshore (Y.) = Calluna Books 94
Gauntlett (M. & J.) = Ian Dyer Cricket Books... 194
Gestetner (J.) = Marlborough Rare Books Ltd... 173
Gibbs (J.) = Hummingbird Books 136
Gibson (J.A.B. & J.L.) = Wayside Books
 & Cards 205
Gilbert (P.) = The Wise Owl Bookshop 61
Giles (D. G.) = Ancient Art Books 163
Gipps (A.) = Woodside Books 133
Gleeson (L.) = Nonsuch Books 234
Gleeson (R.) = Nonsuch Books 234
Glover (S.) = Handsworth Books 110
Goddard (M.) = Rose's Books 287
Golborn (E.M.) = Rosemary Books 186
Golden (E.) = Dorset Bookshop, The 90
Goodenough (M.) = Inprint 114
Goodfellow (A.P.) = Carlton Books 189
Goodrick–Clarke (Dr. N. & C.) = IKON 88
Goodyer (E.) = Eric Goodyer, Natural
 History Books 144
Gosden (S.G.) = Fantastic Literature 109
Goss (G.) = The Dancing Goat Bookshop 188
Goss (M.R.) = Delectus Books 176
Govan (D.) = Armchair Books 268
Gowen (M.) = The Book Jungle 102

Grant (F.) = All Seasons Books 79
Greatwood (J.) = J.G. (Natural History Books) ... 232
Green (J.R.) = Castle Bookshop 107
Green (R.) = The Treasure Chest 226
Green (R.) = Blakes Books 229
Green (W., M. & O.D.) = Angel Books 189
Greenwood (N.) = Right Now Books (Burma) ... 167
Gretton (B.) = Leigh Gallery Books 108
Griffin (C.S.) = Doolin Dinghy Books 275
Grogan (P.) = R.A. Gekoski 177
Gwynne (Mr. N.M.) = Britons Catholic Library .. 279
Habraszewski (T.) = Hab Books 173
Hackett (E.A.) = Boer War Books 196
Hadaway (D. & P.) = The Old Gallery
  Bookshop 136
Hadley (P.J.) = Harwich Old Books 108
Haffner (R.N.) = Postings 233
Halewood (M.) = Preston Book Company 142
Hall (B. & H.) = Books Galore 216
Hall (D.W.) = Cornell Books 114
Hall (D.) = Hanborough Books 207
Hall (J.) = Garretts Antiquarian Books 258
Hallgate (J.) = Lucius Books 196
Hamburger (R.B.) = Riderless Horse Books 187
Hancock (A.) = The George Street Loft 82
Hancock (E.) = Hancock & Monks 286
Hanna (J.) = Blaenavon Books 289
Hanson (D. & M.) = D. & M. Books 248
Harding (J.) = Roundstone Books 141
Hardinge (H.) = The Bookshop 64
Hardman (L.R.) = Broadhurst of Southport Ltd. 186
Hardwick (C.) = Rookery Bookery 223
Hardy (J.) = Butterwick Books 149
Harlow (Dr. B.J. & S.) = Tiger Books 134
Harper (C.) = Torsdag Books 62
Harper (T.) = World War Books 139
Harries (P.) = Boz Books 286
Harris (K.) = Books on Spain 183
Harrison (G.) = The Bookmark 137
Harrison (L.) = Biblion 169
Harrison (L.) = Harrison's Books 173
Harrison (S.J.) = Bracton Books 64
Hartles (D.B. & J.) = Goldsworth Books
  & Prints 234
Haslam (J.) = Brock Books 192
Haslem (J.) = Oakwood Books 113
Hatherell (D.) = The Aviation Bookshop 153
Havercroft (J.) = Havercroft Antiquarian Books 161
Hawes (S. & J.) = Bosco Books 73
Hawkin (S.) = The Staffs Bookshop 222
Hay Cinema Bookshop Ltd = Francis
  Edwards in Hay–on–Wye 286
Hayhoe (M.) = Corfe Books 231
Haylock (B. & J.) = The Idler 227
Hayward (K.) = Burntwood Bookshop 222
Heacock (J.A.) = J.A. Heacock (Antiques
  and Books) 70
Hearn (K.) = Newlyn & New Street Books 75
Heatley (Mr. & Mrs. P.R.) = The Dartmoor
  Bookshop 83
Hebden (M.) = M. & D. Books 254
Hedge (P. & E.) = Hedgerow Books 220
Helstrip (A.) = Oblong Books 197
Hepworth (J.) = Otley Maypole Rare Books 193
Herbert (W.) = Photo Books International 178

Herries (D.) = Find That Book 247
Herron (M.) = The Bookshop 276
Hessey (A.) = Reads 94
Hetherington (P.) = Europa Books 163
Hewitt (M.) = Stride & Son 242
Hill (G. & G.) = Bowdon Books 141
Hill (K.R.) = Stained Glass Books 138
Hinchcliffe (C.) = Empire Books 196
Hinchliffe (Mrs. A.) = Whig Books Ltd. 145
Hinde (H.M.) = Ystwyth Books 281
Hine (J.) = Gresham Books 216
Hiscock (L.) = E. Chalmers Hallam 123
Hitchens (B. & E.) = Silver Trees Books, ... 239
HMV Media Group = Waterstone's 179
Hodgkins (J.R.) = Clifton Books 110
Hoffman (T.) = Tower Bridge Books 162
Holland (J.) = Noel and Holland Books, ... 278
Holman (P.) = Invisible Books 99
Holt (T.) = LyngHeath Books, ... 190
Hooper–Bargery (E.) = Music By The Score 73
Hornseys' (B.,S., &D.) = Hornseys' 194
Horsnell (B.) = Footballana 58
Hougham (M.) = Verandah Books 94
Howard (D.) = Outcast Books 287
Howard (J.) = Photo Books International 178
Howell (N.) = The Chichester Bookshop 241
Hoy (I.) = Ian Hodgkins and Company Limited. 114
Hubbard (P.) = Bufo Books 123
Hudson (H.G.) = The Malvern Bookshop 254
Hudson (P.) = Coracle Books 247
Hughes (A.R.) = Roland Books, ... 137
Hughes (P.) = Vinovium Books 96
Hughes (P.D.) = Deverell Books 61
Hunnings (P.J.M.) = Penn Barn Bookshop 63
Hunt (R. & C.) = Vintage Motorshop 245
Hunter (J.A.) = Hunter and Krageloh 82
Hunter (P.C.) = Hillsborough Bookhunters 260
Hunter (S.) = Major John R. McKenzie 77
Husband (M.) = Merlin Books 243
Hutchison (C. & R.) = Chapter House Books.... 93
Hyslop (D.A.) = Yeoman Books 270
Illsley (R.) = Touchstone Books 190
Ilott (L.) = Cobnar Books 136
Ingram-Hill (R.&S.) = Gaslight Books 149
Ions (B. & G.) = Richmond Books 194
Irvine (J.A.M.) = R.A. Gekoski 177
Irwin (C. & M.) = The Book House 78
Israel (N.) = Nibris Books 165
Ives (B.) = Simon's Books 218
Izzard (S.) = Hall's Bookshop 138
Jackson (D.) = Beware of The Leopard Books... 60
Jackson (R.) = Chapel Books, ... 228
Jackson (S.) = Family Favourites (Books) 104
Jackson–Harris (V.) = Quadrille 174
Jacques (P.) = Professional Book Services 192
Jakubowski (M.) = Murder One 177
James (R. & V.) = Chaucer Head Bookshop 237
Jeffries (J.H.) = Fortune Books 106
Jenks (S. & C.) = Beacon Hill Bookshop 232
Jevon (T.W. & S.) = The Bookbug 129
Johnson (C.R.) = C.R. Johnson Rare Book
  Collections 158
Johnson (C. & C.) = On the Wild Side 255
Johnson (I.A.) = Ian Johnson Natural
  History Books, ... 63

ALPHABETICAL INDEX: Proprietor (J – M)

Johnson (J.) = Reaveley Books 86
Johnson (M.) = Courtyard Books 127
Johnson (M.) = Fineart Photgrapher 127
Johnson (W.F. & C.R.) = Past & Presents 77
Johnstone (P.) = Penzance Rare Books 75
Jolliffe (P.) = Ulysses 178
Jones (A.) = Mindreaders Books 135
Jones (A.) = Museum Bookshop 177
Jones (A. & M.) = Almar Books 247
Jones (H.M. & M.G.) = Books for Content 126
Jones (N.) = Musebookshop 283
Jones (R.) = Ex Libris 250
Jones (R.W.) = Northern Herald Books 245
Jonkers (C. & S.) = Jonkers Rare Books 206
Karloui (P.G.) = Crouch Rare Books 232
Kay (J. & J.) = K Books 72
Kaye (B.J. & S.M.) = K. Books 104
Kelly (L.&L.) = Kelly Books Limited 88
Kelly (M. & L.P.) = Priory Books 256
Kemp (M.) = Marcet Books 161
Kenyon–Thompson (J.) = Spread Eagle Books .. 282
Kerr (D.R. & E.M.) = Russell Books 218
Key (S.) = Sarah Key Books 65
King (R.) = Heatons 252
Kinnaird (J. & J.) = Keswick Bookshop 78
Kinross (J.S.) = Bee Books New and Old 73
Kinsella (W.) = Chapters Bookstore 277
Kirk (M.T.) = Black & White Books 131
Kitchen (J.) = Cygnet Books, ... 105
Knapman (C.) = Collectors Carbooks 199
Knight (I.H. & G.M.) = MilitaryHistory Books.com 136
Kousah (M.G.) = Ely Books 66
Kowalski (S.) = Mereside Books 70
Lafferty (P.) = Gerrards Cross Books 87
Laing (E.) = Blacket Books 269
Laing (E.) = Meadowcroft Books, ... 241
Laithwaite (S.) = Mereside Books 70
Lake (B.) = Jarndyce Antiquarian Booksellers ... 177
Lamb (F.) = Delph Books 116
Lamb (J.) = Tasburgh Books 190
Lamb (J. & E.) = Lamb's Tales 86
Landau (N.) = Murder One 177
Langford (A.) = Book Corner 263
Lannois (G.) = Chiltern Books 172
Laurence (J.) = Anglo-American Rare Books, ... 232
Lawrence (H. & J.) = Peakirk Books 68
Lawson (J.) = Books and Things 241
Lay (J.T.) = Black–Bird Books 157
Laywood (W.R.H.) = Forest Books 147
Layzell (M.) = Othello's Bookshop 108
Ledraw (J.) = J.L. Book Exchange 104
Lee (P.& C.) = The Riverside Bookshop 78
Lee (R.) = Rachel Lee Rare Books 61
Leek (R.J.) = Modern Firsts Etc 140
Leff (L.) = Bookshop Blackheath 160
Lennox–Boyd (The Hon. C.A.) = Sanders of Oxford Limited 208
Levitt (V.) = Newcastle Bookshop 200
Lewis (D. & J.) = Bookshop (Godmanchester) ... 66
Lewis (J. & J.) = Photography at Soldridge Books, ... 120
Lewsey (C.) = Freya Books & Antiques 189
Liddell (S. & E.) = Bookworms 187
Liddle (S.) = Patterson Liddle 214

Lidgett (D.J. & C.) = D.C. Books 148
Lidyard (F.W.) = Ruskin Books 161
Lilly (J.) = Books & Bygones 58
Linsley (Mrs. C.M.) = Archie Miles Bookshop... 79
Loader (I.M. & L.E.) = Armchair Books 238
Longton (Mrs. C.L.) = Moorland Books 118
Loska (J.) = Colin Page Antiquarian Books 99
Lovett (M. J.) = Occultique 198
Lowe (G.B. & H.J.) = Ars Artis 206
Lowe (S.) = Porcupines 84
Luck (S.) = Tooley, Adams & Co. 209
Lumby (J.) = Shearwater Bed & Books 200
Lunt (J.) = Books at the Warehouse 193
Lyon (G.R.) = Bodyline Books 163
McAlister (M.C.) = Prospect House Books 260
McConnell (N.) = McConnell Fine Books 135
McCrory (M.) = Books B.C. 181
MacDonald (N.) = BOOKS4U 282
McElroy (G.) = Castle Frome Books 127
Macey (B.) = Flora Books 151
McGarraghy (J.) = The Little Bookshop 117
McGregor (J.) = Hen Hoose Bookshop 262
MacGregor (N.) = Olynthiacs 212
McKee (C.) = Orlando Booksellers 148
McKenzie (A.) = Goldhold Ltd. 151
Mackey (M.) = Fuchsia Books 276
McKirdy (T.) = Cooks Books 98
Mackrell (J.Q.C.) = San Expedito Books 158
MacMillan (H.) = Mercat Books 267
McRoberts (R.J.) = Maurice Dodd Books 77
MacTaggart (C.) = Charmouth Bookstore 91
Madden (H.) = Cavern Books 69
Madden (H.) = Cavern Books 70
Madden (H.) = Cavern Books 71
Maddison (J.K) = Anvil Books 239
Maddison (J.K.) = J.K. Maddison 238
Maddock (T.) = Alpha Books 153
Magill (S.) = Abbey Books 153
Mair (J.) = Mair Wilkes Books 265
Mallory (S.) = Dead Zone Books, ... 289
Maloney (B.) = Cavan Book Centre 275
Manley (S. & M.) = Barter Books 200
Manning (R.) = R. & A. Books, ... 100
Marks (J.) = Wheatsheaf Antiques 69
Marrin (G.&D.) = G.&D. Marrin & Sons 135
Marshall (A.) = Warsash Nautical Bookshop 124
Marston (E. & V.) = Quayside Bookshop 88
Marten (W.) = Bookstand 93
Martin (J. & B.) = Bryony Books 247
Mather (H.S.G) = Wykeham Books 168
Matthews (J.) = Eddie Baxter - Books 218
Matthews (J. & M.) = Two Jays Bookshop 180
Mattley (J.E.) = Phenotype Books 79
May (E. & D.) = The Eastcote Bookshop 183
Mayall (M. & R.) = Sturford Books 252
Mayes (W.) = Mr. Pickwick of Towcester 199
McGivney (J.) = Kenya Books, ... 99
Meaker (T.M.) = Archive Books and Music 157
Mendel (M.) = Gilham Books 161
Merkel (M.P.) = Chantry Bookshop & Gallery .. 84
M'Garry-Durrant (A. M.) = Bookworm 106
Midgley (C.) = Midas Books & Prints 147
Midgley (T.) = Bookwyze, ... 147
Miles (D.) = The Canterbury Bookshop 133
Miles (H.) = Calendula Horticultural Books, ... 100

ALPHABETICAL INDEX: Proprietor (M – R)

Millard (A.) = R. & A. Books, ... 100
Millard (M.C.) = Cranmer Books 210
Miller (G.) = Resurgam Books 104
Miller (P.) = Ken Spelman 197
Minet (P.P.B.) = Piccadilly Rare Books 103
Missing (C.) = Missing Books 108
Mitchell (A.G.) = Capital Bookshop 280
Mitchell (C.) = Ripping Yarns 155
Mitchell (D.R. & M.E.) = Bruce Main–Smith
 & Co. Ltd. 143
Mitchell (Dr. D.J.) = Scarthin Books 82
Mobsby (S.) = Well–Head Books 91
Moffat (G.R.) = Poor Richard's 226
Monckton (I.) = Kingshead Books, ... 288
Monks (J.) = Hancock & Monks 286
Moore (C.N., E.J. & S.J.) = Castle Bookshop.... 288
Moore (R.) = R M Books 129
Morgan (Dr. D.H. & R.A.) = Turret House...... 191
Morgan (P.) = Coch-y-Bonddu Books............. 288
Morgan–Hughes (A.) = Black Cat Books 188
Morris (G. & B.) = Rhos Point Books............. 281
Morris (P.) = Wiend Books & Collectables 119
Morrish (K. & J.) = Reigate Galleries 233
Mould (B.) = Croft Selections....................... 148
Moy (R.F.) = Spread Eagle Bookshop 162
Mullen (P. & M.) = Yesteryear Railwayana 137
Mullett (G.) = The Eastern Traveller 218
Mundy (D.) = Heritage Antiques 128
Murdoch (G.) = Armchair Auctions 120
Murphie (F.) = The Box of Frogs 263
Murphy (R.P.) = Rods Books 87
Murray (I.C.) = Archways Sports Books......... 268
Murtagh (C.J.) = J.K. Maddison 238
Murtagh (C.J.) = Anvil Books 239
Mustin (L.) = Byre Books............................ 264
Mycock (D. & M.) = Abacus Books and Cards.. 223
Nairn (E.G.) = John Updike Rare Books 270
Nangle (J.) = Words Etcetera, ... 92
Nash (Mrs. D.) = Books & Bygones 94
Nash (M. & V.) = Marine and Cannon Books... 70
Nassau (J.) = Jarndyce Antiquarian Booksellers . 177
Naylor (Rev. A.C.I.) = Bookfare.................... 79
Nearn (Rev. D.H.) = Heritage Books.............. 131
Neil (D.A.) = Westcountry Old Books............ 8
Neville (C.) = Woodbine Books.................... 245
Newbold (R.) = Booktrace International 85
Newland (J.& C.) = Cotswold Internet Books.... 111
Newman (P.) = Castle Hill Books 126
Newton (D.) = Tasburgh Books 190
Nicholls (T.) = Paperbacks Plus.................... 61
Nisbet (D.) = Sterling Books 219
Noble (C. & M.) = Christine's Book Cabin....... 144
Nummelin (S.&A.) = Browning Books 290
Obeney (P.) = Idle Genius Books................... 154
O'Connell (B. & J.) = Schull Books 275
O'Connor (J.&E.) = O'Connor Fine Books...... 142
O'Keeffe (N.S.) = Evergreen Livres 113
Oldham (Dr. T.) = Wyseby House Books........ 57
Oliver (R.) = Empire Books 118
Ollerhead (P.E.) = Copnal Books................... 70
Ondaatje (C.) = Rare Books & Berry 217
O'Neill (A.) = Rees & O'Neill Rare Books 178
Oram (P. & C.) = Menavaur Books 264
Overton Fuller (J.) = Fuller D'Arch Smith........ 172
Owen (J.V.) = Colwyn Books 281

Palmer (E.) = Elmfield Books, ... 238
Papworth (M.J.) = Hunter and Krageloh 82
Park (M.) = Mike Park................................ 183
Parker (H.) = WestField Books, ... 197
Parmoor (Lord) = Bernard Quaritch Ltd.......... 174
Parr (Mrs. C.E.M.) = Far Horizons Books 91
Parr (K.) = Kyrios Books............................. 202
Parry (A.) = Meadowcroft Books,.................. 241
Parry (R.C.) = Exeter Rare Books 85
Partington (F. & J.) = Tennis Collectables....... 69
Pattenden (C.) = Red Star Books................... 128
Patterson (J.) = Patterson Liddle 214
Pavli (P.) = Economia Books........................ 281
Pawson (C.) = Croft Selections..................... 148
Pawson (D. & L.) = Footrope Knots 226
Peace (R.) = Brockwells Bookshop 160
Pearce (P.) = Hencotes Books & Prints............ 200
Pearson (J.) = The Illustrated Book................ 165
Peasgood (A. & M.) = Broadway Books 67
Peggs (K.) = All Books................................ 108
Penney (B.) = Invisible Books...................... 99
Penning (L.) = Arthurian Book 285
Perry (I.) = The Strand Bookshop.................. 288
Perry (M.) = Barn Books 213
Petrie (I.R.) = Bookworms........................... 187
Phil (N.) = Rosanda Books 144
Phillimore (J.F.) = Old World Books 165
Phillips (J.) = Periplus Books....................... 63
Phillips (S.D.) = Bygone Books 272
Piercy (N.S.) = Crimes Ink.......................... 151
Pilborough (D. & L.) = Malmo Books 121
Pither (P.) = Books & Bygones 58
Pizey (J.S.) = P. and P. Books 255
Poklewski–Koziell (S.) = Classic Bindings........ 163
Polczynski (U.K.H.) = Philologus–Fine & Rare
 Books... 166
Pollock (Dr. J.) = Whig Books Ltd................. 145
Poole (S.) = Biblion................................... 169
Potten (H. & D.) = Four Shire Bookshops 113
Potter (R.) = Badgers Books 244
Powell (J. & A.) = Palladour Books................ 124
Pratt (R.J.) = Hereward Books...................... 66
Precious (K. & M.A.) = Moss End Bookshop.... 59
Preene (H.) = Parrott Books......................... 209
Prickett (M.L.) = Haven Booksearch 238
Proctor (C.D. & H.M.) = The Antique Map &
 Bookshop 93
Pugh (D.) = Carta Regis 288
Purkis (H.H. & P.A.) = Harry Holmes Books.... 105
Purkis (N. & S.) = Abbey Bookshop............... 122
Purt (D.) = Anglo-American Rare Books, ... 232
Pye (J. & H.) = The Bookshop...................... 242
Quorn (P. & L.) = Scorpio Books 225
Rajput (M.) = Assassin Books...................... 238
Ralph (A.) = Art Reference Books 123
Ramsden (G.) = Stone Trough Books 197
Raxter (C.) = Lion Books............................. 254
Ray (J.) = Avon Books................................ 60
Read (R.) = The Paperback Reader................ 101
Read (T.) = Home Farm Books 236
Reading (B. & J.) = Oast Books 134
Reding (Mrs. P.F.) = Croydon Bookshop......... 180
Reed (M.) = Sims Reed Limited 167
Rees (P. & D.) = Olio Books......................... 101
Reese (R.W.) = Holdenhurst Books................ 90

ALPHABETICAL INDEX: Proprietor (R – T)

Reiter (K.) = The Great Oak Bookshop 287
Reynold (A.L.) = Stage Door Prints 178
Rhead (J.) = Barnhill Books 272
Richards (D.) = Rugby Relics 284
Richardson (A.) = Afar Books International 238
Richardson (M.) = Books of Note, ... 64
Richmond (M.) = Ming Books 264
Richmond (M.) = AA1 Books 263
Ridgway (H.) = The Old Bookshop 216
Ridler (Dr. A.M.) = Nineteenth Century Books . 209
Rigby (N.) = Green Man Books 81
Riley (A. & J.) = Ryeland Books, ... 198
Ritchie (J.) = Books Afloat 95
Ritchie (P.) = Books 134
Robbins (P.J.) = Elmbury Books 237
Roberts (P.) = Nova Foresta Books 121
Robinson (C.) = The Amwell Book Company ... 152
Robinson (C.) = Books on the Bank 96
Robinson (J.) = Soccer Books Limited 146
Robinson–Brown (P.) = P.R. Brown (Books) 96
Roche (P.) = Pagoda Books, ... 267
Rockall (A.) = Kingswood Books 93
Rogers (D.) = Helion & Company 240
Rogers (P.J.) = Croydon Bookshop 180
Rogers (S.J.) = Chapter and Verse Booksellers... 102
Ronald (A.) = A. & R. Booksearch, ... 75
Ronan (J.) = Chthonios Books 100
Roper (D.) = Adab Books 64
Rose (M.J.) = K. Books 104
Ross (M.C.) = Avonworld Books 215
Rothwell (C.) = Rothwell & Dunworth 216
Routh (S.A.) = Gage Postal Books 109
Rowlinson (D.A.) = Books Ulster 260
Rulton (P.) = Rulton Books 212
Saddington (P.) = Hairpin Books, ... 113
St. Aubyn (H.M. & J.R.) = Woolcott Books 92
St. Clair Smallwood (S. & T.H.) = Smallwood
  Books 148
Salin (P.) = Sarah Key Books 65
Salt (D.T.) = Salsus Books 255
Sames (M.D.) = The Ryde Bookshop 131
Saunders (P. & E.) = Post–Horn Books 192
Scott (Dr. R.) = Quest Booksearch 65
Scott (T.) = Mount's Bay Books 75
Seddon (A.) = Browzers 117
Sedgwick (D.) = Moorside Books 141
Seers (P.R. & C.) = Greensleeves 204
Seton (M.) = Alba Books 267
Sever (T.P.) = Books 282
Seward (P.& G) = The Carnforth Bookshop 140
Sewell (J. & M.) = J & M Books 237
Shackleton (J.K.) = Bookstop Bookshop 193
Shakeshaft (B.L.) = Dr. B. Shakeshaft 72
Sharman (C.E.) = Books Only 226
Sharpe (A.&J.) = Grove Rare Books 195
Shaw (C. & D.) = Bridge Street Bookshop 200
Sheard (D.) = Heckmondwike Book Shop 235
Sheehan (A.) = Darkwood Books 276
Sheehan (M.) = Caissa Books 233
Sheffield (R.) = Roosterbooks 198
Shelley (A. & J.) = Bow Windows Book Shop ... 102
Shepherd (G. & A.) = Arundel Bookshop 241
Sheppard (R.D.) = Fireside Bookshop 80
Shepperd (H.) = Torc Books 190
Sheridan (P.J.) = Books Bought & Sold 231

Sherston–Baker (Sir R.) = Chaucer Bookshop ... 133
Shire (C.) = Theatreshire Books 192
Shouler (P.J.) = Dorset Rare Books 252
Showler (B. & K.) = B. and K. Books 285
Sidwell (R.) = Monmouth House Books 283
Simcock (T.) = The Bookshop Down The Lane . 204
Sims (T.J.) = Bookworms of Evesham 255
Simper (J.I. & S.J.) = Explorer Books 243
Simpson (I.) = Clent Books 254
Simpson (K.M.L.) = Black Five Books 213
Simpson O'Gara (J.P.) = Allhalland Books 83
Sims (G.A.M.) = A Book for All Reasons 227
Singleton (B.) = Bishopston Books 60
Slade (R.) = Restormel Books 256
Slater (K.C.) = Anderson Slater Antiques, ... 195
Slim (R.T.) = Janus Books & Antiques 239
Sloggett (T.) = Leabeck Books 208
Smith (Mr.) = Stanhope Bibliophiles, ... 155
Smith (A.) = Orlando Booksellers 148
Smith (E.) = Bookstand 93
Smith (G.E. & M.K.) = Book End 106
Smith (G.D.) = Great Grandfather's 141
Smith (I.) = Mike Park 183
Smith (M.) = Chelifer Books 79
Smith (M.E & W.A.) = Second Edition 270
Smith (P.M. & R.D.) = Rupert Books 65
Smith (R.) = Burntwood Bookshop 222
Smith (R.W.L.) = Sax Books 228
Somers (J.) = Fine Books Oriental Ltd. 177
Spark (M.S.) = Oval Books 193
Sparkes (J.) = Combat Arts Archive 96
Spence (H.) = BookLovers 217
Spencer (C.) = Lion Fine Arts and Books 287
Spranklins (G.) = Rowan House Books 231
Spurrier (R.) = Post Mortem Books 242
Squires (M.) = The Quarto Bookshop 265
Stallion (M.R.) = Lawful Occasions 106
Starling (R.) = Books Plus 87
Steadman (J.) = The Traveller's Bookshelf 215
Steenson (M.M.) = Books & Things 169
Stemp (I.) = Jade Mountain 123
Steven (G.B. & F.L.) = Batterdale Books 195
Stevens (E.) = Fortune Green Books 157
Stevens (F.) = Collectors Corner 252
Stevens (G.R.) = The Driffield Bookshop 104
Stevens Cox (A.) = The Old Curiosity Shop 257
Stevenson (K.) = Game Advice 207
Stevenson (P.A.) = Boris Books 94
Stewart (K.) = Petersham Books 166
Stinton (R.) = The Idle Booksellers 245
Stoddart (A.) = Hellenic Bookservices 158
Stones (L. A.) = The Bookshelf 194
Stringer (F.) = Jericho Books 208
Strong (E.A.) = McNaughtan's Bookshop 269
Stroud (F.P.A.) = Chaters Motoring Booksellers .. 182
Stuart (E.) = First State Books 172
Suchar (V. & E.) = Camden Books 214
Summers (A. & M.) = The Helston Bookworm .. 74
Sutcliffe (E.) = Pendleside Books 141
Sutherland (S.) = Allhalland Books 83
Suttie (D.S.) = Bowland Bookfinders 140
Sutton (M.) = The Old Celtic Bookshop 86
Swain (A. & C.) = Periwinkle Press 134
Swain (A.) = Faversham Antiques Centre 135
Swindall (J. & R.) = Jiri Books 259

Tait (M.) = Leaf Ends, ... 201
Tall (J. & N.) = Badger Books 218
Tandree (H.) = Rachel Lee Rare Books 61
Tandree (H. & A.) = Anthroposophical Books... 60
Tasker (J.C.) = Ashburton Books 83
Tate (P.) = Satara Books................................ 244
Tatman (C.) = Beverley Old Bookshop............ 104
Taylor (J. & J.) = The Bookshelf 140
Taylor (P.H.) = Farnborough Bookshop
 & Gallery... 121
Taylor (P. & S.) = Greyfriars Books 107
Tebay (K.M.) = Red Rose Books 141
Thatcher (K.) = Foyle Books......................... 260
Thompson (L.) = Portobello Books 174
Thompson (J.) = Saltburn Bookshop 194
Thompson (M. & A.C.) = The Bookshop......... 191
Thomson (G.) = Greta Books........................ 96
Thornhill (J. & M.) = Candle Lane Books........ 213
Thorp (J.D., H.N. & J.H.) = Thomas Thorp 129
Thredder (P.) = Ross Old Books & Prints 127
Tierney (M.) = Wheen O'Books,.................... 261
Tilley (A. & A.) = Tilleys Vintage
 Magazine Shop.. 81
Timothy (D.) = Siop y Morfa 282
Timson (L.) = Humanist Book Services 73
Tindley (J.) = Tindley & Chapman.................. 178
Tobin (D.) = Walden Books.......................... 159
Todd (J.) = Books (For All).......................... 192
Tollerton (J.) = Stacks Bookshop.................... 259
Tomaszewski (C.) = Stella Books 284
Tomlinson (R.K.) = Aviation Book Supply....... 128
Tootell (J.) = Exedra Booksearch Ltd.............. 164
Towns (J.M.) = Dylans Bookstore 289
Townsend–Cardew (J. & B.) = Daisy
 Lane Books 246
Tranter (P.) = Orangeberry Books.................. 206
Traylen (N. & T.) = Ventnor Rare Books......... 132
Treece (M.) = Cornerstone Books 87
Trevitt (J.) = The Weobley Bookshop 127
Trinder (R.) = Trinders' Fine Tools................ 225
Tsunematsu (S.I.) = Japan Books (Y & S
 Company Ltd.).. 180
Tulloch (B & J.) = Abbey Books 187
Turnbull (P.M.) = The Countryman's Gallery.... 143
Turner (B.&G.) = Crime Inc.,...................... 118
Turner (J. & K.) = Wyche Books................... 263
Turner (L.M.) = Bath Book Exchange............. 214
Twitchett (D.E.) = Engaging Gear Ltd............ 106
Tyers (N.A.M., M.G.D. & P.A.) = St. Mary's
 Books & Prints 150
Tynan (P.) = Courtwood Books 278
Tyson (G.) = High Street Books 85
Tyson (L.) = Paper Pleasures........................ 217
Unny (L.) = Broadleaf Books 290
Unsworth (C.) = Unsworths Booksellers Ltd. 178, 209
Unwin (D.) = Eastleach Books...................... 58
Valentine Ketchum (V.A. & B.J.) = Staniland
 (Booksellers)... 150
Valiadis (M. & A.M.) = Anticus.................... 237
Vallely (J.) = Craobh Rua Books 259
Veysey (P.) = www.drivepast.com 114
Wagstaff (A.) = Booksmart 198
Wakeman (P. & F.) = Frances Wakeman Books 202
Wakerley (J. & S.) = Bury Bookshop 225
Waldron (C.) = Bookends............................ 121

Walker (D.) = Chelifer Books....................... 79
Walker (R.) = Fine Art................................ 242
Wallace (N.) = Minster Gate Bookshop.......... 196
Wallbaum (C.) = H. Baron 157
Walsh (J.) = Cahir Cosy Corner Bookshop....... 279
Walsh (M.) = Glenbower Books 277
Walters (H. & G.) = Court Hay Books........... 60
Walters (M.) = Kingfisher Book Service........... 203
Walton (D.W.H. & S.) = Bluntisham Books...... 64
Warwick (D.C.) = The Nautical Antique Centre .. 95
Warwick (N.) = Readers Rest...................... 148
Watson (D.) = Linton Books........................ 262
Watson (J.S.) = John Updike Rare Books 270
Watson (T.) = Church Street Bookshop.......... 153
Watts (N.) = Beaver Booksearch 225
Watts (R.) = Dolphin Books 224
Way (D.) = Diver's & Watersportsman's Library . 86
Way (R.) = Richard Way Booksellers 206
Wayne (J.) = Nicholas Willmott Bookseller....... 280
Wayte (B.) = Deeside Books........................ 266
Weaver (C.A.) = Transformer...................... 264
Weir (D. & J.L.) = Yesterday's Books 91
Weissman (S.) = Ximenes Rare Books Inc. 112
Welford (R.G.M.& M.E.) = Oasis Booksearch... 68
Wesley (P.) = Harlequin.............................. 89
Westall (S.F.J.) = Island Books 86
Weston (J.) = Westons Booksellers Ltd............ 130
West–Skinn (R.) = Golden Goose Books 148
Westwood (F.) = The Petersfield Bookshop..... 122
Whatmore (G.) = Wigley Books 255
Wheeler (M.A.) = W.H. Collectables.............. 172
Wheeler (S.) = Knockhundred Bookshop 243
Whetman (M.) = Isabelline Books.................. 74
Whitaker (J. & M.A.) = Peregrine
 Books (Leeds) 247
Whitaker (S.M.) = Words & Music 70
White (M.J.) = Fun in Books 233
Whitehead (R.) = Arcadia 212
Whitehorn (J.) = Heartland Old Books 88
Whittington (J. & C.) = The Golden Hind
 Bookshop 134
Whitwell (A.L.) = Wolds Book Services.......... 144
Wiberg (C.) = The Book Depot.................... 157
Wicks (J.) = Just Books 76
Wilkes (A.) = Mair Wilkes Books 265
Wilkinson (D. & T.) = The Book Gallery......... 76
Wilkinson (D. & J.) = Autolycus 211
Wilkinson (D.J.) = Intech Books 201
Wilkinson (I.) = The Military Collector 249
Wilkinson (J.B.) = Leeds Bookseller 247
Williams (C. & C.) = Aardvark Books............ 252
Williams (J.) = Bookworm Alley................... 87
Williams (J. & J.) = Octagon Books................ 66
Williams (M.) = Hellenic Bookservices 158
Willmott (N.) = Nicholas Willmott Bookseller ... 280
Wills (T.) = Volumes of Motoring................. 111
Wills (Mrs. V.) = Bridge of Allan Books.......... 262
Wilson (J.) = Halcyon Bookshop 242
Wilson (J.) = John Wilson (Autographs) Ltd..... 112
Wilson (P.D.) = Oriental and African Books 213
Wilson (R.) = The Old Town Bookshop 270
Wilson (R.) = Classic Crime Collections........... 117
Wilyman (G. & J.) = Heritage...................... 238
Winston–Smith (M. & S.) = Dead Mens
 Minds.co.uk... 285

ALPHABETICAL INDEX: Proprietor (W – Z)

Winter (Mrs.J.) = Sedgeberrow Books & Framing 255
Wise (C.) = Atlantis Bookshop 176
Wolff (C.) = Grey House Books 234
Woodell (Dr. S.R.J.) = Bernwode Books 62
Woolley (P. & K.) = Black Cat Bookshop 143
Worms (L.) = Ash Rare Books 152
Worthy (J.S. & S.) = Rochdale Book Company 118
Wratten (M.) = The Woodstock Bookshop 210
Wren (C.) = Annie's Books 220
Wright (C.) = Yarborough House Bookshop 211
Wright (M. & S.) = Roadmaster Books 134
Wyborn (J.) = Chatterton's Books 290
Yablon (G.A.) = Ian Hodgkins and Company Limited 114
Young (I. & S.) = Autumn Leaves 148
Young (R.) = Charmouth Bookstore 91
Zealley (C.J.) = St. Philip's Books 208
Zentner (F.) = The Cinema Bookshop 176

SPECIALITY INDEX

Index of dealers with their speciality subjects

ACADEMIC/SCHOLARLY

Abbey Books, Norfolk................................ 187
Ainslie Books, Scotland 271
Allport (Roy), North Yorkshire................... 195
Alpha Books, London, North 153
Ancient & Modern Bookshop, Dorset 90
Annesley Books of Scottish Interest (Brian), Scotland 272
Antiquary Ltd., (Bar Bookstore), N Yorks 194
Archer (David), Wales 288
Avonbridge Books, Gloucestershire 114
Bell (Peter), Scotland................................. 269
Beware of The Leopard Books, Bristol 60
Biddulph (Joseph), Wales 289
Blanchfield (John), West Yorkshire.............. 247
Boer (Louise), Arthurian Books, Wales.......... 284
Bolland Books (Leslie H.), Bedfordshire......... 55
Book Barrow, Cambridgeshire 64
Book Basket, London, Outer 182
Bookroom (The), Surrey 233
BOOKS4U, Wales...................................... 282
Bookshop (The), Cambridgeshire 64
Bookstop UK, Lancashire 142
Bookwyze, Lincolnshire 147
Bowen (Janice), Wales 286
Bridge of Allan Books, Scotland 262
Brighton Books, East Sussex 98
Burak (Steve), London, West Central 176
Burden Ltd., (Clive A.), Hertfordshire 129
Burgess Booksellers, (J. & J.), Cambridgeshire .. 64
Bush, Bookdealer (John), Gloucestershire 115
Camden Books, Somerset 214
Capes (Books, Maps & Prints) (John L.), N Yorks 195
Carta Regis, Wales 288
Castle Frome Books, Herefordshire 127
Cathach Books Ltd., Republic Of Ireland....... 277
Celtic Bookshop (The), Republic Of Ireland ... 279
Chesters (G. & J.), Staffordshire 223
Church Street Bookshop, London, North 153
Clifton Books, Essex 110
Courtwood Books, Republic Of Ireland 278
Crispin's Day, Antiquarian and Out of Print Military Books, Essex 110
Crouch Rare Books, Surrey........................ 232
Cyclamen Books, Leicestershire 143
Dead Zone Books, Wales 289
Desmond (Arnold), Somerset 217
Dorset Rare Books, Wiltshire 252
Downie Fine Books Ltd., (Robert), Shropshire... 213
Eastern Books of London, London (SW) 163
Eastleach Books, Berkshire 58
English (Toby), Oxfordshire 209
Fin Rare Books, Shropshire 213
Fireside Bookshop, Cumbria 80
Fortune Green Books, London (NW)........... 157
Foster Bookshop (Paul), London (SW)......... 164
Foyle Books, Northern Ireland.................... 260
G C Books, Scotland................................. 264
Galloway & Porter Limited, Cambridgeshire 65
Game Advice, Oxfordshire......................... 207
Glenbower Books, Republic Of Ireland.......... 277
Grampian Books, Scotland 265
Greyfriars Books, Essex 107
Handsworth Books, Essex.......................... 110
Harwich Old Books, Essex......................... 108
Havercroft Antiquarian Books, London (SE).... 161
Hawkes (James), Gloucestershire................. 111
Helion & Company, West Midlands 240
Hellenic Bookservices, London (NW).......... 158
Herb Tandree Philosophy Books, Bristol........ 61
Hornsby, Antiquarian and Secondhand Books (Malcolm), Leicestershire...................... 144
Howes Bookshop, East Sussex 101
Hunter, Bookseller, (K.P.), Cambridgeshire...... 65
Ice House Books...................................... 143
Innes Books, Shropshire............................ 212
Invisible Books, East Sussex 99
Island Books, Devon.................................. 84
Jackdaw Books, Norfolk 189
Jericho Books, Oxfordshire 208
Joppa Books Ltd., Surrey 230
Kelly Books, Devon................................... 88
Key Books (Sarah), Cambridgeshire............... 65
Lee Rare Books (Rachel), Bristol 61
Leeds Bookseller, West Yorkshire 247
Lewcock (John), Cambridgeshire 67
Lewis (J.T. & P.), Cornwall......................... 74
Lloyd (D. Ieuan), Wales............................. 289
Loman, Oriental Books & Manuscripts (David), London (SW) 165
Lowe (John), Norfolk 189
Mair Wilkes Books, Scotland...................... 265
Malvern Bookshop (The), Worcestershire 254
McEwan Fine Books, Scotland.................... 266
Menavaur Books, Scotland......................... 264
Morgan (H.J.), Bedfordshire....................... 56
musebookshop, Wales 283
Northern Herald Books, West Yorkshire......... 245
Oblong Books, N Yorks............................ 197
O'Donoghue Books, London (SW).............. 165
Oriental and African Books, Shropshire.......... 213
Ouse Valley Books, Bedfordshire 56
Outcast Books, Wales 287
Parker Books (Mike), Cambridgeshire 65
Peakirk Books, Cambridgeshire 68
Phillips (Chris), Wiltshire............................ 250
Plurabelle Books, Cambridgeshire 65
Pollak (P.M.), Devon 87
Poole (William), London, West 174
Porter Bookshop (The), South Yorkshire......... 220
Quest Books, East Yorkshire 105
Reading Lasses, Scotland........................... 264
Red Star Books, Hertfordshire 128
Riley–Smith (Hamish), Norfolk 190
Riverside Bookshop (The), Cumbria 78

Rosley Books, Cumbria 79
Roundstone Books, Lancashire 141
St Mary's Books & Prints, Lincolnshire 150
St Philip's Books, Oxfordshire...................... 208
Saunders (Tom), Wales 280
Savery Books, East Sussex 99
Scrivener's Books & Book Binding, Derbyshire ... 81
Shapero Rare Books (Bernard J.), London (W). 174
Smallwood Books, Lincolnshire.................... 148
South Downs Book Service, West Sussex......... 243
Spelman (Ken), N Yorks............................... 197
Spenceley Books (David), West Yorkshire 248
Stacks Bookshop, Northern Ireland 259
Staniland (Booksellers), Lincolnshire.............. 150
Starlord Books, Cheshire............................. 70
Strauss (David), Lincolnshire........................ 147
Studio Bookshop, East Sussex........................ 99
Sue Lowell Natural History Books, London (W). 175
Swan Bookshop (The), Devon........................ 84
Symes Books (Naomi), Cheshire 72
Taylor & Son (Peter), Hertfordshire............... 130
Temple (Robert), London, North................... 155
Thomson (Karen), Scotland 271
Tiffin (Tony and Gill), Durham..................... 96
Till's Bookshop, Scotland 270
Transformer, Scotland 264
Unsworths Booksellers Ltd., London (WC)...... 178
Unsworths Booksellers Ltd., Oxfordshire......... 209
Venables (Morris & Juliet), Bristol 61
Ventnor Rare Books, Isle of Wight................. 132
Victoria Bookshop (The), Devon 83
Vinovium Books, Durham 96
Warrington Book Loft (The), Cheshire 72
Waterfield's, Oxfordshire............................ 209
Waterstone's, London (WC)......................... 179
Wayside Books and Cards, Oxfordshire 206
Woburn Books, London, North..................... 156
Woodstock Bookshop (The), Oxfordshire 210
Worcester Rare Books, Worcestershire 256
Yates (R.A.), Dorset 92

ADVERTISING

Ainslie Books, Scotland 271
Bolland Books (Leslie H.), Bedfordshire.......... 55
Book Barrow, Cambridgeshire 64
Bookroom (The), Surrey 233
Books & Things, London (W)...................... 169
Bookstop UK, Lancashire 142
Bookwyze, Lincolnshire 147
Courtwood Books, Republic Of Ireland 278
Cyclamen Books, Leicestershire 143
Dead Zone Books, Wales 289
Foyle Books, Northern Ireland..................... 260
Franks Booksellers, Greater Manchester 117
Kelly Books, Devon.................................... 88
Malvern Bookshop (The), Worcestershire 254
Menavaur Books, Scotland 264
Parker Books (Mike), Cambridgeshire 65
Prior (Michael), Lincolnshire....................... 149
Riverside Bookshop (The), Cumbria 78
Shipley Specialist Art Booksellers, London (WC). 178
Spread Eagle Bookshop, London (SE)............ 162
Stride & Son, West Sussex 242
Worcester Rare Books, Worcestershire 256

AERONAUTICS

Ainslie Books, Scotland 271
Anchor Books, Lincolnshire 149
Andron (G.W.), London, North 153
Arundel Bookshop, West Sussex.................... 241
Barbican Bookshop, N Yorks 196
Book Barrow, Cambridgeshire 64
Bookroom (The), Surrey 233
Books Bought & Sold, Surrey 231
Bookstop UK, Lancashire 142
Corfe Books, Surrey................................... 231
Dead Zone Books, Wales 289
Duck (William), East Sussex 98
Island Books, Devon................................... 84
Kelly Books, Devon.................................... 88
Key Books (Sarah), Cambridgeshire................ 65
Military Collector (The), West Yorkshire 249
Phelps (Michael), West Sussex...................... 242
Photographery at Soldridge Books, Hampshire . 120
Prior (Michael), Lincolnshire....................... 149
Thin Read Line, Merseyside 186
YSF Books, South Yorkshire........................ 221

AFRICANA

Ainslie Books, Scotland 271
Allsworth Rare Books Ltd., London (SW)....... 163
Armchair Books, Scotland 268
Book Barrow, Cambridgeshire 64
Book Basket, London, Outer 182
Cyclamen Books, Leicestershire 143
Daly (Peter M.), Hampshire 124
Graves–Johnston (Michael), London (SW)...... 164
Hennessey Bookseller (Ray), East Sussex 100
Oriental and African Books, Shropshire.......... 213
Sawyer (Chas. J.), Kent............................... 137
Shapero Rare Books (Bernard J.), London (W). 174
Woburn Books, London, North..................... 156

AGRICULTURE

Barn Books, Shropshire 213
Blest (Peter), Kent..................................... 136
Book Barrow, Cambridgeshire 64
Bookroom (The), Surrey 233
Books for Content, Herefordshire 126
Booth Books, Wales................................... 286
Burmester (James), Bristol 60
Carta Regis, Wales 288
Clifton Books, Essex.................................. 110
Cottage Books, Leicestershire 143
Daly (Peter M.), Hampshire 124
Farquharson, (Hilary), Scotland 273
Ferdinando (Steven), Somerset 217
Guildmaster Books, Cheshire....................... 71
Island Books, Devon................................... 84
Muttonchop Manuscripts, West Sussex........... 243
Phenotype Books, Cumbria 79
Stone, (G.& R.), Scotland........................... 261
Thornber (Peter A.), N Yorks....................... 195

ALCHEMY

Alpha Books, London, North 153
Caduceus Books, Leicestershire 143

SPECIALITY INDEX

Chthonios Books, East Sussex..................... 100
Gilbert (R.A.), Bristol............................... 61
IKON, Devon... 88
Inner Bookshop (The), Oxfordshire 207
Magis Books, Leicestershire....................... 144
Military Collector (The), West Yorkshire 249
Occultique, Northamptonshire 198
Phelps (Michael), West Sussex..................... 242
Quaritch Ltd., (Bernard), London (W)............ 174
Shapero Rare Books (Bernard J.), London (W). 174

ALMANACS

Beighton (Brian), Norfolk........................... 187
Book Basket, London, Outer 182
St Mary's Books & Prints, Lincolnshire 150

ALPINISM/MOUNTAINEERING

All Seasons Books, Cumbria........................ 79
Alpes Livres (Les), Hampshire 120
Ancient & Modern Bookshop, Dorset 90
Askew Books (Vernon), Wiltshire.................. 250
Barnhill Books, Scotland 272
Bonham (J. & S.L.), London (W).................. 169
Book Basket, London, Outer 182
Books, Wales... 282
Bookworld, Shropshire 212
Bosco Books, Cornwall.............................. 73
Bridge of Allan Books, Scotland................... 262
Carnforth Bookshop (The), Lancashire........... 140
Carta Regis, Wales 288
Collectables (W.H.), London (W).................. 172
Coracle Books, West Yorkshire.................... 247
Daly (Peter M.), Hampshire 124
Dartmoor Bookshop (The), Devon................ 83
Eastcote Bookshop (The), London, Outer........ 183
Eastleach Books, Berkshire 58
Fireside Bookshop, Cumbria 80
Glacier Books, Scotland 273
Hill (Peter), Hampshire............................. 121
Hollett and Son (R.F.G.), Cumbria 79
Holmes Books (Harry), East Yorkshire........... 105
Hornsey's, N Yorks 194
Hunter and Krageloh, Derbyshire 82
Jarvis Books (incorporating 'Gaston's Alpine
  Books'), Derbyshire 82
Keel Row Books, Tyne & Wear.................... 235
Main Point Books, Scotland....................... 269
Mother Goose Bookshop, Isle of Wight 131
Mountaineering Books, London, North 154
musebookshop, Wales 283
Page (David), Scotland 270
Post–Horn Books, N Yorks 192
Rhoda (June), Essex................................. 108
Riddell (Peter), East Yorkshire..................... 104
Riverside Bookshop (The), Cumbria 78
Scarthin Books, Derbyshire........................ 82
Shapero Rare Books (Bernard J.), London (W). 174
Spranger (Anthony), Wiltshire..................... 251
Sue Lowell Natural History Books, London (W) 175
Swan Bookshop (The), Devon...................... 84
Vandeleur Antiquarian Books, Surrey 231
Woodstock Bookshop (The), Oxfordshire 210
Yewtree Books, Cumbria............................ 78

YSF Books, South Yorkshire....................... 221

ALTERNATIVE MEDICINE

Alba Books, Scotland................................ 267
Book Basket, London, Outer 182
Dawlish Books, Devon 84
Greensleeves, Oxfordshire.......................... 204
Grieveson (A.), Cheshire 69
Inner Bookshop (The), Oxfordshire 207
Occultique, Northamptonshire 198
Outcast Books, Wales............................... 287
Roundstone Books, Lancashire 141
Starlord Books, Cheshire........................... 70

AMERICAN INDIANS

Americanabooksuk, Cumbria....................... 77
Book Barrow, Cambridgeshire 64
Book Basket, London, Outer 182
Books, Wales... 282
Booth Books, Wales................................. 286
Bracton Books, Cambridgeshire................... 64
Chelifer Books, Cumbria 79
Dancing Goat Bookshop (The), Norfolk 188
Eastcote Bookshop (The), London, Outer........ 183
Emjay Books, Surrey................................ 231
Inner Bookshop (The), Oxfordshire 207
Military Collector (The), West Yorkshire 249
Occultique, Northamptonshire 198
Scarthin Books, Derbyshire........................ 82
Shapero Rare Books (Bernard J.), London (W) .. 174
Sue Lowell Natural History Books, London (W). 175

AMERICANA

Americanabooksuk, Cumbria....................... 77
Anglo-American Rare Books, Surrey.............. 232
Book Basket, London, Outer 182
Dancing Goat Bookshop (The), Norfolk 188
J.K. Bookfinders, London (SW).................... 165
Kenny's Bookshops and Art Galleries Ltd,
  Republic Of Ireland 278
Preston Book Company, Lancashire 142
Shakeshaft (Dr. B.), Cheshire...................... 72
Shakeshaft (Roger & Sylvia), Lincolnshire 146
Shapero Rare Books (Bernard J.), London (W). 174

ANIMALS AND BIRDS

Anderson Slater Antiques, N Yorks............... 195
Annie's Books, South Yorkshire 220
Austwick Hall Books, N Yorks 141
Blest (Peter), Kent................................... 136
Book Corner, Scotland 263
Books & Bygones, Berkshire....................... 58
Buchan Collectibles, Scotland 265
Burgess Booksellers, (J. & J.), Cambridgeshire .. 64
Carta Regis, Wales 288
Castleton (Pat), Kent................................ 135
Catalyst Books, Surrey.............................. 232
Coch-y-Bonddu Books, Wales..................... 288
Collectables (W.H.), London (W).................. 172
Corfe Books, Surrey................................. 231
Crack (Books) (F.N.), Lancashire 140

SPECIALITY INDEX

Daly (Peter M.), Hampshire 124
Demar Books (Grant), Kent 138
Eastleach Books, Berkshire 58
Gate Memorabilia, London, North 153
Goodyer (Nicholas), London, North 154
Ice House Books 143
Island Books, Devon 84
Jackdaw Books, Norfolk 189
Jade Mountain, Hampshire 123
Lewcock (John), Cambridgeshire 67
Liebreich Antique Maps & Prints (Kitty),
  London (W) 173
Mayhew (Veronica), Berkshire 58
McCrone (Audrey), Scotland 272
On the Wild Side, Worcestershire 255
Phenotype Books, Cumbria 79
Popeley (Frank T.), Cambridgeshire 68
R. & A. Books, East Sussex 100
Scarthin Books, Derbyshire 82
Scrivener's Books & Book Binding, Derbyshire . 81
Shapero Rare Books (Bernard J.),
  London (W) 174
Shearwater Bed & Books (formerly John
  Lumby Nat. History Bks), Northumberland ... 200
Spread Eagle Bookshop, London (SE) 162
Stacks Bookshop, Northern Ireland 259
Sue Lowell Natural History Books, London (W) 175
Treasure Island (The), Greater Manchester 118
Way (R.E. & G.B.), Suffolk 227
Wolds Book Services, Leicestershire 144
Wright Trace Books, West Midlands 239

ANNUALS

Armchair Books, Scotland 268
Book Basket, London, Outer 182
BOOKS4U, Wales 282
Buchan Collectibles, Scotland 265
Catalyst Books, Surrey 232
Eastcote Bookshop (The), London, Outer 183
Family Favourites (Books), East Yorkshire 104
Gate Memorabilia, London, North 153
Jade Mountain, Hampshire 123
Katnap Arts, Norfolk 189
Key Books (Sarah), Cambridgeshire 65
Kineton Nooks, Warwickshire 236
Peakirk Books, Cambridgeshire 68
Shacklock Books (David), Suffolk 226
Wright Trace Books, West Midlands 239

ANTHOLOGIES

Addyman Books, Wales 285
Book Basket, London, Outer 182
Cowley, Bookdealer (K.W.), Somerset 215
Eggeling Books (John), West Yorkshire 248
McCrone (Audrey), Scotland 272
Shacklock Books (David), Suffolk 226
Temple (Robert), London, North 155

ANTHROPOLOGY

Afar Books International, West Midlands 238
Austwick Hall Books, N Yorks 141
Book Basket, London, Outer 182

Bowen (Janice), Wales 286
Bracton Books, Cambridgeshire 64
Chalmers Hallam (E.), Hampshire 123
Chesters (G. & J.), Staffordshire 223
Delectus Books, London (WC) 176
Game Advice, Oxfordshire 207
Graves–Johnston (Michael), London (SW) 164
Ice House Books 143
Kenny's Bookshops and Art Galleries Ltd,
  Republic Of Ireland 278
Polczynski (Udo K.H.), London, Outer 183
Rhodes, Bookseller (Peter), Hampshire 124
Sanderson (Edward), Berkshire 58
Shapero Rare Books (Bernard J.), London (W) . 174
Stride & Son, West Sussex 242
Unsworths Booksellers Ltd., London (WC) 178
Whitchurch Books Ltd., Wales 280
Woburn Books, London, North 156
Wolds Book Services, Leicestershire 144
Yesterday's Books, Dorset 91

ANTHROPOSOPHY

Anthroposophical Books, Bristol 60
Bridge of Allan Books, Scotland 262
Greensleeves, Oxfordshire 204
Inner Bookshop (The), Oxfordshire 207
Moray Bookshop (The), Scotland 267

ANTIQUARIAN

Addyman Books, Wales 285
Alastor Books, Hampshire 122
Allsop (Duncan M.), Warwickshire 237
Ancient & Modern Bookshop, Dorset 90
Arcadia, Shropshire 212
Archive Books & Music, London (NW) 157
Arnold (Roy), Suffolk 226
Art Reference Books, Hampshire 123
Atholl Fine Books, Scotland 273
Atticus Books, Essex 109
Autolycus, Shropshire 211
Avonbridge Books, Gloucestershire 114
Bardsley's Books, Suffolk 225
Barmby (C. & A.J.), Kent 138
Bates & Hindmarch, West Yorkshire 247
Baxter (Steve), Surrey 232
Beardsell Books, West Yorkshire 246
Beck Head Books, Cumbria 78
Beckham Books, Suffolk 228
Bell (Peter), Scotland 269
Bertram Rota Ltd., London (WC) 176
Biblion, London (W) 169
Book Basket, London, Outer 182
Booklore, Leicestershire 144
Books on Spain, London, Outer 183
BOOKS4U, Wales 282
Bookshop (The), Republic Of Ireland 276
Bookshop, Kirkstall (The), West Yorkshire 247
Bookwyze, Lincolnshire 147
Booth Books, Wales 286
Bow Windows Book Shop, East Sussex 102
Bridge of Allan Books, Scotland 262
Brinded (Scott), Kent 136
Brockwells Bookshop, London (SE) 160

SPECIALITY INDEX

Burak (Steve), London (WC) 176
Bush, Bookdealer (John), Gloucestershire 115
Capes (Books, Maps & Prints) (John L.),
    N Yorks 195
Capital Bookshop, Wales 280
Cecil Books, Surrey 231
Celtic Bookshop (The), Republic Of Ireland 279
Chantry Bookshop & Gallery, Devon 84
Chapter & Verse, Lincolnshire 148
Chapter and Verse Booksellers, East Sussex 102
Chaucer Bookshop (The), Kent 133
Chelifer Books, Cumbria 79
Cherry (Janet), Dorset 92
Clent Books, Worcestershire 254
Cobnar Books, Kent 136
Cobweb Books, N Yorks 194
Collectable Books, London (SE) 160
Collectables (W.H.), London (W) 172
Cook (R.L.), Norfolk 190
Cox Old & Rare Books (Claude), Suffolk 226
Cox Rare Books (Charles), Cornwall 74
Craobh Rua Books, Northern Ireland 259
Crispin's Day, Antiquarian and Out of
    Print Military Books, Essex 110
Crouch Rare Books, Surrey 232
Dartmoor Bookshop (The), Devon 83
David (G.), Cambridgeshire 64
Davies Fine Books, Worcestershire 256
Dead Mens Minds.co.uk, Wales 285
Dean Byass, Tavistock Books, Devon 86
Dodd Books (Maurice), Cumbria 77
Dorset Rare Books, Wiltshire 252
DoublePlusBooks, Cambridgeshire 68
Doughty Fine Books (Robin), West Midlands ... 238
Drury Rare Books (John), Essex 109
Dylans Bookstore, Wales 289
Eastleach Books, Berkshire 58
Eaton (Booksellers) Limited (Peter),
    Buckinghamshire 62
ECR Books, Dorset 93
Eggle (Mavis), Hertfordshire 128
Emerald Isle Books, Northern Ireland 259
Europa Books, London (SW) 163
Farahar & Dupré (Clive & Sophie),
    Wiltshire 250
Farquharson, (Hilary), Scotland 273
Farringdon (J.M.), Wales 289
Fenning (James), Republic Of Ireland 277
Fine Art, West Sussex 242
Fine Irish Books, Republic Of Ireland 276
Fireside Bookshop, Cumbria 80
Flora Books, London (E) 151
Foster (Stephen), London (NW) 157
Foster Bookshop (Paul), London (SW) 164
Fotheringham (Alex), Northumberland 200
Fox Books (J. & J.), Kent 137
Frew Limited (Robert), London (WC) 177
Gilbert and Son (H.M.), Hampshire 124
Glenbower Books, Republic Of Ireland 277
Goodyer, Natural History Books (Eric),
    Leicestershire 144
Grant Books, Worcestershire 254
Gresham Books, Somerset 216
Guildmaster Books, Cheshire 71
Hanborough Books, Oxfordshire 207

Hancock (Colin), Wales 281
Harrington (Adrian), London (W) 173
Harrington Antiquarian Bookseller (Peter),
    London (SW) 164
Hatchwell (Richard), Wiltshire 251
Havercroft Antiquarian Books, London (SE) 161
Helston Bookworm (The), Cornwall 74
Hennessey Bookseller (Ray), East Sussex 100
Heritage, West Midlands 238
Hodgson (Judith), London (W) 173
Hollett and Son (R.F.G.), Cumbria 79
Holtom (Christopher), Cornwall 76
Honiton Old Bookshop, Devon 85
Hornsby, Antiquarian and Secondhand Books
    (Malcolm), Leicestershire 144
Horsham Bookshop (The), West Sussex 242
Howes Bookshop, East Sussex 101
Humber Books, Lincolnshire 146
Hutchison (Books) (Larry), Scotland 265
Ian Johnson Natural History Books,
    Buckinghamshire 63
Island Books, Devon 84
J.C. Poole Books, Wales 290
Jackdaw Books, Norfolk 189
Jackson (M.W.), Wiltshire 253
Jarndyce Antiquarian Booksellers,
    London (WC) 177
Jericho Books, Oxfordshire 208
Jiri Books, Northern Ireland 259
Joppa Books Ltd., Surrey 230
K. Books, East Yorkshire 104
Kirkman Ltd., (Robert), Bedfordshire 55
Lake (David), Norfolk 189
Lawson & Company (E.M.), Oxfordshire 205
Liebreich Antique Maps & Prints (Kitty),
    London (W) 173
Lion Fine Arts and Books, Wales 287
Lloyd (D. Ieuan), Wales 289
Loman, Oriental Books & Manuscripts (David),
    London (SW) 165
Marine and Cannon Books, Cheshire 70
McConnell Fine Books, Kent 135
McCrone (Audrey), Scotland 272
McKay Rare Books (Barry), Cumbria 77
McNaughtan's Bookshop, Scotland 269
Mead (P.J.), Shropshire 212
Miller (Stephen), London, Outer 184
Moreton Books, Devon 86
Morris (Michael), Staffordshire 222
Museum Bookshop, London (WC) 177
Muttonchop Manuscripts, West Sussex 243
Newby (Valerie), Buckinghamshire 63
Norton Books, Durham 97
Oblong Books, N Yorks 197
Offa's Dyke Books, Shropshire 212
Old Town Bookshop (The), Scotland 270
Paralos Ltd., London (W) 173
Park Gallery & Bookshop (The),
    Northamptonshire 199
Penn Barn Bookshop, Buckinghamshire 63
Phillips (Chris), Wiltshire 250
Phillips (Nigel), London (SW) 166
Philologus–Fine & Rare Books, London (SW) .. 166
Price (John), London, North 155
Pringle Booksellers (Andrew), Scotland 270

SPECIALITY INDEX

Prospect House Books, Northern Ireland 260
Quaritch Ltd., (Bernard), London (W) 174
Rhos Point Books, Wales 281
Riccetti (Margaret), South Yorkshire 220
Riley–Smith (Hamish), Norfolk 190
Robertshaw (John), Cambridgeshire 67
Rogoyski (Old and Rare Books) (Alexander), Lincolnshire 149
Rosley Books, Cumbria 79
Rowan (H. & S.J.), Dorset 91
St Philip's Books, Oxfordshire 208
Sanderson (Edward), Berkshire 58
Scarthin Books, Derbyshire 82
Schulz–Falster Rare Books (Susanne), London (N) 155
Scrivener's Books & Book Binding, Derbyshire . 81
Shapero Rare Books (Bernard J.), London (W) . 174
Sidey, Bookdealer (Philip), Kent 137
Simpson (Dave), Scotland 262
Slavin Rare and Collectable Books (Derek), Warwickshire 237
Smallwood Books, Lincolnshire 148
Smith (Clive), Essex 108
Sokol Books (A.), London (W) 174
South Downs Book Service, West Sussex 243
Spelman (Ken), N Yorks 197
Spooner & Co., Somerset 217
Spread Eagle Bookshop, London (SE) 162
Stacks Bookshop, Northern Ireland 259
Sterling Books, Somerset 219
Stone, (G.& R.), Scotland 261
Stothert Old Books, Cheshire 69
Stride & Son, West Sussex 242
Summersgill (Neil), Lancashire 140
Taylor & Son (Peter), Hertfordshire 130
Temple (Robert), London (N) 155
Thomas (Books) (Leona), Cheshire 71
Thomas Rare Books, Suffolk 226
Thomson (Karen), Scotland 271
Thornber (Peter A.), N Yorks 195
Thorp (Thomas), Hertfordshire 129
Tiger Books, Kent 134
Tobo Books, Hampshire 122
Tower Bridge Books, London (SE) 162
Treglown (Roger J.), Cheshire 71
Turton (John), Durham 97
Unsworths Booksellers Ltd., London (WC) 178
Unsworths Booksellers Ltd., Oxfordshire 209
Vandeleur Antiquarian Books, Surrey 231
Venables (Morris & Juliet), Bristol 61
Ventnor Rare Books, Isle of Wight 132
Waterfield's, Oxfordshire 209
Wayfarer Books, Cornwall 75
Westcountry Old Books, Devon 88
WestField Books, N Yorks 197
Westwood Books (Mark), Wales 287
Wilbraham (J. & S.), London (NW) 159
Woburn Books, London (N) 156
Wolds Book Services, Leicestershire 144
Worcester Rare Books, Worcestershire 256
Ximenes Rare Books Inc., Gloucestershire 112
Yates Antiquarian Books (Tony), Leicestershire 144

ANTIQUES

Abrahams (Mike), Staffordshire 222

Anderson Slater Antiques, N Yorks 195
Arden Books & Cosmographia, Warwickshire ... 236
Arnold (Roy), Suffolk 226
Art Reference Books, Hampshire 123
Autumn Leaves, Lincolnshire 148
Barmby (C. & A.J.), Kent 138
Book Basket, London, Outer 182
Book Corner, Scotland 263
Bookroom (The), Surrey 233
Books, Kent 134
Bookworld, Shropshire 212
Booth Books, Wales 286
Browzers, Greater Manchester 117
Buckland Books, West Sussex 243
Cahir Cosy Corner Bookshop, Republic Of Ireland 279
Camilla's Bookshop, East Sussex 100
Carta Regis, Wales 288
Clark (Nigel A.), London (SE) 160
Classic Crime Collections, Greater Manchester.. 117
Corfe Books, Surrey 231
DoublePlusBooks, Cambridgeshire 68
Eastcote Bookshop (The), London, Outer 183
Foster (Stephen), London (NW) 157
Gloucester Road Bookshop, London (SW) 164
Golden Goose Books, Lincolnshire 148
Gresham Books, Somerset 216
Heneage Art Books (Thomas), London (SW) 164
Hennessey Bookseller (Ray), East Sussex 100
Hollett and Son (R.F.G.), Cumbria 79
Ives Bookseller (John), London, Outer 184
Katharine House Gallery, Wiltshire 251
Kelly Books (Don), London (W) 173
Keswick Bookshop, Cumbria 78
Kim's Bookshop, West Sussex 244
Leabeck Books, Oxfordshire 208
Lion Fine Arts and Books, Wales 287
Malvern Bookshop (The), Worcestershire 254
Moss End Bookshop, Berkshire 59
Mundy (David), Hertfordshire 128
Old Soke Books, Cornwall 74
Olio Books, East Sussex 101
O'Neill (Angus), London (WC) 178
Park Gallery & Bookshop (The), Northamptonshire 199
Phillips of Hitchin (Antiques) Ltd., Hertfordshire 129
Prescott - The Bookseller (John), London, Outer 184
Quadrille at Delehar, London (W) 174
Rees & O'Neill Rare Books, London (WC) 178
Reference Works Ltd., Dorset 94
Rowan (H. & S.J.), Dorset 91
Shipley Specialist Art Booksellers, London (WC) 178
Smith Books, (Sally), Suffolk 225
Studio Bookshop, East Sussex 99
Swan Bookshop (The), Devon 84
Tantalus Antiques & Books, Devon 87
Thin Read Line, Merseyside 186
Thomas (Books) (Leona), Cheshire 71
Trinders' Fine Tools, Suffolk 225
Wolds Book Services, Leicestershire 144

APICULTURE

Bee Books New and Old, Cornwall 73

SPECIALITY INDEX

Mayhew (Veronica), Berkshire 58
Wolds Book Services, Leicestershire 144

APPLIED ART

Amwell Book Company (The), London (EC).... 152
Arnold (Roy), Suffolk................................ 226
Ars Artis, Oxfordshire 206
Art Reference Books, Hampshire 123
Artco, Nottinghamshire 202
Barmby (C. & A.J.), Kent........................... 138
Batterham (David), London (W)................... 169
Biblion, London (W)................................. 169
Books & Things, London (W)...................... 169
Butts Books (Mary), Berkshire..................... 58
Cover to Cover, Merseyside 186
Dew (Roderick), East Sussex 100
DoublePlusBooks, Cambridgeshire 68
Fosters Bookshop, London (W).................... 172
Gardner & Co., (Walter H.), London (N)........ 153
Handsworth Books, Essex.......................... 110
Heneage Art Books (Thomas), London (SW).... 164
Hennessey Bookseller (Ray), East Sussex........ 100
High Street Books, Devon 85
Hodgkins and Company Limited (Ian),
  Gloucestershire.................................... 114
Hogben (Carol), Wales 285
Inprint, Gloucestershire............................ 114
Island Books, Devon................................ 84
Kelly Books (Don), London (W) 173
Keswick Books, Cumbria........................... 78
Martin - Bookseller (Colin), East Yorkshire 105
Peter Lyons Books, Gloucestershire 112
Phillips of Hitchin (Antiques) Ltd.,
  Hertfordshire...................................... 129
Shipley Specialist Art Booksellers, London (WC) 178
Staniland (Booksellers), Lincolnshire............. 150
Studio Bookshop, East Sussex..................... 99
Tasburgh Books, Norfolk 190
Trinders' Fine Tools, Suffolk 225
Wyseby House Books, Berkshire.................. 57
YSF Books, South Yorkshire....................... 221

ARCHAEOLOGY

Aberdeen Rare Books & Caledonian Books,
  Scotland 267
Addyman Books, Wales 285
Arundel Bookshop, West Sussex 241
Atlantis Bookshop, London (WC)................. 176
Baker Limited (A.P. & R.), Scotland.............. 263
Barmby (C. & A.J.), Kent........................... 138
Barn Books, Buckinghamshire..................... 62
Barton (John), Hampshire 124
Book Basket, London, Outer 182
Book House (The), Cumbria....................... 78
Booth Books, Wales................................. 286
Bosco Books, Cornwall............................. 73
Bracton Books, Cambridgeshire................... 64
Cahir Cosy Corner Bookshop, Republic Of
  Ireland.. 279
Castle Bookshop, Wales 288
Castle Bookshop, Essex............................. 107
Cathach Books Ltd., Republic Of Ireland........ 277
Cavan Book Centre, Republic Of Ireland 275

Chaucer Bookshop (The), Kent 133
Clements (R.W.), London, Outer 181
Corfe Books, Surrey................................. 231
Crouch Rare Books, Surrey........................ 232
Curtle Mead Books, Isle of Wight................. 131
Eastleach Books, Berkshire 58
Gate Memorabilia, London (N).................... 153
Graves–Johnston (Michael), London (SW)....... 164
Greyfriars Books, Essex 107
Hancock (Colin), Wales 281
Helion & Company, West Midlands 240
Heneage Art Books (Thomas), London (SW).... 164
Idle Genius Books, London (N).................... 154
Jackdaw Books, Norfolk 189
Joppa Books Ltd., Surrey 230
Kenny's Bookshops and Art Galleries Ltd,
  Republic Of Ireland 278
Kingswood Books, Dorset 93
Larkham Books (Patricia), Gloucestershire 115
Little Bookshop (The), Greater Manchester 117
Lowe (John), Norfolk............................... 189
Malvern Bookshop (The), Worcestershire 254
Manor House Books/John Trotter Books,
  London (N).. 154
Martin - Bookseller (Colin), East Yorkshire 105
McCrone (Audrey), Scotland 272
Moss Books, London (NW) 158
Museum Bookshop, London (WC)................ 177
Naughton Booksellers, Republic Of Ireland...... 277
Nonsuch Books, Surrey............................. 234
Polczynski (Udo K.H.), London, Outer 183
Prescott - The Bookseller (John), London, Outer 184
Quest Books, East Yorkshire 105
St Mary's Books & Prints, Lincolnshire 150
Scrivener's Books & Book Binding, Derbyshire . 81
Spooner & Co., Somerset 217
Staniland (Booksellers), Lincolnshire.............. 150
Stride & Son, West Sussex 242
Taylor & Son (Peter), Hertfordshire............... 130
Unsworths Booksellers Ltd., London (WC)...... 178
Whitchurch Books Ltd., Wales 280
Wiend Books & Collectables, Greater
  Manchester... 119
Winchester Bookshop (The), Hampshire......... 125

ARCHITECTURE

Adams (Judith), Shropshire........................ 211
Addyman Books, Wales 285
Amwell Book Company (The), London (EC).... 152
Ars Artis, Oxfordshire 206
Art Reference Books, Hampshire 123
Ballantyne–Way (Roger), Suffolk.................. 228
Barton (John), Hampshire 124
Batterham (David), London (W)................... 169
Birchden Books, London (E) 151
Book Basket, London, Outer 182
Bookroom (The), Surrey 233
Books, Kent 134
Books & Bygones, Berkshire....................... 58
Booth Books, Wales................................. 286
Bosco Books, Cornwall............................. 73
Bowden Books, Leicestershire 144
Brighton Books, East Sussex 98
Broadhurst of Southport Ltd., Merseyside 186

SPECIALITY INDEX

Buckland Books, West Sussex 243
Butts Books (Mary), Berkshire 58
Cahir Cosy Corner Bookshop, Republic Of
   Ireland 279
Camden Books, Somerset 214
Castle Bookshop, Wales 288
Chapman (Ron), London (SW) 163
Chevin Books, West Yorkshire 248
Classic Bindings, London (SW) 163
Coach House Books, Worcestershire 255
Collectable Books, London (SE) 160
Coombes (A.J.), Surrey 230
Corfe Books, Surrey 231
Cottage Books, Leicestershire 143
Cover to Cover, Merseyside 186
Crook (Chris), Somerset 218
Darkwood Books, Republic Of Ireland 276
Dartmoor Bookshop (The), Devon 83
de Beaumont (Robin), London (SW) 163
Dew (Roderick), East Sussex 100
Dorset Rare Books, Wiltshire 252
DoublePlusBooks, Cambridgeshire 68
Duck (William), East Sussex 98
Eastleach Books, Berkshire 58
Elton Engineering Books, London (W) 172
English (Toby), Oxfordshire 209
Europa Books, London (SW) 163
Finney Antique Books & Prints (Michael),
   London (WC) 177
Foster (Stephen), London (NW) 157
Fosters Bookshop, London (W) 172
Fotheringham (Alex), Northumberland 200
G C Books, Scotland 264
Gloucester Road Bookshop, London (SW) 164
Goodyer (Nicholas), London (N) 154
Grant (Gerald S.), Cheshire 69
Gravity Books, Lincolnshire 147
Gresham Books, Somerset 216
Greyfriars Books, Essex 107
Harrington Antiquarian Bookseller (Peter),
   London (SW) 164
Harwich Old Books, Essex 108
Haskell (R.H. & P.), Dorset 93
Helmsley Antiquarian & Secondhand Books,
   N Yorks 193
Heywood Hill Limited (G.), London (W) 173
Hicks (Ronald C.), Cornwall 74
Hogben (Carol), Wales 285
Hornsey's, N Yorks 194
Hünersdorff Rare Books, London (SW) 165
Inch's Books, N Yorks 194
Island Books, Devon 84
Ives Bookseller (John), London, Outer 184
Jones (Anne), Cornwall 76
Katnap Arts, Norfolk 189
Kenny's Bookshops and Art Galleries Ltd,
   Republic Of Ireland 278
Kerr (Norman), Cumbria 78
Keswick Bookshop, Cumbria 78
Lion Fine Arts and Books, Wales 287
Little Bookshop (The), Greater Manchester 117
Malvern Bookshop (The), Worcestershire 254
Marcan, Bookseller (Peter), London (SE) 161
Marlborough Rare Books Ltd., London (W) 173
Martin - Bookseller (Colin), East Yorkshire 105
McNaughtan's Bookshop, Scotland 269
Mercat Books, Scotland 267
Missing Books, Essex 108
Monmouth House Books, Wales 283
Moss Books, London (NW) 158
Nonsuch Books, Surrey 234
Octagon Books, Cambridgeshire 66
Old Town Bookshop (The), Scotland 270
Pagan Limited (Hugh), London (SW) 166
Patterson Liddle, Somerset 214
Phillips of Hitchin (Antiques) Ltd.,
   Hertfordshire 129
Prescott - The Bookseller (John), London, Outer 184
Quaritch Ltd., (Bernard), London (W) 174
Quest Books, East Yorkshire 105
Reads, Dorset 94
Rochdale Book Company, Greater Manchester 118
Roland Books, Kent 137
Ryeland Books, Northamptonshire 198
St Mary's Books & Prints, Lincolnshire 150
Scarthin Books, Derbyshire 82
Seydi Rare Books (Sevin), London (NW) 159
Shapero Rare Books (Bernard J.), London (W). 174
Shipley Specialist Art Booksellers, London (WC) 178
Sotheran Limited (Henry), London (W) 175
Spooner & Co., Somerset 217
Staniland (Booksellers), Lincolnshire 150
Stewart (Ian), Kent 137
Strauss (David), Lincolnshire 147
Stride & Son, West Sussex 242
Studio Bookshop, East Sussex 99
Sturford Books, Wiltshire 252
Tasburgh Books, Norfolk 190
Tobo Books, Hampshire 122
Tombland Bookshop, Norfolk 190
Trinders' Fine Tools, Suffolk 225
Unsworths Booksellers Ltd., London (WC) 178
Walden Books, London (NW) 159
Wiend Books & Collectables, Greater
   Manchester 119
Woburn Books, London (N) 156
Woodstock Bookshop (The), Oxfordshire 210
Wyseby House Books, Berkshire 57

ARMS & ARMOUR

Atticus Books, Essex 109
Book Basket, London, Outer 182
Burgess Booksellers, (J. & J.), Cambridgeshire .. 64
Chelifer Books, Cumbria 79
Crispin's Day, Antiquarian and Out of Print
   Military Books, Essex 110
DoublePlusBooks, Cambridgeshire 68
Duck (William), East Sussex 98
Empire Books, Greater Manchester 118
Helion & Company, West Midlands 240
Heneage Art Books (Thomas), London (SW).... 164
Lion Fine Arts and Books, Wales 287
Meekins Books (Paul), Warwickshire 237
Military Collector (The), West Yorkshire 249
MilitaryHistoryBooks.com, Kent 136
Prospect Books, Wales 282
Shapero Rare Books (Bernard J.), London (W). 174
Spenceley Books (David), West Yorkshire 248
Stride & Son, West Sussex 242

SPECIALITY INDEX

Thin Read Line, Merseyside 186
Wizard Books, Cambridgeshire 68
Wolds Book Services, Leicestershire 144

ART

Abacus Gallery / The Village Bookshop,
    Staffordshire 223
Abbey Books, Norfolk 187
Adams (Judith), Shropshire 211
Addyman Books, Wales 285
Alba Books, Scotland 267
Americanabooksuk, Cumbria 77
Anderson Slater Antiques, N Yorks 195
Andromeda Books, Buckinghamshire 63
Antiquary Ltd., (Bar Bookstore), N Yorks 194
Anvil Books, West Midlands 239
Anwoth Books, Scotland 263
Arden Books & Cosmographia, Warwickshire... 236
Armchair Books, Scotland 268
Art Reference Books, Hampshire 123
Artco, Nottinghamshire 202
Ashfield Books and Records, Nottinghamshire.. 203
Autumn Leaves, Lincolnshire 148
Avonworld Books, Somerset 215
Ballantyne–Way (Roger), Suffolk 228
Bardsley's Books, Suffolk 225
Barmby (C. & A.J.), Kent 138
Barn Books, Buckinghamshire 62
Beetles Ltd., (Chris), London (SW) 163
Beware of the Leopard Books, Bristol 60
Biblion, London (W) 169
Blaenavon Books, Wales 289
Book Basket, London, Outer 182
Book Corner, Scotland 263
Book Gallery (The), Cornwall 76
Bookroom (The), Surrey 233
Books, Kent 134
Books, Wales 282
Books for Collectors, Gloucestershire 112
Books Galore, Somerset 216
Bookshop (The), Cambridgeshire 64
Bookworms, Norfolk 187
Bookworms of Evesham, Worcestershire 255
Booth (Booksearch Service), (Geoff), Cheshire .. 69
Booth Books, Wales 286
Bosco Books, Cornwall 73
Bowden Books, Leicestershire 144
Brighton Books, East Sussex 98
Broadhurst of Southport Ltd., Merseyside 186
Brock Books, N Yorks 192
Butcher (Pablo), Oxfordshire 205
Butts Books (Mary), Berkshire 58
Cahir Cosy Corner Bookshop, Republic Of
    Ireland 279
Caledonia Books, Scotland 271
Camilla's Bookshop, East Sussex 100
Campbell Art Books (Marcus), London (SE).... 160
Carnforth Bookshop (The), Lancashire 140
Chalk (Old & Out of Print Books)
    (Christine M.), West Midlands 238
Chapter and Verse Booksellers, East Sussex 102
Chaucer Bookshop (The), Kent 133
Chevin Books, West Yorkshire 248
Clark (K.R.), Oxfordshire 205

Classic Bindings, London (SW) 163
Clements (R.W.), London, Outer 181
Cooper Hay Rare Books, Scotland 271
Cover to Cover, Merseyside 186
Croft Selections, Lincolnshire 148
Crook (Chris), Somerset 218
Cross (Ian), Berkshire 57
Cumming Limited (A. & Y.), East Sussex 102
Darkwood Books, Republic Of Ireland 276
Dartmoor Bookshop (The), Devon 83
de Beaumont (Robin), London (SW) 163
Doolin Dinghy Books, Republic Of Ireland 275
Doorbar (P. & D.), Hampshire 122
Dorset Rare Books, Wiltshire 252
DoublePlusBooks, Cambridgeshire 68
Eastcote Bookshop (The), London, Outer 183
Edwards (London) Limited (Francis),
    London (WC) 177
Edwards in Hay–on–Wye (Francis), Wales 286
Ellis, Bookseller (Peter), London (SE) 160
English (Toby), Oxfordshire 209
Europa Books, London (SW) 163
Farnborough Bookshop and Gallery, Hampshire 121
Finch Rare Books Ltd. (Simon), London (W)... 172
fineart-photographer, Herefordshire 127
Fireside Bookshop, Cumbria 80
Fisher & Sperr, London (N) 153
Fortune Green Books, London (NW) 157
Foster Bookshop (Paul), London (SW) 164
Fosters Bookshop, London (W) 172
Fotheringham (Alex), Northumberland 200
Furneaux Books (Lee), Devon 87
Gate Memorabilia, London (N) 153
Gloucester Road Bookshop, London (SW) 164
Golden Goose Books, Lincolnshire 148
Goodyer (Nicholas), London (N) 154
Grant (Gerald S.), Cheshire 69
Greyfriars Books, Essex 107
Hall's Bookshop, Kent 138
Harrington (Adrian), London (W) 173
Heartland Old Books, Devon 88
Helmsley Antiquarian & Secondhand Books, N
    Yorks 193
Heneage Art Books (Thomas), London (SW).... 164
Hennessey Bookseller (Ray), East Sussex 100
Heyman (B.), London, Outer 181
Hicks (Ronald C.), Cornwall 74
Hillside House, Lincolnshire 147
Hodgkins and Company Limited (Ian),
    Gloucestershire 114
Holdsworth Books (Bruce), West Yorkshire 245
Hornsby, Antiquarian and Secondhand Books
    (Malcolm), Leicestershire 144
Horsham Bookshop (The), West Sussex 242
Ice House Books 143
Idler (The), Suffolk 227
Jericho Books, Oxfordshire 208
Katharine House Gallery, Wiltshire 251
Katnap Arts, Norfolk 189
Keel Row Books, Tyne & Wear 235
Keogh's Books, Gloucestershire 113
Keswick Bookshop, Cumbria 78
Leabeck Books, Oxfordshire 208
Leigh Gallery Books, Essex 108
Lion Fine Arts and Books, Wales 287

SPECIALITY INDEX

Malvern Bookshop (The), Worcestershire 254
Marcet Books, London (SE) 161
Martin - Bookseller (Colin), East Yorkshire 105
McNaughtan's Bookshop, Scotland 269
Milne Books (Clifford), Scotland 265
Morley Case, Hampshire 124
Mundy (David), Hertfordshire 128
Mundy (David), Buckinghamshire 62
Naughton Booksellers, Republic Of Ireland...... 277
Newcastle Bookshop, Northumberland 200
Newlyn & New Street Books, Cornwall 75
Niner (Marcus), Gloucestershire 113
Nonsuch Books, Surrey 234
Nova Foresta Books, Hampshire 121
O'Brien Books & Photo Gallery, Republic Of
  Ireland 279
Octagon Books, Cambridgeshire 66
Offa's Dyke Books, Shropshire 212
Old Bookshop (The), West Midlands 240
Old Town Bookshop (The), Scotland 270
Olio Books, East Sussex 101
O'Neill (Angus), London (WC) 178
Ouse Valley Books, Bedfordshire 56
Patterson Liddle, Somerset 214
Penn Barn Bookshop, Buckinghamshire 63
Peter Lyons Books, Gloucestershire 112
Phillips (Chris), Wiltshire 250
Polmorla Books, Cornwall 76
Porcupines, Devon 84
Prescott - The Bookseller (John), London, Outer 184
Quaritch Ltd., (Bernard), London (W) 174
R. & A. Books, East Sussex 100
Riccetti (Margaret), South Yorkshire 220
River Reads Bookshop, Devon 88
Riviera Books, Norfolk 188
Roland Books, Kent 137
Rowan (H. & S.J.), Dorset 91
Russell Books, Somerset 218
Savery Books, East Sussex 99
Sax Books, Suffolk 228
Scorpio Books, Suffolk 225
Shapero Rare Books (Bernard J.), London (W). 174
Shipley Specialist Art Booksellers, London (WC) 178
Silverman (Michael), London (SE) 161
Sims Reed Limited, London (SW) 167
Slaughter & Garratt Rare Books,
  Worcestershire 255
Sotheran Limited (Henry), London (W) 175
Staniland (Booksellers), Lincolnshire 150
Sterling Books, Somerset 219
Stride & Son, West Sussex 242
Studio Bookshop, East Sussex 99
Sturford Books, Wiltshire 252
Tombland Bookshop, Norfolk 190
Treasure Island (The), Greater Manchester 118
Trinders' Fine Tools, Suffolk 225
Unsworths Booksellers Ltd., London (WC) 178
Unsworths Booksellers Ltd., Oxfordshire 209
Upper–Room Books, Somerset 216
Venables (Morris & Juliet), Bristol 61
Walden Books, London (NW) 159
Westwood Books (Mark), Wales 287
Wetherell (Frances), Cambridgeshire 66
Whig Books Ltd., Leicestershire 145
Whitfield (Ken), Essex 109

Wiend Books & Collectables, Greater
  Manchester 119
Woburn Books, London (N) 156
Wolds Book Services, Leicestershire 144
Wood (Peter), Cambridgeshire 66
Woodstock Bookshop (The), Oxfordshire 210
Words & Music, Cheshire 70
Wychwood Books, Gloucestershire 114
Wyseby House Books, Berkshire 57

ART HISTORY

Adams (Judith), Shropshire 211
Ars Artis, Oxfordshire 206
Art Reference Books, Hampshire 123
Ballantyne–Way (Roger), Suffolk 228
Beetles Ltd., (Chris), London (SW) 163
Book Basket, London, Outer 182
Book Gallery (The), Cornwall 76
Books (For All), N Yorks 192
Bosco Books, Cornwall 73
Butts Books (Mary), Berkshire 58
Caledonia Books, Scotland 271
Camden Books, Somerset 214
Carnforth Bookshop (The), Lancashire 140
Chapter and Verse Booksellers, East Sussex 102
Clark (Nigel A.), London (SE) 160
Crook (Chris), Somerset 218
Darkwood Books, Republic Of Ireland 276
Dartmoor Bookshop (The), Devon 83
Dorset Rare Books, Wiltshire 252
DoublePlusBooks, Cambridgeshire 68
Europa Books, London (SW) 163
fineart-photographer, Herefordshire 127
Fisher & Sperr, London (N) 153
Ford Books (David), Hertfordshire 130
Foster (Stephen), London (NW) 157
Grant (Gerald S.), Cheshire 69
Hen Hoose Bookshop, Scotland 262
Heneage Art Books (Thomas), London (SW).... 164
Holdsworth Books (Bruce), West Yorkshire 245
Illustrated Book (The), London (SW) 165
Katnap Arts, Norfolk 189
Kelsall (George), Greater Manchester 117
Keogh's Books, Gloucestershire 113
Kingsgate Books & Prints, Hampshire 125
Kunkler Books (Paul), Cambridgeshire 65
Manheim (Carol), London (W) 173
Martin - Bookseller (Colin), East Yorkshire 105
McCrone (Audrey), Scotland 272
Moreton Books, Devon 86
Newcastle Bookshop, Northumberland 200
Nonsuch Books, Surrey 234
Peter Lyons Books, Gloucestershire 112
Prescott - The Bookseller (John), London, Outer 184
Riccetti (Margaret), South Yorkshire 220
Ryeland Books, Northamptonshire 198
St Philip's Books, Oxfordshire 208
Seydi Rare Books (Sevin), London (NW) 159
Shapero Rare Books (Bernard J.), London (W) . 174
Shipley Specialist Art Booksellers, London (WC) 178
Staniland (Booksellers), Lincolnshire 150
Stevens (Joan), Cambridgeshire 66
Strauss (David), Lincolnshire 147
Tasburgh Books, Norfolk 190

SPECIALITY INDEX 341

Taylor & Son (Peter), Hertfordshire 130
Whitchurch Books Ltd., Wales 280
Wyseby House Books, Berkshire 57
YSF Books, South Yorkshire 221

ART REFERENCE

Abbey Books, Norfolk 187
Adams (Judith), Shropshire 211
Ars Artis, Oxfordshire 206
Art Reference Books, Hampshire 123
Artco, Nottinghamshire 202
Ballantyne–Way (Roger), Suffolk 228
Barlow (Vincent G.), Hampshire 123
Barmby (C. & A.J.), Kent 138
Beetles Ltd., (Chris), London (SW) 163
Book Basket, London, Outer 182
Book Gallery (The), Cornwall 76
Books & Things, London (W) 169
Books at the Warehouse, N Yorks 193
Books on the Bank, Durham 96
Bosco Books, Cornwall 73
Butts Books (Mary), Berkshire 58
Campbell Art Books (Marcus), London (SE) 160
Chapter and Verse Booksellers, East Sussex 102
Clark (Nigel A.), London (SE) 160
Coach House Books, Worcestershire 255
Cox Old & Rare Books (Claude), Suffolk 226
Crook (Chris), Somerset 218
Darkwood Books, Republic Of Ireland 276
Dartmoor Bookshop (The), Devon 83
Dorset Rare Books, Wiltshire 252
DoublePlusBooks, Cambridgeshire 68
Europa Books, London (SW) 163
Firth (Bijou Books & Photography) (Maureen),
 South Yorkshire 221
Foster (Stephen), London (NW) 157
Gardner & Co., (Walter H.), London (N) 153
Greyfriars Books, Essex 107
Harwich Old Books, Essex 108
Hen Hoose Bookshop, Scotland 262
Hodgkins and Company Limited (Ian),
 Gloucestershire 114
Holdsworth Books (Bruce), West Yorkshire 245
Illustrated Book (The), London (SW) 165
Ives Bookseller (John), London, Outer 184
Katnap Arts, Norfolk 189
Kelsall (George), Greater Manchester 117
Kenny's Bookshops and Art Galleries Ltd,
 Republic Of Ireland 278
Keogh's Books, Gloucestershire 113
Kingsgate Books & Prints, Hampshire 125
Manheim (Carol), London (W) 173
Martin - Bookseller (Colin), East Yorkshire 105
Moreton Books, Devon 86
Newcastle Bookshop, Northumberland 200
Nonsuch Books, Surrey 234
Olio Books, East Sussex 101
Peter Lyons Books, Gloucestershire 112
Philologus–Fine & Rare Books, London (SW) .. 166
Rees & O'Neill Rare Books, London (WC) 178
Scrivener's Books & Book Binding, Derbyshire .. 81
Shipley Specialist Art Booksellers,
 London (WC) 178
Staniland (Booksellers), Lincolnshire 150

Stevens (Joan), Cambridgeshire 66
Studio Bookshop, East Sussex 99
Sue Lowell Natural History Books, London (W). 175
Tasburgh Books, Norfolk 190
Trinders' Fine Tools, Suffolk 225
Ventnor Rare Books, Isle of Wight 132
Waddington Books & Prints (Geraldine),
 Northamptonshire 198
Wyseby House Books, Berkshire 57

ARTHURIAN

Addyman Books, Wales 285
Arthurian Book, Wales 285
Boer (Louise), Arthurian Books, Wales 284
Book Basket, London, Outer 182
Byre Books, Scotland 264
Inner Bookshop (The), Oxfordshire 207
Minster Gate Bookshop, N Yorks 196
Whitchurch Books Ltd., Wales 280
Wizard Books, Cambridgeshire 68

ARTISTS

Adams (Judith), Shropshire 211
Ars Artis, Oxfordshire 206
Art Reference Books, Hampshire 123
Artco, Nottinghamshire 202
Arundel Bookshop, West Sussex 241
Ballantyne–Way (Roger), Suffolk 228
Beetles Ltd., (Chris), London (SW) 163
Book Basket, London, Outer 182
Books & Bygones, Berkshire 58
Brown-Studies, Scotland 270
Butts Books (Mary), Berkshire 58
Campbell Art Books (Marcus), London (SE) 160
Chalk (Old & Out of Print Books)
 (Christine M.), West Midlands 238
Clark (Nigel A.), London (SE) 160
Darkwood Books, Republic Of Ireland 276
Dartmoor Bookshop (The), Devon 83
Dorset Rare Books, Wiltshire 252
Ellis, Bookseller (Peter), London (SE) 160
Foster (Stephen), London (NW) 157
Grant (Gerald S.), Cheshire 69
Harwich Old Books, Essex 108
Hodgkins and Company Limited (Ian),
 Gloucestershire 114
Keogh's Books, Gloucestershire 113
Manheim (Carol), London (W) 173
Martin - Bookseller (Colin), East Yorkshire 105
Peter Lyons Books, Gloucestershire 112
Phoenix Fine Books, Essex 110
Rittner Booksearch (Hilary), London (SE) 161
Sephton (A.F.), London (W) 174
Shipley Specialist Art Booksellers, London (WC) . 178
Sims Reed Limited, London (SW) 167
Stevens (Joan), Cambridgeshire 66
Trinders' Fine Tools, Suffolk 225
Upper-Room Books, Somerset 216
Woodbine Books, West Yorkshire 245
Wyseby House Books, Berkshire 57

ARTS, THE

Abbey Books, London (N) 153

SPECIALITY INDEX

Addyman Books, Wales 285
All Books, Essex 108
Anderson Slater Antiques, N Yorks 195
Arcadia, Shropshire 212
Artco, Nottinghamshire 202
Ballantyne–Way (Roger), Suffolk 228
Book Basket, London, Outer 182
Books & Bygones, Berkshire 58
Carta Regis, Wales 288
Collectable Books, London (SE) 160
Dorset Rare Books, Wiltshire 252
Elephant Books, West Yorkshire 247
Ellis, Bookseller (Peter), London (SE) 160
Fine Art, West Sussex 242
Firth (Bijou Books & Photography) (Maureen),
  South Yorkshire 221
Foster (Stephen), London (NW) 157
Harwich Old Books, Essex 108
Hawley (C.L.), N Yorks 195
Holdsworth Books (Bruce), West Yorkshire 245
Howes Bookshop, East Sussex 101
Ice House Books 143
Kerr (Norman), Cumbria 78
Kim's Bookshop, West Sussex 244
Langmaid (Kenneth), Cornwall 76
Little Bookshop (The), Greater Manchester 117
Marcan, Bookseller (Peter), London (SE) 161
Martin - Bookseller (Colin), East Yorkshire 105
Oblong Books, N Yorks 197
Peter Lyons Books, Gloucestershire 112
Sanderson (Edward), Berkshire 58
Segal Books (Joel), Devon 85
Spread Eagle Bookshop, London (SE) 162
Stevens (Joan), Cambridgeshire 66
Trinders' Fine Tools, Suffolk 225
Waterfield's, Oxfordshire 209
Williams (Christopher), Dorset 93
Woburn Books, London (N) 156
Wolds Book Services, Leicestershire 144
Words & Music, Cheshire 70
Wyseby House Books, Berkshire 57
YSF Books, South Yorkshire 221

ASSASSINATIONS

Bolland Books (Leslie H.), Bedfordshire 55
Crimes Ink, London (E) 151
Manor House Books/John Trotter Books,
  London (N) 154

ASTROLOGY

Alpha Books, London (N) 153
Arundel Bookshop, West Sussex 241
Books, Wales 282
Books & Bygones, Berkshire 58
Burgess Booksellers, (J. & J.), Cambridgeshire .. 64
Caduceus Books, Leicestershire 143
Dawlish Books, Devon 84
Delectus Books, London (WC) 176
Greensleeves, Oxfordshire 204
Grieveson (A.), Cheshire 69
Inner Bookshop (The), Oxfordshire 207
Magis Books, Leicestershire 144
Occultique, Northamptonshire 198

Rainger Books (Michael), Wales 285
Shapero Rare Books (Bernard J.), London (W) . 174
Starlord Books, Cheshire 70

ASTRONAUTICS

Duck (William), East Sussex 98
K. Books, Cheshire 72

ASTRONOMY

Addyman Books, Wales 285
Altea Antique Maps & Books, London (WC) ... 169
Andromeda Books, Buckinghamshire 63
Biswell, (Douglas), Kent 134
McCrone (Audrey), Scotland 272
Moorside Books, Lancashire 141
Phelps (Michael), West Sussex 242
Turret House, Norfolk 191
Wayside Books and Cards, Oxfordshire 206
Wayside Books and Cards, Oxfordshire 205

ATLASES

Altea Antique Maps & Books, London (WC) ... 169
Bannister (David), Gloucestershire 111
Barron - The Antique Map Specialist
  (Roderick M.), Kent 137
Booth Books, Wales 286
Burden Ltd., (Clive A.), Hertfordshire 129
Frew Limited (Robert), London (WC) 177
Green (Mrs. D.M.), Surrey 234
Harrington Antiquarian Bookseller (Peter),
  London (SW) 164
Havercroft Antiquarian Books, London (SE) 161
Heritage, West Midlands 238
Hogan (F. & J.), London (N) 154
Kennedy (Peter), Surrey 234
Marshall Rare Books (Bruce), Gloucestershire .. 111
Morris (Michael), Staffordshire 222
Newby (Valerie), Buckinghamshire 63
Nicholson of Chester (Richard), Cheshire 69
Orssich (Paul), London (SW) 166
Paralos Ltd., London (W) 173
Potter Limited (Jonathan), London (W) 174
Preston Book Company, Lancashire 142
Riccetti (Margaret), South Yorkshire 220
Russell (Charles), London (SW) 167
Shapero Rare Books (Bernard J.), London (W). 174
Shaw (David M.), Cheshire 72
Stanhope Bibliophiles, London (N) 155
Stride & Son, West Sussex 242
Summersgill (Neil), Lancashire 140
Tooley, Adams & Co., Oxfordshire 209

AUTHOR
- GENERAL

Anglo-American Rare Books, Surrey 232
Arundel Bookshop, West Sussex 241
Burgess Booksellers, (J. & J.), Cambridgeshire .. 64
Castleton (Pat), Kent 135
Catalyst Books, Surrey 232
DoublePlusBooks, Cambridgeshire 68
Harrington (Adrian), London (W) 173
Langmaid (Kenneth), Cornwall 76

SPECIALITY INDEX

Mother Goose Bookshop, Isle of Wight 131
Olio Books, East Sussex 101
Peakirk Books, Cambridgeshire 68
Stride & Son, West Sussex 242
Swan Bookshop (The), Devon 84

- 20TH CENTURY

Courtyard Books, Herefordshire 127
Hunter, Bookseller, (K.P.), Cambridgeshire 65
Island Books, Devon 84
Kenny's Bookshops and Art Galleries Ltd,
  Republic Of Ireland 278
Rhodes, Bookseller (Peter), Hampshire 124
Shapero Rare Books (Bernard J.), London (W) . 174

- ALDIN, CECIL

Bookmark (Children's Books), Wiltshire 252
Slavin Rare and Collectable Books (Derek),
  Warwickshire 237

- ARDIZZONE, EDWARD

Bookmark (Children's Books), Wiltshire 252
Key Books (Sarah), Cambridgeshire 65
Periwinkle Press, Kent 134
Rittner Booksearch (Hilary), London (SE) 161

- ARNOLD, MATTHEW

Desmond (Arnold), Somerset 217

- AUSTEN, JANE

Hodgkins and Company Limited (Ian),
  Gloucestershire 114
Island Books, Devon 84
Jarndyce Antiquarian Booksellers, London (WC) 177
Sharpe (Mary), West Sussex 241

- BADEN-POWELL, LORD ROBERT

Cahir Cosy Corner Bookshop, Republic
  Of Ireland 279
Hoggarth (John R.), N Yorks 196

- BALLANTYNE, ROBERT M.

Oasis Booksearch, Cambridgeshire 68

- BARING-GOULD, S.

Island Books, Devon 84
Shacklock Books (David), Suffolk 226

- BARKER, CECILY M.

J.K. Bookfinders, London (SW) 165
Key Books (Sarah), Cambridgeshire 65

- BATES, H.E.

Emjay Books, Surrey 231
Heppa (Christopher), Essex 106
Island Books, Devon 86

Park Gallery & Bookshop (The),
  Northamptonshire 199

- BECKETT, S.

Budd (Richard), Somerset 217
McCann (Joe), Oxfordshire 208

- BELLOC, HILAIRE

Island Books, Devon 84
Rosley Books, Cumbria 79

- BETJEMAN, SIR JOHN

Island Books, Devon 84

- BLACKWOOD, A.

Delectus Books, London (WC) 176
Fantastic Literature, Essex 109

- BLAKE, N.

Sutcliffe (Mark), West Yorkshire 246

- BLOOMSBURY GROUP, THE

Criterion Books, London, Outer 182
McKelvie (Ian), London (N) 154
Sharpe (Mary), West Sussex 241

- BLYTON, ENID

Breese Books Ltd., East Sussex 98
Green Meadow Books, Cornwall 75
K. Books, Cheshire 72
Key Books (Sarah), Cambridgeshire 65
Little Stour Books, Kent 133
Roberts (Fine Books) (Julian), Lincolnshire 149
Schutte (David), Hampshire 122
Sesemann (Julia), Kent 133

- BOSWELL, JAMES.

Island Books, Devon 84

- BRAMAH, ERNEST.

Webb Books (John), South Yorkshire 220

- BRENT-DYER, ELINOR M.

Badger Books, Somerset 218
Bookmark (Children's Books), Wiltshire 252
Key Books (Sarah), Cambridgeshire 65
Sims (Sue), Dorset 91
Wilson (J. & M.), Scotland 273

- BRONTES, THE

Hodgkins and Company Limited (Ian),
  Gloucestershire 114
Idle Booksellers (The), West Yorkshire 245
Sharpe (Mary), West Sussex 241

SPECIALITY INDEX

- BUCHAN, JOHN
Armchair Books, Scotland 268
Avonworld Books, Somerset 215
BOOKS4U, Wales 282
Heppa (Christopher), Essex 106

- BUCKERIDGE, A.
Bolland Books (Leslie H.), Bedfordshire 55
Key Books (Sarah), Cambridgeshire 65
Little Stour Books, Kent 133
Schutte (David), Hampshire 122
Wilson (J. & M.), Scotland 273

- BUNYAN, JOHN
Kirkman Ltd., (Robert), Bedfordshire 55
Rosley Books, Cumbria 79

- BURNEY, FANNY
Sharpe (Mary), West Sussex 241

- BURROUGHS, WILLIAM
J.K. Bookfinders, London (SW) 165
Sclanders (Beatbooks), (Andrew), London (EC) 152

- BURTON, R.F.
Campbell Hewson Books (R.), Scotland 265

- BYRON, LORD
Butler – Books (B.), Devon 83
Emjay Books, Surrey 231
Jarndyce Antiquarian Booksellers,
  London (WC) 177
Tobo Books, Hampshire 122
Wise (Derek), East Sussex 102

- CARR, JOHN DICKSON
Sutcliffe (Mark), West Yorkshire 246

- CARROLL, LEWIS
J.K. Bookfinders, London (SW) 165
Key Books (Sarah), Cambridgeshire 65
Thorne (Nick), Gloucestershire 112

- CECIL, H
Sidey, Bookdealer (Philip), Kent 137

- CERVANTES SAAVEDRA, MIGUEL DE
Orssich (Paul), London (SW) 166

- CHARTERIS, LESLIE
K. Books, Cheshire 72

- CHESTERTON, G.K.
Armchair Books, Scotland 268

Rosley Books, Cumbria 79

- CHRISTIE, AGATHA
Classic Crime Collections, Greater Manchester .. 117
Emjay Books, Surrey 231
Harrington (Adrian), London (W) 173
Lucius Books, N Yorks 196
Platt Rare Books (Richard), London (SE) 161
Williams Rare Books (Nigel), London (WC) 179

- CHURCHILL, SIR WINSTON
Frew Limited (Robert), London (WC) 177
Harrington (Adrian), London (W) 173
Island Books, Devon 84
Island Books, Devon 86
Kirkman Ltd., (Robert), Bedfordshire 55
Prior (Michael), Lincolnshire 149
Spread Eagle Bookshop, London (SE) 162
Stanton, (P. & K.), Cornwall 75

- COBBETT, WILLIAM
Island Books, Devon 86
Island Books, Devon 84
Jarndyce Antiquarian Booksellers,
  London (WC) 177
Porcupines, Devon 84

- CONAN DOYLE, SIR ARTHUR
Antique Map and Bookshop (The), Dorset 93
Black Cat Bookshop, Leicestershire 143
Harrington (Adrian), London (W) 173
Island Books, Devon 84
Platt Rare Books (Richard), London (SE) 161
Preston Book Company, Lancashire 142
Rupert Books, Cambridgeshire 65

- CONRAD, JOSEPH
BOOKS4U, Wales 282

- CORELLI, MARIE
Chaucer Head Bookshop, Warwickshire 237

- CORNWELL, BERNARD
Book Bungalow (The), Cornwall 73
Courtyard Books, Herefordshire 127
Harrington (Adrian), London (W) 173

- COWARD, NOEL
Avonworld Books, Somerset 215

- CRANE, HALL
Grant (Gerald S.), Cheshire 69

- CRANE, WALTER
Bookmark (Children's Books), Wiltshire 252
Hodgkins and Company Limited (Ian),

SPECIALITY INDEX

Gloucestershire 114

- **CREASEY, JOHN**
Classic Crime Collections, Greater Manchester.. 117

- **CROFTS, FREEMAN WILLS**
Sutcliffe (Mark), West Yorkshire.................. 246

- **CROMPTON, RICHMAL**
Breese Books Ltd., East Sussex 98
Key Books (Sarah), Cambridgeshire............... 65
Little Stour Books, Kent 133
Roberts (Fine Books) (Julian), Lincolnshire 149
Schutte (David), Hampshire 122
Wilson (J. & M.), Scotland 273

- **CROSBY, HARRY & CARESSE**
Norton Books, Durham 97

- **CROWLEY, ALEISTER**
Occultique, Northamptonshire 198

- **CRUICKSHANK, G.**
Tobo Books, Hampshire............................ 122

- **CUNARD, NANCY**
Norton Books, Durham 97

- **DAHL, ROALD**
Bookmark (Children's Books), Wiltshire 252
Castleton (Pat), Kent................................ 135
Key Books (Sarah), Cambridgeshire............... 65
Roberts (Fine Books) (Julian), Lincolnshire 149
Wilson (J. & M.), Scotland 273

- **DARWIN, CHARLES**
Island Books, Devon 84

- **DICKENS, CHARLES**
Boz Books, Wales 286
Chantry Bookshop & Gallery, Devon............. 84
Childrens Bookshop, West Yorkshire 246
Harrington (Adrian), London (W)................. 173
Jarndyce Antiquarian Booksellers, London (WC) 177
Mr. Pickwick of Towcester, Northamptonshire.. 199
Tiger Books, Kent................................... 134
Tobo Books, Hampshire............................ 122

- **DU MAURIER, DAPHNE**
Bookends of Fowey, Cornwall 74

- **DURRELL, LAWRENCE**
BOOKS4U, Wales.................................... 282
Criterion Books, London, Outer 182

Island Books, Devon 84
Slavin Rare and Collectable Books (Derek), Warwickshire 237

- **DYMOCK POETS, THE**
Smith Books (Keith), Herefordshire............... 127

- **EDWARDS, LIONEL**
BOOKS4U, Wales.................................... 282
Rare Books & Berry, Somerset..................... 217

- **ELIOT, G.**
Sharpe (Mary), West Sussex 241

- **ELIOT, T.S.**
Anglo-American Rare Books, Surrey.............. 232
Rosley Books, Cumbria 79

- **FAIRLIE–BRUCE, D.**
Key Books (Sarah), Cambridgeshire............... 65
Sims (Sue), Dorset................................... 91

- **FARNOL, JEFFERY**
Dusty Books, Wales................................. 287

- **FLEMING, IAN**
Black Cat Bookshop, Leicestershire 143
Book Bungalow (The), Cornwall................... 73
Bookshop Blackheath, London (SE) 160
Classic Crime Collections, Greater Manchester 117
Harrington (Adrian), London (W)................. 173
J.K. Bookfinders, London (SW).................... 165
Jonkers Rare Books, Oxfordshire.................. 206
Lucius Books, N Yorks.............................. 196
Platt Rare Books (Richard), London (SE) 161
St Mary's Books & Prints, Lincolnshire 150
Tobo Books, Hampshire............................ 122
Williams Rare Books (Nigel), London (WC) 179

- **FLINT, WILLIAM RUSSELL**
Slavin Rare and Collectable Books (Derek), Warwickshire 237

- **FOREST, A**
Badger Books, Somerset............................ 218
Key Books (Sarah), Cambridgeshire............... 65
Sims (Sue), Dorset................................... 91

- **FORESTER, C.S.**
Dusty Books, Wales................................. 287
Prior (Michael), Lincolnshire 149

- **FOWLES, JOHN**
BOOKS4U, Wales.................................... 282

- FRANCIS, DICK
Classic Crime Collections, Greater Manchester.. 117
Emjay Books, Surrey................................... 231
Slavin Rare and Collectable Books (Derek),
  Warwickshire.. 237

- FREEMAN, R A
Platt Rare Books (Richard), London (SE) 161

- GASKELL, E.
Hodgkins and Company Limited (Ian),
  Gloucestershire..................................... 114
Sharpe (Mary), West Sussex 241

- GILBERT, MICHAEL
Platt Rare Books (Richard), London (SE) 161

- GILL, ERIC
Grant (Gerald S.), Cheshire........................ 69

- GISSING, GEORGE
BOOKS4U, Wales...................................... 282
Idle Booksellers (The), West Yorkshire........... 245

- GRAVES, ROBERT
Avonworld Books, Somerset........................ 215
Island Books, Devon................................ 84

- GREENE, GRAHAM
Anglo-American Rare Books, Surrey.............. 232
BOOKS4U, Wales...................................... 282
Breese Books Ltd., East Sussex 98
Gloucester Road Bookshop, London (SW) 164
Harrington (Adrian), London (W)................. 173
Slavin Rare and Collectable Books (Derek),
  Warwickshire.. 237
Tobo Books, Hampshire............................. 122
Wayside Books and Cards, Oxfordshire 206
Williams Rare Books (Nigel), London (WC) 179

- GURDJIEFF, W.I.
Yarwood Rare Books (Edward), Cheshire 116

- HAGGARD, SIR HENRY RIDER
Allen (R.), Tyne & Wear 235
BOOKS4U, Wales...................................... 282
Wayside Books and Cards, Oxfordshire 206

- HARDY, THOMAS
Antique Map and Bookshop (The), Dorset 93
Books Afloat, Dorset................................ 95
BOOKS4U, Wales...................................... 282
Ferdinando (Steven), Somerset 217
Island Books, Devon................................ 84
Island Books, Devon................................ 86

Sharpe (Mary), West Sussex 241

- HEMINGWAY, ERNEST
Anglo-American Rare Books, Surrey.............. 232
Courtyard Books, Herefordshire................... 127
Scott (Sporting Books) (John),
  Worcestershire...................................... 256

- HENTY, G.A.
Antique Map and Bookshop (The), Dorset 93
Bookmark (Children's Books), Wiltshire 252
BOOKS4U, Wales...................................... 282
Little Stour Books, Kent 133
Shacklock Books (David), Suffolk 226

- HEYER, GEORGETTE
Allen (R.), Tyne & Wear 235
Book for All Reasons (A.), Suffolk................ 227
Bookseller (The), Suffolk 227
Boris Books, Dorset................................. 94
Dusty Books, Wales................................. 287

- HOUSMAN, A.E.
Antiquary Ltd., (Bar Bookstore), N Yorks 194
Island Books, Devon................................ 84

- INKLINGS, THE
English (Toby), Oxfordshire 209
Rosley Books, Cumbria 79
St Philip's Books, Oxfordshire...................... 208

- JAMES, HENRY
Anglo-American Rare Books, Surrey.............. 232
BOOKS4U, Wales...................................... 282

- JAMES, M.R.
BOOKS4U, Wales...................................... 282
Island Books, Devon................................ 84

- JEFFERIES, R.
Island Books, Devon................................ 84
Island Books, Devon................................ 86

- JOHNS, W.E.
Badger Books, Somerset............................ 218
Harrington (Adrian), London (W)................. 173
Key Books (Sarah), Cambridgeshire.............. 65
Little Stour Books, Kent 133
Lucius Books, N Yorks.............................. 196
Roberts (Fine Books) (Julian), Lincolnshire 149
Schutte (David), Hampshire 122

- JOHNSON, SAMUEL
Staffs Bookshop (The), Staffordshire 222

SPECIALITY INDEX

- JOYCE, JAMES
Courtwood Books, Republic Of Ireland 278
McCann (Joe), Oxfordshire 208
Norton Books, Durham 97
Williams Rare Books (Nigel), London (WC) 179

- KEEPING, CHARLES
Bookmark (Children's Books), Wiltshire 252
Key Books (Sarah), Cambridgeshire............... 65

- KEROUAC, JACK
Courtyard Books, Herefordshire 127
Sclanders (Beatbooks), (Andrew), London (EC) 152

- KING, STEPHEN
Dead Zone Books, Wales 289
Fantastic Literature, Essex 109

- KIPLING, RUDYARD
Avonworld Books, Somerset........................ 215
Faversham Books, Kent 135
Harrington (Adrian), London (W)................. 173
Verandah Books, Dorset 94

- LAITHWAITE, ERIC
KSC Books, Cheshire................................ 71

- LANG, ANDREW
Hodgkins and Company Limited (Ian),
 Gloucestershire..................................... 114

- LAWRENCE, D.H.
BOOKS4U, Wales................................... 282

- LAWRENCE, T.E.
Branksome Books, Dorset 93
Coach House Books, Worcestershire.............. 255
Hunter, Bookseller, (K.P.), Cambridgeshire...... 65
Moorside Books, Lancashire....................... 141

- LE CARRE, JOHN
Courtyard Books, Herefordshire 127

- LEAR, EDWARD
Porcupines, Devon................................... 84

- LEHMANN, J
Criterion Books, London, Outer 182

- LEWIS, C.S.
Armchair Books, Scotland 268
Key Books (Sarah), Cambridgeshire............... 65
Lewis First Editions, Kent 135

- JOYCE, JAMES (cont.)
Oasis Booksearch, Cambridgeshire 68
Rosley Books, Cumbria 79
Saint Philip's Books, Oxfordshire................. 208

- MACDONALD, GEORGE
Rosley Books, Cumbria 79

- MACHEN, ARTHUR
Delectus Books, London (WC)..................... 176

- MACLEAN, ALISTAIR
Little Stour Books, Kent 133

- MADOX FORD, FORD
BOOKS4U, Wales................................... 282

- MAILER, NORMAN
Anglo-American Rare Books, Surrey.............. 232
BOOKS4U, Wales................................... 282

- MASEFIELD, JOHN
Farringdon (J.M.), Wales 289
Prior (Michael), Lincolnshire 149
Smith Books (Keith), Herefordshire............... 127

- MILLER, HENRY
Norton Books, Durham 97

- MILLIGAN, SPIKE
Kineton Nooks, Warwickshire 236

- MILNE, A.A.
BOOKS4U, Wales................................... 282
Harrington (Adrian), London (W)................. 173
Tobo Books, Hampshire............................. 122

- MOORE, JOHN
Cornell Books, Gloucestershire..................... 114
Elmbury Books, Warwickshire 237
Engaging Gear Ltd., Essex.......................... 106
Island Books, Devon................................ 84

- MORRIS, WILLIAM
Hodgkins and Company Limited (Ian),
 Gloucestershire..................................... 114
Upper-Room Books, Somerset..................... 216

- MORTON, H.V.
Fireside Books, Buckinghamshire 63
Island Books, Devon................................ 84
Island Books, Devon................................ 86
Oasis Booksearch, Cambridgeshire 68

SPECIALITY INDEX

- MURDOCH, I.
Anglo-American Rare Books, Surrey.............. 232
Reaveley Books, Devon 86

- NEEDHAM, V
Key Books (Sarah), Cambridgeshire.............. 65
Wilson (J. & M.), Scotland 273

- NEWMAN, CARDINAL
St Philip's Books, Oxfordshire...................... 208

- NIALL, IAN
G C Books, Scotland................................ 264
Island Books, Devon................................ 84

- NIN, ANAIS
Norton Books, Durham 97

- O'BRIAN, PATRICK
BOOKS4U, Wales................................... 282
Harrington (Adrian), London (W)................. 173

- ORWELL, GEORGE
BOOKS4U, Wales................................... 282
Delaney's Books, Republic Of Ireland 275

- OXENHAM, ELSIE
Key Books (Sarah), Cambridgeshire.............. 65
Little Stour Books, Kent 133
Sims (Sue), Dorset................................. 91
Wilson (J. & M.), Scotland 273

- PEPYS, SAMUEL
Island Books, Devon................................ 84

- PETERS, ELLIS
BOOKS4U, Wales................................... 282

- PINTER, HAROLD
Courtyard Books, Herefordshire................... 127
McCann (Joe), Oxfordshire 208

- POTTER, BEATRIX
Bookmark (Children's Books), Wiltshire 252
Hodgkins and Company Limited (Ian),
  Gloucestershire.................................. 114
Jonkers Rare Books, Oxfordshire.................. 206
Key Books (Sarah), Cambridgeshire.............. 65
Sharpe (Mary), West Sussex 241

- POWYS FAMILY, THE
Books Afloat, Dorset............................... 95
Ferdinando (Steven), Somerset 217

- PRATCHETT, TERRY
Fantastic Literature, Essex 109
L.M.S. Books, Hertfordshire 129

- PRIESTLEY, J.B.
Slavin Rare and Collectable Books (Derek),
  Warwickshire.................................... 237

- QUILLER-COUCH, SIR A.T.
Bookends of Fowey, Cornwall 74
Island Books, Devon................................ 84

- RACKHAM, ARTHUR
BOOKS4U, Wales................................... 282
Harrington (Adrian), London (W)................. 173
Key Books (Sarah), Cambridgeshire.............. 65
Little Stour Books, Kent 133
St Mary's Books & Prints, Lincolnshire 150
Slavin Rare and Collectable Books (Derek),
  Warwickshire.................................... 237

- RAISTRICK, ARTHUR
KSC Books, Cheshire.............................. 71

- RAND, AYN
Webb Books (John), South Yorkshire 220

- RANKIN, IAN
Courtyard Books, Herefordshire................... 127
Platt Rare Books (Richard), London (SE) 161

- RANSOME, ARTHUR
Classic Crime Collections, Greater Manchester.. 117
Farringdon (J.M.), Wales 289
Key Books (Sarah), Cambridgeshire.............. 65
Past & Presents, Cumbria 77

- READ, MISS
Baker - Books for the Collector (Colin), Devon. 88
Brown-Studies, Scotland........................... 270

- ROLT, L.T.C.
Baldwin (M. & M.), Shropshire.................... 212
Bird Books (Nigel), Wales.......................... 281
Crosby Nethercott Books, London, Outer 180
Wilson Books (Henry), Cheshire.................. 71

- ROSSETTI, C.
Hodgkins and Company Limited (Ian),
  Gloucestershire.................................. 114

- ROWLING, J.K.
Book Bungalow (The), Cornwall................... 73
Harrington (Adrian), London (W)................. 173
St Mary's Books & Prints, Lincolnshire 150

SPECIALITY INDEX

- RUSHDIE, SALMAN
Courtyard Books, Herefordshire 127

- RUSKIN, JOHN
Hodgkins and Company Limited (Ian),
    Gloucestershire 114
Rosley Books, Cumbria 79

- SABATINI, R.
Dusty Books, Wales................................ 287

- SACKVILLE-WEST, VITA
Bow Windows Book Shop, East Sussex 102
Island Books, Devon................................ 86
Island Books, Devon................................ 84

- SASSOON, SIEGFRIED
Anglo-American Rare Books, Surrey.............. 232
Island Books, Devon................................ 84
Island Books, Devon................................ 86

- SAVILLE, M.
Badger Books, Somerset............................ 218
Green Meadow Books, Cornwall 75
Key Books (Sarah), Cambridgeshire............... 65
Lewis First Editions, Kent 135

- SAYERS, DOROTHY
Avonworld Books, Somerset...................... 215

- SEARLE, RONALD
Grant (Gerald S.), Cheshire........................ 69

- SHAKESPEARE, WILLIAM
BOOKS4U, Wales.................................... 282
Chaucer Head Bookshop, Warwickshire.......... 237

- SHEPARD, E.H.
Key Books (Sarah), Cambridgeshire............... 65

- SHUTE, NEVILLE
Dusty Books, Wales................................ 287
Lewis First Editions, Kent 135
Webb Books (John), South Yorkshire 220

- SIMENON, GEORGES
Wayside Books and Cards, Oxfordshire 206

- SITWELL FAMILY
Slavin Rare and Collectable Books (Derek),
    Warwickshire... 237

- SPARE, AUSTIN OSMAN
Occultique, Northamptonshire 198

- STEADMAN, RALPH
McCann (Joe), Oxfordshire 208

- STEIN, GERTRUDE
Norton Books, Durham 97

- STEINER, RUDOLF
Anthroposophical Books, Bristol 60

- STEVENSON, ROBERT LOUIS
BOOKS4U, Wales.................................... 282

- STOKER, B.
Allen (R.), Tyne & Wear 235
McCann (Joe), Oxfordshire 208

- SWINBURNE, A.C.
Hodgkins and Company Limited (Ian),
    Gloucestershire 114
Seddon (A.C.), West Sussex 244

- TANGYE, D.
Baker - Books for the Collector (Colin), Devon. 88
Emjay Books, Surrey................................ 231
Island Books, Devon................................ 84
Mount's Bay Books, Cornwall 75

- THELWELL, N
Bookstand, Dorset................................... 93

- THOMAS, DYLAN
BOOKS4U, Wales.................................... 282
Dylans Bookstore, Wales........................... 289

- TOLKIEN, J.R.R.
Daeron's Books, Buckinghamshire 63
Harrington (Adrian), London (W)................. 173
Key Books (Sarah), Cambridgeshire............... 65
Rosley Books, Cumbria 79
Tobo Books, Hampshire............................ 122

- TROLLOPE, ANTHONY
Sen Books, Hampshire.............................. 125
Tobo Books, Hampshire............................ 122

- TWAIN, MARK
BOOKS4U, Wales.................................... 282
Harrington (Adrian), London (W)................. 173

- UTTLEY, ALISON
Bookmark (Children's Books), Wiltshire 252
Scarthin Books, Derbyshire 82

SPECIALITY INDEX

- WALLACE, EDGAR
Williams (Bookdealer), (Richard), Lincolnshire . 149

- WALSH, M.
Moray Bookshop (The), Scotland 267

- WATKINS–PITCHFORD, DENYS ('B.B.')
Chalmers Hallam (E.), Hampshire................. 123
Island Books, Devon................................. 84
Key Books (Sarah), Cambridgeshire............... 65
St Mary's Books & Prints, Lincolnshire 150

- WEBB, MARY
Woodbine Books, West Yorkshire................. 245

- WELCH, R.
Key Books (Sarah), Cambridgeshire............... 65

- WELLS, H.G.
BOOKS4U, Wales...................................... 282
Fantastic Literature, Essex 109
Harrington (Adrian), London (W.)................. 173
Slavin Rare and Collectable Books (Derek),
  Warwickshire...................................... 237

- WHEATLEY, DENNIS
Bookstand, Dorset...................................... 93
Heckmondwike Book Shop, West Yorkshire 235

- WHITE, GILBERT
Sen Books, Hampshire................................ 125

- WILDE, OSCAR
Harrington (Adrian), London (W.)................. 173
McCann (Joe), Oxfordshire 208

- WILLIAMS, CHARLES
Rosley Books, Cumbria 79

- WILLIAMSON, HENRY
Island Books, Devon................................. 84
Island Books, Devon................................. 86
Tarka Books, Devon................................. 83

- WILSON, COLIN
Yarwood Rare Books (Edward), Cheshire 116

- WODEHOUSE, P.G.
Classic Crime Collections, Greater Manchester.. 117
Harrington (Adrian), London (W.)................. 173
Heppa (Christopher), Essex......................... 106
Little Stour Books, Kent 133
Olynthiacs, Shropshire............................... 212

Schutte (David), Hampshire 122
Wayside Books and Cards, Oxfordshire 206
Williams Rare Books (Nigel), London (WC) 179

- WOOLF, VIRGINIA
Chapter and Verse Booksellers, East Sussex 102
Sharpe (Mary), West Sussex 241

- WORDSWORTH, WILLIAM
Island Books, Devon................................. 84

- YATES, DORNFORD
Book for All Reasons (A.), Suffolk................ 227

- YEATS, W.B.
McCann (Joe), Oxfordshire 208

- YOUNG, FRANCIS BRETT
Anvil Books, West Midlands 239

- LOCAL
MK Book Services, Cambridgeshire............... 67
R. & B. Graham, Cornwall 74

- WOMEN
Books & Bygones (Pam Taylor), West Midlands.. 240
Crawford (Elizabeth), London (EC)............... 152
dgbbooks, West Sussex 244
Dolphin Books, Suffolk.............................. 224
Harvest Books, Merseyside 185
Hunter, Bookseller, (K.P.), Cambridgeshire...... 65
Johnson Rare Book Collections (C.R.),
  London (NW)...................................... 158
Kenny's Bookshops and Art Galleries Ltd,
  Republic Of Ireland............................... 278
Lane Books (Shirley), Isle of Wight 132
Reading Lasses, Scotland............................ 264
Swan Bookshop (The), Devon...................... 84
Symes Books (Naomi), Cheshire 72
Willmott Bookseller (Nicholas), Wales............ 280

AUTOBIOGRAPHY
Abacus Gallery / The Village Bookshop,
  Staffordshire...................................... 223
Archer (Steve), London, Outer 180
Book Warren, Devon................................. 84
Books & Bygones, Berkshire....................... 58
Bookworld, Shropshire 212
Booth (Booksearch Service), (Geoff), Cheshire .. 69
Castle Frome Books, Herefordshire 127
Castleton (Pat), Kent................................. 135
Chapter and Verse Booksellers, East Sussex 102
Clements (R.W.), London, Outer 181
Dolphin Books, Suffolk.............................. 224
Family Favourites (Books), East Yorkshire...... 104
Fin Rare Books, Shropshire 213
Gate Memorabilia, London (N)..................... 153

SPECIALITY INDEX

Great Oak Bookshop (The), Wales 287
Harris (Books), (Malcolm), West Midlands 239
Kyrios Books, Nottinghamshire 202
Little Bookshop (The), Greater Manchester 117
Moreton Books, Devon 86
Old Bookshop (The), Somerset 216
Old Storytellers Bookshop (The), Scotland 261
Politico's, London (SW) 166
Price (R.D.M. & I.M.) (Books),
   Greater Manchester 119
Reading Lasses, Scotland 264
Satara Books, West Sussex 244
Sax Books, Suffolk 228
Spranger (Anthony), Wiltshire 251
Stacks Bookshop, Northern Ireland 259
Starlord Books, Cheshire 70
Stride & Son, West Sussex 242
Swan Bookshop (The), Devon 84
Willmott Bookseller (Nicholas), Wales 280

AUTOGRAPHS

Baron (H.), London (NW) 157
Bertram Rota Ltd., London (WC) 176
Books & Bygones (Pam Taylor), West Midlands.. 240
Bookstand, Dorset 93
Bristow & Garland, Hampshire 121
Browning (Julian), London (W) 169
Cox Music (Lisa), Devon 85
Cox Rare Books (Charles), Cornwall 74
Davids Ltd., (Roy), Oxfordshire 207
Farahar & Dupré (Clive & Sophie),
   Wiltshire 250
Finch Rare Books Ltd. (Simon), London (W)... 172
Ford (Richard), London (W) 172
Franks Booksellers, Greater Manchester 117
Harrington Antiquarian Bookseller (Peter),
   London (SW) 164
Kirkman Ltd., (Robert), Bedfordshire 55
Maggs Brothers Limited, London (W) 173
Modern Firsts Etc., Lancashire 140
Politico's, London (SW) 166
Rassam (Paul), London (NW) 158
Silverman (Michael), London (SE) 161
Stage Door Prints, London (WC) 178
Summersgill (Neil), Lancashire 140
Wilson (Autographs) Ltd., (John),
   Gloucestershire 112

AVANT-GARDE

Bluntisham Books, Cambridgeshire 64
Sclanders (Beatbooks), (Andrew), London (EC) 152
Woburn Books, London (N) 156

AVIATION

Addendum Books, Scotland 263
All Books, Essex 108
Anchor Books, Lincolnshire 149
Andron (G.W.), London (N) 153
Armchair Auctions, Hampshire 120
Askew Books (Vernon), Wiltshire 250
Atticus Books, Essex 109
Aviation Book Supply, Hertfordshire 128

Aviation Bookshop (The), London (N) 153
Baldwin (M. & M.), Shropshire 212
Barry Meaden (Aviation Books), Hertfordshire . 129
Black Five Books, Shropshire 213
Bonner (John), West Yorkshire 247
Book Corner, Scotland 263
Books Afloat, Dorset 95
Books Bought & Sold, Surrey 231
Bookworms, Norfolk 187
Booth (Booksearch Service), (Geoff), Cheshire .. 69
Booth Books, Wales 286
Bott, (Bookdealers) Ltd., (Martin), Greater
   Manchester 116
Brewin Books Ltd., Warwickshire 237
Burgess Booksellers, (J. & J.), Cambridgeshire .. 64
Camilla's Bookshop, East Sussex 100
Castle Bookshop, Essex 107
Chelifer Books, Cumbria 79
Cobweb Books, N Yorks 194
Cocks Books (Brian), Cambridgeshire 67
Collectables (W.H.), London (W) 172
Cox (Geoff), Devon 89
Cuddy Books (Michael), London (N) 153
de Lotz Books (P.G.), London (NW) 157
Dorset Rare Books, Wiltshire 252
Duck (William), East Sussex 98
Edwards (London) Limited (Francis),
   London (WC) 177
Empire Books, Greater Manchester 118
Falconwood Transport & Military Bookshop,
   London, Outer 184
Fine Books Oriental Ltd., London (WC) 177
Hairpin Books, Gloucestershire 113
Harlequin Books, Bristol 61
Harris (George J.), Worcestershire 254
Hayles Military Books (Derek), Berkshire 57
Helion & Company, West Midlands 240
Hornsby, Antiquarian and Secondhand Books
   (Malcolm), Leicestershire 144
Hornsey's, N Yorks 194
Horsham Bookshop (The), West Sussex 242
J.B. Books, Berkshire 58
Londonline Books, London (SW) 165
Malmo Books, Hampshire 121
Malvern Bookshop (The), Worcestershire 254
Marine and Cannon Books, Cheshire 70
Military Collector (The), West Yorkshire 249
MilitaryHistoryBooks.com, Kent 136
Morley Case, Hampshire 124
Oblong Books, N Yorks 197
Old Gallery Bookshop (The), Kent 136
Patterson Liddle, Somerset 214
Phelps (Michael), West Sussex 242
Photographery at Soldridge Books, Hampshire . 120
Postings, Surrey 233
Prior (Michael), Lincolnshire 149
Quayside Bookshop, Devon 88
Railway Shop (The), Wales 290
Roberts (Booksellers), (Ray), Staffordshire 223
Rowan (H. & S.J.), Dorset 91
Savery Books, East Sussex 99
Scorpio Books, Suffolk 225
Smith Maritime Aviation Books (Frank),
   Tyne & Wear 235
Spooner (John E.), Dorset 90

SPECIALITY INDEX

Thin Read Line, Merseyside 186
Treasure Chest (The), Suffolk 226
Treasure Island (The), Greater Manchester 118
Vanstone - Aviation Books, (Derek), Suffolk 229
Wayfarer Books, Cornwall............................ 75
World War Books, Kent 139
Yeoman Books, Scotland............................. 270
YSF Books, South Yorkshire....................... 221

BANKING & INSURANCE
Abrahams (Mike), Staffordshire.................... 222
Batterdale Books, N Yorks 195
Collectables (W.H.), London (W)................... 172
Downie Fine Books Ltd., (Robert), Shropshire . 213
InterCol London, London (N) 154

BEAT WRITERS
Addyman Books, Wales 285
Ellis, Bookseller (Peter), London (SE) 160
Orlando Booksellers, Lincolnshire 148
Price (R.W.), Nottinghamshire 202
Red Snapper Books, London (WC) 178
Sclanders (Beatbooks), (Andrew), London (EC) 152
Woburn Books, London (N)......................... 156

BELL-RINGING (CAMPANOLOGY)
Church Green Books, Oxfordshire................. 210
Farringdon (J.M.), Wales 289
St Mary's Books & Prints, Lincolnshire 150

BIBLES
Addyman Books, Wales 285
Barbican Bookshop, N Yorks 196
Bardsley's Books, Suffolk 225
Beckham Books, Suffolk............................. 228
Bookwyze, Lincolnshire 147
Chapter Two, London (SE).......................... 160
Golden Age Books, Worcestershire................ 255
Gradwell Concepts, Merseyside 185
Harrington Antiquarian Bookseller (Peter),
  London (SW).. 164
Hennessey Bookseller (Ray), East Sussex......... 100
Humber Books, Lincolnshire 146
Kirkman Ltd., (Robert), Bedfordshire 55
Lund Theological Books, Cambridgeshire........ 65
Manor House Books/John Trotter Books,
  London (N).. 154
Oasis Booksearch, Cambridgeshire 68
Rosley Books, Cumbria 79
St Philip's Books, Oxfordshire..................... 208
Tuft (Patrick), London (W)......................... 175

BIBLIOGRAPHY
Alastor Books, Hampshire 122
Andron (G.W.), London (N) 153
Ash Rare Books, London (EC) 152
Askew Books (Vernon), Wiltshire.................. 250
Biblion, London (W)................................. 169
Brinded (Scott), Kent 136
Broadhurst of Southport Ltd., Merseyside 186

Caledonia Books, Scotland.......................... 271
Cobnar Books, Kent 136
Cox Old & Rare Books (Claude), Suffolk 226
de Lotz Books (P.G.), London (NW) 157
Dew (Roderick), East Sussex 100
Flora Books, London (E) 151
Ford (Richard), London (W) 172
Forest Books, Lincolnshire.......................... 147
Fotheringham (Alex), Northumberland 200
Gildea (Donald), West Sussex 241
Grant (Gerald S.), Cheshire......................... 69
Howes Bookshop, East Sussex 101
Hunter, Bookseller, (K.P.), Cambridgeshire...... 65
Island Books, Devon................................. 84
Island Books, Devon................................. 86
Maggs Brothers Limited, London (W)............ 173
Marcet Books, London (SE)........................ 161
Marlborough Rare Books Ltd., London (W).... 173
McKay Rare Books (Barry), Cumbria 77
Mead (P.J.), Shropshire.............................. 212
Mills Rare Books (Adam), Cambridgeshire 65
Moss Antiquarian Books (V.J.), Lancashire 142
Muttonchop Manuscripts, West Sussex 243
O'Connor Fine Books, Lancashire................. 142
Philologus–Fine & Rare Books, London (SW) .. 166
Prospect House Books, Northern Ireland 260
Quaritch Ltd., (Bernard), London (W)........... 174
Sabin (Printed Works) (P.R. & V.), Kent 133
Sanderson (Edward), Berkshire..................... 58
Sawyer (Chas. J.), Kent.............................. 137
Shapero Rare Books (Bernard J.), London (W).. 174
Smith Books, (Sally), Suffolk 225
Spooner & Co., Somerset 217
Taylor & Son (Peter), Hertfordshire............... 130
Taylor Rare Books (Michael), Norfolk 187
Tuft (Patrick), London (W)......................... 175
Unsworths Booksellers Ltd., London (WC)...... 178
Ventnor Rare Books, Isle of Wight 132
Wakeman Books (Frances), Nottinghamshire ... 202
Ward (K. Anthony), Norfolk....................... 188
Williams (Bookdealer), (Richard), Lincolnshire . 149
Williams (Christopher), Dorset..................... 93
Wykeham Books, London (SW) 168

BINDINGS
Abacus Gallery / The Village Bookshop,
  Staffordshire.. 223
Abbey Books, London (N)......................... 153
Addyman Books, Wales 285
Allsop (Duncan M.), Warwickshire................ 237
Almar Books, West Yorkshire...................... 247
Alpes Livres (Les), Hampshire 120
Atholl Fine Books, Scotland........................ 273
Atticus Books, Essex 109
Bates & Hindmarch, West Yorkshire.............. 247
Baxter (Steve), Surrey................................ 232
Bayntun (George), Somerset 214
Beck Head Books, Cumbria 78
Beckham Books, Suffolk............................. 228
Biblion, London (W)................................. 169
Bicknell, (T.), Herefordshire 126
Booklore, Leicestershire 144
Bookwyze, Lincolnshire 147
Booth Books, Wales.................................. 286

SPECIALITY INDEX

Chapter and Verse Booksellers, East Sussex 102
Chaucer Bookshop (The), Kent 133
Clark (K.R.), Oxfordshire 205
Classic Bindings, London (SW) 163
Cooper Hay Rare Books, Scotland 271
Cox Old & Rare Books (Claude), Suffolk 226
Cumming Limited (A. & Y.), East Sussex 102
David (G.), Cambridgeshire 64
de Beaumont (Robin), London (SW) 163
Dodd Books (Maurice), Cumbria 77
Dorset Rare Books, Wiltshire 252
ECR Books, Dorset 93
Edwards (London) Limited (Francis),
  London (WC) 177
Elgar (Raymond), East Sussex 98
Ely Books, Cambridgeshire 66
Emerald Isle Books, Northern Ireland 259
Eton Antique Bookshop, Berkshire 59
Finch Rare Books Ltd. (Simon), London (W)... 172
Fine Art, West Sussex 242
Forest Books, Lincolnshire 147
Foster Bookshop (Paul), London (SW) 164
Fosters Bookshop, London (W) 172
Frew Limited (Robert), London (WC) 177
Garbett Antiquarian Books (Michael), Bristol... 111
Grove Bookshop (The), N Yorks 195
Hall's Bookshop, Kent 138
Harrington Antiquarian Bookseller (Peter),
  London (SW) 164
Harrison's Books, London (W) 173
Hereward Books, Cambridgeshire 66
Hodgkins and Company Limited (Ian),
  Gloucestershire 114
Honiton Old Bookshop, Devon 85
Horsham Bookshop (The), West Sussex 242
Island Books, Devon 84
J.C. Poole Books, Wales 290
Kay Books Ltd., Surrey 232
Kenny's Bookshops and Art Galleries Ltd,
  Republic Of Ireland 278
Kirkman Ltd., (Robert), Bedfordshire 55
Maggs Brothers Limited, London (W) 173
Mair Wilkes Books, Scotland 265
Malvern Bookshop (The), Worcestershire 254
Marlborough Rare Books Ltd., London (W).... 173
McConnell Fine Books, Kent 135
Mead (P.J.), Shropshire 212
Moorside Books, Lancashire 141
Moss Antiquarian Books (V.J.), Lancashire 142
Muttonchop Manuscripts, West Sussex 243
O'Connor Fine Books, Lancashire 142
Page Antiquarian Books (Colin), East Sussex ... 99
Patterson Liddle, Somerset 214
Penn Barn Bookshop, Buckinghamshire 63
Russell (Charles), London (SW) 167
St Mary's Books & Prints, Lincolnshire 150
Sawyer (Chas. J.), Kent 137
Seydi Rare Books (Sevin), London (NW) 159
Slaughter & Garratt Rare Books, Worcestershire. 255
Sotheran Limited (Henry), London (W) 175
Spread Eagle Bookshop, London (SE) 162
Staniland (Booksellers), Lincolnshire 150
Sterling Books, Somerset 219
Stothert Old Books, Cheshire 69
Summersgill (Neil), Lancashire 140
Thomas (Books) (Leona), Cheshire 71
Tobo Books, Hampshire 122
Turton (John), Durham 97
Unsworths Booksellers Ltd., London (WC) 178
Vandeleur Antiquarian Books, Surrey 231
Ventnor Rare Books, Isle of Wight 132
Wayfarer Books, Cornwall 75
Winchester Bookshop (The), Hampshire 125
Woodbine Books, West Yorkshire 245

BIOGRAPHY

Abacus Gallery / The Village Bookshop,
  Staffordshire 223
Anderson Slater Antiques, N Yorks 195
Applin (Malcolm), Berkshire 57
Archer (Steve), London, Outer 180
Arden Books & Cosmographia, Warwickshire... 236
Arthurian Book, Wales 285
Ashburton Books, Devon 83
Askew Books (Vernon), Wiltshire 250
Beckham Books, Suffolk 228
Bell (Peter), Scotland 269
Beware of The Leopard Books, Bristol 60
Black Five Books, Shropshire 213
Blythswood Bookshop, Scotland 268
Bonner (John), West Yorkshire 247
Book Bungalow (The), Cornwall 73
BookLovers, Somerset 217
Bookroom (The), Surrey 233
Books (For All), N Yorks 192
Books for Writers, Wales 283
Books Galore, Somerset 216
Bookworms, Norfolk 187
Booth (Booksearch Service), (Geoff), Cheshire .. 69
Bosco Books, Cornwall 73
Brighton Books, East Sussex 98
Broadhurst of Southport Ltd., Merseyside 186
Brock Books, N Yorks 192
Brookbanks (P.S.), Cambridgeshire 67
Bush, Bookdealer (John), Gloucestershire 115
Caledonia Books, Scotland 271
Camden Books, Somerset 214
Carnforth Bookshop (The), Lancashire 140
Castle Frome Books, Herefordshire 127
Castleton (Pat), Kent 135
Catalyst Books, Surrey 232
Cavan Book Centre, Republic Of Ireland 275
Cecil Books, Surrey 231
Chapter and Verse Booksellers, East Sussex 102
Charmouth Bookstore, Dorset 91
Chaucer Bookshop (The), Kent 133
Classic Bindings, London (SW) 163
Clements (R.W.), London, Outer 181
Criterion Books, London, Outer 182
Croft Selections, Lincolnshire 148
Darkwood Books, Republic Of Ireland 276
dgbbooks, West Sussex 244
Dolphin Books, Suffolk 224
Doolin Dinghy Books, Republic Of Ireland..... 275
Downie Fine Books Ltd., (Robert), Shropshire . 213
Ellis, Bookseller (Peter), London (SE) 160
Empire Books, Greater Manchester 118
Family Favourites (Books), East Yorkshire 104
Fin Rare Books, Shropshire 213

SPECIALITY INDEX

Firth (Bijou Books & Photography) (Maureen), South Yorkshire ... 221
Frost (Richard), Hertfordshire ... 128
Gate Memorabilia, London (N) ... 153
Gildea (Donald), West Sussex ... 241
Golden Hind Bookshop (The), Kent ... 134
Graham (John), Dorset ... 95
Great Oak Bookshop (The), Wales ... 287
Hab Books, London (W) ... 173
Hall's Bookshop, Kent ... 138
Hawley (C.L.), N Yorks ... 195
Hayles Military Books (Derek), Berkshire ... 57
Holmes Books (Harry), East Yorkshire ... 105
Horsham Bookshop (The), West Sussex ... 242
Ice House Books ... 143
Langmaid (Kenneth), Cornwall ... 76
Llyfraufflur Books, Wales ... 290
LSA Books, Warwickshire ... 236
Malmo Books, Hampshire ... 121
Malvern Bookshop (The), Worcestershire ... 254
McCaughtrie (K.A.), N Yorks ... 192
McCrone (Audrey), Scotland ... 272
Miller, (Dusty), Cornwall ... 73
Missing Books, Essex ... 108
Modlock (Lilian), Dorset ... 92
Mr. Pickwick of Towcester, Northamptonshire ... 199
Nineteenth Century Books, Oxfordshire ... 209
Noel and Holland Books, Republic Of Ireland ... 278
Oblong Books, N Yorks ... 197
O'Brien Books & Photo Gallery, Republic Of Ireland ... 279
O'Donoghue Books, London (SW) ... 165
Old Bookshop (The), Somerset ... 216
Old Storytellers Bookshop (The), Scotland ... 261
Olynthiacs, Shropshire ... 212
Park Gallery & Bookshop (The), Northamptonshire ... 199
Peter Lyons Books, Gloucestershire ... 112
Politico's, London (SW) ... 166
Pooks Motor Books, Leicestershire ... 144
Premier Books & Prints, Lincolnshire ... 146
Price (R.D.M. & I.M.) (Books), Greater Manchester ... 119
Pringle Booksellers (Andrew), Scotland ... 270
Prospect House Books, Northern Ireland ... 260
R. & A. Books, East Sussex ... 100
Reading Lasses, Scotland ... 264
Richmond Books, N Yorks ... 194
Roosterbooks, Northamptonshire ... 198
Rothwell and Dunworth, Somerset ... 216
Roundstone Books, Lancashire ... 141
Sanderson (Edward), Berkshire ... 58
Saunders (Tom), Wales ... 280
Savery Books, East Sussex ... 99
Sax Books, Suffolk ... 228
Shacklock Books (David), Suffolk ... 226
Smith Books, (Sally), Suffolk ... 225
Spranger (Anthony), Wiltshire ... 251
Spread Eagle Books, Wales ... 282
Starlord Books, Cheshire ... 70
Stroma Books, Scotland ... 261
Swan Bookshop (The), Devon ... 84
Tantalus Antiques & Books, Devon ... 87
Target Books, Cambridgeshire ... 68
Taylor & Son (Peter), Hertfordshire ... 130
Thornton (Grahame), Dorset ... 94
Trevorrow (Edwin), Hertfordshire ... 128
Visser Books (de), Cambridgeshire ... 66
Wayside Books and Cards, Oxfordshire ... 205
Wheen O'Blethers Bookshop, Scotland ... 271
Whitfield (Ken), Essex ... 109
Willmott Bookseller (Nicholas), Wales ... 280
Wood (Peter), Cambridgeshire ... 66
Wychwood Books, Gloucestershire ... 114
Yarwood Rare Books (Edward), Cheshire ... 116

BIOLOGY

Alba Books, Scotland ... 267
Austwick Hall Books, N Yorks ... 141
Baron - Scientific Book Sales (P.J.), Somerset ... 215
Bracton Books, Cambridgeshire ... 64
Buchan Collectibles, Scotland ... 265
Ice House Books ... 143
Smith (David & Lynn), London, Outer ... 182
Wyseby House Books, Berkshire ... 57

BLACK STUDIES

Afar Books International, West Midlands ... 238
Black Voices, Merseyside ... 185
Oriental and African Books, Shropshire ... 213
Spurrier (Nick), Kent ... 136
Woburn Books, London (N) ... 156

BOOK OF HOURS

Addyman Books, Wales ... 285
Du Ry Medieval Manuscripts (Marc–Antoine), London (W) ... 172
Shipley Specialist Art Booksellers, London (WC) ... 178

BOOKBINDING

Andron (G.W.), London (N) ... 153
Beverley Old Bookshop, East Yorkshire ... 104
Coupland (Terry W.), Staffordshire ... 222
Island Books, Devon ... 84
McKay Rare Books (Barry), Cumbria ... 77

BOOKS ABOUT BOOKS

Addyman Books, Wales ... 285
Alastor Books, Hampshire ... 122
Andron (G.W.), London (N) ... 153
Arundel Bookshop, West Sussex ... 241
Avonbridge Books, Gloucestershire ... 114
Bardsley's Books, Suffolk ... 225
Bracton Books, Cambridgeshire ... 64
Brinded (Scott), Kent ... 136
Brock Books, N Yorks ... 192
Brockwells Bookshop, London (SE) ... 160
Cowley, Bookdealer (K.W.), Somerset ... 215
Cox Old & Rare Books (Claude), Suffolk ... 226
Deverell Books, Bristol ... 61
Forest Books, Lincolnshire ... 147
Grant (Gerald S.), Cheshire ... 69
Havercroft Antiquarian Books, London (SE) ... 161
Island Books, Devon ... 84
Malvern Bookshop (The), Worcestershire ... 254

SPECIALITY INDEX

McKay Rare Books (Barry), Cumbria 77
Mead (P.J.), Shropshire 212
Mills Rare Books (Adam), Cambridgeshire 65
Moss Antiquarian Books (V.J.), Lancashire 142
Mr. Pickwick of Towcester, Northamptonshire.. 199
Muttonchop Manuscripts, West Sussex 243
Nineteenth Century Books, Oxfordshire 209
Rosemary Books, Merseyside 186
Thomas (Books) (Leona), Cheshire 71
Troath Books (Brian), London (E) 151
Unsworths Booksellers Ltd., London (WC) 178
Updike Rare Books (John), Scotland 270
Wakeman Books (Frances), Nottinghamshire ... 202
Ward (K. Anthony), Norfolk 188
Wykeham Books, London (SW) 168
Zardoz Books, Wiltshire 253

BOTANY

Austwick Hall Books, N Yorks 141
Baron - Scientific Book Sales (P.J.), Somerset ... 215
Bernwode Books, Buckinghamshire 62
Bland (Mary), Herefordshire 126
Blest (Peter), Kent 136
Book Corner, Scotland 263
Brown (Books) (P.R.), Durham 96
Buchan Collectibles, Scotland 265
Buxton Books (Anna), Scotland 269
Calluna Books, Dorset 94
Crack (Books) (F.N.), Lancashire 140
Curtle Mead Books, Isle of Wight 131
Dene Barn Books & Prints, Somerset 218
Goodyer (Nicholas), London (N) 154
Harrington Antiquarian Bookseller (Peter),
  London (SW) 164
Ian Johnson Natural History Books,
  Buckinghamshire 63
Ice House Books 143
Jay Books, Scotland 269
Kennedy (Peter), Surrey 234
Morgan (D. & D.H.W.), Devon 89
On the Wild Side, Worcestershire 255
Park (Mike), London, Outer 183
Phelps (Michael), West Sussex 242
Sue Lowell Natural History Books, London (W) 175
Thin Read Line, Merseyside 186
Woodside Books, Kent 133
Wyseby House Books, Berkshire 57

BREWING

Collectables (W.H.), London (W) 172
Cooksweb, Northamptonshire 198
Lucas (Richard), London (NW) 158
Phelps (Michael), West Sussex 242
Thorne (John), Essex 107
Woodlands Books, West Yorkshire 248

BRIDGE

Beaver Booksearch, Suffolk 225
Jones (Anne), Cornwall 76

BROADCASTING

Kelly Books, Devon 88

Kent T. G., Surrey 230
Wood (Peter), Cambridgeshire 66

BUILDING & CONSTRUCTION

Brown-Studies, Scotland 270
Buckland Books, West Sussex 243
Duck (William), East Sussex 98
Elton Engineering Books, London (W) 172
Ice House Books 143
Inch's Books, N Yorks 194
Staniland (Booksellers), Lincolnshire 150
Trinders' Fine Tools, Suffolk 225

BULL FIGHTING

Askew Books (Vernon), Wiltshire 250
Books on Spain, London, Outer 183
Orssich (Paul), London (SW) 166

BUSES/TRAMS

Bott, (Bookdealers) Ltd., (Martin), Greater
  Manchester 116
Burgess Booksellers, (J. & J.), Cambridgeshire .. 64
Dinnages Transport Publishing, East Sussex 98
Hairpin Books, Gloucestershire 113
Jones (Barry), West Sussex 242
Quayside Bookshop, Devon 88
Roland Books, Kent 137
Simon Lewis Transport Books, Gloucestershire . 112
Wilson Books (Henry), Cheshire 71

BUSINESS STUDIES

Boer (Louise), Arthurian Books, Wales 284
Ice House Books 143
Roland Books, Kent 137
Savery Books, East Sussex 99

BYZANTIUM

Adab Books, Cambridgeshire 64
Askew Books (Vernon), Wiltshire 250
Hellenic Bookservices, London (NW) 158
Loman, Oriental Books & Manuscripts (David),
  London (SW) 165
Unsworths Booksellers Ltd., London (WC) 178
Whitchurch Books Ltd., Wales 280

CALLIGRAPHY

Downie Fine Books Ltd., (Robert), Shropshire . 213
Eggeling Books (John), West Yorkshire 248
McKay Rare Books (Barry), Cumbria 77
Taylor Rare Books (Michael), Norfolk 187
Wheen O'Blethers Bookshop, Scotland 271
Young (D. & J.), Wales 289

CANALS/INLAND WATERWAYS

Abrahams (Mike), Staffordshire 222
Adab Books, Cambridgeshire 64
Anchor Books, Lincolnshire 149
Anvil Books, West Midlands 239
Archer (Steve), London, Outer 180
Arden Books & Cosmographia, Warwickshire... 236

SPECIALITY INDEX

Baldwin (M. & M.), Shropshire 212
Barbican Bookshop, N Yorks 196
Batterdale Books, N Yorks 195
Bird Books (Nigel), Wales 281
Books Afloat, Dorset 95
Bott, (Bookdealers) Ltd., (Martin), Greater
  Manchester 116
Cartographics, Staffordshire 223
Classic Crime Collections, Greater Manchester .. 117
Collectables (W.H.), London (W) 172
Cottage Books, Leicestershire 143
Coulthurst (Richard), Greater Manchester 118
Cox (Geoff), Devon 89
Crosby Nethercott Books, London, Outer 180
Crouch Rare Books, Surrey 232
Duck (William), East Sussex 98
Eastcote Bookshop (The), London, Outer 183
Fine Books Oriental Ltd., London (WC) 177
Hennessey Bookseller (Ray), East Sussex 100
Island Books, Devon 84
Island Books, Devon 86
Jones (Anne), Cornwall 76
Jones (Barry), West Sussex 242
Joppa Books Ltd., Surrey 230
Kingswood Books, Dorset 93
KSC Books, Cheshire 71
Maddison (J.K.), West Midlands 238
Nebulous Books, Hampshire 120
Patterson Liddle, Somerset 214
Roadmaster Books, Kent 134
Rochdale Book Company, Greater Manchester . 118
Shaw (David M.), Cheshire 72
Skyrack Books, West Yorkshire 246
Swan Bookshop (The), Devon 84
Wilson Books (Henry), Cheshire 71
Winchester Antiquarian Books, Hampshire 125

CARICATURE
Batterham (David), London (W) 169
Hogan (F. & J.), London (N) 154

CARPETS
Barmby (C. & A.J.), Kent 138
Byrom Textile Bookroom (Richard), Lancashire .. 140
Heneage Art Books (Thomas), London (SW) 164
Shipley Specialist Art Booksellers, London (WC) . 178
Trinders' Fine Tools, Suffolk 225

CARRIAGES & DRIVING
Adab Books, Cambridgeshire 64
Joppa Books Ltd., Surrey 230
Pennymead Books, N Yorks 193
Phenotype Books, Cumbria 79

CARTOGRAPHY
Archer (David), Wales 288
Bannister (David), Gloucestershire 111
Cartographics, Staffordshire 223
Frew Limited (Robert), London (WC) 177
Heritage, West Midlands 238
Hogan (F. & J.), London (N) 154

InterCol London, London (N) 154
Morris (Michael), Staffordshire 222
Newby (Valerie), Buckinghamshire 63
Orssich (Paul), London (SW) 166
Ouse Valley Books, Bedfordshire 56
Paralos Ltd., London (W) 173
Potter Limited (Jonathan), London (W) 174
Stanhope Bibliophiles, London (N) 155

CARTOONS
Bates & Hindmarch, West Yorkshire 247
D. & M. Books, West Yorkshire 248
Facet Books, Dorset 90
Fine Books Oriental Ltd., London (WC) 177
Hunter and Krageloh, Derbyshire 82
Ice House Books 143
Kingswood Books, Dorset 93

CATALOGUES RAISONNES
Ars Artis, Oxfordshire 206
Barlow (Vincent G.), Hampshire 123
Dorset Rare Books, Wiltshire 252
DoublePlusBooks, Cambridgeshire 68
Garton & Co., Wiltshire 250
Heneage Art Books (Thomas), London (SW) 164
Shipley Specialist Art Booksellers, London (WC) . 178

CATS
Annie's Books, South Yorkshire 220
Archivist (The), Devon 88
Mayhew (Veronica), Berkshire 58
Wise Owl Bookshop (The), Bristol 61

CERAMICS
Abacus Gallery / The Village Bookshop,
  Staffordshire 223
Art Reference Books, Hampshire 123
Barmby (C. & A.J.), Kent 138
Books at the Warehouse, N Yorks 193
Buckland Books, West Sussex 243
Clark (Nigel A.), London (SE) 160
Cover to Cover, Merseyside 186
DoublePlusBooks, Cambridgeshire 68
Firth (Bijou Books & Photography) (Maureen),
  South Yorkshire 221
Heneage Art Books (Thomas), London (SW) 164
Ives Bookseller (John), London, Outer 184
Martin - Bookseller (Colin), East Yorkshire 105
Moss Books, London (NW) 158
Reference Works Ltd., Dorset 94
Shipley Specialist Art Booksellers, London (WC) . 178
Silver Trees Books, West Midlands 239
Studio Bookshop, East Sussex 99

CHEMISTRY
Baron - Scientific Book Sales (P.J.), Somerset ... 215
Beware of The Leopard Books, Bristol 60
Ice House Books 143
Phelps (Michael), West Sussex 242
Weiner (Graham), London (N) 156

SPECIALITY INDEX

CHESS

Abbey Bookshop, Hampshire 122
Bowers Chess Suppliers (Francis), Cambridgeshire 67
Caissa Books, Surrey................................. 233
Ellen, The Bookshop (Barrie E.), Essex........... 110
Gorton Booksearch (John), East Sussex 103
Ice House Books 143
Peterson (Tony), Essex.............................. 109
Saunders (Tom), Wales 280
Savery Books, East Sussex 99
Treglown (Roger J.), Cheshire..................... 71

CHILDREN'S
- GENERAL

AA1 Books, Scotland................................ 263
Abbey Bookshop, Hampshire 122
Abrahams (Mike), Staffordshire.................... 222
Addendum Books, Scotland 263
Altshuler (Jean), Cumbria........................... 78
Annie's Books, South Yorkshire 220
Anwoth Books, Scotland 263
ARC Books, Scotland 272
Arden Books & Cosmographia, Warwickshire... 236
Assinder Books, Bedfordshire 55
Badger Books, Somerset............................. 218
Baker - Books for the Collector (Colin), Devon.. 88
Barlow (Vincent G.), Hampshire.................... 123
Bates Books, London, Outer........................ 181
Bayntun (George), Somerset 214
Beck (John), East Sussex 101
Bee Books New and Old, Cornwall 73
Beverley Old Bookshop, East Yorkshire.......... 104
Biblion, London (W)................................. 169
Black Cat Bookshop, Leicestershire 143
Black Five Books, Shropshire 213
Blacket Books, Scotland............................. 269
Book Bungalow (The), Cornwall................... 73
Book House (The), Cumbria........................ 78
Book Warren, Devon 84
Bookmark (Children's Books), Wiltshire 252
Bookroom (The), Surrey 233
Books & Bygones, Berkshire........................ 58
Books (For All), N Yorks............................ 192
Books Bought & Sold, Surrey....................... 231
Books Galore, Somerset 216
Bookshop (The), Cambridgeshire 64
Bookshop Blackheath, London (SE) 160
Bookworld, Shropshire 212
Book–Worm International, Essex................... 107
Bookworms, Norfolk................................. 187
Booth Books, Wales.................................. 286
Border Bookshop (The), West Yorkshire......... 248
Boris Books, Dorset.................................. 94
Bowers Chess Suppliers (Francis),
  Cambridgeshire..................................... 67
Box of Frogs (The), Scotland....................... 263
Bright (P.G.), Cambridgeshire 66
Brighton Books, East Sussex 98
Broadhurst of Southport Ltd., Merseyside 186
Broadleaf Books, Wales 290
Browning Books, Wales 290
Bryony Books, West Yorkshire 247
Buchan Collectibles, Scotland 265
Bufo Books, Hampshire 123

Burgess Booksellers, (J. & J.), Cambridgeshire .. 64
Butts Books (Mary), Berkshire..................... 58
Bygone Books, Lancashire.......................... 141
Camilla's Bookshop, East Sussex 100
Canterbury Bookshop (The), Kent 133
Castleton (Pat), Kent................................ 135
Catalyst Books, Surrey 232
Charmouth Bookstore, Dorset 91
Childrens Bookshop, West Yorkshire 246
Clarke (J. & D.), Norfolk 189
Clements (R.W.), London, Outer 181
Cornell Books, Gloucestershire.................... 114
Coupland (Terry W.), Staffordshire............... 222
Croft Selections, Lincolnshire...................... 148
Cygnet Books, East Yorkshire 105
D. & M. Books, West Yorkshire................... 248
David (G.), Cambridgeshire........................ 64
Dawson (Modern First Editions), (Philip),
  London, Outer 183
Dean Illustrated Books (Myra), Wales............ 284
Deverell Books, Bristol.............................. 61
Devitt Books (Nial), Warwickshire 236
Doolin Dinghy Books, Republic Of Ireland...... 275
Doorbar (P. & D.), Hampshire..................... 122
Drummond Pleasures of Past Times (David),
  London (WC) 176
Eastcote Bookshop (The), London, Outer........ 183
ECR Books, Dorset.................................. 93
Ellis, Bookseller (Peter), London (SE) 160
Ely Books, Cambridgeshire 66
Everett (Richard), Norfolk......................... 187
Facet Books, Dorset 90
Fin Rare Books, Shropshire 213
Foster Bookshop (Paul), London (SW)........... 164
Fosters Bookshop, London (W).................... 172
Franks Booksellers, Greater Manchester 117
Furneaux Books (Lee), Devon 87
Game Advice, Oxfordshire.......................... 207
Gant (Elizabeth), Surrey............................. 231
Gloucester Road Bookshop, London (SW) 164
Golden Hind Bookshop (The), Kent 134
Green Meadow Books, Cornwall 75
Greer (Robin), London (SW)....................... 164
Harrington (Adrian), London (W)................. 173
Harrington Antiquarian Bookseller (Peter),
  London (SW)...................................... 164
Harrison's Books, London (W) 173
Hawley (C.L.), N Yorks............................. 195
Heppa (Christopher), Essex........................ 106
Heywood Hill Limited (G.), London (W) 173
Hillside House, Lincolnshire....................... 147
Hodgkins and Company Limited (Ian),
  Gloucestershire..................................... 114
Hoggarth (John R.), N Yorks...................... 196
Holtom (Christopher), Cornwall 76
Hornsey's, N Yorks.................................. 194
Hurly Burly Books, Wiltshire...................... 253
Illustrated Book (The), London (SW)............ 165
Innes Books, Shropshire............................. 212
Intech Books, Northumberland.................... 201
J.K. Bookfinders, London (SW)................... 165
Japan Books (Y & S Company Ltd.), Surrey.... 180
JB Books & Collectables, West Sussex........... 243
Jones (J.V.A.), Essex................................ 109
Jonkers Rare Books, Oxfordshire.................. 206

SPECIALITY INDEX

K. Books, Cheshire.................................... 72
Katnap Arts, Norfolk................................ 189
Keel Row Books, Tyne & Wear.................... 235
Kellow Books, Oxfordshire 204
Keswick Bookshop, Cumbria 78
Kevin S. Ogilvie Modern First Editions,
  Scotland... 265
Key Books (Sarah), Cambridgeshire............... 65
Kineton Nooks, Warwickshire 236
Korn Books, (M.E.), London (N) 154
Lane Books (Shirley), Isle of Wight 132
Leabeck Books, Oxfordshire 208
Leaf Ends, Northumberland 201
Little Stour Books, Kent 133
Lloyd-Davies (Sue), Wales 280
Lucius Books, N Yorks................................ 196
Malvern Bookshop (The), Worcestershire 254
March House Books, Dorset 94
McCrone (Audrey), Scotland 272
McNaughtan's Bookshop, Scotland 269
Miller, (Dusty), Cornwall 73
Minster Gate Bookshop, N Yorks................. 196
Modlock (Lilian), Dorset.............................. 92
New Strand Bookshop (The), Herefordshire..... 126
Noel and Holland Books, Republic Of Ireland.. 278
Oblong Books, N Yorks.............................. 197
Old Station Pottery & Bookshop (The),
  Norfolk.. 191
Olio Books, East Sussex 101
Page Antiquarian Books (Colin), East Sussex ... 99
Paperbacks Plus, Bristol.............................. 61
Park Gallery & Bookshop (The),
  Northamptonshire 199
Peakirk Books, Cambridgeshire 68
Periwinkle Press, Kent............................... 134
Peter Lyons Books, Gloucestershire 112
Peter's Bookshop, Norfolk 190
Petersham Books, London (SW) 166
Price (R.W.), Nottinghamshire 202
R. & A. Books, East Sussex 100
Reeve (M. & D.), Oxfordshire..................... 208
Ripping Yarns, London (N) 155
River Reads Bookshop, Devon...................... 88
Riverside Bookshop (The), Cumbria 78
Roberts (Fine Books) (Julian), Lincolnshire 149
Rochdale Book Company, Greater Manchester. 118
Rosemary Books, Merseyside...................... 186
Rose's Books, Wales 287
Roundstone Books, Lancashire 141
Rowan House Books, Surrey 231
Russell Books, Somerset............................ 218
St Mary's Books & Prints, Lincolnshire 150
St Michael at Plea Bookshop, Norfolk 190
Satara Books, West Sussex 244
Saunders (Tom), Wales 280
Savage (Keith A.), Suffolk 228
Savery Books, East Sussex 99
Schutte (David), Hampshire 122
Scrivener's Books & Book Binding, Derbyshire . 81
Second Edition, Scotland 270
Sesemann (Julia), Kent 133
Shakeshaft (Dr. B.), Cheshire....................... 72
Sharpe (Mary), West Sussex 241
Silver Trees Books, West Midlands............... 239
Simpson (Dave), Scotland.......................... 262
Sims (Sue), Dorset.................................... 91
Singleton, (John), London (N) 155
Siri Ellis Books, Greater Manchester............ 116
Smith (Peter Bain), Cumbria 77
Smith Books, (Sally), Suffolk 225
Smith Modern First Editions, (Chris Adam),
  West Sussex.. 243
Sotheran Limited (Henry), London (W) 175
Spread Eagle Bookshop, London (SE).......... 162
Stacks Bookshop, Northern Ireland 259
Staffs Bookshop (The), Staffordshire 222
Stansbury (Rosemary), Devon...................... 87
Stella Books, Wales 284
Stinton (Judith), Dorset............................... 92
Stothert Old Books, Cheshire....................... 69
Thorne (Nick), Gloucestershire 112
Thornton Books (Richard), London (N) 155
Thurston (Barry), Scotland 273
Tiffin (Tony and Gill), Durham 96
Till's Bookshop, Scotland 270
Updike Rare Books (John), Scotland 270
Wiend Books & Collectables,
  Greater Manchester 119
Wilbraham (J. & S.), London (NW).............. 159
Wilson (J. & M.), Scotland 273
Wise Owl Bookshop (The), Bristol 61
Words & Music, Cheshire 70
Wright (Norman), Hertfordshire 130
Yates Antiquarian Books (Tony), Leicestershire 144
Yewtree Books, Cumbria............................ 78

- ILLUSTRATED

Amwell Book Company (The), London (EC).... 152
Art Reference Books, Hampshire 123
Autolycus, Shropshire............................... 211
Baker - Books for the Collector (Colin), Devon. 88
Bayntun (George), Somerset...................... 214
Books & Things, London (W)..................... 169
BOOKS4U, Wales.................................... 282
Browning Books, Wales 290
Castleton (Pat), Kent................................ 135
Catalyst Books, Surrey 232
Doorbar (P. & D.), Hampshire.................... 122
Green Meadow Books, Cornwall 75
Hennessey Bookseller (Ray), East Sussex......... 100
Hurly Burly Books, Wiltshire..................... 253
Lake (David), Norfolk 189
Lloyd-Davies (Sue), Wales 280
Lucius Books, N Yorks.............................. 196
Petersham Books, London (SW) 166
Rhodes, Bookseller (Peter), Hampshire 124
Rose's Books, Wales 287
Shakeshaft (Roger & Sylvia), Lincolnshire 146
Shapero Rare Books (Bernard J.), London (W). 174
Siri Ellis Books, Greater Manchester............ 116
Slavin Rare and Collectable Books (Derek),
  Warwickshire.. 237
Spread Eagle Bookshop, London (SE).......... 162
Unicorn Books, London, Outer 181

CHRISTMAS

Castleton (Pat), Kent................................ 135
Cooksweb, Northamptonshire..................... 198

Nostalgia Unlimited, Merseyside.................. 185

CHURCHILLIANA
Askew Books (Vernon), Wiltshire.................. 250
Baxter (Steve), Surrey.............................. 232
Bicknell, (T.), Herefordshire 126
Guildmaster Books, Cheshire...................... 71
Harrington (Adrian), London (W)................ 173
Harrington Antiquarian Bookseller (Peter),
  London (SW)....................................... 164
Island Books, Devon................................ 84
Sawyer (Chas. J.), Kent............................ 137
Sax Books, Suffolk 228
Sotheran Limited (Henry), London (W) 175
Stride & Son, West Sussex 242
Updike Rare Books (John), Scotland 270

CINEMA/FILM
Ashfield Books and Records, Nottinghamshire.. 203
Bardsley's Books, Suffolk 225
Barn Books, Buckinghamshire..................... 62
Book Basket, London, Outer 182
Bookroom (The), Surrey 233
Books, Wales... 282
Books Plus, Devon 87
Bookworm, Essex................................... 106
Booth Books, Wales................................ 286
Brighton Books, East Sussex 98
Byre Books, Scotland 264
Caledonia Books, Scotland......................... 271
Catalyst Books, Surrey 232
Cinema Bookshop (The), London (WC)......... 176
Cover to Cover, Merseyside 186
Cowley, Bookdealer (K.W.), Somerset 215
Cusack Books, London (W) 172
Downie Fine Books Ltd., (Robert), Shropshire . 213
Eastcote Bookshop (The), London, Outer....... 183
Fitzsimons (Anne), Cumbria....................... 77
Franks Booksellers, Greater Manchester 117
Gate Memorabilia, London (N)................... 153
Ice House Books..................................... 143
Inprint, Gloucestershire............................. 114
Jericho Books, Oxfordshire 208
Kaye - Bookseller (Terence), London (NW) 158
Keel Row Books, Tyne & Wear................... 235
Kelly Books, Devon................................. 88
Kenny's Bookshops and Art Galleries Ltd,
  Republic Of Ireland............................... 278
Kent T. G., Surrey 230
Left Bank (The), Wales............................. 290
McGee (Terence J.), London, Outer.............. 181
Modlock (Lilian), Dorset............................ 92
Moon's Bookshop (Michael), Cumbria 79
Morris (Chris), Oxfordshire........................ 208
Moviedrome, East Sussex 99
Nevitsky (Philip), Greater Manchester 117
Oblong Books, N Yorks............................ 197
O'Brien Books & Photo Gallery, Republic Of
  Ireland... 279
Paramor (C.D.), Suffolk 227
Prescott - The Bookseller (John),
  London, Outer 184
Reads, Dorset 94

Satara Books, West Sussex......................... 244
Savery Books, East Sussex 99
Scrivener's Books & Book Binding, Derbyshire. 81
Singleton, (John), London (N) 155
Spread Eagle Bookshop, London (SE)............ 162
Stage Door Prints, London (WC).................. 178
Till's Bookshop, Scotland........................... 270
Treasure Chest (The), Suffolk 226
Troath Books (Brian), London (E) 151
Unsworths Booksellers Ltd., London (WC)...... 178
Wiend Books & Collectables,
  Greater Manchester 119
Williams (Bookdealer), (Richard), Lincolnshire . 149
Wood (Peter), Cambridgeshire 66
www.drivepast.com, Gloucestershire.............. 114

CIRCUS
Cover to Cover, Merseyside 186
Davis (Peter), Kent.................................. 136
Drummond Pleasures of Past Times (David),
  London (WC) 176
Fitzsimons (Anne), Cumbria....................... 77
Kaye - Bookseller (Terence), London (NW) 158
Webster (D.), Scotland.............................. 272

CITIES
Duck (William), East Sussex....................... 98
Inch's Books, N Yorks 194
Marcan, Bookseller (Peter), London (SE) 161

CITY OF LONDON
Ash Rare Books, London (EC) 152
Missing Books, Essex 108
Sawyer (Chas. J.), Kent............................ 137
Spread Eagle Bookshop, London (SE)............ 162

CIVIL ENGINEERING
Camden Books, Somerset 214
Elton Engineering Books, London (W) 172
Jones (Anne), Cornwall............................. 76
Stewart (Ian), Kent.................................. 137

CLASSICAL STUDIES
Camden Books, Somerset 214
Carnforth Bookshop (The), Lancashire........... 140
Chthonios Books, East Sussex..................... 100
Crouch Rare Books, Surrey........................ 232
Graves–Johnston (Michael), London (SW)....... 164
Hellenic Bookservices, London (NW)............ 158
Hill (Peter), Hampshire............................. 121
Howes Bookshop, East Sussex 101
Ice House Books..................................... 143
Jericho Books, Oxfordshire 208
Lamb (R.W.), Suffolk............................... 227
Loman, Oriental Books & Manuscripts (David),
  London (SW)....................................... 165
Moseley Books, West Midlands................... 238
Museum Bookshop, London (WC)................ 177
Olynthiacs, Shropshire.............................. 212
Paralos Ltd., London (W).......................... 173

Polczynski (Udo K.H.), London, Outer 183
Poole (William), London (W)......................... 174
Quest Books, East Yorkshire 105
Seydi Rare Books (Sevin), London (NW) 159
Smith (Peter Bain), Cumbria.......................... 77
Sokol Books (A.), London (W) 174
Stewart (Andrew), Cornwall 75
Troath Books (Brian), London (E) 151
Unsworths Booksellers Ltd., London (WC)...... 178

COCKFIGHTING

Blest (Peter), Kent..................................... 136
Chalmers Hallam (E.), Hampshire................. 123
Coch-y-Bonddu Books, Wales....................... 288
Home Farm Books, Warwickshire.................. 236
Kilgour (Sporting Books) (Ian), Leicestershire... 145
Scott (Sporting Books) (John), Worcestershire .. 256

COLLECTING

Abrahams (Mike), Staffordshire..................... 222
Art Reference Books, Hampshire................... 123
Barmby (C. & A.J.), Kent............................ 138
Barn Books, Buckinghamshire....................... 62
Books, Kent 134
Browzers, Greater Manchester 117
Buckland Books, West Sussex 243
Clark (Nigel A.), London (SE)...................... 160
Collectors Corner, Wiltshire 252
DoublePlusBooks, Cambridgeshire 68
Heneage Art Books (Thomas), London (SW).... 164
Ives Bookseller (John), London, Outer........... 184
Lion Fine Arts and Books, Wales 287
Moss Antiquarian Books (V.J.), Lancashire 142
Nostalgia Unlimited, Merseyside................... 185
O'Connor Fine Books, Lancashire.................. 142
Porcupines, Devon 84
Restormel Books, Worcestershire 256
Riccetti (Margaret), South Yorkshire 220
Spread Eagle Bookshop, London (SE)............ 162
Trinders' Fine Tools, Suffolk 225
Wiend Books & Collectables,
    Greater Manchester 119

COLONIAL

Afar Books International, West Midlands........ 238
Eggeling Books (John), West Yorkshire 248
Empire Books, Greater Manchester 118
Graves–Johnston (Michael), London (SW)....... 164
Kenny's Bookshops and Art Galleries Ltd,
    Republic Of Ireland 278
Military Collector (The), West Yorkshire 249
Pennymead Books, N Yorks......................... 193
Price (R.D.M. & I.M.) (Books),
    Greater Manchester 119
Thin Read Line, Merseyside 186
Woolcott Books, Dorset............................... 92

COLOUR-PLATE

Artco, Nottinghamshire 202
Aurelian Books, London (NW) 157
Biblion, London (W)................................... 169
Bolton Books, Hampshire............................ 120

Booth (Booksearch Service), (Geoff), Cheshire .. 69
Bowden Books, Leicestershire 144
Chapter and Verse Booksellers, East Sussex 102
Cornell Books, Gloucestershire..................... 114
Eastcote Bookshop (The), London, Outer........ 183
Fine Art, West Sussex 242
Goodyer (Nicholas), London (N) 154
Grayling (David A.H.), Cumbria 78
Halson Books, Cheshire 71
Harrington (Adrian), London (W)................. 173
Harrington Antiquarian Bookseller (Peter),
    London (SW)....................................... 164
Hodgkins and Company Limited (Ian),
    Gloucestershire..................................... 114
Lake (David), Norfolk................................ 189
Marlborough Rare Books Ltd., London (W).... 173
Marshall Rare Books (Bruce), Gloucestershire .. 111
Page Antiquarian Books (Colin), East Sussex ... 99
Preston Book Company, Lancashire 142
Sephton (A.F.), London (W) 174
Shapero Rare Books (Bernard J.), London, (W) 174
Slavin Rare and Collectable Books (Derek),
    Warwickshire....................................... 237
Trafalgar Bookshop (The), East Sussex........... 99

COMEDY

Facet Books, Dorset 90
Ice House Books.. 143
Price (R.W.), Nottinghamshire 202

COMIC BOOKS & ANNUALS

Abrahams (Mike), Staffordshire..................... 222
Armstrongs Books & Collectables,
    West Midlands 239
Beck (John), East Sussex 101
Black Cat Bookshop, Leicestershire 143
Bookmark (Children's Books), Wiltshire 252
Border Bookshop (The), West Yorkshire......... 248
Buchan Collectibles, Scotland 265
Collectables (W.H.), London, West................ 172
D. & M. Books, West Yorkshire.................... 248
Facet Books, Dorset 90
Franks Booksellers, Greater Manchester 117
Intech Books, Northumberland 201
K. Books, Cheshire 72
Keel Row Books, Tyne & Wear..................... 235
Key Books (Sarah), Cambridgeshire............... 65
Nostalgia Unlimited, Merseyside................... 185
Savage (Keith A.), Suffolk 228
Scrivener's Books & Book Binding, Derbyshire . 81
Sesemann (Julia), Kent 133
Starlord Books, Cheshire............................. 70
Tilleys Vintage Magazine Shop,
    South Yorkshire.................................... 220
Tilleys Vintage Magazine Shop, Derbyshire...... 81
Wright (Norman), Hertfordshire 130
Zardoz Books, Wiltshire.............................. 253

COMICS

Armstrongs Books & Collectables,
    West Midlands 239
Arundel Bookshop, West Sussex 241

# SPECIALITY INDEX

Beck (John), East Sussex 101
Black Cat Bookshop, Leicestershire 143
Bookshop (The), Norfolk 191
Border Bookshop (The), West Yorkshire 248
Buchan Collectibles, Scotland 265
D. & M. Books, West Yorkshire 248
Facet Books, Dorset 90
McGee (Terence J.), London, Outer 181
Nostalgia Unlimited, Merseyside 185
Paperback Reader (The), East Sussex 101
Savage (Keith A.), Suffolk 228
Tilleys Vintage Magazine Shop,
  South Yorkshire 220
Wright (Norman), Hertfordshire 130

COMPANY HISTORY

Arundel Bookshop, West Sussex 241
Batterdale Books, N Yorks 195
Bott, (Bookdealers) Ltd., (Martin), Greater
  Manchester 116
Byrom Textile Bookroom (Richard), Lancashire .. 140
Camden Books, Somerset 214
Crosby Nethercott Books, London, Outer 180
Delph Books, Greater Manchester 116
Doro Books, West Sussex 242
Downie Fine Books Ltd., (Robert), Shropshire . 213
Handsworth Books, Essex 110
Jones (Anne), Cornwall 76
Kellow Books, Oxfordshire 204
Roadmaster Books, Kent 134
Rochdale Book Company, Greater Manchester . 118
Spurrier (Nick), Kent 136
Wheen O'Blethers Bookshop, Scotland 271
Wiend Books & Collectables,
  Greater Manchester 119

COMPUTING

Baron - Scientific Book Sales (P.J.), Somerset ... 215
Beware of The Leopard Books, Bristol 60
Downie Fine Books Ltd., (Robert), Shropshire . 213
Game Advice, Oxfordshire 207
Plurabelle Books, Cambridgeshire 65
Smith Booksellers (James), London, Outer 180
Wolds Book Services, Leicestershire 144

CONSERVATION

Aurelian Books, London (NW) 157
Austwick Hall Books, N Yorks 141
Book Corner, Scotland 263
Buchan Collectibles, Scotland 265
Calluna Books, Dorset 94
Coch-y-Bonddu Books, Wales 288
Demar Books (Grant), Kent 138
Elmbury Books, Warwickshire 237
Heneage Art Books (Thomas), London (SW).... 164
Ice House Books 143
Roadmaster Books, Kent 134
Scott (Sporting Books) (John), Worcestershire .. 256
Shipley Specialist Art Booksellers,
  London, West Central 178
Trinders' Fine Tools, Suffolk 225

COOKERY/GASTRONOMY

Abacus Gallery / The Village Bookshop,
  Staffordshire 223
Abrahams (Mike), Staffordshire 222
Autumn Leaves, Lincolnshire 148
Black Cat Books, Norfolk 188
Book Corner, Scotland 263
Book Warren, Devon 84
Books & Bygones, Berkshire 58
Books (For All), N Yorks 192
Books for Content, Herefordshire 126
Books Only, Suffolk 226
Bookworld, Shropshire 212
Book–Worm International, Essex 107
Booth Books, Wales 286
Brown-Studies, Scotland 270
Clarke (Janet), Somerset 214
Cooks Books, East Sussex 98
Cooksweb, Northamptonshire 198
Dusty Books, Wales 287
Elmfield Books, West Midlands 238
Fin Rare Books, Shropshire 213
Firth (Bijou Books & Photography) (Maureen),
  South Yorkshire 221
Fox Books (J. & J.), Kent 137
Gresham Books, Somerset 216
Harrington (Adrian), London, West 173
Harvest Books, Merseyside 185
Heartland Old Books, Devon 88
Island Books, Devon 84
Lane Books (Shirley), Isle of Wight 132
Max Gate Books, Somerset 218
Modlock (Lilian), Dorset 92
Moray Bookshop (The), Scotland 267
Parrott Books, Oxfordshire 209
Price (John), London (N) 155
Quaritch Ltd., (Bernard), London, West 174
R. & B. Graham, Cornwall 74
River Reads Bookshop, Devon 88
Savery Books, East Sussex 99
Seeber (Liz), East Sussex 99
Smith (Clive), Essex 108
Whitchurch Books Ltd., Wales 280
Wiend Books & Collectables,
  Greater Manchester 119
Williams (Christopher), Dorset 93

COUNTERCULTURE

Black Cat Bookshop, Leicestershire 143
Invisible Books, East Sussex 99
McGee (Terence J.), London, Outer 181
Sclanders (Beatbooks), (Andrew), London (EC) 152
Till's Bookshop, Scotland 270

COUNTRIES & REGIONS
- AFGHANISTAN

Bates & Hindmarch, West Yorkshire 247
Traveller's Bookshelf (The), Somerset 215
Verandah Books, Dorset 94

- AFRICA

Adab Books, Cambridgeshire 64

SPECIALITY INDEX

Afar Books International, West Midlands........ 238
Ayre (Peter J.), Somerset 218
Bonham (J. & S.L.), London, West 169
Bracton Books, Cambridgeshire..................... 64
Chalmers Hallam (E.), Hampshire.................. 123
Graves–Johnston (Michael), London (SW)...... 164
Hall, (Anthony C.) Antiquarian Bookseller,
   London, Outer 184
Heritage Books, Isle of Wight 131
Ice House Books... 143
Kenny's Bookshops and Art Galleries Ltd,
   Republic Of Ireland 278
Kenya Books, East Sussex 99
Lawson & Company (E.M.), Oxfordshire 205
Oriental and African Books, Shropshire.......... 213
Popeley (Frank T.), Cambridgeshire............... 68
Post–Horn Books, N Yorks 192
Probsthain (Arthur), London, West Central 178
Woolcott Books, Dorset................................ 92
Yesterday's Books, Dorset 91

- ALBANIA
Traveller's Bookshelf (The), Somerset............. 215
Visser Books (de), Cambridgeshire 66

- AMERICAS, THE
Bracton Books, Cambridgeshire..................... 64
Lawson & Company (E.M.), Oxfordshire 205

- ANDORRA
Books on Spain, London, Outer 183
Orssich (Paul), London (SW)........................ 166

- ANTARCTIC, THE
Bluntisham Books, Cambridgeshire................ 64
Explorer Books, West Sussex....................... 243
McEwan Fine Books, Scotland..................... 266

- ARABIA
Daly (Peter M.), Hampshire 124
Kenny's Bookshops and Art Galleries Ltd,
   Republic Of Ireland 278
Quest Books, East Yorkshire 105
Traveller's Bookshelf (The), Somerset............. 215

- ARCTIC, THE
Bluntisham Books, Cambridgeshire................ 64
Explorer Books, West Sussex....................... 243
J.K. Bookfinders, London (SW).................... 165

- ARMENIA
Traveller's Bookshelf (The), Somerset............. 215

- ASIA
Adab Books, Cambridgeshire....................... 64
Bates & Hindmarch, West Yorkshire.............. 247
Bracton Books, Cambridgeshire..................... 64

Fine Books Oriental Ltd., London,
   West Central... 177
Hall, (Anthony C.) Antiquarian Bookseller,
   London, Outer 184
Kenny's Bookshops and Art Galleries Ltd,
   Republic Of Ireland 278
Post–Horn Books, N Yorks 192
Rayner (Hugh Ashley), Somerset 215

- ASIA MINOR
Quest Books, East Yorkshire 105
Traveller's Bookshelf (The), Somerset............. 215

- AUSTRALASIA
Eggeling Books (John), West Yorkshire 248
Lawson & Company (E.M.), Oxfordshire 205

- AUSTRALIA
Bonham (J. & S.L.), London, West 169
Empire Books, Greater Manchester 118
Londonline Books, London (SW).................. 165
Moore (Peter), Cambridgeshire...................... 65

- AUSTRIA
Visser Books (de), Cambridgeshire 66

- BALKANS, THE
Adab Books, Cambridgeshire....................... 64
Bosphorus Books, London, West Central 176
Cyclamen Books, Leicestershire 143
Kenny's Bookshops and Art Galleries Ltd,
   Republic Of Ireland 278
Quest Books, East Yorkshire 105
Traveller's Bookshelf (The), Somerset............. 215

- BALTIC STATES
MK Book Services, Cambridgeshire............... 67

- BERMUDA
Pennymead Books, N Yorks........................ 193

- BURMA
Rayner (Hugh Ashley), Somerset 215
Right Now Books (Burma), London (SW)....... 167
Verandah Books, Dorset 94

- CARIBBEAN, THE
Afar Books International, West Midlands........ 238
Burton–Garbett (A.), London, Outer 182
Ice House Books... 143
Leapman Ltd. (G. & R.), Hertfordshire 130
Pennymead Books, N Yorks........................ 193

- CENTRAL AMERICA
Books on Spain, London, Outer 183
Burton–Garbett (A.), London, Outer 182
Ice House Books... 143

Orssich (Paul), London (SW)...... 166

- CENTRAL ASIA
Alpes Livres (Les), Hampshire 120
Bates & Hindmarch, West Yorkshire...... 247
Cyclamen Books, Leicestershire 143
Londonline Books, London (SW)...... 165
Rayner (Hugh Ashley), Somerset 215
Riddell (Peter), East Yorkshire 104
Traveller's Bookshelf (The), Somerset...... 215

- CHANNEL ISLANDS, THE
Old Curiosity Shop (The), Channel Islands 257

- CHINA
Ice House Books...... 143
Kenny's Bookshops and Art Galleries Ltd,
  Republic Of Ireland 278
Traveller's Bookshelf (The), Somerset...... 215

- CUBA
Books on Spain, London, Outer 183
Ice House Books...... 143
Pennymead Books, N Yorks...... 193

- CYPRUS
Askew Books (Vernon), Wiltshire...... 250
Charmouth Bookstore, Dorset 91
Hellenic Bookservices, London (NW)...... 158
Quest Books, East Yorkshire 105

- EAST EUROPE
Cyclamen Books, Leicestershire 143
Hab Books, London, West...... 173
Hall, (Anthony C.) Antiquarian Bookseller,
  London, Outer 184

- EGYPT
Afar Books International, West Midlands...... 238
Manor House Books/John Trotter Books,
  London (N)...... 154
Museum Bookshop, London, West Central...... 177
Quest Books, East Yorkshire 105

- ENGLAND
Broadwater Books, Hampshire 124
Island Books, Devon...... 84
Missing Books, Essex 108

- ETHIOPIA
Traveller's Bookshelf (The), Somerset...... 215

- EUROPE
Kenny's Bookshops and Art Galleries Ltd,
  Republic Of Ireland 278
Meinertzhagen (Nicholas), London (SW)...... 165

Shapero Rare Books (Bernard J.), London (W). 174

- FAR EAST, THE
Daly (Peter M.), Hampshire 124
Traveller's Bookshelf (The), Somerset...... 215

- FRANCE
Colwyn Books, Wales...... 281
Cyclamen Books, Leicestershire 143
Langmaid (Kenneth), Cornwall 76

- GERMANY
Helion & Company, West Midlands 240
Visser Books (de), Cambridgeshire 66

- GIBRALTAR
Books on Spain, London, Outer 183
Orssich (Paul), London (SW)...... 166

- GREECE
Charmouth Bookstore, Dorset 91
Crouch Rare Books, Surrey...... 232
Hellenic Bookservices, London (NW)...... 158
Paralos Ltd., London (W)...... 173
Quest Books, East Yorkshire 105
Seydi Rare Books (Sevin), London (NW) 159
Traveller's Bookshelf (The), Somerset...... 215

- GREENLAND
Bluntisham Books, Cambridgeshire...... 64
Explorer Books, West Sussex...... 243

- HIMALAYAS, THE
Rayner (Hugh Ashley), Somerset 215
Traveller's Bookshelf (The), Somerset...... 215
Verandah Books, Dorset 94

- HUNGARY
Meinertzhagen (Nicholas), London (SW)...... 165
Traveller's Bookshelf (The), Somerset...... 215
Visser Books (de), Cambridgeshire 66

- ICELAND
Austwick Hall Books, N Yorks 141

- INDIA
Bates & Hindmarch, West Yorkshire...... 247
Chalmers Hallam (E.), Hampshire...... 123
Donovan Military Books (Tom), East Sussex.... 98
Fine Books Oriental Ltd., London (W) Central. 177
Londonline Books, London (SW)...... 165
Rayner (Hugh Ashley), Somerset 215
Rhodes, Bookseller (Peter), Hampshire 124
Traveller's Bookshelf (The), Somerset...... 215
Verandah Books, Dorset 94
Woolcott Books, Dorset...... 92

SPECIALITY INDEX

- IRAN
Quest Books, East Yorkshire 105
Traveller's Bookshelf (The), Somerset 215

- IRELAND
Armchair Books, Scotland 268
Bell Gallery (The), Northern Ireland 259
Cahir Cosy Corner Bookshop,
  Republic Of Ireland 279
Celtic Bookshop (The), Republic Of Ireland 279
Darkwood Books, Republic Of Ireland 276
Emerald Isle Books, Northern Ireland 259
Fine Irish Books, Republic Of Ireland 276
Foyle Books, Northern Ireland 260
Hyland (C.P.), Republic Of Ireland 276
Kenny's Bookshops and Art Galleries Ltd,
  Republic Of Ireland 278
Kernaghans, Merseyside 186
McCann (Joe), Oxfordshire 208
Naughton Booksellers, Republic Of Ireland...... 277
Prospect House Books, Northern Ireland 260
Tony Skelton, Kent 138
Whelan (P. & F.), Kent............................. 138

- ISLE OF MAN
Garretts Antiquarian Books, Isle of Man 258

- ISLE OF WIGHT
Heritage Books, Isle of Wight 131

- ISLES OF SCILLY
Menavaur Books, Scotland 264

- ITALY
Campbell (Fiona), London (SE) 160
Langmaid (Kenneth), Cornwall 76
Seydi Rare Books (Sevin), London (NW) 159

- JAPAN
Bow Windows Book Shop, East Sussex 102
Fine Books Oriental Ltd., London (W) Central. 177
Japan Books (Y & S Company Ltd.), Surrey 180
Londonline Books, London (SW).................. 165
Traveller's Bookshelf (The), Somerset 215

- KENYA
Kenya Books, East Sussex 99
Popeley (Frank T.), Cambridgeshire............... 68

- KOREA
Londonline Books, London (SW).................. 165
Traveller's Bookshelf (The), Somerset 215

- LATIN AMERICA
Books on Spain, London, Outer 183
Ice House Books..................................... 143

- MALAYSIA
Traveller's Bookshelf (The), Somerset 215

- MALTA
Porcupines, Devon.................................. 84

- MELANESIA
Abbey Bookshop, Hampshire 122
Biblion, London (W)................................ 169
Black Cat Bookshop, Leicestershire 143
Books, Wales.. 282
Bracton Books, Cambridgeshire..................... 64
Broadwater Books, Hampshire..................... 124
Classic Crime Collections, Greater Manchester.. 117
Dead Zone Books, Wales 289
Firsts in Print, Isle of Wight 131
Fortune Books, Essex............................... 106
Golden Hind Bookshop (The), Kent 134
J & M Books, Warwickshire....................... 237
Kevin S. Ogilvie Modern First Editions,
  Scotland 265
L.M.S. Books, Hertfordshire 129
Marjon Books, Essex................................ 110
Morris (Chris), Oxfordshire........................ 208
Murder One, London (WC) 177
Offer (Richard), Cheshire........................... 70
Richmond Books, N Yorks 194
Rosemary Books, Merseyside....................... 186
Russell Books, Somerset............................ 218
Simply Read, East Sussex 100
Trevorrow (Edwin), Hertfordshire 128
Wayside Books and Cards, Oxfordshire 205
Wiend Books & Collectables,
  Greater Manchester 119
Williams Rare Books (Nigel), London (WC) 179
Words & Music, Cheshire.......................... 70
Zardoz Books, Wiltshire............................ 253

- MEXICO
Bardsley's Books, Suffolk 225
Biblion, London (W)................................ 169
Black Cat Bookshop, Leicestershire 143
Books on Spain, London, Outer 183
Book–Worm International, Essex.................. 107
Booth Books, Wales................................. 286
Burton–Garbett (A.), London, Outer 182
Dead Zone Books, Wales 289
Delectus Books, London (WC)..................... 176
J & M Books, Warwickshire....................... 237
Kevin S. Ogilvie Modern First Editions,
  Scotland 265
L.M.S. Books, Hertfordshire 129
Murder One, London (WC) 177
Offer (Richard), Cheshire........................... 70
Orssich (Paul), London (SW)....................... 166
Rods Books, Devon 87
Till's Bookshop, Scotland 270
Williams Rare Books (Nigel), London (WC) 179
Zardoz Books, Wiltshire............................ 253

- MIDDLE EAST, THE
Bosphorus Books, London (WC) 176

SPECIALITY INDEX

Cyclamen Books, Leicestershire 143
Delectus Books, London (WC) 176
Hall, (Anthony C.) Antiquarian Bookseller,
  London, Outer 184
Joppa Books Ltd., Surrey 230
Manor House Books/John Trotter Books,
  London (N) 154
Oriental and African Books, Shropshire 213
Traveller's Bookshelf (The), Somerset 215
Trotter Books (John), London (N) 156

- MONGOLIA
Traveller's Bookshelf (The), Somerset 215

- MOROCCO
Books on Spain, London, Outer 183
Orssich (Paul), London (SW) 166
Traveller's Bookshelf (The), Somerset 215

- NEAR EAST, THE
Traveller's Bookshelf (The), Somerset 215

- NEPAL
Traveller's Bookshelf (The), Somerset 215
Verandah Books, Dorset 94

- PACIFIC, THE
Moore (Peter), Cambridgeshire 65

- PAKISTAN
Traveller's Bookshelf (The), Somerset 215
Verandah Books, Dorset 94

- PALESTINE
Traveller's Bookshelf (The), Somerset 215

- PAPUA NEW GUINEA
Moore (Peter), Cambridgeshire 65
Traveller's Bookshelf (The), Somerset 215

- PHILIPPINES, THE
Traveller's Bookshelf (The), Somerset 215

- POLAND
Bardsley's Books, Suffolk 225
Biblion, London (W) 169
Booth (Booksearch Service), (Geoff), Cheshire .. 69
Caledonia Books, Scotland 271
Cavern Books, Cheshire 70
Meinertzhagen (Nicholas), London (SW) 165
O'Brien Books & Photo Gallery,
  Republic Of Ireland 279
Rochdale Book Company, Greater Manchester . 118
Roundstone Books, Lancashire 141
Savery Books, East Sussex 99

Scrivener's Books & Book Binding, Derbyshire . 81
Visser Books (de), Cambridgeshire 66

- POLAR
Bluntisham Books, Cambridgeshire 64
Bonham (J. & S.L.), London (W) 169
Explorer Books, West Sussex 243
Londonline Books, London (SW) 165
McEwan Fine Books, Scotland 266
Riddell (Peter), East Yorkshire 104

- POLYNESIA
Bracton Books, Cambridgeshire 64

- PORTUGAL
Books on Spain, London, Outer 183
Burton–Garbett (A.), London, Outer 182
Orssich (Paul), London (SW) 166

- PUERTO RICO
Books on Spain, London, Outer 183
Orssich (Paul), London (SW) 166
Pennymead Books, N Yorks 193

- ROMANIA
Traveller's Bookshelf (The), Somerset 215
Visser Books (de), Cambridgeshire 66

- RUSSIA
Cyclamen Books, Leicestershire 143
Hab Books, London (W) 173
Hall, (Anthony C.) Antiquarian Bookseller,
  London, Outer 184
Ice House Books 143
Kenny's Bookshops and Art Galleries Ltd,
  Republic Of Ireland 278
Traveller's Bookshelf (The), Somerset 215

- SANTO DOMINGO
Pennymead Books, N Yorks 193

- SARAWAK
Traveller's Bookshelf (The), Somerset 215

- SCOTLAND
Aberdeen Rare Books & Caledonian Books,
  Scotland 267
Annesley Books of Scottish Interest (Brian),
  Scotland 272
Armchair Books, Scotland 268
Atholl Fine Books, Scotland 273
Bridge of Allan Books, Scotland 262
Broadwater Books, Hampshire 124
Colonsay Bookshop, Scotland 272
Cooper Hay Rare Books, Scotland 271
Farquharson, (Hilary), Scotland 273

Gillies (Benny), Scotland 262
Holmes Books (Harry), East Yorkshire........... 105
Hughes Rare Books (Spike), Scotland 261
Hutchison (Books) (Larry), Scotland.............. 265
MacCormaig (Domhnall), Scotland 269
Milne Books (Clifford), Scotland 265
Moray Bookshop (The), Scotland 267
Quarto Bookshop (The), Scotland 265
Sanderson (Edward), Berkshire...................... 58

- SIAM
Traveller's Bookshelf (The), Somerset.............. 215

- SOUTH AFRICA
Boer War Books, N Yorks............................ 196

- SOUTH AMERICA
Books on Spain, London, Outer 183
Burton–Garbett (A.), London, Outer 182
Hünersdorff Rare Books, London (SW) 165
Orssich (Paul), London (SW)........................ 166
Prescott - The Bookseller (John), London, Outer. 184

- SOUTH ATLANTIC ISLANDS
MK Book Services, Cambridgeshire................ 67

- SOUTH EAST ASIA
Traveller's Bookshelf (The), Somerset.............. 215
Verandah Books, Dorset 94

- SPAIN
Adab Books, Cambridgeshire......................... 64
Books on Spain, London, Outer 183
Burton–Garbett (A.), London, Outer 182
Ice House Books 143
Orssich (Paul), London (SW)........................ 166

- SRI LANKA
Rayner (Hugh Ashley), Somerset 215
Verandah Books, Dorset 94

- STRAITS SETTLEMENTS, THE
Traveller's Bookshelf (The), Somerset.............. 215

- SUDAN, THE
Traveller's Bookshelf (The), Somerset.............. 215

- SWITZERLAND
Alpes Livres (Les), Hampshire 120

- TANZANIA
Popeley (Frank T.), Cambridgeshire................ 68

- TIBET
Alpes Livres (Les), Hampshire 120

Bates & Hindmarch, West Yorkshire.............. 247
Traveller's Bookshelf (The), Somerset.............. 215

- TURKEY
Bosphorus Books, London (WC) 176
Quest Books, East Yorkshire........................ 105
Seydi Rare Books (Sevin), London (NW) 159
Traveller's Bookshelf (The), Somerset.............. 215

- U.S.A.
Americanabooksuk, Cumbria......................... 77

- VIETNAM
Traveller's Bookshelf (The), Somerset.............. 215

- WALES
Capital Bookshop, Wales............................. 280
Castle Bookshop, Wales.............................. 288
Great Oak Bookshop (The), Wales................. 287
Hancock (Colin), Wales 281
Island Books, Devon................................... 84
Modern Welsh Publications Ltd., Merseyside.... 185
Thomas (E. Wyn), Wales............................ 282
Wakeley (A.G. & W.), Wales....................... 285
Whitchurch Books Ltd., Wales...................... 280
Ystwyth Books, Wales................................ 281

- WEST INDIES, THE
Pennymead Books, N Yorks......................... 193

COUNTRY HOUSES
Art Reference Books, Hampshire 123
Duck (William), East Sussex......................... 98
Island Books, Devon................................... 86
Marlborough Rare Books Ltd., London (W).... 173
Morris (Michael), Staffordshire...................... 222
Spenceley Books (David), West Yorkshire 248
Staniland (Booksellers), Lincolnshire.............. 150

COURTESY
Weininger Antiquarian Books (Eva M.),
   London (NW) 159

CRAFTS
Arden Books & Cosmographia, Warwickshire... 236
Baldwin (M. & M.), Shropshire..................... 212
Barn Books, Buckinghamshire........................ 62
Bee Books New and Old, Cornwall 73
Books & Bygones, Berkshire......................... 58
Bookworld, Shropshire................................ 212
Booth Books, Wales................................... 286
Bosco Books, Cornwall................................ 73
Celtica Crafts, Wales.................................. 290
Cooksweb, Northamptonshire....................... 198
Cottage Books, Leicestershire 143
Cover to Cover, Merseyside 186
Crouch Rare Books, Surrey.......................... 232
DoublePlusBooks, Cambridgeshire 68

SPECIALITY INDEX

Dusty Books, Wales.................................. 287
Footrope Knots, Suffolk............................ 226
Furneaux Books (Lee), Devon 87
Holdsworth Books (Bruce), West Yorkshire 245
Ice House Books 143
Jones Books (Russell), Berkshire 57
Max Gate Books, Somerset 218
McCrone (Audrey), Scotland 272
Miller, (Dusty), Cornwall 73
Old Bookshop (The), Somerset................... 216
Savery Books, East Sussex.......................... 99
Scrivener's Books & Book Binding, Derbyshire . 81
Smith Books, (Sally), Suffolk 225
Sterling Books, Somerset 219
Trinders' Fine Tools, Suffolk 225
Upper–Room Books, Somerset.................... 216
Village Bookshop (The), Durham................... 96
Well–Head Books, Dorset........................... 91
Williams (Christopher), Dorset..................... 93

CRIME (TRUE)

Abrahams (Mike), Staffordshire................... 222
Andrews (R.), Gloucestershire..................... 111
Bolland Books (Leslie H.), Bedfordshire.......... 55
Book Bungalow (The), Cornwall................... 73
Book–Worm International, Essex................. 107
Booth (Booksearch Service), (Geoff), Cheshire .. 69
Bradley–Cox (Mary), Dorset....................... 90
Catalyst Books, Surrey 232
Classic Crime Collections, Greater Manchester.. 117
Crimes Ink, London (E)............................ 151
Croft Selections, Lincolnshire...................... 148
Downie Fine Books Ltd., (Robert), Shropshire . 213
Eastcote Bookshop (The), London, Outer........ 183
Elmer Books, (Clifford), Greater Manchester.... 116
Grey House Books, Surrey......................... 234
Keel Row Books, Tyne & Wear................... 235
Lawful Occasions, Essex........................... 106
Lay Books (Loretta), London (NW) 158
McCaughtrie (K.A.), N Yorks 192
Ming Books, Scotland 264
Noel and Holland Books, Republic Of Ireland.. 278
Porter Bookshop (The), South Yorkshire......... 220
Premier Books & Prints, Lincolnshire............. 146
Roland Books, Kent 137
Ruebotham (Kirk), Cheshire........................ 71
Rupert Books, Cambridgeshire..................... 65
Savery Books, East Sussex.......................... 99
Sidey, Bookdealer (Philip), Kent 137
Simply Read, East Sussex 100
Starlord Books, Cheshire............................ 70
Till's Bookshop, Scotland 270
Trinders' Fine Tools, Suffolk 225
Williams (Bookdealer), (Richard), Lincolnshire . 149
Zardoz Books, Wiltshire........................... 253

CRIMINOLOGY

Bolland Books (Leslie H.), Bedfordshire.......... 55
Book Warren, Devon 84
Chesters (G. & J.), Staffordshire 223
Crimes Ink, London (E)............................ 151
Cyclamen Books, Leicestershire 143
Delectus Books, London (WC).................... 176
Elmer Books, (Clifford), Greater Manchester.... 116
Grey House Books, Surrey......................... 234
Ice House Books 143
Lawful Occasions, Essex........................... 106
Lay Books (Loretta), London (NW) 158
Reading Lasses, Scotland........................... 264

CROCHET

Byrom Textile Bookroom (Richard), Lancashire 140
Cover to Cover, Merseyside 186
Mansfield (Judith), West Yorkshire................ 248

CRYPTOGRAPHY

Baldwin (M. & M.), Shropshire 212

CRYPTOZOOLOGY

Inner Bookshop (The), Oxfordshire 207
Wizard Books, Cambridgeshire..................... 68

CULTURE - FOREIGN

Books on Spain, London, Outer 183
Ice House Books 143
Malmo Books, Hampshire 121
Orssich (Paul), London (SW)...................... 166
Visser Books (de), Cambridgeshire 66
Weininger Antiquarian Books (Eva M.),
   London (NW) 159

CULTURE - NATIONAL

Guildmaster Books, Cheshire....................... 71
Hancock (Colin), Wales 281
Ice House Books 143
Kenny's Bookshops and Art Galleries Ltd,
   Republic Of Ireland 278
Llyfraufflur Books, Wales 290
MacCormaig (Domhnall), Scotland 269
Wakeley (A.G. & W.), Wales...................... 285
Weininger Antiquarian Books (Eva M.),
   London (NW) 159

D.I.Y (DO IT YOURSELF)

Brown-Studies, Scotland............................ 270
Spread Eagle Bookshop, London (SE)............ 162
Trinders' Fine Tools, Suffolk 225

DANCE

Barber Music, Kent 136
Baxter - Books (Eddie), Somerset................. 218
Fitzsimons (Anne), Cumbria 77
Gate Memorabilia, London (N).................... 153
Paramor (C.D.), Suffolk 227
Quadrille at Delehar, London (W)................ 174

DECORATIVE ART

Adams (Judith), Shropshire 211
Andromeda Books, Buckinghamshire............. 63
Art Reference Books, Hampshire 123
Ballantyne–Way (Roger), Suffolk 228

Barlow (Vincent G.), Hampshire 123
Barmby (C. & A.J.), Kent........................ 138
Books & Things, London (W)...................... 169
Booth Books, Wales.............................. 286
Buckland Books, West Sussex 243
Butts Books (Mary), Berkshire 58
Chalk (Old & Out of Print Books)
  (Christine M.), West Midlands 238
Cover to Cover, Merseyside 186
DoublePlusBooks, Cambridgeshire 68
Europa Books, London (SW)....................... 163
Foster (Stephen), London (NW) 157
Gardner & Co., (Walter H.), London (N)........ 153
Goodyer (Nicholas), London (N).................. 154
Grant (Gerald S.), Cheshire...................... 69
Heneage Art Books (Thomas), London (SW).... 164
Hodgkins and Company Limited (Ian),
  Gloucestershire................................ 114
Hogben (Carol), Wales 285
Holdsworth Books (Bruce), West Yorkshire 245
Keswick Bookshop, Cumbria....................... 78
Reference Works Ltd., Dorset..................... 94
Shipley Specialist Art Booksellers,
  London (W) Central............................. 178
Spread Eagle Bookshop, London (SE)............ 162
Tasburgh Books, Norfolk 190
Trinders' Fine Tools, Suffolk 225
Wyseby House Books, Berkshire................... 57

DEEP SEA DIVING

Diver's & Watersportsman's Library (The),
  Devon.. 86
Larkham Books (Patricia), Gloucestershire 115
Lewcock (John), Cambridgeshire 67
Rods Books, Devon............................... 87
Sub Aqua Prints and Books, Hampshire 121

DESIGN

Addendum Books, Scotland 263
Art Reference Books, Hampshire 123
Ballantyne–Way (Roger), Suffolk 228
Blaenavon Books, Wales 289
Books for Collectors, Gloucestershire 112
Booth Books, Wales.............................. 286
Broadleaf Books, Wales 290
Brock Books, N Yorks 192
Cover to Cover, Merseyside 186
DoublePlusBooks, Cambridgeshire 68
Duck (William), East Sussex...................... 98
Finch Rare Books Ltd. (Simon), London (W)... 172
Hillside House, Lincolnshire 147
Illustrated Book (The), London (SW)............ 165
Inch's Books, N Yorks 194
Malvern Bookshop (The), Worcestershire 254
Martin - Bookseller (Colin), East Yorkshire 105
O'Connor Fine Books, Lancashire................. 142
Trinders' Fine Tools, Suffolk 225

DIARIES

Arundel Bookshop, West Sussex 241
Camden Books, Somerset 214
Castle Frome Books, Herefordshire 127

Dolphin Books, Suffolk........................... 224
Piccadilly Rare Books, East Sussex 103
Reading Lasses, Scotland......................... 264
South Downs Book Service, West Sussex......... 243

DICTIONARIES

Askew Books (Vernon), Wiltshire................. 250
Beetles Ltd., (Chris), London (SW).............. 163
Books & Bygones (Pam Taylor), West Midlands 240
Bookworld, Shropshire 212
Delectus Books, London (W) Central............. 176
Ice House Books................................. 143
Jade Mountain, Hampshire 123
Loman, Oriental Books & Manuscripts
  (David), London (SW)........................... 165
Malmo Books, Hampshire 121
Orssich (Paul), London (SW)..................... 166
Scrivener's Books & Book Binding, Derbyshire . 81
Stanhope Bibliophiles, London (N)............... 155
Thomson (Karen), Scotland 271

DIVINING

McCrone (Audrey), Scotland 272
Wizard Books, Cambridgeshire.................... 68

DOCUMENTS
- GENERAL

Browning (Julian), London (W).................... 169
Farahar & Dupré (Clive & Sophie),
  Wiltshire...................................... 250
Ford (Richard), London (W) 172
Kenny's Bookshops and Art Galleries Ltd,
  Republic Of Ireland 278
Morris (Michael), Staffordshire.................. 222
Silverman (Michael), London (SE) 161
Spread Eagle Bookshop, London (SE)............ 162
Wilson (Autographs) Ltd., (John),
  Gloucestershire................................ 112

DOGS

Atticus Books, Essex............................ 109
Chalmers Hallam (E.), Hampshire 123
Classic Crime Collections, Greater Manchester.. 117
Coch-y-Bonddu Books, Wales..................... 288
Countrymans Gallery (The), Leicestershire....... 143
Croft Selections, Lincolnshire................... 148
Doorbar (P. & D.), Hampshire.................... 122
Evergreen Livres, Gloucestershire................ 113
Halson Books, Cheshire 71
Home Farm Books, Warwickshire 236
Kilgour (Sporting Books) (Ian), Leicestershire... 145
LyngHeath Books, Norfolk....................... 190
Peel (Valerie), t/a Kiandra Associates Ltd.,
  Berkshire...................................... 57
Rolfe (John), London (SE)....................... 161
Scott (Sporting Books) (John), Worcestershire .. 256
Wright Trace Books, West Midlands............. 239

DOLLS & DOLLS' HOUSES

Art Reference Books, Hampshire 123

SPECIALITY INDEX

Cover to Cover, Merseyside 186
Porcupines, Devon................................. 84
Roadmaster Books, Kent......................... 134
Staffs Bookshop (The), Staffordshire............. 222
Trinders' Fine Tools, Suffolk 225
Well–Head Books, Dorset........................ 91

DRAMA

Ashburton Books, Devon 83
Autumn Leaves, Lincolnshire..................... 148
Brighton Books, East Sussex 64
Caledonia Books, Scotland....................... 271
Catalyst Books, Surrey 232
Chatterton's Books, Wales........................ 290
Clements (R.W.), London, Outer 181
Gate Memorabilia, London (N).................... 153
Ice House Books................................... 143
Heyman (B.), London, Outer...................... 181
Kaye - Bookseller (Terence), London (NW) 158
Kenny's Bookshops and Art Galleries Ltd,
  Republic Of Ireland 278
Kent T. G., Surrey 230
Polmorla Books, Cornwall.......................... 76
Roundstone Books, Lancashire 141
Spread Eagle Bookshop, London (SE)............ 162
Till's Bookshop, Scotland 270
Troath Books (Brian), London (E) 151
Updike Rare Books (John), Scotland 270
Willmott Bookseller (Nicholas), Wales............ 280
Words & Music, Cheshire......................... 70

DRAWING

Family Favourites (Books), East Yorkshire...... 104
Ice House Books................................... 143

DRUGS

Delectus Books, London (W) Central............. 176

EARLY IMPRINTS

David (G.), Cambridgeshire........................ 64
Edwards (Christopher), Berkshire................. 57
Finch Rare Books Ltd. (Simon), London (W)... 172
Fine Art, West Sussex 242
Hatchwell (Richard), Wiltshire 251
House of Figgis Ltd (The), Republic Of Ireland 278
Maggs Brothers Limited, London (W)............ 173
Paralos Ltd., London (W).......................... 173
Quaritch Ltd., (Bernard), London (W)............ 174
Schulz–Falster Rare Books (Susanne),
  London (N)..................................... 155
Seydi Rare Books (Sevin), London (NW) 159
Sokol Books (A.), London (W) 174
Spread Eagle Bookshop, London (SE)............ 162
Treglown (Roger J.), Cheshire..................... 71
Unsworths Booksellers Ltd., London,
  West Central................................... 178
Unsworths Booksellers Ltd., Oxfordshire......... 209
Zardoz Books, Wiltshire........................... 253

EARTH MYSTERIES

Abrahams (Mike), Staffordshire................... 222

Chthonios Books, East Sussex..................... 100
Inner Bookshop (The), Oxfordshire 207
Magis Books, Leicestershire....................... 144
McCrone (Audrey), Scotland 272
Occultique, Northamptonshire 198

ECCLESIASTICAL HISTORY & ARCHITECTURE

Barbican Bookshop, N Yorks 196
Bardsley's Books, Suffolk 225
Beckham Books, Suffolk........................... 228
Birchden Books, London (E) 151
Carter, (Brian), Oxfordshire 205
Cranmer Books, Oxfordshire 210
Crouch Rare Books, Surrey....................... 232
Edwards (Alan & Margaret), Kent 139
Emerald Isle Books, Northern Ireland 259
Gage Postal Books, Essex 109
Gradwell Concepts, Merseyside 185
Island Books, Devon............................... 86
Island Books, Devon............................... 84
Kyrios Books, Nottinghamshire................... 202
Langmaid (Kenneth), Cornwall 76
Lion Fine Arts and Books, Wales 287
Lund Theological Books, Cambridgeshire........ 65
Moss Books, London (NW) 158
Olynthiacs, Shropshire............................. 212
St Philip's Books, Oxfordshire..................... 208
Salsus Books, Worcestershire 255
Shipley Specialist Art Booksellers, London,
  West Central................................... 178
South Downs Book Service, West Sussex........ 243
Spenceley Books (David), West Yorkshire 248
Spooner & Co., Somerset 217
Staniland (Booksellers), Lincolnshire.............. 150
Taylor & Son (Peter), Hertfordshire............... 130
Thornber (Peter A.), N Yorks..................... 195
Trinders' Fine Tools, Suffolk 225
Turton (John), Durham 97
Unsworths Booksellers Ltd., London,
  West Central................................... 178
Whitchurch Books Ltd., Wales.................... 280

ECOLOGY

Baron - Scientific Book Sales (P.J.), Somerset ... 215
Book Corner, Scotland 263
Brown–Studies, Scotland.......................... 270
On the Wild Side, Worcestershire................. 255
Ice House Books................................... 143
Wyseby House Books, Berkshire.................. 57

ECONOMICS

Beware of The Leopard Books, Bristol 60
Billing (Brian), Berkshire 59
Booth Books, Wales................................ 286
Camden Books, Somerset 214
Chesters (G. & J.), Staffordshire.................. 223
Clifton Books, Essex 110
Delectus Books, London (WC)..................... 176
Downie Fine Books Ltd., (Robert),
  Shropshire...................................... 213
Drury Rare Books (John), Essex.................. 109

Economia Books, Wales 281
Edwards in Hay–on–Wye (Francis), Wales 286
Gardner & Co., (Walter H.), London (N) 153
Herb Tandree Philosophy Books, Bristol 61
Ice House Books 143
Jarndyce Antiquarian Booksellers,
　London (WC) 177
Kenny's Bookshops and Art Galleries Ltd,
　Republic Of Ireland 278
Lawson & Company (E.M.), Oxfordshire 205
Lee Rare Books (Rachel), Bristol 61
Malmo Books, Hampshire 121
Meinertzhagen (Nicholas), London (SW) 165
Northern Herald Books, West Yorkshire 245
Pollak (P.M.), Devon 87
Prospect House Books, Northern Ireland 260
Quaritch Ltd., (Bernard), London (W) 174
Riley–Smith (Hamish), Norfolk 190
Rowan (P. & B.), Northern Ireland 259
Schulz–Falster Rare Books (Susanne),
　London (N) 155
South Downs Book Service, West Sussex 243
Spurrier (Nick), Kent 136
Visser Books (de), Cambridgeshire 66
Westwood Books (Mark), Wales 287
Wetherell (Frances), Cambridgeshire 66
Woburn Books, London (N) 156

EDUCATION & SCHOOL

Bates Books, London, Outer 181
Black Five Books, Shropshire 213
Chesters (G. & J.), Staffordshire 223
Downie Fine Books Ltd., (Robert), Shropshire . 213
Drury Rare Books (John), Essex 109
Game Advice, Oxfordshire 207
Holtom (Christopher), Cornwall 76
Jarndyce Antiquarian Booksellers, London,
　West Central 177
Kenny's Bookshops and Art Galleries Ltd,
　Republic Of Ireland 278
McGee (Terence J.), London, Outer 181
Reading Lasses, Scotland 264
Saunders (Tom), Wales 280
Wise (Derek), East Sussex 102
Yates Antiquarian Books (Tony), Leicestershire 144

EGYPTOLOGY

Afar Books International, West Midlands 238
Alpha Books, London (N) 153
Chthonios Books, East Sussex 100
Crouch Rare Books, Surrey 232
Graves–Johnston (Michael), London (SW) 164
Joppa Books Ltd., Surrey 230
Kenny's Bookshops and Art Galleries Ltd,
　Republic Of Ireland 278
Museum Bookshop, London (WC) 177
Occultique, Northamptonshire 198
P. and P. Books, Worcestershire 255
Slavin Rare and Collectable Books (Derek),
　Warwickshire 237
Unsworths Booksellers Ltd.,
　London (WC) 178
Whitchurch Books Ltd., Wales 280

Yesterday's Books, Dorset 91

EMBLEMATA

Parikian, Rare Books (Diana), London (W) 174
Seydi Rare Books (Sevin), London (NW) 159

EMBROIDERY

Black Cat Books, Norfolk 188
Byrom Textile Bookroom (Richard), Lancashire 140
Cooksweb, Northamptonshire 198
Cover to Cover, Merseyside 186
Crouch Rare Books, Surrey 232
Four Shire Bookshops, Gloucestershire 113
Mansfield (Judith), West Yorkshire 248
Max Gate Books, Somerset 218
Old Bookshop (The), W Mids 240
Smith Books (Keith), Herefordshire 127
Traveller's Bookshelf (The), Somerset 215
Trinders' Fine Tools, Suffolk 225
Warnes (Felicity J.), London, Outer 181
Well–Head Books, Dorset 91
Young (D. & J.), Wales 289

ENCYCLOPAEDIAS

Frew Limited (Robert), London (WC) 177

ENGINEERING

Baron - Scientific Book Sales (P.J.), Somerset ... 215
Biblion, London (W) 169
Book House (The), Cumbria 78
Bott, (Bookdealers) Ltd., (Martin), Greater
　Manchester 116
Brockwells Bookshop, London (SE) 160
Courtwood Books, Republic Of Ireland 278
Duck (William), East Sussex 98
Elton Engineering Books, London (W) 172
Falconwood Transport & Military Bookshop,
　London, Outer 184
Jones (Anne), Cornwall 76
Jones Books (Russell), Berkshire 57
Kerr (Norman), Cumbria 78
Penzance Rare Books, Cornwall 75
Phelps (Michael), West Sussex 242
Scrivener's Books & Book Binding, Derbyshire . 81
Theatreshire Books, N Yorks 192
Trinders' Fine Tools, Suffolk 225
Westons, Hertfordshire 130

ENGRAVING

Waddington Books & Prints (Geraldine),
　Northamptonshire 198
Woodbine Books, West Yorkshire 245

ENTERTAINMENT
- GENERAL

Autumn Leaves, Lincolnshire 148
Bookshop (The), Norfolk 191
Cavern Books, Cheshire 71
DaSilva Puppet Books, Oxfordshire 204

SPECIALITY INDEX

Davis (Peter), Kent 136
Downie Fine Books Ltd., (Robert), Shropshire . 213
Jones (J.V.A.), Essex 109
Katnap Arts, Norfolk 189
Kaye - Bookseller (Terence), London (NW) 158
Kent T. G., Surrey 230
Left Bank (The), Wales 290
Nevitsky (Philip), Greater Manchester 117
Noble (Malcolm & Christine), Leicestershire..... 145
Paramor (C.D.), Suffolk 227
Roland Books, Kent 137
Spread Eagle Bookshop, London (SE) 162
Stroma Books, Scotland 261
Till's Bookshop, Scotland 270
Whitfield (Ken), Essex 109
Wood (Peter), Cambridgeshire 66

ENTOMOLOGY

Aurelian Books, London (NW) 157
Austwick Hall Books, N Yorks 141
Blest (Peter), Kent 136
Book Corner, Scotland 263
Buchan Collectibles, Scotland 265
Calluna Books, Dorset 94
Crack (Books) (F.N.), Lancashire 140
Demar Books (Grant), Kent 138
Elmbury Books, Warwickshire 237
Huyton (Peter), Herefordshire 126
Ian Johnson Natural History Books,
 Buckinghamshire 63
Mobbs (A.J.), West Midlands 240
Pendleside Books, Lancashire 141
Shearwater Bed & Books (formerly John Lumby
 Nat. History Bks), Northumberland 200
Woodside Books, Kent 133

ENVIRONMENT, THE

Ice House Books 143
Kenny's Bookshops and Art Galleries Ltd,
 Republic Of Ireland 278
Post–Horn Books, N Yorks 192

EROTICA

Book Basket, London, Outer 182
Chatterton's Books, Wales 290
Collectables (W.H.), London (W) 172
Delectus Books, London (WC) 176
Dylans Bookstore, Wales 289
High Street Books, Devon 85
InterCol London, London (N) 154
Kent T. G., Surrey 230
Muttonchop Manuscripts, West Sussex 243
Occultique, Northamptonshire 198
Paper Pleasures, Somerset 217
Price (R.W.), Nottinghamshire 202

ESOTERIC

Abbey Bookshop, Hampshire 122
Alpha Books, London (N) 153
Armchair Books, Scotland 268
Book Barrow, Cambridgeshire 64
Books (For All), N Yorks 192

Caduceus Books, Leicestershire 143
Eastcote Bookshop (The), London, Outer 183
Far Horizons Books, Dorset 91
Graduate Books, Worcestershire 256
Greensleeves, Oxfordshire 204
IKON, Devon 88
Inner Bookshop (The), Oxfordshire 207
Magis Books, Leicestershire 144
Main Point Books, Scotland 269
Occultique, Northamptonshire 198
Rainger Books (Michael), Wales 285
Starlord Books, Cheshire 70
Treglown (Roger J.), Cheshire 71

ESPIONAGE

AA1 Books, Scotland 263
Baldwin (M. & M.), Shropshire 212
Corfe Books, Surrey 231
Courtyard Books, Herefordshire 127
Crimes Ink, London (E) 151
Empire Books, Greater Manchester 118
Ice House Books 143
Island Books, Devon 84
Military Collector (The), West Yorkshire 249
MilitaryHistoryBooks.com, Kent 136
Ming Books, Scotland 264
Price (R.W.), Nottinghamshire 202
Thornton (Grahame), Dorset 94

ETHNOGRAPHY

Bowen (Janice), Wales 286
Bracton Books, Cambridgeshire 64
Butcher (Pablo), Oxfordshire 205
Campbell Hewson Books (R.), Scotland 265
Delectus Books, London (WC) 176
Graves–Johnston (Michael), London (SW) 164
Traveller's Bookshelf (The), Somerset 215
Yesterday's Books, Dorset 91

ETHNOLOGY

Delectus Books, London (WC) 176
Graves–Johnston (Michael), London (SW) 164

ETIQUETTE

Cooksweb, Northamptonshire 198
Lucas (Richard), London (NW) 158
Weininger Antiquarian Books (Eva M.),
 London (NW) 159

EVOLUTION

Austwick Hall Books, N Yorks 141
Bernwode Books, Buckinghamshire 62
Bracton Books, Cambridgeshire 64
Buchan Collectibles, Scotland 265
Humanist Book Services, Cornwall 73

EX-LIBRIS

Cox Old & Rare Books (Claude), Suffolk 226
Devitt Books (Nial), Warwickshire 236

SPECIALITY INDEX

Heritage, West Midlands 238
Sanderson (Edward), Berkshire 58
Waddington Books & Prints (Geraldine),
  Northamptonshire 198

FABLES
Byre Books, Scotland 264
Eggeling Books (John), West Yorkshire 248
Holtom (Christopher), Cornwall 76
Menavaur Books, Scotland 264
Muttonchop Manuscripts, West Sussex 243
Prescott - The Bookseller (John), London, Outer 184
Roberts (Fine Books) (Julian), Lincolnshire 149
Spread Eagle Bookshop, London (SE) 162

FAIRGROUNDS
Beware of The Leopard Books, Bristol 60
Cottage Books, Leicestershire 143
Cover to Cover, Merseyside 186
Davis (Peter), Kent 136
Kaye - Bookseller (Terence), London (NW) 158
Menavaur Books, Scotland 264

FARMING & LIVESTOCK
Barn Books, Shropshire 213
Evergreen Livres, Gloucestershire 113
Greta Books, Durham 96
Kilgour (Sporting Books) (Ian), Leicestershire... 145
Mayhew (Veronica), Berkshire 58
Muttonchop Manuscripts, West Sussex 243
Phenotype Books, Cumbria 79
Scrivener's Books & Book Binding, Derbyshire . 81
Swan Bookshop (The), Devon 84
Thornber (Peter A.), N Yorks 195

FARRIERS
Austwick Hall Books, N Yorks 141
Phenotype Books, Cumbria 79

FASHION & COSTUME
Abrahams (Mike), Staffordshire 222
Amwell Book Company (The), London (EC).... 152
Art Reference Books, Hampshire 123
Ballantyne–Way (Roger), Suffolk 228
Batterham (David), London (W) 169
Black Cat Books, Norfolk 188
Books for Collectors, Gloucestershire 112
Bowdon Books, Lancashire 141
Byrom Textile Bookroom (Richard), Lancashire 140
Cooksweb, Northamptonshire 198
Dyson (Anthony), West Midlands 239
Goodyer (Nicholas), London (N) 154
Gresham Books, Somerset 216
Hogben (Carol), Wales 285
Hornsey's, N Yorks 194
Ives Bookseller (John), London, Outer 184
Manheim (Carol), London (W) 173
Mansfield (Judith), West Yorkshire 248
Martin - Bookseller (Colin), East Yorkshire 105
Meekins Books (Paul), Warwickshire 237

Shapero Rare Books (Bernard J.), London (W)... 174
Shipley Specialist Art Booksellers, London (WC) . 178
Trinders' Fine Tools, Suffolk 225
Warnes (Felicity J.), London, Outer 181
Young (D. & J.), Wales 289

FEMINISM
Cyclamen Books, Leicestershire 143
Delectus Books, London (WC) 176
Fortune Green Books, London (NW) 157
Kenny's Bookshops and Art Galleries Ltd,
  Republic Of Ireland 278
Lane Books (Shirley), Isle of Wight 132
Reading Lasses, Scotland 264
Roundstone Books, Lancashire 141
Savery Books, East Sussex 99
Spurrier (Nick), Kent 136
Stevens (Joan), Cambridgeshire 66
Swan Bookshop (The), Devon 84
Symes Books (Naomi), Cheshire 72
Till's Bookshop, Scotland 270
Willmott Bookseller (Nicholas), Wales 280

FICTION
- GENERAL
Abacus Gallery / The Village Bookshop,
  Staffordshire 223
Abbey Books, London (N) 153
Anderson Slater Antiques, N Yorks 195
Anglo-American Rare Books, Surrey 232
Applin (Malcolm), Berkshire 57
ARC Books, Scotland 272
Ashburton Books, Devon 83
Atticus Books, Essex 109
Autumn Leaves, Lincolnshire 148
Beaton (Richard), East Sussex 101
Beware of The Leopard Books, Bristol 60
Black Cat Bookshop, Leicestershire 143
Black Five Books, Shropshire 213
Book Corner, Scotland 263
Book for All Reasons (A.), Suffolk 227
Book House (The), Cumbria 78
Book Warren, Devon 84
Bookroom (The), Surrey 233
Books Afloat, Dorset 95
Books for Writers, Wales 283
BOOKS4U, Wales 282
Bookstop UK, Lancashire 142
Booth (Booksearch Service), (Geoff), Cheshire .. 69
Boris Books, Dorset 94
Bosco Books, Cornwall 73
Breese Books Ltd., East Sussex 98
Brighton Books, East Sussex 98
Broadhurst of Southport Ltd., Merseyside 186
Brunner Books, Cambridgeshire 68
Buchan Collectibles, Scotland 265
Bush, Bookdealer (John), Gloucestershire 115
Bygone Books, Lancashire 141
Caledonia Books, Scotland 271
Carnforth Bookshop (The), Lancashire 140
Caron Books, Nottinghamshire 202
Catalyst Books, Surrey 232
Celtic Bookshop (The), Republic Of Ireland 279

SPECIALITY INDEX

Chatterton's Books, Wales 290
Clements (R.W.), London, Outer 181
Corfe Books, Surrey................................... 231
Cox Rare Books (Charles), Cornwall 74
Crimes Ink, London (E)............................. 151
Croft Selections, Lincolnshire..................... 148
Dartmoor Bookshop (The), Devon 83
dgbbooks, West Sussex 244
Doolin Dinghy Books, Republic Of Ireland...... 275
DoublePlusBooks, Cambridgeshire 68
Eastcote Bookshop (The), London, Outer 183
Eggeling Books (John), West Yorkshire 248
Ellis, Bookseller (Peter), London (SE) 160
Ellwood Editions, Hampshire....................... 123
Family Favourites (Books), East Yorkshire...... 104
Fiction First, Cheshire................................ 70
Fireside Bookshop, Cumbria 80
First State Books, London (W) 172
Fortune Green Books, London (NW)............. 157
Freya Books & Antiques, Norfolk................ 189
Gloucester Road Books, London (SW) 164
Golden Hind Bookshop (The), Kent 134
Greta Books, Durham 96
Grove Bookshop (The), N Yorks.................. 195
Harrington (Adrian), London (W)................. 173
Heckmondwike Book Shop, West Yorkshire 235
Ice House Books.. 143
Innes Books, Shropshire............................. 212
Intech Books, Northumberland 201
Jade Mountain, Hampshire 123
Johnson Rare Book Collections (C.R.), London
 (NW)... 158
Jones (J.V.A.), Essex 109
K. Books, Cheshire.................................... 72
Kellow Books, Oxfordshire 204
Kingfisher Book Service, Nottinghamshire 203
L.M.S. Books, Hertfordshire 129
Langmaid (Kenneth), Cornwall 76
Left Bank (The), Wales.............................. 290
Lewis (J.T. & P.), Cornwall........................ 74
Little Bookshop (The), Greater Manchester 117
Little Stour Books, Kent 133
Main Point Books, Scotland........................ 269
Marine Workshop Bookshop, Dorset 92
McKelvie (Ian), London (N)........................ 154
Mercat Books, Scotland 267
Miller, (Dusty), Cornwall 73
Moffat Book Exchange, Scotland 263
Mr. Pickwick of Towcester, Northamptonshire.. 199
Naughton Booksellers, Republic Of Ireland...... 277
New Strand Bookshop (The), Herefordshire 126
Oblong Books, N Yorks.............................. 197
O'Brien Books & Photo Gallery, Republic Of
 Ireland 279
Offer (Richard), Cheshire............................ 70
Old Storytellers Bookshop (The), Scotland....... 261
Olio Books, East Sussex 101
Olynthiacs, Shropshire 212
Park Gallery & Bookshop (The),
 Northamptonshire.................................... 199
Peakirk Books, Cambridgeshire 68
Peter's Bookshop, Norfolk 190
Polmorla Books, Cornwall 76
Premier Books & Prints, Lincolnshire............ 146
Prescott - The Bookseller (John), London, Outer 184

Price (R.D.M. & I.M.) (Books),
 Greater Manchester 119
Price (R.W.), Nottinghamshire 202
Riverside Bookshop (The), Cumbria 78
Roberts (Fine Books) (Julian), Lincolnshire 149
Roland Books, Kent 137
Rosemary Books, Merseyside...................... 186
Russell Books, Somerset............................. 218
St Michael at Plea Bookshop, Norfolk 190
Savery Books, East Sussex 99
Sax Books, Suffolk 228
Scott (T.F.S.), East Sussex 102
Scrivener's Books & Book Binding, Derbyshire. 81
Shacklock Books (David), Suffolk 226
Smith Books, (Sally), Suffolk 225
Stevens (Joan), Cambridgeshire 66
Sturford Books, Wiltshire 252
Swan Bookshop (The), Devon...................... 84
Temple (Robert), London (N)...................... 155
Thomas (E. Wyn), Wales............................ 282
Thornton (Grahame), Dorset 94
Tindley & Chapman, London (WC).............. 178
Trevorrow (Edwin), Hertfordshire 128
Unsworths Booksellers Ltd., London (WC)...... 178
Ventnor Rare Books, Isle of Wight............... 132
Warrington Book Loft (The), Cheshire 72
Whitfield (Ken), Essex 109
Williams (Bookdealer), (Richard), Lincolnshire . 149
Williams Rare Books (Nigel), London (WC) ... 179
Willmott Bookseller (Nicholas), Wales........... 280
Winchester Antiquarian Books, Hampshire...... 125
Woodstock Fabrics & Books, Shropshire......... 212
Zardoz Books, Wiltshire............................. 253

- CRIME, DETECTIVE, SPY, THRILLERS

AA1 Books, Scotland................................. 263
Abbey Bookshop, Hampshire 122
Amwell Book Company (The), London (EC).... 152
Andrews (R.), Gloucestershire..................... 111
Bell (Books) (Mrs. V.S.), Suffolk................. 226
Black–Bird Books, London (NW) 157
Book Warren, Devon 84
Bookshop Blackheath, London (SE) 160
Bookstop UK, Lancashire 142
Bradley–Cox (Mary), Dorset....................... 90
Brunner Books, Cambridgeshire 68
Catalyst Books, Surrey 232
Chevin Books, West Yorkshire 248
Courtyard Books, Herefordshire 127
Cowley, Bookdealer (K.W.), Somerset........... 215
Crime Inc, Greater Manchester 118
Crimes Ink, London (E)............................. 151
Dyson (Anthony), West Midlands................. 239
Eggeling Books (John), West Yorkshire 248
Fantastic Literature, Essex 109
Farringdon Books, Essex............................ 107
Fiction First, Cheshire................................ 70
Gate Memorabilia, London (N).................... 153
Glass Key (The), West Yorkshire 246
Harris (Books), (Malcolm), West Midlands 239
Heckmondwike Book Shop, West Yorkshire 235
Heppa (Christopher), Essex......................... 106
Hight (Norman F.), Bedfordshire.................. 56
Hill (John S.), Devon 85

J & M Books, Warwickshire 237
Jackson (M.W.), Wiltshire 253
Kent (Books) (Mrs. A.), Suffolk 226
Marcet Books, London (SE) 161
Marine Workshop Bookshop, Dorset 92
McCaughtrie (K.A.), N Yorks 192
McKelvie (Ian), London (N) 154
Ming Books, Scotland 264
New Strand Bookshop (The), Herefordshire 126
Platt Rare Books (Richard), London (SE) 161
Porcupine Books, London, Outer 182
Post Mortem Books, West Sussex 242
Price (R.W.), Nottinghamshire 202
Roberts (Fine Books) (Julian), Lincolnshire 149
Ruebotham (Kirk), Cheshire 71
Smith Modern First Editions, (Chris Adam),
   West Sussex 243
Spread Eagle Bookshop, London (SE) 162
Starlord Books, Cheshire 70
Sturgeon (Jamie), West Sussex 244
Sutcliffe (Mark), West Yorkshire 246
Temple (Robert), London (N) 155
Till's Bookshop, Scotland 270
Tindley & Chapman, London (WC) 178
Vokes (Jeremiah), Durham 96
Williams (Bookdealer), (Richard), Lincolnshire . 149
Wilson (J. & M.), Scotland 273
Woodstock Fabrics & Books, Shropshire 212

- FANTASY, HORROR

AA1 Books, Scotland 263
Bookstop UK, Lancashire 142
Chevin Books, West Yorkshire 248
Courtyard Books, Herefordshire 127
Cowley, Bookdealer (K.W.), Somerset 215
Daeron's Books, Buckinghamshire 63
Dalby (Richard), N Yorks 194
Eggeling Books (John), West Yorkshire 248
Fantastic Literature, Essex 109
Fantasy Centre, London (N) 153
Farringdon Books, Essex 107
Fiction First, Cheshire 70
Hight (Norman F.), Bedfordshire 56
Jackson (M.W.), Wiltshire 253
Jericho Books, Oxfordshire 208
Occultique, Northamptonshire 198
Porcupine Books, London, Outer 182
Price (R.W.), Nottinghamshire 202
Roberts (Fine Books) (Julian), Lincolnshire 149
Ruebotham (Kirk), Cheshire 71
Starlord Books, Cheshire 70
Temple (Robert), London (N) 155
Till's Bookshop, Scotland 270
Williams (Bookdealer), (Richard), Lincolnshire . 149

- HISTORICAL

Black Cat Bookshop, Leicestershire 143
Black Five Books, Shropshire 213
Book for All Reasons (A.), Suffolk 227
Bookstop UK, Lancashire 142
Boris Books, Dorset 94
Eggeling Books (John), West Yorkshire 248
Fantastic Literature, Essex 109

Heppa (Christopher), Essex 106
Naughton Booksellers, Republic Of Ireland 277
Roberts (Fine Books) (Julian), Lincolnshire 149
Smith Modern First Editions, (Chris Adam),
   West Sussex 243
Stacks Bookshop, Northern Ireland 259
Temple (Robert), London (N) 155
Trevorrow (Edwin), Hertfordshire 128
Williams Rare Books (Nigel), London (WC) 179

- ROMANTIC

Book for All Reasons (A.), Suffolk 227
Books & Bygones, Berkshire 58
Bookseller (The), Suffolk 227
Chatterton's Books, Wales 290
Eggeling Books (John), West Yorkshire 248
Murder One, London (WC) 177
Price (R.W.), Nottinghamshire 202
Williams (Bookdealer), (Richard),
   Lincolnshire 149

- SCIENCE FICTION

AA1 Books, Scotland 263
Altshuler (Jean), Cumbria 78
Armchair Books, Scotland 268
Armstrongs Books & Collectables,
   West Midlands 239
Black Cat Bookshop, Leicestershire 143
Book Bungalow (The), Cornwall 73
Books & Bygones, Berkshire 58
Books & Bygones (Pam Taylor), W Mids 240
Books (For All), N Yorks 192
Bookstop UK, Lancashire 142
Booth Books, Wales 286
Brunner Books, Cambridgeshire 68
Chevin Books, West Yorkshire 248
Classic Crime Collections, Greater Manchester.. 117
Courtyard Books, Herefordshire 127
Cowley, Bookdealer (K.W.), Somerset 215
Crimes Ink, London (E) 151
Daeron's Books, Buckinghamshire 63
Dead Zone Books, Wales 289
Driffield Bookshop (The), East Yorkshire 104
Eggeling Books (John), West Yorkshire 248
Fantastic Literature, Essex 109
Fantasy Centre, London (N) 153
Farringdon Books, Essex 107
Fiction First, Cheshire 70
Heckmondwike Book Shop, West Yorkshire 235
Hight (Norman F.), Bedfordshire 56
Hill (John S.), Devon 85
J & M Books, Warwickshire 237
Jackson (M.W.), Wiltshire 253
K. Books, Cheshire 72
Left Bank (The), Wales 290
Murder One, London (WC) 177
New Strand Bookshop (The), Herefordshire 126
Offer (Richard), Cheshire 70
Porcupine Books, London, Outer 182
Price (R.W.), Nottinghamshire 202
Roberts (Fine Books) (Julian), Lincolnshire 149
Rods Books, Devon 87
Ruebotham (Kirk), Cheshire 71
Russell Books, Somerset 218

SPECIALITY INDEX

Smith Modern First Editions, (Chris Adam),
  West Sussex 243
Starlord Books, Cheshire 70
Temple (Robert), London (N) 155
Till's Bookshop, Scotland 270
Transformer, Scotland 264
Trevorrow (Edwin), Hertfordshire 128
Wayside Books and Cards, Oxfordshire 205
Wiend Books & Collectables,
  Greater Manchester 119
Williams (Bookdealer), (Richard), Lincolnshire . 149
Woodstock Fabrics & Books, Shropshire 212
Zardoz Books, Wiltshire 253

- WESTERNS

AA1 Books, Scotland 263
Americanabooksuk, Cumbria 77
Books & Bygones, Berkshire 58
Moffat Book Exchange, Scotland 263
Price (R.W.), Nottinghamshire 202
Rods Books, Devon 87
Till's Bookshop, Scotland 270

- WOMEN

Amwell Book Company (The), London (EC) 152
Applin (Malcolm), Berkshire 57
Eggeling Books (John), West Yorkshire 248
Fortune Green Books, London (NW) 157
Gate Memorabilia, London (N) 153
Ice House Books 143
Reading Lasses, Scotland 264
Swan Bookshop (The), Devon 84
Symes Books (Naomi), Cheshire 72
Temple (Robert), London (N) 155
Tiger Books, Kent 134
Till's Bookshop, Scotland 270
Tindley & Chapman, London (WC) 178
Williams (Bookdealer), (Richard), Lincolnshire . 149

FINE & RARE,

Aberdeen Rare Books & Caledonian Books,
  Scotland 267
Allsop (Duncan M.), Warwickshire 237
Almar Books, West Yorkshire 247
Amwell Book Company (The), London (EC) 152
Atholl Fine Books, Scotland 273
Austwick Hall Books, N Yorks 141
Baxter (Steve), Surrey 232
Bayntun (George), Somerset 214
Biblion, London (W) 169
Books on Spain, London, Outer 183
Bookwyze, Lincolnshire 147
Bristow & Garland, Hampshire 121
Broadhurst of Southport Ltd., Merseyside 186
Carnforth Bookshop (The), Lancashire 140
Chantry Bookshop & Gallery, Devon 84
Clent Books, Worcestershire 254
Cox Rare Books (Charles), Cornwall 74
Crispin's Day, Antiquarian and Out of
  Print Military Books, Essex 110
Cygnet Books, East Yorkshire 105
Dartmoor Bookshop (The), Devon 83
David (G.), Cambridgeshire 64

Dorset Rare Books, Wiltshire 252
DoublePlusBooks, Cambridgeshire 68
Eastwood Books (David), Cornwall 73
Ellwood Editions, Hampshire 123
Emerald Isle Books, Northern Ireland 259
Fine Irish Books, Republic Of Ireland 276
Grayling (David A.H.), Cumbria 78
Harrington (Adrian), London (W) 173
Harrington Antiquarian Bookseller (Peter),
  London (SW) 164
Heath (A.R.), Bristol 61
Hughes Rare Books (Spike), Scotland 261
Hutchison (Books) (Larry), Scotland 265
Island Books, Devon 84
Jericho Books, Oxfordshire 208
Kenny's Bookshops and Art Galleries Ltd,
  Republic Of Ireland 278
Kernaghans, Merseyside 186
Lucius Books, N Yorks 196
Mair Wilkes Books, Scotland 265
Marks Limited (Barrie), London (N) 154
Meinertzhagen (Nicholas), London (SW) 165
On the Wild Side, Worcestershire 255
Orlando Booksellers, Lincolnshire 148
Orssich (Paul), London (SW) 166
Paralos Ltd., London (W) 173
Parikian, Rare Books (Diana), London (W) 174
Poole (William), London (W) 174
Riley-Smith (Hamish), Norfolk 190
Rochdale Book Company, Greater Manchester . 118
Rosley Books, Cumbria 79
Rowan (P. & B.), Northern Ireland 259
St Mary's Books & Prints, Lincolnshire 150
Shapero Rare Books (Bernard J.), London (W) . 174
Sokol Books (A.), London (W) 174
Stothert Old Books, Cheshire 69
Taylor & Son (Peter), Hertfordshire 130
Tobo Books, Hampshire 122
Tower Bridge Books, London (SE) 162
Troath Books (Brian), London (E) 151
Updike Rare Books (John), Scotland 270
Venables (Morris & Juliet), Bristol 61
Woodbine Books, West Yorkshire 245

FINE ART

Adams (Judith), Shropshire 211
Ars Artis, Oxfordshire 206
Art Reference Books, Hampshire 123
Beetles Ltd., (Chris), London (SW) 163
Capes (Books, Maps & Prints) (John L.),
  N Yorks 195
Dew (Roderick), East Sussex 100
Dorset Rare Books, Wiltshire 252
fineart-photographer, Herefordshire 127
Garton & Co., Wiltshire 250
Handsworth Books, Essex 110
Heneage Art Books (Thomas), London (SW).... 164
Holdsworth Books (Bruce), West Yorkshire 245
Hollett and Son (R.F.G.), Cumbria 79
Ice House Books 143
Inprint, Gloucestershire 114
Kelly Books (Don), London (W) 173
Kenny's Bookshops and Art Galleries Ltd,
  Republic Of Ireland 278

Marlborough Rare Books Ltd., London (W).... 173
Pagan Limited (Hugh), London (SW)............. 166
Second Edition, Scotland........................... 270
Shipley Specialist Art Booksellers, London (WC) . 178
Slavin Rare and Collectable Books (Derek),
  Warwickshire..................................... 237
Spelman (Ken), N Yorks............................ 197
Sykes (Graham), West Yorkshire 248
Tasburgh Books, Norfolk 190
Trinders' Fine Tools, Suffolk 225
Wyseby House Books, Berkshire................... 57

FINE PRINTING
Bardsley's Books, Suffolk 225
Barlow (Vincent G.), Hampshire................... 123
Cox Old & Rare Books (Claude), Suffolk 226
Grant (Gerald S.), Cheshire......................... 69
J.C. Poole Books, Wales............................ 290
Maggs Brothers Limited, London (W)............ 173
McKay Rare Books (Barry), Cumbria 77
Mills Rare Books (Adam), Cambridgeshire 65
Updike Rare Books (John), Scotland 270

FIRE & FIREFIGHTERS
Premier Books & Prints, Lincolnshire............. 146
Theatreshire Books, N Yorks....................... 192

FIREARMS/GUNS
Americanabooksuk, Cumbria........................ 77
Atticus Books, Essex................................. 109
Books & Bygones, Berkshire....................... 58
Chalmers Hallam (E.), Hampshire................. 123
DoublePlusBooks, Cambridgeshire 68
Duck (William), East Sussex........................ 98
Dyfi Valley Bookshop, Wales....................... 288
Empire Books, Greater Manchester 118
Guildmaster Books, Cheshire....................... 71
Helion & Company, West Midlands 240
Heneage Art Books (Thomas), London (SW).... 164
Home Farm Books, Warwickshire 236
Kilgour (Sporting Books) (Ian), Leicestershire... 145
Meekins Books (Paul), Warwickshire 237
Military Collector (The), West Yorkshire 249
MilitaryHistoryBooks.com, Kent 136
Muttonchop Manuscripts, West Sussex........... 243
Prospect Books, Wales.............................. 282
Scott (Sporting Books) (John),
  Worcestershire..................................... 256
Thin Read Line, Merseyside 186
Trinders' Fine Tools, Suffolk 225

FIRST EDITIONS
Abbey Bookshop, Hampshire 122
Almar Books, West Yorkshire...................... 247
Anderson Slater Antiques, N Yorks 195
Armchair Books, Scotland 268
Armstrongs Books & Collectables,
  West Midlands 239
Ash Rare Books, London (EC) 152
Austwick Hall Books, N Yorks 141
Bates Books, London, Outer....................... 181
Baxter (Steve), Surrey............................... 232
Bayntun (George), Somerset 214
BC Books, Cheshire.................................. 70
Beck Head Books, Cumbria 78
Bertram Rota Ltd., London (WC)................. 176
Beware of The Leopard Books, Bristol 60
Blackman (Martin), Buckinghamshire............. 62
Blythswood Bookshop, Scotland................... 268
Book Barrow, Cambridgeshire 64
Book Gallery (The), Cornwall...................... 76
Books & Bygones, Berkshire....................... 58
Bookshop (The), Republic Of Ireland............. 276
Bookwyze, Lincolnshire 147
Boris Books, Dorset................................. 94
Brighton Books, East Sussex 98
Brunner Books, Cambridgeshire 68
Budd (Richard), Somerset.......................... 217
Bygone Books, Lancashire 141
Carta Regis, Wales................................... 288
Castle Bookshop, Essex............................. 107
Catalyst Books, Surrey 232
Chantry Bookshop & Gallery, Devon............. 84
Chapman (Ron), London (SW) 163
Cobweb Books, N Yorks............................ 194
Courtyard Books, Herefordshire 127
Craobh Rua Books, Northern Ireland 259
Criterion Books, London, Outer 182
Eastcote Bookshop (The), London, Outer........ 183
Ellis, Bookseller (Peter), London (SE) 160
English (Toby), Oxfordshire 209
Farnborough Bookshop and Gallery,
  Hampshire 121
Fiction First, Cheshire............................... 70
Fin Rare Books, Shropshire 213
Fine Art, West Sussex 242
First State Books, London (W) 172
Foster Bookshop (Paul), London (SW)........... 164
Fosters Bookshop, London (W).................... 172
Frost (Richard), Hertfordshire 128
Gate Memorabilia, London (N).................... 153
Gekoski (R.A.), London (WC)..................... 177
Glass Key (The), West Yorkshire.................. 246
Harrington (Adrian), London (W)................. 173
Harrington Antiquarian Bookseller (Peter),
  London (SW) 164
Heathfield Books, Norfolk 188
Heppa (Christopher), Essex........................ 106
Hill (John S.), Devon 85
Hunter, Bookseller (K.P.), Cambridgeshire...... 65
Intech Books, Northumberland 201
Island Books, Devon................................. 84
J & M Books, Warwickshire....................... 237
Jarndyce Antiquarian Booksellers,
  London (WC) 177
Jericho Books, Oxfordshire 208
K. Books, Cheshire.................................. 72
Katnap Arts, Norfolk................................ 189
Kendall–Carpenter (Tim), Greater Manchester.. 117
Kenny's Bookshops and Art Galleries Ltd,
  Republic Of Ireland 278
Keswick Bookshop, Cumbria....................... 78
Kevin S. Ogilvie Modern First Editions,
  Scotland 265
Kirkman Ltd., (Robert), Bedfordshire 55
L.M.S. Books, Hertfordshire 129
Langmaid (Kenneth), Cornwall 76

SPECIALITY INDEX

Leabeck Books, Oxfordshire 208
Little Stour Books, Kent 133
Lloyd-Davies (Sue), Wales 280
Lucius Books, N Yorks............................ 196
Marcet Books, London (SE).................... 161
Marjon Books, Essex............................... 110
McCann (Joe), Oxfordshire 208
McKelvie (Ian), London (N).................... 154
Modern Firsts Etc., Lancashire 140
Nangle (Julian), Dorset............................. 92
Naughton Booksellers, Republic Of Ireland...... 277
Oblong Books, N Yorks........................... 197
Offer (Richard), Cheshire......................... 70
Old Storytellers Bookshop (The), Scotland....... 261
Palladour Books, Hampshire 124
Photographery at Soldridge Books, Hampshire . 120
Platt Rare Books (Richard), London (SE) 161
Prescott - The Bookseller (John), London, Outer 184
Price (R.W.), Nottinghamshire 202
Rassam (Paul), London (NW).................. 158
Red Snapper Books, London (WC) 178
Rees & O'Neill Rare Books, London (WC)...... 178
Riderless Horse Books, Norfolk 187
Riverside Bookshop (The), Cumbria 78
Rosemary Books, Merseyside.................. 186
Roundstone Books, Lancashire 141
Rowan House Books, Surrey 231
Ruebotham (Kirk), Cheshire...................... 71
Russell Books, Somerset......................... 218
Sansovino Books, West Sussex 244
Satara Books, West Sussex..................... 244
Scott (T.F.S.), East Sussex 102
Scrivener's Books & Book Binding, Derbyshire . 81
Second Edition, Scotland........................ 270
Shapero Rare Books (Bernard J.), London (W) . 174
Sillem (Anthony), East Sussex................ 101
Spread Eagle Bookshop, London (SE)..... 162
Studio Bookshop, East Sussex.................. 99
Sutcliffe (Mark), West Yorkshire............. 246
Sykes (Graham), West Yorkshire 248
Temple (Robert), London (N).................. 155
Tindley & Chapman, London (WC)......... 178
Torsdag Books, Buckinghamshire 62
Trevorrow (Edwin), Hertfordshire 128
Troath Books (Brian), London (E) 151
Updike Rare Books (John), Scotland 270
Waterfield's, Oxfordshire 209
Webb Books (John), South Yorkshire 220
Whiteson Ltd., (Edna), Hertfordshire 128
Williams (Bookdealer), (Richard), Lincolnshire . 149
Williams Rare Books (Nigel), London (WC) 179
Woodbine Books, West Yorkshire 245
Words & Music, Cheshire........................ 70

FISHES

Chalmers Hallam (E.), Hampshire........... 123
Coch-y-Bonddu Books, Wales................. 288
Hunter, Bookseller, (K.P.), Cambridgeshire...... 65
On the Wild Side, Worcestershire 255
River Reads Bookshop, Devon................... 88
Scott (Sporting Books) (John), Worcestershire .. 256

FLOWER ARRANGING

Blest (Peter), Kent................................... 136

Calendula Horticultural Books, East Sussex 100
Cooksweb, Northamptonshire.................. 198
Court Hay Books, Bristol.......................... 60
Park (Mike), London, Outer.................... 183
Roadmaster Books, Kent......................... 134

FOLIO SOCIETY, THE

Arundel Bookshop, West Sussex............. 241
Avery (Alan), N Yorks 193
Barbican Bookshop, N Yorks 196
Book Basket, London, Outer................... 182
BOOKS4U, Wales.................................. 282
Chevin Books, West Yorkshire................ 248
Coach House Books, Worcestershire....... 255
Finn (V. & C.), Merseyside 185
Fisher & Sperr, London (N)..................... 153
Oblong Books, N Yorks........................... 197
Prescott - The Bookseller (John),
  London, Outer 184
Ross Old Books & Prints, Herefordshire 127
Spread Eagle Bookshop, London (SE)..... 162
Tasburgh Books, Norfolk 190
Thomas (Books) (Leona), Cheshire........... 71
Waddington Books & Prints (Geraldine),
  Northamptonshire 198

FOLKLORE

Allport (Roy), N Yorks 195
Alpha Books, London (N) 153
Books, Wales.. 282
Books on Spain, London, Outer.............. 183
Bracton Books, Cambridgeshire................ 64
Byre Books, Scotland 264
Cottage Books, Leicestershire................. 143
Dancing Goat Bookshop (The), Norfolk 188
Delectus Books, London (WC)............... 176
Doolin Dinghy Books, Republic Of Ireland...... 275
Dylans Bookstore, Wales........................ 289
Gilbert (R.A.), Bristol............................... 61
Holtom (Christopher), Cornwall 76
Hutchison (Books) (Larry), Scotland....... 265
Inner Bookshop (The), Oxfordshire 207
Lowe (John), Norfolk.............................. 189
Magis Books, Leicestershire.................... 144
Minster Gate Bookshop, N Yorks............ 196
Occultique, Northamptonshire 198
Orssich (Paul), London (SW).................. 166
Polczynski (Udo K.H.), London, Outer 183
Royal Carbery Books Ltd., Republic Of Ireland 275
Wheen O'Blethers Bookshop, Scotland 271

FOOD & DRINK

Arden Books & Cosmographia, Warwickshire... 236
Arundel Bookshop, West Sussex............. 241
Book Corner, Scotland 263
Books & Bygones, Berkshire.................... 58
Clarke (Janet), Somerset......................... 214
Collectable Books, London (SE)............. 160
Cooks Books, East Sussex 98
Cooksweb, Northamptonshire.................. 198
Dusty Books, Wales................................ 287
Elmfield Books, West Midlands.............. 238
Gresham Books, Somerset 216

SPECIALITY INDEX

Harvest Books, Merseyside 185
Jade Mountain, Hampshire 123
Lucas (Richard), London (NW).................... 158
Mercat Books, Scotland 267
Moray Bookshop (The), Scotland 267
Spread Eagle Bookshop, London (SE)........... 162
Words & Music, Cheshire............................ 70
YSF Books, South Yorkshire....................... 221

FORE-EDGE PAINTINGS
Atlantis Bookshop, London (WC)................. 176
Carta Regis, Wales 288
Cox Old & Rare Books (Claude), Suffolk 226
Fine Art, West Sussex 242
Game Advice, Oxfordshire 207
Harrington (Adrian), London (W)................. 173
Harrington Antiquarian Bookseller (Peter),
  London (SW)... 164
Inner Bookshop (The), Oxfordshire 207
Kirkman Ltd., (Robert), Bedfordshire 55
Magis Books, Leicestershire........................ 144
Rainger Books (Michael), Wales.................. 285
Savery Books, East Sussex 99
Smallwood Books, Lincolnshire.................... 148

FOREIGN TEXTS
Artco, Nottinghamshire 202
Books on Spain, London, Outer 183
Chiltern Books, London (W)........................ 172
Classic Bindings, London (SW)..................... 163
Colwyn Books, Wales.................................. 281
Crouch Rare Books, Surrey.......................... 232
Foyle Books, Northern Ireland..................... 260
Hab Books, London (W).............................. 173
Ice House Books.. 143
Hellenic Bookservices, London (NW)............. 158
Malmo Books, Hampshire 121
Meinertzhagen (Nicholas), London (SW)........ 165
Orssich (Paul), London (SW)....................... 166
Parikian, Rare Books (Diana), London (W) 174
Philologus–Fine & Rare Books, London (SW) .. 166
Plurabelle Books, Cambridgeshire 65
Poole (William), London (W)....................... 174
Riley–Smith (Hamish), Norfolk 190
Robertshaw (John), Cambridgeshire............... 67
Sturford Books, Wiltshire 252
Visser Books (de), Cambridgeshire 66

FORESTRY
Coch-y-Bonddu Books, Wales...................... 288
Daly (Peter M.), Hampshire 124
Park (Mike), London, Outer 183

FREE THOUGHT
Humanist Book Services, Cornwall................ 73
Kenny's Bookshops and Art Galleries Ltd,
  Republic Of Ireland 278
Northern Herald Books, West Yorkshire........ 245
Pioneer Books, Hampshire 120
Turton (John), Durham 97

FREEMASONRY & ANTI-MASONRY
Alpha Books, London (N) 153
Fun in Books, Surrey 233
Gilbert (R.A.), Bristol................................ 61
Inner Bookshop (The), Oxfordshire 207
InterCol London, London (N) 154
Magis Books, Leicestershire........................ 144
Occultique, Northamptonshire 198

FURNITURE
Art Reference Books, Hampshire 123
DoublePlusBooks, Cambridgeshire 68
Heneage Art Books (Thomas), London (SW).... 164
Trinders' Fine Tools, Suffolk 225
Upper–Room Books, Somerset..................... 216

GAMBLING
Amos (Denis W.), Hertfordshire 128
Bennetts Books, East Sussex 101
BookLovers, Somerset 217
Delectus Books, London (WC)..................... 176
InterCol London, London (N) 154
Spread Eagle Bookshop, London (SE)........... 162

GAMES
Bookmark (Children's Books), Wiltshire 252
Ellen, The Bookshop (Barrie E.), Essex........... 110
Game Advice, Oxfordshire.......................... 207
Ice House Books....................................... 143
InterCol London, London (N) 154

GARDENING
Abacus Gallery / The Village Bookshop,
  Staffordshire.. 223
Adams (Judith), Shropshire......................... 211
Arden Books & Cosmographia, Warwickshire... 236
Arundel Bookshop, West Sussex 241
Barn Books, Shropshire 213
Barnhill Books, Scotland 272
Beck Head Books, Cumbria 78
Besleys Books, Suffolk 224
Bland (Mary), Herefordshire....................... 126
Blest (Peter), Kent 136
Book Corner, Scotland 263
Book House (The), Cumbria........................ 78
Books, Wales 282
Books & Bygones, Berkshire........................ 58
Books for Content, Herefordshire 126
Bookworld, Shropshire 212
Bosco Books, Cornwall............................... 73
Brighton Books, East Sussex 98
Brown-Studies, Scotland............................. 270
Buxton Books (Anna), Scotland 269
Calendula Horticultural Books, East Sussex ... 100
Carnforth Bookshop (The), Lancashire 140
Castleton (Pat), Kent................................. 135
Cherry (Janet), Dorset 92
Clark (M.R.), West Yorkshire...................... 245
Cooksweb, Northamptonshire 198
Court Hay Books, Bristol............................ 60
Cousens (W.C.), Devon............................... 83

SPECIALITY INDEX

Crack (Books) (F.N.), Lancashire 140
Croft Selections, Lincolnshire...................... 148
Curtle Mead Books, Isle of Wight................ 131
Daly (Peter M.), Hampshire 124
Dartmoor Bookshop (The), Devon 83
Duck (William), East Sussex........................ 98
Dusty Books, Wales.................................. 287
Ellis, Bookseller (Peter), London (SE) 160
Evergreen Livres, Gloucestershire.................. 113
Fin Rare Books, Shropshire 213
Flora Books, London (E) 151
Furneaux Books (Lee), Devon 87
Goodyer (Nicholas), London (N).................. 154
Greyfriars Books, Essex 107
Hennessey Bookseller (Ray), East Sussex........ 100
Hünersdorff Rare Books, London (SW) 165
Hunter, Bookseller, (K.P.), Cambridgeshire...... 65
Ice House Books....................................... 143
Inprint, Gloucestershire............................... 114
Jade Mountain, Hampshire 123
Jay Books, Scotland.................................. 269
Max Gate Books, Somerset 218
Mercat Books, Scotland 267
Merritt (Valerie), Gloucestershire 111
Morgan (D. & D.H.W.), Devon 89
On the Wild Side, Worcestershire.................. 255
Park (Mike), London, Outer........................ 183
Parrott Books, Oxfordshire 209
Prospect House Books, Northern Ireland 260
River Reads Bookshop, Devon...................... 88
Savery Books, East Sussex 99
Scrivener's Books & Book Binding, Derbyshire . 81
Seeber (Liz), East Sussex 99
Silver Trees Books, West Midlands................ 239
Spread Eagle Bookshop, London (SE)............ 162
Staniland (Booksellers), Lincolnshire 150
Sue Lowell Natural History Books, London (W) 175
Thin Read Line, Merseyside 186
Trinders' Fine Tools, Suffolk 225
Wyseby House Books, Berkshire................... 57
YSF Books, South Yorkshire....................... 221

GEMMOLOGY

Barmby (C. & A.J.), Kent........................... 138
J.G. Natural History Books, Surrey................ 232
Nibris Books, London (SW)......................... 165
Trinders' Fine Tools, Suffolk 225

GENEALOGY

Ambra Books, Bristol................................ 60
Booth Books, Wales.................................. 286
Brewin Books Ltd., Warwickshire 237
Cahir Cosy Corner Bookshop, Republic Of
  Ireland 279
Delph Books, Greater Manchester................. 116
Farquharson, (Hilary), Scotland 273
Hawes Books, Norfolk............................... 189
Hutchison (Books) (Larry), Scotland.............. 265
Idle Booksellers (The), West Yorkshire 245
Island Books, Devon................................. 86
Island Books, Devon................................. 84
Kent T. G., Surrey 230
Spooner & Co., Somerset 217

Titford (John), Derbyshire 81
Townsend (John), Berkshire 59
Turton (John), Durham 97

GEOGRAPHY

Archer (David), Wales............................... 288
Cahir Cosy Corner Bookshop, Republic Of
  Ireland 279
Chesters (G. & J.), Staffordshire 223
Harrington Antiquarian Bookseller (Peter),
  London (SW)....................................... 164
Ice House Books....................................... 143
Malmo Books, Hampshire 121
Roadmaster Books, Kent............................ 134

GEOLOGY

Archer (David), Wales............................... 288
Books & Bygones, Berkshire........................ 58
Bott, (Bookdealers) Ltd., (Martin), Greater
  Manchester 116
Bow Windows Book Shop, East Sussex 102
Browne (A.), Cheshire 69
Charmouth Bookstore, Dorset 91
Chesters (G. & J.), Staffordshire 223
Duck (William), East Sussex........................ 98
Earth Science Books, Wiltshire..................... 251
Henly (John), West Sussex 244
Honiton Old Bookshop, Devon.................... 85
Ice House Books....................................... 143
Phelps (Michael), West Sussex..................... 242
Prospect House Books, Northern Ireland 260
Roadmaster Books, Kent............................ 134
Weiner (Graham), London (N)..................... 156
Westwood Books (Mark), Wales................... 287
Whitchurch Books Ltd., Wales..................... 280

GHOSTS

AA1 Books, Scotland................................ 263
Cowley, Bookdealer (K.W.), Somerset 215
Far Horizons Books, Dorset........................ 91
Grieveson (A.), Cheshire 69
Inner Bookshop (The), Oxfordshire 207
Magis Books, Leicestershire......................... 144
Occultique, Northamptonshire 198
Wizard Books, Cambridgeshire..................... 68

GLAMOUR

Book Basket, London, Outer 182
Fun in Books, Surrey 233
Muttonchop Manuscripts, West Sussex........... 243
NostalGia Publications Ltd., N Yorks............ 196
Paper Pleasures, Somerset........................... 217
Tilleys Vintage Magazine Shop, Derbyshire...... 81
Zardoz Books, Wiltshire............................. 253

GLASS

Ancient Art Books, London (SW) 163
Art Reference Books, Hampshire 123
Barmby (C. & A.J.), Kent........................... 138
Heneage Art Books (Thomas), London (SW).... 164

Ives Bookseller (John), London, Outer............ 184
Martin - Bookseller (Colin), East Yorkshire 105
Studio Bookshop, East Sussex...................... 99
Trinders' Fine Tools, Suffolk 225

GNOSTICS
Far Horizons Books, Dorset........................ 91
Gilbert (R.A.), Bristol............................. 61
Rainger Books (Michael), Wales................... 285

GRAPHICS
Lawton (J.), Surrey................................. 232

GUIDE BOOKS
Abrahams (Mike), Staffordshire.................... 222
Arden Books & Cosmographia, Warwickshire... 236
Bookworld, Shropshire 212
Cavern Books, Cheshire 70
Hellenic Bookservices, London (NW).............. 158
Island Books, Devon................................ 84
Langmaid (Kenneth), Cornwall 76
Malmo Books, Hampshire 121
Phoenix Fine Books, Essex......................... 110
Reads, Dorset 94
Royal Carbery Books Ltd., Republic Of Ireland 275
Satara Books, West Sussex......................... 244
Scrivener's Books & Book Binding, Derbyshire . 81
Shacklock Books (David), Suffolk 226
Shapero Rare Books (Bernard J.), London (W). 174
Trinders' Fine Tools, Suffolk 225

GYNAECOLOGY
Alba Books, Scotland............................... 267

GYPSIES
Abrahams (Mike), Staffordshire.................... 222
Allport (Roy), N Yorks 195
Cottage Books, Leicestershire 143
Cover to Cover, Merseyside 186
Delectus Books, London (WC).................... 176
Doorbar (P. & D.), Hampshire..................... 122

HEALTH
Archways Sports Books, Scotland 268
Autumn Leaves, Lincolnshire...................... 148
Bookroom (The), Surrey 233
Chatterton's Books, Wales......................... 290
Collectable Books, London (SE)................... 160
Greensleeves, Oxfordshire 204
Inner Bookshop (The), Oxfordshire 207
Prescott - The Bookseller (John), London, Outer 184
Reading Lasses, Scotland........................... 264
River Reads Bookshop, Devon..................... 88
Savery Books, East Sussex 99
Shapero Rare Books (Bernard J.), London (W). 174
Swan Bookshop (The), Devon..................... 84
Target Books, Cambridgeshire 68
Woburn Books, London (N)....................... 156

HERALDRY
Aberdeen Rare Books & Caledonian Books,
  Scotland.. 267
Biddulph (Joseph), Wales 289
Heritage, West Midlands 238
McEwan Fine Books, Scotland..................... 266
Spooner & Co., Somerset 217
Taylor & Son (Peter), Hertfordshire............... 130
Townsend (John), Berkshire 59
Turton (John), Durham 97

HERBALISM
Blest (Peter), Kent.................................. 136
Brown-Studies, Scotland............................ 270
Calendula Horticultural Books, East Sussex 100
Greensleeves, Oxfordshire 204
Guildmaster Books, Cheshire....................... 71
IKON, Devon....................................... 88
Inner Bookshop (The), Oxfordshire 207
Lucas (Richard), London (NW).................... 158
Occultique, Northamptonshire 198
Park (Mike), London, Outer....................... 183
Phelps (Michael), West Sussex..................... 242

HERMETICISM
Alpha Books, London (N) 153
Chthonios Books, East Sussex...................... 100
Inner Bookshop (The), Oxfordshire 207
Occultique, Northamptonshire 198

HERPETOLOGY
Blest (Peter), Kent.................................. 136
Ian Johnson Natural History Books,
  Buckinghamshire................................. 63
J.G. Natural History Books, Surrey................ 232
Mobbs (A.J.), West Midlands 240

HISTORY
- GENERAL
AA1 Books, Scotland............................... 263
Abacus Gallery / The Village Bookshop,
  Staffordshire..................................... 223
Abbey Books, Norfolk.............................. 187
Abbey Bookshop, Hampshire 122
Addyman Books, Wales 285
All Books, Essex.................................... 108
Anchor Books, Lincolnshire 149
Antiquary Ltd., (Bar Bookstore), N Yorks 194
Arden Books & Cosmographia, Warwickshire... 236
Arundel Bookshop, West Sussex 241
Ashfield Books and Records, Nottinghamshire.. 203
Askew Books (Vernon), Wiltshire.................. 250
Autumn Leaves, Lincolnshire...................... 148
Baker Limited (A.P. & R.), Scotland............... 263
Barbican Bookshop, N Yorks 196
Bardsley's Books, Suffolk 225
Barn Books, Buckinghamshire...................... 62
Barton (John), Hampshire 124
Batstone Books, Wiltshire.......................... 250
Baxter (Steve), Surrey 232
Beardsell Books, West Yorkshire 246
Beckham Books, Suffolk............................ 228
Beware of The Leopard Books, Bristol 60

SPECIALITY INDEX

Entry	Page
Black Five Books, Shropshire	213
Book Warren, Devon	84
BookLovers, Somerset	217
Bookroom (The), Surrey	233
Books, Wales	282
Books & Bygones (Pam Taylor), West Midlands	240
Books (For All), N Yorks	192
Books Bought & Sold, Surrey	231
Bookshop (The), West Sussex	242
Bookstop Bookshop, N Yorks	193
Book–Worm International, Essex	107
Bookworms, Norfolk	187
Bookworms of Evesham, Worcestershire	255
Bookwyze, Lincolnshire	147
Booth Books, Wales	286
Bracton Books, Cambridgeshire	64
Broadhurst of Southport Ltd., Merseyside	186
Broadwater Books, Hampshire	124
Brockwells Bookshop, London (SE)	160
Broughton Books, Scotland	269
Bush, Bookdealer (John), Gloucestershire	115
Cahir Cosy Corner Bookshop, Republic Of Ireland	279
Caledonia Books, Scotland	271
Carnforth Bookshop (The), Lancashire	140
Catalyst Books, Surrey	232
Celtic Bookshop (The), Republic Of Ireland	279
Chatterton's Books, Wales	290
Chaucer Bookshop (The), Kent	133
Chesters (G. & J.), Staffordshire	223
Chevin Books, West Yorkshire	248
Classic Bindings, London (SW)	163
Clements (R.W.), London, Outer	181
Coombes (A.J.), Surrey	230
Corfe Books, Surrey	231
Cox Old & Rare Books (Claude), Suffolk	226
Cranmer Books, Oxfordshire	210
Croft Selections, Lincolnshire	148
Cronin (Jim), Wales	280
Crouch Rare Books, Surrey	232
Curtle Mead Books, Isle of Wight	131
Darkwood Books, Republic Of Ireland	276
Davids Ltd., (Roy), Oxfordshire	207
Dodd Books (Maurice), Cumbria	77
Dolphin Books, Suffolk	224
DoublePlusBooks, Cambridgeshire	68
Downie Fine Books Ltd., (Robert), Shropshire	213
Driffield Bookshop (The), East Yorkshire	104
Eastern Traveller (The), Somerset	218
Edwards (Christopher), Berkshire	57
Emerald Isle Books, Northern Ireland	259
Farnborough Bookshop and Gallery, Hampshire	121
Fin Rare Books, Shropshire	213
Fireside Books, Buckinghamshire	63
Fireside Bookshop, Cumbria	80
Ford Books (David), Hertfordshire	130
Foster (Stephen), London (NW)	157
Frew Limited (Robert), London (WC)	177
Frost (Richard), Hertfordshire	128
Furneaux Books (Lee), Devon	87
Gate Memorabilia, London (N)	153
Gippeswic Books, Suffolk	227
Gloucester Road Bookshop, London (SW)	164
Golden Hind Bookshop (The), Kent	134
Gorton Booksearch (John), East Sussex	103
Graham (John), Dorset	95
Greta Books, Durham	96
Hall's Bookshop, Kent	138
Handsworth Books, Essex	110
Hattle (Anne), Northumberland	200
Hawley (C.L.), N Yorks	195
Helion & Company, West Midlands	240
Heyman (B.), London, Outer	181
Heywood Hill Limited (G.), London (W)	173
Hoggarth (John R.), N Yorks	196
Hornsby, Antiquarian and Secondhand Books (Malcolm), Leicestershire	144
Hornsey's, N Yorks	194
Horsham Bookshop (The), West Sussex	242
Howes Bookshop, East Sussex	101
Hughes Rare Books (Spike), Scotland	261
Hutchison (Books) (Larry), Scotland	265
Ice House Books	143
J.A. Heacock (Antiques and Books), Cheshire	70
Jackdaw Books, Norfolk	189
Jade Mountain, Hampshire	123
Jericho Books, Oxfordshire	208
K. Books, East Yorkshire	104
Katnap Arts, Norfolk	189
Kelsall (George), Greater Manchester	117
Langmaid (Kenneth), Cornwall	76
Leabeck Books, Oxfordshire	208
Lewis (J.T. & P.), Cornwall	74
Little Bookshop (The), Greater Manchester	117
Malmo Books, Hampshire	121
Marine and Cannon Books, Cheshire	70
McCrone (Audrey), Scotland	272
Meekins Books (Paul), Warwickshire	237
Ming Books, Scotland	264
Modern Welsh Publications Ltd., Merseyside	185
Morgan (H.J.), Bedfordshire	56
Naughton Booksellers, Republic Of Ireland	277
Nineteenth Century Books, Oxfordshire	209
Noel and Holland Books, Republic Of Ireland	278
Nonsuch Books, Surrey	234
Oblong Books, N Yorks	197
O'Brien Books & Photo Gallery, Republic Of Ireland	279
Old Bookshop (The), West Midlands	240
Olio Books, East Sussex	101
Olynthiacs, Shropshire	212
Polmorla Books, Cornwall	76
Premier Books & Prints, Lincolnshire	146
R. & A. Books, East Sussex	100
Red Star Books, Hertfordshire	128
Richmond Books, N Yorks	194
Rods Books, Devon	87
Roland Books, Kent	137
Roosterbooks, Northamptonshire	198
Roundstone Books, Lancashire	141
Rowan (P. & B.), Northern Ireland	259
Royal Carbery Books Ltd., Republic Of Ireland	275
Russell Books, Somerset	218
Ryeland Books, Northamptonshire	198
St Philip's Books, Oxfordshire	208
Savery Books, East Sussex	99
Sax Books, Suffolk	228
Scrivener's Books & Book Binding, Derbyshire	81
Shacklock Books (David), Suffolk	226
Shapero Rare Books (Bernard J.), London (W)	174

SPECIALITY INDEX

Silverman (Michael), London (SE) 161
Spelman (Ken), N Yorks 197
Spread Eagle Bookshop, London (SE) 162
Spurrier (Nick), Kent 136
Staffs Bookshop (The), Staffordshire 222
Staniland (Booksellers), Lincolnshire 150
Sterling Books, Somerset 219
Strauss (David), Lincolnshire 147
Studio Bookshop, East Sussex 99
Swan Bookshop (The), Devon 84
Sykes (Graham), West Yorkshire 248
Symes Books (Naomi), Cheshire 72
Target Books, Cambridgeshire 68
Thomas (Books) (Leona), Cheshire 71
Thornton (Grahame), Dorset 94
Till's Bookshop, Scotland 270
Titford (John), Derbyshire 81
Townsend (John), Berkshire 59
Troath Books (Brian), London (E) 151
Tuft (Patrick), London (W) 175
Turner (Robin), Gloucestershire 112
Unsworths Booksellers Ltd., London (WC) 178
Unsworths Booksellers Ltd., Oxfordshire 209
Vinovium Books, Durham 96
Waterfield's, Oxfordshire 209
Wayfarer Books, Cornwall 75
Weiner (Graham), London (N) 156
Westwood Books (Mark), Wales 287
Whig Books Ltd., Leicestershire 145
Whitchurch Books Ltd., Wales 280
Whitfield (Ken), Essex 109
Willmott Bookseller (Nicholas), Wales 280
Wolds Book Services, Leicestershire 144
Woodbine Books, West Yorkshire 245
Words & Music, Cheshire 70
Yesterday's Books, Dorset 91

- 19TH CENTURY

Helion & Company, West Midlands 240
Ice House Books 143
Kenny's Bookshops and Art Galleries Ltd,
  Republic Of Ireland 278
Spread Eagle Bookshop, London (SE) 162
Symes Books (Naomi), Cheshire 72
Thornton (Grahame), Dorset 94
Whitchurch Books Ltd., Wales 280

- AMERICAN

Americanabooksuk, Cumbria 77
Helion & Company, West Midlands 240
Kenny's Bookshops and Art Galleries Ltd,
  Republic Of Ireland 278
Riviera Books, Norfolk 188

- ANARCHISM

Delectus Books, London (WC) 176
Helion & Company, West Midlands 240
Ice House Books 143

- ANCIENT

BC Books, Cheshire 70

Black Five Books, Shropshire 213
Greyfriars Books, Essex 107
Helion & Company, West Midlands 240
Ice House Books 143
Meekins Books (Paul), Warwickshire 237
Museum Bookshop, London (WC) 177
Rods Books, Devon 87
Rosanda Books, Leicestershire 144
Spread Eagle Bookshop, London (SE) 162
Trotter Books (John), London (N) 156
Whitchurch Books Ltd., Wales 280
Wiend Books & Collectables, Greater
  Manchester 119

- BRITISH

Ancient & Modern Bookshop, Dorset 90
BC Books, Cheshire 70
Bell (Peter), Scotland 269
Black Five Books, Shropshire 213
Clifton Books, Essex 110
Coombes (A.J.), Surrey 230
Greyfriars Books, Essex 107
Guildmaster Books, Cheshire 71
Helion & Company, West Midlands 240
Island Books, Devon 84
Jackdaw Books, Norfolk 189
Lowe (John), Norfolk 189
Meekins Books (Paul), Warwickshire 237
Old Storytellers Bookshop (The), Scotland 261
Ouse Valley Books, Bedfordshire 56
Rods Books, Devon 87
Rosanda Books, Leicestershire 144
St Philip's Books, Oxfordshire 208
Spenceley Books (David), West Yorkshire 248
Spread Eagle Bookshop, London (SE) 162
Swan Bookshop (The), Devon 84
Symes Books (Naomi), Cheshire 72
Taylor & Son (Peter), Hertfordshire 130
Whitchurch Books Ltd., Wales 280

- BYZANTINE

Camden Books, Somerset 214
Helion & Company, West Midlands 240
Lund Theological Books, Cambridgeshire 65

- DESIGN

Art Reference Books, Hampshire 123
Inch's Books, N Yorks 194
Stewart (Ian), Kent 137

- EUROPEAN

Books on Spain, London, Outer 183
G C Books, Scotland 264
Helion & Company, West Midlands 240
Ice House Books 143
IKON, Devon 88
Meinertzhagen (Nicholas), London (SW) 165
Rosanda Books, Leicestershire 144
St Philip's Books, Oxfordshire 208

SPECIALITY INDEX

- GUILDS AND LIVERY COMPANIES
Ice House Books 143
Tower Bridge Books, London (SE) 162
Trinders' Fine Tools, Suffolk 225

- INDUSTRIAL
Barbican Bookshop, N Yorks 196
Blanchfield (John), West Yorkshire 247
Book House (The), Cumbria 78
Books & Bygones (Pam Taylor),
   West Midlands 240
Coulthurst (Richard), Greater Manchester 118
Cox (Geoff), Devon 89
Crosby Nethercott Books, London, Outer 180
Duck (William), East Sussex 98
Graham (John), Dorset 95
Hall, (Anthony C.) Antiquarian Bookseller,
   London, Outer 184
Helion & Company, West Midlands 240
Ice House Books 143
Jones (Anne), Cornwall 76
Kelsall (George), Greater Manchester 117
Kenny's Bookshops and Art Galleries Ltd,
   Republic Of Ireland 278
Maddison (J.K.), West Midlands 238
Rochdale Book Company,
   Greater Manchester 118
Scarthin Books, Derbyshire 82
Skyrack Books, West Yorkshire 246
South Downs Book Service, West Sussex 243
Symes Books (Naomi), Cheshire 72
Trinders' Fine Tools, Suffolk 225
Whitchurch Books Ltd., Wales 280
Wilson Books (Henry), Cheshire 71
Winchester Antiquarian Books, Hampshire 125
Ystwyth Books, Wales 281

- IRISH
Armchair Books, Scotland 268
Biblion, London (W) 169
Darkwood Books, Republic Of Ireland 276
Fine Irish Books, Republic Of Ireland 276
Helion & Company, West Midlands 240
Ice House Books 143
Kenny's Bookshops and Art Galleries Ltd,
   Republic Of Ireland 278
Taylor & Son (Peter), Hertfordshire 130

- LABOUR/RADICAL MOVEMENTS
Helion & Company, West Midlands 240
Ice House Books 143
Left on The Shelf, London (E) 151
Symes Books (Naomi), Cheshire 72
Woburn Books, London (N) 156

- LOCAL
Aberdeen Rare Books & Caledonian Books,
   Scotland 267
Abrahams (Mike), Staffordshire 222
Ambra Books, Bristol 60
Angel Books, Norfolk 189

Arden Books & Cosmographia, Warwickshire... 236
Atticus Books, Essex 109
Barbican Bookshop, N Yorks 196
Barn Books, Shropshire 213
Barton (John), Hampshire 124
Beardsell Books, West Yorkshire 246
Beverley Old Bookshop, East Yorkshire 104
Black Five Books, Shropshire 213
Bonython Bookshop 76
Book for All Reasons (A.), Suffolk 227
Bookends of Fowey, Cornwall 74
Bookseller (The), Suffolk 227
Bookshop (The), Republic Of Ireland 276
Bridge of Allan Books, Scotland 262
Bridge Street Bookshop, Northumberland 200
Brown (Books) (P.R.), Durham 96
Carlton Books, Norfolk 189
Carnforth Bookshop (The), Lancashire 140
Castle Bookshop, Essex 107
Clent Books, Worcestershire 254
Coombes (A.J.), Surrey 230
Cottage Books, Leicestershire 143
Courtwood Books, Republic Of Ireland 278
Daly (Peter M.), Hampshire 124
Dinnages Transport Publishing, East Sussex 98
Dobson (Bob), Lancashire 140
Dodd Books (Maurice), Cumbria 77
Dylans Bookstore, Wales 289
Four Shire Bookshops, Gloucestershire 113
G C Books, Scotland 264
Garretts Antiquarian Books, Isle of Man 258
Godmanchester Books, Cambridgeshire 66
Graham (John), Dorset 95
Hancock (Colin), Wales 281
Hawes Books, Norfolk 189
Helion & Company, West Midlands 240
Hicks (Ronald C.), Cornwall 74
Horsham Bookshop (The), West Sussex 242
Hughes Rare Books (Spike), Scotland 261
Huyton (Peter), Herefordshire 126
Ice House Books 143
Island Books, Devon 86
Just Books, Cornwall 76
Kingsgate Books & Prints, Hampshire 125
MacCormaig (Domhnall), Scotland 269
Missing Books, Essex 108
Moon's Bookshop (Michael), Cumbria 79
Nangle (Julian), Dorset 92
Old Soke Books, Cornwall 74
Patterson Liddle, Somerset 214
Polmorla Books, Cornwall 76
Pratt (H.G.), Suffolk 228
Priory Books, Worcestershire 256
Quarto Bookshop (The), Scotland 265
R. & B. Graham, Cornwall 74
Rhoda (June), Essex 108
Rods Books, Devon 87
Rose Books, Greater Manchester 118
Ross Old Books & Prints, Herefordshire 127
Royal Carbery Books Ltd., Republic Of Ireland 275
Scarthin Books, Derbyshire 82
Sedgeberrow Books & Framing, Worcestershire. 255
Skyrack Books, West Yorkshire 246
Smith Books (Keith), Herefordshire 127
South Downs Book Service, West Sussex 243

Sparkes (Books) (Ray), Staffordshire.............. 223
Spooner & Co., Somerset 217
Spread Eagle Books, Wales 282
Swan Bookshop (The), Devon....................... 84
Taylor & Son (Peter), Hertfordshire............... 130
Thomas (E. Wyn), Wales............................ 282
Vinovium Books, Durham 96

- MIDDLE AGES

Camden Books, Somerset 214
Helion & Company, West Midlands 240
Ice House Books.................................. 143
Lund Theological Books, Cambridgeshire........ 65
Rosanda Books, Leicestershire 144
Spenceley Books (David), West Yorkshire 248

- NATIONAL

Barton (John), Hampshire 124
Carnforth Bookshop (The), Lancashire........... 140
Craobh Rua Books, Northern Ireland 259
Crispin's Day, Antiquarian and Out of Print
 Military Books, Essex............................ 110
Davidson Books, Northern Ireland................ 260
Doolin Dinghy Books, Republic Of Ireland..... 275
Dylans Bookstore, Wales.......................... 289
Foyle Books, Northern Ireland.................... 260
Fuchsia Books, Republic Of Ireland 276
G C Books, Scotland.............................. 264
Graham (John), Dorset............................ 95
Hawes Books, Norfolk............................. 189
Helion & Company, West Midlands 240
Hughes Rare Books (Spike), Scotland 261
Ice House Books.................................. 143
Joppa Books Ltd., Surrey 230
Kingswood Books, Dorset 93
Naughton Booksellers, Republic Of Ireland..... 277
Politico's, London (SW)........................... 166
Pringle Booksellers (Andrew), Scotland........... 270
Siop y Morfa, Wales 282
South Downs Book Service, West Sussex......... 243
Whelan (P. & F.), Kent............................ 138
Woolcott Books, Dorset........................... 92

- RENAISSANCE, THE

Art Reference Books, Hampshire 123
Ice House Books.................................. 143
Helion & Company, West Midlands 240
Spenceley Books (David), West Yorkshire 248

- ROMAN

Helion & Company, West Midlands 240

- WOMEN

Dolphin Books, Suffolk............................ 224
Spenceley Books (David), West Yorkshire 248
Swan Bookshop (The), Devon...................... 84

HISTORY OF CIVILISATION

Camden Books, Somerset 214

Crouch Rare Books, Surrey........................ 232
Helion & Company, West Midlands 240
Taylor & Son (Peter), Hertfordshire............... 130

HISTORY OF IDEAS

Arcadia, Shropshire 212
Butler Books, Dorset.............................. 90
Dean Byass, Tavistock Books, Devon............. 86
Downie Fine Books Ltd., (Robert), Shropshire . 213
Drury Rare Books (John), Essex................... 109
Game Advice, Oxfordshire......................... 207
Grampian Books, Scotland 265
Helion & Company, West Midlands 240
Herb Tandree Philosophy Books, Bristol......... 61
Ice House Books.................................. 143
Kenny's Bookshops and Art Galleries Ltd,
 Republic Of Ireland 278
Lee Rare Books (Rachel), Bristol................ 61
Mair Wilkes Books, Scotland...................... 265
Phillips (Nigel), London (SW)..................... 166
Price (John), London (N) 155
Schulz–Falster Rare Books (Susanne),
 London (N)..................................... 155
Seydi Rare Books (Sevin), London (NW) 159
Sokol Books (A.), London (W) 174
Taylor & Son (Peter), Hertfordshire............... 130
Weininger Antiquarian Books (Eva M.),
 London (NW) 159

HOBBIES

ARC Books, Scotland 272
Fin Rare Books, Shropshire 213
River Reads Bookshop, Devon..................... 88

HOLOCAUST

Helion & Company, West Midlands 240
Ice House Books.................................. 143
Island Books, Devon.............................. 84
Military Collector (The), West Yorkshire 249
Third Reich Books, Kent.......................... 134
World War Books, Kent 139

HOMEOPATHY

Greensleeves, Oxfordshire......................... 204
Occultique, Northamptonshire 198
Phelps (Michael), West Sussex.................... 242

HOMOSEXUALITY & LESBIANISM

Chatterton's Books, Wales........................ 290
Delectus Books, London (WC)..................... 176
Ice House Books.................................. 143
Paper Pleasures, Somerset......................... 217
Reading Lasses, Scotland.......................... 264

HORIZON WRITERS

Criterion Books, London, Outer 182

HOROLOGY

Barmby (C. & A.J.), Kent........................ 138

SPECIALITY INDEX 385

Clark (Nigel A.), London (SE) 160
DoublePlusBooks, Cambridgeshire 68
Engaging Gear Ltd., Essex 106
Formby Antiques (Jeffrey), Gloucestershire 113
Nibris Books, London (SW) 165
Trinders' Fine Tools, Suffolk 225

HORTICULTURE

Barn Books, Shropshire 213
Black Five Books, Shropshire 213
Blest (Peter), Kent 136
Book Corner, Scotland 263
Books (For All), N Yorks 192
Calendula Horticultural Books, East Sussex 100
Cherry (Janet), Dorset 92
Coach House Books, Worcestershire 255
Cooksweb, Northamptonshire 198
Court Hay Books, Bristol 60
Eastcote Bookshop (The), London, Outer 183
Evergreen Livres, Gloucestershire 113
Ice House Books 143
Marcan, Bookseller (Peter), London (SE) 161
Merritt (Valerie), Gloucestershire 111
On the Wild Side, Worcestershire 255
Park (Mike), London, Outer 183
Spelman (Ken), N Yorks 197
Thin Read Line, Merseyside 186

HUMANISM

Chthonios Books, East Sussex 100
Humanist Book Services, Cornwall 73
Pioneer Books, Hampshire 120
Poole (William), London (W) 174
Shapero Rare Books (Bernard J.), London (W) . 174

HUMANITIES

Beware of The Leopard Books, Bristol 60
Broughton Books, Scotland 269
Chatterton's Books, Wales 290
Fireside Bookshop, Cumbria 80
Hawley (C.L.), N Yorks 195
Ice House Books 143
Malmo Books, Hampshire 121
Plurabelle Books, Cambridgeshire 65
Porter Bookshop (The), South Yorkshire 220
Studio Bookshop, East Sussex 99
Till's Bookshop, Scotland 270
Unsworths Booksellers Ltd., London (WC) 178
Unsworths Booksellers Ltd., Oxfordshire 209
Waterfield's, Oxfordshire 209
Yates (R.A.), Dorset 92

HUMOUR

Autumn Leaves, Lincolnshire 148
BC Books, Cheshire 70
Beetles Ltd., (Chris), London (SW) 163
Black Five Books, Shropshire 213
Books & Bygones, Berkshire 58
Bookstand, Dorset 93
Bookworld, Shropshire 212
Book-Worm International, Essex 107

Booth Books, Wales 286
Eastcote Bookshop (The), London, Outer 183
Fun in Books, Surrey 233
Golden Hind Bookshop (The), Kent 134
Ice House Books 143
Mercat Books, Scotland 267
Russell Books, Somerset 218
Willmott Bookseller (Nicholas), Wales 280

HYDROGRAPHY

Phelps (Michael), West Sussex 242

ICONOGRAPHY

Bardsley's Books, Suffolk 225
Baron (H.), London (NW) 157
Foster (Stephen), London (NW) 157
Parikian, Rare Books (Diana), London (W) 174

ILLUMINATED MANUSCRIPTS

Bardsley's Books, Suffolk 225
Biblion, London (W) 169
Birchden Books, London (E) 151
Bookwyze, Lincolnshire 147
Cox Old & Rare Books (Claude), Suffolk 226
Du Ry Medieval Manuscripts (Marc-Antoine),
  London (W) 172
Fine Art, West Sussex 242
Maggs Brothers Limited, London (W) 173
Menavaur Books, Scotland 264
Taylor & Son (Peter), Hertfordshire 130

ILLUSTRATED

Addendum Books, Scotland 263
Almar Books, West Yorkshire 247
Arcadia, Shropshire 212
Art Reference Books, Hampshire 123
Artco, Nottinghamshire 202
Autolycus, Shropshire 211
Baker - Books for the Collector (Colin), Devon . 88
Ballantyne-Way (Roger), Suffolk 228
Barlow (Vincent G.), Hampshire 123
Bates Books, London, Outer 181
Batterham (David), London (W) 169
Bayntun (George), Somerset 214
Beetles Ltd., (Chris), London (SW) 163
Besleys Books, Suffolk 224
Beverley Old Bookshop, East Yorkshire 104
Biblion, London (W) 169
Bolton Books, Hampshire 120
Book Bungalow (The), Cornwall 73
Bookends of Fowey, Cornwall 74
Bookmark (Children's Books), Wiltshire 252
Books & Things, London (W) 169
Books Bought & Sold, Surrey 231
Books for Collectors, Gloucestershire 112
Bookstand, Dorset 93
Bookwyze, Lincolnshire 147
Booth Books, Wales 286
Boris Books, Dorset 94
Bright (P.G.), Cambridgeshire 66
Brighton Books, East Sussex 98

SPECIALITY INDEX

Burden Ltd., (Clive A.), Hertfordshire 129
Butts Books (Mary), Berkshire 58
Canterbury Bookshop (The), Kent 133
Chalk (Old & Out of Print Books)
   (Christine M.), West Midlands 238
Cobweb Books, N Yorks 194
Countrymans Gallery (The), Leicestershire 143
Coupland (Terry W.), Staffordshire 222
Cox Old & Rare Books (Claude), Suffolk 226
Criterion Books, London, Outer 182
Cumming Limited (A. & Y.), East Sussex 102
David (G.), Cambridgeshire 64
Davies Fine Books, Worcestershire 256
de Beaumont (Robin), London (SW) 163
Dean Illustrated Books (Myra), Wales 284
Deverell Books, Bristol 61
Devitt Books (Nial), Warwickshire 236
Dodd Books (Maurice), Cumbria 77
Doorbar (P. & D.), Hampshire 122
Doro Books, West Sussex 242
Dorset Rare Books, Wiltshire 252
Doughty Fine Books (Robin), West Midlands ... 238
Drummond Pleasures of Past Times (David),
   London (WC) 176
Eastcote Bookshop (The), London, Outer 183
Eastwood Books (David), Cornwall 73
Elmfield Books, West Midlands 238
Ely Books, Cambridgeshire 66
Embleton (Paul), Essex 109
Everett (Richard), Norfolk 187
Ferdinando (Steven), Somerset 217
Fin Rare Books, Shropshire 213
Fine Art, West Sussex 242
fineart-photographer, Herefordshire 127
Finney Antique Books & Prints (Michael),
   London (WC) 177
Firth (Bijou Books & Photography) (Maureen),
   South Yorkshire 221
Foster Bookshop (Paul), London (SW) 164
Fosters Bookshop, London (W) 172
Frew Limited (Robert), London (WC) 177
Gant (Elizabeth), Surrey 231
Golden Goose Books, Lincolnshire 148
Goodyer (Nicholas), London (N) 154
Grant (Gerald S.), Cheshire 69
Green Meadow Books, Cornwall 75
Greer (Robin), London (SW) 164
Grove Bookshop (The), N Yorks 195
Hanborough Books, Oxfordshire 207
Harrington (Adrian), London (W) 173
Harrington Antiquarian Bookseller (Peter),
   London (SW) 164
Harrison's Books, London (W) 173
Harwich Old Books, Essex 108
Havercroft Antiquarian Books, London (SE) 161
Hennessey Bookseller (Ray), East Sussex 100
Heppa (Christopher), Essex 106
Hereward Books, Cambridgeshire 66
Heritage, West Midlands 238
Heywood Hill Limited (G.), London (W) 173
Hodgkins and Company Limited (Ian),
   Gloucestershire 114
Hummingbird Books, Kent 136
Hurly Burly Books, Wiltshire 253
Illustrated Book (The), London (SW) 165

Innes Books, Shropshire 212
Island Books, Devon 84
Japan Books (Y & S Company Ltd.), Surrey 180
JB Books & Collectables, West Sussex 243
Jonkers Rare Books, Oxfordshire 206
Katharine House Gallery, Wiltshire 251
Kennedy (Peter), Surrey 234
Kerr (Norman), Cumbria 78
Keswick Bookshop, Cumbria 78
Key Books (Sarah), Cambridgeshire 65
Kineton Nooks, Warwickshire 236
Lawton (J.), Surrey 232
Leigh Gallery Books, Essex 108
Little Stour Books, Kent 133
Lloyd-Davies (Sue), Wales 280
Lucius Books, N Yorks 196
March House Books, Dorset 94
Marks Limited (Barrie), London (N) 154
Marlborough Rare Books Ltd., London (W) 173
Martin Bookshop & Gallery (Richard),
   Hampshire 121
McCrone (Audrey), Scotland 272
Menavaur Books, Scotland 264
Mereside Books, Cheshire 70
Miles Book Shop (Archie), Cumbria 79
Mills Rare Books (Adam), Cambridgeshire 65
Minster Gate Bookshop, N Yorks 196
Modlock (Lilian), Dorset 92
Morris (Michael), Staffordshire 222
Nangle (Julian), Dorset 92
Newcastle Bookshop, Northumberland 200
Nonsuch Books, Surrey 234
O'Connor Fine Books, Lancashire 142
Old Storytellers Bookshop (The), Scotland 261
Old Town Bookshop (The), Scotland 270
O'Neill (Angus), London (WC) 178
Page Antiquarian Books (Colin), East Sussex ... 99
Patterson Liddle, Somerset 214
Peakirk Books, Cambridgeshire 68
Penn Barn Bookshop, Buckinghamshire 63
Porcupines, Devon 84
Rees & O'Neill Rare Books, London (WC) 178
Reeve (M. & D.), Oxfordshire 208
Reigate Galleries, Surrey 233
Ripping Yarns, London (N) 155
Rising Tide Books, Scotland 264
Rittner Booksearch (Hilary), London (SE) 161
Rochdale Book Company, Greater Manchester . 118
Rowan House Books, Surrey 231
Sabin (Printed Works) (P.R. & V.), Kent 133
St Mary's Books & Prints, Lincolnshire 150
Scrivener's Books & Book Binding, Derbyshire . 81
Second Edition, Scotland 270
Sephton (A.F.), London (W) 174
Sesemann (Julia), Kent 133
Seydi Rare Books (Sevin), London (NW) 159
Shakeshaft (Dr. B.), Cheshire 72
Shakeshaft (Roger & Sylvia), Lincolnshire 146
Sharpe (Mary), West Sussex 241
Shipley Specialist Art Booksellers, London (WC) . 178
Sillem (Anthony), East Sussex 101
Sims Reed Limited, London (SW) 167
Siri Ellis Books, Greater Manchester 116
Slavin Rare and Collectable Books (Derek),
   Warwickshire 237

SPECIALITY INDEX

Sotheran Limited (Henry), London (W) 175
Spread Eagle Bookshop, London (SE) 162
Stella Books, Wales 284
Stevens (Joan), Cambridgeshire 66
Taylor Rare Books (Michael), Norfolk 187
Ulysses, London (WC)............................... 178
Updike Rare Books (John), Scotland 270
Waddington Books & Prints (Geraldine),
    Northamptonshire 198
Westcountry Old Books, Devon..................... 88
Wilson (J. & M.), Scotland 273
Woodbine Books, West Yorkshire................. 245
Woodstock Fabrics & Books, Shropshire......... 212
Yates Antiquarian Books (Tony), Leicestershire 144

IMPRINTS
McKay Rare Books (Barry), Cumbria 77

INCUNABULA
Fine Art, West Sussex 242
Quaritch Ltd., (Bernard), London (W)............ 174
Seydi Rare Books (Sevin), London (NW) 159
Sokol Books (A.), London (W) 174
Wolds Book Services, Leicestershire............... 144

INDUSTRY
Anvil Books, West Midlands 239
Batterdale Books, N Yorks 195
Blanchfield (John), West Yorkshire................ 247
Bott, (Bookdealers) Ltd., (Martin), Greater
    Manchester 116
Byrom Textile Bookroom (Richard), Lancashire 140
Doro Books, West Sussex 242
Duck (William), East Sussex........................ 98
Fin Rare Books, Shropshire 213
Hogben (Carol), Wales 285
Ice House Books...................................... 143
Jones (Anne), Cornwall.............................. 76
Rochdale Book Company, Greater Manchester . 118
Wheen O'Blethers Bookshop, Scotland 271
Winchester Antiquarian Books, Hampshire...... 125

INTERIOR DESIGN
Barlow (Vincent G.), Hampshire................... 123
Books for Collectors, Gloucestershire............. 112
Buckland Books, West Sussex 243
DoublePlusBooks, Cambridgeshire 68
Foster (Stephen), London (NW) 157
Heneage Art Books (Thomas), London (SW).... 164
Hogben (Carol), Wales 285
Keswick Bookshop, Cumbria....................... 78
Martin - Bookseller (Colin), East Yorkshire 105
Phillips of Hitchin (Antiques) Ltd.,
    Hertfordshire 129
Shipley Specialist Art Booksellers, London (WC)178
Staniland (Booksellers), Lincolnshire.............. 150
Stewart (Ian), Kent.................................... 137
Trinders' Fine Tools, Suffolk 225

INTERNATIONAL AFFAIRS
Ice House Books...................................... 143

Langmaid (Kenneth), Cornwall 76
Tenner (Melvin), London (W)...................... 175

IRISH INTEREST
Abbey Books, London (N).......................... 153
Belfast Book Search, Northern Ireland 259
Bell Gallery (The), Northern Ireland 259
Books Ulster, Northern Ireland 260
Bookshop (The), Republic Of Ireland............ 276
Cahir Cosy Corner Bookshop, Republic Of
    Ireland 279
Caledonia Books, Scotland.......................... 271
Cathach Books Ltd., Republic Of Ireland........ 277
Cavan Book Centre, Republic Of Ireland 275
Clements (R.W.), London, Outer 181
Conry (Ann & Mike), Worcestershire............. 256
Courtwood Books, Republic Of Ireland 278
Craobh Rua Books, Northern Ireland 259
Darkwood Books, Republic Of Ireland........... 276
Davidson Books, Northern Ireland................ 260
Emerald Isle Books, Northern Ireland 259
Ferdinando (Steven), Somerset 217
Fine Irish Books, Republic Of Ireland 276
Foyle Books, Northern Ireland..................... 260
Fuchsia Books, Republic Of Ireland 276
House of Figgis Ltd (The), Republic Of Ireland 278
Hyland (C.P.), Republic Of Ireland 276
Ice House Books...................................... 143
Jackson (M.W.), Wiltshire 253
Jiri Books, Northern Ireland........................ 259
Kenny's Bookshops and Art Galleries Ltd,
    Republic Of Ireland 278
Kernaghans, Merseyside............................. 186
McCann (Joe), Oxfordshire 208
Naughton Booksellers, Republic Of Ireland...... 277
Noel and Holland Books, Republic Of Ireland.. 278
O'Brien Books & Photo Gallery, Republic Of
    Ireland 279
Phillips (Chris), Wiltshire............................ 250
Prospect House Books, Northern Ireland 260
Read Ireland, Republic Of Ireland 277
Rowan (P. & B.), Northern Ireland 259
Royal Carbery Books Ltd., Republic Of Ireland 275
Schull Books, Republic Of Ireland 275
Updike Rare Books (John), Scotland 270
Whelan (P. & F.), Kent.............................. 138

JEWELLERY
Art Reference Books, Hampshire 123
Barmby (C. & A.J.), Kent............................ 138
Heneage Art Books (Thomas), London (SW).... 164
Ives Bookseller (John), London, Outer............ 184
Nibris Books, London (SW)........................ 165
Shipley Specialist Art Booksellers, London (WC)178
Trinders' Fine Tools, Suffolk 225
Warnes (Felicity J.), London, Outer............... 181

JOURNALISM
Anglo-American Rare Books, Surrey.............. 232
Archivist (The), Devon 88
Ice House Books...................................... 143
Kelly Books, Devon.................................. 88

SPECIALITY INDEX

JOURNALS
- GENERAL
Aberdeen Rare Books & Caledonian Books, Scotland 267
Batterham (David), London (W)..................... 169
Downie Fine Books Ltd., (Robert), Shropshire . 213
Gardner & Co., (Walter H.), London (N)........ 153
Ice House Books....................................... 143
Polczynski (Udo K.H.), London, Outer 183
Temple (Robert), London (N)....................... 155
Trafalgar Bookshop (The), East Sussex............ 99
Turton (John), Durham 97
Wayside Books and Cards, Oxfordshire 205

- MARITIME
Nautical Antique Centre (The), Dorset 95

JUDAICA
Bookseekers, London (SW) 163
Fishburn Books, London (NW).................... 157
Ice House Books....................................... 143
Inner Bookshop (The), Oxfordshire 207
Kenny's Bookshops and Art Galleries Ltd, Republic Of Ireland 278
Manor House Books/John Trotter Books, London (N) 154
Occultique, Northamptonshire 198
Scrivener's Books & Book Binding, Derbyshire . 81

JUVENILE
Amwell Book Company (The), London (EC).... 152
Beck (John), East Sussex 101
Beck Head Books, Cumbria 78
Bookmark (Children's Books), Wiltshire 252
Canterbury Bookshop (The), Kent 133
Cavern Books, Cheshire 70
Cook (R.L.), Norfolk 190
Cooper Hay Rare Books, Scotland 271
Coupland (Terry W.), Staffordshire................ 222
Cygnet Books, East Yorkshire 105
Doro Books, West Sussex 242
Freya Books & Antiques, Norfolk................. 189
Game Advice, Oxfordshire.......................... 207
Gate Memorabilia, London (N)..................... 153
Holtom (Christopher), Cornwall 76
Ice House Books....................................... 143
K. Books, Cheshire.................................... 72
Kirkpatrick (Robert J.), London (W) 173
Mead (P.J.), Shropshire.............................. 212
Reeve (M. & D.), Oxfordshire...................... 208
Rosemary Books, Merseyside....................... 186
Sesemann (Julia), Kent 133
Shacklock Books (David), Suffolk 226
Temple (Robert), London (N)....................... 155

KNITTING
Autumn Leaves, Lincolnshire....................... 148
Black Cat Books, Norfolk 188
Brown-Studies, Scotland............................. 270
Byrom Textile Bookroom (Richard), Lancashire 140
Cover to Cover, Merseyside 186
Mansfield (Judith), West Yorkshire................ 248
Warnes (Felicity J.), London, Outer.............. 181
Young (D. & J.), Wales 289

LACE
Black Cat Books, Norfolk 188
Byrom Textile Bookroom (Richard), Lancashire 140
Cover to Cover, Merseyside 186
Crouch Rare Books, Surrey......................... 232
Heneage Art Books (Thomas), London (SW).... 164
Hennessey Bookseller (Ray), East Sussex......... 100
Mansfield (Judith), West Yorkshire................ 248
Warnes (Felicity J.), London, Outer.............. 181
Well–Head Books, Dorset............................ 91
Williams (Christopher), Dorset..................... 93
Young (D. & J.), Wales 289

LANDSCAPE
Buxton Books (Anna), Scotland 269
Calendula Horticultural Books, East Sussex 100
Cottage Books, Leicestershire 143
Duck (William), East Sussex........................ 98
Hünersdorff Rare Books, London (SW).......... 165
Inch's Books, N Yorks 194
Marlborough Rare Books Ltd., London (W).... 173
Modlock (Lilian), Dorset............................. 92
On the Wild Side, Worcestershire.................. 255
Park (Mike), London, Outer........................ 183

LANGUAGES
- AFRICAN
Biddulph (Joseph), Wales 289

- FOREIGN
Assassin Books, West Midlands.................... 238
Autumn Leaves, Lincolnshire....................... 148
Beckham Books, Suffolk............................. 228
Beware of The Leopard Books, Bristol 60
Biddulph (Joseph), Wales 289
Book House (The), Cumbria........................ 78
Books & Bygones, Berkshire........................ 58
Books on Spain, London, Outer 183
Booth Books, Wales.................................. 286
Carnforth Bookshop (The), Lancashire 140
Chiltern Books, London (W) 172
Crouch Rare Books, Surrey......................... 232
Cyclamen Books, Leicestershire 143
Havercroft Antiquarian Books, London (SE).... 161
Hünersdorff Rare Books, London (SW).......... 165
Ice House Books....................................... 143
Jade Mountain, Hampshire 123
Loman, Oriental Books & Manuscripts (David), London (SW)....................................... 165
Malmo Books, Hampshire 121
Orssich (Paul), London (SW)....................... 166
Philologus–Fine & Rare Books, London (SW) .. 166
Robertshaw (John), Cambridgeshire................ 67
Roundstone Books, Lancashire 141
Till's Bookshop, Scotland 270
Transformer, Scotland 264
Walker Fine Books (Steve), London (SW) 167

SPECIALITY INDEX

- NATIONAL

Biddulph (Joseph), Wales 289
Browning Books, Wales 290
Doolin Dinghy Books, Republic Of Ireland...... 275
Hancock (Colin), Wales 281
Hyland (C.P.), Republic Of Ireland 276
Ice House Books...................................... 143
Leeds Bookseller, West Yorkshire 247
Spenceley Books (David), West Yorkshire 248
Treasure Island (The), Greater Manchester 118
Walker Fine Books (Steve), London (SW) 167

LAW

Aberdeen Rare Books & Caledonian Books,
  Scotland 267
Beware of The Leopard Books, Bristol 60
Booth Books, Wales................................. 286
Crimes Ink, London (E)............................. 151
Drury Rare Books (John), Essex................... 109
Edwards in Hay–on–Wye (Francis), Wales....... 286
Langmaid (Kenneth), Cornwall 76
Rowan (P. & B.), Northern Ireland 259
Wayside Books and Cards, Oxfordshire 205
Wayside Books and Cards, Oxfordshire 206

LEPIDOPTEROLOGY / LEPIDOPTERY

Aurelian Books, London (NW) 157
Book Corner, Scotland 263
Ian Johnson Natural History Books,
  Buckinghamshire...................................63
Moss Books, London (NW) 158
On the Wild Side, Worcestershire................. 255
Shearwater Bed & Books (formerly John
  Lumby Nat. History Bks), Northumberland .. 200

LETTERS

Arundel Bookshop, West Sussex................... 241
Baron (H.), London (NW)........................... 157
Camden Books, Somerset 214
Davids Ltd., (Roy), Oxfordshire 207
Farahar & Dupreé (Clive & Sophie),
  Wiltshire... 250
Fergusson Books & Manuscripts (James),
  London (W).. 172
Gekoski (R.A.), London (WC) 177
Hodgkins and Company Limited (Ian),
  Gloucestershire................................... 114
Maggs Brothers Limited, London (W)............ 173
Riley–Smith (Hamish), Norfolk 190
Silverman (Michael), London (SE) 161
Summersgill (Neil), Lancashire 140
Temple (Robert), London (N)...................... 155

LIMITED EDITIONS

Artco, Nottinghamshire 202
Barlow (Vincent G.), Hampshire 123
Biblion, London (W)................................. 169
BOOKS4U, Wales.................................... 282
Budd (Richard), Somerset.......................... 217
Bush, Bookdealer (John), Gloucestershire........ 115
Coach House Books, Worcestershire 255
Courtyard Books, Herefordshire................... 127
Cox Old & Rare Books (Claude), Suffolk 226
Ellis, Bookseller (Peter), London (SE) 160
Fine Art, West Sussex 242
Fine Irish Books, Republic Of Ireland 276
Firth (Bijou Books & Photography) (Maureen),
  South Yorkshire................................... 221
Hanborough Books, Oxfordshire 207
Harwich Old Books, Essex.......................... 108
Ice House Books..................................... 143
Kirkman Ltd., (Robert), Bedfordshire 55
Marks Limited (Barrie), London (N).............. 154
McCann (Joe), Oxfordshire 208
McKelvie (Ian), London (N)........................ 154
Sabin (Printed Works) (P.R. & V.), Kent 133
Temple (Robert), London (N)...................... 155
Troath Books (Brian), London (E) 151
Updike Rare Books (John), Scotland 270
Ward (K. Anthony), Norfolk....................... 188
Whiteson Ltd., (Edna), Hertfordshire............. 128

LINGUISTICS

Chesters (G. & J.), Staffordshire 223
Game Advice, Oxfordshire......................... 207
Ice House Books..................................... 143
Loman, Oriental Books & Manuscripts (David),
  London (SW)...................................... 165
Olynthiacs, Shropshire.............................. 212
Plurabelle Books, Cambridgeshire 65
Schulz–Falster Rare Books (Susanne),
  London (N).. 155
Wheen O'Blethers Bookshop, Scotland 271

LITERARY CRITICISM

Abbey Bookshop, Hampshire 122
Anderson Slater Antiques, N Yorks............... 195
Applin (Malcolm), Berkshire 57
Arcadia, Shropshire 212
Arundel Bookshop, West Sussex................... 241
Autumn Leaves, Lincolnshire...................... 148
Boer (Louise), Arthurian Books, Wales........... 284
Books, Wales.. 282
Bracton Books, Cambridgeshire.................... 64
Broadhurst of Southport Ltd., Merseyside 186
Budd (Richard), Somerset.......................... 217
Caledonia Books, Scotland......................... 271
Carta Regis, Wales 288
Castle Frome Books, Herefordshire 127
Chatterton's Books, Wales 290
Chesters (G. & J.), Staffordshire 223
Delectus Books, London (WC).................... 176
Dyson (Anthony), West Midlands 239
Ellis, Bookseller (Peter), London (SE) 160
Fisher & Sperr, London (N)........................ 153
Fortune Green Books, London (NW)............. 157
Frost (Richard), Hertfordshire 128
Green Man Books, Derbyshire 81
Greyfriars Books, Essex............................ 107
Handsworth Books, Essex.......................... 110
Hawkes (James), Gloucestershire.................. 111
Hawley (C.L.), N Yorks............................. 195
Hellenic Bookservices, London (NW)............. 158
Heyman (B.), London, Outer 181

SPECIALITY INDEX

Island Books, Devon 84
Kingsgate Books & Prints, Hampshire 125
Oblong Books, N Yorks 197
Plurabelle Books, Cambridgeshire 65
Riderless Horse Books, Norfolk 187
Rosley Books, Cumbria 79
Roundstone Books, Lancashire 141
Ryeland Books, Northamptonshire 198
Savery Books, East Sussex 99
Smallwood Books, Lincolnshire 148
Staniland (Booksellers), Lincolnshire 150
Stevens (Joan), Cambridgeshire 66
Strauss (David), Lincolnshire 147
Studio Bookshop, East Sussex 99
Swan Bookshop (The), Devon 84
Symes Books (Naomi), Cheshire 72
Temple (Robert), London (N) 155
Till's Bookshop, Scotland 270
Troath Books (Brian), London (E) 151
Unsworths Booksellers Ltd., London (WC) 178
Venables (Morris & Juliet), Bristol 61
Waterfield's, Oxfordshire 209
Winchester Antiquarian Books, Hampshire 125

LITERARY TRAVEL

Archer (Steve), London, Outer 180
Askew Books (Vernon), Wiltshire 250
Books on Spain, London, Outer 183
Conry (Ann & Mike), Worcestershire 256
Criterion Books, London, Outer 182
Hodgkins and Company Limited (Ian),
  Gloucestershire 114
Ice House Books 143
Old World Books (Tre Archi), London (SW) 165
Orssich (Paul), London (SW) 166
Royal Carbery Books Ltd., Republic Of Ireland 275
Shapero Rare Books (Bernard J.), London (W) . 174
Temple (Robert), London (N) 155
Tiger Books, Kent 134
Yesterday's Books, Dorset 91

LITERATURE

Abbey Books, London (N) 153
Abbey Bookshop, Hampshire 122
Addyman Books, Wales 285
Alba Books, Scotland 267
Almar Books, West Yorkshire 247
Americanabooksuk, Cumbria 77
Anglo-American Rare Books, Surrey 232
Antiquary Ltd., (Bar Bookstore), N Yorks 194
Arcadia, Shropshire 212
Archer (Steve), London, Outer 180
Archivist (The), Devon 88
Armchair Books, Scotland 268
Artco, Nottinghamshire 202
Arundel Bookshop, West Sussex 241
Assassin Books, West Midlands 238
Autumn Leaves, Lincolnshire 148
Avonworld Books, Somerset 215
babelog.books, Herefordshire 126
Barbican Bookshop, N Yorks 196
Baxter (Steve), Surrey 232
Bayntun (George), Somerset 214

BC Books, Cheshire 70
Beck Head Books, Cumbria 78
Bell (Peter), Scotland 269
Bertram Rota Ltd., London (WC) 176
Beware of The Leopard Books, Bristol 60
Black Five Books, Shropshire 213
Bookends of Fowey, Cornwall 74
Books (For All), N Yorks 192
Books on Spain, London, Outer 183
Bookshop (The), Cambridgeshire 64
Book–Worm International, Essex 107
Bookworms, Norfolk 187
Bookworms of Evesham, Worcestershire 255
Booth Books, Wales 286
Boris Books, Dorset 94
Bow Windows Book Shop, East Sussex 102
Boz Books, Wales 286
Bracton Books, Cambridgeshire 64
Bridge of Allan Books, Scotland 262
Bright (P.G.), Cambridgeshire 66
Brinded (Scott), Kent 136
Broadhurst of Southport Ltd., Merseyside 186
Brock Books, N Yorks 192
Broughton Books, Scotland 269
Budd (Richard), Somerset 217
Butts Books (Mary), Berkshire 58
Caledonia Books, Scotland 271
Camden Books, Somerset 214
Carnforth Bookshop (The), Lancashire 140
Carta Regis, Wales 288
Castle Frome Books, Herefordshire 127
Chalk (Old & Out of Print Books)
  (Christine M.), West Midlands 238
Chapman (Ron), London (SW) 163
Charmouth Bookstore, Dorset 91
Chatterton's Books, Wales 290
Chevin Books, West Yorkshire 248
Clark (K.R.), Oxfordshire 205
Clements (R.W.), London, Outer 181
Cook (R.L.), Norfolk 190
Cox Old & Rare Books (Claude), Suffolk 226
Cox Rare Books (Charles), Cornwall 74
Craobh Rua Books, Northern Ireland 259
Criterion Books, London, Outer 182
Crouch Rare Books, Surrey 232
Cumming Limited (A. & Y.), East Sussex 102
Dalby (Richard), N Yorks 194
David (G.), Cambridgeshire 64
Davidson Books, Northern Ireland 260
Dawson (Modern First Editions), (Philip),
  London, Outer 183
Devitt Books (Nial), Warwickshire 236
Dodd Books (Maurice), Cumbria 77
Dolphin Books, Suffolk 224
Doolin Dinghy Books, Republic Of Ireland 275
Doughty Fine Books (Robin), West Midlands . 238
Driffield Bookshop (The), East Yorkshire 104
Dyfi Valley Bookshop, Wales 288
Dylans Bookstore, Wales 289
Dyson (Anthony), West Midlands 239
Eastwood Books (David), Cornwall 73
Edwards (Christopher), Berkshire 57
Edwards (London) Limited (Francis),
  London (WC) 177
Edwards in Hay-on-Wye (Francis), Wales 286

SPECIALITY INDEX

Ellis, Bookseller (Peter), London (SE) 160
Emerald Isle Books, Northern Ireland 259
Farahar & Dupré (Clive & Sophie),
  Wiltshire 250
Ferdinando (Steven), Somerset 217
Finch Rare Books Ltd. (Simon), London (W)... 172
Firsts in Print, Isle of Wight 131
Firth (Bijou Books & Photography)
  (Maureen), South Yorkshire 221
Fortune Green Books, London (NW) 157
Foster (Stephen), London (NW) 157
Fotheringham (Alex), Northumberland 200
Frew Limited (Robert), London (WC) 177
Furneaux Books (Lee), Devon 87
Gate Memorabilia, London (N) 153
Gibbard (A. & T.), East Sussex 100
Gilbert and Son (H.M.), Hampshire 124
Glass Key (The), West Yorkshire 246
Gloucester Road Bookshop, London (SW) 164
Gorton Booksearch (John), East Sussex 103
Green Man Books, Derbyshire 81
Gregory (George), Somerset 214
Greyfriars Books, Essex 107
Grove Bookshop (The), N Yorks 195
Hall's Bookshop, Kent 138
Harrington (Adrian), London (W) 173
Harrington Antiquarian Bookseller (Peter),
  London (SW) 164
Hart (John), Norfolk 190
Harwich Old Books, Essex 108
Hawkes (James), Gloucestershire 111
Hennessey Bookseller (Ray), East Sussex 100
Heppa (Christopher), Essex 106
Heywood Hill Limited (G.), London (W) 173
Holmes Books (Harry), East Yorkshire 105
House of Figgis Ltd (The), Republic Of Ireland 278
Howes Bookshop, East Sussex 101
Hünersdorff Rare Books, London (SW) 165
Hughes Rare Books (Spike), Scotland 261
Hunter, Bookseller, (K.P.), Cambridgeshire..... 65
Hunter–Rare Books (Andrew), London (SW) ... 165
Hutchison (Books) (Larry), Scotland 265
Ice House Books 143
Idle Genius Books, London (N) 154
Innes Books, Shropshire 212
J.A. Heacock (Antiques and Books), Cheshire .. 70
Jackson (M.W.), Wiltshire 253
Jade Mountain, Hampshire 123
Jarndyce Antiquarian Booksellers,
  London (WC) 177
Jericho Books, Oxfordshire 208
Jiri Books, Northern Ireland 259
Johnson Rare Book Collections (C.R.),
  London (NW) 158
Jonkers Rare Books, Oxfordshire 206
K. Books, East Yorkshire 104
Katnap Arts, Norfolk 189
Killeen (John), N Yorks 193
Kingsgate Books & Prints, Hampshire 125
Kirkman Ltd., (Robert), Bedfordshire 55
L.M.S. Books, Hertfordshire 129
Langmaid (Kenneth), Cornwall 76
Lawson & Company (E.M.), Oxfordshire 205
Leabeck Books, Oxfordshire 208
Leigh Gallery Books, Essex 108
Lloyd-Davies (Sue), Wales 280
LSA Books, Warwickshire 236
Lucas (Roger), Lincolnshire 147
Maggs Brothers Limited, London (W) 173
Main Point Books, Scotland 269
Malvern Bookshop (The), Worcestershire 254
Marks Limited (Barrie), London (N) 154
Marlborough Rare Books Ltd., London (W) 173
McCann (Joe), Oxfordshire 208
McCrone (Audrey), Scotland 272
McEwan Fine Books, Scotland 266
McKelvie (Ian), London (N) 154
McNaughtan's Bookshop, Scotland 269
Miles Book Shop (Archie), Cumbria 79
Mills Rare Books (Adam), Cambridgeshire 65
Minster Gate Bookshop, N Yorks 196
Moreton Books, Devon 86
Morgan (H.J.), Bedfordshire 56
Mr. Pickwick of Towcester, Northamptonshire.. 199
Nangle (Julian), Dorset 92
Naughton Booksellers, Republic Of Ireland...... 277
Niner (Marcus), Gloucestershire 113
Nineteenth Century Books, Oxfordshire 209
Nonsuch Books, Surrey 234
Norton Books, Durham 97
Nova Foresta Books, Hampshire 121
Oblong Books, N Yorks 197
O'Brien Books & Photo Gallery, Republic Of
  Ireland 279
Offa's Dyke Books, Shropshire 212
Old Bookshop (The), West Midlands 240
Old Bookshop (The), Somerset 216
Old Town Bookshop (The), Scotland 270
O'Neill (Angus), London (WC) 178
Orangeberry Books, Oxfordshire 206
Orlando Booksellers, Lincolnshire 148
Orssich (Paul), London (SW) 166
Page Antiquarian Books (Colin), East Sussex ... 99
Palladour Books, Hampshire 124
Peter's Bookshop, Norfolk 190
Phoenix Fine Books, Essex 110
Plurabelle Books, Cambridgeshire 65
Polmorla Books, Cornwall 76
Porter Bookshop (The), South Yorkshire 220
Price (John), London (N) 155
Pringle Booksellers (Andrew), Scotland 270
Quaritch Ltd., (Bernard), London (W) 174
Quest Booksearch, Cambridgeshire 65
R. & A. Books, East Sussex 100
Rassam (Paul), London (NW) 158
Rees & O'Neill Rare Books, London (WC)..... 178
Richmond Books, N Yorks 194
Riderless Horse Books, Norfolk 187
Riley–Smith (Hamish), Norfolk 190
Ripping Yarns, London (N) 155
Rosley Books, Cumbria 79
Rothwell and Dunworth, Somerset 216
Roundstone Books, Lancashire 141
Rowan (P. & B.), Northern Ireland 259
Ryeland Books, Northamptonshire 198
St Philip's Books, Oxfordshire 208
Sansovino Books, West Sussex 244
Savery Books, East Sussex 99
Scott (T.F.S.), East Sussex 102
Second Edition, Scotland 270

SPECIALITY INDEX

Seddon (A.C.), West Sussex 244
Segal Books (Joel), Devon 85
Shapero Rare Books (Bernard J.),
　London (W)... 174
Sharpe (Mary), West Sussex 241
Sillem (Anthony), East Sussex 101
Silverman (Michael), London (SE) 161
Simpson (Dave), Scotland............................ 262
Siop y Morfa, Wales 282
Skelly (George B.), London (N)..................... 155
Slavin Rare and Collectable Books (Derek),
　Warwickshire.. 237
Sokol Books (A.), London (W) 174
Sotheran Limited (Henry), London (W) 175
Spelman (Ken), N Yorks 197
Staffs Bookshop (The), Staffordshire 222
Staniland (Booksellers), Lincolnshire............. 150
Stevens (Joan), Cambridgeshire 66
Stone Trough Books, N Yorks....................... 197
Stothert Old Books, Cheshire......................... 69
Studio Bookshop, East Sussex....................... 99
Sturford Books, Wiltshire 252
Swan Bookshop (The), Devon 84
Symes Books (Naomi), Cheshire.................... 72
Temple (Robert), London (N)........................ 155
Thornton Books (Richard), London (N) 155
Tiffin (Tony and Gill), Durham 96
Tiger Books, Kent.. 134
Till's Bookshop, Scotland 270
Tindley & Chapman, London (WC)................ 178
Tony Skelton, Kent 138
Touchstone Books, Norfolk 190
Trafalgar Bookshop (The), East Sussex........... 99
Trevorrow (Edwin), Hertfordshire 128
Troath Books (Brian), London (E) 151
Unsworths Booksellers Ltd., London,
　West Central.. 178
Unsworths Booksellers Ltd., Oxfordshire........ 209
Updike Rare Books (John), Scotland 270
Venables (Morris & Juliet), Bristol 61
Ventnor Rare Books, Isle of Wight................. 132
Visser Books (de), Cambridgeshire 66
Walden Books, London (NW)....................... 159
Walker Fine Books (Steve), London (SW) 167
Ward (K. Anthony), Norfolk.......................... 188
Waterfield's, Oxfordshire 209
Westcountry Old Books, Devon...................... 88
Wetherell (Frances), Cambridgeshire 66
Whig Books Ltd., Leicestershire 145
Wilbraham (J. & S.), London (NW)................ 159
Williams Rare Books (Nigel), London,
　West Central.. 179
Willmott Bookseller (Nicholas), Wales............ 280
Winchester Antiquarian Books, Hampshire...... 125
Winchester Bookshop (The), Hampshire......... 125
Wise (Derek), East Sussex........................... 102
Woodstock Bookshop (The), Oxfordshire 210
Woodstock Fabrics & Books, Shropshire........ 212
Words & Music, Cheshire.............................. 70
Wychwood Books, Gloucestershire 114
Yates Antiquarian Books (Tony), Leicestershire 144
Yesterday's Books, Dorset 91

LITERATURE - VICTORIAN

Beaton (Richard), East Sussex...................... 101

Brock Books, N Yorks 192
Havercroft Antiquarian Books, London (SE).... 161
Jarndyce Antiquarian Booksellers,
　London (WC) 177
Rosley Books, Cumbria 79
Smith Books, (Sally), Suffolk 225
Symes Books (Naomi), Cheshire.................... 72
Temple (Robert), London (N)........................ 155
Tobo Books, Hampshire............................... 122
Winchester Antiquarian Books, Hampshire...... 125

LITERATURE IN TRANSLATION

AA1 Books, Scotland................................... 263
babelog.books, Herefordshire....................... 126
Books on Spain, London, Outer 183
Chthonios Books, East Sussex...................... 100
Havercroft Antiquarian Books, London (SE).... 161
Ice House Books... 143
IKON, Devon 88
MacCormaig (Domhnall), Scotland 269
Malmo Books, Hampshire 121
Modern Welsh Publications Ltd., Merseyside.... 185
Naughton Booksellers, Republic Of Ireland...... 277
Riderless Horse Books, Norfolk 187
Rosley Books, Cumbria 79
Sillem (Anthony), East Sussex 101
Stevens (Joan), Cambridgeshire 66
Studio Bookshop, East Sussex....................... 99
Temple (Robert), London (N)........................ 155
Tiger Books, Kent.. 134
Updike Rare Books (John), Scotland 270

LOCKS & LOCKSMITHS

Book Basket, London, Outer 182

MAGIC & CONJURING

Abrahams (Mike), Staffordshire..................... 222
Bolton Books, Hampshire 120
Book Basket, London, Outer 182
Books & Bygones, Berkshire.......................... 58
Books & Bygones (Pam Taylor), West Midlands 240
Booth (Booksearch Service), (Geoff), Cheshire .. 69
Breese Books Ltd., East Sussex 98
Davis (Peter), Kent...................................... 136
Drummond Pleasures of Past Times (David),
　London (WC) 176
Elgar (Raymond), East Sussex 98
Elmbury Books, Warwickshire....................... 237
Fitzsimons (Anne), Cumbria.......................... 77
Franks Booksellers, Greater Manchester 117
Game Advice, Oxfordshire............................ 207
Harrington (Adrian), London (W).................. 173
Harrington (Adrian), London (W).................. 173
Inner Bookshop (The), Oxfordshire 207
Stage Door Prints, London (WC)................... 178
Vintage Motorshop, West Yorkshire............... 245
Wiend Books & Collectables,
　Greater Manchester 119
Wizard Books, Cambridgeshire...................... 68

SPECIALITY INDEX

MANUALS
- GENERAL
Elmbury Books, Warwickshire 237

- SEAMANSHIP
Elmbury Books, Warwickshire 237
Lewcock (John), Cambridgeshire 67
Nautical Antique Centre (The), Dorset 95

MANUSCRIPTS
Biblion, London (W) 169
Bookstand, Dorset 93
Bookwyze, Lincolnshire 147
Bristow & Garland, Hampshire 121
Browning (Julian), London (W) 169
Collectables (W.H.), London (W) 172
Cox Music (Lisa), Devon 85
Davids Ltd., (Roy), Oxfordshire 207
Drury Rare Books (John), Essex 109
Du Ry Medieval Manuscripts (Marc–Antoine), London (W) 172
Elmbury Books, Warwickshire 237
Farahar & Dupré (Clive & Sophie), Wiltshire 250
Fergusson Books & Manuscripts (James), London (W) 172
Finch Rare Books Ltd. (Simon), London (W)... 172
Fogg Rare Books & Manuscripts (Sam), London (W) 172
Ford (Richard), London (W) 172
Gekoski (R.A.), London (WC) 177
Hatchwell (Richard), Wiltshire 251
Heath (A.R.), Bristol 61
Kenny's Bookshops and Art Galleries Ltd, Republic Of Ireland 278
Kunkler Books (Paul), Cambridgeshire 65
Maggs Brothers Limited, London (W) 173
Marine and Cannon Books, Cheshire 70
Muttonchop Manuscripts, West Sussex 243
Quaritch Ltd., (Bernard), London (W) 174
Rassam (Paul), London (NW) 158
Riley–Smith (Hamish), Norfolk 190
Rowan (P. & B.), Northern Ireland 259
Sabin (Printed Works) (P.R. & V.), Kent 133
Seydi Rare Books (Sevin), London (NW) 159
Silverman (Michael), London (SE) 161
Summersgill (Neil), Lancashire 140
Taylor & Son (Peter), Hertfordshire 130
Townsend (John), Berkshire 59
Williams Rare Books (Nigel), London (WC) 179
Wilson (Autographs) Ltd., (John), Gloucestershire 112

MARINE SCIENCES
Elmbury Books, Warwickshire 237
Ice House Books 143
Sub Aqua Prints and Books, Hampshire 121

MARITIME/NAUTICAL
Abbey Bookshop, Hampshire 122
Alba Books, Scotland 267
All Books, Essex 108
Anchor Books, Lincolnshire 149
Andron (G.W.), London (N) 153
Anvil Books, West Midlands 239
Arden Books & Cosmographia, Warwickshire 236
Arthurian Book, Wales 285
Atticus Books, Essex 109
Avonbridge Books, Gloucestershire 114
Baldwin (M. & M.), Shropshire 212
Barmby (C. & A.J.), Kent 138
Batstone Books, Wiltshire 250
Bookends of Fowey, Cornwall 74
Books Afloat, Dorset 95
Bookworld, Shropshire 212
Booth Books, Wales 286
Bott, (Bookdealers) Ltd., (Martin), Greater Manchester 116
Broadhurst of Southport Ltd., Merseyside 186
Browser's Bookshop, Cornwall 74
Burgess Booksellers, (J. & J.), Cambridgeshire .. 64
Cavan Book Centre, Republic Of Ireland 275
Charmouth Bookstore, Dorset 91
Collectables (W.H.), London (W) 172
Cox (Geoff), Devon 89
Cuddy Books (Michael), London (N) 153
Curtle Mead Books, Isle of Wight 131
Dartmoor Bookshop (The), Devon 83
de Lotz Books (P.G.), London (NW) 157
Duck (William), East Sussex 98
Elmbury Books, Warwickshire 237
Empire Books, Greater Manchester 118
Evans Booksearch, (Lesley), Devon 89
Falconwood Transport & Military Bookshop, London, Outer 184
Fireside Bookshop, Cumbria 80
Fisher Nautical, East Sussex 98
Footrope Knots, Suffolk 226
Fox Books (J. & J.), Kent 137
Greta Books, Durham 96
Guildmaster Books, Cheshire 71
Harrington Antiquarian Bookseller (Peter), London (SW) 164
Helion & Company, West Midlands 240
High Street Books, Devon 85
Island Books, Devon 84
Kellow Books, Oxfordshire 204
Kerr (Norman), Cumbria 78
Kingston (Richard J.), Oxfordshire 206
Larkham Books (Patricia), Gloucestershire 115
Lewcock (John), Cambridgeshire 67
Lewis (John), Essex 107
Londonline Books, London (SW) 165
Maddison (J.K.), West Midlands 238
Malmo Books, Hampshire 121
Marcet Books, London (SE) 161
Marine and Cannon Books, Cheshire 70
Martin Bookshop & Gallery (Richard), Hampshire 121
Menavaur Books, Scotland 264
Military Collector (The), West Yorkshire 249
Mother Goose Bookshop, Isle of Wight 131
Nautical Antique Centre (The), Dorset 95
Oblong Books, N Yorks 197
Old Gallery Bookshop (The), Kent 136
Prior (Michael), Lincolnshire 149

394 SPECIALITY INDEX

Pyke (Robert & Susan), Somerset.................. 214
Quayside Bookshop, Devon 88
Rods Books, Devon.................................. 87
Sansovino Books, West Sussex 244
Savery Books, East Sussex 99
Sea Chest Nautical Bookshop (The), Devon 87
Sidey, Bookdealer (Philip), Kent 137
Skelly (George B.), London (N).................... 155
Smith Maritime Aviation Books (Frank),
   Tyne & Wear 235
Smith Modern First Editions, (Chris Adam),
   West Sussex....................................... 243
South Downs Book Service, West Sussex......... 243
Sub Aqua Prints and Books, Hampshire 121
Swan Bookshop (The), Devon...................... 84
Taylor & Son (Peter), Hertfordshire............... 130
Thin Read Line, Merseyside 186
Treasure Island (The), Greater Manchester 118
Trinders' Fine Tools, Suffolk 225
Vanstone - Aviation Books, (Derek), Suffolk 229
Warsash Nautical Bookshop, Hampshire......... 124
Wayfarer Books, Cornwall.......................... 75
Wiend Books & Collectables,
   Greater Manchester 119
Wise (Derek), East Sussex.......................... 102
World War Books, Kent 139
YSF Books, South Yorkshire....................... 221

MARITIME/NAUTICAL - LOG BOOKS
Nautical Antique Centre (The), Dorset 95
Warsash Nautical Bookshop, Hampshire......... 124

MARQUE HISTORIES
(SEE ALSO MOTORING)
Book Basket, London, Outer 182
Collectors Carbooks, Northamptonshire.......... 199
Knowles (John), Norfolk 188
Pooks Motor Books, Leicestershire................ 144
www.drivepast.com, Gloucestershire............... 114

MARXISM
Ice House Books..................................... 143
Killeen (John), N Yorks............................. 193
Left on The Shelf, London (E) 151
Red Star Books, Hertfordshire 128
Spurrier (Nick), Kent 136
Woburn Books, London (N)........................ 156

MATHEMATICS
Ænigma Designs (Books), Devon.................. 85
Baron - Scientific Book Sales (P.J.), Somerset ... 215
Beware of The Leopard Books, Bristol 60
Camden Books, Somerset 214
Chesters (G. & J.), Staffordshire 223
DoublePlusBooks, Cambridgeshire 68
Downie Fine Books Ltd., (Robert), Shropshire . 213
Eagle Bookshop (The), Bedfordshire 55
Gorton Booksearch (John), East Sussex 103
Greyfriars Books, Essex 107
Holtom (Christopher), Cornwall 76
Ice House Books..................................... 143

Phelps (Michael), West Sussex..................... 242
Savery Books, East Sussex 99
Stroh (M.A.), London (E).......................... 151
Turret House, Norfolk.............................. 191
Westwood Books (Mark), Wales................... 287

MEDIA
Cyclamen Books, Leicestershire 143
Ice House Books..................................... 143
J.C. Poole Books, Wales............................ 290
Kelly Books, Devon................................. 88

MEDICINE
Alba Books, Scotland............................... 267
Ashfield Books and Records, Nottinghamshire.. 203
Austwick Hall Books, N Yorks 141
Baron - Scientific Book Sales (P.J.), Somerset ... 215
Beware of The Leopard Books, Bristol 60
Books & Bygones, Berkshire....................... 58
Bookshop (The), Republic Of Ireland............. 276
Bracton Books, Cambridgeshire.................... 64
Bradley–Cox (Mary), Dorset....................... 90
Burgess Booksellers, (J. & J.), Cambridgeshire .. 64
Carta Regis, Wales 288
Childrens Bookshop, West Yorkshire 246
Collectable Books, London (SE)................... 160
Edwards in Hay-on-Wye (Francis), Wales....... 286
Finch Rare Books Ltd. (Simon), London (W)... 172
Game Advice, Oxfordshire......................... 207
Gaskell Rare Books (Roger), Cambridgeshire ... 67
Hünersdorff Rare Books, London (SW) 165
Hunter–Rare Books (Andrew), London (SW) ... 165
Ice House Books..................................... 143
Kidson (Ruth), East Sussex 102
Lawson & Company (E.M.), Oxfordshire 205
Outcast Books, Wales............................... 287
Phelps (Michael), West Sussex..................... 242
Phillips (Nigel), London (SW)..................... 166
Pollak (P.M.), Devon 87
Pratt (B.A. & C.W.M.), Herefordshire............ 126
Prospect House Books, Northern Ireland 260
Quaritch Ltd., (Bernard), London (W)............ 174
R M Books, Hertfordshire 129
Scrivener's Books & Book Binding, Derbyshire . 81
Smith (Clive), Essex 108
Smith (David & Lynn), London, Outer........... 182
STM Books, London (N) 155
Stroh (M.A.), London (E).......................... 151
Thornton (Grahame), Dorset....................... 94
Treasure Island (The), Greater Manchester 118
Turret House, Norfolk.............................. 191
Weiner (Graham), London (N).................... 156
Westons, Hertfordshire 130
White (David), Cambridgeshire 66
Worcester Rare Books, Worcestershire 256

MEDICINE - HISTORY OF
Alba Books, Scotland............................... 267
Biblion, London (W)............................... 169
Chesters (G. & J.), Staffordshire 223
Childrens Bookshop, West Yorkshire 246
Fireside Bookshop, Cumbria 80
Game Advice, Oxfordshire......................... 207

SPECIALITY INDEX

Mair Wilkes Books, Scotland........................ 265
Phelps (Michael), West Sussex...................... 242
R M Books, Hertfordshire........................... 129
Rowan (P. & B.), Northern Ireland 259
Smith (David & Lynn), London, Outer........... 182
STM Books, London (N) 155
Sue Lowell Natural History Books, London (W) 175
Taylor & Son (Peter), Hertfordshire............... 130
Westwood Books (Mark), Wales.................... 287
White (David), Cambridgeshire 66

MEDIEVAL

Crouch Rare Books, Surrey......................... 232
Du Ry Medieval Manuscripts (Marc–Antoine),
 London (W) 172
Lund Theological Books, Cambridgeshire........ 65
Meekins Books (Paul), Warwickshire 237
Polczynski (Udo K.H.), London, Outer 183
Spenceley Books (David), West Yorkshire 248
Stewart (Andrew), Cornwall 75
Taylor & Son (Peter), Hertfordshire............... 130
Thomson (Karen), Scotland 271
Unsworths Booksellers Ltd., London (WC)...... 178

MEMOIRS

Downie Fine Books Ltd., (Robert), Shropshire . 213
Empire Books, Greater Manchester 118
Firth (Bijou Books & Photography) (Maureen),
 South Yorkshire 221
Gildea (Donald), West Sussex 241
Ice House Books...................................... 143
Kirkpatrick (Robert J.), London (W) 173
Mr. Pickwick of Towcester, Northamptonshire.. 199
Politico's, London (SW)............................. 166
Scott (T.F.S.), East Sussex 102
Sillem (Anthony), East Sussex...................... 101
Third Reich Books, Kent............................ 134

MEMORABILIA

Art Reference Books, Hampshire 123
Dally Books & Collectables, Wales................ 287
Gate Memorabilia, London (N).................... 153
Kent T. G., Surrey 230

METAPHYSICS

Alpha Books, London (N) 153
Far Horizons Books, Dorset........................ 91
Greensleeves, Oxfordshire........................... 204
Inner Bookshop (The), Oxfordshire 207
Starlord Books, Cheshire............................ 70

METEOROLOGY

Duck (William), East Sussex........................ 98
Ice House Books...................................... 143

MICROSCOPY

Phelps (Michael), West Sussex...................... 242
Turret House, Norfolk............................... 191

MILITARY

Abacus Gallery / The Village Bookshop,
 Staffordshire.. 223
Abbey Bookshop, Hampshire 122
Addyman Books, Wales 285
Albion Books, West Midlands...................... 239
Anchor Books, Lincolnshire 149
Andron (G.W.), London (N) 153
Anglo-American Rare Books, Surrey.............. 232
Armchair Auctions, Hampshire 120
Assinder Books, Bedfordshire 55
Atticus Books, Essex................................. 109
Austen (Phillip), Lincolnshire...................... 149
Baldwin (M. & M.), Shropshire.................... 212
Barbican Bookshop, N Yorks 196
Barn Books, Buckinghamshire...................... 62
Barry Meaden (Aviation Books), Hertfordshire . 129
Blacket Books, Scotland............................. 269
Bon Accord Enterprises, Scotland 269
Bonner (John), West Yorkshire 247
Books, Wales.. 282
Books Bought & Sold, Surrey 231
Books Plus, Devon 87
Bookworm, Essex.................................... 106
Bookworms of Evesham, Worcestershire 255
Booth Books, Wales.................................. 286
Bosco Books, Cornwall.............................. 73
Bufo Books, Hampshire 123
Burgess Booksellers, (J. & J.), Cambridgeshire .. 64
Cahir Cosy Corner Bookshop, Republic Of
 Ireland 279
Camilla's Bookshop, East Sussex 100
Castle Bookshop, Essex.............................. 107
Cavern Books, Cheshire............................. 71
Chelifer Books, Cumbria 79
Clent Books, Worcestershire........................ 254
Coach House Books, Worcestershire 255
Cobweb Books, N Yorks............................ 194
Coles (T.V.), Cambridgeshire 67
Collectors Corner, Wiltshire 252
Cox Old & Rare Books (Claude), Suffolk 226
Crispin's Day, Antiquarian and Out of Print
 Military Books, Essex............................. 110
Croft Selections, Lincolnshire....................... 148
Cuddy Books (Michael), London (N)............. 153
Dally Books & Collectables, Wales................ 287
Dartmoor Bookshop (The), Devon................ 83
de Lotz Books (P.G.), London (NW) 157
Deeside Books, Scotland 266
Delph Books, Greater Manchester................. 116
Devanha Military Books, Scotland 267
Donovan Military Books (Tom), East Sussex.... 98
Dorset Rare Books, Wiltshire 252
Eastern Traveller (The), Somerset.................. 218
Edwards (London) Limited (Francis),
 London (WC) 177
Edwards in Hay-on-Wye (Francis), Wales....... 286
Empire Books, Greater Manchester 118
Falconwood Transport & Military Bookshop,
 London, Outer 184
Fin Rare Books, Shropshire 213
Fireside Bookshop, Cumbria 80
Ford Books (David), Hertfordshire................ 130
Fox Books (J. & J.), Kent........................... 137
Golden Hind Bookshop (The), Kent 134

Harlequin Books, Bristol	61
Harris (George J.), Worcestershire	254
Hayles Military Books (Derek), Berkshire	57
Heartland Old Books, Devon	88
Helion & Company, West Midlands	240
High Street Books, Devon	85
Hill (John S.), Devon	85
Horsham Bookshop (The), West Sussex	242
Hutchison (Books) (Larry), Scotland	265
Island Books, Devon	84
Island Books, Devon	86
J.C. Poole Books, Wales	290
Jackson (M.W.), Wiltshire	253
Jones Books (Russell), Berkshire	57
Joppa Books Ltd., Surrey	230
Keegan's Bookshop, Berkshire	58
Keel Row Books, Tyne & Wear	235
Kingfisher Book Service, Nottinghamshire	203
Langmaid (Kenneth), Cornwall	76
Malvern Bookshop (The), Worcestershire	254
Marine and Cannon Books, Cheshire	70
McCrone (Audrey), Scotland	272
McKenzie (Major John R.), Cumbria	77
Meekins Books (Paul), Warwickshire	237
Military Bookworm, London (SE)	161
Military Collector (The), West Yorkshire	249
MilitaryHistoryBooks.com, Kent	136
Morley Case, Hampshire	124
Mother Goose Bookshop, Isle of Wight	131
Mundy (David), Hertfordshire	128
Noel and Holland Books, Republic Of Ireland	278
Oblong Books, N Yorks	197
Old Gallery Bookshop (The), Kent	136
Olio Books, East Sussex	101
Palladour Books, Hampshire	124
Park Gallery & Bookshop (The), Northants.	199
Peakirk Books, Cambridgeshire	68
Polmorla Books, Cornwall	76
Prior (Michael), Lincolnshire	149
Rods Books, Devon	87
Royal Carbery Books Ltd., Republic Of Ireland	275
Russell Books, Somerset	218
Sansovino Books, West Sussex	244
Savery Books, East Sussex	99
Scorpio Books, Suffolk	225
Shacklock Books (David), Suffolk	226
Shapero Rare Books (Bernard J.), London (W)	174
Silver Trees Books, West Midlands	239
Smith (Clive), Essex	108
Spink & Son Limited, London (WC)	178
Spooner (John E.), Dorset	90
Stacks Bookshop, Northern Ireland	259
Stroma Books, Scotland	261
Thin Read Line, Merseyside	186
Thornton (Grahame), Dorset	94
Tiffin (Tony and Gill), Durham	96
Trotman (Ken), Cambridgeshire	66
Turner (Robin), Gloucestershire	112
Vanstone - Aviation Books, (Derek), Suffolk	229
Visser Books (de), Cambridgeshire	66
Warnes (Felicity J.), London, Outer	181
Wayfarer Books, Cornwall	75
Whitfield (Ken), Essex	109
Wise (Derek), East Sussex	102
Wizard Books, Cambridgeshire	68
Woolcott Books, Dorset	92
World War Books, Kent	139
Yeoman Books, Scotland	270
YSF Books, South Yorkshire	221

MILITARY HISTORY

Aardvark Books, Wiltshire	252
Albion Books, West Midlands	239
Americanabooksuk, Cumbria	77
Andron (G.W.), London (N)	153
Armchair Books, Scotland	268
Askew Books (Vernon), Wiltshire	250
Baldwin (M. & M.), Shropshire	212
Barbican Bookshop, N Yorks	196
Biblion, London (W)	169
Black Five Books, Shropshire	213
Book Basket, London, Outer	182
Books Afloat, Dorset	95
Books on Spain, London, Outer	183
Bookstop Bookshop, N Yorks	193
Brockwells Bookshop, London (SE)	160
Cahir Cosy Corner Bookshop, Republic Of Ireland	279
Carnforth Bookshop (The), Lancashire	140
Chelifer Books, Cumbria	79
Chevin Books, West Yorkshire	248
Collectables (W.H.), London (W)	172
Corfe Books, Surrey	231
Crispin's Day, Antiquarian and Out of Print Military Books, Essex	110
Dally Books & Collectables, Wales	287
Dartmoor Bookshop (The), Devon	83
Devanha Military Books, Scotland	267
Donovan Military Books (Tom), East Sussex	98
Downie Fine Books Ltd., (Robert), Shropshire	213
Driffield Bookshop (The), East Yorkshire	104
Eastern Traveller (The), Somerset	218
Empire Books, Greater Manchester	118
Evans Booksearch, (Lesley), Devon	89
Farnborough Bookshop and Gallery, Hampshire	121
G C Books, Scotland	264
Gippeswic Books, Suffolk	227
Guildmaster Books, Cheshire	71
Handsworth Books, Essex	110
Harris (George J.), Worcestershire	254
Hayles Military Books (Derek), Berkshire	57
Helion & Company, West Midlands	240
Heppa (Christopher), Essex	106
Hornsey's, N Yorks	194
Hummingbird Books, Kent	136
Island Books, Devon	84
Keel Row Books, Tyne & Wear	235
Kellow Books, Oxfordshire	204
Kenny's Bookshops and Art Galleries Ltd, Republic Of Ireland	278
Lion Fine Arts and Books, Wales	287
Maggs Brothers Limited, London (W)	173
Malmo Books, Hampshire	121
Marine and Cannon Books, Cheshire	70
McCrone (Audrey), Scotland	272
Meekins Books (Paul), Warwickshire	237
Military Bookworm, London (SE)	161
Military Collector (The), West Yorkshire	249

SPECIALITY INDEX

MilitaryHistoryBooks.com, Kent 136
Morten (Booksellers) (E.J.),
  Greater Manchester 117
O'Brien Books & Photo Gallery, Republic Of
  Ireland 279
Orssich (Paul), London (SW) 166
Parrott Books, Oxfordshire 209
Prescott - The Bookseller (John), London, Outer. 184
Prior (Michael), Lincolnshire 149
Richmond Books, N Yorks 194
Rochdale Book Company, Greater Manchester. 118
Rods Books, Devon 87
Roland Books, Kent 137
Rothwell and Dunworth, Somerset 216
Sax Books, Suffolk 228
Schull Books, Republic Of Ireland 275
Second Edition, Scotland 270
Stanhope Bibliophiles, London (N) 155
Sutcliffe (Victor), London (SW) 167
Swan Bookshop (The), Devon 84
Taylor & Son (Peter), Hertfordshire 130
Thin Read Line, Merseyside 186
Third Reich Books, Kent 134
Tiffin (Tony and Gill), Durham 96
Turton (John), Durham 97
Unsworths Booksellers Ltd., London (WC) ... 178
Ventnor Rare Books, Isle of Wight 132
Vinovium Books, Durham 96
Wiend Books & Collectables,
  Greater Manchester 119
Wise (Derek), East Sussex 102
Wizard Books, Cambridgeshire 68
Yeoman Books, Scotland 270

MIND, BODY & SPIRIT

Far Horizons Books, Dorset 91
Furneaux Books (Lee), Devon 87
Graduate Books, Worcestershire 256
Jericho Books, Oxfordshire 208
Oasis Booksearch, Cambridgeshire 68
Occultique, Northamptonshire 198
Roosterbooks, Northamptonshire 198
Starlord Books, Cheshire 70

MINERALOGY

Browne (A.), Cheshire 69
Henly (John), West Sussex 244
Honiton Old Bookshop, Devon 85
Ice House Books 143
Nibris Books, London (SW) 165
Phelps (Michael), West Sussex 242

MINIATURE BOOKS

Garbett Antiquarian Books (Michael), Bristol ... 111
Hennessey Bookseller (Ray), East Sussex 100
Mead (P.J.), Shropshire 212

MINING

Book House (The), Cumbria 78
Bott, (Bookdealers) Ltd., (Martin), Greater
  Manchester 116

Browne (A.), Cheshire 69
Collectables (W.H.), London (W) 172
Cox (Geoff), Devon 89
Duck (William), East Sussex 98
Ice House Books 143
Jones Books (Russell), Berkshire 57
Phelps (Michael), West Sussex 242
Turton (John), Durham 97
Whitchurch Books Ltd., Wales 280

MODERN FIRST EDITIONS

Addyman Books, Wales 285
Amwell Book Company (The), London (EC) 152
Anglo-American Rare Books, Surrey 232
Annie's Books, South Yorkshire 220
Archer (Steve), London, Outer 180
Askew Books (Vernon), Wiltshire 250
Autolycus, Shropshire 211
Avonworld Books, Somerset 215
babelog.books, Herefordshire 126
Bertram Rota Ltd., London (WC) 176
Biblion, London (W) 169
Blackman (Martin), Buckinghamshire 62
Book Barrow, Cambridgeshire 64
Book Basket, London, Outer 182
Book Bungalow (The), Cornwall 73
BookLovers, Somerset 217
Bookroom (The), Surrey 233
Books & Things, London (W) 169
BOOKS4U, Wales 282
Bookshop Blackheath, London (SE) 160
Bookstand, Dorset 93
Bookstop UK, Lancashire 142
Bookworm, Essex 106
Book-Worm International, Essex 107
Booth (Booksearch Service), (Geoff), Cheshire .. 69
Broadhurst of Southport Ltd., Merseyside 186
Cader Idris Books, Wales 283
Caledonia Books, Scotland 271
Carta Regis, Wales 288
Castle Bookshop, Essex 107
Chiltern Books, London (W) 172
Conry (Ann & Mike), Worcestershire 256
Corfe Books, Surrey 231
Courtyard Books, Herefordshire 127
Criterion Books, London, Outer 182
Dawson (Modern First Editions), (Philip),
  London, Outer 183
Driffield Bookshop (The), East Yorkshire 104
Ellis, Bookseller (Peter), London (SE) 160
Ellwood Editions, Hampshire 123
Family Favourites (Books), East Yorkshire 104
Fin Rare Books, Shropshire 213
Finch Rare Books Ltd. (Simon), London (W) ... 172
Firsts in Print, Isle of Wight 131
Harris (Books), (Malcolm), West Midlands 239
Hawthorn Books, Bristol 61
Heppa (Christopher), Essex 106
Hight (Norman F.), Bedfordshire 56
House of Figgis Ltd (The),
  Republic Of Ireland 278
Idle Genius Books, London (N) 154
Innes Books, Shropshire 212
Island Books, Devon 84
J & M Books, Warwickshire 237

J.K. Bookfinders, London (SW)..................... 165
Jonkers Rare Books, Oxfordshire.................. 206
Katharine House Gallery, Wiltshire 251
Kendall–Carpenter (Tim), Greater Manchester.. 117
Kevin S. Ogilvie Modern First Editions,
 Scotland 265
L.M.S. Books, Hertfordshire 129
Lewis (J.T. & P.), Cornwall.......................... 74
Lewis First Editions, Kent 135
Little Stour Books, Kent 133
Mair Wilkes Books, Scotland....................... 265
McCann (Joe), Oxfordshire 208
McCrone (Audrey), Scotland 272
McKelvie (Ian), London (N)........................ 154
Milne Books (Clifford), Scotland 265
Ming Books, Scotland 264
Moore (Sue), Cornwall 74
Moreton Books, Devon 86
Morris (Chris), Oxfordshire........................ 208
Norton Books, Durham 97
O'Neill (Angus), London (WC) 178
Orlando Booksellers, Lincolnshire 148
Paperbacks Plus, Bristol 61
Parker Books (Mike), Cambridgeshire 65
Peter Lyons Books, Gloucestershire 112
Petersham Books, London (SW) 166
Price (R.W.), Nottinghamshire 202
Pringle Booksellers (Andrew), Scotland........... 270
R. & A. Books, East Sussex 100
Reaveley Books, Devon 86
Rising Tide Books, Scotland........................ 264
Roberts (Fine Books) (Julian), Lincolnshire 149
Roosterbooks, Northamptonshire.................. 198
Sandstone Books, Kent.............................. 134
Satara Books, West Sussex 244
Seddon (A.C.), West Sussex 244
Shakeshaft (Dr. B.), Cheshire....................... 72
Shakeshaft (Roger & Sylvia), Lincolnshire 146
Sidey, Bookdealer (Philip), Kent 137
Sillem (Anthony), East Sussex 101
Silver Trees Books, West Midlands................ 239
Simply Read, East Sussex 100
Simpson (Dave), Scotland........................... 262
Singleton, (John), London (N) 155
Slavin Rare and Collectable Books (Derek),
 Warwickshire.. 237
Smith Modern First Editions, (Chris Adam),
 West Sussex 243
Stroma Books, Scotland............................. 261
Studio Bookshop, East Sussex....................... 99
Temple (Robert), London (N)...................... 155
Thornber (Peter A.), N Yorks....................... 195
Thornton Books (Richard), London (N) 155
Tony Skelton, Kent 138
Touchstone Books, Norfolk 190
Trevorrow (Edwin), Hertfordshire 128
Ulysses, London (WC) 178
Ward (K. Anthony), Norfolk....................... 188
Whiteson Ltd., (Edna), Hertfordshire 128
Willmott Bookseller (Nicholas), Wales............ 280
Wilson (J. & M.), Scotland 273
Winchester Antiquarian Books, Hampshire...... 125
Woodstock Fabrics & Books, Shropshire......... 212
Wright Trace Books, West Midlands.............. 239

MONOGRAPHS

Barlow (Vincent G.), Hampshire................... 123
Campbell Art Books (Marcus), London (SE).... 160
Heneage Art Books (Thomas), London (SW).... 164
Shipley Specialist Art Booksellers, London (WC) 178
Taylor & Son (Peter), Hertfordshire............... 130
Trinders' Fine Tools, Suffolk 225

MOTORBIKES

Book Basket, London, Outer 182
Chaters Motoring Booksellers, London, Outer .. 182
Collectors Carbooks, Northamptonshire.......... 199
Duck (William), East Sussex........................ 98
Falconwood Transport & Military Bookshop,
 London, Outer 184
Hairpin Books, Gloucestershire 113
Holdenhurst Books, Dorset......................... 90
Little Bookshop (The), Greater Manchester 117
Main–Smith & Co. Ltd. (Bruce), Leicestershire . 143
Merlin Books, West Sussex 243
Pooks Motor Books, Leicestershire................ 144
Roadster Motoring Books, Hampshire............ 123
Roberts (Booksellers), (Ray), Staffordshire....... 223
Simon Lewis Transport Books, Gloucestershire . 112
Vintage Motorshop, West Yorkshire 245
Yeoman Books, Scotland........................... 270

MOTORING

Abrahams (Mike), Staffordshire.................... 222
Baldwin (M. & M.), Shropshire.................... 212
Book Basket, London, Outer 182
Book Corner, Scotland 263
Books Bought & Sold, Surrey 231
Booth Books, Wales.................................. 286
Brewin Books Ltd., Warwickshire 237
Camilla's Bookshop, East Sussex................... 100
Chaters Motoring Booksellers, London, Outer .. 182
Cobweb Books, N Yorks............................ 194
Collectables (W.H.), London (W)................. 172
Collectors Carbooks, Northamptonshire.......... 199
Corfe Books, Surrey 231
Cowley, Auto–in–Print (John), Essex 106
Cox (Geoff), Devon 89
David Thomas Motoring Books, Herefordshire. 127
Duck (William), East Sussex........................ 98
Eastcote Bookshop (The), London, Outer........ 183
Emjay Books, Surrey 231
Falconwood Transport & Military Bookshop,
 London, Outer 184
Farquharson, (Hilary), Scotland 273
Hairpin Books, Gloucestershire 113
Harlequin Books, Bristol 61
Heritage, West Midlands 238
Holdenhurst Books, Dorset......................... 90
Hornsey's, N Yorks 194
Horsham Bookshop (The), West Sussex 242
Kerr (Norman), Cumbria 78
Knowles (John), Norfolk 188
Ice House Books..................................... 143
Morris (Chris), Oxfordshire........................ 208
Old Gallery Bookshop (The), Kent................ 136
Pooks Motor Books, Leicestershire................ 144
Roadmaster Books, Kent............................ 134

SPECIALITY INDEX

Roadster Motoring Books, Hampshire............ 123
Roberts (Booksellers), (Ray), Staffordshire....... 223
Rochdale Book Company, Greater Manchester . 118
Roland Books, Kent 137
St Mary's Books & Prints, Lincolnshire 150
Simon Lewis Transport Books, Gloucestershire . 112
Smith Maritime Aviation Books (Frank),
   Tyne & Wear 235
Thompson (Eric), Surrey 233
Vintage Motorshop, West Yorkshire 245
Volumes of Motoring, Gloucestershire............ 111
www.drivepast.com, Gloucestershire................ 114
Yeoman Books, Scotland........................... 270

MOVEABLE & 3D
Kernaghans, Merseyside............................ 186

MUSIC
- GENERAL
AA1 Books, Scotland................................ 263
Abacus Gallery / The Village Bookshop,
   Staffordshire.. 223
Aberdeen Rare Books & Caledonian Books,
   Scotland 267
Anderson Slater Antiques, N Yorks................ 195
Archive Books & Music, London (NW).......... 157
Arundel Bookshop, West Sussex.................... 241
Ashburton Books, Devon 83
Ashfield Books and Records, Nottinghamshire.. 203
Autumn Leaves, Lincolnshire....................... 148
Barber Music, Kent 136
Bardsley's Books, Suffolk 225
Baron (H.), London (NW).......................... 157
Baxter - Books (Eddie), Somerset.................. 218
Beverley Old Bookshop, East Yorkshire.......... 104
Beware of The Leopard Books, Bristol 60
Birchwood Books, West Yorkshire 246
Book Warren, Devon 84
Bookroom (The), Surrey 233
Books, Wales... 282
Books & Bygones, Berkshire....................... 58
Books (For All), N Yorks........................... 192
Bookshop (The), Norfolk 191
Bookworms, Norfolk................................ 187
Boris Books, Dorset................................. 94
Bygone Tunes, Lancashire 142
Carnforth Bookshop (The), Lancashire........... 140
Carta Regis, Wales.................................. 288
Charmouth Bookstore, Dorset 91
Clapham (M. & B.), Hampshire................... 122
Clements (R.W.), London, Outer 181
Croft Selections, Lincolnshire...................... 148
Cronin (Jim), Wales................................. 280
Davids Ltd., (Roy), Oxfordshire................... 207
Dooley (Rosemary), Cumbria 80
Downie Fine Books Ltd., (Robert), Shropshire . 213
Duncan's Books, Devon............................. 88
East Riding Books & Music, East Yorkshire.... 105
Elgar (Raymond), East Sussex 98
Fitzsimons (Anne), Cumbria........................ 77
Gate Memorabilia, London (N).................... 153
Gilham Books, London (SE)....................... 161
Gloucester Road Bookshop, London (SW) 164

Hancock & Monks, Wales.......................... 286
Hancock (Colin), Wales 281
Handsworth Books, Essex........................... 110
Jade Mountain, Hampshire 123
Ice House Books..................................... 143
Kenny's Bookshops and Art Galleries Ltd,
   Republic Of Ireland 278
Kent T. G., Surrey 230
Kim's Bookshop, West Sussex...................... 244
Langmaid (Kenneth), Cornwall 76
Left Bank (The), Wales............................. 290
Malvern Bookshop (The), Worcestershire 254
McGee (Terence J.), London, Outer............... 181
Music By The Score, Cornwall..................... 73
Musicalania, Hertfordshire.......................... 130
Newgate Books, Northumberland 201
Oblong Books, N Yorks............................. 197
Olio Books, East Sussex............................ 101
Paramor (C.D.), Suffolk............................ 227
Price (John), London (N) 155
Price (R.W.), Nottinghamshire 202
Reads, Dorset.. 94
St Mary's Books & Prints, Lincolnshire 150
Scarthin Books, Derbyshire......................... 82
Sherlaw-Johnson (Austin), Oxfordshire 209
Stage Door Prints, London (WC)................... 178
Staniland (Booksellers), Lincolnshire.............. 150
Stevens (Joan), Cambridgeshire 66
Unsworths Booksellers Ltd., London (WC)...... 178
Venables (Morris & Juliet), Bristol 61
Wilbraham (J. & S.), London (NW)............... 159
Willmott Bookseller (Nicholas), Wales........... 280
Wise Owl Bookshop (The), Bristol 61
Wood (Peter), Cambridgeshire...................... 66
Woodlands Books, West Yorkshire................. 248
YSF Books, South Yorkshire....................... 221

- CLASSICAL
Alba Secondhand Music, Scotland 271
Archive Books & Music, London (NW).......... 157
Chesters (G. & J.), Staffordshire 223
East Riding Books & Music, East Yorkshire.... 105
Hancock & Monks, Wales.......................... 286
Marcan, Bookseller (Peter), London (SE) 161
Prescott - The Bookseller (John), London, Outer 184
Willmott Bookseller (Nicholas), Wales........... 280

- COMPOSERS
Boris Books, Dorset..................................94
East Riding Books & Music, East Yorkshire.... 105
Gilham Books, London (SE) 161
Hancock & Monks, Wales.......................... 286
Music By The Score, Cornwall......................73
Musicalania, Hertfordshire.......................... 130
Sherlaw-Johnson (Austin), Oxfordshire 209
Willmott Bookseller (Nicholas), Wales........... 280
Words & Music, Cheshire............................70

- FOLK & IRISH FOLK
Birchwood Books, West Yorkshire 246
Books of Note, Cambridgeshire......................64
Church Green Books, Oxfordshire................. 210

Dancing Goat Bookshop (The), Norfolk 188
Royal Carbery Books Ltd., Republic Of Ireland 275

- JAZZ

Baxter - Books (Eddie), Somerset 218
Books Plus, Devon 87
Bygone Tunes, Lancashire 142
East Riding Books & Music, East Yorkshire 105
Hancock & Monks, Wales 286
Oblong Books, N Yorks 197
Scorpio Books, Suffolk 225
Wiend Books & Collectables,
  Greater Manchester 119
Words & Music, Cheshire 70

- MUSIC HALL

Davis (Peter), Kent 136
Fitzsimons (Anne), Cumbria 77
Hancock & Monks, Wales 286
Kaye - Bookseller (Terence), London (NW) 158
Music By The Score, Cornwall 73
Sanderson (Edward), Berkshire 58

- MUSICIANS

East Riding Books & Music, East Yorkshire 105
Hancock & Monks, Wales 286
Music By The Score, Cornwall 73
Willmott Bookseller (Nicholas), Wales 280
Woodlands Books, West Yorkshire 248

- OPERA

Browne (Christopher I.), West Yorkshire 245
East Riding Books & Music, East Yorkshire 105
Fitzsimons (Anne), Cumbria 77
Gilham Books, London (SE) 161
Hancock & Monks, Wales 286
Hodgkins and Company Limited (Ian),
  Gloucestershire 114
Music By The Score, Cornwall 73
Sanderson (Edward), Berkshire 58
Sherlaw-Johnson (Austin), Oxfordshire 209
Willmott Bookseller (Nicholas), Wales 280
Words & Music, Cheshire 70

- POLITICAL SONGS & BALLADS

Music By The Score, Cornwall 73
Sanderson (Edward), Berkshire 58

- POPULAR

A. & R. Booksearch, Cornwall 75
Archive Books & Music, London (NW) 157
Black Cat Bookshop, Leicestershire 143
Books of Note, Cambridgeshire 64
Cusack Books, London (W) 172
Dancing Goat Bookshop (The), Norfolk 188
Furneaux Books (Lee), Devon 87
Graduate Books, Worcestershire 256
Gravity Books, Lincolnshire 147
Morris (Chris), Oxfordshire 208
Music By The Score, Cornwall 73

Musicalania, Hertfordshire 130
Nevitsky (Philip), Greater Manchester 117
Sanderson (Edward), Berkshire 58
Willmott Bookseller (Nicholas), Wales 280

- PRINTED

Bygone Tunes, Lancashire 142
Cox Music (Lisa), Devon 85

- ROCK

Cusack Books, London (W) 172
Dancing Goat Bookshop (The), Norfolk 188
Fin Rare Books, Shropshire 213
Furneaux Books (Lee), Devon 87
Gravity Books, Lincolnshire 147
Roland Books, Kent 137
Sclanders (Beatbooks), (Andrew), London (EC) 152

MUSICAL INSTRUMENTS

Barber Music, Kent 136
Barmby (C. & A.J.), Kent 138
East Riding Books & Music, East Yorkshire 105
Elgar (Raymond), East Sussex 98
Gilham Books, London (SE) 161
Hancock & Monks, Wales 286
Kitley (A.J.), Bristol 61
KSC Books, Cheshire 71
Lion Fine Arts and Books, Wales 287
Sherlaw-Johnson (Austin), Oxfordshire 209
Trinders' Fine Tools, Suffolk 225

MYCOLOGY

On the Wild Side, Worcestershire 255
Pendleside Books, Lancashire 141

MYSTERIES

Dawlish Books, Devon 84
Furneaux Books (Lee), Devon 87
Inner Bookshop (The), Oxfordshire 207
L.M.S. Books, Hertfordshire 129
Occultique, Northamptonshire 198
Starlord Books, Cheshire 70
Temple (Robert), London (N) 155
Wizard Books, Cambridgeshire 68

MYSTICISM

Bardsley's Books, Suffolk 225
Book Basket, London, Outer 182
Dawlish Books, Devon 84
Facet Books, Dorset 90
Far Horizons Books, Dorset 91
Greensleeves, Oxfordshire 204
Inner Bookshop (The), Oxfordshire 207
Lund Theological Books, Cambridgeshire 65
Magis Books, Leicestershire 144
Occultique, Northamptonshire 198
Rainger Books (Michael), Wales 285
Starlord Books, Cheshire 70
Wizard Books, Cambridgeshire 68

SPECIALITY INDEX

MYTHOLOGY

Alpha Books, London (N) 153
Atlantis Bookshop, London (WC) 176
Brighton Books, East Sussex 98
Byre Books, Scotland 264
Daeron's Books, Buckinghamshire 63
Galloway & Porter Limited, Cambridgeshire 65
Greensleeves, Oxfordshire 204
Inner Bookshop (The), Oxfordshire 207
Linton Books, Scotland 262
Magis Books, Leicestershire 144
Starlord Books, Cheshire 70
Wizard Books, Cambridgeshire 68

NATURAL HEALTH

Dawlish Books, Devon 84
Greensleeves, Oxfordshire 204
IKON, Devon 88
Occultique, Northamptonshire 198

NATURAL HISTORY

AA1 Books, Scotland 263
Abacus Gallery / The Village Bookshop,
    Staffordshire 223
Allhalland Books, Devon 83
Andron (G.W.), London (N) 153
Antique Map and Bookshop (The), Dorset 93
Arden Books & Cosmographia, Warwickshire... 236
Aurelian Books, London (NW) 157
Austwick Hall Books, N Yorks 141
Autumn Leaves, Lincolnshire 148
Ayre (Peter J.), Somerset 218
Barn Books, Buckinghamshire 62
Barnhill Books, Scotland 272
Baron - Scientific Book Sales (P.J.), Somerset ... 215
Bee Books New and Old, Cornwall 73
Bernwode Books, Buckinghamshire 62
Besleys Books, Suffolk 224
Biblion, London (W) 169
Billing (Brian), Berkshire 59
Blest (Peter), Kent 136
Book Corner, Scotland 263
Book Warren, Devon 84
Books (For All), N Yorks 192
Books Galore, Somerset 216
Bookworms, Norfolk 187
Booth (Booksearch Service), (Geoff), Cheshire .. 69
Booth Books, Wales 286
Bow Windows Book Shop, East Sussex 102
Broadhurst of Southport Ltd., Merseyside 186
Broadleaf Books, Wales 290
Brock Books, N Yorks 192
Buchan Collectibles, Scotland 265
Burgess Booksellers, (J. & J.), Cambridgeshire .. 64
Calluna Books, Dorset 94
Camilla's Bookshop, East Sussex 100
Carlton Books, Norfolk 189
Carnforth Bookshop (The), Lancashire 140
Castleton (Pat), Kent 135
Catalyst Books, Surrey 232
Chambers (Barry), Kent 133
Charmouth Bookstore, Dorset 91
Chevin Books, West Yorkshire 248

Clark (M.R.), West Yorkshire 245
Coch-y-Bonddu Books, Wales 288
Collectable Books, London (SE) 160
Cornell Books, Gloucestershire 114
Cox Old & Rare Books (Claude), Suffolk 226
Crack (Books) (F.N.), Lancashire 140
Crook (Chris), Somerset 218
Cumming Limited (A. & Y.), East Sussex 102
Curtle Mead Books, Isle of Wight 131
Daly (Peter M.), Hampshire 124
Dartmoor Bookshop (The), Devon 83
David (G.), Cambridgeshire 64
Dawson (Modern First Editions), (Philip),
    London, Outer 183
Dean Byass, Tavistock Books, Devon 86
Demar Books (Grant), Kent 138
Dene Barn Books & Prints, Somerset 218
Eastcote Bookshop (The), London, Outer 183
Edwards in Hay–on–Wye (Francis), Wales 286
Elmbury Books, Warwickshire 237
Elmfield Books, West Midlands 238
Evergreen Livres, Gloucestershire 113
Fin Rare Books, Shropshire 213
Fine Art, West Sussex 242
Finney Antique Books & Prints (Michael),
    London (WC) 177
Fireside Bookshop, Cumbria 80
Gibbard (A. & T.), East Sussex 100
Gloucester Road Bookshop, London (SW) 164
Goodyer (Nicholas), London (N) 154
Goodyer, Natural History Books (Eric),
    Leicestershire 144
Grahame (Major Iain), Suffolk 225
Grayling (David A.H.), Cumbria 78
Great Grandfather's, Lancashire 141
Green Man Books, Derbyshire 81
Greyfriars Books, Essex 107
Hall's Bookshop, Kent 138
Halson Books, Cheshire 71
Harrington (Adrian), London (W) 173
Henly (John), West Sussex 244
Hereward Books, Cambridgeshire 66
Heywood Hill Limited (G.), London (W) 173
Hollett and Son (R.F.G.), Cumbria 79
Home Farm Books, Warwickshire 236
Hummingbird Books, Kent 136
Huyton (Peter), Herefordshire 126
Ian Johnson Natural History Books,
    Buckinghamshire 63
Ice House Books 143
Island Books, Devon 84
Island Books, Devon 86
J.A. Heacock (Antiques and Books), Cheshire .. 70
Jackson (M.W.), Wiltshire 253
Jay Books, Scotland 269
K. Books, East Yorkshire 104
Katnap Arts, Norfolk 189
Kellow Books, Oxfordshire 204
Kennedy (Peter), Surrey 234
Kernaghans, Merseyside 186
Kerr (Norman), Cumbria 78
Kim's Bookshop, West Sussex 244
Kingsgate Books & Prints, Hampshire 125
Kingshead Books, Wales 288
Korn Books, (M.E.), London (N) 154

Larkham Books (Patricia), Gloucestershire 115
Lion Fine Arts and Books, Wales 287
Maggs Brothers Limited, London (W) 173
Malvern Bookshop (The), Worcestershire 254
Marshall Rare Books (Bruce), Gloucestershire .. 111
McCrone (Audrey), Scotland 272
McEwan Fine Books, Scotland 266
Mercat Books, Scotland 267
Merritt (Valerie), Gloucestershire 111
Mobbs (A.J.), West Midlands 240
Moreton Books, Devon 86
Morgan (D. & D.H.W.), Devon 89
Mount's Bay Books, Cornwall 75
musebookshop, Wales 283
New Strand Bookshop (The), Herefordshire 126
Nineteenth Century Books, Oxfordshire 209
Oblong Books, N Yorks 197
Old Bookshop (The), Somerset 216
On the Wild Side, Worcestershire 255
Page (David), Scotland 270
Page Antiquarian Books (Colin), East Sussex ... 99
Paralos Ltd., London (W) 173
Park (Mike), London, Outer 183
Peakirk Books, Cambridgeshire 68
Peregrine Books (Leeds), West Yorkshire 247
Phelps (Michael), West Sussex 242
Prospect House Books, Northern Ireland 260
R. & B. Graham, Cornwall 74
River Reads Bookshop, Devon 88
Roland Books, Kent 137
Rothwell and Dunworth, Somerset 216
Russell (Charles), London (SW) 167
Ryeland Books, Northamptonshire 198
Segal Books (Joel), Devon 85
Shakeshaft (Dr. B.), Cheshire 72
Shakeshaft (Roger & Sylvia), Lincolnshire 146
Shearwater Bed & Books (formerly John Lumby
  Nat. History Bks), Northumberland 200
Slavin Rare and Collectable Books (Derek),
  Warwickshire 237
Smith (Clive), Essex 108
Smith Books, (Sally), Suffolk 225
Sotheran Limited (Henry), London (W) 175
Stella Books, Wales 284
Stone, (G.& R.), Scotland 261
Sue Lowell Natural History Books, London (W) 175
Summersgill (Neil), Lancashire 140
Sykes (Graham), West Yorkshire 248
Thomas (E. Wyn), Wales 282
Thurston (Barry), Scotland 273
Way (R.E. & G.B.), Suffolk 227
Wheatsheaf Antiques, Cheshire 69
White House Bookshop, Wales 283
Wise (Derek), East Sussex 102
Woodbine Books, West Yorkshire 245
Woodside Books, Kent 133
Woodstock Bookshop (The), Oxfordshire 210
Wychwood Books, Gloucestershire 114
Wyseby House Books, Berkshire 57
YSF Books, South Yorkshire 221

NATURAL SCIENCES
Ayre (Peter J.), Somerset 218
Crack (Books) (F.N.), Lancashire 140

Dean Byass, Tavistock Books, Devon 86
DoublePlusBooks, Cambridgeshire 68
Downie Fine Books Ltd., (Robert), Shropshire . 213
On the Wild Side, Worcestershire 255
Ice House Books 143
Phelps (Michael), West Sussex 242
Pollak (P.M.), Devon 87
Turret House, Norfolk 191
Wyseby House Books, Berkshire 57

NATURISM
Green (Paul), Cambridgeshire 68

NAVAL
AA1 Books, Scotland 263
Anchor Books, Lincolnshire 149
Andron (G.W.), London (N) 153
Armchair Auctions, Hampshire 120
Barry Meaden (Aviation Books), Hertfordshire . 129
Book for All Reasons (A.), Suffolk 227
Bookseller (The), Suffolk 227
Bott, (Bookdealers) Ltd., (Martin), Greater
  Manchester 116
Corfe Books, Surrey 231
Curtle Mead Books, Isle of Wight 131
Edwards (London) Limited (Francis),
  London (WC) 177
Edwards in Hay–on–Wye (Francis), Wales 286
Empire Books, Greater Manchester 118
Evans Booksearch, (Lesley), Devon 89
Harris (George J.), Worcestershire 254
Hayles Military Books (Derek), Berkshire 57
Helion & Company, West Midlands 240
Island Books, Devon 86
Lewcock (John), Cambridgeshire 67
Malmo Books, Hampshire 121
Marcet Books, London (SE) 161
Marine and Cannon Books, Cheshire 70
McCrone (Audrey), Scotland 272
Nautical Antique Centre (The), Dorset 95
Prior (Michael), Lincolnshire 149
Quayside Bookshop, Devon 88
Rods Books, Devon 87
Spooner (John E.), Dorset 90
Thin Read Line, Merseyside 186
Wise (Derek), East Sussex 102

NAVIGATION
Anvil Books, West Midlands 239
Book Warren, Devon 84
Books Afloat, Dorset 95
Curtle Mead Books, Isle of Wight 131
Duck (William), East Sussex 98
Kingston (Richard J.), Oxfordshire 206
Lewcock (John), Cambridgeshire 67
Nautical Antique Centre (The), Dorset 95
Quayside Bookshop, Devon 88
Rods Books, Devon 87
Sea Chest Nautical Bookshop (The), Devon 87
Warsash Nautical Bookshop, Hampshire 124

NEEDLEWORK

Arcadia, Shropshire	212
Arden Books & Cosmographia, Warwickshire...	236
Arundel Bookshop, West Sussex	241
Black Cat Books, Norfolk	188
Books & Bygones, Berkshire	58
Bowdon Books, Lancashire	141
Brown-Studies, Scotland	270
Camilla's Bookshop, East Sussex	100
Cover to Cover, Merseyside	186
Four Shire Bookshops, Gloucestershire	113
Gresham Books, Somerset	216
Heneage Art Books (Thomas), London (SW)....	164
Hennessey Bookseller (Ray), East Sussex	100
Hummingbird Books, Kent	136
Ives Bookseller (John), London, Outer	184
Lane Books (Shirley), Isle of Wight	132
Mansfield (Judith), West Yorkshire	248
Max Gate Books, Somerset	218
Old Bookshop (The), West Midlands	240
Smith Books (Keith), Herefordshire	127
Trinders' Fine Tools, Suffolk	225
Well–Head Books, Dorset	91

NEUROLOGY

Alba Books, Scotland	267
Game Advice, Oxfordshire	207
Mair Wilkes Books, Scotland	265

NEW AGE

Abacus Gallery / The Village Bookshop, Staffordshire	223
Burgess Booksellers, (J. & J.), Cambridgeshire ..	64
Dawlish Books, Devon	84
Greensleeves, Oxfordshire	204
Grieveson (Andrea), Merseyside	185
Ice House Books	143
IKON, Devon	88
Inner Bookshop (The), Oxfordshire	207
Invisible Books, East Sussex	99
Magis Books, Leicestershire	144
Occultique, Northamptonshire	198

NEW NATURALIST

Blest (Peter), Kent	136
Book Corner, Scotland	263
BOOKS4U, Wales	282
musebookshop, Wales	283
Noel and Holland Books, Republic Of Ireland..	278
On the Wild Side, Worcestershire	255
Sue Lowell Natural History Books, London (W)	175

NEWSPAPERS - GENERAL

Empire Books, Greater Manchester	118
Ice House Books	143
Mr. Pickwick of Towcester, Northamptonshire..	199
Nostalgia Unlimited, Merseyside	185
Tilleys Vintage Magazine Shop, Derbyshire	81

NOSTALGIA

Border Bookshop (The), West Yorkshire	248
K. Books, Cheshire	72
McGee (Terence J.), London, Outer	181
Noble (Malcolm & Christine), Leicestershire	145
Nostalgia Unlimited, Merseyside	185
Prior (Michael), Lincolnshire	149
Wheatsheaf Antiques, Cheshire	69

NUMISMATICS

Clark (Nigel A.), London (SE)	160
DoublePlusBooks, Cambridgeshire	68
Heneage Art Books (Thomas), London (SW)....	164
InterCol London, London (N)	154
Porcupines, Devon	84
Spink & Son Limited, London (WC)	178
Taylor & Son (Peter), Hertfordshire	130

OCCULT

Abbey Books, London (N)	153
Alpha Books, London (N)	153
Anthroposophical Books, Bristol	60
Atlantis Bookshop, London (WC)	176
Atticus Books, Essex	109
Book Basket, London, Outer	182
Books, Wales	282
Bygone Books, Scotland	272
Caduceus Books, Leicestershire	143
Camilla's Bookshop, East Sussex	100
Cavern Books, Cheshire	70
Chthonios Books, East Sussex	100
Clegg (David), Staffordshire	222
Dartmoor Bookshop (The), Devon	83
Dawlish Books, Devon	84
Delectus Books, London (WC)	176
Far Horizons Books, Dorset	91
Gilbert (R.A.), Bristol	61
Greensleeves, Oxfordshire	204
Inner Bookshop (The), Oxfordshire	207
Magis Books, Leicestershire	144
Occultique, Northamptonshire	198
Rainger Books (Michael), Wales	285
Starlord Books, Cheshire	70
Till's Bookshop, Scotland	270
Torsdag Books, Buckinghamshire	62
Victoria Bookshop (The), Devon	83
Wizard Books, Cambridgeshire	68
Wyche Books, Scotland	263

ODD & UNUSUAL

Browser's Bookshop, Cornwall	74
Delectus Books, London (WC)	176
Facet Books, Dorset	90
Hartley Books (Caroline), Nottinghamshire	202
Jericho Books, Oxfordshire	208
Lewis (J.T. & P.), Cornwall	74
Moss Books, London (NW)	158
Muttonchop Manuscripts, West Sussex	243
Occultique, Northamptonshire	198
Treglown (Roger J.), Cheshire	71

ORIENTAL

Art Reference Books, Hampshire	123

Books, Wales 282
Butler Books, Dorset 90
Joppa Books Ltd., Surrey 230
Loman, Oriental Books & Manuscripts (David),
London (SW) 165
Malmo Books, Hampshire 121
Probsthain (Arthur), London (WC) 178

ORNITHOLOGY

Anwoth Books, Scotland 263
Barnhill Books, Scotland 272
Blest (Peter), Kent 136
Book Corner, Scotland 263
Bosco Books, Cornwall 73
Brown (Books) (P.R.), Durham 96
Buchan Collectibles, Scotland 265
Calendula Horticultural Books, East Sussex 100
Calluna Books, Dorset 94
Carlton Books, Norfolk 189
Chambers (Barry), Kent 133
Coach House Books, Worcestershire 255
Coch-y-Bonddu Books, Wales 288
Crack (Books) (F.N.), Lancashire 140
Curtle Mead Books, Isle of Wight 131
Daly (Peter M.), Hampshire 124
Dancing Goat Bookshop (The), Norfolk 188
Demar Books (Grant), Kent 138
Family Favourites (Books), East Yorkshire 104
Goodyer (Nicholas), London (N) 154
Ian Johnson Natural History Books,
Buckinghamshire 63
Isabelline Books, Cornwall 74
Kellow Books, Oxfordshire 204
Kerr (Norman), Cumbria 78
Lion Fine Arts and Books, Wales 287
Mayhew (Veronica), Berkshire 58
McEwan Fine Books, Scotland 266
Mobbs (A.J.), West Midlands 240
Morgan (D. & D.H.W.), Devon 89
Moss Books, London (NW) 158
Old Bookshop (The), Somerset 216
Old Gallery Bookshop (The), Kent 136
On the Wild Side, Worcestershire 255
Shearwater Bed & Books (formerly John Lumby
Nat. History Bks), Northumberland 200
Sue Lowell Natural History Books, London (W) 175
Thurston (Barry), Scotland 273
Wheatsheaf Antiques, Cheshire 69
Woodside Books, Kent 133
Wyseby House Books, Berkshire 57

OSTEOPATHY

Phelps (Michael), West Sussex 242

OTTOMAN EMPIRE

Adab Books, Cambridgeshire 64
Bosphorus Books, London (WC) 176
Loman, Oriental Books & Manuscripts (David),
London (SW) 165

OXFORD MOVEMENT

Carter, (Brian), Oxfordshire 205

PACIFISM

Book Basket, London, Outer 182
Cyclamen Books, Leicestershire 143
Ice House Books 143
Left on The Shelf, London (E) 151
Liebreich Antique Maps & Prints (Kitty),
London (W) 173
Moss Books, London (NW) 158
Spurrier (Nick), Kent 136
Woburn Books, London (N) 156
Yesterday's Books, Dorset 91

PAGANISM

Chthonios Books, East Sussex 100
Inner Bookshop (The), Oxfordshire 207
Magis Books, Leicestershire 144
Occultique, Northamptonshire 198
Starlord Books, Cheshire 70

PAINTING

Art Reference Books, Hampshire 123
Butts Books (Mary), Berkshire 58
Ice House Books 143
Heneage Art Books (Thomas), London (SW).... 164
Modern Firsts Etc., Lancashire 140
Shipley Specialist Art Booksellers, London (WC) 178

PALAEOGRAPHY

Brinded (Scott), Kent 136
Island Books, Devon 86
Island Books, Devon 84
Leeds Bookseller, West Yorkshire 247
McKay Rare Books (Barry), Cumbria 77
Taylor & Son (Peter), Hertfordshire 130

PALAEONTOLOGY

Browne (A.), Cheshire 69
Charmouth Bookstore, Dorset 91
Henly (John), West Sussex 244
Sykes (Graham), West Yorkshire 248

PALMISTRY & FORTUNE TELLING

Alpha Books, London (N) 153
Inner Bookshop (The), Oxfordshire 207
Occultique, Northamptonshire 198
Starlord Books, Cheshire 70

PAPERMAKING

Brinded (Scott), Kent 136
Coupland (Terry W.), Staffordshire 222
Cox Old & Rare Books (Claude), Suffolk 226
Duck (William), East Sussex 98
Forest Books, Lincolnshire 147
McKay Rare Books (Barry), Cumbria 77
Moss Antiquarian Books (V.J.), Lancashire 142
O'Connor Fine Books, Lancashire 142
Sabin (Printed Works) (P.R. & V.), Kent 133
Shipley Specialist Art Booksellers, London (WC) 178
Wakeman Books (Frances), Nottinghamshire ... 202

PARAPSYCHOLOGY

Atlantis Bookshop, London (WC) 176
Far Horizons Books, Dorset 91
Greensleeves, Oxfordshire 204
Grieveson (A.), Cheshire 69
Inner Bookshop (The), Oxfordshire 207
Occultique, Northamptonshire 198
Starlord Books, Cheshire 70

PARISH REGISTERS

Delph Books, Greater Manchester 116
Island Books, Devon 84
Stanhope Bibliophiles, London (N) 155
Taylor & Son (Peter), Hertfordshire 130
Townsend (John), Berkshire 59
Turton (John), Durham 97

PERFORMING ARTS

Books & Bygones (Pam Taylor), West Midlands 240
Books for Collectors, Gloucestershire 112
Booth Books, Wales 286
Catalyst Books, Surrey 232
Cover to Cover, Merseyside 186
DaSilva Puppet Books, Oxfordshire 204
Davis (Peter), Kent 136
Dolphin Books, Suffolk 224
Drummond Pleasures of Past Times (David),
  London (WC) 176
Fitzsimons (Anne), Cumbria 77
Franks Booksellers, Greater Manchester 117
Gate Memorabilia, London (N) 153
Gloucester Road Bookshop, London (SW) 164
Ice House Books 143
Inprint, Gloucestershire 114
Jarndyce Antiquarian Booksellers,
  London (WC) 177
Kaye - Bookseller (Terence), London (NW) 158
Kent T. G., Surrey 230
LSA Books, Warwickshire 236
Malvern Bookshop (The), Worcestershire 254
McGee (Terence J.), London, Outer 181
Paramor (C.D.), Suffolk 227
Price (John), London (N) 155
Quadrille at Delehar, London (W) 174
Reads, Dorset 94
Sanderson (Edward), Berkshire 58
Singleton, (John), London (N) 155
Spranger (Anthony), Wiltshire 251
Stage Door Prints, London (WC) 178
Theatreshire Books, N Yorks 192
Till's Bookshop, Scotland 270
Troath Books (Brian), London (E) 151
Unsworths Booksellers Ltd., London (WC) 178
Willmott Bookseller (Nicholas), Wales 280
Wood (Peter), Cambridgeshire 66

PERIODICALS & MAGAZINES

Aberdeen Rare Books & Caledonian Books,
  Scotland 267
Anglo-American Rare Books, Surrey 232
Art Reference Books, Hampshire 123
Black Cat Books, Norfolk 188
Black Cat Bookshop, Leicestershire 143
Book Basket, London, Outer 182
Books & Things, London (W) 169
Border Bookshop (The), West Yorkshire 248
Bracton Books, Cambridgeshire 64
Downie Fine Books Ltd., (Robert), Shropshire . 213
Eggeling Books (John), West Yorkshire 248
Franks Booksellers, Greater Manchester 117
Gardner & Co., (Walter H.), London (N) 153
Ice House Books 143
Lake (Fred), Surrey 234
Langmaid (Kenneth), Cornwall 76
Morgan (D. & D.H.W.), Devon 89
Mr. Pickwick of Towcester, Northamptonshire ... 199
Noble (Malcolm & Christine), Leicestershire 145
NostalGia Publications Ltd., N Yorks 196
Nostalgia Unlimited, Merseyside 185
Omniphil Prints, Buckinghamshire 62
Palladour Books, Hampshire 124
Paper Pleasures, Somerset 217
Phenotype Books, Cumbria 79
Riderless Horse Books, Norfolk 187
Temple (Robert), London (N) 155
Tennis Collectables, Cheshire 69
Tiger Books, Kent 134
Tilleys Vintage Magazine Shop,
  South Yorkshire 220
Tilleys Vintage Magazine Shop, Derbyshire 81
Troath Books (Brian), London (E) 151
Updike Rare Books (John), Scotland 270
Williams (Bookdealer), (Richard), Lincolnshire ... 149
Williams Rare Books (Nigel), London (WC) 179

PHARMACY/PHARMACOLOGY

Alba Books, Scotland 267
Ice House Books 143
Phelps (Michael), West Sussex 242
Smith (David & Lynn), London, Outer 182
White (David), Cambridgeshire 66

PHILATELY

Clark (Nigel A.), London (SE) 160
DoublePlusBooks, Cambridgeshire 68
Frost (Richard), Hertfordshire 128
Ice House Books 143
Pennymead Books, N Yorks 193
Postings, Surrey 233
Treasure Island (The), Greater Manchester 118

PHILOLOGY

Nineteenth Century Books, Oxfordshire 209
Olynthiacs, Shropshire 212
Plurabelle Books, Cambridgeshire 65
Prospect House Books, Northern Ireland 260
Seydi Rare Books (Sevin), London (NW) 159
Thomson (Karen), Scotland 271

PHILOSOPHY

Arcadia, Shropshire 212
Armchair Books, Scotland 268
Batstone Books, Wiltshire 250

Bell (Peter), Scotland................................. 269
Books, Wales... 282
Bookshop (The), Republic Of Ireland............ 276
Booth Books, Wales.................................. 286
Caledonia Books, Scotland........................ 271
Camden Books, Somerset 214
Carter, (Brian), Oxfordshire 205
Chesters (G. & J.), Staffordshire 223
Chthonios Books, East Sussex.................... 100
Downie Fine Books Ltd., (Robert),
 Shropshire.. 213
Drury Rare Books (John), Essex.................. 109
Economia Books, Wales............................. 281
Edwards in Hay–on–Wye (Francis), Wales....... 286
Elephant Books, West Yorkshire 247
Firth (Bijou Books & Photography)
 (Maureen), South Yorkshire 221
Fisher & Sperr, London (N) 153
Game Advice, Oxfordshire......................... 207
Gloucester Road Bookshop, London (SW) 164
Gorton Booksearch (John), East Sussex 103
Graduate Books, Worcestershire 256
Greyfriars Books, Essex 107
Grieveson (A.), Cheshire 69
Handsworth Books, Essex.......................... 110
Herb Tandree Philosophy Books, Bristol......... 61
Howes Bookshop, East Sussex 101
Hughes Rare Books (Spike), Scotland 261
Humanist Book Services, Cornwall............... 73
Ice House Books....................................... 143
Jericho Books, Oxfordshire 208
Kenny's Bookshops and Art Galleries Ltd,
 Republic Of Ireland 278
Killeen (John), N Yorks 193
Kyrios Books, Nottinghamshire.................... 202
Lee Rare Books (Rachel), Bristol 61
Lloyd (D. Ieuan), Wales............................. 289
Lund Theological Books, Cambridgeshire........ 65
Magis Books, Leicestershire........................ 144
Meinertzhagen (Nicholas), London (SW)......... 165
Moseley Books, West Midlands................... 238
Mundy (David), Buckinghamshire................. 62
Oblong Books, N Yorks.............................. 197
Occultique, Northamptonshire 198
O'Donoghue Books, London (SW)................ 165
Philologus–Fine & Rare Books, London (SW) .. 166
Plurabelle Books, Cambridgeshire 65
Price (John), London (N) 155
Prospect House Books, Northern Ireland 260
Quaritch Ltd., (Bernard), London (W)............ 174
Riley–Smith (Hamish), Norfolk 190
Roland Books, Kent................................... 137
Rowan (P. & B.), Northern Ireland 259
Savery Books, East Sussex 99
Schulz–Falster Rare Books (Susanne),
 London (N).. 155
Spurrier (Nick), Kent 136
Staniland (Booksellers), Lincolnshire 150
Strauss (David), Lincolnshire....................... 147
Till's Bookshop, Scotland 270
Unsworths Booksellers Ltd., London (WC)...... 178
Walden Books, London (NW)...................... 159
Waterfield's, Oxfordshire 209
Watson (Kelvin), West Midlands 239
Westwood Books (Mark), Wales.................. 287

Wiend Books & Collectables,
 Greater Manchester 119
Woburn Books, London (N)........................ 156
Worcester Rare Books, Worcestershire 256
Yarwood Rare Books (Edward), Cheshire 116

PHOTOGRAPHY

Abacus Gallery / The Village Bookshop,
 Staffordshire... 223
Allsworth Rare Books Ltd., London (SW)....... 163
Amwell Book Company (The), London (EC).... 152
Ars Artis, Oxfordshire 206
Biblion, London (W).................................. 169
Blaenavon Books, Wales 289
Books, Wales... 282
Books & Things, London (W)...................... 169
Books for Collectors, Gloucestershire............ 112
Books Only, Suffolk.................................. 226
Booth Books, Wales.................................. 286
Brighton Books, East Sussex 98
Broadleaf Books, Wales 290
Butcher (Pablo), Oxfordshire 205
Farahar & Dupré (Clive & Sophie),
 Wiltshire... 250
Finch Rare Books Ltd. (Simon), London (W)... 172
fineart-photographer, Herefordshire............... 127
Firth (Bijou Books & Photography) (Maureen),
 South Yorkshire 221
Holleyman (J.F.), East Sussex...................... 101
Jacobson (Ken & Jenny), Essex 107
Keswick Bookshop, Cumbria....................... 78
Manheim (Carol), London (W) 173
Newcastle Bookshop, Northumberland 200
O'Brien Books & Photo Gallery, Republic Of
 Ireland... 279
Orlando Booksellers, Lincolnshire 148
Paper Pleasures, Somerset.......................... 217
Photo Books International, London (WC) 178
Photographery at Soldridge Books, Hampshire . 120
Pollak (P.M.), Devon 87
Pratt (H.G.), Suffolk 228
Prescott - The Bookseller (John), London, Outer 184
Quaritch Ltd., (Bernard), London (W)............ 174
Rayner (Hugh Ashley), Somerset 215
Red Snapper Books, London (WC) 178
Rhodes, Bookseller (Peter), Hampshire 124
Shipley Specialist Art Booksellers, London (WC) 178
Sykes (Graham), West Yorkshire 248
Treasure Island (The), Greater Manchester 118
Woburn Books, London (N)........................ 156
Wood (Peter), Cambridgeshire 66
YSF Books, South Yorkshire........................ 221

PHRENOLOGY

Austwick Hall Books, N Yorks 141
Phelps (Michael), West Sussex..................... 242

PHYSICAL CULTURE

Archways Sports Books, Scotland 268
Collectables (W.H.), London (W).................. 172
Combat Arts Archive, Durham 96
Webster (D.), Scotland............................... 272

SPECIALITY INDEX

PHYSICS

Camden Books, Somerset 214
DoublePlusBooks, Cambridgeshire 68
Eagle Bookshop (The), Bedfordshire 55
Moorside Books, Lancashire......................... 141
Phelps (Michael), West Sussex...................... 242
Wayside Books and Cards, Oxfordshire 205
Weiner (Graham), London (N)...................... 156

PLANT HUNTING

Barnhill Books, Scotland............................. 272
Blest (Peter), Kent..................................... 136
Buxton Books (Anna), Scotland 269
Calendula Horticultural Books, East Sussex 100
Hunter and Krageloh, Derbyshire 82
Merritt (Valerie), Gloucestershire 111
On the Wild Side, Worcestershire................... 255
Page (David), Scotland 270
Park (Mike), London, Outer......................... 183
Shearwater Bed & Books (formerly John Lumby
  Nat. History Bks), Northumberland 200
Traveller's Bookshelf (The), Somerset............. 215

PLAYS

Bookroom (The), Surrey 233
Ice House Books....................................... 143
Jarndyce Antiquarian Booksellers,
  London (WC) 177
McKelvie (Ian), London (N)......................... 154
Oblong Books, N Yorks.............................. 197
Swan Bookshop (The), Devon....................... 84
Willmott Bookseller (Nicholas), Wales............. 280

POETRY

Abacus Gallery / The Village Bookshop,
  Staffordshire... 223
Aberdeen Rare Books & Caledonian Books,
  Scotland.. 267
Addyman Books, Wales 285
Anderson Slater Antiques, N Yorks................ 195
Anglo-American Rare Books, Surrey............... 232
Anwoth Books, Scotland............................. 263
Applin (Malcolm), Berkshire 57
Arcadia, Shropshire 212
Arden Books & Cosmographia, Warwickshire... 236
Ash Rare Books, London (EC) 152
Ashburton Books, Devon 83
babelog.books, Herefordshire........................ 126
Bayntun (George), Somerset........................ 214
Beck Head Books, Cumbria 78
Beware of The Leopard Books, Bristol 60
Bookroom (The), Surrey 233
Books, Wales... 282
Books & Bygones, Berkshire........................ 58
Books & Bygones (Pam Taylor), West Midlands 240
Bookshop (The), Cambridgeshire 64
Bookstand, Dorset..................................... 93
Book–Worm International, Essex................... 107
Bracton Books, Cambridgeshire..................... 64
Brighton Books, East Sussex 98
Buchan Collectibles, Scotland 265
Budd (Richard), Somerset........................... 217

Catalyst Books, Surrey 232
Cecil Books, Surrey 231
Chalk (Old & Out of Print Books)
  (Christine M.), West Midlands 238
Chatterton's Books, Wales........................... 290
Classic Bindings, London (SW) 163
Clements (R.W.), London, Outer 181
Coracle Books, West Yorkshire..................... 247
Courtyard Books, Herefordshire.................... 127
Cox Rare Books (Charles), Cornwall 74
Criterion Books, London, Outer.................... 182
Dancing Goat Bookshop (The), Norfolk 188
Eastcote Bookshop (The), London, Outer........ 183
Ellwood Editions, Hampshire....................... 123
Gloucester Road Bookshop, London (SW) 164
Golden Hind Bookshop (The), Kent 134
Green (Paul), Cambridgeshire 68
Greyfriars Books, Essex 107
Hellenic Bookservices, London (NW)............. 158
Hennessey Bookseller (Ray), East Sussex......... 100
Ice House Books....................................... 143
Jade Mountain, Hampshire 123
Jiri Books, Northern Ireland........................ 259
Kendall–Carpenter (Tim), Greater Manchester.. 117
Kingsgate Books & Prints, Hampshire 125
Little Bookshop (The), Greater Manchester 117
Main Point Books, Scotland......................... 269
Malvern Bookshop (The), Worcestershire 254
McCann (Joe), Oxfordshire 208
McCrone (Audrey), Scotland 272
McKelvie (Ian), London (N)......................... 154
Mercat Books, Scotland............................... 267
Modlock (Lilian), Dorset............................. 92
Moreton Books, Devon............................... 86
Naughton Booksellers, Republic Of Ireland...... 277
Nineteenth Century Books, Oxfordshire.......... 209
Nova Foresta Books, Hampshire 121
Oblong Books, N Yorks.............................. 197
Old Storytellers Bookshop (The), Scotland....... 261
Orangeberry Books, Oxfordshire................... 206
Orlando Booksellers, Lincolnshire 148
Palladour Books, Hampshire 124
Peakirk Books, Cambridgeshire 68
Peter Lyons Books, Gloucestershire 112
Photography at Soldridge Books, Hampshire . 120
Prescott - The Bookseller (John), London, Outer 184
Priory Books, Worcestershire....................... 256
Prospect House Books, Northern Ireland 260
Quest Booksearch, Cambridgeshire................ 65
Richmond Books, N Yorks.......................... 194
Riderless Horse Books, Norfolk 187
Rosemary Books, Merseyside....................... 186
Roundstone Books, Lancashire 141
Russell Books, Somerset.............................. 218
Singleton, (John), London (N) 155
Smith Books (Keith), Herefordshire............... 127
Staniland (Booksellers), Lincolnshire 150
Stanton, (P. & K.), Cornwall 75
Stevens (Joan), Cambridgeshire 66
Stone, (G.& R.), Scotland........................... 261
Sturford Books, Wiltshire 252
Swan Bookshop (The), Devon....................... 84
Temple (Robert), London (N)...................... 155
Thomas (Books) (Leona), Cheshire................ 71
Tiffin (Tony and Gill), Durham 96

Tindley & Chapman, London (WC) 178
Troath Books (Brian), London (E) 151
Updike Rare Books (John), Scotland 270
Venables (Morris & Juliet), Bristol 61
Watson (Kelvin), West Midlands 239
Willmott Bookseller (Nicholas), Wales 280
Woburn Books, London (N) 156
Woodbine Books, West Yorkshire 245

POLICE FORCE HISTORIES
Bolland Books (Leslie H.), Bedfordshire 55
Crimes Ink, London (E) 151
Delph Books, Greater Manchester 116
Lawful Occasions, Essex 106
Premier Books & Prints, Lincolnshire 146

POLITICS
Abbey Bookshop, Hampshire 122
Ashfield Books and Records, Nottinghamshire .. 203
Barn Books, Buckinghamshire 62
Beware of The Leopard Books, Bristol 60
Books, Wales 282
Books Only, Suffolk 226
Booth Books, Wales 286
Bradley–Cox (Mary), Dorset 90
Brockwells Bookshop, London (SE) 160
Burgess Booksellers, (J. & J.), Cambridgeshire .. 64
Chatterton's Books, Wales 290
Chesters (G. & J.), Staffordshire 223
Croft Selections, Lincolnshire 148
Cronin (Jim), Wales 280
Dolphin Books, Suffolk 224
Drury Rare Books (John), Essex 109
Economia Books, Wales 281
Hab Books, London (W) 173
Ice House Books 143
Invisible Books, East Sussex 99
Jarndyce Antiquarian Booksellers,
 London (WC) 177
Jericho Books, Oxfordshire 208
Joppa Books Ltd., Surrey 230
Keel Row Books, Tyne & Wear 235
Kelsall (George), Greater Manchester 117
Killeen (John), N Yorks 193
Langmaid (Kenneth), Cornwall 76
Malmo Books, Hampshire 121
Modern Welsh Publications Ltd., Merseyside.... 185
Moseley Books, West Midlands 238
Noel and Holland Books, Republic Of Ireland.. 278
Northern Herald Books, West Yorkshire 245
O'Donoghue Books, London (SW) 165
Politico's, London (SW) 166
Premier Books & Prints, Lincolnshire 146
Red Star Books, Hertfordshire 128
Saunders (Tom), Wales 280
Spurrier (Nick), Kent 136
Stevens (Joan), Cambridgeshire 66
Swan Bookshop (The), Devon 84
Till's Bookshop, Scotland 270
Visser Books (de), Cambridgeshire 66
Wiend Books & Collectables,
 Greater Manchester 119
Woburn Books, London (N) 156

POP-UP, 3D, CUT OUT & MOVABLE
Bookmark (Children's Books), Wiltshire 252
Castleton (Pat), Kent 135
Kernaghans, Merseyside 186

POULTRY
Blest (Peter), Kent 136

PRAYER BOOKS
Barbican Bookshop, N Yorks 196
Beckham Books, Suffolk 228
Kyrios Books, Nottinghamshire 202
Lund Theological Books, Cambridgeshire 65
Oasis Booksearch, Cambridgeshire 68

PRECIOUS METALS - SILVER
Art Reference Books, Hampshire 123
Trinders' Fine Tools, Suffolk 225

PRE-RAPHAELITE
Bookstack & D.J. Creece (Bookbinder),
 Shropshire 211

PRINTING
Andron (G.W.), London (N) 153
Ballantyne–Way (Roger), Suffolk 228
Brinded (Scott), Kent 136
Cobnar Books, Kent 136
Coupland (Terry W.), Staffordshire 222
Cox Old & Rare Books (Claude), Suffolk 226
Devitt Books (Nial), Warwickshire 236
Finch Rare Books Ltd. (Simon), London (W)... 172
Forest Books, Lincolnshire 147
Illustrated Book (The), London (SW) 165
K. Books, East Yorkshire 104
McKay Rare Books (Barry), Cumbria 77
Moss Antiquarian Books (V.J.), Lancashire 142
O'Connor Fine Books, Lancashire 142
Sabin (Printed Works) (P.R. & V.), Kent 133
Sanderson (Edward), Berkshire 58
Stewart (Andrew), Cornwall 75
Wakeman Books (Frances), Nottinghamshire ... 202

PRIVATE PRESS
Anticus, Warwickshire 237
Artco, Nottinghamshire 202
Askew Books (Vernon), Wiltshire 250
Atticus Books, Essex 109
Ballantyne–Way (Roger), Suffolk 228
Barlow (Vincent G.), Hampshire 123
Bennetts Books, East Sussex 101
Bertram Rota Ltd., London (WC) 176
Biblion, London (W) 169
Books & Things, London (W) 169
Bookstand, Dorset 93
Broadhurst of Southport Ltd., Merseyside 186
Countrymans Gallery (The), Leicestershire 143
Coupland (Terry W.), Staffordshire 222
Cox Old & Rare Books (Claude), Suffolk 226
Dean Illustrated Books (Myra), Wales 284

SPECIALITY INDEX

Devitt Books (Nial), Warwickshire 236
Doughty Fine Books (Robin), West Midlands... 238
Eastcote Bookshop (The), London, Outer 183
ECR Books, Dorset 93
Ellis, Bookseller (Peter), London (SE) 160
Emjay Books, Surrey 231
English (Toby), Oxfordshire 209
Fine Irish Books, Republic Of Ireland 276
Firth (Bijou Books & Photography) (Maureen),
  South Yorkshire 221
Franks Booksellers, Greater Manchester 117
Grant (Gerald S.), Cheshire 69
Hanborough Books, Oxfordshire 207
Heritage, West Midlands 238
Hodgkins and Company Limited (Ian),
  Gloucestershire 114
Illustrated Book (The), London (SW) 165
Island Books, Devon 86
Marks Limited (Barrie), London (N) 154
McCann (Joe), Oxfordshire 208
Mills Rare Books (Adam), Cambridgeshire 65
O'Connor Fine Books, Lancashire 142
Parrott Books, Oxfordshire 209
Sabin (Printed Works) (P.R. & V.), Kent 133
Sansovino Books, West Sussex 244
Sotheran Limited (Henry), London (W) 175
Stothert Old Books, Cheshire 69
Taylor Rare Books (Michael), Norfolk 187
Temple (Robert), London (N) 155
Thorp (Thomas), Hertfordshire 129
Troath Books (Brian), London (E) 151
Updike Rare Books (John), Scotland 270
Waddington Books & Prints (Geraldine),
  Northamptonshire 198
Wakeman Books (Frances), Nottinghamshire ... 202
Way (R.E. & G.B.), Suffolk 227
Wheen O'Blethers Bookshop, Scotland 271
Williams Rare Books (Nigel), London (WC) 179
Woodbine Books, West Yorkshire 245

PROOF COPIES

Bookstop UK, Lancashire 142
Booth (Booksearch Service), (Geoff), Cheshire .. 69
Brunner Books, Cambridgeshire 68
Dawson (Modern First Editions), (Philip),
  London, Outer 183
Firsts in Print, Isle of Wight 131
Kendall–Carpenter (Tim), Greater Manchester.. 117
McCann (Joe), Oxfordshire 208
McKelvie (Ian), London (N) 154
Temple (Robert), London (N) 155
Williams Rare Books (Nigel), London (WC) 179

PSYCHIC

Alpha Books, London (N) 153
Book Basket, London, Outer 182
Dawlish Books, Devon 84
Facet Books, Dorset 90
Far Horizons Books, Dorset 91
Fine Books Oriental Ltd., London (WC) 177
Gilbert (R.A.), Bristol 61
Greensleeves, Oxfordshire 204
Grieveson (A.), Cheshire 69

Inner Bookshop (The), Oxfordshire 207
Magis Books, Leicestershire 144
Occultique, Northamptonshire 198
Wizard Books, Cambridgeshire 68

PSYCHOANALYSIS

Alba Books, Scotland 267
Delectus Books, London (WC) 176
Game Advice, Oxfordshire 207
Gorton Booksearch (John), East Sussex 103
Inner Bookshop (The), Oxfordshire 207
Oast Books, Kent 134
Outcast Books, Wales 287

PSYCHOLOGY/PSYCHIATRY

Alba Books, Scotland 267
Ashfield Books and Records, Nottinghamshire.. 203
Books & Bygones, Berkshire 58
Bracton Books, Cambridgeshire 64
Chesters (G. & J.), Staffordshire 223
Delectus Books, London (WC) 176
Elephant Books, West Yorkshire 247
Game Advice, Oxfordshire 207
Graduate Books, Worcestershire 256
Greensleeves, Oxfordshire 204
Greyfriars Books, Essex 107
Ice House Books 143
Jade Mountain, Hampshire 123
Mair Wilkes Books, Scotland 265
Mundy (David), Buckinghamshire 62
Oast Books, Kent 134
Occultique, Northamptonshire 198
O'Donoghue Books, London (SW) 165
Outcast Books, Wales 287
Phelps (Michael), West Sussex 242
Reading Lasses, Scotland 264
Savery Books, East Sussex 99
Spurrier (Nick), Kent 136
Unsworths Booksellers Ltd., London (WC) 178
Victoria Bookshop (The), Devon 83
Westwood Books (Mark), Wales 287
Wizard Books, Cambridgeshire 68

PSYCHOTHERAPY

Alba Books, Scotland 267
Bradley–Cox (Mary), Dorset 90
Greensleeves, Oxfordshire 204
Ice House Books 143
Inner Bookshop (The), Oxfordshire 207
Mindreaders Books, Kent 135
Mundy (David), Buckinghamshire 62
Oast Books, Kent 134
Outcast Books, Wales 287

PUBLIC HOUSES

Lucas (Richard), London (NW) 158
Thorne (John), Essex 107
Woodlands Books, West Yorkshire 248

PUBLIC SCHOOLS

Eton Antique Bookshop, Berkshire 59

Kirkpatrick (Robert J.), London (W) 173
Wise (Derek), East Sussex........................... 102

PUBLISHERS
- GENERAL
Dinnages Transport Publishing, East Sussex..... 98
Harper, Books (Berry), East Sussex 100
Ice House Books....................................... 143
Poole (William), London (W)........................ 174
Temple (Robert), London (N)....................... 155
Zardoz Books, Wiltshire............................. 253

- BATSFORD
Book Corner, Scotland 263
Hennessey Bookseller (Ray), East Sussex......... 100
Island Books, Devon................................... 84
Trinders' Fine Tools, Suffolk 225

- BLACK, A. & C.
Bolton Books, Hampshire........................... 120
Bowden Books, Leicestershire 144
Missing Books, Essex 108

- BLACKIE
Bookmark (Children's Books), Wiltshire 252

- CHAMBERS
Premier Books & Prints, Lincolnshire............. 146

- CURWEN PRESS
Illustrated Book (The), London (SW)............. 165

- DAVID & CHARLES
Roadmaster Books, Kent............................ 134

- EDINBURGH UNIVERSITY PRESS
Bell (Peter), Scotland................................ 269

- FOULIS, T.N.
Slavin Rare and Collectable Books (Derek),
  Warwickshire.. 237

- GHOST STORY PRESS
Fantastic Literature, Essex 109

- GUINNESS PUBLISHING LTD.
Premier Books & Prints, Lincolnshire............. 146

- HOGARTH PRESS
Orlando Booksellers, Lincolnshire 148

- JOSEPH LTD., MICHAEL
Archivist (The), Devon 88

- LADYBIRD BOOKS
Book Basket, London, Outer 182
Castleton (Pat), Kent................................. 135
Eden Books, Dorset................................... 92
Harper, Books (Berry), East Sussex 100
Kineton Nooks, Warwickshire 236

- OAKWOOD PRESS
Coulthurst (Richard), Greater Manchester 118

- OXFORD UNIVERSITY PRESS
BOOKS4U, Wales.................................... 282

- PAN
Book Basket, London, Outer 182
Heckmondwike Book Shop, West Yorkshire 235
Orlando Booksellers, Lincolnshire 148

- PELICAN
Book Basket, London, Outer 182
Willmott Bookseller (Nicholas), Wales........... 280

- PENGUIN
Armstrongs Books & Collectables,
  West Midlands 239
Black Cat Bookshop, Leicestershire 143
Book Basket, London, Outer 182
Books at the Warehouse, N Yorks 193
Chiltern Books, London (W) 172
Heckmondwike Book Shop, West Yorkshire 235
Illustrated Book (The), London (SW)............. 165
Marine Workshop Bookshop, Dorset............. 92
Orlando Booksellers, Lincolnshire 148
Peakirk Books, Cambridgeshire 68
Price (R.W.), Nottinghamshire 202
Thornton (Grahame), Dorset....................... 94
Tony Skelton, Kent 138
Willmott Bookseller (Nicholas), Wales........... 280

- PUFFIN
Castleton (Pat), Kent................................. 135
Heckmondwike Book Shop, West Yorkshire 235
Willmott Bookseller (Nicholas), Wales........... 280

- ROUNDWOOD PRESS
Anticus, Warwickshire 237

- STUDIO, THE
Books & Things, London (W)...................... 169

- THAMES & HUDSON
Martin - Bookseller (Colin), East Yorkshire 105

- WARNES
Hine (Anne), Somerset.............................. 216
Southwold Antiques Centre, Suffolk 228

SPECIALITY INDEX

PUBLISHING
Coupland (Terry W.), Staffordshire 222
Ford (Richard), London (W) 172
McKay Rare Books (Barry), Cumbria 77
Moss Antiquarian Books (V.J.), Lancashire 142
O'Connor Fine Books, Lancashire 142
Roadmaster Books, Kent 134
Smith Books, (Sally), Suffolk 225
Wakeman Books (Frances), Nottinghamshire ... 202

PULPS
Askew Books (Vernon), Wiltshire 250
Cowley, Bookdealer (K.W.), Somerset 215
Delectus Books, London (WC) 176

PUPPETS & MARIONETTES
DaSilva Puppet Books, Oxfordshire 204
Davis (Peter), Kent 136
Fitzsimons (Anne), Cumbria 77
Wood (Peter), Cambridgeshire 66

PUZZLES
Ænigma Designs (Books), Devon 85
Wayfarer Books, Cornwall 75

RADICAL ISSUES
Ice House Books 143
Kenny's Bookshops and Art Galleries Ltd,
  Republic Of Ireland 278
Left on The Shelf, London (E) 151
Pioneer Books, Hampshire 120
Red Star Books, Hertfordshire 128
Spurrier (Nick), Kent 136
Tobo Books, Hampshire 122

RADIO/WIRELESS
Book Basket, London, Outer 182
Cover to Cover, Merseyside 186
Kelly Books, Devon 88
Premier Books & Prints, Lincolnshire 146

RAILWAYS
Abacus Gallery / The Village Bookshop,
  Staffordshire 223
Anvil Books, West Midlands 239
Arden Books & Cosmographia, Warwickshire... 236
Baker (Gerald), Bristol 60
Baldwin (M. & M.), Shropshire 212
Barbican Bookshop, N Yorks 196
Batterdale Books, N Yorks 195
Bird Books (Nigel), Wales 281
Black Five Books, Shropshire 213
Book Corner, Scotland 263
Book House (The), Cumbria 78
Books & Bygones, Berkshire 58
Books Afloat, Dorset 95
Books Bought & Sold, Surrey 231
Booth Books, Wales 286
Bott, (Bookdealers) Ltd., (Martin), Greater
  Manchester 116
Brewin Books Ltd., Warwickshire 237
Browser's Bookshop, Cornwall 74
Chichester Bookshop (The), West Sussex 241
Classic Crime Collections, Greater Manchester.. 117
Cobweb Books, N Yorks 194
Collectables (W.H.), London (W) 172
Collectors Corner, Wiltshire 252
Corfe Books, Surrey 231
Coulthurst (Richard), Greater Manchester 118
Cox (Geoff), Devon 89
Crosby Nethercott Books, London, Outer 180
Dinnages Transport Publishing, East Sussex 98
Duck (William), East Sussex 98
Eastcote Bookshop (The), London, Outer 183
Elton Engineering Books, London (W) 172
Falconwood Transport & Military Bookshop,
  London, Outer 184
Gibbard (A. & T.), East Sussex 100
Hairpin Books, Gloucestershire 113
Harlequin Books, Bristol 61
Ice House Books 143
Island Books, Devon 84, 86
Jade Mountain, Hampshire 123
Jones (Barry), West Sussex 242
Jones Books (Russell), Berkshire 57
Keegan's Bookshop, Berkshire 58
Keel Row Books, Tyne & Wear 235
Kerr (Norman), Cumbria 78
Maddison (J.K.), West Midlands 238
Moreton Books, Devon 86
Nebulous Books, Hampshire 120
Nevis Railway Books, Oxfordshire 206
Nevis Railway Bookshops (The Antique & Book
  Collector), Wiltshire 251
Newband (D.M.), Wales 288
Oblong Books, N Yorks 197
Old Gallery Bookshop (The), Kent 136
Park Gallery & Bookshop (The),
  Northamptonshire 199
Patterson Liddle, Somerset 214
Peakirk Books, Cambridgeshire 68
Postings, Surrey 233
Priory Books, Worcestershire 256
Quayside Bookshop, Devon 88
Railway Book and Magazine Search, Berkshire. 58
Railway Shop (The), Wales 290
Rainger Books (Michael), Wales 285
Reads, Dorset 94
Riverside Bookshop (The), Cumbria 78
Roadmaster Books, Kent 134
Rochdale Book Company, Greater Manchester . 118
Roland Books, Kent 137
Sax Books, Suffolk 228
Sedgeberrow Books & Framing, Worcestershire. 255
Simon Lewis Transport Books, Gloucestershire . 112
Skyrack Books, West Yorkshire 246
Spread Eagle Bookshop, London (SE) 162
Stanhope Bibliophiles, London (N) 155
Stella Books, Wales 284
Swan Bookshop (The), Devon 84
Tozer Railway Books (Nick), West Yorkshire... 246
Treasure Island (The), Greater Manchester 118
Trinders' Fine Tools, Suffolk 225
Wiend Books & Collectables,
  Greater Manchester 119

SPECIALITY INDEX

Wilson Books (Henry), Cheshire 71
Yesteryear Railwayana, Kent 137
Yewtree Books, Cumbria 78

REFERENCE

Art Reference Books, Hampshire 123
Bannister (David), Gloucestershire 111
Books, Wales 282
Books for Writers, Wales 283
Downie Fine Books Ltd., (Robert), Shropshire . 213
Emjay Books, Surrey 231
Gardner & Co., (Walter H.), London (N) 153
Ice House Books 143
Malmo Books, Hampshire 121
Potter Limited (Jonathan), London (W) 174
R. & A. Books, East Sussex 100
Shacklock Books (David), Suffolk 226
Sparkes (Books) (Ray), Staffordshire 223
Wiend Books & Collectables,
    Greater Manchester 119

RELIGION
- GENERAL

Armchair Books, Scotland 268
Arundel Bookshop, West Sussex 241
Bardsley's Books, Suffolk 225
Batstone Books, Wiltshire 250
Beckham Books, Suffolk 228
Beware of The Leopard Books, Bristol 60
Blythswood Bookshop, Scotland 268
Books, Wales 282
Books & Bygones, Berkshire 58
Books (For All), N Yorks 192
Broadwater Books, Hampshire 124
Butler Books, Dorset 90
Carta Regis, Wales 288
Cavan Book Centre, Republic Of Ireland 275
Clegg (David), Staffordshire 222
Collectable Books, London (SE) 160
Downie Fine Books Ltd., (Robert), Shropshire . 213
Fin Rare Books, Shropshire 213
G C Books, Scotland 264
Gage Postal Books, Essex 109
Gilbert (R.A.), Bristol 61
Golden Age Books, Worcestershire 255
Handsworth Books, Essex 110
Herb Tandree Philosophy Books, Bristol 61
Ice House Books 143
Jade Mountain, Hampshire 123
Jericho Books, Oxfordshire 208
Kenny's Bookshops and Art Galleries Ltd,
    Republic Of Ireland 278
Kyrios Books, Nottinghamshire 202
Langmaid (Kenneth), Cornwall 76
Lewis (J.T. & P.), Cornwall 74
Little Bookshop (The), Greater Manchester 117
Moss Books, London (NW) 158
Oblong Books, N Yorks 197
Premier Books & Prints, Lincolnshire 146
Prospect House Books, Northern Ireland 260
Reading Lasses, Scotland 264
Russell Books, Somerset 218
St Philip's Books, Oxfordshire 208
Salsus Books, Worcestershire 255

Saunders (Tom), Wales 280
Sax Books, Suffolk 228
Tobo Books, Hampshire 122
Unsworths Booksellers Ltd., London (WC) 178
Walker Fine Books (Steve), London (SW) 167
Wayside Books and Cards, Oxfordshire 205
Wizard Books, Cambridgeshire 68
YSF Books, South Yorkshire 221

- BUDDHISM

Far Horizons Books, Dorset 91
Inner Bookshop (The), Oxfordshire 207
Lund Theological Books, Cambridgeshire 65
Occultique, Northamptonshire 198

- CHRISTIAN

Askew Books (Vernon), Wiltshire 250
Barbican Bookshop, N Yorks 196
Bell (Peter), Scotland 269
Blythswood Bookshop, Scotland 268
Bookshop (The), Republic Of Ireland 276
Bookworm Alley, Devon 87
Butler Books, Dorset 90
Carnforth Bookshop (The), Lancashire 140
Chapter Two, London (SE) 160
Chthonios Books, East Sussex 100
Classic Bindings, London (SW) 163
Crouch Rare Books, Surrey 232
Emerald Isle Books, Northern Ireland 259
Facet Books, Dorset 90
Far Horizons Books, Dorset 91
Golden Age Books, Worcestershire 255
Gradwell Concepts, Merseyside 185
Greensleeves, Oxfordshire 204
Holmes Books (Harry), East Yorkshire 105
Humber Books, Lincolnshire 146
Inner Bookshop (The), Oxfordshire 207
Kernaghans, Merseyside 186
Kyrios Books, Nottinghamshire 202
Lund Theological Books, Cambridgeshire 65
Manor House Books/John Trotter Books,
    London (N) 154
Oasis Booksearch, Cambridgeshire 68
Pratt (H.G.), Suffolk 228
Rose Books, Greater Manchester 118
Rosemary Books, Merseyside 186
St Philip's Books, Oxfordshire 208
Stacks Bookshop, Northern Ireland 259
Thornber (Peter A.), N Yorks 195
Till's Bookshop, Scotland 270
Tuft (Patrick), London (W) 175

- ISLAM

Adab Books, Cambridgeshire 64
Assassin Books, West Midlands 238
Books on Spain, London, Outer 183
Far Horizons Books, Dorset 91
Inner Bookshop (The), Oxfordshire 207
Joppa Books Ltd., Surrey 230
Lund Theological Books, Cambridgeshire 65
Manor House Books/John Trotter Books,
    London (N) 154
Occultique, Northamptonshire 198

SPECIALITY INDEX

Quaritch Ltd., (Bernard), London (W)............ 174

- JEWISH
Books on Spain, London, Outer 183
Bookseekers, London (SW) 163
Butler Books, Dorset................................ 90
Crouch Rare Books, Surrey........................ 232
Cyclamen Books, Leicestershire.................... 143
Golden Age Books, Worcestershire................. 255
Inner Bookshop (The), Oxfordshire 207
Lund Theological Books, Cambridgeshire........ 65
Manor House Books/John Trotter Books,
  London (N).. 154
Occultique, Northamptonshire 198
Trotter Books (John), London (N) 156
Visser Books (de), Cambridgeshire 66

- METHODISM
Barbican Bookshop, N Yorks 196
Beckham Books, Suffolk............................ 228
MK Book Services, Cambridgeshire................ 67
Oasis Booksearch, Cambridgeshire 68
Rosley Books, Cumbria 79

- ORIENTAL
Fine Books Oriental Ltd., London (WC)......... 177
Greensleeves, Oxfordshire........................... 204
Inner Bookshop (The), Oxfordshire 207
Occultique, Northamptonshire 198

- QUAKERS
Barbican Bookshop, N Yorks 196
Post–Horn Books, North Yorkshire............... 192
Rosley Books, Cumbria 79

- ROMAN CATHOLIC
Killeen (John), North Yorkshire 193
Oasis Booksearch, Cambridgeshire 68
St Philip's Books, Oxfordshire...................... 208
Sims (Sue), Dorset................................... 91
Thornton (John), London (SW).................... 167

- TAOISM
Occultique, Northamptonshire 198

- TEXTS
Beckham Books, Suffolk............................ 228

ROYALTY
- GENERAL
Annie's Books, South Yorkshire 220
Barn Books, Buckinghamshire...................... 62
Book–Worm International, Essex.................. 107
Cahir Cosy Corner Bookshop, Republic Of
  Ireland... 279
Croft Selections, Lincolnshire....................... 148
Farahar & Dupré (Clive & Sophie), Wiltshire ... 250
Heritage, West Midlands 238

Malmo Books, Hampshire 121
Piccadilly Rare Books, East Sussex................ 103
Quadrille at Delehar, London (W)................. 174
Sax Books, Suffolk 228
Scrivener's Books & Book Binding, Derbyshire . 81
Shacklock Books (David), Suffolk 226
Ventnor Rare Books, Isle of Wight................ 132

ROYALTY - EUROPEAN
Piccadilly Rare Books, East Sussex................ 103

RUGS
Cover to Cover, Merseyside 186
Smith Books (Keith), Herefordshire............... 127
Trinders' Fine Tools, Suffolk 225

RURAL LIFE
Adkins (Margaret & Geoff), West Midlands..... 240
Allport (Roy), North Yorkshire.................... 195
Arden Books & Cosmographia, Warwickshire... 236
Arnold (Roy), Suffolk............................... 226
Barn Books, Shropshire 213
Blest (Peter), Kent................................... 136
Boer War Books, North Yorkshire................ 196
Books & Bygones, Berkshire........................ 58
Books for Content, Herefordshire 126
Books Galore, Somerset 216
Books on the Bank, Durham....................... 96
Bridge Street Bookshop, Northumberland 200
Campbell Hewson Books (R.), Scotland.......... 265
Coch-y-Bonddu Books, Wales...................... 288
Cottage Books, Leicestershire....................... 143
Countrymans Gallery (The), Leicestershire....... 143
Cover to Cover, Merseyside 186
Dolphin Books, Suffolk.............................. 224
Doorbar (P. & D.), Hampshire..................... 122
Dusty Books, Wales.................................. 287
Dyfi Valley Bookshop, Wales....................... 288
Fin Rare Books, Shropshire 213
Fireside Books, Buckinghamshire................... 63
Fireside Books, Cumbria 80
Furneaux Books (Lee), Devon 87
Gillies (Benny), Scotland............................ 262
Grove Bookshop (The), North Yorkshire 195
Harvest Books, Merseyside 185
Home Farm Books, Warwickshire................. 236
Jones Books (Russell), Berkshire................... 57
Kilgour (Sporting Books) (Ian), Leicestershire... 145
Meekins Books (Paul), Warwickshire 237
Mercat Books, Scotland 267
Missing Books, Essex 108
Moss End Bookshop, Berkshire.................... 59
Mount's Bay Books, Cornwall 75
Old Bookshop (The), Somerset.................... 216
On the Wild Side, Worcestershire................. 255
Park (Mike), London, Outer........................ 183
Pratt (H.G.), Suffolk 228
Roadmaster Books, Kent............................ 134
Rods Books, Devon.................................. 87
Scott (Sporting Books) (John), Worcestershire .. 256
Scrivener's Books & Book Binding, Derbyshire . 81
Swan Bookshop (The), Devon...................... 84
Village Bookshop (The), Durham.................. 96
Woodbine Books, West Yorkshire................. 245

SATIRE

Book Barrow, Cambridgeshire	64
Ice House Books	143
Menavaur Books, Scotland	264

SCHOOL REGISTERS/ROLLS OF HONOUR

Coach House Books, Worcestershire	255
Delph Books, Greater Manchester	116
Military Bookworm, London (SE)	161
Military Collector (The), West Yorkshire	249
Palladour Books, Hampshire	124
Tiffin (Tony and Gill), Durham	96
Townsend (John), Berkshire	59
Turton (John), Durham	97
Wise (Derek), East Sussex	102
World War Books, Kent	139

SCIENCE
- GENERAL

Ænigma Designs (Books), Devon	85
Alba Books, Scotland	267
Ancient & Modern Bookshop, Dorset	90
Austwick Hall Books, North Yorkshire	141
Baron - Scientific Book Sales (P.J.), Somerset	215
Bernwode Books, Buckinghamshire	62
Beware of The Leopard Books, Bristol	60
Bookshop (The), Republic Of Ireland	276
Booth Books, Wales	286
Burgess Booksellers, (J. & J.), Cambridgeshire	64
Camden Books, Somerset	214
Carta Regis, Wales	288
Dodd Books (Maurice), Cumbria	77
Downie Fine Books Ltd., (Robert), Shropshire	213
Eagle Bookshop (The), Bedfordshire	55
Economia Books, Wales	281
Finch Rare Books Ltd. (Simon), London (W)	172
Gaskell Rare Books (Roger), Cambridgeshire	67
Greyfriars Books, Essex	107
Hünersdorff Rare Books, London (SW)	165
Hunter–Rare Books (Andrew), London (SW)	165
Ice House Books	143
Jay Books, Scotland	269
Korn Books, (M.E.), London (N)	154
KSC Books, Cheshire	71
Lawson & Company (E.M.), Oxfordshire	205
Lewis (J.T. & P.), Cornwall	74
Little Stour Books, Kent	133
McGee (Terence J.), London, Outer	181
Meinertzhagen (Nicholas), London (SW)	165
Mollie's Loft, Wales	289
Moorside Books, Lancashire	141
Orangeberry Books, Oxfordshire	206
Phillips (Nigel), London (SW)	166
Pollak (P.M.), Devon	87
Quaritch Ltd., (Bernard), London (W)	174
R M Books, Hertfordshire	129
Riley–Smith (Hamish), Norfolk	190
Smith (David & Lynn), London, Outer	182
Stroh (M.A.), London (E)	151
Transformer, Scotland	264
Turret House, Norfolk	191
Wayside Books and Cards, Oxfordshire	205
Weiner (Graham), London (N)	156
Westons, Hertfordshire	130
Westwood Books (Mark), Wales	287
Worcester Rare Books, Worcestershire	256

- HISTORY OF

Camden Books, Somerset	214
Chesters (G. & J.), Staffordshire	223
Dean Byass, Tavistock Books, Devon	86
DoublePlusBooks, Cambridgeshire	68
Fireside Bookshop, Cumbria	80
Gardner & Co., (Walter H.), London (N)	153
Ice House Books	143
Honiton Old Bookshop, Devon	85
Jay Books, Scotland	269
Kingswood Books, Dorset	93
Mair Wilkes Books, Scotland	265
McGee (Terence J.), London, Outer	181
Moorside Books, Lancashire	141
Phelps (Michael), West Sussex	242
Phillips (Nigel), London (SW)	166
Philologus–Fine & Rare Books, London (SW)	166
Plurabelle Books, Cambridgeshire	65
Pollak (P.M.), Devon	87
R M Books, Hertfordshire	129
Rowan (P. & B.), Northern Ireland	259
Smith (David & Lynn), London, Outer	182
Sokol Books (A.), London (W)	174
Sue Lowell Natural History Books, London (W)	175
Turret House, Norfolk	191
Wayside Books and Cards, Oxfordshire	206
Wayside Books and Cards, Oxfordshire	205
Weiner (Graham), London (N)	156
Worcester Rare Books, Worcestershire	256
Wyseby House Books, Berkshire	57

SCIENTIFIC INSTRUMENTS

Arnold (Roy), Suffolk	226
DoublePlusBooks, Cambridgeshire	68
Formby Antiques (Jeffrey), Gloucestershire	113
Phelps (Michael), West Sussex	242
Pollak (P.M.), Devon	87
Smith (David & Lynn), London, Outer	182
Trinders' Fine Tools, Suffolk	225
Turret House, Norfolk	191

SCOTTISH INTEREST

Addendum Books, Scotland	263
Alba Books, Scotland	267
Anwoth Books, Scotland	263
Armchair Books, Scotland	268
Atholl Browse, Scotland	273
Atholl Fine Books, Scotland	273
Bell (Peter), Scotland	269
Blacket Books, Scotland	269
Buchan Collectibles, Scotland	265
Byre Books, Scotland	264
Caledonia Books, Scotland	271
Chesters (G. & J.), Staffordshire	223
Colonsay Bookshop, Scotland	272
Cooper Hay Rare Books, Scotland	271
Cottage Books, Leicestershire	143
Deeside Books, Scotland	266
Farquharson, (Hilary), Scotland	273

SPECIALITY INDEX

G C Books, Scotland.................................. 264
Gillies (Benny), Scotland 262
Grampian Books, Scotland 265
Grayling (David A.H.), Cumbria 78
Hattle (Anne), Northumberland.................... 200
Houston - Bookseller, (David), London (E)...... 151
Hunter–Rare Books (Andrew), London (SW) ... 165
Linton Books, Scotland.............................. 262
MacCormaig (Domhnall), Scotland 269
Mactaggart (Caroline), Dorset..................... 91
Main Point Books, Scotland........................ 269
Mair Wilkes Books, Scotland....................... 265
McCrone (Audrey), Scotland 272
McNaughtan's Bookshop, Scotland 269
Menavaur Books, Scotland 264
Mercat Books, Scotland 267
Ming Books, Scotland 264
Moray Bookshop (The), Scotland 267
Old Storytellers Bookshop (The), Scotland....... 261
Old Town Bookshop (The), Scotland 270
Price (John), London (N) 155
Pringle Booksellers (Andrew), Scotland........... 270
Prospect House Books, Northern Ireland 260
Reading Lasses, Scotland............................ 264
Riley–Smith (Hamish), Norfolk 190
Rising Tide Books, Scotland....................... 264
Sanderson (Edward), Berkshire.................... 58
Second Edition, Scotland........................... 270
Stroma Books, Scotland............................. 261
Swan Bookshop (The), Devon..................... 84
Temple (Robert), London (N)..................... 155
Thurston (Barry), Scotland 273
Till's Bookshop, Scotland 270
Updike Rare Books (John), Scotland 270
Winram's Bookshop, Scotland 266

SCOUTS & GUIDES

Askew Books (Vernon), Wiltshire................. 250
Books & Bygones (Pam Taylor), West Midlands 240
Collectables (W.H.), London (W).................. 172
Hoggarth (John R.), North Yorkshire 196

SCULPTURE

Birchden Books, London (E) 151
Heneage Art Books (Thomas), London (SW).... 164
Holdsworth Books (Bruce), West Yorkshire 245
Ice House Books.. 143
Jones (Madalyn S.), West Yorkshire 246
Martin - Bookseller (Colin), East Yorkshire 105
Shipley Specialist Art Booksellers, London (WC) 178
Trinders' Fine Tools, Suffolk 225

SELF-SUFFICIENCY

Coch-y-Bonddu Books, Wales..................... 288
Periwinkle Press, Kent 134

SETS OF BOOKS

Baxter (Steve), Surrey................................ 232
Emerald Isle Books, Northern Ireland 259
Eton Antique Bookshop, Berkshire................ 59
Fisher & Sperr, London (N) 153

Fosters Bookshop, London (W)................... 172
Frew Limited (Robert), London (WC)........... 177
Grove Bookshop (The), North Yorkshire 195
Harrington (Adrian), London (W)................ 173
Harrington Antiquarian Bookseller (Peter),
  London (SW).. 164
Kirkman Ltd., (Robert), Bedfordshire 55
Sotheran Limited (Henry), London (W) 175

SEXOLOGY

Chatterton's Books, Wales......................... 290
Delectus Books, London (WC).................... 176
Paper Pleasures, Somerset.......................... 217

SHEEP/SHEPHERDING

Byrom Textile Bookroom (Richard), Lancashire 140

SHERLOCKIANA

Askew Books (Vernon), Wiltshire................. 250
Black Cat Bookshop, Leicestershire 143
Breese Books Ltd., East Sussex 98
Ming Books, Scotland 264
Preston Book Company, Lancashire 142
Rupert Books, Cambridgeshire..................... 65
Vokes (Jeremiah), Durham......................... 96
Williams Rare Books (Nigel), London (WC) 179

SHIP MODELLING

Curtle Mead Books, Isle of Wight................. 131
Prior (Michael), Lincolnshire 149
Quayside Bookshop, Devon 88
Trinders' Fine Tools, Suffolk 225

SHIPBUILDING

Anvil Books, West Midlands 239
Curtle Mead Books, Isle of Wight................. 131
Duck (William), East Sussex....................... 98
Hairpin Books, Gloucestershire 113
Lewcock (John), Cambridgeshire 67
Marine and Cannon Books, Cheshire 70
Nautical Antique Centre (The), Dorset 95
Phelps (Michael), West Sussex..................... 242
Prior (Michael), Lincolnshire 149
Quayside Bookshop, Devon 88
Railway Shop (The), Wales 290
Roadmaster Books, Kent............................ 134
Rods Books, Devon................................... 87
Smith Maritime Aviation Books (Frank),
  Tyne & Wear 235
Trinders' Fine Tools, Suffolk 225

SHORTHAND

Ainslie Books, Scotland 271

SIGILLOGRAPHY

Taylor & Son (Peter), Hertfordshire............... 130

SIGNED EDITIONS

Black Cat Bookshop, Leicestershire 143
Book Barrow, Cambridgeshire 64

SPECIALITY INDEX

Book Bungalow (The), Cornwall................... 73
BOOKS4U, Wales................................... 282
Bookstand, Dorset................................. 93
Corfe Books, Surrey............................... 231
Ellis, Bookseller (Peter), London (SE)........... 160
Farahar & Dupré (Clive & Sophie),
   Wiltshire..................................... 250
Firsts in Print, Isle of Wight................... 131
Fosters Bookshop, London (W)..................... 172
Harrington Antiquarian Bookseller (Peter),
   London (SW)................................... 164
Harris (Books), (Malcolm), West Midlands...... 239
Heppa (Christopher), Essex........................ 106
Kirkman Ltd., (Robert), Bedfordshire............ 55
L.M.S. Books, Hertfordshire....................... 129
Little Stour Books, Kent.......................... 133
McCann (Joe), Oxfordshire......................... 208
McKelvie (Ian), London (N)........................ 154
Platt Rare Books (Richard), London (SE)....... 161
Scrivener's Books & Book Binding, Derbyshire. 81
Simpson (Dave), Scotland......................... 262
Slavin Rare and Collectable Books (Derek),
   Warwickshire.................................. 237
Temple (Robert), London (N)...................... 155
Updike Rare Books (John), Scotland............. 270
Whiteson Ltd., (Edna), Hertfordshire........... 128
Williams Rare Books (Nigel), London (WC).... 179
Woodbine Books, West Yorkshire................. 245

SLAVERY

Charmouth Bookstore, Dorset..................... 91
Ice House Books................................... 143
Kenny's Bookshops and Art Galleries Ltd,
   Republic Of Ireland........................... 278

SOCIAL HISTORY

Abbey Books, Norfolk.............................. 187
Allport (Roy), North Yorkshire................... 195
Bell (Peter), Scotland............................ 269
Beware of The Leopard Books, Bristol........... 60
Black Cat Books, Norfolk......................... 188
Byrom Textile Bookroom (Richard),
   Lancashire.................................... 140
Chesters (G. & J.), Staffordshire................ 223
Clifton Books, Essex.............................. 110
Cottage Books, Leicestershire.................... 143
Cox (Geoff), Devon................................ 89
Cyclamen Books, Leicestershire................... 143
Delectus Books, London (WC)...................... 176
Drury Rare Books (John), Essex................... 109
Duck (William), East Sussex...................... 98
Economia Books, Wales............................. 281
Eggeling Books (John), West Yorkshire.......... 248
Eggle (Mavis), Hertfordshire..................... 128
Emerald Isle Books, Northern Ireland........... 259
Finney Antique Books & Prints (Michael),
   London (WC)................................... 177
Fireside Bookshop, Cumbria....................... 80
Graham (John), Dorset............................. 95
Harvest Books, Merseyside........................ 185
Helion & Company, West Midlands................ 240
Hughes Rare Books (Spike), Scotland............ 261
Ice House Books................................... 143

Jarndyce Antiquarian Booksellers,
   London (WC)................................... 177
Kelsall (George), Greater Manchester............ 117
Malmo Books, Hampshire........................... 121
Marcan, Bookseller (Peter), London (SE)........ 161
Northern Herald Books, West Yorkshire......... 245
Old Bookshop (The), Somerset..................... 216
Pollak (P.M.), Devon.............................. 87
Premier Books & Prints, Lincolnshire........... 146
Reading Lasses, Scotland......................... 264
Red Star Books, Hertfordshire.................... 128
Roadmaster Books, Kent........................... 134
Russell (Charles), London (SW)................... 167
Segal Books (Joel), Devon......................... 85
Sephton (A.F.), London (W)....................... 174
South Downs Book Service, West Sussex......... 243
Stacks Bookshop, Northern Ireland.............. 259
Stevens (Joan), Cambridgeshire.................. 66
Swan Bookshop (The), Devon....................... 84
Symes Books (Naomi), Cheshire................... 72
Unsworths Booksellers Ltd., London (WC)...... 178
Walker Fine Books (Steve), London (SW)....... 167
Warnes (Felicity J.), London, Outer............. 181
Weininger Antiquarian Books (Eva M.),
   London (NW)................................... 159
Wetherell (Frances), Cambridgeshire............ 66
Whitchurch Books Ltd., Wales..................... 280
Woburn Books, London, North...................... 156
YSF Books, South Yorkshire....................... 221

SOCIAL SCIENCES

Chesters (G. & J.), Staffordshire................ 223
Delectus Books, London (WC)...................... 176
Ice House Books................................... 143
Northern Herald Books, West Yorkshire......... 245
Oblong Books, North Yorkshire.................... 197
O'Donoghue Books, London (SW)................... 165
Outcast Books, Wales.............................. 287
Swan Bookshop (The), Devon....................... 84
Woburn Books, London, North...................... 156

SOCIALISM

Cyclamen Books, Leicestershire................... 143
Fin Rare Books, Shropshire....................... 213
Ice House Books................................... 143
Left on The Shelf, London (E).................... 151
Northern Herald Books, West Yorkshire......... 245
Red Star Books, Hertfordshire.................... 128
Spurrier (Nick), Kent............................. 136
Woburn Books, London, North...................... 156

SOCIOLOGY

Chesters (G. & J.), Staffordshire................ 223
Ice House Books................................... 143

SPECIAL COLLECTIONS

Downie Fine Books Ltd., (Robert), Shropshire. 213
Kohler (C.C.), Surrey............................. 230
Temple (Robert), London, North................... 155

SPIRITUALISM

Atticus Books, Essex	109
Cavern Books, Cheshire	71
Cavern Books, Cheshire	70
Chthonios Books, East Sussex	100
Deverell Books, Bristol	61
Facet Books, Dorset	90
Far Horizons Books, Dorset	91
Fine Books Oriental Ltd., London (WC)	177
Greensleeves, Oxfordshire	204
Holmes Books (Harry), East Yorkshire	105
Jade Mountain, Hampshire	123
Magis Books, Leicestershire	144
Nevis Railway Bookshops (The Antique & Book Collector), Wiltshire	251
Occultique, Northamptonshire	198
Railway Book and Magazine Search, Berkshire	58
Rainger Books (Michael), Wales	285
Tilleys Vintage Magazine Shop, South Yorkshire	220
Wizard Books, Cambridgeshire	68

SPORT

- GENERAL

Abacus Gallery / The Village Bookshop, Staffordshire	223
Amos (Denis W.), Hertfordshire	128
Archways Sports Books, Scotland	268
Arundel Bookshop, West Sussex	241
Autumn Leaves, Lincolnshire	148
Book Warren, Devon	84
Books & Bygones, Berkshire	58
Books Galore, Somerset	216
Bookworms, Norfolk	187
Carta Regis, Wales	288
Cavendish Books (Rupert), West Yorkshire	246
Chevin Books, West Yorkshire	248
Clements (R.W.), London, Outer	181
Eastcote Bookshop (The), London, Outer	183
Fin Rare Books, Shropshire	213
Gravity Books, Lincolnshire	147
Hornsey's, North Yorkshire	194
Ice House Books	143
McCrone (Audrey), Scotland	272
Mead (P.J.), Shropshire	212
Morten (Booksellers) (E.J.), Greater Manchester	117
Mr. Pickwick of Towcester, Northamptonshire	199
Oblong Books, North Yorkshire	197
Price (R.W.), Nottinghamshire	202
Roland Books, Kent	137
Swan Bookshop (The), Devon	84
Thornton Books (Richard), London, North	155
Trafalgar Bookshop (The), East Sussex	99

- AMERICAN FOOTBALL

Saunders (Tom), Wales	280

- ANGLING/FISHING

Biblion, London (W)	169
Blest (Peter), Kent	136
Bolland Books (Leslie H.), Bedfordshire	55
Branksome Books, Dorset	93
Castleton (Pat), Kent	135
Chalmers Hallam (E.), Hampshire	123
Coch-y-Bonddu Books, Wales	288
Darkwood Books, Republic Of Ireland	276
Deeside Books, Scotland	266
Diver's & Watersportsman's Library (The), Devon	86
Dusty Books, Wales	287
Eggle (Mavis), Hertfordshire	128
Grayling (David A.H.), Cumbria	78
Grove Bookshop (The), North Yorkshire	195
Harrison's Books, London (W)	173
Hereward Books, Cambridgeshire	66
Home Farm Books, Warwickshire	236
Kilgour (Sporting Books) (Ian), Leicestershire	145
Lion Books, Worcestershire	254
McEwan Fine Books, Scotland	266
Petersfield Bookshop (The), Hampshire	122
Rare Books & Berry, Somerset	217
River Reads Bookshop, Devon	88
Rothwell and Dunworth, Somerset	216
St Mary's Books & Prints, Lincolnshire	150
Scott (Sporting Books) (John), Worcestershire	256
Treasure Island (The), Greater Manchester	118
Vinovium Books, Durham	96
Wheatsheaf Antiques, Cheshire	69
Wigley Books, Worcestershire	255
Winchester Bookshop (The), Hampshire	125
Yesterday Tackle & Books, Dorset	91

- ARCHERY

Chalmers Hallam (E.), Hampshire	123
Dyfi Valley Bookshop, Wales	288
Lake (Fred), Surrey	234
Scott (Sporting Books) (John), Worcestershire	256

- ATHLETICS

Brett (R.C.), Northamptonshire	199
Lewis (Len), Wales	289
Swan Bookshop (The), Devon	84

- BADMINTON

Pennymead Books, North Yorkshire	193

- BALLOONING

J.B. Books, Berkshire	58
Postings, Surrey	233
Roberts (Booksellers), (Ray), Staffordshire	223

- BIG GAME HUNTING

Allsworth Rare Books Ltd., London (SW)	163
Ayre (Peter J.), Somerset	218
Barnhill Books, Scotland	272
Bates & Hindmarch, West Yorkshire	247
Campbell Hewson Books (R.), Scotland	265
Chalmers Hallam (E.), Hampshire	123
Farahar & Dupré (Clive & Sophie), Wiltshire	250
Grayling (David A.H.), Cumbria	78
Home Farm Books, Warwickshire	236
McEwan Fine Books, Scotland	266

Popeley (Frank T.), Cambridgeshire............... 68
Rothwell and Dunworth, Somerset................ 216
Scott (Sporting Books) (John), Worcestershire.... 256
Slaughter & Garratt Rare Books, Worcestershire. 255
Vandeleur Antiquarian Books, Surrey 231
Way (R.E. & G.B.), Suffolk 227

- BILLIARDS/SNOOKER/POOL
Ben–Nathan (Jack), London, Outer 181

- BOXING
Askew Books (Vernon), Wiltshire.................. 250
Combat Arts Archive, Durham 96
Eden Books, Dorset................................ 92
Franks Booksellers, Greater Manchester 117
Hedgerow Books, South Yorkshire................ 220
McInnes (P.F. & J.R.), Dorset 90
Rugby Relics, Wales 284
Thorne (Nick), Gloucestershire.................... 112

- CANOEING/KAYAKS
Baldwin (M. & M.), Shropshire.................... 212
Davis (C. & D.), Devon 83

- CAVING (SPELAEOLOGY)
Post–Horn Books, North Yorkshire............... 192

- CLIMBING & TREKKING
All Seasons Books, Cumbria....................... 79
Coracle Books, West Yorkshire.................... 247
Hunter and Krageloh, Derbyshire 82
Main Point Books, Scotland........................ 269
Swan Bookshop (The), Devon..................... 84

- COURSING
Chalmers Hallam (E.), Hampshire................. 123

- CRICKET
Acumen Books, Staffordshire...................... 223
Archer (Steve), London, Outer 180
Barbican Bookshop, North Yorkshire 196
Bardsley's Books, Suffolk 225
Barmby (C. & A.J.), Kent.......................... 138
Beighton (Brian), Norfolk.......................... 187
Black Five Books, Shropshire 213
Bodyline Books, London (SW).................... 163
Bookseekers, London (SW) 163
Bookshop (The), Cambridgeshire..................64
Border Bookshop (The), West Yorkshire......... 248
Bright (P.G.), Cambridgeshire......................66
Brookbanks (P.S.), Cambridgeshire.................67
Bush, Bookdealer (John), Gloucestershire........ 115
Classic Crime Collections, Greater Manchester.. 117
Coach House Books, Worcestershire............. 255
Dyer Cricket Books (Ian), North Yorkshire 194
Lion Books, Worcestershire........................ 254
Marcet Books, London (SE)....................... 161
McEwan Fine Books, Scotland.................... 266
McKenzie (J.W.), Surrey 231

Prescott - The Bookseller (John), London, Outer 184
Red Rose Books, Lancashire 141
Rugby Relics, Wales 284
St Mary's Books & Prints, Lincolnshire 150
Sax Books, Suffolk 228
Swan Bookshop (The), Devon..................... 84
Tiffin (Tony and Gill), Durham.................... 96
Treasure Island (The), Greater Manchester 118
Wiend Books & Collectables,
   Greater Manchester 119
Wood Cricket Books (Martin), Kent.............. 137

- CROQUET
Slaughter & Garratt Rare Books, Worcestershire. 255

- CYCLING
Angel Books, Norfolk 189
Cronin (Jim), Wales................................ 280
Engaging Gear Ltd., Essex......................... 106
Larkham Books (Patricia), Gloucestershire 115
Ouse Valley Books, Bedfordshire 56
Roberts (Booksellers), (Ray), Staffordshire....... 223
Swan Bookshop (The), Devon..................... 84
Trinders' Fine Tools, Suffolk 225

- DIVING/SUB-AQUA
Diver's & Watersportsman's Library (The),
   Devon... 86
Sidey, Bookdealer (Philip), Kent 137

- DUELLING
Combat Arts Archive, Durham 96
Prospect Books, Wales.............................. 282

- FALCONRY
Barnhill Books, Scotland 272
Chalmers Hallam (E.), Hampshire................. 123
Coch-y-Bonddu Books, Wales..................... 288
Crack (Books) (F.N.), Lancashire 140
Hereward Books, Cambridgeshire 66
Home Farm Books, Warwickshire................. 236
On the Wild Side, Worcestershire.................. 255
Scott (Sporting Books) (John), Worcestershire .. 256
Walker (Adrian), Bedfordshire 55

- FENCING
Chalmers Hallam (E.), Hampshire................. 123
Combat Arts Archive, Durham 96

- FIELD SPORTS
Atticus Books, Essex............................... 109
Barnhill Books, Scotland 272
Branksome Books, Dorset 93
Chalmers Hallam (E.), Hampshire................. 123
Countrymans Gallery (The), Leicestershire....... 143
Crack (Books) (F.N.), Lancashire 140
Daly (Peter M.), Hampshire 124
Deeside Books, Scotland 266
Dyfi Valley Bookshop, Wales...................... 288

SPECIALITY INDEX

Grahame (Major Iain), Suffolk 225
Grayling (David A.H.), Cumbria 78
Grove Bookshop (The), North Yorkshire 195
Heartland Old Books, Devon....................... 88
Hereward Books, Cambridgeshire 66
Hollett and Son (R.F.G.), Cumbria 79
Home Farm Books, Warwickshire................ 236
Kilgour (Sporting Books) (Ian), Leicestershire... 145
Lake (Fred), Surrey 234
McEwan Fine Books, Scotland..................... 266
Moss End Bookshop, Berkshire.................... 59
Rothwell and Dunworth, Somerset 216
Scott (Sporting Books) (John), Worcestershire .. 256
Summersgill (Neil), Lancashire 140
Target Books, Cambridgeshire 68
Vinovium Books, Durham 96
Way (R.E. & G.B.), Suffolk 227

- FOOTBALL (SOCCER)

Amos (Denis W.), Hertfordshire 128
BOOKS4U, Wales...................................... 282
Border Bookshop (The), West Yorkshire......... 248
Brookbanks (P.S.), Cambridgeshire................ 67
Conry (Ann & Mike), Worcestershire............. 256
Eden Books, Dorset.................................... 92
Footballana, Berkshire................................. 58
Forest Books, Lincolnshire.......................... 147
Franks Booksellers, Greater Manchester 117
Hedgerow Books, South Yorkshire................ 220
Lion Books, Worcestershire......................... 254
LyngHeath Books, Norfolk.......................... 190
Red Star Books, Hertfordshire 128
Rugby Relics, Wales 284
Soccer Books Limited, Lincolnshire 146
Swan Bookshop (The), Devon...................... 84
Whitfield (Ken), Essex 109
Wiend Books & Collectables,
  Greater Manchester 119

- GOLF

Abrahams (Mike), Staffordshire.................... 222
Bradley–Cox (Mary), Dorset........................ 90
Classic Crime Collections, Greater Manchester.. 117
Coupland (Terry W.), Staffordshire................ 222
Grant Books, Worcestershire 254
Gresham Books, Somerset 216
Hawthorn Books, Bristol............................. 61
Hennessey Bookseller (Ray), East Sussex......... 100
Intech Books, Northumberland 201
McEwan Golf Books (Rhod), Scotland........... 266
Milne Books (Clifford), Scotland 265
Morley Case, Hampshire............................. 124
Quarto Bookshop (The), Scotland 265
Rugby Relics, Wales 284
Swan Bookshop (The), Devon...................... 84

- GREYHOUND RACING

Bennetts Books, East Sussex........................ 101

- HIGHLAND GAMES

Webster (D.), Scotland................................ 272

- HOCKEY

Bookworld, Shropshire 212
Pennymead Books, North Yorkshire.............. 193
Yesterday's Books, Dorset 91

- HORSE RACING (ALL ASPECTS)

Amos (Denis W.), Hertfordshire 128
Bennetts Books, East Sussex........................ 101
Books & Bygones, Berkshire........................ 58
Brown (Books) (Steve), Staffordshire.............. 222
Browzers, Greater Manchester 117
Carters (Janet), Suffolk 225
Day (J.H.), Hampshire................................ 122
Ice House Books....................................... 143
Leeper (Romilly), London (SW) 165
MK Book Services, Cambridgeshire............... 67
Swan Bookshop (The), Devon...................... 84
Target Books, Cambridgeshire 68
Trafalgar Bookshop (The), East Sussex........... 99
Treasure Island (The), Greater Manchester 118

- HUNTING

Coch-y-Bonddu Books, Wales...................... 288
Countrymans Gallery (The), Leicestershire....... 143
Darkwood Books, Republic Of Ireland........... 276
Grove Bookshop (The), North Yorkshire 195
Ice House Books....................................... 143
Kilgour (Sporting Books) (Ian), Leicestershire... 145
Rare Books & Berry, Somerset..................... 217
Rothwell and Dunworth, Somerset 216
St Mary's Books & Prints, Lincolnshire 150
Scott (Sporting Books) (John), Worcestershire .. 256

- MARTIAL ARTS,

Combat Arts Archive, Durham 96

- MOTOR RACING

Bookworm, Essex...................................... 106
Collectors Carbooks, Northamptonshire.......... 199
Knowles (John), Norfolk............................. 188
Lion Books, Worcestershire......................... 254
Morris (Chris), Oxfordshire......................... 208
Roadster Motoring Books, Hampshire............ 123
Simon Lewis Transport Books, Gloucestershire . 112
Volumes of Motoring, Gloucestershire............ 111
www.drivepast.com, Gloucestershire............... 114

- OLYMPIC GAMES, THE

Amos (Denis W.), Hertfordshire 128
Brett (R.C.), Northamptonshire.................... 199

- PIG-STICKING

Chalmers Hallam (E.), Hampshire................. 123
Scott (Sporting Books) (John), Worcestershire .. 256

- POLO

Askew Books (Vernon), Wiltshire.................. 250
Blacklock's, Surrey 231

SPECIALITY INDEX

Scott (Sporting Books) (John), Worcestershire .. 256

- RACKET SPORTS
Amos (Denis W.), Hertfordshire 128

- ROWING
Tower Bridge Books, London (SE) 162
Vandeleur Antiquarian Books, Surrey 231
Way Booksellers (Richard), Oxfordshire 206

- RUGBY
Eden Books, Dorset 92
Forest Books, Lincolnshire 147
Franks Booksellers, Greater Manchester 117
Lion Books, Worcestershire 254
Oval Books, North Yorkshire 193
Rugby Relics, Wales 284
Saunders (Tom), Wales 280
Swan Bookshop (The), Devon 84
Treasure Island (The), Greater Manchester 118
Wiend Books & Collectables,
 Greater Manchester 119

- SHOOTING
Blest (Peter), Kent 136
Chalmers Hallam (E.), Hampshire 123
Daly (Peter M.), Hampshire 124
Darkwood Books, Republic Of Ireland 276
Dyfi Valley Bookshop, Wales 288
Grayling (David A.H.), Cumbria 78
Kilgour (Sporting Books) (Ian), Leicestershire... 145
Prospect Books, Wales 282
Rothwell and Dunworth, Somerset 216
Scott (Sporting Books) (John), Worcestershire .. 256

- SKIING
Frew Limited (Robert), London (WC) 177

- TENNIS
Amos (Denis W.), Hertfordshire 128
Tennis Collectables, Cheshire 69

- WEIGHTLIFTING/BODYBUILDING
Combat Arts Archive, Durham 96
Webster (D.), Scotland 272

- WRESTLING
Combat Arts Archive, Durham 96
Webster (D.), Scotland 272

- YACHTING
Argent (Alan), Isle of Wight 132
Baldwin (M. & M.), Shropshire 212
Books Afloat, Dorset 95
Clapham (M. & B.), Hampshire 122
Curtle Mead Books, Isle of Wight 131

Footrope Knots, Suffolk 226
Lewcock (John), Cambridgeshire 67
Marcet Books, London (SE) 161
Prior (Michael), Lincolnshire 149
Pyke (Robert & Susan), Somerset 214
Sea Chest Nautical Bookshop (The), Devon 87
Smith Maritime Aviation Books (Frank),
 Tyne & Wear 235

STAINED GLASS
Barmby (C. & A.J.), Kent 138
Birchden Books, London (E) 151
Heneage Art Books (Thomas), London (SW).... 164
Shipley Specialist Art Booksellers, London (WC)178
Staniland (Booksellers), Lincolnshire 150
Studio Bookshop, East Sussex 99
Taylor & Son (Peter), Hertfordshire 130
Trinders' Fine Tools, Suffolk 225
Venables (Morris & Juliet), Bristol 61

STEAM ENGINES
Abrahams (Mike), Staffordshire 222
All Books, Essex 108
Batterdale Books, North Yorkshire 195
Bott, (Bookdealers) Ltd., (Martin), Greater
 Manchester 116
Brewin Books Ltd., Warwickshire 237
Coulthurst (Richard), Greater Manchester 118
Cox (Geoff), Devon 89
Duck (William), East Sussex 98
Jones (Anne), Cornwall 76
Jones Books (Russell), Berkshire 57
Nautical Antique Centre (The), Dorset 95
Newband (D.M.), Wales 288
Penzance Rare Books, Cornwall 75
Quayside Bookshop, Devon 88
Roadmaster Books, Kent 134
Roberts (Booksellers), (Ray), Staffordshire 223
Simon Lewis Transport Books, Gloucestershire . 112
Stanhope Bibliophiles, London, North 155
Wilson Books (Henry), Cheshire 71
Winchester Antiquarian Books, Hampshire 125

SUPERNATURAL
Caduceus Books, Leicestershire 143
Cowley, Bookdealer (K.W.), Somerset 215
Eggeling Books (John), West Yorkshire 248
Facet Books, Dorset 90
Far Horizons Books, Dorset 91
Grieveson (A.), Cheshire 69
Occultique, Northamptonshire 198
Temple (Robert), London, North 155
Till's Bookshop, Scotland 270

SURREALISM
Delectus Books, London (WC) 176
DoublePlusBooks, Cambridgeshire 68
Ellis, Bookseller (Peter), London (SE) 160
Shipley Specialist Art Booksellers, London (WC)178

TAPESTRY
Art Reference Books, Hampshire 123

SPECIALITY INDEX

Byrom Textile Bookroom (Richard), Lancashire 140
DoublePlusBooks, Cambridgeshire 68
Heneage Art Books (Thomas), London (SW).... 164
Hennessey Bookseller (Ray), East Sussex......... 100
Trinders' Fine Tools, Suffolk 225

TAXIDERMY

Blest (Peter), Kent..................................... 136
Chalmers Hallam (E.), Hampshire................. 123
Crack (Books) (F.N.), Lancashire 140
Home Farm Books, Warwickshire................. 236
Scott (Sporting Books) (John), Worcestershire .. 256

TECHNICAL

Addendum Books, Scotland 263
Beware of The Leopard Books, Bristol 60
Duck (William), East Sussex........................ 98
Fin Rare Books, Shropshire 213
Ice House Books...................................... 143
Jones (Anne), Cornwall.............................. 76

TECHNOLOGY

Batterham (David), London (W).................... 169
Book House (The), Cumbria........................ 78
Booth Books, Wales.................................. 286
Bott, (Bookdealers) Ltd., (Martin), Greater
  Manchester 116
Camden Books, Somerset 214
Duck (William), East Sussex........................ 98
Eagle Bookshop (The), Bedfordshire 55
Eggle (Mavis), Hertfordshire........................ 128
Elton Engineering Books, London (W) 172
Gaskell Rare Books (Roger), Cambridgeshire ... 67
Ice House Books...................................... 143
Jay Books, Scotland.................................. 269
Jones (Anne), Cornwall.............................. 76
KSC Books, Cheshire................................ 71
Mollie's Loft, Wales.................................. 289
Orangeberry Books, Oxfordshire................... 206
Phelps (Michael), West Sussex..................... 242
Phillips (Nigel), London (SW)...................... 166
Pollak (P.M.), Devon 87
Stroh (M.A.), London (E)............................ 151
Trinders' Fine Tools, Suffolk 225
Weiner (Graham), London, North.................. 156
Westons, Hertfordshire 130
Westwood Books (Mark), Wales................... 287
Ystwyth Books, Wales............................... 281

TEDDY BEARS

Bookmark (Children's Books), Wiltshire 252

TELEVISION

Byre Books, Scotland 264
Cover to Cover, Merseyside 186
Cusack Books, London (W) 172
Fitzsimons (Anne), Cumbria........................ 77
Kaye - Bookseller (Terence), London (NW) 158
Kelly Books, Devon.................................. 88
Left Bank (The), Wales.............................. 290
McGee (Terence J.), London, Outer............... 181

Morris (Chris), Oxfordshire......................... 208
Mr. Pickwick of Towcester, Northamptonshire.. 199
Paramor (C.D.), Suffolk............................. 227
Premier Books & Prints, Lincolnshire............ 146
Wiend Books & Collectables,
  Greater Manchester 119
Williams (Bookdealer), (Richard), Lincolnshire . 149

TEXTILES

Adams (Judith), Shropshire......................... 211
Art Reference Books, Hampshire.................. 123
Black Cat Books, Norfolk 188
Bowdon Books, Lancashire......................... 141
Brock Books, North Yorkshire..................... 192
Byrom Textile Bookroom (Richard), Lancashire 140
Cover to Cover, Merseyside 186
Crouch Rare Books, Surrey......................... 232
DoublePlusBooks, Cambridgeshire 68
Duck (William), East Sussex........................ 98
Heneage Art Books (Thomas), London (SW).... 164
Hennessey Bookseller (Ray), East Sussex......... 100
Ives Bookseller (John), London, Outer........... 184
Mansfield (Judith), West Yorkshire................ 248
Shipley Specialist Art Booksellers, London (WC)178
Trinders' Fine Tools, Suffolk 225
Warnes (Felicity J.), London, Outer............... 181
Well–Head Books, Dorset........................... 91
Young (D. & J.), Wales 289

THEATRE

Addyman Books, Wales............................. 285
Ashfield Books and Records, Nottinghamshire.. 203
Brock Books, North Yorkshire..................... 192
Byre Books, Scotland 264
Carta Regis, Wales 288
Clark (Nigel A.), London (SE)..................... 160
Cover to Cover, Merseyside 186
Cox Rare Books (Charles), Cornwall 74
DaSilva Puppet Books, Oxfordshire............... 204
Europa Books, London (SW)....................... 163
Fitzsimons (Anne), Cumbria........................ 77
Harris (Books), (Malcolm), West Midlands...... 239
Heyman (B.), London, Outer....................... 181
Jarndyce Antiquarian Booksellers,
  London (WC) 177
Kaye - Bookseller (Terence), London (NW) 158
Keel Row Books, Tyne & Wear.................... 235
Left Bank (The), Wales.............................. 290
McGee (Terence J.), London, Outer............... 181
Paramor (C.D.), Suffolk............................. 227
Prescott - The Bookseller (John), London, Outer 184
Reads, Dorset 94
Rhodes, Bookseller (Peter), Hampshire 124
Sanderson (Edward), Berkshire..................... 58
Spread Eagle Bookshop, London (SE)............ 162
Temple (Robert), London, North................... 155
Theatreshire Books, North Yorkshire............. 192
Wiend Books & Collectables,
  Greater Manchester 119
Willmott Bookseller (Nicholas), Wales............ 280

THEOLOGY

Addyman Books, Wales............................. 285

Barbican Bookshop, North Yorkshire 196
Bardsley's Books, Suffolk 225
Beckham Books, Suffolk.............................. 228
Beverley Old Bookshop, East Yorkshire.......... 104
Beware of The Leopard Books, Bristol 60
Blythswood Bookshop, Scotland................... 268
Bookshop (The), Republic Of Ireland.............. 276
Booth Books, Wales..................................... 286
Broadwater Books, Hampshire...................... 124
Butler Books, Dorset..................................... 90
Carta Regis, Wales 288
Carter, (Brian), Oxfordshire 205
Chesters (G. & J.), Staffordshire 223
Colwyn Books, Wales................................... 281
Cranmer Books, Oxfordshire 210
Crouch Rare Books, Surrey........................... 232
Downie Fine Books Ltd., (Robert), Shropshire . 213
Duncan's Books, Devon................................. 88
ECR Books, Dorset....................................... 93
Edwards (Alan & Margaret), Kent 139
Fotheringham (Alex), Northumberland........... 200
Foyle Books, Northern Ireland...................... 260
Gage Postal Books, Essex 109
Gilbert (R.A.), Bristol.................................... 61
Golden Age Books, Worcestershire................ 255
Gradwell Concepts, Merseyside 185
Hab Books, London (W)............................... 173
Hellenic Bookservices, London (NW)............. 158
Heritage Books, Isle of Wight 131
Howes Bookshop, East Sussex 101
Humber Books, Lincolnshire 146
Jade Mountain, Hampshire 123
Jericho Books, Oxfordshire 208
Kernaghans, Merseyside 186
Kyrios Books, Nottinghamshire..................... 202
Langmaid (Kenneth), Cornwall 76
Lewis (J.T. & P.), Cornwall............................. 74
Lion Fine Arts and Books, Wales 287
Lund Theological Books, Cambridgeshire........ 65
Main Point Books, Scotland......................... 269
Modern Welsh Publications Ltd., Merseyside.... 185
Moss Books, London (NW) 158
Oasis Booksearch, Cambridgeshire 68
Old Bookshop (The), West Midlands 240
Olynthiacs, Shropshire 212
Prospect House Books, Northern Ireland 260
Rose Books, Greater Manchester 118
Rosley Books, Cumbria 79
Ryeland Books, Northamptonshire 198
St Philip's Books, Oxfordshire....................... 208
Salsus Books, Worcestershire 255
Scrivener's Books & Book Binding, Derbyshire . 81
Shacklock Books (David), Suffolk 226
Skelly (George B.), London, North................. 155
Spooner & Co., Somerset 217
Staffs Bookshop (The), Staffordshire 222
Sterling Books, Somerset 219
Stewart (Andrew), Cornwall 75
Strauss (David), Lincolnshire........................ 147
Thornber (Peter A.), North Yorkshire 195

THEOSOPHY

Alpha Books, London, North 153
Inner Bookshop (The), Oxfordshire 207

Occultique, Northamptonshire 198
Starlord Books, Cheshire................................ 70

TOPOGRAPHY
- GENERAL

Abacus Gallery / The Village Bookshop,
   Staffordshire... 223
Addyman Books, Wales................................ 285
Allhalland Books, Devon................................ 83
Altea Antique Maps & Books, London (WC)... 169
Andron (G.W.), London, North 153
Antiquary Ltd., (Bar Bookstore),
   North Yorkshire 194
Arcadia, Shropshire 212
Arden Books & Cosmographia, Warwickshire... 236
Arundel Bookshop, West Sussex 241
Ashfield Books and Records, Nottinghamshire.. 203
Autolycus, Shropshire.................................. 211
Baker - Books for the Collector (Colin), Devon. 88
Bardsley's Books, Suffolk 225
Barton (John), Hampshire 124
Bolton Books, Hampshire............................. 120
Bonham (J. & S.L.), London (W)................... 169
Book Warren, Devon 84
Books, Wales.. 282
Books & Bygones, Berkshire.......................... 58
Books (For All), North Yorkshire 192
Books Afloat, Dorset..................................... 95
Books Galore, Somerset 216
Bookshop (The), Cambridgeshire 64
Bookshop (The), Norfolk 191
Bookworms, Norfolk.................................... 187
Bookwyze, Lincolnshire 147
Booth (Booksearch Service), (Geoff),
   Cheshire 69
Booth Books, Wales.................................... 286
Bowden Books, Leicestershire 144
Brinded (Scott), Kent................................... 136
Broadhurst of Southport Ltd., Merseyside 186
Brock Books, North Yorkshire....................... 192
Browser's Bookshop, Cornwall....................... 74
Bygone Books, Lancashire 141
Carnforth Bookshop (The), Lancashire 140
Carta Regis, Wales 288
Castle Bookshop, Essex............................... 107
Castleton (Pat), Kent................................... 135
Catalyst Books, Surrey 232
Cavern Books, Cheshire 69
Cavern Books, Cheshire 71
Chapter and Verse Booksellers, East Sussex 102
Charmouth Bookstore, Dorset 91
Chaucer Bookshop (The), Kent 133
Chevin Books, West Yorkshire...................... 248
Clarke (J. & D.), Norfolk 189
Classic Bindings, London (SW) 163
Coach House Books, Worcestershire 255
Cobweb Books, North Yorkshire 194
Coombes (A.J.), Surrey................................ 230
Cornell Books, Gloucestershire..................... 114
Countrymans Gallery (The), Leicestershire...... 143
Craobh Rua Books, Northern Ireland 259
Cumming Limited (A. & Y.), East Sussex........ 102
Curiosity Shop (The), Cambridgeshire 67
Dartmoor Bookshop (The), Devon.................. 83

SPECIALITY INDEX

Deeside Books, Scotland 266
Dorset Rare Books, Wiltshire 252
Doughty Fine Books (Robin), West Midlands... 238
Elmfield Books, West Midlands.................... 238
Family Favourites (Books), East Yorkshire 104
Farquharson, (Hilary), Scotland 273
Fin Rare Books, Shropshire 213
Fine Art, West Sussex 242
Fireside Books, Buckinghamshire.................. 63
Fisher & Sperr, London, North 153
Ford Books (David), Hertfordshire................. 130
Frost (Richard), Hertfordshire 128
Gilbert and Son (H.M.), Hampshire................ 124
Golden Hind Bookshop (The), Kent 134
Goodyer (Nicholas), London, North 154
Green (Mrs. D.M.), Surrey 234
Grove Bookshop (The), North Yorkshire 195
Guildmaster Books, Cheshire....................... 71
Hall's Bookshop, Kent................................ 138
Handsworth Books, Essex........................... 110
Harrington Antiquarian Bookseller (Peter),
  London (SW)... 164
Hattle (Anne), Northumberland.................... 200
Hawes Books, Norfolk................................ 189
High Street Books, Devon 85
Hollett and Son (R.F.G.), Cumbria 79
Honiton Old Bookshop, Devon..................... 85
Hook (Arthur), Bristol................................ 61
Hornsey's, North Yorkshire 194
Hummingbird Books, Kent 136
InterCol London, London, North 154
Ice House Books....................................... 143
Island Books, Devon................................. 86
J.A. Heacock (Antiques and Books), Cheshire .. 70
Jackson (M.W.), Wiltshire 253
Jade Mountain, Hampshire......................... 123
K. Books, East Yorkshire............................ 104
Kay Books Ltd., Surrey 232
Keegan's Bookshop, Berkshire 58
Kellow Books, Oxfordshire 204
Kingston (Richard J.), Oxfordshire................ 206
Langmaid (Kenneth), Cornwall 76
Lewis (J.T. & P.), Cornwall......................... 74
Liebreich Antique Maps & Prints (Kitty),
  London (W)... 173
Lowe (John), Norfolk................................. 189
Malvern Bookshop (The), Worcestershire 254
Marcet Books, London (SE)........................ 161
Marlborough Rare Books Ltd., London (W).... 173
Martin Bookshop & Gallery (Richard),
  Hampshire 121
Miles Book Shop (Archie), Cumbria 79
Missing Books, Essex 108
Modlock (Lilian), Dorset............................. 92
Morris (Michael), Staffordshire..................... 222
Mundy (David), Buckinghamshire.................. 62
Mundy (David), Hertfordshire 128
Newlyn & New Street Books, Cornwall 75
Nineteenth Century Books, Oxfordshire 209
Oblong Books, North Yorkshire.................... 197
Old Station Pottery & Bookshop (The), Norfolk 191
Old Storytellers Bookshop (The), Scotland....... 261
Olio Books, East Sussex............................. 101
Ouse Valley Books, Bedfordshire 56
Page Antiquarian Books (Colin), East Sussex ... 99

Paralos Ltd., London (W)........................... 173
Park Gallery & Bookshop (The),
  Northamptonshire 199
Parrott Books, Oxfordshire 209
Patterson Liddle, Somerset......................... 214
Penn Barn Bookshop, Buckinghamshire.......... 63
Phillips (Chris), Wiltshire............................ 250
Prescott - The Bookseller (John), London, Outer 184
Priory Books, Worcestershire....................... 256
R. & A. Books, East Sussex 100
R. & B. Graham, Cornwall 74
Reads, Dorset 94
Reigate Galleries, Surrey 233
Ross Old Books & Prints, Herefordshire 127
Royal Carbery Books Ltd., Republic Of Ireland 275
Russell Books, Somerset............................. 218
St Mary's Books & Prints, Lincolnshire 150
St Michael at Plea Bookshop, Norfolk 190
Satara Books, West Sussex......................... 244
Saunders (Tom), Wales 280
Scott (T.F.S.), East Sussex 102
Scrivener's Books & Book Binding, Derbyshire . 81
Segal Books (Joel), Devon 85
Shacklock Books (David), Suffolk 226
Shakespeare Books (Colin), Staffordshire......... 222
Sharpe (Mary), West Sussex 241
Smith (Clive), Essex 108
Sparkes (Books) (Ray), Staffordshire.............. 223
Spread Eagle Bookshop, London (SE)............ 162
Stella Books, Wales 284
Sterling Books, Somerset............................ 219
Stothert Old Books, Cheshire....................... 69
Swan Bookshop (The), Devon...................... 84
Sykes (Graham), West Yorkshire 248
Titford (John), Derbyshire 81
Townsend (John), Berkshire 59
Trinders' Fine Tools, Suffolk 225
Turton (John), Durham 97
Ventnor Rare Books, Isle of Wight................ 132
Walker Fine Books (Steve), London (SW) 167
Wayfarer Books, Cornwall........................... 75
Wheatsheaf Antiques, Cheshire..................... 69
Whiteson Ltd., (Edna), Hertfordshire 128
Whitfield (Ken), Essex 109
Winchester Bookshop (The), Hampshire.......... 125
Wolds Book Services, Leicestershire............... 144
Wychwood Books, Gloucestershire 114
Yewtree Books, Cumbria 78
YSF Books, South Yorkshire....................... 221

- LOCAL

Abacus Gallery / The Village Bookshop,
  Staffordshire 223
Aberdeen Rare Books & Caledonian Books,
  Scotland 267
Abrahams (Mike), Staffordshire.................... 222
Altea Antique Maps & Books, London (WC)... 169
Ambra Books, Bristol................................ 60
Andron (G.W.), London, North 153
Angel Books, Norfolk 189
Antiquary Ltd., (Bar Bookstore),
  North Yorkshire..................................... 194
Anvil Books, West Midlands 239
Arden Books & Cosmographia, Warwickshire... 236

SPECIALITY INDEX

Atticus Books, Essex 109
Baker - Books for the Collector (Colin), Devon 88
Barbican Bookshop, North Yorkshire 196
Barmby (C. & A.J.), Kent 138
Barn Books, Shropshire 213
Beck Head Books, Cumbria 78
Black Cat Bookshop, Leicestershire 143
Bonython Bookshop 76
Book for All Reasons (A.), Suffolk 227
Book Gallery (The), Cornwall 76
Books Afloat, Dorset 95
Books Bought & Sold, Surrey 231
Books on the Bank, Durham 96
Books Only, Suffolk 226
Bookseller (The), Suffolk 227
Bookshop (The), Republic Of Ireland 276
Bookshop Blackheath, London (SE) 160
Bookworms of Evesham, Worcestershire 255
Bowdon Books, Lancashire 141
Brewin Books Ltd., Warwickshire 237
Bridge of Allan Books, Scotland 262
Capes (Books, Maps & Prints) (John L.), North Yorkshire 195
Carlton Books, Norfolk 189
Carnforth Bookshop (The), Lancashire 140
Cassidy (Bookseller) (P.), Lincolnshire 147
Castle Bookshop, Essex 107
Castleton (Pat), Kent 135
Cavern Books, Cheshire 70
Chapman (Neville), Cornwall 76
Chapter & Verse, Lincolnshire 148
Chapter and Verse Booksellers, East Sussex 102
Chaucer Bookshop (The), Kent 133
Chaucer Head Bookshop, Warwickshire 237
Chevin Books, West Yorkshire 248
Chichester Bookshop (The), West Sussex 241
Church Green Books, Oxfordshire 210
Clark (K.R.), Oxfordshire 205
Clarke (J. & D.), Norfolk 189
Classic Bindings, London (SW) 163
Classic Crime Collections, Greater Manchester .. 117
Clent Books, Worcestershire 254
Coach House Books, Worcestershire 255
Cobnar Books, Kent 136
Collectors Corner, Wiltshire 252
Coombes (A.J.), Surrey 230
Cornell Books, Gloucestershire 114
Courtwood Books, Republic Of Ireland 278
Cousens (W.C.), Devon 83
Cox Old & Rare Books (Claude), Suffolk 226
Curtle Mead Books, Isle of Wight 131
Dartmoor Bookshop (The), Devon 83
Davidson Books, Northern Ireland 260
Debbage (John), Norfolk 189
Deeside Books, Scotland 266
Delph Books, Greater Manchester 116
Dene Barn Books & Prints, Somerset 218
Dobson (Bob), Lancashire 140
Dodd Books (Maurice), Cumbria 77
Dorset Rare Books, Wiltshire 252
Dylans Bookstore, Wales 289
Elmfield Books, West Midlands 238
English (Toby), Oxfordshire 209
Evans Booksearch, (Lesley), Devon 89
Everett (Richard), Norfolk 187
Exeter Rare Books, Devon 85
Farquharson, (Hilary), Scotland 273
Faversham Antiques Centre, Kent 135
Ferdinando (Steven), Somerset 217
Ferrow (David), Norfolk 188
Fine Art, West Sussex 242
Fireside Books, Buckinghamshire 63
Ford Books (David), Hertfordshire 130
Four Shire Bookshops, Gloucestershire 113
Furneaux Books (Lee), Devon 87
Garretts Antiquarian Books, Isle of Man 258
Gibbard (A. & T.), East Sussex 100
Gilbert and Son (H.M.), Hampshire 124
Gillies (Benny), Scotland 262
Gippeswic Books, Suffolk 227
Godmanchester Books, Cambridgeshire 66
Golden Hind Bookshop (The), Kent 134
Graduate Books, Worcestershire 256
Great Grandfather's, Lancashire 141
Greyfriars Books, Essex 107
Grove Bookshop (The), North Yorkshire 195
Hames (Peter), Devon 84
Hancock (Colin), Wales 281
Harlequin Books, Bristol 61
Hatchwell (Richard), Wiltshire 251
Heartland Old Books, Devon 88
Helmsley Antiquarian & Secondhand Books, North Yorkshire 193
Helston Bookworm (The), Cornwall 74
Hennessey Bookseller (Ray), East Sussex 100
Heritage, West Midlands 238
High Street Books, Devon 85
Hollett and Son (R.F.G.), Cumbria 79
Holmes Books (Harry), East Yorkshire 105
Honiton Old Bookshop, Devon 85
Hornsey's, North Yorkshire 194
Horsham Bookshop (The), West Sussex 242
Hutchison (Books) (Larry), Scotland 265
Idle Booksellers (The), West Yorkshire 245
Idle Genius Books, London, North 154
Intech Books, Northumberland 201
Island Books, Devon 86
Jarndyce Antiquarian Booksellers, London (WC) 177
Jonkers Rare Books, Oxfordshire 206
Kellow Books, Oxfordshire 204
Kelsall (George), Greater Manchester 117
Kernaghans, Merseyside 186
Kerr (Norman), Cumbria 78
Key Books (Sarah), Cambridgeshire 65
Killeen (John), North Yorkshire 193
Lake (David), Norfolk 189
Leigh Gallery Books, Essex 108
Lewis (Len), Wales 289
Liebreich Antique Maps & Prints (Kitty), London (W) 173
Lion Books, Worcestershire 254
M. & D. Books, Worcestershire 254
MacCormaig (Domhnall), Scotland 269
Maddison (J.K.), West Midlands 238
Mair Wilkes Books, Scotland 265
Malvern Bookshop (The), Worcestershire 254
Marrin & Sons (G. & D.), Kent 135
McCrone (Audrey), Scotland 272

SPECIALITY INDEX

Missing Books, Essex 108
Modlock (Lilian), Dorset 92
Moon's Bookshop (Michael), Cumbria 79
Moreton Books, Devon 86
Mount's Bay Books, Cornwall 75
Newlyn & New Street Books, Cornwall 75
Niner (Marcus), Gloucestershire 113
Noble (Malcolm & Christine), Leicestershire..... 145
Nova Foresta Books, Hampshire 121
Oakwood Books, Gloucestershire 113
Old Bookshop (The), Somerset 216
Old Bookshop (The), West Midlands 240
Old Soke Books, Cornwall 74
Old Storytellers Bookshop (The), Scotland....... 261
Park Gallery & Bookshop (The),
 Northamptonshire 199
Peakirk Books, Cambridgeshire 68
Pendleside Books, Lancashire 141
Periwinkle Press, Kent 134
Porcupines, Devon 84
Post–Horn Books, North Yorkshire 192
Postings, Surrey 233
Pratt (H.G.), Suffolk 228
Quarto Bookshop (The), Scotland 265
R. & B. Graham, Cornwall 74
Rare Books & Berry, Somerset 217
Reads, Dorset 94
Restormel Books, Worcestershire 256
Richmond Books, North Yorkshire 194
Riverside Bookshop (The), Cumbria 78
Roadmaster Books, Kent 134
Rochdale Book Company, Greater Manchester . 118
Rowan (H. & S.J.), Dorset 91
St Michael at Plea Bookshop, Norfolk 190
Sanders of Oxford Limited, Oxfordshire 208
Satara Books, West Sussex 244
Sax Books, Suffolk 228
Scarthin Books, Derbyshire 82
Scott (T.F.S.), East Sussex 102
Segal Books (Joel), Devon 85
Skyrack Books, West Yorkshire 246
Smallwood Books, Lincolnshire 148
Smith (Clive), Essex 108
Smith (Peter Bain), Cumbria 77
Smith Books (Keith), Herefordshire 127
Spooner & Co., Somerset 217
Spread Eagle Books, Wales 282
Spread Eagle Bookshop, London (SE) 162
Staffs Bookshop (The), Staffordshire 222
Stanhope Bibliophiles, London, North 155
Staniland (Booksellers), Lincolnshire 150
Stella Books, Wales 284
Stinton (Judith), Dorset 92
Stothert Old Books, Cheshire 69
Taylor & Son (Peter), Hertfordshire 130
Thomas (Books) (Leona), Cheshire 71
Thomas (E. Wyn), Wales 282
Tombland Bookshop, Norfolk 190
Townsend (John), Berkshire 59
Treasure Chest (The), Suffolk 226
Turton (John), Durham 97
Ventnor Rare Books, Isle of Wight 132
Village Bookshop (The), Durham 96
Vinovium Books, Durham 96
Wakeley (A.G. & W.), Wales 285
Westcountry Old Books, Devon 88
Whitchurch Books Ltd., Wales 280
Wiend Books & Collectables,
 Greater Manchester 119
Williams (Christopher), Dorset 93
Winchester Bookshop (The), Hampshire 125
Yates Antiquarian Books (Tony), Leicestershire 144
Yewtree Books, Cumbria 78
Ystwyth Books, Wales 281

TOWN PLANNING

Duck (William), East Sussex 98
Inch's Books, North Yorkshire 194

TOYS

Addyman Books, Wales 285
Barmby (C. & A.J.), Kent 138
Bookmark (Children's Books), Wiltshire 252
Porcupines, Devon 84

TRACTION ENGINES

Allport (Roy), North Yorkshire 195
Bott, (Bookdealers) Ltd., (Martin), Greater
 Manchester 116
Collectables (W.H.), London (W) 172
Cottage Books, Leicestershire 143
Cox (Geoff), Devon 89
Duck (William), East Sussex 98
Falconwood Transport & Military Bookshop,
 London, Outer 184
Jones (Anne), Cornwall 76
Jones (Barry), West Sussex 242
Jones Books (Russell), Berkshire 57
Muttonchop Manuscripts, West Sussex 243
Penzance Rare Books, Cornwall 75
Roadmaster Books, Kent 134
Vintage Motorshop, West Yorkshire 245
Wilson Books (Henry), Cheshire 71

TRADE UNIONS

Books Only, Suffolk 226
Byrom Textile Bookroom (Richard),
 Lancashire 140
Clifton Books, Essex 110
Cyclamen Books, Leicestershire 143
Delectus Books, London (WC) 176
Ice House Books 143
Left on The Shelf, London (E) 151
Northern Herald Books, West Yorkshire 245
Red Star Books, Hertfordshire 128
Spurrier (Nick), Kent 136
Woburn Books, London, North 156

TRANSATLANTIC ARTS

Illustrated Book (The), London (SW) 165

TRANSPORT

Addyman Books, Wales 285
Adkins (Margaret & Geoff), W Mids 240
Anvil Books, West Midlands 239
Archer (David), Wales 288

SPECIALITY INDEX

Arden Books & Cosmographia,
  Warwickshire 236
Ashfield Books and Records,
  Nottinghamshire 203
Autumn Leaves, Lincolnshire....................... 148
Baldwin (M. & M.), Shropshire 212
Barbican Bookshop, North Yorkshire 196
Bird Books (Nigel), Wales........................... 281
Black Five Books, Shropshire 213
Book Basket, London, Outer 182
Book Corner, Scotland 263
Book House (The), Cumbria......................... 78
Books, Wales.. 282
Books & Bygones (Pam Taylor), W Mids........ 240
Books Afloat, Dorset.................................. 95
Bookworms, Norfolk................................. 187
Bookworms of Evesham, Worcestershire 255
Booth Books, Wales.................................. 286
Bosco Books, Cornwall................................ 73
Bott, (Bookdealers) Ltd., (Martin), Greater
  Manchester 116
Brewin Books Ltd., Warwickshire 237
Browning Books, Wales 290
Castle Bookshop, Essex.............................. 107
Cavan Book Centre, Republic Of Ireland 275
Cavern Books, Cheshire 69, 70, 71
Clements (R.W.), London, Outer 181
Clifton Books, Essex 110
Cobweb Books, North Yorkshire................... 194
Collectables (W.H.), London (W).................. 172
Collectors Carbooks, Northamptonshire.......... 199
Collectors Corner, Wiltshire 252
Coulthurst (Richard), Greater Manchester 118
Dinnages Transport Publishing, East Sussex..... 98
Duck (William), East Sussex........................ 98
Elton Engineering Books, London (W) 172
Falconwood Transport & Military Bookshop,
  London, Outer 184
Fin Rare Books, Shropshire 213
Fireside Bookshop, Cumbria 80
Gibbard (A. & T.), East Sussex 100
Hairpin Books, Gloucestershire 113
Ice House Books....................................... 143
Jade Mountain, Hampshire 123
Jones (Barry), West Sussex......................... 242
Kelsall (George), Greater Manchester............. 117
Kerr (Norman), Cumbria 78
Kim's Bookshop, West Sussex..................... 244
Knowles (John), Norfolk 188
Maddison (J.K.), West Midlands 238
Malvern Bookshop (The), Worcestershire 254
Marine and Cannon Books, Cheshire 70
Mercat Books, Scotland 267
Mundy (David), Hertfordshire 128
Muttonchop Manuscripts, West Sussex 243
Nebulous Books, Hampshire 120
Newband (D.M.), Wales............................. 288
Noel and Holland Books, Republic Of Ireland.. 278
Old Gallery Bookshop (The), Kent................ 136
Polmorla Books, Cornwall 76
Pooks Motor Books, Leicestershire................ 144
Postings, Surrey....................................... 233
Prior (Michael), Lincolnshire 149
Quayside Bookshop, Devon 88
Railway Shop (The), Wales......................... 290

Roadmaster Books, Kent............................. 134
Roberts (Booksellers), (Ray), Staffordshire....... 223
Rochdale Book Company,
  Greater Manchester 118
Rods Books, Devon................................... 87
Roland Books, Kent 137
Segal Books (Joel), Devon 85
Simon Lewis Transport Books, Gloucestershire . 112
Stacks Bookshop, Northern Ireland 259
Stothert Old Books, Cheshire....................... 69
Ventnor Rare Books, Isle of Wight 132
Vintage Motorshop, West Yorkshire 245
Weiner (Graham), London, North.................. 156
Whitfield (Ken), Essex 109
Wilson Books (Henry), Cheshire.................... 71
Winchester Antiquarian Books, Hampshire 125

TRAVEL
- GENERAL

Abacus Gallery / The Village Bookshop,
  Staffordshire.. 223
Abbey Bookshop, Hampshire 122
Addyman Books, Wales 285
Alastor Books, Hampshire 122
Allsworth Rare Books Ltd., London (SW)....... 163
Altea Antique Maps & Books, London (WC)... 169
Anderson Slater Antiques, North Yorkshire..... 195
Andron (G.W.), London, North 153
Arden Books & Cosmographia, Warwickshire... 236
Arundel Bookshop, West Sussex 241
Ashfield Books and Records, Nottinghamshire.. 203
Askew Books (Vernon), Wiltshire................. 250
Assinder Books, Bedfordshire 55
Atholl Fine Books, Scotland........................ 273
Autolycus, Shropshire................................ 211
Autumn Leaves, Lincolnshire....................... 148
Barnhill Books, Scotland 272
Bernwode Books, Buckinghamshire 62
Biblion, London (W)................................. 169
Billing (Brian), Berkshire 59
Black Five Books, Shropshire 213
Bonham (J. & S.L.), London (W)................. 169
Bookends of Fowey, Cornwall 74
Books & Bygones, Berkshire........................ 58
Books Afloat, Dorset................................. 95
Bookshop (The), Republic Of Ireland............. 276
Bookworld, Shropshire 212
Bookworms, Norfolk................................. 187
Bookworms of Evesham, Worcestershire 255
Bookwyze, Lincolnshire 147
Booth Books, Wales.................................. 286
Bowden Books, Leicestershire 144
Bracton Books, Cambridgeshire.................... 64
Branksome Books, Dorset........................... 93
Broadhurst of Southport Ltd., Merseyside 186
Broadwater Books, Hampshire..................... 124
Brockwells Bookshop, London (SE).............. 160
Burden Ltd., (Clive A.), Hertfordshire............ 129
Cahir Cosy Corner Bookshop, Republic Of
  Ireland 279
Campbell (Fiona), London (SE) 160
Carnforth Bookshop (The), Lancashire........... 140
Catalyst Books, Surrey 232
Cavan Book Centre, Republic Of Ireland 275
Cecil Books, Surrey 231

SPECIALITY INDEX

Chalmers Hallam (E.), Hampshire 123
Chapter and Verse Booksellers, East Sussex 102
Chiltern Books, London (W) 172
Clegg (David), Staffordshire 222
Clements (R.W.), London, Outer 181
Collectable Books, London (SE) 160
Collectables (W.H.), London (W) 172
Cook (R.L.), Norfolk 190
Cornell Books, Gloucestershire 114
Cox Old & Rare Books (Claude), Suffolk 226
Craobh Rua Books, Northern Ireland 259
Croft Selections, Lincolnshire 148
Cumming Limited (A. & Y.), East Sussex 102
Curiosity Shop (The), Cambridgeshire 67
Curtle Mead Books, Isle of Wight 131
D.C. Books, Lincolnshire 148
Dartmoor Bookshop (The), Devon 83
David (G.), Cambridgeshire 64
Davies Fine Books, Worcestershire 256
Deeside Books, Scotland 266
Dodd Books (Maurice), Cumbria 77
Dorset Rare Books, Wiltshire 252
Downie Fine Books Ltd., (Robert), Shropshire . 213
Driffield Bookshop (The), East Yorkshire 104
Duncan's Books, Devon 88
Eastern Traveller (The), Somerset 218
Edwards in Hay–on–Wye (Francis), Wales 286
Ely Books, Cambridgeshire 66
Emerald Isle Books, Northern Ireland 259
Empire Books, North Yorkshire 196
Engaging Gear Ltd., Essex 106
Farahar & Dupré (Clive & Sophie),
 Wiltshire 250
Ferdinando (Steven), Somerset 217
Fin Rare Books, Shropshire 213
Finney Antique Books & Prints (Michael),
 London (WC) 177
Fireside Books, Buckinghamshire 63
Firth (Bijou Books & Photography) (Maureen),
 South Yorkshire 221
Ford Books (David), Hertfordshire 130
Fosters Bookshop, London (W) 172
Frew Limited (Robert), London (WC) 177
Frost (Richard), Hertfordshire 128
Furneaux Books (Lee), Devon 87
Gippeswic Books, Suffolk 227
Gloucester Road Bookshop, London (SW) 164
Goodyer (Nicholas), London, North 154
Greer (Robin), London (SW) 164
Hall's Bookshop, Kent 138
Harrington (Adrian), London (W) 173
Harrington Antiquarian Bookseller (Peter),
 London (SW) 164
Havercroft Antiquarian Books, London (SE) 161
Heartland Old Books, Devon 88
Hereward Books, Cambridgeshire 66
High Street Books, Devon 85
Hill (Peter), Hampshire 121
Hollett and Son (R.F.G.), Cumbria 79
Hook (Arthur), Bristol 61
Howes Bookshop, East Sussex 101
Ice House Books 143
Island Books, Devon 86
J.A. Heacock (Antiques and Books), Cheshire .. 70
Jackson (M.W.), Wiltshire 253

Jade Mountain, Hampshire 123
Jericho Books, Oxfordshire 208
Jiri Books, Northern Ireland 259
Kay Books Ltd., Surrey 232
Kenny's Bookshops and Art Galleries Ltd,
 Republic Of Ireland 278
Kernaghans, Merseyside 186
Kerr (Norman), Cumbria 78
Killeen (John), North Yorkshire 193
Kingston (Richard J.), Oxfordshire 206
Langmaid (Kenneth), Cornwall 76
Larkham Books (Patricia), Gloucestershire 115
Lewis (J.T. & P.), Cornwall 74
Lewis (John), Essex 107
Lloyd-Davies (Sue), Wales 280
Llyfrauflur Books, Wales 290
Lucas (Richard), London (NW) 158
Maggs Brothers Limited, London (W) 173
Malvern Bookshop (The), Worcestershire 254
Marcet Books, London (SE) 161
Marshall Rare Books (Bruce), Gloucestershire .. 111
Martin Bookshop & Gallery (Richard),
 Hampshire 121
Menavaur Books, Scotland 264
Merritt (Valerie), Gloucestershire 111
Modlock (Lilian), Dorset 92
Moreton Books, Devon 86
Morgan (H.J.), Bedfordshire 56
Morrell (Nicholas) Rare Books, London (NW) . 158
Morten (Booksellers) (E.J.), Greater Manchester 117
Mundy (David), Hertfordshire 128
musebookshop, Wales 283
Naughton Booksellers, Republic Of Ireland 277
Niner (Marcus), Gloucestershire 113
Oblong Books, North Yorkshire 197
Old Bookshop (The), Somerset 216
Olio Books, East Sussex 101
Orangeberry Books, Oxfordshire 206
Page (David), Scotland 270
Page Antiquarian Books (Colin), East Sussex ... 99
Paralos Ltd., London (W) 173
Patterson Liddle, Somerset 214
Peregrine Books (Leeds), West Yorkshire 247
Petersfield Bookshop (The), Hampshire 122
Prescott - The Bookseller (John), London, Outer 184
Preston Book Company, Lancashire 142
Price (R.W.), Nottinghamshire 202
Quaritch Ltd., (Bernard), London (W) 174
Quest Books, East Yorkshire 105
Reading Lasses, Scotland 264
Reads, Dorset 94
Reigate Galleries, Surrey 233
Rochdale Book Company, Greater Manchester . 118
Roland Books, Kent 137
Roundstone Books, Lancashire 141
Rowan (P. & B.), Northern Ireland 259
Russell (Charles), London (SW) 167
Second Edition, Scotland 270
Shapero Rare Books (Bernard J.), London (W) . 174
Simply Read, East Sussex 100
Slaughter & Garratt Rare Books, Worcestershire 255
Smith (Clive), Essex 108
Smith Books, (Sally), Suffolk 225
Sokol Books (A.), London (W) 174
Sotheran Limited (Henry), London (W) 175

SPECIALITY INDEX

Spearman Books, East Sussex 102
Spread Eagle Books, Wales 282
Spread Eagle Bookshop, London (SE) 162
Sterling Books, Somerset 219
Stothert Old Books, Cheshire 69
Stroma Books, Scotland 261
Sturford Books, Wiltshire 252
Sue Lowell Natural History Books, London (W) 175
Summersgill (Neil), Lancashire 140
Swan Bookshop (The), Devon 84
Sykes (Graham), West Yorkshire 248
Temple (Robert), London, North 155
Thornton (Grahame), Dorset 94
Till's Bookshop, Scotland 270
Treasure Island (The), Greater Manchester 118
Whiteson Ltd., (Edna), Hertfordshire 128
Whitfield (Ken), Essex 109
Woodstock Bookshop (The), Oxfordshire 210
Yesterday's Books, Dorset 91
Yewtree Books, Cumbria 78
YSF Books, South Yorkshire 221

- AFRICA

Ayre (Peter J.), Somerset 218
Bonham (J. & S.L.), London (W) 169
Bow Windows Book Shop, East Sussex 102
Bowen (Janice), Wales 286
Butcher (Pablo), Oxfordshire 205
Campbell Hewson Books (R.), Scotland 265
Chalmers Hallam (E.), Hampshire 123
Daly (Peter M.), Hampshire 124
Dartmoor Bookshop (The), Devon 83
Eastern Traveller (The), Somerset 218
Empire Books, North Yorkshire 196
Farahar & Dupré (Clive & Sophie),
  Wiltshire 250
Graves–Johnston (Michael), London (SW) 164
Grayling (David A.H.), Cumbria 78
Hall, (Anthony C.) Antiquarian Bookseller,
  London, Outer 184
Joppa Books Ltd., Surrey 230
Kenya Books, East Sussex 99
Lewis (John), Essex 107
Malmo Books, Hampshire 121
Oriental and African Books, Shropshire 213
Page (David), Scotland 270
Prospect House Books, Northern Ireland 260
Scott (Sporting Books) (John), Worcestershire .. 256
Scott (T.F.S.), East Sussex 102
Shapero Rare Books (Bernard J.), London (W). 174
Vandeleur Antiquarian Books, Surrey 231
White (C.R.), London (W) 175
Woolcott Books, Dorset 92
Yesterday's Books, Dorset 91

- AMERICAS

Americanabooksuk, Cumbria 77
Bonham (J. & S.L.), London (W) 169
Books on Spain, London, Outer 183
Bowen (Janice), Wales 286
Butcher (Pablo), Oxfordshire 205
Chalmers Hallam (E.), Hampshire 123
Dartmoor Bookshop (The), Devon 83

Empire Books, North Yorkshire 196
Farahar & Dupré (Clive & Sophie), Wiltshire ... 250
Graves–Johnston (Michael), London (SW) 164
Grayling (David A.H.), Cumbria 78
Leapman Ltd. (G. & R.), Hertfordshire 130
Lewis (John), Essex 107
Orssich (Paul), London (SW) 166
Shapero Rare Books (Bernard J.), London (W). 174
Vandeleur Antiquarian Books, Surrey 231

- ASIA

Allsworth Rare Books Ltd., London (SW) 163
Alpha Books, London, North 153
Bates & Hindmarch, West Yorkshire 247
Bonham (J. & S.L.), London (W) 169
Bow Windows Book Shop, East Sussex 102
Bowen (Janice), Wales 286
Butcher (Pablo), Oxfordshire 205
Chalmers Hallam (E.), Hampshire 123
Daly (Peter M.), Hampshire 124
Dartmoor Bookshop (The), Devon 83
Eastern Traveller (The), Somerset 218
Empire Books, North Yorkshire 196
Farahar & Dupré (Clive & Sophie), Wiltshire ... 250
Fine Books Oriental Ltd., London (WC) 177
Grayling (David A.H.), Cumbria 78
Hall, (Anthony C.) Antiquarian Bookseller,
  London, Outer 184
Honiton Old Bookshop, Devon 85
Hunter and Krageloh, Derbyshire 82
Joppa Books Ltd., Surrey 230
Leeper (Romilly), London (SW) 165
Lewis (John), Essex 107
Moorside Books, Lancashire 141
Page (David), Scotland 270
Prospect House Books, Northern Ireland 260
Rayner (Hugh Ashley), Somerset 215
Scott (T.F.S.), East Sussex 102
Shapero Rare Books (Bernard J.), London (W). 174
Smith (Clive), Essex 108
Traveller's Bookshelf (The), Somerset 215
Vandeleur Antiquarian Books, Surrey 231
Winchester Antiquarian Books, Hampshire 125
Woolcott Books, Dorset 92

- AUSTRALASIA/AUSTRALIA

Bonham (J. & S.L.), London (W) 169
Bowen (Janice), Wales 286
Chalmers Hallam (E.), Hampshire 123
Dartmoor Bookshop (The), Devon 83
Empire Books, North Yorkshire 196
Farahar & Dupré (Clive & Sophie),
  Wiltshire 250
Graves–Johnston (Michael), London (SW) 164
Lewis (John), Essex 107
Moore (Peter), Cambridgeshire 65
Shapero Rare Books (Bernard J.),
  London (W) 174

- EUROPE

Bonham (J. & S.L.), London (W) 169
Book Basket, London, Outer 182

SPECIALITY INDEX 429

Books on Spain, London, Outer 183
Campbell (Fiona), London (SE) 160
Classic Crime Collections, Greater Manchester.. 117
Daly (Peter M.), Hampshire 124
Dartmoor Bookshop (The), Devon 83
Doolin Dinghy Books, Republic Of Ireland...... 275
Empire Books, North Yorkshire 196
Hall, (Anthony C.) Antiquarian Bookseller,
  London, Outer 184
Lewis (John), Essex................................... 107
Old World Books (Tre Archi), London (SW).... 165
Orssich (Paul), London (SW) 166
Prospect House Books, Northern Ireland 260
Scott (T.F.S.), East Sussex 102
Shapero Rare Books (Bernard J.),
  London (W)... 174
Vandeleur Antiquarian Books, Surrey 231

- MIDDLE EAST

Allsworth Rare Books Ltd., London (SW)....... 163
Bonham (J. & S.L.), London (W).................. 169
Chalmers Hallam (E.), Hampshire 123
Cyclamen Books, Leicestershire 143
Daly (Peter M.), Hampshire 124
Dartmoor Bookshop (The), Devon 83
Eastern Traveller (The), Somerset.................. 218
Empire Books, North Yorkshire 196
Farahar & Dupré (Clive & Sophie), Wiltshire ... 250
Fine Books Oriental Ltd., London (WC)......... 177
Hall, (Anthony C.) Antiquarian Bookseller,
  London, Outer 184
Joppa Books Ltd., Surrey 230
Lewis (John), Essex................................... 107
Loman, Oriental Books & Manuscripts (David),
  London (SW)....................................... 165
Moorside Books, Lancashire........................ 141
Museum Bookshop, London (WC) 177
Oriental and African Books, Shropshire 213
Page (David), Scotland 270
Prospect House Books, Northern Ireland 260
Quest Books, East Yorkshire 105
Scott (T.F.S.), East Sussex 102
Shapero Rare Books (Bernard J.), London (W). 174
Traveller's Bookshelf (The), Somerset............. 215
Trotter Books (John), London, North 156
Winchester Antiquarian Books, Hampshire...... 125
Woolcott Books, Dorset............................ 92

- POLAR

Bonham (J. & S.L.), London (W).................. 169
Chalmers Hallam (E.), Hampshire.................. 123
Daly (Peter M.), Hampshire 124
Dartmoor Bookshop (The), Devon 83
Empire Books, North Yorkshire 196
Explorer Books, West Sussex 243
Farahar & Dupré (Clive & Sophie),
  Wiltshire... 250
Glacier Books, Scotland 273
Graves–Johnston (Michael), London (SW)....... 164
Holmes Books (Harry), East Yorkshire............ 105
Hunter and Krageloh, Derbyshire 82
Lewis (John), Essex................................... 107
Page (David), Scotland 270
Prospect House Books, Northern Ireland 260

Shapero Rare Books (Bernard J.), London (W). 174
Vandeleur Antiquarian Books, Surrey 231
White (C.R.), London (W).......................... 175

TRIBAL

Bowen (Janice), Wales 286
Bracton Books, Cambridgeshire.................... 64
Popeley (Frank T.), Cambridgeshire............... 68
Traveller's Bookshelf (The), Somerset............. 215
Yesterday's Books, Dorset 91

TYPOGRAPHY

Andron (G.W.), London, North 153
Batterham (David), London (W)................... 169
Brinded (Scott), Kent 136
Canterbury Bookshop (The), Kent 133
ECR Books, Dorset 93
English (Toby), Oxfordshire 209
Fox Books (J. & J.), Kent............................ 137
Hanborough Books, Oxfordshire 207
Illustrated Book (The), London (SW)............. 165
Katnap Arts, Norfolk................................ 189
Mills Rare Books (Adam), Cambridgeshire 65
Moss Antiquarian Books (V.J.), Lancashire 142
O'Connor Fine Books, Lancashire................. 142
Taylor Rare Books (Michael), Norfolk 187
Wakeman Books (Frances), Nottinghamshire ... 202

U.F.O.S

Alpha Books, London, North 153
Croft Selections, Lincolnshire....................... 148
Dawlish Books, Devon 84
Facet Books, Dorset 90
Greensleeves, Oxfordshire 204
Inner Bookshop (The), Oxfordshire 207
Occultique, Northamptonshire 198
Scrivener's Books & Book Binding, Derbyshire . 81
Starlord Books, Cheshire............................ 70
Till's Bookshop, Scotland 270
Wizard Books, Cambridgeshire..................... 68

UNEXPLAINED, THE

Chevin Books, West Yorkshire...................... 248
Fantastic Literature, Essex 109
Inner Bookshop (The), Oxfordshire 207
Occultique, Northamptonshire 198

UNIVERSITY TEXTS

Castle Frome Books, Herefordshire 127
Downie Fine Books Ltd., (Robert), Shropshire . 213
Ice House Books....................................... 143
Warrington Book Loft (The), Cheshire 72

URBAN HISTORY

Ice House Books....................................... 143
Inch's Books, North Yorkshire...................... 194
Marcan, Bookseller (Peter), London (SE) 161
Stanhope Bibliophiles, London, North............ 155

VATICAN AND PAPAL HISTORY, THE
Jericho Books, Oxfordshire 208
Lund Theological Books, Cambridgeshire 65
Shapero Rare Books (Bernard J.), London (W). 174
Taylor & Son (Peter), Hertfordshire................ 130
Tuft (Patrick), London (W)......................... 175

VENTRILOQUISM
Wood (Peter), Cambridgeshire 66

VETERINARY
Alba Books, Scotland................................ 267
Ice House Books...................................... 143
Phenotype Books, Cumbria.......................... 79
STM Books, London, North 155

VICTORIANA
Art Reference Books, Hampshire 123
Bosco Books, Cornwall............................... 73
Collectables (W.H.), London (W).................. 172
de Beaumont (Robin), London (SW).............. 163
DoublePlusBooks, Cambridgeshire 68
Kenny's Bookshops and Art Galleries Ltd,
  Republic Of Ireland 278
Sanderson (Edward), Berkshire..................... 58
Shacklock Books (David), Suffolk 226

VINTAGE CARS
Baldwin (M. & M.), Shropshire..................... 212
Brewin Books Ltd., Warwickshire 237
Collectables (W.H.), London (W).................. 172
Collectors Carbooks, Northamptonshire........... 199
Cox (Geoff), Devon 89
Falconwood Transport & Military Bookshop,
  London, Outer 184
Hairpin Books, Gloucestershire 113
Jones Books (Russell), Berkshire.................... 57
Pooks Motor Books, Leicestershire................. 144
Roadmaster Books, Kent............................. 134
Roadster Motoring Books, Hampshire............. 123
Simon Lewis Transport Books, Gloucestershire . 112
Vintage Motorshop, West Yorkshire 245
www.drivepast.com, Gloucestershire............... 114
YSF Books, South Yorkshire........................ 221

VINTAGE PAPERBACKS
Black Cat Bookshop, Leicestershire 143
Books for Collectors, Gloucestershire 112
Cowley, Bookdealer (K.W.), Somerset 215
Dancing Goat Bookshop (The), Norfolk 188
Eggeling Books (John), West Yorkshire 248
Heckmondwike Book Shop, West Yorkshire 235
Illustrated Book (The), London (SW)............. 165
Jericho Books, Oxfordshire 208
Katnap Arts, Norfolk................................. 189
Paperbacks Plus, Bristol.............................. 61
Ruebotham (Kirk), Cheshire........................ 71
Seddon (A.C.), West Sussex 244
Till's Bookshop, Scotland 270
Trevorrow (Edwin), Hertfordshire 128

VITICULTURE
Cooksweb, Northamptonshire...................... 198
Ice House Books...................................... 143
Thorne (John), Essex................................. 107

VOYAGES & DISCOVERY
Afar Books International, West Midlands........ 238
Allsworth Rare Books Ltd., London (SW)....... 163
Altea Antique Maps & Books, London (WC) ... 169
Americanabooksuk, Cumbria........................ 77
Austwick Hall Books, North Yorkshire 141
Barn Books, Buckinghamshire...................... 62
Bookends of Fowey, Cornwall 74
Books on Spain, London, Outer 183
Brockwells Bookshop, London (SE).............. 160
Campbell Hewson Books (R.), Scotland.......... 265
Cherry (Janet), Dorset 92
Collectables (W.H.), London (W).................. 172
Dartmoor Bookshop (The), Devon................ 83
Eastern Traveller (The), Somerset................. 218
Edwards (London) Limited (Francis),
  London (WC) 177
Explorer Books, West Sussex 243
Farahar & Dupré (Clive & Sophie),
  Wiltshire.. 250
Glacier Books, Scotland 273
Graves–Johnston (Michael), London (SW)....... 164
Harrington (Adrian), London (W)................. 173
Harrington Antiquarian Bookseller (Peter),
  London (SW)...................................... 164
Holmes Books (Harry), East Yorkshire........... 105
Keel Row Books, Tyne & Wear.................... 235
Lawson & Company (E.M.), Oxfordshire 205
Lewcock (John), Cambridgeshire 67
Lewis (John), Essex.................................. 107
Marine and Cannon Books, Cheshire 70
Newby (Valerie), Buckinghamshire 63
Orssich (Paul), London (SW)....................... 166
Paralos Ltd., London (W)........................... 173
Prior (Michael), Lincolnshire 149
Prospect House Books, Northern Ireland 260
Quayside Bookshop, Devon 88
Rothwell and Dunworth, Somerset................ 216
Rowan (P. & B.), Northern Ireland 259
St Mary's Books & Prints, Lincolnshire 150
Shapero Rare Books (Bernard J.), London (W). 174
Slaughter & Garratt Rare Books, Worcestershire 255
Smith (Clive), Essex 108
Vandeleur Antiquarian Books, Surrey 231

WAR
- GENERAL
Albion Books, West Midlands...................... 239
Andron (G.W.), London, North 153
Arundel Bookshop, West Sussex.................... 241
Ashfield Books and Records, Nottinghamshire.. 203
Barbican Bookshop, North Yorkshire 196
Books & Bygones, Berkshire........................ 58
Bookworms, Norfolk................................. 187
Broadhurst of Southport Ltd., Merseyside 186
Brockwells Bookshop, London (SE)............... 160
Bufo Books, Hampshire 123
Chapter and Verse Booksellers, East Sussex 102

SPECIALITY INDEX

Chelifer Books, Cumbria 79
Cherry (Janet), Dorset 92
Collectables (W.H.), London (W) 172
Crispin's Day, Antiquarian and Out of Print
   Military Books, Essex 110
Dally Books & Collectables, Wales 287
Daly (Peter M.), Hampshire 124
Dartmoor Bookshop (The), Devon 83
de Lotz Books (P.G.), London (NW) 157
Devanha Military Books, Scotland 267
Downie Fine Books Ltd., (Robert), Shropshire . 213
Eastcote Bookshop (The), London, Outer 183
Empire Books, Greater Manchester 118
Fin Rare Books, Shropshire 213
Gate Memorabilia, London, North 153
Golden Hind Bookshop (The), Kent 134
Handsworth Books, Essex 110
Harrington Antiquarian Bookseller (Peter),
   London (SW) 164
Harris (George J.), Worcestershire 254
Hayles Military Books (Derek), Berkshire 57
Ice House Books 143
Keel Row Books, Tyne & Wear 235
Lewis (J.T. & P.), Cornwall 74
Malmo Books, Hampshire 121
Marine and Cannon Books, Cheshire 70
McCrone (Audrey), Scotland 272
Meekins Books (Paul), Warwickshire 237
Mercat Books, Scotland 267
Military Collector (The), West Yorkshire 249
MilitaryHistoryBooks.com, Kent 136
Palladour Books, Hampshire 124
Peakirk Books, Cambridgeshire 68
Prior (Michael), Lincolnshire 149
Rods Books, Devon 87
Russell Books, Somerset 218
Scorpio Books, Suffolk 225
Scrivener's Books & Book Binding, Derbyshire . 81
Shapero Rare Books (Bernard J.), London (W) . 174
Smith Books, (Sally), Suffolk 225
Spurrier (Nick), Kent 136
Stacks Bookshop, Northern Ireland 259
Stevens (Joan), Cambridgeshire 66
Stothert Old Books, Cheshire 69
Thin Read Line, Merseyside 186
Turner (Robin), Gloucestershire 112
Wolds Book Services, Leicestershire 144
World War Books, Kent 139
Yeoman Books, Scotland 270
Zardoz Books, Wiltshire 253

- AMERICAN CIVIL WAR

Americanabooksuk, Cumbria 77
Broadhurst of Southport Ltd., Merseyside 186
Crispin's Day, Antiquarian and Out of Print
   Military Books, Essex 110
Empire Books, Greater Manchester 118
Harris (George J.), Worcestershire 254
Helion & Company, West Midlands 240
Meekins Books (Paul), Warwickshire 237
Military Collector (The), West Yorkshire 249
Rods Books, Devon 87

- BOER, THE

Crispin's Day, Antiquarian and Out of Print
   Military Books, Essex 110
Empire Books, Greater Manchester 118
Helion & Company, West Midlands 240
Military Collector (The), West Yorkshire 249

- ENGLISH CIVIL WARS

Crispin's Day, Antiquarian and Out of Print
   Military Books, Essex 110
Empire Books, Greater Manchester 118
Helion & Company, West Midlands 240
Honiton Old Bookshop, Devon 85
Ice House Books 143
Meekins Books (Paul), Warwickshire 237
Military Collector (The), West Yorkshire 249
Spenceley Books (David), West Yorkshire 248
Taylor & Son (Peter), Hertfordshire 130
Thomas (Books) (Leona), Cheshire 71

- NAPOLEONIC

Chevin Books, West Yorkshire 248
Donovan Military Books (Tom), East Sussex.... 98
Empire Books, Greater Manchester 118
Helion & Company, West Midlands 240
Military Collector (The), West Yorkshire 249
Prior (Michael), Lincolnshire 149

- SPANISH CIVIL WAR

Books on Spain, London, Outer 183
Cyclamen Books, Leicestershire 143
Empire Books, Greater Manchester 118
Helion & Company, West Midlands 240
Ice House Books 143
Left on The Shelf, London (E) 151
Orssich (Paul), London (SW) 166
Red Star Books, Hertfordshire 128

- VIETNAM

Anglo-American Rare Books, Surrey 232
Empire Books, Greater Manchester 118
Helion & Company, West Midlands 240
Ice House Books 143
Military Collector (The), West Yorkshire 249

- WORLD WAR I

Aardvark Books, Wiltshire 252
Albion Books, West Midlands 239
Anglo-American Rare Books, Surrey 232
Armchair Auctions, Hampshire 120
Barbican Bookshop, North Yorkshire 196
Chevin Books, West Yorkshire 248
Crispin's Day, Antiquarian and Out of Print
   Military Books, Essex 110
Dally Books & Collectables, Wales 287
Empire Books, Greater Manchester 118
Harris (George J.), Worcestershire 254
Helion & Company, West Midlands 240
Heppa (Christopher), Essex 106
Ice House Books 143
Island Books, Devon 86

Joppa Books Ltd., Surrey 230
Marrin & Sons (G. & D.), Kent 135
Meekins Books (Paul), Warwickshire 237
Military Collector (The), West Yorkshire 249
Palladour Books, Hampshire 124
Prior (Michael), Lincolnshire 149
Rods Books, Devon 87
Smith Books (Keith), Herefordshire 127
Thornton (Grahame), Dorset 94
Tiffin (Tony and Gill), Durham 96
Updike Rare Books (John), Scotland 270

- WORLD WAR II
Aardvark Books, Wiltshire 252
Baldwin (M. & M.), Shropshire 212
Barbican Bookshop, North Yorkshire 196
Book for All Reasons (A.), Suffolk 227
Bookseller (The), Suffolk 227
Chevin Books, West Yorkshire 248
Crispin's Day, Antiquarian and Out of Print
  Military Books, Essex 110
Dally Books & Collectables, Wales 287
Donovan Military Books (Tom), East Sussex.... 98
Empire Books, Greater Manchester 118
G C Books, Scotland 264
Harris (George J.), Worcestershire 254
Helion & Company, West Midlands 240
Ice House Books 143
Island Books, Devon 86
Meekins Books (Paul), Warwickshire 237
Military Collector (The), West Yorkshire 249
Palladour Books, Hampshire 124
Prior (Michael), Lincolnshire 149
Rods Books, Devon 87
Thin Read Line, Merseyside 186
Third Reich Books, Kent 134
Thornton (Grahame), Dorset 94
Updike Rare Books (John), Scotland 270
Wolds Book Services, Leicestershire 144

WARGAMES
Bardsley's Books, Suffolk 225
Chelifer Books, Cumbria 79
Helion & Company, West Midlands 240
Ice House Books 143
Meekins Books (Paul), Warwickshire 237
Military Collector (The), West Yorkshire 249
MilitaryHistoryBooks.com, Kent 136

WEIRD & WONDERFUL
Delectus Books, London (WC) 176
Far Horizons Books, Dorset 91
Inner Bookshop (The), Oxfordshire 207
Starlord Books, Cheshire 70

WELSH INTEREST
BOOKS4U, Wales 282
Cader Idris Books, Wales 283
Carta Regis, Wales 288
Castle Bookshop, Wales 288
Chatterton's Books, Wales 290

Coch-y-Bonddu Books, Wales 288
Dally Books & Collectables, Wales 287
Dusty Books, Wales 287
Great Oak Bookshop (The), Wales 287
Hancock (Colin), Wales 281
Kingshead Books, Wales 288
Mollie's Loft, Wales 289
Rhos Point Books, Wales 281
Siop y Morfa, Wales 282
Spread Eagle Books, Wales 282
Willmott Bookseller (Nicholas), Wales 280

WHALING
Bluntisham Books, Cambridgeshire 64
Marine and Cannon Books, Cheshire 70
Prior (Michael), Lincolnshire 149

WHISKY
Cooksweb, Northamptonshire 198
Moray Bookshop (The), Scotland 267
Thorne (John), Essex 107

WINDMILLS & WATERMILLS
Allport (Roy), North Yorkshire 195
Arnold (Roy), Suffolk 226
Cottage Books, Leicestershire 143
Duck (William), East Sussex 98
Island Books, Devon 84
Just Books, Cornwall 76
Satara Books, West Sussex 244

WINE
Clarke (Janet), Somerset 214
Collectable Books, London (SE) 160
Cooksweb, Northamptonshire 198
Dusty Books, Wales 287
Gresham Books, Somerset 216
Ice House Books 143
Thorne (John), Essex 107

WITCHCRAFT
Alpha Books, London, North 153
Book Basket, London, Outer 182
Burgess Booksellers, (J. & J.), Cambridgeshire .. 64
Caduceus Books, Leicestershire 143
Chthonios Books, East Sussex 100
Dawlish Books, Devon 84
Far Horizons Books, Dorset 91
Gilbert (R.A.), Bristol 61
Inner Bookshop (The), Oxfordshire 207
Magis Books, Leicestershire 144
Occultique, Northamptonshire 198
Rainger Books (Michael), Wales 285
Shapero Rare Books (Bernard J.), London (W). 174
Starlord Books, Cheshire 70
Wizard Books, Cambridgeshire 68

WOMEN
Black Cat Books, Norfolk 188
Books & Bygones (Pam Taylor), West Midlands 240

Chatterton's Books, Wales 290
Chesters (G. & J.), Staffordshire 223
Crawford (Elizabeth), London (EC) 152
Dolphin Books, Suffolk 224
Fortune Green Books, London (NW) 157
Ice House Books 143
Jarndyce Antiquarian Booksellers,
   London (WC) 177
Lane Books (Shirley), Isle of Wight 132
Max Gate Books, Somerset 218
Northern Herald Books, West Yorkshire 245
Orlando Booksellers, Lincolnshire 148
Reading Lasses, Scotland 264
Scorpio Books, Suffolk 225
Shapero Rare Books (Bernard J.),
   London (W) 174
Spurrier (Nick), Kent 136
Stevens (Joan), Cambridgeshire 66
Stone, (G.& R.), Scotland 261
Swan Bookshop (The), Devon 84
Symes Books (Naomi), Cheshire 72
Taylor Books (Susan), West Yorkshire 246
Till's Bookshop, Scotland 270
Willmott Bookseller (Nicholas), Wales 280
Woburn Books, London, North 156

WOODWORK

Arnold (Roy), Suffolk 226
Brown-Studies, Scotland 270
Ice House Books 143
Phillips of Hitchin (Antiques) Ltd.,
   Hertfordshire 129
Trinders' Fine Tools, Suffolk 225
Upper–Room Books, Somerset 216
Well–Head Books, Dorset 91

YOGA

Far Horizons Books, Dorset 91
Greensleeves, Oxfordshire 204
Inner Bookshop (The), Oxfordshire 207
Occultique, Northamptonshire 198

ZOOLOGY

Alba Books, Scotland 267
Baron - Scientific Book Sales (P.J.), Somerset ... 215
Blest (Peter), Kent 136
Book Corner, Scotland 263
Bracton Books, Cambridgeshire 64
Daly (Peter M.), Hampshire 124
Demar Books (Grant), Kent 138
Grayling (David A.H.), Cumbria 78
Harrington Antiquarian Bookseller (Peter),
   London (SW) 164
Ian Johnson Natural History Books,
   Buckinghamshire 63
Ice House Books 143
On the Wild Side, Worcestershire 255
Phelps (Michael), West Sussex 242
Scott (Sporting Books) (John), Worcestershire .. 256
Sue Lowell Natural History Books, London (W) 175
Wyseby House Books, Berkshire 57

Looking for out-of-print, rare, or secondhand books?

We have over 45 million. From 11,000 booksellers. Out of 42 countries.

Try Abebooks!

www.abebooks.co.uk

BOOKSEARCH SERVICE

Index of dealers who offer a booksearch service

Dealer	Page
Afar Books International, West Midlands	238
Ainslie Books, Scotland	271
Albion Books, West Midlands	239
All Seasons Books, Cumbria	79
Allen (R.), Tyne & Wear	235
Alton Secondhand Books, Hampshire	120
Americanabooksuk, Cumbria	77
Amos (Denis W.), Hertfordshire	128
Angel Books, Norfolk	189
Anglo-American Rare Books, Surrey	232
Annie's Books, South Yorkshire	220
Antiquary Ltd., (Bar Bookstore), North Yorkshire	194
Anvil Books, West Midlands	239
Aquarius Books Ltd., Gloucestershire	114
Archer (Steve), London, Outer	180
Armchair Auctions, Hampshire	120
Armchair Books, West Midlands	238
Arnold (Roy), Suffolk	226
Ashfield Books and Records, Nottinghamshire	203
Askew Books (Vernon), Wiltshire	250
Atticus Books, Essex	109
Austwick Hall Books, North Yorkshire	141
Ayre (Peter J.), Somerset	218
Ballantyne–Way (Roger), Suffolk	228
Bardsley's Books, Suffolk	225
Barn Books, Buckinghamshire	62
Barnard (Colin), Kent	138
Barry Meaden (Aviation Books), Hertfordshire	129
Bath Book Exchange, Somerset	214
Baxter - Books (Eddie), Somerset	218
Baxter (Steve), Surrey	232
Beaver Booksearch, Suffolk	225
Beckham Books, Suffolk	228
Beckham Books, Suffolk	228
Belfast Book Search, Northern Ireland	259
Bell (Books) (Mrs. V.S.), Suffolk	226
Ben–Nathan (Jack), London, Outer	181
Bertram Rota Ltd., London (WC)	176
Bird Books (Nigel), Wales	281
Black & White Books, Isle of Wight	131
Black Cat Bookshop, Leicestershire	143
Black Voices, Merseyside	185
Bolland Books (Leslie H.), Bedfordshire	55
Book Depot (The), London (NW)	157
Book House (The), Cumbria	78
Bookmark (Children's Books), Wiltshire	252
Bookquest, Devon	83
Books and Things, West Sussex	241
Books Bought & Sold, Surrey	231
Books for Writers, Wales	283
Bookseekers, London (SW)	163
Bookshop (The), West Sussex	242
Bookshop (The), Republic Of Ireland	276
Booktrace International, Devon	85
Bookworld, Shropshire	212
Bookwyze, Lincolnshire	147
Booth (Booksearch Service), (Geoff), Cheshire	69
Boris Books, Dorset	94
Bott, (Bookdealers) Ltd., (Martin), Greater Manchester	116
Bowers Chess Suppliers (Francis), Cambridgeshire	67
Bowland Bookfinders, Lancashire	140
Bridge of Allan Books, Scotland	262
Broadhurst of Southport Ltd., Merseyside	186
Brown (K.C.), Berkshire	58
Bryant (Mrs. Muriel J.), Devon	84
Buchan Collectibles, Scotland	265
Butts Books (Mary), Berkshire	58
Bygone Books, Lancashire	141
Camilla's Bookshop, East Sussex	100
Candle Lane Books, Shropshire	213
Capital Bookshop, Wales	280
Carta Regis, Wales	288
Castle Bookshop, Essex	107
Catalyst Books, Surrey	232
Cathach Books Ltd., Republic Of Ireland	277
Cavan Book Centre, Republic Of Ireland	275
Cecil Books, Surrey	231
Chaldon Books & Records, Surrey	230
Chapter and Verse Booksellers, East Sussex	102
Chapter House Books, Dorset	93
Chapters Bookstore, Republic Of Ireland	277
Chaters Motoring Booksellers, London, Outer	182
Chichester Bookshop (The), West Sussex	241
Christine's Book Cabin, Leicestershire	144
Chthonios Books, East Sussex	100
Church Green Books, Oxfordshire	210
Clark (M.R.), West Yorkshire	245
Clark (Nigel A.), London (SE)	160
Classic Crime Collections, Greater Manchester	117
Coach House Books, Worcestershire	255
Coch-y-Bonddu Books, Wales	288
Cocks Books (Brian), Cambridgeshire	67
Collectors Carbooks, Northamptonshire	199
Colwyn Books, Wales	281
Cooksweb, Northamptonshire	198
Corfe Books, Surrey	231
Cornell Books, Gloucestershire	114
Coulthurst (Richard), Greater Manchester	118
Cousens (W.C.), Devon	83
Cowley, Auto–in–Print (John), Essex	106
Craobh Rua Books, Northern Ireland	259
Crispin's Day, Antiquarian and Out of Print Military Books, Essex	110
Croft Selections, Lincolnshire	148
Cuddy Books (Michael), London, North	153
Curtle Mead Books, Isle of Wight	131
Cygnet Books, East Yorkshire	105
D. & M. Books, West Yorkshire	248
Davis (C. & D.), Devon	83
Delaney's Books, Republic Of Ireland	275
Delph Books, Greater Manchester	116
Dolphin Books, Suffolk	224

Dorset Rare Books, Wiltshire 252
Doughty Fine Books (Robin), West Midlands... 238
Dusty Books, Wales.................................. 287
Dyfi Valley Bookshop, Wales....................... 288
Eastern Books of London, London (SW) 163
ECR Books, Dorset..................................... 93
Elmbury Books, Warwickshire 237
Embleton (Paul), Essex 109
Emjay Books, Surrey................................. 231
English (Toby), Oxfordshire 209
Eton Antique Bookshop, Berkshire................. 59
Evans Booksearch, (Lesley), Devon 89
Exedra Booksearch Ltd., London (SW) 164
Facet Books, Dorset 90
Family Favourites (Books), East Yorkshire...... 104
Fantastic Literature, Essex 109
Farnborough Bookshop and Gallery, Hampshire 121
Farquharson, (Hilary), Scotland 273
Farringdon (J.M.), Wales 289
Faversham Antiques Centre, Kent................. 135
Ferguson (Elizabeth), Scotland.................... 265
Fin Rare Books, Shropshire 213
Find That Book, West Yorkshire.................. 247
Fireside Books, Buckinghamshire................... 63
Firth (Bijou Books & Photography) (Maureen),
    South Yorkshire 221
Fisher Nautical, East Sussex........................ 98
Four Shire Bookshops, Gloucestershire........... 113
Four Tees Booksearch, Dorset 90
Foyle Books, Northern Ireland.................... 260
Freya Books & Antiques, Norfolk................. 189
Fuchsia Books, Republic Of Ireland 276
Fullerton's Booksearch, Norfolk................... 188
Game Advice, Oxfordshire......................... 207
Gilham Books, London (SE) 161
Glass Key (The), West Yorkshire................. 246
Gloucester Road Bookshop, London (SW) 164
Godmanchester Books, Cambridgeshire 66
Goldsworth Books & Prints, Surrey............... 234
Gorton Booksearch (John), East Sussex 103
Gradwell Concepts, Merseyside 185
Graham (John), Dorset............................... 95
Grahame (Major Iain), Suffolk..................... 225
Grant (Gerald S.), Cheshire......................... 69
Gravity Books, Lincolnshire 147
Great Oak Bookshop (The), Wales................ 287
Greensleeves, Oxfordshire 204
Guildmaster Books, Cheshire........................ 71
Hairpin Books, Gloucestershire 113
Hall's Bookshop, Kent............................... 138
Hancock (Colin), Wales 281
Harries (Pauline), Hampshire...................... 122
Harris (Books), (Malcolm), West Midlands...... 239
Harvest Books, Merseyside 185
Haven Booksearch, West Midlands................ 238
Hawley (C.L.), North Yorkshire 195
Helion & Company, West Midlands 240
Hen Hoose Bookshop, Scotland 262
Hencotes Books & Prints, Northumberland...... 200
Heneage Art Books (Thomas), London (SW).... 164
Heppa (Christopher), Essex........................ 106
Heywood Hill Limited (G.), London (W) 173
Hicks (Ronald C.), Cornwall 74
Hill (John S.), Devon 85
Hillsborough Bookhunters, Northern Ireland.... 260

Holdsworth Books (Bruce), West Yorkshire 245
Holmes Books (Harry), East Yorkshire........... 105
Home Farm Books, Warwickshire................. 236
Hoovey's Books, East Sussex....................... 101
Howell, Photographic Books (Jill), Kent 137
HP Bookfinders, Scotland.......................... 262
Hutchison (Books) (Larry), Scotland............. 265
Ice House Books..................................... 143
Idler (The), Suffolk 227
Intech Books, Northumberland 201
Island Books, Devon.................................. 86
Jobson (N.W.), Oxfordshire........................ 205
Jones (Anne), Cornwall.............................. 76
Jones (Madalyn S.), West Yorkshire 246
Jones Books (Russell), Berkshire................... 57
K. Books, East Yorkshire........................... 104
Katnap Arts, Norfolk................................ 189
Kaye - Bookseller (Terence), London (NW) 158
Kenny's Bookshops and Art Galleries Ltd,
    Republic Of Ireland 278
Kent (Books) (Mrs. A.), Suffolk 226
Kent T. G., Surrey 230
Kingfisher Book Service, Nottinghamshire....... 203
Kitley (A.J.), Bristol.................................. 61
Knockhundred Bookshop, West Sussex.......... 243
Korn Books, (M.E.), London, North 154
KSC Books, Cheshire................................. 71
Leaf Ends, Northumberland 201
Leapman Ltd. (G. & R.), Hertfordshire 130
Lee Rare Books (Rachel), Bristol.................. 61
Left on The Shelf, London (E).................... 151
Lewis (John), Essex.................................. 107
Lloyd-Davies (Sue), Wales 280
Luckman (Bill), London, Outer 183
LyngHeath Books, Norfolk 190
Maddison (J.K.), West Midlands 238
Malmo Books, Hampshire 121
Malvern Bookshop (The),
    Worcestershire................................... 254
Manor House Books/John Trotter Books,
    London, North................................... 154
Marine and Cannon Books, Cheshire.............. 70
Martin - Bookseller (Colin), East Yorkshire 105
Mayhew Books, Norfolk 187
McKenzie (Major John R.), Cumbria.............. 77
Meadowcroft Books, West Sussex 241
Meekins Books (Paul), Warwickshire 237
Mercat Books, Scotland............................. 267
Merlin Books, West Sussex 243
Miles Book Shop (Archie), Cumbria 79
Military Collector (The), West Yorkshire 249
MilitaryHistoryBooks.com, Kent.................. 136
Minster Gate Bookshop, North Yorkshire....... 196
MK Book Services, Cambridgeshire................ 67
Modlock (Lilian), Dorset............................ 92
Monmouth House Books, Wales.................. 283
Moon's Bookshop (Michael), Cumbria 79
Moore (Sue), Cornwall............................... 74
Moorland Books, Greater Manchester............ 118
Moss Antiquarian Books (V.J.), Lancashire 142
Mr. Pickwick of Towcester, Northamptonshire.. 199
Museum Bookshop, London (WC)................ 177
Naughton Booksellers, Republic Of Ireland..... 277
Newband (D.M.), Wales............................ 288
Newgate Books, Northumberland 201

Nineteenth Century Books, Oxfordshire 209
Noble (Malcolm & Christine), Leicestershire..... 145
Noel and Holland Books, Republic Of Ireland.. 278
Occultique, Northamptonshire 198
Old Bookshop (The), Somerset..................... 216
Palladour Books, Hampshire 124
Paramor (C.D.), Suffolk 227
Park (Mike), London, Outer........................ 183
Park Gallery & Bookshop (The),
   Northamptonshire 199
Peakirk Books, Cambridgeshire 68
Pedlar's Pack Books, Devon......................... 89
Peel (Valerie), t/a Kiandra Associates Ltd.,
   Berkshire 57
Petersfield Bookshop (The), Hampshire........... 122
Phillips of Hitchin (Antiques) Ltd.,
   Hertfordshire 129
Philologus–Fine & Rare Books, London (SW) .. 166
Pioneer Books, Hampshire.......................... 120
Pratt (H.G.), Suffolk 228
Premier Books & Prints, Lincolnshire............. 146
Price (R.D.M. & I.M.) (Books),
   Greater Manchester 119
Quarto Bookshop (The), Scotland................. 265
Quest Books, East Yorkshire 105
Quest Booksearch, Cambridgeshire................ 65
Railway Book and Magazine Search, Berkshire . 58
Rainger Books (Michael), Wales.................... 285
Right Now Books (Burma), London (SW)....... 167
Rittner Booksearch (Hilary), London (SE)....... 161
Roadmaster Books, Kent............................ 134
Roberts (Booksellers), (Ray), Staffordshire....... 223
Rods Books, Devon.................................. 87
Roosterbooks, Northamptonshire.................. 198
Roundstone Books, Lancashire 141
Rowan (H. & S.J.), Dorset.......................... 91
Ruskin Books, London (SE)........................ 161
Russell Books, Somerset............................. 218
Sabin (Printed Works) (P.R. & V.), Kent 133
St Mary's Books & Prints, Lincolnshire 150
Saltburn Bookshop, North Yorkshire............. 194
San Expedito Books, London (NW)............... 158
Sansovino Books, West Sussex 244
Sax Books, Suffolk 228
Scarthin Books, Derbyshire......................... 82
Scott (Sporting Books) (John), Worcestershire .. 256
Sea Chest Nautical Bookshop (The), Devon..... 87
Seeber (Liz), East Sussex 99
Sen Books, Hampshire.............................. 125
Shacklock Books (David), Suffolk 226
Shapero Rare Books (Bernard J.),
   London (W)....................................... 174
Shearwater Bed & Books (formerly John
   Lumby Nat. History Bks), Northumberland ... 200
Shipley Specialist Art Booksellers, London (WC)178
Simply Read, East Sussex 100
Sims (Sue), Dorset................................... 91
Skelly (George B.), London, North................ 155
Skyrack Books, West Yorkshire.................... 246
Smallwood Books, Lincolnshire.................... 148
Smith Booksellers (James), London, Outer....... 180
Spelman (Ken), North Yorkshire 197
Spenceley Books (David), West Yorkshire 248
Spooner & Co., Somerset 217
Spread Eagle Books, Wales......................... 282
Spurrier (Nick), Kent 136
Stella Books, Wales 284
Sterling Books, Somerset 219
Sturford Books, Wiltshire........................... 252
Sturgeon (Jamie), West Sussex 244
Symes Books (Naomi), Cheshire................... 72
Tarka Books, Devon................................. 83
Taylor Books (Susan), West Yorkshire 246
Tenner (Melvin), London (W)..................... 175
Tennis Collectables, Cheshire....................... 69
Thin Read Line, Merseyside........................ 186
Thompson (Eric), Surrey 233
Thornton (Grahame), Dorset....................... 94
Tiger Books, Kent.................................... 134
Titford (John), Derbyshire 81
Tombland Bookshop, Norfolk 190
Tony Skelton, Kent 138
Tozer Railway Books (Nick), West Yorkshire... 246
Trafalgar Bookshop (The), East Sussex........... 99
Trevorrow (Edwin), Hertfordshire 128
Trotter Books (John), London, North 156
Twiggers Booksearch, London (SW) 167
Vokes (Jeremiah), Durham......................... 96
Walden Books, London (NW)..................... 159
Warsash Nautical Bookshop, Hampshire......... 124
Wayfarer Books, Cornwall.......................... 75
Webster (D.), Scotland.............................. 272
Well–Head Books, Dorset.......................... 91
Wells (Mary), London (SW)....................... 167
Weobley Bookshop (The), Herefordshire......... 127
Wetherell (Frances), Cambridgeshire.............. 66
Whitchurch Books Ltd., Wales.................... 280
Whiteson Ltd., (Edna), Hertfordshire 128
Wilson Books (Henry), Cheshire 71
Winchester Bookshop (The), Hampshire.......... 125
Woolcott Books, Dorset............................. 92
Wright Trace Books, West Midlands.............. 239
www.drivepast.com, Gloucestershire.............. 114
Wyche Books, Scotland............................. 263

LARGE PRINT BOOKS
Index of dealers with stocks in large print

Arden Books & Cosmographia, Warwickshire... 236
Fin Rare Books, Shropshire 213
Peter's Bookshop, Norfolk 190
Shapero Rare Books (Bernard J.), London (W). 174

DISPLAY ADVERTISMENTS

Index of Advertisers

abebooks.com 433	Paul Orssich 166
Abrams – Books, Harvey 54	Parchment Printers 42
Antiquarian Book Monthly 25	Period Bookbinders 43
atlanticweb.co.uk 46	P.B.F.A 21, 41
Bardsley's Books 224	Project Portmanteaux 205
Biblion 170	M & D Reeve Children's Books 208
Bloomsbury Book Auctions 38	The Old Town Bookshop 268
Bonhams 34	Rhod McEwan Golf 266
Book Collector 27	Ripping Yarns 155
Bookdealer 29	Snowden Smith 167
Carol Hogben 274	Stella Books 284
Game Advice 207	Scottish Book Collector 31
Adrian Harrington 171	Spranger, Anthony 251
HD Fairs 39	TL Dallas (City) Ltd 35
Humber Books 146	